GUINNESS
BRITI
HIT SINGLES

Editorial Associate: Steve Smith

Dedicated to Bob Geldof, Midge Ure and those artists
who participated in the recording of Band Aid's
'Do They Know It's Christmas'?

Photo: Duncan Paul Associates

ACKNOWLEDGEMENTS

The four authors would like to thank many of the artists featured in this book for their interest and cooperation and also to the following: BBC Photos, BBC Record Library, BPI, Graham Betts, Steve Earnshaw, Eileen Heinink, Sheila Goldsmith, Robert Heesom, Jan Rice and Wayne Tilling.

We also thank the *New Musical Express* and *Music Week* for the use of their charts and the many record company press offices for their patient help and for photographs.

Hits from this book can be heard by dialling the GRRR Golden Hit Line on 01-246-8044. The authors would like to express their gratitude to Bill Heath for this service.

Editor: Alex E. Reid

Design and layout: David Roberts

Fifth edition 1985

© GRRR Books Ltd. and Guinness Superlatives Ltd. 1985

First edition 1977, reprinted three times
Second edition 1979, reprinted three times
Third edition 1981, reprinted three times
Fourth edition 1983, reprinted three times

Published in Great Britain by
Guinness Superlatives Ltd.,
2 Cecil Court, London Road, Enfield, Middlesex

British Library Cataloguing in Publication Data

The Guinness book of British hit singles.—
    5th ed.
    1. Music, Popular (Songs, etc.)—Great
    Britain—Discography
    I. Rice, Jo
    016.7899'12   ML156.4.P6

    ISBN 0-85112-429-1

'Guinness' is a registered trade mark of Guinness Superlatives Ltd.

Typeset by BPCC Information Services Ltd, Derby and by
Hazell Watson & Viney Limited, Aylesbury.
Printed and bound in Great Britain by
Hazell Watson & Viney Limited,
Member of the BPCC Group,
Aylesbury, Bucks

CONTENTS

Acknowledgements
Introductions

All statistics and information cover the period 14 November 1952 to 31 December 1984, and are as follows:

PART 1 Alphabetically by Artist 8

About 3000 chart acts listed alphabetically with chronological title list showing date disc first hit the chart, title, label, catalogue number, highest position reached, number of weeks on chart. Top ten placings and number ones highlighted.

PART 2 Alphabetically by Title 246

Approximately 9500 hits listed alphabetically by title with artists' names and year of initial chart entry. Different versions of the same song are indicated.

PART 3 Facts and Feats...................... 285

INTRODUCTION

Welcome to one of the few pieces of entertainment that can honestly claim it contains more hits every time it appears. This is the fifth edition of *The Guinness Book of British Hit Singles*, **and it keeps getting bigger. By the time we reach the twentieth edition only weightlifters will be able to carry the book home from the shop.**

We are 750 hits heavier this time around, and what hits some of them have been. It is always a great pleasure for us when the music business is on an upswing, and during the 1983–4 period the sales slump of the early eighties was halted. Part of the reason lay with the astonishing success of Michael Jackson and Frankie Goes to Hollywood, who not only sold large numbers of singles but other products that got buyers into the stores. Once there, of course, they were more likely to buy singles by other artists. We recently added *British Hit Albums* to our list of titles and expect to issue a second edition in 1986. The phenomenal sales of *The Making of Michael Jackson's 'Thriller'* and the subsequent sales surge in other pop music videocassettes suggests we may one day be tabulating music video charts. If the unprecedented Frankie T-shirt boom of the summer of '84 was merely the beginning of a new kind of music spin-off we may also have to chart clothes. The 12-inch single strengthened its position as a major mass market force, especially with Gary Byrd and New Order reaching the Top 10 in a 12-inch-only format and Frankie selling large numbers of various 12-inch mixes.

The British music business also profited during our two-year survey period from increased sales in overseas markets. American number ones were achieved by a plethora of British artists, including David Bowie, Phil Collins, Culture Club, Dexy's Midnight Runners, Duran Duran, Eurythmics, Paul McCartney (with Michael Jackson), Billy Ocean, the Police, Bonnie Tyler, John Waite and Wham! In West Germany, a bigger market than Britain, Kajagoogoo were number one for 5 weeks, Paul Young reigned, Talk Talk placed two in the Top Twenty at the same time, and Bronski Beat went Top Three first time out. Queen wowed the continent, and Frankie Goes to Hollywood reached number one on the Euro-chart with both their first two singles.

This international success follows by exactly two decades what Americans call 'the British invasion'. That Beatle-led boom extended through the middle of the decade, and there is no reason to suspect that the talents mentioned above and numerous others cannot sustain their careers until our sixth edition.

We cherish our old friends and welcome the new. First-time readers may be intrigued to hear that our original volume was planned in 1974. It was finally finished and printed in 1977. We have been publishing updated editions every two years, and last time increased the height of the book to accommodate the growing text. Since the expansion of the official chart from a Top 50 to a 75 in 1978 there have been more new hits per year.

We have decided not to go lower than the 75 in our listings, though both *Music Week* and *Record Mirror* print a top 100 from Gallup. Our reason is that positions 76–100 are not genuine reflections of sales. Records that have been going down by at least a certain rate are dropped from this Gallup section, allowing others to move up artificially. If a dying single has a slight increase in sales one week it will appear as a re-entry when in fact it has only gone up a couple of places. Unless and until the lower list is as accurate as the top table, we will stick to the 75. One of our number finds this decision correct but frustrating. He has been placed between 76 and 100 with three different releases, but continues to be denied a listing in these pages.

Though there are many groups whose names include the number 'four', the Seasons and Tops being merely the best-known, there are strangely few who incorporate 'five'. For our fifth celebration mascot we turn to the American act the Jive Five, whose repertoire included 'I'm a Happy Man'. Our book dates back to the fifties, when the jive was popular, and we are happy that we are still here and healthy. Thank you for your continued support.

THE CHARTS

In the compilation of this book, we have used the charts published by the *New Musical Express* and then by *Record Retailer/Music Week*. This chart has grown over 32 years from a Top 12 to a Top 75, as explained below. If ever a week went by without a chart being compiled, the previous week's chart was used again for the purposes of all the information and statistics used in this book. In many years, no chart was compiled for the Christmas week. If ever a chart was compiled but not published, this chart has been found and used.

1 NEW MUSICAL EXPRESS

14 Nov 52	First ever chart, a Top 12 only
1 Oct 54	Chart becomes a Top 20
30 Dec 55	Top 25 published, for this week only
13 Apr 56	Chart becomes a Top 30
26 Feb 60	Last *NME* Top 30 used by British Hit Singles

2 RECORD RETAILER/MUSIC WEEK

10 Mar 60	Top 50 inaugurated. This is a publication date, the chart date being 5 March, which is why the 4 March *NME* chart is not used.
3 Jan 63	Top 50 now independently audited
13 Feb 69	Top 50 now 'compiled for *RR* and BBC by British Market Research Bureau'.
6 Feb 71	Top 40 only, caused by postal strike, for 7 weeks.
27 Mar 71	Top 50 resumes
6 Jan 73	Top 30 only, for 1 week
22 Dec 73	Top 30 only, for 1 week
6 May 78	Top 75 begins
8 Jan 83	Charts compilation taken over by Gallup, now described as 'The British Record Industry charts © Social Surveys (Gallup Poll) Ltd.' A 'next 25' also published, but NOT used in the compilation of this book.

83 84

1983

A man called Boy and a former child star dominated the 1983 single charts. The artist of the year was clearly **Michael Jackson**, with **Culture Club** the homegrown heroes.

■ Jackson became the first act to draw five Top Ten singles from one album. His source was the best-selling long player of 1983, *Thriller*. When 1983 began his Top Ten duet with **Paul McCartney**, 'The Girl Is Mine', was still in the charts. He followed it with a number one, 'Billie Jean', and a number three, 'Beat It'. 'Wanna Be Startin' Something' and 'Thriller' made it five top tenners. In scraping in at number ten 'Thriller' enabled Michael to break the mark he and the Electric Light Orchestra had shared of lifting four top tenners from one LP. He had done it with *Off The Wall*, they with *Discovery*.

■ Michael was also represented this year by his most successful duet with McCartney, 'Say Say Say', which netted them a number two, and by three odd examples of songwriting success. **Lydia Murdock** made the Top Twenty with 'Superstar', an answer record replying to 'Billie Jean', while the latter title was coupled with Steely Dan's 'Do It Again' for a hit medley by Italian disco group **Club House**. **Ashaye** got into the chart-making act with his own Michael medley.

■ In only one sense was the former Motown star surpassed. A Polydor promotional push brought thirteen former **Jam** hits back to the lower levels of the list. Their combined short stays, plus the declining days of the group's swan song 'Beat Surrender', a 1982 number one, gave the trio a total of 55 weeks on chart, the top figure of the year. Jackson had 46, plus 14 with McCartney.

Michael Jackson

Wham! Two of George Michael's 1984 releases sold over a million; one under the 'Wham' banner with Andrew Ridgely and one as a soloist.

It was unheard of for an act to be a year's weeks-on-chart champ without having any new hits. The Jam also set a new record for most chart break-ins in one week. Eight **Elvis Presley** re-issues came into the fifty in the week of 3 September, 1977, shortly after the artist's death. Nine Jam discs, eight re-entries and one re-issue, came into the expanded seventy-five the week of 22 January, 1983. The occasion this time was the termination of the act. Of its three ex-members Paul Weller fared best in 1983, leading the **Style Council** to four hits, two of them top tenners.

Culture Club was the Group of the Year, however, bagging the best-seller of 1983, 'Karma Chameleon'. George, John, Mikey and Roy released three singles and peaked at one, two and three, an orderly way to conduct a year's business. No act had more than one chart-topper, but they came close. **David Bowie** was nearest, notching up two number twos in addition to his list leader 'Let's Dance'.

It was a fine year for British groups who went on to dominate international hit parades. **Kajagoogoo** began the long march with 'Too Shy', a number one with their first attempt. Despite the subsequent sacking of lead singer **Limahl** they managed to make it three top tenners by year's end. Since for all their fame they had never nabbed a number one, **Duran Duran** may have been irked that 'Too Shy' had been co-produced by their keyboard man Nick Rhodes and former studio mentor Colin Thurston. Any such feelings would have been assuaged when 'Is There Something I Should Know' came straight in at number one the week of 26 March, the fifteenth 45 in history to enter at the top.

In Top Ten terms **Eurythmics** batted four-for-four, tying Michael Jackson for most Top Ten titles. The **Thompson Twins**, whose previous best had been 67, good for golf but mediocre for music, came on strong with three top tenners. Other groups who made noteworthy gains included **Spandau Ballet** and **UB40**, who scored their first number ones, **Modern Romance**, who had their best year with three top tenners, and **Wham**, who achieved three Top Ten placings and 47 weeks on the chart. Breakouts were achieved by **Heaven 17** and **Tears For Fears**, both of whom visited the Top Five twice. The **Police** went all the way with 'Every Breath You Take', America's number one of the year, moving into a tie for eighth in the all-time most number one hits category.

David Bowie, the runner-up to Michael Jackson for top Male Vocalist, was himself nearly caught by **Paul Young**, whose debut solo album yielded three Top Five hits. Otherwise this category proved vital for veterans, with **David Essex, Elton John** and **Rod Stewart** joining Bowie in having their best years since the seventies. Stewart's 'Baby Jane' moved him to joint sixth in the all-time most number ones.

Billy Joel, long America's favourite soloist, finally cracked the British market in a big way, his 'Uptown Girl' finishing second only to 'Karma Chameleon' in the year-end sales tally. Intriguing successes by male vocalists included a Top Ten 12" by **Gary Byrd**, the highest placing by a record issued only in that configuration, and a top ten rap parody by **Kenny Everett**. **Phil Collins** found his first solo number with a Supremes cover and **Elvis Costello** did better under a pseudonym, **The Imposter**, than he did under his real name.

The top female vocalist was someone who was previously considered strictly a comedienne. **Tracey Ullman** had her breakout with 'Breakaway' and proceeded to garner three top

Tracey Ullman not needing her sunglasses.

tenners. The female group **Bananarama** earned two such hits.

Christmas again proved a season unto itself. The year began with 1982's Christmas number one, 'Save Your Love' by **Renée and Renato**, and ended with the **Flying Pickets'** *a cappella* reading of Yazoo's 'Only You'. Neither record started a trend.

1984

No matter how tightly they fastened their seat belts, list lovers had a thrilling ride in 1984. Chart and sales records that had stood for years were broken with impunity. There was no trend in the nature of the standards or the type of artist involved – it was just a great year for record-breaking.

The most coveted title of all, Best Selling Single in British History, changed hands. **Band Aid**, a supergroup assembled by Bob Geldof to benefit Ethiopian famine victims, came straight in at number one with 'Do They Know It's Christmas?'. Combined sales of the 7- and 12-inch versions exceeded three million by year's end, the first time that figure had been reached. In less than 3 weeks the single overtook the previous number one, Wings' 'Mull of Kintyre'.

Oddly, **Paul McCartney** was the leader of Wings, a member of the Beatles, who held the best-selling title for 14 years with 'She Loves You', and a guest artist on 'Do They Know It's Christmas?'. His spoken message was featured on both the B-side of the 7-inch, 'Feed the World', and on the extended 12-inch of the A-side. This means that McCartney has appeared on the three most recent discs to hold the Best Selling Single distinction.

■ Paul set another mark when his 'Pipes of Peace' was a January number one. He became the first artist to top the British chart as a soloist ('Pipes of Peace') and as part of a duo ('Ebony and Ivory' with Stevie Wonder), a trio ('Mull of Kintyre' by Wings), a quartet (16 titles by the Beatles) and a quintet ('Get Back' by the Beatles with Billy Preston). This achievement is unlikely to be surpassed unless McCartney himself makes a record with a fivesome like **Duran Duran** or **Frankie Goes To Hollywood**.

■ The latter Liverpudlians were the act of 1984. Their feats startled even the jaded. By reaching number one with their first three releases, 'Relax', 'Two Tribes' and 'The Power of Love', Frankie equalled the seemingly invincible opening pace of Gerry and the Pacemakers, who had made the debut hat trick in 1963. This earlier lot of Liverpool lads experienced the irony of seeing their 'Ferry Cross the Mersey' on the B-side of 'Relax', a profitable position for writer Gerry Marsden.

■ Frankie spent more weeks on the chart than any other act this year, registering 68 weeks between their three hits. The longest-lived was 'Relax', which spent 5 weeks at number one before dropping down but not out and then surging back to the runner-up position behind 'Two Tribes'. The latter mighty hit entered at number one and totalled 9 weeks on top, the longest run since 'You're the One That I Want' by John Travolta and Olivia Newton-John in 1978. Only two singles, 'Cara Mia' by David Whitfield (10 weeks in 1953) and 'Rose Marie' by Slim Whitman (11 in 1955) have had lengthier uninterrupted stretches at the summit. The FGTH figure of 15 cumulative weeks at number one in a calendar year was the highest since John and Newton-John spent 16 weeks of 1978 together at the top. The British boys were the first act to snare the two top titles in the same week since the slain John Lennon achieved the feat posthumously in 1981.

Frankie Goes To Hollywood

■ In almost any other year **Wham** would have been the top act. George Michael and Andrew Ridgeley tallied two number ones as a duo, 'Wake Me Up Before You Go Go' and 'Freedom'. Michael had a solo number one, 'Careless Whisper', co-written by Ridgeley, and the pair had the Christmas number two, 'Last Christmas/Everything She Wants'. Even these statistics did not tell the full story. The two latter hits sold over a million copies each. The double A-side was the first million seller not to get to number one since the 1962 instrumental 'Stranger on the Shore' by Acker Bilk. It was blocked by the Band Aid side on which Michael himself sang, giving him vocal performances on the two top tracks at Christmas. This was a distinction of note since 1984 was the first year in which the two hottest hits at Christmas were both actually about Christmas. Michael was the first artist to score number ones in a year both as a soloist and as a group member since Gary Numan went all the way in 1979 with Tubeway Army's 'Are "Friends" Electric?' and his own 'Cars'.

■ The sales statistics of Frankie Goes to Hollywood and Wham led British pop in a year when the artists who did well did very well indeed. Six singles sold over a million copies, the most seven-digit sellers in any calendar year. Joining 'Relax', 'Two Tribes', 'Careless Whisper', 'Do They Know It's Christmas?' and 'Last Christmas' was **Stevie Wonder's** 'I Just Called to Say I Love You'. This glorious return after two years of silence gave Wonder his greatest success ever. It sold over 1·8 million by the end of the year, second only to the Band Aid bonanza, and gave the Motown marvel his first number one after over 18 years of chart activity. As detailed in Part 3 of this book, the gap between his first British hit, 'Uptight', and his first number one was the longest waiting period of all-time, eclipsing that of previous record holder Johnny Mathis by one day.

■ 'I Just Called To Say I Love You' was also noteworthy for spending 6 weeks at number one. Before 'Karma Chameleon' did that in late 1983 no disc had led so long in the decade of the eighties. This year 'I Just Called to Say I Love You' and **Lionel Richie's** 'Hello' both went for six and 'Two Tribes' had four and a half weeks for each tribe.

■ Long runs were also a feature of the chart as a whole. 'Relax' had Britain buzzing with yo-yo movements that resulted in 48 weeks on chart, but an only slightly less exciting phenomenon was 'White Lines' by **Grandmaster and Melle Mel.** This New York rap record took months even to get out of the 41–75 bracket. Once it hit the Top Forty it stayed, showing a special affinity for the upper reaches of the Top Ten and the low teens. 'White Lines' zig-zagged for 42 weeks in all and joined 'Relax' in our all-time table of most Consecutive Weeks on Chart (see p. 312). 1984 was the first year since 1973 when more than one hit qualified for this list. 'Agadoo' by **Black Lace** and 'Ghost-busters' by **Ray Parker Jr.,** both among the year's Top Ten sellers, had achieved lengthy runs by year's end and with the Wonder winner seemed poised to join the list in 1985.

■ Another of the year's awesome achievements did not involve spectacular sales, merely the survival and adaptability of the artist. **Eartha Kitt** had her first hit since 1955, easily becoming the act with the greatest gap between hits. 'Where Is My Man?' could easily have been 'Where Is My A&R Man?'

■ Despite her comeback Kitt was not the top female artist of the year. That distinction fell to 45 years-old Annie Mae Bullock a.k.a. **Tina Turner. Nik Kershaw**, who scored five Top 20 hits in 1984 including three which made the Top Five, was the years leading male star.

PART ONE

The British Hit Singles: Alphabetically by Artist

The information given in this part of the book is as follows: Date disc first hit the chart, title, label, catalogue number, highest position reached on chart, number of weeks on the chart, individually by single and in total by artist. Number one records are highlighted with a star, other top ten records by a dot and a dagger indicates hits still on chart at 31 December 1984, as follows:

★ **Number one single**

● **Top ten single**

† **Single still on chart at 31 December 1984**

For the purposes of this book, a record is considered a re-issue if it hits the chart for a second time with a new catalogue number. Otherwise the reappearance of any record is considered a mere re-entry.

Describing a recording act in one sentence is often fraught with danger, but we have attempted to do so above each act's list of hits. Although we are aware that many of the 'vocalists' thus described also play an instrument, we have only mentioned this fact where the artist's instrumental skills were an important factor in the record's success.

For the first time we have calculated the total weeks spent on the chart by every single act to have graced the British Singles charts. This figure appears at the top right of each act's entry. Alert readers will notice that some acts (e.g. Elvis Presley and Cliff Richard) have a weeks grand total that is slightly less than the figure obtained by adding up the weeks totals of each of their hit titles. This is because in the early days of the charts used herein (the *NME* charts of 1951–60) opposite sides of the same disc were sometimes listed simultaneously in different positions (e.g. Cliff's 'Travellin' Light' and 'Dynamite'). In these instances the two sides score 1 week towards the act's total, not 2. A list of all the acts to have registered 100 weeks or more on the chart is to be found at the beginning of Part Three. Catalogue numbers throughout are those of the 7-inch version of the single

A

ABBA
Sweden, male/female vocal/instrumental group   *247 wks*

20 Apr 74	★	WATERLOO	Epic EPC 2240		1	9 wks
13 Jul 74		RING RING	Epic EPC 2452		32	5 wks
12 Jul 75		I DO I DO I DO I DO I DO	Epic EPC 3229		38	6 wks
20 Sep 75	●	S. O. S.	Epic EPC 3576		6	10 wks
13 Dec 75	★	MAMMA MIA	Epic EPC 3790		1	14 wks
27 Mar 76	★	FERNANDO	Epic EPC 4036		1	15 wks
21 Aug 76	★	DANCING QUEEN	Epic EPC 4499		1	15 wks
20 Nov 76	●	MONEY MONEY MONEY	Epic EPC 4713		3	12 wks
26 Feb 77	★	KNOWING ME KNOWING YOU	Epic EPC 4955		1	13 wks
22 Oct 77	★	THE NAME OF THE GAME	Epic EPC 5750		1	12 wks
4 Feb 78	★	TAKE A CHANCE ON ME	Epic EPC 5950		1	10 wks
16 Sep 78	●	SUMMER NIGHT CITY	Epic EPC 6595		5	9 wks
3 Feb 79	●	CHIQUITITA	Epic EPC 7030		2	9 wks
5 May 79	●	DOES YOUR MOTHER KNOW	Epic EPC 7316		4	9 wks
14 Jul 79	●	ANGELEYES/VOULEZ-VOUS	Epic EPC 7499		3	11 wks
20 Oct 79	●	GIMME GIMME GIMME (A MAN AFTER MIDNIGHT)	Epic EPC 7914		3	12 wks
15 Dec 79	●	I HAVE A DREAM	Epic EPC 8088		2	10 wks
2 Aug 80	★	THE WINNER TAKES IT ALL	Epic EPC 8835		1	10 wks
15 Nov 80	★	SUPER TROUPER	Epic EPC 9089		1	12 wks
18 Jul 81	●	LAY ALL YOUR LOVE ON ME	Epic EPC A 1456		7	7 wks
12 Dec 81	●	ONE OF US	Epic EPC A 1740		3	10 wks
20 Feb 82		HEAD OVER HEELS	Epic EPC A 2037		25	7 wks
23 Oct 82		THE DAY BEFORE YOU CAME	Epic EPC A 2847		32	6 wks
11 Dec 82		UNDER ATTACK	Epic EPC A 2971		26	8 wks
12 Nov 83		THANK YOU FOR THE MUSIC	CBS A 3894		33	6 wks

Russ ABBOTT   *UK, male vocalist*   *3 wks*

6 Feb 82	A DAY IN THE LIFE OF VINCE PRINCE	EMI 5249	61	1 wk
20 Feb 82	A DAY IN THE LIFE OF VINCE PRINCE (re-entry) EMI 5249		75	1 wk
29 Dec 84	ATMOSPHERE	Spirit FIRE 4	61†	1 wk

ABC   *UK, male vocal/instrumental group*   *52 wks*

31 Oct 81		TEARS ARE NOT ENOUGH	Neutron NT 101	19	8 wks
20 Feb 82	●	POISON ARROW	Neutron/Phonogram NT 102	6	11 wks
15 May 82	●	THE LOOK OF LOVE	Neutron/Phonogram NT 103	4	11 wks
4 Sep 82	●	ALL OF MY HEART	Neutron/Phonogram NT 104	5	8 wks
15 Jan 83		THE LOOK OF LOVE (re-entry) Neutron/Phonogram NT 103		71	1 wk
5 Nov 83		THAT WAS THEN BUT THIS IS NOW Neutron/Phonogram NT 105		18	4 wks
21 Jan 84		S. O. S.	Neutron/Phonogram NT 106	39	5 wks
10 Nov 84		HOW TO BE A MILLIONAIRE Neutron/Phonogram NT 107		49	4 wks

Father ABRAHAM and the SMURFS
Holland, male vocalist as himself and Smurfs   *36 wks*

3 Jun 78	●	THE SMURF SONG	Decca F 13759	2	17 wks
30 Sep 78		DIPPETY DAY	Decca F 13798	13	12 wks
2 Dec 78		CHRISTMAS IN SMURFLAND	Decca F 13819	19	7 wks

Father ABRAPHART and the SMURPS
UK, male vocal group (Jonathan King under an assumed name)   4 wks

16 Dec 78	LICK A SMURP FOR CHRISTMAS (ALL FALL DOWN) *Petrol GAS 1*	58	4 wks

Hit transferred to Magnet MAG 139 after first week on chart. See also Jonathan King.

AC/DC
Australia/UK, male vocal/instrumental group   74 wks

10 Jun 78	ROCK 'N' ROLL DAMNATION *Atlantic K 11142*	24	9 wks
1 Sep 79	HIGHWAY TO HELL *Atlantic K 11321*	56	4 wks
2 Feb 80	TOUCH TOO MUCH *Atlantic K 11435*	29	9 wks
28 Jun 80	DIRTY DEEDS DONE DIRT CHEAP *Atlantic HM 2*	47	3 wks
28 Jun 80	WHOLE LOTTA ROSIE *Atlantic HM 4*	36	8 wks
28 Jun 80	HIGH VOLTAGE (LIVE VERSION) *Atlantic HM 1*	48	3 wks
28 Jun 80	IT'S A LONG WAY TO THE TOP (IF YOU WANNA ROCK'N'ROLL) *Atlantic HM 3*	55	3 wks
13 Sep 80	YOU SHOOK ME ALL NIGHT LONG *Atlantic K 11600*	38	6 wks
29 Nov 80	ROCK 'N' ROLL AIN'T NOISE POLLUTION *Atlantic K 11630*	15	8 wks
6 Feb 82	LET'S GET IT UP *Atlantic K 11706*	13	6 wks
3 Jul 82	FOR THOSE ABOUT TO ROCK (WE SALUTE YOU) *Atlantic K 11721*	15	6 wks
29 Oct 83	GUNS FOR HIRE *Atlantic A 9774*	37	4 wks
4 Aug 84	NERVOUS SHAKEDOWN *Atlantic A 9651*	35	5 wks

Group Australia only for first 7 hits.

ACE
UK, male vocal/instrumental group   10 wks

9 Nov 74	HOW LONG *Anchor ANC 1002*	20	10 wks

Richard ACE
Jamaica, male vocalist   2 wks

2 Dec 78	STAYIN' ALIVE *Blue Inc. INC 2*	66	2 wks

ACES - *See Desmond DEKKER and the ACES*

ACT ONE
US, male/female vocal/instrumental group   6 wks

18 May 74	TOM THE PEEPER *Mercury 6008 005*	40	6 wks

ADAM and the ANTS
UK, male vocal/instrumental group   182 wks

2 Aug 80	KINGS OF THE WILD FRONTIER *CBS 8877*	48	5 wks
11 Oct 80 ●	DOG EAT DOG *CBS 9039*	4	16 wks
6 Dec 80 ●	ANTMUSIC *CBS 9352*	2	18 wks
27 Dec 80 ●	YOUNG PARISIANS *Decca F13803*	9	13 wks
24 Jan 81	ZEROX *Do It DUN 8*	45	9 wks
24 Jan 81	CARTROUBLE *Do It DUN 10*	33	9 wks
21 Feb 81	KINGS OF THE WILD FRONTIER (re-entry) *CBS 8877*	2	13 wks
9 May 81 ★	STAND AND DELIVER *CBS A 1065*	1	15 wks
12 Sep 81 ★	PRINCE CHARMING *CBS A 1408*	1	12 wks
12 Dec 81	ANT RAP *CBS A 1738*	3	10 wks
27 Feb 82	DEUTSCHER GIRLS *Ego 5*	13	6 wks
13 Mar 82	THE ANTMUSIC EP (THE B-SIDES) *Do It DUN 20*	46	4 wks
22 May 82 ★	GOODY TWO SHOES *CBS A 2367*	1	11 wks
18 Sep 82 ●	FRIEND OR FOE *CBS A 2736*	9	8 wks
27 Nov 82	DESPERATE BUT NOT SERIOUS *CBS A 2892*	33	7 wks
29 Oct 83 ●	PUSS 'N BOOTS *CBS A 3614*	5	12 wks
10 Dec 83	STRIP *CBS A 3589*	41	6 wks
22 Sep 84	APOLLO 9 *CBS A 4719*	13	8 wks

Credited as Adam Ant from Goody Two Shoes onwards. Tracks on The Antmusic EP (The B-sides): Friends/Kick/ Physical.

Arthur ADAMS
US, male vocalist   5 wks

24 Oct 81	YOU GOT THE FLOOR *RCA 146*	38	5 wks

Cliff ADAMS
UK, orchestra   2 wks

28 Apr 60	LONELY MAN THEME *Pye International 7N 25056*	39	2 wks

Gayle ADAMS
US, female vocalist   1 wk

26 Jul 80	STRETCHIN' OUT *Epic EPC 8791*	64	1 wk

Marie ADAMS - *See Johnny OTIS SHOW*

ADDRISI BROTHERS
US, male vocal duo   3 wks

6 Oct 79	GHOST DANCER *Scotti Brothers K 11361*	57	3 wks

ADICTS
UK, male vocal/instrumental group   1 wk

14 May 83	BAD BOY *Razor RZS 104*	75	1 wk

ADVENTURES
UK, male vocal/instrumental group   6 wks

15 Sep 84	ANOTHER SILENT DAY *Chrysalis CHS 2000*	71	2 wks
1 Dec 84	SEND MY HEART *Chrysalis CHS 2001*	62	4 wks

ADVERTS
UK, male/female vocal/instrumental group   11 wks

27 Aug 77	GARY GILMORE'S EYES *Anchor ANC 1043*	18	7 wks
4 Feb 78	NO TIME TO BE 21 *Bright BRI*	38	4 wks

AFTER THE FIRE
UK, male vocal/instrumental group   12 wks

9 Jun 79	ONE RULE FOR YOU *CBS 7025*	40	6 wks
8 Sep 79	LASER LOVE *CBS 7769*	62	2 wks
9 Apr 83	DER KOMMISSAR *CBS A 2399*	47	4 wks

AFTERNOON BOYS - *See YOUNG STEVE and the AFTERNOON BOYS*

AIR SUPPLY
Australia, male vocal/instrumental group   15 wks

27 Sep 80	ALL OUT OF LOVE *Arista ARIST 362*	11	11 wks
2 Oct 82	EVEN THE NIGHTS ARE BETTER *Arista ARIST 474*	44	4 wks

Laurel AITKEN and the UNITONE
Jamaica/Cuba, male vocal/instrumental group   3 wks

17 May 80	RUDI GOT MARRIED *I-Spy SEE 6*	60	3 wks

Jewel AKENS   US, male vocalist   8 wks

25 Mar 65	**THE BIRDS AND THE BEES** *London HLN 9954*		**29**	8 wks

ALARM   UK, male vocal/instrumental group   21 wks

24 Sep 83	**68 GUNS** *I.R.S/A & M PFP 1023*		**17**	7 wks
21 Jan 84	**WHERE WERE YOU HIDING WHEN THE STORM BROKE** *I.R.S IRS 101*		**22**	6 wks
31 Mar 84	**THE DECEIVER** *I.R.S IRS 103*		**51**	4 wks
3 Nov 84	**THE CHANT HAS JUST BEGUN** *I.R.S IRS 114*		**49**	4 wks

Morris ALBERT   Brazil, male vocalist   10 wks

27 Sep 75	● **FEELINGS** *Decca F 13591*		**4**	10 wks

ALBERTO Y LOST TRIOS PARANOIAS
UK, male vocal/instrumental group   5 wks

23 Sep 78	**HEADS DOWN NO NONSENSE MINDLESS BOOGIE** *Logo GO 323*		**47**	5 wks

ALESSI   US, male vocal duo   11 wks

11 Jun 77	● **OH LORI** *A&M AMS 7289*		**8**	11 wks

ALFI and HARRY   US, male vocalist,
David Seville under two false names   5 wks

23 Mar 56	**THE TROUBLE WITH HARRY** *London HLU 8242*		**15**	5 wks

See also David Seville; Chipmunks.

ALL STARS - *See Louis ARMSTRONG*

ALL-STARS - *See Junior WALKER and the ALL-STARS*

Richard ALLAN   UK, male vocalist   1 wk

24 Mar 60	**AS TIME GOES BY** *Parlophone R 4634*		**44**	1 wk

Steve ALLAN   UK, male vocalist   2 wks

27 Jan 79	**TOGETHER WE ARE BEAUTIFUL** *Creole CR 164*		**67**	1 wk
10 Feb 79	**TOGETHER WE ARE BEAUTIFUL** (re-entry) *Creole CR 164*		**70**	1 wk

ALLISONS   UK, male vocal duo   27 wks

23 Feb 61	● **ARE YOU SURE** *Fontana H 294*		**2**	16 wks
18 May 61	**WORDS** *Fontana H 304*		**34**	5 wks
15 Feb 62	**LESSONS IN LOVE** *Fontana H 362*		**30**	6 wks

ALLNIGHT BAND
UK, male instrumental group   3 wks

3 Feb 79	**THE JOKER (THE WIGAN JOKER)** *Casino Classics CC 6*		**50**	3 wks

Marc ALMOND   UK, male vocalist   8 wks

2 Jun 84	**THE BOY WHO CAME BACK** *Some Bizarre/Phonogram BZS 23*		**52**	5 wks
1 Sep 84	**YOU HAVE** *Some Bizarre/Phonogram BZS 24*		**57**	3 wks

Herb ALPERT
US, male instrumentalist - trumpet   90 wks

3 Jan 63	**THE LONELY BULL** *Stateside SS 138*		**22**	9 wks
9 Dec 65	● **SPANISH FLEA** *Pye International 7 N 25335*		**3**	20 wks
24 Mar 66	**TIJUANA TAXI** *Pye International 7 N 25352*		**37**	4 wks
27 Apr 67	**CASINO ROYALE** *A & M AMS 700*		**27**	14 wks
3 Jul 68	● **THIS GUY'S IN LOVE WITH YOU** *A & M AMS 727*		**3**	16 wks
26 Mar 69	**THIS GUY'S IN LOVE WITH YOU** (re-entry) *A & M AMS 727*		**47**	1 wk
9 Apr 69	**THIS GUY'S IN LOVE WITH YOU** (2nd re-entry) *A & M AMS 727*		**49**	1 wk
7 May 69	**THIS GUY'S IN LOVE WITH YOU** (3rd re-entry) *A & M AMS 727*		**50**	1 wk
18 Jun 69	**WITHOUT HER** *A & M AMS 755*		**36**	5 wks
12 Dec 70	**JERUSALEM** *A & M AMS 810*		**47**	1 wk
2 Jan 71	**JERUSALEM** (re-entry) *A & M AMS 810*		**42**	2 wks
13 Oct 79	**RISE** *A & M AMS 7465*		**13**	13 wks
19 Jan 80	**ROTATION** *A & M AMS 7500*		**46**	3 wks

Spanish Flea, Tijuana Taxi, Casino Royale, Without Her and Jerusalem credit Herb Alpert and The Tijuana Brass. The Lonely Bull credits only The Tijuana Brass. Alpert vocalises on This Guy's in Love with You and Without Her.

ALPHABETA - *See Izhar COHEN and ALPHABETA*

ALPHAVILLE
Germany, male vocal/instrumental group   13 wks

18 Aug 84	● **BIG IN JAPAN** *WEA Int. X9505*		**8**	13 wks

ALTERED IMAGES
UK, male/female vocal/instrumental group   60 wks

28 Mar 81	**DEAD POP STARS** *Epic EPC A 1023*		**67**	2 wks
26 Sep 81	● **HAPPY BIRTHDAY** *Epic EPC A 1522*		**2**	17 wks
12 Dec 81	● **I COULD BE HAPPY** *Epic EPC A 1834*		**7**	12 wks
27 Mar 82	**SEE THOSE EYES** *Epic EPC A 2198*		**11**	7 wks
22 May 82	**PINKY BLUE** *Epic EPC A 2426*		**35**	6 wks
19 Mar 83	● **DON'T TALK TO ME ABOUT LOVE** *Epic EPC A 3083*		**7**	7 wks
28 May 83	**BRING ME CLOSER** *Epic EPC A 3398*		**29**	6 wks
16 Jul 83	**LOVE TO STAY** *Epic EPC A 3582*		**46**	3 wks

ALTHIA and DONNA
Jamaica, female vocal duo   11 wks

24 Dec 77	★ **UP TOWN TOP RANKING** *Lightning LIG 506*		**1**	11 wks

AMEN CORNER
UK, male vocal/instrumental group   67 wks

26 Jul 67	**GIN HOUSE BLUES** *Deram DM 136*		**12**	10 wks
11 Oct 67	**WORLD OF BROKEN HEARTS** *Deram DM 151*		**26**	6 wks
17 Jan 68	● **BEND ME SHAPE ME** *Deram DM 172*		**3**	12 wks
31 Jul 68	**HIGH IN THE SKY** *Deram DM 197*		**6**	13 wks
29 Jan 69	★ **(IF PARADISE IS) HALF AS NICE** *Immediate IM 073*		**1**	11 wks
25 Jun 69	● **HELLO SUZIE** *Immediate IM 081*		**4**	10 wks
14 Feb 76	**(IF PARADISE IS) HALF AS NICE** (re-issue) *Immediate IMS 103*		**34**	5 wks

BAY CITY ROLLERS (top left) Barry Blue presents them with silver discs for their fourth hit, 'Summerlove Sensation'.

AMERICAN BREED (top right) Members of this group went on to be part of Rufus.

THE ALARM (below left) Dylan-influenced, Rhyl-based quartet.

ASWAD (below right) Brinsley Forde of the British reggae band who scored first in the Album chart (Photo: Clare Muller.)

AMERICA US, male vocal/instrumental group · 20 wks

Date	Title	Label	Pos	Wks
18 Dec 71	HORSE WITH NO NAME Warner Bros. K 16128		49	2 wks
8 Jan 72 ●	HORSE WITH NO NAME (re-entry) Warner Bros. K 16128		3	11 wks
25 Nov 72	VENTURA HIGHWAY Warner Bros. K 16219		43	4 wks
6 Nov 82	YOU CAN DO MAGIC Capitol CL 264		59	3 wks

AMERICAN BREED
US, male vocal/instrumental group · 6 wks

Date	Title	Label	Pos	Wks
7 Feb 68	BEND ME SHAPE ME Stateside SS 2078		24	6 wks

AMES BROTHERS US, male vocal group · 6 wks

Date	Title	Label	Pos	Wks
4 Feb 55 ●	NAUGHTY LADY OF SHADY LANE HMV B 10800		6	6 wks

Laurie ANDERSON
US, female vocalist/multi-instrumentalist · 6 wks

Date	Title	Label	Pos	Wks
17 Oct 81 ●	O SUPERMAN Warner Bros. K 17870		2	6 wks

Leroy ANDERSON US, orchestra · 4 wks

Date	Title	Label	Pos	Wks
28 Jun 57	FORGOTTEN DREAMS Brunswick 05485		28	1 wk
12 Jul 57	FORGOTTEN DREAMS (re-entry) Brunswick 05485		30	1 wk
6 Sep 57	FORGOTTEN DREAMS (2nd re-entry) Brunswick 05485		24	2 wks

Lynn ANDERSON US, female vocalist · 20 wks

Date	Title	Label	Pos	Wks
20 Feb 71 ●	ROSE GARDEN CBS 5360		3	20 wks

Moira ANDERSON UK, female vocalist · 2 wks

Date	Title	Label	Pos	Wks
27 Dec 69	HOLY CITY Decca F 12989		43	2 wks

Chris ANDREWS UK, male vocalist · 36 wks

Date	Title	Label	Pos	Wks
7 Oct 65 ●	YESTERDAY MAN Decca F 12236		3	15 wks
2 Dec 65	TO WHOM IT CONCERNS Decca F 22285		13	10 wks
14 Apr 66	SOMETHING ON MY MIND Decca F 22365		45	1 wk
28 Apr 66	SOMETHING ON MY MIND (re-entry) Decca F 22365		41	2 wks
2 Jun 66	WHATCHA GONNA DO NOW Decca F 22404		40	4 wks
25 Aug 66	STOP THAT GIRL Decca F 22472		36	4 wks

Eamonn ANDREWS
Ireland, male vocalist · 3 wks

Date	Title	Label	Pos	Wks
20 Jan 56	SHIFTING WHISPERING SANDS (PARTS 1 & 2) Parlophone R 4106		18	3 wks

ANEKA UK, female vocalist · 16 wks

Date	Title	Label	Pos	Wks
8 Aug 81 ★	JAPANESE BOY Hansa HANSA 5		1	12 wks
7 Nov 81	LITTLE LADY Hansa/Ariola HANSA 8		50	4 wks

ANGELETTES UK, female vocal group · 5 wks

Date	Title	Label	Pos	Wks
13 May 72	DON'T LET HIM TOUCH YOU Decca F 13284		35	5 wks

ANGELIC UPSTARTS
UK, male vocal/instrumental group · 30 wks

Date	Title	Label	Pos	Wks
21 Apr 79	I'M AN UPSTART Warner Bros. K 17354		31	8 wks
11 Aug 79	TEENAGE WARNING Warner Bros. K 17426		29	6 wks
3 Nov 79	NEVER 'AD NOTHIN' Warner Bros. K 17476		52	4 wks
9 Feb 80	OUT OF CONTROL Warner Bros. K 17558		58	3 wks
22 Mar 80	WE GOTTA GET OUT OF THIS PLACE Warner Bros. K 17576		65	2 wks
2 Aug 80	LAST NIGHT ANOTHER SOLDIER EMI-Angelic Upstarts Z 7		51	4 wks
7 Feb 81	KIDS ON THE STREET Zonophone Z 16		57	3 wks

Bobby ANGELO and the TUXEDOS
UK, male vocal/instrumental group · 6 wks

Date	Title	Label	Pos	Wks
10 Aug 61	BABY SITTIN' HMV POP 892		30	6 wks

ANGELS US, female vocal group · 1 wk

Date	Title	Label	Pos	Wks
3 Oct 63	MY BOYFRIEND'S BACK Mercury AMT 1211		50	1 wk

ANGELWITCH
UK, male vocal/instrumental group · 1 wk

Date	Title	Label	Pos	Wks
7 Jun 80	SWEET DANGER EMI 5064		75	1 wk

ANIMAL NIGHTLIFE
UK, male/female vocal/instrumental group · 15 wks

Date	Title	Label	Pos	Wks
13 Aug 83	NATURE BOY (UPTOWN) Innervision A3584		60	3 wks
18 Aug 84	MR. SOLITAIRE Island IS 193		25	12 wks

ANIMALS UK, male vocal/instrumental group · 105 wks

Date	Title	Label	Pos	Wks
16 Apr 64	BABY LET ME TAKE YOU HOME Columbia DB 7247		21	8 wks
25 Jun 64 ★	HOUSE OF THE RISING SUN Columbia DB 7301		1	12 wks
17 Sep 64 ●	I'M CRYING Columbia DB 7354		8	10 wks
4 Feb 65 ●	DON'T LET ME BE MISUNDERSTOOD Columbia DB 7445		3	9 wks
8 Apr 65 ●	BRING IT ON HOME TO ME Columbia DB 7539		7	11 wks
15 Jul 65 ●	WE'VE GOTTA GET OUT OF THIS PLACE Columbia DB 7639		2	12 wks
28 Oct 65 ●	IT'S MY LIFE Columbia DB 7741		7	11 wks
17 Feb 66	INSIDE - LOOKING OUT Decca F 12332		12	8 wks
2 Jun 66 ●	DON'T BRING ME DOWN Decca F 12407		6	8 wks
7 Oct 72	HOUSE OF THE RISING SUN (re-issue) RAK RR 1		25	6 wks
18 Sep 82	HOUSE OF THE RISING SUN (re-entry of re-issue) RAK RR 1		11	10 wks

See also Eric Burdon.

Paul ANKA Canada, male vocalist · 123 wks

Date	Title	Label	Pos	Wks
9 Aug 57 ★	DIANA Columbia DB 3980		1	25 wks
8 Nov 57 ●	I LOVE YOU BABY Columbia DB 4022		3	15 wks
8 Nov 57	TELL ME THAT YOU LOVE ME Columbia DB 4022		25	2 wks
31 Jan 58 ●	YOU ARE MY DESTINY Columbia DB 4063		6	13 wks
30 May 58	CRAZY LOVE Columbia DB 4110		26	1 wk
26 Sep 58	MIDNIGHT Columbia DB 4172		26	1 wk
30 Jan 59 ●	(ALL OF A SUDDEN) MY HEART SINGS Columbia DB 4241		10	13 wks
10 Jul 59 ●	LONELY BOY Columbia DB 4324		3	17 wks
1 Jan 60	PUT YOUR HEAD ON MY SHOULDER Columbia DB 4355		17	3 wks

26 Feb 60		IT'S TIME TO CRY	Columbia DB 4390	....	**28**	1 wk
31 Mar 60		PUPPY LOVE	Columbia DB 4434	....	**33**	4 wks
14 Apr 60		IT'S TIME TO CRY	(re-entry) Columbia DB 4390		**47**	1 wk
5 May 60		PUPPY LOVE	(re-entry) Columbia DB 4434	.....	**37**	3 wks
15 Sep 60		HELLO YOUNG LOVERS	Columbia DB 4504	......	**44**	1 wk
15 Mar 62		LOVE ME WARM AND TENDER	RCA 1276	..	**19**	11 wks
26 Jul 62		A STEEL GUITAR AND A GLASS OF WINE				
			RCA 1292	....	**41**	4 wks
28 Sep 74	●	(YOU'RE) HAVING MY BABY				
			United Artists UP 35713	....	**6**	10 wks

ANKLEBITERS - *See Fogwell FLAX and the ANKLEBITERS from FREEHOLD
JUNIOR SCHOOL*

Billie ANTHONY *UK, female vocalist* *16 wks*

| 15 Oct 54 | ● | THIS OLE HOUSE | Columbia DB 3519 | .... | **4** | 16 wks |

Miki ANTHONY *UK, male vocalist* *7 wks*

| 3 Feb 73 | | IF IT WASN'T FOR THE REASON THAT I LOVE | | | | |
| | | YOU | Bell 1275 | .... | **27** | 7 wks |

Ray ANTHONY *US, orchestra* *2 wks*

| 4 Dec 53 | ● | DRAGNET | Capitol CL 13983 | .... | **7** | 1 wk |
| 8 Jan 54 | | DRAGNET | (re-entry) Capitol CL 13983 | .... | **11** | 1 wk |

Richard ANTHONY

France, male vocalist *15 wks*

12 Dec 63		WALKING ALONE	Columbia DB 7133	....	**37**	5 wks
2 Apr 64		IF I LOVED YOU	Columbia DB 7235	....	**48**	1 wk
23 Apr 64		IF I LOVED YOU	(re-entry) Columbia DB 7235	..	**18**	9 wks

ANTI-NOWHERE LEAGUE

UK, male vocal/instrumental group *10 wks*

23 Jan 82		STREETS OF LONDON	WXYZ ABCD 1	.....	**48**	5 wks
20 Mar 82		I HATE ... PEOPLE	WXYZ ABCD 2	....	**46**	3 wks
3 Jul 82		WOMAN	WXYZ ABCD 4	....	**72**	2 wks

ANTI-PASTI - *See EXPLOITED and ANTI-PASTI*

ANTS - *See ADAM and the ANTS*

APHRODITE'S CHILD

Greece, male vocal/instrumental group *7 wks*

| 6 Nov 68 | | RAIN AND TEARS | Mercury MF 1039 | .... | **30** | 7 wks |

APPLEJACKS

UK, male/female vocal/instrumental group *29 wks*

5 Mar 64	●	TELL ME WHEN	Decca F 11833	....	**7**	13 wks
11 Jun 64		LIKE DREAMERS DO	Decca F 11916	....	**20**	11 wks
15 Oct 64		THREE LITTLE WORDS	Decca F 11981	......	**23**	5 wks

Charlie APPLEWHITE

US, male vocalist *1 wk*

| 23 Sep 55 | | BLUE STAR (THE MEDIC THEME) | | | | |
| | | | Brunswick 05416 | .... | **20** | 1 wk |

Helen APRIL - *See John DUMMER and Helen APRIL*

APRIL WINE

Canada, male vocal/instrumental group *9 wks*

15 Mar 80		I LIKE TO ROCK	Capitol CL 16121	....	**41**	5 wks
11 Apr 81		JUST BETWEEN YOU AND ME				
			Capitol CL 16184	....	**52**	4 wks

AQUARIAN DREAM

US, male/female vocal/instrumental group *1 wk*

| 24 Feb 79 | | YOU'RE A STAR | Elektra LV 7 | .... | **67** | 1 wk |

ARCHIES *US, male/female vocal group* *26 wks*

| 11 Oct 69 | ★ | SUGAR SUGAR | RCA 1872 | .... | **1** | 26 wks |

ARGENT *UK, male vocal/instrumental group* *27 wks*

4 Mar 72	●	HOLD YOUR HEAD UP	Epic EPC 7786	....	**5**	12 wks
10 Jun 72		TRAGEDY	Epic EPC 8115	....	**34**	7 wks
24 Mar 73		GOD GAVE ROCK & ROLL TO YOU				
			Epic EPC 1243	....	**18**	8 wks

Ship's Company and Royal Marine band of H.M.S. ARK ROYAL

UK, male choir and Marine band *6 wks*

| 23 Dec 78 | | THE LAST FAREWELL | BBC RESL 61 | .... | **46** | 6 wks |

Joan ARMATRADING

UK, female vocalist *48 wks*

16 Oct 76	●	LOVE AND AFFECTION	A & M AMS 7249	..	**10**	9 wks
23 Feb 80		ROSIE	A & M AMS 7506	....	**49**	5 wks
14 Jun 80		ME MYSELF I	A & M AMS 7527	....	**21**	11 wks
6 Sep 80		ALL THE WAY FROM AMERICA				
			A & M AMS 7552	....	**54**	3 wks
12 Sep 81		I'M LUCKY	A & M AMS 8163	....	**46**	5 wks
16 Jan 82		NO LOVE	A & M AMS 8179	....	**50**	5 wks
19 Feb 83		DROP THE PILOT	A & M AMS 8306	....	**11**	10 wks

ARMOURY SHOW

UK, male vocal/instrumental group *2 wks*

| 25 Aug 84 | | CASTLES IN SPAIN | Parlophone R 6079 | .... | **69** | 2 wks |

Louis ARMSTRONG

US, male band leader/trumpet and vocals *75 wks*

19 Dec 52	●	TAKES TWO TO TANGO	Brunswick 04995	.....	**6**	10 wks
13 Apr 56	●	THEME FROM THE THREEPENNY OPERA				
			Philips PB 574	....	**8**	11 wks
15 Jun 56		TAKE IT SATCH (EP)	Philips BBE 12035	......	**29**	1 wk
13 Jul 56		THE FAITHFUL HUSSAR	Philips PB 604	......	**27**	2 wks
6 Nov 59		MACK THE KNIFE	Philips PB 967	....	**24**	1 wk
4 Jun 64	●	HELLO DOLLY	London HLR 9878	....	**4**	14 wks
7 Feb 68	★	WHAT A WONDERFUL WORLD/CABARET				
			HMV POP 1615	....	**1**	29 wks
26 Jun 68		SUNSHINE OF LOVE	Stateside SS 2116	....	**41**	7 wks

Take It Satch tracks: *Tiger Rag/Mack the Knife/ The Faithful Hussar/Back O' Town Blues*.
Mack the Knife *is a re-issue of* Theme From the Threepenny Opera *under a different
title*. Cabaret *was not listed with* What a Wonderful World *until 14 Feb 68. The four hits
on Philips are all credited to Louis Armstrong with his All Stars.*

ARNIE'S LOVE
US, male/female vocal/instrumental group — *3 wks*

26 Nov 83	I'M OUT OF YOUR LIFE	*Streetwave WAVE 9* ..	67	3 wks

Eddy ARNOLD *US, male vocalist* — *21 wks*

17 Feb 66	● MAKE THE WORLD GO AWAY	*RCA 1496* ...	8	17 wks
26 May 66	I WANT TO GO WITH YOU	*RCA 1519*	49	1 wk
9 Jun 66	I WANT TO GO WITH YOU (re-entry) *RCA 1519*		46	2 wks
28 Jul 66	IF YOU WERE MINE MARY	*RCA 1529*	49	1 wk

P. P. ARNOLD *US, female vocalist* — *27 wks*

4 May 67	FIRST CUT IS THE DEEPEST	*Immediate IM 047*	18	10 wks
2 Aug 67	THE TIME HAS COME	*Immediate IM 055*	47	2 wks
24 Jan 68	GROOVY	*Immediate IM 061*	41	4 wks
10 Jul 68	ANGEL OF THE MORNING	*Immediate IM 067*	29	11 wks

ARPEGGIO *US, male/female vocal group* — *3 wks*

31 Mar 79	LOVE AND DESIRE (PART 1)	*Polydor POSP 40*	63	3 wks

ARRIVAL
UK, male/female vocal/instrumental group — *20 wks*

10 Jan 70	● FRIENDS	*Decca F 12986*	8	9 wks
6 Jun 70	I WILL SURVIVE	*Decca F 13026*	16	11 wks

ARROW *Monserrat, male vocalist* — *5 wks*

28 Jul 84	HOT HOT HOT	*Cool Tempo/Chrysalis ARROW 1*	59	5 wks

ARROWS
US/UK, male vocal/instrumental group — *16 wks*

25 May 74	● A TOUCH TOO MUCH	*RAK 171*	8	9 wks
1 Feb 75	MY LAST NIGHT WITH YOU	*RAK 189*	25	7 wks

ARSENAL F.C. FIRST TEAM SQUAD *UK, male football team vocalists* — *7 wks*

8 May 71	GOOD OLD ARSENAL	*Pye 7N 45067*	16	7 wks

ART COMPANY
Holland, male vocal/instrumental group — *11 wks*

26 May 84	SUSANNA	*Epic A 4174*	12	11 wks

ASHAYE *UK, male vocalist* — *3 wks*

15 Oct 83	MICHAEL JACKSON MEDLEY *Record Shack SOHO 10*		45	3 wks

Tracks on medley: Don't Stop Til You Get Enough, Wanna Be Startin' Something, Shake Your Body Down To The Ground, Blame It On The Boogie.

John ASHER *UK, male vocalist* — *6 wks*

15 Nov 75	LET'S TWIST AGAIN	*Creole CR 112*	14	6 wks

ASHFORD and SIMPSON
US, male/female vocal duo — *4 wks*

18 Nov 78	IT SEEMS TO HANG ON	*Warner Bros. K 17237*	48	4 wks

ASHTON, GARDNER AND DYKE
UK, male vocal/instrumental group — *14 wks*

16 Jan 71	● RESURRECTION SHUFFLE	*Capitol CL 15665* ..	3	14 wks

ASIA *UK, male vocal/instrumental group* — *13 wks*

3 Jul 82	HEAT OF THE MOMENT	*Geffen GEF A2494*	46	5 wks
18 Sep 82	ONLY TIME WILL TELL	*Geffen GEF A2228*	54	3 wks
13 Aug 83	DON'T CRY	*Geffen A 3580*	33	5 wks

ASSEMBLY
UK, male vocal/instrumental group — *10 wks*

12 Nov 83	● NEVER NEVER	*Mute TINY 1*	4	10 wks

ASSOCIATES
UK, male vocal/instrumental group — *38 wks*

20 Feb 82	● PARTY FEARS TWO	*Associates ASC 1*	9	10 wks
8 May 82	CLUB COUNTRY	*Associates ASC 2*	13	10 wks
7 Aug 82	18 CARAT LOVE AFFAIR/LOVE HANGOVER *Associates ASC 3*		21	8 wks
16 Jun 84	THOSE FIRST IMPRESSIONS	*WEA YZ 6*	43	6 wks
1 Sep 84	WAITING FOR THE LOVE BOAT	*WEA YZ 16*	53	4 wks

18 Carat Love Affair *listed until 28 Aug only. Act was duo on 1982 hits*

ASSOCIATION
US, male vocal/instrumental group — *8 wks*

22 May 68	TIME FOR LIVING	*Warner Bros. WB 7195*	23	8 wks

ASWAD *UK, male vocal/instrumental group* — *6 wks*

3 Mar 84	CHASING FOR THE BREEZE	*Island IS 160* ...	51	3 wks
6 Oct 84	54-46 (WAS MY NUMBER)	*Island IS 170*	70	3 wks

Gali ATARI - *See MILK AND HONEY*

Chet ATKINS
US, male instrumentalist – guitar — *2 wks*

17 Mar 60	TEENSVILLE	*RCA 1174*	46	1 wk
5 May 60	TEENSVILLE (re-entry) *RCA 1174*		49	1 wk

ATLANTA RHYTHM SECTION
US, male vocal/instrumental group — *4 wks*

27 Oct 79	SPOOKY	*Polydor POSP 74*	48	4 wks

ATLANTIC STARR
US, male/female vocal/instrumental group — *3 wks*

9 Sep 78	GIMME YOUR LOVIN'	*A & M AMS 7380*	66	3 wks

ATMOSFEAR
UK, male vocal/instrumental group   *7 wks*

17 Nov 79	**DANCING IN OUTER SPACE** *MCA 543*	**46**	7 wks

ATOMIC ROOSTER
UK, male vocal/instrumental group   *25 wks*

6 Feb 71	**TOMORROW NIGHT** *B & C CB 131*	**11**	12 wks
10 Jul 71	● **THE DEVIL'S ANSWER** *B & C CB 157*	**4**	13 wks

ATTRACTIONS - *See Elvis COSTELLO and the ATTRACTIONS*

Winifred ATWELL
UK, female instrumentalist - piano   *117 wks*

12 Dec 52	**BRITANNIA RAG** *Decca F 10015*	**11**	1 wk
9 Jan 53	● **BRITANNIA RAG** (re-entry) *Decca F 10015*	**5**	5 wks
15 May 53	● **CORONATION RAG** *Decca F 10110*	**12**	1 wk
29 May 53	● **CORONATION RAG** (re-entry) *Decca F 10110* ..	**5**	5 wks
25 Sep 53	● **FLIRTATION WALTZ** *Decca F 10181*	**12**	1 wk
9 Oct 53	● **FLIRTATION WALTZ** (re-entry) *Decca F 10181*	**10**	1 wk
6 Nov 53	**FLIRTATION WALTZ** (2nd re-entry) *Decca F10181*	**12**	1 wk
4 Dec 53	● **LET'S HAVE A PARTY** *Philips PB 213*	**2**	9 wks
23 Jul 54	● **RACHMANINOFF'S 18TH VARIATION ON A THEME BY PAGANINI** *Philips PB 234*	**9**	7 wks
1 Oct 54	**RACHMANINOFF'S 18TH VARIATION ON A THEME BY PAGANINI** (re-entry) *Philips PB 234*	**19**	2 wks
26 Nov 54	**LET'S HAVE A PARTY** (re-entry) *Philips PB 213*	**14**	6 wks
26 Nov 54	★ **LET'S HAVE ANOTHER PARTY** *Philips PB 268*	**1**	8 wks
4 Nov 55	● **LET'S HAVE A DING DONG** *Decca F 10634* ...	**3**	10 wks
16 Mar 56	★ **POOR PEOPLE OF PARIS** *Decca F 10681*	**1**	16 wks
18 May 56	**PORT AU PRINCE** *Decca F 10727*	**18**	6 wks
20 Jul 56	**LEFT BANK** *Decca F 10762*	**14**	7 wks
26 Oct 56	● **MAKE IT A PARTY** *Decca F 10796*	**7**	12 wks
22 Feb 57	**LET'S ROCK 'N ROLL** *Decca F 10852*	**28**	2 wks
15 Mar 57	**LET'S ROCK 'N ROLL** (re-entry) *Decca F 10852*	**24**	2 wks
6 Dec 57	● **LET'S HAVE A BALL** *Decca F 10956*	**4**	6 wks
7 Aug 59	**SUMMER OF THE SEVENTEENTH DOLL** *Decca F 11143*	**24**	2 wks
27 Nov 59	● **PIANO PARTY** *Decca F 11183*	**10**	7 wks

Various hits listed above were medleys as follows: Let's Have a Party: Boomps A Daisy/Daisy Bell/If You Knew Suzie/ Knees Up Mother Brown/The More We Are Together/She Was One Of The Early Birds/That's My Weakness Now/Three O'Clock In The Morning. Let's Have Another Party: Another Little Drink/Broken Doll/Bye Bye Blackbird/Honeysuckle And The Bee/I Wonder Where My Baby Is Tonight/Lily of Laguna/Nellie Dean/Sheik of Araby/Somebody Stole My Gal/When The Red Red Robin. Let's Have a Ding Dong: Happy Days Are Here Again/Oh Johnny Oh Johnny Oh/Oh You Beautiful Doll/Ain't She Sweet/Yes We Have No Bananas/I'm Forever Blowing Bubbles/I'll Be Your Sweetheart/ If These Lips Could Only Speak/Who's Taking You Home Tonight. Make It a Party: Who Were You With Last Night/Hello Hello Who's Your Lady Friend/Yes Sir That's My Baby/Don't Dilly Dally On The Way/Beer Barrel Polka/After The Ball/ Peggy O'Neil/Meet Me Tonight In Dreamland/I Belong To Glasgow/Down At The Old Bull And Bush. Let's Rock 'n Roll: Singin' The Blues/Green Door/See You Later Alligator/Shake Rattle and Roll/Rock Around The Clock/Razzle Dazzle. Let's Have a Ball: Music Music Music/This Ole House/Heartbreaker/Woody Woodpecker/Last Train to San Fernando/Bring A Little Water Sylvie/ Puttin' On The Style/Don't You Rock Me Daddy-O. Piano Party: Baby Face/Comin' Thru' The Rye/Annie Laurie/Little Brown Jug/Let Him Go Let Him Tarry/Put Your Arms Around Me Honey/ I'll Be With You In Apple Blossom Time/Shine On Harvest Moon/Blue Skies/I'll Never Say Never Again/I'll See You In My Dreams. See also Various Artists - All Star Hit Parade.

Brian AUGER - *See Julie DRISCOLL, Brian AUGER and the TRINITY*

David AUSTIN *UK, male vocalist*   *3 wks*

21 Jul 84	**TURN TO GOLD** *Parlophone R 6068*	**68**	3 wks

Patti AUSTIN and James INGRAM
US, female/male vocal duo   *10 wks*

12 Feb 83	**BABY, COME TO ME** *Qwest K 15005*	**11**	10 wks

AUTUMN *UK, male vocal/instrumental group*   *6 wks*

16 Oct 71	**MY LITTLE GIRL** *Pye 7N 45090*	**37**	6 wks

Frankie AVALON *US, male vocalist*   *15 wks*

10 Oct 58	**GINGERBREAD** *HMV POP 517*	**30**	1 wk
24 Apr 59	**VENUS** *HMV POP 603*	**16**	6 wks
22 Jan 60	**WHY** *HMV POP 688*	**20**	4 wks
28 Apr 60	**DON'T THROW AWAY ALL THOSE TEARDROPS** *HMV POP 727*	**37**	4 wks

AVALON BOYS - *See LAUREL and HARDY with the AVALON BOYS*

AVERAGE WHITE BAND
UK, male vocal/instrumental vocal group   *45 wks*

22 Feb 75	● **PICK UP THE PIECES** *Atlantic K 10489*	**6**	9 wks
26 Apr 75	**CUT THE CAKE** *Atlantic K 10605*	**31**	4 wks
9 Oct 76	**QUEEN OF MY SOUL** *Atlantic K 10825*	**23**	7 wks
28 Apr 79	**WALK ON BY** *RCA XC 1087*	**46**	5 wks
25 Aug 79	**WHEN WILL YOU BE MINE** *RCA XB 1096*	**49**	5 wks
26 Apr 80	**LET'S GO ROUND AGAIN PT.1** *RCA AWB 1*	**12**	11 wks
26 Jul 80	**FOR YOU FOR LOVE** *RCA AWB 2*	**46**	4 wks

AVONS *UK, male/female vocal group*   *22 wks*

13 Nov 59	● **SEVEN LITTLE GIRLS SITTING IN THE BACK SEAT** *Columbia DB 4363*	**3**	13 wks
7 Jul 60	**WE'RE ONLY YOUNG ONCE** *Columbia DB 4461*	**49**	1 wk
21 Jul 60	**WE'RE ONLY YOUNG ONCE** (re-entry) *Columbia DB 4461*	**45**	1 wk
27 Oct 60	**FOUR LITTLE HEELS** *Columbia DB 4522*	**45**	2 wks
1 Dec 60	**FOUR LITTLE HEELS** (re-entry) *Columbia DB 4522*	**49**	1 wk
26 Jan 61	**RUBBER BALL** *Columbia DB 4569*	**30**	4 wks

Hoyt AXTON *US, male vocalist*   *4 wks*

7 Jun 80	**DELLA AND THE DEALER** *Young Blood YB 82*	**48**	4 wks

Roy AYERS
US, male vocalist/instrumentalist - vibraphone   *7 wks*

21 Oct 78	**GET ON UP, GET ON DOWN** *Polydor AYERS 7*	**41**	4 wks
2 Feb 80	**DON'T STOP THE FEELING** *Polydor STEP 6* ..	**56**	3 wks

See also Roy Ayers and Wayne Henderson.

Roy AYERS and Wayne HENDERSON *US, male duo (Ayers vocalist/instrumentalist - vibraphone, Henderson instrumentalist - trombone)*   *5 wks*

13 Jan 79	**HEAT OF THE BEAT** *Polydor POSP 16*	**43**	5 wks

See also Roy Ayers.

Charles AZNAVOUR
France, male vocalist   *29 wks*

22 Sep 73	THE OLD FASHIONED WAY *Barclay BAR 20*	50	1 wk
20 Oct 73	THE OLD FASHIONED WAY (re-entry)		
	Barclay BAR 20	38	12 wks
22 Jun 74	★ SHE *Barclay BAR 26*	1	14 wks
27 Jul 74	THE OLD FASHIONED WAY (2nd re-entry)		
	Barclay BAR 20	47	2 wks

AZTEC CAMERA
UK, male vocal/instrumental group   *27 wks*

19 Feb 83	OBLIVIOUS *Rough Trade RT 122*	46	6 wks
4 Jun 83	WALK OUT TO WINTER *Rough Trade RT 132*	64	4 wks
5 Nov 83	OBLIVIOUS (re-issue) *WEA AZTEC 1*	18	11 wks
1 Sep 84	ALL I NEED IS EVERYTHING *WEA AC 1*	34	6 wks

AZYMUTH   *Brazil, male instrumental group*   *8 wks*

| 12 Jan 80 | JAZZ CARNIVAL *Milestone MSP 101* | 19 | 8 wks |

Bob AZZAM   *Egypt, singing orchestra*   *14 wks*

| 26 May 60 | MUSTAPHA *Decca F 21235* | 23 | 14 wks |

B

B, B, and Q BAND
US, male vocal/instrumental group   *5 wks*

| 18 Jul 81 | ON THE BEAT *Capitol CL 202* | 41 | 5 wks |

B. B. S. UNLIMITED - *See Eddie DRENNON and B. B. S. UNLIMITED*

B-52'S
US, male/female vocal/instrumental group   *10 wks*

11 Aug 79	ROCK LOBSTER *Island WIP 6506*	37	5 wks
9 Aug 80	GIVE ME BACK MY MAN *Island WIP 6579*	61	3 wks
7 May 83	FUTURE GENERATION *Island IS 107*	63	2 wks

B-MOVIE   *UK, male vocal/instrumental group*   *7 wks*

| 18 Apr 81 | REMEMBRANCE DAY *Deram DM 437* | 61 | 3 wks |
| 27 Mar 82 | NOWHERE GIRL *Some Bizzare BZZ 8* | 67 | 4 wks |

B. T. EXPRESS
US, male instrumental/vocal group   *10 wks*

29 Mar 75	EXPRESS *Pye International 7N 25674*	34	6 wks
26 Jul 80	DOES IT FEEL GOOD/GIVE UP THE FUNK		
	(LET'S DANCE) *Calibre CAB 503*	52	4 wks

Alice BABS   *Sweden, female vocalist*   *1 wk*

| 15 Aug 63 | AFTER YOU'VE GONE *Fontana TF 409* | 43 | 1 wk |

BABY O
US, male/female vocal/instrumental group   *5 wks*

| 26 Jul 80 | IN THE FOREST *Calibre CAB 505* | 46 | 5 wks |

BABYS   *US/UK, male vocal/instrumental group*   *3 wks*

| 21 Jan 78 | ISN'T IT TIME *Chrysalis CHS 2173* | 45 | 3 wks |

BACCARA   *Spain, female vocal duo*   *25 wks*

| 17 Sep 77 | ★ YES SIR I CAN BOOGIE *RCA PB 5526* | 1 | 16 wks |
| 14 Jan 78 | ● SORRY I'M A LADY *RCA PB 5555* | 8 | 9 wks |

Burt BACHARACH
US, orchestra and chorus   *11 wks*

| 20 May 65 | ● TRAINS AND BOATS AND PLANES | | |
| | *London HL 9968* | 4 | 11 wks |

BACHELORS   *Ireland, male vocal group*   *187 wks*

24 Jan 63	● CHARMAINE *Decca F 11559*	6	19 wks
4 Jul 63	FARAWAY PLACES *Decca F 11666*	36	3 wks
29 Aug 63	WHISPERING *Decca F 11712*	18	10 wks
23 Jan 64	★ DIANE *Decca F 11799*	1	19 wks
19 Mar 64	● I BELIEVE *Decca F 11857*	2	17 wks
4 Jun 64	● RAMONA *Decca F 11910*	4	13 wks
13 Aug 64	● I WOULDN'T TRADE YOU FOR THE WORLD		
	Decca F 11949	4	16 wks
3 Dec 64	● NO ARMS CAN EVER HOLD YOU		
	Decca F 12034	7	12 wks
1 Apr 65	TRUE LOVE FOR EVER MORE *Decca F 12108*	34	6 wks
20 May 65	● MARIE *Decca F 12156*	9	12 wks
28 Oct 65	IN THE CHAPEL IN THE MOONLIGHT		
	Decca F 12256	27	10 wks
6 Jan 66	HELLO DOLLY *Decca F 12309*	38	4 wks
17 Mar 66	● THE SOUND OF SILENCE *Decca F 12351*	3	13 wks
7 Jul 66	CAN I TRUST YOU *Decca F 12417*	26	7 wks
1 Dec 66	WALK WITH FAITH IN YOUR HEART		
	Decca F 22523	22	9 wks
6 Apr 67	OH HOW I MISS YOU *Decca F 22592*	30	8 wks
5 Jul 67	MARTA *Decca F 22634*	20	9 wks

BACHMAN-TURNER OVERDRIVE
Canada, male vocal/instrumental group   *18 wks*

16 Nov 74	● YOU AIN'T SEEN NOTHIN' YET		
	Mercury 6167 025	2	12 wks
1 Feb 75	ROLL ON DOWN THE HIGHWAY		
	Mercury 6167 071	22	6 wks

BAD COMPANY
UK, male vocal/instrumental group   *23 wks*

1 Jun 74	CAN'T GET ENOUGH *Island WIP 6191*	15	8 wks
22 Mar 75	GOOD LOVIN' GONE BAD *Island WIP 6223*	31	6 wks
30 Aug 75	FEEL LIKE MAKIN' LOVE *Island WIP 6242*	20	9 wks

BAD MANNERS
UK, male vocal/instrumental group   *111 wks*

1 Mar 80	NE-NE NA-NA NA-NA NU-NU		
	Magnet MAG 164	28	14 wks
14 Jun 80	LIP UP FATTY *Magnet MAG 175*	15	14 wks
27 Sep 80	● SPECIAL BREW *Magnet MAG 180*	3	13 wks
6 Dec 80	LORRAINE *Magnet MAG 181*	21	12 wks
28 Mar 81	JUST A FEELING *Magnet MAG 187*	13	9 wks
27 Jun 81	● CAN CAN *Magnet MAG 190*	3	13 wks
26 Sep 81	● WALKING IN THE SUNSHINE		
	Magnet MAG 197	10	9 wks
21 Nov 81	BUONA SERA *Magnet MAG 211*	34	9 wks
1 May 82	GOT NO BRAINS *Magnet MAG 216*	44	5 wks

BEATLES (top) In front of a couple of dozen people at a hall in Aldershot in 1961 – the year they changed their name from the Silver Beatles. **BAD COMPANY** (left) Simon Kirke started with Paul Kossoff in London's Blues Band Black Cat Bones (1967–8) before they formed Free with Andy Fraser and Paul Rodgers. After a brief interlude Rodgers and Kirke joined with Boz Burrell and Mick Ralphs, under the name Bad Company.

JOE BROWN and BILLY FURY (above) 'A Picture of You' in a 'Wonderous Place!' Bespectacled Billy Fury and Joe Brown bump into three fans out shopping.

31 Jul 82	●	MY GIRL LOLLIPOP (MY BOY LOLLIPOP)			
		Magnet MAG 232		9	7 wks
30 Oct 82		SAMSON AND DELILAH	Magnet MAG 236	58	3 wks
14 May 83		THAT'LL DO NICELY	Magnet MAG 243	49	3 wks

BADFINGER
UK, male vocal/instrumental group   *34 wks*

10 Jan 70	●	COME AND GET IT	Apple 20	4	11 wks
9 Jan 71	●	NO MATTER WHAT	Apple 31	5	12 wks
29 Jan 72	●	DAY AFTER DAY	Apple 40	10	11 wks

Joan BAEZ   *US, female vocalist*   *47 wks*

6 May 65		WE SHALL OVERCOME	Fontana TF 564	26	10 wks
8 Jul 65	●	THERE BUT FOR FORTUNE	Fontana TF 587	8	12 wks
2 Sep 65		IT'S ALL OVER NOW BABY BLUE			
		Fontana TF 604		22	8 wks
23 Dec 65		FAREWELL ANGELINA	Fontana TF 639	35	3 wks
20 Jan 66		FAREWELL ANGELINA (re-entry)			
		Fontana TF 639		49	1 wk
28 Jul 66		PACK UP YOUR SORROWS	Fontana TF 727	50	1 wk
9 Oct 71	●	THE NIGHT THEY DROVE OLD DIXIE DOWN			
		Vanguard VS 35138		6	12 wks

Adrian BAKER   *UK, male vocalist*   *8 wks*

19 Jul 75	●	SHERRY	Magnet MAG 34	10	8 wks

Hylda BAKER and Arthur MULLARD   *UK, female/male vocal duo*   *6 wks*

9 Sep 78		YOU'RE THE ONE THAT I WANT			
		Pye 7N 46121		22	6 wks

George BAKER SELECTION
Holland, male/female vocal/instrumental group   *10 wks*

6 Sep 75	●	PALOMA BLANCA	Warner Bros. K 16541	10	10 wks

Long John BALDRY   *UK, male vocalist*   *36 wks*

8 Nov 67	★	LET THE HEARTACHES BEGIN	Pye 7N 17385	1	13 wks
28 Aug 68		WHEN THE SUN COMES SHININ' THRU			
		Pye 7N 17593		29	7 wks
23 Oct 68		MEXICO	Pye 7N 17563	15	8 wks
29 Jan 69		IT'S TOO LATE NOW	Pye 7N 17664	21	8 wks

Kenny BALL and his JAZZMEN
UK, male band, Kenny Ball vocals and trumpet   *136 wks*

23 Feb 61		SAMANTHA	Pye Jazz Today 7NJ 2040	13	15 wks
11 May 61		I STILL LOVE YOU ALL	Pye Jazz 7NJ 2042	24	6 wks
31 Aug 61		SOMEDAY	Pye Jazz 7NJ 2047	28	6 wks
9 Nov 61	●	MIDNIGHT IN MOSCOW	Pye Jazz 7NJ 2049	2	21 wks
15 Feb 62	●	MARCH OF THE SIAMESE CHILDREN			
		Pye Jazz 7NJ 2051		4	13 wks
17 May 62	●	THE GREEN LEAVES OF SUMMER			
		Pye Jazz 7NJ 2054		7	14 wks
23 Aug 62		SO DO I	Pye Jazz 7NJ 2056	14	8 wks
18 Oct 62		THE PAY OFF	Pye Jazz 7NJ 2061	23	6 wks
17 Jan 63	●	SUKIYAKI	Pye Jazz 7NJ 2062	10	13 wks
25 Apr 63		CASABLANCA	Pye Jazz 7NJ 2064	21	11 wks
13 Jun 63		RONDO	Pye Jazz 7NJ 2065	24	8 wks
22 Aug 63		ACAPULCO 1922	Pye Jazz 7NJ 2067	27	6 wks
11 Jun 64		HELLO DOLLY	Pye Jazz 7NJ 2071	30	7 wks
19 Jul 67		WHEN I'M 64	Pye 7N 17348	43	2 wks

Afrika BAMBAATA and James BROWN   *US, male vocal duo*   *5 wks*

1 Sep 84		UNITY (PART 1-THE THIRD COMING)		
		Tommy Boy/Polydor AFR 2	49	5 wks

See also James Brown.

Afrika BAMBAATA and the SOUL SONIC FORCE   *US, male vocalist and male vocal/instumental backing group*   *7 wks*

28 Aug 82		PLANET BOOK	21/Polydor POSP 497	53	3 wks
10 Mar 84		RENEGADES OF FUNK			
		Tommy Boy/Polydor AFR 1	30	4 wks

BANANARAMA   *UK, female vocal group*   *68 wks*

10 Apr 82	●	REALLY SAYING SOMETHING			
		Deram NANA 1		5	10 wks
3 Jul 82	●	SHY BOY	London NANA 2	4	11 wks
4 Dec 82		CHEERS THEN	London NANA 3	45	7 wks
26 Feb 83	●	NA NA HEY HEY KISS HIM GOODBYE			
		London NANA 4		5	10 wks
9 Jul 83	●	CRUEL SUMMER	London NANA 5	8	10 wks
3 Mar 84	●	ROBERT DE NIRO'S WAITING			
		London NANA 6		3	11 wks
26 May 84		ROUGH JUSTICE	London NANA 7	23	7 wks
24 Nov 84		HOTLINE TO HEAVEN	London NANA 8	58	2 wks

Really Saying Something *credited to Bananarama with Funboy Three. See also Funboy Three; Funboy Three and Bananarama.*

BAND   *Canada, male vocal/instrumental group*   *18 wks*

18 Sep 68	THE WEIGHT	Capitol CL 15559	21	9 wks
4 Apr 70	RAG MAMA RAG	Capitol CL 15629	16	9 wks

BAND AID   *International, male/female vocal/instrumental group*   *3 wks*

15 Dec 84	★	DO THEY KNOW IT'S CHRISTMAS?		
		Mercury/Phonogram FEED 1	1†	3 wks

BAND AKA
US, male vocal/instrumental group   *12 wks*

15 May 82	GRACE	Epic EPC A2376	41	5 wks
5 Mar 83	JOY	Epic EPC A 3145	24	7 wks

BAND OF GOLD
Holland, male/female vocal/instrumental group   *11 wks*

14 Jul 84	LOVE SONGS ARE BACK AGAIN (MEDLEY)			
	RCA 428		24	11 wks

BANDITS - *See Billy COTTON and his BAND*

BANDWAGON - *See Johnny JOHNSON and the BANDWAGON*

Honey BANE   *UK, female vocalist*   *8 wks*

24 Jan 81	TURN ME ON TURN ME OFF	Zonophone Z 15	37	5 wks
18 Apr 81	BABY LOVE	Zonophone Z 19	58	3 wks

BANNED   UK, male vocal/instrumental group   6 wks

17 Dec 77	**LITTLE GIRL**	*Harvest HAR 5145*	36	6 wks

BANSHEES   - See SIOUXSIE and the BANSHEES

Chris BARBER'S JAZZ BAND
UK, male band, Chris Barber trombone   *30 wks*

13 Feb 59	● **PETITE FLEUR**	*Pye Nixa NJ 2026*	3	22 wks
31 Jul 59	**PETITE FLEUR**	(re-entry) *Pye Nixa NJ 2026*	22	2 wks
9 Oct 59	**LONESOME**	*Columbia DB 4333*	27	2 wks
4 Jan 62	**REVIVAL**	*Columbia SCD 2166*	50	2 wks
1 Feb 62	**REVIVAL**	(re-entry) *Columbia SCD 2166*	43	2 wks

BARBRA and NEIL
US, female/male vocal duo   *12 wks*

25 Nov 78	● **YOU DON'T BRING ME FLOWERS**	*CBS 6803*	5	12 wks

See also Barbra Streisand; Neil Diamond; Donna Summer and Barbra Streisand; Barbra Streisand and Barry Gibb

BARCLAY JAMES HARVEST
UK, male vocal/instrumental group   *9 wks*

2 Apr 77	**LIVE** (EP)	*Polydor 2229 198*	49	1 wk
16 Apr 77	**LIVE** (EP)	(re-entry) *Polydor 2229 198*	49	1 wk
26 Jan 80	**LOVE ON THE LINE**	*Polydor POSP 97*	63	1 wk
22 Nov 80	**LIFE IS FOR LIVING**	*Polydor POSP 195*	61	3 wks
21 May 83	**JUST A DAY AWAY**	*Polydor POSP 585*	68	2 wks

Tracks on Live EP: Rock'n'Roll Star/Medicine Man (Parts 1 & 2).

BARDO   UK, male/female vocal duo   8 wks

10 Apr 82	● **ONE STEP FURTHER**	*Epic EPC A2265*	2	8 wks

BAR-KAYS
US, male vocal/instrumental group   *11 wks*

23 Aug 67	**SOUL FINGER**	*Stax 601 014*	33	7 wks
22 Jan 77	**SHAKE YOUR RUMP TO THE FUNK** *Mercury 6167 417*		41	4 wks

Richard BARNES   UK, male vocalist   10 wks

23 May 70	**TAKE TO THE MOUNTAINS**	*Philips BF 1840*	35	6 wks
24 Oct 70	**GO NORTH**	*Philips 6006 039*	49	1 wk
7 Nov 70	**GO NORTH**	(re-entry) *Philips 6006 039*	38	3 wks

BARRACUDAS
UK/US, male vocal/instrumental group   *6 wks*

16 Aug 80	**SUMMER FUN**	*EMI-Wipe Out Z 5*	37	6 wks

Wild Willy BARRETT   - *See John OTWAY and Wild Willy BARRETT*

J. J. BARRIE   Canada, male vocalist   11 wks

24 Apr 76	★ **NO CHARGE**	*Power Exchange PX 209*	1	11 wks

Ken BARRIE   UK, male vocalist   15 wks

10 Jul 82	**POSTMAN PAT**	*Post Music PP 001*	44	8 wks
25 Dec 82	**POSTMAN PAT**	(re-entry) *Post Music PP 001* ...	54	3 wks
24 Dec 83	**POSTMAN PAT**	(2nd re-entry) *Post Music PP 001*	59	4 wks

BARRON KNIGHTS
UK, male vocal/instrumental group   *92 wks*

9 Jul 64	● **CALL UP THE GROUPS**	*Columbia DB 7317* ...	3	13 wks
22 Oct 64	**COME TO THE DANCE**	*Columbia DB 7375* ...	42	2 wks
25 Mar 65	● **POP GO THE WORKERS**	*Columbia DB 7525* ...	5	13 wks
16 Dec 65	● **MERRY GENTLE POPS**	*Columbia DB 7780*	9	7 wks
1 Dec 66	**UNDER NEW MANAGEMENT** *Columbia DB 8071*		15	9 wks
23 Oct 68	**AN OLYMPIC RECORD**	*Columbia DB 8485* ...	35	4 wks
29 Oct 77	● **LIVE IN TROUBLE**	*Epic EPC 5752*	7	10 wks
2 Dec 78	● **A TASTE OF AGGRO**	*Epic EPC 6829*	3	10 wks
8 Dec 79	**FOOD FOR THOUGHT**	*Epic EPC 8011*	46	6 wks
4 Oct 80	**THE SIT SONG**	*Epic EPC 8994*	44	4 wks
6 Dec 80	**NEVER MIND THE PRESENTS**	*Epic EPC 9070* ...	17	7 wks
5 Dec 81	**BLACKBOARD JUMBLE**	*CBS A 1795*	52	4 wks
19 Mar 83	**BUFFALO BILL'S LAST SCRATCH** *Epic EPC A 3208*		49	3 wks

Joe BARRY   US, male vocalist   1 wk

24 Aug 61	**I'M A FOOL TO CARE**	*Mercury AMT 1149*	49	1 wk

John BARRY
UK, male instrumental group/orchestra   *78 wks*

10 Mar 60	● **HIT AND MISS**	*Columbia DB 4414*	10	12 wks
28 Apr 60	**BEAT FOR BEATNIKS**	*Columbia DB 4446*	40	2 wks
9 Jun 60	**HIT AND MISS**	(re-entry) *Columbia DB 4414*	45	1 wk
14 Jul 60	**NEVER LET GO**	*Columbia DB 4480*	49	1 wk
18 Aug 60	**BLUEBERRY HILL**	*Columbia DB 4480*	34	3 wks
8 Sep 60	**WALK DON'T RUN**	*Columbia DB 4505*	49	1 wk
22 Sep 60	**WALK DON'T RUN**	(re-entry) *Columbia DB 4505*	11	13 wks
8 Dec 60	**BLACK STOCKINGS**	*Columbia DB 4554*	27	9 wks
2 Mar 61	**THE MAGNIFICENT SEVEN**	*Columbia DB 4598*	48	1 wk
16 Mar 61	**THE MAGNIFICENT SEVEN**	(re-entry) *Columbia DB 4598*	45	2 wks
6 Apr 61	**THE MAGNIFICENT SEVEN**	(2nd re-entry) *Columbia DB 4598*	50	1 wk
8 Jun 61	**THE MAGNIFICENT SEVEN**	(3rd re-entry) *Columbia DB 4598*	47	1 wk
26 Apr 62	**CUTTY SARK**	*Columbia DB 4816*	35	2 wks
1 Nov 62	**JAMES BOND THEME**	*Columbia DB 4898* ...	13	11 wks
21 Nov 63	**FROM RUSSIA WITH LOVE**	*Ember S 181* ...	44	1 wk
19 Dec 63	**FROM RUSSIA WITH LOVE**	(re-entry) *Ember S 181*	39	2 wks
11 Dec 71	**THE PERSUADERS**	*CBS 7469*	13	15 wks

Billed as the John Barry Seven on Hit and Miss, Walk Don't Run, Black Stockings, The Magnificent Seven and Cutty Sark. Others John Barry Orchestra.

Len BARRY   US, male vocalist   24 wks

4 Nov 65	● **1-2-3**	*Brunswick 05942*	3	14 wks
13 Jan 66	● **LIKE A BABY**	*Brunswick 05949*	10	10 wks

Count BASIE   - *See Frank SINATRA*

Toni BASIL   US, female vocalist   16 wks

6 Feb 82	● **MICKEY**	*Radialchoice TIC 4*	2	12 wks
1 May 82	**NOBODY**	*Radialchoice/Virgin TIC 2*	52	4 wks

Alfie BASS – *See Michael MEDWIN/Bernard BRESSLAW/Alfie BASS and Leslie FYSON*

Fontella BASS *US, female vocalist* 15 wks

2 Dec 65	**RESCUE ME**	*Chess CRS 8023*	....	11	10 wks
20 Jan 66	**RECOVERY**	*Chess CRS 8027*	....	32	5 wks

Shirley BASSEY *UK, female vocalist* 313 wks

15 Feb 57	● **BANANA BOAT SONG**	*Philips PB 668*	....	8	10 wks
23 Aug 57	**FIRE DOWN BELOW**	*Philips PB 723*	....	30	1 wk
6 Sep 57	**YOU YOU ROMEO**	*Philips PB 723*	....	29	2 wks
19 Dec 58	**AS I LOVE YOU**	*Philips PB 845*	....	27	2 wks
26 Dec 58	● **KISS ME HONEY KISS ME**				
		Philips PB 860		3	17 wks
9 Jan 59	★ **AS I LOVE YOU** (re-entry)	*Philips PB 845*	......	1	17 wks
31 Mar 60	**WITH THESE HANDS**	*Columbia DB 4422*		38	2 wks
21 Apr 60	**WITH THESE HANDS** (re-entry)				
		Columbia DB 4422		31	2 wks
12 May 60	**WITH THESE HANDS** (2nd re-entry)				
		Columbia DB 4422		41	2 wks
4 Aug 60	● **AS LONG AS HE NEEDS ME**	*Columbia DB 4490*		2	30 wks
11 May 61	● **YOU'LL NEVER KNOW**	*Columbia DB 4643*	....	6	17 wks
27 Jul 61	★ **REACH FOR THE STARS/CLIMB EV'RY**				
	MOUNTAIN	*Columbia DB 4685*	.....	1	16 wks
23 Nov 61	**REACH FOR THE STARS/CLIMB EV'RY**				
	MOUNTAIN (re-entry)	*Columbia DB 4685*	.....	40	2 wks
23 Nov 61	● **I'LL GET BY**	*Columbia DB 4737*	....	10	8 wks
15 Feb 62	**TONIGHT**	*Columbia DB 4777*	....	21	8 wks
26 Apr 62	**AVE MARIA**	*Columbia DB 4816*	....	34	4 wks
31 May 62	**FAR AWAY**	*Columbia DB 4836*	....	24	13 wks
30 Aug 62	● **WHAT NOW MY LOVE**	*Columbia DB 4882*	....	5	17 wks
28 Feb 63	**WHAT KIND OF FOOL AM I?**	*Columbia DB 4974*		47	2 wks
26 Sep 63	● **I (WHO HAVE NOTHING)**	*Columbia DB 7113*	..	6	20 wks
23 Jan 64	**MY SPECIAL DREAM**	*Columbia DB 7185*	.....	32	7 wks
9 Apr 64	**GONE**	*Columbia DB 7248*	....	36	5 wks
15 Oct 64	**GOLDFINGER**	*Columbia DB 7360*	....	21	9 wks
20 May 65	**NO REGRETS**	*Columbia DB 7535*	.....	39	4 wks
11 Oct 67	**BIG SPENDER**	*United Artists UP 1192*	...	21	15 wks
20 Jun 70	● **SOMETHING**	*United Artists UP 35125*	..	4	21 wks
2 Jan 71	**THE FOOL ON THE HILL**				
		United Artists UP 35156	....	48	1 wk
23 Jan 71	**SOMETHING** (re-entry)	*United Artists UP 35125*		50	1 wk
27 Mar 71	**(WHERE DO I BEGIN) LOVE STORY**				
		United Artists UP 35194	.....	34	9 wks
7 Aug 71	**FOR ALL WE KNOW**	*United Artists UP 35267*	.	46	1 wk
21 Aug 71	● **FOR ALL WE KNOW** (re-entry)				
		United Artists UP 35267	....	6	23 wks
15 Jan 72	**DIAMONDS ARE FOREVER**				
		United Artists UP 35293	.....	38	6 wks
3 Mar 73	● **NEVER NEVER NEVER**	*United Artists UP 35490*		8	18 wks
14 Jul 73	**NEVER NEVER NEVER** (re-entry)				
		United Artists UP 35490	.....	48	1 wk

Mike BATT *UK, male vocalist* 8 wks

16 Aug 75	● **SUMMERTIME CITY**	*Epic EPC 3460*	....	4	8 wks

Mike Batt is, among other things, the voice behind the Wombles - see Wombles. On this hit, billed as Mike Batt (with the New Edition.)

BAUHAUS
UK, male vocal/instrumental group 35 wks

18 Apr 81	**KICK IN THE EYE**	*Beggars Banquet BEG 54*	.....	59	3 wks
4 Jul 81	**THE PASSIONS OF LOVERS**				
		Beggars Banquet BEG 59		51	2 wks
6 Mar 82	**KICK IN THE EYE** (EP)	*Beggars Banquet BEG 74*		45	4 wks
19 Jun 82	**SPIRIT**	*Beggars Banquet BEG 79*	......	42	5 wks
9 Oct 82	**ZIGGY STARDUST**	*Beggars Banquet BEG 83*	...	15	7 wks
22 Jan 83	**LAGARTIJA NICK**	*Beggars Banquet BEG 88*	...	44	4 wks
9 Apr 83	**SHE'S IN PARTIES**	*Beggars Banquet BEG 91*	.....	26	6 wks

29 Oct 83	**THE SINGLES 1981-83**	*Beggars Banquet BEG 100E*		52	4 wks

Tracks on Kick In The Eye EP: Kick In The Eye (Searching For Satori)/Harry/Earwax.

Les BAXTER *US, orchestra and chorus* 9 wks

13 May 55	● **UNCHAINED MELODY**	*Capitol CL 14257*	.....	10	9 wks

BAY CITY ROLLERS
UK, male vocal/instrumental group 113 wks

18 Sep 71	● **KEEP ON DANCING**	*Bell 1164*	....	9	13 wks
9 Feb 74	● **REMEMBER (SHA-LA-LA)**	*Bell 1338*	.....	6	12 wks
27 Apr 74	● **SHANG-A-LANG**	*Bell 1355*	....	2	10 wks
27 Jul 74	● **SUMMERLOVE SENSATION**	*Bell 1369*	.....	3	10 wks
12 Oct 74	● **ALL OF ME LOVES ALL OF YOU**	*Bell 1382*	..	4	10 wks
8 Mar 75	★ **BYE BYE BABY**	*Bell 1409*	....	1	16 wks
12 Jul 75	★ **GIVE A LITTLE LOVE**	*Bell 1425*	....	1	9 wks
22 Nov 75	● **MONEY HONEY**	*Bell 1461*	....	3	9 wks
10 Apr 76	● **LOVE ME LIKE I LOVE YOU**	*Bell 1477*	....	4	6 wks
11 Sep 76	● **I ONLY WANNA BE WITH YOU**	*Bell 1493*	...	4	9 wks
7 May 77	**IT'S A GAME**	*Arista 108*	....	16	6 wks
30 Jul 77	**YOU MADE ME BELIEVE IN MAGIC**				
		Arista 127	....	34	3 wks

BE BOP DELUXE
UK, male vocal/instrumental group 13 wks

21 Feb 76	**SHIPS IN THE NIGHT**	*Harvest HAR 5104*	.....	23	8 wks
13 Nov 76	**HOT VALVES** (EP)	*Harvest HAR 5117*	....	36	5 wks

Hot Valves EP contains the following tracks: Maid In Heaven/Blazing Apostles/Jet Silver And The Dolls Of Venus/ Bring Back The Spark.

BEACH BOYS
US, male vocal/instrumental group 253 wks

1 Aug 63	**SURFIN' USA**	*Capitol CL 15305*	....	34	7 wks
9 Jul 64	● **I GET AROUND**	*Capitol CL 15350*	....	7	13 wks
29 Oct 64	**WHEN I GROW UP (TO BE A MAN)**				
		Capitol CL 15361	....	44	2 wks
19 Nov 64	**WHEN I GROW UP (TO BE A MAN)** (re-entry)				
		Capitol CL 15361	....	27	5 wks
21 Jan 65	**DANCE DANCE DANCE**	*Capitol CL 15370*	.....	24	6 wks
3 Jun 65	**HELP ME RHONDA**	*Capitol CL 15392*	.....	27	10 wks
2 Sep 65	**CALIFORNIA GIRLS**	*Capitol CL 15409*	....	26	8 wks
17 Feb 66	● **BARBARA ANN**	*Capitol CL 15432*	....	3	10 wks
21 Apr 66	● **SLOOP JOHN B**	*Capitol CL 15441*	....	2	15 wks
28 Jul 66	● **GOD ONLY KNOWS**	*Capitol CL 15459*	.....	2	14 wks
3 Nov 66	★ **GOOD VIBRATIONS**	*Capitol CL 15475*	....	1	13 wks
4 May 67	● **THEN I KISSED HER**	*Capitol CL 15502*	.....	4	11 wks
23 Aug 67	● **HEROES AND VILLAINS**	*Capitol CL 15510*	..	8	9 wks
22 Nov 67	**WILD HONEY**	*Capitol CL 15521*	....	29	6 wks
17 Jan 68	**DARLIN'**	*Capitol CL 15527*	....	11	14 wks
8 May 68	**FRIENDS**	*Capitol CL 15545*	....	25	7 wks
24 Jul 68	★ **DO IT AGAIN**	*Capitol CL 15554*	....	1	14 wks
25 Dec 68	**BLUEBIRDS OVER THE MOUNTAIN**				
		Capitol CL 15572	....	33	5 wks
26 Feb 69	● **I CAN HEAR MUSIC**	*Capitol CL 15584*	.....	10	13 wks
11 Jun 69	● **BREAK AWAY**	*Capitol CL 15598*	....	6	11 wks
16 May 70	● **COTTONFIELDS**	*Capitol CL 15640*	....	5	17 wks
3 Mar 73	**CALIFORNIA SAGA - CALIFORNIA**				
		Reprise K 14232	....	37	5 wks
3 Jul 76	**GOOD VIBRATIONS** (re-issue)	*Capitol CL 15875*		18	7 wks
10 Jul 76	**ROCK AND ROLL MUSIC**	*Reprise K 14440*	...	36	4 wks
31 Mar 79	**HERE COMES THE NIGHT**	*Caribou CRB 7204*		37	8 wks
16 Jun 79	● **LADY LYNDA**	*Caribou CRB 7427*	....	6	11 wks
29 Sep 79	**SUMAHAMA**	*Caribou CRB 7846*	....	45	4 wks
29 Aug 81	**BEACH BOYS MEDLEY**	*Capitol CL 213*	......	47	4 wks

BEAKY – *See Dave DEE, DOZY, BEAKY, MICK and TICH*

BRONSKI BEAT (above) Smalltown boys – Larry, Jimi and Steve whose first concert was at the Bell pub in London's King's Cross.

SARAH BRIGHTMAN (right) Ex-Hot Gossip dancer who lost her heart to Andrew Lloyd Webber.

THE BLUEBELLS (above) 'We don't mind if in 2 years' time people don't remember us because they'll have the records in their collection and in 10 years' time maybe people will appreciate them again.'

BOW WOW WOW (below) Annabella Lwin, of the group whose debut single was about cassettes, and whose follow-up was available only as a cassette.

BLANCMANGE (below) Neil Arthur and Steven Luscombe's first musical venture was an independent single under the name Irene Mavis and the Blancmange.

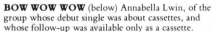

The BEAT

UK, male vocal/instrumental group 90 wks

8 Dec 79	● TEARS OF A CLOWN/RANKING FULL STOP 2 Tone CHS TT 6	6	11 wks
23 Feb 80	● HANDS OFF – SHE'S MINE Go Feet FEET 1	9	9 wks
3 May 80	● MIRROR IN THE BATHROOM Go Feet FEET 2	4	9 wks
16 Aug 80	BEST FRIEND/STAND DOWN MARGARET (DUB) Go Feet FEET 3	22	9 wks
13 Dec 80	● TOO NICE TO TALK TO Go Feet FEET 4	7	11 wks
18 Apr 81	DROWNING/ALL OUT TO GET YOU Go Feet FEET 6	22	8 wks
20 Jun 81	DOORS OF YOUR HEART Go Feet FEET 9	33	6 wks
5 Dec 81	HIT IT Go Feet FEET 11	70	2 wks
17 Apr 82	SAVE IT FOR LATER Go Feet FEET 333	47	4 wks
18 Sep 82	JEANETTE Go Feet FEET 15	45	3 wks
4 Dec 82	I CONFESS Go Feet FEET 16	54	3 wks
30 Apr 83	● CAN'T GET USED TO LOSING YOU Go Feet FEET 17	3	11 wks
2 Jul 83	ACKEE 1-2-3 Go Feet FEET 18	54	4 wks

BEATLES *UK, male vocal/instrumental group* 419 wks

11 Oct 62	LOVE ME DO Parlophone R 4949	17	18 wks
17 Jan 63	● PLEASE PLEASE ME Parlophone R 4983	2	18 wks
18 Apr 63	● FROM ME TO YOU Parlophone R 5015	1	21 wks
29 Aug 63	★ SHE LOVES YOU Parlophone R 5055	1	31 wks
5 Dec 63	★ I WANT TO HOLD YOUR HAND Parlophone R 5084	1	21 wks
26 Mar 64	★ CAN'T BUY ME LOVE Parlophone R 5114	1	14 wks
9 Apr 64	SHE LOVES YOU (re-entry) Parlophone R 5055	42	2 wks
14 May 64	I WANT TO HOLD YOUR HAND (re-entry) Parlophone R 5084	48	1 wk
11 Jun 64	AIN'T SHE SWEET Polydor 52 317	29	6 wks
9 Jul 64	CAN'T BUY ME LOVE (re-entry) Parlophone R 5114	47	1 wk
16 Jul 64	★ A HARD DAY'S NIGHT Parlophone R 5160	1	13 wks
3 Dec 64	★ I FEEL FINE Parlophone R 5200	1	13 wks
15 Apr 65	★ TICKET TO RIDE Parlophone R 5265	1	12 wks
29 Jul 65	★ HELP! Parlophone R 5305	1	14 wks
9 Dec 65	★ DAY TRIPPER/WE CAN WORK IT OUT Parlophone R 5389	1	12 wks
16 Jun 66	★ PAPERBACK WRITER Parlophone R 5452	1	11 wks
11 Aug 66	★ YELLOW SUBMARINE/ELEANOR RIGBY Parlophone R 5493	1	13 wks
23 Feb 67	● PENNY LANE/STRAWBERRY FIELDS FOREVER Parlophone R 5570	2	11 wks
12 Jul 67	★ ALL YOU NEED IS LOVE Parlophone R 5620	1	13 wks
29 Nov 67	★ HELLO GOODBYE Parlophone R 5655	1	12 wks
13 Dec 67	● MAGICAL MYSTERY TOUR (DOUBLE EP) Parlophone SMMT/MMT 1	2	12 wks
20 Mar 68	★ LADY MADONNA Parlophone R 5675	1	8 wks
4 Sep 68	★ HEY JUDE Apple R 5722	1	16 wks
23 Apr 69	★ GET BACK Apple R 5777	1	17 wks
4 Jun 69	★ BALLAD OF JOHN AND YOKO Apple R 5786	1	14 wks
8 Nov 69	● SOMETHING /COME TOGETHER Apple R 5814	4	12 wks
14 Mar 70	● LET IT BE Apple R 5833	2	9 wks
24 Oct 70	LET IT BE (re-entry) Apple R 5833	43	1 wk
13 Mar 76	● YESTERDAY Apple R 6013	8	7 wks
27 Mar 76	HEY JUDE (re-entry) Apple R 5722	12	7 wks
27 Mar 76	PAPERBACK WRITER (re-entry) Parlophone R 5452	23	5 wks
3 Apr 76	STRAWBERRY FIELDS FOREVER (re-entry) Parlophone R 5570	32	3 wks
3 Apr 76	GET BACK (re-entry) Apple R 5777	28	5 wks
10 Apr 76	HELP! (re-entry) Parlophone R 5305	37	3 wks
10 Jul 76	BACK IN THE U.S.S.R. Parlophone R 6016	19	6 wks
7 Oct 78	SGT. PEPPER'S LONELY HEARTS CLUB BAND – WITH A LITTLE HELP FROM MY FRIENDS Parlophone R 6022	63	3 wks
5 Jun 82	● BEATLES MOVIE MEDLEY Parlophone R 6055	10	9 wks
16 Oct 82	● LOVE ME DO (re-entry) Parlophone R 4949	4	7 wks
22 Jan 83	PLEASE PLEASE ME (re-entry) Parlophone R 4983	29	4 wks
23 Apr 83	FROM ME TO YOU (re-entry) Parlophone R 5015	40	4 wks
3 Sep 83	SHE LOVES YOU (2nd re-entry) Parlophone R 5055	45	3 wks
26 Nov 83	I WANT TO HOLD YOUR HAND (2nd re-entry) Parlophone R 5084	62	2 wks
31 Mar 84	CAN'T BUY ME LOVE (2nd re-entry) R 5114	53	2 wks
21 Jul 84	A HARD DAY'S NIGHT (re-entry) Parlophone R 5160	52	2 wks
8 Dec 84	I FEEL FINE (re-entry) Parlophone R 5200	65	1 wk

Get Back is with Billy Preston. See also Billy Preston; Billy Preston and Syreeta; Tony Sheridan and the Beatles. Tracks on Magical Mystery Tour EP: Magical Mystery Tour/Your Mother Should Know/I Am The Walrus/Fool On The Hill/ Flying/Blue Jay Way.

Gilbert BECAUD *France, male vocalist* 12 wks

29 Mar 75	● A LITTLE LOVE AND UNDERSTANDING Decca F 13537	10	12 wks

Jeff BECK

UK, male vocalist/instrumentalist - guitar 39 wks

23 Mar 67	HI-HO SILVER LINING Columbia DB 8151	14	14 wks
2 Aug 67	TALLYMAN Columbia DB 8227	30	3 wks
28 Feb 68	LOVE IS BLUE Columbia DB 8359	23	7 wks
4 Nov 72	HI-HO SILVER LINING (re-issue) Rak RR 3	17	11 wks
9 Oct 82	HI-HO SILVER LINING (re-entry of re-issue) RAK RR	62	4 wks

See also Jeff Beck and Rod Stewart.

Jeff BECK and Rod STEWART

UK, male vocal/instrumental duo 6 wks

5 May 73	I'VE BEEN DRINKING Rak RR 4	27	6 wks

See also Jeff Beck; Rod Stewart; Donovan with Jeff Beck Group.

BEDROCKS

UK, male vocal/instrumental group 7 wks

18 Dec 68	OB-LA-DI OB-LA-DA Columbia DB 8516	20	7 wks

Celi BEE and the BUZZY BUNCH

US, male/female vocal/instrumental group 1 wk

17 Jun 78	HOLD YOUR HORSES BABE TK TKR 6032	72	1 wk

BEE GEES

UK, male vocal/instrumental group 266 wks

27 Apr 67	NEW YORK MINING DISASTER 1941 Polydor 56 161	12	10 wks
12 Jul 67	TO LOVE SOMEBODY Polydor 56 178	50	1 wk
26 Jul 67	TO LOVE SOMEBODY (re-entry) Polydor 56 178	41	4 wks
20 Sep 67	★ MASSACHUSETTS Polydor 56 192	1	17 wks
22 Nov 67	● WORLD Polydor 56 220	9	16 wks
31 Jan 68	● WORDS Polydor 56 229	8	10 wks
27 Mar 68	JUMBO/THE SINGER SANG HIS SONG Polydor 56 242	25	7 wks
7 Aug 68	★ I'VE GOTTA GET A MESSAGE TO YOU Polydor 56 273	1	15 wks
19 Feb 69	● FIRST OF MAY Polydor 56 304	6	11 wks
4 Jun 69	TOMORROW TOMORROW Polydor 56 331	23	8 wks
16 Aug 69	● DON'T FORGET TO REMEMBER Polydor 56 343	2	15 wks
28 Mar 70	I.O.I.O. Polydor 56 377	49	1 wk
5 Dec 70	LONELY DAYS Polydor 2001 104	33	9 wks
29 Jan 72	MY WORLD Polydor 2058 185	16	9 wks
22 Jul 72	● RUN TO ME Polydor 2058 255	9	10 wks
28 Jun 75	JIVE TALKIN' RSO 2090 160	5	11 wks
31 Jul 76	● YOU SHOULD BE DANCING RSO 2090 195	5	10 wks

13 Nov 76		LOVE SO RIGHT *RSO 2090 207*	41	4 wks
29 Oct 77	●	HOW DEEP IS YOUR LOVE *RSO 2090 259* ...	3	15 wks
4 Feb 78	●	STAYIN' ALIVE *RSO 2090 267*	4	20 wks
15 Apr 78	★	NIGHT FEVER *RSO 002*	1	20 wks
13 May 78		STAYIN' ALIVE (re-entry) *RSO 2090 267* ...	63	6 wks
25 Nov 78	●	TOO MUCH HEAVEN *RSO 25*	3	13 wks
17 Feb 79	★	TRAGEDY *RSO 27*	1	10 wks
14 Apr 79		LOVE YOU INSIDE OUT *RSO 31*	13	9 wks
5 Jan 80		SPIRITS (HAVING FLOWN) *RSO 52*	16	7 wks
17 Sep 83		SOMEONE BELONGING TO SOMEONE *RSO/Polydor 96*	49	6 wks

Act was UK/Australia up to and including Tomorrow Tomorrow.

BEGGAR and CO
UK, male vocal/instrumental group　　　　　　　*15 wks*

7 Feb 81		(SOMEBODY) HELP ME OUT *Ensign ENY 201*	15	10 wks
12 Sep 81		MULE (CHANT NO.2) *RCA 130*	37	5 wks

BEGINNING OF THE END
US, male vocal/instrumental group　　　　　　　*6 wks*

23 Feb 74		FUNKY NASSAU *Atlantic K 10021*	31	6 wks

Harry BELAFONTE　*US, male vocalist*　　　*79 wks*

1 Mar 57	●	BANANA BOAT SONG *HMV POP 308*	2	18 wks
14 Jun 57		ISLAND IN THE SUN *HMV POP 360*	3	25 wks
6 Sep 57		SCARLET RIBBONS *HMV POP 360*	18	18 wks
1 Nov 57	★	MARY'S BOY CHILD *RCA 1022*	1	12 wks
22 Aug 58		LITTLE BERNADETTE *RCA 1072*	16	7 wks
28 Nov 58	●	MARY'S BOY CHILD (re-entry) *RCA 1022*	10	6 wks
12 Dec 58		SON OF MARY *RCA 1084*	18	4 wks
11 Dec 59		MARY'S BOY CHILD (2nd re-entry) *RCA 1022*	30	1 wk

See also Harry Belafonte and Odetta.

Harry BELAFONTE and ODETTA
US, male/female vocal duo　　　　　　　*8 wks*

21 Sep 61		HOLE IN THE BUCKET *RCA 1247*	32	2 wks
12 Oct 61		HOLE IN THE BUCKET (re-entry) *RCA 1247* ..	34	6 wks

See also Harry Belafonte.

BELL and JAMES　*US, male vocal duo*　*3 wks*

31 Mar 79		LIVIN' IT UP (FRIDAY NIGHT) *A & M AMS 7424*	68	1 wk
14 Apr 79		LIVIN' IT UP (FRIDAY NIGHT) (re-entry) *A & M AMS 7424*	59	2 wks

Archie BELL and the DRELLS
US, male vocal group　　　　　　　*29 wks*

7 Oct 72		HERE I GO AGAIN *Atlantic K 10210*	11	10 wks
27 Jan 73		THERE'S GONNA BE A SHOWDOWN *Atlantic K 10263*	36	5 wks
8 May 76		SOUL CITY WALK *Philadelphia International PIR 4250*	13	10 wks
11 Jun 77		EVERYBODY HAVE A GOOD TIME *Philadelphia International PIR 5179*	43	4 wks

See also Philadelphia International All-Stars.

Freddie BELL and the BELLBOYS
US, male vocal/instrumental group　　　　*10 wks*

28 Sep 56	●	GIDDY-UP-A-DING-DONG *Mercury MT 122* ..	4	10 wks

Maggie BELL　*UK, female vocalist*　　*4 wks*

15 Apr 78		HAZELL *Swan Song SSK 19412*	37	3 wks
13 May 78		HAZELL (re-entry) *Swan Song SSK 19412*	74	1 wk

See also B.A. Robertson and Maggie Bell.

William BELL　*US, male vocalist*　　　*7 wks*

29 May 68		TRIBUTE TO A KING *Stax 601 038*	31	7 wks

See also Judy Clay and William Bell.

BELLAMY BROTHERS
US, male vocal duo　　　　　　　*29 wks*

17 Apr 76	●	LET YOUR LOVE FLOW *Warner Bros. K 16690*	7	12 wks
21 Aug 76		SATIN SHEETS *Warner Bros. K 16775*	43	3 wks
11 Aug 79	●	IF I SAID YOU HAVE A BEAUTIFUL BODY WOULD YOU HOLD IT AGAINST ME *Warner Bros. K 17405*	3	14 wks

BELLBOYS - *See Freddie BELL and the BELLBOYS*

BELLE and the DEVOTIONS
UK, female vocal group　　　　　　　*8 wks*

21 Apr 84		LOVE GAMES *CBS A 4332*	11	8 wks

La BELLE EPOQUE
France, female vocal duo　　　　　　*14 wks*

27 Aug 77		BLACK IS BLACK *Harvest HAR 5133*	48	1 wk
10 Sep 77	●	BLACK IS BLACK (re-entry) *Harvest HAR 5133*	2	13 wks

BELLE STARS
UK, female vocal/instrumental group　　*42 wks*

5 Jun 82		IKO IKO *Stiff BUY 150*	35	6 wks
17 Jul 82		THE CLAPPING SONG *Stiff BUY 155*	11	9 wks
16 Oct 82		MOCKINGBIRD *Stiff BUY 159*	51	3 wks
15 Jan 83	●	SIGN OF THE TIMES *Stiff BUY 167*	3	11 wks
16 Apr 83		SWEET MEMORY *Stiff BUY 174*	22	9 wks
13 Aug 83		INDIAN SUMMER *Stiff BUY 185*	52	3 wks
14 Jul 84		80'S ROMANCE *Stiff BUY 200*	71	1 wk

BELMONTS - *See DION and the BELMONTS*

Pat BENATAR　*US, female vocalist*　　*5 wks*

21 Jan 84		LOVE IS A BATTLEFIELD *Chrysalis CHS 2747*	49	5 wks

David BENDETH
Canada, male vocalist and multi-instrumentalist　*5 wks*

8 Sep 79		FEEL THE REAL *Sidewalk SID 113*	44	5 wks

BENELUX and Nancy DEE
Belgium/Holland/Luxembourg, female vocal group　*4 wks*

25 Aug 79		SWITCH *Scope/Hansa SC 4*	52	4 wks

Boyd BENNETT US, male vocalist — 2 wks

23 Dec 55	SEVENTEEN Parlophone R 4063	16	2 wks

Chris BENNETT - See MUNICH MACHINE

Cliff BENNETT and the REBEL ROUSERS UK, male vocal/instrumental group — 23 wks

1 Oct 64	● ONE WAY LOVE Parlophone R 5173	9	9 wks
4 Feb 65	I'LL TAKE YOU HOME Parlophone R 5229	42	3 wks
11 Aug 66	● GOT TO GET YOU INTO MY LIFE Parlophone R 5489	6	11 wks

Peter E. BENNETT UK, male vocalist — 1 wk

7 Nov 70	THE SEAGULL'S NAME WAS NELSON RCA 1991	45	1 wk

Tony BENNETT US, male vocalist — 61 wks

15 Apr 55	★ STRANGER IN PARADISE Philips PB 420	1	16 wks
16 Sep 55	CLOSE YOUR EYES Philips PB 445	18	1 wk
13 Apr 56	COME NEXT SPRING Philips PB 537	29	1 wk
5 Jan 61	TILL/SERENATA Philips PB 1079	35	2 wks
18 Jul 63	THE GOOD LIFE CBS AAG 153	27	13 wks
6 May 65	IF I RULED THE WORLD CBS 201735	40	5 wks
27 May 65	I LEFT MY HEART IN SAN FRANCISCO CBS 201730	46	2 wks
30 Sep 65	I LEFT MY HEART IN SAN FRANCISCO (re-entry) CBS 201730	40	5 wks
9 Dec 65	I LEFT MY HEART IN SAN FRANCISCO (2nd re-entry) CBS 201730	25	7 wks
23 Dec 65	THE VERY THOUGHT OF YOU CBS 202021	21	9 wks

Gary BENSON UK, male vocalist — 8 wks

9 Aug 75	DON'T THROW IT ALL AWAY State STAT 10	20	8 wks

George BENSON
US, male vocalist/instrumentalist - guitar — 104 wks

25 Oct 75	SUPERSHIP CTI CTSP 002	30	6 wks
4 Jun 77	NATURE BOY Warner Bros. K 16921	26	6 wks
24 Sep 77	THE GREATEST LOVE OF ALL Arista 133	27	7 wks
31 Mar 79	LOVE BALLAD Warner Bros. K 17333	29	9 wks
26 Jul 80	● GIVE ME THE NIGHT Warner Bros. K 17673	7	10 wks
4 Oct 80	● LOVE X LOVE Warner Bros. K 17699	10	8 wks
7 Feb 81	WHAT'S ON YOUR MIND Warner Bros. K 17748	45	5 wks
14 Nov 81	TURN YOUR LOVE AROUND Warner Bros. K 17877	29	11 wks
23 Jan 82	NEVER GIVE UP ON A GOOD THING Warner Bros. K 17902	14	10 wks
21 May 83	LADY LOVE ME (ONE MORE TIME) Warner Bros. W 9614	11	10 wks
16 Jul 83	FEEL LIKE MAKIN' LOVE Warner Bros. W 9551	28	7 wks
24 Sep 83	● IN YOUR EYES Warner Bros. W 9487	7	10 wks
17 Dec 83	INSIDE LOVE (SO PERSONAL) WEA Int. W 9427	57	5 wks

Billed as George 'Bad' Benson on first hit. See also Aretha Franklin and George Benson.

Brook BENTON US, male vocalist — 18 wks

10 Jul 59	ENDLESSLY Mercury AMT 1043	28	2 wks
6 Oct 60	KIDDIO Mercury AMT 1109	42	3 wks
3 Nov 60	KIDDIO (re-entry) Mercury AMT 1109	41	3 wks
16 Feb 61	FOOLS RUSH IN Mercury AMT 1121	50	1 wk
13 Jul 61	BOLL WEEVIL SONG Mercury AMT 1148	30	9 wks

Ingrid BERGMAN - See Dooley WILSON

Elmer BERNSTEIN US, orchestra — 9 wks

1 Jan 60	● STACCATO'S THEME Capitol CL 15101	4	8 wks
10 Mar 60	STACCATO'S THEME (re-entry) Capitol CL 15101	40	1 wk

Chuck BERRY US, male vocalist/guitarist — 91 wks

21 Jun 57	SCHOOL DAY Columbia DB 3951	24	2 wks
12 Jul 57	SCHOOL DAY (re-entry) Columbia DB 3951	24	2 wks
25 Apr 58	SWEET LITTLE SIXTEEN London HLM 8585	16	5 wks
11 Jul 63	GO GO GO Pye International 7N 25209	38	6 wks
10 Oct 63	● LET IT ROCK/MEMPHIS TENNESSEE Pye International 7N 25218	6	13 wks
19 Dec 63	RUN RUDOLPH RUN Pye International 7N 25228	36	6 wks
13 Feb 64	NADINE (IS IT YOU) Pye International 7N 25236	27	6 wks
2 Apr 64	NADINE (IS IT YOU) (re-entry) Pye International 7N 25236	43	1 wk
7 May 64	● NO PARTICULAR PLACE TO GO Pye International 7N 25242	3	12 wks
20 Aug 64	YOU NEVER CAN TELL Pye International 7N 25257	23	8 wks
14 Jan 65	PROMISED LAND Pye International 7N 25285	26	6 wks
28 Oct 72	★ MY DING-A-LING Chess 6145 019	1	17 wks
3 Feb 73	REELIN' AND ROCKIN' Chess 6145 020	18	7 wks

Dave BERRY UK, male vocalist — 76 wks

19 Sep 63	MEMPHIS TENNESSEE Decca F 11734	19	13 wks
9 Jan 64	MY BABY LEFT ME Decca F 11803	41	1 wk
23 Jan 64	MY BABY LEFT ME (re-entry) Decca F 11803	37	8 wks
30 Apr 64	BABY IT'S YOU Decca F 11876	24	6 wks
6 Aug 64	● THE CRYING GAME Decca F 11937	5	12 wks
26 Nov 64	ONE HEART BETWEEN TWO Decca F 12020	41	2 wks
25 Mar 65	● LITTLE THINGS Decca F 12103	5	12 wks
22 Jul 65	THIS STRANGE EFFECT Decca F 12188	37	6 wks
30 Jun 66	● MAMA Decca F 12435	5	16 wks

Billed as Dave Berry and The Cruisers on the first two hits.

Mike BERRY UK, male vocalist — 51 wks

12 Oct 61	TRIBUTE TO BUDDY HOLLY HMV POP 912	24	6 wks
3 Jan 63	● DON'T YOU THINK IT'S TIME HMV POP 1105	6	12 wks
11 Apr 63	MY LITTLE BABY HMV POP 1142	34	7 wks
2 Aug 80	● THE SUNSHINE OF YOUR SMILE Polydor 2059 261	9	12 wks
29 Nov 80	IF I COULD ONLY MAKE YOU CARE Polydor POSP 202	37	9 wks
5 Sep 81	MEMORIES Polydor POSP 287	55	5 wks

HMV hits credited to Mike Berry with the Outlaws. See also Outlaws.

BEVERLEY SISTERS
UK, female vocal trio — 34 wks

27 Nov 53	I SAW MOMMY KISSING SANTA CLAUS Philips PB 188	11	1 wk
11 Dec 53	● I SAW MOMMY KISSING SANTA CLAUS (re-entry) Philips PB 188	6	4 wks
13 Apr 56	WILLIE CAN Decca F 10705	23	4 wks
1 Feb 57	I DREAMED Decca F 10832	24	2 wks
13 Feb 59	● LITTLE DRUMMER BOY Decca F 11107	6	13 wks
1 Jan 60	LITTLE DONKEY Decca F 11172	14	7 wks
23 Jun 60	GREEN FIELDS Columbia DB 4444	48	1 wk
7 Jul 60	GREEN FIELDS (re-entry) Columbia DB 4444	29	2 wks

See also Various Artists - All Star Hit Parade No. 2.

BIDDU *UK, orchestra* *13 wks*

2 Aug 75	**SUMMER OF '42** *Epic EPC 3318*		14	8 wks
17 Apr 76	**RAIN FOREST** *Epic EPC 4084*		39	4 wks
11 Feb 78	**JOURNEY TO THE MOON** *Epic EPC 5910*		41	1 wk

BIG APPLE BAND - *See Walter MURPHY and the BIG APPLE BAND*

BIG BEN BANJO BAND
UK, instrumental group *6 wks*

10 Dec 54	● **LET'S GET TOGETHER NO. 1** *Columbia DB 3549*		6	4 wks
9 Dec 55	**LET'S GET TOGETHER AGAIN** *Columbia DB 3676*		19	1 wk
30 Dec 55	**LET'S GET TOGETHER AGAIN** (re-entry) *Columbia DB 3676*		18	1 wk

These hits were both medleys as follows: Let's Get Together No. 1: I'm Just Wild About Harry/April Showers/Rock-a-Bye Your Baby/Swanee/Darktown Strutters Ball/ For Me And My Gal/Oh You Beautiful Doll/Yes Sir That's My Baby. Let's Get Together Again: I'm Looking Over A Four-leafed Clover/ By The Light Of The Silvery Moon/Oh Susannah/Baby Face/ I'm Sitting On Top Of The World/My Mammy/Dixie's Land/Margie.

BIG BOPPER *US, male vocalist* *8 wks*

26 Dec 58	**CHANTILLY LACE** *Mercury AMT 1002*		30	1 wk
9 Jan 59	**CHANTILLY LACE** (re-entry) *Mercury AMT 1002*	12	7 wks

BIG COUNTRY
UK, male vocal/instrumental group *47 wks*

26 Feb 83	● **FIELDS OF FIRE (400 MILES)** *Mercury/Phonogram COUNT 2*		10	12 wks
28 May 83	**IN A BIG COUNTRY** *Mercury/Phonogram COUNT 3*		17	7 wks
3 Sep 83	● **CHANCE** *Mercury/Phonogram COUNT 4*		9	9 wks
21 Jan 84	● **WONDERLAND** *Mercury/Phonogram COUNT 5*	8	8 wks
29 Sep 84	**EAST OF EDEN** *Mercury/Phonogram MER 175*		17	6 wks
1 Dec 84	**WHERE THE ROSE IS SOWN** *Mercury/Phonogram MER 185*		29†	5 wks

BIG ROLL BAND - *See Zoot MONEY and the BIG ROLL BAND*

BIG SOUND - *See Simon DUPREE and the BIG SOUND*

BIG THREE *UK, vocal/instrumental group* *17 wks*

11 Apr 63	**SOME OTHER GUY** *Decca F 11614*		37	7 wks
11 Jul 63	**BY THE WAY** *Decca F 11689*		22	10 wks

Barry BIGGS *Jamaica, male vocalist* *46 wks*

28 Aug 76	**WORK ALL DAY** *Dynamic DYN 101*		38	5 wks
4 Dec 76	● **SIDESHOW** *Dynamic DYN 118*		3	16 wks
23 Apr 77	**YOU'RE MY LIFE** *Dynamic DYN 127*		36	4 wks
9 Jul 77	**THREE RING CIRCUS** *Dynamic DYN 128*		22	8 wks
15 Dec 79	**WHAT'S YOUR SIGN GIRL** *Dynamic DYN 150*		55	7 wks
20 Jun 81	**WIDE AWAKE IN A DREAM** *Dynamic DYN 10*		44	6 wks

Ivor BIGGUN *UK, male vocalist* *15 wks*

2 Sep 78	**WINKER'S SONG (MISPRINT)** *Beggars Banquet BOP 1*		22	12 wks
12 Sep 81	**BRAS ON 45 (FAMILY VERSION)** *Dead Badger BOP 6*		50	3 wks

First hit gives minor credit to Ivor's backing group the Red Nosed Burglars, (UK, male instrumentalists). Second hit credited to Ivor Biggun and the D Cups.

BILBO *UK, male vocal/instrumental group* *7 wks*

26 Aug 78	**SHE'S GONNA WIN** *Lightning LIG 548*		42	7 wks

Mr. Acker BILK *UK, male band leader, vocalist/instrumentalist - clarinet* *171 wks*

22 Jan 60	● **SUMMER SET** *Columbia DB 4382*		5	19 wks
9 Jun 60	**GOODNIGHT SWEET PRINCE** *Melodisc MEL 1547*		50	1 wk
18 Aug 60	**WHITE CLIFFS OF DOVER** *Columbia DB 4492*		30	9 wks
8 Dec 60	**BUONA SERA** *Columbia DB 4544*		7	18 wks
13 Jul 61	● **THAT'S MY HOME** *Columbia DB 4673*		7	17 wks
2 Nov 61	**STARS AND STRIPES FOREVER/CREOLE JAZZ** *Columbia SCD 2155*		22	10 wks
30 Nov 61	● **STRANGER ON THE SHORE** *Columbia DB 4750*		2	55 wks
15 Mar 62	**FRANKIE AND JOHNNY** *Columbia DB 4795*		42	2 wks
26 Jul 62	**GOTTA SEE BABY TONIGHT** *Columbia SCD 2176*		24	9 wks
27 Sep 62	**LONELY** *Columbia DB 4897*		14	11 wks
24 Jan 63	**A TASTE OF HONEY** *Columbia DB 4949*		16	9 wks
21 Aug 76	● **ARIA** *Pye 7N 45607*		5	11 wks

Stranger On The Shore, Lonely and A Taste Of Honey credit Mr Acker Bilk with the Leon Young String Chorale. Aria credits Acker Bilk (no 'Mr.') His Clarinet And Strings. All others Mr. Acker Bilk and his Paramount Jazz Band.

BIMBO JET
France, male/female vocal/instrumental group *10 wks*

26 Jul 75	**EL BIMBO** *EMI 2317*		12	10 wks

Umberto BINDI *Italy, male vocalist* *1 wk*

10 Nov 60	**IL NOSTRO CONCERTO** *Oriole CB 1577*		47	1 wk

La BIONDA *Italy, male/female vocal group* *4 wks*

7 Oct 78	**ONE FOR YOU ONE FOR ME** *Philips 6198 227*		54	4 wks

BIRDS *UK, male vocal/instrumental group* *1 wk*

27 May 65	**LEAVING HERE** *Decca F 12140*		45	1 wk

Jane BIRKIN and Serge GAINSBOURG
UK/France, female/male vocal duo *34 wks*

30 Jul 69	● **JE T'AIME. . . MOI NON PLUS** *Fontana TF 1042*		2	11 wks
4 Oct 69	★ **JE T'AIME. . . MOI NON PLUS** (re-issue) *Major Minor MM 645*		1	14 wks
7 Dec 74	**JE T'AIME. . . MOI NON PLUS** (2nd re-issue) *Atlantic K 11511*		31	9 wks

Elvin BISHOP
US, male instrumentalist - guitar *4 wks*

15 May 76	**FOOLED AROUND AND FELL IN LOVE** *Capricorn 2089 204*		34	4 wks

Cilla BLACK *UK, female vocalist* *192 wks*

17 Oct 63	**LOVE OF THE LOVED** *Parlophone R 5065*		35	6 wks
6 Feb 64	★ **ANYONE WHO HAD A HEART** *Parlophone R 5101*		1	17 wks
7 May 64	★ **YOU'RE MY WORLD** *Parlophone R 5133*		1	17 wks

Date		Title	Label/Number		Pos	Wks
6 Aug 64	●	IT'S FOR YOU	Parlophone R 5162	....	7	10 wks
14 Jan 65	●	YOU'VE LOST THAT LOVIN' FEELIN'	Parlophone R 5225	....	2	9 wks
22 Apr 65		I'VE BEEN WRONG BEFORE	Parlophone R 5296		17	8 wks
13 Jan 66	●	LOVE'S JUST A BROKEN HEART	Parlophone R 5395		5	11 wks
31 Mar 66	●	ALFIE	Parlophone R 5427		9	12 wks
9 Jun 66	●	DON'T ANSWER ME	Parlophone R 5463	......	6	10 wks
20 Oct 66		A FOOL AM I	Parlophone R 5515		13	9 wks
8 Jun 67		WHAT GOOD AM I	Parlophone R 5608		24	7 wks
29 Nov 67		I ONLY LIVE TO LOVE YOU	Parlophone R 5652		26	11 wks
13 Mar 68	●	STEP INSIDE LOVE	Parlophone R 5674		8	9 wks
12 Jun 68		WHERE IS TOMORROW	Parlophone R 5706	....	40	3 wks
12 Feb 69	●	SURROUND YOURSELF WITH SORROW	Parlophone R 5759		3	12 wks
9 Jul 69	●	CONVERSATIONS	Parlophone R 5785	.....	7	12 wks
13 Dec 69		IF I THOUGHT YOU'D EVER CHANGE YOUR MIND	Parlophone R 5820	....	20	9 wks
20 Nov 71	●	SOMETHING TELLS ME (SOMETHING IS GONNA HAPPEN TONIGHT)	Parlophone R 5924		3	14 wks
2 Feb 74		BABY WE CAN'T GO WRONG	EMI 2107	....	36	6 wks

Jeanne BLACK   US, female vocalist   4 wks

23 Jun 60	HE'LL HAVE TO STAY	Capitol CL 15131	.....	41	4 wks

BLACK GORILLA
UK, male/female vocal/instrumental group   6 wks

27 Aug 77	GIMME DAT BANANA	Response SR 502	......	29	6 wks

BLACK LACE
UK, male vocal/instrumental group   55 wks

31 Mar 79		MARY ANN	EMI 2919	....	42	4 wks
24 Sep 83	●	SUPERMAN (GIOCA JOUER)	Flair FLA 105	...	9	18 wks
30 Jun 84	●	AGADOO	Flair FLA 107		2†	27 wks
24 Nov 84	●	DO THE CONGA	Flair FLA 108		10†	6 wks

BLACK SABBATH
UK/US, male vocal/instrumental group   67 wks

29 Aug 70	●	PARANOID	Vertigo 6059 010	....	4	18 wks
3 Jun 78		NEVER SAY DIE	Vertigo SAB 001		21	8 wks
14 Oct 78		HARD ROAD	Vertigo SAB 002		33	4 wks
5 Jul 80		NEON KNIGHTS	Vertigo SAB 3		22	9 wks
16 Aug 80		PARANOID (re-issue)	Nems BSS 101	....	14	12 wks
6 Dec 80		DIE YOUNG	Vertigo SAB 4	....	41	7 wks
7 Nov 81		MOB RULES	Vertigo SAB 5		46	4 wks
13 Feb 82		TURN UP THE NIGHT	Vertigo/Phonogram SAB 6		37	5 wks

Group UK only for first 3 hits and re-issue of Paranoid.

BLACK SLATE
UK/Jamaica, male vocal/instrumental group   15 wks

20 Sep 80	●	AMIGO	Ensign ENY 42		9	9 wks
6 Dec 80		BOOM BOOM	Ensign ENY 47		51	6 wks

BLACK UHURU
Jamaica, male vocal/instrumental group   6 wks

8 Sep 84	WHAT IS LIFE?	Island IS 150		56	6 wks

Band of the BLACK WATCH
UK, military band   22 wks

30 Aug 75	●	SCOTCH ON THE ROCKS	Spark SRL 1128	....	8	14 wks
13 Dec 75		DANCE OF THE CUCKOOS	Spark SRL 1135	..	37	8 wks

Tony BLACKBURN   UK, male vocalist   7 wks

24 Jan 68	SO MUCH LOVE	MGM 1375	....	31	4 wks
26 Mar 69	IT'S ONLY LOVE	MGM 1467	....	42	3 wks

BLACKBYRDS
US, male vocal/instrumental group   6 wks

31 May 75	WALKING IN RHYTHM	Fantasy FTC 114	.....	23	6 wks

BLACKFOOT
US, male vocal/instrumental group   5 wks

6 Mar 82	DRY COUNTY	Atco K 11686	....	43	4 wks
18 Jun 83	SEND ME AN ANGEL	Atco B 9880	....	66	1 wk

J BLACKFOOT   US, male vocalist   4 wks

17 Mar 84	TAXI	Allegiance ALES 2	....	48	4 wks

BLACKFOOT SUE
UK, male vocal/instrumental group   15 wks

12 Aug 72	●	STANDING IN THE ROAD	Jam 13	....	4	10 wks
16 Dec 72		SING DON'T SPEAK	Jam 29	....	36	5 wks

BLACKHEARTS - *See Joan JETT and the BLACKHEARTS*

Bill BLACK'S COMBO
US, male instrumental group, Bill Black, bass   8 wks

8 Sep 60	WHITE SILVER SANDS	London HLU 9090	....	50	1 wk
3 Nov 60	DON'T BE CRUEL	London HLU 9212	....	32	7 wks

BLACKWELLS   US, male vocal group   2 wks

18 May 61	LOVE OR MONEY	London HLW 9334	....	46	2 wks

Vivian BLAINE   US, female vocalist   1 wk

10 Jul 53	BUSHEL AND A PECK	Brunswick 05100	....	12	1 wk

Joyce BLAIR - *See Miss X*

Peter BLAKE   UK, male vocalist   4 wks

8 Oct 77	LIPSMACKIN' ROCK 'N' ROLLIN'	Pepper UP 36295		40	4 wks

BLANCMANGE
UK, male vocal/instrumental group   64 wks

17 Apr 82		GOD'S KITCHEN/I'VE SEEN THE WORD	London BLANC 1	....	65	2 wks
31 Jul 82		FEEL ME	London BLANC 2	....	46	5 wks
30 Oct 82	●	LIVING ON THE CEILING	London BLANC 3	..	7	14 wks

LAURA BRANIGAN (right) Gloria be to Laura B.

BREAK MACHINE (below left) Their big break came in 1984.

BROWN SAUCE (below right) Noel Edmunds of the *Swap Shop* hit trio about to do the trip with a pith-helmeted Dave Lee Travis.

JAMES BROWN (bottom left) Papa's got a brand new poodle.

CLIFF BENNETT (bottom right) Trying to remember the words on stage at Liverpool's Cavern.

19 Feb 83	**WAVES** *London BLANC 4*	**19**	9 wks
7 May 83 ●	**BLIND VISION** *London BLANC 5*	**10**	8 wks
26 Nov 83	**THAT'S LOVE, THAT IT IS** *London BLANC 6*	**33**	8 wks
14 Apr 84 ●	**DON'T TELL ME** *London BLANC 7*	**8**	10 wks
21 Jul 84	**THE DAY BEFORE YOU CAME** *London BLANC 8*	**22**	8 wks

Billy BLAND   *US, male vocalist*   *10 wks*

19 May 60	**LET THE LITTLE GIRL DANCE** *London HL 9096*	**15**	10 wks

BLOCKHEADS   – *See Ian DURY and the BLOCKHEADS*

BLONDIE
US/UK, female/male vocal/instrumental group   *140 wks*

18 Feb 78 ●	**DENIS** *Chrysalis CHS 2204*	**2**	14 wks
6 May 78 ●	**(I'M ALWAYS TOUCHED BY YOUR) PRESENCE DEAR** *Chrysalis CHS 2217*	**10**	9 wks
26 Aug 78	**PICTURE THIS** *Chrysalis CHS 2242*	**12**	11 wks
11 Nov 78	**HANGING ON THE TELEPHONE** *Chrysalis CHR 2266*	**5**	12 wks
27 Jan 79 ★	**HEART OF GLASS** *Chrysalis CHE 2275*	**1**	12 wks
19 May 79 ★	**SUNDAY GIRL** *Chrysalis CHS 2320*	**1**	13 wks
29 Sep 79 ●	**DREAMING** *Chrysalis CHS 2350*	**2**	8 wks
24 Nov 79	**UNION CITY BLUE** *Chrysalis CHS 2400*	**13**	10 wks
23 Feb 80 ★	**ATOMIC** *Chrysalis CHS 2410*	**1**	9 wks
12 Apr 80 ★	**CALL ME** *Chrysalis CHS 2414*	**1**	9 wks
8 Nov 80 ★	**THE TIDE IS HIGH** *Chrysalis CHS 2465*	**1**	12 wks
24 Jan 81 ●	**RAPTURE** *Chrysalis CHS 2485*	**5**	8 wks
8 May 82	**ISLAND OF LOST SOULS** *Chrysalis CHS 2608*	**11**	9 wks
24 Jul 82	**WAR CHILD** *Chrysalis CHS 2624*	**39**	4 wks

BLOOD SWEAT AND TEARS
US/Canada, male vocal/instrumental group   *6 wks*

30 Apr 69	**YOU'VE MADE ME SO VERY HAPPY** *CBS 4116*	**35**	6 wks

BLOODSTONE
US, male vocal/instrumental group   *4 wks*

18 Aug 73	**NATURAL HIGH** *Decca F 13382*	**40**	4 wks

Bobby BLOOM   *US, male vocalist*   *24 wks*

29 Aug 70 ●	**MONTEGO BAY** *Polydor 2058 051*	**3**	14 wks
12 Dec 70	**MONTEGO BAY** (re-entry) *Polydor 2058 051*	**42**	3 wks
9 Jan 71	**MONTEGO BAY** (2nd re-entry) *Polydor 2058 051*	**47**	2 wks
9 Jan 71	**HEAVY MAKES YOU HAPPY** *Polydor 2001 122*	**31**	5 wks

BLOOMSBURY SET
UK, male vocal/instrumental group   *3 wks*

25 Jun 83	**HANGING AROUND WITH THE BIG BOYS** *Stiletto/RCA STL 13*	**56**	3 wks

Kurtis BLOW   *US, male vocalist*   *10 wks*

15 Dec 79	**CHRISTMAS RAPPIN'** *Mercury BLOW 7*	**30**	6 wks
11 Oct 80	**THE BREAKS** *Mercury BLOW 8*	**47**	4 wks

BLUE   *UK, male vocal/instrumental group*   *8 wks*

30 Apr 77	**GONNA CAPTURE YOUR HEART** *Rocket ROKN 522*	**18**	8 wks

Babbity BLUE   *UK, female vocalist*   *2 wks*

11 Feb 65	**DON'T MAKE ME** *Decca F 12053*	**48**	2 wks

Barry BLUE   *UK, male vocalist*   *48 wks*

28 Jul 73 ●	**(DANCING) ON A SATURDAY NIGHT** *Bell 1295*	**2**	15 wks
3 Nov 73 ●	**DO YOU WANNA DANCE** *Bell 1336*	**7**	12 wks
2 Mar 74	**SCHOOL LOVE** *Bell 1345*	**11**	9 wks
3 Aug 74	**MISS HIT AND RUN** *Bell 1364*	**26**	7 wks
26 Oct 74	**HOT SHOT** *Bell 1379*	**23**	5 wks

BLUEBELLS
UK, male vocal/instrumental group   *34 wks*

12 Mar 83	**CATH** *London LON 20*	**62**	2 wks
9 Jul 83	**SUGAR BRIDGE (IT WILL STAND)** *London LON 27*	**72**	1 wk
24 Mar 84	**I'M FALLING** *London LON 45*	**11**	12 wks
23 Jun 84 ●	**YOUNG AT HEART** *London LON 49*	**8**	12 wks
1 Sep 84	**CATH/WILL SHE ALWAYS BE WAITING** *London LON 54*	**38**	7 wks

LON 54 version of Cath is a re-issue of LON 20.

BLUE FEATHER
Holland, male vocal/instrumental group   *4 wks*

3 Jul 82	**LET'S FUNK TONIGHT** *Mercury/Phonogram MER 109*	**50**	4 wks

BLUE FLAMES   – *See Georgie FAME*

BLUE GRASS BOYS   – *See Johnny DUNCAN and the BLUE GRASS BOYS*

BLUE HAZE
UK, male vocal/instrumental group   *6 wks*

18 Mar 72	**SMOKE GETS IN YOUR EYES** *A & M AMS 891*	**32**	6 wks

BLUE JEANS   – *See Bob B. SOXX and the BLUE JEANS*

BLUE MINK
UK/US, male/female vocal/instrumental group   *83 wks*

15 Nov 69 ●	**MELTING POT** *Philips BF 1818*	**3**	15 wks
28 Mar 70 ●	**GOOD MORNING FREEDOM** *Philips BF 1838*	**10**	10 wks
19 Sep 70	**OUR WORLD** *Philips 6006 042*	**17**	9 wks
29 May 71 ●	**BANNER MAN** *Regal Zonophone RZ 3034*	**3**	14 wks
11 Nov 72	**STAY WITH ME** *Regal Zonophone RZ 3064*	**11**	13 wks
17 Feb 73	**STAY WITH ME** (re-entry) *Regal Zonophone RZ 3064*	**43**	2 wks
3 Mar 73	**BY THE DEVIL** *EMI 2007*	**26**	9 wks
23 Jun 73 ●	**RANDY** *EMI 2028*	**9**	11 wks

BLUE OYSTER CULT
US, male vocal/instrumental group   *14 wks*

20 May 78	**(DON'T FEAR) THE REAPER** *CBS 6333*	**16**	14 wks

BLUE RONDO a la TURK
UK, male vocal/instrumental group   9 wks

| 14 Nov 81 | ME AND MR SANCHEZ | *Virgin VS 463* .... | **40** | 4 wks |
| 13 Mar 82 | KLACTOVEESEDSTEIN | *Virgin VS 476* .... | **50** | 5 wks |

BLUE ZOO
UK, male vocal/instrumental group   17 wks

12 Jun 82	I'M YOUR MAN	*Magnet MAG 224*	**55**	3 wks
16 Oct 82	CRY BOY CRY	*Magnet MAG 234*	**13**	10 wks
28 May 83	I JUST CAN'T (FORGIVE AND FORGET)			
		Magnet MAG 241	**60**	4 wks

BLUENOTES - *See Harold MELVIN and the BLUENOTES*

BLUES BAND
UK, male vocal/instrumental group   2 wks

| 12 Jul 80 | BLUES BAND (EP) | *Arista BOOT 2* .... | **68** | 2 wks |

Tracks on Blues Band EP: Maggie's Farm/Ain't it Tuff/ Diddy Wah Diddy/Back Door Man.

Colin BLUNSTONE   UK, male vocalist   19 wks

12 Feb 72	SAY YOU DON'T MIND	*Epic EPC 7765*	**15**	9 wks
11 Nov 72	I DON'T BELIEVE IN MIRACLES			
		Epic EPC 8434	**31**	6 wks
17 Feb 73	HOW COULD WE DARE TO BE WRONG			
		Epic EPC 1197	**45**	2 wks
29 May 82	TRACKS OF MY TEARS	*PRT 7P 236*	**60**	2 wks

See also Neil MacArthur; Dave Stewart

BOB and EARL   US, male vocal duo   13 wks

| 12 Mar 69 | ● HARLEM SHUFFLE | *Island WIP 6053* .... | **7** | 13 wks |

BOB and MARCIA
Jamaica, male/female vocal duo   25 wks

| 14 Mar 70 | ● YOUNG GIFTED AND BLACK | *Harry J HJ 6605* ... | **5** | 12 wks |
| 5 Jun 71 | PIED PIPER | *Trojan TR 7818* .... | **11** | 13 wks |

BODYSNATCHERS
UK, female vocal/instrumental group   12 wks

| 15 Mar 80 | LET'S DO ROCK STEADY | *2Tone CHS TT 9* .. | **22** | 9 wks |
| 19 Jul 80 | EASY LIFE | *2Tone CHS TT 12* .... | **50** | 3 wks |

Humphrey BOGART - *See Dooley WILSON*

Hamilton BOHANNON
US, male vocalist/instrumentalist - drums   38 wks

15 Feb 75	SOUTH AFRICAN MAN	*Brunswick BR 16*	**22**	8 wks
24 May 75	● DISCO STOMP	*Brunswick BR 19*	**6**	12 wks
5 Jul 75	FOOT STOMPIN' MUSIC	*Brunswick BR 21*	**23**	6 wks
6 Sep 75	HAPPY FEELING	*Brunswick BR 24*	**49**	3 wks
26 Aug 78	LET'S START THE DANCE	*Mercury 6167 700* ..	**56**	4 wks
13 Feb 82	LET'S START TO DANCE AGAIN			
		London HL 10582	**49**	5 wks

BOILING POINT
US, male vocal/instrumental group   6 wks

| 27 May 78 | LET'S GET FUNKTIFIED | *Bang BANG 1312* .... | **41** | 6 wks |

Marc BOLAN   UK, male vocalist   8 wks

9 May 81	RETURN OF THE ELECTRIC WARRIOR (EP)			
		Ram MBSF 001	**50**	4 wks
19 Sep 81	YOU SCARE ME TO DEATH			
		Cherry Red CHERRY 29	**51**	4 wks

Tracks on Return Of The Electric Warrior EP: Sing Me A Song/Endless Sleep/The Lilac Hand Of Menthol Dan. See also T. Rex.

BOMBERS
US, male/female vocal/instrumental group   10 wks

| 5 May 79 | (EVERYBODY) GET DANCIN' | *Flamingo FM 1* | **37** | 7 wks |
| 18 Aug 79 | LET'S DANCE | *Flamingo FM 4* .... | **58** | 3 wks |

Ronnie BOND   UK, male vocalist   5 wks

| 31 May 80 | IT'S WRITTEN ON YOUR BODY | | | |
| | | *Mercury MER 13* .... | **52** | 5 wks |

Gary 'U.S.' BONDS   US, male vocalist   39 wks

19 Jan 61	NEW ORLEANS	*Top Rank JAR 527*	**16**	11 wks
20 Jul 61	● QUARTER TO THREE	*Top Rank JAR 575* ...	**7**	13 wks
30 May 81	THIS LITTLE GIRL	*EMI AMERICA EA 122* ...	**43**	6 wks
22 Aug 81	JOLÉ BLON	*EMI AMERICA EA 127*	**51**	3 wks
31 Oct 81	IT'S ONLY LOVE	*EMI AMERICA EA 128*	**43**	3 wks
17 Jul 82	SOUL DEEP	*EMI AMERICA EA 140*	**59**	3 wks

Known as U.S. Bonds on his 1961 hits.

Elbow BONES and the RACKETEERS
US, male group leader with female backing group   9 wks

| 14 Jan 84 | A NIGHT IN NEW YORK | *EMI America EA 165* | **33** | 9 wks |

BONEY M
Various West Indian Islands male/female vocal group   152 wks

18 Dec 76	● DADDY COOL	*Atlantic K 10827*	**6**	13 wks
12 Mar 77	● SUNNY	*Atlantic K 10892*	**3**	10 wks
25 Jun 77	● MA BAKER	*Atlantic K 10965*	**2**	13 wks
29 Oct 77	BELFAST	*Atlantic K 11020*	**8**	13 wks
29 Apr 78	★ RIVERS OF BABYLON/BROWN GIRL IN THE RING	*Atlantic/Hansa K 11120* ...	**1**	40 wks
7 Oct 78	● RASPUTIN	*Atlantic/Hansa K 11192*	**2**	10 wks
2 Dec 78	★ MARY'S BOY CHILD - OH MY LORD			
		Atlantic/Hansa K 11221	**1**	8 wks
3 Mar 79	● PAINTER MAN	*Atlantic/Hansa K 11255*	**10**	6 wks
28 Apr 79	HOORAY HOORAY IT'S A HOLI-HOLIDAY			
		Atlantic/Hansa K 11279	**3**	9 wks
11 Aug 79	GOTTA GO HOME/EL LUTE			
		Atlantic/Hansa K 11351	**12**	11 wks
15 Dec 79	I'M BORN AGAIN	*Atlantic/Hansa K 11410*	**35**	7 wks
26 Apr 80	MY FRIEND JACK	*Atlantic/Hansa K 11463*	**57**	5 wks
14 Feb 81	CHILDREN OF PARADISE			
		Atlantic/Hansa K 11637	**66**	2 wks
21 Nov 81	WE KILL THE WORLD (DON'T KILL THE WORLD)	*Atlantic/Hansa K 11689*	**39**	5 wks

El Lute only listed with Gotta Go Home from 29 Sep 79. Brown Girl in The Ring only listed with Rivers of Babylon from 5 Aug 78.

BIG COUNTRY (top left) Led by ex-Skid Stuart Adamson – 'As far as I'm concerned people who buy our records and come to our gigs are as much a part of the group as us' **BREAD** (top right) Changed their name from 'Pleasure Faire' to make it with five Top 40 hits in Britain and 12 in America. **BUGGLES** (lower left) Yes, Geoff Downes joined Asia and Trevor Horn produced Frankie Goes To Hollywood **BOOKER T. AND THE M.G.'s** (lower right) Their 'Soul Limbo' became the BBC Cricket theme

Graham BONNET   UK, male vocalist — 15 wks

21 Mar 81	●	NIGHT GAMES	Vertigo VER 1		6	11 wks
13 Jun 81		LIAR	Vertigo VER 2		51	4 wks

Graham BONNEY   UK, male vocalist — 8 wks

24 Mar 66	SUPERGIRL	Columbia DB 7843	19	8 wks

BONNIE - See DELANEY and BONNIE and FRIENDS featuring Eric CLAPTON

BONZO DOG DOO-DAH BAND
UK, male vocal/instrumental group — 14 wks

6 Nov 68	●	I'M THE URBAN SPACEMAN	Liberty LBF 15144		5	14 wks

BOOKER T. and the M. G.'S
US, male instrumental group — 43 wks

11 Dec 68		SOUL LIMBO	Stax 102		30	9 wks
7 May 69	●	TIME IS TIGHT	Stax 119		4	18 wks
30 Aug 69		SOUL CLAP '69	Stax 127		35	4 wks
15 Dec 79	●	GREEN ONIONS	Atlantic K 10109		7	12 wks

BOOMTOWN RATS
Ireland, male vocal/instrumental group — 120 wks

27 Aug 77		LOOKING AFTER NO. 1	Ensign ENY 4		11	9 wks
19 Nov 77		MARY OF THE FOURTH FORM	Ensign ENY 9		15	9 wks
15 Apr 78		SHE'S SO MODERN	Ensign ENY 13		12	11 wks
17 Jun 78	●	LIKE CLOCKWORK	Ensign ENY 14		6	13 wks
14 Oct 78	★	RAT TRAP	Ensign ENY 16		1	15 wks
21 Jul 79	★	I DON'T LIKE MONDAYS	Ensign ENY 30		1	12 wks
17 Nov 79		DIAMOND SMILES	Ensign ENY 33		13	10 wks
26 Jan 80	●	SOMEONE'S LOOKING AT YOU	Ensign EN 34		4	9 wks
22 Nov 80	●	BANANA REPUBLIC	Ensign BONGO 1		3	11 wks
31 Jan 81		THE ELEPHANT'S GRAVEYARD (GUILTY) Ensign BONGO 2			26	6 wks
12 Dec 81		NEVER IN A MILLION YEARS Mercury MER 87			62	3 wks
20 Mar 82		HOUSE ON FIRE	Mercury/Phonogram MER 91		24	8 wks
18 Feb 84		TONIGHT	Mercury/Phonogram MER 154		73	1 wk
19 May 84		DRAG ME DOWN	Mercury/Phonogram MER 163		50	3 wks

Daniel BOONE   UK, male vocalist — 25 wks

14 Aug 71	DADDY DON'T YOU WALK SO FAST Penny Farthing PEN 764		17	15 wks
1 Apr 72	BEAUTIFUL SUNDAY	Penny Farthing PEN 781	48	1 wk
15 Apr 72	BEAUTIFUL SUNDAY (re-entry) Penny Farthing PEN 781		21	9 wks

Debby BOONE   US, female vocalist — 2 wks

24 Dec 77	YOU LIGHT UP MY LIFE	Warner Bros. K 17043	48	2 wks

Pat BOONE   US, male vocalist — 296 wks

18 Nov 55	●	AIN'T THAT A SHAME	London HLD 8173		7	9 wks
27 Apr 56	★	I'LL BE HOME	London HLD 8253		1	22 wks
27 Jul 56		LONG TALL SALLY	London HLD 8291		27	3 wks
17 Aug 56		I ALMOST LOST MY MIND	London HLD 8303		14	7 wks
24 Aug 56		LONG TALL SALLY (re-entry) London HLD 8291			18	4 wks
7 Dec 56	●	FRIENDLY PERSUASION	London HLD 8346		3	21 wks
11 Jan 57		I'LL BE HOME (re-entry) London HLD 8253			19	2 wks
11 Jan 57		AIN'T THAT A SHAME (re-entry) London HLD 8173			22	2 wks
1 Feb 57	●	DON'T FORBID ME	London HLD 8370		2	16 wks
26 Apr 57		WHY BABY WHY	London HLD 8404		17	7 wks
5 Jul 57	●	LOVE LETTERS IN THE SAND London HLD 8445			2	21 wks
27 Sep 57	●	REMEMBER YOU'RE MINE/THERE'S A GOLDMINE IN THE SKY London HLD 8479			5	18 wks
6 Dec 57	●	APRIL LOVE	London HLD 8512		7	23 wks
13 Dec 57		WHITE CHRISTMAS	London HLD 8520		29	1 wk
4 Apr 58	●	A WONDERFUL TIME UP THERE London HLD 8574			2	17 wks
11 Apr 58	●	IT'S TOO SOON TO KNOW London HLD 8574			7	12 wks
27 Jun 58	●	SUGAR MOON	London HLD 8640		6	12 wks
29 Aug 58		IF DREAMS CAME TRUE	London HLD 8675		16	11 wks
5 Dec 58		GEE BUT IT'S LONELY	London HLD 8739		30	1 wk
16 Jan 59		I'LL REMEMBER TONIGHT	London HLD 8775		28	1 wk
6 Feb 59		I'LL REMEMBER TONIGHT (re-entry) London HLD 8775			21	1 wk
20 Feb 59		I'LL REMEMBER TONIGHT (2nd re-entry) London HLD 8775			18	7 wks
10 Apr 59		WITH THE WIND AND THE RAIN IN YOUR HAIR London HLD 8824			21	3 wks
22 May 59		FOR A PENNY	London HLD 8855		28	3 wks
26 Jun 59		FOR A PENNY (re-entry) London HLD 8855			19	6 wks
31 Jul 59		'TWIXT TWELVE AND TWENTY London HLD 8910			18	6 wks
18 Sep 59		'TWIXT TWELVE AND TWENTY (re-entry) London HLD 8910			26	1 wk
23 Jun 60		WALKING THE FLOOR OVER YOU London HLD 9138			40	2 wks
14 Jul 60		WALKING THE FLOOR OVER YOU (re-entry) London HLD 9138			46	1 wk
4 Aug 60		WALKING THE FLOOR OVER YOU (2nd re-entry) London HLD 9138			39	2 wks
6 Jul 61		MOODY RIVER	London HLD 9350		18	10 wks
7 Dec 61	●	JOHNNY WILL	London HLD 9461		4	13 wks
15 Feb 62		I'LL SEE YOU IN MY DREAMS London HLD 9504			27	9 wks
24 May 62		QUANDO QUANDO QUANDO London HLD 9543			41	4 wks
12 Jul 62	●	SPEEDY GONZALES	London HLD 9573		2	19 wks
15 Nov 62		THE MAIN ATTRACTION	London HLD 9620		12	11 wks

There's A Goldmine In The Sky was only credited for the week of 27 Sep 57 with Remember You're Mine.

Duke BOOTEE - See Melle MEL and Duke BOOTEE

Ken BOOTHE   Jamaica, male vocalist — 22 wks

21 Sep 74	★	EVERYTHING I OWN	Trojan TR 7920		1	12 wks
14 Dec 74		CRYING OVER YOU	Trojan TR 7944		11	10 wks

BOOTHILL FOOTAPPERS
UK, male/female vocal/instrumental group — 3 wks

14 Jul 84	GET YOUR FEET OUT OF MY SHOES Go Discs TAP 1		64	3 wks

BOOTSY'S RUBBER BAND
US, male vocal/instrumental group — 3 wks

8 Jul 78	BOOTZILLA	Warner Bros. K 17196	43	3 wks

BOSTON   US, male vocal/instrumental group — 13 wks

29 Jan 77	MORE THAN A FEELING	Epic EPC 4658	22	8 wks
7 Oct 78	DON'T LOOK BACK	Epic EPC 6653	43	5 wks

Eve BOSWELL   Hungary, female vocalist — 13 wks

30 Dec 55	●	PICKIN' A CHICKEN	Parlophone R 4082		9	7 wks
2 Mar 56		PICKIN' A CHICKEN (re-entry) Parlophone R 4082			16	3 wks

6 Apr 56	PICKIN' A CHICKEN (2nd re-entry) *Parlophone R 4082*			20	3 wks

BOUNCING CZECKS
UK, male vocal/instrumental group *1 wk*

29 Dec 84	I'M A LITTLE CHRISTMAS CRACKER *RCA 463*			72†	1 wk

BOURGIE BOURGIE
UK, male vocal/instrumental group *4 wks*

3 Mar 84	BREAKING POINT *MCA BOU 1*			48	4 wks

BOW WOW WOW
UK, female/male vocal/instrumental group *54 wks*

26 Jul 80	C30, C60, C90, GO *EMI 5088*			34	7 wks
6 Dec 80	YOUR CASSETTE PET *EMI WOW 1*			58	6 wks
28 Mar 81	W.O.R.K. (N.O. NAH NO NO MY DADDY DON'T) *EMI 5153*			62	3 wks
15 Aug 81	PRINCE OF DARKNESS *RCA 100*			58	4 wks
7 Nov 81	CHIHUAHUA *RCA 144*			51	4 wks
30 Jan 82	● GO WILD IN THE COUNTRY *RCA 175*			7	13 wks
1 May 82	SEE JUNGLE (JUNGLE BOY) TV SAVAGE *RCA 220*			45	3 wks
5 Jun 82	● I WANT CANDY *RCA 238*			9	8 wks
31 Jul 82	LOUIS QUATORZE *RCA 263*			66	2 wks
12 Mar 83	DO YOU WANNA HOLD ME *RCA 314*			47	4 wks

Your Cassette Pet listed as Louis Quatorze on 6 Dec 80 only. Tracks on Your Cassette Pet (available only as a cassette) are: Louis Quatorze/Gold He Said/Umo-Sex-Al Apache/I Want My Baby On Mars/Sexy Eiffel Towers/Giant Sized Baby Thing/Fools Rush In/Radio G.String. RCA 263 is disc version of track on EMI WOW 1 Cassette.

David BOWIE *UK, male vocalist* *317 wks*

6 Sep 69	SPACE ODDITY *Philips BF 1801*			48	1 wk
20 Sep 69	● SPACE ODDITY (re-entry) *Philips BF 1801*			5	13 wks
24 Jun 72	● STARMAN *RCA 2199*			10	11 wks
16 Sep 72	JOHN I'M ONLY DANCING *RCA 2263*			12	10 wks
9 Dec 72	● THE JEAN GENIE *RCA 2302*			2	13 wks
14 Apr 73	● DRIVE-IN SATURDAY *RCA 2352*			3	10 wks
30 Jun 73	● LIFE ON MARS *RCA 2316*			3	13 wks
15 Sep 73	THE LAUGHING GNOME *Deram DM 123*			6	12 wks
20 Oct 73	SORROW *RCA 2424*			3	9 wks
5 Jan 74	SORROW (re-entry) *RCA 2424*			30	4 wks
23 Feb 74	● REBEL REBEL *RCA LPBO 5009*			5	7 wks
20 Apr 74	ROCK AND ROLL SUICIDE *RCA LPBO 5021*			22	7 wks
22 Jun 74	DIAMOND DOGS *RCA APBO 0293*			21	6 wks
28 Sep 74	● KNOCK ON WOOD *RCA 2466*			10	6 wks
1 Mar 75	YOUNG AMERICANS *RCA 2523*			18	7 wks
2 Aug 75	FAME *RCA 2579*			17	8 wks
11 Oct 75	★ SPACE ODDITY (re-issue) *RCA 2593*			1	10 wks
29 Nov 75	● GOLDEN YEARS *RCA 2640*			8	10 wks
22 May 76	TVC 15 *RCA 2682*			33	4 wks
19 Feb 77	● SOUND AND VISION *RCA PB 0905*			3	11 wks
15 Oct 77	HEROES *RCA PB 1121*			24	8 wks
21 Jan 78	BEAUTY AND THE BEAST *RCA PB 1190*			39	3 wks
2 Dec 78	BREAKING GLASS (EP) *RCA BOW 1*			54	7 wks
5 May 79	BOYS KEEP SWINGING *RCA BOW 2*			7	10 wks
21 Jul 79	D.J. *RCA BOW 3*			29	5 wks
15 Dec 79	JOHN I'M ONLY DANCING (AGAIN) (1975)/JOHN I'M ONLY DANCING (1972) *RCA BOW 4*			12	8 wks
1 Mar 80	ALABAMA SONG *RCA BOW 5*			23	5 wks
16 Aug 80	★ ASHES TO ASHES *RCA BOW 6*			1	10 wks
1 Nov 80	● FASHION *RCA BOW 7*			5	11 wks
10 Jan 81	SCARY MONSTERS (AND SUPER CREEPS) *RCA BOW 8*			20	6 wks
28 Mar 81	UP THE HILL BACKWARDS *RCA BOW 9*			32	6 wks
28 Nov 81	WILD IS THE WIND *RCA BOW 10*			24	10 wks

6 Mar 82	BAAL'S HYMN (EP) *RCA BOW 11*			29	5 wks
10 Apr 82	● CAT PEOPLE (PUTTING OUT FIRE) *MCA 770*			26	6 wks
26 Mar 83	★ LET'S DANCE *EMI America EA 152*			1	14 wks
11 Jun 83	● CHINA GIRL *EMI America EA 157*			2	8 wks
24 Sep 83	● MODERN LOVE *EMI America EA 158*			2	8 wks
5 Nov 83	WHITE LIGHT, WHITE HEAT *RCA 372*			46	3 wks
22 Sep 84	● BLUE JEAN *EMI America EA 181*			6	8 wks
8 Dec 84	TONIGHT *EMI America EA 187*			53†	4 wks

Tracks on Breaking Glass EP: Breaking Glass/Art Decade/ Ziggy Stardust. All 3 versions of John I'm Only Dancing are different versions. Tracks on Baal's Hymn EP: Baal's Hymn/ The Drowned Girl/Remembering Marie/The Dirty Song/Ballad of the Adventurers. See also Queen and David Bowie; David Bowie and Bing Crosby.

David BOWIE and Bing CROSBY
UK/US, male vocal duo *8 wks*

27 Nov 82	● PEACE ON EARTH - LITTLE DRUMMER BOY *RCA BOW 12*			3	8 wks

See also David Bowie; Queen and David Bowie; Bing Crosby; Bing Crosby and Grace Kelly; Bing Crosby and Jane Wyman.

BOX TOPS
US, male vocal/instrumental group *33 wks*

13 Sep 67	● THE LETTER *Stateside SS 2044*			5	12 wks
20 Mar 68	CRY LIKE A BABY *Bell 1001*			15	12 wks
23 Aug 69	SOUL DEEP *Bell 1068*			22	9 wks

Jimmy BOYD *US, male vocalist* *6 wks*

27 Nov 53	● I SAW MOMMY KISSING SANTA CLAUS *Columbia DB 3365*			3	6 wks

See also Frankie Laine and Jimmy Boyd.

Jacqueline BOYER *France, female vocalist* *2 wks*

28 Apr 60	TOM PILLIBI *Columbia DB 4452*			33	2 wks

BOYSTOWN GANG
US, male/female vocal group *20 wks*

22 Aug 81	AIN'T NO MOUNTAIN HIGH ENOUGH *WEA DICK 1*			46	6 wks
31 Jul 82	● CAN'T TAKE MY EYES OFF YOU *ERC 101*			4	11 wks
9 Oct 82	SIGNED SEALED DELIVERED (I'M YOURS) *ERC 102*			50	3 wks

Wilfred BRAMBELL and Harry H. CORBETT *UK, male vocal duo* *12 wks*

28 Nov 63	AT THE PALACE (PARTS 1 & 2) *Pye 7N 15588*			25	12 wks

Johnny BRANDON *UK, male vocalist* *12 wks*

11 Mar 55	● TOMORROW *Polygon P 1131*			8	6 wks
29 Apr 55	TOMORROW (re-entry) *Polygon P 1131*			16	2 wks
1 Jul 55	DON'T WORRY *Polygon P 1163*			18	4 wks

Laura BRANIGAN *US, female vocalist* *33 wks*

18 Dec 82	● GLORIA *Atlantic K 11759*			6	13 wks
7 Jul 84	● SELF CONTROL *Atlantic A 9676*			5	17 wks
6 Oct 84	THE LUCKY ONE *Atlantic A 9636*			56	3 wks

BRASS CONSTRUCTION
US, male vocal/instrumental group   *28 wks*

3 Apr 76	**MOVIN'** *United Artists UP 36090*	**23**	6 wks
5 Feb 77	**HA CHA CHA (FUNKTION)**	**37**	5 wks
	United Artists UP 36205		
26 Jan 80	**MUSIC MAKES YOU FEEL LIKE DANCING**	**39**	6 wks
	United Artists UP 615		
28 Mar 83	**WALKIN' THE LINE** *Capitol CL 292*	**47**	3 wks
16 Jul 83	**WE CAN WORK IT OUT** *Capitol CL 299*	**70**	2 wks
7 Jul 84	**PARTYLINE** *Capitol CL 335*	**56**	4 wks
27 Oct 84	**INTERNATIONAL** *Capitol CL 341*	**70**	2 wks

BRAT
UK, male vocalist   *8 wks*

10 Jul 82	**CHALK DUST - THE UMPIRE STRIKES BACK**	**19**	8 wks
	Hansa SMASH 1		

BREAD
US, male vocal/instrumental group   *46 wks*

1 Aug 70	● **MAKE IT WITH YOU** *Elektra 2101 010*	**5**	14 wks
15 Jan 72	**BABY I'M A WANT YOU** *Elektra K 12033*	**14**	10 wks
29 Apr 72	**EVERYTHING I OWN** *Elektra K 12041*	**32**	6 wks
30 Sep 72	**GUITAR MAN** *Elektra K 12066*	**16**	9 wks
25 Dec 76	**LOST WITHOUT YOUR LOVE** *Elektra K 12241*	**27**	7 wks

BREAK MACHINE
US, male vocal/dance group   *32 wks*

4 Feb 84	● **STREET DANCE** *Record Shack SOHO 13*	**3**	14 wks
12 May 84	● **BREAKDANCE PARTY** *Record Shack SOHO 20*	**9**	8 wks
14 Jul 84	**BREAKDANCE PARTY** (re-entry)	**65**	2 wks
	Record Shack SOHO 20		
11 Aug 84	**ARE YOU READY?** *Record Shack SOHO 24*	**27**	8 wks

Freddy BRECK   *Germany, male vocalist*   *4 wks*

13 Apr 74	**SO IN LOVE WITH YOU** *Decca F 13481*	**44**	4 wks

BRECKER BROTHERS
US, male vocal/instrumental group   *5 wks*

4 Nov 78	**EAST RIVER** *Arista ARIST 211*	**34**	5 wks

BREEKOUT KREW   *US, male vocal duo*   *3 wks*

24 Nov 84	**MATT'S MOOD** *Next Plateau/London LON 59* ...	**51**	3 wks

Ann BREEN   *Ireland, female vocalist*   *2 wks*

19 Mar 83	**PAL OF MY CRADLE DAYS** *Homespun HS 052*	**69**	1 wk
7 Jan 84	**PAL OF MY CRADLE DAYS** (re-entry)	**74**	1 wk
	Homespun HS 052		

BRENDON   *UK, male vocalist*   *9 wks*

19 Mar 77	**GIMME SOME** *Magnet MAG 80*	**14**	9 wks

Rose BRENNAN   *UK, female vocalist*   *9 wks*

7 Dec 61	**TALL DARK STRANGER** *Philips PB 1193*	**31**	9 wks

Walter BRENNAN   *US, male vocalist*   *3 wks*

28 Jun 62	**OLD RIVERS** *Liberty LIB 55436*	**38**	3 wks

Tony BRENT   *UK, male vocalist*   *52 wks*

19 Dec 52	● **WALKIN' TO MISSOURI** *Columbia DB 3147* ...	**9**	2 wks
2 Jan 53	● **MAKE IT SOON** *Columbia DB 3187*	**9**	4 wks
9 Jan 53	● **WALKIN' TO MISSOURI** (re-entry)	**7**	5 wks
	Columbia DB 3147		
23 Jan 53	**GOT YOU ON MY MIND** *Columbia DB 3226* ...	**12**	1 wk
13 Mar 53	● **MAKE IT SOON** (re-entry) *Columbia DB 3187* ...	**9**	3 wks
30 Nov 56	**CINDY OH CINDY** *Columbia DB 3844*	**16**	6 wks
8 Feb 57	**CINDY OH CINDY** (re-entry) *Columbia DB 3844* ...	**30**	1 wk
28 Jun 57	**DARK MOON** *Columbia DB 3950*	**17**	14 wks
28 Feb 58	**THE CLOUDS WILL SOON ROLL BY**	**24**	3 wks
	Columbia DB 4066		
9 May 58	**THE CLOUDS WILL SOON ROLL BY** (re-entry)	**20**	2 wks
	Columbia DB 4066		
5 Sep 58	**GIRL OF MY DREAMS** *Columbia DB 4177*	**16**	7 wks
24 Jul 59	**WHY SHOULD I BE LONELY**	**24**	4 wks
	Columbia DB 4304		

Bernard BRESSLAW   *UK, male vocalist*   *11 wks*

5 Sep 58	● **MAD PASSIONATE LOVE** *HMV POP 522*	**6**	11 wks

See also Michael Medwin, Bernard Bresslaw, Alfie Bass and Leslie Fyson.

Teresa BREWER   *US, female vocalist*   *53 wks*

11 Feb 55	● **LET ME GO LOVER** *Vogue/Coral Q 72043*	**9**	10 wks
13 Apr 56	● **A TEAR FELL** *Vogue/Coral Q 72146*	**2**	15 wks
13 Jul 56	● **SWEET OLD-FASHIONED GIRL**	**3**	15 wks
	Vogue/Coral Q 72172		
10 May 57	**NORA MALONE** *Vogue/Coral Q 72224*	**26**	2 wks
23 Jun 60	**HOW DO YOU KNOW IT'S LOVE**	**21**	11 wks
	Coral Q 72396		

BRIAN AND MICHAEL
UK, male vocal duo   *19 wks*

25 Feb 78	★ **MATCHSTALK MEN AND MATCHSTALK CATS**	**1**	19 wks
	AND DOGS *Pye 7N 46035*		

BRICK   *US, male vocal/instrumental group*   *4 wks*

5 Feb 77	**DAZZ** *Bang 004*	**36**	4 wks

Alicia BRIDGES   *US, female vocalist*   *10 wks*

11 Nov 78	**I LOVE THE NIGHT LIFE (DISCO ROUND)**	**32**	10 wks
	Polydor 2066 936		

BRIGHOUSE AND RASTRICK
BRASS BAND   *UK, male brass band*   *13 wks*

12 Nov 77	● **THE FLORAL DANCE** *Transatlantic BIG 548* ...	**2**	13 wks

Bette BRIGHT   *UK, female vocalist*   *5 wks*

8 Mar 80	**HELLO I AM YOUR HEART** *Korova KOW 3* ..	**50**	5 wks

Sarah BRIGHTMAN *UK, female vocalist* 23 wks

11 Nov 78 ●	I LOST MY HEART TO A STARSHIP TROOPER		
	Ariola/Hansa AHA 527	6	14 wks
7 Apr 79	THE ADVENTURES OF THE LOVE CRUSADER		
	Ariola/Hansa AHA 538	53	5 wks
30 Jul 83	HIM *Polydor POSP 625*	55	4 wks

First hit credited to Sarah Brightman and Hot Gossip, second to Sarah Brightman and the Starship Troopers. Him credited to Sarah Brightman and the Royal Philharmonic Orchestra.

BRIGHTON and HOVE ALBION
F.C. *UK, male football team vocalists* 2 wks

28 May 83	THE BOYS IN THE OLD BRIGHTON BLUE		
	Energy NRG 2	65	2 wks

Johnny BRISTOL *US, male vocalist* 11 wks

24 Aug 74 ●	HANG ON IN THERE BABY *MGM 2006 443*	3	11 wks

See also Amii Stewart and Johnny Bristol.

BRONKSI BEAT
UK, male vocal/instrumental group 28 wks

2 Jun 84 ●	SMALLTOWN BOY *Forbidden Fruit/London BITE 1*	3	13 wks
22 Sep 84 ●	WHY? *Forbidden Fruit/London BITE 2*	6	10 wks
1 Dec 84	IT AIN'T NECCESSARILY SO		
	Forbidden Fruit/London BITE 3	30†	5 wks

Jet BRONX and the FORBIDDEN
UK, male vocal/instrumental group 1 wk

17 Dec 77	AIN'T DOIN' NOTHIN' *Lightning L1G 507*	49	1 wk

BROOK BROTHERS
UK, male vocal duo 35 wks

30 Mar 61 ●	WARPAINT *Pye 7N 15333*	5	14 wks
24 Aug 61	AIN'T GONNA WASH FOR A WEEK		
	Pye 7N 15369	13	10 wks
25 Jan 62	HE'S OLD ENOUGH TO KNOW BETTER		
	Pye 7N 15409	37	1 wk
16 Aug 62	WELCOME HOME BABY *Pye 7N 15453*	33	6 wks
21 Feb 63	TROUBLE IS MY MIDDLE NAME		
	Pye 7N 15498	38	4 wks

Elkie BROOKS *UK, female vocalist* 71 wks

2 Apr 77 ●	PEARL'S A SINGER *A & M AMS 7275*	8	9 wks
20 Aug 77 ●	SUNSHINE AFTER THE RAIN		
	A & M AMS 7306	10	9 wks
25 Feb 78	LILAC WINE *A & M AMS 7333*	16	7 wks
3 Jun 78	ONLY LOVE CAN BREAK YOUR HEART		
	A & M AMS 7353	43	5 wks
11 Nov 78	DON'T CRY OUT LOUD *A & M AMS 7395*	12	11 wks
5 May 79	THE RUNAWAY *A & M AMS 7428*	50	5 wks
16 Jan 82	FOOL IF YOU THINK IT'S OVER		
	A & M AMS 8187	17	10 wks
1 May 82	OUR LOVE *A & M AMS 8214*	43	5 wks
17 Jul 82	NIGHTS IN WHITE SATIN *A & M AMS 8235*	33	5 wks
22 Jan 83	GASOLINE ALLEY *A & M AMS 8305*	52	5 wks

Mel BROOKS *US, male vocalist* 10 wks

18 Feb 84	TO BE OR NOT TO BE (THE HITLER RAP)		
	Island IS 158	12	10 wks

Norman BROOKS *US, male vocalist* 1 wk

12 Nov 54	A SKY BLUE SHIRT AND A RAINBOW TIE		
	London L 1228	17	1 wk

BROTHERHOOD OF MAN
UK, male/female vocal group 97 wks

14 Feb 70 ●	UNITED WE STAND *Deram DM 284*	10	9 wks
4 Jul 70	WHERE ARE YOU GOING TO MY LOVE		
	Deram DM 298	22	10 wks
13 Mar 76 ★	SAVE YOUR KISSES FOR ME *Pye 7N 45569*	1	16 wks
19 Jun 76	MY SWEET ROSALIE *Pye 7N 45602*	30	7 wks
26 Feb 77 ●	OH BOY (THE MOOD I'M IN) *Pye 7N 45656*	8	12 wks
9 Jul 77 ★	ANGELO *Pye 7N 45699*	1	12 wks
14 Jan 78 ★	FIGARO *Pye 7N 46037*	1	11 wks
27 May 78	BEAUTIFUL LOVER *Pye 7N 46071*	15	12 wks
30 Sep 78	MIDDLE OF THE NIGHT *Pye 7N 46117*	41	6 wks
3 Jul 82	LIGHTNING FLASH *EMI 5309*	67	2 wks

BROTHERLOVE - *See PRATT and McLAIN with BROTHERLOVE*

BROTHERS *UK, male vocal group* 9 wks

29 Jan 77 ●	SING ME *Bus Stop BUS 1054*	8	9 wks

BROTHERS FOUR *US, male vocal group* 2 wks

23 Jun 60	GREENFIELDS *Philips PB 1009*	49	1 wk
7 Jul 60	GREENFIELDS (re-entry) *Philips PB 1009*	40	1 wk

BROTHERS JOHNSON
US, male vocal /instrumental duo 34 wks

9 July 77	STRAWBERRY LETTER 23 *A & M AMS 7297*	35	5 wks
2 Sep 78	AIN'T WE FUNKIN' NOW *A & M AMS 7379*	43	6 wks
4 Nov 78	RIDE-O-ROCKET *A & M AMS 7400*	50	4 wks
23 Feb 80 ●	STOMP *A & M AMS 7509*	6	12 wks
31 May 80	LIGHT UP THE NIGHT *A & M AMS 7526*	47	4 wks
25 Jul 81	THE REAL THING *A & M AMS 8149*	50	3 wks

Edgar BROUGHTON BAND
UK, male vocal/instrumental group 10 wks

18 Apr 70	OUT DEMONS OUT *Harvest HAR 5015*	39	5 wks
23 Jan 71	APACHE DROPOUT *Harvest HAR 5032*	49	1 wk
6 Feb 71	APACHE DROPOUT (re-entry)		
	Harvest HAR 5032	35	2 wks
13 Mar 71	APACHE DROPOUT (2nd re-entry)		
	Harvest HAR 5032	35	1 wk
27 Mar 71	APACHE DROPOUT (3rd re-entry)		
	Harvest HAR 5032	33	1 wk

Crazy World of Arthur BROWN
UK, male vocal/instrumental group 14 wks

26 Jun 68 ★	FIRE *Track 604 022*	1	14 wks

Dennis BROWN *Jamaica, male vocalist* 18 wks

3 Mar 79	MONEY IN MY POCKET *Lightning LV 5*	14	9 wks
3 Jul 82	LOVE HAS FOUND ITS WAY		
	A & M AMS 8226	47	6 wks
11 Sep 82	HALFWAY UP HALFWAY DOWN		
	A & M AMS 8250	56	3 wks

James BROWN *US, male vocalist*   51 wks

23 Sep 65	PAPA'S GOT A BRAND NEW BAG		25	7 wks
	London HL 9990			
24 Feb 66	I GOT YOU *Pye International 7N 25350*		29	6 wks
16 Jun 66	IT'S A MAN'S MAN'S MAN'S WORLD		13	9 wks
	Pye International 7N 25371			
10 Oct 70	GET UP I FEEL LIKE BEING A SEX MACHINE		32	7 wks
	Polydor 2001 071			
27 Nov 71	HEY AMERICA *Mojo 2093 006*		47	3 wks
18 Sep 76	GET UP OFFA THAT THING *Polydor 2066 687*		22	6 wks
29 Jan 77	BODY HEAT *Polydor 2066 763*		36	4 wks
10 Jan 81	RAPP PLAYBACK (WHERE IZ MOSES?)		39	5 wks
	RCA 28			
2 Jul 83	BRING IT ON ... BRING IT ON		45	4 wks
	Sonet/Churchill/Augusta SON 2258			

Billed as James Brown and The Famous Flames on the first three hits. See also Africa Bambaata and James Brown

Joanne BROWN - *See Tony OSBORNE*

Jocelyn BROWN *US, female vocalist*   12 wks

21 Apr 84	SOMEBODY ELSE'S GUY		13	9 wks
	Fourth and Broadway/Island BRW 5			
22 Sep 84	I WISH YOU WOULD		51	3 wks
	Fourth and Broadway/Island BRW 14			

Joe BROWN
UK, male vocalist/instrumentalist - guitar   92 wks

17 Mar 60	DARKTOWN STRUTTERS BALL *Decca F 11207*		34	6 wks
26 Jan 61	SHINE *Pye 7N 15322*		33	6 wks
11 Jan 62	WHAT A CRAZY WORLD WE'RE LIVING IN		37	2 wks
	Piccadilly 7N 35024			
17 May 62 ●	A PICTURE OF YOU *Piccadilly 7N 35047*		2	19 wks
13 Sep 62	YOUR TENDER LOOK *Piccadilly 7N 35058*		31	6 wks
15 Nov 62 ●	IT ONLY TOOK A MINUTE *Piccadilly 7N 35082*		6	13 wks
7 Feb 63 ●	THAT'S WHAT LOVE WILL DO		3	14 wks
	Piccadilly 7N 35106			
21 Feb 63	IT ONLY TOOK A MINUTE (re-entry)		50	1 wk
	Piccadilly 7N 35082			
27 Jun 63	NATURE'S TIME FOR LOVE *Piccadilly 7N 35129*		26	6 wks
26 Sep 63	SALLY ANN *Piccadilly 7N 35138*		28	9 wks
29 Jun 67	WITH A LITTLE HELP FROM MY FRIENDS		32	4 wks
	Pye 7N 17339			
14 Apr 73	HEY MAMA *Ammo AMO 101*		33	6 wks

Joe Brown's male vocal/instrumental backing group, the Bruvvers, were credited on all his hits except Shine, With A Little Help From My Friends *and* Hey Mama.

Miguel BROWN *US, female vocalist*   4 wks

| 18 Feb 84 | HE'S A SAINT, HE'S A SINNER | | 68 | 4 wks |
| | *Record Shack SOHO 15* . . . . | | | |

Peter BROWN *US, male vocalist*   9 wks

11 Feb 78	DO YA WANNA GET FUNKY WITH ME		43	4 wks
	TK TKR 6009			
17 Jun 78	DANCE WITH ME *TK TKR 6027*		57	5 wks

Polly BROWN *UK, female vocalist*   5 wks

| 14 Sep 74 | UP IN A PUFF OF SMOKE *GTO GT 2* . . . . . . | | 43 | 5 wks |

Sharon BROWN *UK, female vocalist*   9 wks

| 17 Apr 82 | I SPECIALIZE IN LOVE *Virgin VS 494* . . . . . . | | 38 | 9 wks |

BROWN SAUCE
UK, male/female vocal group   12 wks

| 12 Dec 81 | I WANNA BE A WINNER *BBC RESL 101* . . . . . | | 15 | 12 wks |

Duncan BROWNE *UK, male vocalist*   8 wks

19 Aug 72	JOURNEY *RAK 135*		23	6 wks
22 Dec 84	THEME FROM 'THE TRAVELLING MAN'		68	2 wks
	Towerbell TOW 64			

Jackson BROWNE *US, male vocalist*   11 wks

| 1 Jul 78 | STAY *Asylum K 13128* . . . . | | 12 | 11 wks |

Tom BROWNE *US, male vocalist*   20 wks

19 Jul 80 ●	FUNKIN' FOR JAMAICA (N.Y.)		10	11 wks
	Arista ARIST 357			
25 Oct 80	THIGHS HIGH (GRIP YOUR HIPS AND MOVE)		45	5 wks
	Arista ARIST 367			
30 Jan 82	FUNGI MAMA (BEBOPAFUNKADISCOLYPSO)		58	4 wks
	Arista ARIST 450			

BROWNS *US, male/female vocal group*   13 wks

| 18 Sep 59 ● | THE THREE BELLS *RCA 1140* . . . . . . | | 6 | 13 wks |

BROWNSVILLE STATION
US, male vocal/instrumental group   6 wks

| 2 Mar 74 | SMOKIN' IN THE BOY'S ROOM | | 27 | 6 wks |
| | *Philips 6073 834* . . . . | | | |

Dave BRUBECK QUARTET
US, male instrumental group   30 wks

26 Oct 61 ●	TAKE FIVE *Fontana H 339*		6	15 wks
8 Feb 62	IT'S A RAGGY WALTZ *Fontana H 352*		36	3 wks
17 May 62	UNSQUARE DANCE *CBS AAG 102*		14	12 wks

Tommy BRUCE *UK, male vocalist*   21 wks

26 May 60 ●	AIN'T MISBEHAVIN' *Columbia DB 4453*		3	16 wks
8 Sep 60	BROKEN DOLL *Columbia DB 4498*		36	4 wks
22 Feb 62	BABETTE *Columbia DB 4776*		50	1 wk

First two hits credit the Bruisers, Tommy's backing group. See also Bruisers.

BRUISERS
UK, male vocal/instrumental group   7 wks

| 8 Aug 63 | BLUE GIRL *Parlophone R 5042* . . . . . . | | 31 | 6 wks |
| 26 Sep 63 | BLUE GIRL (re-entry) *Parlophone R 5042* . . . . | | 47 | 1 wk |

See also Tommy Bruce.

Tyrone BRUNSON
US, male instrumentalist-bass   5 wks

| 25 Dec 82 | THE SMURF *Epic EPC A 3024* . . . . . . | | 52 | 5 wks |

BRUVVERS - *See Joe BROWN*

Dora BRYAN *UK, female vocalist* — 6 wks

| 5 Dec 63 | ALL I WANT FOR CHRISTMAS IS A BEATLE | | | |
| | *Fontana TF 427* .... | 20 | 6 wks |

Anita BRYANT *US, female vocalist* — 6 wks

26 May 60	PAPER ROSES	*London HLL 9144*	49	1 wk
30 Jun 60	PAPER ROSES	(re-entry) *London HLL 9144*	45	1 wk
14 Jul 60	PAPER ROSES	(2nd re-entry) *London HLL 9144*	24	2 wks
6 Oct 60	MY LITTLE CORNER OF THE WORLD			
	London HLL 9171	48	2 wks

Peabo BRYSON and Roberta FLACK *US, male/female vocal duo* — 13 wks

| 20 Aug 83 | ● TONIGHT I CELEBRATE MY LOVE | | | |
| | *Capitol CL 302* .... | 2 | 13 wks |

See also Roberta Flack; Roberta Flack and Donny Hathaway

BUBBLEROCK
UK, male vocalist, Jonathan King under false name — 5 wks

| 26 Jan 74 | (I CAN'T GET NO) SATISFACTION | *UK 53* ... | 29 | 5 wks |

See also Jonathan King.

Roy BUCHANAN
US, male instrumentalist - guitar — 3 wks

| 31 Mar 73 | SWEET DREAMS | *Polydor 2066 307* .... | 40 | 3 wks |

Lindsey BUCKINGHAM
US, male vocalist — 7 wks

| 16 Jan 82 | TROUBLE | *Mercury MER 85* .... | 31 | 7 wks |

BUCKS FIZZ *UK, male/female vocal group* — 116 wks

28 Mar 81	★ MAKING YOUR MIND UP	*RCA 56*	1	12 wks
6 Jun 81	PIECE OF THE ACTION	*RCA 88*	12	9 wks
15 Aug 81	ONE OF THOSE NIGHTS	*RCA 114*	20	10 wks
28 Nov 81	★ THE LAND OF MAKE BELIEVE	*RCA 163*	1	16 wks
27 Mar 82	★ MY CAMERA NEVER LIES	*RCA 202*	1	8 wks
19 Jun 82	● NOW THOSE DAYS ARE GONE	*RCA 241* ..	8	9 wks
27 Nov 82	● IF YOU CAN'T STAND THE HEAT	*RCA 300*	10	11 wks
12 Mar 83	RUN FOR YOUR LIFE	*RCA FIZ 1*	14	7 wks
18 Jun 83	● WHEN WE WERE YOUNG	*RCA 342* ...	10	8 wks
1 Oct 83	LONDON TOWN	*RCA 363*	34	6 wks
17 Dec 83	RULES OF THE GAME	*RCA 380*	57	6 wks
25 Aug 84	TALKING IN YOUR SLEEP	*RCA FIZ 2*	15	9 wks
27 Oct 84	GOLDEN DAYS	*RCA FIZ 3*	42	4 wks
29 Dec 84	I HEAR TALK	*RCA FIZ 4*	53†	1 wk

BUDGIE *UK, male vocal/instrumental group* — 2 wks

| 3 Oct 81 | KEEPING A RENDEZVOUS | *RCA BUDGIE 3* | 71 | 2 wks |

BUGGLES *UK, male vocal/instrumental duo* — 28 wks

22 Sep 79	★ VIDEO KILLED THE RADIO STAR			
	Island WIP 6524	1	11 wks
26 Jan 80	THE PLASTIC AGE	*Island WIP 6540*	16	8 wks
5 Apr 80	CLEAN CLEAN	*Island WIP 6584*	38	5 wks

| 8 Nov 80 | ELSTREE | *Island WIP 6624* .... | 55 | 4 wks |

B. BUMBLE and the STINGERS
US, male instrumental group — 26 wks

| 19 Apr 62 | ★ NUT ROCKER | *Top Rank JAR 611* .... | 1 | 15 wks |
| 3 Jun 72 | NUT ROCKER | (re-issue) *Stateside SS 2203* ...... | 19 | 11 wks |

BUNNYMEN - *See ECHO and the BUNNYMEN*

Eric BURDON *UK, male vocalist* — 42 wks

27 Oct 66	HELP ME GIRL	*Decca F 12502*	14	10 wks
15 Jun 67	WHEN I WAS YOUNG	*MGM 1340*	45	3 wks
6 Sep 67	GOOD TIMES	*MGM 1344*	20	11 wks
18 Oct 67	● SAN FRANCISCAN NIGHTS	*MGM 1359*	7	10 wks
14 Feb 68	SKY PILOT	*MGM 1373*	40	3 wks
15 Jan 69	RING OF FIRE	*MGM 1461*	35	5 wks

Help Me Girl, When I Was Young, Good Times *and* Ring Of Fire *are credited to Eric Burdon and the Animals. See also the Animals.*

Geoffrey BURGON *UK, orchestra* — 4 wks

| 26 Dec 81 | BRIDESHEAD THEME | *Chrysalis CHS 2562* .... | 48 | 4 wks |

Keni BURKE *US, male vocalist* — 3 wks

| 27 Jun 81 | LET SOMEBODY LOVE YOU | *RCA 93* | 59 | 3 wks |

Hank C. BURNETTE
Sweden, male multi-instrumentalist — 8 wks

| 30 Oct 76 | SPINNING ROCK BOOGIE | *Sonet SON 2094* ... | 21 | 8 wks |

Johnny BURNETTE *US, male vocalist* — 48 wks

29 Sep 60	● DREAMIN'	*London HLG 9172*	5	16 wks
12 Jan 61	● YOU'RE SIXTEEN	*London HLG 9254*	3	12 wks
13 Apr 61	LITTLE BOY SAD	*London HLG 9315*	12	12 wks
10 Aug 61	GIRLS	*London HLG 9388*	37	5 wks
17 May 62	CLOWN SHOES	*Liberty LIB 55416*	35	3 wks

Rocky BURNETTE *US, male vocalist* — 7 wks

| 17 Nov 79 | TIRED OF TOEIN' THE LINE | *EMI 2992* ...... | 58 | 7 wks |

Ray BURNS *UK, male vocalist* — 19 wks

11 Feb 55	● MOBILE	*Columbia DB 3563*	4	13 wks
26 Aug 55	THAT'S HOW A LOVE SONG WAS BORN			
	Columbia DB 3640	14	6 wks

BURUNDI STEIPHENSON BLACK
Burundi, drummers and chanters with orchestral additions by Mike Steiphenson of France — 14 wks

| 13 Nov 71 | BURUNDI BLACK | *Barclay BAR 3* .... | 31 | 14 wks |

Lou BUSCH *US, orchestra* — 17 wks

| 27 Jan 56 | ● ZAMBESI | *Capitol CL 14504* .... | 2 | 17 wks |

See also Joe 'Fingers' Carr.

CLASSIX NOUVEAUX (below) Dental telepathy – Sal Solo about to give himself a filling.

LLOYD COLE and the COMMOTIONS (bottom) 'I am a commotion, a logical anomaly' . . .Lloyd Cole

CAPTAIN SENSIBLE (left) Damned bass player gave Rodgers and Hammerstein their first number one since 'You'll Never Walk Alone'.

CHAS and DAVE (below) In non-rabbitting mood.

Kate BUSH   UK, female vocalist   92 wks

11 Feb 78	★	WUTHERING HEIGHTS EMI 2719	1	12 wks
13 May 78		WUTHERING HEIGHTS (re-entry) EMI 2719 ..	75	1 wk
10 Jun 78	●	MAN WITH THE CHILD IN HIS EYES EMI 2806	6	11 wks
11 Nov 78		HAMMER HORROR EMI 2887	44	6 wks
17 Mar 79		WOW EMI 2911	14	10 wks
15 Sep 79	●	KATE BUSH ON STAGE (EP) EMI MIEP 2991	10	9 wks
26 Apr 80		BREATHING EMI 5058	16	7 wks
5 Jul 80	●	BABOOSHKA EMI 5085	5	10 wks
4 Oct 80		ARMY DREAMERS EMI 5106	16	9 wks
6 Dec 80		DECEMBER WILL BE MAGIC AGAIN EMI 5121	29	7 wks
11 Jul 81		SAT IN YOUR LAP EMI 5201	11	7 wks
7 Aug 82		THE DREAMING EMI 5296	48	3 wks

Tracks on On Stage EP: *Them Heavy People/ Don't Push Your Foot on the Heartbrake/James and the Cold Gun/ L'Amour Looks Something Like You.*

BUSTER   UK, male vocal/instrumental group   1 wk

19 Jun 76	SUNDAY RCA 2678	49	1 wk

Prince BUSTER   Jamaica, male vocalist   13 wks

23 Feb 67	AL CAPONE Blue Beat BB 324	18	13 wks

BUTTERSCOTCH   UK, male vocal group   11 wks

2 May 70	DON'T YOU KNOW RCA 1937	17	11 wks

BUZZCOCKS
UK, male vocal/instrumental group   53 wks

18 Feb 78	WHAT DO I GET United Artists UP 36348	37	3 wks
13 May 78	I DON'T MIND United Artists UP 36386	55	2 wks
15 Jul 78	LOVE YOU MORE United Artists UP 36433	34	6 wks
23 Sep 78	EVER FALLEN IN LOVE (WITH SOMEONE YOU SHOULDN'T'VE HAVE) United Artists UP 36455	12	11 wks
25 Nov 78	PROMISES United Artists UP 36471	20	10 wks
10 Mar 79	EVERYBODY'S HAPPY NOWADAYS United Artists UP 36499	29	6 wks
21 Jul 79	HARMONY IN MY HEAD United Artists UP 36541	32	6 wks
25 Aug 79	SPIRAL SCRATCH (EP) New Hormones ORG 1	31	6 wks
6 Sep 80	ARE EVERYTHING/WHY SHE'S A GIRL FROM THE CHAINSTORE United Artists BP 365	61	3 wks

Tracks on Spiral Scratch EP: *Breakdown/Time's Up/ Boredom/Friends Of Mine.* Sleeve of EP (not the label) credits 'Buzzcocks with Howard Devoto'. Why She's A Girl From The Chainstore listed from 13 Sep 80.

BUZZY BUNCH   - *See Celi BEE and the BUZZY BUNCH*

Max BYGRAVES   UK, male vocalist   127 wks

14 Nov 52	COWPUNCHER'S CANTATA HMV B 10250 ..	11	1 wk
2 Jan 53	● COWPUNCHER'S CANTATA (re-entry) HMV B 10250	8	1 wk
23 Jan 53	● COWPUNCHER'S CANTATA (2nd re-entry) HMV B 10250	6	5 wks
6 Mar 53	● COWPUNCHER'S CANTATA (3rd re-entry) HMV B 10250	10	1 wk
14 May 54	● HEART OF MY HEART HMV B 10654	7	8 wks
10 Sep 54	GILLY GILLY OSSENFEFFER KATZENELLEN BOGEN BY THE SEA HMV B 10734	7	7 wks
5 Nov 54	GILLY GILLY OSSENFEFFER KATZENELLEN BOGEN BY THE SEA (re-entry) HMV B 10734	20	1 wk
21 Jan 55	MR. SANDMAN HMV B 10821	16	1 wk
18 Nov 55	● MEET ME ON THE CORNER HMV POP 116	2	11 wks

17 Feb 56	BALLAD OF DAVY CROCKETT HMV POP 153	20	1 wk
25 May 56	OUT OF TOWN HMV POP 164	18	7 wks
5 Apr 57	HEART Decca F 10862	14	8 wks
2 May 58	● YOU NEED HANDS/TULIPS FROM AMSTERDAM Decca F 11004	3	25 wks
22 Aug 58	LITTLE TRAIN/GOTTA HAVE RAIN Decca F 11096	28	2 wks
2 Jan 59	MY UKELELE Decca F 11077	19	4 wks
18 Dec 59	● JINGLE BELL ROCK Decca F 11176	7	4 wks
10 Mar 60	● FINGS AIN'T WOT THEY USED T'BE Decca F 11214	5	15 wks
28 Jul 60	CONSIDER YOURSELF Decca F 11251 ...	50	1 wk
1 Jun 61	BELLS OF AVIGNON Decca F 11350 ...	36	5 wks
19 Feb 69	YOU'RE MY EVERYTHING Pye 7N 17705 ...	50	1 wk
5 Mar 69	YOU'RE MY EVERYTHING (re-entry) Pye 7N 17705	34	3 wks
6 Oct 73	DECK OF CARDS Pye 7N 45276	13	15 wks

See also Various Artists - All Star Hit Parade No. 2. Cowpuncher's Cantata is a medley with the following songs: *Cry Of The Wild Goose/Riders In The Sky/Mule Train/Jezebel.* You Need Hands was listed by itself on 2 May 58. Tulips From Amsterdam was first listed on 9 May 58 and both sides continued to be listed until the end of the record's chart run.

Charlie BYRD   - *See Stan GETZ and Charlie BYRD*

Donald BYRD
US, male vocalist/instrumentalist - trumpet   6 wks

26 Sep 81	LOVE HAS COME AROUND/LOVING YOU Elektra K 12559	41	6 wks

Gary BYRD and the GB EXPERIENCE
US, male vocalist and male/female vocal group   9 wks

28 Jul 83	● THE CROWN Motown TMGT 1312	6	9 wks

BYRDS   US, male vocal/instrumental group   52 wks

17 Jun 65	★	MR. TAMBOURINE MAN CBS 201765	1	14 wks
12 Aug 65	●	ALL I REALLY WANT TO DO CBS 201796 ...	4	10 wks
11 Nov 65		TURN! TURN! TURN! CBS 202008	26	8 wks
5 May 66		EIGHT MILES HIGH CBS 202067 ...	24	9 wks
5 Jun 68		YOU AIN'T GOIN' NOWHERE CBS 3411 ...	45	3 wks
13 Feb 71		CHESTNUT MARE CBS 5322	19	8 wks

Edward BYRNES and Connie STEVENS   US, male/female vocal duo   8 wks

5 May 60	KOOKIE KOOKIE (LEND ME YOUR COMB) Warner Bros. WB 5	27	8 wks

See also Connie Stevens.

BYSTANDERS
UK, male vocal/instrumental group   1 wk

9 Feb 67	98.6 Piccadilly 7N 35363	45	1 wk

C

C. C. S.   UK, male vocal/instrumental group   55 wks

31 Oct 70		WHOLE LOTTA LOVE RAK 104	13	13 wks
27 Feb 71	●	WALKIN' RAK 109	7	16 wks
4 Sep 71	●	TAP TURNS ON THE WATER RAK 119	5	13 wks
4 Mar 72		BROTHER RAK 126	25	8 wks

4 Aug 73	BAND PLAYED THE BOOGIE	RAK 154	36	5 wks

ÇA VA ÇA VA
UK, male vocal/instrumental group — *8 wks*

18 Sep 82	WHERE'S ROMEO?	Regard RG 103	49	5 wks
19 Feb 83	BROTHER BRIGHT	Regard RG 105	65	3 wks

CADETS   UK, male/female vocal group — *1 wk*

3 Jun 65	JEALOUS HEART	Pye 7N 15852	42	1 wk

Hit has credit 'with Eileen Read lead vocal.'

Susan CADOGAN   UK, female vocalist — *19 wks*

5 Apr 75	● HURT SO GOOD	Magnet MAG 23	4	12 wks
19 Jul 75	LOVE ME BABY	Magnet MAG 36	22	7 wks

Al CAIOLA   US, orchestra — *6 wks*

15 Jun 61	THE MAGNIFICENT SEVEN	HMV POP 889 ..	34	6 wks

CALIBRE CUTS
Montage of 16 other discs, see footnote — *2 wks*

17 May 80	CALIBRE CUTS	Calibre CAB 502	75	2 wks

Calibre Cuts *is a montage of 13 singles and 3 re-makes of hit titles by session musicians. The titles are : Big Apple Rock by Black Ivory, Don't Hold Back by Chanson, The River Drive by Jupiter Beyond, Dancing At The Disco by L.A.X., Girls Mellow Right On by Lowrell, Pata Pata by Osibisa, I Like It by Players Association, We Got The Funk by Positive Force, Holdin' On by Tony Rallo and the Midnight Band, Can You Feel The Force by Real Thing, Miami Heatwave by Seventh Avenue, Rappers Delight by Sugarhill Gang, Que Tal America by Two Man Sound. The three re-makes by session musicians are Ain't No Stopping Us Now, Bad Girls and We Are Family. Act descriptions are, of course, various.*

Eddie CALVERT
UK, male instrumentalist - trumpet — *80 wks*

18 Dec 53	★ OH MEIN PAPA	Columbia DB 3337	1	21 wks
8 Apr 55	★ CHERRY PINK & APPLE BLOSSOM WHITE			
		Columbia DB 3581	1	21 wks
13 May 55	STRANGER IN PARADISE	Columbia DB 3594 ..	14	4 wks
29 Jul 55	● JOHN AND JULIE	Columbia DB 3624	6	11 wks
2 Mar 56	ZAMBESI	Columbia DB 3747	18	1 wk
23 Mar 56	ZAMBESI (re-entry)	Columbia DB 3747	13	6 wks
7 Feb 58	● MANDY	Columbia DB 3956	9	14 wks
20 Jun 58	LITTLE SERENADE	Columbia DB 4139	28	2 wks

CAMEO   UK, male vocal/instrumental group — *8 wks*

31 Mar 84	SHE'S STRANGE	Club/Phonogram JAB 2	37	8 wks

Andy CAMERON   UK, male vocalist — *8 wks*

4 Mar 78	● ALLY'S TARTAN ARMY	Klub 03	6	8 wks

Tony CAMILLO'S BAZUKA
US, male instrumental/vocal group — *5 wks*

31 May 75	DYNOMITE (PART 1.)	A & M AMS 7168	28	5 wks

CAMOUFLAGE featuring MYSTI
UK, male/female vocal/instrumental group — *3 wks*

24 Sep 77	BEE STING	State STAT 58	48	3 wks

Ethna CAMPBELL   UK, female vocalist — *11 wks*

27 Dec 75	THE OLD RUGGED CROSS	Philips 6006 475 ...	33	11 wks

Glen CAMPBELL   US, male vocalist — *84 wks*

29 Jan 69	● WICHITA LINEMAN	Ember EMBS 261	7	13 wks
7 May 69	GALVESTON	Ember EMBS 263	14	10 wks
7 Feb 70	TRY A LITTLE KINDNESS	Capitol CL 15622	45	2 wks
9 May 70	● HONEY COME BACK	Capitol CL 15638	4	19 wks
26 Sep 70	EVERYTHING A MAN COULD EVER NEED			
		Capitol CL 15653	32	5 wks
21 Nov 70	● IT'S ONLY MAKE BELIEVE	Capitol CL 15663	4	14 wks
27 Mar 71	DREAM BABY	Capitol CL 15674	39	3 wks
4 Oct 75	● RHINESTONE COWBOY	Capitol CL 15824	4	12 wks
26 Mar 77	SOUTHERN NIGHTS	Capitol CL 15907	28	6 wks

See also Bobbie Gentry and Glen Campbell.

Jo Ann CAMPBELL   US, female vocalist — *3 wks*

8 Jun 61	MOTORCYCLE MICHAEL	HMV POP 873	41	3 wks

Junior CAMPBELL   UK, male vocalist — *18 wks*

14 Oct 72	● HALLELUJAH FREEDOM	Deram DM 364	10	9 wks
2 Jun 73	SWEET ILLUSION	Deram DM 387	15	9 wks

Pat CAMPBELL   Ireland, male vocalist — *5 wks*

15 Nov 69	THE DEAL	Major Minor MM 648	31	5 wks

Ian CAMPBELL FOLK GROUP
UK, male vocal/instrumental group — *5 wks*

11 Mar 65	THE TIMES THEY ARE A-CHANGIN'			
		Transatlantic SP 5	42	2 wks
1 Apr 65	THE TIMES THEY ARE A-CHANGIN' (re-entry)			
		Transatlantic SP 5	47	1 wk
15 Apr 65	THE TIMES THEY ARE A-CHANGIN'			
		(2nd re-entry) Transatlantic SP 5	46	2 wks

CAN   Germany, male vocal/instrumental group — *10 wks*

28 Aug 76	I WANT MORE	Virgin VS 153	26	10 wks

CANDIDO   US, male multi-instrumentalist — *3 wks*

18 Jul 81	JINGO	Excaliber EXC 102	55	3 wks

CANDLEWICK GREEN
UK, vocal/instrumental group — *8 wks*

23 Feb 74	WHO DO YOU THINK YOU ARE			
		Decca F 13480	21	8 wks

CANNED HEAT
US, vocal/instrumental group — 41 wks

Date		Title	Label	Pos	Wks
24 Jul	68	● ON THE ROAD AGAIN Liberty LBS 15090		8	15 wks
1 Jan	69	GOING UP THE COUNTRY Liberty LBF 15169		19	10 wks
17 Jan	70	● LET'S WORK TOGETHER Liberty LBF 15302		2	15 wks
11 Jul	70	SUGAR BEE Liberty LBF 15350		49	1 wk

Freddy CANNON
US, male vocalist — 51 wks

Date		Title	Label	Pos	Wks
14 Aug	59	TALLAHASSEE LASSIE Top Rank JAR 135		17	8 wks
1 Jan	60	● WAY DOWN YONDER IN NEW ORLEANS Top Rank JAR 247		3	16 wks
10 Mar	60	CALIFORNIA HERE I COME Top Rank JAR 309		33	1 wk
17 Mar	60	INDIANA Top Rank JAR 309		42	1 wk
24 Mar	60	CALIFORNIA HERE I COME (re-entry) Top Rank JAR 309		46	1 wk
19 May	60	THE URGE Top Rank JAR 369		18	10 wks
20 Apr	61	MUSKRAT RAMBLE Top Rank JAR 548		32	5 wks
28 Jun	62	PALISADES PARK Stateside SS 101		20	9 wks

Jim CAPALDI
UK, male vocalist — 17 wks

Date		Title	Label	Pos	Wks
27 Jul	74	IT'S ALL UP TO YOU Island WIP 6198		27	6 wks
25 Oct	75	● LOVE HURTS Island WIP 6246		4	11 wks

Tony CAPSTICK and the CARLTON MAIN/FRICKLEY COLLIERY BAND
UK, male vocalist and male instrumental band — 8 wks

Date		Title	Label	Pos	Wks
21 Mar	81	● THE SHEFFIELD GRINDER/CAPSTICK COMES HOME Dingles SID 27		3	8 wks

CAPTAIN and TENNILLE
US, male instrumentalist-keyboards/female vocalist — 24 wks

Date		Title	Label	Pos	Wks
2 Aug	75	LOVE WILL KEEP US TOGETHER A & M AMS 7165		32	5 wks
24 Jan	76	THE WAY I WANT TO TOUCH YOU A & M AMS 7203		28	6 wks
4 Nov	78	YOU NEVER DONE IT LIKE THAT A & M AMS 7384		63	3 wks
16 Feb	80	● DO THAT TO ME ONE MORE TIME Casablanca CAN 175		7	10 wks

CAPTAIN BEAKY - See Keith MICHELL, CAPTAIN BEAKY and his BAND

CAPTAIN SENSIBLE
UK, male vocalist — 30 wks

Date		Title	Label	Pos	Wks
26 Jun	82	★ HAPPY TALK A & M CAP 1		1	8 wks
14 Aug	82	WOT A & M CAP 2		26	7 wks
24 Mar	84	● GLAD IT'S ALL OVER/DAMNED ON 45 A & M CAP 6		6	10 wks
28 Jul	84	THERE ARE MORE SNAKES THAN LADDERS A & M CAP 7		57	5 wks

Irene CARA
US, female vocalist — 33 wks

Date		Title	Label	Pos	Wks
3 Jul	82	★ FAME RSO 90		1	16 wks
4 Sep	82	OUT HERE ON MY OWN Polydor/RSO 66		58	3 wks
4 Jun	83	● FLASHDANCE...WHAT A FEELING Casablanca/Phonogram CAN 1016		2	14 wks

CARAMBA
Sweden, male vocal/multi-instrumentalist/dog impersonator, Michael Tretow under false group name — 6 wks

Date		Title	Label	Pos	Wks
12 Nov	83	FEDORA (I'LL BE YOUR DAWG) Billco BILL 101		56	6 wks

CARAVELLES
UK, female vocal duo — 13 wks

Date		Title	Label	Pos	Wks
8 Aug	63	● YOU DON'T HAVE TO BE A BABY TO CRY Decca F 11697		6	13 wks

CARE
UK, male vocal/instrumental duo — 3 wks

Date		Title	Label	Pos	Wks
12 Nov	83	FLAMING SWORD Arista KBIRD 2		65	3 wks

Carl CARLTON
US, male vocalist — 8 wks

Date		Title	Label	Pos	Wks
18 Jul	81	SHE'S A BAD MAMA JAMA (SHE'S BUILT, SHE'S STACKED) 20th Century TC 2488		34	8 wks

Larry CARLTON - See Mike POST featuring Larry CARLTON

CARMEL
UK, female/male vocal/instrumental group — 16 wks

Date		Title	Label	Pos	Wks
6 Aug	83	BAD DAY London LON 29		15	9 wks
11 Feb	84	MORE, MORE, MORE London LON 44		23	7 wks

Eric CARMEN
US, male vocalist — 7 wks

Date		Title	Label	Pos	Wks
10 Apr	76	ALL BY MYSELF Arista 42		12	7 wks

Kim CARNES
US, female vocalist — 15 wks

Date		Title	Label	Pos	Wks
9 May	81	● BETTE DAVIS EYES EMI America EA 121		10	9 wks
8 Aug	81	DRAW OF THE CARDS EMI America EA 125		49	4 wks
9 Oct	82	VOYEUR EMI America EA 143		68	2 wks

Renato CAROSONE and his SEXTET
Italy, male vocalist and instrumental backing group — 1 wk

Date		Title	Label	Pos	Wks
4 Jul	58	TORERO - CHA CHA CHA Parlophone R 4433		25	1 wk

CARPENTERS
US, male/female vocal/instrumental duo — 164 wks

Date		Title	Label	Pos	Wks
5 Sep	70	● (THEY LONG TO BE) CLOSE TO YOU A & M AMS 800		6	18 wks
9 Jan	71	WE'VE ONLY JUST BEGUN A & M AMS 813		28	7 wks
18 Sep	71	SUPERSTAR /FOR ALL WE KNOW A & M AMS 864		18	13 wks
1 Jan	72	MERRY CHRISTMAS DARLING A & M AME 601		45	1 wk
23 Sep	72	● I WON'T LAST A DAY WITHOUT YOU/GOODBYE TO LOVE A & M AMS 7023		9	16 wks
7 Jul	73	● YESTERDAY ONCE MORE A & M AMS 7073		2	17 wks
20 Oct	73	● TOP OF THE WORLD A & M AMS 7086		5	18 wks
2 Mar	74	JAMBALAYA (ON THE BAYOU)/MR. GUDER A & M AMS 7098		12	11 wks
8 Jun	74	I WON'T LAST A DAY WITHOUT YOU (re-issue) A & M AMS 7111		32	5 wks
18 Jan	75	● PLEASE MR. POSTMAN A & M AMS 7141		2	12 wks

19 Apr 75	● ONLY YESTERDAY *A & M AMS 7159*	7	10 wks
30 Aug 75	SOLITAIRE *A & M AMS 7187*	32	5 wks
20 Dec 75	SANTA CLAUS IS COMIN' TO TOWN		
	A & M AMS 7144	37	4 wks
27 Mar 76	THERE'S A KIND OF HUSH (ALL OVER THE		
	WORLD) *A & M AMS 7219*	22	6 wks
3 Jul 76	I NEED TO BE IN LOVE *A & M AMS 7238* ...	36	5 wks
8 Oct 77	● CALLING OCCUPANTS OF INTERPLANETARY		
	CRAFT (THE RECOGNIZED ANTHEM OF		
	WORLD CONTACT DAY)		
	A & M AMS 7318	9	9 wks
11 Feb 78	SWEET SWEET SMILE *A & M AMS 7327*	40	4 wks
22 Oct 83	MAKE BELIEVE IT'S YOUR FIRST TIME		
	A & M AM 147	60	3 wks

I Won't Last A Day Without You *AMS 7023* listed by itself 23 Sep 72. Goodbye To
Love, *the other side, listed by itself from 30 Sep 72 until the end of the record's chart run.* Mr
Guder *listed with* Jambalaya *from 16 Mar 74 until end of the record's chart run.*

Joe 'Fingers' CARR *US, male*
instrumentalist – piano, Lou Busch under a false name   *5 wks*

29 Jun 56	PORTUGUESE WASHERWOMAN		
	Capitol CL 14587	20	5 wks

See also Lou Busch.

Linda CARR and the LOVE SQUAD
US, female vocalist, female vocal backing group   *8 wks*

12 Jul 75	HIGHWIRE *Chelsea 2005 025*	15	8 wks

See also Linda and the Funky Boys – it's the same Linda.

Pearl CARR and Teddy JOHNSON
UK, female/male vocal duo   *19 wks*

20 Mar 59	SING LITTLE BIRDIE *Columbia DB 4275*	12	8 wks
6 Apr 61	HOW WONDERFUL TO KNOW		
	Columbia DB 4603	23	11 wks

Valerie CARR *UK, female vocalist*   *2 wks*

4 Jul 58	WHEN THE BOYS TALK ABOUT THE GIRLS		
	Columbia DB 4131	29	1 wk
18 Jul 58	WHEN THE BOYS TALK ABOUT THE GIRLS		
	(re-entry) *Columbia DB 4131*	30	1 wk

Vikki CARR *US, female vocalist*   *26 wks*

1 Jun 67	● IT MUST BE HIM (SEUL SUR SON ETOILE)		
	Liberty LIB 55917	2	20 wks
30 Aug 67	THERE I GO *Liberty LBF 15022*	50	1 wk
12 Mar 69	WITH PEN IN HAND *Liberty LBF 15166*	43	1 wk
26 Mar 69	WITH PEN IN HAND (re-entry)		
	Liberty LBF 15166	40	2 wks
30 Apr 69	WITH PEN IN HAND (2nd re-entry)		
	Liberty LBF 15166	40	2 wks

Raffaella CARRA *Italy, female vocalist*   *12 wks*

15 Apr 78	● DO IT DO IT AGAIN *Epic EPC 6094*	9	12 wks

Ronnie CARROLL *UK, male vocalist*   *50 wks*

27 Jul 56	WALK HAND IN HAND *Philips PB 603*	13	8 wks
29 Mar 57	THE WISDOM OF A FOOL *Philips PB 667*	20	2 wks
31 Mar 60	FOOTSTEPS *Philips PB 1004*	36	3 wks
22 Feb 62	RING A DING GIRL *Philips PB 1222*	46	3 wks

2 Aug 62	● ROSES ARE RED *Philips 326532 BF*	3	16 wks
15 Nov 62	IF ONLY TOMORROW *Philips 326550 BF*	33	4 wks
7 Mar 63	● SAY WONDERFUL THINGS *Philips 326574 BF*	6	14 wks

Jasper CARROTT *UK, male vocalist*   *15 wks*

16 Aug 75	● FUNKY MOPED/MAGIC ROUNDABOUT		
	DJM DJS 388	5	15 wks

CARS *US, male vocal/instrumental group*   *39 wks*

11 Nov 78	● MY BEST FRIEND'S GIRL *Elektra K 12301*	3	10 wks
17 Feb 79	JUST WHAT I NEEDED *Elektra K 12312*	17	10 wks
28 Jul 79	LET'S GO *Elektra K 12371*	51	4 wks
5 Jun 82	SINCE YOU'RE GONE *Elektra K 13177*	37	4 wks
29 Sep 84	● DRIVE *Elektra E 9706*	5	11 wks

Clarence CARTER *US, male vocalist*   *13 wks*

10 Oct 70	● PATCHES *Atlantic 2091 030*	2	13 wks

CARVELLS *UK, male vocalist/instrumentalist*
(Alan Carvell under a group name)   *4 wks*

26 Nov 77	THE L.A. RUN *Creole CR 143*	31	4 wks

CASCADES *US, male vocal group*   *16 wks*

28 Feb 63	● RHYTHM OF THE RAIN *Warner Bros. WB 88* ..	5	16 wks

Natalie CASEY *UK, female vocalist*   *1 wk*

7 Jan 84	CHICK CHICK CHICKEN *Polydor CHICK 1* ...	72	1 wk

Johnny CASH *US, male vocalist*   *59 wks*

3 Jun 65	IT AIN'T ME BABE *CBS 201760*	28	8 wks
6 Sep 69	● A BOY NAMED SUE *CBS 4460*	4	19 wks
23 May 70	WHAT IS TRUTH *CBS 4934*	21	11 wks
15 Apr 72	● A THING CALLED LOVE *CBS 7797*	4	13 wks
22 Jul 72	A THING CALLED LOVE (re-entry) *CBS 7797*	48	1 wk
3 Jul 76	ONE PIECE AT A TIME *CBS 4287*	32	7 wks

A Thing Called Love *with the Evangel Temple Choir.* One Piece At A Time *with The
Tennessee Three.*

CASINOS *US, male vocal group*   *7 wks*

23 Feb 67	THEN YOU CAN TELL ME GOODBYE		
	President PT 123	28	7 wks

Mama CASS *US, female vocalist*   *27 wks*

14 Aug 68	DREAM A LITTLE DREAM OF ME *RCA 1726*	11	12 wks
16 Aug 69	● IT'S GETTING BETTER *Stateside SS 8021*	8	15 wks

See also Mamas and the Papas.

David CASSIDY *US, male vocalist*   *94 wks*

8 Apr 72	● COULD IT BE FOREVER *Bell 1224*	2	17 wks
16 Sep 72	★ HOW CAN I BE SURE *Bell 1258*	1	11 wks
25 Nov 72	ROCK ME BABY *Bell 1268*	11	9 wks
24 Mar 73	● I'M A CLOWN/SOME KIND OF A SUMMER		
	Bell MABEL 4	3	12 wks
13 Oct 73	★ DAYDREAMER/THE PUPPY SONG *Bell 1334*	1	15 wks
11 May 74	● IF I DIDN'T CARE *Bell 1350*	9	8 wks

27 Jul 74	**PLEASE PLEASE ME** *Bell 1371*	**16**	6 wks
5 Jul 75	**I WRITE THE SONGS/GET IT UP FOR LOVE** *RCA 2571*	**11**	8 wks
25 Oct 75	**DARLIN'** *RCA 2622*	**16**	8 wks

See also Partridge Family starring Shirley Jones featuring David Cassidy.

CAST OF IDIOTS - *See Rick DEES and his CAST OF IDIOTS*

Roy CASTLE *UK, male vocalist*   *3 wks*

22 Dec 60	**LITTLE WHITE BERRY** *Philips PB 1087*	**40**	3 wks

CASUALS *UK, male vocal/instrumental group*   *26 wks*

14 Aug 68 ●	**JESAMINE** *Decca F 22784*	**2**	18 wks
4 Dec 68	**TOY** *Decca F 22852*	**30**	8 wks

CATS *UK, male instrumental group*   *2 wks*

9 Apr 69	**SWAN LAKE** *BAF 1*	**48**	1 wk
21 May 69	**SWAN LAKE** (re-entry) *BAF 1*	**50**	1 wk

CATS U.K. *UK, female vocal group*   *8 wks*

6 Oct 79	**LUTON AIRPORT** *WEA K 18075*	**22**	8 wks

CENTRAL LINE
UK, male vocal/instrumental group   *30 wks*

31 Jan 81	**(YOU KNOW) YOU CAN DO IT** *Mercury LINE 7*	**67**	3 wks
15 Aug 81	**WALKING INTO SUNSHINE** *Mercury MER 78*	**42**	10 wks
30 Jan 82	**DON'T TELL ME** *Mercury MER 90*	**55**	3 wks
20 Nov 82	**YOU'VE SAID ENOUGH** *Mercury/Phonogram MER 117*	**58**	3 wks
22 Jan 83	**NATURE BOY** *Mercury/Phonogram MER 131*	**21**	8 wks
11 Jun 83	**SURPRISE SURPRISE** *Mercury/Phonogram MER 133*	**48**	3 wks

CERRONE
France, male producer and multi- instrumentalist   *20 wks*

5 Mar 77	**LOVE IN C MINOR** *Atlantic K 10895*	**31**	4 wks
29 Jul 78 ●	**SUPER NATURE** *Atlantic K 11089*	**8**	12 wks
13 Jan 79	**JE SUIS MUSIC** *CBS 6918*	**39**	4 wks

Frank CHACKSFIELD *UK, orchestra*   *35 wks*

3 Apr 53 ●	**LITTLE RED MONKEY** *Parlophone R 3658*	**10**	3 wks
22 May 53 ●	**LIMELIGHT** *Decca F 10106*	**2**	24 wks
12 Feb 54 ●	**EBB TIDE** *Decca F 10122*	**9**	2 wks
24 Feb 56	**IN OLD LISBON** *Decca F 10689*	**15**	4 wks
31 Aug 56	**DONKEY CART** *Decca F 10743*	**26**	2 wks

Little Red Monkey credited to Frank Chacksfield's Tunesmiths.

CHAIRMEN OF THE BOARD
US, male vocal group   *74 wks*

22 Aug 70 ●	**GIVE ME JUST A LITTLE MORE TIME** *Invictus INV 501*	**3**	13 wks
14 Nov 70 ●	**YOU'VE GOT ME DANGLING ON A STRING** *Invictus INV 504*	**5**	13 wks
20 Feb 71	**EVERYTHING'S TUESDAY** *Invictus INV 507* ..	**12**	9 wks
15 May 71	**PAY TO THE PIPER** *Invictus INV 511*	**34**	7 wks
4 Sep 71	**CHAIRMAN OF THE BOARD** *Invictus INV 516*	**48**	2 wks

15 Jul 72	**WORKING ON A BUILDING OF LOVE** *Invictus INV 519*	**20**	8 wks
7 Oct 72	**ELMO JAMES** *Invictus INV 524*	**21**	7 wks
16 Dec 72	**I'M ON MY WAY TO A BETTER PLACE** *Invictus INV 527*	**38**	1 wk
13 Jan 73	**I'M ON MY WAY TO A BETTER PLACE** (re-entry) *Invictus INV 527*	**30**	5 wks
23 Jun 73	**FINDERS KEEPERS** *Invictus INV 530*	**21**	9 wks

CHAKACHAS
Belgium, male/female vocal/instrumental group   *8 wks*

11 Jan 62	**TWIST TWIST** *RCA 1264*	**48**	1 wk
27 May 72	**JUNGLE FEVER** *Polydor 2121 064*	**29**	7 wks

George CHAKIRIS *US, male vocalist*   *1 wk*

2 Jun 60	**HEART OF A TEENAGE GIRL** *Triumph RGM 1010*	**49**	1 wk

Richard CHAMBERLAIN
US, male vocalist   *36 wks*

7 Jun 62	**THEME FROM 'DR. KILDARE' (THREE STARS WILL SHINE TONIGHT)** *MGM 1160*	**12**	10 wks
1 Nov 62	**LOVE ME TENDER** *MGM 1173*	**15**	11 wks
21 Feb 63	**HI-LILI HI-LO** *MGM 1189*	**20**	9 wks
18 Jul 63	**TRUE LOVE** *MGM 1205*	**30**	6 wks

CHAMELEONS - *See LORI and the CHAMELEONS*

CHAMPAIGN
US, male/female vocal/instrumental group   *13 wks*

9 May 81 ●	**HOW 'BOUT US** *CBS A 1046*	**5**	13 wks

CHAMPS *US, male instrumental group*   *10 wks*

4 Apr 58 ●	**TEQUILA** *London HLU 8580*	**5**	9 wks
17 Mar 60	**TOO MUCH TEQUILA** *London HLH 9052*	**49**	1 wk

CHAMPS BOYS
France, male instrumental group   *6 wks*

19 Jun 76	**TUBULAR BELLS** *Philips 6006 519*	**41**	6 wks

Gene CHANDLER *US, male vocalist*   *29 wks*

5 Jun 68	**NOTHING CAN STOP ME** *Soul City SC 102* ..	**41**	4 wks
3 Feb 79	**GET DOWN** *20th Century BTC 1040*	**11**	11 wks
1 Sep 79	**WHEN YOU'RE NUMBER 1** *20th Century TC 2411*	**43**	5 wks
28 Jun 80	**DOES SHE HAVE A FRIEND** *20th Century/Chi-Sound TC 2451*	**28**	9 wks

CHANGE
US, male/female vocal/instrumental group   *32 wks*

28 Jun 80	**A LOVER'S HOLIDAY/GLOW OF LOVE** *WEA K 79141*	**14**	8 wks
6 Sep 80	**SEARCHING** *WEA K 79156*	**11**	10 wks
2 Jun 84	**CHANGE OF HEART** *WEA YZ 7*	**17**	10 wks
11 Aug 84	**YOU ARE MY MELODY** *WEA YZ 14*	**48**	4 wks

COLOUR FIELD (above) From The Specials via Fun Boy Three to the Colour Field. Terry Hall is on the right.

BILLY CONNOLLY (below) Just about to 'beet' his chest.

NATALIE COLE Nattily dressed daughter of Old King Cole.

CORONETS The group that got together in 1953 while travelling on a train as five separate singers.

Bruce CHANNEL   *US, male vocalist*   *28 wks*

22 Mar 62	● **HEY! BABY** *Mercury AMT 1171*	**2**	12 wks
26 Jun 68	**KEEP ON** *Bell 1010*	**12**	16 wks

CHANSON   *US, male/female vocal group*   *7 wks*

13 Jan 79	**DON'T HOLD BACK** *Ariola ARO 140*	**33**	7 wks

CHANTAYS   *US, male instrumental group*   *14 wks*

18 Apr 63	**PIPELINE** *London HLD 9696*	**16**	14 wks

CHANTER SISTERS
UK, female vocal group   *5 wks*

17 Jul 76	**SIDE SHOW** *Polydor 2058 734*	**43**	5 wks

Harry CHAPIN   *US, male vocalist*   *5 wks*

11 May 74	**W. O. L. D.** *Elektra K 12133*	**34**	5 wks

CHAQUITO   *UK, male arranger/conductor*
Johnny Gregory under false name   *1 wk*

27 Oct 60	**NEVER ON SUNDAY** *Fontana H 265*	**50**	1 wk

CHARLENE   *US, female vocalist*   *12 wks*

15 May 82	★ **I'VE NEVER BEEN TO ME** *Motown TMG 1260*	**1**	12 wks

Don CHARLES   *UK, male vocalist*   *5 wks*

22 Feb 62	**WALK WITH ME MY ANGEL** *Decca F 11424* ..	**39**	5 wks

Ray CHARLES
US, male vocalist/instrumentalist – piano   *123 wks*

1 Dec 60	**GEORGIA ON MY MIND** *HMV POP 792*	**47**	1 wk
15 Dec 60	**GEORGIA ON MY MIND** (re-entry)		
	HMV POP 792	**24**	7 wks
19 Oct 61	● **HIT THE ROAD JACK** *HMV POP 935*	**6**	12 wks
14 Jun 62	★ **I CAN'T STOP LOVING YOU** *HMV POP 1034*	**1**	17 wks
13 Sep 62	● **YOU DON'T KNOW ME** *HMV POP 1064*	**9**	13 wks
13 Dec 62	**YOUR CHEATING HEART** *HMV POP 1099* ..	**13**	8 wks
28 Mar 63	**DON'T SET ME FREE** *HMV POP 1133*	**37**	3 wks
16 May 63	● **TAKE THESE CHAINS FROM MY HEART**		
	HMV POP 1161	**5**	20 wks
12 Sep 63	**NO ONE** *HMV POP 1202*	**35**	7 wks
31 Oct 63	**BUSTED** *HMV POP 1221*	**21**	10 wks
24 Sep 64	**NO ONE TO CRY TO** *HMV POP 1333*	**38**	3 wks
21 Jan 65	**MAKIN' WHOOPEE** *HMV POP 1383*	**42**	4 wks
10 Feb 66	**CRYIN' TIME** *HMV POP 1502*	**50**	1 wk
21 Apr 66	**TOGETHER AGAIN** *HMV POP 1519*	**48**	1 wk
5 Jul 67	**HERE WE GO AGAIN** *HMV POP 1595*	**38**	1 wk
19 Jul 67	**HERE WE GO AGAIN** (re-entry) *HMV POP 1595*	**45**	2 wks
20 Dec 67	**YESTERDAY** *Stateside SS 2071*	**44**	4 wks
31 Jul 68	**ELEANOR RIGBY** *Stateside SS 2120*	**36**	9 wks

Tina CHARLES   *UK, female vocalist*   *60 wks*

7 Feb 76	★ **I LOVE TO LOVE (BUT MY BABY LOVES TO**		
	DANCE) *CBS 3937*	**1**	12 wks
1 May 76	**LOVE ME LIKE A LOVER** *CBS 4237*	**28**	7 wks
21 Aug 76	● **DANCE LITTLE LADY DANCE** *CBS 4480*	**6**	13 wks

4 Dec 76	● **DR. LOVE** *CBS 4779*	**4**	10 wks
14 May 77	**RENDEZVOUS** *CBS 5174*	**27**	6 wks
29 Oct 77	**LOVE BUG-SWEETS FOR MY SWEET** (MEDLEY)		
	CBS 5680	**26**	4 wks
11 Mar 78	**I'LL GO WHERE YOUR MUSIC TAKES ME**		
	CBS 6062	**27**	8 wks

Dick CHARLESWORTH and his CITY GENTS   *UK, male instrumental group,*
Dick Charlesworth clarinet   *1 wk*

4 May 61	**BILLY BOY** *Top Rank JAR 558*	**43**	1 wk

CHARLEY   -   *See JOHNNY and CHARLEY*

CHARME   *US, male/female vocal group*   *2 wks*

17 Nov 84	**GEORGY PORGY** *RCA 464*	**68**	2 wks

CHARO and the SALSOUL ORCHESTRA
US, female vocalist and orchestra   *4 wks*

29 Apr 78	**DANCE A LITTLE BIT CLOSER**		
	Salsoul SSOL 101	**44**	4 wks

CHAS and DAVE
UK, male vocal/instrumental duo   *57 wks*

11 Nov 78	**STRUMMIN'** *EMI 2874*	**52**	3 wks
26 May 79	**GERTCHA** *EMI 2947*	**20**	8 wks
1 Sep 79	**THE SIDEBOARD SONG (GOT MY BEER IN**		
	THE SIDEBOARD HERE) *EMI 2986*	**55**	3 wks
29 Nov 80	● **RABBIT** *Rockney 9*	**8**	11 wks
12 Dec 81	**STARS OVER 45** *Rockney KOR 12*	**21**	8 wks
13 Mar 82	● **AIN'T NO PLEASING YOU** *Rockney KOR 14*	**2**	11 wks
17 Jul 82	**MARGATE** *Rockney KOR 15*	**46**	4 wks
19 Mar 83	**LONDON GIRLS** *Rockney/Towerbell KOR 17*	**63**	3 wks
3 Dec 83	**MY MELANCHOLY BABY**		
	Rockney/Towerbell KOR 21	**51**	6 wks

See also Tottenham Hotspur FA Cup Squad. Strummin' by Chas and Dave, with Rockney. UK male instrumental backing group.

CHEAP TRICK
US, male vocal/instrumental group   *14 wks*

5 May 79	**I WANT YOU TO WANT ME** *Epic EPC 7258*	**29**	9 wks
2 Feb 80	**WAY OF THE WORLD** *Epic EPC 8114*	**73**	2 wks
31 Jul 82	**IF YOU WANT MY LOVE** *Epic EPC A 2406* ...	**57**	3 wks

Oliver CHEATHAM   *US, male vocalist*   *5 wks*

2 Jul 83	**GET DOWN SATURDAY NIGHT** *MCA 828* ..	**38**	5 wks

Chubby CHECKER   *US, male vocalist*   *97 wks*

22 Sep 60	**THE TWIST** *Columbia DB 4503*	**49**	1 wk
6 Oct 60	**THE TWIST** (re-entry) *Columbia DB 4503*	**44**	1 wk
30 Mar 61	**PONY TIME** *Columbia DB 4591*	**27**	6 wks
17 Aug 61	**LET'S TWIST AGAIN** *Columbia DB 4691*	**37**	3 wks
28 Dec 61	● **LET'S TWIST AGAIN** (re-entry)		
	Columbia DB 4691	**2**	27 wks
11 Jan 62	**THE TWIST** (2nd re-entry) *Columbia DB 4503* ..	**14**	10 wks
4 Apr 62	**SLOW TWISTIN'** *Columbia DB 4808*	**23**	8 wks
9 Aug 62	**DANCIN' PARTY** *Columbia DB 4876*	**19**	13 wks

23 Aug 62	LET'S TWIST AGAIN (2nd re-entry) *Columbia DB 4691*	46	1 wk
13 Sep 62	LET'S TWIST AGAIN (3rd re-entry) *Columbia DB 4691*	49	3 wks
1 Nov 62	LIMBO ROCK *Cameo-Parkway P 849*	32	10 wks
31 Oct 63	WHAT DO YA SAY *Cameo-Parkway P 806*	37	4 wks
29 Nov 75	● LET'S TWIST AGAIN/THE TWIST (re-issue) *London HL 10512*	5	10 wks

See also Chubby Checker and Bobby Rydell.

Chubby CHECKER and Bobby RYDELL US, *male vocal duo* *4 wks*

19 Apr 62	TEACH ME TO TWIST *Columbia DB 4802*	45	1 wk
20 Dec 62	JINGLE BELL ROCK *Cameo-Parkway C 205*	40	3 wks

See also Chubby Checker; Bobby Rydell.

CHECKMATES - *See Emile FORD and the CHECKMATES*

CHECKMATES LTD.
US, *male vocal/instrumental group* *8 wks*

15 Nov 69	PROUD MARY *A & M AMS 769*	30	8 wks

CHEETAHS
UK, *male vocal/instrumental group* *6 wks*

1 Oct 64	MECCA *Philips BF 1362*	36	3 wks
21 Jan 65	SOLDIER BOY *Philips BF 1383*	39	3 wks

CHELSEA F.C.
UK, *male football team vocalists* *12 wks*

26 Feb 72	● BLUE IS THE COLOUR *Penny Farthing PEN 782*	5	12 wks

CHEQUERS
UK, *male vocal/instrumental group* *10 wks*

18 Oct 75	ROCK ON BROTHER *Creole CR 111*	21	5 wks
28 Feb 76	HEY MISS PAYNE *Creole CR 116*	32	5 wks

CHER US, *female vocalist* *46 wks*

19 Aug 65	● ALL I REALLY WANT TO DO *Liberty LIB 66114*	9	10 wks
31 Mar 66	● BANG BANG (MY BABY SHOT ME DOWN) *Liberty LIB 66160*	3	12 wks
4 Aug 66	I FEEL SOMETHING IN THE AIR *Liberty LIB 12034*	43	2 wks
22 Sep 66	SUNNY *Liberty LIB 12083*	32	5 wks
6 Nov 71	● GYPSIES TRAMPS AND THIEVES *MCA MU 1142*	4	13 wks
16 Feb 74	DARK LADY *MCA 101*	36	3 wks
16 Mar 74	DARK LADY (re-entry) *MCA 101*	45	1 wk

See also Sonny and Cher.

CHERI UK, *female vocal duo* *9 wks*

19 Jun 82	MURPHY'S LAW *Polydor POSP 459*	13	9 wks

CHEROKEES
UK, *male vocal/instrumental group* *5 wks*

3 Sep 64	SEVEN DAFFODILS *Columbia DB 7341*	33	5 wks

Don CHERRY US, *male vocalist* *11 wks*

10 Feb 56	● BAND OF GOLD *Philips PB 549*	6	11 wks

CHIC US, *male/female vocal/instrumental group* *79 wks*

26 Nov 77	● DANCE DANCE DANCE (YOWSAH YOWSAH YOWSAH) *Atlantic K 11038*	6	12 wks
1 Apr 78	● EVERYBODY DANCE *Atlantic K 11097*	9	11 wks
18 Nov 78	● LE FREAK *Atlantic K 11209*	7	16 wks
24 Feb 79	● I WANT YOUR LOVE *Atlantic LV 16*	4	11 wks
30 Jun 79	● GOOD TIMES *Atlantic K 11310*	5	11 wks
13 Oct 79	MY FORBIDDEN LOVER *Atlantic K 11385*	15	8 wks
8 Dec 79	MY FEET KEEP DANCING *Atlantic K 11415*	21	9 wks
12 Mar 83	HANGIN' *Atlantic A 9898*	64	1 wk

CHICAGO US, *male vocal/instrumental group* *68 wks*

10 Jan 70	● I'M A MAN *CBS 4715*	8	11 wks
18 Jul 70	● 25 OR 6 TO 4 *CBS 5076*	7	13 wks
9 Oct 76	★ IF YOU LEAVE ME NOW *CBS 4603* ...	1	16 wks
5 Nov 77	BABY WHAT A BIG SURPRISE *CBS 5672*	41	3 wks
21 Aug 82	● HARD TO SAY I'M SORRY *Full Moon K 79301*	4	15 wks
27 Oct 84	● HARD HABIT TO BREAK *FullMoon/WEA W 9214*	8†	10 wks

CHICKEN SHACK
UK, *male/female vocal/instrumental group* *19 wks*

7 May 69	I'D RATHER GO BLIND *Blue Horizon 57-3153* ..	14	13 wks
6 Sep 69	TEARS IN THE WIND *Blue Horizon 57-3160* ...	29	6 wks

CHICORY TIP
UK, *male vocal/instrumental group* *34 wks*

29 Jan 72	★ SON OF MY FATHER *CBS 7737*	1	13 wks
20 May 72	WHAT'S YOUR NAME *CBS 8021*	13	8 wks
31 Mar 73	GOOD GRIEF CHRISTINA *CBS 1258*	17	13 wks

CHIFFONS US, *female vocal group* *40 wks*

11 Apr 63	HE'S SO FINE *Stateside SS 172*	16	12 wks
18 Jul 63	ONE FINE DAY *Stateside SS 202*	29	6 wks
26 May 66	SWEET TALKIN' GUY *Stateside SS 512*	31	8 wks
18 Mar 72	● SWEET TALKIN' GUY (re-issue) *London HL 10271*	4	14 wks

CHILD UK, *male vocal/instrumental group* *22 wks*

29 Apr 78	WHEN YOU WALK IN THE ROOM *Ariola Hansa AHA 511*	38	5 wks
22 Jul 78	● IT'S ONLY MAKE BELIEVE *Ariola Hansa AHA 522*	10	12 wks
28 Apr 79	ONLY YOU (AND YOU ALONE) *Ariola Hansa AHA 536*	33	5 wks

CHI-LITES US, *male vocal group* *89 wks*

28 Aug 71	(FOR GOD'S SAKE) GIVE MORE POWER TO THE PEOPLE *MCA MU 1138*	32	6 wks
15 Jan 72	● HAVE YOU SEEN HER *MCA MU 1146*	3	12 wks
27 May 72	OH GIRL *MCA MU 1156*	14	9 wks
23 Mar 74	● HOMELY GIRL *Brunswick BR 9*	5	13 wks
20 Jul 74	I FOUND SUNSHINE *Brunswick BR 12*	35	5 wks
2 Nov 74	● TOO GOOD TO BE FORGOTTEN *Brunswick BR 13*	10	11 wks
21 Jun 75	● HAVE YOU SEEN HER/OH GIRL (re-issue) *Brunswick BR 20*	5	9 wks

13 Sep 75 ●	IT'S TIME FOR LOVE *Brunswick BR 25*	5	10 wks
31 Jul 76 ●	YOU DON'T HAVE TO GO *Brunswick BR 34* ..	3	11 wks
13 Aug 83	CHANGING FOR YOU *R & B RBS 215*	61	3 wks

CHILL FAC-TOR
US, male vocal/instrumental group   *8 wks*

2 Apr 83	TWIST (ROUND 'N' ROUND) *Phillyworld PWS 109*	37	8 wks

CHINA CRISIS
UK, male vocal/instrumental group   *36 wks*

7 Aug 82	AFRICAN AND WHITE *Inevitable/Virgin INEV 011*	45	5 wks
22 Jan 83	CHRISTIAN *Virgin VS 562*	12	9 wks
21 May 83	TRAGEDY AND MYSTERY *Virgin VS 587*	46	6 wks
15 Oct 83	WORKING WITH FIRE AND STEEL *Virgin VS 620*	48	5 wks
14 Jan 84 ●	WISHFUL THINKING *Virgin VS 647*	9	8 wks
10 Mar 84	HANNA HANNA *Virgin VS 665*	44	3 wks

Johnny CHINGAS *US, male vocalist*   *6 wks*

19 Feb 83	PHONE HOME *CBS A 3121*	43	6 wks

CHIPMUNKS *US, male vocalist, David*
Seville as a chipmunk vocal group   *8 wks*

24 Jul 59	RAGTIME COWBOY JOE *London HLU 8916* ...	11	8 wks

See also David Seville; Alfi and Harry.

CHORDETTES *US, female vocal group*   *25 wks*

17 Dec 54	MR. SANDMAN *Columbia DB 3553*	11	8 wks
31 Aug 56 ●	BORN TO BE WITH YOU *London HLA 8302* ..	8	9 wks
18 Apr 58 ●	LOLLIPOP *London HLA 8584*	6	8 wks

CHORDS *UK, male vocal/instrumental group*   *17 wks*

6 Oct 79	NOW IT'S GONE *Polydor 2059 141*	63	2 wks
2 Feb 80	MAYBE TOMORROW *Polydor POSP 101*	40	5 wks
26 Apr 80	SOMETHING'S MISSING *Polydor POSP 146*	55	3 wks
12 Jul 80	THE BRITISH WAY OF LIFE *Polydor 2059 258*	54	3 wks
18 Oct 80	IN MY STREET *Polydor POSP 185*	50	4 wks

Neil CHRISTIAN *UK, male vocalist*   *10 wks*

7 Apr 66	THAT'S NICE *Strike JH 301*	14	10 wks

CHRISTIE
UK, male vocal/instrumental group   *37 wks*

2 May 70 ★	YELLOW RIVER *CBS 4911*	1	22 wks
10 Oct 70	SAN BERNADINO *CBS 5169*	49	1 wk
24 Oct 70 ●	SAN BERNADINO (re-entry) *CBS 5169*	7	13 wks
25 Mar 72	IRON HORSE *CBS 7747*	47	1 wk

David CHRISTIE *France, male vocalist*   *12 wks*

14 Aug 82 ●	SADDLE UP *KR KR 9*	9	12 wks

John CHRISTIE *Australia, male vocalist*   *6 wks*

25 Dec 76	HERE'S TO LOVE (AULD LANG SYNE) *EMI 2554*	24	6 wks

Lou CHRISTIE *US, male vocalist*   *35 wks*

24 Feb 66	LIGHTNIN' STRIKES *MGM 1297*	11	8 wks
28 Apr 66	RHAPSODY IN THE RAIN *MGM 1308*	37	2 wks
13 Sep 69 ●	I'M GONNA MAKE YOU MINE *Buddah 201 057*	2	17 wks
27 Dec 69	SHE SOLD ME MAGIC *Buddah 201 073*	25	8 wks

Tony CHRISTIE *UK, male vocalist*   *47 wks*

9 Jan 71	LAS VEGAS *MCA MK 5058*	21	9 wks
8 May 71 ●	I DID WHAT I DID FOR MARIA *MCA MK 5064*	2	17 wks
20 Nov 71	IS THIS THE WAY TO AMARILLO *MCA MKS 5073*	18	13 wks
10 Feb 73	AVENUES AND ALLEYWAYS *MCA MKS 5101*	37	4 wks
17 Jan 76	DRIVE SAFELY DARLIN' *MCA 219*	35	4 wks

CHRISTMAS TREES - *See SANTA CLAUS and the CHRISTMAS TREES*

CHUCKS *UK, male/female vocal group*   *7 wks*

24 Jan 63	LOO-BE-LOO *Decca F 11569*	22	7 wks

CINDY and the SAFFRONS
UK, female vocal group   *3 wks*

15 Jan 83	PAST, PRESENT AND FUTURE *Disques Bleus/Stilletto STL 9*	56	3 wks

Gigliola CINQUETTI
Italy, female vocalist   *27 wks*

23 Apr 64	NON HO L'ETA PER AMARTI *Decca F 21882*	17	17 wks
4 May 74 ●	GO (BEFORE YOU BREAK MY HEART) *CBS 2294*	8	10 wks

CIRRUS *UK, disco aggregation*   *1 wk*

30 Sep 78	ROLLIN' ON *Jet 123*	62	1 wk

CITY BOY
UK, male vocal/instrumental group   *20 wks*

8 Jul 78 ●	5-7-0-5 *Vertigo 6059 207*	8	12 wks
28 Oct 78	WHAT A NIGHT *Vertigo 6059 211*	39	5 wks
15 Sep 79	THE DAY THE EARTH CAUGHT FIRE *Vertigo 6059 238*	67	3 wks

CITY GENTS - *See Dick CHARLESWORTH and his CITY GENTS*

C.J.& CO. *US, male vocal/instrumental group*   *2 wks*

30 Jul 77	DEVIL'S GUN *Atlantic K 10956*	43	2 wks

CLANNAD *Ireland, male/female vocal group*   *16 wks*

6 Nov 82 ●	THEME FROM HARRY'S GAME *RCA 292*	5	10 wks
2 Jul 83	NEW GRANGE *RCA 340*	65	1 wk
12 May 84	ROBIN (THE HOODED MAN) *RCA HOOD 1*	42	5 wks

JACKIE DENNIS (above) Charted with covers of Billie and Lilke and Sheb Wooley

PHIL COLLINS (below left) He joined Genesis from Flaming Youth, replacing drummer John Mayhew. (Photo: Allan Ballard.)

ARTHUR CONLEY (below right) 'Sweet Soul Music' was a re-write of Sam Cooke's 'Yeah Man' and provided Otis Redding's protegée with a Top 10 hit.

THE CURE Lol and Robert first wielded their chart axes in 'A Forest'.

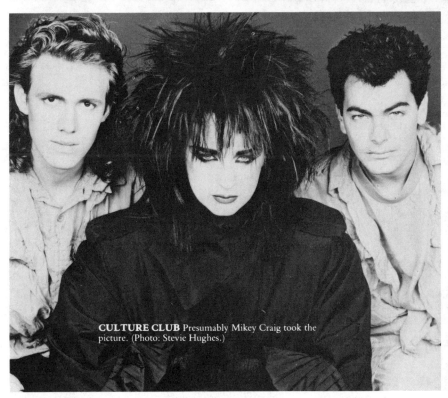

DETROIT SPINNERS To avoid confusion with the long-established English folk singers The Spinners, these Spinners became the Motown Spinners and ultimately the Detroit Spinners for UK purposes.

CULTURE CLUB Presumably Mikey Craig took the picture. (Photo: Stevie Hughes.)

Jimmy CLANTON *US, male vocalist*   *1 wk*

21 Jul 60	**ANOTHER SLEEPLESS NIGHT**			
	Top Rank JAR 382	**50**	1 wk

Eric CLAPTON
UK, male vocalist/instrumentalist-guitar   *38 wks*

27 Jul 74 ●	**I SHOT THE SHERIFF** *RSO 2090 132*	**9**	9 wks
10 May 75	**SWING LOW SWEET CHARIOT** *RSO 2090 158*	**19**	9 wks
16 Aug 75	**KNOCKIN' ON HEAVEN'S DOOR**		
	RSO 2090 166	**38**	4 wks
24 Dec 77	**LAY DOWN SALLY** *RSO 2090 264*	**39**	6 wks
21 Oct 78	**PROMISES** *RSO 21*	**37**	7 wks
5 Jun 82 ●	**I SHOT THE SHERIFF** (re-issue) *RSO 88*	**64**	2 wks
23 Apr 83	**THE SHAPE YOU'RE IN**		
	Duck/Warner Bros. W 9701	**75**	1 wk

See also Derek and the Dominos; Delaney and Bonnie and Friends featuring Eric Clapton

Dee CLARK *US, male vocalist*   *9 wks*

2 Oct 59	**JUST KEEP IT UP** *London HL 8915*	**26**	1 wk
11 Oct 75	**RIDE A WILD HORSE** *Chelsea 2005 037*	**16**	8 wks

Petula CLARK *UK, female vocalist*   *236 wks*

11 Jun 54	**THE LITTLE SHOEMAKER** *Polygon P 1117* ...	**12**	1 wk
25 Jun 54 ●	**THE LITTLE SHOEMAKER** (re-entry)		
	Polygon P 1117	**7**	9 wks
18 Feb 55	**MAJORCA** *Polygon P 1146*	**12**	4 wks
25 Mar 55	**MAJORCA** (re-entry) *Polygon P 1146*	**18**	1 wk
25 Nov 55	**SUDDENLY THERE'S A VALLEY**		
	Pye Nixa N 15013	**7**	10 wks
26 Jul 57 ●	**WITH ALL MY HEART** *Pye Nixa N 15096*	**4**	18 wks
15 Nov 57 ●	**ALONE** *Pye Nixa N 15112*	**8**	12 wks
28 Feb 58	**BABY LOVER** *Pye Nixa N 15126*	**12**	7 wks
26 Jan 61 ★	**SAILOR** *Pye 7N 15324*	**1**	15 wks
13 Apr 61	**SOMETHING MISSING** *Pye 7N 15337*	**44**	1 wk
13 Jul 61 ●	**ROMEO** *Pye 7N 15361*	**3**	15 wks
16 Nov 61 ●	**MY FRIEND THE SEA** *Pye 7N 15387*	**7**	13 wks
8 Feb 62	**I'M COUNTING ON YOU** *Pye 7N 15407*	**41**	2 wks
28 Jun 62	**YA YA TWIST** *Pye 7N 15448*	**14**	11 wks
20 Sep 62	**YA YA TWIST** (re-entry) *Pye 7N 15448*	**45**	2 wks
2 May 63	**CASANOVA /CHARIOT** *Pye 7N 15522*	**39**	7 wks
12 Nov 64 ●	**DOWNTOWN** *Pye 7N 15722*	**2**	15 wks
11 Mar 65	**I KNOW A PLACE** *Pye 7N 15772*	**17**	8 wks
12 Aug 65	**YOU BETTER COME HOME** *Pye 7N 15864* ...	**44**	3 wks
14 Oct 65	**ROUND EVERY CORNER** *Pye 7N 15945*	**43**	3 wks
4 Nov 65	**YOU'RE THE ONE** *Pye 7N 15991*	**23**	9 wks
10 Feb 66 ●	**MY LOVE** *Pye 7N 17038*	**4**	9 wks
21 Apr 66	**A SIGN OF THE TIMES** *Pye 7N 17071*	**49**	1 wk
30 Jun 66 ●	**I COULDN'T LIVE WITHOUT YOUR LOVE**		
	Pye 7N 17133	**6**	11 wks
2 Feb 67 ★	**THIS IS MY SONG** *Pye 7N 17258*	**1**	14 wks
25 May 67	**DON'T SLEEP IN THE SUBWAY** *Pye 7N 17325*	**12**	11 wks
13 Dec 67	**THE OTHER MAN'S GRASS** *Pye 7N 17416* ...	**20**	9 wks
6 Mar 68	**KISS ME GOODBYE** *Pye 7N 17466*	**50**	1 wk
30 Jan 71	**THE SONG OF MY LIFE** *Pye 7N 45026*	**41**	1 wk
13 Feb 71	**THE SONG OF MY LIFE** (re-entry) *Pye 7N 45026*	**32**	11 wks
15 Jan 72	**I DON'T KNOW HOW TO LOVE HIM**		
	Pye 7N 45112	**47**	1 wk
29 Jan 72	**I DON'T KNOW HOW TO LOVE HIM** (re-entry)		
	Pye 7N 45112	**49**	1 wk

Dave CLARK FIVE
UK, male vocal/instrumental group   *171 wks*

3 Oct 63	**DO YOU LOVE ME** *Columbia DB 7112*	**30**	6 wks
21 Nov 63 ★	**GLAD ALL OVER** *Columbia DB 7154*	**1**	19 wks
20 Feb 64 ●	**BITS AND PIECES** *Columbia DB 7210*	**2**	11 wks
28 May 64 ●	**CAN'T YOU SEE THAT SHE'S MINE**		
	Columbia DB 7291	**10**	11 wks

13 Aug 64	**THINKING OF YOU BABY** *Columbia DB 7335*	**26**	4 wks
22 Oct 64	**ANYWAY YOU WANT IT** *Columbia DB 7377* ..	**25**	5 wks
14 Jan 65	**EVERYBODY KNOWS** *Columbia DB 7453*	**37**	4 wks
11 Mar 65	**REELIN' AND ROCKIN'** *Columbia DB 7503*	**24**	8 wks
27 May 65	**COME HOME** *Columbia DB 7580*	**16**	8 wks
15 Jul 65 ●	**CATCH US IF YOU CAN** *Columbia DB 7625* ...	**5**	11 wks
11 Nov 65	**OVER AND OVER** *Columbia DB 7744*	**45**	4 wks
19 May 66	**LOOK BEFORE YOU LEAP** *Columbia DB 7909*	**50**	1 wk
16 Mar 67	**YOU GOT WHAT IT TAKES** *Columbia DB 8152*	**28**	8 wks
1 Nov 67 ●	**EVERYBODY KNOWS** *Columbia DB 8286*	**2**	14 wks
28 Feb 68	**NO ONE CAN BREAK A HEART LIKE YOU**		
	Columbia DB 8342	**28**	7 wks
18 Sep 68	**RED BALLOON** *Columbia DB 8465*	**7**	11 wks
27 Nov 68	**LIVE IN THE SKY** *Columbia DB 8505*	**39**	6 wks
25 Oct 69	**PUT A LITTLE LOVE IN YOUR HEART**		
	Columbia DB 8624	**31**	4 wks
6 Dec 69 ●	**GOOD OLD ROCK 'N ROLL** *Columbia DB 8638*	**7**	12 wks
7 Mar 70 ●	**EVERYBODY GET TOGETHER**		
	Columbia DB 8660	**8**	8 wks
4 Jul 70	**HERE COMES SUMMER** *Columbia DB 8689*	**44**	3 wks
7 Nov 70	**MORE GOOD OLD ROCK 'N ROLL**		
	Columbia DB 8724	**34**	6 wks

(Everybody Knows *on DB 7453* and Everybody Knows *on DB 8286 are two different songs. The two Rock 'N' Roll titles are medleys as follows:* Good Old Rock 'N' Roll: *Good Old Rock 'N' Roll/Sweet Little Sixteen/ Long Tall Sally/Whole Lotta Shakin' Goin' On/Blue Suede Shoes/ Lucille/Reelin' and Rockin'/Memphis Tennessee.* More Good Old Rock 'N Roll: *Rock And Roll Music/Blueberry Hill/Good Golly Miss Molly/My Blue Heaven/Keep A Knockin'/Loving You/ One Night/Lawdy Miss Clawdy.*

John Cooper CLARKE
UK, male vocalist   *3 wks*

10 Mar 79	**GIMMIX! PLAY LOUD** *Epic EPC 7009*	**39**	3 wks

CLASH
UK, male vocal and instrumental group   *102 wks*

2 Apr 77	**WHITE RIOT** *CBS 5058*	**38**	3 wks
8 Oct 77	**COMPLETE CONTROL** *CBS 5664*	**28**	2 wks
4 Mar 78	**CLASH CITY ROCKERS** *CBS 5834*	**35**	4 wks
24 Jun 78	**(WHITE MAN) IN HAMMERSMITH PALAIS**		
	CBS 6383	**32**	7 wks
2 Dec 78	**TOMMY GUN** *CBS 6788*	**19**	10 wks
3 Mar 79	**ENGLISH CIVIL WAR (JOHNNY COMES**		
	MARCHING HOME) *CBS 7082*	**25**	6 wks
19 May 79	**THE COST OF LIVING** (EP) *CBS 7324*	**22**	8 wks
15 Dec 79	**LONDON CALLING** *CBS 8087*	**11**	10 wks
9 Aug 80	**BANKROBBER** *CBS 8323*	**12**	10 wks
6 Dec 80	**THE CALL UP** *CBS 9339*	**40**	6 wks
24 Jan 81	**HITSVILLE UK** *CBS 9480*	**56**	4 wks
25 Apr 81	**THE MAGNIFICENT SEVEN** *CBS 1133*	**34**	5 wks
28 Nov 81	**THIS IS RADIO CLASH** *CBS A 1797*	**47**	5 wks
1 May 82	**KNOW YOUR RIGHTS** *CBS A 2309*	**43**	3 wks
26 Jan 82	**ROCK THE CASBAH** *CBS A 2429*	**30**	10 wks
25 Sep 82	**SHOULD I STAY OR SHOULD I GO/STRAIGHT**		
	TO HELL *CBS A 2645*	**17**	9 wks

Tracks on Cost Of Living EP: *I Fought The Law /Groovy Times/Gates Of The West/Capital Radio.*

CLASS ACTION featuring Chris WILTSHIRE *US, female vocal group*   *3 wks*

7 May 83	**WEEKEND** *Jive JIVE 35*	**49**	3 wks

CLASSICS IV
US, male vocal/instrumental group   *1 wk*

28 Feb 68	**SPOOKY** *Liberty LBS 15051*	**46**	1 wk

CLASSIX NOUVEAUX
UK, male vocal/instrumental group   *34 wks*

28 Feb 81	**GUILTY** *Liberty BP 388*	**43**	7 wks
16 May 81	**TOKYO** *Liberty BP 397*	**67**	3 wks
8 Aug 81	**INSIDE OUTSIDE** *Liberty BP 403*	**46**	5 wks
7 Nov 81	**NEVER AGAIN (THE DAYS TIME ERASED)** *Liberty BP 406*	**44**	4 wks
13 Mar 82	**IS IT A DREAM** *Liberty BP 409*	**11**	9 wks
29 May 82	**BECAUSE YOU'RE YOUNG** *Liberty BP 411* ...	**43**	4 wks
30 Oct 82	**THE END ... OR THE BEGINNING** *Liberty BP 414*	**60**	2 wks

Judy CLAY and William BELL
US, female/male vocal duo   *14 wks*

20 Nov 68 ●	**PRIVATE NUMBER** *Stax 101*	**8**	14 wks

See also William Bell.

Jimmy CLIFF   *Jamaica, male vocalist*   *28 wks*

25 Oct 69 ●	**WONDERFUL WORLD BEAUTIFUL PEOPLE** *Trojan TR 690*	**6**	13 wks
14 Feb 70	**VIETNAM** *Trojan TR 7722*	**47**	1 wk
28 Feb 70	**VIETNAM** (re-entry) *Trojan TR 7722*	**46**	2 wks
8 Aug 70 ●	**WILD WORLD** *Island WIP 6087*	**8**	12 wks

Buzz CLIFFORD   *US, male vocalist*   *13 wks*

2 Mar 61	**BABY SITTIN' BOOGIE** *Fontana H 297*	**17**	13 wks

Linda CLIFFORD   *US, female vocalist*   *12 wks*

10 Jun 78	**IF MY FRIENDS COULD SEE ME NOW** *Curtom K 17163*	**50**	5 wks
5 May 79	**BRIDGE OVER TROUBLED WATER** *RSO 30*	**28**	7 wks

CLIMAX BLUES BAND
UK, male vocal/instrumental group   *9 wks*

9 Oct 76 ●	**COULDN'T GET IT RIGHT** *BTM SBT 105*	**10**	9 wks

Patsy CLINE   *US, female vocalist*   *6 wks*

26 Apr 62	**SHE'S GOT YOU** *Brunswick 05866*	**43**	1 wk
29 Nov 62	**HEARTACHES** *Brunswick 05878*	**31**	5 wks

George CLINTON   *US, male vocalist*   *5 wks*

4 Dec 82	**LOOPZILLA** *Capitol CL 271*	**57**	5 wks

Rosemary CLOONEY
US, female vocalist   *81 wks*

14 Nov 52 ●	**HALF AS MUCH** *Columbia DB 3129*	**3**	9 wks
5 Feb 54 ●	**MAN** *Philips PB 220*	**7**	5 wks
8 Oct 54 ★	**THIS OLE HOUSE** *Philips PB 336*	**1**	18 wks
17 Dec 54 ★	**MAMBO ITALIANO** *Philips PB 382*	**1**	16 wks
20 May 55 ●	**WHERE WILL THE BABY'S DIMPLE BE** *Philips PB 428*	**6**	13 wks
30 Sep 55 ●	**HEY THERE** *Philips PB 494*	**4**	11 wks
29 Mar 57	**MANGOS** *Philips PB 671*	**25**	2 wks
26 Apr 57	**MANGOS** (re-entry) *Philips PB 671*	**17**	7 wks

From 19 Feb 54 other side of Man, Woman by José Ferrer was also credited. See José Ferrer.

CLOUD   *UK, male instrumental group*   *1 wk*

31 Jan 81	**ALL NIGHT LONG/TAKE IT TO TOP** *UK Champagne FUNK 1*	**72**	1 wk

CLOUT
South Africa, female vocal/instrumental group   *15 wks*

17 Jun 78 ●	**SUBSTITUTE** *Carrere EMI 2788*	**2**	15 wks

CLUB HOUSE
Italy, male vocal/instrumental group   *9 wks*

23 Jul 83	**DO IT AGAIN-BILLIE JEAN** *Island IS 132*	**11**	6 wks
3 Dec 83	**SUPERSTITION-GOOD TIMES** *Island IS 147* ...	**59**	3 wks

Jeremy CLYDE   -   *See Chad STUART and Jeremy CLYDE*

CLYDE VALLEY STOMPERS
UK, male instrumental group   *8 wks*

9 Aug 62	**PETER AND THE WOLF** *Parlophone R 4928* ...	**25**	8 wks

COAST TO COAST
UK, male vocal/instrumental group   *22 wks*

31 Jan 81 ●	**(DO) THE HUCKLEBUCK** *Polydor POSP 214* ...	**5**	15 wks
23 May 81	**LET'S JUMP THE BROOMSTICK** *Polydor POSP 249*	**28**	7 wks

COASTERS   *US, male vocal group*   *28 wks*

27 Sep 57	**SEARCHIN'** *London HLE 8450*	**30**	1 wk
15 Aug 58	**YAKETY YAK** *London HLE 8665*	**12**	8 wks
27 Mar 59 ●	**CHARLIE BROWN** *London HLE 8819*	**6**	12 wks
30 Oct 59	**POISON IVY** *London HLE 8938*	**15**	7 wks

Eddie COCHRAN   *US, male vocalist*   *83 wks*

7 Nov 58	**SUMMERTIME BLUES** *London HLU 8702*	**18**	6 wks
13 Mar 59 ●	**C'MON EVERYBODY** *London HLU 8792*	**6**	13 wks
16 Oct 59	**SOMETHIN' ELSE** *London HLU 8944*	**22**	3 wks
22 Jan 60	**HALLELUJAH I LOVE HER SO** *London HLW 9022*	**28**	1 wk
5 Feb 60	**HALLELUJAH I LOVE HER SO** (re-entry) *London HLW 9022*	**22**	3 wks
12 May 60 ★	**THREE STEPS TO HEAVEN** *London HLG 9115*	**1**	15 wks
6 Oct 60	**SWEETIE PIE** *London HLG 9196*	**38**	3 wks
3 Nov 60	**LONELY** *London HLG 9196*	**41**	1 wk
15 Jun 61	**WEEKEND** *London HLG 9362*	**15**	16 wks
30 Nov 61	**JEANNIE, JEANNIE, JEANNIE** *London HLG 9460*	**31**	4 wks
25 Apr 63	**MY WAY** *Liberty LIB 10088*	**23**	10 wks
24 Apr 68	**SUMMERTIME BLUES** (re-issue) *Liberty LBF 15071*	**34**	8 wks

Joe COCKER   *UK, male vocalist*   *31 wks*

22 May 68	**MARJORINE** *Regal-Zonophone RZ 3006*	**48**	1 wk
2 Oct 68 ★	**WITH A LITTLE HELP FROM MY FRIENDS** *Regal-Zonophone RZ 3013*	**1**	13 wks
27 Sep 69 ●	**DELTA LADY** *Regal-Zonophone RZ 3024*	**10**	11 wks
4 Jul 70	**THE LETTER** *Regal-Zonophone RZ 3027*	**39**	6 wks

See also Joe Cocker and Jennifer Warnes.

Joe COCKER and Jennifer WARNES UK/US, male/female vocal duo   13 wks

15 Jan 83	● UP WHERE WE BELONG *Island WIP 6831*	7	13 wks

See also Joe Cocker.

COCKEREL CHORUS UK, male vocal group   12 wks

24 Feb 73	NICE ONE CYRIL *Youngblood YB 1017*	14	12 wks

COCKNEY REBEL - *See Steve HARLEY*

COCKNEY REJECTS UK, male vocal/instrumental group   22 wks

1 Dec 79	I'M NOT A FOOL *EMI 5008*	65	2 wks
16 Feb 80	BADMAN *EMI 5035*	65	3 wks
26 Apr 80	THE GREATEST COCKNEY RIPOFF *EMI Z 2*	21	7 wks
17 May 80	I'M FOREVER BLOWING BUBBLES *EMI Z 4*	35	5 wks
12 Jul 80	WE CAN DO ANYTHING		
	EMI-Cockney Rejects Z 6	65	2 wks
25 Oct 80	WE ARE THE FIRM *EMI-Cockney Rejects Z 10* . .	54	3 wks

CO-CO UK, male/female vocal/instrumental group   7 wks

22 Apr 78	BAD OLD DAYS *Ariola Hansa AHA 513*	13	7 wks

El COCO US, male vocal/instrumental group   4 wks

14 Jan 78	COCOMOTION *Pye International 7N 25761*	31	4 wks

COCONUTS US, female vocal group   3 wks

11 Jun 83	DID YOU HAVE TO LOVE ME LIKE YOU DID		
	EMI America EA 156	60	3 wks

See also Kid Creole and the Coconuts.

COFFEE US, female vocal group   13 wks

27 Sep 80	CASANOVA *De-Lite MER 38*	13	10 wks
6 Dec 80	SLIP AND DIP/I WANNA BE WITH YOU		
	De-Lite DE 1	57	3 wks

COCTEAU TWINS UK, male/female vocal duo   5 wks

28 Apr 84	PEARLY-DEW DROPS DROPS *4AD 405*	29	5 wks

C.O.D. US, male vocal/instrumental group   2 wks

14 May 83	IN THE BOTTLE *Streetwave WAVE 2*	54	2 wks

Alma COGAN UK, female vocalist   109 wks

19 Mar 54	● BELL BOTTOM BLUES *HMV B 10653*	4	9 wks
27 Aug 54	LITTLE THINGS MEAN A LOT *HMV B 10717*	11	2 wks
8 Oct 54	LITTLE THINGS MEAN A LOT (re-entry)		
	HMV B 10717	19	1 wk
22 Oct 54	LITTLE THINGS MEAN A LOT (2nd re-entry)		
	HMV B 10717	18	2 wks

3 Dec 54	● I CAN'T TELL A WALTZ FROM A TANGO		
	HMV B 10786	6	11 wks
27 May 55	★ DREAMBOAT *HMV B 10872*	1	16 wks
23 Sep 55	BANJO'S BACK IN TOWN *HMV B 10917* . .	17	1 wk
14 Oct 55	GO ON BY *HMV B 10917*	16	4 wks
16 Dec 55	TWENTY TINY FINGERS *HMV POP 129*	17	1 wk
23 Dec 55	● NEVER DO A TANGO WITH AN ESKIMO		
	HMV POP 129	6	5 wks
30 Mar 56	WILLIE CAN *HMV POP 187*	13	8 wks
13 Jul 56	THE BIRDS AND THE BEES *HMV POP 223* . .	25	4 wks
10 Aug 56	WHY DO FOOLS FALL IN LOVE		
	HMV POP 223	22	3 wks
2 Nov 56	IN THE MIDDLE OF THE HOUSE		
	HMV POP 261	26	1 wk
23 Nov 56	IN THE MIDDLE OF THE HOUSE (re-entry)		
	HMV POP 261	20	3 wks
18 Jan 57	YOU ME AND US *HMV POP 284*	18	6 wks
29 Mar 57	WHATEVER LOLA WANTS *HMV POP 317* . .	26	2 wks
31 Jan 58	THE STORY OF MY LIFE *HMV POP 433* . . .	25	2 wks
14 Feb 58	SUGARTIME *HMV POP 450*	16	10 wks
2 May 58	SUGARTIME (re-entry) *HMV POP 450*	30	1 wk
23 Jan 59	LAST NIGHT ON THE BACK PORCH		
	HMV POP 573	27	2 wks
18 Dec 59	WE GOT LOVE *HMV POP 670*	26	4 wks
11 Aug 60	TRAIN OF LOVE *HMV POP 760*	27	5 wks
20 Apr 61	COWBOY JIMMY JOE *Columbia DB 4607*	37	6 wks

Shaye COGAN US, female vocalist   1 wk

24 Mar 60	MEAN TO ME *MGM 1063*	43	1 wk

Izhar COHEN and ALPHABETA Israel, male/female vocal group   7 wks

13 May 78	A BA NI BI *Polydor 2001 781*	20	7 wks

Cozy COLE US, male instrumentalist - drums   1 wk

5 Dec 58	TOPSY (PARTS 1 AND 2) *London HL 8750*	29	1 wk

Lloyd COLE and the COMMOTIONS UK, male vocalist and instrumental backing group   17 wks

26 May 84	PERFECT SKIN *Polydor COLE 1*	71	1 wk
9 Jun 84	PERFECT SKIN (re-entry) *Polydor COLE 1*	26	8 wks
25 Aug 84	FOREST FIRE *Polydor COLE 2*	41	6 wks
17 Nov 84	RATTLESNAKES *Polydor COLE 3*	65	2 wks

Nat 'King' COLE US, male vocalist   225 wks

14 Nov 52	● SOMEWHERE ALONG THE WAY		
	Capitol CL 13774	3	7 wks
19 Dec 52	● BECAUSE YOU'RE MINE *Capitol CL 13811* . . .	6	2 wks
2 Jan 53	FAITH CAN MOVE MOUNTAINS		
	Capitol CL 13811	11	1 wk
16 Jan 53	FAITH CAN MOVE MOUNTAINS (re-entry)		
	Capitol CL 13811	12	2 wks
23 Jan 53	● BECAUSE YOU'RE MINE (re-entry)		
	Capitol CL 13811	10	1 wk
6 Feb 53	● FAITH CAN MOVE MOUNTAINS (2nd re-entry)		
	Capitol CL 13811	10	1 wk
13 Feb 53	BECAUSE YOU'RE MINE (2nd re-entry)		
	Capitol CL 13811	11	1 wk
24 Apr 53	● PRETEND *Capitol CL 13878*	2	18 wks
14 Aug 53	● CAN'T I? *Capitol CL 13937*	9	3 wks
18 Sep 53	CAN'T I? (re-entry) *Capitol CL 13937*	6	4 wks
18 Sep 53	● MOTHER NATURE AND FATHER TIME		
	Capitol CL 13912	7	7 wks
30 Oct 53	● CAN'T I? (2nd re-entry) *Capitol CL 13937*	10	1 wk

16 Apr 54	● TENDERLY *Capitol CL 14061*	10	1 wk
10 Sep 54	● SMILE *Capitol CL 14149*	2	14 wks
8 Oct 54	MAKE HER MINE *Capitol CL 14149*	11	2 wks
25 Feb 55	● A BLOSSOM FELL *Capitol CL 14235*	3	10 wks
26 Aug 55	MY ONE SIN *Capitol CL 14327*	18	1 wk
16 Sep 55	MY ONE SIN (re-entry) *Capitol CL 14327* ...	17	1 wk
27 Jan 56	● DREAMS CAN TELL A LIE *Capitol CL 14513* ..	10	9 wks
11 May 56	● TOO YOUNG TO GO STEADY *Capitol CL 14573*	8	14 wks
14 Sep 56	LOVE ME AS IF THERE WERE NO TOMORROW *Capitol CL 14621*	24	2 wks
5 Oct 56	LOVE ME AS IF THERE WERE NO TOMORROW (re-entry) *Capitol CL 14621*	11	13 wks
19 Apr 57	● WHEN I FALL IN LOVE *Capitol CL 14709* ...	2	20 wks
5 Jul 57	WHEN ROCK 'N ROLL CAME TO TRINIDAD *Capitol CL 14733*	28	1 wk
18 Oct 57	MY PERSONAL POSSESSION *Capitol CL 14765*	21	2 wks
25 Oct 57	STARDUST *Capitol CL 14787*	24	2 wks
29 May 59	YOU MADE ME LOVE YOU *Capitol CL 15017*	22	3 wks
4 Sep 59	MIDNIGHT FLYER *Capitol CL 15056*	27	1 wk
18 Sep 59	MIDNIGHT FLYER (re-entry) *Capitol CL 15056*	23	3 wks
12 Feb 60	TIME AND THE RIVER *Capitol CL 15111*	29	1 wk
26 Feb 60	TIME AND THE RIVER (re-entry) *Capitol CL 15111*	23	2 wks
31 Mar 60	TIME AND THE RIVER (2nd re-entry) *Capitol CL 15111*	47	1 wk
26 May 60	● THAT'S YOU *Capitol CL 15129*	10	8 wks
10 Nov 60	JUST AS MUCH AS EVER *Capitol CL 15163* ...	18	10 wks
2 Feb 61	THE WORLD IN MY ARMS *Capitol CL 15178* ..	36	10 wks
16 Nov 61	LET TRUE LOVE BEGIN *Capitol CL 15224*	29	10 wks
22 Mar 62	BRAZILIAN LOVE SONG *Capitol CL 15241* ...	34	4 wks
31 May 62	THE RIGHT THING TO SAY *Capitol CL 15250* ..	42	4 wks
19 Jul 62	LET THERE BE LOVE *Capitol CL 15257*	11	14 wks
27 Sep 62	● RAMBLIN' ROSE *Capitol CL 15270*	5	14 wks
20 Dec 62	DEAR LONELY HEARTS *Capitol CL 15280*	37	3 wks

Let There Be Love *with George Shearing male instrumentalist - piano. See also George Shearing.*

Natalie COLE *US, female vocalist* 5 *wks*

11 Oct 75	THIS WILL BE *Capitol CL 15834*	32	5 wks

John Ford COLEY *- See ENGLAND DAN and John Ford COLEY*

Dave and Ansil COLLINS

Jamaica, male vocal duo 27 *wks*

27 Mar 71	★ DOUBLE BARREL *Technique TE 901*	1	15 wks
26 Jun 71	● MONKEY SPANNER *Technique TE 914*	7	12 wks

Edwyn COLLINS *- See Paul QUINN and Edwyn COLLINS*

Jeff COLLINS *UK, male vocalist* 8 *wks*

18 Nov 72	ONLY YOU *Polydor 2058 287*	40	8 wks

Judy COLLINS *US, female vocalist* 86 *wks*

17 Jan 70	BOTH SIDES NOW *Elektra EKSN 45043*	14	11 wks
5 Dec 70	● AMAZING GRACE *Elektra 2101 020*	5	32 wks
24 Jul 71	AMAZING GRACE (re-entry) *Elektra 2101 020*	48	1 wk
4 Sep 71	AMAZING GRACE (2nd re-entry) *Elektra 2101 020*	40	7 wks
20 Nov 71	AMAZING GRACE (3rd re-entry) *Elektra 2101 020*	50	1 wk
18 Dec 71	AMAZING GRACE (4th re-entry) *Elektra 2101 020*	48	2 wks
22 Apr 72	AMAZING GRACE (5th re-entry) *Elektra 2101 020*	20	19 wks
9 Sep 72	AMAZING GRACE (6th re-entry) *Elektra 2101 020*	46	2 wks
23 Dec 72	AMAZING GRACE (7th re-entry) *Elektra 2101 020*	49	3 wks
17 May 75	● SEND IN THE CLOWNS *Elektra K 12177*	6	8 wks

Phil COLLINS *UK, male vocalist* 63 *wks*

17 Jan 81	● IN THE AIR TONIGHT *Virgin VSK 102*	2	10 wks
7 Mar 81	I MISSED AGAIN *Virgin VS 402*	14	8 wks
30 May 81	IF LEAVING ME IS EASY *Virgin VS 423*	17	8 wks
23 Oct 82	THRU' THESE WALLS *Virgin VS 524*	56	2 wks
4 Dec 82	★ YOU CAN'T HURRY LOVE *Virgin VS 531*	1	16 wks
19 Mar 83	DON'T LET HIM STEAL YOUR HEART AWAY *Virgin VS 572*	45	5 wks
7 Apr 84	● AGAINST ALL ODDS (TAKE A LOOK AT ME NOW) *Virgin VS 674*	2	14 wks

Don't Let Him Steal Your Heart Away *has credit: With the Martyn Ford Orchestra.*

Rodger COLLINS *US, male vocalist* 6 *wks*

3 Apr 76	YOU SEXY SUGAR PLUM (BUT I LIKE IT) *Fantasy FTC 132*	22	6 wks

COLORADO *UK, female vocal group* 3 *wks*

21 Oct 78	CALIFORNIA DREAMIN' *Pinnacle PIN 67*	45	3 wks

COLOUR FIELD
UK, male vocal/instrumental group 5 *wks*

21 Jan 84	THE COLOUR FIELD *Chrysalis COLF 1*	43	4 wks
28 Jul 84	TAKE *Chrysalis COLF 2*	70	1 wk

COMETS *- See Bill HALEY and his COMETS*

COMMODORES
US, male vocal/instrumental group 91 *wks*

24 Aug 74	MACHINE GUN *Tamla Motown TMG 902*	20	11 wks
23 Nov 74	THE ZOO (THE HUMAN ZOO) *Tamla Motown TMG 924*	44	2 wks
2 Jul 77	● EASY *Motown TMG 1073*	9	10 wks
8 Oct 77	BRICK HOUSE/SWEET LOVE *Motown TMG 1086*	32	6 wks
11 Mar 78	TOO HOT TO TROT /ZOOM *Motown TMG 1096*	38	4 wks
24 Jun 78	FLYING HIGH *Motown TMG 1111*	37	7 wks
5 Aug 78	★ THREE TIMES A LADY *Motown TMG 1113* ...	1	14 wks
25 Nov 78	JUST TO BE CLOSE TO YOU *Motown TMG 1127*	62	4 wks
25 Aug 79	● SAIL ON *Motown TMG 1155*	8	10 wks
3 Nov 79	● STILL *Motown TMG 1166*	4	11 wks
19 Jan 80	WONDERLAND *Motown TMG 1172*	40	4 wks
1 Aug 81	LADY (YOU BRING ME UP) *Motown TMG 1238*	56	5 wks
21 Nov 81	OH NO *Motown TMG 1245*	44	3 wks

COMMOTIONS *- See Lloyd COLE and the COMMOTIONS*

Perry COMO *US, male vocalist* 294 *wks*

16 Jan 53	★ DON'T LET THE STARS GET IN YOUR EYES *HMV B 10400*	1	15 wks
4 Jun 54	● WANTED *HMV B 10691*	4	14 wks
25 Jun 54	● IDLE GOSSIP *HMV B 10710*	3	15 wks
1 Oct 54	WANTED (re-entry) *HMV B 10691*	18	1 wk
10 Dec 54	PAPA LOVES MAMBO *HMV B 10776*	16	1 wk
30 Dec 55	TINA MARIE *HMV POP 103*	24	1 wk
27 Apr 56	JUKE BOX BABY *HMV POP 191*	22	6 wks
25 May 56	● HOT DIGGITY *HMV POP 212*	4	13 wks
21 Sep 56	● MORE *HMV POP 240*	10	11 wks
28 Sep 56	GLENDORA *HMV POP 240*	18	6 wks
14 Dec 56	MORE (re-entry) *HMV POP 240*	29	1 wk
7 Feb 58	★ MAGIC MOMENTS *RCA 1036*	1	17 wks
7 Mar 58	● CATCH A FALLING STAR *RCA 1036*	9	10 wks

HAZELL DEAN (top left) Thirty-three weeks on chart in her debut year.

SKEETER DAVIS (top right) Her first American hit '(I Can't Help You) I'm Falling Too', was the answer record to Hank Locklin's 'Please Help Me I'm Falling'.

BOBBY DARIN (above) He changed musical styles in 1959 against expert advice, but results proved him right.

DUFFO (left) A brief reign for the age of the brain.

CRAIG DOUGLAS The ex-milkman seen in motion at the Billy Fury Memorial concert.

9 May 58 ●	KEWPIE DOLL *RCA 1055*	9	7 wks
30 May 58	I MAY NEVER PASS THIS WAY AGAIN		
	RCA 1062	15	8 wks
5 Sep 58	MOON TALK *RCA 1071*	17	11 wks
7 Nov 58 ●	LOVE MAKES THE WORLD GO ROUND		
	RCA 1086	6	14 wks
21 Nov 58	MANDOLINS IN THE MOONLIGHT *RCA 1086*	13	12 wks
27 Feb 59 ●	TOMBOY *RCA 1111*	10	12 wks
10 Jul 59	I KNOW *RCA 1126*	13	16 wks
26 Feb 60 ●	DELAWARE *RCA 1170*	3	13 wks
10 May 62	CATERINA *RCA 1283*	37	4 wks
14 Jun 62	CATERINA (re-entry) *RCA 1283*	45	2 wks
30 Jan 71 ●	IT'S IMPOSSIBLE *RCA 2043*	4	23 wks
15 May 71	I THINK OF YOU *RCA 2075*	14	11 wks
21 Apr 73 ●	AND I LOVE YOU SO *RCA 2346*	3	31 wks
25 Aug 73 ●	FOR THE GOOD TIMES *RCA 2402*	7	27 wks
8 Dec 73	WALK RIGHT BACK *RCA 2432*	33	10 wks
12 Jan 74	AND I LOVE YOU SO (re-entry) *RCA 2346*	40	4 wks
25 May 74	I WANT TO GIVE *RCA LPBO 7518*	31	4 wks

COMPAGNONS DE LA CHANSON
France, male vocal group   *3 wks*

9 Oct 59	THE THREE BELLS *Columbia DB 4358*	27	1 wk
23 Oct 59	THE THREE BELLS (re-entry) *Columbia DB 4358*	21	2 wks

Song is sub-titled 'The Jimmy Brown Song'.

COMSAT ANGELS
UK, male vocal/instrumental group   *2 wks*

21 Jan 84	INDEPENDENCE DAY *Jive JIVE 54*	75	1 wk
4 Feb 84	INDEPENDENCE DAY (re-entry) *Jive JIVE 54*	71	1 wk

CONGREGATION *UK, male/female choir*   *14 wks*

27 Nov 71 ●	SOFTLY WHISPERING I LOVE YOU		
	Columbia DB 8830	4	14 wks

Arthur CONLEY *US, male vocalist*   *15 wks*

27 Apr 67 ●	SWEET SOUL MUSIC *Atlantic 584 083*	7	14 wks
10 Apr 68	FUNKY STREET *Atlantic 583 175*	46	1 wk

Billy CONNOLLY *UK, male vocalist*   *22 wks*

1 Nov 75 ★	D. I. V. O. R. C. E. *Polydor 2058 652*	1	10 wks
17 Jul 76	NO CHANCE (NO CHARGE) *Polydor 2058 748*	24	5 wks
25 Aug 79	IN THE BROWNIES *Polydor 2059 160*	38	7 wks

Jess CONRAD *UK, male vocalist*   *13 wks*

30 Jun 60	CHERRY PIE *Decca F 11236*	39	1 wk
26 Jan 61	MYSTERY GIRL *Decca F 11315*	44	1 wk
9 Feb 61	MYSTERY GIRL (re-entry) *Decca F 11315*	18	9 wks
11 Oct 62	PRETTY JENNY *Decca F 11511*	50	2 wks

CONSORTIUM *UK, male vocal group*   *9 wks*

12 Feb 69	ALL THE LOVE IN THE WORLD		
	Pye 7N 17635	22	9 wks

CONTOURS *US, male vocal group*   *6 wks*

24 Jan 70	JUST A LITTLE MISUNDERSTANDING		
	Tamla Motown TMG 723	31	6 wks

Russ CONWAY
UK, male instrumentalist - piano   *168 wks*

29 Nov 57	PARTY POPS *Columbia DB 4031*	24	5 wks
29 Aug 58	GOT A MATCH *Columbia DB 4166*	30	1 wk
28 Nov 58 ●	MORE PARTY POPS *Columbia DB 4204*	10	7 wks
23 Jan 59	THE WORLD OUTSIDE *Columbia DB 4234* •••	24	1 wk
20 Feb 59 ★	SIDE SADDLE *Columbia DB 4256*	1	30 wks
6 Mar 59	THE WORLD OUTSIDE (re-entry)		
	Columbia DB 4234	24	3 wks
15 May 59 ★	ROULETTE *Columbia DB 4298*	1	19 wks
21 Aug 59	CHINA TEA *Columbia DB 4337*	5	13 wks
13 Nov 59	SNOW COACH *Columbia DB 4368*	7	9 wks
20 Nov 59 ●	MORE AND MORE PARTY POPS		
	Columbia DB 4373	5	8 wks
10 Mar 60	ROYAL EVENT *Columbia DB 4418*	15	7 wks
21 Apr 60	FINGS AIN'T WOT THEY USED T'BE		
	Columbia DB 4422	47	1 wk
19 May 60	LUCKY FIVE *Columbia DB 4457*	14	9 wks
29 Sep 60	PASSING BREEZE *Columbia DB 4508*	16	10 wks
24 Nov 60	EVEN MORE PARTY POPS *Columbia DB 4535*	27	4 wks
19 Jan 61	PEPE *Columbia DB 4564*	19	9 wks
25 May 61	PABLO *Columbia DB 4649*	45	2 wks
30 Nov 61 ●	TOY BALLOONS *Columbia DB 4738*	7	11 wks
22 Feb 62	LESSON ONE *Columbia DB 4784*	21	7 wks
29 Nov 62	ALWAYS YOU AND ME *Columbia DB 4934* •••	33	4 wks
3 Jan 63	ALWAYS YOU AND ME (re-entry)		
	Columbia DB 4934	35	3 wks

See also Dorothy Squires and Russ Conway. Always You And Me featured Russ Conway talking as well as playing piano. Several of the discs were medleys as follows: Party Pops: When You're Smiling/I'm Looking Over a Four-Leafed Clover/When You Wore a Tulip/Row Row Row/For Me And My Girl/Shine On Harvest Moon/ By The Light Of The Silvery Moon/Side By Side. More Party Pops: Music Music Music/If You Were The Only Girl In The World/Nobody's Sweetheart/Yes Sir That's My Baby/Some Of These Days/Honeysuckle And The Bee/Hello Hello Who's Your Lady Friend/Shanty In Old Shanty Town. More And More Party Pops: Sheik of Araby/Who Were You With Last Night/Any Old Iron/Tiptoe Through The Tulips/If You Were The Only Girl In The World/ When I Leave The World Behind. Even More Party Pops: Ain't She Sweet/I Can't Give You Anything But Love/Yes We Have No Bananas/I May Be Wrong/Happy Days And Lonely Nights/Glad Rag Doll. He really did feature If You Were The Only Girl In The World on two different hits.

Martin COOK - *See Richard DENTON and Martin COOK*

Peter COOK *UK, male vocalist*   *5 wks*

15 Jul 65	THE BALLAD OF SPOTTY MULDOON		
	Decca F 12182	34	5 wks

See also Peter Cook and Dudley Moore.

Peter COOK and Dudley MOORE
UK, male vocal duo, Dudley Moore featured pianist   *10 wks*

17 Jun 65	GOODBYE-EE *Decca F 12158*	18	10 wks

See also Peter Cook.

Sam COOKE *US, male vocalist*   *70 wks*

17 Jan 58	YOU SEND ME *London HLU 8506*	29	1 wk
14 Aug 59	ONLY SIXTEEN *HMV POP 642*	23	4 wks
7 Jul 60	WONDERFUL WORLD *HMV POP 754*	27	8 wks
29 Sep 60 ●	CHAIN GANG *RCA 1202*	9	11 wks
27 Jul 61 ●	CUPID *RCA 1242*	7	14 wks
8 Mar 62 ●	TWISTIN' THE NIGHT AWAY *RCA 1277*	6	14 wks
16 May 63	ANOTHER SATURDAY NIGHT *RCA 1341* ...	23	12 wks
5 Sep 63	FRANKIE AND JOHNNY *RCA 1361* ...	30	6 wks

COOKIES *US, female vocal group*   *1 wk*

10 Jan 63	CHAINS *London HLU 9634*	50	1 wk

Rita COOLIDGE US, female vocalist   24 wks

25 Jun 77	● WE'RE ALL ALONE A & M AMS 7295	6	13 wks
15 Oct 77	(YOUR LOVE HAS LIFTED ME) HIGHER AND HIGHER A & M AMS 7315	49	1 wk
29 Oct 77	(YOUR LOVE HAS LIFTED ME) HIGHER AND HIGHER (re-entry) A & M AMS 7315	48	1 wk
4 Feb 78	WORDS A & M AMS 7330	25	8 wks
25 Jun 83	ALL TIME HIGH A & M AM 007	75	1 wk

COOLNOTES
UK, male/female vocal/instrumental group   7 wks

| 18 Aug 84 | YOU'RE NEVER TOO YOUNG Abstract Dance AD 1 .... | 42 | 5 wks |
| 17 Nov 84 | I FORGOT Abstract Dance AD 2 .... | 63 | 2 wks |

Alice COOPER US, male vocalist   64 wks

15 Jul 72	★ SCHOOL'S OUT Warner Bros. K 16188	1	12 wks
7 Oct 72	● ELECTED Warner Bros. K 16214	4	10 wks
10 Feb 73	● HELLO HURRAY Warner Bros. K 16248	6	12 wks
21 Apr 73	● NO MORE MR. NICE GUY Warner Bros. K 16262	10	10 wks
19 Jan 74	TEENAGE LAMENT '74 Warner Bros. K 16345 ..	12	7 wks
21 May 77	(NO MORE) LOVE AT YOUR CONVENIENCE Warner Bros. K 16935	44	2 wks
23 Dec 78	HOW YOU GONNA SEE ME NOW Warner Bros. K 17270	61	6 wks
6 Mar 82	SEVEN AND SEVEN IS (LIVE VERSION) Warner Bros. K 17924	62	3 wks
8 May 82	FOR BRITAIN ONLY/UNDER MY WHEELS Warner Bros. K 17940	66	2 wks

For the first 5 hits, 'Alice Cooper' was the name of the entire group, not just of the lead vocalist.

Tommy COOPER UK, male vocalist   3 wks

| 29 Jun 61 | DON'T JUMP OFF THE ROOF DAD Palette PG 9019 .... | 40 | 2 wks |
| 20 Jul 61 | DON'T JUMP OFF THE ROOF DAD (re-entry) Palette PG 9019 .... | 50 | 1 wk |

Julian COPE UK, male vocalist   6 wks

| 19 Nov 83 | SUNSHINE PLAYROOM Mercury/Phonogram COPE 1 .... | 64 | 1 wk |
| 31 Mar 84 | THE GREATNESS AND PERFECTION OF LOVE Mercury MER 155 .... | 52 | 5 wks |

Harry H. CORBETT - *See Wilfred BRAMBELL and Harry H. CORBETT*

Frank CORDELL UK, orchestra   4 wks

| 24 Aug 56 | SADIE'S SHAWL HMV POP 229 .... | 29 | 2 wks |
| 16 Feb 61 | BLACK BEAR HMV POP 824 .... | 44 | 2 wks |

Phil CORDELL - *See SPRINGWATER*

Louise CORDET France, female vocalist   13 wks

| 5 Jul 62 | I'M JUST A BABY Decca F 11476 .... | 13 | 13 wks |

Don CORNELL US, male vocalist   23 wks

| 3 Sep 54 | ★ HOLD MY HAND Vogue Q 2013 .... | 1 | 21 wks |
| 22 Apr 55 | STRANGER IN PARADISE Vogue Q 72073 .... | 19 | 2 wks |

Lynn CORNELL UK, female vocalist   9 wks

| 20 Oct 60 | NEVER ON SUNDAY Decca F 11277 .... | 30 | 9 wks |

Charlotte CORNWELL - *See Julie COVINGTON, Rula LENSKA, Charlotte CORNWELL and Sue JONES-DAVIES*

CORONETS UK, male/female vocal group   1 wk

| 25 Nov 55 | TWENTY TINY FINGERS Columbia DB 3671 .. | 20 | 1 wk |

Vladimir COSMA Hungary, orchestra   1 wk

| 14 Jul 79 | DAVID'S SONG (MAIN THEME FROM 'KIDNAPPED') Decca FR 13841 .... | 64 | 1 wk |

Don COSTA US, orchestra   10 wks

| 13 Oct 60 | NEVER ON SUNDAY London HLT 9195 ..... | 27 | 9 wks |
| 22 Dec 60 | NEVER ON SUNDAY (re-entry) London HLT 9195 .... | 41 | 1 wk |

Elvis COSTELLO and the ATTRACTIONS
UK, male vocalist/instrumentalist - guitar   136 wks

5 Nov 77	WATCHING THE DETECTIVES Stiff BUY 20	15	11 wks
11 Mar 78	(I DON'T WANNA GO TO) CHELSEA Radar ADA 3	16	10 wks
13 May 78	PUMP IT UP Radar ADA 10	24	10 wks
28 Oct 78	RADIO RADIO Radar ADA 24	29	7 wks
10 Feb 79	● OLIVER'S ARMY Radar ADA 31	2	12 wks
12 May 79	ACCIDENTS WILL HAPPEN Radar ADA 35 ..	28	8 wks
16 Feb 80	● I CAN'T STAND UP FOR FALLING DOWN F. Beat XX 1	4	8 wks
12 Apr 80	HI FIDELITY F. Beat XX 3	30	5 wks
7 Jun 80	NEW AMSTERDAM F. Beat XX 5	36	6 wks
20 Dec 80	CLUBLAND F. Beat XX 12	60	4 wks
3 Oct 81	● A GOOD YEAR FOR THE ROSES F. Beat XX 17	6	11 wks
12 Dec 81	SWEET DREAMS F. Beat XX 19	42	8 wks
10 Apr 82	I'M YOUR TOY F. Beat XX 21	51	3 wks
19 Jun 82	YOU LITTLE FOOL F. Beat XX 26	52	3 wks
31 Jul 82	MAN OUT OF TIME F. Beat XX 28	58	2 wks
25 Sep 82	FROM HEAD TO TOE F. Beat XX 30	43	4 wks
11 Dec 82	PARTY PARTY A & M AMS 8267	48	6 wks
9 Jul 83	EVERYDAY I WRITE THE BOOK F. Beat XX 32	28	8 wks
17 Sep 83	LET THEM ALL TALK F. Beat XX 33	59	2 wks
16 Jun 84	I WANNA BE LOVED/TURNING THE TOWN RED F. Beat XX 35	25	6 wks
28 Aug 84	THE ONLY FLAME IN TOWN F. Beat XX 37	71	2 wks

Billed as Elvis Costello on hits in 1977 and 1980 with the exception of Clubland. I'm Your Toy credits Elvis Costello and the Attractions with the Royal Philharmonic Orchestra. See Royal Philharmonic Orchestra. See also Imposter.

COTTAGERS - *See Tony REES and the COTTAGERS*

Billy COTTON and his BAND
UK, male bandleader, vocalist, with band and chorus   25 wks

1 May 53	● IN A GOLDEN COACH Decca F 10058	3	10 wks
18 Dec 53	I SAW MOMMY KISSING SANTA CLAUS Decca F 10206	11	3 wks
30 Apr 54	FRIENDS AND NEIGHBOURS Decca F 10299 ..	12	1 wk
14 May 54	● FRIENDS AND NEIGHBOURS (re-entry) Decca F 10299	3	11 wks

In a Golden Coach has the credit 'Vocal by Doreen Stephens' but also featured Billy Cotton as an unbilled narrator. I Saw Mommy Kissing Santa Claus has the credits 'Vocals by the

Mill Girls and the Bandits', Friends and Neighbours 'Vocal by the Bandits'. See also Various Artists - All Star Hit Parade No. 2.

Mike COTTON'S JAZZMEN
UK, male instrumental band, Mike Cotton trumpet　　　*4 wks*

| 20 Jun 63 | **SWING THAT HAMMER** *Columbia DB 7029* ... | 36 | 4 wks |

John COUGAR *US, male vocalist*　　*8 wks*

| 23 Oct 82 | **JACK AND DIANE** *Riva RIVA 37* .... | 25 | 8 wks |

COUGARS *UK, male instrumental group*　　*8 wks*

| 28 Feb 63 | **SATURDAY NITE AT THE DUCK POND** *Parlophone R 4989* .... | 33 | 8 wks |

COUNCIL COLLECTIVE
UK/US, male/female vocal/instrumental group　　*2 wks*

| 22 Dec 84 | **SOUL DEEP** (PART 1) *Polydor MINE 1* .... | 24† | 2 wks |

COUNTRYMEN *UK, male vocal group*　　*2 wks*

| 3 May 62 | **I KNOW WHERE I'M GOING** *Piccadilly 7N 35029* | 45 | 2 wks |

Don COVAY *US, male vocalist*　　*6 wks*

| 7 Sep 74 | **IT'S BETTER TO HAVE (AND DON'T NEED)** *Mercury 6052 634* .... | 29 | 6 wks |

Julie COVINGTON *UK, female vocalist*　　*29 wks*

25 Dec 76	★ **DON'T CRY FOR ME ARGENTINA** *MCA 260*	1	15 wks
3 Dec 77	**ONLY WOMEN BLEED** *Virgin VS 196*	12	11 wks
15 Jul 78	**DON'T CRY FOR ME ARGENTINA** (re-entry) *MCA 260*	63	3 wks

See also Julie Covington, Rula Lenska, Charlotte Cornwell and Sue Jones-Davies.

Julie COVINGTON, Rula LENSKA, Charlotte CORNWELL and Sue JONES-DAVIES
UK, female vocal group　　*6 wks*

| 21 May 77 | ● **O.K?** *Polydor 2001 714* .... | 10 | 6 wks |

See also Julie Covington.

Warren COVINGTON - *See Tommy DORSEY Orchestra starring Warren COVINGTON*

Patrick COWLEY - *See SYLVESTER with Patrick COWLEY*

Michael COX *UK, male vocalist*　　*15 wks*

| 9 Jun 60 | ● **ANGELA JONES** *Triumph RGM 1011* .... | 7 | 13 wks |
| 20 Oct 60 | **ALONG CAME CAROLINE** *HMV POP 789* ... | 41 | 2 wks |

Floyd CRAMER
US, male instrumentalist - piano　　*24 wks*

| 13 Apr 61 | ★ **ON THE REBOUND** *RCA 1231* .... | 1 | 14 wks |

| 20 Jul 61 | **SAN ANTONIO ROSE** *RCA 1241* .... | 36 | 8 wks |
| 23 Aug 62 | **HOT PEPPER** *RCA 1301* .... | 46 | 2 wks |

Les CRANE *US, male vocalist*　　*14 wks*

| 19 Feb 72 | ● **DESIDERATA** *Warner Bros. K 16119* .... | 7 | 14 wks |

Jimmy CRAWFORD *UK, male vocalist*　　*11 wks*

| 8 Jun 61 | **LOVE OR MONEY** *Columbia DB 4633* .... | 49 | 1 wk |
| 16 Nov 61 | **I LOVE HOW YOU LOVE ME** *Columbia DB 4717* .... | 18 | 10 wks |

Randy CRAWFORD *US, female vocalist*　　*50 wks*

21 Jun 80	**LAST NIGHT AT DANCELAND** *Warner Bros. K 17631*	61	2 wks
30 Aug 80	● **ONE DAY I'LL FLY AWAY** *Warner Bros. K 17680*	2	11 wks
30 May 81	**YOU MIGHT NEED SOMEBODY** *Warner Bros. K 17803*	11	13 wks
8 Aug 81	**RAINY NIGHT IN GEORGIA** *Warner Bros. K 17840*	18	9 wks
31 Oct 81	**SECRET COMBINATION** *Warner Bros. K 17872*	48	3 wks
30 Jan 82	**IMAGINE** *Warner Bros. K 17906*	60	1 wk
13 Feb 82	**IMAGINE** (re-entry) *Warner Bros. K 17906*	75	1 wk
5 Jun 82	**ONE HELLO** *Warner Bros. K 17948*	48	4 wks
19 Feb 83	**HE REMINDS ME** *Warner Bros. K 17970*	65	2 wks
8 Oct 83	**NIGHT LINE** *Warner Bros. W 9530*	51	4 wks

See also Crusaders.

CRAZY ELEPHANT
US, male vocal group　　*13 wks*

| 21 May 69 | **GIMME GIMME GOOD LOVIN'** *Major Minor MM 609* .... | 12 | 13 wks |

CREAM *UK, male vocal/instrumental group*　　*59 wks*

20 Oct 66	**WRAPPING PAPER** *Reaction 591 007*	34	6 wks
15 Dec 66	**I FEEL FREE** *Reaction 591 011*	11	12 wks
8 Jun 67	**STRANGE BREW** *Reaction 591 015*	17	9 wks
5 Jun 68	**ANYONE FOR TENNIS (THE SAVAGE SEVEN THEME)** *Polydor 56 258*	40	3 wks
9 Oct 68	**SUNSHINE OF YOUR LOVE** *Polydor 56 286* ...	25	7 wks
15 Jan 69	**WHITE ROOM** *Polydor 56 300*	28	8 wks
9 Apr 69	**BADGE** *Polydor 56 315*	18	10 wks
28 Oct 72	**BADGE** (re-issue) *Polydor 2058 285*	42	4 wks

CREATION
UK, male vocal/instrumental group　　*3 wks*

| 7 Jul 66 | **MAKING TIME** *Planet PLF 116* .... | 49 | 1 wk |
| 3 Nov 66 | **PAINTER MAN** *Planet PLF 119* .... | 36 | 2 wks |

CREATURES
UK, male/female vocal/instrumental group　　*24 wks*

3 Oct 81	**MAD EYED SCREAMER** *Polydor POSPD 354* ..	24	7 wks
23 Apr 83	**MISS THE GIRL** *Wonderland/Polydor SHE 1*	21	7 wks
16 Jul 83	**RIGHT NOW** *Wonderland/Polydor SHE 2*	14	10 wks

Creatures are Siouxsie and Budgie who is the Banshees' drummer. See Siouxsie and the Banshees.

CREEDENCE CLEARWATER REVIVAL   US, male vocal/instrumental group   93 wks

28 May 69	● PROUD MARY Liberty LBF 15223		8	13 wks
16 Aug 69	★ BAD MOON RISING Liberty LBF 15230		1	15 wks
15 Nov 69	GREEN RIVER Liberty LBF 15250		19	11 wks
14 Feb 70	DOWN ON THE CORNER Liberty LBF 15283		31	6 wks
4 Apr 70	● TRAVELLIN' BAND Liberty LBF 15310		8	12 wks
20 Jun 70	UP AROUND THE BEND Liberty LBF 15354		3	12 wks
4 Jul 70	TRAVELLIN' BAND (re-entry) Liberty LBF 15310		46	1 wk
5 Sep 70	LONG AS I CAN SEE THE LIGHT Liberty LBF 15384		20	9 wks
20 Mar 71	HAVE YOU EVER SEEN THE RAIN Liberty LBF 15440		36	6 wks
24 Jul 71	SWEET HITCH-HIKER United Artists UP 35261		36	8 wks

Kid CREOLE and the COCONUTS
US, male vocalist and female vocal group   50 wks

13 Jun 81	ME NO POP I Ze/Island WIP 6711		32	7 wks
15 May 82	● I'M A WONDERFUL THING, BABY Ze/Island WIP 6756		4	11 wks
24 Jul 82	STOOL PIGEON Ze/Island WIP 6793		7	9 wks
9 Oct 82	● ANNIE I'M NOT YOUR DADDY Ze/Island WIP 6801		2	8 wks
11 Dec 82	DEAR ADDY Ze/Island WIP 6840		29	7 wks
10 Sep 83	THERE'S SOMETHING WRONG IN PARADISE Island IS 130		35	4 wks
19 Nov 83	THE LIFEBOAT PARTY Island IS 142		49	4 wks

Me No Pop I billed as 'Kid Creole and the Coconuts present Coati Mundi'. Coati Mundi US, male vocalist. See also Coconuts.

CREW CUTS   Canada, male vocal group   29 wks

1 Oct 54	SH-BOOM Mercury MB 3140		12	9 wks
15 Apr 55	● EARTH ANGEL Mercury MB 3202		4	20 wks

Bernard CRIBBINS   UK, male vocalist   29 wks

15 Feb 62	● HOLE IN THE GROUND Parlophone R 4869		9	13 wks
5 Jul 62	● RIGHT SAID FRED Parlophone R 4923		10	10 wks
13 Dec 62	GOSSIP CALYPSO Parlophone R 4961		25	6 wks

CRICKETS   US, male vocal/instrumental group   90 wks

27 Sep 57	★ THAT'LL BE THE DAY Vogue Coral Q 72279		1	14 wks
27 Dec 57	● OH BOY Coral Q 72298		3	15 wks
10 Jan 58	THAT'LL BE THE DAY (re-entry) Vogue Coral Q 72279		29	1 wk
14 Mar 58	● MAYBE BABY Coral Q 72307		4	10 wks
25 Jul 58	THINK IT OVER Coral Q 72329		11	7 wks
24 Apr 59	LOVE'S MADE A FOOL OF YOU Coral Q 72365		26	1 wk
8 May 59	LOVE'S MADE A FOOL OF YOU (re-entry) Coral Q 72365		30	1 wk
15 Jan 60	WHEN YOU ASK ABOUT LOVE Coral Q 72382		27	1 wk
26 May 60	BABY MY HEART Coral Q 72395		33	4 wks
21 Jun 62	DON'T EVER CHANGE Liberty LIB 55441		5	13 wks
24 Jan 63	MY LITTLE GIRL Liberty LIB 10067		17	9 wks
6 Jun 63	DON'T TRY TO CHANGE ME Liberty LIB 10092		37	4 wks
2 Jul 64	(THEY CALL HER) LA BAMBA Liberty LIB 55696		21	10 wks

Although not credited on the records, Buddy Holly was featured on the first 4 hits. See also Buddy Holly.

CRISPY AND COMPANY
US, male vocal/instrumental group   11 wks

16 Aug 75	BRAZIL Creole CR 109		26	5 wks

27 Dec 75	GET IT TOGETHER Creole CR 114		21	6 wks

CRITTERS
US, male vocal/instrumental group   5 wks

30 Jun 66	YOUNGER GIRL London HL 10047		38	5 wks

Tony CROMBIE and his ROCKETS   UK, male vocal/instrumental group,
Tony Crombie drums   2 wks

19 Oct 56	TEACH YOU TO ROCK/SHORT'NIN' BREAD Columbia DB 3822		25	2 wks

Bing CROSBY   US, male vocalist   51 wks

14 Nov 52	● ISLE OF INNISFREE Brunswick 04900		3	12 wks
19 Dec 52	● SILENT NIGHT Brunswick 03929		8	2 wks
19 Mar 54	● CHANGING PARTNERS Brunswick 05244		10	1 wk
2 Apr 54	CHANGING PARTNERS (re-entry) Brunswick 05244		9	1 wk
23 Apr 54	CHANGING PARTNERS (2nd re-entry) Brunswick 05244		11	1 wk
7 Jan 55	COUNT YOUR BLESSINGS Brunswick 05339		18	1 wk
21 Jan 55	COUNT YOUR BLESSINGS (re-entry) Brunswick 05339		11	2 wks
29 Apr 55	STRANGER IN PARADISE Brunswick 05410		17	2 wks
27 Apr 56	IN A LITTLE SPANISH TOWN Brunswick 05543		22	3 wks
24 May 57	● AROUND THE WORLD Brunswick 05674		5	15 wks
9 Aug 75	THAT'S WHAT LIFE IS ALL ABOUT United Artists UP 35852		41	4 wks
3 Dec 77	● WHITE CHRISTMAS MCA 111		5	7 wks

See also Bing Crosby and Grace Kelly; Bing Crosby and Jane Wyman; David Bowie and Bing Crosby.

Bing CROSBY and Grace KELLY
US, male/female vocal duo   30 wks

23 Nov 56	● TRUE LOVE Capitol CL 14645		4	27 wks
17 Dec 83	TRUE LOVE (re-issue) Capitol CL 315		70	3 wks

See also Bing Crosby; Bing Crosby and Jane Wyman; David Bowie and Bing Crosby.

Bing CROSBY and Jane WYMAN
US, male/female vocal duo   2 wks

5 Dec 52	● ZING A LITTLE ZONG Brunswick 04981		10	2 wks

See also Bing Crosby; Bing Crosby and Grace Kelly; David Bowie and Bing Crosby.

CROSBY, STILLS and NASH
US/UK, male vocal/instrumental group   9 wks

16 Aug 69	MARRAKESH EXPRESS Atlantic 584 283		17	9 wks

See also Stephen Stills.

Christopher CROSS   US, male vocalist   27 wks

19 Apr 80	RIDE LIKE THE WIND Warner Bros. K 17582		69	1 wk
14 Feb 81	SAILING Warner Bros. K 17695		48	6 wks
17 Oct 81	ARTHUR'S THEME (BEST THAT YOU CAN DO) Warner Bros. K 17847		56	4 wks
9 Jan 82	● ARTHUR'S THEME (BEST THAT YOU CAN DO) (re-entry) Warner Bros. K 17847		7	11 wks
5 Feb 83	ALL RIGHT Warner Bros. W 9843		51	5 wks

CROWN HEIGHTS AFFAIR
US, male vocal/instrumental group   *34 wks*

19 Aug 78	**GALAXY OF LOVE** *Philips 6168 801*		**24**	10 wks
11 Nov 78	**I'M GONNA LOVE YOU FOREVER**			
	Mercury 6188 808		**47**	4 wks
14 Apr 79	**DANCE LADY DANCE** *Mercury 6168 804*		**44**	4 wks
3 May 80	● **YOU GAVE ME LOVE** *De-Lite MER 9*		**10**	12 wks
9 Aug 80	**YOU'VE BEEN GONE** *De-Lite MER 28*		**44**	4 wks

CRUISERS   - *See Dave BERRY*

CRUSADERS
US, male vocal/instrumental group   *16 wks*

18 Aug 79	● **STREET LIFE** *MCA 513*		**5**	11 wks
26 Sep 81	**I'M SO GLAD I'M STANDING HERE TODAY**			
	MCA 741		**61**	3 wks
7 Apr 84	**NIGHT LADIES** *MCA MCA 853*		**55**	2 wks

Vocalist on Street Life *was Randy Crawford, though uncredited - see also Randy Crawford.* I'm So Glad I'm Standing Here Today *credits 'featured vocalist Joe Cocker'. See Joe Cocker.*

Bobby CRUSH
UK, male instrumentalist - piano   *4 wks*

4 Nov 72	**BORSALINO** *Philips 6006 248*		**37**	4 wks

CRYIN' SHAMES
UK, male vocal/instrumental group   *7 wks*

31 Mar 66	**PLEASE STAY** *Decca F 12340*		**26**	7 wks

CRYPT-KICKERS   - *See Bobby 'Boris' PICKETT and the CRYPT-KICKERS*

CRYSTALS   *US, female vocal group*   *54 wks*

22 Nov 62	**HE'S A REBEL** *London HLU 9611*		**19**	13 wks
20 Jun 63	● **DA DOO RON RON** *London HLU 9732*		**5**	16 wks
19 Sep 63	● **THEN HE KISSED ME** *London HLU 9773*		**2**	14 wks
5 Mar 64	**I WONDER** *London HLU 9852*		**36**	3 wks
19 Oct 74	**DA DOO RON RON** (re-issue)			
	Warner Spector K 19010		**15**	8 wks

CUFF-LINKS   *US, male vocal group*   *30 wks*

29 Nov 69	● **TRACY** *MCA MU 1101*		**4**	16 wks
14 Mar 70	● **WHEN JULIE COMES AROUND**			
	MCA MU 1112		**10**	14 wks

CULT   *UK, male vocal/instrumental group*   *2 wks*

22 Dec 84	**RESURRECTION JOE** *Beggars Banquet BEG 122*		**74†**	2 wks

Smiley CULTURE   *UK, male vocalist*   *3 wks*

15 Dec 84	**POLICE OFFICER** *Fashion FAD 7012*		**40†**	3 wks

CULTURE CLUB
UK, male vocal/instrumental group   *90 wks*

18 Sep 82	★ **DO YOU REALLY WANT TO HURT ME**			
	Virgin VS 518		**1**	18 wks
27 Nov 82	● **TIME (CLOCK OF THE HEART)** *Virgin VS 558*		**3**	12 wks
9 Apr 83	● **CHURCH OF THE POISON MIND**			
	Virgin VS 571		**2**	9 wks
17 Sep 83	★ **KARMA CHAMELEON** *Virgin VS 612*		**1**	20 wks
10 Dec 83	● **VICTIMS** *Virgin VS 641*		**3**	10 wks
24 Mar 84	● **IT'S A MIRACLE** *Virgin VS 662*		**4**	9 wks
6 Oct 84	● **THE WAR SONG** *Virgin VS 694*		**2**	8 wks
1 Dec 84	**THE MEDAL SONG** *Virgin VS 730*		**32**	4 wks

Larry CUNNINGHAM and the MIGHTY AVONS
Ireland, male vocal/instrumental group   *11 wks*

10 Dec 64	**TRIBUTE TO JIM REEVES** *King KG 1016*		**40**	8 wks
25 Feb 65	**TRIBUTE TO JIM REEVES** (re-entry)			
	King KG 1016		**46**	3 wks

CUPID'S INSPIRATION
UK, male vocal/instrumental group   *19 wks*

19 Jun 68	● **YESTERDAY HAS GONE** *Nems 56 3500*		**4**	11 wks
2 Oct 68	**MY WORLD** *Nems 56 3702*		**33**	8 wks

CURE   *UK, male vocal/instrumental group*   *53 wks*

12 Apr 80	**A FOREST** *Fiction FICS 10*		**31**	8 wks
4 Apr 81	**PRIMARY** *Fiction FICS 12*		**43**	6 wks
17 Oct 81	**CHARLOTTE SOMETIMES** *Fiction FICS 14* ...		**44**	4 wks
24 Jul 82	**HANGING GARDEN** *Fiction FICS 15*		**34**	4 wks
27 Nov 82	**LET'S GO TO BED** *Fiction FICS 17*		**44**	4 wks
8 Jan 83	**LET'S GO TO BED** (re-entry) *Fiction FICS 17* ...		**75**	1 wk
9 Jul 83	**THE WALK** *Fiction FICS 18*		**12**	8 wks
29 Oct 83	● **THE LOVE CATS** *Fiction FICS 19*		**7**	11 wks
7 Apr 84	**THE CATERPILLAR** *Fiction FICS 20*		**14**	7 wks

CURLS   - *See Paul EVANS and the CURLS*

Chantal CURTIS   *France, female vocalist*   *3 wks*

14 Jul 79	**GET ANOTHER LOVE** *Pye 7P 5003*		**51**	3 wks

CURVED AIR
UK, male/female vocal/instrumental group   *12 wks*

7 Aug 71	● **BACK STREET LUV** *Warner Bros. K 16092*		**4**	12 wks

Adge CUTLER and the WURZELS
UK, male vocal/instrumental group   *1 wk*

2 Feb 67	**DRINK UP THY ZIDER** *Columbia DB 8081*		**45**	1 wk

See also Wurzels.

Johnny CYMBAL   *UK, male vocalist*   *10 wks*

14 Mar 63	**MR. BASS MAN** *London HLR 9682*		**24**	10 wks

D

Vicky D   *UK, female vocalist*   *6 wks*

13 Mar 82	**THIS BEAT IS MINE** *Virgin VS 486*		**42**	6 wks

DICKIES (top left) Tongue-in-cheek punk group who took everything from Christmas carols to Moody Blues ballads at 90 m.p.h.

ECHO AND THE BUNNYMEN (top right) In a Beatlish situation. *Help!*

SHEENA EASTON (above) Became a one-man woman and went to live and work permanently in the States. (Photo: Brian Aris.)

DURAN DURAN (right) In the fifties they screamed at Elvis, the sixties the Beatles, the seventies the Bay City Rollers and the eighties Duran Duran. (Photo: Mike Owen.)

D, B, M and T
UK, male vocal/instrumental group — 8 wks

1 Aug 70	**MR. PRESIDENT**	Fontana 6007 022	. . . .	33	8 wks

See also Dave Dee; Dave Dee, Dozy, Beaky, Mick and Tich.

D TRAIN
US, male vocalist/multi-instrumentalist — 23 wks

6 Feb 82	**YOU'RE THE ONE FOR ME**	Epic EPC A 2016		30	8 wks
8 May 82	**WALK ON BY**	Epic EPC A 2298	. . . .	44	6 wks
7 May 83	**MUSIC PART 1**	Prelude A 3332		23	7 wks
16 Jul 83	**KEEP GIVING ME LOVE**	Prelude A 3497	. . . . . .	65	2 wks

Paul DA VINCI
UK, male vocalist — 8 wks

20 Jul 74	**YOUR BABY AIN'T YOUR BABY ANYMORE**			
	Penny Farthing PEN 843	. . . .	20	8 wks

Terry DACTYL and the DINOSAURS
UK, male vocal/instrumental group — 16 wks

15 Jul 72	● **SEASIDE SHUFFLE**	UK 5		2	12 wks
13 Jan 73	**ON A SATURDAY NIGHT**	UK 21	. . . .	45	4 wks

DAKOTAS
UK, male instrumental group — 13 wks

11 Jul 63	**THE CRUEL SEA**	Parlophone R 5044	. . . .	18	13 wks

See also Billy J. Kramer and the Dakotas.

Jim DALE
UK, male vocalist — 22 wks

11 Oct 57	● **BE MY GIRL**	Parlophone R 4343	. . . .	2	16 wks
10 Jan 58	**JUST BORN**	Parlophone R 4376		27	1 wk
17 Jan 58	**CRAZY DREAM**	Parlophone R 4376		24	2 wks
7 Mar 58	**SUGARTIME**	Parlophone R 4402		25	3 wks

DALE AND GRACE
US, male/female vocal duo — 2 wks

9 Jan 64	**I'M LEAVING IT UP TO YOU**	London HL 9807		42	2 wks

DALE SISTERS
UK, female vocal group — 6 wks

23 Nov 61	**MY SUNDAY BABY**	Ember S 140	. . . .	36	6 wks

DALI'S CAR
UK, male vocal/instrumental duo — 2 wks

3 Nov 84	**THE JUDGEMENT IS THE MIRROR**			
	Paradox DOX 1	. . . .	66	2 wks

Roger DALTREY
UK, male vocalist — 36 wks

14 Apr 73	● **GIVING IT ALL AWAY**	Track 2094 110	. . . .	5	11 wks
4 Aug 73	**I'M FREE**	Ode ODS 66302		13	10 wks
14 May 77	**WRITTEN ON THE WIND**	Polydor 2121 319	. . .	46	2 wks
2 Aug 80	**FREE ME**	Polydor 2001 980		39	6 wks
11 Oct 80	**WITHOUT YOUR LOVE**	Polydor POSP 181	. . . .	55	4 wks
3 Mar 84	**WALKING IN MY SLEEP**	WEA U 9686	. . . . . .	56	3 wks

DAMNED
UK, male vocal/instrumental group — 31 wks

5 May 79	**LOVE SONG**	Chiswick CHIS 112	. . . .	20	8 wks
20 Oct 79	**SMASH IT UP**	Chiswick CHIS 116	. . . .	35	5 wks
1 Dec 79	**I JUST CAN'T BE HAPPY TODAY**				
	Chiswick CHIS 120	. . . .	46	5 wks	
4 Oct 80	**HISTORY OF THE WORLD** (PART 1)				
	Chiswick CHIS 135	. . . .	51	4 wks	
28 Nov 81	**FRIDAY 13TH** (EP)	Stale One TRY 1		50	4 wks
10 Jul 82	**LOVELY MONEY**	Bronze BRO 149	. . . .	42	4 wks
9 Jun 84	**THANKS FOR THE NIGHT**				
	Damned DAMNED 1		42	1 wk	

Tracks on EP; Disco Man/The Limit Club/Billy Bad Breaks/Citadel.

Kenny DAMON
US, male vocalist — 1 wk

19 May 66	**WHILE I LIVE**	Mercury MF 907	. . . .	48	1 wk

Vic DAMONE
US, male vocalist — 22 wks

6 Dec 57	**AN AFFAIR TO REMEMBER**	Philips PB 745	. . .	29	1 wk
31 Jan 58	**AN AFFAIR TO REMEMBER** (re-entry)				
	Philips PB 745	. . . .	30	1 wk	
9 May 58	★ **ON THE STREET WHERE YOU LIVE**				
	Philips PB 819	. . . .	1	17 wks	
1 Aug 58	**THE ONLY MAN ON THE ISLAND**				
	Philips PB 837	. . . .	24	3 wks	

DANA
Ireland, female vocalist — 75 wks

4 Apr 70	★ **ALL KINDS OF EVERYTHING**	Rex R 11054	. .	1	15 wks
25 Jul 70	**ALL KINDS OF EVERYTHING** (re-entry)				
	Rex R 11054	. . . .	47	1 wk	
13 Feb 71	**WHO PUT THE LIGHTS OUT**	Rex R 11062	. . .	14	11 wks
25 Jan 75	● **PLEASE TELL HIM THAT I SAID HELLO**				
	GTO GT 6	. . . .	8	14 wks	
13 Dec 75	● **IT'S GONNA BE A COLD COLD CHRISTMAS**				
	GTO GT 45	. . . .	4	6 wks	
6 Mar 76	**NEVER GONNA FALL IN LOVE AGAIN**				
	GTO GT 55	. . . .	31	4 wks	
16 Oct 76	**FAIRYTALE**	GTO GT 66	. . . .	13	16 wks
31 Mar 79	**SOMETHING'S COOKIN' IN THE KITCHEN**				
	GTO GT 243	. . . .	44	5 wks	
15 May 82	**I FEEL LOVE COMIN' ON**	Creole CR 32	. . . . . .	66	3 wks

DAN-I
UK, male vocalist — 9 wks

10 Nov 79	**MONKEY CHOP**	Island WIP 6520	. . . .	30	9 wks

Charlie DANIELS BAND
US, male vocal/instrumental group — 10 wks

22 Sep 79	**THE DEVIL WENT DOWN TO GEORGIA**				
	Epic EPC 7737	. . . .	14	10 wks	

Johnny DANKWORTH
UK, male orchestral/group leader/instrumentalist - alto sax — 33 wks

22 Jun 56	● **EXPERIMENTS WITH MICE**	Parlophone R 4185		7	12 wks
23 Feb 61	● **AFRICAN WALTZ**	Columbia DB 4590	. . . . .	9	21 wks

DANNY and the JUNIORS
US, male vocal group — 19 wks

17 Jan 58	● **AT THE HOP**	HMV POP 436	. . . .	3	14 wks
10 Jul 76	**AT THE HOP** (re-issue)	ABC 4123	. . . .	39	5 wks

DANSE SOCIETY
UK, male vocal/instrumental group   *5 wks*

27 Aug 83	WAKE UP *Society/Arista SOC 5*	62	3 wks
5 Nov 83	HEAVEN IS WAITING *Society/Arista SOC 6*	60	2 wks

Bobby DARIN   *US, male vocalist*   *161 wks*

1 Aug 58	SPLISH SPLASH *London HLE 8666*	28	1 wk
15 Aug 58	SPLISH SPLASH (re-entry) *London HLE 8666* ...	18	6 wks
9 Jan 59	QUEEN OF THE HOP *London HLE 8737*	24	2 wks
29 May 59 ★	DREAM LOVER *London HLE 8867*	1	19 wks
25 Sept 59 ★	MACK THE KNIFE *London HLE 8939*	1	16 wks
22 Jan 60	MACK THE KNIFE (re-entry) *London HLE 8939*	30	1 wk
29 Jan 60 ●	LA MER (BEYOND THE SEA) *London HLE 9034*	8	10 wks
10 Mar 60	MACK THE KNIFE (2nd re-entry) *London HLE 8939*	50	1 wk
31 Mar 60 ●	CLEMENTINE *London HLK 9086*	8	12 wks
21 Apr 60	LA MER (BEYOND THE SEA) (re-entry) *London HLE 9034*	40	2 wks
30 Jun 60	BILL BAILEY *London HLK 9142*	36	1 wk
14 Jul 60	BILL BAILEY (re-entry) *London HLK 9142* ...	34	1 wk
16 Mar 61 ●	LAZY RIVER *London HLK 9303*	2	13 wks
6 Jul 61	NATURE BOY *London HLK 9375*	24	7 wks
12 Oct 61 ●	YOU MUST HAVE BEEN A BEAUTIFUL BABY *London HLK 9429*	10	11 wks
26 Oct 61	COME SEPTEMBER *London HLK 9407*	50	1 wk
21 Dec 61 ●	MULTIPLICATION *London HLK 9474*	5	13 wks
19 Jul 62 ●	THINGS *London HLK 9575*	2	17 wks
4 Oct 62	IF A MAN ANSWERS *Capitol CL 15272*	24	6 wks
29 Nov 62	BABY FACE *London HLK 9624*	40	4 wks
25 Jul 63	EIGHTEEN YELLOW ROSES *Capitol CL 15306*	37	4 wks
13 Oct 66 ●	IF I WERE A CARPENTER *Atlantic 584 051*	9	12 wks
14 Apr 79	DREAM LOVER/MACK THE KNIFE (re-issue) *Lightning LIG 9017*	64	1 wk

Come September is an instrumental credited to the Bobby Darin Orchestra.

Guy DARRELL   *UK, male vocalist*   *13 wks*

18 Aug 73	I'VE BEEN HURT *Santa Ponsa PNS 4*	12	13 wks

James DARREN   *US, male vocalist*   *25 wks*

11 Aug 60	BECAUSE THEY'RE YOUNG *Pye International 7N 25059*	29	7 wks
14 Dec 61	GOODBYE CRUEL WORLD *Pye International 7N 25116*	28	9 wks
29 Mar 62	HER ROYAL MAJESTY *Pye International 7N 25125*	36	3 wks
21 Jun 62	CONSCIENCE *Pye International 7N 25138*	30	6 wks

DARTS
UK, male/female vocal/instrumental group   *117 wks*

5 Nov 77 ●	DADDY COOL - THE GIRL CAN'T HELP IT *Magnet MAG 100*	6	13 wks
28 Jan 78 ●	COME BACK MY LOVE *Magnet MAG 110*	2	12 wks
6 May 78 ●	BOY FROM NEW YORK CITY *Magnet MAG 116*	2	13 wks
5 Aug 78 ●	IT'S RAINING *Magnet MAG 126*	2	11 wks
11 Nov 78	DON'T LET IT FADE AWAY *Magnet MAG 134*	18	11 wks
10 Feb 79 ●	GET IT *Magnet MAG 140*	10	9 wks
21 Jul 79 ●	DUKE OF EARL *Magnet MAG 147*	6	11 wks
20 Oct 79	CAN'T GET ENOUGH OF YOUR LOVE *Magnet MAG 156*	43	6 wks
1 Dec 79	REET PETITE *Magnet MAG 160*	51	7 wks
31 May 80	LET'S HANG ON *Magnet MAG 174*	11	14 wks
6 Sep 80	PEACHES *Magnet MAG 179*	66	3 wks
29 Nov 80	WHITE CHRISTMAS/SH-BOOM (LIFE COULD BE A DREAM) *Magnet MAG 184*	48	7 wks

DAVE - *See SAM and DAVE*

DAVE - *See CHAS and DAVE*

DAVID and JONATHAN
UK, male vocal duo   *22 wks*

13 Jan 66	MICHELLE *Columbia DB 7800*	11	6 wks
7 Jul 66 ●	LOVERS OF THE WORLD UNITE *Columbia DB 7950*	7	16 wks

Anne-Marie DAVID
France, female vocalist   *9 wks*

28 Apr 73	WONDERFUL DREAM *Epic EPC 1446*	13	9 wks

F.R. DAVID   *France, male vocalist*   *14 wks*

2 Apr 83 ●	WORDS *Carrere CAR 248*	2	12 wks
18 Jun 83	MUSIC *Carrere CAR 282*	71	2 wks

Jim DAVIDSON   *UK, male vocalist*   *4 wks*

27 Dec 80	WHITE CHRISTMAS/TOO RISKY *Scratch SCR 001*	52	4 wks

Paul DAVIDSON   *Jamaica, male vocalist*   *10 wks*

27 Dec 75 ●	MIDNIGHT RIDER *Tropical ALO 56*	10	10 wks

Dave DAVIES   *UK, male vocalist*   *17 wks*

19 Jul 67 ●	DEATH OF A CLOWN *Pye 7N 17356*	3	10 wks
6 Dec 67	SUSANNAH'S STILL ALIVE *Pye 7N 17429*	20	7 wks

Windsor DAVIES and Don ESTELLE   *UK, male vocal duo*   *16 wks*

17 May 75 ★	WHISPERING GRASS *EMI 2290*	1	12 wks
25 Oct 75	PAPER DOLL *EMI 2361*	41	4 wks

Billie DAVIS   *UK, female vocalist*   *23 wks*

7 Feb 63 ●	TELL HIM *Decca F 11572*	10	12 wks
30 May 63	HE'S THE ONE *Decca F 11658*	40	3 wks
9 Oct 68	I WANT YOU TO BE MY BABY *Decca F 12823*	33	8 wks

See also Mike Sarne.

John DAVIS and the MONSTER ORCHESTRA
US, male vocal/instrumental group   *2 wks*

10 Feb 79	AIN'T THAT ENOUGH FOR YOU *Miracle M 2*	70	2 wks

Mac DAVIS   *US, male vocalist*   *22 wks*

4 Nov 72	BABY DON'T GET HOOKED ON ME *CBS 8250*	29	6 wks
15 Nov 80	IT'S HARD TO BE HUMBLE *Casablanca CAN 210* ...	27	16 wks

Ruth DAVIS - *See Bo KIRKLAND and Ruth DAVIS*

Skeeter DAVIS *US, female vocalist*   *13 wks*

14 Mar 63	END OF THE WORLD *RCA 1328*	18	13 wks

Spencer DAVIS GROUP
UK, male vocal/instrumental group   *71 wks*

5 Nov 64	I CAN'T STAND IT *Fontana TF 499*	47	3 wks
25 Feb 65	EVERY LITTLE BIT HURTS *Fontana TF 530* . .	43	2 wks
18 Mar 65	EVERY LITTLE BIT HURTS (re-entry) *Fontana TF 530*	41	1 wk
10 Jun 65	STRONG LOVE *Fontana TF 571*	50	1 wk
24 Jun 65	STRONG LOVE (re-entry) *Fontana TF 571*	44	3 wks
2 Dec 65	★ KEEP ON RUNNING *Fontana TF 632*	1	14 wks
24 Mar 66	★ SOMEBODY HELP ME *Fontana TF 679* . .	1	10 wks
1 Sep 66	WHEN I COME HOME *Fontana TF 739* . .	12	9 wks
3 Nov 66	● GIMME SOME LOVING *Fontana TF 762*	2	12 wks
26 Jan 67	● I'M A MAN *Fontana TF 785*	9	7 wks
9 Aug 67	TIME SELLER *Fontana TF 854*	30	5 wks
10 Jan 68	MR. SECOND CLASS *United Artists UP 1203*	35	4 wks

Billy DAVIS JR. - *See Marilyn McCOO and Billy DAVIS JR.*

Sammy DAVIS JR. *US, male vocalist*   *25 wks*

29 Jul 55	SOMETHING'S GOTTA GIVE *Brunswick 05428*	19	2 wks
19 Aug 55	SOMETHING'S GOTTA GIVE (re-entry) *Brunswick 05428*	11	5 wks
9 Sep 55	● LOVE ME OR LEAVE ME *Brunswick 05428*	8	6 wks
30 Sep 55	THAT OLD BLACK MAGIC *Brunswick 05450* . . .	16	1 wk
7 Oct 55	HEY THERE *Brunswick 05469*	19	1 wk
4 Nov 55	LOVE ME OR LEAVE ME (re-entry) *Brunswick 05428*	18	2 wks
20 Apr 56	IN A PERSIAN MARKET *Brunswick 05518*	28	1 wk
28 Dec 56	ALL OF YOU *Brunswick 05629*	28	1 wk
22 Mar 62	WHAT KIND OF FOOL AM I?/GONNA BUILD A MOUNTAIN *Reprise R 20048*	26	8 wks

See also Sammy Davis Jr. and Carmen McRae; Frank Sinatra and Sammy Davis Jr.

Sammy DAVIS JR. and Carmen McRAE *US, male/female vocal duo*   *1 wk*

16 Jun 60	HAPPY TO MAKE YOUR ACQUAINTANCE *Brunswick 05830*	46	1 wk

See also Sammy Davis Jr.; Frank Sinatra and Sammy Davis Jr.

DAWN *US, male/female vocal group*   *109 wks*

16 Jan 71	● CANDIDA *Bell 1118*	9	11 wks
10 Apr 71	★ KNOCK THREE TIMES *Bell 1146*	1	27 wks
31 Jul 71	● WHAT ARE YOU DOING SUNDAY *Bell 1169*	3	12 wks
10 Mar 73	★ TIE A YELLOW RIBBON ROUND THE OLD OAK TREE *Bell 1287*	1	39 wks
4 Aug 73	SAY, HAS ANYBODY SEEN MY SWEET GYPSY ROSE *Bell 1322*	12	15 wks
5 Jan 74	TIE A YELLOW RIBBON ROUND THE OLE OAK TREE (re-entry) *Bell 1287*	41	1 wk
9 Mar 74	WHO'S IN THE STRAWBERRY PATCH WITH SALLY *Bell 1343*	37	4 wks

First two hits credit Dawn, the next three Dawn featuring Tony Orlando, and the final one Tony Orlando and Dawn. See also Tony Orlando.

Bobby DAY *US, male vocalist*   *2 wks*

7 Nov 58	ROCKIN' ROBIN *London HL 8726*	29	2 wks

Doris DAY *US, female vocalist*   *116 wks*

21 Nov 52	● MY LOVE AND DEVOTION *Columbia DB 3157*	10	2 wks
2 Apr 54	★ SECRET LOVE *Philips PB 230*	1	29 wks
27 Aug 54	● BLACK HILLS OF DAKOTA *Philips PB 287* . . .	7	8 wks
1 Oct 54	● IF I GIVE MY HEART TO YOU *Philips PB 325*	4	11 wks
8 Apr 55	● READY WILLING AND ABLE *Philips PB 402* . .	7	9 wks
9 Sep 55	LOVE ME OR LEAVE ME *Philips PB 479*	20	1 wk
21 Oct 55	I'LL NEVER STOP LOVING YOU *Philips PB 497*	17	2 wks
25 Nov 55	I'LL NEVER STOP LOVING YOU (re-entry) *Philips PB 497*	19	1 wk
29 Jun 56	★ WHATEVER WILL BE WILL BE *Philips PB 586*	1	22 wks
13 Jun 58	A VERY PRECIOUS LOVE *Philips PB 799*	16	11 wks
15 Aug 58	EVERYBODY LOVES A LOVER *Philips PB 843*	25	3 wks
26 Sep 58	EVERYBODY LOVES A LOVER (re-entry) *Philips PB 843*	27	1 wk
12 Mar 64	● MOVE OVER DARLING *CBS AAG 183*	8	16 wks

See also Doris Day and Frankie Laine; Doris Day and Johnnie Ray.

Doris DAY and Frankie LAINE
US, female/male vocal duo   *8 wks*

14 Nov 52	● SUGARBUSH *Columbia DB 3123*	8	2 wks
5 Dec 52	● SUGARBUSH (re-entry) *Columbia DB 3123*	8	6 wks

See also Doris Day; Frankie Laine; Doris Day and Johnnie Ray; Frankie Laine and Jimmy Boyd; Frankie Laine and Johnnie Ray.

Doris DAY and Johnnie RAY
US, female/male vocal duo   *16 wks*

3 Apr 53	MA SAYS PA SAYS *Columbia DB 3242*	12	1 wk
17 Apr 53	FULL TIME JOB *Columbia DB 3242*	11	1 wk
24 Jul 53	● LET'S WALK THATA-WAY *Philips PB 157* . . .	4	14 wks

See also Doris Day; Johnnie Ray; Doris Day and Frankie Laine; Frankie Laine and Johnnie Ray.

DAYTON *US, male vocalist*   *1 wk*

10 Dec 83	THE SOUND OF MUSIC *Capitol CL 318*	75	1 wk

DAZZ BAND
US, male vocal/instrumental group   *9 wks*

3 Nov 84	LET IT ALL BLOW *Motown TMG 1361*	12†	9 wks

D.B.M.
German, male/female vocal/instrumental group   *3 wks*

12 Nov 77	DISCO BEATLEMANIA *Atlantic K 11027*	45	3 wks

Nino DE ANGELO
Germany, male vocalist   *5 wks*

21 Jul 84	GUARDIAN ANGEL *Carrere CAR 335*	57	5 wks

Chris DE BURGH *Ireland, male vocalist*   *10 wks*

23 Oct 82	DON'T PAY THE FERRYMAN *A & M AMS 8256*	48	5 wks
12 May 84	HIGH ON EMOTION *A & M AM 190*	44	5 wks

DE CASTRO SISTERS
US, female vocal group   *1 wk*

11 Feb 55		**TEACH ME TONIGHT** *London HL 8104*	20	1 wk

Lynsey DE PAUL   UK, *female vocalist*   *47 wks*

19 Aug 72	●	**SUGAR ME** *MAM 81*	5	11 wks
2 Dec 72		**GETTING A DRAG** *MAM 88*	18	8 wks
27 Oct 73		**WON'T SOMEBODY DANCE WITH ME** *MAM 109*	14	7 wks
8 Jun 74		**OOH I DO** *Warner Bros. K 16401* ...	25	6 wks
2 Nov 74	●	**NO HONESTLY** *Jet 747* .... ··	7	11 wks
22 Mar 75		**MY MAN AND ME** *Jet 750*	40	4 wks

See also Lynsey De Paul and Mike Moran.

Lynsey DE PAUL and Mike MORAN
UK, *female/male vocal and instrumental duo, pianos*   *7 wks*

26 Mar 77		**ROCK BOTTOM** *Polydor 2058 859*	19	7 wks

See also Lynsey De Paul.

Terri DE SARIO   US, *female vocalist*   *5 wks*

2 Sep 78		**AIN'T NOTHIN' (GONNA KEEP ME FROM YOU)** *Casablanca CAN 128*	52	5 wks

Stephanie DE SYKES
UK, *female vocalist*   *17 wks*

20 Jul 74	●	**BORN WITH A SMILE ON MY FACE** *Bradley's BRAD 7409*	2	10 wks
19 Apr 75		**WE'LL FIND OUR DAY** *Bradley's BRAD 7509* ..	17	7 wks

Born With A Smile On My Face credits Stephanie De Sykes With Rain, UK male vocal group.

William DE VAUGHN
US, *male vocalist*   *10 wks*

6 Jul 74		**BE THANKFUL FOR WHAT YOU'VE GOT** *Chelsea 2005 002*	31	5 wks
20 Sep 80		**BE THANKFUL FOR WHAT YOU'VE GOT** *EMI 5101*	44	5 wks

EMI version of hit is a new recording.

DEAD END KIDS
UK, *male vocal and instrumental group*   *10 wks*

26 Mar 77	●	**HAVE I THE RIGHT** *CBS 4972*	6	10 wks

DEAD KENNEDYS
US, *male vocal/instrumental group*   *9 wks*

1 Nov 80		**KILL THE POOR** *Cherry Red CHERRY 16*	49	3 wks
30 May 81		**TOO DRUNK TO FUCK** *Cherry Red CHERRY 24*	36	6 wks

DEAD OR ALIVE
UK, *male vocal/instrumental group*   *14 wks*

24 Mar 84		**THAT'S THE WAY (I LIKE IT)** *Epic A 4271* ...	22	9 wks
1 Dec 84		**YOU SPIN ME ROUND (LIKE A RECORD)** *Epic A 4861*	49†	5 wks

---

DEAN   - *See JAN and DEAN*

Hazell DEAN   UK, *female vocalist*   *33 wks*

18 Feb 84		**EVERGREEN/JEALOUS LOVE** *Proto ENA 114*	63	3 wks
21 Apr 84	●	**SEARCHIN'** *Proto ENA 109*	6	15 wks
28 Jul 84	●	**WHATEVER I DO (WHEREVER I GO)** *Proto ENA 119*	4	11 wks
3 Nov 84		**BACK IN MY ARMS ONCE AGAIN** *Proto ENA 122*	41	4 wks

Jimmy DEAN   US, *male vocalist*   *17 wks*

26 Oct 61	●	**BIG BAD JOHN** *Philips PB 1187*	2	13 wks
8 Nov 62		**LITTLE BLACK BOOK** *CBS AAG 122*	33	4 wks

Diana DECKER   US, *female vocalist*   *10 wks*

23 Oct 53	●	**POPPA PICCOLINO** *Columbia DB 3325*	2	8 wks
8 Jan 54	●	**POPPA PICCOLINO** (re-entry) *Columbia DB 3325*	5	2 wks

Dave DEE   UK, *male vocalist*   *4 wks*

14 Mar 70		**MY WOMAN'S MAN** *Fontana TF 1074*	42	4 wks

See also D, B, M and T; Dave Dee, Dozy, Beaky, Mick and Tich.

Dave DEE, DOZY, BEAKY, MICK and TICH   UK, *male vocal/instrumental group*   *141 wks*

23 Dec 65		**YOU MAKE IT MOVE** *Fontana TF 630*	26	8 wks
3 Mar 66	●	**HOLD TIGHT** *Fontana TF 671*	4	17 wks
9 Jun 66	●	**HIDEAWAY** *Fontana TF 711*	10	11 wks
15 Sep 66	●	**BEND IT** *Fontana TF 746*	2	12 wks
8 Dec 66	●	**SAVE ME** *Fontana TF 775*	4	10 wks
9 Mar 67		**TOUCH ME TOUCH ME** *Fontana TF 798* ...	13	9 wks
18 May 67	●	**OKAY!** *Fontana TF 830*	4	11 wks
11 Oct 67	●	**ZABADAK!** *Fontana TF 873*	3	14 wks
14 Feb 68	★	**LEGEND OF XANADU** *Fontana TF 903*	1	12 wks
3 Jul 68	●	**LAST NIGHT IN SOHO** *Fontana TF 953*	8	11 wks
2 Oct 68		**WRECK OF THE ANTOINETTE** *Fontana TF 971*	14	9 wks
5 Mar 69		**DON JUAN** *Fontana TF 1000*	23	9 wks
14 May 69		**SNAKE IN THE GRASS** *Fontana TF 1020*	23	8 wks

See also Dave Dee; D, B, M and T.

Jazzy DEE   US, *male vocalist*   *5 wks*

5 Mar 83		**GET ON UP** *Laurie LRS 101*	53	5 wks

Joey DEE and the STARLITERS
US, *male vocal/instrumental group*   *8 wks*

8 Feb 62		**PEPPERMINT TWIST** *Columbia DB 4758*	33	8 wks

Kiki DEE   UK, *female vocalist*   *55 wks*

10 Nov 73		**AMOUREUSE** *Rocket PIG 4*	13	13 wks
7 Sep 74		**I GOT THE MUSIC IN ME** *Rocket PIG 9* ...	19	8 wks
12 Apr 75		**(YOU DONT KNOW) HOW GLAD I AM** *Rocket PIG 16*	33	4 wks
11 Sep 76		**LOVING AND FREE/AMOUREUSE** (re-issue of AMOUREUSE) *Rocket ROKN 515*	13	8 wks
19 Feb 77		**FIRST THING IN THE MORNING** *Rocket ROKN 520*	32	5 wks
11 Jun 77		**CHICAGO** *Rocket ROKN 526*	28	4 wks
21 Feb 81		**STAR** *Ariola ARO 251*	13	10 wks

23 May 81	**PERFECT TIMING** *Ariola ARO 257*	**66**	3 wks

Amoureuse, when re-issued on the same record as a new title, Loving and Free, was only listed on the charts for 5 weeks of the record's eight-week run. On 18 Sep, 25 Sep and 2 Oct 1976, Loving And Free was the only title mentioned. I Got The Music In Me and (You Don't Know) How Glad I Am credited to The Kiki Dee Band. Chicago was one side of a double sided chart entry, the other being Bite Your Lip (Get Up and Dance) by Elton John. See also Elton John; Elton John and Kiki Dee.

Nancy DEE - *See BENELUX and Nancy DEE*

DEEDEE - *See DICK and DEEDEE*

Carol DEENE   *UK, female vocalist*   *25 wks*

26 Oct 61	**SAD MOVIES** *HMV POP 922*	**44**	3 wks
25 Jan 62	**NORMAN** *HMV POP 973*	**24**	8 wks
5 Jul 62	**JOHNNY GET ANGRY** *HMV POP 1027*	**32**	4 wks
23 Aug 62	**SOME PEOPLE** *HMV POP 1058*	**25**	10 wks

DEEP FEELING
UK, male vocal/instrumental group   *5 wks*

25 Apr 70	**DO YOU LOVE ME** *Page One POF 165*	**45**	1 wk
9 May 70	**DO YOU LOVE ME** (re-entry) *Page One POF 165*	**34**	4 wks

DEEP PURPLE
UK, male vocal/instrumental group   *75 wks*

15 Aug 70	● **BLACK NIGHT** *Harvest HAR 5020*	**2**	21 wks
27 Feb 71	● **STRANGE KIND OF WOMAN** *Harvest HAR 5033*	**8**	12 wks
13 Nov 71	**FIREBALL** *Harvest HAR 5045*	**15**	13 wks
1 Apr 72	**NEVER BEFORE** *Purple PUR 102*	**35**	6 wks
16 Apr 77	**SMOKE ON THE WATER** *Purple PUR 132*	**21**	7 wks
15 Oct 77	**NEW LIVE AND RARE** *Purple PUR 135*	**31**	4 wks
7 Oct 78	**NEW LIVE AND RARE II** (EP) *Purple PUR 137*	**45**	3 wks
2 Aug 80	**BLACK NIGHT** (re-issue) *Harvest HAR 5210*	**43**	6 wks
1 Nov 80	**NEW LIVE AND RARE VOLUME 3** *Harvest SHEP 101*	**48**	3 wks

Tracks on New Live And Rare: Black Night (live)/Painted Horse/When A Blind Man Cries. New Live And Rare II EP: Burn (Edited version)/Coronarias Redig/Mistreated (live)/Rock Me Baby. New Live And Rare Volume 3 EP: Smoke On The Water/Bird Has Flown/Grabsplatter.

DEEP RIVER BOYS
UK, male vocal group   *1 wk*

7 Dec 56	**THAT'S RIGHT** *HMV POP 263*	**29**	1 wk

Rick DEES and his CAST OF IDIOTS   *US, male vocalist with male/female vocal/instrumental group*   *9 wks*

18 Sep 76	● **DISCO DUCK** *RSO 2090 204*	**6**	9 wks

DEF LEPPARD
UK, male vocal/instrumental group   *14 wks*

17 Nov 79	**WASTED** *Vertigo 6059 247*	**61**	3 wks
23 Feb 80	**HELLO AMERICA** *Vertigo LEPP 1*	**45**	4 wks
5 Feb 83	**PHOTOGRAPH** *Vertigo/Phonogram VER 5*	**66**	3 wks
27 Aug 83	**ROCK OF AGES** *Vertigo/Phonogram VER 6*	**41**	4 wks

Desmond DEKKER and the ACES
Jamaica, male vocal/instrumental group   *71 wks*

12 Jul 67	**007** *Pyramid PYR 6004*	**14**	11 wks
19 Mar 69	★ **ISRAELITES** *Pyramid PYR 6058*	**1**	14 wks
25 Jun 69	● **IT MIEK** *Pyramid PYR 6068*	**7**	11 wks
2 Jul 69	**ISRAELITES** (re-entry) *Pyramid PYR 6058*	**45**	1 wk
10 Jan 70	**PICKNEY GAL** *Pyramid PYR 6078*	**42**	3 wks
22 Aug 70	● **YOU CAN GET IT IF YOU REALLY WANT** *Trojan TR 7777*	**2**	15 wks
10 May 75	● **ISRAELITES** (re-issue) *Cactus CT 57*	**10**	9 wks
30 Aug 75	**SING A LITTLE SONG** *Cactus CT 73*	**16**	7 wks

You Can Get It If You Really Want credited only to Desmond Dekker.

DELANEY and BONNIE and FRIENDS featuring Eric CLAPTON
US male/female vocal/instrumental group   *9 wks*

20 Dec 69	**COMIN' HOME** *Atlantic 584 308*	**16**	9 wks

DELEGATION
UK, male vocal/instrumental group   *7 wks*

23 Apr 77	**WHERE IS THE LOVE (WE USED TO KNOW)** *State STAT 40*	**22**	6 wks
20 Aug 77	**YOU'VE BEEN DOING ME WRONG** *State STAT 55*	**49**	1 wk

DELFONICS   *US, male vocal group*   *23 wks*

10 Apr 71	**DIDN'T I (BLOW YOUR MIND THIS TIME)** *Bell 1099*	**43**	1 wk
24 Apr 71	**DIDN'T I (BLOW YOUR MIND THIS TIME)** (re-entry) *Bell 1099*	**22**	8 wks
10 Jul 71	**LA-LA MEANS I LOVE YOU** *Bell 1165*	**19**	10 wks
16 Oct 71	**READY OR NOT HERE I COME** *Bell 1175*	**41**	4 wks

'DELIVERANCE' SOUNDTRACK
US, male instrumental duo, Eric Weissberg and Steve Mandell, banjos   *7 wks*

31 Mar 73	**DUELLING BANJOS** *Warner Bros. K 16223*	**17**	7 wks

DELLS   *US, male vocal group*   *9 wks*

16 Jul 69	**I CAN SING A RAINBOW - LOVE IS BLUE** (MEDLEY) *Chess CRS 8099*	**15**	9 wks

DELRONS - *See REPARATA and the DELRONS*

Terry DENE   *UK, male vocalist*   *20 wks*

7 Jun 57	**A WHITE SPORT COAT** *Decca F 10895*	**18**	6 wks
19 Jul 57	**START MOVIN'** *Decca F 10914*	**15**	8 wks
26 Jul 57	**A WHITE SPORT COAT** (re-entry) *Decca F 10895*	**30**	1 wk
16 May 58	**STAIRWAY OF LOVE** *Decca F 11016*	**16**	5 wks

Jackie DENNIS   *UK, male vocalist*   *10 wks*

14 Mar 58	● **LA DEE DAH** *Decca F 10992*	**4**	9 wks
27 Jun 58	**PURPLE PEOPLE EATER** *Decca F 11033*	**29**	1 wk

DENNISONS
UK, male vocal/instrumental group   *13 wks*

15 Aug 63	BE MY GIRL *Decca F 11691*		46	6 wks
7 May 64	WALKIN' THE DOG *Decca F 11880*		36	7 wks

Richard DENTON and Martin COOK *UK, male orchestral leaders/instrumental duo, guitar and keyboards*   *7 wks*

15 Apr 78	THEME FROM THE HONG KONG BEAT			
	BBC RESL 52		25	7 wks

John DENVER *US, male vocalist*   *13 wks*

17 Aug 74	★ ANNIE'S SONG *RCA APBO 0295*		1	13 wks

See also Placido Domingo and John Denver.

Karl DENVER *UK, male vocalist*   *124 wks*

22 Jun 61	● MARCHETA *Decca F 11360*		8	20 wks
19 Oct 61	● MEXICALI ROSE *Decca F 11395*		8	11 wks
25 Jan 62	● WIMOWEH *Decca F 11420*		4	17 wks
22 Feb 62	● NEVER GOODBYE *Decca F 11431*		9	18 wks
7 Jun 62	A LITTLE LOVE A LITTLE KISS *Decca F 11470*		19	10 wks
20 Sep 62	BLUE WEEKEND *Decca F 11505*		33	5 wks
21 Mar 63	CAN YOU FORGIVE ME *Decca F 11608*		32	8 wks
13 Jun 63	INDIAN LOVE CALL *Decca F 11674*		32	8 wks
22 Aug 63	STILL *Decca F 11720*		13	15 wks
5 Mar 64	MY WORLD OF BLUE *Decca F 11828*		29	6 wks
4 Jun 64	LOVE ME WITH ALL YOUR HEART			
	Decca F 11905		37	6 wks

DEODATO *US, orchestra*   *9 wks*

5 May 73	● ALSO SPRACH ZARATHUSTRA (2001)			
	Creed Taylor CTI 4000		7	9 wks

DEPARTMENT S
UK, male vocal/instrumental group   *13 wks*

4 Apr 81	IS VIC THERE? *Demon D 1003*		22	10 wks
11 Jul 81	GOING LEFT RIGHT *Stiff BUY 118*		55	3 wks

DEPECHE MODE
UK, male vocal/instrumental group   *108 wks*

4 Apr 81	DREAMING OF ME *Mute MUTE 013*		57	4 wks
13 Jun 81	NEW LIFE *Mute MUTE 014*		11	15 wks
19 Sep 81	● JUST CAN'T GET ENOUGH *Mute MUTE 016*		8	10 wks
13 Feb 82	● SEE YOU *Mute MUTE 018*		6	10 wks
8 May 82	THE MEANING OF LOVE *Mute MUTE 022* ...		12	8 wks
28 Aug 82	LEAVE IN SILENCE *Mute BONG 1*		18	10 wks
12 Feb 83	GET THE BALANCE RIGHT *Mute 7 BONG 2*		13	8 wks
23 Jul 83	● EVERYTHING COUNTS *Mute 7 BONG 3*		6	11 wks
1 Oct 83	LOVE IN ITSELF.2 *Mute 7 BONG 4*		21	7 wks
24 Mar 84	● PEOPLE ARE PEOPLE *Mute 7 BONG 5*		4	10 wks
1 Sep 84	● MASTER AND SERVANT *Mute 7 BONG 6* ...		9	9 wks
10 Nov 84	SOMEBODY/BLASPHEMOUS RUMOURS			
	Mute 7 BONG 7		16	6 wks

DEREK and the DOMINOS
UK/US, male vocal/instrumental group   *21 wks*

12 Aug 72	● LAYLA *Polydor 2058 130*		7	11 wks
6 Mar 82	● LAYLA (re-issue) *RSO 87*		4	10 wks

Derek being Eric Clapton under a false name, see also Eric Clapton.

DETROIT EMERALDS
US, male vocal group   *44 wks*

10 Feb 73	● FEEL THE NEED IN ME *Janus 6146 020*		4	15 wks
5 May 73	YOU WANT IT YOU GOT IT			
	Westbound 6146 103		12	9 wks
11 Aug 73	I THINK OF YOU *Westbound 6146 104*		27	9 wks
18 Jun 77	FEEL THE NEED IN ME *Atlantic K 10945*		12	11 wks

The second Feel The Need In Me was a re-recording.

DETROIT SPINNERS
US, male vocal group   *83 wks*

14 Nov 70	IT'S A SHAME *Tamla Motown TMG 755*		20	11 wks
21 Apr 73	COULD IT BE I'M FALLING IN LOVE			
	Atlantic K 10283		11	11 wks
29 Sep 73	● GHETTO CHILD *Atlantic K 10359*		7	10 wks
11 Sep 76	THE RUBBERBAND MAN *Atlantic K 10807* ...		16	11 wks
29 Jan 77	WAKE UP SUSAN *Atlantic K 10799*		29	6 wks
7 May 77	COULD IT BE I'M FALLING IN LOVE (EP)			
	Atlantic K 10935		32	3 wks
23 Feb 80	★ WORKING MY WAY BACK TO YOU			
	Atlantic K 11432		1	14 wks
10 May 80	BODY LANGUAGE *Atlantic K 11392*		40	7 wks
28 Jun 80	● CUPID – I'VE LOVED YOU FOR A LONG TIME			
	(MEDLEY) *Atlantic K 11498*		4	10 wks

See also Dionne Warwicke and the Detroit Spinners. Group is known simply as the Spinners in the US. On It's A Shame they were called the Motown Spinners in the UK. Tracks on Could It Be I'm Falling In Love EP: Could It Be I'm Falling In Love/You're Throwing A Good Love Away/Games People Play/ Lazy Susan.

DETROIT WHEELS – *See Mitch RYDER and the DETROIT WHEELS*

Sidney DEVINE *UK, male vocalist*   *1 wk*

1 Apr 78	SCOTLAND FOREVER *Philips SCOT 1*		48	1 wk

DEVO *US, male vocal/instrumental group*   *23 wks*

22 Apr 78	(I CAN'T ME GET NO) SATISFACTION			
	Stiff BOY 1		41	8 wks
13 May 78	JOCKO HOMO *Stiff DEV 1*		62	3 wks
12 Aug 78	BE STIFF *Stiff BOY 2*		71	1 wk
2 Sep 78	COME BACK JONEE *Virgin VS 223*		60	4 wks
22 Nov 80	WHIP IT *Virgin VS 383*		51	7 wks

DEVOTIONS – *See BELLE and the DEVOTIONS*

Howard DEVOTO – *See BUZZCOCKS*

DEXY'S MIDNIGHT RUNNERS
UK, male vocal/instrumental group   *83 wks*

19 Jan 80	DANCE STANCE *Oddball Productions R 6028*		40	6 wks
22 Mar 80	★ GENO *Late Night Feelings R 6033*		1	14 wks
12 July 80	● THERE THERE MY DEAR			
	Late Night Feelings R 6038		7	9 wks
21 Mar 81	PLAN B *Parlophone R 6046*		58	2 wks
11 Jul 81	SHOW ME *Mercury DEXYS 6*		16	9 wks
20 Mar 82	THE CELTIC SOUL BROTHERS			
	Mercury/Phonogram DEXYS 8		45	4 wks
3 Jul 82	★ COME ON EILEEN *Mercury/Phonogram DEXYS 9*		1	17 wks
2 Oct 82	● JACKIE WILSON SAID			
	Mercury/Phonogram DEXYS 10		5	7 wks
4 Dec 82	LET'S GET THIS STRAIGHT (FROM THE			
	START)/OLD *Mercury/Phonogram DEXYS 11* ...		17	9 wks

2 Apr 83 **THE CELTIC SOUL BROTHERS**
Mercury/Phonogram DEXYS 12 .... **20** 6 wks

The first entries of The Celtic Soul Brothers and Come On Eileen are credited to Dexy's Midnight Runners with the Emerald Express (female vocal/instrumental group). Jackie Wilson Said, Let's Get This Straight and the second-issue of The Celtic Soul Brothers are credited to Kevin Rowland and Dexy's Midnight Runners. DEXYS 12 is a different version from DEXYS 8.

Jim DIAMOND   UK, *male vocalist*   *9 wks*

3 Nov 84	★ I SHOULD HAVE KNOWN BETTER		
	A & M AM 220	**1†**	9 wks

Neil DIAMOND   US, *male vocalist*   *107 wks*

7 Nov 70	● CRACKLIN' ROSIE *Uni UN 529*	**3**	17 wks
20 Feb 71	● SWEET CAROLINE *Uni UN 531*	**8**	11 wks
8 May 71	● I AM . . . I SAID *Uni UN 532*	**4**	12 wks
13 May 72	SONG SUNG BLUE *Uni UN 538*	**14**	13 wks
14 Aug 76	IF YOU KNOW WHAT I MEAN *CBS 4398*	**35**	4 wks
23 Oct 76	BEAUTIFUL NOISE *CBS 4601*	**13**	9 wks
24 Dec 77	DESIREE *CBS 5869*	**39**	6 wks
3 Mar 79	FOREVER IN BLUE JEANS *CBS 7047*	**16**	12 wks
15 Nov 80	LOVE ON THE ROCKS *Capitol CL 16173*	**17**	12 wks
14 Feb 81	HELLO AGAIN *Capitol CL 16176*	**51**	4 wks
20 Nov 82	HEARTLIGHT *CBS A 2814*	**47**	7 wks

See also Barbra and Neil.

Gregg DIAMOND BIONIC BOOGIE
US, *male/female vocal group*   *3 wks*

20 Jan 79	CREAM (ALWAYS RISES TO THE TOP)		
	Polydor POSP 18	**61**	3 wks

DIAMOND HEAD
UK, *male vocal/instrumental group*   *2 wks*

11 Sep 82	IN THE HEAT OF THE NIGHT		
	MCA DHM 102	**67**	2 wks

DIAMONDS   Canada, *male vocal group*   *17 wks*

31 May 57	● LITTLE DARLIN' *Mercury MT 148*	**3**	17 wks

DICK and DEEDEE
US, *male/female vocal duo*   *3 wks*

26 Oct 61	THE MOUNTAIN'S HIGH *London HLG 9408* ...	**37**	3 wks

Charles DICKENS   UK, *male vocalist*   *8 wks*

1 Jul 65	THAT'S THE WAY LOVE GOES *Pye 7N 15887*	**37**	8 wks

Neville DICKIE
UK, *male instrumentalist - piano*   *10 wks*

25 Oct 69	ROBIN'S RETURN *Major Minor MM 644*	**33**	7 wks
20 Dec 69	ROBIN'S RETURN (re-entry)		
	Major Minor MM 644	**43**	3 wks

DICKIES   US, *male vocal/instrumental group*   *28 wks*

16 Dec 78	SILENT NIGHT *A & M AMS 7403*	**47**	4 wks
21 Apr 79	● BANANA SPLITS (TRA LA LA SONG)		
	A & M AMS 7431	**7**	8 wks

21 Jul 79	PARANOID *A & M AMS 7368*	**45**	6 wks
15 Sep 79	NIGHTS IN WHITE SATIN *A & M AMS 7469*	**39**	5 wks
16 Feb 80	FAN MAIL *A & M AMS 7504*	**57**	3 wks
19 Jul 80	GIGANTOR *A & M AMS 7544*	**72**	2 wks

Barbara DICKSON   UK, *female vocalist*   *33 wks*

17 Jan 76	● ANSWER ME *RSO 2090 174*	**9**	7 wks
26 Feb 77	ANOTHER SUITCASE IN ANOTHER HALL		
	MCA 266	**18**	7 wks
19 Jan 80	CARAVAN SONG *Epic EPC 8103*	**41**	7 wks
15 Mar 80	JANUARY FEBRUARY *Epic EPC 8115*	**11**	10 wks
14 Jun 80	IN THE NIGHT *Epic EPC 8593*	**48**	2 wks

DICTATORS
US, *male vocal/instrumental group*   *2 wks*

17 Sep 77	SEARCH AND DESTROY *Asylum K 13091*	**49**	1 wk
1 Oct 77	SEARCH AND DESTROY (re-entry)		
	Asylum K 13091	**50**	1 wk

Bo DIDDLEY
US, *male vocalist/instrumentalist - guitar*   *10 wks*

10 Oct 63	PRETTY THING *Pye International 7N 25217*	**34**	6 wks
18 Mar 65	HEY GOOD LOOKIN' *Chess 8000*	**39**	4 wks

DIFFORD and TILBROOK
UK, *male vocal/instrumental duo*   *2 wks*

30 Jun 84	LOVE'S CRASHING WAVES *A & M AM 193*	**57**	2 wks

Mark DINNING   US, *male vocalist*   *4 wks*

10 Mar 60	TEEN ANGEL *MGM 1053*	**37**	3 wks
7 Apr 60	TEEN ANGEL (re-entry) *MGM 1053*	**42**	1 wk

DINOSAURS - *See Terry DACTYL and the DINOSAURS*

DIO   UK/US, *male vocal/instrumental group*   *12 wks*

20 Aug 83	HOLY DIVER *Vertigo/Phonogram DIO 1*	**72**	2 wks
29 Oct 83	RAINBOW IN THE DARK		
	Vertigo/Phonogram DIO 2	**46**	3 wks
11 Aug 84	WE ROCK *Vertigo/Phonogram DIO 3* ....,.....	**42**	3 wks
29 Sep 84	MYSTERY *Vertigo/Phonogram DIO 4*	**34**	4 wks

DION   US, *male vocalist*   *31 wks*

19 Jan 61	LONELY TEENAGER *Top Rank JAR 521*	**47**	1 wk
2 Nov 61	RUNAROUND SUE *Top Rank JAR 586*	**11**	9 wks
15 Feb 62	● THE WANDERER *HMV POP 971*	**10**	12 wks
22 May 76	THE WANDERER (re-issue) *Philips 6146 700*	**16**	9 wks

See also Dion and the Belmonts.

DION and the BELMONTS
US, *male vocal group*   *2 wks*

26 Jun 59	A TEENAGER IN LOVE *London HLU 8874*	**28**	2 wks

See also Dion.

DIPSTICKS - *See Laurie LINGO and the DIPSTICKS*

DIRE STRAITS
UK, male vocal/instrumental group   *54 wks*

10 Mar 79	● SULTANS OF SWING *Vertigo 6059 206*	8	11 wks
28 Jul 79	LADY WRITER *Vertigo 6059 230*	51	6 wks
17 Jan 81	● ROMEO AND JULIET *Vertigo MOVIE 1*	8	11 wks
4 Apr 81	SKATEAWAY *Vertigo MOVIE 2*	37	5 wks
10 Oct 81	TUNNEL OF LOVE *Vertigo MUSIC 3*	54	3 wks
4 Sep 82	● PRIVATE INVESTIGATIONS *Vertigo/Phonogram DSTR 1*	2	8 wks
22 Jan 83	TWISTING BY THE POOL *Vertigo/Phonogram DSTR 2*	14	7 wks
18 Feb 84	LOVE OVER GOLD (LIVE) /SOLID ROCK (LIVE) *Vertigo/Phonogram DSTR A12*	50	3 wks

DISCHARGE
UK, male vocal/instrumental group   *3 wks*

24 Oct 81	NEVER AGAIN *Clay CLAY 6*	64	3 wks

DISCO TEX and the SEX-O-LETTES
US, male vocalist/female vocal group   *22 wks*

23 Nov 74	● GET DANCING *Chelsea 2005 013*	8	12 wks
26 Apr 75	● I WANNA DANCE WIT CHOO *Chelsea 2005 024*	6	10 wks

Second hit has credit 'featuring Sir Monti Rock III' – the lead vocalist.

Sacha DISTEL   *France, male vocalist*   *27 wks*

10 Jan 70	RAINDROPS KEEP FALLING ON MY HEAD *Warner Bros. WB 7345*	50	1 wk
24 Jan 70	● RAINDROPS KEEP FALLING ON MY HEAD (re-entry) *Warner Bros. WB 7345*	10	20 wks
27 Jun 70	RAINDROPS KEEP FALLING ON MY HEAD (2nd re-entry) *Warner Bros. WB 7345*	43	4 wks
1 Aug 70	RAINDROPS KEEP FALLING ON MY HEAD (3rd re-entry) *Warner Bros. WB 7345*	47	1 wk
15 Aug 70	RAINDROPS KEEP FALLING ON MY HEAD (4th re-entry) *Warner Bros. WB 7345*	44	1 wk

DIVERSIONS
UK, male/female vocal/instrumental group   *3 wks*

20 Sep 75	FATTIE BUM BUM *Gull GULS 18*	34	3 wks

DIVINE   *US, male vocalist*   *14 wks*

15 Oct 83	LOVE REACTION *Design Communications DES 4*	65	2 wks
14 Jul 84	YOU THINK YOU'RE A MAN *Proto ENA 118*	16	10 wks
20 Oct 84	I'M SO BEAUTIFUL *Proto ENA 121*	52	2 wks

DIXIE CUPS   *US, female vocal group*   *16 wks*

18 Jun 64	CHAPEL OF LOVE *Pye International 7N 25245* ..	22	8 wks
13 May 65	IKO IKO *Red Bird RB 10024*	23	8 wks

DIZZY HEIGHTS
UK, male vocal/instrumental group   *4 wks*

18 Dec 82	CHRISTMAS RAPPING *Polydor WRAP 1*	49	4 wks

Carl DOBKINS JR.   *US, male vocalist*   *1 wk*

31 Mar 60	LUCKY DEVIL *Brunswick 05817*	44	1 wk

DR. FEELGOOD
UK, male vocal/instrumental group   *29 wks*

11 Jun 77	SNEAKIN' SUSPICION *United Artists UP 36255*	47	3 wks
24 Sep 77	SHE'S A WIND UP *United Artists UP 36304*	34	5 wks
30 Sep 78	DOWN AT THE DOCTOR'S *United Artists UP 36444*	48	5 wks
20 Jan 79	● MILK AND ALCOHOL *United Artists UP 36468*	9	9 wks
5 May 79	AS LONG AS THE PRICE IS RIGHT *United Artists YUP 36506*	40	6 wks
8 Dec 79	PUT HIM OUT OF YOUR MIND *United Artists BP 306*	73	1 wk

DR. HOOK
US, male vocal/instrumental group   *96 wks*

24 Jun 72	● SYLVIA'S MOTHER *CBS 7929*	2	13 wks
26 Jun 76	● A LITTLE BIT MORE *Capitol CL 15871* ...	2	14 wks
30 Oct 76	● IF NOT YOU *Capitol CL 15885*	5	10 wks
25 Mar 78	MORE LIKE THE MOVIES *Capitol CL 15967*	14	10 wks
22 Sep 79	★ WHEN YOU'RE IN LOVE WITH A BEAUTIFUL WOMAN *Capitol CL 16039*	1	17 wks
5 Jan 80	● BETTER LOVE NEXT TIME *Capitol CL 16112*	8	8 wks
29 Mar 80	● SEXY EYES *Capitol CL 16127*	4	9 wks
23 Aug 80	YEARS FROM NOW *Capitol CL 16154*	47	6 wks
8 Nov 80	SHARING THE NIGHT TOGETHER *Capitol CL 16171*	43	4 wks
22 Nov 80	GIRLS CAN GET IT *Mercury MER 51*	40	5 wks

Group billed as Dr. Hook And The Medicine Show on CBS.

Ken DODD   *UK, male vocalist*   *233 wks*

7 Jul 60	● LOVE IS LIKE A VIOLIN *Decca F 11248*	8	18 wks
15 Jun 61	ONCE IN EVERY LIFETIME *Decca F 11355* ...	28	7 wks
10 Aug 61	ONCE IN EVERY LIFETIME (re-entry) *Decca F 11355*	47	1 wk
24 Aug 61	ONCE IN EVERY LIFETIME (2nd re-entry) *Decca F 11355*	31	10 wks
1 Feb 62	PIANISSIMO *Decca F 11422*	21	15 wks
29 Aug 63	STILL *Columbia DB 7094*	35	10 wks
6 Feb 64	EIGHT BY TEN *Columbia DB 7191*	22	11 wks
23 Jul 64	HAPPINESS *Columbia DB 7325*	31	13 wks
26 Nov 64	SO DEEP IS THE NIGHT *Columbia DB 7398* ...	31	7 wks
2 Sep 65	★ TEARS *Columbia DB 7659*	1	24 wks
18 Nov 65	● THE RIVER (LE COLLINE SONO IN FIORO) *Columbia DB 7750*	3	14 wks
12 May 66	● PROMISES *Columbia DB 7914*	6	14 wks
4 Aug 66	MORE THAN LOVE *Columbia DB 7976*	14	11 wks
27 Oct 66	IT'S LOVE *Columbia DB 8031*	36	7 wks
19 Jan 67	LET ME CRY ON YOUR SHOULDER *Columbia DB 8101*	11	10 wks
30 Jul 69	TEARS WON'T WASH AWAY MY HEARTACHE *Columbia DB 8600*	22	11 wks
5 Dec 70	BROKEN HEARTED *Columbia DB 8725*	15	9 wks
13 Feb 71	BROKEN HEARTED (re-entry) *Columbia DB 8725*	38	1 wk
10 Jul 71	WHEN LOVE COMES ROUND AGAIN (L'ARCA DI NOE) *Columbia DB 8796*	19	16 wks
18 Nov 72	JUST OUT OF REACH (OF MY TWO EMPTY ARMS) *Columbia DB 8947*	29	11 wks
29 Nov 75	(THINK OF ME) WHEREVER YOU ARE *EMI 2342*	21	8 wks
26 Dec 81	HOLD MY HAND *Images IMGS 0002*	44	5 wks

Joe DOLAN   *Ireland, male vocalist*   *40 wks*

25 Jun 69	● MAKE ME AN ISLAND *Pye 7N 17731*	3	18 wks
1 Nov 69	TERESA *Pye 7N 17833*	20	7 wks
8 Nov 69	MAKE ME AN ISLAND (re-entry) *Pye 7N 17731*	48	1 wk
28 Feb 70	YOU'RE SUCH A GOOD LOOKING WOMAN *Pye 7N 17891*	17	13 wks
17 Sep 77	I NEED YOU *Pye 7N 45702*	43	1 wk

DAVID ESSEX Not only a consistent hitmaker but stage star via *Godspell*, *Byron* and *Evita*, screen star via *That'll Be The Day*, *Stardust* and *Silver Dream Racer*.

SHIRLEY ELLIS Her husband Lincoln Chase composed her three best-known songs – 'The Name Game', 'The Clapping Song' and 'The Nitty Gritty'.

FABIAN Hound dog man with the Elvis looks.

EURYTHMICS Here come The Tourists again. (Photo: Gary Gershoff, Retna Pictures.)

Thomas DOLBY

UK, male vocalist/instrumentalist - computers 33 wks

3 Oct 81	**EUROPA AND THE PIRATE TWINS** *Parlophone R 6051*	48	3 wks
14 Aug 82	**WINDPOWER** *Venice In Peril VIPS 103*	31	8 wks
6 Nov 82	**SHE BLINDED ME WITH SCIENCE** *Venice In Peril VIPS 104*	49	4 wks
16 Jul 83	**SHE BLINDED ME WITH SCIENCE** (re-issue) *Venice In Peril VIP 105*	56	4 wks
21 Jan 84	**HYPERACTIVE** *Parlophone ODEON R 6065*	17	9 wks
31 Mar 84	**I SCARE MYSELF** *Parlophone ODEON R 6067*	46	5 wks

Joe DOLCE MUSIC THEATRE

US, male vocalist 10 wks

7 Feb 81	★ **SHADDAP YOU FACE** *Epic EPC 9518*	1	10 wks

DOLL

UK, male/female vocal/instrumental group 8 wks

13 Jan 79	**DESIRE ME** *Beggars Banquet BEG 11*	28	8 wks

DOLLAR *UK, male/female vocal duo* 110 wks

11 Nov 78	**SHOOTING STAR** *EMI 2871*	14	12 wks
19 May 79	**WHO WERE YOU WITH IN THE MOONLIGHT** *Carrere CAR 110*	14	12 wks
18 Aug 79 ●	**LOVE'S GOTTA HOLD ON ME** *Carrere CAR 122*	4	13 wks
24 Nov 79 ●	**I WANNA HOLD YOUR HAND** *Carrere CAR 131*	9	14 wks
25 Oct 80	**TAKIN' A CHANCE ON YOU** *WEA K 18353*	62	3 wks
15 Aug 81	**HAND HELD IN BLACK AND WHITE** *WEA BUCK 1*	19	12 wks
14 Nov 81 ●	**MIRROR MIRROR (MON AMOUR)** *WEA BUCK 2*	4	17 wks
20 Mar 82	**RING RING** *Carrere CAR 225*	61	2 wks
27 Mar 82 ●	**GIVE ME BACK MY HEART** *WEA BUCK 3*	4	9 wks
19 Jun 82	**VIDEOTHEQUE** *WEA BUCK 4*	17	10 wks
18 Sep 82	**GIVE ME SOME KINDA MAGIC** *WEA BUCK 5*	34	6 wks

Placido DOMINGO with John DENVER *Spain, male vocalist with US, male vocalist/instrumentalist - guitar* 9 wks

12 Dec 81	**PERHAPS LOVE** *CBS A 1905*	46	9 wks

See also John Denver.

Fats DOMINO

US, male vocalist/instrumentalist, piano 110 wks

27 Jul 56	**I'M IN LOVE AGAIN** *London HLU 8280*	28	1 wk
17 Aug 56	**I'M IN LOVE AGAIN** (re-entry) *London HLU 8280*	12	13 wks
30 Nov 56	**BLUEBERRY HILL** *London HLU 8330*	26	1 wk
21 Dec 56 ●	**BLUEBERRY HILL** (re-entry) *London HLU 8330*	6	14 wks
25 Jan 57	**AIN'T THAT A SHAME** *London HLU 8173*	23	2 wks
1 Feb 57	**HONEY CHILE** *London HLU 8356*	29	1 wk
29 Mar 57	**BLUE MONDAY** *London HLP 8377*	23	1 wk
19 Apr 57	**BLUE MONDAY** (re-entry) *London HLP 8377*	30	1 wk
19 Apr 57	**I'M WALKIN'** *London HLP 8407*	19	7 wks
21 Jul 57	**VALLEY OF TEARS** *London HLP 8449*	25	1 wk
28 Mar 58	**THE BIG BEAT** *London HLP 8575*	20	4 wks
4 Jul 58	**SICK AND TIRED** *London HLP 8628*	26	1 wk
22 May 59	**MARGIE** *London HLP 8865*	18	5 wks
16 Oct 59	**I WANT TO WALK YOU HOME** *London HLP 8942*	14	5 wks
18 Dec 59	**BE MY GUEST** *London HLP 9005*	11	8 wks
19 Feb 60	**BE MY GUEST** (re-entry) *London HLP 9005*	19	4 wks
17 Mar 60	**COUNTRY BOY** *London HLP 9073*	19	11 wks
21 Jul 60	**WALKING TO NEW ORLEANS** *London HLP 9163*	19	10 wks
10 Nov 60	**THREE NIGHTS A WEEK** *London HLP 9198*	45	2 wks
5 Jan 61	**MY GIRL JOSEPHINE** *London HLP 9244*	32	3 wks
27 Jul 61	**IT KEEPS RAININ'** *London HLP 9374*	49	1 wk
30 Nov 61	**WHAT A PARTY** *London HLP 9456*	43	1 wk
29 Mar 62	**JAMBALAYA** *London HLP 9520*	41	1 wk
31 Oct 63	**RED SAILS IN THE SUNSET** *HMV POP 1219*	34	6 wks
24 Apr 76	**BLUEBERRY HILL** (re-issue) *United Artists UP 35797*	41	5 wks

DOMINOS - *See DEREK and the DOMINOS*

Lonnie DONEGAN *UK, male vocalist* 321 wks

6 Jan 56 ●	**ROCK ISLAND LINE** *Decca F 10647*	8	13 wks
13 Apr 56	**ROCK ISLAND LINE** (re-entry) *Decca F 10647*	16	3 wks
20 Apr 56	**STEWBALL** *Pye Nixa N 15036*	27	1 wk
27 Apr 56	**LOST JOHN/STEWBALL** *Pye Nixa N 15036*	2	17 wks
11 May 56	**ROCK ISLAND LINE** (2nd re-entry) *Decca F 10647*	19	6 wks
6 Jul 56	**SKIFFLE SESSION** (EP) *Pye Nixa NJE 1017*	20	2 wks
7 Sep 56 ●	**BRING A LITTLE WATER SYLVIE/DEAD OR ALIVE** *Pye Nixa N 15071*	7	12 wks
21 Dec 56	**LONNIE DONEGAN SHOWCASE** (LP) *Pye Nixa NPT 19012*	26	3 wks
11 Jan 57	**BRING A LITTLE WATER SYLVIE/DEAD OR ALIVE** (re-entry) *Pye Nixa N 15071*	30	1 wk
18 Jan 57 ●	**DON'T YOU ROCK ME DADDY-O** *Pye Nixa N 15080*	4	17 wks
5 Apr 57 ★	**CUMBERLAND GAP** *Pye Nixa B 15087*	1	12 wks
7 Jun 57 ★	**GAMBLIN' MAN/PUTTING ON THE STYLE** *Pye Nixa N 15093*	1	19 wks
11 Oct 57 ●	**MY DIXIE DARLING** *Pye Nixa N 15108*	10	15 wks
20 Dec 57	**JACK O' DIAMONDS** *Pye Nixa N 15116*	14	7 wks
11 Apr 58 ●	**GRAND COOLIE DAM** *Pye Nixa N 15129*	6	15 wks
11 Jul 58	**SALLY DON'T YOU GRIEVE/BETTY BETTY BETTY** *Pye Nixa N 15148*	11	7 wks
26 Sep 58	**LONESOME TRAVELLER** *Pye Nixa N 15158*	28	1 wk
14 Nov 58	**LONNIE'S SKIFFLE PARTY** *Pye Nixa N 15165*	23	5 wks
21 Nov 58 ●	**TOM DOOLEY** *Pye Nixa 7N 15172*	3	14 wks
6 Feb 59 ●	**DOES YOUR CHEWING GUM LOSE ITS FLAVOUR** *Pye Nixa 7N 15181*	3	12 wks
8 May 59	**FORT WORTH JAIL** *Pye Nixa 7N 15198*	14	5 wks
26 Jun 59 ●	**BATTLE OF NEW ORLEANS** *Pye 7N 15206*	2	16 wks
11 Sep 59	**SAL'S GOT A SUGAR LIP** *Pye 7N 15223*	13	4 wks
4 Dec 59	**SAN MIGUEL** *Pye 7N 15237*	19	4 wks
24 Mar 60 ★	**MY OLD MAN'S A DUSTMAN** *Pye 7N 15256*	1	13 wks
26 May 60	**I WANNA GO HOME** *Pye 7N 15267*	5	17 wks
25 Aug 60 ●	**LORELEI** *Pye 7N 15275*	10	8 wks
24 Nov 60	**LIVELY** *Pye 7N 15312*	13	9 wks
8 Dec 60	**VIRGIN MARY** *Pye 7N 15315*	27	5 wks
11 May 61 ●	**HAVE A DRINK ON ME** *Pye 7N 15354*	8	15 wks
31 Aug 61 ●	**MICHAEL ROW THE BOAT/LUMBERED** *Pye 7N 15371*	6	11 wks
18 Jan 62	**THE COMANCHEROS** *Pye 7N 15410*	14	10 wks
5 Apr 62 ●	**THE PARTY'S OVER** *Pye 7N 15424*	9	12 wks
16 Aug 62	**PICK A BALE OF COTTON** *Pye 7N 15455*	11	10 wks

Stewball had one week on the chart by itself on 20 Apr 56. Lost John, the other side, replaced it on 27 Apr 56 but Stewball was given co-billing with Lost John for the weeks of 11, 18 and 25 May only, during Lost John's 17-week run. Dead Or Alive was not listed for the week 7 Sep 56 with Bring A Little Water Sylvie. Putting On The Style was not listed for the weeks of 7 and 14 June 56 with Gamblin' Man. Tracks on Skiffle Session EP: Railroad Bill/Stackalee/Ballad of Jesse James/Ol' Riley. Tracks on Lonnie Donegan Showcase LP: Wabash Cannonball/How Long How Long Blues/Nobody's Child/I Shall Not Be Moved/I'm Alabammy Bound/I'm A Rambling Man/Wreck Of The Old '97/Frankie And Johnny. Lonnie's Skiffle Party was a medley as follows: Little Liza Jane/Putting' On The Style/Camptown Races/Knees Up Mother Brown/So Long/On Top Of Old Smokey/Down In The Valley/So Long. Yes, there are two versions of So Long on this disc.

DONNA - *See ALTHIA and DONNA*

Ral DONNER *US, male vocalist* *10 wks*

21 Sep 61	**YOU DON'T KNOW WHAT YOU'VE GOT**			
	Parlophone R 4820	**25**	10 wks

DONOVAN *UK, male vocalist* *90 wks*

25 Mar 65	● **CATCH THE WIND** *Pye 7N 15801*	**4**	13 wks
3 Jun 65	● **COLOURS** *Pye 7N 15866*	**4**	12 wks
11 Nov 65	**TURQUOISE** *Pye 7N 15984*	**30**	6 wks
8 Dec 66	● **SUNSHINE SUPERMAN** *Pye 7N 17241*	**3**	11 wks
9 Feb 67	● **MELLOW YELLOW** *Pye 7N 17267*	**8**	8 wks
25 Oct 67	● **THERE IS A MOUNTAIN** *Pye 7N 17403* . . .	**8**	11 wks
21 Feb 68	● **JENNIFER JUNIPER** *Pye 7N 17457*	**5**	11 wks
29 May 68	● **HURDY GURDY MAN** *Pye 7N 17537* . . .	**4**	10 wks
4 Dec 68	**ATLANTIS** *Pye 7N 17660*	**23**	8 wks

See also Donovan with The Jeff Beck Group.

DONOVAN with the Jeff BECK GROUP *UK, male vocalist/instrumental group* *9 wks*

9 Jul 69	**GOO GOO BARABAJAGAL (LOVE IS HOT)**			
	Pye 7N 17778	**12**	9 wks

See also Donovan; Jeff Beck; Jeff Beck and Rod Stewart.

DOOBIE BROTHERS
US, male vocal/instrumental group *27 wks*

9 Mar 74	**LISTEN TO THE MUSIC** *Warner Bros. K 16208*	**29**	7 wks
7 Jun 75	**TAKE ME IN YOUR ARMS**			
	Warner Bros. K 16559	**29**	5 wks
17 Feb 79	**WHAT A FOOL BELIEVES**			
	Warner Bros. K 17314	**31**	10 wks
5 May 79	**WHAT A FOOL BELIEVES** (re-entry)			
	Warner Bros. K 17314	**72**	1 wk
14 Jul 79	**MINUTE BY MINUTE** *Warner Bros. K 17411* . . .	**47**	4 wks

---

DOOLEYS
UK, male/female vocal/instrumental group *83 wks*

13 Aug 77	**THINK I'M GONNA FALL IN LOVE WITH YOU**			
	GTO GT 95	**13**	10 wks
12 Nov 77	● **LOVE OF MY LIFE** *GTO GT 110*	**9**	11 wks
13 May 78	**DON'T TAKE IT LYIN' DOWN** *GTO GT 220*	**60**	3 wks
2 Sep 78	**A ROSE HAS TO DIE** *GTO GT 229* . . .	**11**	11 wks
10 Feb 79	**HONEY I'M LOST** *GTO GT 242*	**24**	9 wks
16 Jun 79	● **WANTED** *GTO GT 249*	**3**	14 wks
22 Sep 79	● **THE CHOSEN FEW** *GTO GT 258* . . .	**7**	11 wks
8 Mar 80	**LOVE PATROL** *GTO GT 260*	**29**	7 wks
6 Sep 80	**BODY LANGUAGE** *GTO GT 276*	**46**	4 wks
10 Oct 81	**AND I WISH** *GTO GT 300*	**52**	3 wks

---

Val DOONICAN *Ireland, male vocalist* *143 wks*

15 Oct 64	● **WALK TALL** *Decca F 11982*	**3**	21 wks
21 Jan 65	● **THE SPECIAL YEARS** *Decca F 12049*	**7**	12 wks
8 Apr 65	**I'M GONNA GET THERE SOMEHOW**			
	Decca F 12118	**25**	5 wks
22 Apr 65	**THE SPECIAL YEARS** (re-entry) *Decca F 12049*	**49**	1 wk
17 Mar 66	● **ELUSIVE BUTTERFLY** *Decca F 12358* . .	**5**	12 wks
3 Nov 66	● **WHAT WOULD I BE** *Decca F 12505* . . .	**2**	17 wks
23 Feb 67	**MEMORIES ARE MADE OF THIS** *Decca F 12566*	**11**	12 wks
25 May 67	**TWO STREETS** *Decca F 12608*	**39**	4 wks
18 Oct 67	● **IF THE WHOLE WORLD STOPPED LOVING**			
	Pye 7N 17396	**3**	19 wks
21 Feb 68	**YOU'RE THE ONLY ONE** *Pye 7N 17465*	**37**	4 wks

---

12 Jun 68	**NOW** *Pye 7N 17534*	**43**	2 wks
23 Oct 68	**IF I KNEW THEN WHAT I KNOW NOW**			
	Pye 7N 17616	**14**	13 wks
23 Apr 69	**RING OF BRIGHT WATER** *Pye 7N 17713*	**48**	1 wk
4 Dec 71	**MORNING** *Philips 6006 177*	**12**	13 wks
10 Mar 73	**HEAVEN IS MY WOMAN'S LOVE**			
	Philips 6028 031	**34**	6 wks
28 Apr 73	**HEAVEN IS MY WOMAN'S LOVE** (re-entry)			
	Philips 6028 031	**47**	1 wk

DOORS *US, male vocal/instrumental group* *31 wks*

16 Aug 67	**LIGHT MY FIRE** *Elektra EKSN 45014*	**49**	1 wk
28 Aug 68	**HELLO I LOVE YOU** *Elektra EKSN 45037* . . .	**15**	12 wks
16 Oct 71	**RIDERS ON THE STORM** *Elektra K 12021*	**50**	1 wk
30 Oct 71	**RIDERS ON THE STORM** (re-entry)			
	Elektra K 12021	**22**	10 wks
20 Mar 76	**RIDERS ON THE STORM** (re-issue)			
	Elektra K 12203	**33**	5 wks
3 Feb 79	**HELLO I LOVE YOU** (re-issue) *Elektra K 12215*	**71**	2 wks

---

Charlie DORE *UK, female vocalist* *2 wks*

17 Nov 79	**PILOT OF THE AIRWAVES** *Island WIP 6526* . .	**66**	2 wks

---

Lee DORSEY *US, male vocalist* *36 wks*

3 Feb 66	**GET OUT OF MY LIFE WOMAN**			
	Stateside SS 485	**22**	7 wks
5 May 66	**CONFUSION** *Stateside SS 506*	**38**	6 wks
11 Aug 66	● **WORKING IN THE COALMINE** *Stateside SS 528*	**8**	11 wks
27 Oct 66	● **HOLY COW** *Stateside SS 552*	**6**	12 wks

---

Tommy DORSEY ORCHESTRA starring Warren COVINGTON
US, orchestra, Warren Covington, male, leader *19 wks*

17 Oct 58	● **TEA FOR TWO CHA CHA** *Brunswick 05757*	**3**	19 wks

---

Carl DOUGLAS *UK, male vocalist* *28 wks*

17 Aug 74	★ **KUNG FU FIGHTING** *Pye 7N 45377*	**1**	13 wks
30 Nov 74	**DANCE THE KUNG FU** *Pye 7N 45418*	**35**	5 wks
3 Dec 77	**RUN BACK** *Pye 7N 46018*	**25**	10 wks

---

Carol DOUGLAS *US, female vocalist* *4 wks*

22 Jul 78	**NIGHT FEVER** *Gull GULS 61*	**66**	4 wks

---

Craig DOUGLAS *UK, male vocalist* *112 wks*

12 Jun 59	**A TEENAGER IN LOVE** *Top Rank JAR 133* . . .	**13**	11 wks
7 Aug 59	★ **ONLY SIXTEEN** *Top Rank JAR 159*	**1**	15 wks
22 Jan 60	● **PRETTY BLUE EYES** *Top Rank JAR 268*	**4**	14 wks
28 Apr 60	● **THE HEART OF A TEENAGE GIRL**			
	Top Rank JAR 340	**10**	9 wks
11 Aug 60	**OH! WHAT A DAY** *Top Rank JAR 406* . . .	**43**	1 wk
20 Apr 61	● **A HUNDRED POUNDS OF CLAY**			
	Top Rank JAR 555	**9**	9 wks
29 Jun 61	● **TIME** *Top Rank JAR 569*	**9**	14 wks
22 Mar 62	● **WHEN MY LITTLE GIRL IS SMILING**			
	Top Rank JAR 610	**9**	13 wks
28 Jun 62	● **OUR FAVOURITE MELODIES**			
	Columbia DB 4854	**9**	10 wks
18 Oct 62	**OH LONESOME ME** *Decca F 11523*	**15**	12 wks
28 Feb 63	**TOWN CRIER** *Decca F 11575*	**36**	4 wks

DOWLANDS *UK, male vocal duo*   *7 wks*

9 Jan 64	**ALL MY LOVING** *Oriole CB 1897*	33	7 wks

Don DOWNING *US, male vocalist*   *10 wks*

10 Nov 73	**LONELY DAYS, LONELY NIGHTS** *People PEO 102*	32	10 wks

Lamont DOZIER - *See HOLLAND-DOZIER*

DOZY - *See Dave DEE, DOZY, BEAKY, MICK and TICH*

Charlie DRAKE *UK, male vocalist*   *37 wks*

8 Aug 58 ●	**SPLISH SPLASH** *Parlophone R 4461*	7	11 wks
24 Oct 58	**VOLARE** *Parlophone R 4478*	28	2 wks
27 Oct 60	**MR. CUSTER** *Parlophone R 4699*	12	12 wks
5 Oct 61	**MY BOOMERANG WON'T COME BACK** *Parlophone R 4824*	14	11 wks
1 Jan 72	**PUCKWUDGIE** *Columbia DB 8829*	47	1 wk

DRAMATIS
UK, male vocal/instrumental group   *1 wk*

13 Nov 82	**I CAN SEE HER NOW** *Rocket/Phonogram XPRES 83*	57	1 wk

See also Gary Numan.

Rusty DRAPER *US, male vocalist*   *4 wks*

11 Aug 60	**MULE SKINNER BLUES** *Mercury AMT 1101* ...	39	4 wks

DREAMERS - *See FREDDIE and the DREAMERS*

DREAMWEAVERS
US, male/female vocal group   *18 wks*

10 Feb 56 ★	**IT'S ALMOST TOMORROW** *Brunswick 05515* ...	1	18 wks

DRELLS - *See Archie BELL and the DRELLS*

Eddie DRENNON and B. B. S. UNLIMITED
US, male vocal/instrumental group   *6 wks*

28 Feb 76	**LET'S DO THE LATIN HUSTLE** *Pye International 7N 25702*	20	6 wks

Alan DREW *UK, male vocalist*   *2 wks*

26 Sep 63	**ALWAYS THE LONELY ONE** *Columbia DB 7090*	48	2 wks

DRIFTERS *US, male vocal group*   *176 wks*

8 Jan 60	**DANCE WITH ME** *London HLE 8988*	17	4 wks
10 Mar 60	**DANCE WITH ME** (re-entry) *London HLE 8988* ..	35	1 wk
3 Nov 60 ●	**SAVE THE LAST DANCE FOR ME** *London HLK 9201*	2	18 wks
16 Mar 61	**I COUNT THE TEARS** *London HLK 9287*	28	6 wks
5 Apr 62	**WHEN MY LITTLE GIRL IS SMILING** *London HLK 9522*	31	3 wks
10 Oct 63	**I'LL TAKE YOU HOME** *London HLK 9785*	37	5 wks
24 Sep 64	**UNDER THE BOARDWALK** *Atlantic AT 4001*	45	4 wks
8 Apr 65	**AT THE CLUB** *Atlantic AT 4019*	35	7 wks
29 Apr 65	**COME ON OVER TO MY PLACE** *Atlantic AT 4023*	40	5 wks
2 Feb 67	**BABY WHAT I MEAN** *Atlantic 584 065*	49	1 wk
25 Mar 72	**AT THE CLUB** (re-issue) *Atlantic K 10148*	39	1 wk
8 Apr 72 ●	**AT THE CLUB/SATURDAY NIGHT AT THE MOVIES** (re-entry of re-issue) *Atlantic K 10148*	3	19 wks
26 Aug 72 ●	**COME ON OVER TO MY PLACE** (re-issue) *Atlantic K 10216*	9	11 wks
4 Aug 73 ●	**LIKE SISTER AND BROTHER** *Bell 1313*	7	12 wks
15 Jun 74 ●	**KISSIN' IN THE BACK ROW OF THE MOVIES** *Bell 1358*	2	13 wks
12 Oct 74 ●	**DOWN ON THE BEACH TONIGHT** *Bell 1381*	7	9 wks
8 Feb 75	**LOVE GAMES** *Bell 1396*	33	6 wks
6 Sep 75 ●	**THERE GOES MY FIRST LOVE** *Bell 1433* ...	3	12 wks
29 Nov 75	**CAN I TAKE YOU HOME LITTLE GIRL** *Bell 1462*	10	10 wks
13 Mar 76	**HELLO HAPPINESS** *Bell 1469*	12	8 wks
11 Sep 76	**EVERY NITE'S A SATURDAY NIGHT WITH YOU** *Bell 1491*	29	7 wks
18 Dec 76 ●	**YOU'RE MORE THAN A NUMBER IN MY LITTLE RED BOOK** *Arista 78*	5	12 wks
14 Apr 79	**SAVE THE LAST DANCE FOR ME/WHEN MY LITTLE GIRL IS SMILING** (re-issue) *Lightning LIG 9014*	69	2 wks

Saturday Night At The Movies only received chart credit with At The Club after the re-issue's return to the chart on 8 Apr 72.

Julie DRISCOLL, Brian AUGER and the TRINITY
UK, female vocalist/male instrumental group   *16 wks*

17 Apr 68 ●	**THIS WHEEL'S ON FIRE** *Marmalade 598 006* ...	5	16 wks

DRIVER 67 *UK, male vocalist*   *12 wks*

23 Dec 78 ●	**CAR 67** *Logo GO 336*	7	12 wks

Driver 67 is Paul Phillips.

Frank D'RONE *US, male vocalist*   *6 wks*

22 Dec 60	**STRAWBERRY BLONDE** *Mercury AMT 1123* ..	24	6 wks

DRUPI *Italy, male vocalist*   *12 wks*

1 Dec 73	**VADO VIA** *A & M AMS 7083*	17	12 wks

John DU CANN *UK, male vocalist*   *6 wks*

22 Sep 79	**DON'T BE A DUMMY** *Vertigo 6059 241*	33	6 wks

DUBLINERS
Ireland, male vocal/instrumental group   *35 wks*

30 Mar 67 ●	**SEVEN DRUNKEN NIGHTS** *Major Minor MM 506*	7	17 wks
30 Aug 67	**BLACK VELVET BAND** *Major Minor MM 530*	15	15 wks
20 Dec 67	**NEVER WED AN OLD MAN** *Major Minor MM 551*	43	3 wks

DUFFO *Australia, male vocalist*   *2 wks*

24 Mar 79	**GIVE ME BACK ME BRAIN** *Beggars Banquet BEG 15*	60	2 wks

George DUKE
US, male vocal/instrumentalist   *6 wks*

| 12 Jul 80 | **BRAZILIAN LOVE AFFAIR** | *Epic EPC 8751* | .... | **36** | 6 wks |

DUKES *UK, male vocal duo*   *13 wks*

| 17 Oct 81 | **MYSTERY GIRL** | *WEA K 18867* | .... | **47** | 7 wks |
| 1 May 82 | **THANK YOU FOR THE PARTY** | *WEA K 19136* | | **53** | 6 wks |

John DUMMER and Helen APRIL
UK, male/female vocal duo   *3 wks*

| 28 Aug 82 | **BLUE SKIES** | *Speed SPEED 8* | .... | **54** | 3 wks |

Johnny DUNCAN and the BLUE GRASS BOYS
US, male vocal/instrumental group   *20 wks*

26 Jul 57	● **LAST TRAIN TO SAN FERNANDO**				
	Columbia DB 3959	....	**2**	17 wks
25 Oct 57	**BLUE BLUE HEARTACHES**	*Columbia DB 3996*	**27**	1 wk
29 Nov 57	**FOOTPRINTS IN THE SNOW**	*Columbia DB 4029*	**27**	1 wk
3 Jan 58	**FOOTPRINTS IN THE SNOW**	(re-entry)		
	Columbia DB 4029	....	**28**	1 wk

David DUNDAS *UK, male vocalist*   *14 wks*

24 Jul 76	● **JEANS ON**	*Air CHS 2094*	....	**3**	9 wks
9 Apr 77	**ANOTHER FUNNY HONEYMOON**				
	Air CHS 2136	....	**29**	5 wks

Erroll DUNKLEY *Jamaica, male vocalist*   *14 wks*

| 22 Sep 79 | **O.K. FRED** | *Scope SC 6* | .... | **11** | 11 wks |
| 2 Feb 80 | **SIT DOWN AND CRY** | *Scope SC 11* | | **52** | 3 wks |

Clive DUNN *UK, male vocalist*   *28 wks*

| 28 Nov 70 | ★ **GRANDAD** | *Columbia DB 8726* | .... | **1** | 27 wks |
| 26 Jun 71 | **GRANDAD** | (re-entry) *Columbia D8 8726* | .... | **50** | 1 wk |

Simon DUPREE and The BIG SOUND
UK, male vocal/instrumental group   *16 wks*

22 Nov 67	● **KITES**	*Parlophone R 5646*	....	**9**	13 wks
3 Apr 68	**FOR WHOM THE BELL TOLLS**				
	Parlophone R 5670	....	**43**	3 wks

DURAN DURAN
UK, male vocal/instrumental group   *122 wks*

21 Feb 81	**PLANET EARTH**	*EMI 5137*	....	**12**	11 wks
9 May 81	**CARELESS MEMORIES**	*EMI 5168*	......	**37**	7 wks
25 Jul 81	● **GIRLS ON FILM**	*EMI 5206*	....	**5**	11 wks
28 Nov 81	**MY OWN WAY**	*EMI 5254*	....	**14**	11 wks
15 May 82	● **HUNGRY LIKE THE WOLF**	*EMI 5295*		**5**	12 wks
21 Aug 82	● **SAVE A PRAYER**	*EMI 5327*	....	**2**	9 wks
13 Nov 82	● **RIO**	*EMI 5346*	....	**9**	11 wks
26 Mar 83	★ **IS THERE SOMETHING I SHOULD KNOW**				
	EMI 5371	....	**1**	9 wks
29 Oct 83	● **UNION OF THE SNAKE**	*EMI 5429*	....	**3**	7 wks
24 Dec 83	**UNION OF THE SNAKE**	(re-entry) *EMI 5429*		**66**	4 wks
4 Feb 84	● **NEW MOON ON MONDAY**	*EMI DURAN 1*		**9**	7 wks
28 Apr 84	★ **THE REFLEX**	*EMI DURAN 2*	....	**1**	14 wks
3 Nov 84	● **WILD BOYS**	*Parlophone DURAN 3*	....	**2†**	9 wks

Judith DURHAM
Australia, female vocalist   *5 wks*

| 15 Jun 67 | **OLIVE TREE** | *Columbia DB 8207* | .... | **33** | 5 wks |

Ian DURY and the BLOCKHEADS
UK, male vocal/instrumental group   *45 wks*

29 Apr 78	● **WHAT A WASTE**	*Stiff BUY 27*	......	**9**	12 wks
9 Dec 78	★ **HIT ME WITH YOUR RHYTHM STICK**				
	Stiff BUY 38	....	**1**	15 wks
4 Aug 79	● **REASONS TO BE CHEERFUL, (PT. 3)**				
	Stiff BUY 50	....	**3**	8 wks
30 Aug 80	**I WANT TO BE STRAIGHT**	*Stiff BUY 90*		**22**	7 wks
15 Nov 80	**SUEPERMAN'S BIG SISTER**	*Stiff BUY 100*	....	**51**	3 wks

Hit Me With Your Rhythm Stick *credits Ian and the Blockheads.*

Slim DUSTY *Australia, male vocalist*   *15 wks*

| 30 Jan 59 | ● **A PUB WITH NO BEER** | *Columbia DB 4212* | | **3** | 15 wks |

DYKE - *See ASHTON, GARDNER and DYKE*

Bob DYLAN *US, male vocalist*   *133 wks*

25 Mar 65	● **TIMES THEY ARE A-CHANGIN'**	*CBS 201751*		**9**	11 wks
29 Apr 65	● **SUBTERRANEAN HOMESICK BLUES**				
	CBS 201753		**9**	9 wks
17 Jun 65	**MAGGIE'S FARM**	*CBS 201781*		**22**	8 wks
19 Aug 65	● **LIKE A ROLLING STONE**	*CBS 201811*	....	**4**	12 wks
28 Oct 65	● **POSITIVELY FOURTH STREET**	*CBS 201824*	..	**8**	12 wks
27 Jan 66	**CAN YOU PLEASE CRAWL OUT YOUR WINDOW**	*CBS 201900*		**17**	5 wks
14 Apr 66	**ONE OF US MUST KNOW (SOONER OR LATER)**	*CBS 202053*	....	**33**	5 wks
12 May 66	● **RAINY DAY WOMEN NOS. 12 & 35**				
	CBS 202307		**7**	8 wks
21 Jul 66	**I WANT YOU**	*CBS 202258*		**16**	9 wks
14 May 69	**I THREW IT ALL AWAY**	*CBS 4219*		**30**	6 wks
13 Sep 69	● **LAY LADY LAY**	*CBS 4434*		**5**	12 wks
10 Jul 71	**WATCHING THE RIVER FLOW**	*CBS 7329*		**24**	9 wks
6 Oct 73	**KNOCKIN' ON HEAVEN'S DOOR**	*CBS 1762*	..	**14**	9 wks
7 Feb 76	**HURRICANE**	*CBS 3879*	....	**43**	4 wks
29 Jul 78	**BABY STOP CRYING**	*CBS 6499*		**13**	11 wks
28 Oct 78	**IS YOUR LOVE IN VAIN**	*CBS 6718*		**56**	3 wks

DYNASTY
US, male vocal/instrumental group   *20 wks*

13 Oct 79	**I DON'T WANT TO BE A FREAK (BUT I CAN'T HELP MYSELF)**	*Solar FB 1694*		**20**	13 wks
9 Aug 80	**I'VE JUST BEGUN TO LOVE YOU**	*Solar SO 10*		**51**	4 wks
21 May 83	**DOES THAT RING A BELL**	*Solar E 9911*	.....	**53**	3 wks

Ronnie DYSON *US, male vocalist*   *6 wks*

| 4 Dec 71 | **WHEN YOU GET RIGHT DOWN TO IT** | | | | |
| | *CBS 7449* | .... | **34** | 6 wks |

E

EAGLES *US, male vocal/instrumental group*   *50 wks*

| 9 Aug 75 | **ONE OF THESE NIGHTS** | *Asylum AYM 543* | ... | **23** | 7 wks |

1 Nov 75	LYIN' EYES *Asylum AYM 548*	. . . .	23	7 wks
6 Mar 76	TAKE IT TO THE LIMIT *Asylum K 13029*	. . . . .	12	7 wks
15 Jan 77	NEW KID IN TOWN *Asylum K 13069*	. . . .	20	7 wks
16 Apr 77 ●	HOTEL CALIFORNIA *Asylum K 13079*	. . . .	8	10 wks
16 Dec 78	PLEASE COME HOME FOR CHRISTMAS			
	Asylum K 13145		30	5 wks
13 Oct 79	HEARTACHE TONIGHT *Asylum K 12394*	. . . .	40	5 wks
1 Dec 79	THE LONG RUN *Elektra K 12404*	. . . .	66	2 wks

EARL - *See BOB and EARL*

Robert EARL *UK, male vocalist*   27 wks

25 Apr 58	I MAY NEVER PASS THIS WAY AGAIN			
	Philips PB 805	14	13 wks
24 Oct 58	MORE THAN EVER (COME PRIMA)			
	Philips PB 867	26	2 wks
21 Nov 58	MORE THAN EVER (COME PRIMA) (re-entry)			
	Philips PB 867	28	2 wks
13 Feb 59	WONDERFUL SECRET OF LOVE			
	Philips PB 891	17	10 wks

Charles EARLAND
US, male instrumentalist - keyboards   5 wks

19 Aug 78	LET THE MUSIC PLAY *Mercury 6167 703*	46	5 wks

Hit features uncredited male vocalist.

EARLY MUSIC CONSORT,
Directed by David Munrow
UK, male/female instrumental group   1 wk

3 Apr 71	MUSIC FROM 'THE SIX WIVES OF HENRY VIII'			
	BBC RESL 1	49	1 wk

EARTH WIND AND FIRE
US, male vocal/instrumental group   109 wks

12 Feb 77	SATURDAY NITE *CBS 4835*	17	9 wks
11 Feb 78	FANTASY *CBS 6056*	14	10 wks
13 May 78	JUPITER *CBS 6267*	41	5 wks
29 Jul 78	MAGIC MIND *CBS 6490*	75	1 wk
12 Aug 78	MAGIC MIND (re-entry) *CBS 6490*	54	4 wks
7 Oct 78	GOT TO GET YOU INTO MY LIFE *CBS 6553* . .	33	7 wks
9 Dec 78 ●	SEPTEMBER *CBS 6922*	3	13 wks
28 Jul 79 ●	AFTER THE LOVE HAS GONE *CBS 7721*	4	10 wks
6 Oct 79	STAR *CBS 7092*	16	8 wks
15 Dec 79	CAN'T LET GO *CBS 8077*	46	7 wks
8 Mar 80	IN THE STONE *CBS 8252*	53	3 wks
11 Oct 80	LET ME TALK *CBS 8982*	29	5 wks
20 Dec 80	BACK ON THE ROAD *CBS 9377*	63	4 wks
7 Nov 81 ●	LET'S GROOVE *CBS A 1679*	3	13 wks
6 Feb 82	IVE HAD ENOUGH *CBS A 1959*	29	6 wks
5 Feb 83	FALL IN LOVE WITH ME *CBS A 2927*	47	4 wks

See also Earth Wind and Fire with the Emotions.

EARTH WIND AND FIRE with the
EMOTIONS *US, male vocal/instrumental*
group, female vocal group   13 wks

12 May 79 ●	BOOGIE WONDERLAND *CBS 7292*	4	13 wks

See also Earth Wind and Fire; Emotions.

EAST OF EDEN
UK, male instrumental group   12 wks

17 Apr 71 ●	JIG A JIG *Deram DM 297*	7	12 wks

Sheena EASTON *UK, female vocalist*   78 wks

5 Apr 80	MODERN GIRL *EMI 5042*	56	3 wks
19 Jul 80 ●	9 TO 5 *EMI 5066*	3	15 wks
9 Aug 80 ●	MODERN GIRL (re-entry) *EMI 5042*	8	12 wks
25 Oct 80	ONE MAN WOMAN *EMI 5114*	14	6 wks
14 Feb 81	TAKE MY TIME *EMI 5135*	44	5 wks
2 May 81	WHEN HE SHINES *EMI 5166*	12	8 wks
27 Jun 81 ●	FOR YOUR EYES ONLY *EMI 5195*	8	13 wks
12 Sep 81	JUST ANOTHER BROKEN HEART *EMI 5232* . .	33	8 wks
5 Dec 81	YOU COULD HAVE BEEN WITH ME			
	EMI 5252	54	3 wks
31 Jul 82	MACHINERY *EMI 5326*	38	5 wks

See also Kenny Rogers and Sheena Easton.

EASTSIDE CONNECTION
US, disco aggregation   3 wks

8 Apr 78	YOU'RE SO RIGHT FOR ME *Creole CR 149* . . .	44	3 wks

Clint EASTWOOD *US, male vocalist*   2 wks

7 Feb 70	I TALK TO THE TREES *Paramount PARA 3004*	18	2 wks

This is the flip of Wand'rin Star by Lee Marvin and was listed with Marvin's A-side for 2 weeks only. See also Lee Marvin.

Clint EASTWOOD and General
SAINT *UK, male vocal duo*   3 wks

29 Sep 84	LAST PLANE (ONE WAY TICKET)			
	MCA MCA 910	51	3 wks

EASYBEATS
Australia, male vocal/instrumental group   24 wks

27 Oct 66 ●	FRIDAY ON MY MIND *United Artists UP 1157*	6	15 wks
10 Apr 68	HELLO HOW ARE YOU *United Artists UP 2209*	20	9 wks

Cleveland EATON
US, male instrumentalist - keyboards   6 wks

23 Sep 78	BAMA BOOGIE WOOGIE *Gull GULS 63*	35	6 wks

ECHO and the BUNNYMEN
UK, male vocal/instrumental group   49 wks

17 May 80	RESCUE *Korova KOW 1*	62	1 wk
18 Apr 81	CROCODILES *Korova ECHO 1*	37	4 wks
18 Jul 81	A PROMISE *Korova KOW 15*	49	4 wks
29 May 82	THE BACK OF LOVE *Korova KOW 24*	19	7 wks
22 Jan 83 ●	THE CUTTER *Korova KOW 26*	8	8 wks
16 Jul 83	NEVER STOP *Korova KOW 28*	15	7 wks
28 Jan 84 ●	THE KILLING MOON *Korova KOW 32*	9	6 wks
21 Apr 84	SILVER *Korova KOW 34*	30	5 wks
14 Jul 84	SEVEN SEAS *Korova KOW 35*	16	7 wks

Billy ECKSTINE *US, male vocalist*   31 wks

12 Nov 54 ●	NO ONE BUT YOU *MGM 763*	3	17 wks

| 13 Feb 59 | ● GIGI | Mercury AMT 1018 | 8 | 14 wks |

See also Billy Eckstine and Sarah Vaughan.

Billy ECKSTINE and Sarah VAUGHAN US, male/female vocal duo
17 wks

| 27 Sep 57 | PASSING STRANGERS | Mercury MT 164 | 22 | 2 wks |
| 12 Mar 69 | PASSING STRANGERS (re-issue) Mercury MF 1082 | | 20 | 15 wks |

See also Billy Eckstine; Sarah Vaughan.

EDDIE and the HOTRODS UK, male vocal/instrumental group
26 wks

11 Sep 76	LIVE AT THE MARQUEE (EP)	Island IEP 2	43	5 wks
13 Nov 76	TEENAGE DEPRESSION	Island WIP 6354	35	4 wks
23 Apr 77	I MIGHT BE LYING	Island WIP 6388	44	3 wks
13 Aug 77	● DO ANYTHING YOU WANNA DO Island WIP 6401		9	10 wks
21 Jan 78	QUIT THIS TOWN	Island WIP 6411	36	4 wks

Do Anything You Wanna Do *credited simply to Rods. Tracks on EP: 96 Tears/Get Out Of Denver/Medley: Gloria/Satisfaction.*

Duane EDDY US, male instrumentalist-guitar
187 wks

5 Sep 58	REBEL ROUSER	London HL 8669	19	10 wks
2 Jan 59	CANNONBALL	London HL 8764	22	4 wks
19 Jun 59	● PETER GUNN THEME	London HLW 8879	6	10 wks
24 Jul 59	YEP	London HLW 8879	17	5 wks
4 Sep 59	FORTY MILES OF BAD ROAD London HLW 8929		11	9 wks
11 Sep 59	PETER GUNN THEME (re-entry) London HLW 8879		27	1 wk
18 Dec 59	SOME KINDA EARTHQUAKE London HLW 9007		12	5 wks
19 Feb 60	BONNIE CAME BACK	London HLW 9050	12	10 wks
28 Apr 60	● SHAZAM! London HLW 9104		4	13 wks
21 Jul 60	● BECAUSE THEY'RE YOUNG London HLW 9162		2	18 wks
10 Nov 60	KOMMOTION	London HLW 9225	13	10 wks
12 Jan 61	● PEPE London HLW 9257		2	14 wks
20 Apr 61	● THEME FROM DIXIE London HLW 9324		7	10 wks
22 Jun 61	RING OF FIRE London HLW 9370		17	10 wks
14 Sep 61	DRIVIN' HOME	London HLW 9406	30	4 wks
5 Oct 61	CARAVAN	Parlophone R 4826	42	3 wks
24 May 62	DEEP IN THE HEART OF TEXAS	RCA 1288	19	8 wks
23 Aug 62	● BALLAD OF PALADIN	RCA 1300	10	10 wks
8 Nov 62	● DANCE WITH THE GUITAR MAN	RCA 1316	4	16 wks
14 Feb 63	BOSS GUITAR	RCA 1329	27	8 wks
30 May 63	LONELY BOY LONELY GUITAR	RCA 1344	35	4 wks
29 Aug 63	YOUR BABY'S GONE SURFIN'	RCA 1357	49	1 wk
8 Mar 75	● PLAY ME LIKE YOU PLAY YOUR GUITAR GTO GT 11		9	9 wks

The London hits featured Duane Eddy and the Rebels. Dance With The Guitar Man, Boss Guitar and Play Me Like You Play Your Guitar featured Duane Eddy and the Rebelettes.

Randy EDELMAN US, male vocalist
18 wks

6 Mar 76	CONCRETE AND CLAY	20th Century BTC 2261	11	7 wks
18 Sep 76	UPTOWN UPTEMPO WOMAN 20th Century BTC 2225		25	7 wks
15 Jan 77	YOU	20th Century BTC 2253	49	2 wks
12 Jul 82	NOBODY MADE ME	Rocket/Phonogram XPRES 81	60	2 wks

EDISON LIGHTHOUSE UK, male vocal/instrumental group
13 wks

| 24 Jan 70 | ★ LOVE GROWS (WHERE MY ROSEMARY GOES) Bell 1091 | | 1 | 12 wks |

| 30 Jan 71 | IT'S UP TO YOU PETULA | Bell 1136 | 49 | 1 wk |

Dave EDMUNDS UK, male vocalist/multi-instrumentalist
84 wks

21 Nov 70	★ I HEAR YOU KNOCKING	MAM 1	1	14 wks
20 Jan 73	● BABY I LOVE YOU	Rockfield ROC 1	8	13 wks
9 Jun 73	● BORN TO BE WITH YOU	Rockfield ROC 2	5	12 wks
2 Jul 77	I KNEW THE BRIDE	Swan Song SSK 19411	26	8 wks
30 Jun 79	● GIRLS TALK	Swan Song SSK 19418	4	11 wks
22 Sep 79	QUEEN OF HEARTS	Swansong SSK 19419	11	9 wks
24 Nov 79	CRAWLING FROM THE WRECKAGE Swan Song SSK 19420		59	4 wks
9 Feb 80	SINGING THE BLUES	Swan Song SSK 19422	28	8 wks
28 Mar 81	ALMOST SATURDAY NIGHT Swan Song SSK 19424		58	3 wks
26 Mar 83	SLIPPING AWAY	Arista ARIST 522	60	2 wks

See also Dave Edmunds and Stray Cats.

Dave EDMUNDS and the STRAY CATS UK, male vocalist/instrumentalists and male vocal/instrumental group
6 wks

| 20 Jun 81 | THE RACE IS ON | Swansong SSK 19425 | 34 | 6 wks |

See also Dave Edmunds; Stray Cats.

Alton EDWARDS UK, male vocalist
9 wks

| 9 Jan 82 | I JUST WANNA (SPEND SOME TIME WITH YOU) Streetwave STRA 1897 | | 20 | 9 wks |

Dennis EDWARDS US, male vocalist
5 wks

| 24 Mar 84 | DON'T LOOK ANY FURTHER Gordy TMG 1334 | | 45 | 5 wks |

Rupie EDWARDS Jamaica, male vocalist
16 wks

| 23 Nov 74 | ● IRE FEELINGS (SKANGA) | Cactus CT 38 | 9 | 10 wks |
| 8 Feb 75 | LEGO SKANGA | Cactus CT 51 | 32 | 6 wks |

Tommy EDWARDS US, male vocalist
18 wks

| 3 Oct 58 | ★ IT'S ALL IN THE GAME | MGM 989 | 1 | 17 wks |
| 7 Aug 59 | MY MELANCHOLY BABY | MGM 1020 | 29 | 1 wk |

Donnie ELBERT US, male vocalist
29 wks

8 Jan 72	● WHERE DID OUR LOVE GO?	London HL 10352	8	10 wks
26 Feb 72	I CAN'T HELP MYSELF	Avco 6105 009	11	10 wks
29 Apr 72	LITTLE PIECE OF LEATHER	London HL 10370	27	9 wks

ELECTRIC LIGHT ORCHESTRA UK, male vocal/instrumental group
236 wks

29 Jul 72	● 10538 OVERTURE	Harvest HAR 5053	9	8 wks
27 Jan 73	● ROLL OVER BEETHOVEN	Harvest HAR 5063	6	10 wks
6 Oct 73	SHOWDOWN	Harvest HAR 5077	12	10 wks
9 Mar 74	MA-MA-MA-BELLE	Warner Bros K 16349	22	8 wks
10 Jan 76	● EVIL WOMAN	Jet 764	10	8 wks
3 Jul 76	STRANGE MAGIC	Jet 779	38	3 wks
13 Nov 76	● LIVIN' THING	Jet UP 36184	4	12 wks
19 Feb 77	● ROCKARIA!	Jet UP 36209	9	9 wks
21 May 77	● TELEPHONE LINE	Jet UP 36254	8	10 wks
29 Oct 77	TURN TO STONE	Jet UP 36313	18	12 wks
28 Jan 78	● MR. BLUE SKY	Jet UP 36342	6	11 wks

SHANE FENTON (left) Before becoming Alvin Stardust, Shane Fenton demonstrates his bongo-playing technique to the Fentones.

BRYAN FERRY (right) His first three solo hits were covers of Bob Dylan, Dobie Gray and The Platters.

FOUNDATIONS (left) Seventies charts were entirely without Foundation.

FREEEZ (right) They didn't keep in touch.

FATBACK BAND (left) The party disco outfit had just become Fatback by 1980.

FAIRPORT CONVENTION (right) Originally formed in Muswell Hill in 1967 as an English answer to Jefferson Airplane, they appeared at London Underground clubs such as Middle Earth and the U.F.O.

10 Jun 78	●	WILD WEST HERO	*Jet JET 109*	**6**	14 wks
7 Oct 78	●	SWEET TALKIN' WOMAN	*Jet 121*	**6**	9 wks
9 Dec 78		ELO EP (EP)	*Jet ELO 1*	**34**	8 wks
19 May 79	●	SHINE A LITTLE LOVE	*Jet 144*	**6**	10 wks
21 Jul 79	●	THE DIARY OF HORACE WIMP	*Jet 150* ...	**8**	9 wks
1 Sep 79	●	DON'T BRING ME DOWN	*Jet 153*	**3**	9 wks
17 Nov 79	●	CONFUSION /LAST TRAIN TO LONDON			
			Jet 166	**8**	10 wks
24 May 80		I'M ALIVE	*Jet 179*	**20**	9 wks
2 Aug 80		ALL OVER THE WORLD	*Jet 195*	**11**	9 wks
22 Nov 80		DON'T WALK AWAY	*Jet 7004*	**21**	10 wks
1 Aug 81	●	HOLD ON TIGHT	*Jet 7011*	**4**	12 wks
24 Oct 81		TWILIGHT	*Jet 7015*	**30**	7 wks
9 Jan 82		TICKET TO THE MOON/HERE IS THE NEWS			
			Jet 7018	**24**	8 wks
18 Jun 83		ROCK 'N' ROLL IS KING	*Jet A 3500* ...	**13**	9 wks
3 Sep 83		SECRET MESSAGES	*Jet A 3720*	**48**	3 wks

Here Is The News *listed from 16 Jan 82. See also Olivia Newton-John and Electric Light Orchestra. Tracks on ELO EP are: Out of My Head/Strange Magic/ Ma-Ma-Ma-Belle/Evil Woman.*

ELECTRIC PRUNES
US, male vocal/instrumental group 5 wks

9 Feb 67	I HAD TOO MUCH TO DREAM LAST NIGHT			
	Reprise RS 20532	**49**	1 wk
11 May 67	GET ME TO THE WORLD ON TIME			
	Reprise RS 20564	**42**	4 wks

ELECTRONICAS
Belgium, male instrumental group 8 wks

19 Sep 81	ORIGINAL BIRD DANCE	*Polydor POSP 360* ...	**22**	8 wks

ELEGANTS *US, male vocal group* 2 wks

26 Sep 58	LITTLE STAR	*HMV POP 520*	**25**	2 wks

ELGINS *US, male/female vocal group* 20 wks

1 May 71	●	HEAVEN MUST HAVE SENT YOU			
		Tamla Motown TMG 771	**3**	13 wks
9 Oct 71		PUT YOURSELF IN MY PLACE			
		Tamla Motown TMG 787	**28**	7 wks

ELIAS and his ZIGZAG JIVE FLUTES
South Africa, male instrumental group 14 wks

25 Apr 58	●	TOM HARK	*Columbia DB 4109*	**2** 14 wks

Yvonne ELLIMAN *US, female vocalist* 44 wks

29 Jan 72		I DON'T KNOW HOW TO LOVE HIM			
		MCA MMKS 5077	**47**	1 wk
6 Nov 76	●	LOVE ME	*RSO 2090 205*	**6**	13 wks
7 May 77		HELLO STRANGER	*RSO 2090 236*	**26**	5 wks
13 Aug 77		I CAN'T GET YOU OUT OF MY MIND			
		RSO 2090 251	**17**	13 wks
6 May 78	●	IF I CAN'T HAVE YOU	*RSO 2090 266*	**4**	12 wks

I Don't Know How To Love Him *was one of 4 tracks on a Maxi-Single, 2 of which were credited during the disc's one week on the chart. The other track credited was Superstar by Murray Head. See also Murray Head.*

Duke ELLINGTON *US, orchestra* 4 wks

5 Mar 54	●	SKIN DEEP	*Philips PB 243*	**7**	4 wks

Ray ELLINGTON *UK, orchestra* 4 wks

15 Nov 62	THE MADISON	*Ember S 102*	**41**	2 wks
20 Dec 62	THE MADISON	(re-entry) *Ember S 102*	**36**	2 wks

Bern ELLIOTT and the FENMEN
UK, male vocalist, male vocal/instrumental backing group 22 wks

21 Nov 63	MONEY	*Decca F 11770*	**14**	13 wks
19 Mar 64	NEW ORLEANS	*Decca F 11852*	**24**	9 wks

Shirley ELLIS *US, female vocalist* 17 wks

6 May 65	●	THE CLAPPING SONG	*London HLR 9961*	**6**	13 wks
8 Jul 78		THE CLAPPING SONG (EP)	*MCA MCEP 1* ...	**59**	4 wks

Tracks on Clapping Song EP: *The Clapping Song/Ever See a Diver Kiss His Wife While The Bubbles Bounce Above The Water/ The Name Game/The Nitty Gritty. The Clapping Song itself qualifies as a re-issue.*

Keith EMERSON
UK, male instrumentalist - piano 5 wks

10 Apr 76	HONKY TONK TRAIN BLUES			
	Manticore K 13513	**21**	5 wks

See also Emerson, Lake and Palmer.

EMERSON, LAKE AND PALMER
UK, male instrumental group 13 wks

4 Jun 77	●	FANFARE FOR THE COMMON MAN			
		Atlantic K 10946	**2**	13 wks

See also Keith Emerson; Greg Lake.

Dick EMERY *UK, male vocalist* 8 wks

26 Feb 69	IF YOU LOVE HER	*Pye 7N 17644*	**32**	4 wks
13 Jan 73	YOU ARE AWFUL	*Pye 7N 45202*	**43**	4 wks

EMOTIONS *US, female vocal group* 15 wks

10 Sep 77	●	BEST OF MY LOVE	*CBS 5555*	**4**	10 wks
24 Dec 77		I DON'T WANNA LOSE YOUR LOVE			
		CBS 5819	**40**	5 wks

See also Earth Wind and Fire with the Emotions.

ENGLAND DAN and John Ford COLEY *US, male vocal duo* 12 wks

25 Sep 76	I'D REALLY LOVE TO SEE YOU TONIGHT			
	Atlantic K 10810	**26**	7 wks
23 Jun 79	LOVE IS THE ANSWER	*Big Tree K 11296*	**45**	5 wks

ENGLAND SISTERS
UK, female vocal group 1 wk

17 Mar 60	HEARTBEAT	*HMV POP 710*	**33**	1 wk

ENGLAND WORLD CUP SQUAD
UK, male football team vocalists 30 wks

18 Apr 70	★	BACK HOME	*Pye 7N 17920*	**1**	16 wks

15 Aug 70	**BACK HOME** (re-entry) *Pye 7N 17920*	46	1 wk
10 Apr 82	● **THIS TIME (WE'LL GET IT RIGHT)/ENGLAND WE'LL FLY THE FLAG** *England ER 1*	2	13 wks

Scott ENGLISH *US, male vocalist* — *10 wks*

9 Oct 71	**BRANDY** *Horse HOSS 7*	12	10 wks

ENIGMA *UK, male vocal/instrumental group* — *15 wks*

23 May 81	**AIN'T NO STOPPING** *Creole CR 9*	11	8 wks
8 Aug 81	**I LOVE MUSIC** *Creole CR 14*	25	7 wks

EQUALS *UK, male vocal/instrumental group* — *69 wks*

21 Feb 68	**I GET SO EXCITED** *President PT 180*	44	4 wks
1 May 68	**BABY COME BACK** *President PT 135*	50	1 wk
15 May 68	★ **BABY COME BACK** (re-entry) *President PT 135* ..	1	17 wks
21 Aug 68	**LAUREL & HARDY** *President PT 200*	35	5 wks
27 Nov 68	**SOFTLY SOFTLY** *President PT 222*	48	3 wks
2 Apr 69	**MICHAEL & THE SLIPPER TREE** *President PT 240*	24	7 wks
30 Jul 69	● **VIVA BOBBY JOE** *President PT 260*	6	14 wks
27 Dec 69	**RUB A DUB DUB** *President PT 275*	34	7 wks
19 Dec 70	● **BLACK SKIN BLUE EYED BOYS** *President PT 325*	9	11 wks

EROTIC DRUM BAND
Canada, male/female vocal/instrumental group — *3 wks*

9 Jun 79	**LOVE DISCO STYLE** *Scope SC 1*	47	3 wks

ERUPTION
US, male/female vocal/instrumental group — *21 wks*

18 Feb 78	● **I CAN'T STAND THE RAIN** *Atlantic K 11068* ..	5	11 wks
21 Apr 79	● **ONE WAY TICKET** *Atlantic/Hansa K 11266*	9	10 wks

I Can't Stand The Rain *has credit Eruption featuring Precious Wilson.*

ESCORTS *UK, male vocal/instrumental group* — *2 wks*

2 Jul 64	**THE ONE TO CRY** *Fontana TF 474*	49	2 wks

ESSEX *US, male/female vocal group* — *5 wks*

8 Aug 63	**EASIER SAID THAN DONE** *Columbia DB 7077*	41	5 wks

David ESSEX *UK, male vocalist* — *182 wks*

18 Aug 73	● **ROCK ON** *CBS 1693*	3	11 wks
10 Nov 73	● **LAMPLIGHT** *CBS 1902*	7	15 wks
11 May 74	**AMERICA** *CBS 2176*	32	5 wks
12 Oct 74	★ **GONNA MAKE YOU A STAR** *CBS 2492* ..	1	17 wks
14 Dec 74	**STARDUST** *CBS 2828*	7	10 wks
5 Jul 75	● **ROLLIN' STONE** *CBS 3425*	5	7 wks
13 Sep 75	★ **HOLD ME CLOSE** *CBS 3572*	1	10 wks
6 Dec 75	**IF I COULD** *CBS 3776*	13	8 wks
20 Mar 76	**CITY LIGHTS** *CBS 4050*	24	4 wks
16 Oct 76	**COMING HOME** *CBS 4486*	24	6 wks
17 Sep 77	**COOL OUT TONIGHT** *CBS 5495*	23	6 wks
11 Mar 78	**STAY WITH ME BABY** *CBS 6063*	45	5 wks
19 Aug 78	● **OH WHAT A CIRCUS** *Mercury 6007 185* ..	3	11 wks
21 Oct 78	**BRAVE NEW WORLD** *CBS 6705*	55	3 wks
3 Mar 79	**IMPERIAL WIZARD** *Mercury 6007 202*	32	8 wks
5 Apr 80	● **SILVER DREAM MACHINE** (PART 1) *Mercury BIKE 1*	4	11 wks
14 Jun 80	**HOT LOVE** *Mercury HOT 11*	57	4 wks
26 Jun 82	**ME AND MY GIRL (NIGHT-CLUBBING)** *Mercury/Phonogram MER 107*	13	10 wks
11 Dec 82	● **A WINTER'S TALE** *Mercury/Phonogram MER 127*	2	10 wks
4 Jun 83	**THE SMILE** *Mercury/Phonogram ESSEX 1*	52	4 wks
27 Aug 83	● **TAHITI** *Mercury/Phonogram BOUNT 1*	8	11 wks
26 Nov 83	**YOU'RE IN MY HEART** *Mercury/Phonogram ESSEX 2*	67	2 wks
17 Dec 83	**YOU'RE IN MY HEART** (re-entry) *Mercury/Phonogram ESSEX 2*	59	4 wks

Don ESTELLE - *See Windsor DAVIES and Don ESTELLE*

ETHIOPIANS
Jamaica, male vocal/instrumental group — *6 wks*

13 Sep 67	**TRAIN TO SKAVILLE** *Rio RIO 130*	40	6 wks

Tony ETORIA *UK, male vocalist* — *8 wks*

4 Jun 77	**I CAN PROVE IT** *GTO GT 89*	21	8 wks

EURYTHMICS
UK, male/female vocal/instrumental group — *67 wks*

4 Jul 81	**NEVER GONNA CRY AGAIN** *RCA 68*	63	3 wks
20 Nov 82	**LOVE IS A STRANGER** *RCA DA 1*	54	4 wks
12 Feb 83	● **SWEET DREAMS (ARE MADE OF THIS)** *RCA DA 2*	2	14 wks
9 Apr 83	● **LOVE IS A STRANGER** (re-entry) *RCA DA 1* ..	6	8 wks
9 Jul 83	● **WHO'S THAT GIRL?** *RCA DA 3*	3	10 wks
5 Nov 83	● **RIGHT BY YOUR SIDE** *RCA DA 4*	10	11 wks
21 Jan 84	● **HERE COMES THE RAIN AGAIN** *RCA DA 5*	8	8 wks
3 Nov 84	● **SEXCRIME (NINETEEN EIGHTY FOUR)** *Virgin VS 728*	4†	9 wks

EVANGEL TEMPLE CHOIR - *See Johnny CASH*

EVANS - *See ZAGER and EVANS*

Maureen EVANS *UK, female vocalist* — *37 wks*

22 Jan 60	**THE BIG HURT** *Oriole CB 1533*	26	2 wks
17 Mar 60	**LOVE KISSES & HEARTACHES** *Oriole CB 1540*	44	1 wk
2 Jun 60	**PAPER ROSES** *Oriole CB 1550*	40	5 wks
29 Nov 62	● **LIKE I DO** *Oriole CB 1763*	3	18 wks
27 Feb 64	**I LOVE HOW YOU LOVE ME** *Oriole CB 1906*	34	10 wks
14 May 64	**I LOVE HOW YOU LOVE ME** (re-entry) *Oriole CB 1906*	50	1 wk

Paul EVANS *US, male vocalist* — *14 wks*

27 Nov 59	**SEVEN LITTLE GIRLS SITTING IN THE BACK SEAT** *London HLL 8968*	25	1 wk
31 Mar 60	**MIDNIGHT SPECIAL** *London HLL 9045*	41	1 wk
16 Dec 78	● **HELLO THIS IS JOANIE (THE TELEPHONE ANSWERING MACHINE SONG)** *Spring 2066 932*	6	12 wks

Seven Little Girls Sitting in the Back Seat *credits Paul Evans and The Curls, The Curls being a female vocal group.*

EVASIONS
UK, male/female vocal/instrumental group — *8 wks*

13 Jun 81	**WIKKA WRAP** *Groove GP 107*	20	8 wks

Betty EVERETT   *US, female vocalist*   *14 wks*

14 Jan 65	**GETTING MIGHTY CROWDED** *Fontana TF 520*	**29**	7 wks
30 Oct 68	**IT'S IN HIS KISS** *President PT 215*	**34**	7 wks

Kenny EVERETT   *UK, male vocalist*   *8 wks*

26 Mar 83	● **SNOT RAP** *RCA KEN 1*	**9**	8 wks

See also Kenny Everett and Mike Vickers.

Kenny EVERETT and Mike VICKERS
UK, male vocalist and multi-instrumentalist   *4 wks*

12 Nov 77	**CAPTAIN KREMMEN (RETRIBUTION)** *DJM DJS 10810*	**32**	4 wks

Phil EVERLY   *US, male vocalist*   *6 wks*

6 Nov 82	**LOUISE** *Capitol CL 266*	**47**	6 wks

See also Everly Brothers; Phil Everly and Cliff Richard.

Phil EVERLY and Cliff RICHARD
US/UK, male vocal duo   *9 wks*

19 Feb 83	● **SHE MEANS NOTHING TO ME** *Capitol CL 276*	**9**	9 wks

See also Cliff Richard; Phil Everly; Everly Brothers.

EVERLY BROTHERS
US, male vocal duo   *337 wks*

12 Jul 57	● **BYE BYE LOVE** *London HLA 8440*	**6**	16 wks
8 Nov 57	● **WAKE UP LITTLE SUSIE** *London HLA 8498* ...	**2**	13 wks
23 May 58	★ **ALL I HAVE TO DO IS DREAM/CLAUDETTE** *London HLA 8618*	**1**	21 wks
12 Sep 58	● **BIRD DOG** *London HLA 8685*	**2**	16 wks
23 Jan 59	● **PROBLEMS** *London HLA 8781*	**6**	12 wks
22 May 59	**TAKE A MESSAGE TO MARY** *London HLA 8863*	**29**	1 wk
29 May 59	**POOR JENNY** *London HLA 8863*	**14**	11 wks
19 Jun 59	**TAKE A MESSAGE TO MARY** (re-entry) *London HLA 8863*	**27**	1 wk
3 Jul 59	**TAKE A MESSAGE TO MARY** (2nd re-entry) *London HLA 8863*	**20**	8 wks
11 Sep 59	● **('TIL) I KISSED YOU** *London HLA 8934*	**2**	15 wks
12 Feb 60	**LET IT BE ME** *London HLA 9039*	**13**	5 wks
31 Mar 60	**LET IT BE ME** (re-entry) *London HLA 9039*	**26**	4 wks
14 Apr 60	★ **CATHY'S CLOWN** *Warner Bros. WB 1*	**1**	18 wks
14 Jul 60	● **WHEN WILL I BE LOVED** *London HLA 9157*	**4**	16 wks
22 Sep 60	● **LUCILLE /SO SAD (TO WATCH GOOD LOVE GO BAD)** *Warner Bros. WB 19*	**4**	15 wks
15 Dec 60	**LIKE STRANGERS** *London HLA 9250*	**11**	10 wks
9 Feb 61	★ **WALK RIGHT BACK** *Warner Bros. WB 33*	**1**	16 wks
15 Jun 61	★ **TEMPTATION** *Warner Bros. WB 42*	**1**	15 wks
5 Oct 61	● **MUSKRAT** *Warner Bros. WB 50*	**20**	6 wks
18 Jan 62	● **CRYIN' IN THE RAIN** *Warner Bros. WB 56*	**6**	15 wks
17 May 62	**HOW CAN I MEET HER** *Warner Bros. WB 67* ..	**12**	10 wks
25 Oct 62	**NO ONE CAN MAKE MY SUNSHINE SMILE** *Warner Bros. WB 79*	**11**	11 wks
21 Mar 63	**SO IT WILL ALWAYS BE** *Warner Bros. WB 94*	**23**	11 wks
13 Jun 63	**IT'S BEEN NICE** *Warner Bros. WB 99*	**26**	5 wks
17 Oct 63	**THE GIRL SANG THE BLUES** *Warner Bros. WB 109*	**25**	9 wks
16 Jul 64	**FERRIS WHEEL** *Warner Bros. WB 135*	**22**	10 wks
3 Dec 64	**GONE GONE GONE** *Warner Bros. WB 146*	**36**	7 wks
6 May 65	**THAT'LL BE THE DAY** *Warner Bros. WB 158*	**30**	4 wks
20 May 65	● **THE PRICE OF LOVE** *Warner Bros. WB 161* ...	**2**	14 wks
26 Aug 65	**I'LL NEVER GET OVER YOU** *Warner Bros. WB 5639*	**35**	5 wks

21 Oct 65	**LOVE IS STRANGE** *Warner Bros. WB 5649*	**11**	9 wks
8 May 68	**IT'S MY TIME** *Warner Bros. WB 7192*	**39**	6 wks
22 Sep 84	**ON THE WINGS OF A NIGHTINGALE** *Mercury/Phonogram MER 170*	**41**	9 wks

All I Have To Do Is Dream was listed without Claudette for its first week on the chart, but from 30 May 58 both sides were charted for 20 more weeks. See also Phil Everly; Phil Everly and Cliff Richard.

EVERYTHING BUT THE GIRL
UK, male/female vocal/instrumental group   *11 wks*

12 May 84	**EACH AND EVERYONE** *blanco y negro NEG 1*	**28**	7 wks
21 Jul 84	**MINE** *blanco y negro NEG 3*	**58**	2 wks
6 Oct 84	**NATIVE LAND** *blanco y negro NEG 6*	**73**	2 wks

EXCITERS   *US, male/female vocal group*   *7 wks*

21 Feb 63	**TELL HIM** *United Artists UP 1011*	**46**	1 wk
4 Oct 75	**REACHING FOR THE BEST** *20th Century BTC 1005*	**31**	6 wks

EXILE   *US, male vocal/instrumental group*   *18 wks*

19 Aug 78	● **KISS YOU ALL OVER** *RAK 279*	**6**	12 wks
12 May 79	**HOW COULD THIS GO WRONG** *RAK 293* ...	**67**	2 wks
12 Sep 81	**HEART AND SOUL** *RAK 333*	**54**	4 wks

EXPLOITED
UK, male vocal/instrumental group   *12 wks*

18 Apr 81	**DOGS OF WAR** *Secret SHH 110*	**63**	4 wks
17 Oct 81	**DEAD CITIES** *Secret SHH 120*	**31**	5 wks
8 May 82	**ATTACK** *Secret SHH 130*	**50**	3 wks

See also Exploited and Anti-Pasti.

EXPLOITED and ANTI-PASTI
UK, male vocal/instrumental group   *1 wk*

5 Dec 81	**DON'T LET 'EM GRIND YOU DOWN** *Superville EXP 1003*	**70**	1 wk

See also Exploited.

EXPRESSOS
UK, male/female vocal/instrumental group   *5 wks*

14 Mar 81	**HEY GIRL** *WEA K 18246*	**60**	3 wks
	TANGO IN MONO *WEA K 18431*	**70**	2 wks

F

Shelley FABARES   *US, female vocalist*   *4 wks*

26 Apr 62	**JOHNNY ANGEL** *Pye International 7N 25132*	**41**	4 wks

FABIAN   *US, male vocalist*   *1 wk*

10 Mar 60	**HOUND DOG MAN** *HMV POP 695*	**46**	1 wk

FACES   *UK, male vocal/instrumental group*   *46 wks*

18 Dec 71	● **STAY WITH ME** *Warner Bros. K 16136*	**6**	14 wks
17 Feb 73	● **CINDY INCIDENTALLY** *Warner Bros. K 16247*	**2**	9 wks

8 Dec 73	● POOL HALL RICHARD/I WISH IT WOULD RAIN *Warner Bros. K 16341*	8	11 wks
7 Dec 74	YOU CAN MAKE ME DANCE SING OR ANYTHING *Warner Bros. K 16494*	12	9 wks
4 Jun 77	THE FACES (EP) *Riva 8*	41	3 wks

Tracks on Faces EP: Memphis/You Can Make Me Dance Sing or Anything/Stay With Me/Cindy Incidentally. You Can Make Me Dance Sing or Anything credited to Rod Stewart and the Faces. See also Rod Stewart; Small Faces.

Joe FAGIN UK, male vocalist   11 wks

| 7 Jan 84 | ● THAT'S LIVIN' ALRIGHT *Towerbell TOW 46* | 3 | 11 wks |

Yvonne FAIR US, female vocalist   11 wks

| 24 Jan 76 | ● IT SHOULD HAVE BEEN ME *Tamla Motown TMG 1013* | 5 | 11 wks |

FAIR WEATHER
UK, male vocal/instrumental group   12 wks

| 18 Jul 70 | ● NATURAL SINNER *RCA 1977* | 6 | 12 wks |

FAIRPORT CONVENTION
UK, male/female vocal/instrumental group   9 wks

| 23 Jul 69 | SI TU DOIS PARTIR *Island WIP 6064* | 21 | 8 wks |
| 27 Sep 69 | SI TU DOIS PARTIR (re-entry) *Island WIP 6064* | 49 | 1 wk |

Andy FAIRWEATHER-LOW
UK, male vocalist   18 wks

| 21 Sep 74 | ● REGGAE TUNE *A & M AMS 7129* | 10 | 8 wks |
| 6 Dec 75 | ● WIDE EYED AND LEGLESS *A & M AMS 7202* | 6 | 10 wks |

Adam FAITH UK, male vocalist   251 wks

20 Nov 59	★ WHAT DO YOU WANT *Parlophone R 4591*	1	15 wks
22 Jan 60	★ POOR ME *Parlophone R 4623*	1	17 wks
10 Mar 60	WHAT DO YOU WANT (re-entry) *Parlophone R 4591*	24	4 wks
14 Apr 60	● SOMEONE ELSE'S BABY *Parlophone R 4643*	2	13 wks
30 Jun 60	● WHEN JOHNNY COMES MARCHING HOME/MADE YOU *Parlophone R 4665*	5	13 wks
15 Sep 60	● HOW ABOUT THAT *Parlophone R 4689*	4	14 wks
17 Nov 60	● LONELY PUP (IN A CHRISTMAS SHOP) *Parlophone R 4708*	4	11 wks
9 Feb 61	● THIS IS IT /WHO AM I *Parlophone R 4735*	5	14 wks
27 Apr 61	EASY GOING ME *Parlophone R 4766*	12	10 wks
20 Jul 61	DON'T YOU KNOW IT *Parlophone R 4807*	12	10 wks
26 Oct 61	● THE TIME HAS COME *Parlophone R 4837*	4	14 wks
18 Jan 62	LONESOME *Parlophone R 4864*	12	9 wks
3 May 62	● AS YOU LIKE IT *Parlophone R 4896*	5	15 wks
30 Aug 62	● DON'T THAT BEAT ALL *Parlophone R 4930*	8	11 wks
13 Dec 62	BABY TAKE A BOW *Parlophone R 4964*	22	6 wks
31 Jan 63	WHAT NOW *Parlophone R 4990*	31	5 wks
11 Jul 63	WALKIN' TALL *Parlophone R 5039*	23	6 wks
19 Sep 63	● THE FIRST TIME *Parlophone R 5061*	5	13 wks
12 Dec 63	WE ARE IN LOVE *Parlophone R 5091*	11	12 wks
12 Mar 64	IF HE TELLS YOU *Parlophone R 5109*	25	9 wks
28 May 64	I LOVE BEING IN LOVE WITH YOU *Parlophone R 5138*	33	6 wks
26 Nov 64	MESSAGE TO MARTHA (KENTUCKY BLUEBIRD) *Parlophone R 5201*	12	11 wks
11 Feb 65	STOP FEELING SORRY FOR YOURSELF *Parlophone R 5235*	23	6 wks
17 Jun 65	SOMEONE'S TAKEN MARIA AWAY *Parlophone R 5289*	34	5 wks

| 20 Oct 66 | CHERYL'S GOIN' HOME *Parlophone R 5516* | 46 | 2 wks |

The following hits featured the Roulettes, UK, male vocal/ instrumental group, backing Adam Faith: The First Time, We Are In Love, If He Tells You, I Love Being In Love With You.

Horace FAITH Jamaica, male vocalist   10 wks

| 12 Sep 70 | BLACK PEARL *Trojan TR 7790* | 13 | 10 wks |

Percy FAITH US, orchestra   30 wks

| 10 Mar 60 | ● THEME FROM 'A SUMMER PLACE' *Philips PB 989* | 2 | 30 wks |

FAITH, HOPE and CHARITY
US, male/female vocal group   4 wks

| 31 Jan 76 | JUST ONE LOOK *RCA 2632* | 38 | 4 wks |

Marianne FAITHFULL
UK, female vocalist   59 wks

13 Aug 64	● AS TEARS GO BY *Decca F 11923*	9	13 wks
18 Feb 65	● COME AND STAY WITH ME *Decca F 12075*	4	13 wks
6 May 65	● THIS LITTLE BIRD *Decca F 12162*	6	11 wks
22 Jul 65	● SUMMER NIGHTS *Decca F 12193*	10	10 wks
4 Nov 65	YESTERDAY *Decca F 12268*	36	4 wks
9 Mar 67	IS THIS WHAT I GET FOR LOVING YOU *Decca F 22524*	43	2 wks
24 Nov 79	THE BALLAD OF LUCY JORDAN *Island WIP 6491*	48	6 wks

Agnetha FALTSKOG
Sweden, female vocalist   12 wks

28 May 83	THE HEAT IS ON *Epic A 3436*	36	6 wks
13 Aug 83	WRAP YOUR ARMS AROUND ME *Epic A 3622*	44	5 wks
22 Oct 83	CAN'T SHAKE LOOSE *Epic A 3812*	63	1 wk

FAME and PRICE TOGETHER
UK, male vocal/instrumental duo – piano   10 wks

| 10 Apr 71 | ROSETTA *CBS 7108* | 11 | 10 wks |

See also Georgie Fame; Alan Price.

Georgie FAME UK, male vocalist   105 wks

17 Dec 64	★ YEH YEH *Columbia DB 7428*	1	12 wks
4 Mar 65	IN THE MEANTIME *Columbia DB 7494*	22	8 wks
29 Jul 65	LIKE WE USED TO BE *Columbia DB 7633*	33	7 wks
28 Oct 65	SOMETHING *Columbia DB 7727*	23	7 wks
23 Jun 66	★ GET AWAY *Columbia DB 7946*	1	11 wks
22 Sep 66	SUNNY *Columbia DB 8015*	13	8 wks
22 Dec 66	SITTING IN THE PARK *Columbia DB 8096*	12	10 wks
23 Mar 67	BECAUSE I LOVE YOU *CBS 202587*	15	8 wks
13 Sep 67	TRY MY WORLD *CBS 2945*	37	5 wks
13 Dec 67	● BALLAD OF BONNIE & CLYDE *CBS 3124*	1	13 wks
9 Jul 69	PEACEFUL *CBS 4295*	16	9 wks
13 Dec 69	SEVENTH SON *CBS 4659*	25	7 wks

All Columbia hits except Sunny credit The Blue Flames backing Georgie Fame. See also Fame and Price Together.

FAMILY UK, male vocal/instrumental group   44 wks

| 1 Nov 69 | NO MULE'S FOOL *Reprise RS 27001* | 29 | 7 wks |
| 22 Aug 70 | STRANGE BAND *Reprise RS 27009* | 11 | 12 wks |

CONNIE FRANCIS (above left) No hits since 1966 yet still the second most successful female soloist in British charts.

STAN GETZ (left) The jazz great had two hits with two different partners.

GENERATION X (above right) Billy Idol drinks to his own future solo success.

GARY GLITTER (below left) Seen here in his Paul Raven days.

ANDY GIBB (right) Bee Gee Barry Gibb coaxes small psychedelic-shirted brother Andy into his first steps to becoming a pop star.

ROBIN GIBB (below right) His 'Juliet' became number one on the Eurochart even without cracking the British seventy-five.

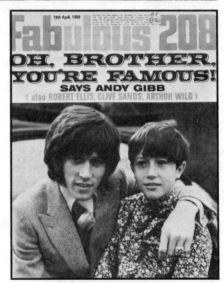

19th April, 1969

Fabulous 208

OH, BROTHER, YOU'RE FAMOUS!
SAYS ANDY GIBB
(also ROBERT ELLIS, CLIVE SANDS, ARTHUR WILD)

José FELICIANO
US, male vocalist/instrumentalist – guitar · · · · · · · · · · · · 23 wks

18 Sep 68	● LIGHT MY FIRE *RCA 1715*	**6**	16 wks
18 Oct 69	AND THE SUN WILL SHINE *RCA 1871*	25	7 wks

Julie FELIX US, female vocalist · · · · · · · · · 19 wks

18 Apr 70	IF I COULD (EL CONDOR PASA) *RAK 101* ..	**19**	11 wks
17 Oct 70	HEAVEN IS HERE *RAK 105*	22	8 wks

FENDERMEN
US, male vocal/instrumental duo, guitars · · · · · · · · 9 wks

18 Aug 60	MULE SKINNER BLUES *Top Rank JAR 395* ...	**50**	1 wk
1 Sep 60	MULE SKINNER BLUES (re-entry)		
	Top Rank JAR 395	37	2 wks
29 Sep 60	MULE SKINNER BLUES (2nd re-entry)		
	Top Rank JAR 395	32	6 wks

FENMEN - *See Bern ELLIOTT and the FENMEN*

Peter FENTON UK, male vocalist · · · · · · 3 wks

10 Nov 66	MARBLE BREAKS IRON BENDS		
	Fontana TF 748	**46**	3 wks

Shane FENTON and the FENTONES
UK, male vocal/instrumental group · · · · · · · · · · 28 wks

26 Oct 61	I'M A MOODY GUY *Parlophone R 4827*	**22**	8 wks
1 Feb 62	WALK AWAY *Parlophone R 4866*	38	5 wks
5 Apr 62	IT'S ALL OVER NOW *Parlophone R 4883*	29	7 wks
12 Jul 62	CINDY'S BIRTHDAY *Parlophone R 4921*	19	8 wks

Fenton later became Alvin Stardust - see also Alvin Stardust. See also Fentones.

FENTONES UK, male instrumental group · · · · · 4 wks

19 Apr 62	THE MEXICAN *Parlophone R 4899*	**41**	3 wks
27 Sep 62	THE BREEZE & I *Parlophone R 4937*	48	1 wk

See also Shane Fenton and the Fentones.

FERKO STRING BAND
US, male vocal/instrumental group · · · · · · · · · · 2 wks

12 Aug 55	ALABAMA JUBILEE *London HL 8140*	**20**	2 wks

Luisa FERNANDEZ
Spain, female vocalist · · · · · · · · · · · · · · · · · 8 wks

11 Nov 78	LAY LOVE ON YOU *Warner Bros. K 17061*	**31**	8 wks

FERRANTE and TEICHER
US, male instrumental duo - pianos · · · · · · · · · 18 wks

18 Aug 60	THEME FROM 'THE APARTMENT'		
	London HLT 9164	**44**	1 wk
9 Mar 61	● THEME FROM 'EXODUS'		
	London HLT 9298 and HMV POP 881	6	17 wks

Theme From Exodus available first on London, then on HMV when the American label, United Artists, changed its UK outlet.

José FERRER US, male vocalist · · · · · · · 3 wks

19 Feb 54	● WOMAN *Philips PB 220*	**7**	3 wks

Woman coupled with Man by Rosemary Clooney. See Rosemary Clooney.

Bryan FERRY UK, male vocalist · · · · · · · 71 wks

29 Sep 73	● A HARD RAIN'S GONNA FALL		
	Island WIP 6170	**10**	9 wks
25 May 74	THE IN CROWD *Island WIP 6196*	13	6 wks
31 Aug 74	SMOKE GETS IN YOUR EYES *Island WIP 6205* ..	17	8 wks
5 Jul 75	YOU GO TO MY HEAD *Island WIP 6234*	33	3 wks
12 Jun 76	● LET'S STICK TOGETHER *Island WIP 6307*	4	10 wks
7 Aug 76	● EXTENDED PLAY (EP) *Island IEP 1*	7	9 wks
5 Feb 77	◎ THIS IS TOMORROW *Polydor 2001 704*	9	9 wks
14 May 77	TOKYO JOE *Polydor 2001 711*	15	7 wks
13 May 78	WHAT GOES ON *Polydor POSP 3*	67	2 wks
5 Aug 78	SIGN OF THE TIMES *Polydor 2001 798*	37	8 wks

Tracks on EP: Price Of Love/Shame Shame Shame/Heart On My Sleeve/ It's Only Love.

Karel FIALKA
UK, male vocalist and multi-instrumentalist · · · · · · · 4 wks

17 May 80	THE EYES HAVE IT *Blueprint BLU 2005*	**52**	4 wks

FIAT LUX
UK, male vocal/instrumental group · · · · · · · · · · 4 wks

28 Jan 84	SECRETS *Polydor FIAT 2*	**65**	3 wks
17 Mar 84	BLUE EMOTION *Polydor FIAT 3*	59	1 wk

FICTION FACTORY
UK, male vocal/instrumental group · · · · · · · · · 11 wks

14 Jan 84	● (FEELS LIKE) HEAVEN · *CBS A 3996*	**6**	9 wks
17 Mar 84	GHOST OF YOU *CBS A 3819*	64	2 wks

FIDDLER'S DRAM
UK, male/female vocal/instrumental group · · · · · · 9 wks

15 Dec 79	● DAY TRIP TO BANGOR (DIDN'T WE HAVE A		
	LOVELY TIME) *Dingles SID 211*	**3**	9 wks

Billy FIELD Australia, male vocalist · · · · · 3 wks

12 Jun 82	YOU WEREN'T IN LOVE WITH ME		
	CBS A 2344	**67**	3 wks

Ernie FIELDS US, orchestra · · · · · · · · · 8 wks

25 Dec 59	IN THE MOOD *London HL 8985*	**13**	8 wks

Gracie FIELDS UK, female vocalist · · · · · 15 wks

31 May 57	● AROUND THE WORLD *Columbia DB 3953*	**8**	8 wks
2 Aug 57	AROUND THE WORLD (re-entry)		
	Columbia DB 3953	24	1 wk
6 Nov 59	LITTLE DONKEY *Columbia DB 4360*	30	1 wk
20 Nov 59	LITTLE DONKEY (re-entry) *Columbia DB 4360*	20	5 wks

Richard 'Dimples' FIELDS
US, male vocalist   4 wks

20 Feb 82	I'VE GOT TO LEARN TO SAY NO		
	Epic EPC A 1918	56	4 wks

FIFTH DIMENSION
US, male/female vocal group   20 wks

23 Apr 69	AQUARIUS - LET THE SUNSHINE IN		
	(MEDLEY) Liberty LBF 15198	11	11 wks
17 Jan 70	WEDDING BELL BLUES Liberty LBF 15288	16	9 wks

53RD and 3RD   UK, male vocal group plus
Jonathan King much in evidence on vocals   4 wks

20 Sep 75	CHICK A BOOM (DON'T YA JES LOVE IT)		
	UK 2012 002	36	4 wks

Hit featured The Sound Of Shag. See also Shag; Jonathan King.

FIREBALLS   US, male instrumental group   9 wks

27 Jul 61	QUITE A PARTY Pye International 7N 25092	29	9 wks

See also Jimmy Gilmer and the Fireballs.

FIRM   UK, male vocal/instrumental group   9 wks

17 Jul 82	ARTHUR DALEY ('E'S ALRIGHT)		
	Bark/Stiff HID 1	14	9 wks

FIRST CHOICE   US, female vocal group   21 wks

19 May 73	ARMED & EXTREMELY DANGEROUS		
	Bell 1297	16	10 wks
4 Aug 73 ●	SMARTY PANTS Bell 1324	9	11 wks

FIRST CLASS   UK, male vocal group   10 wks

15 Jun 74	BEACH BABY UK 66	13	10 wks

FIRST EDITION - See Kenny ROGERS

FIRST LIGHT
UK, male vocal/instrumental duo   5 wks

21 May 83	EXPLAIN THE REASONS London/Oval LON 26	65	3 wks
28 Jan 84	WISH YOU WERE HERE London/Oval LON 43	71	2 wks

FISCHER-Z
UK, male vocal/instrumental group   7 wks

26 May 79	THE WORKER United Artists UP 36509	53	5 wks
3 May 80	SO LONG United Artists BP 342	72	2 wks

Eddie FISHER   US, male vocalist   105 wks

2 Jan 53 ★	OUTSIDE OF HEAVEN HMV B 10362	1	16 wks
23 Jan 53	EVERYTHING I HAVE IS YOURS		
	HMV B 10398	12	1 wk
6 Feb 53 ●	EVERYTHING I HAVE IS YOURS (re-entry)		
	HMV B 10398	8	4 wks
1 May 53	OUTSIDE OF HEAVEN (re-entry) HMV B 10362	12	1 wk
1 May 53 ●	DOWNHEARTED HMV B 10450	3	15 wks

22 May 53 ★	I'M WALKING BEHIND YOU HMV B 10489 ..	1	18 wks
6 Nov 53 ●	WISH YOU WERE HERE HMV B 10564	8	9 wks
22 Jan 54 ●	OH MEIN PAPA HMV B 10614	9	1 wk
5 Feb 54 ●	OH MEIN PAPA (re-entry) HMV B 10614	11	1 wk
26 Feb 54 ●	OH MEIN PAPA (2nd re-entry) HMV B 10614 ..	10	1 wk
12 Mar 54 ●	OH MEIN PAPA (3rd re-entry) HMV B 10614 ..	11	1 wk
29 Oct 54	I NEED YOU NOW HMV B 10755	16	2 wks
19 Nov 54	I NEED YOU NOW (re-entry) HMV B 10755 ...	13	7 wks
21 Jan 55	I NEED YOU NOW (2nd re-entry) HMV B 10755	19	1 wk
18 Mar 55 ●	WEDDING BELLS HMV B 10839	5	11 wks
23 Nov 56 ●	CINDY OH CINDY HMV POP 273	5	16 wks

Toni FISHER   US, female vocalist   1 wk

12 Feb 60	THE BIG HURT Top Rank JAR 261	30	1 wk

Ella FITZGERALD   US, female vocalist   29 wks

23 May 58	SWINGIN' SHEPHERD BLUES HMV POP 486	15	5 wks
16 Oct 59	BUT NOT FOR ME HMV POP 657	25	2 wks
25 Dec 59	BUT NOT FOR ME (re-entry) HMV POP 657 ..	29	1 wk
21 Apr 60	MACK THE KNIFE HMV POP 736	19	9 wks
6 Oct 60	HOW HIGH THE MOON HMV POP 782	46	1 wk
22 Nov 62	DESAFINADO Verve VS 502	38	4 wks
27 Dec 62	DESAFINADO (re-entry) Verve VS 502	41	2 wks
30 Apr 64	CAN'T BUY ME LOVE Verve VS 519	34	5 wks

Scott FITZGERALD and Yvonne KEELY   UK/Holland, male/female vocal duo   10 wks

14 Jan 78 ●	IF I HAD WORDS Pepper UP 36333	3	10 wks

Hit credits St. Thomas Moore School Choir.

FIVE SMITH BROTHERS
UK, male vocal group   1 wk

22 Jul 55	I'M IN FAVOUR OF FRIENDSHIP		
	Decca F 10527	20	1 wk

5000 VOLTS
UK, male/female vocal/instrumental group   18 wks

6 Sep 75 ●	I'M ON FIRE Philips 6006 464	4	9 wks
24 Jul 76 ●	DR. KISS KISS Philips 6006 533	8	9 wks

FIXX   UK, male vocal/instrumental group   8 wks

24 Apr 82	STAND OR FALL MCA FIXX 2	54	4 wks
17 Jul 82	RED SKIES MCA FIXX 3	57	4 wks

Roberta FLACK   US, female vocalist   42 wks

27 May 72	THE FIRST TIME EVER I SAW YOUR FACE		
	Atlantic K 10161	14	14 wks
17 Feb 73 ●	KILLING ME SOFTLY WITH HIS SONG		
	Atlantic K 10282	6	14 wks
24 Aug 74	FEEL LIKE MAKING LOVE Atlantic K 10467 ..	34	7 wks
30 Aug 80	DON'T MAKE ME WAIT TOO LONG		
	Atlantic K 11555	44	7 wks

See also Roberta Flack and Donny Hathaway.

Roberta FLACK and Donny HATHAWAY   US, female/male vocal duo   22 wks

5 Aug 72	WHERE IS THE LOVE Atlantic K 10202	29	7 wks
6 May 78	THE CLOSER I GET TO YOU Atlantic K 11099	42	4 wks

17 May 80	● BACK TOGETHER AGAIN	Atlantic K 11481	...	3	11 wks

See also Roberta Flack.

FLAMINGOS US, male vocal group   5 wks

4 Jun 69	BOOGALOO PARTY	Philips BF 1786	....	26	5 wks

Michael FLANDERS UK, male vocalist   3 wks

27 Feb 59	LITTLE DRUMMER BOY	Parlophone R 4528	...	20	2 wks
17 Apr 59	LITTLE DRUMMER BOY	(re-entry)			
		Parlophone R 4528	....	24	1 wk

FLASH AND THE PAN
Australia, male vocal/instrumental group   15 wks

23 Sep 78	AND THE BAND PLAYED ON (DOWN AMONG THE DEAD MEN)	Ensign ENY 15	....	54	4 wks
21 May 83	● WAITING FOR A TRAIN	Easybeat EASY 1	....	7	11 wks

Lester FLATT and Earl SCRUGGS
US, male instrumental duo, banjos   6 wks

15 Nov 67	FOGGY MOUNTAIN BREAKDOWN				
		CBS 3038 and Mercury MF 1007	....	39	6 wks

The versions on the two labels were not the same cuts; CBS had a 1965 recording, Mercury a 1967. The chart did not differentiate and listed both together.

Fogwell FLAX and the ANKLEBITERS from FREEHOLD JUNIOR SCHOOL
UK, male vocalist and school choir   1 wk

26 Dec 81	ONE NINE FOR SANTA	EMI 5255	....	68	1 wk

F.L.B. US, male vocal/instrumental group   4 wks

10 Mar 79	BOOGIE TOWN	Fantasy FTC 168	....	46	4 wks

See also Fat Larry's Band.

FLEE-REKKERS
UK, male instrumental group   13 wks

19 May 60	GREEN JEANS	Triumph RGM 1008	....	23	13 wks

FLEETWOOD MAC
UK/US, male/female vocal/instrumental group   169 wks

10 Apr 68	BLACK MAGIC WOMAN	Blue Horizon 57 3138		37	7 wks
17 Jul 68	NEED YOUR LOVE SO BAD				
		Blue Horizon 57 3139	....	31	13 wks
4 Dec 68	★ ALBATROSS	Blue Horizon 57 3145	...	1	20 wks
16 Apr 69	● MAN OF THE WORLD	Immediate IM 080	......	2	14 wks
23 Jul 69	NEED YOUR LOVE SO BAD	(re-issue)			
		Blue Horizon 57 3157	....	32	6 wks
13 Sep 69	NEED YOUR LOVE SO BAD	(re-entry of re-issue)			
		Blue Horizon 57 3157	....	42	3 wks
4 Oct 69	● OH WELL	Reprise RS 27000	......	2	16 wks
23 May 70	● THE GREEN MANALISHI (WITH THE TWO-PRONG CROWN)	Reprise RS 27007	...	10	12 wks
12 May 73	● ALBATROSS	(re-issue) CBS 8306	......	2	15 wks
13 Nov 76	SAY YOU LOVE ME	Reprise K 14447	....	40	4 wks

19 Feb 77	GO YOUR OWN WAY	Warner Bros. K 16872	...	38	4 wks
30 Apr 77	DON'T STOP	Warner Bros. K 16930	....	32	5 wks
9 Jul 77	DREAMS	Warner Bros. K 16969		24	9 wks
22 Oct 77	YOU MAKE LOVING FUN	Warner Bros. K 17013		45	2 wks
11 Mar 78	RHIANNON	Reprise K 14430		46	3 wks
6 Oct 79	● TUSK	Warner Bros. K 17468		6	10 wks
22 Dec 79	SARA	Warner Bros. K 17533		37	8 wks
25 Sep 82	GYPSY	Warner Bros. K 17997		46	3 wks
18 Dec 82	● OH DIANE	Warner Bros. FLEET 1	....	9	15 wks

Group were UK and male only up to and including the re-issue of Albatross.

FLEETWOODS
US, male/female vocal group   8 wks

24 Apr 59	● COME SOFTLY TO ME	London HL 8841	......	6	8 wks

La FLEUR
Dutch, male/female vocal/instrumental group   4 wks

30 Jul 83	BOOGIE NIGHTS	Proto ENA 111	....	51	4 wks

Berni FLINT UK, male vocalist   11 wks

19 Mar 77	● I DON'T WANT TO PUT A HOLD ON YOU				
		EMI 2599	....	3	10 wks
23 Jul 77	SOUTHERN COMFORT	EMI 2621	....	48	1 wk

FLINTLOCK
UK, male vocal/instrumental group   5 wks

29 May 76	DAWN	Pinnacle P 8419	....	30	5 wks

F.L.O. - See Rahni HARRIS and F.L.O.

FLOATERS
US, male vocal/instrumental group   11 wks

23 Jul 77	★ FLOAT ON	ABC 4187	....	1	11 wks

A FLOCK OF SEAGULLS
UK, male vocal/instrumental group   43 wks

27 Mar 82	I RAN	Jive JIVE 14	....	43	6 wks
12 Jun 82	SPACE AGE LOVE SONG	Jive JIVE 17	...	34	6 wks
6 Nov 82	● WISHING (IF I HAD A PHOTOGRAPH OF YOU)				
		Jive JIVE 25	....	10	12 wks
23 Apr 83	NIGHTMARES	Jive JIVE 33	....	53	3 wks
25 Jun 83	TRANSFER AFFECTION	Jive JIVE 41	......	38	5 wks
14 Jul 84	THE MORE YOU LIVE, THE MORE YOU LOVE				
		Jive JIVE 62	....	26	11 wks

FLOWERPOT MEN
UK, male vocal group   12 wks

23 Aug 67	● LET'S GO TO SAN FRANCISCO	Deram DM 142		4	12 wks

Eddie FLOYD US, male vocalist   29 wks

2 Feb 67	KNOCK ON WOOD	Atlantic 584 041	....	50	1 wk
2 Mar 67	KNOCK ON WOOD	(re-entry) Atlantic 584 041	..	19	17 wks
16 Mar 67	RAISE YOUR HAND	Stax 601 001	....	42	3 wks
9 Aug 67	THINGS GET BETTER	Stax 601 016	....	31	8 wks

FLYING LIZARDS
UK, male/female vocal/instrumental group   *16 wks*

4 Aug 79 ●	MONEY *Virgin VS 276*		5	10 wks
9 Feb 80	T.V. *Virgin VS 325*		43	6 wks

FLYING PICKETS   *UK, male vocal group*   *20 wks*

26 Nov 83 ★	ONLY YOU *10 Records/Virgin TEN 14*		1	11 wks
21 Apr 84 ●	WHEN YOU'RE YOUNG AND IN LOVE			
	10 Records/Virgin TEN 20		7	8 wks
8 Dec 84	WHO'S THAT GIRL *10 Records/Virgin GIRL 1* ..		71	1 wk

FOCUS   *Holland, male instrumental group*   *21 wks*

20 Jan 73	HOCUS POCUS *Polydor 2001 211*		20	10 wks
27 Jan 73 ●	SYLVIA *Polydor 2001 422*		4	11 wks

Dan FOGELBERG   *US, male vocalist*   *4 wks*

15 Mar 80	LONGER *Full Moon/Epic EPC 8230*		59	4 wks

Wayne FONTANA   *UK, male vocalist*   *31 wks*

9 Dec 65	IT WAS EASIER TO HURT HER			
	Fontana TF 642		36	6 wks
21 Apr 66	COME ON HOME *Fontana TF 684*		16	12 wks
25 Aug 66	GOODBYE BLUEBIRD *Fontana TF 737*		49	1 wk
8 Dec 66	PAMELA PAMELA *Fontana TF 770*		11	12 wks

See also Wayne Fontana and the Mindbenders.

Wayne FONTANA and the MINDBENDERS   *UK, male vocalist, male*
vocal/instrumental backing group   *45 wks*

11 Jul 63	HELLO JOSEPHINE *Fontana TF 404*		46	2 wks
28 May 64	STOP LOOK & LISTEN *Fontana TF 451*		37	4 wks
8 Oct 64	UM UM UM UM UM UM *Fontana TF 497*		5	15 wks
4 Feb 65 ●	GAME OF LOVE *Fontana TF 535*		2	11 wks
17 Jun 65	JUST A LITTLE BIT TOO LATE			
	Fontana TF 579		20	7 wks
30 Sep 65	SHE NEEDS LOVE *Fontana TF 611*		32	6 wks

See also Wayne Fontana; Mindbenders.

Bill FORBES   *UK, male vocalist*   *1 wk*

15 Jan 60	TOO YOUNG *Columbia DB 4386*		29	1 wk

FORBIDDEN - *See Jet BRONX and the FORBIDDEN*

Clinton FORD   *UK, male vocalist*   *25 wks*

23 Oct 59	OLD SHEP *Oriole CB 1500*		27	1 wk
17 Aug 61	TOO MANY BEAUTIFUL GIRLS			
	Oriole CB 1623		48	1 wk
8 Mar 62	FANLIGHT FANNY *Oriole CB 1706*		22	10 wks
5 Jan 67	RUN TO THE DOOR *Piccadilly 7N 35361*		25	13 wks

Emile FORD and the CHECKMATES
UK, male vocal/instrumental group   *88 wks*

30 Oct 59 ★	WHAT DO YOU WANT TO MAKE THOSE			
	EYES AT ME FOR *Pye 7N 15225*		1	26 wks

5 Feb 60 ●	ON A SLOW BOAT TO CHINA *Pye 7N 15245*		3	14 wks
26 May 60	YOU'LL NEVER KNOW WHAT YOU'RE			
	MISSING *Pye 7N 15268*		12	9 wks
1 Sep 60	THEM THERE EYES *Pye 7N 15282*		18	16 wks
8 Dec 60 ●	COUNTING TEARDROPS *Pye 7N 15314*		4	12 wks
2 Mar 61	WHAT AM I GONNA DO *Pye 7N 15331*		33	6 wks
18 May 61	HALF OF MY HEART *Piccadilly 7N 35003*		50	1 wk
22 Jun 61	HALF OF MY HEART (re-entry)			
	Piccadilly 7N 35003		42	3 wks
8 Mar 62	I WONDER WHO'S KISSING HER NOW			
	Piccadilly 7N 35033		43	1 wk

Checkmates not on Them There Eyes *or the two Piccadilly hits.*

Martyn FORD   *UK, orchestra*   *3 wks*

14 May 77	LET YOUR BODY GO DOWNTOWN			
	Mountain TOP 26		38	3 wks

Mary FORD - *See Les PAUL and Mary FORD*

Tennessee Ernie FORD
US, male vocalist   *42 wks*

21 Jan 55 ★	GIVE ME YOUR WORD *Capitol CL 14005*		1	24 wks
6 Jan 56 ★	SIXTEEN TONS *Capitol CL 14500*		1	11 wks
13 Jan 56 ●	THE BALLAD OF DAVY CROCKETT			
	Capitol CL 14506		3	7 wks

FOREIGNER
UK/US, male vocal/instrumental group   *53 wks*

6 May 78	FEELS LIKE THE FIRST TIME *Atlantic K 11086*		39	6 wks
15 July 78	COLD AS ICE *Atlantic K 10986*		24	10 wks
28 Oct 78	HOT BLOODED *Atlantic K 11167*		42	3 wks
24 Feb 79	BLUE MORNING BLUE DAY *Atlantic K 11236*		45	4 wks
29 Aug 81	URGENT *Atlantic K 11665*		54	4 wks
10 Oct 81	JUKE BOX HERO *Atlantic K 11678*		48	4 wks
12 Dec 81 ●	WAITING FOR A GIRL LIKE YOU			
	Atlantic K 11696		8	13 wks
8 May 82	URGENT (re-issue) *Atlantic K 11728*		45	5 wks
8 Dec 84	I WANT TO KNOW WHAT LOVE IS			
	Atlantic A 9596		11†	4 wks

FORMATIONS   *US, male vocal group*   *11 wks*

31 Jul 71	AT THE TOP OF THE STAIRS *Mojo 2027 001*		50	1 wk
14 Aug 71	AT THE TOP OF THE STAIRS (re-entry)			
	Mojo 2027 001		28	10 wks

George FORMBY
UK, male vocalist/instrumentalist - ukelele   *3 wks*

21 Jul 60	HAPPY GO LUCKY ME/BANJO BOY			
	Pye 7N 15269		40	3 wks

FORREST   *US, male vocalist*   *20 wks*

26 Feb 83 ●	ROCK THE BOAT *CBS A 3121*		4	10 wks
14 May 83	FEEL THE NEED IN ME *CBS A 3411*		17	8 wks
17 Sep 83	ONE LOVER (DON'T STOP THE SHOW)			
	CBS A 3734		67	2 wks

Lance FORTUNE   *UK, male vocalist*   *17 wks*

19 Feb 60 ●	BE MINE *Pye 7N 15240*		4	12 wks
5 May 60	THIS LOVE I HAVE FOR YOU *Pye 7N 15260*		26	5 wks

EDDY GRANT (left) He led The Equals to fame before having greater success as a solo artist.

BOBBY GOLDSBORO (right) Almost the number one position twice with the same song. The records that denied him a place at the top were The Union Gap's 'Young Girl' in 1968 and the Bay City Roller's 'Bye Bye Baby' in 1975.

GRAND FUNK RAILROAD (below) The US heavy metal outfit with a string of successful albums in the States during the early seventies – first came to prominence after an appearance at the 1969 Atlantic Pop Festival.

GO-GOS (left) Belinda Carlisle, Charlotte Caffey, Gina Schock, Jane Wiedlin and Kathy Valentine.

FORTUNES

UK, male vocal/instrumental group   *65 wks*

8 Jul	65	● YOU'VE GOT YOUR TROUBLES			
		Decca F 12173		2	14 wks
7 Oct	65	● HERE IT COMES AGAIN *Decca F 12243*		4	14 wks
3 Feb	66	THIS GOLDEN RING *Decca F 12321*		15	9 wks
11 Sep	71	● FREEDOM COME FREEDOM GO			
		Capitol CL 15693		6	17 wks
29 Jan	72	● STORM IN A TEACUP *Capitol CL 15707*		7	11 wks

FOSTER and ALLEN

Ireland, male vocal duo   *40 wks*

27 Feb	82	A BUNCH OF THYME *Ritz RITZ 5*		18	11 wks
30 Oct	82	OLD FLAMES *Ritz RITZ 028*		51	8 wks
19 Feb	83	MAGGIE *Ritz RITZ 025*		27	9 wks
29 Oct	83	I WILL LOVE YOU ALL MY LIFE			
		Ritz RITZ 056		49	6 wks
30 Jun	84	JUST FOR OLD TIME'S SAKE *Ritz RITZ 066*		47	6 wks

FOUNDATIONS

UK, male vocal/instrumental group   *56 wks*

27 Sep	67	★ BABY NOW THAT I'VE FOUND YOU			
		Pye 7N 17366		1	16 wks
24 Jan	68	BACK ON MY FEET AGAIN *Pye 7N 17417*		18	10 wks
1 May	68	ANY OLD TIME *Pye 7N 17503*		48	1 wk
15 May	68	ANY OLD TIME (re-entry) *Pye 7N 17503*		50	1 wk
20 Nov	68	● BUILD ME UP BUTTERCUP *Pye 7N 17638* ...		2	15 wks
12 Mar	69	● IN THE BAD BAD OLD DAYS *Pye 7N 17702*		8	10 wks
13 Sep	69	BORN TO LIVE AND BORN TO DIE			
		Pye 7N 17809		46	3 wks

FOUR ACES   *US, male vocal group*   *40 wks*

30 Jul	54	● THREE COINS IN THE FOUNTAIN			
		Brunswick 05308		5	5 wks
22 Oct	54	THREE COINS IN THE FOUNTAIN (re-entry)			
		Brunswick 05308		17	1 wk
7 Jan	55	● MR. SANDMAN *Brunswick 05355*		9	5 wks
20 May	55	● STRANGER IN PARADISE *Brunswick 05418*		6	6 wks
18 Nov	55	● LOVE IS A MANY SPLENDOURED THING			
		Brunswick 05480		2	13 wks
19 Oct	56	WOMAN IN LOVE *Brunswick 05589*		19	3 wks
4 Jan	57	FRIENDLY PERSUASION *Brunswick 05623*		29	1 wk
23 Jan	59	THE WORLD OUTSIDE *Brunswick 05773*		18	6 wks

FOUR BUCKETEERS

UK, male/female vocal group   *6 wks*

3 May	80	BUCKET OF WATER SONG *CBS 8393*		26	6 wks

FOUR ESQUIRES   *US, male vocal group*   *2 wks*

31 Jan	58	LOVE ME FOREVER *London HLO 8533*		23	2 wks

FOUR KNIGHTS   *US, male vocal group*   *11 wks*

4 Jun	54	● I GET SO LONELY *Capitol CL 14076*		5	7 wks
30 Jul	54	● I GET SO LONELY (re-entry) *Capitol CL 14076*		10	4 wks

FOUR LADS   *US, male vocal group*   *4 wks*

28 Apr	60	STANDING ON THE CORNER *Philips PB 1000*	34	4 wks

FOUR PENNIES

UK, male vocal/instrumental group   *56 wks*

16 Jan	64	DO YOU WANT ME TO *Philips BF 1296*		47	1 wk
6 Feb	64	DO YOU WANT ME TO (re-entry)			
		Philips BF 1296		49	1 wk
2 Apr	64	★ JULIET *Philips BF 1322*		1	15 wks
16 Jul	64	I FOUND OUT THE HARD WAY			
		Philips BF 1349		14	11 wks
29 Oct	64	BLACK GIRL *Philips BF 1366*		20	12 wks
7 Oct	65	UNTIL IT'S TIME FOR YOU TO GO			
		Philips BF 1435		19	11 wks
17 Feb	66	TROUBLE IS MY MIDDLE NAME			
		Philips BF 1469		32	5 wks

FOUR PREPS   *US, male vocal group*   *23 wks*

13 Jun	58	● BIG MAN *Capitol CL 14873*		2	13 wks
19 Sep	58	BIG MAN (re-entry) *Capitol CL 14873*		22	1 wk
26 May	60	GOT A GIRL *Capitol CL 15128*		28	6 wks
14 Jul	60	GOT A GIRL (re-entry) *Capitol CL 15128*		47	1 wk
2 Nov	61	MORE MONEY FOR YOU AND ME (MEDLEY)			
		Capitol CL 15217		39	2 wks

Tracks of medley: Mr. Blue/Alley Oop/Smoke Gets In Your Eyes/ In This Whole Wide World/A Worried Man/Tom Dooley/A Teenager In Love, all with new lyrics.

FOUR SEASONS   *US, male vocal group*   *147 wks*

4 Oct	62	● SHERRY *Stateside SS 122*		8	16 wks
17 Jan	63	BIG GIRLS DON'T CRY *Stateside SS 145*		13	10 wks
28 Mar	63	WALK LIKE A MAN *Stateside SS 169*		12	12 wks
27 Jun	63	AIN'T THAT A SHAME *Stateside SS 194*		38	3 wks
27 Aug	64	● RAG DOLL *Philips BF 1347*		2	13 wks
18 Nov	65	● LET'S HANG ON *Philips BF 1439*		4	16 wks
31 Mar	66	WORKIN' MY WAY BACK TO YOU			
		Philips BF 1474		50	3 wks
2 Jun	66	OPUS 17 (DON'T YOU WORRY 'BOUT ME)			
		Philips BF 1493		20	9 wks
29 Sep	66	I'VE GOT YOU UNDER MY SKIN			
		Philips BF 1511		12	11 wks
12 Jan	67	TELL IT TO THE RAIN *Philips BF 1538*		37	5 wks
19 Apr	75	● NIGHT *Mowest MW 3024*		7	9 wks
20 Sep	75	● WHO LOVES YOU *Warner Bros. K 16602*		6	9 wks
31 Jan	76	★ DECEMBER '63 (OH WHAT A NIGHT)			
		Warner Bros. K 16688		1	10 wks
24 Apr	76	SILVER STAR *Warner Bros. K 16742*		3	9 wks
27 Nov	76	WE CAN WORK IT OUT *Warner Bros. K 16845*		34	4 wks
18 Jun	77	RHAPSODY *Warner Bros. K 16932*		37	3 wks
20 Aug	77	DOWN THE HALL *Warner Bros. K 16982*		34	5 wks

First two Philips hits 'with the sound of Frankie Valli', last four Philips hits 'with Frankie Valli'. Mowest hit 'Frankie Valli and the Four Seasons'. See also Frankie Valli.

FOUR TOPS   *US, male vocal group*   *265 wks*

1 Jul	65	I CAN'T HELP MYSELF			
		Tamla Motown TMG 515		23	9 wks
2 Sep	65	IT'S THE SAME OLD SONG			
		Tamla Motown TMG 528		34	8 wks
21 Jul	66	LOVING YOU IS SWEETER THAN EVER			
		Tamla Motown TMG 568		21	12 wks
13 Oct	66	★ REACH OUT I'LL BE THERE			
		Tamla Motown TMG 579		1	16 wks
12 Jan	67	STANDING IN THE SHADOWS OF LOVE			
		Tamla Motown TMG 589		6	8 wks
30 Mar	67	● BERNADETTE *Tamla Motown TMG 601*		8	10 wks
15 Jun	67	SEVEN ROOMS OF GLOOM			
		Tamla Motown TMG 612		12	9 wks
11 Oct	67	YOU KEEP RUNNING AWAY			
		Tamla Motown TMG 623		26	7 wks
13 Dec	67	● WALK AWAY RENEE *Tamla Motown TMG 634*		3	11 wks
13 Mar	68	● IF I WERE A CARPENTER			
		Tamla Motown TMG 647		7	11 wks

21 Aug 68	YESTERDAY'S DREAMS			
	Tamla Motown TMG 665		23	15 wks
13 Nov 68	I'M IN A DIFFERENT WORLD			
	Tamla Motown TMG 675		27	13 wks
28 May 69	WHAT IS A MAN	*Tamla Motown TMG 698*	16	11 wks
27 Sep 69	DO WHAT YOU GOTTA DO			
	Tamla Motown TMG 710		11	11 wks
21 Mar 70 ●	I CAN'T HELP MYSELF (re-issue)			
	Tamla Motown TMG 732		10	11 wks
30 May 70 ●	IT'S ALL IN THE GAME			
	Tamla Motown TMG 736		5	14 wks
12 Sep 70	IT'S ALL IN THE GAME (re-entry)			
	Tamla Motown TMG 736		48	2 wks
3 Oct 70 ●	STILL WATER (LOVE)	*Tamla Motown TMG 752*	10	10 wks
19 Dec 70	STILL WATER (LOVE) (re-entry)			
	Tamla Motown TMG 752		44	2 wks
1 May 71	JUST SEVEN NUMBERS (CAN STRAIGHTEN			
	OUT MY LIFE) *Tamla Motown TMG 770*		36	5 wks
25 Sep 71 ●	SIMPLE GAME *Tamla Motown TMG 785*		3	11 wks
11 Mar 72	BERNADETTE (re-issue) *Tamla Motown TMG 803*	23	7 wks
5 Aug 72	WALK WITH ME TALK WITH ME DARLING			
	Tamla Motown TMG 823		32	6 wks
18 Nov 72	KEEPER OF THE CASTLE *Probe PRO 575*	18	9 wks
10 Nov 73	SWEET UNDERSTANDING LOVE			
	Probe PRO 604		29	10 wks
17 Oct 81 ●	WHEN SHE WAS MY GIRL			
	Casablanca CAN 1005		3	10 wks
19 Dec 81	DON'T WALK AWAY *Casablanca CAN 1006*	16	11 wks
6 Mar 82	TONIGHT I'M GONNA LOVE YOU ALL OVER			
	Casablanca/Phonogram CAN 1008		43	4 wks
26 Jun 82	BACK TO SCHOOL AGAIN *RSO 89*	62	2 wks

See also Supremes and the Four Tops.

FOURMOST
UK, male vocal/instrumental group — 64 wks

12 Sep 63 ●	HELLO LITTLE GIRL *Parlophone R 5056*	9	17 wks
26 Dec 63	I'M IN LOVE *Parlophone R 5078*	17	12 wks
23 Apr 64 ●	A LITTLE LOVING *Parlophone R 5128*	6	13 wks
13 Aug 64	HOW CAN I TELL HER *Parlophone R 5157*	33	4 wks
26 Nov 64	BABY I NEED YOUR LOVIN' *Parlophone R 5194*	24	12 wks
9 Dec 65	GIRLS GIRLS GIRLS *Parlophone R 5379*	33	6 wks

14-18
UK, male vocalist, Peter Waterman, under false group name — 4 wks

| 1 Nov 75 | GOODBYE-EE *Magnet MAG 48* | 33 | 4 wks |

FOX
UK, male/female vocal/instrumental group — 29 wks

15 Feb 75 ●	ONLY YOU CAN *GTO GT 8*	3	11 wks
10 May 75	IMAGINE ME IMAGINE YOU *GTO GT 21*	15	8 wks
10 Apr 76 ●	S-S-S-SINGLE BED *GTO GT 57*	4	10 wks

Noosha FOX
UK, female vocalist — 6 wks

| 12 Nov 77 | GEORGINA BAILEY *GTO GT 106* | 31 | 6 wks |

Bruce FOXTON
UK, male vocalist — 9 wks

30 Jul 83	FREAK *Arista BFOX 1*	23	5 wks
29 Oct 83	THIS IS THE WAY *Arista BFOX 2*	56	3 wks
21 Apr 84	IT MAKES ME WONDER *Arista BFOX 3*	74	1 wk

Inez FOXX
US, female vocalist — 3 wks

| 23 Jul 64 | HURT BY LOVE *Sue WI 323* | 40 | 3 wks |

See also Inez and Charlie Foxx.

Inez and Charlie FOXX
US, female/male vocal/instrumental duo, Charlie Foxx guitar — 5 wks

| 19 Feb 69 | MOCKINGBIRD *United Artists UP 2269* | 36 | 2 wks |
| 19 Mar 69 | MOCKINGBIRD (re-entry) *United Artists UP 2269* | 34 | 3 wks |

See also Inez Foxx.

John FOXX
UK, male vocalist — 31 wks

26 Jan 80	UNDERPASS *Virgin/Metal Beat VS 318*	31	8 wks
29 Mar 80	NO-ONE DRIVING (Double single)		
	Virgin/Metal Beat VS 338	32	4 wks
19 Jul 80	BURNING CAR *Virgin/Metal Beat VS 360*	35	7 wks
8 Nov 80	MILES AWAY *Virgin/Metal Beat VS 382*	51	3 wks
29 Aug 81	EUROPE - AFTER THE RUN *Virgin VS 393*	40	5 wks
2 Jul 83	ENDLESSLY *Virgin VS 543*	66	3 wks
17 Sep 83	YOUR DRESS *Virgin VS 615*	61	1 wk

Tracks on double single: No-One Driving/Glimmer/Mr. No/This City.

FRAGGLES
UK/US, puppets — 8 wks

| 18 Feb 84 | FRAGGLE ROCK THEME *RCA 389* | 33 | 8 wks |

Peter FRAMPTON
UK, male vocalist — 24 wks

1 May 76 ●	SHOW ME THE WAY *A & M AMS 7218*	10	12 wks
11 Sep 76	BABY I LOVE YOUR WAY *A & M AMS 7246*	43	5 wks
6 Nov 76	DO YOU FEEL LIKE WE DO		
	A & M AMS 7260	39	4 wks
23 Jul 77	I'M IN YOU *A & M AMS 7298*	41	3 wks

Connie FRANCIS
US, female vocalist — 241 wks

4 Apr 58 ★	WHO'S SORRY NOW *MGM 975*	1	25 wks
27 Jun 58	I'M SORRY I MADE YOU CRY *MGM 982*	11	10 wks
22 Aug 58 ★	CAROLINA MOON/STUPID CUPID *MGM 985*	1	19 wks
31 Oct 58	I'LL GET BY *MGM 993*	19	6 wks
21 Nov 58	FALLIN' *MGM 993*	20	5 wks
26 Dec 58	YOU ALWAYS HURT THE ONE YOU LOVE		
	MGM 998	13	7 wks
13 Feb 59 ●	MY HAPPINESS *MGM 1001*	4	14 wks
29 May 59	MY HAPPINESS (re-entry) *MGM 1001*	30	1 wk
3 Jul 59 ●	LIPSTICK ON YOUR COLLAR *MGM 1018*	3	16 wks
11 Sep 59	PLENTY GOOD LOVIN' *MGM 1036*	18	6 wks
4 Dec 59	AMONG MY SOUVENIRS *MGM 1046*	11	10 wks
17 Mar 60	VALENTINO *MGM 1060*	27	8 wks
19 May 60 ●	MAMA /ROBOT MAN *MGM 1076*	2	19 wks
18 Aug 60 ●	EVERYBODY'S SOMEBODY'S FOOL		
	MGM 1086	5	13 wks
3 Nov 60 ●	MY HEART HAS A MIND OF ITS OWN		
	MGM 1100	3	15 wks
12 Jan 61	MANY TEARS AGO *MGM 1111*	12	9 wks
16 Mar 61 ●	WHERE THE BOYS ARE/BABY ROO		
	MGM 1121	5	14 wks
15 Jun 61	BREAKIN' IN A BRAND NEW BROKEN HEART		
	MGM 1136	12	11 wks
14 Sep 61 ●	TOGETHER *MGM 1138*	6	11 wks
14 Dec 61	BABY'S FIRST CHRISTMAS *MGM 1145*	30	4 wks
26 Apr 62	DON'T BREAK THE HEART THAT LOVES		
	YOU *MGM 1157*	39	3 wks
2 Aug 62 ●	VACATION *MGM 1165*	10	9 wks
20 Dec 62	I'M GONNA BE WARM THIS WINTER		
	MGM 1185	48	1 wk
10 Jun 65	MY CHILD *MGM 1271*	26	6 wks
20 Jan 66	JEALOUS HEART *MGM 1293*	44	2 wks

Claude FRANCOIS
France, male vocalist — 4 wks

| 10 Jan 76 | TEARS ON THE TELEPHONE | | |
| | *Bradley's BRAD 7528* | 35 | 4 wks |

Joe FRANK - *See HAMILTON, Joe FRANK and REYNOLDS*

FRANKIE GOES TO HOLLYWOOD
UK, male vocal/instrumental group   *74 wks*

26 Nov 83	★	RELAX *ZTT/Island ZTAS 1*	1	48 wks
16 Jun 84	★	TWO TRIBES *ZTT/Island ZTAS 3*	1	20 wks
10 Nov 84		TWO TRIBES (re-entry) *ZTT/Island ZTAS 3* ...	73	1 wk
4 Dec 84	★	THE POWER OF LOVE *ZTT/Island ZTAS 5* ...	1†	5 wks

Aretha FRANKLIN *US, female vocalist*   *96 wks*

8 Jun 67	●	RESPECT *Atlantic 584 115*	10	14 wks
23 Aug 67		BABY I LOVE YOU *Atlantic 584 127*	39	4 wks
20 Dec 67		CHAIN OF FOOLS/SATISFACTION *Atlantic 584 157*	43	2 wks
10 Jan 68		SATISFACTION (re-entry) *Atlantic 584 157*	37	5 wks
13 Mar 68		SINCE YOU'VE BEEN GONE *Atlantic 584 172*	47	1 wk
22 May 68		THINK *Atlantic 584 186*	26	9 wks
7 Aug 68	●	I SAY A LITTLE PRAYER *Atlantic 584 206*	4	14 wks
22 Aug 70		DON'T PLAY THAT SONG *Atlantic 2091 027*	13	11 wks
2 Oct 71		SPANISH HARLEM *Atlantic 2091 138*	14	9 wks
8 Sep 73		ANGEL *Atlantic K 10346*	37	5 wks
16 Feb 74		UNTIL YOU COME BACK TO ME (THAT'S WHAT I'M GONNA DO) *Atlantic K 10399* ...	26	8 wks
6 Dec 80		WHAT A FOOL BELIEVES *Arista ARIST 377* ..	46	7 wks
4 Sep 82		JUMP TO IT *Arista ARIST 479*	42	5 wks
23 Jul 83		GET IT RIGHT *Arista ARIST 537*	74	2 wks

See also Aretha Franklin and George Benson.

Aretha FRANKLIN and George BENSON *US, female vocalist and male vocalist/instrumentalist - guitar*   *3 wks*

19 Sep 81	LOVE ALL THE HURT AWAY *Arista ARIST 428*	49	3 wks

See also Aretha Franklin; George Benson.

Rodney FRANKLIN
US, male instrumentalist - piano   *9 wks*

19 Apr 80	●	THE GROOVE *CBS 8529*	7	9 wks

FRANTIC FIVE - *See Don LANG*

FRANTIQUE *US, female vocal group*   *12 wks*

11 Aug 79	◉	STRUT YOUR FUNKY STUFF *Philadelphia International PIR 7728*	10	12 wks

Stan FREBERG *US, male vocalist*   *4 wks*

19 Nov 54	SH-BOOM *Capitol CL 14187*	15	2 wks
27 Jul 56	ROCK ISLAND LINE/HEARTBREAK HOTEL *Capitol CL 14608*	24	1 wk
10 Aug 56	ROCK ISLAND LINE/HEARTBREAK HOTEL (re-entry) *Capitol CL 14608*	29	1 wk

John FRED and the PLAYBOY BAND *US, male vocal/instrumental group*   *12 wks*

3 Jan 68	●	JUDY IN DISGUISE (WITH GLASSES) *Pye International 7N 25442*	3	12 wks

FREDDIE and the DREAMERS
UK, male vocal/instrumental group   *85 wks*

9 May 63	●	IF YOU GOTTA MAKE A FOOL OF SOMEBODY *Columbia DB 7032*	3	14 wks
8 Aug 63	●	I'M TELLING YOU NOW *Columbia DB 7068* ..	2	11 wks
7 Nov 63	●	YOU WERE MADE FOR ME *Columbia DB 7147*	3	15 wks
20 Feb 64		OVER YOU *Columbia DB 7214*	13	11 wks
14 May 64		I LOVE YOU BABY *Columbia DB 7286*	16	8 wks
16 Jul 64		JUST FOR YOU *Columbia DB 7322*	41	3 wks
5 Nov 64	●	I UNDERSTAND *Columbia DB 7381*	5	15 wks
22 Apr 65		A LITTLE YOU *Columbia DB 7526*	26	5 wks
4 Nov 65		THOU SHALT NOT STEAL *Columbia DB 7720*	44	3 wks

FREDERICK - *See NINA and FREDERICK*

FREE *UK, male vocal/instrumental group*   *66 wks*

6 Jun 70	●	ALL RIGHT NOW *Island WIP 6082*	2	16 wks
1 May 71	●	MY BROTHER JAKE *Island WIP 6100*	4	11 wks
27 May 72		LITTLE BIT OF LOVE *Island WIP 6129*	13	10 wks
13 Jan 73	●	WISHING WELL *Island WIP 6146*	7	10 wks
21 Jul 73		ALL RIGHT NOW (re-entry) *Island WIP 6082*	15	9 wks
18 Feb 78		FREE (EP) *Island IEP 6*	11	7 wks
23 Oct 82		FREE (EP) (re-entry) *Island IEP 6*	57	3 wks

Tracks on Free EP: All Right Now/My Brother Jake/ Wishing Well.

FREEEZ *UK, male instrumental group*   *40 wks*

7 Jun 80		KEEP IN TOUCH *Calibre CAB 103*	49	3 wks
7 Feb 81	●	SOUTHERN FREEEZ *Beggars Banquet BEG 51* ..	8	11 wks
18 Apr 81		FLYING HIGH *Beggars Banquet BEG 55*	35	5 wks
18 Jun 83		I.O.U. *Beggars Banquet BEG 96*	2	15 wks
1 Oct 83		POP GOES MY LOVE *Beggars Banquet BEG 98* ..	26	6 wks

FREEHOLD JUNIOR SCHOOL - *See Fogwell FLAX and the ANKLEBITERS from FREEHOLD JUNIOR SCHOOL*

FRESHIES
UK, male vocal/instrumental group   *3 wks*

14 Feb 81	I'M IN LOVE WITH THE GIRL ON A CERTAIN MANCHESTER MEGASTORE CHECKOUT DESK *MCA 760*	54	3 wks

Matt FRETTON *UK, male vocalist*   *5 wks*

11 Jun 83	IT'S SO HIGH *Chrysalis MATT 1*	50	5 wks

⌇⌇⌇ (FREUR)
UK, male vocal/instrumental group   *4 wks*

23 Apr 83	DOOT DOOT *CBS A 3141*	59	4 wks

FRIDA *Norway, female vocalist*   *7 wks*

21 Aug 82	I KNOW THERE'S SOMETHING GOING ON *Epic EPC A2603*	43	7 wks

See also Frida and B. A. Robertson.

FRIDA and B. A. ROBERTSON
Norway/UK, female/male vocal duo   *5 wks*

17 Dec 83	TIME *Epic A 3983*	45	5 wks

See also Frida; B.A. Robertson; B.A. Robertson and Maggie Bell.

Dean FRIEDMAN *US, male vocalist*   *22 wks*

3 Jun 78	WOMAN OF MINE *Lifesong LS 401*	52	5 wks
23 Sep 78	● LUCKY STARS *Lifesong LS 402*	3	10 wks
18 Nov 78	LYDIA *Lifesong LS 403*	31	7 wks

FRIENDS - *See DELANEY and BONNIE and FRIENDS featuring Eric CLAPTON*

FRIENDS - *See Brian MAY and FRIENDS*

FRIENDS AGAIN *UK, male vocal/instrumental group*   *3 wks*

| 4 Aug 84 | THE FRIENDS AGAIN (EP) | | |
| | *Mercury/Phonogram FA 1* .... | 59 | 3 wks |

Tracks on EP: *Lullaby On Board/Wand You Wave/Thank You For Being an Angel.*

FRIJID PINK *US, male vocal/instrumental group*   *16 wks*

| 28 Mar 70 | ● HOUSE OF THE RISING SUN *Deram DM 288* | 4 | 16 wks |

Jane FROMAN *US, female vocalist*   *4 wks*

| 17 Jun 55 | I WONDER *Capitol CL 14254* .... | 14 | 4 wks |

Bobby FULLER FOUR *US, male vocal/instrumental group*   *4 wks*

| 14 Apr 66 | I FOUGHT THE LAW *London HL 10030* .... | 33 | 4 wks |

FUNBOY THREE *UK, male vocal/instrumental group*   *50 wks*

7 Nov 81	THE LUNATICS (HAVE TAKEN OVER THE		
	ASYLUM) *Chrysalis CHS 2563*	20	12 wks
8 May 82	THE TELEPHONE ALWAYS RINGS		
	Chrysalis CHS 2609	17	9 wks
31 Jul 82	SUMMERTIME *Chrysalis CHS 2629*	18	8 wks
15 Jan 83	THE MORE I SEE (THE LESS I BELIEVE)		
	Chrysalis CHS 2554	68	1 wk
5 Feb 83	● TUNNEL OF LOVE *Chrysalis CHS 2678*	10	10 wks
30 Apr 83	● OUR LIPS ARE SEALED *Chrysalis FUNB 1*	7	10 wks

See also Funboy Three and Bananarama.

FUNBOY THREE and BANANARAMA *UK, male vocal group and female vocal group*   *10 wks*

| 13 Feb 82 | ● IT AIN'T WHAT YOU DO IT'S THE WAY THAT | | |
| | YOU DO IT *Chrysalis CHS 2570* .... | 4 | 10 wks |

See also Funboy Three; Bananarama.

FUNK MASTERS *UK, male/female vocal/instrumental group*   *12 wks*

| 18 Jun 83 | ● IT'S OVER *Master Funk Records 7MP 004* .... | 8 | 12 wks |

FUNKADELIC *US, male vocal/instrumental group*   *12 wks*

| 9 Dec 78 | ● ONE NATION UNDER A GROOVE - (PART 1) | | |
| | *Warner Bros. K 17246* .... | 9 | 12 wks |

FUNKAPOLITAN *UK, male vocal/instrumental group*   *7 wks*

| 22 Aug 81 | AS TIME GOES BY (VOCALS) *London LON 001* | 41 | 7 wks |

FUNKY BOYS - *See LINDA and the FUNKY BOYS*

FUREYS *Ireland, male vocal group*   *14 wks*

10 Oct 81	WHEN YOU WERE SWEET SIXTEEN		
	Ritz RITZ 003	14	11 wks
3 Apr 82	I WILL LOVE YOU (EVERY TIME WHEN WE		
	ARE GONE) *Ritz RITZ 012*	54	3 wks

When You Were Sweet Sixteen *credits the Fureys with Davey Arthur.*

FURIOUS FIVE - *See GRANDMASTER FLASH, Melle MEL and the FURIOUS FIVE*

Billy FURY *UK, male vocalist*   *281 wks*

27 Feb 59	MAYBE TOMORROW *Decca F 11102*	22	3 wks
27 Mar 59	MAYBE TOMORROW (re-entry) *Decca F 11102*	18	6 wks
26 Jun 59	MARGOT *Decca F 11128*	28	1 wk
10 Mar 60	● COLETTE *Decca F 11200*	9	10 wks
26 May 60	THAT'S LOVE *Decca F 11237*	19	11 wks
22 Sep 60	WONDROUS PLACE *Decca F 11267*	25	9 wks
19 Jan 61	A THOUSAND STARS *Decca F 11311*	14	10 wks
27 Apr 61	DON'T WORRY *Decca F 11334*	40	2 wks
11 May 61	● HALFWAY TO PARADISE *Decca F 11349*	3	23 wks
7 Sep 61	● JEALOUSY *Decca F 11384*	2	12 wks
14 Dec 61	● I'D NEVER FIND ANOTHER YOU		
	Decca F 11409	5	15 wks
15 Mar 62	LETTER FULL OF TEARS *Decca F 11437*	32	6 wks
3 May 62	● LAST NIGHT WAS MADE FOR LOVE		
	Decca F 11458	4	16 wks
19 Jul 62	● ONCE UPON A DREAM *Decca F 11485*	7	13 wks
25 Oct 62	BECAUSE OF LOVE *Decca F 11508*	18	14 wks
14 Feb 63	● LIKE I'VE NEVER BEEN GONE *Decca F11582*	3	15 wks
16 May 63	● WHEN WILL YOU SAY I LOVE YOU		
	Decca F 11655	3	12 wks
25 Jul 63	● IN SUMMER *Decca F 11701*	5	11 wks
3 Oct 63	SOMEBODY ELSE'S GIRL *Decca F 11744*	18	7 wks
2 Jan 64	DO YOU REALLY LOVE ME TOO		
	Decca F 11792	13	10 wks
30 Apr 64	I WILL *Decca F 118888*	14	12 wks
23 Jul 64	● IT'S ONLY MAKE BELIEVE *Decca F 11939*	10	10 wks
14 Jan 65	I'M LOST WITHOUT YOU *Decca F 12048*	16	10 wks
22 Jul 65	● IN THOUGHTS OF YOU *Decca F 12178*	9	11 wks
16 Sep 65	RUN TO MY LOVIN' ARMS *Decca F 12230* ...	25	7 wks
10 Feb 66	I'LL NEVER QUITE GET OVER YOU		
	Decca F 12325	35	5 wks
4 Aug 66	GIVE ME YOUR WORD *Decca F 12459*	27	7 wks
4 Sep 82	LOVE OR MONEY *Polydor POSP 488*	57	5 wks
13 Nov 82	DEVIL OR ANGEL *Polydor POSP 528*	58	4 wks
4 Jun 83	FORGET HIM *Polydor POSP 558*	59	4 wks

Leslie FYSON - *See Michael MEDWIN, Bernard BRESSLAW, Alfie BASS and Leslie FYSON*

G

Bobby G   UK, male vocalist
4 wks

| 1 Dec 84 | BIG DEAL | BBC RESL 151 | 75 | 1 wk |
| 15 Dec 84 | BIG DEAL | (re-entry) BBC RESL 151 | 66† | 3 wks |

Kenny G
US, male instrumentalist - saxophone
3 wks

| 21 Apr 84 | HI! HOW YA DOIN'? | Arista ARIST 561 | 70 | 3 wks |

GBH   UK, male vocal/instrumental group
5 wks

| 6 Feb 82 | NO SURVIVORS | Clay CLAY 8 | 63 | 2 wks |
| 20 Nov 82 | GIVE ME FIRE | Clay CLAY 16 | 69 | 3 wks |

G. F. BAND   -   See Gene FARROW and G. F. BAND

G. Q.   US, male vocal/instrumental group
6 wks

| 10 Mar 79 | DISCO NIGHTS (ROCK FREAK) | | | |
| | Arista ARIST 245 | | 42 | 6 wks |

Peter GABRIEL   UK, male vocalist
40 wks

9 Apr 77	SOLSBURY HILL	Charisma CB 301	13	9 wks
9 Feb 80 ●	GAMES WITHOUT FRONTIERS			
	Charisma CB 354		4	11 wks
10 May 80	NO SELF CONTROL	Charisma CB 360	33	6 wks
23 Aug 80	BIKO	Charisma CB 370	38	3 wks
25 Sep 82	SHOCK THE MONKEY			
	Charisma/Phonogram SHOCK 1		58	5 wks
9 Jul 83	I DON'T REMEMBER	Charisma/Phonogram GAB 1	62	3 wks
2 Jun 84	WALK THROUGH THE FIRE	Virgin US 689	69	3 wks

Yvonne GAGE   US, female vocalist
4 wks

| 16 Jun 84 | DOIN' IT IN A HAUNTED HOUSE | Epic A 4519 | 45 | 4 wks |

Serge GAINSBOURG   -   See Jane BIRKIN and Serge GAINSBOURG

GALAXY   -   See Phil FEARON and GALAXY

GALLAGHER and LYLE
UK, male vocal/instrumental duo
27 wks

28 Feb 76 ●	I WANNA STAY WITH YOU			
	A & M AMS 7211		6	9 wks
22 May 76 ●	HEART ON MY SLEEVE	A & M AMS 7227	6	10 wks
11 Sep 76	BREAKAWAY	A & M AMS 7245	35	4 wks
29 Jan 77	EVERY LITTLE TEARDROP			
	A & M AMS 7274		32	4 wks

Patsy GALLANT   Canada, female vocalist
9 wks

| 10 Sep 77 ● | FROM NEW YORK TO L.A. | EMI 2620 | 6 | 9 wks |

James GALWAY
Ireland, male instrumentalist - flute
13 wks

| 27 May 78 ● | ANNIE'S SONG | RCA Red Seal RB 5085 | 3 | 13 wks |

GANG OF FOUR
UK, male vocal/instrumental group
5 wks

| 16 Jun 79 | AT HOME HE'S A TOURIST | EMI 2956 | 58 | 3 wks |
| 22 May 82 | I LOVE A MAN IN UNIFORM | EMI 5299 | 65 | 2 wks |

GAP BAND
US, male vocal/instrumental group
58 wks

12 Jul 80 ●	OOPS UP SIDE YOUR HEAD	Mercury MER 22	6	14 wks
27 Sep 80	PARTY LIGHTS	Mercury MER 37	30	8 wks
27 Dec 80	BURN RUBBER ON ME (WHY YOU WANNA HURT ME)	Mercury MER 52	22	11 wks
11 Apr 81	HUMPIN'	Mercury MER 63	36	6 wks
27 Jun 81	YEARNING FOR YOUR LOVE	Mercury MER 73	47	4 wks
5 Jun 82	EARLY IN THE MORNING			
	Mercury/Phonogram MER 97		55	3 wks
19 Feb 83	OUTSTANDING			
	Total Experience/Phonogram TE 001		68	2 wks
31 Mar 84	SOMEDAY	Total Experience/Phonogram TE 5	17	8 wks
23 Jun 84	JAMMIN' IN AMERICA			
	Total Experience/Phonogram TE 6		64	2 wks

Paul GARDINER
UK, male instrumentalist - bass
4 wks

| 25 Jul 81 | STORMTROOPER IN DRAG | | | |
| | Beggars Banquet BEG 61 | | 49 | 4 wks |

Featuring Gary Numan on vocals. See also Gary Numan.

GARDNER   -   See ASHTON, GARDNER and DYKE

Boris GARDNER
Jamaica, male instrumentalist - organ
14 wks

| 17 Jan 70 | ELIZABETHAN REGGAE | Duke DU 39 | 48 | 1 wk |
| 31 Jan 70 | ELIZABETHAN REGGAE | (re-entry) Duke DU 39 | 14 | 13 wks |

Art GARFUNKEL   US, male vocalist
37 wks

13 Sep 75	★ I ONLY HAVE EYES FOR YOU	CBS 3575	1	11 wks
3 Mar 79	★ BRIGHT EYES	CBS 6947	1	19 wks
7 Jul 79	SINCE I DON'T HAVE YOU	CBS 7371	38	7 wks

See also Simon and Garfunkel.

Judy GARLAND   US, female vocalist
2 wks

| 10 Jun 55 | THE MAN THAT GOT AWAY | Philips PB 366 | 18 | 2 wks |

Lee GARRETT   US, male vocalist
7 wks

| 29 May 76 | YOU'RE MY EVERYTHING | Chrysalis CHS 2087 | 15 | 7 wks |

Leif GARRETT   US, male vocalist
14 wks

20 Jan 79 ●	I WAS MADE FOR DANCIN'			
	Scotti Brothers K 11202		4	10 wks
21 Apr 79	FEEL THE NEED	Scotti Brothers K 11274	38	4 wks

David GARRICK   UK, male vocalist
16 wks

| 9 Jun 66 | LADY JANE | Piccadilly 7N 35317 | 28 | 7 wks |
| 22 Sep 66 | DEAR MRS. APPLEBEE | Piccadilly 7N 35335 | 22 | 9 wks |

GARY'S GANG
US, male vocal/instrumental group   *18 wks*

24 Feb	79	● KEEP ON DANCIN' *CBS 7109*	**8**	10 wks
2 Jun	79	LET'S LOVE DANCE TONIGHT *CBS 7328* ...	**49**	4 wks
6 Nov	82	KNOCK ME OUT *Arista ARIST 499*	**45**	4 wks

Barbara GASKIN - *See Dave STEWART with Barbara GASKIN*

David GATES *US, male vocalist*   *2 wks*

22 Jul	78	TOOK THE LAST TRAIN *Elektra K 12307*	**50**	2 wks

Marvin GAYE *US, male vocalist*   *89 wks*

10 Dec	64	HOW SWEET IT IS *Stateside SS 360*	**49**	1 wk
29 Sep	66	LITTLE DARLIN' *Tamla Motown TMG 574*	**50**	1 wk
12 Feb	69	★ I HEARD IT THROUGH THE GRAPEVINE *Tamla Motown TMG 686*	**1**	15 wks
23 Jul	69	● TOO BUSY THINKING 'BOUT MY BABY *Tamla Motown TMG 705*	**5**	16 wks
9 May	70	● ABRAHAM MARTIN & JOHN *Tamla Motown TMG 734*	**9**	14 wks
11 Dec	71	SAVE THE CHILDREN *Tamla Motown TMG 796*	**41**	6 wks
22 Sep	73	LET'S GET IT ON *Tamla Motown TMG 868*	**31**	7 wks
7 May	77	● GOT TO GIVE IT UP *Motown TMG 1069* ...	**7**	10 wks
30 Oct	82	(SEXUAL) HEALING *CBS A 2855*	**4**	14 wks
8 Jan	83	MY LOVE IS WAITING *CBS A 3048*	**34**	5 wks

See also Diana Ross and Marvin Gaye; Marvin Gaye and Tammi Terrell; Marvin Gaye and Mary Wells; Marvin Gaye and Kim Weston; Diana Ross, Marvin Gaye, Smokey Robinson and Stevie Wonder.

Marvin GAYE and Tammi TERRELL *US, male/female vocal duo*   *61 wks*

17 Jan	68	IF I COULD BUILD MY WHOLE WORLD AROUND YOU *Tamla Motown TMG 635*	**41**	7 wks
12 Jun	68	AIN'T NOTHIN' LIKE THE REAL THING *Tamla Motown TMG 655*	**34**	7 wks
2 Oct	68	YOU'RE ALL I NEED TO GET BY *Tamla Motown TMG 668*	**19**	19 wks
22 Jan	69	YOU AIN'T LIVIN' TILL YOU'RE LOVIN' *Tamla Motown TMG 681*	**21**	8 wks
4 Jun	69	GOOD LOVIN' AIN'T EASY TO COME BY *Tamla Motown TMG 697*	**26**	7 wks
30 Jul	69	GOOD LOVIN' AIN'T EASY TO COME BY (re-entry) *Tamla Motown TMG 697*	**48**	1 wk
15 Nov	69	● ONION SONG *Tamla Motown TMG 715*	**9**	12 wks

See also Marvin Gaye; Diana Ross and Marvin Gaye; Marvin Gaye and Mary Wells; Marvin Gaye and Kim Weston; Diana Ross, Marvin Gaye, Smokey Robinson and Stevie Wonder.

Marvin GAYE and Mary WELLS
US, male/female vocal duo   *1 wk*

30 Jul	64	ONCE UPON A TIME *Stateside SS 316*	**50**	1 wk

See also Marvin Gaye; Mary Wells; Marvin Gaye and Tammi Terrell; Marvin Gaye and Kim Weston; Diana Ross and Marvin Gaye; Diana Ross, Marvin Gaye, Smokey Robinson and Stevie Wonder.

Marvin GAYE and Kim WESTON
US, male/female vocal duo   *11 wks*

26 Jan	67	IT TAKES TWO *Tamla Motown TMG 590*	**16**	11 wks

See also Marvin Gaye; Marvin Gaye and Tammi Terrell; Marvin Gaye and Mary Wells; Diana Ross and Marvin Gaye; Diana Ross, Marvin Gaye, Smokey Robinson and Stevie Wonder.

Crystal GAYLE *US, female vocalist*   *28 wks*

12 Nov	77	● DON'T IT MAKE MY BROWN EYES BLUE *United Artists UP 36307*	**5**	14 wks
26 Aug	78	TALKING IN YOUR SLEEP *United Artists UP 36422*	**11**	14 wks

Gloria GAYNOR *US, female vocalist*   *62 wks*

7 Dec	74	● NEVER CAN SAY GOODBYE *MGM 2006 463*	**2**	13 wks
8 Mar	75	REACH OUT I'LL BE THERE *MGM 2006 499*	**14**	8 wks
9 Aug	75	ALL I NEED IS YOUR SWEET LOVIN' *MGM 2006 531*	**44**	3 wks
17 Jan	76	HOW HIGH THE MOON *MGM 2006 558*	**33**	4 wks
3 Feb	79	★ I WILL SURVIVE *Polydor 2095 017*	**1**	15 wks
6 Oct	79	LET ME KNOW (I HAVE A RIGHT) *Polydor STEP 5*	**32**	7 wks
24 Dec	83	I AM WHAT I AM *Chrysalis CHS 2765*	**13**	12 wks

GAZ *US, male vocal/instrumental group*   *4 wks*

24 Feb	79	SING SING *Salsoul SSOL 116*	**60**	4 wks

GB EXPERIENCE - *See Gary BYRD and the GB EXPERIENCE*

G-CLEFS *US, male vocal group*   *12 wks*

30 Nov	61	I UNDERSTAND *London HLU 9433*	**17**	12 wks

J. GEILS BAND
US, male vocal/instrumental group   *20 wks*

9 Jun	79	ONE LAST KISS *EMI AMERICA AM 507*	**74**	1 wk
13 Feb	82	● CENTERFOLD *EMI AMERICA EA 135*	**3**	9 wks
10 Apr	82	FREEZE-FRAME *EMI AMERICA EA 134*	**27**	7 wks
26 Jun	82	ANGEL IN BLUE *EMI AMERICA EA 138*	**55**	3 wks

GENERAL PUBLIC
UK, male vocal/instrumental group   *3 wks*

10 Mar	84	GENERAL PUBLIC *Virgin VS 659*	**60**	3 wks

GENERATION X
UK, male vocal/instrumental group   *31 wks*

17 Sep	77	YOUR GENERATION *Chrysalis CHS 2165*	**36**	4 wks
11 Mar	78	READY STEADY GO *Chrysalis CHS 2207*	**47**	3 wks
20 Jan	79	KING ROCKER *Chrysalis CHS 2261*	**11**	9 wks
7 Apr	79	VALLEY OF THE DOLLS *Chrysalis CHS 2310*	**23**	7 wks
30 Jun	79	FRIDAY'S ANGELS *Chrysalis CHS 2330*	**62**	2 wks
18 Oct	80	DANCING WITH MYSELF *Chrysalis CHS 2444*	**62**	2 wks
24 Jan	81	DANCING WITH MYSELF (EP) *Chrysalis CHS 2488*	**60**	4 wks

From Dancing With Myself, group is billed as Gen X. Dancing With Myself EP contains the following tracks: Dancing with Myself/Untouchables/Rock On/King Rocker.

GENESIS *UK, male vocal/instrumental group*   *105 wks*

6 Apr	74	I KNOW WHAT I LIKE (IN YOUR WARDROBE) *Charisma CB 224*	**21**	7 wks
26 Feb	77	YOUR OWN SPECIAL WAY *Charisma CB 300*	**43**	3 wks
28 May	77	SPOT THE PIGEON (EP) *Charisma GEN 001* ...	**14**	7 wks
11 Mar	78	● FOLLOW YOU FOLLOW ME *Charisma CB 309*	**7**	13 wks
8 Jul	78	MANY TOO MANY *Charisma CB 315*	**43**	5 wks
15 Mar	80	● TURN IT ON AGAIN *Charisma CB 356*	**8**	10 wks
17 May	80	DUCHESS *Charisma CB 363*	**46**	5 wks
13 Sep	80	MISUNDERSTANDING *Charisma CB 369*	**42**	5 wks

22 Aug 81	● **ABACAB** *Charisma CB 388*	**9**	8 wks
31 Oct 81	**KEEP IT DARK** *Charisma CB 391*	**33**	4 wks
13 Mar 82	**MAN ON THE CORNER** *Charisma CB 393*	**41**	5 wks
22 May 82	● **3 X 3** (EP) *Charisma/Phonogram GEN 1*	**10**	8 wks
3 Sep 83	● **MAMA** *Virgin/Charisma MAMA 1*	**4**	10 wks
12 Nov 83	**THAT'S ALL** *Charisma/Virgin TATA 1*	**16**	11 wks
11 Feb 84	**ILLEGAL ALIEN** *Charisma/Virgin AL1*	**46**	3 wks
10 Mar 84	**ILLEGAL ALIEN** (re-entry) *Charisma/Virgin AL1*	**70**	1 wk

Tracks on Spot The Pigeon EP: Match Of The Day/Pigeons/Inside and Out. Tracks on 3 x 3 EP: Paper Late/ You Might Recall/Me And Virgil.

GENEVIEVE *France, female vocalist*   1 wk

5 May 66	**ONCE** *CBS 202061*	**43**	1 wk

Bobbie GENTRY *US, female vocalist*   34 wks

13 Sep 67	**ODE TO BILLY JOE** *Capitol CL 15511*	**13**	11 wks
30 Aug 69	★ **I'LL NEVER FALL IN LOVE AGAIN** *Capitol CL 15606*	**1**	19 wks
21 Feb 70	**RAINDROPS KEEP FALLIN' ON MY HEAD** *Capitol CL 15626*	**40**	4 wks

See also Bobbie Gentry and Glen Campbell.

Bobbie GENTRY and Glen CAMPBELL *US, female/male vocal duo*   14 wks

6 Dec 69	● **ALL I HAVE TO DO IS DREAM** *Capitol CL 15619*	**3**	14 wks

See also Bobbie Gentry; Glen Campbell.

GEORDIE *UK, vocal/instrumental group*   35 wks

2 Dec 72	**DON'T DO THAT** *Regal Zonophone RZ 3067* ...	**32**	7 wks
17 Mar 73	● **ALL BECAUSE OF YOU** *EMI 2008*	**6**	13 wks
16 Jun 73	**CAN YOU DO IT** *EMI 2031*	**13**	9 wks
25 Aug 73	**ELECTRIC LADY** *EMI 2047*	**32**	6 wks

Danyel GERARD *France, male vocalist*   12 wks

18 Sep 71	**BUTTERFLY** *CBS 7453*	**11**	12 wks

---

GERRY and the PACEMAKERS
UK, male vocal/instrumental group   114 wks

14 Mar 63	★ **HOW DO YOU DO IT?** *Columbia DB 4987*	**1**	18 wks
30 May 63	★ **I LIKE IT** *Columbia DB 7041*	**1**	15 wks
10 Oct 63	★ **YOU'LL NEVER WALK ALONE** *Columbia DB 7126*	**1**	19 wks
16 Jan 64	● **I'M THE ONE** *Columbia DB 7189*	**2**	15 wks
16 Apr 64	● **DON'T LET THE SUN CATCH YOU CRYING** *Columbia DB 7268*	**6**	11 wks
3 Sep 64	**IT'S GONNA BE ALL RIGHT** *Columbia DB 7353*	**24**	7 wks
17 Dec 64	● **FERRY ACROSS THE MERSEY** *Columbia DB 7437*	**8**	13 wks
25 Mar 65	**I'LL BE THERE** *Columbia DB 7504*	**15**	9 wks
18 Nov 65	**WALK HAND IN HAND** *Columbia DB 7738*	**29**	7 wks

---

Stan GETZ and Charlie BYRD
US, male instrumental duo, sax and guitar   13 wks

8 Nov 62	**DESAFINADO** *HMV POP 1061*	**11**	13 wks

See also Stan Getz and Joao Gilberto.

Stan GETZ and Joao GILBERTO
US/Brazil, male instrumentalist - tenor sax/male vocalist   10 wks

23 Jul 64	**THE GIRL FROM IPANEMA (GAROTA DE IPANEMA)** *Verve VS 520*	**29**	10 wks

See also Stan Getz and Charlie Byrd. Joao Gilberto did not actually appear on this hit. The vocalist is in fact Astrud, his wife. See also Astrud Gilberto.

Andy GIBB *UK, male vocalist*   30 wks

25 Jun 77	**I JUST WANNA BE YOUR EVERYTHING** *RSO 2090 237*	**26**	7 wks
13 May 78	**SHADOW DANCING** *RSO 001*	**42**	6 wks
12 Aug 78	● **AN EVERLASTING LOVE** *RSO 015*	**10**	10 wks
27 Jan 79	**(OUR LOVE) DON'T THROW IT ALL AWAY** *RSO 26*	**32**	7 wks

---

Barry GIBB - See Barbra STREISAND and Barry GIBB

Robin GIBB *UK, male vocalist*   21 wks

9 Jul 69	● **SAVED BY THE BELL** *Polydor 56-337*	**2**	16 wks
15 Nov 69	**SAVED BY THE BELL** (re-entry) *Polydor 56-337*	**49**	1 wk
7 Feb 70	**AUGUST OCTOBER** *Polydor 56-371*	**45**	3 wks
11 Feb 84	**ANOTHER LONELY NIGHT IN NEW YORK** *Polydor POSP 668*	**71**	1 wk

---

Steve GIBBONS BAND
UK, male vocal/instrumental group   14 wks

6 Aug 77	**TULANE** *Polydor 2058 889*	**12**	10 wks
13 May 78	**EDDY VORTEX** *Polydor 2059 017*	**56**	4 wks

---

Georgia GIBBS *US, female vocalist*   2 wks

22 Apr 55	**TWEEDLE DEE** *Mercury MB 3196*	**20**	1 wk
13 Jul 56	**KISS ME ANOTHER** *Mercury MT 110*	**24**	1 wk

---

Don GIBSON *US, male vocalist*   16 wks

31 Aug 61	**SEA OF HEARTBREAK** *RCA 1243*	**14**	13 wks
1 Feb 62	**LONESOME NUMBER ONE** *RCA 1272*	**47**	3 wks

---

Wayne GIBSON *UK, male vocalist*   13 wks

3 Sep 64	**KELLY** *Pye 7N 15680*	**48**	2 wks
23 Nov 74	**UNDER MY THUMB** *Pye Disco Demand DDS 2001*	**17**	11 wks

---

GIBSON BROTHERS
Martinique, male vocal/instrumental group   54 wks

10 Mar 79	**CUBA** *Island WIP 6483*	**41**	9 wks
21 Jul 79	● **OOH! WHAT A LIFE** *Island WIP 6503*	**10**	12 wks
17 Nov 79	● **QUE SERA MI VIDA (IF YOU SHOULD GO)** *Island WIP 6525*	**5**	11 wks
23 Feb 80	**CUBA** (re-issue) /**BETTER DO IT SALSA** *Island WIP 6561*	**12**	9 wks
12 July 80	**MARIANA** *Island WIP 6617*	**11**	10 wks
9 Jul 83	**MY HEART'S BEATING WILD (TIC TAC TIC TAC)** *Stiff BUY 184*	**56**	3 wks

GIDEA PARK *UK, male vocal/instrumental*
group, Adrian Baker under false group name.　　　　　*19 wks*

4 Jul 81	**BEACHBOY GOLD** *Stone SON 2162*	**11**	13 wks
12 Sep 81	**SEASONS OF GOLD** *Polo POLO 14*	**28**	6 wks

See also Adrian Baker.

Astrud GILBERTO
Brazil, female vocalist　　　　　*6 wks*

25 Aug 84	**THE GIRL FROM IPANEMA** *Verve/Polydor IPA 1*	**55**	6 wks

See also Stan Getz and Joao Gilberto. Re-issue of The Girl From Ipanema (Garota De Ipanema) on Verve VS 520 by Stan Getz and Joao Gilberta.

Joao GILBERTO - *See Stan GETZ and Joao GILBERTO*

GILLAN *UK, male vocal/instrumental group*　　　*46 wks*

14 Jun 80	**SLEEPIN' ON THE JOB** *Virgin VS 355*	**55**	3 wks
4 Oct 80	**TROUBLE** *Virgin VS 377*	**14**	6 wks
14 Feb 81	**MUTUALLY ASSURED DESTRUCTION**		
	Virgin VS 103	**32**	5 wks
21 Mar 81	**NEW ORLEANS** *Virgin VS 406*	**17**	10 wks
20 Jun 81	**NO LAUGHING IN HEAVEN** *Virgin VS 425*	**31**	6 wks
10 Oct 81	**NIGHTMARE** *Virgin VS 441*	**36**	6 wks
23 Jan 82	**RESTLESS** *Virgin VS 465*	**25**	7 wks
4 Sep 82	**LIVING FOR THE CITY** *Virgin VS 519*	**50**	3 wks

Stuart GILLIES *UK, male vocalist*　　　*10 wks*

31 Mar 73	**AMANDA** *Philips 6006 293*	**13**	10 wks

Jimmy GILMER and the FIREBALLS
US, male vocalist/instrumental backing group　　　*8 wks*

14 Nov 63	**SUGAR SHACK** *London HLD 9789*	**45**	4 wks
19 Dec 63	**SUGAR SHACK** (re-entry) *London HLD 9789*	**46**	4 wks

See also Fireballs.

James GILREATH *US, male vocalist*　　　*10 wks*

2 May 63	**LITTLE BAND OF GOLD**		
	Pye International 7N 25190	**29**	10 wks

Jim GILSTRAP *US, male vocalist*　　　*11 wks*

15 Mar 75	● **SWING YOUR DADDY** *Chelsea 2005 021*	**4**	11 wks

Gordon GILTRAP
UK, male instrumentalist - guitar　　　*10 wks*

14 Jan 78	**HEARTSONG** *Electric WOT 19*	**21**	7 wks
28 Apr 79	**FEAR OF THE DARK** *Electric WOT 29*	**58**	3 wks

Fear Of The Dark credited to the Gordon Giltrap Band.

GINGERBREADS - *See GOLDIE and the GINGERBREADS*

GIRL *UK, male vocal/instrumental group*　　　*3 wks*

12 Apr 80	**HOLLYWOOD TEASE** *Jet 176*	**50**	3 wks

GIRLSCHOOL
UK, female vocal/instrumental group　　　*17 wks*

2 Aug 80	**RACE WITH THE DEVIL** *Bronze BRO 100*	**49**	6 wks
11 Apr 81	**HIT AND RUN** *Bronze BRO 118*	**32**	6 wks
11 Jul 81	**C'MON LET'S GO** *Bronze BRO 126*	**42**	3 wks
3 Apr 82	**DON'T CALL IT LOVE (WILDLIFE EP)**		
	Bronze BRO 144	**58**	2 wks

See also Headgirl. Tracks on Wildlife EP: Don't Call it Love/Wildlife/Don't Stop.

GLADIATORS - *See NERO and the GLADIATORS*

Mayson GLEN ORCHESTRA - *See Paul HENRY and the Mayson GLEN ORCHESTRA*

Gary GLITTER *UK, male vocalist*　　　*160 wks*

10 Jun 72	● **ROCK & ROLL** (PARTS 1 & 2) *Bell 1216*	**2**	15 wks
23 Sep 72	● **I DIDN'T KNOW I LOVED YOU (TILL I SAW YOU ROCK N ROLL)** *Bell 1259*	**4**	11 wks
20 Jan 73	● **DO YOU WANNA TOUCH ME (OH YEAH)** *Bell 1280*	**2**	11 wks
7 Apr 73	● **HELLO HELLO I'M BACK AGAIN** *Bell 1299* ..	**2**	14 wks
21 Jul 73	★ **I'M THE LEADER OF THE GANG (I AM)** *Bell 1321*	**1**	12 wks
17 Nov 73	★ **I LOVE YOU LOVE ME LOVE** *Bell 1337* ..	**1**	14 wks
30 Mar 74	● **REMEMBER ME THIS WAY** *Bell 1349*	**3**	8 wks
15 Jun 74	★ **ALWAYS YOURS** *Bell 1359*	**1**	9 wks
23 Nov 74	● **OH YES! YOU'RE BEAUTIFUL** *Bell 1391*	**2**	10 wks
3 May 75	● **LOVE LIKE YOU AND ME** *Bell 1423*	**10**	6 wks
21 Jun 75	● **DOING ALRIGHT WITH THE BOYS** *Bell 1429*	**6**	7 wks
8 Nov 75	● **PAPA OOM MOW MOW** *Bell 1451*	**38**	5 wks
13 Mar 76	**YOU BELONG TO ME** *Bell 1473*	**40**	5 wks
22 Jan 77	**IT TAKES ALL NIGHT LONG** *Arista 85*	**25**	6 wks
16 Jul 77	**A LITTLE BOOGIE WOOGIE IN THE BACK OF MY MIND** *Arista 112*	**31**	5 wks
20 Sep 80	**GARY GLITTER** (EP) *GTO GT 282*	**57**	3 wks
10 Oct 81	**AND THEN SHE KISSED ME** *Bell BELL 1497* ...	**39**	5 wks
5 Dec 81	**ALL THAT GLITTERS** *Bell (Eagle) BELL 1498* ..	**48**	4 wks
23 Jun 84	**DANCE ME UP** *Arista/MLM ARIST 570*	**25**	5 wks
1 Dec 84	● **ANOTHER ROCK AND ROLL CHRISTMAS** *Arista/MLM ARIST 592*	**7†**	5 wks

Rock & Roll Part 1 not listed with Part 2 for weeks of 10 and 17 Jan 72. Tracks on Gary Glitter EP: I'm The Leader Of The Gang (I Am)/Rock And Roll (Part 2) Hello Hello I'm Back Again/ Do You Wanna Touch Me? (Oh Yeah). All were re-issues.

GLITTER BAND
UK, male vocal/instrumental group　　　*60 wks*

23 Mar 74	● **ANGEL FACE** *Bell 1348*	**4**	10 wks
3 Aug 74	● **JUST FOR YOU** *Bell 1368*	**10**	8 wks
19 Oct 74	● **LET'S GET TOGETHER AGAIN** *Bell 1383*	**8**	8 wks
18 Jan 75	● **GOODBYE MY LOVE** *Bell 1395*	**2**	9 wks
12 Apr 75	● **THE TEARS I CRIED** *Bell 1416*	**8**	8 wks
9 Aug 75	**LOVE IN THE SUN** *Bell 1437*	**15**	8 wks
28 Feb 76	● **PEOPLE LIKE YOU AND PEOPLE LIKE ME** *Bell 1471*	**5**	9 wks

GLOVE *UK, male vocal/instrumental group*　　*3 wks*

20 Aug 83	**LIKE AN ANIMAL** *Wonderland/Polydor SHE 3* ...	**52**	3 wks

GODIEGO
Japan/US, male vocal/instrumental group　　　*11 wks*

15 Oct 77	**THE WATER MARGIN** *BBC RESL 50*	**37**	4 wks
16 Feb 80	**GANDHARA** *BBC RESL 66*	**56**	7 wks

The Water Margin is the English version of the song, which shared chart credit with the Japanese language version by Peter Mac Junior. See also Peter Mac Junior.

GODLEY and CREME
UK, male audiovisual duo   *22 wks*

12 Sep 81 ●	UNDER YOUR THUMB	*Polydor POSP 322*	3	11 wks
21 Nov 81 ●	WEDDING BELLS	*Polydor POSP 369*	7	11 wks

GO-GOS   *US, female vocal/instrumental group*   *6 wks*

15 May 82	OUR LIPS ARE SEALED			
	I.R.S./A & M GDN 102		47	6 wks

Andrew GOLD
US, male vocalist and instrumentalist - piano   *36 wks*

2 Apr 77	LONELY BOY	*Asylum K 13076*	11	9 wks
25 Mar 78 ●	NEVER LET HER SLIP AWAY	*Asylum K 13112*	5	13 wks
24 Jun 78	HOW CAN THIS BE LOVE	*Asylum K 13126* ...	19	10 wks
14 Oct 78	THANK YOU FOR BEING A FRIEND			
	Asylum K 13135		42	4 wks

GOLDEN EARRING
Holland, male vocal/instrumental group   *16 wks*

8 Dec 73 ●	RADAR LOVE	*Track 2094 116*	7	13 wks
8 Oct 77	RADAR LOVE	*Polydor 2121 335*	44	3 wks

These are two different recordings of the same song.

GOLDIE   *UK, male vocal/instrumental group*   *11 wks*

27 May 78 ●	MAKING UP AGAIN	*Bronze BRO 50*	7	11 wks

GOLDIE and the GINGERBREADS
US, female vocal/instrumental group   *5 wks*

25 Feb 65	CAN'T YOU HEAR MY HEART BEAT?			
	Decca F 12070		25	5 wks

Bobby GOLDSBORO   *US, male vocalist*   *47 wks*

17 Apr 68 ●	HONEY	*United Artists UP2215*	2	15 wks
4 Aug 73 ●	SUMMER (THE FIRST TIME)			
	United Artists UP35558		9	10 wks
3 Aug 74	HELLO SUMMERTIME	*United Artists UP35705* .	14	10 wks
29 Mar 75 ●	HONEY	(re-issue) *United Artists UP35633*	2	12 wks

Leroy GOMEZ   -   *See SANTA ESMERALDA and Leroy GOMEZ*

GONZALEZ
UK, male vocal/instrumental group   *11 wks*

31 Mar 79 ●	HAVEN'T STOPPED DANCING YET			
	Sidewalk SID 102		15	11 wks

GOODIES   *UK, male vocal group*   *38 wks*

7 Dec 74 ●	THE IN BETWEENIES/FATHER CHRISTMAS			
	DO NOT TOUCH ME *Bradley's BRAD 7421* ..		7	9 wks
15 Mar 75 ●	FUNKY GIBBON/SICK MAN BLUES			
	Bradley's BRAD 7504		4	10 wks
21 Jun 75	BLACK PUDDING BERTHA			
	Bradley's BRAD 7517		19	7 wks
27 Sep 75	NAPPY LOVE/WILD THING			
	Bradley's BRAD 7524		21	6 wks
13 Dec 75	MAKE A DAFT NOISE FOR CHRISTMAS			
	Bradley's BRAD 7533		20	6 wks

Cuba GOODING   *US, male vocalist*   *2 wks*

19 Nov 83	HAPPINESS IS JUST AROUND THE BEND			
	Streetwise/London LON 41		72	2 wks

Ron GOODWIN   *UK, orchestra*   *24 wks*

15 May 53 ●	LIMELIGHT	*Parlophone R 3686*	3	23 wks
28 Oct 55	BLUE STAR (THE MEDIC THEME)			
	Parlophone R 4074		20	1 wk

GOODY GOODY   *US, female vocal duo*   *5 wks*

2 Dec 78	NUMBER ONE DEE JAY	*Atlantic LV 3*	55	5 wks

GOOMBAY DANCE BAND
Germany/Montserrat, male/female vocal/instrumental group   *16 wks*

27 Feb 82 ★	SEVEN TEARS	*Epic EPC A 1242*	1	12 wks
15 May 82	SUN OF JAMAICA	*Epic EPC A 2345*	50	4 wks

GOONS   *UK, male vocal group*   *30 wks*

29 Jun 56 ●	I'M WALKING BACKWARDS FOR			
	CHRISTMAS/BLUEBOTTLE BLUES			
	Decca F 10756		4	10 wks
14 Sep 56 ●	BLOODNOK'S ROCK N ROLL/YING TONG			
	SONG *Decca E 10780*		3	10 wks
21 Jul 73 ●	YING TONG SONG	(re-issue) *Decca F 13414*	9	10 wks

Bluebottle Blues only listed from 13 Jul 56.

GORDON   -   *See PETER and GORDON*

Lesley GORE   *US, female vocalist*   *20 wks*

20 Jun 63 ●	IT'S MY PARTY	*Mercury AMT 1205*	9	12 wks
24 Sep 64	MAYBE I KNOW	*Mercury MF 829*	20	8 wks

Eydie GORMÉ   *US, female vocalist*   *20 wks*

24 Jan 58	LOVE ME FOREVER	*HMV POP 432*	21	5 wks
21 Jun 62 ●	YES MY DARLING DAUGHTER	*CBS AAG 105*	10	9 wks
31 Jan 63	BLAME IT ON THE BOSSA NOVA			
	CBS AAG 131		32	6 wks

See also Steve and Eydie.

Graham GOULDMAN
UK, male vocalist   *4 wks*

23 Jun 79	SUNBURN	*Mercury SUNNY 1*	52	4 wks

GRACE   -   *See DALE and GRACE*

Charlie GRACIE   *US, male vocalist*   *39 wks*

19 Apr 57	BUTTERFLY	*Parlophone R 4290*	12	8 wks
14 Jun 57 ●	FABULOUS	*Parlophone R 4313*	8	16 wks
23 Aug 57	I LOVE YOU SO MUCH IT HURTS/WANDERIN'			
	EYES *London HL 8467*		14	2 wks
6 Sep 57	I LOVE YOU SO MUCH IT HURTS			
	London HL 8467		20	2 wks
6 Sep 57 ●	WANDERIN' EYES	*London HL 8467*	6	12 wks

10 Jan 58	**COOL BABY** London HLU 8521	**26**	1 wk

I Love You So Much It Hurts and Wanderin' Eyes were listed together for 2 weeks, then listed separately for a further 2 and 12 weeks respectively.

Eve GRAHAM - See NEW SEEKERS

Larry GRAHAM   US, male vocalist   4 wks

3 Jul 82	**SOONER OR LATER** Warner Bros. K 17925	**54**	4 wks

Ron GRAINER ORCHESTRA
UK, orchestra   7 wks

9 Dec 78	**A TOUCH OF VELVET A STING OF BRASS** Casino Classics CC 5	**60**	7 wks

GRAND FUNK RAILROAD
US, male vocal/instrumental group   1 wk

6 Feb 71	**INSIDE LOOKING OUT** Capitol CL 15668	**40**	1 wk

GRANDMASTER FLASH, Melle MEL and the FURIOUS FIVE
US, male vocal duo and male vocal group   65 wks

28 Aug 82	● **THE MESSAGE** Sugarhill SHL 117	**8**	9 wks
19 Nov 83	**WHITE LINES (DON'T DON'T DO IT)** Sugarhill SH 130	**60**	3 wks
11 Feb 84	● **WHITE LINES (DON'T DON'T DO IT)** (re-entry) Sugarhill SH 130	**7**	38 wks
30 Jun 84	**BEAT STREET BREAKDOWN** Atlantic A9659	**42**	7 wks
22 Sep 84	**WE DON'T WORK FOR FREE** Sugarhill SH 136	**45**	4 wks
24 Nov 84	**WHITE LINES (DON'T DON'T DO IT)** (2nd re-entry) Sugarhill SH 130	**75**	1 wk
15 Dec 84	**STEP OFF (PART 1)** Sugarhill SH 139	**35†**	3 wks

Act billed as Grandmaster Flash and the Furious Five on The Message; as Grandmaster Flash and Melle Mel on White Lines (Don't Don't Do It), and as Grandmaster Melle Mel and the Furious Five on other hits. See also Melle Mel and Duke Bootee.

GRANDMIXER   US, male 'scratch' DJ   3 wks

24 Dec 83	**CRAZY CUTS** Celluloid/Island IS 146	**73**	2 wks
14 Jan 84	**CRAZY CUTS** (re-entry) Celluloid/Island IS 146	**71**	1 wk

GRAND PRIX
UK, male vocal/instrumental group   1 wk

27 Feb 82	**KEEP ON BELIEVING** RCA 162	**75**	1 wk

Gerri GRANGER   US, female vocalist   3 wks

30 Sep 78	**I GO TO PIECES (EVERYTIME)** Casino Classics CC3	**50**	3 wks

Boysie GRANT - See Ezz RECO and the LAUNCHERS with Boysie GRANT

David GRANT   UK, male vocalist   32 wks

30 Apr 83	**STOP AND GO** Chrysalis GRAN 1	**19**	9 wks
16 Jul 83	● **WATCHING YOU WATCHING ME** Chrysalis GRAN 2	**10**	13 wks
8 Oct 83	**LOVE WILL FIND A WAY** Chrysalis GRAN 3	**24**	6 wks
26 Nov 83	**ROCK THE MIDNIGHT** Chrysalis GRAN 4	**46**	4 wks

Eddy GRANT
Guyana, male vocalist/instrumentalist   80 wks

2 Jun 79	**LIVING ON THE FRONT LINE** Ensign ENY 26	**11**	11 wks
15 Nov 80	● **DO YOU FEEL MY LOVE** Ensign ENY 45	**8**	11 wks
4 Apr 81	**CAN'T GET ENOUGH OF YOU** Ice/Ensign ENY 207	**13**	10 wks
25 Jul 81	**I LOVE YOU, YES I LOVE YOU** Ice/Ensign ENY 216	**37**	6 wks
16 Oct 82	★ **I DON'T WANNA DANCE** Ice ICE 56	**1**	15 wks
15 Jan 83	● **ELECTRIC AVENUE** Ice ICE 57	**2**	9 wks
19 Mar 83	**LIVING ON THE FRONTLINE/DO YOU FEEL MY LOVE** (re-issue) Mercury/Phonogram MER 135	**47**	4 wks
23 Apr 83	**WAR PARTY** Ice ICE 58	**42**	4 wks
29 Oct 83	**TILL I CAN'T TAKE LOVE NO MORE** Ice ICE 60	**42**	7 wks
19 May 84	**ROMANCING THE STONE** Ice ICE 61	**52**	3 wks

Gogi GRANT   US, female vocalist   11 wks

29 Jun 56	● **WAYWARD WIND** London HLB 8282	**9**	11 wks

Julie GRANT   UK, female vocalist   17 wks

3 Jan 63	**UP ON THE ROOF** Pye 7N 15483	**33**	3 wks
28 Mar 63	**COUNT ON ME** Pye 7N 15508	**24**	9 wks
24 Sep 64	**COME TO ME** Pye 7N 15684	**31**	5 wks

Rudy GRANT   Guyana, male vocalist   3 wks

14 Feb 81	**LATELY** Ensign ENY 202	**58**	3 wks

GRAPEFRUIT
UK, male vocal/instrumental group   19 wks

14 Feb 68	**DEAR DELILAH** RCA 1656	**21**	9 wks
14 Aug 68	**C'MON MARIANNE** RCA 1716	**31**	10 wks

Dobie GRAY   US, male vocalist   11 wks

25 Feb 65	**THE IN CROWD** London HL 9953	**25**	7 wks
27 Sep 75	**OUT ON THE FLOOR** Black Magic BM 107	**42**	4 wks

Dorian GRAY   UK, male vocalist   7 wks

27 Mar 68	**I'VE GOT YOU ON MY MIND** Parlophone R 5667	**36**	7 wks

Les GRAY   UK, male vocalist   5 wks

26 Feb 77	**A GROOVY KIND OF LOVE** Warner Bros. K 16883	**32**	5 wks

Barry GRAY ORCHESTRA
UK, orchestra   2 wks

11 Jul 81	**THUNDERBIRDS** PRT 7P 216	**61**	2 wks

Buddy GRECO   US, male vocalist   8 wks

7 Jul 60	**LADY IS A TRAMP** Fontana H 225	**26**	8 wks

STEVE HARLEY (above) Self-confessed Harley admirers Duran Duran covered his number one 'Make Me Smile' on the B-side of their number one 'The Reflex'.

HELLO (above left) They said goodbye in '75, apart from Keith Marshall who had a solo hit in the Spring of '81.

HEATWAVE (left) Many of this group's hits were penned by future Michael Jackson Cleffer Rod Temperton.

HERMAN'S HERMITS (below left) Peter Noone was christened Herman by the rest of the group after Sherman, a character in the TV cartoon show *Bullwinkle*.

RUSS HAMILTON (below centre) The Everton-born ex-Butlins Redcoat wrote his debut hit in a 5-minute tea break during his time as a costing clerk.

NICK HEYWARD (below right) Monkee fan Nick takes time off from learning to play the giant electric violin.

GREEDIES
Ireland/UK/US, male vocal/instrumental group   5 wks

15 Dec 79	**A MERRY JINGLE** *Vertigo GREED 1*	28	5 wks

GREEK SERENADERS - *See MAKADOPOULOS and his GREEK SERENADERS*

Al GREEN   *US, male vocalist*   53 wks

9 Oct 71	● **TIRED OF BEING ALONE** *London HL 10337* ...	4	13 wks
8 Jan 72	● **LET'S STAY TOGETHER** *London HL 10348*	7	12 wks
20 May 72	**LOOK WHAT YOU DONE FOR ME** *London HL 10369*	44	4 wks
19 Aug 72	**I'M STILL IN LOVE WITH YOU** *London HL 10382*	35	5 wks
16 Nov 74	**SHA-LA-LA (MAKE ME HAPPY)** *London HL 10470*	20	11 wks
15 Mar 75	**L. O. V. E.** *London HL 10482*	24	8 wks

Jesse GREEN   *US, male vocalist*   26 wks

7 Aug 76	**NICE AND SLOW** *EMI 2492*	17	12 wks
18 Dec 76	**FLIP** *EMI 2564*	26	8 wks
11 Jun 77	**COME WITH ME** *EMI 2615*	29	6 wks

Norman GREENBAUM
US, male vocalist   20 wks

21 Mar 70	★ **SPIRIT IN THE SKY** *Reprise RS 20885*	1	20 wks

Lorne GREENE   *US, male vocalist*   8 wks

17 Dec 64	**RINGO** *RCA 1428*	22	8 wks

Lee GREENWOOD   *US, male vocalist*   6 wks

19 May 84	**THE WIND BENEATH MY WINGS** *MCA 877*	49	6 wks

Iain GREGORY   *UK, male vocalist*   2 wks

4 Jan 62	**CAN'T YOU HEAR THE BEAT OF A BROKEN HEART** *Pye 7N 15397*	39	2 wks

Johnny GREGORY - *See CHAQUITO*

GREYHOUND
Jamaica, male vocal/instrumental group   33 wks

26 Jun 71	● **BLACK AND WHITE** *Trojan TR 7820*	6	13 wks
8 Jan 72	**MOON RIVER** *Trojan TR 7848*	12	11 wks
25 Mar 72	**I AM WHAT I AM** *Trojan TR 7853*	20	9 wks

Zaine GRIFF   *New Zealand, male vocalist*   6 wks

16 Feb 80	**TONIGHT** *Automatic K 17547*	54	3 wks
31 May 80	**ASHES AND DIAMONDS** *Automatic K 17610* ...	68	3 wks

Billy GRIFFIN   *US, male vocalist*   12 wks

8 Jan 83	**HOLD ME TIGHTER IN THE RAIN** *CBS A 2935*	17	9 wks
14 Jan 84	**SERIOUS** *CBS A 4053*	64	3 wks

Ronnie GRIFFITH   *US, female vocalist*   4 wks

30 Jun 84	**(THE BEST PART OF) BREAKING UP** *Making Waves/Priority SURF 101*	63	4 wks

Henry GROSS   *US, male vocalist*   4 wks

28 Aug 76	**SHANNON** *Life Song ELS 45002*	32	4 wks

GUESS WHO
Canada, male vocal/instrumental group   14 wks

16 Feb 67	**HIS GIRL** *King KG 1044*	45	1 wk
9 May 70	**AMERICAN WOMAN** *RCA 1943*	45	2 wks
30 May 70	**AMERICAN WOMAN** (re-entry) *RCA 1943*	19	11 wks

GUN   *UK, male vocal/instrumental group*   11 wks

20 Nov 68	● **RACE WITH THE DEVIL** *CBS 3764*	8	11 wks

Adrian GURVITZ   *UK, male vocalist*   16 wks

30 Jan 82	● **CLASSIC** *RAK 339*	8	13 wks
12 Jun 82	**YOUR DREAM** *RAK 343*	61	3 wks

GUYS and DOLLS
UK, male/female vocal group   33 wks

1 Mar 75	● **THERE'S A WHOLE LOT OF LOVING** *Magnet MAG 20*	2	11 wks
17 May 75	**HERE I GO AGAIN** *Magnet MAG 30*	33	5 wks
21 Feb 76	● **YOU DON'T HAVE TO SAY YOU LOVE ME** *Magnet MAG 50*	5	8 wks
6 Nov 76	**STONEY GROUND** *Magnet MAG 76*	38	4 wks
13 May 78	**ONLY LOVIN' DOES IT** *Magnet MAG 115*	42	5 wks

H

H_2O *UK, male vocal/instrumental group*   16 wks

21 May 83	**DREAM TO SLEEP** *RCA 330*	17	10 wks
13 Aug 83	**JUST OUTSIDE OF HEAVEN** *RCA 349*	38	6 wks

Steve HACKETT
UK, male vocalist/instrumentalist - guitar   2 wks

2 Apr 83	**CELL 151** *Charisma/Phonogram CELL 1*	66	2 wks

Sammy HAGAR
US, male vocalist/instrumentalist - guitar   15 wks

15 Dec 79	**THIS PLANET'S ON FIRE/SPACE STATION NO.5** *Capitol CL 16114*	52	5 wks
16 Feb 80	**I'VE DONE EVERYTHING FOR YOU** *Capitol CL 16120*	36	5 wks
24 May 80	**HEARTBEAT /LOVE OR MONEY** *Capitol RED 1*	67	2 wks
16 Jan 82	**PIECE OF MY HEART** *Geffen GEFA 1884*	67	1 wk
30 Jan 82	**PIECE OF MY HEART** (re-entry) *Geffen GEFA 1884*	67	2 wks

Paul HAIG   UK, male vocalist   *3 wks*

28 May 83	HEAVEN SENT *Island IS 111*	74	3 wks

HAIRCUT 100
UK, male vocal/instrumental group   *47 wks*

24 Oct 81	● FAVOURITE SHIRTS (BOY MEETS GIRL)			
	Arista CLIP 1	4	14 wks
30 Jan 82	● LOVE PLUS ONE *Arista CLIP 2*	3	12 wks
10 Apr 82	● FANTASTIC DAY *Arista CLIP 3*	9	9 wks
21 Aug 82	● NOBODY'S FOOL *Arista CLIP 4*	9	7 wks
6 Aug 83	PRIME TIME *Polydor HC 1*	46	5 wks

Curtis HAIRSTON   US, male vocalist   *5 wks*

15 Oct 83	I WANT YOU (ALL TONIGHT) *RCA 368*	44	5 wks

Bill HALEY and his COMETS
US, male vocalist/instrumentalist – guitar, and male vocal/instrumental backing group   *199 wks*

17 Dec 54	● SHAKE RATTLE AND ROLL *Brunswick 05338* ..	4	14 wks
7 Jan 55	ROCK AROUND THE CLOCK *Brunswick 05317*	17	2 wks
15 Apr 55	MAMBO ROCK *Brunswick 05405*	14	2 wks
14 Oct 55	★ ROCK AROUND THE CLOCK (re-entry)			
	Brunswick 05317	1	17 wks
30 Dec 55	● ROCK-A-BEATIN' BOOGIE *Brunswick 05509* ..	4	9 wks
9 Mar 56	● SEE YOU LATER ALLIGATOR *Brunswick 05530*	7	13 wks
25 May 56	● THE SAINTS ROCK 'N ROLL *Brunswick 05565*	5	24 wks
17 Aug 56	● ROCKIN' THROUGH THE RYE *Brunswick 05582*	3	18 wks
14 Sep 56	RAZZLE DAZZLE *Brunswick 05453*	13	8 wks
21 Sep 56	● ROCK AROUND THE CLOCK (2nd re-entry)			
	Brunswick 05317	5	11 wks
21 Sep 56	SEE YOU LATER ALLIGATOR (re-entry)			
	Brunswick 05530	12	8 wks
9 Nov 56	● RIP IT UP *Brunswick 05615*	4	18 wks
9 Nov 56	ROCK 'N ROLL STAGE SHOW (LP)			
	Brunswick LAT 8139	30	1 wk
23 Nov 56	RUDY'S ROCK *Brunswick 05616*	30	1 wk
14 Dec 56	RUDY'S ROCK (re-entry) *Brunswick 05616*	26	4 wks
14 Dec 56	ROCK AROUND THE CLOCK (3rd re-entry)			
	Brunswick 05317	24	2 wks
4 Jan 57	ROCKIN' THROUGH THE RYE (re-entry)			
	Brunswick 05582	19	5 wks
4 Jan 57	ROCK AROUND THE CLOCK (4th re-entry)			
	Brunswick 05317	25	2 wks
25 Jan 57	ROCK AROUND THE CLOCK (5th re-entry)			
	Brunswick 05317	22	2 wks
1 Feb 57	ROCK THE JOINT *London HLF 8371*	20	4 wks
8 Feb 57	● DON'T KNOCK THE ROCK *Brunswick 05640* ...	7	8 wks
3 Apr 68	ROCK AROUND THE CLOCK (re-issue)			
	MCA MU 1013	20	11 wks
16 Mar 74	ROCK AROUND THE CLOCK (2nd re-issue)			
	MCA 128	12	10 wks
25 Apr 81	HALEY'S GOLDEN MEDLEY *MCA 694*	50	5 wks

Tracks on Rock 'N Roll Stage Show LP: Calling All Comets/Rockin' Through The Rye/A Rockin' Little Tune/Hide And Seek/Hey There Now/Goofin' Around/Hook Line And Sinker/Rudy's Rock/Choo Choo Ch'Boogie/Blue Comets Rock/Hot Dog Buddy Buddy/Tonight's The Night. Occasionally, some of the Rock Around The Clock labels billed the song as (We're Gonna) Rock Around The Clock.

Daryl HALL and John OATES
US, male vocal/instrumental duo   *69 wks*

16 Oct 76	SHE'S GONE *Atlantic K 10828*	42	4 wks
14 Jun 80	RUNNING FROM PARADISE *RCA RUN 1* ...	41	6 wks
20 Sep 80	YOU'VE LOST THAT LOVIN' FEELIN' *RCA 1*	55	3 wks
15 Nov 80	KISS ON MY LIST *RCA 15*	33	8 wks
23 Jan 82	● I CAN'T GO FOR THAT (NO CAN DO)			
	RCA 172	8	10 wks
10 Apr 82	PRIVATE EYES *RCA 134*	32	7 wks
30 Oct 82	● MANEATER *RCA 290*	6	11 wks
22 Jan 83	ONE ON ONE *RCA 305*	63	3 wks
30 Apr 83	FAMILY MAN *RCA 323*	15	7 wks
12 Nov 83	SAY IT ISN'T SO *RCA 375*	69	3 wks
10 Mar 84	ADULT EDUCATION *RCA 396*	63	2 wks
20 Oct 84	OUT OF TOUCH *RCA 449*	48	5 wks

HAMILTON, Joe FRANK and REYNOLDS   US, male vocal group   *6 wks*

13 Sep 75	FALLIN' IN LOVE *Pye International 7N 25690* ...	33	6 wks

Russ HAMILTON   UK, male vocalist   *26 wks*

24 May 57	● WE WILL MAKE LOVE *Oriole CB 1359*	2	20 wks
27 Sep 57	WEDDING RING *Oriole CB 1388*	20	6 wks

George HAMILTON IV
US, male vocalist   *13 wks*

7 Mar 58	WHY DON'T THEY UNDERSTAND			
	HMV POP 429	22	9 wks
18 Jul 58	I KNOW WHERE I'M GOING *HMV POP 505*	29	1 wk
8 Aug 58	I KNOW WHERE I'M GOING (re-entry)			
	HMV POP 505	23	3 wks

Marvin HAMLISCH
US, male instrumentalist – piano   *13 wks*

30 Mar 74	THE ENTERTAINER *MCA 121*	25	13 wks

Albert HAMMOND   UK, male vocalist   *11 wks*

30 Jun 73	FREE ELECTRIC BAND *Mums 1494*	19	11 wks

Herbie HANCOCK
US, male vocalist/instrumentalist – keyboards   *41 wks*

26 Aug 78	I THOUGHT IT WAS YOU *CBS 6530*	15	9 wks
3 Feb 79	YOU BET YOUR LOVE *CBS 7010*	18	10 wks
30 Jul 83	● ROCKIT *CBS A 3577*	8	12 wks
8 Oct 83	AUTO DRIVE *CBS A 3802*	33	4 wks
21 Jan 84	FUTURE SHOCK *CBS A 4075*	54	3 wks
4 Aug 84	HARDROCK *CBS A 4616*	65	3 wks

HANDLEY FAMILY
UK, male/female vocal group   *7 wks*

7 Apr 73	WAM BAM *GL 100*	30	7 wks

HANDS OF DR. TELENY   -   See Peter STRAKER and the HANDS OF DR. TELENY.

HANOI ROCKS
US, male vocal/instrumental group   *2 wks*

7 Jul 84	UP AROUND THE BEND *CBS A 4513*	61	2 wks

HAPPENINGS   US, male vocal group   *14 wks*

18 May 67	I GOT RHYTHM *Stateside SS 2013*	28	9 wks

| 16 Aug 67 | **MY MAMMY** | | |
| | *Pye International 7N 25501 & B.T.Puppy BTS 45530* | **34** | 5 wks |

Pye gave the American B. T. Puppy label its own identification halfway through the success of My Mammy.

Paul HARDCASTLE
UK, male instrumentalist - keyboards — 16 wks

7 Apr 84	**YOU'RE THE ONE FOR ME-DAYBREAK - A.M.**		
	Total Control TOCO 1	**41**	4 wks
28 Jul 84	**GUILTY** *Total Control TOCO 2*	**55**	3 wks
22 Sep 84	**RAIN FOREST** *Bluebird BR 8*	**41**	5 wks
17 Nov 84	**EAT YOUR HEART OUT**		
	Cool Tempo/Chrysalis COOL 102	**59**	4 wks

Tim HARDIN *US, male vocalist* — 1 wk

| 5 Jan 67 | **HANG ON TO A DREAM** *Verve VS 1504* . . . . . | **50** | 1 wk |

Mike HARDING *UK, male vocalist* — 8 wks

| 2 Aug 75 | **ROCHDALE COWBOY** *Rubber ADUB 3* . . . . | **22** | 8 wks |

Francoise HARDY *France, female vocalist* — 26 wks

25 Jun 64	**TOUS LES GARCONS ET LES FILLES**		
	Pye 7N 15653	**36**	7 wks
7 Jan 65	**ET MEME** *Pye 7N 15740*	**31**	4 wks
25 Mar 65	**ALL OVER THE WORLD** *Pye 7N 15802*	**16**	15 wks

HARLEM COMMUNITY CHOIR - *See John LENNON*

Steve HARLEY and COCKNEY REBEL *UK, male vocalist and male vocal/instrumental backing group* — 54 wks

11 May 74	● **JUDY TEEN** *EMI 2128*	**5**	11 wks
10 Aug 74	● **MR. SOFT** *EMI 2191*	**8**	9 wks
8 Feb 75	★ **MAKE ME SMILE (COME UP AND SEE ME)**		
	EMI 2263	**1**	9 wks
7 Jun 75	**MR. RAFFLES (MAN IT WAS MEAN)** *EMI 2299*	**13**	6 wks
31 Jul 76	● **HERE COMES THE SUN** *EMI 2505*	**10**	7 wks
6 Nov 76	**LOVE'S A PRIMA DONNA** *EMI 2539*	**41**	4 wks
20 Oct 79	**FREEDOM'S PRISONER** *EMI 2994*	**58**	3 wks
13 Aug 83	**BALLERINA (PRIMA DONNA)**		
	Stilletto/RCA STL 14	**51**	5 wks

First two hits are credited simply to Cockney Rebel, the next two to Steve Harley and Cockney Rebel, the remaining hits to Steve Harley.

HARLEY QUINNE
UK, male vocal group — 8 wks

| 14 Oct 72 | **NEW ORLEANS** *Bell 1255* . . . . | **19** | 8 wks |

HARMONY GRASS
UK, male vocal/instrumental group — 7 wks

| 29 Jan 69 | **MOVE IN A LITTLE CLOSER** *RCA 1772* . . . . . | **24** | 7 wks |

Charlie HARPER *UK, male vocalist* — 1 wk

| 19 Jul 80 | **BARMY LONDON ARMY** *Gem GEMS 35* . . . . . | **68** | 1 wk |

HARPERS BIZARRE
US, male vocal group — 13 wks

30 Mar 67	**59TH STREET BRIDGE SONG (FEELING**		
	GROOVY) *Warner Bros. WB 5890*	**34**	7 wks
4 Oct 67	**ANYTHING GOES** *Warner Bros. WB 7063*	**33**	6 wks

HARPO *Sweden, male vocalist* — 6 wks

| 17 Apr 76 | **MOVIE STAR** *DJM DJS 400* . . . . | **24** | 6 wks |

T. HARRINGTON - *See Rahni HARRIS and F.L.O.*

Anita HARRIS *UK, female vocalist* — 50 wks

29 Jun 67	● **JUST LOVING YOU** *CBS 2724*	**6**	30 wks
11 Oct 67	**PLAYGROUND** *CBS 2991*	**46**	3 wks
24 Jan 68	**ANNIVERSARY WALTZ** *CBS 3211*	**21**	9 wks
14 Aug 68	**DREAM A LITTLE DREAM OF ME** *CBS 3637*	**33**	8 wks

Emmylou HARRIS *US, female vocalist* — 6 wks

| 6 Mar 76 | **HERE THERE AND EVERYWHERE** | | |
| | *Reprise K 14415* . . . . | **30** | 6 wks |

Jet HARRIS
UK, male instrumentalist - bass guitar — 18 wks

24 May 62	**BESAME MUCHO** *Decca F 11466*	**22**	7 wks
16 Aug 62	**MAIN TITLE THEME FROM 'MAN WITH THE**		
	GOLDEN ARM' *Decca F 11488*	**12**	11 wks

See also Jet Harris and Tony Meehan.

Jet HARRIS and Tony MEEHAN
UK, male instrumental duo - bass guitar and drums — 39 wks

10 Jan 63	★ **DIAMONDS** *Decca F 11563*	**1**	13 wks
25 Apr 63	● **SCARLETT O'HARA** *Decca F 11644*	**2**	13 wks
5 Sep 63	● **APPLEJACK** *Decca F 11710*	**4**	13 wks

See also Jet Harris; Tony Meehan.

Keith HARRIS and ORVILLE
UK, male ventriloquist vocalist with feathered dummy — 15 wks

| 18 Dec 82 | ● **ORVILLE'S SONG** *BBC RESL 124* . . . . | **4** | 11 wks |
| 24 Dec 83 | **COME TO MY PARTY** *BBC RESL 138* . . . . | **44** | 4 wks |

Come To My Party also credits Dippy (Prehistoric Dummy).

Major HARRIS *US, male vocalist* — 9 wks

| 9 Aug 75 | **LOVE WON'T LET ME WAIT** *Atlantic K 10585* | **37** | 7 wks |
| 5 Nov 83 | **ALL MY LIFE** *London LON 37* . . . . | **61** | 2 wks |

Max HARRIS *UK, orchestra* — 10 wks

| 1 Dec 60 | **GURNEY SLADE** *Fontana H 282* . . . . | **11** | 10 wks |

Rahni HARRIS and F.L.O.
US, male instrumental group   *7 wks*

16 Dec 78   **SIX MILLION STEPS (WEST RUNS SOUTH)**
     Mercury 6007 198 .... **43**   7 wks

Hit has credit 'Vocals by T. Harrington and O. Rasbury'.

Richard HARRIS   *Ireland, male vocalist*   *18 wks*

26 Jun 68 ● **MACARTHUR PARK**   *RCA 1699* .... **4**   12 wks
8 Jul 72   **MACARTHUR PARK** (re-issue) *Probe GFF 101* .. **38**   6 wks

Rolf HARRIS   *Australia, male vocalist*   *64 wks*

21 Jul 60 ● **TIE ME KANGAROO DOWN SPORT**
     Columbia DB 4483 .... **9**   13 wks
25 Oct 62 ● **SUN ARISE** *Columbia DB 4888* .... **3**   16 wks
28 Feb 63   **JOHNNY DAY** *Columbia DB 4979* ...... **44**   2 wks
16 Apr 69   **BLUER THAN BLUE** *Columbia DB 8553* .. **30**   8 wks
22 Nov 69 ★ **TWO LITTLE BOYS** *Columbia DB 8630* .. **1**   24 wks
20 Jun 70   **TWO LITTLE BOYS** (re-entry) *Columbia DB 8630* **50**   1 wk

Ronnie HARRIS   *UK, male vocalist*   *3 wks*

24 Sep 54   **STORY OF TINA** *Columbia DB 3499* .... **12**   3 wks

George HARRISON   *UK, male vocalist*   *58 wks*

23 Jan 71 ★ **MY SWEET LORD** *Apple R 5884* .... **1**   17 wks
14 Aug 71 ● **BANGLA DESH** *Apple R 5912* .... **10**   9 wks
2 Jun 73 ● **GIVE ME LOVE (GIVE ME PEACE ON EARTH)**
     Apple R 5988 .... **8**   10 wks
21 Dec 74   **DING DONG** *Apple R 6002* .... **38**   5 wks
11 Oct 75   **YOU** *Apple R 6007* .... **38**   5 wks
10 Mar 79   **BLOW AWAY** *Dark Horse K 17327* .... **51**   5 wks
23 May 81   **ALL THOSE YEARS AGO** *Dark Horse 3 K 17807* **13**   7 wks

Noel HARRISON   *UK, male vocalist*   *14 wks*

26 Feb 69 ● **WINDMILLS OF YOUR MIND** *Reprise RS 20758* **8**   14 wks

HARRY - *See ALFI and HARRY*

Debbie HARRY   *US, female vocalist*   *6 wks*

1 Aug 81   **BACKFIRED** *Chrysalis CHS 2526* .... **32**   6 wks

HARRY J. ALL STARS
Jamaica, male instrumental group   *25 wks*

25 Oct 69 ● **LIQUIDATOR** *Trojan TR 675* .... **9**   20 wks
29 Mar 80   **LIQUIDATOR** (re-issue) *Trojan TRO 9063* ...... **42**   5 wks

Re-issue of Liquidator coupled with re-issue of Long Shot Kick De Bucket by The Pioneers. See also The Pioneers.

Richard HARTLEY and the Michael REED ORCHESTRA
UK, male instrumentalist - synthesisor, and orchestra   *10 wks*

25 Feb 84 ● **THE MUSIC OF TORVILL AND DEAN EP**
     Safari SKATE 1 .... **9**   10 wks

Tracks on EP: Bolero/Capriccio Espagnole Opus. 34 (Nos.4 & 5) by Richard Hartley; Barnum On Ice/Discoskate by the Michael Reed Orchestra.

Dan HARTMAN   *US, male vocalist*   *23 wks*

21 Oct 78 ● **INSTANT REPLAY** *Sky 6706* .... **8**   15 wks
13 Jan 79   **THIS IS IT** *Blue Sky SKY 6999* .... **17**   8 wks

Steve HARVEY   *UK, male vocalist*   *6 wks*

28 May 83   **SOMETHING SPECIAL** *London LON 25* .... **46**   4 wks
29 Oct 83   **TONIGHT** *London LON 36* .... **63**   2 wks

Sensational Alex HARVEY BAND
UK, male vocal/instrumental group   *25 wks*

26 Jul 75 ● **DELILAH** *Vertigo ALEX 001* .... **7**   7 wks
22 Nov 75   **GAMBLIN' BAR ROOM BLUES**
     Vertigo ALEX 002 .... **38**   8 wks
19 Jun 76   **THE BOSTON TEA PARTY** *Mountain TOP 12* **13**   10 wks

Tony HATCH   *UK, orchestra*   *1 wk*

4 Oct 62   **OUT OF THIS WORLD** *Pye 7N 15460* .... **50**   1 wk

Donny HATHAWAY - *See Roberta FLACK and Donny HATHAWAY*

Edwin HAWKINS SINGERS
US, male/female vocal group   *13 wks*

21 May 69 ● **OH HAPPY DAY** *Buddah 201 048* .... **2**   12 wks
23 Aug 69   **OH HAPPY DAY** (re-entry) *Buddah 201 048* ..... **43**   1 wk

Hit credits soloist : Dorothy Combs Morrison.

HAWKWIND   *UK, male vocal/instrumental group with female dancer*   *28 wks*

1 Jul 72 ● **SILVER MACHINE** *United Artists UP 35381* ... **3**   15 wks
11 Aug 73   **URBAN GUERRILLA** *United Artists UP 35566* .. **39**   3 wks
21 Oct 78   **SILVER MACHINE** (re-entry)
     United Artists UP 35381 .... **34**   5 wks
19 Jul 80   **SHOT DOWN IN THE NIGHT** *Bronze BRO 98* **59**   3 wks
15 Jan 83   **SILVER MACHINE** (2nd re-entry)
     United Artists UP 35381 .... **67**   2 wks

Bill HAYES   *US, male vocalist*   *9 wks*

6 Jan 56 ● **BALLAD OF DAVY CROCKETT**
     London HLA 8220 .... **2**   9 wks

Isaac HAYES
US, male vocalist/multi-instrumentalist   *21 wks*

4 Dec 71 ● **THEME FROM 'SHAFT'** *Stax 2025 069* .... **4**   12 wks
3 Apr 76 ● **DISCO CONNECTION** *ABC 4100* .... **10**   9 wks

Billed as Isaac Hayes Movement on Disco Connection.

HAYSI FANTAYZEE
UK, male/female vocal duo   *25 wks*

24 Jul 82   **JOHN WAYNE IS BIG LEGGY** *Regard RG 100* **11**   10 wks
13 Nov 82   **HOLY JOE** *Regard RG 104* .... **51**   3 wks
22 Jan 83   **SHINY SHINY** *Regard RG 106* .... **16**   10 wks
25 Jun 83   **SISTER FRICTION** *Regard RG 108* .... **62**   2 wks

Justin HAYWARD   UK, male vocalist   13 wks

8 Jul 78	● FOREVER AUTUMN CBS 6368	5	13 wks

See also Justin Hayward and John Lodge.

Justin HAYWARD and John LODGE   UK, male vocal/instrumental duo   7 wks

25 Oct 75	● BLUE GUITAR Threshold TH 21	8	7 wks

See also Justin Hayward.

Leon HAYWOOD   US, male vocalist   11 wks

15 Mar 80	DON'T PUSH IT, DON'T FORCE IT 20th Century Fox TC 2443	12	11 wks

HAYWOODE   UK, male vocalist   11 wks

17 Sep 83	A TIME LIKE THIS CBS A 3651	48	7 wks
29 Sep 84	I CAN'T LET YOU GO CBS A 4664	63	4 wks

Lee HAZLEWOOD - *See Nancy SINATRA and Lee HAZLEWOOD*

Murray HEAD   UK, male vocalist   9 wks

29 Jan 72	SUPERSTAR MCA MMKS 5077	47	1 wk
10 Nov 84	ONE NIGHT IN BANGKOK RCA CHESS 1	12†	8 wks

Superstar was one of 4 tracks on a maxi-single, 2 of which were credited during the disc's one week on the chart. The other track credited was I Don't Know How To Love Him by Yvonne Elliman. See also Yvonne Elliman.

Roy HEAD   US, male vocalist   5 wks

4 Nov 65	TREAT HER RIGHT Vocalion V-P 9248	30	5 wks

HEADBANGERS
UK, male vocal/instrumental group   3 wks

10 Oct 81	STATUS ROCK Magnet MAG 206	60	3 wks

HEADBOYS
UK, male vocal/instrumental group   8 wks

22 Sep 79	THE SHAPE OF THINGS TO COME RSO 40	45	8 wks

HEADGIRL
UK, male/female vocal/instrumental group   8 wks

21 Feb 81	● ST. VALENTINE'S DAY MASSACRE (EP) Bronze BRO 116	5	8 wks

Headgirl is Motorhead and Girlschool together. See Motorhead; Girlschool. Tracks on St. Valentine's Day Massacre EP Please Don't Touch/Emergency/Bomber.

HEARTBREAKERS - *See Stevie NICKS with Tom PETTY and the HEARTBREAKERS; Tom PETTY and the HEARTBREAKERS*

Ted HEATH   UK, orchestra   56 wks

16 Jan 53	VANESSA Decca F 9983	11	1 wk
3 Jul 53	● HOT TODDY Decca F 10093	6	11 wks
23 Oct 53	DRAGNET Decca F 10176	12	1 wk
27 Nov 53	● DRAGNET (re-entry) Decca F 10176	9	1 wk
11 Dec 53	DRAGNET (2nd re-entry) Decca F 10176	11	1 wk
15 Jan 54	DRAGNET (3rd re-entry) Decca F 10176	11	1 wk
5 Feb 54	DRAGNET (4th re-entry) Decca F 10176	12	1 wk
12 Feb 54	● SKIN DEEP Decca F 10246	9	3 wks
6 Jul 56	THE FAITHFUL HUSSAR Decca F 10746	18	9 wks
14 Mar 58	● SWINGIN' SHEPHERD BLUES Decca F 11000	3	14 wks
11 Apr 58	TEQUILA Decca F 11003	21	6 wks
4 Jul 58	TOM HARK Decca F 11025	24	2 wks
5 Oct 61	SUCU SUCU Decca F 11392	36	4 wks
9 Nov 61	SUCU SUCU (re-entry) Decca F 11392	47	1 wk

HEATWAVE
UK/US, male vocal and instrumental group   78 wks

22 Jan 77	● BOOGIE NIGHTS GTO GT 77	2	14 wks
7 May 77	TOO HOT TO HANDLE/SLIP YOUR DISC TO THIS GTO GT 91	15	11 wks
14 Jan 78	THE GROOVE LINE GTO GT 115	12	8 wks
3 Jun 78	MIND BLOWING DECISIONS GTO GT 226	12	11 wks
4 Nov 78	● ALWAYS AND FOREVER/MIND BLOWING DECISIONS GTO GT 236	9	14 wks
26 May 79	RAZZLE DAZZLE GTO GT 248	43	5 wks
17 Jan 81	GANGSTERS OF THE GROOVE GTO GT 285	19	8 wks
21 Mar 81	JITTERBUGGIN' GTO GT 290	34	7 wks

Mind Blowing Decisions on GT 236 is an extended remixed version of GT 226.

HEAVEN 17
UK, male vocal/instrumental group   65 wks

21 Mar 81	(WE DON'T NEED THIS) FASCIST GROOVE THANG Virgin VS 400	45	5 wks
5 Sep 81	PLAY TO WIN Virgin VS 433	46	7 wks
14 Nov 81	PENTHOUSE AND PAVEMENT Virgin VS 455	57	3 wks
30 Oct 82	LET ME GO B.E.F./Virgin VS 532	41	6 wks
16 Apr 83	● TEMPTATION B.E.F/Virgin VS 570	2	13 wks
25 Jun 83	● COME LIVE WITH ME B.E.F./Virgin VS 607	5	11 wks
10 Sep 83	CRUSHED BY THE WHEELS OF INDUSTRY B.E.F/Virgin VS 628	17	7 wks
1 Sep 84	SUNSET NOW Virgin VS 708	24	6 wks
27 Oct 84	THIS IS MINE Virgin VS 722	23	7 wks

HEAVY PETTIN'
UK, male vocal/instrumental group   2 wks

17 Mar 84	LOVE TIMES LOVE Polydor HEP 3	69	2 wks

Bobby HEBB   US, male vocalist   15 wks

8 Sep 66	SUNNY Philips BF 1503	12	9 wks
19 Aug 72	LOVE LOVE LOVE Philips 6051 023	32	6 wks

HEDGEHOPPERS ANONYMOUS
UK, male vocal/instrumental group   12 wks

30 Sep 65	● IT'S GOOD NEWS WEEK Decca F 12241	5	12 wks

Den HEGARTY   UK, male vocalist   2 wks

31 Mar 79	VOODOO VOODOO Magnet MAG 143	73	2 wks

HEINZ   UK, male vocalist   35 wks

8 Aug 63	● JUST LIKE EDDIE Decca F 11693	5	15 wks
28 Nov 63	COUNTRY BOY Decca F 11768	26	9 wks
27 Feb 64	YOU WERE THERE Decca F 11831	26	8 wks
15 Oct 64	QUESTIONS I CAN'T ANSWER Columbia DB 7374	39	2 wks
18 Mar 65	DIGGIN' MY POTATOES Columbia DB 7482	49	1 wk

HUMAN LEAGUE Three Top 20 hits in 1984 and one Top 10 hit for lead singer Philip Oakey with Producer/Writer Giorgio Moroder. (Photo: Simon Fowler.)

BUDDY HOLLY He was only with us until February, 1959 but left a legacy of recordings, since covered by dozens of artists including The Beatles, The Rolling Stones, Cliff Richard, The Clash, the Everly Brothers, Don McLean, Peter and Gordon, Mud, Blondie and Showaddywaddy.

TAB HUNTER (below) As Arthur Gelien he was a Californian skating champion in 1949 and 1950 before changing his name when a film career called.

THE SENSATIONAL ALEX HARVEY BAND (right) Wild man of pop Alex Harvey (at the top, middle) died during a European tour.

HELLO UK, male vocal/instrumental group — 21 wks

9 Nov 74	● TELL HIM Bell 1377	6	12 wks
18 Oct 75	● NEW YORK GROOVE Bell 1438	9	9 wks

Bobby HELMS US, male vocalist — 7 wks

29 Nov 57	MY SPECIAL ANGEL Brunswick 05721	22	3 wks
21 Feb 58	NO OTHER BABY Brunswick 05730	30	1 wk
1 Aug 58	JACQUELINE Brunswick 05748	20	3 wks

Jimmy HELMS UK, male vocalist — 10 wks

24 Feb 73	● GONNA MAKE YOU AN OFFER YOU CAN'T REFUSE Cube BUG 27	8	10 wks

Eddie HENDERSON
US, male vocalist/instrumentalist - trumpet — 6 wks

28 Oct 78	PRANCE ON Capitol CL 16015	44	6 wks

Joe 'Mr. Piano' HENDERSON
UK, male instrumentalist - piano — 23 wks

3 Jun 55	SING IT WITH JOE Polygon P 1167	14	4 wks
2 Sep 55	SING IT AGAIN WITH JOE Polygon P 1184	18	3 wks
25 Jul 58	TRUDIE Pye Nixa N 15147	14	12 wks
24 Oct 58	TRUDIE (re-entry) Pye Nixa N 15147	23	2 wks
23 Oct 59	TREBLE CHANCE Pye 7N 15224	28	1 wk
24 Mar 60	OOH LA LA Pye 7N 15257	46	1 wk

First two hits are medleys as follows: Sing It With Joe : *Margie/I'm Nobody's Sweetheart Now/Somebody Stole My Gal/Moonlight Bay/By The Light Of The Silvery Moon/Cuddle Up A Little Closer.* Sing It Again With Joe: *Put Your Arms Around Me Honey/Ain't She Sweet/When You're Smiling/Shine On Harvest Moon/My Blue Heaven/Show Me The Way To Go Home.*

Wayne HENDERSON - *See Roy AYERS and Wayne HENDERSON*

Jimi HENDRIX EXPERIENCE
US/UK, male vocal/instrumental group, Jimi Hendrix, vocalist/ instrumentalist - guitar — 81 wks

5 Jan 67	● HEY JOE Polydor 56 139	6	10 wks
23 Mar 67	● PURPLE HAZE Track 604 001	3	14 wks
11 May 67	● THE WIND CRIES MARY Track 604 004	6	11 wks
30 Aug 67	BURNING OF THE MIDNIGHT LAMP Track 604 007	18	9 wks
23 Oct 68	● ALL ALONG THE WATCHTOWER Track 604 025	5	11 wks
16 Apr 69	CROSSTOWN TRAFFIC Track 604 029	37	3 wks
7 Nov 70	★ VOODOO CHILE Track 2095 001	1	13 wks
30 Oct 71	GYPSY EYES/REMEMBER Track 2094 010	35	5 wks
12 Feb 72	JOHNNY B. GOODE Polydor 2001 277	35	5 wks

On Polydor the act is simply billed as Jimi Hendrix.

Don HENLEY US, male vocalist — 3 wks

12 Feb 83	DIRTY LAUNDRY Asylum E 9894	59	3 wks

Clarence 'Frogman' HENRY
US, male vocalist — 33 wks

4 May 61	● BUT I DO Pye international 7N 25078	3	19 wks
13 Jul 61	● YOU ALWAYS HURT THE ONE YOU LOVE Pye International 7N 25089	6	12 wks
21 Sep 61	LONELY STREET/WHY CAN'T YOU Pye International 7N 25108	42	2 wks

Paul HENRY and the Mayson GLEN ORCHESTRA
UK, male vocalist/orchestra — 2 wks

14 Jan 78	BENNY'S THEME Pye 7N 46027	39	2 wks

HERB - *See PEACHES and HERB*

HERD UK, male vocal/instrumental group — 35 wks

13 Sep 67	● FROM THE UNDERWORLD Fontana TF 856	6	13 wks
20 Dec 67	PARADISE LOST Fontana TF 887	15	9 wks
10 Apr 68	● I DON'T WANT OUR LOVING TO DIE Fontana TF 925	5	13 wks

HERMAN'S HERMITS
UK, male vocal/instrumental group — 211 wks

20 Aug 64	★ I'M INTO SOMETHING GOOD Columbia DB 7338	1	15 wks
19 Nov 64	SHOW ME GIRL Columbia DB 7408	19	9 wks
18 Feb 65	● SILHOUETTES Columbia DB 7475	3	12 wks
29 Apr 65	● WONDERFUL WORLD Columbia DB 7546	7	9 wks
2 Sep 65	JUST A LITTLE BIT BETTER Columbia DB 7670	15	9 wks
23 Dec 65	● A MUST TO AVOID Columbia DB 7791	6	11 wks
24 Mar 66	YOU WON'T BE LEAVING Columbia DB 7861	20	7 wks
23 Jun 66	THIS DOOR SWINGS BOTH WAYS Columbia DB 7947	18	7 wks
6 Oct 66	● NO MILK TODAY Columbia DB 8012	7	11 wks
1 Dec 66	EAST WEST Columbia DB 8076	37	7 wks
9 Feb 67	● THERE'S A KIND OF HUSH Columbia DB 8123	7	11 wks
17 Jan 68	I CAN TAKE OR LEAVE YOUR LOVING Columbia DB 8327	11	9 wks
1 May 68	SLEEPY JOE Columbia DB 8404	12	10 wks
17 Jul 68	● SUNSHINE GIRL Columbia DB 8446	8	14 wks
18 Dec 68	SOMETHING'S HAPPENING Columbia DB 8504	6	15 wks
23 Apr 69	● MY SENTIMENTAL FRIEND Columbia DB 8563	2	12 wks
8 Nov 69	HERE COMES THE STAR Columbia DB 8626	33	9 wks
7 Feb 70	● YEARS MAY COME, YEARS MAY GO Columbia DB 8656	7	11 wks
2 May 70	YEARS MAY COME YEARS MAY GO (re-entry) Columbia DB 8656	45	1 wk
23 May 70	BET YER LIFE I DO RAK 102	22	10 wks
14 Nov 70	LADY BARBARA RAK 106	13	12 wks

On Lady Barbara billed as Peter Noone and Herman's Hermits. See also Peter Noone.

Patrick HERNANDEZ
Germany, male vocalist — 14 wks

16 Jun 79	● BORN TO BE ALIVE Gem/Aquarius GEM 4	10	14 wks

HERREYS
Sweden, male vocal/instrumental group — 3 wks

26 May 84	DIGGI LOO-DIGGI LEY MCA/Panther PAN 5	46	3 wks

Nick HEYWARD UK, male vocalist — 46 wks

19 Mar 83	WHISTLE DOWN THE WIND Arista HEY 1	13	8 wks
4 Jun 83	TAKE THAT SITUATION Arista HEY 2	11	10 wks
24 Sep 83	BLUE HAT FOR A BLUE DAY Arista HEY 3	14	8 wks
3 Dec 83	ON A SUNDAY Arista HEY 4	52	5 wks
2 Jun 84	LOVE ALL DAY Arista HEY 5	31	6 wks
3 Nov 84	WARNING SIGN Arista HEY 6	25†	9 wks

HI GLOSS *US, disco aggregation*   *13 wks*

8 Aug 81	**YOU'LL NEVER KNOW** *Epic EPC A 1387*	12	13 wks

HI TENSION
UK, male vocal/instrumental group   *23 wks*

6 May 78	**HI TENSION** *Island WIP 6422*	13	12 wks
12 Aug 78	● **BRITISH HUSTLE/PEACE ON EARTH**		
	Island WIP 6446	8	11 wks

Peace On Earth credited with British Hustle from 2 Sep 78 to end of record's chart run.

Al HIBBLER *US, male vocalist*   *17 wks*

13 May 55	● **UNCHAINED MELODY** *Brunswick 05420*	2	17 wks

Bertie HIGGINS *US, male vocalist*   *4 wks*

5 Jun 82	**KEY LARGO** *Epic EPC A 2168*	60	4 wks

HIGH NUMBERS
UK, male vocal/instrumental group   *4 wks*

5 Apr 80	**I'M THE FACE** *Back Door DOOR 4*	49	4 wks

The High Numbers were an early version of the Who. See also the Who.

HIGH SOCIETY
UK, male vocal/instrumental group   *4 wks*

15 Nov 80	**I NEVER GO OUT IN THE RAIN** *Eagle ERS 002*	53	4 wks

HIGHLY LIKELY
UK, male vocal/instrumental group   *4 wks*

21 Apr 73	**WHATEVER HAPPENED TO YOU (LIKELY**		
	LADS THEME) *BBC RESL 10*	35	4 wks

HIGHWAYMEN *US, male vocal group*   *18 wks*

7 Sep 61	★ **MICHAEL** *HMV POP 910*	1	14 wks
7 Dec 61	**GYPSY ROVER** *HMV POP 948*	41	3 wks
11 Jan 62	**GYPSY ROVER** (re-entry) *HMV POP 948*	43	1 wk

Benny HILL *UK, male vocalist*   *39 wks*

16 Feb 61	**GATHER IN THE MUSHROOMS** *Pye 7N 15327*	12	8 wks
1 Jun 61	**TRANSISTOR RADIO** *Pye 7N 15359*	24	6 wks
16 May 63	**HARVEST OF LOVE** *Pye 7N 15520*	20	8 wks
13 Nov 71	★ **ERNIE (THE FASTEST MILKMAN IN THE**		
	WEST) *Columbia DB 8833*	1	17 wks

Chris HILL
UK, male vocalist plus extracts from other hit records   *14 wks*

6 Dec 75	● **RENTA SANTA** *Philips 6006 491*	10	7 wks
4 Dec 76	● **BIONIC SANTA** *Philips 6006 551*	10	7 wks

Dan HILL *Canada, male vocalist*   *13 wks*

18 Feb 78	**SOMETIMES WHEN WE TOUCH**		
	20th Century BTC 2355	46	1 wk

4 Mar 78	**SOMETIMES WHEN WE TOUCH** (re-entry)		
	20th Century BTC 2355	13	12 wks

Roni HILL *US, female vocalist*   *4 wks*

7 May 77	**YOU KEEP ME HANGIN' ON - STOP IN THE**		
	NAME OF LOVE (MEDLEY) *Creole CR 138* ..	36	4 wks

Vince HILL *UK, male vocalist*   *91 wks*

7 Jun 62	**THE RIVER'S RUN DRY** *Piccadilly 7N 35043* ...	49	1 wk
28 Jun 62	**THE RIVER'S RUN DRY** (re-entry)		
	Piccadilly 7N 35043	41	1 wk
6 Jan 66	**TAKE ME TO YOUR HEART AGAIN**		
	Columbia DB 7781	13	11 wks
17 Mar 66	**HEARTACHES** *Columbia DB 7852*	28	5 wks
2 Jun 66	**MERCI CHERI** *Columbia DB 7924*	36	6 wks
9 Feb 67	● **EDELWEISS** *Columbia DB 8127*	2	17 wks
11 May 67	**ROSES OF PICARDY** *Columbia DB 8185*	13	11 wks
27 Sep 67	**LOVE LETTERS IN THE SAND**		
	Columbia DB 8268	23	9 wks
26 Jun 68	**IMPORTANCE OF YOUR LOVE**		
	Columbia DB 8414	32	12 wks
12 Feb 69	**DOESN'T ANYBODY KNOW MY NAME?**		
	Columbia DB 8515	50	1 wk
25 Oct 69	**LITTLE BLUE BIRD** *Columbia DB 8616*	42	1 wk
25 Sep 71	**LOOK AROUND** *Columbia DB 8804*	12	16 wks

HILLTOPPERS *US, male vocal group*   *30 wks*

27 Jan 56	● **ONLY YOU** *London HLD 8221*	3	22 wks
10 Aug 56	**ONLY YOU** (re-entry) *London HLD 8221*	24	1 wk
14 Sep 56	**TRYIN'** *London HLD 8298*	30	1 wk
5 Apr 57	**MARIANNE** *London HLD 8381*	20	2 wks
26 Apr 57	**MARIANNE** (re-entry) *London HLD 8381*	23	4 wks

Ronnie HILTON *UK, male vocalist*   *128 wks*

26 Nov 54	● **I STILL BELIEVE** *HMV B 10785*	3	14 wks
10 Dec 54	**VENI VIDI VICI** *HMV B 10785*	12	8 wks
11 Mar 55	● **A BLOSSOM FELL** *HMV B 10808*	10	5 wks
26 Aug 55	**STARS SHINE IN YOUR EYES** *HMV B 10901*	13	7 wks
11 Nov 55	**YELLOW ROSE OF TEXAS** *HMV B 10924*	15	2 wks
10 Feb 56	**YOUNG AND FOOLISH** *HMV POP 154*	17	1 wk
24 Feb 56	**YOUNG AND FOOLISH** (re-entry)		
	HMV POP 154	20	1 wk
9 Mar 56	**YOUNG AND FOOLISH** (2nd re-entry)		
	HMV POP 154	19	1 wk
20 Apr 56	★ **NO OTHER LOVE** *HMV POP 198*	1	14 wks
29 Jun 56	● **WHO ARE WE** *HMV POP 221*	6	12 wks
21 Sep 56	**WOMAN IN LOVE** *HMV POP 248*	30	1 wk
9 Nov 56	**TWO DIFFERENT WORLDS** *HMV POP 274* ...	13	13 wks
24 May 57	● **AROUND THE WORLD** *HMV POP 338*	4	18 wks
2 Aug 57	**WONDERFUL WONDERFUL** *HMV POP 364* ...	27	2 wks
21 Feb 58	**MAGIC MOMENTS** *HMV POP 446*	22	2 wks
18 Apr 58	**I MAY NEVER PASS THIS WAY AGAIN**		
	HMV POP 468	30	1 wk
2 May 58	**I MAY NEVER PASS THIS WAY AGAIN**		
	(re-entry) *HMV POP 468*	30	1 wk
6 Jun 58	**I MAY NEVER PASS THIS WAY AGAIN**		
	(2nd re-entry) *HMV POP 468*	27	1 wk
9 Jan 59	**THE WORLD OUTSIDE** *HMV POP 559*	18	6 wks
21 Aug 59	**THE WONDER OF YOU** *HMV POP 638*	22	3 wks
21 May 64	**DON'T LET THE RAIN COME DOWN**		
	HMV POP 1291	21	10 wks
11 Feb 65	**A WINDMILL IN OLD AMSTERDAM**		
	HMV POP 1378	23	13 wks

Edmund HOCKRIDGE
Canada, male vocalist   *18 wks*

17 Feb 56	● **YOUNG AND FOOLISH** *Nixa N 15039*	10	7 wks

13 Apr 56	YOUNG AND FOOLISH (re-entry) Nixa N 15039	28	1 wk
4 May 56	YOUNG AND FOOLISH (2nd re-entry) Nixa N 15039	26	1 wk
11 May 56	NO OTHER LOVE Nixa N 15046	24	2 wks
1 Jun 56	NO OTHER LOVE (re-entry) Nixa N 15046	29	1 wk
15 Jun 56	NO OTHER LOVE (2nd re-entry) Nixa N 15046	30	1 wk
31 Aug 56	BY THE FOUNTAINS OF ROME Pye Nixa N 15063	17	5 wks

Eddie HODGES *US, male vocalist* *10 wks*

| 28 Sep 61 | I'M GONNA KNOCK ON YOUR DOOR London HLA 9369 | 37 | 6 wks |
| 9 Aug 62 | MADE TO LOVE (GIRLS GIRLS GIRLS) London HLA 9576 | 37 | 4 wks |

HOLLAND-DOZIER
US, male vocal duo *5 wks*

| 28 Oct 72 | WHY CAN'T WE BE LOVERS Invictus INV 525 | 29 | 5 wks |

Hit has credit 'featuring Lamont Dozier'

Jennifer HOLLIDAY *US, female vocalist* *6 wks*

| 4 Sep 82 | AND I'M TELLING YOU I'M NOT GOING Geffen GEF A 2644 | 32 | 6 wks |

Michael HOLLIDAY *UK, male vocalist* *63 wks*

30 Mar 56	NOTHIN' TO DO Columbia DB 3746	20	1 wk
27 Apr 56	NOTHIN' TO DO (re-entry) Columbia DB 3746	23	2 wks
15 Jun 56	GAL WITH THE YALLER SHOES Columbia DB 3783	13	3 wks
22 Jun 56	HOT DIGGITY Columbia DB 3783	14	5 wks
3 Aug 56	HOT DIGGITY/GAL WITH THE YALLER SHOES (re-entry) Columbia DB 3783	17	3 wks
5 Oct 56	TEN THOUSAND MILES Columbia DB 3813	24	3 wks
17 Jan 58	★ THE STORY OF MY LIFE Columbia DB 4058	1	15 wks
14 Mar 58	IN LOVE Columbia DB 4087	26	3 wks
16 May 58	● STAIRWAY OF LOVE Columbia DB 4121	3	13 wks
11 Jul 58	I'LL ALWAYS BE IN LOVE WITH YOU Columbia DB 4155	27	1 wk
1 Jan 60	★ STARRY EYED Columbia DB 4378	1	12 wks
14 Apr 60	SKYLARK Columbia DB 4437	39	3 wks
1 Sep 60	LITTLE BOY LOST Columbia DB 4475	50	1 wk

When Hot Diggity/Gal With The Yaller Shoes re-entered the chart on 3 Aug 56, Hot Diggity was listed by itself on 3 Aug and 10 Aug. Both sides were listed on 17 Aug.

HOLLIES *UK, male vocal/instrumental group* *300 wks*

30 May 63	JUST LIKE ME Parlophone R 5030	25	10 wks
29 Aug 63	SEARCHIN' Parlophone R 5052	12	14 wks
21 Nov 63	● STAY Parlophone R 5077	8	16 wks
27 Feb 64	● JUST ONE LOOK Parlophone R 5104	2	13 wks
21 May 64	● HERE I GO AGAIN Parlophone R 5137	4	12 wks
17 Sep 64	● WE'RE THROUGH Parlophone R 5178	7	11 wks
28 Jan 65	● YES I WILL Parlophone R 5232	9	13 wks
27 May 65	★ I'M ALIVE Parlophone R 5287	1	14 wks
2 Sep 65	● LOOK THROUGH ANY WINDOW Parlophone R 5322	4	11 wks
9 Dec 65	IF I NEEDED SOMEONE Parlophone R 5392	20	9 wks
24 Feb 66	● I CAN'T LET GO Parlophone R 5409	2	10 wks
23 Jun 66	● BUS STOP Parlophone R 5469	5	9 wks
13 Oct 66	● STOP STOP STOP Parlophone R 5508	2	12 wks
16 Feb 67	● ON A CAROUSEL Parlophone R 5562	4	11 wks
1 Jun 67	● CARRIE-ANNE Parlophone R 5602	3	11 wks
27 Sep 67	KING MIDAS IN REVERSE Parlophone R 5637	18	8 wks
27 Mar 68	● JENNIFER ECCLES Parlophone R 5680	7	11 wks
2 Oct 68	LISTEN TO ME Parlophone R 5733	11	11 wks

5 Mar 69	● SORRY SUZANNE Parlophone R 5765	3	12 wks
4 Oct 69	● HE AIN'T HEAVY HE'S MY BROTHER Parlophone R 5806	3	15 wks
18 Apr 70	● I CAN'T TELL THE BOTTOM FROM THE TOP Parlophone R 5837	7	10 wks
3 Oct 70	GASOLINE ALLEY BRED Parlophone R 5862	14	7 wks
22 May 71	HEY WILLY Parlophone R 5905	22	7 wks
26 Feb 72	THE BABY Polydor 2058 199	26	6 wks
2 Sep 72	LONG COOL WOMAN IN A BLACK DRESS Parlophone R 5939	32	8 wks
13 Oct 73	THE DAY THAT CURLY BILLY SHOT CRAZY SAM MCGHEE Polydor 2058 403	24	6 wks
9 Feb 74	● THE AIR THAT I BREATHE Polydor 2058 435	2	13 wks
14 Jun 80	SOLDIER'S SONG Polydor 2059 246	58	3 wks
29 Aug 81	HOLLIEDAZE (MEDLEY) EMI 5229	28	7 wks

HOLLY and the IVY'S
UK, male/female vocal/instrumental group *4 wks*

| 19 Dec 81 | CHRISTMAS ON 45 Decca SANTA 1 | 40 | 4 wks |

Buddy HOLLY *US, male vocalist* *186 wks*

6 Dec 57	● PEGGY SUE Coral Q 72293	6	17 wks
14 Mar 58	LISTEN TO ME Coral Q 72288	16	2 wks
20 Jun 58	● RAVE ON Coral Q 72325	5	14 wks
29 Aug 58	EARLY IN THE MORNING Coral Q 72333	17	4 wks
16 Jan 59	HEARTBEAT Coral Q 72346	30	1 wk
27 Feb 59	★ IT DOESN'T MATTER ANYMORE Coral Q 72360	1	21 wks
31 Jul 59	MIDNIGHT SHIFT Brunswick 05800	26	3 wks
11 Sep 59	PEGGY SUE GOT MARRIED Coral Q 72376	13	10 wks
28 Apr 60	HEARTBEAT (re-issue) Coral Q 72392	30	3 wks
26 May 60	TRUE LOVE WAYS Coral Q 72397	25	7 wks
20 Oct 60	LEARNIN' THE GAME Coral Q 72411	36	3 wks
26 Jan 61	WHAT TO DO Coral Q 72419	34	6 wks
6 Jul 61	BABY I DON'T CARE/VALLEY OF TEARS Coral Q 72432	12	14 wks
15 Mar 62	LISTEN TO ME (re-issue) Coral Q 72449	48	1 wk
13 Sep 62	REMINISCING Coral Q 72455	17	11 wks
14 Mar 63	● BROWN-EYED HANDSOME MAN Coral Q 72459	3	17 wks
6 Jun 63	● BO DIDDLEY Coral Q 72463	4	12 wks
5 Sep 63	● WISHING Coral Q 72466	10	11 wks
19 Dec 63	WHAT TO DO (re-issue) Coral Q 72469	27	8 wks
14 May 64	YOU'VE GOT LOVE Coral Q 72472	40	6 wks
10 Sep 64	LOVE'S MADE A FOOL OF YOU Coral Q 72475	39	6 wks
3 Apr 68	PEGGY SUE/RAVE ON (re-issue) MCA MU 1012	32	9 wks

Buddy Holly's version of Love's Made A Fool Of You is not the same version as the Crickets' hit of 1959, on which Holly did not appear. You've Got Love was released with credit to Buddy Holly and The Crickets. Valley Of Tears was not listed together with Baby I Don't Care until 13 Jul 61. See also Crickets.

HOLLYWOOD ARGYLES
US, male vocal group *10 wks*

| 21 Jul 60 | ALLEY OOP London HLU 9146 | 24 | 10 wks |

Eddie HOLMAN *US, male vocalist* *13 wks*

| 19 Oct 74 | ● (HEY THERE) LONELY GIRL ABC 4012 | 4 | 13 wks |

Rupert HOLMES *US, male vocalist* *14 wks*

| 12 Jan 80 | ESCAPE (THE PINA COLADA SONG) Infinity INF 120 | 23 | 7 wks |
| 22 Mar 80 | HIM MCA 565 | 31 | 7 wks |

John HOLT *Jamaica, male vocalist* *14 wks*

14 Dec 74 ●	**HELP ME MAKE IT THROUGH THE NIGHT**			
	Trojan TR 7909		**6**	14 wks

HONEYBUS *UK, male vocal/instrumental group* *12 wks*

20 Mar 68 ●	**I CAN'T LET MAGGIE GO** *Deram DM 182*		**8**	12 wks

HONEYCOMBS *UK, male/female vocal/instrumental group* *39 wks*

23 Jul 64 ★	**HAVE I THE RIGHT** *Pye 7N 15664*		**1**	15 wks
22 Oct 64	**IS IT BECAUSE** *Pye 7N 15705*		**38**	6 wks
29 Apr 65	**SOMETHING BETTER BEGINNING**			
	Pye 7N 15827		**39**	4 wks
5 Aug 65	**THAT'S THE WAY** *Pye 7N 15890*		**12**	14 wks

HONKY *UK, male vocal/instrumental group* *5 wks*

28 May 77	**JOIN THE PARTY** *Creole CR 137*		**28**	5 wks

Frank HOOKER and POSITIVE PEOPLE *US, male vocal/instrumental group* *4 wks*

5 Jul 80	**THIS FEELIN'** *DJM DJS 10947*		**48**	4 wks

John Lee HOOKER *US, male vocalist* *10 wks*

11 Jun 64	**DIMPLES** *Stateside SS 297*		**23**	10 wks

Mary HOPKIN *UK, female vocalist* *74 wks*

4 Sep 68 ★	**THOSE WERE THE DAYS** *Apple 2*		**1**	21 wks
2 Apr 69 ●	**GOODBYE** *Apple 10*		**2**	14 wks
31 Jan 70 ●	**TEMMA HARBOUR** *Apple 22*		**6**	11 wks
28 Mar 70 ●	**KNOCK KNOCK WHO'S THERE** *Apple 26*		**2**	14 wks
31 Oct 70	**THINK ABOUT YOUR CHILDREN** *Apple 30* ..		**19**	7 wks
2 Jan 71	**THINK ABOUT YOUR CHILDREN** (re-entry)			
	Apple 30		**46**	2 wks
31 Jul 71	**LET MY NAME BE SORROW** *Apple 34* ...		**46**	1 wk
20 Mar 76	**IF YOU LOVE ME** *Good Earth GD 2*		**32**	4 wks

Johnny HORTON *US, male vocalist* *15 wks*

26 Jun 59	**BATTLE OF NEW ORLEANS** *Philips PB 932* ...		**16**	4 wks
19 Jan 61	**NORTH TO ALASKA** *Philips PB 1062*		**23**	11 wks

HOT BLOOD *France, male instrumental group* *5 wks*

9 Oct 76	**SOUL DRACULA** *Creole CR 132*		**32**	5 wks

HOT BUTTER *US, male instrumental group* *19 wks*

22 Jul 72 ●	**POPCORN** *Pye International 7N 25583*		**5**	16 wks
23 Dec 72	**POPCORN** (re-entry) *Pye International 7N 25583* ..		**50**	3 wks

HOT CHOCOLATE *UK, male vocal/instrumental group* *255 wks*

15 Aug 70 ●	**LOVE IS LIFE** *RAK 103*		**6**	12 wks
6 Mar 71	**YOU COULD HAVE BEEN A LADY** *RAK 110*		**22**	9 wks
28 Aug 71 ●	**I BELIEVE (IN LOVE)** *RAK 118*		**8**	11 wks
28 Oct 72	**YOU'LL ALWAYS BE A FRIEND** *RAK 139*		**23**	8 wks
14 Apr 73 ●	**BROTHER LOUIE** *RAK 149*		**7**	10 wks
18 Aug 73	**RUMOURS** *RAK 157*		**44**	3 wks
16 Mar 74 ●	**EMMA** *RAK 168*		**3**	10 wks
30 Nov 74	**CHERI BABE** *RAK 188*		**31**	9 wks
24 May 75	**DISCO QUEEN** *RAK 202*		**11**	7 wks
9 Aug 75 ●	**A CHILD'S PRAYER** *RAK 212*		**7**	10 wks
8 Nov 75 ●	**YOU SEXY THING** *RAK 221*		**2**	12 wks
20 Mar 76	**DON'T STOP IT NOW** *RAK 230*		**11**	8 wks
26 Jun 76	**MAN TO MAN** *RAK 238*		**14**	8 wks
21 Aug 76	**HEAVEN IS IN THE BACK SEAT OF MY**			
	CADILLAC *RAK 240*		**25**	8 wks
18 Jun 77 ★	**SO YOU WIN AGAIN** *RAK 259*		**1**	11 wks
26 Nov 77 ●	**PUT YOUR LOVE IN ME** *RAK 266*		**10**	9 wks
4 Mar 78	**EVERY 1'S A WINNER** *RAK 270*		**12**	11 wks
2 Dec 78	**I'LL PUT YOU TOGETHER AGAIN** *RAK 286*		**13**	11 wks
19 May 79	**MINDLESS BOOGIE** *RAK 292*		**46**	5 wks
28 Jul 79	**GOING THROUGH THE MOTIONS** *RAK 296* ..		**53**	4 wks
3 May 80 ●	**NO DOUBT ABOUT IT** *RAK 310*		**2**	11 wks
19 Jul 80	**ARE YOU GETTING ENOUGH OF WHAT**			
	MAKES YOU HAPPY *RAK 318*		**17**	7 wks
13 Dec 80	**LOVE ME TO SLEEP** *RAK 324*		**50**	5 wks
30 May 81	**YOU'LL NEVER BE SO WRONG** *RAK 331* ...		**52**	4 wks
17 Apr 82 ●	**GIRL CRAZY** *RAK 341*		**7**	11 wks
10 Jul 82 ●	**IT STARTED WITH A KISS** *RAK 344*		**5**	12 wks
25 Sep 82	**CHANCES** *RAK 350*		**32**	5 wks
7 May 83 ●	**WHAT KINDA BOY YOU LOOKING FOR**			
	(GIRL) *RAK 357*		**10**	9 wks
17 Sep 83	**TEARS ON THE TELEPHONE** *RAK 363*		**37**	5 wks
4 Feb 84	**I GAVE YOU MY HEART (DIDN'T I)** *RAK 369*		**13**	10 wks

HOT GOSSIP - *See Sarah BRIGHTMAN*

HOTLEGS *UK, male vocal/instrumental group* *14 wks*

4 Jul 70 ●	**NEANDERTHAL MAN** *Fontana 6007 019*		**2**	14 wks

HOTRODS - *See EDDIE and the HOTRODS*

HOTSHOTS *UK, male vocal group* *15 wks*

2 Jun 73 ●	**SNOOPY VS. THE RED BARON**			
	Mooncrest MOON 5		**4**	15 wks

HOT STREAK *US, male vocal/instrumental group* *8 wks*

10 Sep 83	**BODY WORK** *Polydor POSP 642*		**19**	8 wks

Thelma HOUSTON *US, female vocalist* *17 wks*

5 Feb 77	**DON'T LEAVE ME THIS WAY**			
	Motown TMG 1060		**13**	8 wks
27 Jun 81	**IF YOU FEEL IT** *RCA 77*		**48**	4 wks
1 Dec 84	**YOU USED TO HOLD ME SO TIGHT**			
	MCA MCA 932		**49†**	5 wks

Billy HOWARD *UK, male vocalist* *12 wks*

13 Dec 75 ●	**KING OF THE COPS** *Penny Farthing PEN 892* ..		**6**	12 wks

HOWLIN' WOLF US, male vocalist — 5 wks

4 Jun 64	SMOKESTACK LIGHTNIN'	Pye International 7N 25244	42	5 wks

Al HUDSON and the PARTNERS
US, male/female vocal/instrumental group — 14 wks

9 Sep 78	DANCE, GET DOWN/HOW DO YOU DO	ABC 4229	57	4 wks
15 Sep 79	YOU CAN DO IT	MCA 511	15	10 wks

First hit credited to Al Hudson – US, male vocalist. See also One Way featuring Al Hudson.

HUDSON-FORD UK, male vocal/instrumental duo — 20 wks

18 Aug 73	● PICK UP THE PIECES	A & M AMS 7078	8	9 wks
16 Feb 74	BURN BABY BURN	A & M AMS 7096	15	9 wks
29 Jun 74	FLOATING IN THE WIND	A & M AMS 7116	35	2 wks

See also Monks.

HUES CORPORATION US, male/female vocal group — 16 wks

27 Jul 74	● ROCK THE BOAT	RCA APBO 0232	6	10 wks
19 Oct 74	ROCKIN' SOUL	RCA PB 10066	24	6 wks

David HUGHES UK, male vocalist — 1 wk

21 Sep 56	BY THE FOUNTAINS OF ROME	Philips PB 606	27	1 wk

HUGO and LUIGI US, male vocal duo — 2 wks

24 Jul 59	LA PLUME DE MA TANTE	RCA 1127	29	2 wks

HUMAN LEAGUE UK, male/female vocal/instrumental group — 109 wks

3 May 80	HOLIDAY 80 (Double single)	Virgin SV 105	56	5 wks
21 Jun 80	EMPIRE STATE HUMAN	Virgin VS 351	62	2 wks
28 Feb 81	BOYS AND GIRLS	Virgin VS 395	48	4 wks
2 May 81	THE SOUND OF THE CROWD	Virgin VS 416	12	10 wks
8 Aug 81	● LOVE ACTION (I BELIEVE IN LOVE) Virgin VS 435		3	13 wks
10 Oct 81	● OPEN YOUR HEART	Virgin VS 453	6	9 wks
5 Dec 81	★ DON'T YOU WANT ME	Virgin VS 466	1	13 wks
9 Jan 82	● BEING BOILED	EMI FAST 4	6	9 wks
6 Feb 82	HOLIDAY 80 (Double single) (re-entry) Virgin SV 105		46	5 wks
20 Nov 82	● MIRROR MAN	Virgin VS 522	2	10 wks
23 Apr 83	● (KEEP FEELING) FASCINATION	Virgin VS 569	2	9 wks
5 May 84	THE LEBANON	Virgin VS 672	11	6 wks
23 Jun 84	THE LEBANON (re-entry) Virgin VS 672		75	1 wk
30 Jun 84	LIFE ON YOUR OWN	Virgin VS 688	16	6 wks
17 Nov 84	LOUISE	Virgin VS 723	13†	7 wks

Tracks on double single: Being Boiled/Marianne/Rock And Roll - Nightclubbing/Dancevision.

HUMBLE PIE UK, male vocal/instrumental group — 10 wks

23 Aug 69	● NATURAL BORN BUGIE	Immediate IM 082	4	10 wks

Engelbert HUMPERDINCK
UK, male vocalist — 235 wks

26 Jan 67	★ RELEASE ME	Decca F 12541	1	56 wks
25 May 67	● THERE GOES MY EVERYTHING	Decca F 12610	2	29 wks
23 Aug 67	★ THE LAST WALTZ	Decca F 12655	1	27 wks
10 Jan 68	● AM I THAT EASY TO FORGET	Decca F 12722	3	13 wks
24 Apr 68	● A MAN WITHOUT LOVE	Decca F 12770	2	15 wks
25 Sep 68	● LES BICYCLETTES DE BELSIZE	Decca F 12834	5	15 wks
5 Feb 69	● THE WAY IT USED TO BE	Decca F 12879	3	14 wks
9 Aug 69	I'M A BETTER MAN	Decca F 12957	15	13 wks
15 Nov 69	● WINTER WORLD OF LOVE	Decca F 12980	7	13 wks
30 May 70	MY MARIE	Decca F 13032	31	7 wks
12 Sep 70	SWEETHEART	Decca F 13068	22	6 wks
31 Oct 70	SWEETHEART (re-entry) Decca F 13068		50	1 wk
11 Sep 71	ANOTHER TIME ANOTHER PLACE Decca F 13212		13	12 wks
4 Mar 72	TOO BEAUTIFUL TO LAST	Decca F 13281	14	10 wks
20 Oct 73	LOVE IS ALL	Decca F 13443	44	3 wks
17 Nov 73	LOVE IS ALL (re-entry) Decca F 13443		45	1 wk

Geraldine HUNT Canada, female vocalist — 5 wks

25 Oct 80	CAN'T FAKE THE FEELING	Champagne FIZZ 5001	44	5 wks

Marsha HUNT US, female vocalist — 3 wks

21 May 69	WALK ON GILDED SPLINTERS	Track 604 030	46	2 wks
2 May 70	KEEP THE CUSTOMER SATISFIED	Track 604 037	41	1 wk

Tommy HUNT US, male vocalist — 17 wks

11 Oct 75	CRACKIN' UP	Spark SRL 1132	39	5 wks
21 Aug 76	LOVING ON THE LOSING SIDE	Spark SRL 1146	28	9 wks
4 Dec 76	ONE FINE MORNING	Spark SRL 1148	44	3 wks

Ian HUNTER UK, male vocalist — 10 wks

3 May 75	ONCE BITTEN TWICE SHY	CBS 3194	14	10 wks

Tab HUNTER US, male vocalist — 30 wks

8 Feb 57	★ YOUNG LOVE	London HLD 8380	1	18 wks
12 Apr 57	● 99 WAYS	London HLD 8410	5	11 wks
5 Jul 57	99 WAYS (re-entry) London HLD 8410		29	1 wk

HURRICANES - *See JOHNNY and the HURRICANES*

Phil HURTT US, male vocalist — 5 wks

11 Nov 78	GIVING IT BACK	Fantasy FTC 161	36	5 wks

Willie HUTCH US, male vocalist — 7 wks

4 Dec 82	IN AND OUT	Motown TMG 1285	51	7 wks

June HUTTON US, female vocalist — 7 wks

7 Aug 53	● SAY YOU'RE MINE AGAIN	Capitol CL 13918	10	3 wks
4 Sep 53	● SAY YOU'RE MINE AGAIN (re-entry) Capitol CL 13918		6	4 wks

JEAN-MICHEL JARRE (above) Far-eastern fans study his synthesizer with a view to knocking up a cheaper model.

MICHAEL JACKSON (below) White glove at the White House.

MILLIE JACKSON (above) Run of the mille – two weeks.

JANIS IAN (below) She had her first song published at 13. She released her first single at 15. When she was 24 she won a grammy with 'At Seventeen'.

MICK JAGGER (above) Outside the Stones, Jagger has also appeared on records by The Beatles, The Jacksons, Peter Tosh, Dr. John, Carly Simon, Leslie West – as well as the soundtracks of *Ned Kelly* and the film that gave him his solo hit single – *Performance*.

PETER JAY (above) Great Yarmouth drummer and leader of The Jaywalkers. He admitted in an in-depth interview to his addiction to Chinese food and Coca-Cola.

Brian HYLAND   *US, male vocalist*   *72 wks*

7 Jul 60	● ITSY BITSY TEENY WEENY YELLOW POLKA DOT BIKINI *London HLR 9161*	**8**	13 wks
20 Oct 60	**FOUR LITTLE HEELS** *London HLR 9203*	**29**	6 wks
10 May 62	● **GINNY COME LATELY** *HMV POP 1013*	**5**	15 wks
2 Aug 62	● **SEALED WITH A KISS** *HMV POP 1051*	**3**	15 wks
8 Nov 62	**WARMED OVER KISSES** *HMV POP 1079*	**28**	6 wks
27 Mar 71	**GYPSY WOMAN** *Uni UN 530*	**45**	1 wk
10 Apr 71	**GYPSY WOMAN** (re-entry) *Uni UN 530*	**42**	5 wks
28 Jun 75	● **SEALED WITH A KISS** (re-issue) *ABC 4059*	**7**	11 wks

Sheila HYLTON   *Jamaica, female vocalist*   *12 wks*

15 Sep 79	**BREAKFAST IN BED** *United Artists BP 304*	**57**	5 wks
17 Jan 81	**THE BED'S TOO BIG WITHOUT YOU** *Island WIP 6671*	**35**	7 wks

Phyllis HYMAN   *US, female vocalist*   *9 wks*

16 Feb 80	**YOU KNOW HOW TO LOVE ME** *Arista ARIST 323*	**47**	6 wks
12 Sep 81	**YOU SURE LOOK GOOD TO ME** *Arista ARIST 424*	**56**	3 wks

Dick HYMAN TRIO   *US, male instrumental group, Dick Hyman, keyboards*   *10 wks*

16 MAR 56	● **THEME FROM 'THE THREEPENNY OPERA'** *MGM 890*	**9**	10 wks

HYSTERICS   *UK, male vocal/instrumental group*   *5 wks*

12 Dec 81	**JINGLE BELLS LAUGHING ALL THE WAY** *Record Delivery KA 5*	**44**	5 wks

I

Janis IAN   *US, female vocalist*   *10 wks*

17 Nov 79	**FLY TOO HIGH** *CBS 7936*	**44**	7 wks
28 Jun 80	**THE OTHER SIDE OF THE SUN** *CBS 8611* ...	**44**	3 wks

IAN AND THE BLOCKHEADS   - *See Ian DURY*

ICE HOUSE   *Australia, male vocal/instrumental group*   *14 wks*

5 Feb 83	**HEY LITTLE GIRL** *Chrysalis CHS 2670*	**17**	10 wks
23 Apr 83	**STREET CAFE** *Chrysalis COOL 1*	**62**	4 wks

ICICLE WORKS   *UK, male vocal/instrumental group*   *12 wks*

24 Dec 83	**LOVE IS A WONDERFUL COLOUR** *Beggars Banquet BEG 99*	**15**	8 wks
10 Mar 84	**BIRDS FLY/IN THE CAULDRON OF LOVE** *Beggars Banquet BEG 108*	**53**	4 wks

IDES OF MARCH   *US, male vocal/instrumental group*   *9 wks*

6 Jun 70	**VEHICLE** *Warner Bros. WB 7378*	**31**	9 wks

Billy IDOL   *UK, male vocalist*   *20 wks*

11 Sep 82	**HOT IN THE CITY** *Chrysalis CHS 2625*	**58**	4 wks
24 Mar 84	**REBEL YELL** *Chrysalis IDOL 2*	**62**	2 wks
30 Jun 84	**EYES WITHOUT A FACE** *Chrysalis IDOL 3* ...	**18**	11 wks
29 Sep 84	**FLESH FOR FANTASY** *Chrysalis IDOL 4*	**54**	3 wks

Frank IFIELD   *UK, male vocalist*   *155 wks*

19 Feb 60	**LUCKY DEVIL** *Columbia DB 4399*	**22**	2 wks
7 Apr 60	**LUCKY DEVIL** (re-entry) *Columbia DB 4399* ...	**33**	2 wks
29 Sep 60	**GOTTA GET A DATE** *Columbia DB 4496*	**49**	1 wk
5 Jul 62	★ **I REMEMBER YOU** *Columbia DB 4856*	**1**	28 wks
25 Oct 62	★ **LOVESICK BLUES** *Columbia DB 4913*	**1**	17 wks
24 Jan 63	★ **WAYWARD WIND** *Columbia DB 4960*	**1**	13 wks
11 Apr 63	● **NOBODY'S DARLIN' BUT MINE** *Columbia DB 7007*	**4**	16 wks
27 Jun 63	★ **CONFESSIN'** *Columbia DB 7062*	**1**	16 wks
17 Oct 63	**MULE TRAIN** *Columbia DB 7131*	**22**	6 wks
9 Jan 64	● **DON'T BLAME ME** *Columbia DB 7184*	**8**	13 wks
23 Apr 64	**ANGRY AT THE BIG OAK TREE** *Columbia DB 7263*	**25**	8 wks
23 Jul 64	**I SHOULD CARE** *Columbia DB 7319*	**33**	3 wks
1 Oct 64	**SUMMER IS OVER** *Columbia DB 7355*	**25**	6 wks
19 Aug 65	**PARADISE** *Columbia DB 7655*	**26**	9 wks
23 Jun 66	**NO ONE WILL EVER KNOW** *Columbia DB 7940*	**25**	4 wks
8 Dec 66	**CALL HER YOUR SWEETHEART** *Columbia DB 8078*	**24**	11 wks

Julio IGLESIAS   *Spain, male vocalist*   *37 wks*

24 Oct 81	★ **BEGIN THE BEGUINE (VOLVER A EMPEZAR)** *CBS A 1612*	**1**	14 wks
6 Mar 82	● **QUIEREME MUCHO (YOURS)** *CBS A 1939* ...	**3**	9 wks
9 Oct 82	**AMOR** *CBS A 2801*	**32**	7 wks
9 Apr 83	**HEY!** *CBS JULIO 1*	**31**	7 wks

See also Julio Iglesias and Diana Ross; Julio Iglesias and Willie Nelson.

Julio IGLESIAS and Diana ROSS   *Spain/US, male/female vocal duo*   *8 wks*

7 Jul 84	**ALL OF YOU** *CBS A 4522*	**43**	8 wks

See also Diana Ross; Diana Ross and Marvin Gaye; Diana Ross, Marvin Gaye, Smokey Robinson and Stevie Wonder; Diana Ross and Michael Jackson; Diana Ross and Lionel Richie; Diana Ross and the Supremes and the Temptations; Julio Iglesias; Julio Iglesias and Willie Nelson.

Julio IGLESIAS and Willie NELSON   *Spain/US, male vocal duo*   *10 wks*

7 Apr 84	**TO ALL THE GIRLS I'VE LOVED BEFORE** *CBS A 4252*	**17**	10 wks

See also Willie Nelson; Julio Iglesias; Julio Iglesias and Diana Ross.

I-LEVEL   *UK, male vocal/instrumental group*   *9 wks*

16 Apr 83	**MINEFIELD** *Virgin VS 563*	**52**	6 wks
18 Jun 83	**TEACHER** *Virgin VS 595*	**56**	3 wks

IMAGINATION   *UK, male vocal group*   *94 wks*

16 May 81	● **BODY TALK** *R & B RBS 201*	**4**	18 wks
5 Sep 81	**IN AND OUT OF LOVE** *R & B RBS 202*	**16**	9 wks
14 Nov 81	**FLASHBACK** *R & B RBS 206*	**16**	13 wks
6 Mar 82	● **JUST AN ILLUSION** *R & B RBS 208*	**2**	11 wks
26 Jun 82	● **MUSIC AND LIGHTS** *R & B RBS 210*	**5**	9 wks
25 Sep 82	**IN THE HEAT OF THE NIGHT** *R & B RBS 211*	**22**	8 wks
11 Dec 82	**CHANGES** *R & B RBS 213*	**31**	8 wks

4 Jun 83	**LOOKING AT MIDNIGHT** *R & B RBS 214* ...	29	7 wks
5 Nov 83	**NEW DIMENSIONS** *R & B/Red Bus RBS 216* ...	56	3 wks
26 May 84	**STATE OF LOVE** *R & B/Red Bus RBS 218*	67	2 wks
27 Nov 84	**THANK YOU MY LOVE** *R & B/Red Bus RBS 219*	60†	6 wks

IMPALAS *US, male vocal group* 1 wk

21 Aug 59	**SORRY (I RAN ALL THE WAY HOME)** *MGM 1015*	28	1 wk

IMPERIALS *US, male vocal group* 9 wks

24 Dec 77	**WHO'S GONNA LOVE ME** *Power Exchange PX-266*	17	9 wks

See also Little Anthony and the Imperials.

IMPOSTER *UK, male vocalist, Elvis Costello under an assumed name* 7 wks

11 Jun 83	**PILLS AND SOAP** *Imp/Demon IMP 001*	16	4 wks
28 Apr 84	**PEACE IN OUR TIME** *Imposter TRUCE 1*	48	3 wks

IMPRESSIONS *US, male vocal group* 10 wks

22 Nov 75	**FIRST IMPRESSIONS** *Curtom K 16638*	16	10 wks

IN CROWD *UK, male vocal/instrumental group* 1 wk

20 May 65	**THAT'S HOW STRONG MY LOVE IS** *Parlophone R 5276*	48	1 wk

IN DEEP *US, male/female vocal duo* 11 wks

22 Jan 83	**LAST NIGHT A DJ SAVED MY LIFE** *Sound of New York SNY 1*	13	9 wks
14 May 83	**WHEN BOYS TALK** *Sound of New York SNY 3*	67	2 wks

INCANTATION *UK, male instrumental group* 12 wks

4 Dec 82	**CACHARPAYA (ANDES PUMPSA DAESI)** *Beggars Banquet BEG 84*	12	12 wks

INCOGNITO *France, male instrumental group* 2 wks

15 Nov 80	**PARISIENNE GIRL** *Ensign ENY 44*	73	2 wks

INGRAM *US, male vocal/instrumental group* 2 wks

11 Jun 83	**SMOOTHIN' GROOVIN'** *Streetwave WAVE 3* ...	56	2 wks

James INGRAM With Michael McDONALD *US, male vocal duo* 8 wks

18 Feb 84	**YAH MO B THERE** *Qwest W 9394*	44	5 wks
7 Apr 84	**YAH MO B THERE** (re-entry) *Qwest W 9394* ...	69	3 wks

See also Patti Austin and James Ingram.

INK SPOTS *US, male vocal group* 4 wks

29 Apr 55	● **MELODY OF LOVE** *Parlophone MSP 6152*	10	4 wks

John INMAN *UK, male vocalist* 6 wks

25 Oct 75	**ARE YOU BEING SERVED SIR** *DJM DJS 602*	39	6 wks

INMATES *UK, male vocal/instrumental group* 9 wks

8 Dec 79	**THE WALK** *Radar ADA 47*	36	9 wks

INNER CIRCLE *Jamaica, male vocal/instrumental group* 11 wks

24 Feb 79	**EVERYTHING IS GREAT** *Island WIP 6472*	37	8 wks
12 May 79	**STOP BREAKING MY HEART** *Island WIP 6488*	50	3 wks

INSPIRATIONAL CHOIR *US, male/female choir* 2 wks

22 Dec 84	**ABIDE WITH ME** *Epic A 4997*	44†	2 wks

INSTANT FUNK *US, male vocal/instrumental group* 5 wks

20 Jan 79	**GOT MY MIND MADE UP** *Salsoul SSOL 114* ..	46	5 wks

INTRUDERS *US, male vocal group* 18 wks

13 Apr 74	**I'LL ALWAYS LOVE MY MAMA** *Philadelphia International PIR 2147*	32	7 wks
6 Jul 74	**(WIN PLACE OR SHOW) SHE'S A WINNER** *Philadelphia International PIR 2212*	14	9 wks
22 Dec 84	**WHO DO YOU LOVE?** *Streetwave KHAN 34* ...	69†	2 wks

INVISIBLE GIRLS - *See Pauline MURRAY and the INVISIBLE GIRLS*

IRON MAIDEN *UK, male vocal/instrumental group* 68 wks

23 Feb 80	**RUNNING FREE** *EMI 5032*	34	5 wks
7 Jun 80	**SANCTUARY** *EMI 5065*	29	5 wks
8 Nov 80	**WOMEN IN UNIFORM** *EMI 5105*	35	4 wks
14 Mar 81	**TWILIGHT ZONE/WRATH CHILD** *EMI 5145* ..	31	5 wks
27 Jun 81	**PURGATORY** *EMI 5184*	52	3 wks
26 Sep 81	**MAIDEN JAPAN** *EMI 5219*	43	4 wks
20 Feb 82	● **RUN TO THE HILLS** *EMI 5263*	7	10 wks
15 May 82	**THE NUMBER OF THE BEAST** *EMI 5287*	18	8 wks
23 Apr 83	**FLIGH OF ICARUS** *EMI 5378*	11	6 wks
2 Jul 83	**THE TROOPER** *EMI 5397*	12	7 wks
18 Aug 84	**2 MINUTES TO MIDNIGHT** *EMI 5849*	11	6 wks
3 Nov 84	**ACES HIGH** *EMI 5502*	20	5 wks

IRONHORSE *Canada, male vocal/instrumental group* 3 wks

5 May 79	**SWEET LUI-LOUISE** *Scotti Brothers K 11271*	60	3 wks

Big Dee IRWIN *US, male vocalist* 17 wks

21 Nov 63	● **SWINGING ON A STAR** *Colpix PX 11010*	7	17 wks

This hit was in fact a vocal duet by Big Dee Irwin and Little Eva, though Little Eva was not credited. See also Little Eva.

ISLEY BROTHERS
US, male vocal/instrumental group — 108 wks

Date	Title	Pos	Wks
25 Jul 63	TWIST AND SHOUT *Stateside SS 112*	42	1 wk
28 Apr 66	THIS OLD HEART OF MINE *Tamla Motown TMG 555*	47	1 wk
1 Sep 66	I GUESS I'LL ALWAYS LOVE YOU *Tamla Motown TMG 572*	45	2 wks
23 Oct 68 ●	THIS OLD HEART OF MINE (re-entry) *Tamla Motown TMG 555*	3	16 wks
15 Jan 69	I GUESS I'LL ALWAYS LOVE YOU (re-issue) *Tamla Motown TMG 683*	11	9 wks
16 Apr 69 ●	BEHIND A PAINTED SMILE *Tamla Motown TMG 693*	5	12 wks
25 Jun 69	IT'S YOUR THING *Major Minor MM 621*	30	5 wks
30 Aug 69	PUT YOURSELF IN MY PLACE *Tamla Motown TMG 708*	13	11 wks
22 Sep 73	THAT LADY *Epic EPC 1704*	14	9 wks
19 Jan 74	HIGHWAY OF MY LIFE *Epic EPC 1980*	25	8 wks
25 May 74	SUMMER BREEZE *Epic EPC 2244*	16	8 wks
10 Jul 76 ●	HARVEST FOR THE WORLD *Epic EPC 4369*	10	8 wks
13 May 78	TAKE ME TO THE NEXT PHASE *Epic EPC 6292*	50	4 wks
3 Nov 79	IT'S A DISCO NIGHT (ROCK DON'T STOP) *Epic EPC 7911*	14	11 wks
16 Jul 83	BETWEEN THE SHEETS *Epic A 3513*	52	3 wks

Burl IVES
US, male vocalist — 25 wks

Date	Title	Pos	Wks
25 Jan 62 ●	A LITTLE BITTY TEAR *Brunswick 05863*	9	15 wks
17 May 62	FUNNY WAY OF LAUGHIN' *Brunswick 05868*	29	10 wks

IVY LEAGUE
UK, male vocal group — 31 wks

Date	Title	Pos	Wks
4 Feb 65 ●	FUNNY HOW LOVE CAN BE *Piccadilly 7N 35222*	8	9 wks
6 May 65	THAT'S WHY I'M CRYING *Piccadilly 7N 35228*	22	8 wks
24 Jun 65 ●	TOSSING AND TURNING *Piccadilly 7N 35251*	3	13 wks
14 Jul 66	WILLOW TREE *Piccadilly 7N 35326*	50	1 wk

IVY'S - *See HOLLY and the IVY'S*

J

J. A. L. N. BAND
UK/Jamaica, male vocal/instrumental group — 17 wks

Date	Title	Pos	Wks
11 Sep 76	DISCO MUSIC /I LIKE IT *Magnet MAG 73*	21	9 wks
27 Aug 77	I GOT TO SING *Magnet MAG 97*	40	4 wks
1 Jul 78	GET UP *Magnet MAG 118*	53	4 wks

JBs ALL STARS
UK, male/female vocal/instrumental group — 4 wks

Date	Title	Pos	Wks
11 Feb 84	BACKFIELD IN MOTION *RCA Victor RCA 384*	48	4 wks

Terry JACKS
Canada, male vocalist — 21 wks

Date	Title	Pos	Wks
23 Mar 74 ★	SEASONS IN THE SUN *Bell 1344*	1	12 wks
29 Jun 74 ●	IF YOU GO AWAY *Bell 1362*	8	9 wks

Dee D. JACKSON
UK, female vocalist — 14 wks

Date	Title	Pos	Wks
22 Apr 78 ●	AUTOMATIC LOVER *Mercury 6007 171*	4	9 wks
2 Sep 78	METEOR MAN *Mercury 6007 182*	48	5 wks

Jermaine JACKSON
US, male vocalist — 26 wks

Date	Title	Pos	Wks
10 May 80 ●	LET'S GET SERIOUS *Motown TMG 1183*	8	11 wks
26 Jul 80	BURNIN' HOT *Motown TMG 1194*	32	6 wks
30 May 81	YOU LIKE ME DON'T YOU *Motown TMG 1222*	41	5 wks
12 May 84	SWEETEST SWEETEST *Arista JJK 1*	52	4 wks

See also Jackson Five; Jacksons; Jermaine Jackson and Pia Zadora

Jermaine JACKSON and Pia ZADORA
US, male/female vocal duo — 2 wks

Date	Title	Pos	Wks
27 Oct 84	WHEN THE RAIN BEGINS TO FALL *Arista ARIST 584*	68	2 wks

See also Jermaine Jackson; Jackson Five; Jacksons.

Joe JACKSON
UK, male vocalist — 40 wks

Date	Title	Pos	Wks
4 Aug 79	IS SHE REALLY GOING OUT WITH HIM? *A & M AMS 7459*	13	9 wks
12 Jan 80 ●	IT'S DIFFERENT FOR GIRLS *A & M AMS 7493*	5	9 wks
4 Jul 81	JUMPIN' JIVE *A & M AMS 8145*	43	5 wks
8 Jan 83 ●	STEPPIN' OUT *A & M AMS 8262*	6	8 wks
12 Mar 83	BREAKING US IN TWO *A & M AM 101*	59	4 wks
28 Apr 84	HAPPY ENDING *A & M AM 186*	58	3 wks
7 Jul 84	BE MY NUMBER TWO *A & M AM 200*	70	2 wks

Jumpin' Jive credited to Joe Jackson's Jumpin' Jive.

Michael JACKSON
US, male vocalist — 198 wks

Date	Title	Pos	Wks
12 Feb 72 ●	GOT TO BE THERE *Tamla Motown TMG 797*	5	11 wks
20 May 72 ●	ROCKIN' ROBIN *Tamla Motown TMG 816*	3	14 wks
19 Aug 72 ●	AIN'T NO SUNSHINE *Tamla Motown TMG 826*	8	11 wks
25 Nov 72 ●	BEN *Tamla Motown TMG 834*	7	14 wks
15 Sep 79 ●	DON'T STOP TILL YOU GET ENOUGH *Epic EPC 7763*	3	12 wks
24 Nov 79 ●	OFF THE WALL *Epic EPC 8045*	7	10 wks
9 Feb 80 ●	ROCK WITH YOU *Epic EPC 8206*	7	9 wks
3 May 80 ●	SHE'S OUT OF MY LIFE *Epic EPC 8384*	3	9 wks
26 Jul 80	GIRLFRIEND *Epic EPC 8782*	41	5 wks
23 May 81 ★	ONE DAY IN YOUR LIFE *Motown TMG 976*	1	14 wks
1 Aug 81	WE'RE ALMOST THERE *Motown TMG 977*	46	4 wks
29 Jan 83 ★	BILLIE JEAN *Epic EPC A 3084*	1	15 wks
9 Apr 83 ●	BEAT IT *Epic EPC A 3258*	3	12 wks
11 Jun 83 ●	WANNA BE STARTIN' SOMETHING *Epic A 3427*	8	9 wks
23 Jul 83	HAPPY (LOVE THEME FROM 'LADY SINGS THE BLUES') *Tamla Motown TMG 986*	52	3 wks
19 Nov 83 ●	THRILLER *Epic A 3643*	10	18 wks
31 Mar 84 ●	P.Y.T (PRETTY YOUNG THING) *Epic A 4136*	11	8 wks
2 Jun 84 ●	FAREWELL MY SUMMER LOVE *Motown TMG 1342*	7	12 wks
11 Aug 84	GIRL YOU'RE SO TOGETHER *Motown TMG 1355*	33	8 wks

See also Jackson Five; Jacksons; Diana Ross and Michael Jackson; Michael Jackson and Paul McCartney.

Michael JACKSON and Paul McCARTNEY
US/UK, male vocal duo — 25 wks

Date	Title	Pos	Wks
6 Nov 82 ●	THE GIRL IS MINE *Epic EPC A2729*	8	9 wks
15 Jan 83	THE GIRL IS MINE (re-entry) *Epic EPC 2729*	75	1 wk
15 Oct 83 ●	SAY SAY SAY *Parlophone R 6062*	2	15 wks

See also Michael Jackson; Jackson Five; Jacksons; Diana Ross and Michael Jackson; Paul McCartney; Paul McCartney with Stevie Wonder; Wings.

Mick JACKSON
UK, male vocalist — 16 wks

Date	Title	Pos	Wks
30 Sep 78	BLAME IT ON THE BOOGIE *Atlantic K 11102*	15	8 wks

JAPAN (above) The now defunct Japan pose for a gentleman taking a Polaroid.

HOWARD JONES (below left) meets Peter Gabriel at *Top of the Pops*.

PAUL JONES (below right) Originally known as blues singer P. P. Pond, Jones signs page 103 of *The Guinness Book of British Hit Singles* third edition for Donovan. (Photo: Rex Features.)

3 Feb 79	WEEKEND	*Atlantic K 11224*	....	38	8 wks

Millie JACKSON   *US, female vocalist*   *3 wks*

18 Nov 72	MY MAN A SWEET MAN	*Mojo 2093 022*	.....	50	1 wk
10 Mar 84	I FEEL LIKE WALKIN' IN THE RAIN				
	Sire W 9348	....		55	2 wks

Stonewall JACKSON   *US, male vocalist*   *2 wks*

17 Jul 59	WATERLOO	*Philips PB 941*	....	24	2 wks

Tony JACKSON and the VIBRATIONS
UK, male vocal/instrumental group   *3 wks*

8 Oct 64	BYE BYE BABY	*Pye 7N 15685*	....	38	3 wks

Wanda JACKSON   *US, female vocalist*   *11 wks*

1 Sep 60	LET'S HAVE A PARTY	*Capitol CL 15147*	.....	32	8 wks
26 Jan 61	MEAN MEAN MAN	*Capitol CL 15176*		46	1 wk
9 Feb 61	MEAN MEAN MAN	(re-entry) *Capitol CL 15176*		40	2 wks

JACKSON FIVE   *US, male vocal group*   *104 wks*

31 Jan 70	● I WANT YOU BACK	*Tamla Motown TMG 724*	..	2	13 wks
16 May 70	● ABC	*Tamla Motown TMG 738*	..	8	11 wks
1 Aug 70	● THE LOVE YOU SAVE	*Tamla Motown TMG 746*	..	7	9 wks
21 Nov 70	● I'LL BE THERE	*Tamla Motown TMG 758*	......	4	16 wks
10 Apr 71	MAMA'S PEARL	*Tamla Motown TMG 769*	.....	25	7 wks
17 Jul 71	NEVER CAN SAY GOODBYE				
	Tamla Motown TMG 778	....		33	7 wks
11 Nov 72	◉ LOOKIN' THROUGH THE WINDOWS				
	Tamla Motown TMG 833	....		9	11 wks
23 Dec 72	SANTA CLAUS IS COMING TO TOWN				
	Tamla Motown TMG 837	....		43	3 wks
17 Feb 73	● DOCTOR MY EYES	*Tamla Motown TMG 842*	..	9	10 wks
9 Jun 73	HALLELUJAH DAY	*Tamla Motown TMG 856*	..	20	9 wks
8 Sep 73	SKYWRITER	*Tamla Motown TMG 865*	....	25	8 wks

80 per cent of the group became part of the Jacksons and moved to Epic records. See also Jacksons; Diana Ross and Michael Jackson; Michael Jackson; Michael Jackson and Paul McCartney; Jermaine Jackson.

JACKSONS   *US, male vocal group*   *115 wks*

9 Apr 77	ENJOY YOURSELF	*Epic EPC 5063*	....	42	4 wks
4 Jun 77	★ SHOW YOU THE WAY TO GO	*Epic EPC 5266*		1	10 wks
13 Aug 77	DREAMER	*Epic EPC 5458*	....	22	9 wks
5 Nov 77	GOIN' PLACES	*Epic EPC 5732*	....	26	7 wks
11 Feb 78	EVEN THOUGH YOU'VE GONE	*Epic EPC 5919*		31	4 wks
23 Sep 78	● BLAME IT ON THE BOOGIE	*Epic EPC 6683*	..	8	12 wks
3 Feb 79	DESTINY	*Epic EPC 6983*		39	6 wks
24 Mar 79	SHAKE YOUR BODY (DOWN TO THE				
	GROUND)	*Epic EPC 7181*	....	4	12 wks
25 Oct 80	LOVELY ONE	*Epic EPC 9302*	....	29	6 wks
13 Dec 80	HEARTBREAK HOTEL	*Epic EPC 9391*	.....	44	6 wks
28 Feb 81	● CAN YOU FEEL IT	*Epic EPC 9554*	......	6	15 wks
4 Jul 81	● WALK RIGHT NOW	*Epic EPC A 1294*	......	7	11 wks
7 Jul 84	STATE OF SHOCK	*Epic A 4431*	....	14	8 wks
8 Sep 84	TORTURE	*Epic A 4675*	....	26	5 wks

The Jacksons were the Jackson Five minus Jermaine, plus other relatives too young to perform in Jackson Five days but Jermaine Jackson did appear on Epic A4675. State Of Shock credits lead vocal to Mick Jagger and Michael Jackson. See also Jackson Five; Michael Jackson; Michael Jackson and Paul McCartney; Diana Ross and Michael Jackson; Michael Jackson; Mick Jagger.

JACKY   *UK, female vocalist*   *14 wks*

10 Apr 68	● WHITE HORSES	*Philips BF 1674*	....	10	14 wks

Jacky is Jackie Lee. See also Jackie Lee.

Mick JAGGER   *UK, male vocalist*   *5 wks*

14 Nov 70	MEMO FROM TURNER	*Decca F 13067*	....	32	5 wks

JAGS   *UK, male vocal/instrumental group*   *11 wks*

8 Sep 79	BACK OF MY HAND	*Island WIP 6501*	....	17	10 wks
2 Feb 80	WOMAN'S WORLD	*Island WIP 6531*	....	75	1 wk

JAM   *UK, male vocal/instrumental group*   *201 wks*

7 May 77	IN THE CITY	*Polydor 2058 866*	....	40	6 wks
23 Jul 77	ALL AROUND THE WORLD	*Polydor 2058 903*		13	8 wks
5 Nov 77	THE MODERN WORLD	*Polydor 2058 945*	.....	36	4 wks
11 Mar 78	NEWS OF THE WORLD	*Polydor 2058 995*	.....	27	5 wks
26 Aug 78	DAVID WATTS/'A' BOMB IN WARDOUR				
	STREET	*Polydor 2059 054*	....	25	8 wks
21 Oct 78	DOWN IN THE TUBE STATION AT MIDNIGHT				
	Polydor POSP 8			15	7 wks
17 Mar 79	STRANGE TOWN	*Polydor POSP 34*	....	15	9 wks
25 Aug 79	WHEN YOU'RE YOUNG	*Polydor POSP 69*	..	17	7 wks
3 Nov 79	● THE ETON RIFLES	*Polydor POSP 83*	......	3	12 wks
22 Mar 80	★ GOING UNDERGROUND/THE DREAMS OF				
	CHILDREN	*Polydor POSP 113*	....	1	9 wks
26 Apr 80	STRANGE TOWN	(re-entry) *Polydor POSP 34*	..	44	4 wks
26 Apr 80	ALL AROUND THE WORLD	(re-entry)			
	Polydor 2058 903	....		43	3 wks
26 Apr 80	THE MODERN WORLD	(re-entry)			
	Polydor 2058 945	....		52	3 wks
26 Apr 80	NEWS OF THE WORLD	(re-entry)			
	Polydor 2058 995	....		53	3 wks
26 Apr 80	DAVID WATTS	(re-entry) *Polydor 2059 054*	...	54	3 wks
23 Aug 80	★ START	*Polydor 2059 266*	....	1	8 wks
26 Apr 80	IN THE CITY	(re-entry) *Polydor 2058 866*	..	40	4 wks
7 Feb 81	THAT'S ENTERTAINMENT	*Metronome 0030 364*		21	7 wks
6 Jun 81	● FUNERAL PYRE	*Polydor POSP 257*	......	4	6 wks
24 Oct 81	● ABSOLUTE BEGINNERS	*Polydor POSP 350*	..	4	6 wks
13 Feb 82	★ TOWN CALLED MALICE/PRECIOUS				
	Polydor POSP 400	....		1	8 wks
3 Jul 82	● JUST WHO IS THE FIVE O'CLOCK HERO				
	Polydor 2059 504	....		8	5 wks
18 Sep 82	● THE BITTEREST PILL (I EVER HAD TO				
	SWALLOW)	*Polydor POSP 505*	....	2	7 wks
4 Dec 82	★ BEAT SURRENDER	*Polydor POSP 540*	....	1	9 wks
22 Jan 83	NEWS OF THE WORLD	(2nd re-entry)			
	Polydor 2058 995	....		39	4 wks
22 Jan 83	DOWN IN THE TUBE STATION AT MIDNIGHT				
	(re-entry) *Polydor POSP 8*	....		30	6 wks
22 Jan 83	ALL AROUND THE WORLD	(2nd re-entry)			
	Polydor 2058 903	....		38	4 wks
22 Jan 83	GOING UNDERGROUND/DREAMS OF				
	CHILDREN	(re-entry) *Polydor POSP 113*	......	21	6 wks
22 Jan 83	IN THE CITY	(2nd re-entry) *Polydor 2058 866*	...	47	4 wks
22 Jan 83	STRANGE TOWN	(re-entry) *Polydor POSP 34*	..	42	5 wks
22 Jan 83	THE MODERN WORLD	(2nd re-entry)			
	Polydor 2058 945	....		51	4 wks
22 Jan 83	DAVID WATTS/A-BOMB IN WARDOUR				
	STREET	(2nd re-entry) *Polydor 2059 054*	.....	50	4 wks
22 Jan 83	WHEN YOU'RE YOUNG	(re-entry)			
	Polydor POSP 69	....		53	4 wks
29 Jan 83	THAT'S ENTERTAINMENT	*Polydor POSP 482*		60	3 wks
5 Feb 83	ETON RIFLES	(re-entry) *Polydor POSP 83*	.....	54	3 wks
5 Feb 83	START	(re-entry) *Polydor 2059 266*	....	62	2 wks
5 Feb 83	TOWN CALLED MALICE/PRECIOUS	(re-entry)			
	Polydor POSP 400	....		73	1 wk

Dreams of Children was only listed with the re-entry of Going Underground from 5 Feb 83. Metronome 0030 364 was an import.

JAMES - *See BELL and JAMES*

Dick JAMES *UK, male vocalist*　13 wks

20 Jan 56	**ROBIN HOOD** *Parlophone R 4117*	14	8 wks
18 May 56	**ROBIN HOOD/BALLAD OF DAVY CROCKETT**		
	(re-entry) *Parlophone R 4117*	29	1 wk
11 Jan 57	**GARDEN OF EDEN** *Parlophone R 4255*	18	4 wks

Freddie JAMES *US, male vocalist*　3 wks

| 24 Nov 79 | **GET UP AND BOOGIE** *Warner Bros. K 17478* .. | 54 | 3 wks |

Jimmy JAMES and the VAGABONDS
UK, male vocal/instrumental group　25 wks

11 Sep 68	**RED RED WINE** *Pye 7N 17579*	36	8 wks
24 Apr 76	**I'LL GO WHERE YOUR MUSIC TAKES ME**		
	Pye 7N 45585	23	8 wks
17 Jul 76	● **NOW IS THE TIME** *Pye 7N 45606*	5	9 wks

Joni JAMES *US, female vocalist*　2 wks

| 6 Mar 53 | **WHY DON'T YOU BELIEVE ME** *MGM 582* .. | 11 | 1 wk |
| 30 Jan 59 | **THERE MUST BE A WAY** *MGM 1002* .... | 24 | 1 wk |

Rick JAMES *Canada, male vocalist*　19 wks

8 Jul 78	**YOU AND I** *Motown TMG 1110*	46	7 wks
6 Sep 80	**BIG TIME** *Motown TMG 1198*	41	6 wks
4 Jul 81	**GIVE IT TO ME BABY** *Motown TMG 1229* ...	47	3 wks
3 Jul 82	**DANCE WIT' ME** *Motown TMG 1266*	53	3 wks

See also Teena Marie; Temptations.

Sonny JAMES *US, male vocalist*　8 wks

| 30 Nov 56 | **THE CAT CAME BACK** *Capitol CL 14635* ..... | 30 | 1 wk |
| 8 Feb 57 | **YOUNG LOVE** *Capitol CL 14683* .... | 11 | 7 wks |

Tommy JAMES and the SHONDELLS
US, male vocal/instrumental group　25 wks

| 21 Jul 66 | **HANKY PANKY** *Roulette RK 7000* .... | 38 | 7 wks |
| 5 Jun 68 | ★ **MONY MONY** *Major Minor MM 567* .... | 1 | 18 wks |

JAMES BOYS *UK, male vocal duo*　6 wks

| 19 May 73 | **OVER AND OVER** *Penny Farthing PEN 806* .... | 39 | 6 wks |

JAMMERS *US, male vocal/instrumental group*　4 wks

| 29 Jan 83 | **BE MINE TONIGHT** *Salsoul SAL 101* .... | 59 | 4 wks |

JAN and DEAN *US, male vocal duo*　18 wks

| 24 Aug 61 | **HEART AND SOUL** *London HLH 9395* ...... | 24 | 8 wks |
| 15 Aug 63 | **SURF CITY** *Liberty LIB 55580* .... | 26 | 10 wks |

JAN and KJELD
Denmark, male vocal duo　4 wks

| 21 Jul 60 | **BANJO BOY** *Ember S 101* .... | 36 | 4 wks |

Horst JANKOWSKI
Germany, male instrumentalist - piano　18 wks

| 29 Jul 65 | ● **A WALK IN THE BLACK FOREST** | | |
| | *Mercury MF 861* .... | 3 | 18 wks |

Philip JAP *UK, male vocalist*　8 wks

| 31 Jul 82 | **SAVE US** *A & M AMS 8217* .... | 53 | 4 wks |
| 25 Sep 82 | **TOTAL ERASURE** *A & M JAP 1* .... | 41 | 4 wks |

JAPAN *UK, male vocal/instrumental group*　81 wks

18 Oct 80	**GENTLEMEN TAKE POLAROIDS**		
	Virgin VS 379	60	2 wks
9 May 81	**THE ART OF PARTIES** *Virgin VS 409*	48	5 wks
19 Sep 81	**QUIET LIFE** *Hansa HANSA 6*	19	9 wks
7 Nov 81	**VISIONS OF CHINA** *Virgin VS 436*	32	12 wks
23 Jan 82	**EUROPEAN SON** *Hansa/Ariola HANSA 10*	31	6 wks
20 Mar 82	● **GHOSTS** *Virgin VS 472*	5	8 wks
22 May 82	**CANTONESE BOY** *Virgin VS 502*	24	6 wks
3 Jul 82	● **I SECOND THAT EMOTION** *Hansa HANSA 12*	9	11 wks
9 Oct 82	**LIFE IN TOKYO** *Hansa HANSA 17*	28	6 wks
20 Nov 82	**NIGHT PORTER** *Virgin VS 554*	29	9 wks
12 Mar 83	**ALL TOMORROW'S PARTIES**		
	Hansa HANSA 18	38	4 wks
21 May 83	**CANTON (LIVE)** *Virgin VS 581*	42	3 wks

Jean-Michel JARRE
France, male instrumentalist/producer　14 wks

| 27 Aug 77 | ● **OXYGENE PART IV** *Polydor 2001 721* .... | 4 | 9 wks |
| 20 Jan 79 | **EQUINOXE PART 5** *Polydor POSP 20* .... | 45 | 5 wks |

Al JARREAU *US, male vocalist*　18 wks

26 Sep 81	**WE'RE IN THIS LOVE TOGETHER**		
	Warner Bros. K 17849	55	4 wks
14 May 83	**MORNIN'** *WEA U9929*	28	6 wks
16 Jul 83	**TROUBLE IN PARADISE** *WEA Int. U9871*	36	5 wks
24 Sep 83	**BOOGIE DOWN** *WEA U9814*	63	3 wks

JAVELLS featuring Nosmo KING
UK, male/female vocal group　8 wks

| 9 Nov 74 | **GOODBYE NOTHING TO SAY** | | |
| | *Pye Disco Demand DDS 2003* .... | 26 | 8 wks |

Peter JAY and the JAYWALKERS
UK, male instrumental group, Peter Jay, drums　11 wks

| 8 Nov 62 | **CAN CAN 62** *Decca F 11531* .... | 31 | 11 wks |

JAYWALKERS - *See Peter JAY and the JAYWALKERS*

JEFFERSON *UK, male vocalist*　8 wks

| 9 Apr 69 | **COLOUR OF MY LOVE** *Pye 7N 17706* .... | 22 | 8 wks |

JEFFERSON STARSHIP
US, male vocal/instrumental group — 9 wks

26 Jan 80	**JANE** Grunt FB 1750	**21**	9 wks

JERRY - See OLLIE and JERRY

JETHRO TULL
UK, male vocal/instrumental group — 58 wks

1 Jan 69	**LOVE STORY** Island WIP 6048	**29**	8 wks
14 May 69	● **LIVING IN THE PAST** Island WIP 6056	**3**	14 wks
1 Nov 69	● **SWEET DREAM** Chrysalis WIP 6070	**7**	11 wks
24 Jan 70	● **THE WITCH'S PROMISE/TEACHER** Chrysalis WIP 6077	**4**	9 wks
18 Sep 71	**LIFE IS A LONG SONG/UP THE POOL** Chrysalis WIP 6106	**11**	8 wks
11 Dec 76	**RING OUT SOLSTICE BELLS** (EP) Chrysalis CXP 2	**28**	6 wks
15 Sep 84	**LAP OF LUXURY** Chrysalis TULL 1	**70**	2 wks

Tracks on EP : Ring Out Solstice Bells/March the Mad Scientist/ The Christmas Song/Pan Dance.

JETS
UK, male vocal/instrumental group — 38 wks

22 Aug 81	**SUGAR DOLL** EMI 5211	**55**	3 wks
31 Oct 81	**YES TONIGHT JOSEPHINE** EMI 5247	**25**	11 wks
6 Feb 82	**LOVE MAKES THE WORLD GO ROUND** EMI 5262	**21**	9 wks
24 Apr 82	**THE HONEYDRIPPER** EMI 5289	**58**	3 wks
9 Oct 82	**SOMEBODY TO LOVE** EMI 5342	**56**	3 wks
6 Aug 83	**BLUE SKIES** EMI 5405	**53**	3 wks
17 Dec 83	**ROCKIN' AROUND THE CHRISTMAS TREE** PRT 7P 297	**62**	4 wks
13 Oct 84	**PARTY DOLL** PRT JETS 2	**72**	2 wks

Joan JETT and the BLACKHEARTS
US, female vocalist with male vocal/instrumental group — 13 wks

24 Apr 82	● **I LOVE ROCK 'N' ROLL** Epic EPC A 2087	**4**	10 wks
10 Jul 82	**CRIMSON AND CLOVER** Epic EPC A 2485	**60**	3 wks

JIGSAW
UK, male vocal/instrumental group — 16 wks

1 Nov 75	● **SKY HIGH** Splash CP1 1	**9**	11 wks
6 Aug 77	**IF I HAVE TO GO AWAY** Splash CP 11	**36**	5 wks

JILTED JOHN
UK, male vocalist — 12 wks

12 Aug 78	● **JILTED JOHN** EMI International INT 567	**4**	12 wks

JIMMY the HOOVER
UK, male/female vocal/instrumental group — 8 wks

25 Jun 83	**TANTALISE (WO WO EE YEH YEH)** Innervision A 3406	**18**	8 wks

JINGLE BELLS
US/UK, female vocal group — 4 wks

17 Dec 83	**CHRISTMAS SPECTRE** Passion PASH 14	**37**	4 wks

JKD BAND
UK, male vocal/instrumental group — 4 wks

1 Jul 78	**DRAGON POWER** Satril SAT 132	**58**	4 wks

JO BOXERS
UK, male vocal/instrumental group — 33 wks

19 Feb 83	● **BOXER BEAT** RCA BOXX 1	**3**	15 wks
21 May 83	● **JUST GOT LUCKY** RCA BOXX 2	**7**	9 wks
13 Aug 83	**JOHNNY FRIENDLY** RCA BOXX 3	**31**	8 wks
12 Nov 83	**JEALOUS LOVE** RCA BOXX 4	**72**	1 wk

JO JO GUNNE
US, male vocal/instrumental group — 12 wks

25 Mar 72	● **RUN RUN RUN** Asylum AYM 501	**6**	12 wks

John Paul JOANS
UK, male vocalist — 7 wks

19 Dec 70	**MAN FROM NAZARETH** RAK 107	**41**	3 wks
16 Jan 71	**MAN FROM NAZARETH** (re-entry) RAK 107	**25**	4 wks

JOCKO
US, male vocalist — 3 wks

23 Feb 80	**RHYTHM TALK** Philadelphia International PIR 8222	**56**	3 wks

Billy JOEL
US, male vocalist/instrumentalist - piano — 100 wks

11 Feb 78	**JUST THE WAY YOU ARE** CBS 5872	**19**	9 wks
24 Jun 78	**MOVIN' OUT (ANTHONY'S SONG)** CBS 6412	**35**	6 wks
2 Dec 78	**MY LIFE** CBS 6821	**12**	15 wks
28 Apr 79	**UNTIL THE NIGHT** CBS 7242	**50**	3 wks
12 Apr 80	**ALL FOR LEYNA** CBS 8325	**40**	4 wks
9 Aug 80	**IT'S STILL ROCK AND ROLL TO ME** CBS 8753	**14**	11 wks
15 Oct 83	★ **UPTOWN GIRL** CBS A 3775	**1**	17 wks
10 Dec 83	● **TELL HER ABOUT IT** CBS A 3655	**4**	10 wks
18 Feb 84	● **AN INNOCENT MAN** CBS A 4142	**8**	10 wks
28 Apr 84	**THE LONGEST TIME** CBS A 4280	**25**	8 wks
23 Jun 84	**LEAVE A TENDER MOMENT ALONE/GOODNIGHT SAIGON** CBS A 4521	**29**	7 wks

Goodnight Saigon only listed from 30 Jun 84.

Elton JOHN
UK, male vocalist/instrumentalist - piano — 306 wks

23 Jan 71	● **YOUR SONG** DJM DJS 233	**7**	12 wks
22 Apr 72	● **ROCKET MAN** DJM DJS 501	**2**	13 wks
9 Sep 72	**HONKY CAT** DJM DJS 269	**31**	6 wks
4 Nov 72	● **CROCODILE ROCK** DJM DJS 271	**5**	14 wks
20 Jan 73	● **DANIEL** DJM DJS 275	**4**	10 wks
7 Jul 73	● **SATURDAY NIGHT'S ALRIGHT FOR FIGHTING** DJM DJX 502	**7**	9 wks
29 Sep 73	● **GOODBYE YELLOW BRICK ROAD** DJM DJS 285	**6**	16 wks
8 Dec 73	**STEP INTO CHRISTMAS** DJM DJS 290	**24**	7 wks
2 Mar 74	**CANDLE IN THE WIND** DJM DJS 297	**11**	9 wks
1 Jun 74	**DON'T LET THE SUN GO DOWN ON ME** DJM DJS 302	**16**	8 wks
14 Sep 74	**THE BITCH IS BACK** DJM DJS 322	**15**	7 wks
23 Nov 74	● **LUCY IN THE SKY WITH DIAMONDS** DJM DJS 340	**10**	10 wks
8 Mar 75	**PHILADELPHIA FREEDOM** DJM DJS 354	**12**	9 wks
28 Jun 75	**SOMEONE SAVED MY LIFE TONIGHT** DJM DJS 385	**22**	5 wks
4 Oct 75	**ISLAND GIRL** DJM DJS 610	**14**	8 wks

20 Mar 76	●	**PINBALL WIZARD** *DJM DJS 652*		7	7 wks
25 Sep 76		**BENNIE AND THE JETS** *DJM DJS 10705*		37	5 wks
13 Nov 76		**SORRY SEEMS TO BE THE HARDEST WORD** *Rocket ROKN 517*		11	10 wks
26 Feb 77		**CRAZY WATER** *Rocket ROKN 521*		27	6 wks
11 Jun 77		**BITE YOUR LIP (GET UP AND DANCE)** *Rocket ROKN 526*		28	4 wks
15 Apr 78		**EGO** *Rocket ROKN 539*		34	6 wks
21 Oct 78		**PART TIME LOVE** *Rocket XPRES 1*		15	13 wks
16 Dec 78	●	**SONG FOR GUY** *Rocket XPRES 5*		4	10 wks
12 May 79		**ARE YOU READY FOR LOVE** *Rocket XPRES 13*		42	6 wks
24 May 80		**LITTLE JEANNIE** *Rocket XPRES 32*		33	7 wks
23 Aug 80		**SARTORIAL ELOQUENCE** *Rocket XPRES 41* ..		44	5 wks
23 May 81		**NOBODY WINS** *Rocket XPRES 54*		42	5 wks
27 Mar 82	●	**BLUE EYES** *Rocket XPRES 71*		8	10 wks
12 Jun 82		**EMPTY GARDEN** *Rocket/Phonogram XPRES 77* ..		51	4 wks
30 Apr 83	●	**I GUESS THAT'S WHY THEY CALL IT THE BLUES** *Rocket/Phonogram XPRES 91*		5	15 wks
30 Jul 83	●	**I'M STILL STANDING** *Rocket/Phonogram EJS 1* ..		4	11 wks
15 Oct 83		**KISS THE BRIDE** *Rocket/Phonogram EJS 2*		20	7 wks
10 Dec 83		**COLD AS CHRISTMAS** *Rocket/Phonogram EJS 3*		33	6 wks
26 May 84	●	**SAD SONGS (SAY SO MUCH)** *Rocket/Phonogram PH 7*		7	12 wks
11 Aug 84	●	**PASSENGERS** *Rocket/Phonogram EJS 5*		5	11 wks
20 Oct 84		**WHO WEARS THESE SHOES** *Rocket/Phonogram EJS 6*		50	3 wks

See also Elton John and Kiki Dee. Philadelphia Freedom credits The Elton John Band. Bite Your Lip (Get Up and Dance) was one side of a double-sided chart entry, the other being Chicago by Kiki Dee. See also Kiki Dee, Elton John Band featuring John Lennon and the Muscle Shoals Horns.

Elton JOHN and Kiki DEE
UK, male/female vocal duo   *14 wks*

3 Jul 76	★	**DON'T GO BREAKING MY HEART** *Rocket ROKN 512*		1	14 wks

See also Elton John; Kiki Dee; Elton John Band featuring John Lennon and the Muscle Shoals Horns

Robert JOHN   *US, male vocalist*   *13 wks*

17 Jul 68	**IF YOU DON'T WANT MY LOVE** *CBS 3436* ..		42	5 wks
20 Oct 79	**SAD EYES** *EMI American EA 101*		31	8 wks

Elton JOHN BAND featuring John LENNON and the MUSCLE SHOALS HORNS
UK, male vocalists/instrumentalists with US, male instrumental group   *4 wks*

21 Mar 81	**I SAW HER STANDING THERE** *DJM DJS 10965*		40	4 wks

See also Elton John; Elton John and Kiki Dee; John Lennon.

JOHNNY - *See SANTO and JOHNNY*

JOHNNY and CHARLEY
Spain, male vocal duo   *1 wk*

14 Oct 65	**LA YENKA** *Pye International 7N 25326*		49	1 wk

JOHNNY and the HURRICANES
US, male instrumental group   *88 wks*

9 Oct 59	●	**RED RIVER ROCK** *London HL 8948*		3	16 wks
25 Dec 59		**REVEILLE ROCK** *London HL 9017*		14	5 wks
17 Mar 60	●	**BEATNIK FLY** *London HLI 9072*		8	19 wks

16 Jun 60	●	**DOWN YONDER** *London HLX 9134*		8	11 wks
29 Sep 60	●	**ROCKING GOOSE** *London HLX 9190*		3	20 wks
2 Mar 61		**JA-DA** *London HLX 9289*		14	9 wks
6 Jul 61		**OLD SMOKEY/HIGH VOLTAGE** *London HLX 9378*		24	8 wks

Bryan JOHNSON   *UK, male vocalist*   *11 wks*

10 Mar 60	**LOOKING HIGH HIGH HIGH** *Decca F 11213*		20	11 wks

Howard JOHNSON   *US, male vocalist*   *6 wks*

4 Sep 82	**KEEPIN' LOVE NEW/SO FINE** *A & M USA 1221*		45	6 wks

Keepin' Love New listed 4 Sep only.

Johnny JOHNSON and the BANDWAGON
US, male vocal group   *50 wks*

16 Oct 68	●	**BREAKIN' DOWN THE WALLS OF HEARTACHE** *Direction 58-3670*		4	15 wks
5 Feb 69		**YOU** *Direction 58-3923*		34	4 wks
28 May 69		**LET'S HANG ON** *Direction 58-4180*		36	6 wks
25 Jul 70	●	**SWEET INSPIRATION** *Bell 1111*		10	12 wks
24 Oct 70		**SWEET INSPIRATION** (re-entry) *Bell 1111*		46	1 wk
28 Nov 70	●	**BLAME IT ON THE PONY EXPRESS** *Bell 1128*		7	12 wks

Listed as Bandwagon on Direction hits.

Kevin JOHNSON   *Australia, male vocalist*   *6 wks*

11 Jan 75	**ROCK 'N ROLL (I GAVE YOU THE BEST YEARS OF MY LIFE)** *UK UKR 84*		23	6 wks

L. J. JOHNSON   *US, male vocalist*   *6 wks*

7 Feb 76	**YOUR MAGIC PUT A SPELL ON ME** *Philips 6006 492*		27	6 wks

Laurie JOHNSON   *UK, orchestra*   *12 wks*

28 Sep 61	●	**SUCU SUCU** *Pye 7N 15383*		9	12 wks

Lou JOHNSON   *US, male vocalist*   *2 wks*

26 Nov 64	**MESSAGE TO MARTHA** *London HL 9929*		36	2 wks

Marv JOHNSON   *US, male vocalist*   *39 wks*

12 Feb 60	●	**YOU GOT WHAT IT TAKES** *London HLT 9013*		5	16 wks
5 May 60		**I LOVE THE WAY YOU LOVE** *London HLT 9109*		35	3 wks
11 Aug 60		**AIN'T GONNA BE THAT WAY** *London HLT 9156*		50	1 wk
22 Jan 69		**I'LL PICK A ROSE FOR MY ROSE** *Tamla Motown TMG 680*		10	11 wks
25 Oct 69		**I MISS YOU BABY** *Tamla Motown TMG 713* ...		25	8 wks

Teddy JOHNSON - *See Pearl CARR and Teddy JOHNSON*

Bruce JOHNSTON
US, male instrumentalist - keyboards   *4 wks*

27 Aug 77	**PIPELINE** *CBS 5514*		33	4 wks

JOHNSTON BROTHERS
UK, male vocal group — *30 wks*

3 Apr 53	●	OH HAPPY DAY *Decca F 10071*		4	8 wks
7 Oct 55	★	HERNANDO'S HIDEAWAY *Decca F 10608*		1	13 wks
30 Dec 55	●	JOIN IN AND SING AGAIN *Decca F 10636*		9	1 wk
13 Apr 56		NO OTHER LOVE *Decca F 10721*		22	1 wk
30 Nov 56		IN THE MIDDLE OF THE HOUSE *Decca F 10781*		27	1 wk
7 Dec 56		JOIN IN AND SING (NO. 3) *Decca F 10814*		30	1 wk
28 Dec 56		JOIN IN AND SING (NO. 3) (re-entry) *Decca F 10814*		24	1 wk
8 Feb 57		GIVE HER MY LOVE *Decca F 10828*		27	1 wk
19 Apr 57		HEART *Decca F 10860*		23	3 wks

The following two hits were medleys: Join In And Sing Again: *Sheik of Araby/Yes Sir That's My Baby/California Here I Come/Some Of These Days/Charleston/Margie.* Join In And Sing (No. 3): *Coal Black Morning/When You're Smiling/Alexander's Ragtime Band/Sweet Sue Just You/When You Wore A Tulip/If You Were The Only Girl In The World.* See also Joan Regan and the Johnston Brothers; Various Artists - All Star Hit Parade No. 2.

JOLLY BROTHERS
Jamaica, male vocal/instrumental group — *7 wks*

28 Jul 79	CONSCIOUS MAN *United Artists UP 36415*		46	7 wks

JON and VANGELIS
UK, male vocalist/Greece, male multi-instrumentalist — *28 wks*

5 Jan 80	●	I HEAR YOU NOW *Polydor POSP 96*		8	11 wks
12 Dec 81	●	I'LL FIND MY WAY HOME *Polydor JV 1*		6	13 wks
30 Jul 83		HE IS SAILING *Polydor JV 4*		61	2 wks
18 Aug 84		STATE OF INDEPENDENCE *Polydor JV 5*		67	2 wks

See also Vangelis.

JONATHAN - See DAVID and JONATHAN

Barbara JONES *Jamaica, female vocalist* — *7 wks*

31 Jan 81	JUST WHEN I NEEDED YOU MOST *Sonet SON 2221*		31	7 wks

Grace JONES *US, female vocalist* — *19 wks*

26 Jul 80	PRIVATE LIFE *Island WIP 6629*		17	8 wks
20 Jun 81	PULL UP TO THE BUMPER *Island WIP 6696*		53	4 wks
30 Oct 82	THE APPLE STRETCHING/NIPPLE TO THE BOTTLE *Island WIP 6779*		50	4 wks
9 Apr 83	MY JAMAICAN GUY *Island IS 103*		56	3 wks

Howard JONES *UK, male vocalist* — *61 wks*

17 Sep 83	●	NEW SONG *WEA HOW 1*		3	12 wks
26 Nov 83	●	WHAT IS LOVE *WEA HOW 2*		2	15 wks
14 Jan 84		NEW SONG (re-entry) *WEA HOW 1*		60	3 wks
18 Feb 84	●	HIDE AND SEEK *WEA HOW 3*		12	9 wks
26 May 84	●	PEARL IN SHELL *WEA HOW 4*		7	10 wks
11 Aug 84	●	LIKE TO GET TO KNOW YOU WELL *WEA HOW 5*		4	12 wks

Janie JONES *UK, female vocalist* — *3 wks*

27 Jan 66	WITCHES' BREW *HMV POP 1495*		46	3 wks

Jimmy JONES *US, male vocalist* — *47 wks*

17 Mar 60	●	HANDY MAN *MGM 1051*	3	21 wks

16 Jun 60	★	GOOD TIMIN' *MGM 1078*		1	15 wks
18 Aug 60		HANDY MAN (re-entry) *MGM 1051*		32	3 wks
8 Sep 60		I JUST GO FOR YOU *MGM 1091*		35	4 wks
17 Nov 60		READY FOR LOVE *MGM 1103*		46	1 wk
30 Mar 61		I TOLD YOU SO *MGM 1123*		33	3 wks

Juggy JONES
US, male multi-instrumentalist — *4 wks*

7 Feb 76	INSIDE AMERICA *Contempo CS 2080*		39	4 wks

Paul JONES *UK, male vocalist* — *34 wks*

6 Oct 66	●	HIGH TIME *HMV POP 1554*		4	15 wks
19 Jan 67	●	I'VE BEEN A BAD BAD BOY *HMV POP 1576*		5	9 wks
23 Aug 67		THINKIN' AIN'T FOR ME *HMV POP 1602*		47	1 wk
13 Sep 67		THINKIN' AIN'T FOR ME (re-entry) *HMV POP 1602*		32	7 wks
5 Feb 69		AQUARIUS *Columbia DB 8514*		45	2 wks

See also Manfred Mann.

Quincy JONES
US, male arranger/instrumentalist - keyboards — *31 wks*

29 Jul 78	STUFF LIKE THAT *A & M AMS 7367*		34	9 wks
11 Apr 81	AI NO CORRIDA (I-NO-KO-REE-DA) *A & M AMS 8109*		14	10 wks
20 Jun 81	RAZZAMATAZZ *A & M AMS 8140*		11	9 wks
5 Sep 81	BETCHA' WOULDN'T HURT ME *A & M AMS 8157*		52	3 wks

Uncredited lead singer on Razzamatazz is Patti Austin.

Rickie Lee JONES *US, female vocalist* — *9 wks*

23 Jun 79	CHUCK E.'S IN LOVE *Warner Bros. K 17390*		18	9 wks

Shirley JONES - See PARTRIDGE FAMILY starring Shirley JONES featuring David CASSIDY; VARIOUS ARTISTS (Carousel Soundtrack).

Tammy JONES *UK, female vocalist* — *10 wks*

26 Apr 75	●	LET ME TRY AGAIN *Epic EPC 3211*	5	10 wks

Tom JONES *UK, male vocalist* — *306 wks*

11 Feb 65	★	IT'S NOT UNUSUAL *Decca F 12062*		1	14 wks
6 May 65		ONCE UPON A TIME *Decca F 12121*		32	4 wks
8 Jul 65		WITH THESE HANDS *Decca F 12191*		13	11 wks
12 Aug 65		WHAT'S NEW PUSSYCAT *Decca F 12203*		11	10 wks
13 Jan 66		THUNDERBALL *Decca F 12292*		35	4 wks
19 May 66		ONCE THERE WAS A TIME/NOT RESPONSIBLE *Decca F 12390*		18	9 wks
18 Aug 66		THIS AND THAT *Decca F 12461*		44	3 wks
10 Nov 66	★	GREEN GREEN GRASS OF HOME *Decca F 22511*		1	22 wks
16 Feb 67	●	DETROIT CITY *Decca F 22555*		8	10 wks
13 Apr 67	●	FUNNY FAMILIAR FORGOTTEN FEELINGS *Decca F 12599*		7	15 wks
26 Jul 67	●	I'LL NEVER FALL IN LOVE AGAIN *Decca F 12639*		2	25 wks
22 Nov 67	●	I'M COMING HOME *Decca F 12693*		2	16 wks
28 Feb 68	●	DELILAH *Decca F 12747*		2	17 wks
17 Jul 68	●	HELP YOURSELF *Decca F 12812*		5	26 wks
27 Nov 68		A MINUTE OF YOUR TIME *Decca F 12854*		14	15 wks
14 May 69	●	LOVE ME TONIGHT *Decca F 12924*		9	12 wks
13 Dec 69	●	WITHOUT LOVE *Decca F 12990*		10	11 wks
14 Mar 70		WITHOUT LOVE (re-entry) *Decca F 12990*		49	1 wk
18 Apr 70	●	DAUGHTER OF DARKNESS *Decca F 13013*		5	15 wks
15 Aug 70		I (WHO HAVE NOTHING) *Decca F 13061*		16	8 wks

17 Oct 70	**I (WHO HAVE NOTHING)** (re-entry)			
	Decca F 13061	47	3 wks
16 Jan 71	**SHE'S A LADY** *Decca F 13113*	13	9 wks
27 Mar 71	**SHE'S A LADY** (re-entry) *Decca F 13113*	47	1 wk
5 Jun 71	**PUPPET MAN** *Decca F 13183*	49	1 wk
19 Jun 71	**PUPPET MAN** (re-entry) *Decca F 13183*	50	1 wk
23 Oct 71	● **TILL** *Decca F 13236*	2	15 wks
1 Apr 72	● **THE YOUNG NEW MEXICAN PUPPETEER**		
	Decca F 13298	6	12 wks
14 Apr 73	**LETTER TO LUCILLE** *Decca F 13393*	31	8 wks
7 Sep 74	**SOMETHING 'BOUT YOU BABY I LIKE**		
	Decca F 13550	36	5 wks
16 Apr 77	**SAY YOU'LL STAY UNTIL TOMORROW**		
	EMI 2583	40	3 wks

Sue JONES-DAVIES - *See Julie COVINGTON, Rula LENSKA Charlotte CORNWELL and Sue JONES-DAVIES*

Dick JORDAN *UK, male vocalist* *4 wks*

17 Mar 60	**HALLELUJAH I LOVE HER SO** *Oriole CB 1534*	47	1 wk
9 Jun 60	**LITTLE CHRISTINE** *Oriole CB 1548*	39	3 wks

David JOSEPH *UK, male vocalist* *16 wks*

26 Feb 83	**YOU CAN'T HIDE (YOUR LOVE FROM ME)**		
	Island IS 101	13	9 wks
28 May 83	**LET'S LIVE IT UP (NITE PEOPLE)**		
	Island IS 116	26	5 wks
18 Feb 84	**JOYS OF LIFE** *Island IS 153*	61	2 wks

JOURNEY *US, male vocal/instrumental group* *9 wks*

27 Feb 82	**DON'T STOP BELIEVIN'** *CBS A 1728*	62	4 wks
11 Sep 82	**WHO'S CRYING NOW** *CBS A 2725*	46	5 wks

JOY DIVISION
UK, male vocal/instrumental group *16 wks*

28 Jun 80	**LOVE WILL TEAR US APART** *Factory FAC 23*	13	9 wks
29 Oct 83	**LOVE WILL TEAR US APART** (re-entry)		
	Factory FAC 23	19	7 wks

JOY STRINGS
UK, male/female vocal/instrumental group *11 wks*

27 Feb 64	**IT'S AN OPEN SECRET** *Regal-Zonophone RZ 501*	32	7 wks
17 Dec 64	**A STARRY NIGHT** *Regal-Zonophone RZ 504*	35	4 wks

JUDAS PRIEST
UK, male vocal/instrumental group *46 wks*

20 Jan 79	**TAKE ON THE WORLD** *CBS 6915*	14	10 wks
12 May 79	**EVENING STAR** *CBS 7312*	53	4 wks
29 Mar 80	**LIVING AFTER MIDNIGHT** *CBS 8379*	12	7 wks
7 Jun 80	**BREAKING THE LAW** *CBS 8644*	12	6 wks
23 Aug 80	**UNITED** *CBS 8897*	26	8 wks
21 Feb 81	**DON'T GO** *CBS 9520*	51	3 wks
25 Apr 81	**HOT ROCKIN'** *CBS 1153*	60	3 wks
21 Aug 82	**YOU'VE GOT ANOTHER THING COMIN'**		
	CBS A 2611	66	2 wks
21 Jan 84	**FREEWHEEL BURNIN'** *CBS A 4054*	42	3 wks

JUDGE DREAD *UK, male vocalist* *95 wks*

26 Aug 72	**BIG SIX** *Big Shot BI 608*	11	27 wks
9 Dec 72	● **BIG SEVEN** *Big Shot BI 613*	8	18 wks
21 Apr 73	**BIG EIGHT** *Big Shot BI 619*	14	10 wks
5 Jul 75	● **JE T'AIME (MOI NON PLUS)** *Cactus CT 65* ...	9	9 wks
27 Sep 75	**BIG TEN** *Cactus CT 77*	14	7 wks
6 Dec 75	**CHRISTMAS IN DREADLAND/COME OUTSIDE**		
	Cactus CT 80	14	7 wks
8 May 76	**THE WINKLE MAN** *Cactus CT 90*	35	4 wks
28 Aug 76	**Y VIVA SUSPENDERS** *Cactus CT 99*	27	4 wks
2 Apr 77	**5TH ANNIVERSARY** (EP) *Cactus CT 98*	31	4 wks
14 Jan 78	**UP WITH THE COCK/BIG PUNK**		
	Cactus CT 110	49	1 wk
16 Dec 78	**HOKEY COKEY/JINGLE BELLS** *EMI 2881* ...	59	4 wks

Tracks On 5th Anniversary EP: Jamaica Jerk (off)/Bring Back The Skins/End Of The World/Big Everything.

JUICY LUCY
UK, male vocal/instrumental group *17 wks*

7 Mar 70	**WHO DO YOU LOVE** *Vertigo V 1*	14	12 wks
10 Oct 70	**PRETTY WOMAN** *Vertigo 6059 015*	45	2 wks
31 Oct 70	**PRETTY WOMAN** (re-entry) *Vertigo 6059 015* ...	44	3 wks

JULIA and COMPANY
US, male/female vocal group *8 wks*

3 Mar 84	**BREAKIN' DOWN (SUGAR SAMBA)**		
	London LON 46	15	8 wks

JULUKA
South Africa, male/female vocal/instrumental group *4 wks*

12 Feb 83	**SCATTERLINGS OF AFRICA** *Safari ZULU 1* ..	44	4 wks

JUMPING JACKS - *See Danny PEPPERMINT and the JUMPING JACKS*

Rosemary JUNE *US, female vocalist* *9 wks*

23 Jan 59	**APPLE BLOSSOM TIME**		
	Pye International 7N 25005	14	9 wks

JUNIOR *UK, male vocalist* *30 wks*

24 Apr 82	● **MAMA USED TO SAY (AMERICAN REMIX)**		
	Mercury/Phonogram MER 98	7	13 wks
10 Jul 82	**TOO LATE** *Mercury/Phonogram MER 112*	20	9 wks
25 Sep 82	**LET ME KNOW/I CAN'T HELP IT**		
	Mercury/Phonogram MER 116	53	3 wks
23 Apr 83	**COMMUNICATION BREAKDOWN**		
	Mercury/Phonogram MER 134	57	3 wks
8 Sep 84	**SOMEBODY** *London LON 50*	64	2 wks

JUNIORS - *See DANNY and the JUNIORS*

Jimmy JUSTICE *UK, male vocalist* *35 wks*

29 Mar 62	● **WHEN MY LITTLE GIRL IS SMILING**		
	Pye 7N 15421	9	13 wks
14 Jun 62	● **AIN'T THAT FUNNY** *Pye 7N 15443*	8	11 wks
23 Aug 62	**SPANISH HARLEM** *Pye 7N 15457*	20	11 wks

Bill JUSTIS
US, male instrumentalist - alto sax *8 wks*

10 Jan 58	**RAUNCHY** *London HLS 8517*	24	2 wks
31 Jan 58	**RAUNCHY** (re-entry) *London HLS 8517*	11	6 wks

NIK KERSHAW (left) His favourite single is Judy Tzuke's 'Stay With Me Till Dawn'.

KINKS (right) The original publicity hand out for 'You Really Got Me' proclaimed, 'The A side has a beat which Cannonball Adderley would be proud of though the lyrics are fully within the rhythm and blues idiom'.

ANNABEL LAMB (left) The chart opened to her version of a Doors classic.

KILLING JOKE (right) Their other hits followed 'Follow The Leaders'.

CYNDI LAUPER (left) She charted time after time in 1984. (Photo: Chuck Sillery).

KANE GANG (right) A trio of hits in 1984 for Dave, Paul and Martin.

Patrick JUVET — France, male vocalist — 19 wks

2 Sep 78	GOT A FEELING Casablanca CAN 127	34	7 wks
4 Nov 78	I LOVE AMERICA Casablanca CAN 132	12	12 wks

K

Bert KAEMPFERT — Germany, orchestra — 10 wks

23 Dec 65	BYE BYE BLUES Polydor BM 56 504	24	10 wks

KAJAGOOGOO
UK, male vocal/instrumental group — 47 wks

22 Jan 83	★ TOO SHY EMI 5359	1	13 wks
2 Apr 83	● OOH TO BE AH EMI 5383	7	8 wks
4 Jun 83	HANG ON NOW EMI 5394	13	7 wks
17 Sep 83	● BIG APPLE EMI 5425	8	8 wks
3 Mar 84	THE LION'S MOUTH EMI 5449	25	7 wks
5 May 84	TURN YOUR BACK ON ME EMI 5646 ...	47	4 wks

KALIN TWINS — US, male vocal duo — 18 wks

18 Jul 58	★ WHEN Brunswick 05751	1	18 wks

Kitty KALLEN — US, female vocalist — 23 wks

2 Jul 54	★ LITTLE THINGS MEAN A LOT Brunswick 05287	1	23 wks

Gunther KALLMAN CHOIR
Germany, male/female vocal group — 3 wks

24 Dec 64	ELISABETH SERENADE Polydor NH 24678	45	3 wks

KANDIDATE
UK, male vocal/instrumental group — 28 wks

19 Aug 78	DON'T WANNA SAY GOODNIGHT RAK 280	47	6 wks
17 Mar 79	I DON'T WANNA LOSE YOU RAK 289	11	12 wks
4 Aug 79	GIRLS GIRLS GIRLS RAK 295	34	7 wks
22 Mar 80	LET ME ROCK YOU RAK 306	58	3 wks

Eden KANE — UK, male vocalist — 73 wks

1 Jun 61	★ WELL I ASK YOU Decca F 11353	1	21 wks
14 Sep 61	● GET LOST Decca F 11381	10	11 wks
18 Jan 62	● FORGET ME NOT Decca F 11418	3	14 wks
10 May 62	● I DON'T KNOW WHY Decca F 11460	7	13 wks
30 Jan 64	● BOYS CRY Fontana TF 438	8	14 wks

KANE GANG
UK, male vocal/instrumental group — 21 wks

19 May 84	SMALL TOWN CREED Kitchenware/London SK 11	60	2 wks
7 Jul 84	CLOSEST THING TO HEAVEN		
	Kitchenware/London SK 15	12	11 wks
10 Nov 84	RESPECT YOURSELF Kitchenware/London SK 16	21†	8 wks

KANSAS — US, male vocal/instrumental group — 7 wks

1 Jul 78	CARRY ON WAYWARD SON Kirshner KIR 4932	51	7 wks

KASENETZ-KATZ SINGING ORCHESTRAL CIRCUS
US, male vocal/instrumental group — 15 wks

20 Nov 68	QUICK JOEY SMALL (RUN JOEY RUN)		
	Buddah 201 022	19	15 wks

Janet KAY — UK, female vocalist — 14 wks

9 Jun 79	● SILLY GAMES Scope SC 2	2	14 wks

Danny KAYE — US, male vocalist — 10 wks

27 Feb 53	● WONDERFUL COPENHAGEN Brunswick 05023	5	10 wks

KAYE SISTERS — UK, female vocal group — 20 wks

3 Jan 58	SHAKE ME I RATTLE/ALONE Philips PB 752	27	1 wk
7 Jul 60	● PAPER ROSES Philips PB 1024	7	19 wks

See also Frankie Vaughan and The Kaye Sisters; Three Kayes.

KC and THE SUNSHINE BAND
US, male vocal/instrumental group — 102 wks

17 Aug 74	● QUEEN OF CLUBS Jayboy BOY 88	7	12 wks
23 Nov 74	SOUND YOUR FUNKY HORN Jayboy BOY 83	17	9 wks
29 Mar 75	GET DOWN TONIGHT Jayboy BOY 93	21	9 wks
2 Aug 75	● THAT'S THE WAY (I LIKE IT) Jayboy BOY 99	4	10 wks
22 Nov 75	I'M SO CRAZY Jayboy BOY 101	34	3 wks
17 Jul 76	(SHAKE SHAKE SHAKE) SHAKE YOUR BOOTY		
	Jayboy BOY 110	22	8 wks
11 Dec 76	KEEP IT COMIN' LOVE Jayboy BOY 112	31	8 wks
30 Apr 77	I'M YOUR BOOGIE MAN TK XB 2167	41	4 wks
6 May 78	BOOGIE SHOES TK TKR 6025	34	5 wks
22 Jul 78	IT'S THE SAME OLD SONG TK TKR 6037 ...	49	5 wks
8 Dec 79	● PLEASE DON'T GO TK TKR 7558	3	12 wks
16 Jul 83	★ GIVE IT UP Epic EPC A 3017	1	14 wks
24 Sep 83	(YOU SAID) YOU'D GIMME SOME MORE		
	Epic A 2760	41	3 wks

Ernie K-DOE — US, male vocalist — 7 wks

11 May 61	MOTHER-IN-LAW London HLU 9330	29	7 wks

Johnny KEATING — UK, orchestra — 14 wks

1 Mar 62	● THEME FROM 'Z CARS' Piccadilly 7N 35032 ...	8	14 wks

Kevin KEEGAN — UK, male vocalist — 6 wks

9 Jun 79	HEAD OVER HEELS IN LOVE EMI 2965	31	6 wks

Yvonne KEELY - *See Scott FITZGERALD and Yvonne KEELY*

Nelson KEENE — UK, male vocalist — 5 wks

25 Aug 60	IMAGE OF A GIRL HMV POP 771	37	4 wks
29 Sep 60	IMAGE OF A GIRL (re-entry) HMV POP 771 ...	45	1 wk

KEITH — US, male vocalist — 8 wks

26 Jan 67	98.6 Mercury MF 955	24	7 wks
16 Mar 67	TELL ME TO MY FACE Mercury MF 968	50	1 wk

Jerry KELLER   US, male vocalist   55 wks → 14 wks

28 Aug 59	★ HERE COMES SUMMER London HLR 8890	1	14 wks

Frank KELLY   Ireland, male vocalist   5 wks

24 Dec 83	CHRISTMAS COUNTDOWN Ritz RITZ 062 ..	26	4 wks
29 Dec 84	CHRISTMAS COUNTDOWN (re-entry)		
	Ritz RITZ 062	54†	1 wk

Grace KELLY - *See Bing CROSBY and Grace KELLY*

Keith KELLY   UK, male vocalist   5 wks

5 May 60	TEASE ME Parlophone R 4640	46	1 wk
19 May 60	TEASE ME (re-entry) Parlophone R 4640	27	3 wks
18 Aug 60	LISTEN LITTLE GIRL Parlophone R 4676	47	1 wk

Roberta KELLY   US, female vocalist   3 wks

| 21 Jan 78 | ZODIACS   Oasis/Hansa 3   .... | 48 | 1 wk |
| 4 Feb 78 | ZODIACS   (re-entry) Oasis/Hansa 3   .... | 44 | 2 wks |

Eddie KENDRICKS   US, male vocalist   18 wks

| 3 Nov 73 | KEEP ON TRUCKIN'   Tamla Motown TMG 873 | 18 | 14 wks |
| 16 Mar 74 | BOOGIE DOWN   Tamla Motown TMG 888   ..... | 39 | 4 wks |

Jane KENNAWAY and STRANGE BEHAVIOUR
UK, female vocalist, male instrumental group   3 wks

| 24 Jan 81 | I.O.U.   Deram DM 436   .... | 65 | 3 wks |

KENNY   Ireland, male vocalist   16 wks

| 3 Mar 73 | HEART OF STONE   RAK 144   .... | 11 | 13 wks |
| 30 Jun 73 | GIVE IT TO ME NOW   RAK 153   .... | 38 | 3 wks |

KENNY   UK, male vocal/instrumental group   39 wks

7 Dec 74	● THE BUMP RAK 186	3	15 wks
8 Mar 75	● FANCY PANTS RAK 196	4	9 wks
7 Jun 75	BABY I LOVE YOU OK RAK 207	12	7 wks
16 Aug 75	● JULIE ANN RAK 214	10	8 wks

Gerard KENNY   US, male vocalist   18 wks

9 Dec 78	NEW YORK, NEW YORK RCA PB 5117	43	8 wks
21 Jun 80	FANTASY RCA PB 5256	65	1 wk
5 Jul 80	FANTASY (re-entry) RCA PB 5256	34	5 wks
18 Feb 84	THE OTHER WOMAN, THE OTHER MAN		
	Impression IMS 3	69	4 wks

Klark KENT
US, male vocalist/multi-instrumentalist   4 wks

| 26 Aug 78 | DON'T CARE   A & M AMS 7376   .... | 48 | 4 wks |

KERRI and MICK
Australia, female/male vocal duo   3 wks

| 28 Apr 84 | SONS AND DAUGHTERS THEME   A-1 A1 286 | 68 | 3 wks |

Nik KERSHAW   UK, male vocalist   55 wks

19 Nov 83	I WON'T LET THE SUN GO DOWN ON ME		
	MCA MCA 816	47	5 wks
28 Jan 84	● WOULDN'T IT BE GOOD MCA NIK 2	4	14 wks
14 Apr 84	DANCING GIRLS MCA NIK 3	13	9 wks
16 Jun 84	● I WON'T LET THE SUN GO DOWN ON ME		
	(re-issue) MCA NIK 4	2	13 wks
15 Sep 84	HUMAN RACING MCA NIK 5	19	7 wks
17 Nov 84	● THE RIDDLE MCA NIK 6	3†	7 wks

KEVIN THE GERBIL
UK, male gerbil vocalist   6 wks

| 4 Aug 84 | SUMMER HOLIDAY   Rodent/Magnet RAT 3   .... | 50 | 6 wks |

Chaka KHAN   US, female vocalist   24 wks

| 2 Dec 78 | I'M EVERY WOMAN   Warner Bros. K 17269 | 11 | 13 wks |
| 20 Oct 84 | ★ I FEEL FOR YOU   Warner Bros. W 9209 | 1† | 11 wks |

See also Rufus and Chaka Khan.

K.I.D.
Antilles, male/female vocal/instrumental group   4 wks

| 28 Feb 81 | DON'T STOP   EMI 5143   .... | 49 | 4 wks |

Johnny KIDD and the PIRATES
UK, male vocal/instrumental group   62 wks

12 Jun 59	PLEASE DON'T TOUCH HMV POP 615	26	3 wks
17 Jul 59	PLEASE DON'T TOUCH (re-entry)		
	HMV POP 615	25	2 wks
12 Feb 60	YOU GOT WHAT IT TAKES HMV POP 698 ..	25	3 wks
16 Jun 60	★ SHAKIN' ALL OVER HMV POP 753	1	19 wks
6 Oct 60	RESTLESS HMV POP 790	22	7 wks
13 Apr 61	LINDA LU HMV POP 853	47	1 wk
10 Jan 63	SHOT OF RHYTHM & BLUES HMV POP 1088	48	1 wk
25 Jul 63	● I'LL NEVER GET OVER YOU HMV POP 1173	4	15 wks
28 Nov 63	HUNGRY FOR LOVE HMV POP 1228	20	10 wks
30 Apr 64	ALWAYS AND EVER HMV POP 1269	46	1 wk

Please Don't Touch without the Pirates.

KIDS FROM 'FAME'
US, male/female vocal group   36 wks

14 Aug 82	● HI-FIDELITY RCA 254	5	10 wks
2 Oct 82	★ STARMAKER RCA 280	3	10 wks
11 Dec 82	MANNEQUIN RCA 299	50	6 wks
9 Apr 83	FRIDAY NIGHT (LIVE VERSION) RCA 320 ..	15	10 wks

Hi-Fidelity is 'featuring Valerie Landsberg'. Mannequin is 'featuring Gene Anthony Ray'.

Greg KIHN BAND
US, male vocal/instrumental group   2 wks

| 23 Apr 83 | JEOPARDY   Beserkley E 9847   .... | 63 | 2 wks |

KILLING JOKE
UK, male vocal/instrumental group   22 wks

23 May 81	FOLLOW THE LEADERS		
	Malicious Damage/Polydor EGMDS 101	55	5 wks
20 Mar 82	EMPIRE SONG Malicious Damage/Polydor EGO 4	43	4 wks
30 Oct 82	BIRDS OF A FEATHER E.G./Polydor EGO 10 ...	64	2 wks

25 Jun 83	LET'S ALL (GO TO THE FIRE DANCES)			
	EG/Polydor EGO 11		51	3 wks
15 Oct 83	ME OR YOU? EG/Polydor EGO 14		57	1 wk
7 Apr 84	EIGHTIES EG/Polydor EGO 16		60	5 wks
21 Jul 84	A NEW DAY EG/Polydor EGO 17		56	2 wks

Andy KIM *Canada, male vocalist* *12 wks*

24 Aug 74 ●	ROCK ME GENTLY Capitol CL 15787	2	12 wks

KING KURT
UK, male vocal/instrumental group *14 wks*

15 Oct 83	DESTINATION ZULULAND Stiff BUY 189	36	6 wks
28 Apr 84	MACK THE KNIFE Stiff BUY 199	55	4 wks
4 Aug 84	BANANA BANANA Stiff BUY 206	54	4 wks

Ben E. KING *US, male vocalist* *22 wks*

2 Feb 61	FIRST TASTE OF LOVE London HLK 9258	27	11 wks
22 Jun 61	STAND BY ME London HLK 9358	50	1 wk
6 Jul 61	STAND BY ME (re-entry) London HLK 9358	27	6 wks
5 Oct 61	AMOR AMOR London HLK 9416	38	4 wks

Carole KING *US, female vocalist* *29 wks*

20 Sep 62 ●	IT MIGHT AS WELL RAIN UNTIL SEPTEMBER		
	London HLU 9591	3	13 wks
7 Aug 71 ●	IT'S TOO LATE A & M AMS 849	6	12 wks
28 Oct 72	IT MIGHT AS WELL RAIN UNTIL SEPTEMBER		
	(re-issue) London HL 10391	43	4 wks

Dave KING *Canada, male vocalist* *29 wks*

17 Feb 56 ●	MEMORIES ARE MADE OF THIS Decca F 10684	5	15 wks
13 Apr 56	YOU CAN'T BE TRUE TO TWO Decca F 10720	11	9 wks
21 Dec 56	CHRISTMAS AND YOU Decca F 10791	23	2 wks
24 Jan 58	THE STORY OF MY LIFE Decca F 10973	20	3 wks

See also Various Artists - All Star Hit Parade.

Evelyn KING *US, female vocalist* *64 wks*

13 May 78	SHAME RCA PC 1122	39	23 wks
3 Feb 79	I DON'T KNOW IF IT'S RIGHT RCA PB 1386	67	2 wks
27 Jun 81	I'M IN LOVE RCA 95	27	11 wks
26 Sep 81	IF YOU WANT MY LOVIN' RCA 131	43	6 wks
28 Aug 82 ●	LOVE COME DOWN RCA 249	7	13 wks
20 Nov 82	BACK TO LOVE RCA 287	40	4 wks
19 Feb 83	GET LOOSE RCA 315	45	5 wks

Act billed as Evelyn Champagne King for first two hits.

Jonathan KING *UK, male vocalist* *67 wks*

29 Jul 65 ●	EVERYONE'S GONE TO THE MOON		
	Decca F 12187	4	11 wks
10 Jan 70	LET IT ALL HANG OUT Decca F 12988	26	7 wks
29 May 71	LAZY BONES Decca F 13177	23	8 wks
20 Nov 71	HOOKED ON A FEELING Decca F 13241	23	10 wks
5 Feb 72	FLIRT Decca F 13276	22	9 wks
6 Sep 75 ●	UNA PALOMA BLANCA UK 105	5	11 wks
7 Oct 78	ONE FOR YOU ONE FOR ME GTO GT 237	29	6 wks
16 Jun 79	YOU'RE THE GREATEST LOVER		
	UK International INT 586	67	2 wks
3 Nov 79	GLORIA Ariola ARO 198	65	3 wks

See also Bubblerock; 53rd and 3rd; Sakkarin; Shag; 100 Ton and A Feather; Weathermen; Sound 9418; Father Abraphart and the Smurps.

Nosmo KING - *See JAVELLS featuring Nosmo KING*

Solomon KING *US, male vocalist* *28 wks*

3 Jan 68 ●	SHE WEARS MY RING Columbia DB 8325	3	18 wks
1 May 68	WHEN WE WERE YOUNG Columbia DB 8402	21	10 wks

KING BROTHERS
UK, male vocal/instrumental group *74 wks*

31 May 57 ●	A WHITE SPORT COAT Parlophone R 4310	6	14 wks
9 Aug 57	IN THE MIDDLE OF AN ISLAND		
	Parlophone R 4338	19	13 wks
6 Dec 57	WAKE UP LITTLE SUSIE Parlophone R 4367	22	3 wks
31 Jan 58	PUT A LIGHT IN THE WINDOW		
	Parlophone R 4389	29	1 wk
14 Feb 58	PUT A LIGHT IN THE WINDOW (re-entry)		
	Parlophone R 4389	28	1 wk
28 Feb 58	PUT A LIGHT IN THE WINDOW (2nd re-entry)		
	Parlophone R 4389	25	2 wks
14 Apr 60 ●	STANDING ON THE CORNER		
	Parlophone R 4639	4	11 wks
28 Jul 60	MAIS OUI Parlophone R 4672	16	10 wks
12 Jan 61	DOLL HOUSE Parlophone R 4715	21	8 wks
2 Mar 61	76 TROMBONES Parlophone R 4737	19	11 wks

KING TRIGGER
UK, male/female vocal/instrumental group *4 wks*

14 Aug 82	THE RIVER Chrysalis CHS 2623	57	4 wks

KINGS OF SWING ORCHESTRA
Australia, orchestra *5 wks*

1 May 82	SWITCHED ON SWING Philips SWING 1	48	5 wks

KINGSMEN
US, male vocal/instrumental group *7 wks*

30 Jan 64	LOUIE LOUIE Pye International 7N 25231	26	7 wks

KINGSTON TRIO
US, male vocal/instrumental group *15 wks*

21 Nov 58 ●	TOM DOOLEY Capitol CL 14951	5	14 wks
4 Dec 59	SAN MIGUEL Capitol CL 15073	29	1 wk

KINKS *UK, male vocal/instrumental group* *213 wks*

13 Aug 64 ★	YOU REALLY GOT ME Pye 7N 15673	1	12 wks
29 Oct 64 ●	ALL DAY AND ALL OF THE NIGHT		
	Pye 7N 15714	2	14 wks
21 Jan 65 ★	TIRED OF WAITING FOR YOU Pye 7N 15759	1	10 wks
25 Mar 65	EVERYBODY'S GONNA BE HAPPY		
	Pye 7N 15813	17	8 wks
27 May 65 ●	SET ME FREE Pye 7N 15854	9	11 wks
5 Aug 65 ●	SEE MY FRIEND Pye 7N 15919	10	9 wks
2 Dec 65 ●	TILL THE END OF THE DAY Pye 7N 15981	8	12 wks
3 Mar 66 ●	DEDICATED FOLLOWER OF FASHION		
	Pye 7N 17064	4	11 wks
9 Jun 66 ★	SUNNY AFTERNOON Pye 7N 17125	1	13 wks
24 Nov 66 ●	DEAD END STREET Pye 7N 17222	5	11 wks
11 May 67 ●	WATERLOO SUNSET Pye 7N 17321	2	11 wks
18 Oct 67 ●	AUTUMN ALMANAC Pye 7N 17400	3	11 wks
17 Apr 68	WONDERBOY Pye 7N 17468	36	5 wks
17 Jul 68	DAYS Pye 7N 17573	12	10 wks
16 Apr 69	PLASTIC MAN Pye 7N 17724	31	4 wks
10 Jan 70	VICTORIA Pye 7N 17865	33	4 wks

4 Jul 70	● **LOLA** *Pye 7N 17961*	**2**	14 wks
12 Dec 70	● **APEMAN** *Pye 7N 45016*	**5**	14 wks
27 May 72	**SUPERSONIC ROCKET SHIP** *RCA 2211*	**16**	8 wks
27 Jun 81	**BETTER THINGS** *Arista ARIST 415*	**46**	5 wks
6 Aug 83	**COME DANCING** *Arista ARIST 502*	**12**	9 wks
15 Oct 83	**YOU REALLY GOT ME** (re-issue) *PRT KD1* ...	**47**	4 wks
15 Oct 83	**DON'T FORGET TO DANCE** *Arista ARIST 524*	**58**	3 wks

Fern KINNEY US, *female vocalist*　　11 wks

16 Feb 80	★ **TOGETHER WE ARE BEAUTIFUL** *WEA K 79111*	**1**	11 wks

KINSHASA BAND　- See Johnny WAKELIN

Kathy KIRBY UK, *female vocalist*　　54 wks

15 Aug 63	**DANCE ON** *Decca F 11682*	**11**	13 wks
7 Nov 63	● **SECRET LOVE** *Decca F 11759*	**4**	18 wks
20 Feb 64	● **LET ME GO LOVER** *Decca F 11832*	**10**	11 wks
7 May 64	**YOU'RE THE ONE** *Decca F 11892*	**17**	9 wks
4 Mar 65	**I BELONG** *Decca F 12087*	**36**	3 wks

Bo KIRKLAND and Ruth DAVIS
US, *male/female vocal duo*　　9 wks

4 Jun 77	**YOU'RE GONNA GET NEXT TO ME** *EMI International INT 532*	**12**	9 wks

KISS US, *male vocal/instrumental group*　　22 wks

30 Jun 79	**I WAS MADE FOR LOVIN' YOU** *Casablanca CAN 152*	**50**	7 wks
20 Feb 82	**A WORLD WITHOUT HEROES** *Casablanca/Phonogram KISS 002*	**55**	3 wks
30 Apr 83	**CREATURES OF THE NIGHT** *Casablanca/Phonogram KISS 4*	**34**	4 wks
29 Oct 83	**LICK IT UP** *Vertigo/Phonogram KISS 5*	**31**	5 wks
8 Sep 84	**HEAVEN'S ON FIRE** *Vertigo/Phonogram VER 12*	**43**	3 wks

KISSING THE PINK
UK, *male/female vocal/instrumental group*　　14 wks

5 Mar 83	**LAST FILM** *Magnet KTP 3*	**19**	14 wks

Mac and Katie KISSOON
UK, *male/female vocal duo*　　33 wks

19 Jun 71	**CHIRPY CHIRPY CHEEP CHEEP** *Young Blood YB 1026*	**41**	1 wk
18 Jan 75	● **SUGAR CANDY KISSES** *Polydor 2058 531*	**3**	10 wks
3 May 75	● **DON'T DO IT BABY** *State STAT 4*	**9**	8 wks
30 Aug 75	**LIKE A BUTTERFLY** *State STAT 9*	**18**	9 wks
15 May 76	**THE TWO OF US** *State STAT 21*	**46**	5 wks

Eartha KITT US, *female vocalist*　　24 wks

1 Apr 55	● **UNDER THE BRIDGES OF PARIS** *HMV B 10647*	**7**	9 wks
10 Jun 55	**UNDER THE BRIDGES OF PARIS** (re-entry) *HMV B 10647*	**20**	1 wk
3 Dec 83	**WHERE IS MY MAN** *Record Shack SOHO 11* ...	**36**	11 wks
7 Jul 84	**I LOVE MEN** *Record Shack SOHO 21*	**50**	3 wks

KJELD　- *See JAN and KJELD*

KLAXONS
Belgium, *male vocal/instrumental group*　　6 wks

10 Dec 83	**THE CLAP CLAP SOUND** *PRT 7P 290*	**45**	6 wks

KLEEER
US, *male/female vocal/instrumental group*　　10 wks

17 Mar 79	**KEEP YOUR BODY WORKING** *Atlantic LV 21*	**51**	6 wks
14 Mar 81	**GET TOUGH** *Atlantic 11560*	**49**	4 wks

KNACK US, *male vocal/instrumental group*　　12 wks

30 Jun 79	● **MY SHARONA** *Capitol CL 16087*	**6**	10 wks
13 Oct 79	**GOOD GIRLS DON'T** *Capitol CL 16097*	**66**	2 wks

Frederick KNIGHT US, *male vocalist*　　10 wks

10 Jun 72	**I'VE BEEN LONELY SO LONG** *Stax 2025 098*	**22**	10 wks

Gladys KNIGHT and the PIPS
US, *female vocalist/male vocal backing group*　　161 wks

8 Jun 67	**TAKE ME IN YOUR ARMS & LOVE ME** *Tamla Motown TMG 604*	**13**	15 wks
27 Dec 67	**I HEARD IT THROUGH THE GRAPEVINE** *Tamla Motown TMG 629*	**47**	1 wk
17 Jun 72	**JUST WALK IN MY SHOES** *Tamla Motown TMG 813*	**35**	8 wks
25 Nov 72	**HELP ME MAKE IT THROUGH THE NIGHT** *Tamla Motown TMG 830*	**11**	17 wks
3 Mar 73	**LOOK OF LOVE** *Tamla Motown TMG 844*	**21**	9 wks
26 May 73	**NEITHER ONE OF US** *Tamla Motown TMG 855*	**31**	7 wks
5 Apr 75	● **THE WAY WE WERE/TRY TO REMEMBER** (MEDLEY) *Buddah BDS 428*	**4**	15 wks
2 Aug 75	● **BEST THING THAT EVER HAPPENED TO ME** *Buddah BDS 432*	**7**	10 wks
15 Nov 75	**PART TIME LOVE** *Buddah BDS 438*	**30**	5 wks
8 May 76	● **MIDNIGHT TRAIN TO GEORGIA** *Buddah BDS 444*	**10**	9 wks
21 Aug 76	**MAKE YOURS A HAPPY HOME** *Buddah BDS 447*	**35**	4 wks
6 Nov 76	**SO SAD THE SONG** *Buddah BDS 448*	**20**	9 wks
15 Jan 77	**NOBODY BUT YOU** *Buddah BDS 451*	**34**	2 wks
28 May 77	● **BABY DON'T CHANGE YOUR MIND** *Buddah BDS 458*	**4**	12 wks
24 Sep 77	**HOME IS WHERE THE HEART IS** *Buddah BDS 460*	**35**	4 wks
8 Apr 78	**THE ONE AND ONLY** *Buddah BDS 470*	**32**	4 wks
13 May 78	**THE ONE AND ONLY** (re-entry) *Buddah BDS 478*	**66**	1 wk
24 Jun 78	**COME BACK AND FINISH WHAT YOU STARTED** *Buddah BDS 473*	**15**	13 wks
30 Sep 78	**IT'S A BETTER THAN GOOD TIME** *Buddah BDS 478*	**59**	4 wks
30 Aug 80	**TASTE OF BITTER LOVE** *CBS 8890*	**35**	6 wks
8 Nov 80	**BOURGIE BOURGIE** *CBS 9081*	**32**	6 wks

See also Johnny Mathis and Gladys Knight.

Robert KNIGHT US, *male vocalist*　　26 wks

17 Jan 68	**EVERLASTING LOVE** *Monument MON 1008* ...	**40**	2 wks
24 Nov 73	● **LOVE ON A MOUNTAIN TOP** *Monument MNT 1875*	**10**	16 wks
9 Mar 74	**EVERLASTING LOVE** (re-issue) *Monument MNT 2106*	**19**	8 wks

Mark KNOPFLER
UK, male vocalist/instrumentalist - guitar — *3 wks*

12 Mar 83	**GOING HOME** *Vertigo/Phonogram DSTR 4*	56	3 wks

Buddy KNOX *US, male vocalist* — *5 wks*

10 May 57	**PARTY DOLL** *Columbia DB 3914*	29	3 wks
16 Aug 62	**SHE'S GONE** *Liberty LIB 55473*	45	2 wks

Moe KOFFMAN QUARTETTE
Canada, male instrumental group, Moe Koffman, flute — *2 wks*

28 Mar 58	**SWINGIN' SHEPHERD BLUES** *London HLJ 8549*	23	2 wks

KOKOMO *US, male instrumentalist - piano* — *7 wks*

13 Apr 61	**ASIA MINOR** *London HLU 9305*	35	7 wks

KOKOMO
UK, male/female vocal/instrumental group — *3 wks*

29 May 82	**A LITTLE BIT FURTHER AWAY** *CBS A 2064*	45	3 wks

John KONGOS
South Africa, male vocalist/multi-instrumentalist — *25 wks*

22 May 71	● **HE'S GONNA STEP ON YOU AGAIN** *Fly BUG 8*	4	14 wks
20 Nov 71	● **TOKOLOSHE MAN** *Fly BUG 14*	4	11 wks

KOOL and the GANG
US, male vocal/instrumental group — *149 wks*

27 Oct 79	● **LADIES NIGHT** *Mercury KOOL 7*	9	12 wks
19 Jan 80	**TOO HOT** *Mercury KOOL 8*	23	8 wks
12 Jul 80	**HANGIN' OUT** *De-Lite KOOL 9*	52	4 wks
1 Nov 80	● **CELEBRATION** *De-Lite KOOL 10*	7	13 wks
21 Feb 81	**JONES VS JONES/SUMMER MADNESS/FUNKY STUFF/HOLLYWOOD SWINGING** *De-Lite KOOL 112, KOOL 11, Gang 11*	17	11 wks
30 May 81	**TAKE IT TO THE TOP** *De-Lite DE 2*	15	9 wks
31 Oct 81	**STEPPIN' OUT** *De-Lite DE 4*	12	13 wks
19 Dec 81	● **GET DOWN ON IT** *De-Lite DE 5*	3	12 wks
6 Mar 82	**TAKE MY HEART (YOU CAN HAVE IT IF YOU WANT IT)** *De-Lite/Phonogram DE 6*	29	7 wks
7 Aug 82	**BIG FUN** *De-Lite/Phonogram DE 7*	14	8 wks
16 Oct 82	● **OOH LA LA (LET'S GO DANCIN')** *De-Lite/Phonogram DE 9*	6	9 wks
4 Dec 82	**HI DE HI, HI DE HO** *De-Lite/Phonogram DE 14* ..	29	8 wks
10 Dec 83	**STRAIGHT AHEAD** *De-Lite/Phonogram DE 15* ...	15	10 wks
11 Feb 84	● **JOANNA/TONIGHT** *De-Lite/Phonogram DE 16*	2	11 wks
14 Apr 84	● **(WHEN YOU SAY YOU LOVE SOMEBODY) FROM THE HEART** *De-Lite/Phonogram DE 17*	7	8 wks
24 Nov 84	**FRESH** *De-Lite/Phonogram DE 18*	11†	6 wks

Jones vs Jones/Summer Madness was issued in three versions, a 7-inch single, a 12-inch single and an EP sales of which were combined for chart purposes. The 7-inch single De-Lite KOOL 11, does not contain Funky Stuff or Hollywood Swinging.

KORGIS *UK, male vocal/instrumental duo* — *27 wks*

23 Jun 79	**IF I HAD YOU** *Rialto TREB 103*	13	12 wks
24 May 80	● **EVERYBODY'S GOT TO LEARN SOMETIME** *Rialto TREB 115*	5	12 wks
30 Aug 80	**IF IT'S ALRIGHT WITH YOU BABY** *Rialto TREB 118*	56	3 wks

KRAFTWERK
Germany, male instrumental/vocal group — *63 wks*

10 May 75	**AUTOBAHN** *Vertigo 6147 012*	11	9 wks
28 Oct 78	**NEON LIGHTS** *Capitol CL 15998*	53	3 wks
9 May 81	**POCKET CALCULATOR** *EMI 5175*	39	6 wks
11 Jul 81	**COMPUTER LOVE/THE MODEL** *EMI 5207*	36	8 wks
26 Dec 81	★ **COMPUTER LOVE/THE MODEL** (re-entry) *EMI 5207*	1	13 wks
20 Feb 82	**SHOWROOM DUMMIES** *EMI 5272*	25	5 wks
6 Aug 83	**TOUR DE FRANCE** *EMI 5413*	22	8 wks
25 Aug 84	**TOUR DE FRANCE** (re-entry) *EMI 5413*	24	11 wks

Billy J. KRAMER and the DAKOTAS
UK, male vocalist/male instrumental backing group — *71 wks*

2 May 63	● **DO YOU WANT TO KNOW A SECRET?** *Parlophone R 5023*	2	15 wks
1 Aug 63	★ **BAD TO ME** *Parlophone R 5049*	1	14 wks
7 Nov 63	● **I'LL KEEP YOU SATISFIED** *Parlophone R 5073*	4	13 wks
27 Feb 64	★ **LITTLE CHILDREN** *Parlophone R 5105*	1	13 wks
23 Jul 64	● **FROM A WINDOW** *Parlophone R 5156*	10	8 wks
20 May 65	**TRAINS AND BOATS AND PLANES** *Parlophone R 5285*	12	8 wks

See also Dakotas.

KRANKIES *UK, male/female vocal duo* — *6 wks*

7 Feb 81	**FAN'DABI'DOZI** *Monarch MON 21*	71	1 wk
7 Mar 81	**FAN'DABI'DOZI** (re-entry) *Monarch MON 21* ...	46	5 wks

KREW-KATS *UK, male instrumental group* — *10 wks*

9 Mar 61	**TRAMBONE** *HMV POP 840*	33	9 wks
18 May 61	**TRAMBONE** (re-entry) *HMV POP 840*	49	1 wk

KROKUS
Switzerland/Malta, male vocal/instrumental group — *2 wks*

16 May 81	**INDUSTRIAL STRENGTH** (EP) *Ariola ARO 258*	62	2 wks

Tracks on Industrial Strength EP: Bedside Radio/Easy Rocker/ Celebration/Bye Bye Baby.

Charlie KUNZ
US, male instrumentalist - piano — *4 wks*

17 Dec 54	**PIANO MEDLEY NO. 114** *Decca F 10419*	20	3 wks
14 Jan 55	**PIANO MEDLEY NO. 114** (re-entry) *Decca F 10419*	16	1 wk

Medley titles: There Must Be A Reason/Hold My Hand/If I Give My Heart To You/Little Things Mean A Lot/Make Her Mine/My Son My Son.

KURSAAL FLYERS
UK, male vocal/instrumental group — *10 wks*

20 Nov 76	**LITTLE DOES SHE KNOW** *CBS 4689*	14	10 wks

L

Danny LA RUE *UK, male vocalist* — *9 wks*

18 Dec 68	**ON MOTHER KELLY'S DOORSTEP** *Page One POF 108*	33	9 wks

JOHN D. LOUDERMILK (above left) The writer of hits including 'Angela Jones', and 'Ebony Eyes'; duets here with Mike Read on 'The Language Of Love' at the Wembley Festival 1983. (Photo: Graham Barker).

JERRY LEE LEWIS (above right) in high spirits whooping it up with some distant acquaintances.

LEVEL 42 (below) The 'not quite so level' four.

LABELLE US, female vocal group　　9 wks

22 Mar 75	**LADY MARMALADE (VOULEZ-VOUS COUCHER AVEC MOI CE SOIR?)** *Epic EPC 2852*		**17**	9 wks

Cleo LAINE UK, female vocalist　　14 wks

29 Dec 60	**LET'S SLIP AWAY** *Fontana H 269*		**42**	1 wk
14 Sep 61	● **YOU'LL ANSWER TO ME** *Fontana H 326*		**5**	13 wks

Frankie LAINE US, male vocalist　　253 wks

14 Nov 52	● **HIGH NOON** *Columbia DB 3113*		**7**	7 wks
20 Mar 53	● **GIRL IN THE WOOD** *Columbia DB 2907*		**11**	1 wk
3 Apr 53	★ **I BELIEVE** *Philips PB 117*		**1**	36 wks
4 Sep 53	● **WHERE THE WIND BLOWS** *Philips PB 167*		**2**	12 wks
16 Oct 53	★ **HEY JOE** *Philips PB 172*		**1**	8 wks
30 Oct 53	★ **ANSWER ME** *Philips PB 196*		**1**	17 wks
8 Jan 54	● **BLOWING WILD** *Philips PB 207*		**2**	12 wks
26 Mar 54	● **GRANADA** *Philips PB 242*		**10**	1 wk
9 Apr 54	● **GRANADA** (re-entry) *Philips PB 242*		**9**	1 wk
16 Apr 54	● **THE KID'S LAST FIGHT** *Philips PB 258*		**3**	10 wks
13 Aug 54	● **MY FRIEND** *Philips PB 316*		**3**	15 wks
8 Oct 54	● **THERE MUST BE A REASON** *Philips PB 306*		**9**	9 wks
22 Oct 54	● **RAIN RAIN RAIN** *Philips PB 311*		**8**	16 wks
11 Mar 55	**IN THE BEGINNING** *Philips PB 311*		**20**	1 wk
24 Jun 55	● **COOL WATER** *Philips PB 465*		**2**	22 wks
15 Jul 55	● **STRANGE LADY IN TOWN** *Philips PB 478*		**6**	13 wks
11 Nov 55	**HUMMING BIRD** *Philips PB 498*		**16**	1 wk
25 Nov 55	**HAWKEYE** *Philips PB 519*		**7**	8 wks
20 Jan 56	**SIXTEEN TONS** *Philips PB 539*		**10**	3 wks
4 May 56	**HELL HATH NO FURY** *Philips PB 585*		**28**	1 wk
7 Sep 56	★ **A WOMAN IN LOVE** *Philips PB 617*		**1**	21 wks
28 Dec 56	● **MOONLIGHT GAMBLER** *Philips PB 638*		**13**	12 wks
29 Mar 57	**MOONLIGHT GAMBLER** (re-entry) *Philips PB 638*		**28**	1 wk
26 Apr 57	**LOVE IS A GOLDEN RING** *Philips PB 676*		**19**	5 wks
13 Nov 59	● **RAWHIDE** *Philips PB 965*		**6**	17 wks
31 Mar 60	**RAWHIDE** (re-entry) *Philips PB 965*		**41**	2 wks
11 May 61	**GUNSLINGER** *Philips PB 1135*		**50**	1 wk

See also Frankie Laine and Jimmy Boyd; Frankie Laine and Johnnie Ray; Doris Day and Frankie Laine.

Frankie LAINE and Jimmy BOYD US, male vocal duo　　16 wks

8 May 53	● **TELL ME A STORY** *Philips PB 126*		**5**	15 wks
11 Sep 53	**TELL ME A STORY** (re-entry) *Philips PB 126*		**12**	1 wk

See also Frankie Laine; Jimmy Boyd; Frankie Laine and Johnnie Ray; Doris Day and Frankie Laine.

Frankie LAINE and Johnnie RAY US, male vocal duo　　4 wks

4 Oct 57	**GOOD EVENING FRIENDS/UP ABOVE MY HEAD** *Philips PB 708*		**25**	4 wks

See also Frankie Laine; Johnnie Ray; Frankie Laine and Jimmy Boyd; Doris Day and Frankie Laine; Doris Day and Johnnie Ray.

Greg LAKE UK, male vocalist　　12 wks

6 Dec 75	● **I BELIEVE IN FATHER CHRISTMAS** *Manticore K 13511*		**2**	7 wks
25 Dec 82	**I BELIEVE IN FATHER CHRISTMAS** (re-entry) *Manticore K 13511*		**72**	3 wks
24 Dec 83	**I BELIEVE IN FATHER CHRISTMAS** (2nd re-entry) *Manticore K 13511*		**65**	2 wks

See also Emerson, Lake and Palmer.

Annabel LAMB UK, female vocalist　　7 wks

27 Aug 83	**RIDERS ON THE STORM** *A & M AM 131*		**27**	7 wks

LAMBRETTAS UK, male vocal/instrumental group　　24 wks

1 Mar 80	● **POISON IVY** *Rocket XPRESS 25*		**7**	12 wks
24 May 80	**D-A-A-ANCE** *Rocket XPRESS 33*		**12**	8 wks
23 Aug 80	**ANOTHER DAY (ANOTHER GIRL)** *Rocket XPRESS 36*		**49**	4 wks

LANCASTRIANS UK, male vocal/instrumental group　　2 wks

24 Dec 64	**WE'LL SING IN THE SUNSHINE** *Pye 7N 15732*		**47**	2 wks

Major LANCE US, male vocalist　　2 wks

13 Feb 64	**UM UM UM UM UM UM** *Columbia DB 7205*		**40**	2 wks

LANDSCAPE UK, male vocal/instrumental group　　20 wks

28 Feb 81	● **EINSTEIN A GO-GO** *RCA 22*		**5**	13 wks
23 May 81	**NORMAN BATES** *RCA 60*		**40**	7 wks

Ronnie LANE UK, male vocalist　　12 wks

12 Jan 74	**HOW COME** *GM GMS 011*		**11**	8 wks
15 Jun 74	**THE POACHER** *GM GMS 024*		**36**	4 wks

Both hits have the credit 'accompanied by the band Slim Chance'.

Don LANG UK, male vocalist　　18 wks

4 Nov 55	**CLOUDBURST** *HMV POP 115*		**16**	2 wks
2 Dec 55	**CLOUDBURST** (re-entry) *HMV POP 115*		**18**	1 wk
13 Jan 56	**CLOUDBURST** (2nd re-entry) *HMV POP 115*		**20**	1 wk
5 Jul 57	**SCHOOL DAY** *HMV POP 350*		**26**	2 wks
23 May 58	● **WITCH DOCTOR** *HMV POP 488*		**5**	11 wks
10 Mar 60	**SINK THE BISMARCK** *HMV POP 714*		**43**	1 wk

School Day and Witch Doctor credit Don Lang and his Frantic Five.

Mario LANZA US, male vocalist　　32 wks

14 Nov 52	● **BECAUSE YOU'RE MINE** *HMV DA 2017*		**3**	24 wks
4 Feb 55	**DRINKING SONG** *HMV DA 2065*		**13**	1 wk
18 Feb 55	**I'LL WALK WITH GOD** *HMV DA 2062*		**18**	1 wk
22 Apr 55	**SERENADE** *HMV DA 2065*		**19**	1 wk
6 May 55	**SERENADE** (re-entry) *HMV DA 2065*		**15**	2 wks
6 May 55	**I'LL WALK WITH GOD** (re-entry) *HMV DA 2062*		**20**	1 wk
14 Sep 56	**SERENADE** *HMV DA 2085*		**25**	1 wk
12 oct 56	**SERENADE** (re-entry) *HMV DA 2085*		**29**	1 wk

DA 2065 and DA 2085 are two different songs.

Julius LAROSA US, male vocalist　　9 wks

4 Jul 58	**TORERO** *RCA 1063*		**15**	9 wks

James LAST BAND
Germany, male instrumental group   *4 wks*

3 May 80	**THE SEDUCTION (LOVE THEME)**			
	Polydor PD 2071		**48**	4 wks

The LATE SHOW
UK, male vocal/instrumental group   *6 wks*

3 Mar 79	**BRISTOL STOMP** *Decca F 13822*		**40**	6 wks

Stacy LATTISAW   *US, female vocalist*   *14 wks*

14 Jun 80 ●	**JUMP TO THE BEAT** *Atlantic/Cotillion K 11496*		**3**	11 wks
30 Aug 80	**DYNAMITE** *Atlantic K 11554*		**51**	3 wks

LAUNCHERS - *See Ezz RECO and the LAUNCHERS with Boysie GRANT*

Cyndi LAUPER   *US, female vocalist*   *36 wks*

14 Jan 84 ●	**GIRLS JUST WANT TO HAVE FUN**			
	Portrait/Epic A 3943		**2**	12 wks
24 Mar 84	**TIME AFTER TIME** *Portrait/Epic A 4290*		**54**	4 wks
16 Jun 84 ●	**TIME AFTER TIME** (re-entry) *Portrait/Epic A 4290*		**3**	13 wks
1 Sep 84	**SHE BOP** *Portrait/Epic A 4620*		**46**	5 wks
17 Nov 84	**ALL THROUGH THE NIGHT**			
	Portrait/Epic A 4849		**64**	2 wks

LAUREL and HARDY
UK, male vocal/instrumental duo   *2 wks*

2 Apr 83	**CLUNK CLINK** *CBS A 3213*		**65**	2 wks

LAUREL and HARDY with the AVALON BOYS
UK/US, male vocal duo and male vocal group   *10 wks*

22 Nov 75 ●	**THE TRAIL OF THE LONESOME PINE**			
	United Artists UP 36026		**2**	10 wks

Has credit: featuring Chill Wills.

Lee LAWRENCE   *UK, male vocalist*   *10 wks*

20 Nov 53	**CRYING IN THE CHAPEL** *Decca F 10177*		**11**	1 wk
11 Dec 53 ●	**CRYING IN THE CHAPEL** (re-entry)			
	Decca F 10177		**7**	5 wks
2 Dec 55	**SUDDENLY THERE'S A VALLEY**			
	Columbia DB 3681		**19**	1 wk
16 Dec 55	**SUDDENLY THERE'S A VALLEY** (re-entry)			
	Columbia DB 3681		**14**	3 wks

Steve LAWRENCE   *US, male vocalist*   *14 wks*

21 Apr 60 ●	**FOOTSTEPS** *HMV POP 726*		**4**	13 wks
18 Aug 60	**GIRLS GIRLS GIRLS** *London HLT 9166*		**49**	1 wk

See also Steve and Eydie.

Vicky LEANDROS
Greece, female vocalist   *29 wks*

8 Apr 72 ●	**COME WHAT MAY** *Philips 6000 049*		**2**	16 wks
23 Dec 72	**THE LOVE IN YOUR EYES** *Philips 6000 081*		**48**	3 wks
20 Jan 73	**THE LOVE IN YOUR EYES** (re-entry)			
	Philips 6000 081		**40**	4 wks
7 Apr 73	**THE LOVE IN YOUR EYES** (2nd re-entry)			
	Philips 6000 081		**46**	1 wk
7 Jul 73	**WHEN BOUZOUKIS PLAYED** *Philips 6000 111*		**44**	2 wks
28 Jul 73	**WHEN BOUZOUKIS PLAYED** (re-entry)			
	Philips 6000 111		**45**	3 wks

LEE - *See PETERS and LEE*

Brenda LEE   *US, female vocalist*   *210 wks*

17 Mar 60	**SWEET NOTHIN'S** *Brunswick 05819*		**45**	1 wk
7 Apr 60 ●	**SWEET NOTHIN'S** (re-entry) *Brunswick 05819*		**4**	18 wks
30 Jun 60	**I'M SORRY** *Brunswick 05833*		**12**	16 wks
20 Oct 60	**I WANT TO BE WANTED** *Brunswick 05839*		**31**	6 wks
19 Jan 61	**LET'S JUMP THE BROOMSTICK**			
	Brunswick 05823		**12**	15 wks
6 Apr 61	**EMOTIONS** *Brunswick 05847*		**45**	1 wk
20 Jul 61	**DUM DUM** *Brunswick 05854*		**22**	8 wks
16 Nov 61	**FOOL NUMBER ONE** *Brunswick 05860*		**38**	3 wks
8 Feb 62	**BREAK IT TO ME GENTLY** *Brunswick 05864*		**46**	2 wks
5 Apr 62 ●	**SPEAK TO ME PRETTY** *Brunswick 05867*		**3**	12 wks
21 Jun 62 ●	**HERE COMES THAT FEELING** *Brunswick 05871*		**5**	12 wks
13 Sep 62	**IT STARTED ALL OVER AGAIN**			
	Brunswick 05876		**15**	11 wks
29 Nov 62 ●	**ROCKIN' AROUND THE CHRISTMAS TREE**			
	Brunswick 05880		**6**	7 wks
17 Jan 63 ●	**ALL ALONE AM I** *Brunswick 05882*		**7**	17 wks
28 Mar 63 ●	**LOSING YOU** *Brunswick 05886*		**10**	16 wks
18 Jul 63	**I WONDER** *Brunswick 05891*		**14**	9 wks
31 Oct 63	**SWEET IMPOSSIBLE YOU** *Brunswick 05896*		**28**	6 wks
9 Jan 64 ●	**AS USUAL** *Brunswick 05899*		**5**	15 wks
9 Apr 64	**THINK** *Brunswick 05903*		**26**	8 wks
10 Sep 64	**IS IT TRUE** *Brunswick 05915*		**17**	8 wks
10 Dec 64	**CHRISTMAS WILL BE JUST ANOTHER LONELY DAY** *Brunswick 05921*		**29**	5 wks
4 Feb 65	**THANKS A LOT** *Brunswick 05927*		**41**	2 wks
29 Jul 65	**TOO MANY RIVERS** *Brunswick 05936*		**22**	12 wks

Curtis LEE   *US, male vocalist*   *2 wks*

31 Aug 61	**PRETTY LITTLE ANGEL EYES**			
	London HLX 9397		**47**	1 wk
14 Sep 61	**PRETTY LITTLE ANGEL EYES** (re-entry)			
	London HLX 9397		**48**	1 wk

Jackie LEE   *UK, female vocalist*   *17 wks*

2 Jan 71	**RUPERT** *Pye 7N 45003*		**14**	17 wks

See also Jacky.

Leapy LEE   *UK, male vocalist*   *28 wks*

21 Aug 68 ●	**LITTLE ARROWS** *MCA MU 1028*		**2**	21 wks
20 Dec 69	**GOOD MORNING** *MCA MK 5021*		**47**	1 wk
10 Jan 70	**GOOD MORNING** (re-entry) *MCA MK 5021*		**29**	6 wks

Peggy LEE   *US, female vocalist*   *28 wks*

24 May 57 ●	**MR. WONDERFUL** *Brunswick 05671*		**5**	13 wks
15 Aug 58 ●	**FEVER** *Capitol CL 14902*		**5**	11 wks
23 Mar 61	**TILL THERE WAS YOU** *Capitol CL 15184*		**40**	1 wk
6 Apr 61	**TILL THERE WAS YOU** (re-entry)			
	Capitol CL 15184		**30**	3 wks

Toney LEE   *US, male vocalist*   *4 wks*

29 Jan 83	**REACH UP** *TMT TMT 2*		**64**	4 wks

LEEDS UNITED FC
UK, male football team vocalists — 10 wks

29 Apr 72 ●	LEEDS UNITED	Chapter One SCH 168	10	10 wks

Raymond LEFEVRE   *France, orchestra* — 2 wks

15 May 68	SOUL COAXING	Major Minor MM 559	46	2 wks

LEMON PIPERS
US, male vocal/instrumental group — 16 wks

7 Feb 68 ●	GREEN TAMBOURINE			
	Pye International 7N 25444		7	11 wks
1 May 68	RICE IS NICE	Pye International 7N 25454	41	5 wks

John LENNON   *UK, male vocalist* — 173 wks

9 Jul 69 ●	GIVE PEACE A CHANCE	Apple 13	2	13 wks
1 Nov 69	COLD TURKEY	Apple APPLES 1001	14	8 wks
21 Feb 70 ●	INSTANT KARMA	Apple APPLES 1003	5	9 wks
20 Mar 71 ●	POWER TO THE PEOPLE	Apple R 5892	7	9 wks
9 Dec 72 ●	HAPPY XMAS (WAR IS OVER)	Apple R 5970	4	8 wks
24 Nov 73	MIND GAMES	Apple R 5994	26	9 wks
19 Oct 74	WHATEVER GETS YOU THROUGH THE			
	NIGHT	Apple R 5998	36	4 wks
4 Jan 75	HAPPY XMAS (WAR IS OVER) (re-entry)			
	Apple R 5970		48	1 wk
8 Feb 75	NUMBER 9 DREAM	Apple R 6003	23	8 wks
3 May 75	STAND BY ME	Apple R 6005	30	7 wks
1 Nov 75 ●	IMAGINE	Apple R 6009	6	11 wks
8 Nov 80 ★	(JUST LIKE) STARTING OVER	Geffen K 79186	1	15 wks
20 Dec 80 ●	HAPPY XMAS (WAR IS OVER) (2nd re-entry)			
	Apple R 5970		2	9 wks
27 Dec 80 ★	IMAGINE (re-entry) Apple R 6009		1	13 wks
24 Jan 81 ★	WOMAN	Geffen K 79195	1	11 wks
24 Jan 81	GIVE PEACE A CHANCE (re-entry) Apple 13 ..		33	5 wks
4 Apr 81	WATCHING THE WHEELS	Geffen K 79207 ...	30	6 wks
19 Dec 81	HAPPY XMAS (WAR IS OVER) (3rd re-entry)			
	Apple R 5970		28	5 wks
20 Nov 82	LOVE	Parlophone R 6059	41	6 wks
25 Dec 82	HAPPY XMAS (WAR IS OVER) (4th re-entry)			
	Apple R 5970		56	3 wks
1 Jan 83	LOVE	Parlophone R 6059	62	1 wk
21 Jan 84 ●	NOBODY TOLD ME			
	Ono Music/Polydor POSP 700		6	6 wks
17 Mar 84	BORROWED TIME	Polydor POSP 701	32	6 wks

Instant Karma *is by Lennon,* Ono *and the Plastic Ono Band,* Power To The People *by John Lennon/Plastic Ono Band,* Happy Xmas War Is Over *by John and Yoko/Plastic Ono Band with The Harlem Community Choir,* Whatever Gets You Through The Night *by John Lennon with The Plastic Ono Nuclear Band, and the others simply John Lennon. The* Yoko *and the* Ono *in these credits refer to Yoko Ono, Japanese female vocalist. See also Elton John Band featuring John Lennon and the Muscle Shoals Horns.*

Julian LENNON   *UK, male vocalist* — 14 wks

6 Oct 84 ●	TOO LATE FOR GOODBYES			
	Charisma/Virgin JL 1		6	11 wks
15 Dec 84	VALOTTE	Charisma/Virgin JL 2	55†	3 wks

Rula LENSKA - *See Julie COVINGTON, Rula LENSKA, Charlotte CORNWELL and Sue JONES-DAVIES*

Ketty LESTER   *US, female vocalist* — 16 wks

19 Apr 62 ●	LOVE LETTERS	London HLN 9527	4	12 wks
19 Jul 62	BUT NOT FOR ME	London HLN 9574	45	4 wks

LETTERMEN   *US, male vocal group* — 3 wks

23 Nov 61	THE WAY YOU LOOK TONIGHT			
	Capitol CL 15222		36	3 wks

LEVEL 42
UK/France, male vocal/instrumental group — 72 wks

30 Aug 80	LOVE MEETING LOVE	Polydor POSP 170	61	4 wks
18 Apr 81	LOVE GAMES	Polydor POSP 234	39	6 wks
8 Aug 81	TURN IT ON	Polydor POSP 286	57	6 wks
14 Nov 81	STARCHILD	Polydor POSP 343	47	4 wks
8 May 82	ARE YOU HEARING (WHAT I HEAR)?			
	Polydor POSP 396		49	5 wks
2 Oct 82	WEAVE YOUR SPELL	Polydor POSP 500	43	4 wks
15 Jan 83	THE CHINESE WAY	Polydor POSP 538	24	8 wks
16 Apr 83	OUT OF SIGHT, OUT OF MIND			
	Polydor POSP 570		41	4 wks
30 Jul 83 ●	THE SUN GOES DOWN (LIVING IT UP)			
	Polydor POSP 622		10	12 wks
22 Oct 83	MICRO KIDS	Polydor POSP 643	37	5 wks
1 Sep 84	HOT WATER	Polydor POSP 697	18	9 wks
3 Nov 84	THE CHANT HAS BEGUN	Polydor POSP 710 ..	41	5 wks

Hank LEVINE   *US, orchestra* — 4 wks

21 Dec 61	IMAGE	HMV POP 947	45	4 wks

Jona LEWIE   *UK, male vocalist* — 20 wks

10 May 80	YOU'LL ALWAYS FIND ME IN THE KITCHEN			
	AT PARTIES Stiff BUY 73		16	9 wks
29 Nov 80 ●	STOP THE CAVALRY	Stiff BUY 104	3	11 wks

On some copies first title was simply Kitchen At Parties.

Gary LEWIS and the PLAYBOYS
US, male vocal/instrumental group, Gary Lewis lead vocals and drums — 7 wks

8 Feb 75	MY HEART'S SYMPHONY			
	United Artists UP 35780		36	7 wks

Huey LEWIS and the NEWS
US, male vocal/instrumental group — 10 wks

27 Oct 84 ●	IF THIS IS IT	Chrysalis CHS 2829	7†	10 wks

Jerry LEWIS   *US, male vocalist* — 8 wks

8 Feb 57	ROCK-A-BYE YOUR BABY (WITH A DIXIE			
	MELODY) Brunswick 05636		12	7 wks
5 Apr 57	ROCK-A-BYE YOUR BABY (WITH A DIXIE			
	MELODY) (re-entry) Brunswick 05636		22	1 wk

Jerry Lee LEWIS
US, male vocalist/instrumentalist - piano — 68 wks

27 Sep 57 ●	WHOLE LOTTA SHAKIN' GOIN' ON			
	London HLS 8457		8	10 wks
20 Dec 57 ★	GREAT BALLS OF FIRE	London HLS 8529	1	12 wks
27 Dec 57	WHOLE LOTTA SHAKIN' GOIN' ON (re-entry)			
	London HLS 8457		26	1 wk
11 Apr 58 ●	BREATHLESS	London HLS 8592	8	7 wks
23 Jan 59	HIGH SCHOOL CONFIDENTIAL			
	London HLS 8780		12	6 wks
1 May 59	LOVIN' UP A STORM	London HLS 8840	28	1 wk

9 Jun 60	BABY BABY BYE BYE *London HLS 9131*	47	1 wk
4 May 61 ●	WHAT'D I SAY *London HLS 9335*	10	12 wks
3 Aug 61	WHAT'D I SAY (re-entry) *London HLS 9335*	49	2 wks
6 Sep 62	SWEET LITTLE SIXTEEN *London HLS 9584*	38	5 wks
14 Mar 63	GOOD GOLLY MISS MOLLY *London HLS 9688*	31	6 wks
6 May 72	CHANTILLY LACE *Mercury 6052 141*	33	5 wks

Linda LEWIS *UK, female vocalist* *30 wks*

2 Jun 73	ROCK-A-DOODLE-DOO *Raft RA 18502*	15	11 wks
12 Jul 75 ●	IT'S IN HIS KISS *Arista 17*	6	8 wks
17 Apr 76	BABY I'M YOURS *Arista 43*	33	6 wks
2 Jun 79	I'D BE SURPRISINGLY GOOD FOR YOU *Ariola ARO 166*	40	5 wks

Ramsey LEWIS
US, male instrumentalist - piano *8 wks*

15 Apr 72	WADE IN THE WATER *Chess 6145 004*	31	8 wks

John LEYTON *UK, male vocalist* *70 wks*

3 Aug 61 ★	JOHNNY REMEMBER ME *Top Rank JAR 577*	1	15 wks
5 Oct 61 ●	WILD WIND *Top Rank JAR 585*	2	10 wks
28 Dec 61	SON THIS IS SHE *HMV POP 956*	15	10 wks
15 Mar 62	LONE RIDER *HMV POP 992*	40	5 wks
3 May 62	LONELY CITY *HMV POP 1014*	14	11 wks
23 Aug 62	DOWN THE RIVER NILE *HMV POP 1054*	42	3 wks
21 Feb 63	CUPBOARD LOVE *HMV POP 1122*	22	12 wks
18 Jul 63	I'LL CUT YOUR TAIL OFF *HMV POP 1175*	50	1 wk
8 Aug 63	I'LL CUT YOUR TAIL OFF (re-entry) *HMV POP 1175*	36	2 wks
20 Feb 64	MAKE LOVE TO ME *HMV POP 1264*	49	1 wk

LEYTON BUZZARDS
UK, male vocal/instrumental group *5 wks*

3 Mar 79	SATURDAY NIGHT (BENEATH THE PLASTIC PALM TREES) *Chrysalis CHS 2288*	53	5 wks

LIBERACE *US, male instrumentalist - piano* *2 wks*

17 Jun 55	UNCHAINED MELODY *Philips PB 430*	20	1 wk
19 Oct 56	I DON'T CARE *Columbia DB 3834*	28	1 wk

I Don't Care *featured Liberace as vocalist too.*

LIEUTENANT PIGEON
UK, male/female instrumental group *29 wks*

16 Sep 72 ★	MOULDY OLD DOUGH *Decca F 13278*	1	19 wks
16 Dec 72	DESPERATE DAN *Decca F 13365*	17	10 wks

LIGHT OF THE WORLD
UK, male vocal/instrumental group *25 wks*

14 Apr 79	SWINGIN' *Ensign ENY 22*	45	5 wks
14 Jul 79	MIDNIGHT GROOVIN' *Ensign ENY 29*	72	1 wk
18 Oct 80	LONDON TOWN *Ensign ENY 43*	41	5 wks
17 Jan 81	I SHOT THE SHERIFF *Ensign ENY 46*	40	5 wks
28 Mar 81	I'M SO HAPPY *Mercury/Ensign MER 64*	35	6 wks
21 Nov 81	RIDE THE LOVE TRAIN *EMI 5242*	49	3 wks

Gordon LIGHTFOOT
Canada, male vocalist *26 wks*

19 Jun 71	IF YOU COULD READ MY MIND *Reprise RS 20974*	30	9 wks
3 Aug 74	SUNDOWN *Reprise K 14327*	33	7 wks
15 Jan 77	THE WRECK OF THE EDMUND FITZGERALD *Reprise K 14451*	40	4 wks
16 Sep 78	DAYLIGHT KATY *Warner Bros. K 17214*	41	6 wks

Terry LIGHTFOOT and his NEW ORLEANS JAZZMEN *UK, male*
vocal/instrumental group, Terry Lightfoot clarinet and vocals *17 wks*

7 Sep 61	TRUE LOVE *Columbia DB 4696*	33	4 wks
23 Nov 61	KING KONG *Columbia SCD 2165*	29	12 wks
3 May 62	TAVERN IN THE TOWN *Columbia DB 4822*	49	1 wk

LIMAHL *UK, male vocalist* *23 wks*

5 Nov 83	ONLY FOR LOVE *EMI LML 1*	16	8 wks
2 Jun 84	TOO MUCH TROUBLE *EMI LML 2*	64	3 wks
13 Oct 84 ●	NEVER ENDING STORY *EMI LML 3*	4†	12 wks

LIMMIE and the FAMILY COOKIN' *US, male/female vocal group* *28 wks*

21 Jul 73 ●	YOU CAN DO MAGIC *Avco 6105 019*	3	13 wks
20 Oct 73	DREAMBOAT *Avco 6105 025*	31	5 wks
6 Apr 74 ●	A WALKIN' MIRACLE *Avco 6105 027*	6	10 wks

Bob LIND *US, male vocalist* *10 wks*

10 Mar 66 ●	ELUSIVE BUTTERFLY *Fontana TF 670*	5	9 wks
26 May 66	REMEMBER THE RAIN *Fontana TF 702*	46	1 wk

LINDA and the FUNKY BOYS *US,*
female vocalist, male vocal/instrumental backing group *4 wks*

5 Jun 76	SOLD MY SOUL FOR ROCK 'N ROLL *Spark SRL 1139*	36	4 wks

Linda is Linda Carr. *See also Linda Carr and the Love Squad.*

LINDISFARNE
UK, male vocal/instrumental group *46 wks*

26 Feb 72 ●	MEET ME ON THE CORNER *Charisma CB 173*	5	11 wks
13 May 72 ●	LADY ELEANOR *Charisma CB 153*	3	11 wks
23 Sep 72	ALL FALL DOWN *Charisma CB 191*	34	5 wks
3 Jun 78 ●	RUN FOR HOME *Mercury 6007 177*	10	15 wks
7 Oct 78	JUKE BOX GYPSY *Mercury 6007 187*	56	4 wks

LINER *UK, male vocal/instrumental group* *6 wks*

10 Mar 79	KEEP REACHING OUT FOR LOVE *Atlantic K 11235*	49	3 wks
26 May 79	YOU AND ME *Atlantic K 11285*	44	3 wks

LOS BRAVOS (from the top) Miguel, Pablo, Antonio, Mike and Manolo.

HANK LOCKLIN (right) His new tuning process.

LITTLE EVA (right) Gerry Goffin and Carole King's former babysitter snapped on a visit to Liverpool.

LIMAHL (below) Former Kajagoogoo man Chris Hamill, whose professional name is an anagram of his surname.

Laurie LINGO and the DIPSTICKS
UK, male vocal duo, disc jockeys Dave Lee Travis and Paul Burnett   *7 wks*

17 Apr	76	● CONVOY G. B. *State STAT 23*	4	7 wks

LINX   *UK, male vocal/instrumental group*   *45 wks*

20 Sep	80	YOU'RE LYING *Chrysalis CHS 2461*	15	10 wks
7 Mar	81	● INTUITION *Chrysalis CHS 2500*	7	11 wks
13 Jun	81	THROW AWAY THE KEY *Chrysalis CHS 2519*	21	9 wks
5 Sep	81	SO THIS IS ROMANCE *Chrysalis CHS 2546*	15	9 wks
21 Nov	81	CAN'T HELP MYSELF *Chrysalis CHS 2565* ..	55	3 wks
10 Jul	82	PLAYTHING *Chrysalis CHS 2621*	48	3 wks

LIPPS INC.
US, male/female vocal/instrumental group   *13 wks*

17 May	80	● FUNKYTOWN *Casablanca CAN 194*	2	13 wks

LIQUID GOLD
UK, male/female vocal/instrumental group   *46 wks*

2 Dec	78	ANYWAY YOU DO IT *Creole CR 159*	41	7 wks
23 Feb	80	● DANCE YOURSELF DIZZY *Polo 1*	2	14 wks
31 May	80	● SUBSTITUTE *Polo POLO 4*	8	9 wks
1 Nov	80	THE NIGHT THE WINE AND THE ROSES *POLO 6*	32	7 wks
28 Mar	81	DON'T PANIC *Polo POLO 8*	42	5 wks
21 Aug	82	WHERE DID WE GO WRONG *Polo POLO 23*	56	4 wks

De Etta LITTLE and Nelson PIGFORD   *US, female/male vocal duo*   *5 wks*

13 Aug	77	YOU TAKE MY HEART AWAY *United Artists UP 36257*	35	5 wks

LITTLE ANTHONY and the IMPERIALS   *US, male vocal group*   *4 wks*

31 Jul	76	BETTER USE YOUR HEAD *United Artists UP 36118*	42	4 wks

See also Imperials

LITTLE EVA   *US, female vocalist*   *44 wks*

6 Sep	62	● THE LOCO-MOTION *London HL 9581*	2	17 wks
3 Jan	63	KEEP YOUR HANDS OFF MY BABY *London HLU 9633*	30	4 wks
7 Mar	63	LET'S TURKEY TROT *London HLU 9687*	13	12 wks
29 Jul	72	THE LOCO-MOTION (re-entry) *London HL 9581*	11	11 wks

See also Big Dee Irwin.

LITTLE RICHARD
US, male vocalist/instrumentalist - piano   *104 wks*

14 Dec	56	RIP IT UP *London HLO 8336*	30	1 wk
8 Feb	57	● LONG TALL SALLY *London HLO 8366*	3	16 wks
22 Feb	57	TUTTI FRUTTI *London HLO 8366*	29	1 wk
8 Mar	57	SHE'S GOT IT *London HLO 8382*	15	7 wks
15 Mar	57	● THE GIRL CAN'T HELP IT *London HLO 8382*	9	11 wks
24 May	57	SHE'S GOT IT (re-entry) *London HLO 8382*	28	2 wks
28 Jun	57	● LUCILLE *London HLO 8446*	10	9 wks
13 Sep	57	JENNY JENNY *London HLO 8470*	11	5 wks
29 Nov	57	KEEP A KNOCKIN' *London HLO 8509*	21	7 wks

28 Feb	58	● GOOD GOLLY MISS MOLLY *London HLU 8560*	8	9 wks
11 Jul	58	OOH MY SOUL *London HLO 8647*	30	1 wk
25 Jul	58	OOH MY SOUL (re-entry) *London HLO 8647*	22	3 wks
2 Jan	59	● BABY FACE *London HLU 8770*	2	15 wks
3 Apr	59	BY THE LIGHT OF THE SILVERY MOON *London HLU 8831*	17	5 wks
5 Jun	59	KANSAS CITY *London HLU 8868*	26	5 wks
11 Oct	62	HE GOT WHAT HE WANTED *Mercury AMT 1189*	38	4 wks
4 Jun	64	BAMA LAMA BAMA LOO *London HL 9896*	20	7 wks
2 Jul	77	GOOD GOLLY MISS MOLLY/RIP IT UP *Creole CR 140*	37	4 wks

The versions of Good Golly Miss Molly and Rip It Up on Creole are re-recordings.

LITTLE TONY   *Italy, male vocalist*   *3 wks*

15 Jan	60	TOO GOOD *Decca F 11190*	19	3 wks

LIVERPOOL EXPRESS
UK, male vocal/instrumental group   *26 wks*

26 Jun	76	YOU ARE MY LOVE *Warner Bros. K 16743*	11	9 wks
16 Oct	76	HOLD TIGHT *Warner Bros. K 16799*	46	2 wks
18 Dec	76	EVERY MAN MUST HAVE A DREAM *Warner Bros. K 16854*	17	11 wks
4 Jun	77	DREAMIN' *Warner Bros. K 16933*	40	4 wks

LIVERPOOL FOOTBALL TEAM
UK, male football team vocalists   *8 wks*

28 May	77	WE CAN DO IT (EP) *State STAT 50*	15	4 wks
23 Apr	83	LIVERPOOL (WE'RE NEVER...)/ANTHEM *Mow MEAN 102*	54	4 wks

Tracks on We Can Do It EP: We Can Do It/Liverpool Lou/ We Shall Not Be Moved/You'll Never Walk Alone.

Dandy LIVINGSTONE
Jamaica, male vocalist   *19 wks*

2 Sep	72	SUZANNE BEWARE OF THE DEVIL *Horse HOSS 16*	14	11 wks
13 Jan	73	BIG CITY/THINK ABOUT THAT *Horse HOSS 25*	26	8 wks

LOBO   *US, male vocalist*   *25 wks*

19 Jun	71	● ME AND YOU AND A DOG NAMED BOO *Philips 6073 801*	4	14 wks
8 Jun	74	● I'D LOVE YOU TO WANT ME *UK 68*	5	11 wks

LOBO   *Holland, male vocalist*   *11 wks*

25 Jul	81	● THE CARIBBEAN DISCO SHOW *Polydor POSP 302*	8	11 wks

Hank LOCKLIN   *US, male vocalist*   *41 wks*

11 Aug	60	● PLEASE HELP ME I'M FALLING *RCA 1188* ..	9	19 wks
15 Feb	62	FROM HERE TO THERE TO YOU *RCA 1273*	44	3 wks
15 Nov	62	WE'RE GONNA GO FISHIN' *RCA 1305*	18	11 wks
5 May	66	I FEEL A CRY COMING ON *RCA 1510*	28	8 wks

LOCKSMITH
US, male vocal/instrumental group   *6 wks*

23 Aug	80	UNLOCK THE FUNK *Arista ARIST 364*	42	6 wks

LOCOMOTIVE
UK, male vocal/instrumental group — 8 wks

16 Oct 68	**RUDI'S IN LOVE** Parlophone R 5718	**25**	8 wks

John LODGE - See Justin HAYWARD and John LODGE

Johnny LOGAN Australia, male vocalist — 8 wks

3 May 80	★ **WHAT'S ANOTHER YEAR** Epic EPC 8572	**1**	8 wks

Johnny Logan, although Australian, represented Ireland in the 1980 Eurovision Song Contest.

Kenny LOGGINS US, male vocalist — 10 wks

28 Apr 84	● **FOOTLOOSE** CBS A 4101	**6**	10 wks

Julie LONDON US, female vocalist — 3 wks

5 Apr 57	**CRY ME A RIVER** London HLU 8240	**22**	3 wks

Laurie LONDON UK, male vocalist — 12 wks

8 Nov 57	**HE'S GOT THE WHOLE WORLD IN HIS HANDS** Parlophone R 4359	**12**	12 wks

LONDON STRING CHORALE
UK, orchestra/choir — 13 wks

15 Dec 73	**GALLOPING HOME** Polydor 2058 280	**49**	3 wks
19 Jan 74	**GALLOPING HOME** (re-entry) Polydor 2058 280	**31**	10 wks

LONDON SYMPHONY ORCHESTRA UK, orchestra — 5 wks

6 Jan 79	**THEME FROM 'SUPERMAN'** (MAIN TITLE) Warner Bros. K 17292	**32**	5 wks

Orchestra conducted by John Williams.

Shorty LONG US, male vocalist — 7 wks

17 Jul 68	**HERE COMES THE JUDGE** Tamla Motown TMG 663	**30**	7 wks

LONG AND THE SHORT
UK, male vocal/instrumental group — 8 wks

10 Sep 64	**THE LETTER** Decca F 11959	**30**	5 wks
24 Dec 64	**CHOC ICE** Decca F 12043	**49**	3 wks

LOOK UK, male vocal/instrumental group — 15 wks

20 Dec 80	● **I AM THE BEAT** MCA 647	**6**	12 wks
29 Aug 81	**FEEDING TIME** MCA 736	**50**	3 wks

LOOSE ENDS
UK, male/female vocal/instrumental group — 10 wks

25 Feb 84	**TELL ME WHAT YOU WANT** Virgin VS 658	**74**	1 wk
28 Apr 84	**EMERGENCY (DIAL 999)** Virgin VS 677	**41**	6 wks
21 Jul 84	**CHOOSE ME (RESCUE ME)** Virgin VS 697	**59**	3 wks

Trini LOPEZ US, male vocalist — 37 wks

12 Sep 63	● **IF I HAD A HAMMER** Reprise R 20198	**4**	17 wks
12 Dec 63	**KANSAS CITY** Reprise R 20236	**35**	5 wks
12 May 66	**I'M COMING HOME CINDY** Reprise R 20455 ..	**28**	5 wks
6 Apr 67	**GONNA GET ALONG WITHOUT YA NOW** Reprise R 20547	**41**	5 wks
19 Dec 81	**TRINI TRACKS** RCA 154	**59**	5 wks

Jerry LORDAN UK, male vocalist — 15 wks

8 Jan 60	**I'LL STAY SINGLE** Parlophone R 4588	**26**	2 wks
26 Feb 60	**WHO COULD BE BLUER** Parlophone R 4627 ...	**17**	9 wks
10 Mar 60	**I'LL STAY SINGLE** (re-entry) Parlophone R 4588	**41**	1 wk
19 May 60	**WHO COULD BE BLUER** (re-entry) Parlophone R 4627	**45**	1 wk
2 Jun 60	**SING LIKE AN ANGEL** Parlophone R 4653	**36**	2 wks

Sophia LOREN - See Peter SELLERS and Sophia LOREN

LORI and the CHAMELEONS
UK, male/female vocal/instrumental group — 1 wk

8 Dec 79	**TOUCH** Sire SIR 4025	**70**	1 wk

LOS INDIOS TABAJARAS
Brazil, male instrumental duo - guitars — 17 wks

31 Oct 63	● **MARIA ELENA** RCA 1365	**5**	17 wks

LOS BRAVOS
Spain/Germany, male vocal/instrumental group — 24 wks

30 Jun 66	● **BLACK IS BLACK** Decca F 22419	**2**	13 wks
8 Sep 66	**I DON'T CARE** Decca F 13367	**16**	11 wks

Joe LOSS UK, orchestra — 53 wks

29 Jun 61	**WHEELS CHA CHA** HMV POP 880	**21**	21 wks
19 Oct 61	**SUCU SUCU** HMV POP 937	**48**	1 wk
29 Mar 62	**THE MAIGRET THEME** HMV POP 995	**20**	10 wks
1 Nov 62	**MUST BE MADISON** HMV POP 1075	**20**	13 wks
5 Nov 64	**MARCH OF THE MODS** HMV POP 1351	**35**	4 wks
24 Dec 64	**MARCH OF THE MODS** (re-entry) HMV POP 1351	**31**	4 wks

LOTUS EATERS
UK, male vocal/instrumental group — 16 wks

2 Jul 83	**FIRST PICTURE OF YOU** Sylvan/Arista SYL 1	**15**	12 wks
8 Oct 83	**YOU DON'T NEED SOMEONE NEW** Sylvan/Arista SYL 2	**53**	4 wks

Bonnie LOU US, female vocalist — 10 wks

5 Feb 54	● **TENNESSEE WIG WALK** Parlophone R 3730 ...	**4**	10 wks

John D. LOUDERMILK
US, male vocalist — 10 wks

4 Jan 62	**THE LANGUAGE OF LOVE** RCA 1269	**13**	10 wks

Geoff LOVE - See MANUEL and his MUSIC OF THE MOUNTAINS

LOVE AFFAIR
UK, male vocal/instrumental group   *56 wks*

3 Jan 68	★ EVERLASTING LOVE *CBS 3125*	**1**	12 wks
17 Apr 68	● RAINBOW VALLEY *CBS 3366*	**5**	13 wks
11 Sep 68	● A DAY WITHOUT LOVE *CBS 3674*	**6**	12 wks
19 Feb 69	ONE ROAD *CBS 3994*	**16**	9 wks
16 Jul 69	● BRINGING ON BACK THE GOOD TIMES *CBS 4300*	**9**	10 wks

LOVE SCULPTURE
UK, instrumental group   *14 wks*

27 Nov 68	● SABRE DANCE *Parlophone R 5744*	**5**	14 wks

LOVE SQUAD   - *See Linda CARR and the LOVE SQUAD*

LOVE UNLIMITED
US, female vocal group   *19 wks*

17 Jun 72	WALKIN' IN THE RAIN WITH THE ONE I LOVE *Uni UN 539*	**14**	10 wks
25 Jan 75	IT MAY BE WINTER OUTSIDE (BUT IN MY HEART IT'S SPRING) *20th Century BTC 2149*	**11**	9 wks

LOVE UNLIMITED ORCHESTRA
US, orchestra   *10 wks*

2 Feb 74	● LOVE'S THEME *Pye International 7N 25635*	**10**	10 wks

Bill LOVELADY   *UK, male vocalist*   *10 wks*

18 Aug 79	REGGAE FOR IT NOW *Charisma CB 337*	**12**	10 wks

Lene LOVICH   *US, female vocalist*   *38 wks*

17 Feb 79	● LUCKY NUMBER *Stiff BUY 42*	**3**	11 wks
12 May 79	SAY WHEN *Stiff BUY 46*	**19**	10 wks
20 Oct 79	BIRD SONG *Stiff BUY 53*	**39**	7 wks
29 Mar 80	WHAT WILL I DO WITHOUT YOU *Stiff BUY 69*	**58**	3 wks
14 Mar 81	NEW TOY *Stiff BUY 97*	**53**	5 wks
27 Nov 82	IT'S YOU, ONLY YOU (MEIN SCHMERZ) *Stiff BUY 164*	**68**	2 wks

LOVIN' SPOONFUL
US/Canada, male vocal/instrumental group   *33 wks*

14 Apr 66	● DAYDREAM *Pye International 7N 25361*	**2**	13 wks
14 Jul 66	● SUMMER IN THE CITY *Kama Sutra KAS 200* ..	**8**	11 wks
5 Jan 67	NASHVILLE CATS *Kama Sutra KAS 204*	**26**	7 wks
9 Mar 67	DARLING BE HOME SOON *Kama Sutra KAS 207*	**44**	2 wks

Gary LOW   *UK, male vocalist*   *3 wks*

8 Oct 83	I WANT YOU *Savoir Faire FAIS 004*	**52**	3 wks

Jim LOWE   *US, male vocalist*   *9 wks*

26 Oct 56	● THE GREEN DOOR *London HLD 8317*	**8**	9 wks

Nick LOWE   *UK, male vocalist*   *27 wks*

11 Mar 78	● I LOVE THE SOUND OF BREAKING GLASS *Radar ADA 1*	**7**	8 wks
9 Jun 79	CRACKIN' UP *Radar ADA 34*	**34**	5 wks
25 Aug 79	CRUEL TO BE KIND *Radar ADA 43*	**12**	11 wks
26 May 84	HALF A BOY HALF A MAN *F. Beat XX 34* ...	**53**	3 wks

LOWRELL   *US, male vocalist*   *9 wks*

24 Nov 79	MELLOW MELLOW RIGHT ON *AVI AVIS 108*	**37**	9 wks

L.T.D.   *US, male vocal/instrumental group*   *3 wks*

9 Sep 78	HOLDING ON *A & M AMS 7378*	**70**	3 wks

Carrie LUCAS   *US, female vocalist*   *6 wks*

16 Jun 79	DANCE WITH YOU *Solar FB 1482*	**40**	6 wks

LUIGI   - *See HUGO and LUIGI*

Robin LUKE   *US, male vocalist*   *6 wks*

17 Oct 58	SUSIE DARLIN' *London HLD 8676*	**24**	3 wks
21 Nov 58	SUSIE DARLIN' (re-entry) *London HLD 8676*	**23**	1 wk
5 Dec 58	SUSIE DARLIN' (2nd re-entry) *London HLD 8676*	**23**	2 wks

LULU   *UK, female vocalist*   *122 wks*

14 May 64	● SHOUT *Decca F 11884*	**7**	13 wks
12 Nov 64	HERE COMES THE NIGHT *Decca F 12017* ...	**50**	1 wk
17 Jun 65	● LEAVE A LITTLE LOVE *Decca F 12169*	**8**	11 wks
2 Sep 65	TRY TO UNDERSTAND *Decca F 12214*	**25**	8 wks
13 Apr 67	● THE BOAT THAT I ROW *Columbia DB 8169* ..	**6**	11 wks
29 Jun 67	LET'S PRETEND *Columbia DB 8221*	**11**	11 wks
8 Nov 67	LOVE LOVES TO LOVE LOVE *Columbia DB 8295*	**32**	6 wks
28 Feb 68	● ME THE PEACEFUL HEART *Columbia DB 8358*	**9**	9 wks
5 Jun 68	BOY *Columbia DB 8425*	**15**	7 wks
6 Nov 68	● I'M A TIGER *Columbia DB 8500*	**9**	13 wks
12 Mar 69	● BOOM BANG-A-BANG *Columbia DB 8550*	**2**	13 wks
22 Nov 69	OH ME OH MY (I'M A FOOL FOR YOU BABY) *Atco 226 008*	**47**	2 wks
26 Jan 74	● THE MAN WHO SOLD THE WORLD *Polydor 2001 490*	**3**	9 wks
19 Apr 75	TAKE YOUR MAMA FOR A RIDE *Chelsea 2005 022*	**37**	4 wks
12 Dec 81	I COULD NEVER MISS YOU (MORE THAN I DO) *Alfa ALFA 1700*	**62**	3 wks
16 Jan 82	I COULD NEVER MISS YOU (MORE THAN I DO) (re-entry) *Alfa ALFA 1700*	**63**	1 wk

Shout *credited to Lulu and The Luvvers.*

Bob LUMAN   *US, male vocalist*   *21 wks*

8 Sep 60	● LET'S THINK ABOUT LIVING *Warner Bros. WB 18*	**6**	18 wks
15 Dec 60	WHY WHY BYE BYE *Warner Bros. WB 28*	**46**	1 wk
4 May 61	THE GREAT SNOWMAN *Warner Bros. WB 37*	**49**	2 wks

LURKERS
UK, male vocal/instrumental group   *11 wks*

3 Jun 78	AIN'T GOT A CLUE *Beggars Banquet BEG 6*	**45**	3 wks
5 Aug 78	I DON'T NEED TO TELL HER *Beggars Banquet BEG 9*	**49**	4 wks
3 Feb 79	JUST THIRTEEN *Beggars Banquet BEG 14*	**66**	2 wks

9 Jun 79	**OUT IN THE DARK/CYANIDE**		
	Beggars Banquet BEG 19	**72**	1 wk
17 Nov 79	**NEW GUITAR IN TOWN**		
	Beggars Banquet BEG 28	**72**	1 wk

LUVVERS - *See LULU*

LYLE - *See GALLAGHER and LYLE*

Frankie LYMON and the TEENAGERS *US, male vocal group* 38 wks

29 Jun 56 ★	**WHY DO FOOLS FALL IN LOVE**		
	Columbia DB 3772	**1**	16 wks
29 Mar 57	**I'M NOT A JUVENILE DELINQUENT**		
	Columbia DB 3878	**12**	7 wks
12 Apr 57 ●	**BABY BABY** Columbia DB 3878	**4**	12 wks
20 Sep 57	**GOODY GOODY** Columbia DB 3983	**24**	3 wks

First hit billed the group as The Teenagers Featuring Frankie Lymon.

Kenny LYNCH *UK, male vocalist* 59 wks

30 Jun 60	**MOUNTAIN OF LOVE** HMV POP 751	**33**	3 wks
13 Sep 62	**PUFF** HMV POP 1057	**33**	5 wks
25 Oct 62	**PUFF** (re-entry) HMV POP 1057	**46**	1 wk
6 Dec 62 ●	**UP ON THE ROOF** HMV POP 1090	**10**	12 wks
20 Jun 63 ●	**YOU CAN NEVER STOP ME LOVING YOU**		
	HMV POP 1165	**10**	14 wks
16 Apr 64	**STAND BY ME** HMV POP 1280	**39**	7 wks
27 Aug 64	**WHAT AM I TO DO** HMV POP 1321	**37**	4 wks
1 Oct 64	**WHAT AM I TO DO** (re-entry) HMV POP 1321	**44**	2 wks
17 Jun 65	**I'LL STAY BY YOU** HMV POP 1430	**29**	7 wks
20 Aug 83	**HALF THE DAY'S GONE AND WE HAVN'T EARNED A PENNY** Satril SAT 510	**50**	4 wks

Cheryl LYNN *US, female vocalist* 2 wks

8 Sep 84	**ENCORE** Streetwave KHAN 23	**68**	2 wks

Patti LYNN *UK, female vocalist* 5 wks

10 May 62	**JOHNNY ANGEL** Fontana H 391	**37**	5 wks

Tami LYNN *US, female vocalist* 20 wks

22 May 71 ●	**I'M GONNA RUN AWAY FROM YOU**		
	Mojo 2092 001	**4**	14 wks
3 May 75	**I'M GONNA RUN AWAY FROM YOU** (re-issue)		
	Contempo Raries CS 9026	**36**	6 wks

Vera LYNN *UK, female vocalist* 46 wks

14 Nov 52 ●	**HOMING WALTZ** Decca F 9959	**9**	3 wks
14 Nov 52 ●	**AUF WIEDERSEHEN** Decca F 9927	**10**	1 wk
14 Nov 52 ●	**FORGET ME NOT** Decca F 9985	**7**	1 wk
28 Nov 52 ●	**FORGET ME NOT** (re-entry) Decca F 9985	**5**	5 wks
5 Jun 53	**WINDSOR WALTZ** Decca F 10092	**11**	1 wk
15 Oct 54 ★	**MY SON MY SON** Decca F 10372	**1**	14 wks
8 Jun 56	**WHO ARE WE** Decca F 10715	**30**	1 wk
26 Oct 56	**A HOUSE WITH LOVE IN IT** Decca F 10799 ..	**17**	13 wks
15 Mar 57	**THE FAITHFUL HUSSAR (DON'T CRY MY LOVE)** Decca F 10846	**29**	2 wks
21 Jun 57	**TRAVELLIN' HOME** Decca F 10903	**20**	5 wks

Carol LYNN TOWNES
US, female vocalist 4 wks

4 Aug 84	**99 1/2** Polydor POSP 693	**47**	4 wks

Philip LYNOTT *Ireland, male vocalist* 24 wks

5 Apr 80	**DEAR MISS LONELY HEARTS** Vertigo SOLO 1	**32**	6 wks
21 Jun 80	**KING'S CALL** Vertigo SOLO 2	**35**	6 wks
21 Mar 81	**YELLOW PEARL** Vertigo SOLO 3	**56**	3 wks
26 Dec 81	**YELLOW PEARL** (re-entry) Vertigo SOLO 3	**14**	9 wks

LYNYRD SKYNYRD
US, male vocal/instrumental group 21 wks

11 Sep 76	**FREE BIRD** (EP) MCA 251	**31**	4 wks
22 Dec 79	**FREE BIRD** (EP) (re-entry) MCA 251	**43**	8 wks
19 Jun 82	**FREE BIRD** (EP) (2nd re-entry) MCA 251	**21**	9 wks

Tracks on EP: Free Bird/Sweet Home Alabama/Double Trouble

Barbara LYON *US, female vocalist* 12 wks

24 Jun 55	**STOWAWAY** Columbia DB 3619	**12**	8 wks
21 Dec 56	**LETTER TO A SOLDIER** Columbia DB 3685 ...	**27**	4 wks

Humphrey LYTTELTON BAND
UK, male instrumental group, Humphrey Lyttelton - trumpet 6 wks

12 Jul 56	**BAD PENNY BLUES** Parlophone R 4184	**19**	6 wks

M

M *UK, male vocalist/multi-instrumentalist* 30 wks

7 Apr 79 ●	**POP MUZIK** MCA 413	**2**	14 wks
8 Dec 79	**MOONLIGHT AND MUZAK** MCA 541	**33**	9 wks
15 Mar 80	**THAT'S THE WAY THE MONEY GOES**		
	MCA 570	**45**	5 wks
22 Nov 80	**OFFICIAL SECRETS** MCA 650	**64**	2 wks

M is Robin Scott.

M + M *Canada, male/female vocal duo* 4 wks

28 Jul 84	**BLACK STATIONS WHITE STATIONS**		
	RCA 426	**46**	4 wks

M and O BAND
US, male vocal/instrumental group 6 wks

28 Feb 76	**LET'S DO THE LATIN HUSTLE** Creole CR 120	**16**	6 wks

Bobby M
US, male/female vocal/instrumental duo 3 wks

29 Jan 83	**LET'S STAY TOGETHER** Gordy TMG 1288 ...	**53**	3 wks

Hit has credit: featuring Jean Carn

Lorin MAAZEL - *See PHILHARMONIA ORCHESTRA, conductor Lorin MAAZEL*

Neil MacARTHUR *UK, male vocalist* 5 wks

5 Feb 69	**SHE'S NOT THERE** Deram DM 225	**34**	5 wks

Neil MacArthur is Colin Blunstone under a false name. See also Colin Blunstone; Dave Stewart.

HANK MARVIN (right) In his busking days (1984): 31 hits with The Shadows, 30 with Cliff Richard, and one solo success.

KEITH MARSHALL (above) Former member of Hello scored with 'Only Crying' but lost out with his cover of the Temptations – 'Since I Lost My Baby'.

MALCOLM McCLAREN (above) The man behind the Sex Pistols and Bow Wow Wow hits clocked up five of his own by the end of 1984.

MARILYN (right) A little application to cover the stubble.

MARTHA AND THE VANDELLAS (above) The first record that the former Motown secretary and her colleagues appeared on was Marvin Gaye's 'Stubborn Kind Of Fellow'.

MASSIEL (above) She won the 13th Eurovision Song Contest in 1968 with 'La La La' beating the British entry Cliff Richard's 'Congratulations'.

David MacBETH   UK, male vocalist   4 wks

30 Oct 59	**MR. BLUE**	Pye 7N 15231	....	18	4 wks

Kirsty MacCOLL   UK, female vocalist   9 wks

13 Jun 81	**THERE'S A GUY WORKS DOWN THE CHIPSHOP SWEARS HE'S ELVIS**				
	Polydor POSP 250	....	14	9 wks	

Frankie McBRIDE   Ireland, male vocalist   15 wks

9 Aug 67	**FIVE LITTLE FINGERS**	Emerald MD 1081	.....	19	15 wks

Dan McCAFFERTY   UK, male vocalist   3 wks

13 Sep 75	**OUT OF TIME**	Mountain TOP 1	....	41	3 wks

C. W. McCALL   US, male vocalist   10 wks

14 Feb 76	● **CONVOY**	MGM 2006 560	....	2	10 wks

David McCALLUM   UK, male vocalist   4 wks

14 Apr 66	**COMMUNICATION**	Capitol CL 15439	....	32	4 wks

Linda **McCARTNEY**   - See Paul McCARTNEY

Paul McCARTNEY   UK, male vocalist   85 wks

27 Feb 71	● **ANOTHER DAY**	Apple R 5889	....	2	12 wks
28 Aug 71	**BACK SEAT OF MY CAR**	Apple R 5914	....	39	5 wks
1 Dec 79	● **WONDERFUL CHRISTMASTIME**				
	Parlophone R 6029			6	8 wks
19 Apr 80	● **COMING UP**	Parlophone R 6035	......	2	9 wks
21 Jun 80	● **WATERFALLS**	Parlophone R 6037	......	9	8 wks
3 Jul 82	**TAKE IT AWAY**	Parlophone R 6056	......	15	10 wks
9 Oct 82	**TUG OF WAR**	Parlophone R 6057	......	53	3 wks
17 Dec 83	★ **PIPES OF PEACE**	Parlophone R 6064	......	1	11 wks
6 Oct 84	● **NO MORE LONELY NIGHTS**	Parlophone R 6080		2†	13 wks
24 Nov 84	● **WE ALL STAND TOGETHER**	Parlophone R 6086		3†	6 wks

See also Paul McCartney with Stevie Wonder; Michael Jackson and Paul McCartney;
Beatles; Wings; Back Seat Of My Car credited to Paul and Linda McCartney.

Paul McCARTNEY with Stevie WONDER   UK/US, male vocal duo   10 wks

10 Apr 82	★ **EBONY AND IVORY**	Panophone R 6054	....	1	10 wks

See also Paul McCartney; Beatles; Wings; Michael Jackson and Paul McCartney; Stevie
Wonder; Diana Ross, Marvin Gaye, Smokey Robinson and Stevie Wonder.

Marilyn McCOO and Billy DAVIS JR.   US, female/male vocal duo   9 wks

19 Mar 77	● **YOU DON'T HAVE TO BE A STAR (TO BE IN MY SHOW)**	ABC 4147	....	7	9 wks

Van McCOY   US, orchestra   36 wks

31 May 75	● **THE HUSTLE**	Avco 6105 037	....	3	12 wks
1 Nov 75	**CHANGE WITH THE TIMES**	Avco 6105 042	...	36	4 wks
12 Feb 77	**SOUL CHA CHA**	H & L 6105 065	......	34	6 wks
9 Apr 77	● **THE SHUFFLE**	H & L 6105 076	......	4	14 wks

First hit featured the Soul City Symphony.

McCOYS   US, male vocal/instrumental group   18 wks

2 Sep 65	● **HANG ON SLOOPY**	Immediate IM 001	....	5	14 wks
16 Dec 65	**FEVER**	Immediate IM 021	....	44	4 wks

George McCRAE   US, male vocalist   62 wks

29 Jun 74	★ **ROCK YOUR BABY**	Jayboy BOY 85	....	1	14 wks
5 Oct 74	● **I CAN'T LEAVE YOU ALONE**	Jayboy BOY 90		9	9 wks
14 Dec 74	**YOU CAN HAVE IT ALL**	Jayboy BOY 92		23	9 wks
22 Mar 75	**SING A HAPPY SONG**	Jayboy BOY 95		38	4 wks
19 Jul 75	● **IT'S BEEN SO LONG**	Jayboy BOY 100		4	11 wks
18 Oct 75	**I AIN'T LYIN'**	Jayboy BOY 105		12	7 wks
24 Jan 76	**HONEY I**	Jayboy BOY 107	....	33	4 wks
25 Feb 84	**ONE STEP CLOSER (TO LOVE)**				
	President PT 522	....	57	4 wks	

McCRARYS
US, male vocal/instrumental group   4 wks

31 Jul 82	**LOVE ON A SUMMER NIGHT**	Capitol CL 251		52	4 wks

Ian McCULLOCH   UK, male vocalist   3 wks

15 Dec 84	**SEPTEMBER SONG**	Korova KOW 40	....	51†	3 wks

Gene McDANIELS   US, male vocalist   2 wks

16 Nov 61	**TOWER OF STRENGTH**	London HLG 9448	....	49	1 wk
30 Nov 61	**TOWER OF STRENGTH**	(re-entry)		49	1 wk
	London HLG 9448	....			

Charles McDEVITT SKIFFLE GROUP featuring Nancy WHISKEY
UK, male/female vocal/instrumental group   20 wks

12 Apr 57	● **FREIGHT TRAIN**	Oriole CB 1352	....	5	17 wks
14 Jun 57	**GREENBACK DOLLAR**	Oriole CB 1371		28	1 wk
5 Jun 57	**GREENBACK DOLLAR**	(re-entry) Oriole CB 1371		30	1 wk
20 Sep 57	**FREIGHT TRAIN**	(re-entry) Oriole CB 1352	.....	27	1 wk

Michael **McDONALD**   - See James INGRAM with Michael McDONALD

McFADDEN and WHITEHEAD
US, male vocal duo   10 wks

19 May 79	● **AIN'T NO STOPPIN' US NOW**				
	Philadelphia International PIR 7365	....	5	10 wks	

Mike McGEAR   UK, male vocalist   4 wks

5 Oct 74	**LEAVE IT**	Warner Bros. K 16446	....	36	4 wks

Maureen McGOVERN
US, female vocalist   8 wks

5 Jun 76	**THE CONTINENTAL**	20th Century BTC 2222	..	16	8 wks

Mary MacGREGOR   US, female vocalist   10 wks

19 Feb 77	● **TORN BETWEEN TWO LOVERS**				
	Ariola America AA 111	....	4	10 wks	

McGUINNESS FLINT
UK, male vocal/instrumental group — 26 wks

21 Nov 70 ●	WHEN I'M DEAD AND GONE *Capitol CL 15662*	2	14 wks
1 May 71 ●	MALT AND BARLEY BLUES *Capitol CL 15682*	5	12 wks

Barry McGUIRE *US, male vocalist* — 13 wks

9 Sep 65 ●	EVE OF DESTRUCTION *RCA 1469*	3	13 wks

McGUIRE SISTERS
US, female vocal group — 24 wks

1 Apr 55	NO MORE *Vogue Coral Q 72050*	20	1 wk
15 Jul 55	SINCERELY *Vogue Coral Q 72050*	14	4 wks
1 Jun 56	DELILAH JONES *Vogue Coral Q 72161*	24	2 wks
14 Feb 58	SUGARTIME *Coral Q 72305*	14	6 wks
1 May 59	MAY YOU ALWAYS *Coral Q 72356*	15	10 wks
17 Jul 59	MAY YOU ALWAYS (re-entry) *Coral Q 72356* ..	28	1 wk

Peter MacJUNIOR *US, male vocalist* — 4 wks

15 Oct 77	THE WATER MARGIN *BBC RESL 50*	37	4 wks

This is the Japanese version of the song which shared chart credit with the English language version by Godiego. See also Godiego

Lonnie MACK
US, male instrumentalist - guitar — 3 wks

14 Apr 79	MEMPHIS *Lightning LIG 9011*	47	3 wks

Memphis was coupled with Let's Dance by Chris Montez as a double A-side. See also Chris Montez.

Kenneth McKELLAR *UK, male vocalist* — 4 wks

10 Mar 66	A MAN WITHOUT LOVE *Decca F 12341*	30	4 wks

Gisele McKENZIE
Canada, female vocalist — 6 wks

17 Jul 53	SEVEN LONELY DAYS *Capitol CL 13920*	12	1 wk
31 Jul 53	SEVEN LONELY DAYS (re-entry) *Capitol CL 13920*	11	1 wk
21 Aug 53 ●	SEVEN LONELY DAYS (2nd re-entry) *Capitol CL 13920*	6	4 wks

Scott McKENZIE *US, male vocalist* — 18 wks

12 Jul 67 ★	SAN FRANCISCO (BE SURE TO WEAR FLOWERS IN YOUR HAIR) *CBS 2816*	1	17 wks
1 Nov 67	LIKE AN OLD TIME MOVIE *CBS 3009*	50	1 wk

Second hit credited to The Voice Of Scott McKenzie.

Ken MACKINTOSH *UK, orchestra* — 9 wks

15 Jan 54	THE CREEP *HMV BD 1295*	12	1 wk
29 Jan 54 ●	THE CREEP (re-entry) *HMV BD 1295*	10	1 wk
7 Feb 58	RAUNCHY *HMV POP 426*	19	6 wks
10 Mar 60	NO HIDING PLACE *HMV POP 713*	45	1 wk

Tommy McLAIN *US, male vocalist* — 1 wk

8 Sep 66	SWEET DREAMS *London HL 10065*	49	1 wk

McLAIN - *See PRATT and McLAIN with BROTHERLOVE*

Malcolm McLAREN *UK, male vocalist* — 44 wks

4 Dec 82 ●	BUFFALO GALS *Charisma/Phonogram MALC 1* ..	9	12 wks
26 Feb 83	SOWETO *Charisma MALC 2*	32	5 wks
2 Jul 83 ●	DOUBLE DUTCH *Charisma/Phonogram MALC 3*	3	13 wks
17 Dec 83	DUCK FOR THE OYSTER *Charisma/Virgin MALC 4*	54	5 wks
1 Sep 84	MADAM BUTTERFLY *Charisma/Virgin MALC 5*	13	9 wks

First hit credited to Malcolm McLaren and the World's Famous Supreme Team, second to Malcolm McLaren and the McLarenettes.

Don McLEAN *US, male vocalist* — 58 wks

22 Jan 72 ●	AMERICAN PIE *United Artists UP 35325*	2	16 wks
13 May 72 ★	VINCENT *United Artists UP 35359*	1	15 wks
14 Apr 73	EVERYDAY *United Artists UP 35519*	38	5 wks
10 May 80 ★	CRYING *EMI 5051*	1	14 wks
17 Apr 82	CASTLES IN THE AIR *EMI 5258*	47	8 wks

Phil McLEAN *US, male vocalist* — 4 wks

18 Jan 62	SMALL SAD SAM *Top Rank JAR 597*	34	4 wks

Jackie McLEAN *US, male instrumentalist - alto sax, with male/female vocal backing group* — 4 wks

7 Jul 79	DR. JACKYLL AND MISTER FUNK *RCA PB 1575*	53	4 wks

MACNEAL - *See MOUTH and MACNEAL*

Clyde McPHATTER *US, male vocalist* — 1 wk

24 Aug 56	TREASURE OF LOVE *London HLE 8293*	27	1 wk

Carmen McRAE - *See Sammy DAVIS JR. and Carmen McRAE*

Gordon MACRAE - *See VARIOUS ARTISTS (Carousel Soundtrack)*

Ralph McTELL *UK, male vocalist* — 18 wks

7 Dec 74 ●	STREETS OF LONDON *Reprise K 14380*	2	12 wks
20 Dec 75	DREAMS OF YOU *Warner Bros. K 16648*	36	6 wks

MADNESS
UK, male vocal/instrumental group — 187 wks

1 Sep 79	THE PRINCE *2-Tone TT 3*	16	11 wks
10 Nov 79 ●	ONE STEP BEYOND *Stiff BUY 56*	7	14 wks
5 Jan 80 ●	MY GIRL *Stiff BUY 62*	3	10 wks
5 Apr 80 ●	WORK REST AND PLAY EP *Stiff BUY 71*	6	8 wks
13 Sep 80 ●	BAGGY TROUSERS *Stiff BUY 84*	3	20 wks
22 Nov 80 ●	EMBARRASSMENT *Stiff BUY 102*	4	6 wks
24 Jan 81 ●	THE RETURN OF THE LOS PALMAS SEVEN *Stiff BUY 108*	7	11 wks
25 Apr 81 ●	GREY DAY *Stiff BUY 112*	4	10 wks
26 Sep 81 ●	SHUT UP *Stiff BUY 126*	7	9 wks
5 Dec 81 ●	IT MUST BE LOVE *Stiff BUY 134*	4	12 wks
20 Feb 82	CARDIAC ARREST *Stiff BUY 140*	14	10 wks
22 May 82 ★	HOUSE OF FUN *Stiff BUY 146*	1	9 wks
24 Jul 82 ●	DRIVING IN MY CAR *Stiff BUY 153*	4	8 wks
27 Nov 82 ●	OUR HOUSE *Stiff BUY 163*	5	5 wks
19 Feb 83 ●	TOMORROW'S (JUST ANOTHER DAY)/MADNESS (IS ALL IN THE MIND) *Stiff BUY 169*	8	9 wks

20 Aug 83	●	**WINGS OF A DOVE** *Stiff BUY 181*	**2**	10 wks
5 Nov 83	●	**THE SUN AND THE RAIN** *Stiff BUY 192*	**5**	10 wks
11 Feb 84		**MICHAEL CAINE** *Stiff BUY 196*	**11**	8 wks
2 Jun 84		**ONE BETTER DAY** *Stiff BUY 201*	**17**	7 wks

Tracks on Work Rest and Play EP: Night Boat to Cairo/Deceives The Eye/The Young And The Old/Don't Quote Me On That.

MADONNA *US, female vocalist* *31 wks*

14 Jan 84	● **HOLIDAY** *Sire W 9405*	**6**	11 wks
17 Mar 84	**LUCKY STAR** *Sire W 9522*	**14**	9 wks
2 Jun 84	**BORDERLINE** *Sire W 9260*	**56**	4 wks
17 Nov 84	● **LIKE A VIRGIN** *Sire W 9210*	**4†**	7 wks

MAGAZINE
UK, male vocal/instrumental group *7 wks*

11 Feb 78	**SHOT BY BOTH SIDES** *Virgin VS 200* ...	**41**	4 wks
26 Jul 80	**SWEET HEART CONTRACT** *Virgin VS 368* ...	**54**	3 wks

MAGIC LANTERNS
UK, male vocal/instrumental group *3 wks*

7 Jul 66	**EXCUSE ME BABY** *CBS 202094*	**46**	1 wk
28 Jul 66	**EXCUSE ME BABY** (re-entry) *CBS 202094*	**44**	1 wk
11 Aug 66	**EXCUSE ME BABY** (2nd re-entry) *CBS 202094*	**46**	1 wk

MAGNUM
UK, male vocal/instrumental group *6 wks*

22 Mar 80	**MAGNUM** (Double single) *Jet 175*	**47**	6 wks

Tracks on double single: Invasion/Kingdom of Madness/All of My Life/Great Adventure.

MAIN INGREDIENT
US, male vocal group *7 wks*

29 Jun 74	**JUST DON'T WANT TO BE LONELY** *RCA APBO 0205*	**27**	7 wks

MAISONETTES
UK, male/female vocal group *11 wks*

11 Dec 82	● **HEARTACHE AVENUE** *Ready Steady Go! RSG 1*	**7**	11 wks

MAKADOPULOS and his GREEK SERENADERS
Greece, male vocal/instrumental group *14 wks*

20 Oct 60	**NEVER ON SUNDAY** *Palette PG 9005*	**36**	14 wks

Carl MALCOLM *Jamaica, male vocalist* *8 wks*

13 Sep 75	● **FATTIE BUM BUM** *UK 108*	**8**	8 wks

MAMAS and the PAPAS
US, female/male vocal group *64 wks*

28 Apr 66	**CALIFORNIA DREAMIN'** *RCA 1503*	**23**	9 wks
12 May 66	**MONDAY MONDAY** *RCA 1516*	**3**	13 wks
28 Jul 66	**I SAW HER AGAIN** *RCA 1533*	**11**	11 wks
9 Feb 67	**WORDS OF LOVE** *RCA 1564*	**47**	3 wks
6 Apr 67	● **DEDICATED TO THE ONE I LOVE** *RCA 1576*	**2**	17 wks

26 Jul 67	● **CREEQUE ALLEY** *RCA 1613*	**9**	11 wks

See also Mama Cass.

MAMBAS - *See MARC and the MAMBAS*

MANCHESTER UNITED FOOTBALL CLUB
UK, male football team vocalists *6 wks*

8 May 76	**MANCHESTER UNITED** *Decca F 13633*	**50**	1 wk
21 May 83	**GLORY GLORY MAN. UNITED** *EMI 5390*	**13**	5 wks

Henry MANCINI *US, orchestra/chorus* *23 wks*

7 Dec 61	**MOON RIVER** *RCA 1256*	**46**	2 wks
28 Dec 61	**MOON RIVER** (re-entry) *RCA 1256*	**44**	1 wk
24 Sep 64	● **HOW SOON** *RCA 1414*	**10**	12 wks
25 Mar 72	**THEME FROM 'CADE'S COUNTY'** *RCA 2182*	**42**	1 wk
11 Feb 84	**MAIN THEME FROM 'THE THORNBIRDS'** *Warner Bros. 9677*	**23**	7 wks

Steve MANDELL - *See 'DELIVERANCE' SOUNDTRACK*

MANFRED MANN
South Africa/UK, male vocal/instrumental group *176 wks*

23 Jan 64	● ★ **5-4-3-2-1** *HMV POP 1252*	**5**	13 wks
16 Apr 64	**HUBBLE BUBBLE TOIL AND TROUBLE** *HMV POP 1282*	**11**	8 wks
16 Jul 64	★ **DO WAH DIDDY DIDDY** *HMV POP 1320*	**1**	14 wks
15 Oct 64	**SHA LA LA** *HMV POP 1346*	**3**	12 wks
14 Jan 65	● **COME TOMORROW** *HMV POP 1381*	**4**	9 wks
15 Apr 65	**OH NO NOT MY BABY** *HMV POP 1413*	**11**	10 wks
16 Sep 65	● **IF YOU GOTTA GO GO NOW** *HMV POP 1466*	**2**	12 wks
21 Apr 66	★ **PRETTY FLAMINGO** *HMV POP 1523*	**1**	12 wks
7 Jul 66	**YOU GAVE ME SOMEBODY TO LOVE** *HMV POP 1541*	**36**	4 wks
4 Aug 66	● **JUST LIKE A WOMAN** *Fontana TF 730*	**10**	10 wks
27 Oct 66	● **SEMI-DETACHED SUBURBAN MR. JAMES** *Fontana TF 757*	**2**	12 wks
30 Mar 67	● **HA HA SAID THE CLOWN** *Fontana TF 812* ...	**4**	11 wks
25 May 67	**SWEET PEA** *Fontana TF 828*	**36**	4 wks
24 Jan 68	★ **MIGHTY QUINN** *Fontana TF 897*	**1**	11 wks
12 Jun 68	● **MY NAME IS JACK** *Fontana TF 943*	**8**	11 wks
18 Dec 68	● **FOX ON THE RUN** *Fontana TF 985*	**5**	12 wks
30 Apr 69	● **RAGAMUFFIN MAN** *Fontana TF 1013*	**8**	11 wks

The HMV hits featured Paul Jones as lead vocalist and the Fontana hits Mike d'Abo, except for Sweet Pea, an instrumental disc. See also Paul Jones; Manfred Mann's Earth Band.

MANFRED MANN'S EARTH BAND
South Africa/UK, male vocal/instrumental group *41 wks*

8 Sep 73	● **JOYBRINGER** *Vertigo 6059 083*	**9**	10 wks
28 Aug 76	● **BLINDED BY THE LIGHT** *Bronze BRO 29*	**6**	10 wks
20 May 78	● **DAVY'S ON THE ROAD AGAIN** *Bronze BRO 52*	**6**	12 wks
17 Mar 79	**YOU ANGEL YOU** *Bronze BRO 68*	**54**	5 wks
7 Jul 79	**DON'T KILL IT CAROL** *Bronze BRO 77*	**45**	4 wks

See also Manfred Mann.

MANHATTAN TRANSFER
US, male/female vocal group *72 wks*

7 Feb 76	**TUXEDO JUNCTION** *Atlantic K 10670*	**24**	6 wks
5 Feb 77	★ **CHANSON D'AMOUR** *Atlantic K 10886*	**1**	13 wks
28 May 77	**DON'T LET GO** *Atlantic K 10930*	**32**	6 wks
18 Feb 78	**WALK IN LOVE** *Atlantic K 11075*	**48**	1 wk
4 Mar 78	**WALK IN LOVE** (re-entry) *Atlantic K 11075*	**12**	11 wks

20 May 78   **ON A LITTLE STREET IN SINGAPORE**   *Atlantic K 11136*   **20**   9 wks

16 Sep 78   **WHERE DID OUR LOVE GO/JE VOULAIS TE DIRE (QUE JE T'ATTENDS)**   *Atlantic K 11182*   **40**   4 wks

23 Dec 78   **WHO WHAT WHEN WHERE WHY**   *Atlantic K 11233*   **49**   6 wks

17 May 80   **TWILIGHT ZONE-TWILIGHT TONE (MEDLEY)**   *Atlantic K 11476*   **25**   8 wks

21 Jan 84   **SPICE OF LIFE**   *Atlantic A 9728*   **19**   8 wks

MANHATTANS   *US, male vocal group*   *31 wks*

Date	Title	Pos	Wks
19 Jun 76	● KISS AND SAY GOODBYE *CBS 4317*	4	11 wks
2 Oct 76	● HURT *CBS 4562*	4	11 wks
23 Apr 77	IT'S YOU *CBS 5093*	43	3 wks
26 Jul 80	SHINING STAR *CBS 8624*	45	4 wks
6 Aug 83	CRAZY *CBS A 3578*	63	2 wks

Barry MANILOW   *US, male vocalist*   *123 wks*

Date	Title	Pos	Wks
22 Feb 75	MANDY *Arista 1*	11	9 wks
6 May 78	CAN'T SMILE WITHOUT YOU *Arista 176*	43	7 wks
29 Jul 78	SOMEWHERE IN THE NIGHT/COPACABANA (AT THE COPA) *Arista 196*	42	10 wks
23 Dec 78	COULD IT BE MAGIC *Arista ARIST 229*	25	10 wks
8 Nov 80	LONELY TOGETHER *Arista ARIST 373*	12	13 wks
7 Feb 81	I MADE IT THROUGH THE RAIN *Arista ARIST 384*	37	6 wks
11 Apr 81	BERMUDA TRIANGLE *Arista ARIST 406*	15	9 wks
26 Sep 81	LET'S HANG ON *Arista ARIST 429*	12	11 wks
12 Dec 81	THE OLD SONGS *Arista ARIST 443*	48	8 wks
20 Feb 82	IF I SHOULD LOVE AGAIN *Arista ARIST 453*	66	2 wks
17 Apr 82	STAY (LIVE) *Arista ARIST 464*	23	8 wks
16 Oct 82	● I WANNA DO IT WITH YOU *Arista ARIST 495*	8	8 wks
4 Dec 82	I'M GONNA SIT RIGHT DOWN AND WRITE MYSELF A LETTER *Arista ARIST 503*	36	7 wks
25 Jun 83	SOME KIND OF FRIEND *Arista ARIST 516*	48	2 wks
27 Aug 83	YOU'RE LOOKING HOT TONIGHT *Arista ARIST 542*	47	6 wks
10 Dec 83	READ 'EM AND WEEP *Arista ARIST 551*	17	7 wks

MANKIND   *UK, male instrumental group*   *12 wks*

Date	Title	Pos	Wks
25 Nov 78	DR. WHO *Pinnacle PIN 71*	25	12 wks

Johnny MANN SINGERS
US, male/female vocal group   *13 wks*

Date	Title	Pos	Wks
12 Jul 67	● UP, UP AND AWAY *Liberty LIB 55972*	6	13 wks

MANTOVANI   *UK, orchestra*   *52 wks*

Date	Title	Pos	Wks
19 Dec 52	● WHITE CHRISTMAS *Decca F 10017*	6	3 wks
29 May 53	★ MOULIN ROUGE *Decca F 10094*	1	21 wks
23 Oct 53	● SWEDISH RHAPSODY *Decca F 10168*	2	17 wks
13 Nov 53	● MOULIN ROUGE (re-entry) *Decca F 10094*	10	1 wk
4 Dec 53	MOULIN ROUGE (2nd re-entry) *Decca F 10094*	12	1 wk
26 Feb 54	SWEDISH RHAPSODY (re-entry) *Decca F 10168*	12	1 wk
11 Feb 55	LONELY BALLERINA *Decca F 10395*	16	3 wks
18 Mar 55	LONELY BALLERINA (re-entry) *Decca F 10395*	18	1 wk
31 May 57	AROUND THE WORLD *Decca F 10888*	20	4 wks

MANUEL and his MUSIC OF THE MOUNTAINS
UK, orchestra, leader Geoff Love   *31 wks*

Date	Title	Pos	Wks
28 Aug 59	THEME FROM HONEYMOON *Columbia DB 4323*	29	2 wks
25 Sep 59	THEME FROM HONEYMOON (re-entry) *Columbia DB 4323*	22	5 wks
6 Nov 59	THEME FROM HONEYMOON (2nd re-entry) *Columbia DB 4323*	27	2 wks
13 Oct 60	NEVER ON SUNDAY *Columbia DB 4515*	29	10 wks
13 Oct 66	SOMEWHERE MY LOVE *Columbia DB 7969*	42	2 wks
31 Jan 76	● RODRIGO'S GUITAR CONCERTO DE ARANJUEZ (THEME FROM 2ND MOVEMENT) *EMI 2383*	3	10 wks

MARAUDERS   *UK, male vocal/instrumental group*   *4 wks*

Date	Title	Pos	Wks
8 Aug 63	THAT'S WHAT I WANT *Decca F 11695*	48	1 wk
22 Aug 63	THAT'S WHAT I WANT (re-entry) *Decca F 11695*	43	3 wks

MARBLES   *UK, male vocal duo*   *18 wks*

Date	Title	Pos	Wks
25 Sep 68	● ONLY ONE WOMAN *Polydor 56 272*	5	12 wks
26 Mar 69	THE WALLS FELL DOWN *Polydor 56 310*	28	6 wks

MARC and the MAMBAS
UK, male/female vocal/instrumental group   *3 wks*

Date	Title	Pos	Wks
25 Jun 83	BLACK HEART *Some Bizarre/Phonogram BZS 19*	49	3 wks

MARCELS   *US, male vocal group*   *17 wks*

Date	Title	Pos	Wks
13 Apr 61	★ BLUE MOON *Pye International 7N 25073*	1	13 wks
8 Jun 61	SUMMERTIME *Pye International 7N 25083*	46	4 wks

Little Peggy MARCH
US, female vocalist   *7 wks*

Date	Title	Pos	Wks
12 Sep 63	HELLO HEARTACHE GOODBYE LOVE *RCA 1362*	29	7 wks

MARCIA - See BOB and MARCIA

MARDI GRAS   *UK, male vocal/instrumental group*   *9 wks*

Date	Title	Pos	Wks
5 Aug 72	TOO BUSY THINKING 'BOUT MY BABY *Bell 1226*	19	9 wks

Kelly MARIE   *UK, female vocalist*   *36 wks*

Date	Title	Pos	Wks
2 Aug 80	★ FEELS LIKE I'M IN LOVE *Calibre PLUS 1*	1	16 wks
18 Oct 80	LOVING JUST FOR FUN *Calibre PLUS 4*	21	7 wks
7 Feb 81	HOT LOVE *Calibre PLUS 5*	22	10 wks
30 May 81	TRIAL *Calibre PLUS 7*	51	3 wks

Rose MARIE   *UK, female vocalist*   *5 wks*

Date	Title	Pos	Wks
19 Nov 83	WHEN I LEAVE MY WORLD BEHIND *A1 284*	75	1 wk
3 Dec 83	WHEN I LEAVE MY WORLD BEHIND (re-entry) *A1 284*	63	2 wks
24 Dec 83	WHEN I LEAVE MY WORLD BEHIND (2nd re-entry) *A1 284*	66	2 wks

Teena MARIE   *US, female vocalist*   *24 wks*

Date	Title	Pos	Wks
7 Jul 79	I'M A SUCKER FOR YOUR LOVE *Motown TMG 1146*	43	8 wks
31 May 80	● BEHIND THE GROOVE *Motown TMG 1185*	6	10 wks

RUBY MURRAY (left) She made her first TV appearance at the age of 12, and her London Palladium debut when she was 20. In March 1955 she brought off the unique achievement of having five records in the Top 20 simultaneously.

JONI MITCHELL (centre) Alberta born, former art student, perfecting her Marlene Dietrich impression.

ALISON MOYET (right) Successful as half of Yazoo with ex-Depeche Mode man Vince Clarke, she was voted top female singer of 1984.

THE MOVE (above) From left to right – Roy Wood who went on to form Wizzard and E.L.O.; Trevor Burton, who later teamed up with Steve Gibbons, Carl Wayne, who went solo; and Ace Kefford, who formed Ace Kefford's Stand. Bev Bevan (not in picture) became E.L.O.'s drummer.

MODERN ROMANCE (left) On the 1981 charts for 22 weeks; the 1982 chart for 23 weeks; and the 1983 hit parades for 32 weeks; but no love in 1984.

MUD (right) Les, Ray, Rob and Dave topped the chart three times in the mid-seventies.

11 Oct 80		**I NEED YOUR LOVIN'** *Motown TMG 1203*	28	6 wks

First hit has credit 'Co-lead vocals: Rick James'. See also Rick James.

MARILLION
UK, male vocal/instrumental group   *26 wks*

20 Nov 82		**MARKET SQUARE HEROES** *EMI 5351*	60	2 wks
12 Feb 83		**HE KNOWS YOU KNOW** *EMI 5362*	35	4 wks
16 Apr 83		**MARKET SQUARE HEROES** (re-entry) *EMI 5351*	53	6 wks
18 Jun 83		**GARDEN PARTY** *EMI 5393*	16	5 wks
11 Feb 84		**PUNCH AND JUDY** *EMI MARIL 1*	29	4 wks
12 May 84		**ASSASSING** *EMI MARIL 2*	22	5 wks

MARILYN *UK, male vocalist*   *25 wks*

5 Nov 83	●	**CALLING YOUR NAME** *Mercury/Phonogram MAZ 1*	4	12 wks
11 Feb 84		**CRY AND BE FREE** *Mercury/Phonogram MAZ 2*	31	6 wks
21 Apr 84		**YOU DON'T LOVE ME** *Mercury/Phonogram MAZ 3*	40	7 wks

Marino MARINI *Italy, male vocalist*   *23 wks*

3 Oct 58		**VOLARE** *Durium DC 16632*	13	7 wks
10 Oct 58	●	**COME PRIMA** *Durium DC 16632*	2	14 wks
20 Mar 59		**CIAO CIAO BAMBINA** *Durium DC 16636*	25	1 wk
3 Apr 59		**CIAO CIAO BAMBINA** (re-entry) *Durium DC 16636*	24	1 wk

Pigmeat MARKHAM *US, male vocalist*   *8 wks*

17 Jul 68		**HERE COMES THE JUDGE** *Chess CRS 8077* . . .	19	8 wks

Yannis MARKOPOULOS
Greece, orchestra   *8 wks*

17 Dec 77		**WHO PAYS THE FERRYMAN** *BBC RESL 51* . .	11	8 wks

Guy MARKS *Australia, male vocalist*   *8 wks*

13 May 78		**LOVING YOU HAS MADE ME BANANAS** *ABC 4211*	25	8 wks

Bob MARLEY and the WAILERS
Jamaica, male vocal/instrumental group   *121 wks*

27 Sep 75		**NO WOMAN NO CRY** *Island WIP 6244*	22	7 wks
25 Jun 77		**EXODUS** *Island WIP 6390*	14	9 wks
10 Sep 77		**WAITING IN VAIN** *Island WIP 6402*	27	6 wks
10 Dec 77	●	**JAMMING/PUNKY REGGAE PARTY** *Island WIP 6410*	9	12 wks
25 Feb 78	●	**IS THIS LOVE** *Island WIP 6420*	9	9 wks
10 Jun 78		**SATISFY MY SOUL** *Island WIP 6440*	21	10 wks
20 Oct 79		**SO MUCH TROUBLE IN THE WORLD** *Island WIP 6510*	56	4 wks
21 Jun 80	●	**COULD YOU BE LOVED** *Island WIP 6610*	5	12 wks
13 Sep 80		**THREE LITTLE BIRDS** *Island WIP 6641*	17	9 wks
13 Jun 81	●	**NO WOMAN NO CRY** (re-entry) *Island WIP 6244*	8	11 wks
7 May 83	●	**BUFFALO SOLDIER** *Island/Tuff Gong IS 108* . . .	4	12 wks
21 Apr 84	●	**ONE LOVE/PEOPLE GET READY** *Island IS 169*	5	11 wks
23 Jun 84		**WAITING IN VAIN** (re-issue) *Island IS 180*	31	7 wks
8 Dec 84		**COULD YOU BE LOVED** (re-issue) *Island IS 210*	71	2 wks

MARMALADE *UK, male vocal group*   *130 wks*

22 May 68	●	**LOVIN' THINGS** *CBS 3412*	6	13 wks

23 Oct 68		**WAIT FOR ME MARIANNE** *CBS 3708*	30	5 wks
4 Dec 68	★	**OB-LA-DI OB-LA-DA** *CBS 3892*	1	20 wks
11 Jun 69	●	**BABY MAKE IT SOON** *CBS 4287*	9	13 wks
20 Dec 69		**REFLECTIONS OF MY LIFE** *Decca F 12982*	3	12 wks
18 Jul 70		**RAINBOW** *Decca F 13035*	3	14 wks
27 Mar 71		**MY LITTLE ONE** *Decca F 13135*	15	11 wks
4 Sep 71		**COUSIN NORMAN** *Decca F 13214*	6	11 wks
27 Nov 71		**BACK ON THE ROAD** *Decca F 13251*	35	7 wks
22 Jan 72		**BACK ON THE ROAD** (re-entry) *Decca F 13251*	50	1 wk
1 Apr 72		**RADANCER** *Decca F 13297*	6	12 wks
21 Feb 76	●	**FALLING APART AT THE SEAMS** *Target TGT 105*	9	11 wks

Stevie MARSH *UK, female vocalist*   *4 wks*

4 Dec 59		**THE ONLY BOY IN THE WORLD** *Decca F 11181*	29	2 wks
25 Dec 59		**THE ONLY BOY IN THE WORLD** (re-entry) *Decca F 11181*	24	2 wks

Joy MARSHALL *UK, female vocalist*   *2 wks*

23 Jun 66		**THE MORE I SEE YOU** *Decca F 12422*	34	2 wks

Keith MARSHALL *UK, male vocalist*   *10 wks*

4 Apr 81		**ONLY CRYING** *Arrival PIK 2*	12	10 wks

MARSHALL HAIN
UK, male/female vocal/instrumental duo   *19 wks*

3 Jun 78	●	**DANCING IN THE CITY** *Harvest HAR 5157* . . .	3	15 wks
14 Oct 78		**COMING HOME** *Harvest HAR 5168*	39	4 wks

Lena MARTELL *UK, female vocalist*   *18 wks*

29 Sep 79	★	**ONE DAY AT A TIME** *Pye 7N 46021*	1	18 wks

MARTHA and the MUFFINS
Canada, female/male vocal/instrumental group   *10 wks*

1 Mar 80	●	**ECHO BEACH** *Dindisc DIN 9*	10	10 wks

MARTHA and the VANDELLAS - *See Martha REEVES and the VANDELLAS*

Dean MARTIN *US, male vocalist*   *154 wks*

18 Sep 53	●	**KISS** *Capitol CL 13893*	9	1 wk
2 Oct 53	●	**KISS** (re-entry) *Capitol CL 13893*	5	7 wks
22 Jan 54	●	**THAT'S AMORE** *Capitol CL 14008*	2	11 wks
1 Oct 54	●	**SWAY** *Capitol CL 14138*	6	7 wks
22 Oct 54		**HOW DO YOU SPEAK TO AN ANGEL** *Capitol CL 14150*	15	2 wks
19 Nov 54		**HOW DO YOU SPEAK TO AN ANGEL** (re-entry) *Capitol CL 14150*	17	4 wks
28 Jan 55	●	**NAUGHTY LADY OF SHADY LANE** *Capitol CL 14226*	5	10 wks
4 Feb 55		**MAMBO ITALIANO** *Capitol CL 14227*	14	2 wks
25 Feb 55	●	**LET ME GO LOVER** *Capitol CL 14226*	3	9 wks
1 Apr 55	●	**UNDER THE BRIDGES OF PARIS** *Capitol CL 14255*	6	8 wks
10 Feb 56	★	**MEMORIES ARE MADE OF THIS** *Capitol CL 14523*	1	16 wks
2 Mar 56		**YOUNG AND FOOLISH** *Capitol CL 14519*	20	1 wk
27 Apr 56		**INNAMORATA** *Capitol CL 14507*	21	3 wks
22 Mar 57		**THE MAN WHO PLAYS THE MANDOLINO** *Capitol CL 14690*	21	2 wks
13 Jun 58	●	**RETURN TO ME** *Capitol CL 14844*	2	22 wks

29 Aug 58	● VOLARE Capitol CL 14910		2	14 wks
27 Aug 64	EVERYBODY LOVES SOMEBODY		11	13 wks
	Reprise R 20281			
12 Nov 64	THE DOOR IS STILL OPEN TO MY HEART		42	4 wks
	Reprise R 20307			
5 Feb 69	● GENTLE ON MY MIND Reprise RS 23343		2	23 wks
30 Aug 69	GENTLE ON MY MIND (re-entry)		49	1 wk
	Reprise RS 23343			

Juan MARTIN
Spain, male instrumentalist - guitar   *7 wks*

28 Jan 84	● LOVE THEME FROM 'THE THORN BIRDS'		10	7 wks
	WEA X 9518			

Ray MARTIN *UK, orchestra*   *11 wks*

14 Nov 52	● BLUE TANGO Columbia DB 3051		8	1 wk
28 Nov 52	● BLUE TANGO (re-entry) Columbia DB 3051		10	3 wks
4 Dec 53	● SWEDISH RHAPSODY Columbia DB 3346		10	1 wk
18 Dec 53	● SWEDISH RHAPSODY (re-entry)		4	3 wks
	Columbia DB 3346			
15 Jun 56	CAROUSEL WALTZ Columbia DB 3771		28	1 wk
3 Aug 56	CAROUSEL WALTZ (re-entry) Columbia DB 3771		24	2 wks

Tony MARTIN *US, male vocalist*   *28 wks*

22 Apr 55	● STRANGER IN PARADISE HMV B 10849		6	13 wks
13 Jul 56	● WALK HAND IN HAND HMV POP 222		2	15 wks

Vince MARTIN *US, male vocalist*   *1 wk*

14 Dec 56	CINDY OH CINDY London HLN 8340		26	1 wk

Wink MARTINDALE *US, male vocalist*   *41 wks*

4 Dec 59	DECK OF CARDS London HLD 8962		18	5 wks
15 Jan 60	DECK OF CARDS (re-entry) London HLD 8962		28	2 wks
31 Mar 60	DECK OF CARDS (2nd re-entry)		45	1 wk
	London HLD 8962			
18 Apr 63	● DECK OF CARDS (3rd re-entry)		5	21 wks
	London HLD 8962			
20 Oct 73	DECK OF CARDS (re-issue) Dot DOT 109		22	12 wks

Al MARTINO *US, male vocalist*   *87 wks*

14 Nov 52	★ HERE IN MY HEART Capitol CL 13779		1	18 wks
21 Nov 52	● TAKE MY HEART Capitol CL 13769		9	1 wk
30 Jan 53	● NOW Capitol CL 13835		3	12 wks
10 Jul 53	● RACHEL Capitol CL 13879		10	4 wks
11 Sep 53	RACHEL (re-entry) Capitol CL 13879		12	1 wk
4 Jun 54	WANTED Capitol CL 14128		12	1 wk
18 Jun 54	● WANTED (re-entry) Capitol CL 14128		4	14 wks
1 Oct 54	WANTED (2nd re-entry) Capitol CL 14128		17	1 wk
1 Oct 54	● THE STORY OF TINA Capitol CL 14163		10	8 wks
23 Sep 55	THE MAN FROM LARAMIE Capitol CL 14347		19	2 wks
28 Oct 55	THE MAN FROM LARAMIE (re-entry)		20	1 wk
	Capitol CL 14347			
31 Mar 60	SUMMERTIME Top Rank JAR 312		49	1 wk
29 Aug 63	I LOVE YOU BECAUSE Capitol CL 15300		48	1 wk
22 Aug 70	SPANISH EYES Capitol CL 15430		49	1 wk
14 Jul 73	● SPANISH EYES (re-entry) Capitol CL 15430		5	21 wks

MARVELETTES *US, female vocal group*   *10 wks*

15 Jun 67	WHEN YOU'RE YOUNG AND IN LOVE		13	10 wks
	Tamla Motown TMG 609			

MARVIN *UK, robot*   *4 wks*

16 May 81	MARVIN THE PARANOID ANDROID		53	4 wks
	Polydor POSP 261			

Hank MARVIN
UK, male vocalist/instrumentalist-guitar   *4 wks*

6 Mar 82	DON'T TALK Polydor POSP 420		49	4 wks

See also Cliff Richard.

Lee MARVIN *US, male vocalist*   *23 wks*

7 Feb 70	★ WAND'RIN' STAR Paramount PARA 3004		1	18 wks
20 Jun 70	WAND'RIN' STAR (re-entry)		42	3 wks
	Paramount PARA 3004			
15 Aug 70	WAND'RIN' STAR (2nd re-entry)		47	2 wks
	Paramount PARA 3004			

I Talk To The Trees, by Clint Eastwood, the flip side of Wand'rin' Star, was listed with Wand'rin' Star for 7 Feb 70 and 14 Feb 70 only. See also Clint Eastwood.

MARY JANE GIRLS
US, female vocal group   *14 wks*

21 May 83	CANDY MAN Motown TMG 1301		60	4 wks
25 Jun 83	ALL NIGHT LONG Gordy TMG 1309		13	9 wks
8 Oct 83	BOYS Gordy TMG 1315		74	1 wk

MARY - *See PETER, PAUL and MARY*

Carolyne MAS *US, female vocalist*   *2 wks*

2 Feb 80	QUOTE GOODBYE QUOTE Mercury 6167 873		71	2 wks

MASH *US, male vocal/instrumental group*   *12 wks*

10 May 80	★ THEME FROM M*A*S*H* (SUICIDE IS PAINLESS) CBS 8536		1	12 wks

Barbara MASON *US, female vocalist*   *5 wks*

21 Jan 84	ANOTHER MAN		45	5 wks
	Streetwave/Arista/West End KHAN 3			

Glen MASON *UK, male vocalist*   *7 wks*

28 Sep 56	GLENDORA Parlophone R 4203		28	2 wks
16 Nov 56	GREEN DOOR Parlophone R 4244		24	5 wks

Mary MASON *UK, female vocalist*   *6 wks*

8 Oct 77	ANGEL OF THE MORNING - ANY WAY THAT YOU WANT ME (MEDLEY) Epic EPC 5552		27	6 wks

MASS PRODUCTION
US, male vocal/instrumental group   *7 wks*

12 Mar 77	WELCOME TO OUR WORLD (OF MERRY MUSIC) Atlantic K 10898		44	3 wks
17 May 80	SHANTE Atlantic/Cotillion K 11475		59	4 wks

MASSIEL *Spain, female vocalist* *4 wks*

24 Apr 68	LA LA LA	*Philips BF 1667*	35	4 wks

MASTER SINGERS
UK, male vocal group *7 wks*

14 Apr 66	HIGHWAY CODE	*Parlophone R 5428*	25	6 wks
17 Nov 66	WEATHER FORECAST	*Parlophone R 5523*	50	1 wk

Sammy MASTERS *US, male vocalist* *5 wks*

9 Jun 60	ROCKIN' RED WING	*Warner Bros. WB 10*	36	5 wks

MATCH *UK, male vocal/instrumental group* *3 wks*

16 Jun 79	BOOGIE MAN	*Flamingo FM 2*	48	3 wks

MATCHBOX
UK, male vocal/instrumental group *66 wks*

3 Nov 79	ROCKABILLY REBEL	*Magnet MAG 155*	18	12 wks
19 Jan 80	BUZZ BUZZ A DIDDLE IT	*Magnet MAG 157*	22	8 wks
10 May 80	MIDNITE DYNAMOS	*Magnet MAG 169*	14	12 wks
27 Sep 80 ●	WHEN YOU ASK ABOUT LOVE			
	Magnet MAG 191		4	12 wks
29 Nov 80	OVER THE RAINBOW - YOU BELONG TO ME			
	(MEDLEY) *Magnet MAG 192*		15	11 wks
4 Apr 81	BABES IN THE WOOD	*Magnet MAG 193*	46	6 wks
1 Aug 81	LOVE'S MADE A FOOL OF YOU			
	Magnet MAG 194		63	3 wks
29 May 82	ONE MORE SATURDAY NIGHT			
	Magnet MAG 223		63	2 wks

Mireille MATHIEU
France, female vocalist *7 wks*

13 Dec 67	LA DERNIERE VALSE	*Columbia DB 8323*	26	7 wks

Johnny MATHIS *US, male vocalist* *113 wks*

23 May 58	TEACHER TEACHER	*Fontana H 130*	27	5 wks
26 Sep 58 ●	A CERTAIN SMILE	*Fontana H 142*	4	16 wks
19 Dec 58	WINTER WONDERLAND	*Fontana H 165*	17	3 wks
7 Aug 59 ●	SOMEONE	*Fontana H 199*	6	15 wks
27 Nov 59	THE BEST OF EVERYTHING	*Fontana H 218* ..	30	1 wk
29 Jan 60	MISTY	*Fontana H 219*	12	7 wks
24 Mar 60	YOU ARE BEAUTIFUL	*Fontana H 234*	38	8 wks
14 Apr 60	MISTY	(re-entry) *Fontana H 219*	46	2 wks
26 May 60	YOU ARE BEAUTIFUL	(re-entry) *Fontana H 234*	46	1 wk
28 Jul 60	STARBRIGHT	*Fontana H 254*	47	2 wks
6 Oct 60 ●	MY LOVE FOR YOU	*Fontana H 267*	9	18 wks
4 Apr 63	WHAT WILL MY MARY SAY	*CBS AAG 127* ...	49	1 wk
25 Jan 75 ●	I'M STONE IN LOVE WITH YOU	*CBS 2653* ..	10	12 wks
13 Nov 76 ★	WHEN A CHILD IS BORN (SOLEADO)			
	CBS 4599		1	12 wks
11 Aug 79	GONE GONE GONE	*CBS 7730*	15	10 wks

See also Johnny Mathis and Deniece Williams; Johnny Mathis and Gladys Knight.

Johnny MATHIS and Gladys KNIGHT *US, male/female vocal duo* *1 wk*

26 Dec 81	WHEN A CHILD IS BORN	*CBS S 1758*	74	1 wk

See also Johnny Mathis; Gladys Knight and the Pips; Johnny Mathis and Deniece Williams.

Johnny MATHIS and Deniece WILLIAMS *US, male/female vocal duo* *20 wks*

25 Mar 78 ●	TOO MUCH TOO LITTLE TOO LATE			
	CBS 6164		3	14 wks
29 Jul 78	YOU'RE ALL I NEED TO GET BY	*CBS 6483*	45	6 wks

See also Johnny Mathis; Deniece Williams; Johnny Mathis and Gladys Knight.

MATT BIANCO
UK/Poland, male/female vocal/instrumental group *23 wks*

11 Feb 84	GET OUT OF YOUR LAZY BED			
	WEA BIANCO 1		15	8 wks
14 Apr 84	SNEAKING OUT OF THE BACK DOOR/MATT'S			
	MOOD *WEA YZ 3*		44	7 wks
10 Nov 84	HALF A MINUTE *WEA YZ 26*		23†	8 wks

Matt's Mood only credited from 5 May 84.

Al MATTHEWS *US, male vocalist* *8 wks*

23 Aug 75	FOOL	*CBS 3429*	16	8 wks

MATTHEWS SOUTHERN COMFORT
UK, male vocal/instrumental group *18 wks*

26 Sep 70 ★	WOODSTOCK	*Uni UNS 526*	1	18 wks

MATUMBI
UK, male vocal/instrumental group *7 wks*

29 Sep 79	POINT OF VIEW	*Matumbi RIC 101*	35	7 wks

Susan MAUGHAN *UK, female vocalist* *25 wks*

11 Oct 62 ●	BOBBY'S GIRL	*Philips 326544 BF*	3	19 wks
14 Feb 63	HAND A HANDKERCHIEF TO HELEN			
	Philips 326562 BF		41	3 wks
9 May 63	SHE'S NEW TO YOU	*Philips 326586 BF*	45	3 wks

Paul MAURIAT *France, orchestra* *14 wks*

21 Feb 68	LOVE IS BLUE (L'AMOUR EST BLEU)			
	Philips BF 1637		12	14 wks

Billy MAY *US, orchestra* *10 wks*

27 Apr 56 ●	MAIN TITLE THEME FROM MAN WITH THE			
	GOLDEN ARM *Capitol CL 14551*		9	10 wks

Brian MAY and FRIENDS *UK, male vocalist/instrumentalist-guitar, and male instrumental group* *3 wks*

5 Nov 83	STAR FLEET	*EMI 5436*	65	3 wks

Mary MAY *UK, female vocalist* *1 wk*

27 Feb 64	ANYONE WHO HAD A HEART	*Fontana TF 440*	49	1 wk

Simon MAY *UK, male vocalist*   *10 wks*

9 Oct 76	● SUMMER OF MY LIFE *Pye 7N 45627*	7	8 wks
21 May 77	WE'LL GATHER LILACS-ALL MY LOVING (MEDLEY) *Pye 7N 45688*	49	1 wk
4 Jun 77	WE'LL GATHER LILACS-ALL MY LOVING (MEDLEY) (re-entry) *Pye 7N 45688*	50	1 wk

Curtis MAYFIELD *US, male vocalist*   *13 wks*

| 31 Jul 71 | MOVE ON UP *Buddah 2011 080* .... | 12 | 10 wks |
| 2 Dec 78 | NO GOODBYES *Atlantic LV 1* .... | 65 | 3 wks |

MAYTALS
Jamaica, male vocal/instrumental group   *4 wks*

| 25 Apr 70 | MONKEY MAN *Trojan TR 7711* .... | 50 | 1 wk |
| 9 May 70 | MONKEY MAN (re-entry) *Trojan TR 7711* ..... | 47 | 3 wks |

ME AND YOU
Jamaica/UK, male/female vocal duo   *9 wks*

| 28 Jul 79 | YOU NEVER KNOW WHAT YOU'VE GOT *Laser LAS 8* .... | 31 | 9 wks |

Has credit: featuring We The People Band.

MEAT LOAF *US, male vocalist*   *67 wks*

20 May 78	YOU TOOK THE WORDS RIGHT OUT OF MY MOUTH *Epic EPC 5980*	33	8 wks
19 Aug 78	TWO OUT OF THREE AIN'T BAD *Epic EPC 6281*	32	8 wks
10 Feb 79	BAT OUT OF HELL *Epic EPC 7018*	15	7 wks
26 Sep 81	I'M GONNA LOVE HER FOR BOTH OF US *Epic EPCA 1580*	62	3 wks
28 Nov 81	● DEAD RINGER FOR LOVE *Epic EPCA 1697* ...	5	17 wks
28 May 83	IF YOU REALLY WANT TO *Cleveland Int./Epic A 3357*	59	2 wks
24 Sep 83	MIDNIGHT AT THE LOST AND FOUND *Cleveland Int./Epic A 3748*	17	8 wks
14 Jan 84	RAZOR'S EDGE *Cleveland Int./Epic A 4080*	41	3 wks
6 Oct 84	MODERN GIRL *Arista ARIST 585*	17	9 wks
22 Dec 84	NOWHERE FAST *Arista ARIST 600*	67†	2 wks

Dead Ringer For Love features Cher as uncredited co-vocalist. See Cher; Sonny and Cher.

MECO *US, orchestra*   *9 wks*

| 1 Oct 77 | ● STAR WARS THEME-CANTINA BAND *RCA XB 1028* .... | 7 | 9 wks |

MEDICINE HEAD
UK, male vocal/instrumental duo   *37 wks*

26 Jun 71	(AND THE) PICTURES IN THE SKY *Dandelion DAN 7003*	22	8 wks
5 May 73	● ONE AND ONE IS ONE *Polydor 2001 432*	3	13 wks
4 Aug 73	RISING SUN *Polydor 2058 389*	11	9 wks
9 Feb 74	SLIP AND SLIDE *Polydor 2058 436*	22	7 wks

MEDICINE SHOW - *See* DR. HOOK

Michael MEDWIN, Bernard BRESSLAW, Alfie BASS and Leslie FYSON *UK, male vocal group*   *9 wks*

| 30 May 58 | ● THE SIGNATURE TUNE OF THE ARMY GAME *HMV POP 490* .... | 5 | 9 wks |

See also Bernard Bresslaw.

Tony MEEHAN COMBO
UK, male instrumentalist - drums   *4 wks*

| 16 Jan 64 | SONG OF MEXICO *Decca F 11801* .... | 39 | 4 wks |

See also Jet Harris and Tony Meehan.

Melle MEL - *See* GRANDMASTER FLASH, *Melle MEL and the* FURIOUS FIVE

Melle MEL and Duke BOOTEE
US, male/vocal duo   *2 wks*

| 22 Jan 83 | MESSAGE II (SURVIVAL) *Sugarhill SH 119* .... | 74 | 2 wks |

See also Grandmaster Flash, Melle Mel and the Furious Five.

MELACHRINO ORCHESTRA
UK, orchestra, conductor George Melachrino   *9 wks*

| 12 Oct 56 | AUTUMN CONCERTO *HMV B 10958* .... | 18 | 9 wks |

MELANIE *US, female vocalist*   *35 wks*

26 Sep 70	● RUBY TUESDAY *Buddah 2011 038*	9	14 wks
9 Jan 71	RUBY TUESDAY (re-entry) *Buddah 2011 038* ...	43	1 wk
16 Jan 71	WHAT HAVE THEY DONE TO MY SONG MA *Buddah 2011 038*	39	1 wk
1 Jan 72	● BRAND NEW KEY *Buddah 2011 105* ...	4	12 wks
16 Feb 74	WILL YOU LOVE ME TOMORROW *Neighbourhood NBH 9*	37	5 wks
24 Sep 83	EVERY BREATH OF THE WAY *Neighbourhood HOOD NB1*	70	2 wks

MELODIANS
Jamaica, male vocal/instrumental group   *1 wk*

| 10 Jan 70 | SWEET SENSATION *Trojan TR 695* .... | 41 | 1 wk |

Harold MELVIN and the BLUENOTES *US, male vocal group*   *52 wks*

13 Jan 73	● IF YOU DON'T KNOW ME BY NOW *CBS 8496*	9	9 wks
12 Jan 74	THE LOVE I LOST *Philadelphia International PIR 1879*	21	8 wks
13 Apr 74	SATISFACTION GUARANTEED (OR TAKE YOUR LOVE BACK) *Philadelphia International PIR 2187*	32	6 wks
31 May 75	GET OUT *Route RT 06*	35	5 wks
28 Feb 76	WAKE UP EVERYBODY *Philadelphia PIR 3866*	23	7 wks
22 Jan 77	● DON'T LEAVE ME THIS WAY *Philadelphia International PIR 4909*	5	10 wks
2 Apr 77	REACHING FOR THE WORLD *ABC 4161*	48	1 wk
28 Apr 84	DON'T GIVE ME UP *Phillyworld/London LON 47*	59	4 wks
4 Aug 84	TODAY'S YOUR LUCKY DAY *Phillyworld/London LON 52*	66	2 wks

MEMBERS

UK, male vocal/instrumental group   *14 wks*

3 Feb 79		THE SOUND OF THE SUBURBS *Virgin VS 242*		12	9 wks
7 Apr 79		OFFSHORE BANKING BUSINESS *Virgin VS 248*		31	5 wks

MEN AT WORK

Australia, male vocal/instrumental group   *39 wks*

30 Oct 82		WHO CAN IT BE NOW? *Epic EPC A 2392*		45	5 wks
8 Jan 83	★	DOWN UNDER *Epic EPC A 1980*		1	12 wks
9 Apr 83		OVERKILL *Epic EPC A 3220*		21	10 wks
10 Sep 83		DR. HECKYLL AND MR. JIVE *Epic EPC A 3668*		31	6 wks
2 Jul 83		IT'S A MISTAKE *Epic EPC A 3475*		33	6 wks

MEN WITHOUT HATS

Canada, male vocal/instrumental group   *11 wks*

8 Oct 83	●	THE SAFETY DANCE *Statik TAK 1*		6	11 wks

Sergio MENDES   *US, male conductor*   *5 wks*

9 Jul 83	NEVER GONNA LET YOU GO *A & M AM 118*		45	5 wks

Freddie MERCURY   *UK, male vocalist*   *9 wks*

22 Sep 84	●	LOVE KILLS *CBS A 4735*		10	9 wks

Tony MERRICK   *UK, male vocalist*   *1 wk*

2 Jun 66	LADY JANE *Columbia DB 7913*		49	1 wk

MERSEYBEATS

UK, male vocal/instrumental group   *64 wks*

12 Sep 63		IT'S LOVE THAT REALLY COUNTS *Fontana TF 412*		24	12 wks
16 Jan 64	●	I THINK OF YOU *Fontana TF 431*		5	17 wks
16 Apr 64		DON'T TURN AROUND *Fontana TF 459*		13	11 wks
9 Jul 64		WISHIN' AND HOPIN' *Fontana TF 482*		13	10 wks
5 Nov 64		LAST NIGHT *Fontana TF 504*		40	3 wks
14 Oct 65		I LOVE YOU, YES I DO *Fontana TF 607*		22	8 wks
20 Jan 66		I STAND ACCUSED *Fontana TF 645*		38	3 wks

MERSEYS   *UK, male vocal duo*   *13 wks*

28 Apr 66	●	SORROW *Fontana TF 694*		4	13 wks

MERTON PARKAS

UK, male vocal/instrumental group   *6 wks*

4 Aug 79	YOU NEED WHEELS *Beggars Banquet BEG 22*		40	6 wks

METEORS

UK, male vocal/instrumental group   *2 wks*

26 Feb 83	JOHNNY REMEMBER ME *I.D. EYE 1*		66	2 wks

MEZZOFORTE

Iceland, male instrumental group   *10 wks*

5 Mar 83	GARDEN PARTY *Steinar STE 705*		17	9 wks
11 Jun 83	ROCKALL *Steinar STE 710*		75	1 wk

MFSB   *US, orchestra*   *18 wks*

27 Apr 74	TSOP (THE SOUND OF PHILADELPHIA) *Philadelphia International PIR 2289*		22	9 wks
26 Jul 75	SEXY *Philadelphia International PIR 3381*		37	5 wks
31 Jan 81	MYSTERIES OF THE WORLD *The Sound of Philadelphia, PIR 9501*		41	4 wks

TSOP billed as MFSB featuring the Three Degrees. See also Three Degrees.

M.G.'S - *See BOOKER T. and the M.G.'s*

MIAMI SOUND MACHINE

US, male/female vocal group   *14 wks*

11 Aug 84	●	DR BEAT *Epic A 4614*		6	14 wks

Keith MICHELL   *Australia, male vocalist*   *21 wks*

27 Mar 71	I'LL GIVE YOU THE EARTH (TOUS LES BATEUX, TOUS LES OISEAUX) *Spark SRL 1046*		43	1 wk
17 Apr 71	I'LL GIVE YOU THE EARTH (TOUS LES BATEUX, TOUS LES OISEAUX) (re-entry) *Spark SRL 1046*		30	10 wks
26 Jan 80 ●	CAPTAIN BEAKY/WILFRED THE WEASEL *Polydor POSP 106*		5	10 wks

See also Keith Michell, Captain Beaky and his Band.

Keith MICHELL, CAPTAIN BEAKY and his BAND

Australia, male vocalist/UK, instrumental group   *4 wks*

29 Mar 80	THE TRIAL OF HISSING SID *Polydor HISS 1*		53	4 wks

See also Keith Michell.

Lloyd MICHELS - *See MISTURA with Lloyd MICHELS*

MICK - *See Dave DEE, DOZY, BEAKY, MICK and TICH*

MICK - *See KERRI and MICK*

George MICHAEL   *UK, male vocalist*   *17 wks*

4 Aug 84	★	CARELESS WHISPER *Epic A 4603*		1	17 wks

MICROBE   *UK, male vocalist*   *7 wks*

14 May 69	GROOVY BABY *CBS 4158*		29	7 wks

MIDDLE OF THE ROAD

UK, male/female vocal/instrumental group   *76 wks*

5 Jun 71	★	CHIRPY CHIRPY CHEEP CHEEP *RCA 2047*		1	34 wks
4 Sep 71	●	TWEEDLE DEE TWEEDLE DUM *RCA 2110*		2	17 wks
11 Dec 71	●	SOLEY SOLEY *RCA 2151*		5	12 wks
25 Mar 72		SACRAMENTO *RCA 2184*		49	1 wk
8 Apr 72		SACRAMENTO (re-entry) *RCA 2184*		23	6 wks
29 Jul 72		SAMSON & DELILAH *RCA 2237*		26	6 wks

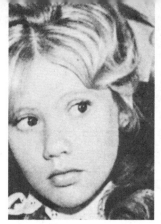

MATT BIANCO (above left) A matt glossy.

HAYLEY MILLS (above centre) An early film fanzine fact sheet reads – Real name: Haley Mills; Born: 18 April 1946; Personal Secret: Her bedroom is decorated in shocking pink with candy stripes.

MEATLOAF (above right) . . . You took the words right out of my mouth.

SUSAN MAUGHAN (left) Belting 'Bobby's Girl' into a Reslo microphone on stage at Liverpool's Cavern Club.

MILK AND HONEY (below) Eurovision winners in 1979 from Israel. The British entry that year was Black Lace's 'Mary Ann'. (Photo: Press Association.)

MIDNIGHT BAND - *See Tony RALLO and the MIDNIGHT BAND*

MIDNIGHT COWBOY SOUNDTRACK *US, orchestra*   *4 wks*

8 Nov 80	**MIDNIGHT COWBOY**	*United Artists UP 634*	...	**47**	4 wks

MIGHTY AVENGERS
UK, male vocal/instrumental group   *2 wks*

26 Nov 64	**SO MUCH IN LOVE**	*Decca F 11962*	....	**46**	2 wks

MIGHTY AVONS - *See Larry CUNNINGHAM and the MIGHTY AVONS*

MIGHTY WAH
UK, male vocal/instrumental group   *9 wks*

30 Jun 84	**COME BACK**	*Eternal/Beggars Banquet BEG 111*	...	**20**	9 wks

See also Wah!

MIGIL FIVE
UK, male vocal/instrumental group   *20 wks*

19 Mar 64	● **MOCKINGBIRD HILL**	*Pye 7N 15597*	....	**10**	13 wks
4 Jun 64	**NEAR YOU**	*Pye 7N 15645*	....	**31**	7 wks

MIKI and GRIFF
UK, male/female vocal duo   *25 wks*

2 Oct 59	**HOLD BACK TOMORROW**	*Pye 7N 15213*	....	**26**	2 wks
13 Oct 60	**ROCKIN' ALONE**	*Pye 7N 15296*	....	**44**	3 wks
1 Feb 62	**LITTLE BITTY TEAR**	*Pye 7N 15412*	.....	**16**	13 wks
22 Aug 63	**I WANNA STAY HERE**	*Pye 7N 15555*	....	**23**	7 wks

John MILES
UK, male vocalist/multi-instrumentalist   *30 wks*

18 Oct 75	**HIGH FLY**	*Decca F 13595*	......	**17**	6 wks
20 Mar 76	● **MUSIC**	*Decca F 13627*	....	**3**	9 wks
16 Oct 76	**REMEMBER YESTERDAY**	*Decca F 13667*	.....	**32**	5 wks
18 Jun 77	● **SLOW DOWN**	*Decca F 13709*	....	**10**	10 wks

MILK AND HONEY
Israel, male/female vocal/instrumental group   *8 wks*

14 Apr 79	● **HALLELUJAH**	*Polydor 2001 870*	....	**5**	8 wks

Hit has credit 'featuring Gali Atari'.

MILL GIRLS - *See Billy COTTON and his BAND*

Frankie MILLER *UK, male vocalist*   *26 wks*

4 Jun 77	**BE GOOD TO YOURSELF**	*Chrysalis CHS 2147*		**27**	6 wks
14 Oct 78	● **DARLIN'**	*Chrysalis CHS 2255*	....	**6**	15 wks
20 Jan 79	**WHEN I'M AWAY FROM YOU** *Chrysalis CHS 2276*	....		**42**	5 wks

Gary MILLER *UK, male vocalist*   *35 wks*

21 Oct 55	**YELLOW ROSE OF TEXAS**	*Nixa N 15004*	....	**13**	5 wks
13 Jan 56	● **ROBIN HOOD**	*Nixa N 15020*	....	**10**	6 wks
11 Jan 57	**GARDEN OF EDEN**	*Pye Nixa N 15070*	....	**14**	6 wks
1 Mar 57	**GARDEN OF EDEN** (re-entry)	*Pye Nixa N 15070*		**27**	1 wk

---

19 Jul 57	**WONDERFUL WONDERFUL**	*Pye Nixa N 15094*	**29**	1 wk
17 Jan 58	**STORY OF MY LIFE**	*Pye Nixa N 15120*	....	**14**	6 wks
21 Dec 61	**THERE GOES THAT SONG AGAIN/THE NIGHT IS YOUNG**	*Pye 7N 15404*	....	**29**	9 wks
1 Mar 62	**THERE GOES THAT SONG AGAIN** (re-entry) *Pye 7N 15404*	....		**48**	1 wk

The Night Is Young only listed with There Goes That Song Again for weeks 21 and 28 Dec 61 and 4 Jan 62.

Glenn MILLER
US, orchestra, Glenn Miller, trombone   *9 wks*

12 Mar 54	**MOONLIGHT SERENADE**	*HMV BD 5942*	....	**12**	1 wk
24 Jan 76	**MOONLIGHT SERENADE/LITTLE BROWN JUG/IN THE MOOD** (re-issue)	*RCA 2644*	.....	**13**	8 wks

Jody MILLER *US, female vocalist*   *1 wk*

21 Oct 65	**HOME OF THE BRAVE**	*Capitol CL 15415*	.....	**49**	1 wk

Mitch MILLER *US, orchestra and chorus*   *13 wks*

7 Oct 55	● **YELLOW ROSE OF TEXAS**	*Philips PB 505*	....	**2**	13 wks

Ned MILLER *US, male vocalist*   *22 wks*

14 Feb 63	● **FROM A JACK TO A KING**	*London HL 9648*	...	**2**	21 wks
18 Feb 65	**DO WHAT YOU DO DO WELL** *London HL 9937*	....		**48**	1 wk

Roger MILLER *US, male vocalist*   *42 wks*

18 Mar 65	★ **KING OF THE ROAD**	*Philips BF 1397*	....	**1**	15 wks
3 Jun 65	**ENGINE ENGINE NO. 9**	*Philips BF 1416*		**33**	5 wks
21 Oct 65	**KANSAS CITY STAR**	*Philips BF 1437*	....	**48**	1 wk
16 Dec 65	**ENGLAND SWINGS**	*Philips BF 1456*		**45**	1 wk
6 Jan 66	**ENGLAND SWINGS** (re-entry)	*Philips BF 1456*		**13**	7 wks
27 Mar 68	**LITTLE GREEN APPLES**	*Mercury MF 1021*	...	**19**	10 wks
2 Apr 69	**LITTLE GREEN APPLES** (re-entry) *Mercury MF 1021*			**48**	1 wk
7 May 69	**LITTLE GREEN APPLES** (2nd re-entry) *Mercury MF 1021*			**39**	2 wks

Suzi MILLER *UK, female vocalist*   *2 wks*

21 Jan 55	**HAPPY DAYS & LONELY NIGHTS** *Decca F 10389*	....		**14**	2 wks

Steve MILLER BAND
US, male vocal/instrumental group   *23 wks*

23 Oct 76	**ROCK'N ME**	*Mercury 6078 804*	....	**11**	9 wks
19 Jun 82	● **ABRACADABRA**	*Mercury/Phonogram STEVE 3*	.	**2**	11 wks
4 Sep 82	**KEEPS ME WONDERING WHY** *Mercury/Phonogram STEVE 4*	....		**52**	3 wks

MILLICAN and NESBITT
UK, male vocal duo   *14 wks*

1 Dec 73	**VAYA CON DIOS**	*Pye 7N 45310*	....	**20**	11 wks
18 May 74	**FOR OLD TIME'S SAKE**	*Pye 7N 45357*	....	**38**	3 wks

MILLIE *Jamaica, female vocalist*   *28 wks*

12 Mar 64	● **MY BOY LOLLIPOP**	*Fontana TF 449*	....	**2**	18 wks
25 Jun 64	**SWEET WILLIAM**	*Fontana TF 479*	....	**30**	9 wks

11 Nov 65	**BLOODSHOT EYES** *Fontana TF 617*	**48**	1 wk

---

Garry MILLS *UK, male vocalist* — *31 wks*

7 Jul 60 ●	**LOOK FOR A STAR** *Top Rank JAR 336*	**7**	14 wks
20 Oct 60	**TOP TEEN BABY** *Top Rank JAR 500*	**24**	12 wks
22 Jun 61	**I'LL STEP DOWN** *Decca F 11358*	**39**	5 wks

---

Hayley MILLS *UK, female vocalist* — *11 wks*

19 Oct 61	**LET'S GET TOGETHER** *Decca F 21396*	**17**	11 wks

---

Mrs. MILLS
UK, female instrumentalist - piano — *5 wks*

14 Dec 61	**MRS MILLS' MEDLEY** *Parlophone R 4856*	**18**	5 wks

Mrs Mills' Medley *consisted of the following tunes: I Want To Be Happy/Sheik Of Araby/Baby Face/Somebody Stole My Gal/ Ma (He's Making Eyes At Me)/Swanee/Ain't She Sweet/California Here I Come.*

Stephanie MILLS *US, female vocalist* — *27 wks*

18 Oct 80 ●	**NEVER KNEW LOVE LIKE THIS BEFORE** *20th Century TC 2460*	**4**	14 wks
23 May 81	**TWO HEARTS** *20th Century TC 2492*	**49**	5 wks
15 Sep 84	**THE MEDICINE SONG** *Club/Phonogram JAB 8* ..	**29**	8 wks

Two Hearts *is 'featuring Teddy Pendergrass'. See Teddy Pendergrass.*

MILLS BROTHERS
US, male vocal group — *1 wk*

30 Jan 53 ●	**GLOW WORM** *Brunswick 05007*	**10**	1 wk

---

Garnet MIMMS and TRUCKIN' CO.
US, male vocalist and male instrumental group — *1 wk*

25 Jun 77	**WHAT IT IS** *Arista 109*	**44**	1 wk

---

MINDBENDERS
UK, male vocal/instrumental group — *34 wks*

13 Jan 66 ●	**A GROOVY KIND OF LOVE** *Fontana TF 644* ..	**2**	14 wks
5 May 66	**CAN'T LIVE WITH YOU (CAN'T LIVE WITHOUT YOU)** *Fontana TF 697*	**28**	7 wks
25 Aug 66	**ASHES TO ASHES** *Fontana TF 731*	**14**	9 wks
20 Sep 67	**THE LETTER** *Fontana TF 869*	**42**	4 wks

See also Wayne Fontana and The Mindbenders.

Sal MINEO *US, male vocalist* — *11 wks*

12 Jul 57	**START MOVIN'** *Philips PB 707*	**16**	11 wks

---

Marcello MINERBI *Italy, orchestra* — *16 wks*

22 Jul 65 ●	**ZORBA'S DANCE** *Durium DRS 54001*	**6**	16 wks

---

MINK DE VILLE
US, male vocal/instrumental group — *9 wks*

6 Aug 77	**SPANISH STROLL** *Capitol CLX 103*	**20**	9 wks

---

Sugar MINOTT *UK, male vocalist* — *16 wks*

28 Mar 81 ●	**GOOD THING GOING (WE'VE GOT A GOOD THING GOING)** *RCA 58*	**4**	12 wks
17 Oct 81	**NEVER MY LOVE** *RCA 138*	**52**	4 wks

---

MIRACLES *US, male vocal group* — *10 wks*

10 Jan 76 ●	**LOVE MACHINE** *Tamla Motown TMG 1015*	**3**	10 wks

See also Smokey Robinson and the Miracles.

MIRAGE *US, male vocal instrumental group* — *4 wks*

14 Jan 84	**GIVE ME THE NIGHT** (MEDLEY) *Passion PASH 15*	**49**	4 wks

Record has credit; featuring Roy Gayle

Danny MIRROR *Holland, male vocalist* — *9 wks*

17 Sep 77 ●	**I REMEMBER ELVIS PRESLEY (THE KING IS DEAD)** *Sonet SON 2121*	**4**	9 wks

---

MR. BIG *UK, male vocal/instrumental group* — *14 wks*

12 Feb 77 ●	**ROMEO** *EMI 2567*	**4**	10 wks
21 May 77	**FEEL LIKE CALLING HOME** *EMI 2610*	**35**	4 wks

---

MR BLOE
UK, male instrumentalist - harmonica — *18 wks*

9 May 70 ●	**GROOVIN' WITH MR. BLOE** *DJM DJS 216* ...	**2**	18 wks

---

MISTURA *US, male instrumental group* — *10 wks*

15 May 76	**THE FLASHER** *Route RT 30*	**23**	10 wks

Has credit: Featuring Lloyd Michels (trumpet).

Cameron **MITCHELL** - See VARIOUS ARTISTS (Carousel Soundtrack)

Guy MITCHELL *US, male vocalist* — *163 wks*

14 Nov 52 ●	**FEET UP** *Columbia DB 3151*	**2**	10 wks
13 Feb 53 ★	**SHE WEARS RED FEATHERS** *Columbia DB 3238*	**1**	15 wks
24 Apr 53 ●	**PRETTY LITTLE BLACK EYED SUSIE** *Columbia DB 3255*	**2**	11 wks
12 Jun 53	**SHE WEARS RED FEATHERS** (re-entry) *Columbia DB 3238*	**12**	1 wk
28 Aug 53 ★	**LOOK AT THAT GIRL** *Philips PB 162*	**1**	14 wks
6 Nov 53 ●	**CHICKA BOOM** *Philips PB 178*	**5**	9 wks
18 Dec 53 ●	**CLOUD LUCKY SEVEN** *Philips PB 210*	**2**	16 wks
15 Jan 54 ●	**CHICKA BOOM** (re-entry) *Philips PB 178*	**4**	6 wks
19 Feb 54 ●	**CUFF OF MY SHIRT** *Philips PB 225*	**9**	1 wk
26 Feb 54	**SIPPIN' SODA** *Philips PB 210*	**11**	1 wk
19 Mar 54	**CUFF OF MY SHIRT** (re-entry) *Philips PB 225*	**12**	1 wk
2 Apr 54	**CUFF OF MY SHIRT** (2nd re-entry) *Philips PB 225*	**11**	1 wk
30 Apr 54 ●	**DIME AND A DOLLAR** *Philips PB 248*	**8**	1 wk
14 May 54 ●	**DIME AND A DOLLAR** (re-entry) *Philips PB 248*	**8**	4 wks
7 Dec 56 ★	**SINGING THE BLUES** *Philips PB 650*	**1**	22 wks
15 Feb 57 ●	**KNEE DEEP IN THE BLUES** *Philips PB 669* ...	**3**	12 wks
26 Apr 57 ★	**ROCK-A-BILLY** *Philips PB 685*	**1**	14 wks
26 Jul 57	**IN THE MIDDLE OF A DARK DARK NIGHT/SWEET STUFF** *Philips PB 712* ...	**27**	2 wks
23 Aug 57	**IN THE MIDDLE OF A DARK DARK NIGHT/SWEET STUFF** (re-entry) *Philips PB 712*	**25**	2 wks

11 Oct 57	**CALL ROSIE ON THE PHONE** *Philips PB 743*	**17**	6 wks
27 Nov 59	**HEARTACHES BY THE NUMBER** *Philips PB 964*	**26**	2 wks
18 Dec 59 ●	**HEARTACHES BY THE NUMBER** (re-entry) *Philips PB 964*	**5**	13 wks

Joni MITCHELL   *Canada, female vocalist*   *15 wks*

13 Jun 70	**BIG YELLOW TAXI** *Reprise RS 20906*	**11**	15 wks

Willie MITCHELL
US, male instrumentalist - guitar   *3 wks*

24 Apr 68	**SOUL SERENADE** *London HLU 10186*	**43**	1 wk
11 Dec 76	**THE CHAMPION** *London HL 10545*	**47**	2 wks

MIXTURES
Australia, male vocal/instrumental group   *21 wks*

16 Jan 71 ●	**THE PUSHBIKE SONG** *Polydor 2058 083*	**2**	21 wks

Hank MIZELL   *US, male vocalist*   *13 wks*

20 Mar 76 ●	**JUNGLE ROCK** *Charly CS 1005*	**3**	13 wks

MOBILES
UK, male/female vocal/instrumental group   *14 wks*

9 Jan 82 ●	**DROWNING IN BERLIN** *Rialto RIA 3*	**9**	10 wks
27 Mar 82	**AMOUR AMOUR** *Rialto RIA 5*	**45**	4 wks

MODERN LOVERS
US, male vocal/instrumental group   *4 wks*

21 Jan 78	**MORNING OF OUR LIVES** *Beserkley BZZ 7*	**29**	4 wks

See also Jonathan Richman and the Modern Lovers.

MODERN ROMANCE
UK, male vocal/instrumental group   *77 wks*

15 Aug 81	**EVERYBODY SALSA** *WEA K 18815*	**12**	10 wks
7 Nov 81 ●	**AY AY AY AY MOOSEY** *WEA K 18883*	**10**	12 wks
30 Jan 82	**QUEEN OF THE RAPPING SCENE (NOTHING EVER GOES THE WAY YOU PLAN)** *WEA K 18928*	**37**	8 wks
14 Aug 82	**CHERRY PINK AND APPLE BLOSSOM WHITE** *WEA K 19245*	**15**	8 wks
13 Nov 82 ●	**BEST YEARS OF OUR LIVES** *WEA ROM 1*	**4**	13 wks
26 Feb 83 ●	**HIGH LIFE** *WEA ROM 2*	**8**	8 wks
7 May 83	**DON'T STOP THAT CRAZY RHYTHM** *WEA ROM 3*	**14**	6 wks
6 Aug 83 ●	**WALKING IN THE RAIN** *WEA X 9733*	**7**	12 wks

Cherry Pink And Apple Blossom White *has credit featuring 'John du Prez'.*

MODETTES
UK, female vocal/instrumental group   *6 wks*

12 Jul 80	**PAINT IT BLACK** *Deram DET-R 1*	**42**	5 wks
18 Jul 81	**TONIGHT** *Deram DET 3*	**68**	1 wk

Domenico MODUGNO
Italy, male vocalist   *13 wks*

5 Sep 58 ●	**VOLARE** *Oriole CB 5000*	**10**	12 wks
27 Mar 59	**CIAO CIAO BAMBINA** *Oriole CB 1489*	**29**	1 wk

MOJO   *UK, male instrumental group*   *3 wks*

22 Aug 81	**DANCE ON** *Creole CR 17*	**70**	3 wks

MOJOS   *UK, male vocal/instrumental group*   *26 wks*

26 Mar 64 ●	**EVERYTHING'S ALRIGHT** *Decca F 11853*	**9**	11 wks
11 Jun 64	**WHY NOT TONIGHT** *Decca F 11918*	**25**	10 wks
10 Sep 64	**SEVEN DAFFODILS** *Decca F 11959*	**30**	5 wks

MOMENTS   *US, male vocal group*   *22 wks*

19 Jul 75 ●	**DOLLY MY LOVE** *All Platinum 6146 306*	**10**	9 wks
25 Oct 75	**LOOK AT ME (I'M IN LOVE)** *All Platinum 6146 309*	**42**	4 wks
22 Jan 77 ●	**JACK IN THE BOX** *All Platinum 6146 318*	**7**	9 wks

See also Moments and Whatnauts.

MOMENTS and WHATNAUTS
US, male vocal group, male instrumental group   *10 wks*

8 Mar 75 ●	**GIRLS** *All Platinum 6146 302*	**3**	10 wks

See also Moments.

Zoot MONEY and the BIG ROLL BAND
UK, male vocalist/instrumentalist - keyboards, male instrumental backing group   *8 wks*

18 Aug 66	**BIG TIME OPERATOR** *Columbia DB 7975*	**25**	8 wks

T S MONK
US, male/female vocal/instrumental group   *6 wks*

7 Mar 81	**BON BON VIE** *Mirage K 11653*	**63**	2 wks
25 Apr 81	**CANDIDATE FOR LOVE** *Mirage K 11648*	**58**	4 wks

MONKEES
US/UK, male vocal/instrumental group   *98 wks*

5 Jan 67 ★	**I'M A BELIEVER** *RCA 1560*	**1**	17 wks
26 Jan 67	**LAST TRAIN TO CLARKSVILLE** *RCA 1547*	**23**	7 wks
6 Apr 67 ●	**A LITTLE BIT ME A LITTLE BIT YOU** *RCA 1580*	**3**	12 wks
22 Jun 67 ●	**ALTERNATE TITLE** *RCA 1604*	**2**	12 wks
16 Aug 67	**PLEASANT VALLEY SUNDAY** *RC 1620*	**11**	8 wks
15 Nov 67 ●	**DAYDREAM BELIEVER** *RCA 1645*	**5**	17 wks
27 Mar 68	**VALLERI** *RCA 1679*	**12**	8 wks
26 Jun 68	**D. W. WASHBURN** *RCA 1706*	**17**	6 wks
26 Mar 69	**TEARDROP CITY** *RCA 1802*	**46**	1 wk
25 Jun 69	**SOMEDAY MAN** *RCA 1824*	**47**	1 wk
15 Mar 80	**THE MONKEES EP** (re-issue of 4 hits) *Arista ARIST 326*	**33**	9 wks

Tracks on EP: I'm a Believer/Daydream Believer/Last Train to Clarksville/A Little Bit Me A Little Bit You.

MONKS UK, male vocal/instrumental group   9 wks

21 Apr 79	NICE LEGS SHAME ABOUT HER FACE		
	Carrere CAR 104	19	9 wks

The Monks are Hudson-Ford under new name. See also Hudson-Ford.

Matt MONRO UK, male vocalist   127 wks

15 Dec 60	● PORTRAIT OF MY LOVE Parlophone R 4714 ...	3	16 wks
9 Mar 61	● MY KIND OF GIRL Parlophone R 4755	5	12 wks
18 May 61	WHY NOT NOW/CAN THIS BE LOVE		
	Parlophone R 4775	24	9 wks
28 Sep 61	GONNA BUILD A MOUNTAIN		
	Parlophone R 4819	44	3 wks
8 Feb 62	● SOFTLY AS I LEAVE YOU Parlophone R 4868 ..	10	18 wks
14 Jun 62	WHEN LOVE COMES ALONG		
	Parlophone R 4911	46	3 wks
8 Nov 62	MY LOVE AND DEVOTION Parlophone R 4954	29	5 wks
14 Nov 63	FROM RUSSIA WITH LOVE Parlophone R 5068	20	13 wks
17 Sep 64	● WALK AWAY Parlophone R 5171	4	20 wks
24 Dec 64	FOR MAMA Parlophone R 5215	36	4 wks
25 Mar 65	WITHOUT YOU Parlophone R 5251	37	4 wks
21 Oct 65	● YESTERDAY Parlophone R 5348	8	12 wks
24 Nov 73	AND YOU SMILED EMI 2091	28	8 wks

Gerry MONROE UK, male vocalist   57 wks

23 May 70	● SALLY Chapter One CH 122	4	20 wks
19 Sep 70	CRY Chapter One CH 128	38	5 wks
14 Nov 70	● MY PRAYER Chapter One CH 132	9	12 wks
17 Apr 71	IT'S A SIN TO TELL A LIE Chapter One CH 144	13	12 wks
21 Aug 71	LITTLE DROPS OF SILVER		
	Chapter One CH 152	37	6 wks
12 Feb 72	GIRL OF MY DREAMS Chapter One CH 159 ...	43	2 wks

MONSOON
UK, male/female vocal/instrumental group   12 wks

3 Apr 82	EVER SO LONELY Phonogram CORP 2	12	9 wks
5 Jun 82	SHAKTI (THE MEANING OF WITHIN)		
	Mobile Suit Corp/Phonogram CORP 4	41	3 wks

MONSTER ORCHESTRA - See John DAVIS and the MONSTER
    ORCHESTRA

Hugo MONTENEGRO US, orchestra   26 wks

11 Sep 68	★ THE GOOD THE BAD & THE UGLY		
	RCA 1727	1	24 wks
8 Jan 69	HANG 'EM HIGH RCA 1771	50	1 wk
19 Mar 69	THE GOOD THE BAD & THE UGLY (re-entry)		
	RCA 1727	48	1 wk

MONTANA SEXTET US, male vocal and
male/female vocal/instrumental group   1 wk

15 Jan 83	HEAVY VIBES Virgin VS 560	59	1 wk

Chris MONTEZ US, male vocalist   61 wks

4 Oct 62	● LET'S DANCE London HLU 9596	2	18 wks
17 Jan 63	● SOME KINDA FUN London HLU 9650	10	9 wks
30 Jun 66	● THE MORE I SEE YOU		
	Pye International 7N 25369	3	13 wks
22 Sep 66	THERE WILL NEVER BE ANOTHER YOU		
	Pye International 7N 25381	37	4 wks
14 Oct 72	● LET'S DANCE (re-issue) London HL 10205	9	14 wks

14 Apr 79	LET'S DANCE (2nd re-issue) Lightning LIG 9011	47	3 wks

The second re-issue of Let's Dance on Lightning was coupled with Memphis by Lonnie Mack as a double A-side. See also Lonnie Mack.

MONTROSE
US, male vocal/instrumental group   2 wks

28 Jun 80	SPACE STATION NO. 5/GOOD ROCKIN'		
	TONIGHT WB HM 9	71	2 wks

MONYAKA
US, male vocal/instrumental group   8 wks

10 Sep 83	GO DEH YAKA (GO TO THE TOP)		
	Polydor POSP 641	14	8 wks

MOOD UK, male vocal/instrumental group   10 wks

6 Feb 82	DON'T STOP RCA 171	59	4 wks
22 May 82	PARIS IS ONE DAY AWAY RCA 211	42	5 wks
30 Oct 82	PASSION IN DARK ROOMS RCA 276	74	1 wk

MOODY BLUES
UK, male vocal/instrumental group   110 wks

10 Dec 64	★ GO NOW Decca F 12022	1	14 wks
4 Mar 65	I DON'T WANT TO GO ON WITHOUT YOU		
	Decca F 12095	33	9 wks
10 Jun 65	FROM THE BOTTOM OF MY HEART		
	Decca F 12166	22	9 wks
18 Nov 65	EVERYDAY Decca F 12266	44	2 wks
27 Dec 67	NIGHTS IN WHITE SATIN Deram DM 161	19	11 wks
7 Aug 68	VOICES IN THE SKY Deram DM 196	27	10 wks
4 Dec 68	RIDE MY SEE-SAW Deram DM 213	42	1 wk
2 May 70	● QUESTION Threshold TH 4	2	12 wks
6 May 72	ISN'T LIFE STRANGE Threshold TH 9	13	10 wks
2 Dec 72	● NIGHTS IN WHITE SATIN (re-entry)		
	Deram DM 161	9	11 wks
10 Feb 73	I'M JUST A SINGER (IN A ROCK 'N ROLL		
	BAND) Threshold TH 13	36	4 wks
10 Nov 79	NIGHTS IN WHITE SATIN (2nd re-entry)		
	Deram DM 161	14	12 wks
20 Aug 83	BLUE WORLD Threshold TH 30	35	5 wks

MOONTREKKERS
UK, male instrumental group   1 wk

2 Nov 61	NIGHT OF THE VAMPIRE Parlophone R 4814 ..	50	1 wk

Dorothy MOORE US, female vocalist   24 wks

19 Jun 76	● MISTY BLUE Contempo CS 2087	5	12 wks
16 Oct 76	FUNNY HOW TIME SLIPS AWAY		
	Contempo CS 2092	38	3 wks
15 Oct 77	I BELIEVE YOU Epic EPC 5573	20	9 wks

Dudley MOORE - See Peter COOK and Dudley MOORE

Gary MOORE
UK, male vocalist/instrumentalist - guitar   19 wks

21 Apr 79	● PARISIENNE WALKWAYS MCA 419	8	11 wks
12 Jan 84	HOLD ON TO YOUR LOVE		
	10 Records/Virgin TEN 13	65	3 wks
11 Aug 84	EMPTY ROOMS 10 Records/Virgin TEN 25	51	5 wks

GILBERT O'SULLIVAN (left) While at art school Irish-born Raymond O'Sullivan played with semi-pro group Rick's Blues, whose Richard Davies co-founded Supertramp with Rodger Hodgson.

OUTLAWS (above) Their 'Ambush' was successful in 1961.

JEFFREY OSBORNE (right) Four hits but his 'Wings' took him highest.

NENA The German group named themselves after their lead singer.

Jackie MOORE · US, female vocalist · 5 wks

15 Sep 79	THIS TIME BABY	CBS 7722	....	49	5 wks

Melba MOORE · US, female vocalist · 29 wks

15 May 76	● THIS IS IT	Buddah BDS 443	....	9	8 wks
26 May 79	PICK ME UP I'LL DANCE	Epic EPC 7234	.....	48	5 wks
9 Oct 82	LOVE'S COMIN' AT YA	EMI America EA 146	..	15	8 wks
15 Jan 83	MIND UP TONIGHT	Capitol CL 272	....	22	6 wks
5 Mar 83	UNDERLOVE	Capitol CL 281	....	60	2 wks

Mike MORAN - See Lynsey DE PAUL and Mike MORAN

MORE · UK, male vocal/instrumental group · 2 wks

14 Mar 81	WE ARE THE BAND	Atlantic K 11561	......	59	2 wks

Derrick MORGAN · Jamaica, male vocalist · 1 wk

17 Jan 70	MOON HOP	Crab 32	....	49	1 wk

Jane MORGAN · US, female vocalist · 21 wks

5 Dec 58	★ THE DAY THE RAINS CAME	London HLR 8751		1	15 wks
22 May 59	IF ONLY I COULD LIVE MY LIFE AGAIN				
		London HLR 8810	....	27	1 wk
21 Jul 60	ROMANTICA	London HLR 9120	....	39	5 wks

Ray MORGAN · UK, male vocalist · 6 wks

25 Jul 70	THE LONG AND WINDING ROAD				
		B & C CB 128	....	32	6 wks

Giorgio MORODER · Italy, male instrumentalist - keyboard synthesisers · 16 wks

24 Sep 77	FROM HERE TO ETERNITY	Oasis 1	....	16	10 wks
17 Mar 79	CHASE	Casablanca CAN 144	....	48	6 wks

First hit credited simply to Giorgio.

Georgio MORODER and Phil OAKEY · Italy/UK, male instrumental/vocal duo · 13 wks

22 Sep 84	● TOGETHER IN ELECTRIC DREAMS				
		Virgin VS 713	....	3	13 wks

See also Georgio Moroder.

Ennio MORRICONE · Italy, orchestra · 12 wks

11 Apr 81	● CHI MAI (THEME FROM THE TV SERIES THE LIFE AND TIMES OF DAVID LLOYD GEORGE)	BBC RESL 92		2	12 wks

Van MORRISON · UK, male vocalist · 3 wks

20 Oct 79	BRIGHT SIDE OF THE ROAD	Mercury 6001 121		63	3 wks

Dorothy Combs MORRISON - See Edwin HAWKINS SINGERS

Buddy MORROW · US, orchestra · 1 wk

20 Mar 53	NIGHT TRAIN	HMV B 10347	....	12	1 wk

Mickie MOST · UK, male vocalist · 1 wk

25 Jul 63	MISTER PORTER	Decca F 11664	....	45	1 wk

MOTELS · US/UK, male/female vocal/instrumental group · 7 wks

11 Oct 80	WHOSE PROBLEM?	Capitol CL 16162	....	42	4 wks
10 Jan 81	DAYS ARE O.K.	Capitol CL 16149	....	41	3 wks

MOTORHEAD · UK, male vocal/instrumental group · 61 wks

16 Sep 78	LOUIE LOUIE	Bronze BRO 60	....	75	1 wk
30 Sep 78	LOUIE LOUIE (re-entry)	Bronze BRO 60	....	68	1 wk
10 Mar 79	OVERKILL	Bronze BRO 67	....	39	4 wks
14 Apr 79	OVERKILL (re-entry)	Bronze BRO 67	....	57	3 wks
30 Jun 79	NO CLASS	Bronze BRO 78	....	61	4 wks
1 Dec 79	BOMBER	Bronze BRO 85	....	34	7 wks
3 May 80	● THE GOLDEN YEARS (EP)	Bronze BRO 92	..	8	7 wks
1 Nov 80	ACE OF SPADES	Bronze BRO 106	....	15	12 wks
22 Nov 80	BEER DRINKERS AND HELL RAISERS				
		Big Beat SWT 61	....	43	4 wks
11 Jul 81	● MOTORHEAD LIVE	Bronze BRO 124	....	6	7 wks
3 Apr 82	IRON FIST	Bronze BRO 146	....	29	5 wks
21 May 83	I GOT MINE	Bronze BRO 165	....	46	2 wks
30 Jul 83	SHINE	Bronze BRO 167	....	59	2 wks
1 Sep 84	KILLED BY DEATH	Bronze BRO 185	......	51	2 wks

Tracks on EP: Dead Men Tell No Tales/Too Late Too Late/Leaving Here/Stone Dead Forever. See also Headgirl, Young and Moody Band.

MOTORS · UK, male vocal/instrumental group · 29 wks

24 Sep 77	DANCING THE NIGHT AWAY	Virgin VS 186		42	4 wks
10 Jun 78	● AIRPORT	Virgin VS 219	....	4	13 wks
19 Aug 78	FORGET ABOUT YOU	Virgin VS 222	....	13	9 wks
12 Apr 80	LOVE AND LONELINESS	Virgin VS 263	.....	58	3 wks

MOTOWN SPINNERS - See DETROIT SPINNERS

MOTT THE HOOPLE · UK, male vocal/instrumental group · 55 wks

12 Aug 72	● ALL THE YOUNG DUDES	CBS 8271		3	11 wks
16 Jun 73	HONALOOCHIE BOOGIE	CBS 1530		12	9 wks
8 Sep 73	ALL THE WAY FROM MEMPHIS	CBS 1764	..	10	8 wks
24 Nov 73	● ROLL AWAY THE STONE	CBS 1895	.....	8	12 wks
30 Mar 74	GOLDEN AGE OF ROCK AND ROLL				
		CBS 2177	....	16	7 wks
22 Jun 74	FOXY FOXY	CBS 2439	....	33	5 wks
2 Nov 74	SATURDAY GIG	CBS 2754	....	41	3 wks

MOUTH and MACNEAL · Holland, male/female vocal duo · 10 wks

4 May 74	● I SEE A STAR	Decca F 13504	....	8	10 wks

MOVE · UK, male vocal/instrumental group · 110 wks

5 Jan 67	● NIGHT OF FEAR	Deram DM 109	....	2	10 wks
6 Apr 67	● I CAN HEAR THE GRASS GROW				
		Deram DM 117	....	5	10 wks
6 Sep 67	● FLOWERS IN THE RAIN				
		Regal Zonophone RZ3001	....	2	13 wks
7 Feb 68	● FIRE BRIGADE	Regal Zonophone RZ3005	....	3	11 wks
25 Dec 68	★ BLACKBERRY WAY	Regal Zonophone RZ3015	..	1	12 wks
23 Jul 69	CURLY	Regal Zonophone RZ3021	..	12	12 wks
25 Apr 70	● BRONTOSAURUS	Regal Zonophone RZ3026	...	7	10 wks

3 Jul 71	TONIGHT *Harvest HAR 5038*	11	10 wks
23 Oct 71	CHINATOWN *Harvest HAR 5043*	23	8 wks
13 May 72 ●	CALIFORNIA MAN *Harvest HAR 5050*	7	14 wks

Alison MOYET *UK, female vocalist*   *27 wks*

23 Jun 84 ●	LOVE RESURRECTION *CBS A 4497*	10	11 wks
13 Oct 84 ●	ALL CRIED OUT *CBS A 4757*	8	11 wks
1 Dec 84 ●	INVISIBLE *CBS A 4930*	23†	5 wks

MTUME
US, male/female vocal/instrumental group   *12 wks*

14 May 83	JUICY FRUIT *Epic A 3424*	34	9 wks
22 Sep 84	PRIME TIME *Epic A 4720*	57	3 wks

MUD *UK, male vocal/instrumental group*   *136 wks*

10 Mar 73	CRAZY *RAK 146*	12	12 wks
23 Jun 73	HYPNOSIS *RAK 152*	16	13 wks
27 Oct 73 ●	DYNA-MITE *RAK 159*	4	12 wks
19 Jan 74 ★	TIGER FEET *RAK 166*	1	11 wks
13 Apr 74 ●	THE CAT CREPT IN *RAK 170*	2	9 wks
27 Jul 74 ●	ROCKET *RAK 178*	6	9 wks
30 Nov 74 ★	LONELY THIS CHRISTMAS *RAK 187* ...	1	10 wks
15 Feb 75 ●	THE SECRETS THAT YOU KEEP *RAK 194* ..	3	9 wks
26 Apr 75 ★	OH BOY *RAK 201*	1	9 wks
21 Jun 75 ●	MOONSHINE SALLY *RAK 208*	10	7 wks
2 Aug 75	ONE NIGHT *RAK 213*	32	4 wks
4 Oct 75 ●	L-L-LUCY *Private Stock PVT 41*	10	6 wks
29 Nov 75 ●	SHOW ME YOU'RE A WOMAN		
	Private Stock PVT 45	8	8 wks
15 May 76	SHAKE IT DOWN *Private Stock PVT 65*	12	8 wks
27 Nov 76 ●	LEAN ON ME *Private Stock PVT 85*	7	9 wks

MUDLARKS *UK, male/female vocal group*   *19 wks*

2 May 58 ●	LOLLIPOP *Columbia DB 4099*	2	9 wks
6 Jun 58 ●	BOOK OF LOVE *Columbia DB 4133*	8	9 wks
27 Feb 59	THE LOVE GAME *Columbia DB 4250*	30	1 wk

MUFFINS - *See MARTHA and the MUFFINS*

Idris MUHAMMAD *US, male vocalist*   *3 wks*

17 Sep 77	COULD HEAVEN EVER BE LIKE THIS		
	Kudu 935	42	3 wks

Maria MULDAUR *US, female vocalist*   *8 wks*

29 Jun 74	MIDNIGHT AT THE OASIS *Reprise K 14331* ...	21	8 wks

Arthur MULLARD - *See Hylda BAKER and Arthur MULLARD*

MUNGO JERRY
UK, male vocal/instrumental group   *87 wks*

6 Jun 70 ★	IN THE SUMMERTIME *Dawn DNX 2502*	1	20 wks
6 Feb 71	BABY JUMP *Dawn DNX 2505*	32	1 wk
20 Feb 71 ★	BABY JUMP (re-entry) *Dawn DNX 2505*	1	12 wks
29 May 71 ●	LADY ROSE *Dawn DNX 2510*	5	12 wks
18 Sep 71	YOU DON'T HAVE TO BE IN THE ARMY TO		
	FIGHT IN THE WAR *Dawn DNX 2513*	13	8 wks
22 Apr 72	OPEN UP *Dawn DNX 2514*	21	8 wks
7 Jul 73 ●	ALRIGHT ALRIGHT ALRIGHT		
	Dawn DNS 1037	3	12 wks
10 Nov 73	WILD LOVE *Dawn DNS 1051*	32	5 wks

6 Apr 74	LONGLEGGED WOMAN DRESSED IN BLACK		
	Dawn DNS 1061	13	9 wks

MUNICH MACHINE
Germany, male instrumental group   *8 wks*

10 Dec 77	GET ON THE FUNK TRAIN *Oasis 2*	41	4 wks
4 Nov 78	A WHITER SHADE OF PALE		
	Oasis/Hansa OASIS 5	42	4 wks

A Whiter Shade Of Pale *billed as Munich Machine introducing Chris Bennett.*

David MUNROW - *See EARLY MUSIC CONSORT*

MUPPETS *US, puppets*   *15 wks*

28 May 77 ●	HALFWAY DOWN THE STAIRS *Pye 7N 45698*	7	8 wks
17 Dec 77	THE MUPPET SHOW MUSIC HALL EP		
	PYE 7NX 8004	19	7 wks

Halfway Down the Stairs *is sung by Jerry Nelson as Kermit the Frog's nephew, Robin. Tracks of EP: Don't Dilly Dally On The Way/Waiting At The Church/The Boy In The Gallery/Wotcher (Knocked 'Em In The Old Kent Road).*

Lydia MURDOCK *US, female vocalist*   *9 wks*

24 Sep 83	SUPERSTAR *Korova KOW 30*	14	9 wks

Walter MURPHY and the BIG APPLE BAND *US, orchestra*   *9 wks*

10 Jul 76	A FIFTH OF BEETHOVEN *Private Stock PVT 59*	28	9 wks

Anne MURRAY *Canada, female vocalist*   *40 wks*

24 Oct 70	SNOWBIRD *Capitol CL 15654*	23	17 wks
21 Oct 72	DESTINY *Capitol CL 15734*	41	4 wks
9 Dec 78	YOU NEEDED ME *Capitol CL 16011*	22	14 wks
21 Apr 79	I JUST FALL IN LOVE AGAIN *Capitol CL 16069*	58	2 wks
19 Apr 80	DAYDREAM BELIEVER *Capitol CL 16123*	61	3 wks

Pauline MURRAY and the INVISIBLE GIRLS *UK, female vocalist with*
male (really) vocal/instrumental group   *2 wks*

2 Aug 80	DREAM SEQUENCE (ONE) *Illusive IVE 1*	67	2 wks

Ruby MURRAY *Ireland, female vocalist*   *110 wks*

3 Dec 54 ●	HEARTBEAT *Columbia DB 3542*	3	16 wks
28 Jan 55 ★	SOFTLY SOFTLY *Columbia DB 3558*	1	22 wks
4 Feb 55 ●	HAPPY DAYS & LONELY NIGHTS		
	Columbia DB 3577	6	8 wks
4 Mar 55 ●	LET ME GO LOVER *Columbia DB 3577*	5	7 wks
18 Mar 55 ●	IF ANYONE FINDS THIS I LOVE YOU		
	Columbia DB 3580	4	11 wks
1 Jul 55 ●	EVERMORE *Columbia DB 3617*	3	17 wks
8 Jul 55	SOFTLY SOFTLY (re-entry) *Columbia DB 3558* ..	20	1 wk
14 Oct 55 ●	I'LL COME WHEN YOU CALL		
	Columbia DB 3643	6	7 wks
31 Aug 56	YOU ARE MY FIRST LOVE *Columbia DB 3770*	16	4 wks
5 Oct 56	YOU ARE MY FIRST LOVE (re-entry)		
	Columbia DB 3770	21	1 wk
12 Dec 58	REAL LOVE *Columbia DB 4192*	18	6 wks
5 Jun 59 ●	GOODBYE JIMMY GOODBYE		
	Columbia DB 4305	10	13 wks
9 Oct 59	GOODBYE JIMMY GOODBYE (re-entry)		
	Columbia DB 4305	26	1 wk

Junior MURVIN *Jamaica, male vocalist* 9 wks

| 3 May 80 | POLICE AND THIEVES *Island WIP 6539* ...... | 23 | 9 wks |

MUSICAL YOUTH
UK, male vocal/instrumental group 55 wks

25 Sep 82 ★	PASS THE DUTCHIE *MCA YOU 1*	1	12 wks
20 Nov 82	YOUTH OF TODAY *MCA YOU 2*	13	9 wks
8 Jan 83	PASS THE DUTCHIE (re-entry) *MCA YOU 1* ..	65	1 wk
12 Feb 83 ●	NEVER GONNA GIVE YOU UP *MCA YOU 3*	6	10 wks
16 Apr 83	HEARTBREAKER *MCA YOU 4*	44	3 wks
9 Jul 83	TELL MY WHY *MCA YOU 5*	33	6 wks
22 Oct 83	007 *MCA YOU 6*	26	6 wks
14 Jan 84	SIXTEEN *MCA YOU 7*	23	8 wks

MUSIQUE *US, female vocal group* 12 wks

| 18 Nov 78 | IN THE BUSH *CBS 6791* .... | 16 | 12 wks |

MUSTAFAS - *See STAIFFI and his MUSTAFAS*

Tim MYCROFT - *See SOUNDS NICE*

Richard MYHILL *UK, male vocalist* 9 wks

| 1 Apr 78 | IT TAKES TWO TO TANGO *Mercury TANGO 1* .... | 17 | 9 wks |

Alicia MYERS *US, female vocalist* 3 wks

| 1 Sep 84 | YOU GET THE BEST FROM ME (SAY SAY SAY) *MCA MCA 914* .... | 58 | 3 wks |

Marie MYRIAM *France, female vocalist* 4 wks

| 28 May 77 | L'OISEAU ET L'ENFANT *Polydor 2056 634* .... | 42 | 4 wks |

MYSTERIANS - *See ?(QUESTION MARK) and the MYSTERIANS*

MYSTI - *See CAMOUFLAGE featuring MYSTI*

MYSTIC MERLIN
US, male vocal/instrumental and magic group 9 wks

| 26 Apr 80 | JUST CAN'T GIVE YOU UP *Capitol CL 16133* | 20 | 9 wks |

N

NAKED EYES
UK, male vocal/instrumental duo 2 wks

| 23 Jul 83 | ALWAYS SOMETHING THERE TO REMIND ME *RCA 348* .... | 60 | 2 wks |

NAPOLEON XIV *US, male vocalist* 10 wks

| 4 Aug 66 ● | THEY'RE COMING TO TAKE ME AWAY HA-HAAA! *Warner Bros. WB 5831* .... | 4 | 10 wks |

NASH - *See CROSBY, STILLS and NASH*

Johnny NASH *US, male vocalist* 97 wks

7 Aug 68 ●	HOLD ME TIGHT *Regal Zonophone RZ 3010* ...	5	16 wks
8 Jan 69 ●	YOU GOT SOUL *Major Minor MM 586*	6	12 wks
2 Apr 69 ●	CUPID *Major Minor MM 603*	6	11 wks
25 Jun 69	CUPID (re-entry) *Major Minor MM 603* ...	50	1 wk
1 Apr 72	STIR IT UP *CBS 7800*	13	12 wks
24 Jun 72 ●	I CAN SEE CLEARLY NOW *CBS 8113* ...	5	15 wks
7 Oct 72 ●	THERE ARE MORE QUESTIONS THAN ANSWERS *CBS 8351*	9	9 wks
14 Jun 75 ★	TEARS ON MY PILLOW *CBS 3220* ...	1	11 wks
11 Oct 75	LET'S BE FRIENDS *CBS 3597*	42	3 wks
12 Jun 76	(WHAT A) WONDERFUL WORLD *Epic EPC 4294*	25	7 wks

NASHVILLE TEENS
UK, male vocal/instrumental group 37 wks

9 Jul 64 ●	TOBACCO ROAD *Decca F 11930*	6	13 wks
22 Oct 64 ●	GOOGLE EYE *Decca F 12000*	10	11 wks
4 Mar 65	FIND MY WAY BACK HOME *Decca F 12089* ..	34	6 wks
20 May 65	THIS LITTLE BIRD *Decca F 12143* ...	38	4 wks
3 Feb 66	THE HARD WAY *Decca F 12316*	45	2 wks
24 Feb 66	THE HARD WAY (re-entry) *Decca F 12316* ...	48	1 wk

NATASHA *UK, female vocalist* 16 wks

| 5 Jun 82 ● | IKO IKO *Towerbell TOW 22* .... | 10 | 11 wks |
| 4 Sep 82 | THE BOOM BOOM ROOM *Towerbell TOW 25* | 44 | 5 wks |

NATURALS
UK, male vocal/instrumental group 9 wks

| 20 Aug 64 | I SHOULD HAVE KNOWN BETTER *Parlophone R 5165* .... | 24 | 9 wks |

David NAUGHTON *US, male vocalist* 6 wks

| 25 Aug 79 | MAKIN' IT *RSO 32* .... | 44 | 6 wks |

NAZARETH
UK, male vocal/instrumental group 75 wks

5 May 73 ●	BROKEN DOWN ANGEL *Mooncrest MOON 1* ..	9	11 wks
21 Jul 73 ●	BAD BAD BOY *Mooncrest MOON 9*	10	9 wks
13 Oct 73	THIS FLIGHT TONIGHT *Mooncrest MOON 14*	11	13 wks
23 Mar 74	SHANGHAI'D IN SHANGHAI *Mooncrest MOON 22*	41	4 wks
14 Jun 75	MY WHITE BICYCLE *Mooncrest MOON 47* ...	14	8 wks
15 Nov 75	HOLY ROLLER *Mountain TOP 3*	36	4 wks
24 Sep 77	HOT TRACKS (EP) *Mountain NAZ 1*	15	11 wks
18 Feb 78	GONE DEAD TRAIN *Mountain NAZ 002*	49	2 wks
13 May 78	PLACE IN YOUR HEART *Mountain TOP 37* ...	70	1 wk
27 May 78	PLACE IN YOUR HEART (re-entry) *Mountain TOP 37*	74	1 wk
27 Jan 79	MAY THE SUN SHINE *Mountain NAZ 003*	22	8 wks
28 Jul 79	STAR *Mountain TOP 45*	54	3 wks

Tracks on Hot Tracks EP: Love Hurts/ This Flight Tonight/Broken Down Angel/Hair of the Dog.

NEIL - *See BARBRA and NEIL*

neil *UK, male vocalist* 10 wks

| 14 Jul 84 ● | HOLE IN MY SHOE *WEA YZ 10* .... | 2 | 10 wks |

Bill NELSON *UK, male*
vocalist/instrumentalist - guitars and synthesisers **12 wks**

24 Feb 79	**FURNITURE MUSIC** *Harvest HAR 5176*	59	3 wks
5 May 79	**REVOLT INTO STYLE** *Harvest HAR 5183*	69	2 wks
5 Jul 80	**DO YOU DREAM IN COLOUR?** *Cocteau COQ 1*	52	4 wks
13 Jun 81	**YOUTH OF NATION ON FIRE** *Mercury WILL 2*	73	3 wks

Furniture Music and Revolt Into Style credited to Bill Nelson's Red Noise

Rick NELSON *US, male vocalist* **132 wks**

21 Feb 58	**STOOD UP** *London HLP 8542*	27	1 wk
7 Mar 58	**STOOD UP** (re-entry) *London HLP 8542*	29	1 wk
22 Aug 58	● **POOR LITTLE FOOL** *London HLP 8670*	4	13 wks
7 Nov 58	● **SOMEDAY** *London HLP 8732*	9	13 wks
21 Nov 58	**I GOT A FEELING** *London HLP 8732*	27	1 wk
28 Nov 58	**POOR LITTLE FOOL** (re-entry) *London HLP 8670*	28	1 wk
17 Apr 59	● **IT'S LATE** *London HLP 8817*	3	20 wks
15 May 59	**NEVER BE ANYONE ELSE BUT YOU** *London HLP 8817*	19	1 wk
5 Jun 59	**NEVER BE ANYONE ELSE BUT YOU** (re-entry) *London HLP 8817*	14	9 wks
4 Sep 59	**SWEETER THAN YOU** *London HLP 8927*	19	3 wks
11 Sep 59	**JUST A LITTLE TOO MUCH** *London HLP 8927*	11	8 wks
15 Jan 60	**I WANNA BE LOVED** *London HLP 9021*	30	1 wk
7 Jul 60	**YOUNG EMOTIONS** *London HLP 9121*	48	1 wk
1 Jun 61	● **HELLO MARY LOU/TRAVELLIN' MAN** *London HLP 9347*	2	18 wks
16 Nov 61	**EVERLOVIN'** *London HLP 9440*	23	5 wks
29 Mar 62	**YOUNG WORLD** *London HLP 9524*	19	13 wks
30 Aug 62	**TEENAGE IDOL** *London HLP 9583*	39	4 wks
17 Jan 63	**IT'S UP TO YOU** *London HLP 9648*	22	9 wks
17 Oct 63	**FOOLS RUSH IN** *Brunswick 05895*	12	9 wks
30 Jan 64	**FOR YOU** *Brunswick 05900*	14	10 wks
21 Oct 72	**GARDEN PARTY** *MCA MU 1165*	41	4 wks

Billed as Ricky Nelson on all the hits up to and including Hello Mary Lou/Travellin' Man.

Sandy NELSON
US, male instrumentalist - drums **42 wks**

6 Nov 59	● **TEEN BEAT** *Top Rank JAR 197*	9	11 wks
5 Feb 60	**TEEN BEAT** (re-entry) *Top Rank JAR 197*	25	1 wk
14 Dec 61	● **LET THERE BE DRUMS** *London HLP 9466*	3	16 wks
22 Mar 62	**DRUMS ARE MY BEAT** *London HLP 9521*	30	6 wks
7 Jun 62	**DRUMMIN' UP A STORM** *London HLP 9558* ...	39	8 wks

Willie NELSON *US, male vocalist* **3 wks**

31 Jul 82	**ALWAYS ON MY MIND** *CBS A 2511*	49	3 wks

See also Julio Iglesias and Willie Nelson.

NENA
Germany, female/male vocal/instrumental group **14 wks**

4 Feb 84	★ **99 RED BALLOONS** *Epic A 4074*	1	12 wks
5 May 84	**JUST A DREAM** *Epic H 3249*	70	2 wks

NERO and the GLADIATORS
UK, male instrumental group **6 wks**

23 Mar 61	**ENTRY OF THE GLADIATORS** *Decca F 11329*	50	1 wk
6 Apr 61	**ENTRY OF THE GLADIATORS** (re-entry) *Decca F 11329*	37	4 wks
27 Jul 61	**IN THE HALL OF THE MOUNTAIN KING** *Decca F 11367*	48	1 wk

---

NESBITT - *See MILLICAN and NESBITT*

Michael NESMITH *US, male vocalist* **6 wks**

26 Mar 77	**RIO** *Island WIP 6373*	28	6 wks

NEVADA
UK, male/female vocal/instrumental group **1 wk**

8 Jan 83	**IN THE BLEAK MID WINTER** *Polydor POSP 203*	71	1 wk

NEW EDITION *US, male vocal group* **18 wks**

16 Apr 83	★ **CANDY GIRL** *London LON 21*	1	13 wks
13 Aug 83	**POPCORN LOVE** *Streetwise/London LON 31*	44	5 wks

NEW GENERATION
UK, male vocal/instrumental group **5 wks**

26 Jun 68	**SMOKEY BLUES AWAY** *Spark SRL 1007*	38	5 wks

NEW MUSIK
UK, male vocal/instrumental group **27 wks**

6 Oct 79	**STRAIGHT LINES** *GTO GT 255*	53	5 wks
19 Jan 80	**LIVING BY NUMBERS** *GTO GT 261*	13	8 wks
26 Apr 80	**THIS WORLD OF WATER** *GTO GT 268*	31	7 wks
12 Jul 80	**SANCTUARY** *GTO GT 275*	31	7 wks

NEW ORDER
UK, male/female vocal/instrumental group **67 wks**

14 Mar 81	**CEREMONY** *Factory FAC 33*	34	5 wks
3 Oct 81	**PROCESSION/EVERYTHING'S GONE GREEN** *Factory FAC 53*	38	5 wks
22 May 82	**TEMPTATION** *Factory FAC 63*	29	7 wks
19 Mar 83	**BLUE MONDAY** *Factory FAC 7312*	12	17 wks
13 Aug 83	● **BLUE MONDAY** (re-entry) *Factory FAC 7312* ...	9	17 wks
3 Sep 83	**CONFUSION** *Factory FAC 93*	12	7 wks
7 Jan 84	**BLUE MONDAY** (2nd re-entry) *Factory FAC 7312*	52	4 wks
28 Apr 84	**THIEVES LIKE US** *Factory FAC 103*	18	5 wks

Group male only on first hit.

NEW ORLEANS JAZZMEN - *See Terry LIGHTFOOT and his NEW ORLEANS JAZZMEN*

NEW SEEKERS
UK, male/female vocal/instrumental group **143 wks**

17 Oct 70	**WHAT HAVE THEY DONE TO MY SONG MA** *Philips 6006 027*	48	1 wk
31 Oct 70	**WHAT HAVE THEY DONE TO MY SONG MA** (re-entry) *Philips 6006 027*	44	1 wk
10 Jul 71	● **NEVER ENDING SONG OF LOVE** *Philips 6006 125*	2	19 wks
18 Dec 71	★ **I'D LIKE TO TEACH THE WORLD TO SING** *Polydor 2058 184*	1	21 wks
4 Mar 72	● **BEG STEAL OR BORROW** *Polydor 2058 201* ...	2	13 wks
10 Jun 72	● **CIRCLES** *Polydor 2058 242*	4	16 wks
2 Dec 72	**COME SOFTLY TO ME** *Polydor 2058 313*	20	11 wks
24 Feb 73	**PINBALL WIZARD - SEE ME FEEL ME** (MEDLEY) *Polydor 2058 338*	16	8 wks
7 Apr 73	**NEVERTHELESS** *Polydor 2068 340*	34	5 wks
16 Jun 73	**GOODBYE IS JUST ANOTHER WORD** *Polydor 2058 368*	36	5 wks

24 Nov 73 ★	YOU WON'T FIND ANOTHER FOOL LIKE ME			
	Polydor 2058 421		1	16 wks
9 Mar 74 ●	I GET A LITTLE SENTIMENTAL OVER YOU			
	Polydor 2058 439		5	9 wks
14 Aug 76	IT'S SO NICE (TO HAVE YOU HOME)			
	CBS 4391		44	4 wks
29 Jan 77	I WANNA GO BACK CBS 4786		25	4 wks
15 Jul 78	ANTHEM (ONE DAY IN EVERY WEEK)			
	CBS 6413		21	10 wks

Come Softly To Me has credit 'featuring Marty Kristian'. Nevertheless billed as 'by Eve Graham and the New Seekers'.

NEW VAUDEVILLE BAND

UK, male vocal/instrumental group　　　　　　　　　　　　*43 wks*

8 Sep 66 ●	WINCHESTER CATHEDRAL Fontana TF 741		4	19 wks
26 Jan 67 ●	PEEK-A-BOO Fontana TF 784		7	11 wks
11 May 67	FINCHLEY CENTRAL Fontana TF 824		11	9 wks
2 Aug 67	GREEN STREET GREEN Fontana TF 853		37	4 wks

Peek-A-Boo has credit: Featuring Tristram.

NEW WORLD

Australia, male vocal/instrumental group　　　　　　　*53 wks*

27 Feb 71	ROSE GARDEN RAK 111		15	11 wks
3 Jul 71 ★	TOM TOM TURNAROUND RAK 117		6	15 wks
4 Dec 71	KARA KARA RAK 123		17	13 wks
13 May 72 ●	SISTER JANE RAK 130		9	13 wks
12 May 73	ROOF TOP SINGING RAK 148		50	1 wk

NEW YORK CITY *US, male vocal group*　　*11 wks*

21 Jul 73	I'M DOING FINE NOW RCA 2351		20	11 wks

NEW YORK SKYY

US, male/female vocal/instrumental group　　　　　　*2 wks*

16 Jan 82	LET'S CELEBRATE Epic EPC A 1898		71	1 wk
30 Jan 82	LET'S CELEBRATE (re-entry) Epic EPC A 1898		67	1 wk

NEWBEATS *US, male vocal group*　　*22 wks*

10 Sep 64	BREAD AND BUTTER Hickory 1269		15	9 wks
23 Oct 71 ●	RUN BABY RUN London HL 10341		10	13 wks

Booker NEWBURY III

US, male vocalist　　　　　　　　　　　　　　　　*13 wks*

28 May 83 ●	LOVE TOWN Polydor POSP 613		6	8 wks
8 Oct 83	TEDDY BEAR Polydor/Montage POSP 637		44	5 wks

Mickey NEWBURY *US, male vocalist*　　*5 wks*

1 Jul 72	AMERICAN TRILOGY Elektra K 12047		42	5 wks

NEWCLEUS

US, male vocal/instrumental group　　　　　　　　　*6 wks*

3 Sep 83	JAM ON REVENGE (THE WIKKI WIKKI SONG)			
	Beckett BKS 8		44	6 wks

Anthony NEWLEY *UK, male vocalist*　　*129 wks*

1 May 59 ●	I'VE WAITED SO LONG Decca F 11127		3	15 wks

8 May 59	IDLE ON PARADE (EP) Decca DFE 6566		13	4 wks
12 Jun 59 ●	PERSONALITY Decca F 11142		6	12 wks
15 Jun 60 ★	WHY Decca F 11194		1	17 wks
24 Mar 60 ★	DO YOU MIND Decca F 11220		1	15 wks
14 Jul 60 ●	IF SHE SHOULD COME TO YOU			
	Decca F 11254		6	15 wks
24 Nov 60 ●	STRAWBERRY FAIR Decca F 11295		3	11 wks
16 Mar 61 ●	AND THE HEAVENS CRIED Decca F 11331		6	12 wks
15 Jun 61	POP GOES THE WEASEL/BEE BOM			
	Decca F 11362		12	9 wks
3 Aug 61	WHAT KIND OF FOOL AM I? Decca F 11376		36	8 wks
25 Jan 62	D-DARLING Decca F 11419		25	6 wks
26 Jul 62	THAT NOISE Decca F 11486		34	5 wks

Bee Bom only listed together with Pop Goes The Weasel for weeks of 15 and 22 June 61. Tracks on Idle On Parade EP: I've Waited So Long/Idle Rock-A-Boogie/Idle On Parade/Saturday Night Rock-A-Boogie.

Alfred NEWMAN - *See VARIOUS ARTISTS (Carousel Soundtrack)*

Brad NEWMAN *UK, male vocalist*　　　*1 wk*

22 Feb 62	SOMEBODY TO LOVE Fontana H 357		47	1 wk

Dave NEWMAN *UK, male vocalist*　　*6 wks*

15 Apr 72	THE LION SLEEPS TONIGHT Pye 7N 45134		48	1 wk
29 Apr 72	THE LION SLEEPS TONIGHT (re-entry)			
	Pye 7N 45134		34	5 wks

NEWS *US, male vocal/instrumental group*　　*3 wks*

29 Aug 81	AUDIO VIDEO George GEORGE 1		52	3 wks

NEWS - *See Huey LEWIS and the NEWS*

Juice NEWTON *US, female vocalist*　　*6 wks*

2 May 81	ANGEL OF THE MORNING Capitol CL 16189		43	6 wks

Olivia NEWTON-JOHN

UK, female vocalist　　　　　　　　　　　　　　*145 wks*

20 Mar 71 ●	IF NOT FOR YOU Pye International 7N 25543		7	11 wks
23 Oct 71 ●	BANKS OF THE OHIO Pye International 7N 25568		6	17 wks
11 Mar 72	WHAT IS LIFE Pye International 7N 25575		16	8 wks
13 Jan 73	TAKE ME HOME COUNTRY ROADS			
	Pye International 7N 25599		15	13 wks
16 Mar 74	LONG LIVE LOVE Pye International 7N 25638		11	8 wks
12 Oct 74	I HONESTLY LOVE YOU EMI 2216		22	6 wks
11 Jun 77 ●	SAM EMI 2616		6	11 wks
4 Nov 78 ●	HOPELESSLY DEVOTED TO YOU RSO 17		2	11 wks
16 Dec 78 ●	A LITTLE MORE LOVE EMI 2879		4	12 wks
30 Jun 79	DEEPER THAN THE NIGHT EMI 2954		64	3 wks
23 Aug 80	MAGIC Jet 196		32	7 wks
10 Oct 81 ●	PHYSICAL EMI 5234		7	16 wks
16 Jan 82	LANDSLIDE EMI 5257		18	9 wks
17 Apr 82	MAKE A MOVE ON ME EMI 5291		43	3 wks
23 Oct 82	HEART ATTACK EMI 5347		46	4 wks
15 Jan 83	I HONESTLY LOVE YOU (re-issue) EMI 5360		52	4 wks
12 Nov 83	TWIST OF FATE EMI 5438		57	2 wks

See also Olivia Newton-John and Electric Light Orchestra; Olivia Newton-John and Cliff Richard; John Travolta and Olivia Newton-John.

Olivia NEWTON-JOHN and ELECTRIC LIGHT ORCHESTRA
UK, female vocalist, male vocal/instrumental group   *11 wks*

| 21 Jun 80 | ★ XANADU *Jet 185* | 1 | 11 wks |

See also Olivia Newton-John; John Travolta and Olivia Newton-John; Olivia Newton-John and Cliff Richard; Electric Light Orchestra.

Olivia NEWTON-JOHN and Cliff RICHARD
UK, female/male vocal duo   *7 wks*

| 25 Oct 80 | SUDDENLY *Jet 7002* | 15 | 7 wks |

See also Olivia Newton-John; Cliff Richard; Olivia Newton-John and Electric Light Orchestra; John Travolta and Olivia Newton-John.

NICE
UK, male instrumental group   *15 wks*

| 10 Jul 68 | AMERICA *Immediate IM 068* | 21 | 15 wks |

Paul NICHOLAS
UK, male vocalist   *31 wks*

17 Apr 76	REGGAE LIKE IT USED TO BE *RSO 2090 185*	17	8 wks
9 Oct 76	● DANCING WITH THE CAPTAIN *RSO 2090 206*	8	9 wks
4 Dec 76	● GRANDMA'S PARTY *RSO 2090 216*	9	11 wks
9 Jul 77	HEAVEN ON THE 7TH FLOOR *RSO 2090 249*	40	3 wks

Sue NICHOLS
UK, female vocalist   *8 wks*

| 3 Jul 68 | WHERE WILL YOU BE *Pye 7N 17565* | 17 | 8 wks |

Stevie NICKS with Tom PETTY and the HEARTBREAKERS
US, female vocalist with male vocal/instrumental group   *4 wks*

| 15 Aug 81 | STOP DRAGGIN' MY HEART AROUND *WEA K 79231* | 50 | 4 wks |

See also Tom Petty and the Heartbreakers.

NICOLE
Germany, female vocalist   *10 wks*

| 8 May 82 | ★ A LITTLE PEACE *CBS A 2365* | 1 | 9 wks |
| 21 Aug 82 | GIVE ME MORE TIME *CBS A 2467* | 75 | 1 wk |

Maxine NIGHTINGALE
UK, female vocalist   *16 wks*

| 1 Nov 75 | ● RIGHT BACK WHERE WE STARTED FROM *United Artists UP 36015* | 8 | 8 wks |
| 12 Mar 77 | LOVE HIT ME *United Artists UP 36215* | 11 | 8 wks |

NILSSON
US, male vocalist   *51 wks*

27 Sep 69	EVERYBODY'S TALKIN' *RCA 1876*	50	1 wk
11 Oct 69	EVERYBODY'S TALKIN' (re-entry) *RCA 1876*	23	9 wks
14 Mar 70	EVERYBODY'S TALKIN' (2nd re-entry) *RCA 1876*	39	5 wks
5 Feb 72	★ WITHOUT YOU *RCA 2165*	1	20 wks
3 Jun 72	COCONUT *RCA 2214*	42	5 wks
16 Oct 76	WITHOUT YOU (re-issue) *RCA 2733*	22	8 wks
20 Aug 77	ALL I THINK ABOUT IS YOU *RCA PB 9104*	43	3 wks

NINA and FREDERICK
Denmark, female/male vocal duo   *29 wks*

18 Dec 59	MARY'S BOY CHILD *Columbia DB 4375*	26	1 wk
10 Mar 60	LISTEN TO THE OCEAN *Columbia DB 4332*	47	1 wk
7 Apr 60	LISTEN TO THE OCEAN (re-entry) *Columbia DB 4332*	46	1 wk
17 Nov 60	● LITTLE DONKEY *Columbia DB 4536*	3	10 wks
28 Sep 61	LONGTIME BOY *Columbia DB 4703*	43	3 wks
5 Oct 61	SUCU SUCU *Columbia DB 4632*	23	13 wks

999
UK, male vocal/instrumental group   *13 wks*

25 Nov 78	HOMICIDE *United Artists UP 36467*	40	3 wks
27 Oct 79	FOUND OUT TOO LATE *Radar ADA 46*	69	2 wks
16 May 81	OBSESSED *Albion ION 1011*	71	1 wk
18 Jul 81	LIL RED RIDING HOOD *Albion ION 1017*	59	3 wks
14 Nov 81	INDIAN RESERVATION *Albion ION 1023*	51	4 wks

1910 FRUITGUM CO.
US, male vocal/instrumental group   *16 wks*

| 20 Mar 68 | ● SIMON SAYS *Pye International 7N 25447* | 2 | 16 wks |

NIRVANA
UK, male vocal/instrumental duo   *6 wks*

| 15 May 68 | RAINBOW CHASER *Island WIP 6029* | 34 | 6 wks |

NO DICE
UK, male vocal/instrumental group   *2 wks*

| 5 May 79 | COME DANCING *EMI 2927* | 65 | 2 wks |

NOLANS
Ireland, female vocal group   *89 wks*

6 Oct 79	SPIRIT BODY AND SOUL *Epic EPC 7796*	34	6 wks
22 Dec 79	● I'M IN THE MOOD FOR DANCING *Epic EPC 8068*	3	15 wks
12 Apr 80	DON'T MAKE WAVES *Epic EPC 8349*	12	11 wks
13 Sep 80	● GOTTA PULL MYSELF TOGETHER *Epic EPC 8878*	9	13 wks
6 Dec 80	WHO'S GONNA ROCK YOU *Epic EPC 9325*	12	11 wks
14 Mar 81	● ATTENTION TO ME *Epic EPC 9571*	9	13 wks
15 Aug 81	CHEMISTRY *Epic EPC A1485*	15	8 wks
20 Feb 82	DON'T LOVE ME TOO HARD *Epic EPC A 1927*	14	12 wks

First hit billed as Nolan Sisters. See also Young and Moody Band.

Peter NOONE
UK, male vocalist   *9 wks*

| 22 May 71 | OH YOU PRETTY THING *RAK 114* | 12 | 9 wks |

See also Herman's Hermits.

Freddie NOTES and the RUDIES
Jamaica, male vocal/instrumental group   *2 wks*

| 10 Oct 70 | MONTEGO BAY *Trojan TR 7791* | 45 | 2 wks |

NOTTINGHAM FOREST F.C. and PAPER LACE
UK, football team vocalists and UK, male vocal/instrumental group   *6 wks*

| 4 Mar 78 | WE'VE GOT THE WHOLE WORLD IN OUR HANDS *Warner Bros. K 17710* | 24 | 6 wks |

See also Paper Lace.

Nancy NOVA   US, female vocalist   2 wks

| 4 Sep 82 | NO NO NO | EMI 5328 | .... | 63 | 2 wks |

Gary NUMAN   UK, male vocalist   99 wks

19 May 79	★ ARE FRIENDS ELECTRIC				
	Beggars Banquet BEG 18	....	1	16 wks
1 Sep 79	★ CARS Beggars Banquet BEG 23	....	1	11 wks
24 Nov 79	● COMPLEX Beggars Banquet BEG 29	....	6	9 wks
24 May 80	● WE ARE GLASS Beggars Banquet BEG 35	......	5	7 wks
30 Aug 80	● I DIE: YOU DIE Beggars Banquet BEG 46	....	6	7 wks
20 Dec. 80	THIS WRECKAGE Beggars Banquet BEG 50	....	20	7 wks
29 Aug 81	● SHE'S GOT CLAWS Beggars Banquet BEG 62	....	6	6 wks
5 Dec 81	LOVE NEEDS NO DISGUISE				
	Beggars Banquet BEG 68	....	33	7 wks
6 Mar 82	MUSIC FOR CHAMELEONS				
	Beggars Banquet BEG 70	....	19	7 wks
19 Jun 82	● WE TAKE MYSTERY (TO BED)				
	Beggars Banquet BEG 77	....	9	4 wks
28 Aug 82	WHITE BOYS AND HEROES				
	Beggars Banquet BEG 81	....	20	4 wks
3 Sep 83	WARRIORS Beggars Banquet BEG 95	....	20	5 wks
22 Oct 83	SISTER SURPRISE Beggars Banquet BEG 101	....	32	3 wks
3 Nov 84	BERSERKER Numa NU 4	....	32	5 wks
22 Dec 84	MY DYING MACHINE Numa NU 6	....	66	1 wk

Are Friends Electric by Gary Numan under the group name Tubeway Army. Love Needs No Disguise *credited to Gary Numan and Dramatis. See also Dramatis.*

Bobby NUNN
US, male vocalist/multi-instrumentalist   3 wks

| 4 Feb 84 | DON'T KNOCK IT (UNTIL YOU TRY IT) | | | | |
| | Motown TMG 1323 | .... | 65 | 3 wks |

O

Phil OAKEY   - *See Georgio MORODER and Phil OAKEY*

John OATES   - *See Daryl HALL and John OATES*

OBERNKIRCHEN CHILDREN'S CHOIR   Germany, children's choir   26 wks

| 22 Jan 54 | ● HAPPY WANDERER   Parlophone R 3799 | .... | 2 | 23 wks |
| 9 Jul 54 | ● HAPPY WANDERER   (re-entry) Parlophone R 3799 | .. | 8 | 3 wks |

Dermot O'BRIEN   Ireland, male vocalist   2 wks

20 Oct 66	THE MERRY PLOUGHBOY Envoy ENV 016	..	46	1 wk
3 Nov 66	THE MERRY PLOUGHBOY (re-entry)				
	Envoy ENV 016	....	50	1 wk

Billy OCEAN   UK, male vocalist   63 wks

21 Feb 76	● LOVE REALLY HURTS WITHOUT YOU				
	GTO GT 52	....	2	10 wks
10 Jul 76	L.O.D. (LOVE ON DELIVERY) GTO GT 62	..	19	8 wks
13 Nov 76	STOP ME (IF YOU'VE HEARD IT ALL BEFORE)				
	GTO GT 72	....	12	11 wks
19 Mar 77	● RED LIGHT SPELLS DANGER GTO GT 85	..	2	10 wks
1 Sep 79	AMERICAN HEARTS GTO GT 244	....	54	5 wks
19 Jan 80	ARE YOU READY GTO GT 259	....	42	7 wks
13 Oct 84	● CARIBBEAN QUEEN (NO MORE LOVE ON THE RUN) Jive JIVE 77	....	6†	12 wks

Des O'CONNOR   UK, male vocalist   107 wks

1 Nov 67	● CARELESS HANDS Columbia DB 8275	....	6	17 wks
8 May 68	★ I PRETEND Columbia DB 8397	....	1	36 wks
20 Nov 68	● 1-2-3 O'LEARY Columbia DB 8492	....	4	11 wks
7 May 69	DICK-A-DUM-DUM (KING'S ROAD)				
	Columbia DB 8566	....	14	10 wks
29 Nov 69	LONELINESS Columbia DB 8632	....	18	11 wks
14 Mar 70	I'LL GO ON HOPING Columbia DB 8661	....	30	7 wks
26 Sep 70	THE TIPS OF MY FINGERS Columbia DB 8713	....	15	15 wks

Hazel O'CONNOR   UK, female vocalist   46 wks

16 Aug 80	● EIGHTH DAY A & M AMS 7553	....	5	11 wks
25 Oct 80	GIVE ME AN INCH A & M AMS 7569	......	41	4 wks
21 Mar 81	● D-DAYS Albion ION 1009	....	10	9 wks
23 May 81	● WILL YOU A & M AMS 8131	....	8	10 wks
1 Aug 81	(COVER PLUS) WE'RE ALL GROWN UP				
	Albion ION 1018	....	41	6 wks
3 Oct 81	HANGING AROUND Albion ION 1022	....	45	3 wks
23 Jan 82	CALLS THE TUNE A & M AMS 8203	....	60	3 wks

Alan O'DAY   US, male vocalist   3 wks

| 2 Jul 77 | UNDERCOVER ANGEL   Atlantic K 10926 | ...... | 43 | 3 wks |

ODETTA   - *See Harry BELAFONTE and ODETTA*

ODYSSEY   US, male/female vocal group   78 wks

24 Dec 77	● NATIVE NEW YORKER RCA PC 1129	....	5	11 wks
21 Jun 80	★ USE IT UP AND WEAR IT OUT RCA PB 1962		1	12 wks
13 Sep 80	● IF YOU'RE LOOKIN' FOR A WAY OUT				
	RCA 5	....	6	15 wks
17 Jan 81	HANG TOGETHER RCA 23	....	36	7 wks
30 May 81	● GOING BACK TO MY ROOTS RCA 85	....	4	12 wks
19 Sep 81	IT WILL BE ALRIGHT RCA 128	....	43	5 wks
12 Jun 82	● INSIDE OUT RCA 226	....	3	11 wks
11 Sep 82	MAGIC TOUCH RCA 275	....	41	5 wks

Esther and Abi OFARIM
Israel, female/male vocal duo   22 wks

| 14 Feb 68 | ★ CINDERELLA ROCKEFELLA   Philips BF 1640 | .. | 1 | 13 wks |
| 19 Jun 68 | ONE MORE DANCE   Philips BF 1678 | .... | 13 | 9 wks |

OHIO EXPRESS
US, male vocal/instrumental group   15 wks

| 5 Jun 68 | ● YUMMY YUMMY YUMMY | | | | |
| | Pye International 7N 25459 | .... | 5 | 15 wks |

OHIO PLAYERS
US, male vocal/instrumental group   4 wks

| 10 Jul 76 | WHO'D SHE COO   Mercury PLAY 001 | .... | 43 | 4 wks |

O'JAYS   US, male vocal group   72 wks

23 Sep 72	BACK STABBERS CBS 8270	....	14	9 wks
3 Mar 73	● LOVE TRAIN CBS 1181	....	9	13 wks
31 Jan 76	I LOVE MUSIC Philadelphia International PIR 3879		13	9 wks
12 Feb 77	DARLIN' DARLIN' BABY (SWEET, TENDER, LOVE) Philadelphia International PIR 4834		24	6 wks
8 Apr 78	I LOVE MUSIC (re-issue)				
	Philadelphia International PIR 6093	....	36	3 wks

ORANGE JUICE (left) Despite production by Dennis Bovell the title of their last single '84 proved to be fairly prophetic.

PALE FOUNTAINS (above). just sprayed the charts (Photo: Baker and Trasmundi.)

TOM PETTY (above) Del Shannon shows Tom the chords to 'Runaway'. (Photo: Dennis Callahan.)

ROBERT PALMER (right) Yorkshire born, he joined The Alan Bown Set, before becoming a member of Dada. The latter group evolved into Vinegar Joe, in which Palmer shared lead vocals with Elkie Brooks and Peter Gage. (Photo: Peter Ashworth.)

17 Jun 78	USED TA BE MY GIRL			
	Philadelphia International PIR 6332	12	12 wks
30 Sep 78	BRANDY *Philadelphia International PIR 6658*	21	9 wks
29 Sep 79	SING A HAPPY SONG			
	Philadelphia International PIR 7825	39	6 wks
30 Jul 83	PUT OUR HEADS TOGETHER			
	Philadelphia International A 3642	45	5 wks

Mike OLDFIELD
UK, male multi-instrumentalist/vocalist 86 wks

13 Jul 74	MIKE OLDFIELD'S SINGLE (THEME FROM TUBULAR BELLS) *Virgin VS 101*	31	6 wks
20 Dec 75 ●	IN DULCE JUBILO/ON HORSEBACK *Virgin VS 131*	4	10 wks
27 Nov 76 ●	PORTSMOUTH *Virgin VS 163*	3	12 wks
23 Dec 78	TAKE 4 (EP) *Virgin VS 238*	72	3 wks
21 Apr 79	GUILTY *Virgin VS 245*	22	8 wks
8 Dec 79	BLUE PETER *Virgin VS 317*	19	9 wks
20 Mar 82	FIVE MILES OUT *Virgin VS 464*	43	6 wks
12 Jun 82	FAMILY MAN *Virgin VS 489*	45	6 wks
28 May 83 ●	MOONLIGHT SHADOW *Virgin VS 586*	4	17 wks
14 Jan 84	CRIME OF PASSION *Virgin VS 648*	61	3 wks
30 Jun 84	TO FRANCE *Virgin VS 686*	48	7 wks

Tracks on Take 4 EP: Portsmouth/In Dulce Jubilo/ Wrekorder Wrondo/Sailors Hornpipe.

Sally OLDFIELD   *UK, female vocalist*   13 wks

9 Dec 78	MIRRORS *Bronze BRO 66*	19	13 wks

OLIVER   *US, male vocalist*   18 wks

9 Aug 69 ●	GOOD MORNING STARSHINE *CBS 4435*	6	16 wks
27 Dec 69	GOOD MORNING STARSHINE (re-entry) *CBS 4435*	39	2 wks

OLLIE and JERRY   *US, male vocal duo*   11 wks

23 Jun 84 ●	BREAKIN'...THERE'S NO STOPPING US *Polydor POSP 690*	5	11 wks

OLYMPIC ORCHESTRA
UK, orchestra   15 wks

1 Oct 83	REILLY *Red Bus RBUS 82*	26	15 wks

OLYMPIC RUNNERS
UK, male vocal/instrumental group   21 wks

13 May 78	WHATEVER IT TAKES *RCA PC 5078*	61	2 wks
14 Oct 78	GET IT WHILE YOU CAN *Polydor RUN 7*	35	6 wks
20 Jan 79	SIR DANCEALOT *Polydor POSP 17*	35	6 wks
28 Jul 79	THE BITCH *Polydor POSP 63*	37	7 wks

OLYMPICS   *US, male vocal group*   9 wks

3 Oct 58	WESTERN MOVIES *HMV POP 528*	12	8 wks
19 Jan 61	I WISH I COULD SHIMMY LIKE MY SISTER KATE *Vogue V 9174*	45	1 wk

ONE HUNDRED TON AND A FEATHER
UK, male vocalist, Jonathan King under false name   9 wks

26 Jun 76 ●	IT ONLY TAKES A MINUTE *UK 135*	9	9 wks

See also Jonathan King.

ONE THE JUGGLER
UK, male vocal/instrumental group   1 wk

19 Feb 83	PASSION KILLER *Regard RG 107*	71	1 wk

ONE WAY featuring Al HUDSON
US, male/female vocal/instrumental group   6 wks

8 Dec 79	MUSIC *MCA 542*	56	6 wks

See also Al Hudson and the Partners.

Yoko ONO   *Japan, female vocalist*   5 wks

28 Feb 81	WALKING ON THIN ICE *Geffen K 79202*	35	5 wks

See also John Lennon.

ORANGE JUICE
UK, male vocal/instrumental group   34 wks

7 Nov 81	L.O.V.E...LOVE *Polydor POSP 357*	65	2 wks
30 Jan 82	FELICITY *Polydor POSP 386*	63	3 wks
21 Aug 82	TWO HEARTS TOGETHER/HOKOYO *Polydor POSP 470*	60	2 wks
23 Oct 82	I CAN'T HELP MYSELF *Polydor POSP 522*	42	3 wks
19 Feb 83 ●	RIP IT UP *Polydor POSP 547*	8	11 wks
4 Jun 83	FLESH OF MY FLESH *Black/Polydor OJ 4*	41	6 wks
25 Feb 84	BRIDGE *Polydor OJ 5*	67	2 wks
12 May 84	WHAT PRESENCE? *Polydor OJ 6*	47	4 wks
27 Oct 84	LEAN PERIOD *Polydor OJ 7*	74	1 wk

Roy ORBISON   *US, male vocalist*   309 wks

28 Jul 60	ONLY THE LONELY *London HLU 9149*	36	1 wk
11 Aug 60 ★	ONLY THE LONELY (re-entry) *London HLU 9149*	1	23 wks
27 Oct 60	BLUE ANGEL *London HLU 9207*	11	16 wks
25 May 61 ●	RUNNING SCARED *London HLU 9342*	9	15 wks
21 Sep 61	CRYIN' *London HLU 9405*	25	9 wks
8 Mar 62 ●	DREAM BABY *London HLU 9511*	2	14 wks
28 Jun 62	THE CROWD *London HLU 9561*	40	4 wks
8 Nov 62	WORKIN' FOR THE MAN *London HLU 9607*	50	1 wk
28 Feb 63 ●	IN DREAMS *London HLU 9676*	6	23 wks
30 May 63 ●	FALLING *London HLU 9727*	9	11 wks
19 Sep 63 ●	BLUE BAYOU/MEAN WOMAN BLUES *London HLU 9777*	3	19 wks
20 Feb 64	BORNE ON THE WIND *London HLU 9845*	15	10 wks
30 Apr 64 ★	IT'S OVER *London HLU 9882*	1	18 wks
10 Sep 64 ★	OH PRETTY WOMAN *London HLU 9919* ...	1	18 wks
19 Nov 64 ●	PRETTY PAPER *London HLU 9930*	6	11 wks
11 Feb 65	GOODNIGHT *London HLU 9951*	14	9 wks
22 Jul 65	(SAY) YOU'RE MY GIRL *London HLU 9978* ...	23	8 wks
9 Sep 65	RIDE AWAY *London HLU 9986*	34	6 wks
4 Nov 65	CRAWLIN' BACK *London HLU 10000*	19	9 wks
27 Jan 66	BREAKIN' UP IS BREAKIN' MY HEART *London HL 10015*	22	6 wks
7 Apr 66	TWINKLE TOES *London HLU 10034*	29	5 wks
16 Jun 66	LANA *London HL 10051*	15	9 wks
18 Aug 66 ●	TOO SOON TO KNOW *London HLU 10067*	3	17 wks
1 Dec 66	THERE WON'T BE MANY COMING HOME *London HL 10096*	18	9 wks
23 Feb 67	SO GOOD *London HL 10113*	32	6 wks
24 Jul 68	WALK ON *London HLU 10206*	39	10 wks
25 Sep 68	HEARTACHE *London HLU 10222*	44	4 wks
30 Apr 69	MY FRIEND *London HL 10261*	35	4 wks
13 Sep 69	PENNY ARCADE *London HL 10285*	40	3 wks
11 Oct 69	PENNY ARCADE (re-entry) *London HL 10285* ...	27	11 wks

ORCHESTRAL MANOEUVRES in the DARK
UK, male vocal/instrumental duo — 107 wks

9 Feb 80	RED FRAME WHITE LIGHT	Dindisc DIN 6	67	2 wks
10 May 80	MESSAGES	Dindisc DIN 15	13	11 wks
4 Oct 80 ●	ENOLA GAY	Dindisc DIN 22	8	15 wks
29 Aug 81 ●	SOUVENIR	Dindisc DIN 24	3	12 wks
24 Oct 81 ●	JOAN OF ARC	Dindisc DIN 36	5	14 wks
23 Jan 82 ●	MAID OF ORLEANS (THE WALTZ JOAN OF ARC)	Dindisc DIN 40	4	10 wks
19 Feb 83	GENETIC ENGINEERING	Telegraph/Virgin VS 527	20	8 wks
9 Apr 83	TELEGRAPH	Telegraph/Virgin VS 580	42	4 wks
14 Apr 84 ●	LOCOMOTION	Virgin VS 660	5	11 wks
16 Jun 84	TALKING LOUD AND CLEAR	Virgin VS 685	11	10 wks
8 Sep 84	TESLA GIRLS	Virgin VS 705	21	8 wks
10 Nov 84	NEVER TURN AWAY	Virgin VS 727	70	2 wks

Tony ORLANDO
US, male vocalist — 11 wks

5 Oct 61 ●	BLESS YOU	Fontana H 330	5	11 wks

See also Dawn.

ORLONS
US, female/male vocal group — 3 wks

27 Dec 62	DON'T HANG UP	Cameo Parkway C 231	50	1 wk
10 Jan 63	DON'T HANG UP (re-entry)	Cameo Parkway C 231	39	2 wks

Tony OSBORNE SOUND
UK, orchestra — 3 wks

23 Feb 61	MAN FROM MADRID	HMV POP 827	50	1 wk
3 Feb 73	THE SHEPHERD'S SONG	Philips 6006 266	46	2 wks

Hit has credit; featuring Joanne Brown (UK female vocalist).

Jeffrey OSBOURNE
US, male vocalist — 29 wks

17 Sep 83	DON'T YOU GET SO MAD	A & M AM 140	54	2 wks
14 Apr 84	STAY WITH ME TONIGHT	A & M AM 188	18	11 wks
23 Jun 84	ON THE WINGS OF LOVE	A & M AM 198	11	14 wks
20 Oct 84	DON'T STOP	A & M AM 222	61	2 wks

Ozzy OSBOURNE BLIZZARD OF OZZ
UK, male vocal/instrumental group — 24 wks

13 Sep 80	CRAZY TRAIN	Jet 197	49	4 wks
15 Nov 80	MR. CROWLEY	Jet 7003	46	3 wks
26 Nov 83	BARK AT THE MOON	Epic A 3915	21	8 wks
2 Jun 84	SO TIRED	Epic A 4452	20	9 wks

Last two hits credited to Ozzy Osbourne only.

OSIBISA
Ghana/Nigeria, male vocal/instrumental group — 12 wks

17 Jan 76	SUNSHINE DAY	Bronze BRO 20	17	6 wks
5 Jun 76	DANCE THE BODY MUSIC	Bronze BRO 26	31	6 wks

Donny OSMOND
US, male vocalist — 105 wks

17 Jun 72 ★	PUPPY LOVE	MGM 2006 104	1	17 wks
16 Sep 72 ●	TOO YOUNG	MGM 2006 113	5	12 wks
21 Oct 72	PUPPY LOVE (re-entry)	MGM 2006 104	45	2 wks
11 Nov 72 ●	WHY	MGM 2006 119	3	20 wks
23 Dec 72	PUPPY LOVE (2nd re-entry)	MGM 2006 104	46	1 wk
23 Dec 72	TOO YOUNG (re-entry)	MGM 2006 113	47	3 wks
27 Jan 73	PUPPY LOVE (3rd re-entry)	MGM 2006 104	48	1 wk
10 Mar 73 ★	THE TWELFTH OF NEVER	MGM 2006 199	1	14 wks
18 Aug 73 ●	YOUNG LOVE	MGM 2006 300	1	10 wks
10 Nov 73 ●	WHEN I FALL IN LOVE	MGM 2006 365	4	13 wks
9 Nov 74	WHERE DID ALL THE GOOD TIMES GO	MGM 2006 468	18	10 wks

See also Donny and Marie Osmond; Osmonds.

Donny and Marie OSMOND
US, male/female vocal duo — 37 wks

3 Aug 74 ●	I'M LEAVING IT (ALL) UP TO YOU	MGM 2006 446	2	12 wks
14 Dec 74 ●	MORNING SIDE OF THE MOUNTAIN	MGM 2006 474	5	12 wks
21 Jun 75	MAKE THE WORLD GO AWAY	MGM 2006 523	18	6 wks
17 Jan 76	DEEP PURPLE	MGM 2006 561	25	7 wks

See also Donny Osmond; Marie Osmond; Osmonds.

Little Jimmy OSMOND
US, male vocalist — 50 wks

25 Nov 72 ★	LONG HAIRED LOVER FROM LIVERPOOL	MGM 2006 109	1	24 wks
31 Mar 73 ●	TWEEDLE DEE	MGM 2006 175	4	13 wks
19 May 73	LONG HAIRED LOVER FROM LIVERPOOL (re-entry)	MGM 2006 109	41	3 wks
23 Mar 74	I'M GONNA KNOCK ON YOUR DOOR	MGM 2006 389	11	10 wks

Marie OSMOND
US, female vocalist — 15 wks

17 Nov 73 ●	PAPER ROSES	MGM 2006 315	2	15 wks

See also Donny and Marie Osmond.

OSMONDS
US, male vocal/instrumental group — 91 wks

25 Mar 72	DOWN BY THE LAZY RIVER	MGM 2006 096	40	5 wks
11 Nov 72 ●	CRAZY HORSES	MGM 2006 142	2	18 wks
14 Jul 73 ●	GOING HOME	MGM 2006 288	4	10 wks
27 Oct 73 ●	LET ME IN	MGM 2006 321	2	14 wks
20 Apr 74	I CAN'T STOP	MCA 129	12	10 wks
24 Aug 74 ★	LOVE ME FOR A REASON	MGM 2006 458	1	9 wks
1 Mar 75	HAVING A PARTY	MGM 2006 492	28	8 wks
24 May 75	THE PROUD ONE	MGM 2006 520	5	8 wks
15 Nov 75	I'M STILL GONNA NEED YOU	MGM 2006 551	32	4 wks
30 Oct 76	I CAN'T LIVE A DREAM	Polydor 2391 236	37	5 wks

See also Donny Osmond; Donny and Marie Osmond.

Gilbert O'SULLIVAN
Ireland, male vocalist — 143 wks

28 Nov 70 ●	NOTHING RHYMED	MAM 3	8	11 wks
3 Apr 71	UNDERNEATH THE BLANKET GO	MAM 13	40	1 wk
17 Apr 71	UNDERNEATH THE BLANKET GO (re-entry)	MAM 13	42	3 wks
24 Jul 71	WE WILL	MAM 30	16	11 wks
27 Nov 71 ●	NO MATTER HOW I TRY	MAM 53	5	15 wks
4 Mar 72 ●	ALONE AGAIN (NATURALLY)	MAM 66	3	12 wks
17 Jun 72 ●	OOH-WAKKA-DOO-WAKKA-DAY	MAM 78	8	11 wks
21 Oct 72 ★	CLAIR	MAM 84	1	14 wks
17 Mar 73 ★	GET DOWN	MAM 96	1	13 wks
15 Sep 73	OOH BABY	MAM 107	18	7 wks
10 Nov 73 ●	WHY OH WHY OH WHY	MAM 111	6	14 wks
9 Feb 74	HAPPINESS IS ME AND YOU	MAM 114	19	7 wks
24 Aug 74	A WOMAN'S PLACE	MAM 122	42	3 wks
14 Dec 74	CHRISTMAS SONG	MAM 124	12	6 wks

14 Jun 75	I DON'T LOVE YOU BUT I THINK I LIKE YOU		
	MAM 130	14	6 wks
27 Sep 80	WHAT'S IN A KISS? CBS 8929	19	9 wks

Johnny OTIS SHOW
US, orchestra and chorus — *22 wks*

22 Nov 57 ●	MA HE'S MAKING EYES AT ME		
	Capitol CL 14794	2	15 wks
10 Jan 58	BYE BYE BABY Capitol CL 14817	20	7 wks

Ma He's Making Eyes At Me *credits Johnny Otis and his orchestra with Marie Adams and the Three Tons of Joy.* Bye Bye Baby *features vocals by Marie Adams and Johnny Otis.*

OTTAWAN *France, male/female vocal duo* — *45 wks*

13 Sep 80 ●	D.I.S.C.O. Carrere CAR 161	2	18 wks
13 Dec 80	YOU'RE O.K. Carrere CAR 168	56	6 wks
29 Aug 81 ●	HANDS UP (GIVE ME YOUR HEART)		
	Carrere CAR 183	3	15 wks
5 Dec 81	HELP, GET ME SOME HELP! Carrere CAR 215	49	6 wks

John OTWAY and Wild Willy BARRETT *UK, male vocal/instrumental duo* — *12 wks*

3 Dec 77	REALLY FREE Polydor 2058 951	27	8 wks
5 Jul 80	DK 50-80 Polydor 2059 250	45	4 wks

DK 50-80 *credited simply to Otway and Barrett.*

OUR DAUGHTER'S WEDDING
US, male vocal/instrumental group — *6 wks*

1 Aug 81	LAWNCHAIRS EMI America EA 124	49	6 wks

OUR KID *UK, male vocal group* — *11 wks*

29 May 76 ●	YOU JUST MIGHT SEE ME CRY		
	Polydor 2058 729	2	11 wks

OUTLAWS *UK, male instrumental group* — *4 wks*

13 Apr 61	SWINGIN' LOW HMV POP 844	46	2 wks
8 Jun 61	AMBUSH HMV POP 877	43	2 wks

See also Mike Berry with the Outlaws.

OVERLANDERS
UK, male vocal/instrumental group — *10 wks*

13 Jan 66 ★	MICHELLE Pye 7N 17034	1	10 wks

Reg OWEN *UK, orchestra* — *10 wks*

27 Feb 59	MANHATTAN SPIRITUAL		
	Pye International 7N 25009	20	8 wks
27 Oct 60	OBSESSION Palette PG 9004	43	2 wks

P

Thom PACE *US, male vocalist* — *15 wks*

19 May 79	MAYBE RSO 34	14	15 wks

PACEMAKERS – *See GERRY and the PACEMAKERS*

PACKABEATS
UK, male instrumental group — *1 wk*

23 Feb 61	GYPSY BEAT Parlophone R 4729	49	1 wk

Hal PAGE and the WHALERS
US, male vocal/instrumental group — *1 wk*

25 Aug 60	GOING BACK TO MY HOME TOWN		
	Melodisc MEL 1553	50	1 wk

Patti PAGE *US, female vocalist* — *5 wks*

27 Mar 53 ●	(HOW MUCH IS) THAT DOGGIE IN THE WINDOW Oriole CB 1156	9	5 wks

PAGLIARO *Canada, male vocalist* — *6 wks*

19 Feb 72	LOVING YOU AIN'T EASY Pye 7N 45111	31	6 wks

Elaine PAIGE *UK, female vocalist* — *21 wks*

21 Oct 78	DON'T WALK AWAY TILL I TOUCH YOU		
	EMI 2862	46	5 wks
6 Jun 81 ●	MEMORY Polydor POSP 279	6	12 wks
30 Jan 82	MEMORY (re-entry) Polydor POSP 279	67	3 wks
14 Apr 84	SOMETIMES (THEME FROM CHAMPIONS)		
	Island IS 174	72	1 wk

PALE FOUNTAINS
UK, male vocal/instrumental group — *6 wks*

27 Nov 82	THANK YOU Virgin VS 557	48	6 wks

Robert PALMER *UK, male vocalist* — *37 wks*

20 May 78	EVERY KINDA PEOPLE Island WIP 6425	53	4 wks
7 Jul 79	BAD CASE OF LOVIN' YOU (DOCTOR DOCTOR) Island WIP 6481	61	2 wks
6 Sep 80	JOHNNY AND MARY Island WIP 6638	44	8 wks
22 Nov 80	LOOKING FOR CLUES Island WIP 6651	33	9 wks
13 Feb 82	SOME GUYS HAVE ALL THE LUCK		
	Island WIP 6754	16	8 wks
2 Apr 83	YOU ARE IN MY SYSTEM Island IS 104	53	4 wks
18 Jun 83	YOU CAN HAVE IT (TAKE MY HEART)		
	Island IS 121	74	2 wks

PAPER DOLLS *UK, female vocal group* — *13 wks*

13 Mar 68	SOMETHING HERE IN MY HEART (KEEPS A-TELLIN' ME NO) Pye 7N 17456	11	13 wks

PAPER LACE
UK, male vocal/instrumental group — *35 wks*

23 Feb 74 ★	BILLY DON'T BE A HERO Bus Stop BUS 1014	1	14 wks
4 May 74 ●	THE NIGHT CHICAGO DIED		
	Bus Stop BUS 1016	3	11 wks
24 Aug 74	THE BLACK EYED BOYS Bus Stop BUS 1019	11	10 wks

See also Nottingham Forest F.C. with Paper Lace

PARADISE
UK, male vocal/instrumental group   4 wks

10 Sep 83	**ONE MIND, TWO HEARTS**	*Priority P 1*	......	42	4 wks

Norrie PARAMOR   *UK, orchestra*   8 wks

17 Mar 60	**THEME FROM 'A SUMMER PLACE'**				
	Columbia DB 4419	....		36	2 wks
22 Mar 62	**THEME FROM 'Z CARS'**	*Columbia DB 4789*	....	33	6 wks

PARAMOUNT JAZZ BAND   - *See Mr. Acker BILK*

PARAMOUNTS
UK, male vocal/instrumental group   7 wks

16 Jan 64	**POISON IVY**	*Parlophone R 5093*	....	35	7 wks

PARCHMENT
UK, male/female vocal/instrumental group   5 wks

16 Sep 72	**LIGHT UP THE FIRE**	*Pye 7N 45178*	....	31	5 wks

PARIS   *UK, male/female vocal group*   4 wks

19 Jun 82	**NO GETTING OVER YOU**	*RCA 222*	....	49	4 wks

Ryan PARIS   *France, male vocalist*   10 wks

3 Sep 83	● **DOLCE VITA**	*Clever/Carrere CAR 289*	....	5	10 wks

Simon PARK   *UK, orchestra*   22 wks

25 Nov 72	**EYE LEVEL**	*Columbia DB 8946*		41	2 wks
15 Sep 73	★ **EYE LEVEL**	(re-entry) *Columbia DB 8946*	......	1	14 wks
5 Jan 74	**EYE LEVEL**	(2nd re-entry) *Columbia DB 8946*	...	31	6 wks

Graham PARKER   *UK, male vocalist*   4 wks

20 Mar 82	**TEMPORARY BEAUTY**	*RCA PARK 100*	.....	50	4 wks

See also Graham Parker and the Rumour.

Graham PARKER and the RUMOUR
UK, male vocal and instrumental group   12 wks

19 Mar 77	**THE PINK PARKER** (EP)	*Vertigo PARK 001*	....	24	5 wks
22 Apr 78	**HEY LORD DON'T ASK ME QUESTIONS**				
	Vertigo PARK 002	....		32	7 wks

Tracks on The Pink Parker EP: Hold Back The Night/ (Let Me Get) Sweet On You/White Honey/Soul Shoes. See also Graham Parker.

Ray PARKER JUNIOR
US, male vocalist   19 wks

25 Aug 84	● **GHOSTBUSTERS**	*Arista ARIST 580*	....	2†	19 wks

Robert PARKER   *US, male vocalist*   8 wks

4 Aug 66	**BAREFOOTIN'**	*Island WI 286*	....	24	8 wks

Jimmy PARKINSON
Australia, male vocalist   19 wks

2 Mar 56	● **THE GREAT PRETENDER**	*Columbia DB 3729*	..	9	13 wks
17 Aug 56	**WALK HAND IN HAND**	*Columbia DB 3775*	....	30	1 wk
5 Oct 56	**WALK HAND IN HAND**	(re-entry)			
	Columbia DB 3775	....		26	1 wk
9 Nov 56	**IN THE MIDDLE OF THE HOUSE**				
	Columbia DB 3833	....		26	2 wks
30 Nov 56	**IN THE MIDDLE OF THE HOUSE**	(re-entry)			
	Columbia DB 3833	....		20	2 wks

Dean PARRISH   *US, male vocalist*   5 wks

8 Feb 75	**I'M ON MY WAY**	*UK USA 2*		38	5 wks

Man PARRISH   *US, mixer*   6 wks

26 Mar 83	**HIP HOP, BE BOP (DON'T STOP)**				
	Polydor POSP 575	....		41	6 wks

Alan PARSONS PROJECT
UK, male vocal instrumental group   4 wks

15 Jan 83	**OLD & WISE**	*Arista ARIST 494*	....	74	1 wk
10 Mar 84	**DON'T ANSWER ME**	*Arista ARIST 553*	....	58	3 wks

Bill PARSONS   *US, male vocalist*   2 wks

10 Apr 59	**ALL AMERICAN BOY**	*London HL 8798*	....	22	2 wks

PARTNERS   - *See Al HUDSON and the PARTNERS*

David PARTON   *UK, male vocalist*   9 wks

15 Jan 77	● **ISN'T SHE LOVELY**	*Pye 7N 45663*	....	4	9 wks

Dolly PARTON   *US, female vocalist*   16 wks

15 May 76	● **JOLENE**	*RCA 2675*	....	7	10 wks
21 Feb 81	**9 TO 5**	*RCA 25*	....	47	5 wks
7 Apr 84	**HERE YOU COME AGAIN**	*RCA 395*	....	75	1 wk

See also Kenny Rogers and Dolly Parton.

Stella PARTON   *US, female vocalist*   4 wks

22 Oct 77	**THE DANGER OF A STRANGER**				
	Elektra K 12272	....		35	4 wks

Don PARTRIDGE   *UK, male vocalist*   32 wks

7 Feb 68	● **ROSIE**	*Columbia DB 8330*	....	4	12 wks
29 May 68	● **BLUE EYES**	*Columbia DB 8416*	....	3	13 wks
19 Feb 69	**BREAKFAST ON PLUTO**	*Columbia DB 8538*	...	26	7 wks

PARTRIDGE FAMILY starring Shirley JONES featuring David CASSIDY   *US, male/female vocal group*   53 wks

13 Feb 71	**I THINK I LOVE YOU**	*Bell 1130*	....	18	9 wks
26 Feb 72	**IT'S ONE OF THOSE NIGHTS (YES LOVE)**				
	Bell 1203			11	11 wks
8 Jul 72	● **BREAKING UP IS HARD TO DO**	*Bell MABEL 1*		3	13 wks

3 Feb 73	● **LOOKING THROUGH THE EYES OF LOVE**			
	Bell 1278	9	9 wks	
19 May 73	● **WALKING IN THE RAIN** *Bell 1293*	10	11 wks	

See also David Cassidy, Various Artists - Carousel Soundtrack, on which Shirley Jones appears. Last two hits are simply 'starring David Cassidy' - no Shirley Jones credit.

PASSIONS
UK, male/female vocal/instrumental group — *8 wks*

31 Jan 81	**I'M IN LOVE WITH A GERMAN FILM STAR**			
	Polydor POSP 222	25	8 wks	

PATIENCE and PRUDENCE
US, female vocal duo — *8 wks*

2 Nov 56	**TONIGHT YOU BELONG TO ME**			
	London HLU 8321	28	3 wks	
1 Mar 57	**GONNA GET ALONG WITHOUT YA NOW**			
	London HLU 8369	22	4 wks	
12 Apr 57	**GONNA GET ALONG WITHOUT YA NOW**			
	(re-entry) *London HLU 8369*	24	1 wk	

Kellee PATTERSON *US, female vocalist* — *7 wks*

18 Feb 78	**IF IT DON'T FIT DON'T FORCE IT**			
	EMI International INT 558	44	7 wks	

PAUL - *See PETER, PAUL and MARY*

PAUL and PAULA
US, male/female vocal duo — *31 wks*

14 Feb 63	● **HEY PAULA** *Philips 304012 BF*	8	12 wks	
18 Apr 63	● **YOUNG LOVERS** *Philips 304016 BF*	9	14 wks	
16 May 63	**HEY PAULA** (re-entry) *Philips 304012 BF*	37	5 wks	

Billy PAUL *US, male vocalist* — *44 wks*

13 Jan 73	**ME & MRS JONES** *Epic EPC 1055*	12	9 wks	
12 Jan 74	**THANKS FOR SAVING MY LIFE**			
	Philadelphia International PIR 1928	33	6 wks	
22 May 76	**LET'S MAKE A BABY**			
	Philadelphia International PIR 4144	30	5 wks	
30 Apr 77	**LET 'EM IN** *Philadelphia International PIR 5143*	26	5 wks	
16 Jul 77	**YOUR SONG** *Philadelphia International PIR 5391*	37	7 wks	
19 Nov 77	**ONLY THE STRONG SURVIVE**			
	Philadelphia International PIR 5699	33	7 wks	
14 Jul 79	**BRING THE FAMILY BACK**			
	Philadelphia International PIR 7456	51	5 wks	

See also Philadelphia International All-Stars.

Les PAUL and Mary FORD
US, male instrumentalist - guitar, and female vocalist — *4 wks*

20 Nov 53	● **VAYA CON DIOS** *Capitol CL 13943*	7	4 wks	

Lyn PAUL *UK, female vocalist* — *6 wks*

28 Jun 75	**IT OUGHTA SELL A MILLION** *Polydor 2058 602*	37	6 wks	

PAULA - *See PAUL and PAULA*

Rita PAVONE *Italy, female vocalist* — *19 wks*

1 Dec 66	**HEART** *RCA 1553*	27	12 wks	

19 Jan 67	**YOU ONLY YOU** *RCA 1561*	21	7 wks	

Freda PAYNE *US, female vocalist* — *30 wks*

5 Sep 70	★ **BAND OF GOLD** *Invictus INV 502*	1	19 wks	
21 Nov 70	**DEEPER & DEEPER** *Invictus INV 505*	33	9 wks	
27 Mar 71	**CHERISH WHAT IS DEAR TO YOU**			
	Invictus INV 509	46	2 wks	

PEACHES and HERB
US, female/male vocal duo — *23 wks*

20 Jan 79	**SHAKE YOUR GROOVE THING**			
	Polydor 2066 992	26	10 wks	
21 Apr 79	● **REUNITED** *Polydor POSP 43*	4	13 wks	

PEARLS *UK, female vocal duo* — *24 wks*

27 May 72	**THIRD FINGER, LEFT HAND** *Bell 1217*	31	6 wks	
23 Sep 72	**YOU CAME YOU SAW YOU CONQUERED**			
	Bell 1254	32	5 wks	
24 Mar 73	**YOU ARE EVERYTHING** *Bell 1284*	41	3 wks	
1 Jun 74	● **GUILTY** *Bell 1352*	10	10 wks	

Johnny PEARSON
UK, orchestra, Johnny Pearson featured pianist — *15 wks*

18 Dec 71	● **SLEEPY SHORES** *Penny Farthing PEN 778*	8	15 wks	

PEDDLERS
UK, male vocal/instrumental group — *14 wks*

7 Jan 65	**LET THE SUNSHINE IN** *Philips BF 1375*	50	1 wk	
23 Aug 69	**BIRTH** *CBS 4449*	17	9 wks	
31 Jan 70	**GIRLIE** *CBS 4720*	34	4 wks	

Ann PEEBLES *US, female vocalist* — *3 wks*

20 Apr 74	**I CAN'T STAND THE RAIN** *London HL 10428*	50	1 wk	
4 May 74	**I CAN'T STAND THE RAIN** (re-entry)			
	London HL 10428	41	2 wks	

PEECH BOYS
UK, male vocal/instrumental group — *3 wks*

30 Oct 82	**DON'T MAKE ME WAIT** *TMT TMT 7001*	49	3 wks	

Donald PEERS *UK, male vocalist* — *27 wks*

18 Dec 68	● **PLEASE DON'T GO** *Columbia DB 8502*	3	18 wks	
30 Apr 69	**PLEASE DON'T GO** (re-entry) *Columbia DB 8502*	38	3 wks	
24 Jun 72	**GIVE ME ONE MORE CHANCE** *Decca F 13302*	36	6 wks	

Teddy PENDERGRASS
US, male vocalist — *9 wks*

21 May 77	**THE WHOLE TOWN'S LAUGHING AT ME**			
	Philadelphia International PIR 5116	44	3 wks	
28 Oct 78	**ONLY YOU /CLOSE THE DOOR**			
	Philadelphia International S PIR 6713	41	6 wks	

See also Philadelphia International All-Stars.

P. J. PROBY Photographed getting to grips with his pony tail before his appearance at the Billy Fury Memorial Concert.

COZY POWELL Cozy's the one on the right.

POLICE Your very own cardboard cut-out picture disc.

PENTANGLE
UK, male/female vocal/instrumental group   4 wks

28 May 69	ONCE I HAD A SWEETHEART Big T BIG 124	46	1 wk
14 Feb 70	LIGHT FLIGHT Big T BIG 128	43	1 wk
28 Feb 70	LIGHT FLIGHT (re-entry) Big T BIG 128	45	2 wks

PEOPLES - See YARBROUGH and PEOPLES

PEOPLES CHOICE
US, male vocal/instrumental group   9 wks

| 20 Sep 75 | DO IT ANYWAY YOU WANNA Philadelphia International PIR 3500 .... | 36 | 5 wks |
| 21 Jan 78 | JAM JAM JAM Philadelphia International PIR 5891 | 40 | 4 wks |

Danny PEPPERMINT and the JUMPING JACKS
US, male vocal/instrumental group   8 wks

| 18 Jan 62 | PEPPERMINT TWIST London HLL 9478 .... | 26 | 8 wks |

PEPPERS France, male instrumental group   12 wks

| 26 Oct 74 ● | PEPPER BOX Spark SRL 1100 .... | 6 | 12 wks |

Lance PERCIVAL UK, male vocalist   3 wks

| 28 Oct 65 | SHAME AND SCANDAL IN THE FAMILY Parlophone R 5335 .... | 37 | 3 wks |

Emilio PERICOLI Italy, male vocalist   14 wks

| 28 Jun 62 | AL DI LA Warner Bros. WB 69 .... | 30 | 14 wks |

Carl PERKINS US, male vocalist   8 wks

| 18 May 56 ● | BLUE SUEDE SHOES London HLU 8271 ...... | 10 | 8 wks |

Steve PERRY UK, male vocalist   1 wk

| 4 Aug 60 | STEP BY STEP HMV POP 745 | 41 | 1 wk |

Jon PERTWEE UK, male vocalist   7 wks

| 1 Mar 80 | WORZEL'S SONG Decca F 13885 .... | 33 | 7 wks |

PETER and GORDON
UK, male vocal duo   77 wks

12 Mar 64 ★	A WORLD WITHOUT LOVE Columbia DB 7225	1	14 wks
4 Jun 64 ●	NOBODY I KNOW Columbia DB 7292	10	11 wks
8 Apr 65 ●	TRUE LOVE WAYS Columbia DB 7524	2	15 wks
24 Jun 65 ●	TO KNOW YOU IS TO LOVE YOU Columbia DB 7617	5	10 wks
21 Oct 65	BABY I'M YOURS Columbia DB 7729	19	9 wks
24 Feb 66	WOMAN Columbia DB 7834	28	7 wks
22 Sep 66	LADY GODIVA Columbia DB 8003	16	11 wks

PETER, PAUL and MARY
US, male/female vocal/instrumental group   38 wks

10 Oct 63	BLOWING IN THE WIND Warner Bros. WB 104	13	16 wks
16 Apr 64	TELL IT ON THE MOUNTAIN Warner Bros. WB 127	33	4 wks
15 Oct 64	THE TIMES THEY ARE A-CHANGIN' Warner Bros. WB 142	44	2 wks
17 Jan 70 ●	LEAVIN' ON A JET PLANE Warner Bros. WB 7340	2	16 wks

PETERS and LEE
UK, male/female vocal duo   57 wks

26 May 73 ★	WELCOME HOME Philips 6006 307	1	24 wks
3 Nov 73	BY YOUR SIDE Philips 6006 339	39	4 wks
20 Apr 74 ●	DON'T STAY AWAY TOO LONG Philips 6006 388	3	15 wks
17 Aug 74	RAINBOW Philips 6006 406	17	7 wks
6 Mar 76	HEY MR. MUSIC MAN Philips 6006 502	16	7 wks

Ray PETERSON US, male vocalist   9 wks

4 Sep 59	THE WONDER OF YOU RCA 1131	23	1 wk
24 Mar 60	ANSWER ME RCA 1175	47	1 wk
19 Jan 61	CORRINE, CORRINA London HLX 9246	48	1 wk
2 Feb 61	CORRINE, CORRINA (re-entry) London HLX 9246	41	6 wks

Tom PETTY and the HEARTBREAKERS
US, male vocal/instrumental group   8 wks

| 25 Jun 77 | ANYTHING THAT'S ROCK 'N' ROLL Shelter WIP 6396 .... | 36 | 3 wks |
| 13 Aug 77 | AMERICAN GIRL Shelter WIP 6403 .... | 40 | 5 wks |

See also Stevie Nicks with Tom Petty and the Heartbreakers.

PHARAOHS - See SAM THE SHAM and the PHARAOHS

PhD UK, male vocal/instrumental duo   14 wks

| 3 Apr 82 ● | I WON'T LET YOU DOWN WEA K 79209 .... | 3 | 14 wks |

PHILADELPHIA INTERNATIONAL ALL-STARS
US, amalgamation of various acts   8 wks

| 13 Aug 77 | LET'S CLEAN UP THE GHETTO Philadelphia International PIR 5451 .... | 34 | 8 wks |

The All-Stars include Archie Bell, Dee Dee Sharp Gamble, O'Jays, Billy Paul, Teddy Pendergrass and Lou Rawls. See also the separate hit lists of each of these artists. Dee Dee Sharp Gamble, see Dee Dee Sharp. Archie Bell, see Archie Bell and the Drells.

PHILHARMONIA ORCHESTRA, conductor Lorin MAAZEL
UK, orchestra, US, male conductor   7 wks

| 30 Jul 69 | THUS SPAKE ZARATHUSTRA Columbia DB 8607 .... | 33 | 7 wks |

Esther PHILLIPS   US, female vocalist   *8 wks*

4 Oct 75 ●	WHAT A DIFFERENCE A DAY MADE	*Kudu 925*	6	8 wks

Paul PHILLIPS - *See DRIVER 67*

Paul PHOENIX   UK, male vocalist   *4 wks*

3 Nov 79	NUNC DIMITTIS	*Different HAVE 20*	56	4 wks

Full artist credit on hit as follows: Paul Phoenix (treble) with Instrumental Ensemble-James Watson (trumpet) John Scott (organ) conducted by Barry Rose.

PHOTOS
UK, male/female vocal/instrumental group   *4 wks*

17 May 80	IRENE	*Epic EPC 8517*	56	4 wks

Edith PIAF   France, female vocalist   *15 wks*

12 May 60	MILORD	*Columbia DC 754*	41	4 wks
3 Nov 60	MILORD	(re-entry) *Columbia DC 754*	24	11 wks

Bobby 'Boris' PICKETT and the CRYPT-KICKERS   US, male vocalist, male vocal/instrumental backing group   *13 wks*

1 Sep 73 ●	MONSTER MASH	*London HL 10320*	3	13 wks

Wilson PICKETT   US, male vocalist   *58 wks*

23 Sep 65	IN THE MIDNIGHT HOUR	*Atlantic AT 4036*	12	11 wks
25 Nov 65	DON'T FIGHT IT	*Atlantic AT 4052*	29	8 wks
10 Mar 66	634-5789	*Atlantic AT 4072*	36	5 wks
1 Sep 66	LAND OF 1000 DANCES	*Atlantic 584-039*	22	9 wks
15 Dec 66	MUSTANG SALLY	*Atlantic 584-066*	28	7 wks
27 Sep 67	FUNKY BROADWAY	*Atlantic 584-130*	43	3 wks
11 Sep 68	IN THE MIDNIGHT HOUR (re-issue) *Atlantic 584-203*		38	6 wks
8 Jan 69	HEY JUDE	*Atlantic 584-236*	16	9 wks

PICKETTYWITCH
UK, male/female vocal/instrumental group   *34 wks*

28 Feb 70 ●	THAT SAME OLD FEELING	*Pye 7N 17887*	5	14 wks
4 Jul 70	(IT'S LIKE A) SAD OLD KINDA MOVIE *Pye 7N 17951*		16	10 wks
7 Nov 70	BABY I WON'T LET YOU DOWN *Pye 7N 45002*		27	10 wks

PIGBAG   UK, male instrumental group   *20 wks*

7 Nov 81	SUNNY DAY	*Y RECORDS Y 12*	53	3 wks
27 Feb 82	GETTING UP	*Y RECORDS Y 16*	61	3 wks
3 Apr 82 ●	PAPA'S GOT A BRAND NEW PIGBAG *Y RECORDS Y 10*		3	11 wks
10 Jul 82	THE BIG BEAN	*Y RECORDS Y 24*	40	3 wks

Nelson PIGFORD - *See De Etta LITTLE and Nelson PIGFORD*

PIGLETS   UK, female vocal group   *12 wks*

6 Nov 71 ●	JOHNNY REGGAE	*Bell 1180*	3	12 wks

PILOT   UK, male vocal/instrumental group   *29 wks*

2 Nov 74	MAGIC	*EMI 2217*	11	11 wks
18 Jan 75 ★	JANUARY	*EMI 2255*	1	10 wks
19 Apr 75	CALL ME ROUND	*EMI 2287*	34	4 wks
27 Sep 75	JUST A SMILE	*EMI 2338*	31	4 wks

PILTDOWN MEN
US, male instrumental group   *36 wks*

8 Sep 60	MACDONALD'S CAVE	*Capitol CL 15149*	14	18 wks
12 Jan 61	PILTDOWN RIDES AGAIN	*Capitol CL 15175*	14	10 wks
9 Mar 61	GOODNIGHT MRS. FLINTSTONE *Capitol CL 15186*		18	8 wks

PING PING and Al VERLAINE
Belgium, male vocal duo   *4 wks*

28 Sep 61	SUCU SUCU	*Oriole CB 1589*	41	4 wks

PINK FLOYD
UK, male vocal/instrumental group   *41 wks*

30 Mar 67	ARNOLD LAYNE	*Columbia DB 8156*	20	8 wks
22 Jun 67 ●	SEE EMILY PLAY	*Columbia DB 8214*	6	12 wks
1 Dec 79 ★	ANOTHER BRICK IN THE WALL (PART 2) *Harvest HAR 5194*		1	12 wks
7 Aug 82	WHEN THE TIGERS BROKE FREE *Harvest HAR 5222*		39	5 wks
7 May 83	NOT NOW JOHN	*Harvest HAR 5224*	30	4 wks

PINKEES   UK, male vocal/instrumental group   *9 wks*

18 Sep 82 ●	DANGER GAMES	*Creole CR 39*	8	9 wks

PINKERTON'S ASSORTED COLOURS
UK, male vocal/instrumental group   *12 wks*

13 Jan 66 ●	MIRROR MIRROR	*Decca F 12307*	9	11 wks
21 Apr 66	DON'T STOP LOVIN' ME BABY	*Decca F 12377*	50	1 wk

PIONEERS
Jamaica, male vocal/instrumental group   *34 wks*

18 Oct 69	LONG SHOT KICK DE BUCKET	*Trojan TR 672*	21	10 wks
10 Jan 70	LONG SHOT KICK DE BUCKET (re-entry) *Trojan TR 672*		40	1 wk
31 Jul 71 ●	LET YOUR YEAH BE YEAH	*Trojan TR 7824*	5	12 wks
15 Jan 72	GIVE AND TAKE	*Trojan TR 7846*	35	6 wks
29 Mar 80	LONG SHOT KICK DE BUCKET (re-issue) *Trojan TRO 9063*		42	5 wks

Re-issue of Long Shot Kick De Bucket coupled with re-issue of Liquidator by Harry J. All Stars. See also Harry J. All Stars.

PIPKINS   UK, male vocal duo   *10 wks*

28 Mar 70 ●	GIMME DAT DING	*Columbia DB 8662*	6	10 wks

PIPS - *See Gladys KNIGHT and the PIPS*

PIRANHAS
UK, male vocal/instrumental group   21 wks

2 Aug 80	●	TOM HARK	*Sire/Hansa SIR 4044*	6	12 wks
16 Oct 82		ZAMBESI	*Dakota DAK 6*	17	9 wks

Zambezi is 'featuring Boring Bob Grover'.

PIRATES - *See Johnny KIDD and the PIRATES*

Gene PITNEY *US, male vocalist*   200 wks

23 Mar 61	I WANNA LOVE MY LIFE AWAY			
	London HL 9270	26	11 wks	
8 Mar 62	TOWN WITHOUT PITY *HMV POP 952*	32	6 wks	
5 Dec 63 ●	TWENTY FOUR HOURS FROM TULSA			
	United Artists UP 1035	5	19 wks	
5 Mar 64 ●	THAT GIRL BELONGS TO YESTERDAY			
	United Artists UP 1045	7	12 wks	
15 Oct 64	IT HURTS TO BE IN LOVE			
	United Artists UP 1063	36	4 wks	
12 Nov 64 ●	I'M GONNA BE STRONG *Stateside SS 358*	2	14 wks	
18 Feb 65 ●	I MUST BE SEEING THINGS *Stateside SS 390* ..	6	10 wks	
10 Jun 65 ●	LOOKING THROUGH THE EYES OF LOVE			
	Stateside SS 420	3	12 wks	
4 Nov 65 ●	PRINCESS IN RAGS *Stateside SS 471*	9	12 wks	
17 Feb 66 ●	BACKSTAGE *Stateside SS 490*	4	10 wks	
9 Jun 66 ●	NOBODY NEEDS YOUR LOVE *Stateside SS 518*	2	13 wks	
10 Nov 66 ●	JUST ONE SMILE *Stateside SS 558*	8	12 wks	
23 Feb 67	COLD LIGHT OF DAY *Stateside SS 597*	38	6 wks	
15 Nov 67 ●	SOMETHING'S GOTTEN HOLD OF MY HEART			
	Stateside SS 2060	5	13 wks	
3 Apr 68	SOMEWHERE IN THE COUNTRY			
	Stateside SS 2013	19	9 wks	
27 Nov 68	YOURS UNTIL TOMORROW *Stateside SS 2131*	34	7 wks	
5 Mar 69	MARIA ELENA *Stateside SS 2142*	25	6 wks	
14 Mar 70	A STREET CALLED HOPE *Stateside SS 2164* ...	37	5 wks	
3 Oct 70	SHADY LADY *Stateside SS 2177*	29	8 wks	
28 Apr 73	24 SYCAMORE *Pye International 7N 25606*	34	7 wks	
2 Nov 74	BLUE ANGEL *Bronze BRO 11*	49	1 wk	
16 Nov 74	BLUE ANGEL (re-entry) *Bronze BRO 11*	39	3 wks	

PLANET PATROL
US, male vocal/instrumental group   3 wks

17 Sep 83	CHEAP THRILLS *Polydor POSP 639*	64	3 wks

PLANETS *UK, male vocal/instrumental group*   8 wks

18 Aug 79	LINES *Rialto TREB 104*	36	6 wks
25 Oct 80	DON'T LOOK DOWN *Rialto TREB 116*	66	2 wks

Robert PLANT *UK, male vocalist*   11 wks

9 Oct 82	BURNING DOWN ONE SIDE		
	Swansong SSK 19429	73	1 wk
16 Jul 83	BIG LOG *WEA B 9848*	11	10 wks

PLASMATICS
UK, female/male vocal/instrumental group   4 wks

26 Jul 80	BUTCHER BABY *Stiff BUY 76*	55	4 wks

PLASTIC BERTRAND
Belgium, male vocalist   17 wks

13 May 78 ●	CA PLANE POUR MOI *Sire 6078 616*	8	12 wks
5 Aug 78	SHA LA LA LA LEE *Vertigo 6059 209*	39	5 wks

---

PLASTIC ONO BAND - *See John LENNON*

PLASTIC ONO NUCLEAR BAND - *See John LENNON*

PLASTIC PENNY
UK, male vocal/instrumental group   10 wks

3 Jan 68 ●	EVERYTHING I AM *Page One POF 051*	6	10 wks

PLATINUM HOOK
US, male vocal/instrumental group   1 wk

2 Sep 78	STANDING ON THE VERGE (OF GETTING IT		
	ON) *Motown TMG 1115*	72	1 wk

PLATTERS *US, male/female vocal group*   91 wks

7 Sep 56 ●	THE GREAT PRETENDER/ONLY YOU		
	Mercury MT 117	5	12 wks
2 Nov 56 ●	MY PRAYER *Mercury MT 120*	4	10 wks
7 Dec 56	THE GREAT PRETENDER/ONLY YOU		
	(re-entry) *Mercury MT 117*	21	1 wk
18 Jan 57	MY PRAYER (re-entry) *Mercury MT 120*	28	2 wks
25 Jan 57	YOU'LL NEVER NEVER KNOW/IT ISN'T		
	RIGHT *Mercury MT 130*	23	1 wk
8 Feb 57	YOU'LL NEVER NEVER KNOW/IT ISN'T		
	RIGHT (re-entry) *Mercury MT 130*	29	1 wk
29 Mar 57	ONLY YOU (2nd re-entry) *Mercury MT 117*	18	3 wks
29 Mar 57	MY PRAYER (2nd re-entry) *Mercury MT 120*	22	1 wk
12 Apr 57	YOU'LL NEVER NEVER KNOW/IT ISN'T		
	RIGHT (2nd re-entry) *Mercury MT 130*	29	1 wk
17 May 57	I'M SORRY *Mercury MT 145*	18	6 wks
5 Jul 57	I'M SORRY (re-entry) *Mercury MT 145*	23	1 wk
19 Jul 57	I'M SORRY (2nd re-entry) *Mercury MT 145*	22	1 wk
16 May 58 ●	TWILIGHT TIME *Mercury MT 214*	3	18 wks
16 Jan 59 ★	SMOKE GETS IN YOUR EYES		
	Mercury AMT 1016	1	20 wks
28 Aug 59	REMEMBER WHEN *Mercury AMT 1053*	25	2 wks
29 Jan 60	HARBOUR LIGHTS *Mercury AMT 1081*	11	11 wks

PLAYBOY BAND - *See John FRED and the PLAYBOY BAND*

PLAYBOYS - *See Gary LEWIS and the PLAYBOYS*

PLAYER
US/UK, male vocal/instrumental group   7 wks

25 Feb 78	BABY COME BACK *RSO 2090 254*	32	7 wks

PLAYERS ASSOCIATION
US, male/female vocal/instrumental group   17 wks

10 Mar 79 ●	TURN THE MUSIC UP *Vanguard VS 5011*	8	9 wks
5 May 79	RIDE THE GROOVE *Vanguard VS 5012*	42	5 wks
9 Feb 80	WE GOT THE GROOVE *Vanguard VS 5016*	61	3 wks

POETS *UK, male vocal/instrumental group*   5 wks

29 Oct 64	NOW WE'RE THRU *Decca F 11995*	31	5 wks

POINTER SISTERS
US, female vocal group   70 wks

3 Feb 79	EVERYBODY IS A STAR *Planet K 12324*	61	3 wks
17 Mar 79	FIRE *Planet K 12339*	34	8 wks
22 Aug 81 ●	SLOWHAND *Planet K 12530*	10	11 wks
5 Dec 81	SHOULD I DO IT? *Reprise K 12578*	50	4 wks

14 Apr 84 ● AUTOMATIC	Planet RPS 105	....	2	15 wks
23 Jun 84 ● JUMP (FOR MY LOVE)	Planet RPS 106	....	6	10 wks
11 Aug 84 I NEED YOU	Planet RPS 107	....	25	9 wks
27 Oct 84 I'M SO EXCITED	Planet RPS 108	....	11†	10 wks

POLECATS
UK, male vocal/instrumental group   *18 wks*

7 Mar 81	JOHN I'M ONLY DANCING/BIG GREEN CAR			
	Mercury POLE 1	....	35	8 wks
16 May 81	ROCKABILLY GUY Mercury POLE 2	....	35	6 wks
22 Aug 81	JEEPSTER/MARIE CELESTE Mercury POLE 3		53	4 wks

POLICE
UK/US, male vocal/instrumental group   *138 wks*

7 Oct 78	CAN'T STAND LOSING YOU			
	A & M AMS 7381	....	42	5 wks
28 Apr 79	ROXANNE A & M AMS 7348	....	12	9 wks
7 Jul 79 ●	CAN'T STAND LOSING YOU (re-entry)			
	A & M AMS 7381		2	11 wks
22 Sep 79 ★	MESSAGE IN A BOTTLE A & M AMS 7474	..	1	11 wks
17 Nov 79	FALL OUT Illegal IL 001	....	47	4 wks
1 Dec 79 ★	WALKING ON THE MOON A & M AMS 7494		1	10 wks
16 Feb 80 ●	SO LONELY A & M AMS 7402	....	6	10 wks
14 Jun 80	SIX PACK A & M AMPP 6001	....	17	4 wks
27 Sep 80 ★	DON'T STAND SO CLOSE TO ME			
	A & M AMS 7564	....	1	10 wks
13 Dec 80 ●	DE DO DO DO, DE DA DA DA			
	A & M AMS 7578	....	5	8 wks
26 Sep 81 ●	INVISIBLE SUN A & M AMS 8164	....	2	8 wks
24 Oct 81 ★	EVERY LITTLE THING SHE DOES IS MAGIC			
	A & M AMS 8174	....	1	13 wks
12 Dec 81	SPIRITS IN THE MATERIAL WORLD			
	A & M AMS 8194	....	12	8 wks
28 May 83 ★	EVERY BREATH YOU TAKE A & M AM 117		1	11 wks
23 Jul 83 ●	WRAPPED AROUND YOUR FINGER			
	A & M AM 127	....	7	7 wks
5 Nov 83 ●	SYNCHRONICITY II A & M AM 153	......	17	4 wks
14 Jan 84	KING OF PAIN A & M AM 176	....	17	5 wks

*Six Pack consists of six separate Police singles as follows: The Bed's Too Big Without You;
Roxanne; Message in a Bottle; Walking on the Moon; So Lonely; Can't Stand Losing You.
The last five titles were re-issues.*

PONI-TAILS
US, female vocal group   *14 wks*

19 Sep 58 ●	BORN TOO LATE HMV POP 516	....	5	11 wks
10 Apr 59	EARLY TO BED HMV POP 596	....	26	3 wks

Brian POOLE and the TREMELOES
UK, male vocalist, male
vocal/instrumental backing group   *90 wks*

4 Jul 63 ●	TWIST AND SHOUT Decca F 11694	....	4	14 wks
12 Sep 63 ★	DO YOU LOVE ME Decca F 11739	....	1	14 wks
28 Nov 63	I CAN DANCE Decca F 11771	....	31	8 wks
30 Jan 64 ●	CANDY MAN Decca F 11823	....	6	13 wks
7 May 64 ●	SOMEONE SOMEONE Decca F 11893	......	2	17 wks
20 Aug 64	TWELVE STEPS TO LOVE Decca F 11951	...	32	7 wks
7 Jan 65	THREE BELLS Decca F 12037	....	17	9 wks
22 Jul 65	I WANT CANDY Decca F 12197	....	25	8 wks

See also Tremeloes.

Glyn POOLE
UK, male vocalist   *8 wks*

20 Oct 73	MILLY MOLLY MANDY York SYK 565	......	35	8 wks

POP TOPS
Spain, male vocal group   *6 wks*

9 Oct 71	MAMY BLUE A & M AMS 859	....	34	6 wks

POPPY FAMILY
Canada, male/female vocal/instrumental group   *14 wks*

15 Aug 70 ●	WHICH WAY YOU GOIN' BILLY			
	Decca F 22976		7	14 wks

Gary PORTNOY
US, male vocalist   *3 wks*

25 Feb 84	THEME FROM 'CHEERS' Starblend CHEER 1	..	58	3 wks

PORTSMOUTH SINFONIA
UK, orchestra   *4 wks*

12 Sep 81	CLASSICAL MUDDLEY			
	Springtime/Island WIP 6736	....	38	4 wks

Sandy POSEY
US, female vocalist   *32 wks*

15 Sep 66	BORN A WOMAN MGM 1321	....	24	11 wks
5 Jan 67	SINGLE GIRL MGM 1330	....	15	13 wks
13 Apr 67	WHAT A WOMAN IN LOVE WON'T DO			
	MGM 1335		48	3 wks
6 Sep 75	SINGLE GIRL (re-issue) MGM 2006 533		35	5 wks

POSITIVE FORCE
US, female vocal duo   *9 wks*

22 Dec 79	WE GOT THE FUNK Sugarhill SHL 102	....	18	9 wks

POSITIVE PEOPLE - *See Frank HOOKER and POSITIVE PEOPLE*

Mike POST featuring Larry CARLTON
US, conductor and instrumentalist - guitar   *11 wks*

16 Jan 82	THEME FROM 'HILL STREET BLUES'			
	Elektron K 12576	....	25	11 wks

See also Mike Post.

Mike POST
US, orchestra   *7 wks*

9 Aug 75	AFTERNOON OF THE RHINO			
	Warner Bros. K 16588	....	48	1 wk
23 Aug 75	AFTERNOON OF THE RHINO (re-entry)			
	Warner Bros. K 16588	....	47	1 wk
29 Sep 84	THE A TEAM RCA 443	....	45	5 wks

*Group credited to 'Mike Post Coalition' for the first hit only. See also Mike Post featuring
Larry Carlton.*

POTTERS
UK, male vocal group   *2 wks*

1 Apr 72	WE'LL BE WITH YOU Pye JT 100	....	34	2 wks

Cozy POWELL
UK, male instrumentalist - drums   *35 wks*

8 Dec 73 ●	DANCE WITH THE DEVIL RAK 165	....	3	15 wks
25 Mar 74	THE MAN IN BLACK RAK 173	....	18	8 wks
10 Aug 74 ●	NA NA NA RAK 180	....	10	10 wks
10 Nov 79	THEME ONE Ariola ARO 189	....	62	2 wks

Will POWERS US, female vocalist *9 wks*

1 Oct 83	**KISSING WITH CONFIDENCE** *Island IS 134* ..	17	9 wks

Perez PRADO US, orchestra *33 wks*

25 Mar 55	★ **CHERRY PINK & APPLE BLOSSOM WHITE** *HMV B 10833*	1	17 wks
25 Jul 58	● **PATRICIA** *RCA 1067*	8	16 wks

Billed on first hit as Perez 'Prez' Prado and His Orchestra, The King of the Mambo.

PRATT and McLAIN with BROTHERLOVE
US, male vocal duo, male instrumental group *6 wks*

1 Oct 77	**HAPPY DAYS** *Reprise K 14435*	31	6 wks

PRAYING MANTIS
UK, male vocal/instrumental group *2 wks*

31 Jan 81	**CHEATED** *Arista ARIST 378*	69	2 wks

PREFAB SPROUT
UK, male vocal/instrumental group *2 wks*

28 Jan 84	**DON'T SING** *Kitchenware/CBS SK 9*	62	2 wks

PRELUDE *UK, male/female vocal group* *26 wks*

26 Jan 74	**AFTER THE GOLDRUSH** *Dawn DNS 1052*	21	9 wks
26 Apr 80	**PLATINUM BLONDE** *EMI 5046*	45	7 wks
22 May 82	**AFTER THE GOLDRUSH** (re-issue) *After Hours AFT 02*	28	7 wks
31 Jul 82	**ONLY THE LONELY** *After Hours AFT 06*	55	3 wks

Elvis PRESLEY US, male vocalist *1124 wks*

11 May 56	● **HEARTBREAK HOTEL** *HMV POP 182*	2	21 wks
25 May 56	● **BLUE SUEDE SHOES** *HMV POP 213*	9	8 wks
13 Jul 56	**I WANT YOU I NEED YOU I LOVE YOU** *HMV POP 235*	25	2 wks
3 Aug 56	**I WANT YOU I NEED YOU I LOVE YOU** (re-entry) *HMV POP 235*	14	9 wks
17 Aug 56	**BLUE SUEDE SHOES** (re-entry) *HMV POP 213*	26	2 wks
21 Sep 56	● **HOUND DOG** *HMV POP 249*	2	23 wks
26 Oct 56	**HEARTBREAK HOTEL** (re-entry) *HMV POP 182*	23	1 wk
16 Nov 56	● **BLUE MOON** *HMV POP 272*	9	11 wks
23 Nov 56	**I DON'T CARE IF THE SUN DON'T SHINE** *HMV POP 272*	29	1 wk
7 Dec 56	**LOVE ME TENDER** *HMV POP 253* ..	11	9 wks
21 Dec 56	**I DON'T CARE IF THE SUN DON'T SHINE** (re-entry) *HMV POP 272*	23	3 wks
15 Feb 57	**MYSTERY TRAIN** *HMV POP 295* ..	25	5 wks
8 Mar 57	**RIP IT UP** *HMV POP 305*	27	1 wk
10 May 57	● **TOO MUCH** *HMV POP 330*	6	8 wks
14 Jun 57	**ALL SHOOK UP** *HMV POP 359*	24	1 wk
28 Jun 57	★ **ALL SHOOK UP** (re-entry) *HMV POP 359*	1	20 wks
12 Jul 57	**TOO MUCH** (re-entry) *HMV POP 330* ...	26	1 wk
12 Jul 57	● **TEDDY BEAR** *RCA 1013*	3	19 wks
30 Aug 57	● **PARALYSED** *HMV POP 378*	8	10 wks
4 Oct 57	● **PARTY** *RCA 1020*	2	15 wks
18 Oct 57	**GOT A LOT O' LIVIN' TO DO** *RCA 1020*	17	4 wks
1 Nov 57	**LOVING YOU** *RCA 1013*	24	2 wks
1 Nov 57	**TRYING TO GET TO YOU** *HMV POP 408* ...	16	4 wks
8 Nov 57	**LAWDY MISS CLAWDY** *HMV POP 408*	15	5 wks
15 Nov 57	● **SANTA BRING MY BABY BACK TO ME** *RCA 1025*	7	8 wks
17 Jan 58	**I'M LEFT YOU'RE RIGHT SHE'S GONE** *HMV POP 428*	21	2 wks
24 Jan 58	★ **JAILHOUSE ROCK** *RCA 1028*	1	14 wks
31 Jan 58	**JAILHOUSE ROCK** (EP) *RCA RCX 106*	18	5 wks
7 Feb 58	**I'M LEFT YOU'RE RIGHT SHE'S GONE** (re-entry) *HMV POP 428*	29	1 wk
28 Feb 58	● **DON'T** *RCA 1043*	2	11 wks
2 May 58	● **WEAR MY RING AROUND YOUR NECK** *RCA 1058*	3	10 wks
25 Jul 58	● **HARD HEADED WOMAN** *RCA 1070*	2	11 wks
3 Oct 58	● **KING CREOLE** *RCA 1081*	2	15 wks
23 Jan 59	★ **ONE NIGHT/I GOT STUNG** *RCA 1100*	1	12 wks
24 Apr 59	★ **A FOOL SUCH AS I/I NEED YOUR LOVE TONIGHT** *RCA 1113*	1	15 wks
24 Jul 59	● **A BIG HUNK O' LOVE** *RCA 1136*	4	9 wks
12 Feb 60	**STRICTLY ELVIS** (EP) *RCA RCX 175*	26	1 wk
7 Apr 60	● **STUCK ON YOU** *RCA 1187*	3	14 wks
28 Jul 60	**A MESS OF BLUES** *RCA 1194*	2	18 wks
3 Nov 60	★ **IT'S NOW OR NEVER** *RCA 1207*	1	19 wks
19 Jan 61	★ **ARE YOU LONESOME TONIGHT** *RCA 1216*	1	15 wks
9 Mar 61	★ **WOODEN HEART** *RCA 1226*	1	27 wks
25 May 61	★ **SURRENDER** *RCA 1227*	1	15 wks
7 Sep 61	● **WILD IN THE COUNTRY/I FEEL SO BAD** *RCA 1244*	4	12 wks
2 Nov 61	★ **HIS LATEST FLAME/LITTLE SISTER** *RCA 1258*	1	13 wks
1 Feb 62	★ **ROCK A HULA BABY/CAN'T HELP FALLING IN LOVE** *RCA 1270*	1	20 wks
10 May 62	★ **GOOD LUCK CHARM** *RCA 1280*	1	17 wks
21 Jun 62	**FOLLOW THAT DREAM** (EP) *RCA RCX 211*	34	2 wks
30 Aug 62	★ **SHE'S NOT YOU** *RCA 1303*	1	14 wks
29 Nov 62	★ **RETURN TO SENDER** *RCA 1320*	1	14 wks
28 Feb 63	**ONE BROKEN HEART FOR SALE** *RCA 1337*	12	9 wks
4 Jul 63	★ **DEVIL IN DISGUISE** *RCA 1355*	1	12 wks
24 Oct 63	**BOSSA NOVA BABY** *RCA 1374*	13	8 wks
19 Dec 63	**KISS ME QUICK** *RCA 1375*	14	10 wks
12 Mar 64	**VIVA LAS VEGAS** *RCA 1390*	17	12 wks
25 Jun 64	● **KISSIN' COUSINS** *RCA 1404*	10	11 wks
20 Aug 64	**SUCH A NIGHT** *RCA 1411*	13	10 wks
29 Oct 64	**AIN'T THAT LOVIN' YOU BABY** *RCA 1422*	15	8 wks
3 Dec 64	**BLUE CHRISTMAS** *RCA 1430*	11	7 wks
11 Mar 65	**DO THE CLAM** *RCA 1443*	19	8 wks
27 May 65	★ **CRYING IN THE CHAPEL** *RCA 1455*	1	15 wks
11 Nov 65	**TELL ME WHY** *RCA 1489*	15	10 wks
24 Feb 66	**BLUE RIVER** *RCA 1504*	22	7 wks
7 Apr 66	● **FRANKIE AND JOHNNY** *RCA 1509*	21	9 wks
7 Jul 66	● **LOVE LETTERS** *RCA 1526*	6	10 wks
13 Oct 66	**ALL THAT I AM** *RCA 1545*	18	8 wks
1 Dec 66	**IF EVERY DAY WAS LIKE CHRISTMAS** *RCA 1557*	13	7 wks
9 Feb 67	**INDESCRIBABLY BLUE** *RCA 1565*	21	5 wks
11 May 67	**YOU GOTTA STOP/LOVE MACHINE** *RCA 1593*	38	5 wks
16 Aug 67	**LONG LEGGED GIRL** *RCA Victor RCA 1616*	49	2 wks
21 Feb 68	**GUITAR MAN** *RCA 1663*	19	9 wks
15 May 68	**U. S. MALE** *RCA 1673*	15	8 wks
17 Jul 68	**YOUR TIME HASN'T COME YET BABY** *RCA 1714*	22	11 wks
16 Oct 68	**YOU'LL NEVER WALK ALONE** *RCA 1747* ...	44	3 wks
26 Feb 69	**IF I CAN DREAM** *RCA 1795*	11	10 wks
11 Jun 69	● **IN THE GHETTO** *RCA 1831*	2	16 wks
6 Sep 69	**CLEAN UP YOUR OWN BACK YARD** *RCA 1869*	21	7 wks
18 Oct 69	**IN THE GHETTO** (re-entry) *RCA 1831* ...	50	1 wk
29 Nov 69	● **SUSPICIOUS MINDS** *RCA 1900*	2	14 wks
28 Feb 70	● **DON'T CRY DADDY** *RCA 1916*	8	11 wks
16 May 70	**KENTUCKY RAIN** *RCA 1949*	21	11 wks
11 Jul 70	★ **THE WONDER OF YOU** *RCA 1974*	1	20 wks
8 Aug 70	**KENTUCKY RAIN** (re-entry) *RCA 1949*	46	1 wk
14 Nov 70	● **I'VE LOST YOU** *RCA 1999*	9	12 wks
9 Jan 71	● **YOU DON'T HAVE TO SAY YOU LOVE ME** *RCA 2046*	9	7 wks
23 Jan 71	**THE WONDER OF YOU** (re-entry) *RCA 1974* ..	47	1 wk
6 Mar 71	**YOU DON'T HAVE TO SAY YOU LOVE ME** (re-entry) *RCA 2046*	35	3 wks
20 Mar 71	● **THERE GOES MY EVERYTHING** *RCA 2060* ..	6	11 wks
15 May 71	● **RAGS TO RICHES** *RCA 2084*	9	11 wks
17 Jul 71	● **HEARTBREAK HOTEL/HOUND DOG** (re-issue) *RCA MAXIMILLION 2104*	10	12 wks

DOROTHY PROVINE (above) 'You can bring Pearl, she's a damn nice girl, but don't bring Lulu'.

PRINCE (right) He reigned in 1984. (Photo: Gary Garshoff Retna Pictures.)

ELVIS PRESLEY (below) 'C'mon do Le Rock Du Bagne with me . . .'

METRO · GOLDWYN · MAYER

ELVIS PRESLEY

le Rock du bagne

JUDY TYLER

MICKEY SHAUGHNESSY · DEAN JONES · JENNIFER HOLDEN

GUY TROSPER

RICHARD THORPE · PANDRO S. BERMAN

UNE PRODUCTION AVON · EN CINEMASCOPE

PREFAB SPROUT (right) They did sing and got to 64 in '84. (Photo: Bleddvn Butcher.)

2 Oct 71	I'M LEAVIN' RCA 2125	23	9 wks
4 Dec 71	● I JUST CAN'T HELP BELIEVING RCA 2158	6	16 wks
11 Dec 71	JAILHOUSE ROCK (re-issue) RCA MAXIMILLION 2153	42	5 wks
1 Apr 72	● UNTIL IT'S TIME FOR YOU TO GO RCA 2188	5	9 wks
17 Jun 72	● AMERICAN TRILOGY RCA 2229	8	11 wks
30 Sep 72	● BURNING LOVE RCA 2267	7	9 wks
16 Dec 72	● ALWAYS ON MY MIND RCA 2304	9	13 wks
26 May 73	POLK SALAD ANNIE RCA 2359	23	7 wks
11 Aug 73	FOOL RCA 2393	15	10 wks
24 Nov 73	RAISED ON ROCK RCA 2435	36	7 wks
16 Mar 74	I'VE GOT A THING ABOUT YOU BABY RCA APBO 0196	33	5 wks
13 Jul 74	IF YOU TALK IN YOUR SLEEP RCA APBO 0280	40	3 wks
16 Nov 74	MY BOY RCA 2458	5	13 wks
18 Jan 75	● PROMISED LAND RCA PB 10074	9	8 wks
24 May 75	T. R. O. U. B. L. E. RCA 2562	31	4 wks
29 Nov 75	GREEN GREEN GRASS OF HOME RCA 2635	29	7 wks
1 May 76	HURT RCA 2674	37	5 wks
4 Sep 76	● GIRL OF MY BEST FRIEND RCA 2729	9	12 wks
25 Dec 76	● SUSPICION RCA 2768	9	12 wks
5 Mar 77	● MOODY BLUE RCA PB 0857	6	9 wks
13 Aug 77	★ WAY DOWN RCA PB 0998	1	13 wks
3 Sep 77	IT'S NOW OR NEVER (re-issue) RCA PB 2698	39	2 wks
3 Sep 77	ALL SHOOK UP (re-issue) RCA 2694	41	2 wks
3 Sep 77	CRYING IN THE CHAPEL (re-issue) RCA PB 2708	43	2 wks
3 Sep 77	JAILHOUSE ROCK (2nd re-issue) RCA PB 2695	44	2 wks
3 Sep 77	ARE YOU LONESOME TONIGHT (re-issue) RCA PB 2699	46	1 wk
3 Sep 77	THE WONDER OF YOU (re-issue) RCA PB 2709	48	1 wk
3 Sep 77	WOODEN HEART (re-issue) RCA PB 2700	49	1 wk
3 Sep 77	RETURN TO SENDER (re-issue) RCA PB 2706	42	3 wks
10 Dec 77	● MY WAY RCA PB 1165	9	8 wks
24 Jun 78	DON'T BE CRUEL RCA PB 9265	24	12 wks
15 Dec 79	IT WON'T SEEM LIKE CHRISTMAS (WITHOUT YOU) RCA PB 9464	13	6 wks
30 Aug 80	● IT'S ONLY LOVE /BEYOND THE REEF RCA 4	3	10 wks
6 Dec 80	SANTA CLAUS IS BACK IN TOWN RCA 16	41	6 wks
14 Feb 81	GUITAR MAN RCA 43	43	4 wks
18 Apr 81	LOVING ARMS RCA 48	47	6 wks
13 Mar 82	ARE YOU LONESOME TONIGHT RCA 196	25	7 wks
26 Jun 82	THE SOUND OF YOUR CRY RCA 232	59	2 wks
5 Feb 83	JAILHOUSE ROCK (re-entry) RCA 1078	27	6 wks
7 May 83	BABY I DON'T CARE RCA 332	61	3 wks
3 Dec 83	I CAN HELP RCA 369	30	9 wks
10 Nov 84	THE LAST FAREWELL RCA 459	48	6 wks

Tracks on Jailhouse Rock EP: Jailhouse Rock/Young And Beautiful/I Want To Be Free/Don't Leave Me Now/Baby I Don't Care. On Strictly Elvis EP: Old Shep/Any Place Is Paradise/ Paralysed/Is It So Strange. On Follow That Dream EP: Follow That Dream/Angel/What A Wonderful Life/I'm Not The Marrying Kind. On 5 July 62 a note on the Top 50 for that week stated 'Due to difficulties in assessing returns of Follow That Dream EP, it has been decided not to include it in Britain's Top 50. It is of course No.1 in the EP charts'. Therefore this EP only had a 2 week run on the chart when its sales would certainly have justified a much longer one. Beyond The Reef listed only 30 Aug to 13 Sep 80. Are You Lonesome Tonight on RCA 196 is a live version. Can't Help Falling In Love credited with Rock-a-Hula Baby from 1 Mar 62.

Billy PRESTON

US, male vocalist/instrumentalist - keyboards 13 wks

2 Jul 69	THAT'S THE WAY GOD PLANNED IT Apple 12	11	10 wks
16 Sep 72	OUTA SPACE A & M AMS 7007	44	3 wks

See also Beatles; Billy Preston and Syreeta.

Billy PRESTON and SYREETA

US, male/female vocal duo 15 wks

15 Dec 79	● WITH YOU I'M BORN AGAIN Motown TMG 1159	2	11 wks

8 Mar 80	IT WILL COME IN TIME Motown TMG 1175	47	4 wks

See also Billy Preston; Syreeta; Beatles.

Johnny PRESTON

US, male vocalist 45 wks

12 Feb 60	★ RUNNING BEAR Mercury AMT 1079	1	14 wks
21 Apr 60	● CRADLE OF LOVE Mercury AMT 1092	2	16 wks
2 Jun 60	RUNNING BEAR (re-entry) Mercury AMT 1079	41	1 wk
28 Jul 60	I'M STARTING TO GO STEADY Mercury AMT 1104	49	1 wk
11 Aug 60	FEEL SO FINE Mercury AMT 1104	18	10 wks
8 Dec 60	CHARMING BILLY Mercury AMT 1114	34	1 wk
22 Dec 60	CHARMING BILLY (re-entry) Mercury AMT 1114	42	2 wks

Mike PRESTON

UK, male vocalist 33 wks

30 Oct 59	MR. BLUE Decca F 11167	12	8 wks
25 Aug 60	I'D DO ANYTHING Decca F 11255	23	10 wks
22 Dec 60	TOGETHERNESS Decca F 11287	41	5 wks
9 Mar 61	MARRY ME Decca F 11335	14	10 wks

PRETENDERS

UK/US, male/female vocal/instrumental group 83 wks

10 Feb 79	STOP YOUR SOBBING Real ARE 6	34	9 wks
14 Jul 79	KID Real ARE 9	33	7 wks
17 Nov 79	★ BRASS IN POCKET Real ARE 11	1	17 wks
5 Apr 80	● TALK OF THE TOWN Real ARE 12	8	8 wks
14 Feb 81	MESSAGE OF LOVE Real ARE 15	11	7 wks
12 Sep 81	DAY AFTER DAY Real ARE 17	45	4 wks
14 Nov 81	● I GO TO SLEEP Real ARE 18	7	10 wks
2 Oct 82	BACK ON THE CHAIN GANG Real ARE 19	17	9 wks
26 Nov 83	2000 MILES Real ARE 20	15	9 wks
9 Jun 84	THIN LINE BETWEEN LOVE AND HATE Real ARE 22	49	3 wks

PRETTY THINGS

UK, male vocal/instrumental group 41 wks

18 Jun 64	ROSALYN Fontana TF 469	41	5 wks
22 Oct 64	● DON'T BRING ME DOWN Fontana TF 503	10	11 wks
25 Feb 65	HONEY I NEED Fontana TF 537	13	10 wks
15 Jul 65	CRY TO ME Fontana TF 585	28	7 wks
20 Jan 66	MIDNIGHT TO SIX MAN Fontana TF 647	46	1 wk
5 May 66	COME SEE ME Fontana TF 688	43	5 wks
21 Jul 66	A HOUSE IN THE COUNTRY Fontana TF 722	50	1 wk
4 Aug 66	A HOUSE IN THE COUNTRY (re-entry) Fontana TF 722	50	1 wk

Alan PRICE

UK, male vocalist/instrumentalist - keyboards 74 wks

31 Mar 66	● I PUT A SPELL ON YOU Decca F 12367	9	10 wks
14 Jul 66	HI LILI HI LO Decca F 12442	11	12 wks
2 Mar 67	● SIMON SMITH & HIS AMAZING DANCING BEAR Decca F 12570	4	12 wks
2 Aug 67	● THE HOUSE THAT JACK BUILT Decca F 12641	4	10 wks
15 Nov 67	SHAME Decca F 12691	45	2 wks
31 Jan 68	DON'T STOP THE CARNIVAL Decca F 12731	13	8 wks
25 May 74	● JARROW SONG Warner Bros. K 16372	6	9 wks
29 Apr 78	JUST FOR YOU Jet UP 36358	43	8 wks
17 Feb 79	BABY OF MINE/JUST FOR YOU (re-issue) Jet 135	32	3 wks

The Decca hits are credited to the Alan Price Set. See also Fame and Price Together.

Lloyd PRICE

US, male vocalist 36 wks

13 Feb 59	● STAGGER LEE HMV POP 580	7	14 wks
15 May 59	WHERE WERE YOU HMV POP 598	15	6 wks

12 Jun 59 ●	PERSONALITY	HMV POP 626	9	8 wks
14 Aug 59	PERSONALITY	(re-entry) HMV POP 626	25	2 wks
11 Sep 59	I'M GONNA GET MARRIED	HMV POP 650 ..	23	5 wks
21 Apr 60	LADY LUCK	HMV POP 712	45	1 wk

Dickie PRIDE UK, male vocalist *1 wk*

30 Oct 59	PRIMROSE LANE	Columbia DB 4340	28	1 wk

Louis PRIMA US, male vocalist *1 wk*

21 Feb 58	BUONA SERA	Capitol CL 14841	25	1 wk

PRIMA DONNA
UK, male/female vocal group *4 wks*

26 Apr 80	LOVE ENOUGH FOR TWO	Ariola ARO 221 ...	48	4 wks

PRINCE
US, male vocalist/instrumentalist - guitar *46 wks*

19 Jan 80	I WANNA BE YOUR LOVER			
	Warner Bros. K 17537		41	3 wks
29 Jan 83	1999 Warner Bros. W 9896		25	7 wks
30 Apr 83	LITTLE RED CORVETTE Warner Bros. W 9688		54	6 wks
26 Nov 83	LITTLE RED CORVETTE (re-issue)			
	Warner Bros. W 9436		66	2 wks
30 Jun 84 ●	WHEN DOVES CRY Warner Bros. W 9286 ...		4	15 wks
22 Sep 84 ●	PURPLE RAIN Warner Bros. W 9174		8	9 wks
8 Dec 84	I WOULD DIE 4 U Warner Bros. W 9121		64†	4 wks

PRIVATE LIVES
UK, male vocal/instrumental duo *4 wks*

11 Feb 84	LIVING IN A WORLD (TURNED UPSIDE DOWN) EMI PRIV 2		53	4 wks

P. J. PROBY US, male vocalist *89 wks*

28 May 64 ●	HOLD ME Decca F 11904		3	15 wks
3 Sep 64 ●	TOGETHER Decca F 11967		8	11 wks
10 Dec 64	SOMEWHERE Liberty LIB 10182		6	12 wks
25 Feb 65	I APOLOGISE Liberty LIB 10188		11	8 wks
8 Jul 65	LET THE WATER RUN DOWN			
	Liberty LIB 10206		19	8 wks
30 Sep 65	THAT MEANS A LOT Liberty LIB 10215		30	6 wks
25 Nov 65	MARIA Liberty LIB 10218		8	9 wks
10 Feb 66	YOU'VE COME BACK Liberty LIB 10223		25	7 wks
16 Jun 66	TO MAKE A BIG MAN CRY Liberty LIB 10236		34	3 wks
27 Oct 66	I CAN'T MAKE IT ALONE Liberty LIB 10250 ..		37	5 wks
6 Mar 68	IT'S YOUR DAY TODAY Liberty LBF 15046 ...		32	5 wks

PROCOL HARUM
UK, male vocal/instrumental group *56 wks*

25 May 67 ★	A WHITER SHADE OF PALE Deram DM 126		1	15 wks
4 Oct 67 ●	HOMBURG Regal Zonophone RZ 3003		6	10 wks
24 Apr 68	QUITE RIGHTLY SO Regal Zonophone RZ 3007		50	1 wk
18 Jun 69	SALTY DOG Regal Zonophone RZ 3019		44	1 wk
2 Jul 69	SALTY DOG (re-entry) Regal Zonophone RZ 3019		44	1 wk
16 Jul 69	SALTY DOG (2nd re-entry)			
	Regal Zonophone RZ 3019		44	1 wk
22 Apr 72	A WHITER SHADE OF PALE (re-issue)			
	Magnifly ECHO 10		13	13 wks
5 Aug 72	CONQUISTADOR Chrysalis CHS 2003		22	7 wks
23 Aug 75	PANDORA'S BOX Chrysalis CHS 2073		16	7 wks

PROFESSIONALS
UK, male vocal/instrumental group *4 wks*

11 Oct 80	1-2-3 Virgin VS 376		43	4 wks

PROPAGANDA
Germany, male/female vocal/instrumental group *9 wks*

17 Mar 84	DR MABUSE ZTT/Island ZTAS 2		27	9 wks

Brian PROTHEROE UK, male vocalist *6 wks*

7 Sep 74	PINBALL Chrysalis CHS 2043		22	6 wks

Dorothy PROVINE US, female vocalist *15 wks*

7 Dec 61	DON'T BRING LULU Warner Bros. WB 53		17	12 wks
28 Jun 62	CRAZY WORDS CRAZY TUNE			
	Warner Bros. WB 70		45	3 wks

PRUDENCE - See PATIENCE and PRUDENCE

PSYCHEDELIC FURS
UK, male vocal/instrumental group *21 wks*

2 May 81	DUMB WAITERS CBS 1166		59	2 wks
27 Jun 81	PRETTY IN PINK CBS A 1327		43	5 wks
31 Jul 82	LOVE MY WAY CBS A 2549		42	6 wks
31 Mar 84	HEAVEN CBS A 4300		29	6 wks
16 Jun 84	GHOST IN YOU CBS A 4470		68	2 wks

PUBLIC IMAGE LTD.
UK, male vocal/instrumental group *36 wks*

21 Oct 78 ●	PUBLIC IMAGE Virgin VS 228		9	8 wks
7 Jul 79	DEATH DISCO (PARTS 1 & 2) Virgin VS 274 ...		20	7 wks
20 Oct 79	MEMORIES Virgin VS 299		60	2 wks
4 Apr 81	FLOWERS OF ROMANCE Virgin VS 397		24	7 wks
17 Sep 83 ●	THIS IS NOT A LOVE SONG Virgin VS 529 ...		5	10 wks
19 May 84	BAD LIFE Virgin VS 675		71	2 wks

Act billed as P.I.L. on all but first hit.

Gary PUCKETT and the UNION GAP US, male vocalist, male vocal/instrumental backing group *47 wks*

17 Apr 68 ★	YOUNG GIRL CBS 3365		1	17 wks
7 Aug 68 ●	LADY WILLPOWER CBS 3551		5	16 wks
28 Aug 68	WOMAN WOMAN CBS 3100		48	1 wk
15 Jun 74 ●	YOUNG GIRL (re-issue) CBS 8202		6	13 wks

Billed as The Union Gap featuring Gary Puckett on the original issue of Young Girl and Lady Willpower.

James and Bobby PURIFY
US, male vocal duo *16 wks*

24 Apr 76	I'M YOUR PUPPET Mercury 6167 324		12	10 wks
7 Aug 76	MORNING GLORY Mercury 6167 380		27	6 wks

PURPLE HEARTS
UK, male vocal/instrumental group *5 wks*

22 Sep 79	MILLIONS LIKE US Fiction FICS 003		57	3 wks

8 Mar 80	**JIMMY**	*Fiction FICS 9*	60	2 wks

PUSSYCAT
Holland, male/female vocal/instrumental group 30 wks

28 Aug 76	★ **MISSISSIPPI**	*Sonet SON 2077*	1	22 wks
25 Dec 76	**SMILE**	*Sonet SON 2096*	24	8 wks

PYRAMIDS
Jamaica, male vocal/instrumental group 4 wks

22 Nov 67	**TRAIN TOUR TO RAINBOW CITY** *President PT 161*	35	4 wks

PYTHON LEE JACKSON
UK, male vocal/instrumental group 12 wks

30 Sep 72	● **IN A BROKEN DREAM**	*Youngblood YB 1002* . . .	3	12 wks

Q

QUADS   *UK, male vocal/instrumental group* 2 wks

22 Sep 79	**THERE MUST BE THOUSANDS**	*Big Bear BB 23*	66	2 wks

QUANTUM JUMP
UK, male vocal/instrumental group 10 wks

2 Jun 79	● **THE LONE RANGER**	*Electric WOT 33*	5	10 wks

QUARTERFLASH
US, male/female vocal/instrumental group 5 wks

27 Feb 82	**HARDEN MY HEART**	*Geffen GEF A 1838*	49	5 wks

Suzi QUATRO
US, female vocalist/instrumentalist - bass guitar 114 wks

19 May 73	★ **CAN THE CAN**	*RAK 150*	1	14 wks
28 Jul 73	● **48 CRASH**	*RAK 158*	3	9 wks
27 Oct 73	**DAYTONA DEMON**	*RAK 161*	14	13 wks
9 Feb 74	★ **DEVIL GATE DRIVE**	*RAK 167*	1	11 wks
29 Jun 74	**TOO BIG**	*RAK 175*	14	6 wks
9 Nov 74	● **THE WILD ONE**	*RAK 185*	7	10 wks
8 Feb 75	**YOUR MAMA WON'T LIKE ME**	*RAK 191*	31	5 wks
5 Mar 77	**TEAR ME APART**	*RAK 248*	27	6 wks
18 Mar 78	● **IF YOU CAN'T GIVE ME LOVE**	*RAK 271*	4	13 wks
22 Jul 78	**THE RACE IS ON**	*RAK 278*	43	5 wks
20 Oct 79	**SHE'S IN LOVE WITH YOU**	*RAK 299*	11	9 wks
19 Jan 80	**MAMA'S BOY**	*RAK 303*	34	5 wks
5 Apr 80	**I'VE NEVER BEEN IN LOVE**	*RAK 307*	56	3 wks
25 Oct 80	**ROCK HARD**	*Dreamland DLSP 6*	68	2 wks
13 Nov 82	**HEART OF STONE**	*Polydor POSP 477*	60	3 wks

See Suzi Quatro and Chris Norman.

Suzi QUATRO and Chris NORMAN   *UK/US, female/male vocal duo* 8 wks

11 Nov 78	**STUMBLIN' IN**	*Rak RAK 285*	41	8 wks

See also Suzi Quatro.

QUEEN   *UK, male vocal/instrumental group* 230 wks

9 Mar 74	● **SEVEN SEAS OF RHYE**	*EMI 2121*	10	10 wks
26 Oct 74	● **KILLER QUEEN**	*EMI 2229*	2	12 wks
25 Jan 75	**NOW I'M HERE**	*EMI 2256*	11	7 wks
8 Nov 75	★ **BOHEMIAN RHAPSODY**	*EMI 2375*	1	17 wks
3 Jul 76	● **YOU'RE MY BEST FRIEND**	*EMI 2494*	7	8 wks
27 Nov 76	● **SOMEBODY TO LOVE**	*EMI 2565*	2	9 wks
19 Mar 77	**TIE YOUR MOTHER DOWN**	*EMI 2593*	31	4 wks
4 Jun 77	**QUEEN'S FIRST EP** (EP)	*EMI 2623*	17	10 wks
22 Oct 77	● **WE ARE THE CHAMPIONS**	*EMI 2708*	2	11 wks
25 Feb 78	**SPREAD YOUR WINGS**	*EMI 2757*	34	4 wks
28 Oct 78	**BICYCLE RACE/FAT BOTTOMED GIRLS** *EMI 2870*	11	12 wks
10 Feb 79	● **DON'T STOP ME NOW**	*EMI 2910*	9	12 wks
14 Jul 79	**LOVE OF MY LIFE**	*EMI 2959*	63	2 wks
20 Oct 79	● **CRAZY LITTLE THING CALLED LOVE** *EMI 5001*	2	14 wks
2 Feb 80	**SAVE ME**	*EMI 5022*	11	6 wks
14 Jun 80	**PLAY THE GAME**	*EMI 5076*	14	8 wks
6 Sep 80	● **ANOTHER ONE BITES THE DUST**	*EMI 5102*	7	9 wks
6 Dec 80	● **FLASH**	*EMI 5126*	10	13 wks
1 May 82	**BODY LANGUAGE**	*EMI 5293*	25	6 wks
12 Jun 82	**LAS PALABRAS DE AMOR**	*EMI 5316*	17	8 wks
21 Aug 82	**BACKCHAT**	*EMI 5325*	40	4 wks
4 Feb 84	● **RADIO GAGA**	*EMI QUEEN 1*	2	9 wks
14 Apr 84	● **I WANT TO BREAK FREE**	*EMI QUEEN 2* . .	3	15 wks
28 Jul 84	● **IT'S A HARD LIFE**	*EMI QUEEN 3*	6	9 wks
22 Sep 84	**HAMMER TO FALL**	*EMI QUEEN 4*	13	7 wks
8 Dec 84	**THANK GOD IT'S CHRISTMAS**	*EMI QUEEN 5*	21†	4 wks

See also Queen and David Bowie. Tracks on Queen's First EP: Good Old Fashioned Lover Boy/Death On Two Legs (Dedicated To...)/Tenement Funster/White Queen (As it Began).

QUEEN and David BOWIE
UK, male vocal/instrumental group and male vocalist 11 wks

14 Nov 81	★ **UNDER PRESSURE**	*EMI 5250*	1	11 wks

See also Queen; David Bowie; David Bowie and Bing Crosby.

QUESTIONS
UK, male vocal/instrumental group 8 wks

23 Apr 83	**PRICE YOU PAY**	*Respond KOB 702*	56	3 wks
17 Sep 83	**TEAR SOUP**	*Respond KOB 705*	66	1 wk
10 Mar 84	**TUESDAY SUNSHINE**	*Respond KOB 707*	46	4 wks

? (QUESTION MARK) and the MYSTERIANS
US, male vocal/instrumental group 4 wks

17 Nov 66	**96 TEARS**	*Cameo Parkway C 428*	37	4 wks

QUICK   *UK, male vocal/instrumental group* 7 wks

15 May 82	**RHYTHM OF THE JUNGLE**	*Epic EPC A 2013*	41	7 wks

Tommy QUICKLY   *UK, male vocalist* 8 wks

22 Oct 64	**WILD SIDE OF LIFE**	*Pye 7N 15708*	33	8 wks

QUIET FIVE
UK, male vocal/instrumental group 3 wks

13 May 65	**WHEN THE MORNING SUN DRIES THE DEW** *Parlophone R 5273*	45	1 wk
21 Apr 66	**HOMEWARD BOUND**	*Parlophone R 5421*	44	2 wks

QUIET RIOT
US, male vocal/instrumental group · *5 wks*

3 Dec 83	**METAL HEALTH/CUM ON FEEL THE NOIZE**			
	Epic A 3968	45	5 wks

Cum on Feel the Noize *only credited from 10 Dec 83*.

Paul QUINN and Edwyn COLLINS
UK, male vocal duo · *2 wks*

11 Aug 84	**PALE BLUE EYES**	*Swamplands/London SWP 1* ...	72	2 wks

QUIVER - *See SUTHERLAND BROTHERS*

R

Eddie RABBITT *US, male vocalist* · *14 wks*

27 Jan 79	**EVERY WHICH WAY BUT LOOSE**			
	Elektra K 12331	41	9 wks
28 Feb 81	**I LOVE A RAINY NIGHT**	*Elektra K 12498*	53	5 wks

Steve RACE
UK, male instrumentalist - piano · *9 wks*

28 Feb 63	**PIED PIPER (THE BEEJE)**	*Parlophone R 4981* ...	29	9 wks

RACEY *UK, male vocal/instrumental group* · *44 wks*

25 Nov 78 ●	**LAY YOUR LOVE ON ME**	*Rak RAK 284*	3	14 wks
31 Mar 79	**SOME GIRLS**	*RAK 291*	2	11 wks
18 Aug 79	**BOY OH BOY**	*RAK 297*	22	9 wks
20 Dec 80	**RUNAROUND SUE**	*RAK 325*	13	10 wks

RACING CARS
UK, male vocal/instrumental group · *7 wks*

12 Feb 77	**THEY SHOOT HORSES DON'T THEY**			
	Chrysalis CHS 2129	14	7 wks

RACKETEERS - *See Elbow BONES and the RACKETEERS*

Jimmy RADCLIFFE *US, male vocalist* · *2 wks*

4 Feb 65	**LONG AFTER TONIGHT IS ALL OVER**			
	Stateside SS 374	40	2 wks

RADHA KRISHNA TEMPLE
Oxford Street, male/female vocal/instrumental group · *17 wks*

13 Sep 69	**HARE KRISHNA MANTRA**	*Apple 15*	12	9 wks
28 Mar 70	**GOVINDA**	*Apple 25*	23	8 wks

RADIO REVELLERS - *See Anthony STEEL and the RADIO REVELLERS*

RADIO STARS
UK, male vocal/instrumental group · *3 wks*

4 Feb 78	**NERVOUS WRECK**	*Chiswick NS 23*	39	3 wks

Fonda RAE *US, female vocalist* · *4 wks*

6 Oct 84	**TUCH ME**	*Streetwave KHAN 28*	49	4 wks

Gerry RAFFERTY *UK, male vocalist* · *43 wks*

18 Feb 78 ●	**BAKER STREET**	*United Artists UP 36346*	3	15 wks
26 May 79 ●	**NIGHT OWL**	*United Artists UP 36512*	5	13 wks
18 Aug 79	**GET IT RIGHT NEXT TIME**			
	United Artists BP 301	30	9 wks
22 Mar 80	**BRING IT ALL HOME**	*United Artists BP 340* ...	54	4 wks
21 Jun 80	**ROYAL MILE**	*United Artists BP 354*	67	2 wks

RAGTIMERS *UK, male instrumental group* · *8 wks*

16 Mar 74	**THE STING**	*Pye 7N 45323*	46	1 wk
30 Mar 74	**THE STING**	(re-entry) *Pye 7N 45323*	31	7 wks

RAH BAND *UK, instrumental group* · *38 wks*

9 Jul 77 ●	**THE CRUNCH**	*Good Earth GD 7*	6	12 wks
1 Nov 80	**FALCON**	*DJM DJS 10954*	35	7 wks
7 Feb 81	**SLIDE**	*DJM DJS 10964*	50	7 wks
1 May 82	**PERFUMED GARDEN**	*KR KR 5*	45	7 wks
9 Jul 83	**MESSAGES FROM THE STARS**	*TMT TMT 5* ...	42	5 wks

RAIN - *See Stephanie DE SYKES*

RAINBOW
UK, male vocal/instrumental group · *62 wks*

17 Sep 77	**KILL THE KING**	*Polydor 2066 845*	44	3 wks
8 Apr 78	**LONG LIVE ROCK 'N' ROLL**	*Polydor 2066 913*	33	3 wks
30 Sep 78	**L. A. CONNECTION**	*Polydor 2066 968*	40	4 wks
15 Sep 79 ●	**SINCE YOU'VE BEEN GONE**	*Polydor POSP 70*	6	10 wks
16 Feb 80	**ALL NIGHT LONG**	*Polydor POSP 104*	5	11 wks
31 Jan 81 ●	**I SURRENDER**	*Polydor POSP 221*	3	10 wks
20 Jun 81	**CAN'T HAPPEN HERE**	*Polydor POSP 251*	20	8 wks
11 Jul 81	**KILL THE KING**	(re-issue) *Polydor POSP 274*	41	4 wks
3 Apr 82	**STONE COLD**	*Polydor POSP 421*	34	4 wks
27 Aug 83	**STREET OF DREAMS**	*Polydor POSP 631*	52	3 wks
5 Nov 83	**CAN'T LET YOU GO**	*Polydor POSP 654*	43	2 wks

RAINBOW COTTAGE
UK, male vocal/instrumental group · *4 wks*

6 Mar 76	**SEAGULL**	*Penny Farthing PEN 906*	33	4 wks

Marvin RAINWATER
US, male vocalist · *22 wks*

7 Mar 58 ★	**WHOLE LOTTA WOMAN**	*MGM 974*	1	15 wks
6 Jun 58	**I DIG YOU BABY**	*MGM 980*	19	7 wks

Tony RALLO and the MIDNIGHT BAND *France, instrumentalist-guitar with US male vocal/instrumental group* · *8 wks*

23 Feb 80	**HOLDIN' ON**	*Calibre CAB 1*	34	8 wks

RAM JAM *US, male vocal/instrumental group* · *12 wks*

10 Sep 77 ●	**BLACK BETTY**	*Epic EPC 5492*	7	12 wks

RAM JAM BAND - *See Geno WASHINGTON and the RAM JAM BAND*

QUEEN Freddie, John Roger and Brian had more weeks on the chart in 1984 than in any other year.

JOHNNIE RAY (below left) One of many J. R. bubblegum cards.

QUESTIONS (below right) Their sun shone for four Tuesdays.

No. 7   JOHNNIE RAY
stars in the 20th Century-Fox
CinemaScope picture
"There's no Business like Show Business"

RAMBLERS (from the Abbey Hey Junior School) *UK, children's choir*   *15 wks*

13 Oct 79	**THE SPARROW** *Decca F 13860*	**11**	15 wks

RAMONES
US, male vocal/instrumental group   *29 wks*

21 May 77	**SHEENA IS A PUNK ROCKER** *Sire RAM 001*	**22**	7 wks
6 Aug 77	**SWALLOW MY PRIDE** *Sire 6078 607*	**36**	3 wks
30 Sep 78	**DON'T COME CLOSE** *Sire SRE 1031*	**39**	5 wks
8 Sep 79	**ROCK 'N' ROLL HIGH SCHOOL** *Sire SIR 4021*	**67**	2 wks
26 Jan 80 ●	**BABY I LOVE YOU** *Sire SIR 4031*	**8**	9 wks
19 Apr 80	**DO YOU REMEMBER ROCK 'N' ROLL RADIO**		
	Sire SIR 4037	**54**	3 wks

RAMRODS
US, male/female instrumental group   *12 wks*

23 Feb 61 ●	**RIDERS IN THE SKY** *London HLU 9282*	**8**	12 wks

RARE BIRD
UK, male vocal/instrumental group   *8 wks*

14 Feb 70	**SYMPATHY** *Charisma CB 120*	**27**	8 wks

O. RASBURY - *See Rahni HARRIS and F.L.O.*

Roland RAT SUPERSTAR
UK, male rat vocalist   *19 wks*

19 Nov 83	**RAT RAPPING** *Rodent/Magnet RAT 1*	**14**	12 wks
28 Apr 84	**LOVE ME TENDER** *Rodent/Magnet RAT 2*	**32**	7 wks

RATTLES
Germany, male vocal/instrumental group   *15 wks*

3 Oct 70 ●	**THE WITCH** *Decca F 23058*	**8**	15 wks

RAW SILK   *US, female vocal group*   *12 wks*

16 Oct 82	**DO IT TO THE MUSIC** *KR KR 14*	**18**	9 wks
10 Sep 83	**JUST IN TIME** *West End/Arista WEND 2*	**49**	3 wks

Lou RAWLS   *US, male vocalist*   *10 wks*

31 Jul 76 ●	**YOU'LL NEVER FIND ANOTHER LOVE LIKE**		
	MINE *Philadelphia International PIR 4372*	**10**	10 wks

See also Philadelphia International All-Stars.

Johnnie RAY   *US, male vocalist*   *132 wks*

14 Nov 52	**WALKING MY BABY BACK HOME**		
	Columbia DB 3060	**12**	1 wk
19 Dec 52 ●	**FAITH CAN MOVE MOUNTAINS**		
	Columbia DB 3154	**7**	2 wks
9 Jan 53 ●	**FAITH CAN MOVE MOUNTAINS** (re-entry)		
	Columbia DB 3154	**9**	1 wk
10 Apr 53 ●	**SOMEBODY STOLE MY GAL** *Philips PB 123* ..	**6**	1 wk
24 Apr 53 ●	**SOMEBODY STOLE MY GAL** (re-entry)		
	Philips PB 123	**6**	4 wks
29 May 53	**SOMEBODY STOLE MY GAL** (2nd re-entry)		
	Philips PB 123	**12**	1 wk
7 Aug 53	**SOMEBODY STOLE MY GAL** (3rd re-entry)		
	Philips PB 123	**11**	1 wk
9 Apr 54 ★	**SUCH A NIGHT** *Philips PB 244*	**1**	18 wks
8 Apr 55	**IF YOU BELIEVE** *Philips PB 379*	**15**	1 wk
13 May 55 ●	**IF YOU BELIEVE** (re-entry) *Philips PB 379*	**7**	10 wks
20 May 55	**PATHS OF PARADISE** *Philips PB 441*	**20**	1 wk
7 Oct 55	**HERNANDO'S HIDEAWAY** *Philips PB 495*	**11**	5 wks
14 Oct 55 ●	**HEY THERE** *Philips PB 495*	**5**	9 wks
28 Oct 55 ●	**SONG OF THE DREAMER** *Philips PB 516* ...	**10**	5 wks
17 Feb 56	**WHO'S SORRY NOW** *Philips PB 546*	**17**	2 wks
20 Apr 56	**AIN'T MISBEHAVIN'** *Philips PB 580*	**17**	6 wks
8 Jun 56	**AIN'T MISBEHAVIN'** (re-entry) *Philips PB 580* ..	**24**	1 wk
12 Oct 56 ★	**JUST WALKIN' IN THE RAIN** *Philips PB 624* .	**1**	19 wks
18 Jan 57	**YOU DON'T OWE ME A THING** *Philips PB 655*	**12**	15 wks
8 Feb 57 ●	**LOOK HOMEWARD ANGEL** *Philips PB 655* ..	**7**	16 wks
10 May 57 ★	**YES TONIGHT JOSEPHINE** *Philips PB 686*	**1**	16 wks
6 Sep 57	**BUILD YOUR LOVE** *Philips PB 721*	**17**	7 wks
4 Dec 59	**I'LL NEVER FALL IN LOVE AGAIN**		
	Philips PB 952	**26**	4 wks
8 Jan 60	**I'LL NEVER FALL IN LOVE AGAIN** (re-entry)		
	Philips PB 952	**26**	1 wk
5 Feb 60	**I'LL NEVER FALL IN LOVE AGAIN**		
	(2nd re-entry) *Philips PB 952*	**28**	1 wk

See also Doris Day and Johnnie Ray; Frankie Laine and Johnnie Ray. The chart history of You Don't Owe Me A Thing/Look Homeward Angel is complicated, as follows; You Don't Owe Me A Thing entered the chart by itself on 18 Jan 57. On 8 and 15 Feb 57 Look Homeward Angel was coupled with You Don't Owe Me A Thing but from 22 Feb 57 the two sides went their individual ways on the chart and were listed separately, You Don't Owe Me A Thing for a further 10 weeks and Look Homeward Angel for a further 14.

RAYDIO
US, male/female vocal/instrumental group   *21 wks*

8 Apr 78	**JACK AND JILL** *Arista 161*	**11**	12 wks
8 Jul 78	**IS THIS A LOVE THING** *Arista 193*	**27**	9 wks

Chris REA   *UK, male vocalist*   *17 wks*

7 Oct 78	**FOOL (IF YOU THINK IT'S OVER)**		
	Magnet MAG 111	**30**	7 wks
21 Apr 79	**DIAMONDS** *Magnet MAG 144*	**44**	3 wks
27 Mar 82	**LOVING YOU** *Magnet MAG 215*	**65**	3 wks
1 Oct 83	**I CAN HEAR YOUR HEARTBEAT**		
	Magnet MAG 244	**60**	2 wks
17 Mar 84	**I DON'T KNOW WHAT IT IS BUT I LOVE IT**		
	Magnet MAG 255	**65**	2 wks

Eileen READ - *See CADETS*

REAL THING
UK, male vocal/instrumental group   *80 wks*

5 Jun 76 ★	**YOU TO ME ARE EVERYTHING**		
	Pye International 7N 25709	**1**	11 wks
4 Sep 76 ●	**CAN'T GET BY WITHOUT YOU** *Pye 7N 45618*	**2**	10 wks
12 Feb 77	**YOU'LL NEVER KNOW WHAT YOU'RE**		
	MISSING *Pye 7N 45662*	**16**	9 wks
30 Jul 77	**LOVE'S SUCH A WONDERFUL THING**		
	Pye 7N 45701	**33**	5 wks
4 Mar 78	**WHENEVER YOU WANT MY LOVE**		
	Pye 7N 46045	**18**	9 wks
3 Jun 78	**LET'S GO DISCO** *Pye 7N 46078*	**39**	7 wks
12 Aug 78	**RAININ' THROUGH MY SUNSHINE**		
	Pye 7N 46113	**40**	8 wks
17 Feb 79 ●	**CAN YOU FEEL THE FORCE** *Pye 7N 46147*	**5**	11 wks
21 Jul 79	**BOOGIE DOWN (GET FUNKY NOW)**		
	Pye 7P 109	**33**	6 wks
22 Nov 80	**SHE'S A GROOVY FREAK** *Calibre CAB 105* ...	**52**	4 wks

REAL TO REEL
US, male vocal/instrumental group · 2 wks

| 21 Apr 84 | LOVE ME LIKE THIS | Arista ARIST 565 | 68 | 2 wks |

REBEL ROUSERS - *See Cliff BENNETT and the REBEL ROUSERS*

REBELETTES - *See Duane EDDY*

REBELS - *See Duane EDDY*

Ezz RECO and the LAUNCHERS with Boysie GRANT
Jamaica, male vocal/instrumental group · 4 wks

| 5 Mar 64 | KING OF KINGS | Columbia DB 7217 | 44 | 4 wks |

REDBONE
US, male vocal/instrumental group · 12 wks

| 25 Sep 71 | ● WITCH QUEEN OF NEW ORLEANS Epic EPC 7351 | 2 | 12 wks |

Sharon REDD US, female vocalist · 27 wks

28 Feb 81	CAN YOU HANDLE IT	Epic EPC 9572	31	8 wks
2 Oct 82	NEVER GIVE YOU UP	Prelude PRL A2755	20	9 wks
15 Jan 83	IN THE NAME OF LOVE	Prelude PRL A2905	31	5 wks
22 Oct 83	LOVE HOW YOU FEEL	Prelude A3868	39	5 wks

Otis REDDING US, male vocalist · 108 wks

25 Nov 65	MY GIRL	Atlantic AT 4050	11	16 wks
7 Apr 66	SATISFACTION	Atlantic AT 4080	33	4 wks
14 Jul 66	MY LOVER'S PRAYER	Atlantic 584 019	37	6 wks
25 Aug 66	I CAN'T TURN YOU LOOSE	Atlantic 584 030	29	8 wks
24 Nov 66	FA FA FA FA FA (SAD SONG)	Atlantic 584 049	23	9 wks
26 Jan 67	TRY A LITTLE TENDERNESS	Atlantic 584 070	46	4 wks
23 Mar 67	DAY TRIPPER	Stax 601 005	43	6 wks
4 May 67	LET ME COME ON HOME	Stax 601 007	48	1 wk
15 Jun 67	SHAKE	Stax 601 011	28	10 wks
14 Feb 68	MY GIRL (re-issue)	Atlantic 584 092	36	9 wks
21 Feb 68	● (SITTIN' ON) THE DOCK OF THE BAY Stax 601 031	3	15 wks
29 May 68	HAPPY SONG	Stax 601 040	24	5 wks
31 Jul 68	HARD TO HANDLE	Atlantic 584 199	15	12 wks
9 Jul 69	LOVE MAN	Atco 226 001	43	3 wks

See also Otis Redding and Carla Thomas.

Otis REDDING and Carla THOMAS US, male/female vocal duo · 16 wks

| 19 Jul 67 | TRAMP | Stax 601 012 | 18 | 11 wks |
| 11 Oct 67 | KNOCK ON WOOD | Stax 601 021 | 35 | 5 wks |

See also Otis Redding.

Helen REDDY Australia, female vocalist · 18 wks

| 18 Jan 75 | ● ANGIE BABY | Capitol CL 15799 | 5 | 10 wks |
| 28 Nov 81 | I CAN'T SAY GOODBYE TO YOU | MCA 744 | 43 | 8 wks |

REDSKINS
UK, male vocal/instrumental group · 5 wks

| 10 Nov 84 | KEEP ON KEEPIN' ON | Decca F 1 | 43 | 5 wks |

Jimmy REED US, male vocalist · 2 wks

| 10 Sep 64 | SHAME SHAME SHAME | Stateside SS 330 | 45 | 2 wks |

Lou REED US, male vocalist · 9 wks

| 12 May 73 | ● WALK ON THE WILD SIDE | RCA 2303 | 10 | 9 wks |

Michael REED ORCHESTRA - *See Richard HARLEY and the Michael REED ORCHESTRA*

Tony REES and the COTTAGERS
UK, male vocal group · 1 wk

| 10 May 75 | VIVA EL FULHAM | Sonet SON 2059 | 46 | 1 wk |

Jim REEVES US, male vocalist · 322 wks

24 Mar 60	HE'LL HAVE TO GO	RCA 1168	36	1 wk
7 Apr 60	HE'LL HAVE TO GO (re-entry)	RCA 1168	12	30 wks
16 Mar 61	WHISPERING HOPE	RCA 1223	50	1 wk
23 Nov 61	YOU'RE THE ONLY GOOD THING	RCA 1261	17	19 wks
28 Jun 62	ADIOS AMIGO	RCA 1293	23	21 wks
22 Nov 62	I'M GONNA CHANGE EVERYTHING RCA 1317	42	2 wks
13 Jun 63	● WELCOME TO MY WORLD	RCA 1342	6	15 wks
17 Oct 63	GUILTY	RCA 1364	29	7 wks
20 Feb 64	● I LOVE YOU BECAUSE	RCA 1385	5	39 wks
18 Jun 64	● I WON'T FORGET YOU	RCA 1400	3	25 wks
5 Nov 64	● THERE'S A HEARTACHE FOLLOWING ME RCA 1423	6	13 wks
7 Jan 65	I WON'T FORGET YOU (re-entry)	RCA 1400	47	1 wk
4 Feb 65	● IT HURTS SO MUCH	RCA 1437	8	10 wks
15 Apr 65	NOT UNTIL THE NEXT TIME	RCA 1446	13	12 wks
6 May 65	HOW LONG HAS IT BEEN	RCA 1445	45	5 wks
15 Jul 65	THIS WORLD IS NOT MY HOME	RCA 1412	22	9 wks
11 Nov 65	IS IT REALLY OVER	RCA 1488	17	9 wks
18 Aug 66	★ DISTANT DRUMS	RCA 1537	1	25 wks
2 Feb 67	I WON'T COME IN WHILE HE'S THERE RCA 1563	12	11 wks
26 Jul 67	TRYING TO FORGET	RCA 1611	33	5 wks
22 Nov 67	I HEARD A HEART BREAK LAST NIGHT RCA 1643	38	6 wks
27 Mar 68	PRETTY BROWN EYES	RCA 1672	33	5 wks
25 Jun 68	WHEN TWO WORLDS COLLIDE	RCA 1830	17	17 wks
6 Dec 69	BUT YOU LOVE ME DADDY	RCA 1899	15	16 wks
21 Mar 70	NOBODY'S FOOL	RCA 1915	32	5 wks
12 Sep 70	ANGELS DON'T LIE	RCA 1997	44	1 wk
26 Sep 70	ANGELS DON'T LIE (re-entry)	RCA 1997	32	2 wks
26 Jun 71	I LOVE YOU BECAUSE (re-issue)/HE'LL HAVE TO GO (re-issue)/MOONLIGHT & ROSES RCA Maximillion 2092	34	8 wks
19 Feb 72	YOU'RE FREE TO GO	RCA 2174	48	2 wks

Martha REEVES and the VANDELLAS US, female vocal group · 82 wks

29 Oct 64	DANCING IN THE STREET	Stateside SS 345	28	8 wks
1 Apr 65	NOWHERE TO RUN	Tamla Motown TMG 502	26	8 wks
1 Dec 66	I'M READY FOR LOVE	Tamla Motown TMG 582	29	8 wks
30 Mar 67	JIMMY MACK	Tamla Motown TMG 599	21	9 wks
17 Jan 68	HONEY CHILE	Tamla Motown TMG 636	30	9 wks
15 Jan 69	● DANCING IN THE STREET (re-issue) Tamla Motown TMG 684	4	12 wks

16 Apr 69	NOWHERE TO RUN (re-issue)			
	Tamla Motown TMG 694		42	3 wks
29 Aug 70	JIMMY MACK (re-entry) Tamla Motown TMG 599		21	12 wks
13 Feb 71	FORGET ME NOT Tamla Motown TMG 762 ...		11	8 wks
8 Jan 72	BLESS YOU Tamla Motown TMG 794		33	5 wks

The group is billed as Martha and the Vandellas – no Reeves – for Dancing In The Street *on Stateside,* Nowhere To Run *on Tamla Motown TMG 502,* I'm Ready For Love *and* Jimmy Mack.

RE-FLEX   *UK, male vocal/instrumental group*   *9 wks*

28 Jan 84	THE POLITICS OF DANCING EMI FLEX 2 ...		28	9 wks

Joan REGAN   *UK, female vocalist*   *61 wks*

11 Dec 53	● RICOCHET Decca F 10193		8	1 wk
8 Jan 54	● RICOCHET (re-entry) Decca F 10193		9	4 wks
14 May 54	● SOMEONE ELSE'S ROSES Decca F 10257		5	8 wks
1 Oct 54	IF I GIVE MY HEART TO YOU Decca F 10373		20	1 wk
29 Oct 54	● IF I GIVE MY HEART TO YOU (re-entry)			
	Decca F 10373		3	10 wks
25 Mar 55	● PRIZE OF GOLD Decca F 10432		6	8 wks
6 May 55	OPEN UP YOUR HEART Decca F 10474		19	1 wk
1 May 59	● MAY YOU ALWAYS HMV POP 593		9	16 wks
5 Feb 60	HAPPY ANNIVERSARY Pye 7N 15238		29	1 wk
19 Feb 60	HAPPY ANNIVERSARY (re-entry) Pye 7N 15238		29	1 wk
28 Jul 60	PAPA LOVES MAMA Pye 7N 15278		29	8 wks
24 Nov 60	ONE OF THE LUCKY ONES Pye 7N 15310 ...		47	1 wk
5 Jan 61	MUST BE SANTA Pye 7N 15303		42	1 wk

Ricochet *credited to Joan Regan with the Squadronaires. See also Joan Regan and The Johnston Brothers, Various Artists – All Star Hit Parade.*

Joan REGAN and the JOHNSTON BROTHERS
UK, female vocalist, male vocal group   *1 wk*

5 Nov 54	WAIT FOR ME Decca F 10362		18	1 wk

See also Joan Regan; Johnston Brothers; Various Artists – All Star Hit Parade and All Star Hit Parade No. 2.

REGENTS   *UK, male/female vocal/instrumental group*   *14 wks*

22 Dec 79	7 TEEN Rialto TREB 111		11	12 wks
7 Jun 80	SEE YOU LATER Arista ARIST 350		55	2 wks

Mike REID   *UK, male vocalist*   *8 wks*

22 Mar 75	● THE UGLY DUCKLING Pye 7N 45434		10	8 wks

Nothing to do with any of this book's co-authors.

Neil REID   *UK, male vocalist*   *26 wks*

1 Jan 72	● MOTHER OF MINE Decca F 13264		2	20 wks
8 Apr 72	THAT'S WHAT I WANT TO BE Decca F 13300		49	1 wk
22 Apr 72	THAT'S WHAT I WANT TO BE (re-entry)			
	Decca F 13300		45	5 wks

Keith RELF   *UK, male vocalist*   *1 wk*

26 May 66	MR. ZERO Columbia DB 7920		50	1 wk

RENAISSANCE
UK, male/female vocal/instrumental group   *11 wks*

15 Jul 78	● NORTHERN LIGHTS Warner Bros. K 17177		10	11 wks

RENÉE AND RENATO
UK/Italy, female/male vocal duo   *21 wks*

30 Oct 82	★ SAVE YOUR LOVE Hollywood HWD 003		1	15 wks
12 Feb 83	JUST ONE MORE KISS Hollywood HWD 006 ..		48	6 wks

REO SPEEDWAGON
US, male vocal/instrumental group   *28 wks*

11 Apr 81	● KEEP ON LOVING YOU Epic EPC 9544		7	14 wks
27 Jun 81	TAKE IT ON THE RUN Epic EPC A 1207		19	14 wks

REPARATA   *US, female vocalist*   *2 wks*

18 Oct 75	SHOES Dart 2066 562		43	2 wks

See also Reparata and the Delrons.

REPARATA and the DELRONS
US, female vocal group   *10 wks*

20 Mar 68	CAPTAIN OF YOUR SHIP Bell 1002		13	10 wks

See also Reparata.

REUNION   *US, male vocal group*   *4 wks*

21 Sep 74	LIFE IS A ROCK (BUT THE RADIO ROLLED ME) RCA PB 10056		33	4 wks

REVILLOS - *See REZILLOS*

REYNOLDS - *See HAMILTON, Joe FRANK and REYNOLDS*

Debbie REYNOLDS   *US, female vocalist*   *17 wks*

30 Aug 57	● TAMMY Vogue-Coral Q 72274		2	17 wks

Jody REYNOLDS   *US, male vocalist*   *1 wk*

14 Apr 79	ENDLESS SLEEP Lightning LIG 9015		66	1 wk

Endless Sleep was coupled with To Know Him Is To Love Him *by the Teddy Bears as a double A-side. See also the Teddy Bears.*

L J REYNOLDS   *US, male vocalist*   *3 wks*

30 Jun 84	DON'T LET NOBODY HOLD YOU DOWN Club/Phonogram JAB 5		53	3 wks

REZILLOS
UK, male/female vocal/instrumental group   *21 wks*

12 Aug 78	TOP OF THE POPS Sire SIR 4001		17	9 wks
25 Nov 78	DESTINATION VENUS Sire SIR 4008		43	4 wks
18 Aug 79	I WANNA BE YOUR MAN/I CAN'T STAND MY BABY Sensible SAB 1		71	1 wk
1 Sep 79	I WANNA BE YOUR MAN/I CAN'T STAND MY BABY (re-entry) Sensible SAB 1		75	1 wk

26 Jan 80 **MOTORBIKE BEAT** *Dindisc DIN 5* .... 45 6 wks

Motorbike Beat *credited to the Revillos.*

RHODA with the SPECIAL A.K.A.
UK, female vocalist with male vocal/instrumental group 5 wks

23 Jan 82 **THE BOILER** *2-Tone CHSTT 18* .... 35 5 wks

See also Specials.

Charlie RICH *US, male vocalist* 29 wks

16 Feb 74 ●	**THE MOST BEAUTIFUL GIRL** *CBS 1897*	2	14 wks
13 Apr 74	**BEHIND CLOSED DOORS** *Epic EPC 1539* ...	16	10 wks
1 Feb 75	**WE LOVE EACH OTHER** *Epic EPC 2868*	37	5 wks

RICH KIDS
UK, male vocal/instrumental group 5 wks

28 Jan 78 **RICH KIDS** *EMI 2738* .... 24 5 wks

Cliff RICHARD *UK, male vocalist* 902 wks

12 Sep 58 ●	**MOVE IT** *Columbia DB 4178*	2	17 wks
21 Nov 58 ●	**HIGH CLASS BABY** *Columbia DB 4203*	7	10 wks
30 Jan 59	**LIVIN' LOVIN' DOLL** *Columbia DB 4249*	20	6 wks
8 May 59 ●	**MEAN STREAK** *Columbia DB 4290*	10	9 wks
15 May 59	**NEVER MIND** *Columbia DB 4290*	21	2 wks
10 Jul 59 ●	**LIVING DOLL** *Columbia DB 4306*	1	21 wks
9 Oct 59 ★	**TRAVELLIN' LIGHT** *Columbia DB 4351*	1	17 wks
9 Oct 59	**DYNAMITE** *Columbia DB 4351*	16	2 wks
30 Oct 59	**DYNAMITE** (re-entry) *Columbia DB 4351*	21	2 wks
11 Dec 59	**LIVING DOLL** (re-entry) *Columbia DB 4306*	26	1 wk
1 Jan 60	**LIVING DOLL** (2nd re-entry) *Columbia DB 4306*	28	1 wk
15 Jan 60	**EXPRESSO BONGO** (EP) *Columbia SEG 7971* ..	14	7 wks
22 Jan 60 ●	**VOICE IN THE WILDERNESS** *Columbia DB 4398*	2	13 wks
24 Mar 60 ●	**FALL IN LOVE WITH YOU** *Columbia DB 4431*	2	15 wks
5 May 60	**VOICE IN THE WILDERNESS** (re-entry) *Columbia DB 4398*	36	2 wks
30 Jun 60 ★	**PLEASE DON'T TEASE** *Columbia DB 4479*	1	18 wks
22 Sep 60 ●	**NINE TIMES OUT OF TEN** *Columbia DB 4506*	3	12 wks
1 Dec 60 ★	**I LOVE YOU** *Columbia DB 4547*	1	16 wks
2 Mar 61 ●	**THEME FOR A DREAM** *Columbia DB 4593*	3	14 wks
30 Mar 61 ●	**GEE WHIZ IT'S YOU** *Columbia DC 756*	4	14 wks
22 Jun 61 ●	**A GIRL LIKE YOU** *Columbia DB 4667*	3	14 wks
19 Oct 61 ●	**WHEN THE GIRL IN YOUR ARMS IS THE GIRL IN YOUR HEART** *Columbia DB 4716*	3	15 wks
11 Jan 62 ★	**THE YOUNG ONES** *Columbia DB 4761*	1	21 wks
10 May 62 ●	**I'M LOOKING OUT THE WINDOW/DO YOU WANNA DANCE** *Columbia DB 4828*	2	17 wks
6 Sep 62 ●	**IT'LL BE ME** *Columbia DB 4886*	2	12 wks
6 Dec 62 ★	**THE NEXT TIME/BACHELOR BOY** *Columbia DB 4950*	1	18 wks
21 Feb 63 ★	**SUMMER HOLIDAY** *Columbia DB 4977*	1	18 wks
9 May 63 ●	**LUCKY LIPS** *Columbia DB 7034*	4	15 wks
22 Aug 63 ●	**IT'S ALL IN THE GAME** *Columbia DB 7089*	2	13 wks
7 Nov 63 ●	**DON'T TALK TO HIM** *Columbia DB 7150*	2	13 wks
6 Feb 64 ●	**I'M THE LONELY ONE** *Columbia DB 7203*	8	10 wks
13 Feb 64	**DON'T TALK TO HIM** (re-entry) *Columbia DB 7150*	50	1 wk
30 Apr 64 ●	**CONSTANTLY** *Columbia DB 7272*	4	13 wks
2 Jul 64 ●	**ON THE BEACH** *Columbia DB 7305*	7	13 wks
8 Oct 64 ●	**THE TWELFTH OF NEVER** *Columbia DB 7372*	8	11 wks
10 Dec 64 ●	**I COULD EASILY FALL** *Columbia DB 7420*	9	11 wks
11 Mar 65 ★	**THE MINUTE YOU'RE GONE** *Columbia DB 7496*	1	14 wks
10 Jun 65 ●	**ON MY WORD** *Columbia DB 7596*	12	10 wks
19 Aug 65	**THE TIME IN BETWEEN** *Columbia DB 7660*	22	8 wks
4 Nov 65 ●	**WIND ME UP (LET ME GO)** *Columbia DB 7745*	2	16 wks
24 Mar 66	**BLUE TURNS TO GREY** *Columbia DB 7866* ...	15	9 wks
21 Jul 66 ●	**VISIONS** *Columbia DB 7968*	7	12 wks

13 Oct 66 ●	**TIME DRAGS BY** *Columbia DB 8017*	10	12 wks
15 Dec 66 ●	**IN THE COUNTRY** *Columbia DB 8094*	6	10 wks
16 Mar 67 ●	**IT'S ALL OVER** *Columbia DB 8150*	9	10 wks
8 Jun 67	**I'LL COME RUNNING** *Columbia DB 8210* ...	26	8 wks
16 Aug 67 ●	**THE DAY I MET MARIE** *Columbia DB 8245* ..	10	14 wks
15 Nov 67 ●	**ALL MY LOVE** *Columbia DB 8293*	6	12 wks
20 Mar 68 ★	**CONGRATULATIONS** *Columbia DB 8376* ...	1	13 wks
26 Jun 68	**I'LL LOVE YOU FOREVER TODAY** *Columbia DB 8437*	27	6 wks
25 Sep 68	**MARIANNE** *Columbia DB 8476*	22	8 wks
27 Nov 68	**DON'T FORGET TO CATCH ME** *Columbia DB 8503*	21	10 wks
26 Feb 69	**GOOD TIMES (BETTER TIMES)** *Columbia DB 8548*	12	11 wks
28 May 69 ●	**BIG SHIP** *Columbia DB 8581*	8	10 wks
13 Sep 69 ●	**THROW DOWN A LINE** *Columbia DB 8615*	7	9 wks
6 Dec 69 ●	**WITH THE EYES OF A CHILD** *Columbia DB 8641*	20	11 wks
21 Feb 70	**JOY OF LIVING** *Columbia DB 8657*	25	8 wks
6 Jun 70 ●	**GOODBYE SAM HELLO SAMANTHA** *Columbia DB 8685*	6	15 wks
5 Sep 70	**I AIN'T GOT TIME ANYMORE** *Columbia DB 8708*	21	7 wks
23 Jan 71	**SUNNY HONEY GIRL** *Columbia DB 8747* ...	19	8 wks
10 Apr 71	**SILVERY RAIN** *Columbia DB 8774*	27	6 wks
17 Jul 71	**FLYING MACHINE** *Columbia DB 8797* ...	37	7 wks
13 Nov 71	**SING A SONG OF FREEDOM** *Columbia DB 8836*	13	12 wks
11 Mar 72	**JESUS** *Columbia DB 8864*	35	3 wks
26 Aug 72	**LIVING IN HARMONY** *Columbia DB 8917*	12	10 wks
17 Mar 73 ●	**POWER TO ALL OUR FRIENDS** *EMI 2012* ...	4	12 wks
12 May 73	**HELP IT ALONG/TOMORROW RISING** *EMI 2022*	29	6 wks
1 Dec 73	**TAKE ME HIGH** *EMI 2088*	27	12 wks
18 May 74	**(YOU KEEP ME) HANGIN' ON** *EMI 2150*	13	8 wks
7 Feb 76	**MISS YOU NIGHTS** *EMI 2376*	15	10 wks
8 May 76 ●	**DEVIL WOMAN** *EMI 2458*	9	8 wks
21 Aug 76	**I CAN'T ASK FOR ANYMORE THAN YOU** *EMI 2499*	17	8 wks
4 Dec 76	**HEY MR. DREAM MAKER** *EMI 2559*	31	5 wks
5 Mar 77	**MY KINDA LIFE** *EMI 2584*	15	8 wks
16 Jul 77	**WHEN TWO WORLDS DRIFT APART** *EMI 2633*	46	3 wks
31 Mar 79	**GREEN LIGHT** *EMI 2920*	57	3 wks
21 Jul 79 ★	**WE DON'T TALK ANYMORE** *EMI 2975*	1	14 wks
3 Nov 79	**HOT SHOT** *EMI 5003*	46	5 wks
2 Feb 80 ●	**CARRIE** *EMI 5006*	4	10 wks
16 Aug 80 ●	**DREAMIN'** *EMI 5095*	8	10 wks
24 Jan 81	**A LITTLE IN LOVE** *EMI 5123*	15	8 wks
29 Aug 81 ●	**WIRED FOR SOUND** *EMI 5221*	4	9 wks
21 Nov 81 ●	**DADDY'S HOME** *EMI 5251*	2	12 wks
17 Jul 82 ●	**THE ONLY WAY OUT** *EMI 5318*	10	8 wks
25 Sep 82	**WHERE DO WE GO FROM HERE** *EMI 5341*	60	3 wks
4 Dec 82	**LITTLE TOWN** *EMI 5348*	11	7 wks
16 Apr 83 ●	**TRUE LOVE WAYS** *EMI 5385*	8	8 wks
3 Sep 83	**NEVER SAY DIE (GIVE A LITTLE BIT MORE)** *EMI 5415*	15	7 wks
26 Nov 83 ●	**PLEASE DON'T FALL IN LOVE** *EMI 5437*	7	9 wks
31 Mar 84	**BABY YOU'RE DYNAMITE/OCEAN DEEP** *EMI 5457*	27	6 wks
19 May 84	**OCEAN DEEP/BABY YOU'RE DYNAMITE** (re-entry) *EMI 5457*	72	1 wk
3 Nov 84	**SHOOTING FROM THE HEART** *EMI RICH 1*	51	4 wks

The Shadows appear on all Cliff's hits from Move It to A Girl Like You. After that they are on the following hits: The Young Ones, Do You Wanna Dance, It'll Be Me, The Next Time, Bachelor Boy, Summer Holiday, Lucky Lips, Don't Talk To Him, I'm The Lonely One, On The Beach, I Could Easily Fall, The Time In Between, Blue Turns To Grey, Time Drags By, In The Country and Don't Forget To Catch Me. Throw Down A Line and Joy Of Living are credited to 'Cliff and Hank', Hank being Hank B. Marvin of the Shadows, who played guitar and sang on these two hits. The tracks on the Expresso Bongo EP: Love/A Voice in The Wilderness/The Shrine On The Second Floor/Bongo Blues. Bongo Blues features only the Shadows. The Shadows were the Drifters on Cliff's hits before Living Doll. See also the Shadows. See also Olivia Newton-John and Cliff Richard; Phil Everly and Cliff Richard; Sheila Walsh and Cliff Richard. True Love Ways credits the London Philharmonic Orchestra. Ocean Deep listed from 28 Apr 84 onwards.

Wendy RICHARD - *See Mike SARNE*

CLIFF RICHARD (top left) 27 April 1959 – Cliff has just been voted Best New Singer in the annual *New Musical Express* poll, has recorded 'Mean Streak/Never Mind' and is poised to top the bill at the Chiswick Empire. The compere that night went on to have seven hits himself years later. (Photo: Harry Hammond.)

OTIS REDDING (top right) His first venture into the music business was a roadie for R and B group Johnny Jenkins and the Pinetoppers.

RAINBOW (above) The group was formed in 1975 by former Deep Purple, Outlaws and Lord Sutch's Savages guitarist Richie Blackmore and former 'Elf' vocalist Ronnie James Dio.

ROCKWELL (right) The son of Motown boss Berry Gordy Jnr. covered George Harrison's 'Taxman' originally on the Beatles album 'Revolver'.

Lionel RICHIE — US, male vocalist — 83 wks

Date		Title	Label	Pos	Wks
20 Nov 82	●	TRULY	Motown TMG 1284	6	11 wks
29 Jan 83		YOU ARE	Motown TMG 1290	43	7 wks
7 May 83		MY LOVE	Motown TMG 1300	70	3 wks
1 Oct 83	●	ALL NIGHT LONG (ALL NIGHT) Motown TMG 1319		2	16 wks
3 Dec 83	●	RUNNING WITH THE NIGHT Motown TMG 1324		9	12 wks
10 Mar 84	★	HELLO	Motown TMG 1330	1	15 wks
23 Jun 84		STUCK ON YOU	Motown TMG 1341	12	12 wks
20 Oct 84		PENNY LOVER	Motown TMG 1356	18	7 wks

See also Diana Ross and Lionel Richie.

Jonathan RICHMAN and the MODERN LOVERS
US, male vocal/instrumental group — 23 wks

Date		Title	Label	Pos	Wks
16 Jul 77		ROADRUNNER	Beserkley BZZ 1	11	9 wks
29 Oct 77	●	EGYPTIAN REGGAE	Beserkley BZZ 3	5	14 wks

See also Modern Lovers.

RICO - See the SPECIALS

RIGHEIRA — Italy, male vocal duo — 3 wks

Date	Title	Label	Pos	Wks
24 Sep 83	VAMOS A LA PLAYA	A & M AM 137	53	3 wks

RIGHTEOUS BROTHERS
US, male vocal duo — 63 wks

Date		Title	Label	Pos	Wks
14 Jan 65	★	YOU'VE LOST THAT LOVIN' FEELIN' London HLU 9943		1	10 wks
12 Aug 65		UNCHAINED MELODY	London HL 9975	14	12 wks
13 Jan 66		EBB TIDE	London HL 10011	48	2 wks
14 Apr 66		(YOU'RE MY) SOUL AND INSPIRATION Verve VS 535		15	10 wks
10 Nov 66		WHITE CLIFFS OF DOVER	London HL 10086	21	9 wks
22 Dec 66		ISLAND IN THE SUN	Verve VS 547	36	5 wks
12 Feb 69	●	YOU'VE LOST THAT LOVIN' FEELIN' (re-issue) London HL 10241		10	11 wks
19 Nov 77		YOU'VE LOST THAT LOVIN' FEELIN' (2nd re-issue) Phil Spector International 2010 022		42	4 wks

Jeannie C. RILEY — US, female vocalist — 15 wks

Date	Title	Label	Pos	Wks
16 Oct 68	HARPER VALLEY P. T. A.	Polydor 56 148	12	15 wks

RIMSHOTS
US, male instrumental/vocal group — 5 wks

Date	Title	Label	Pos	Wks
19 Jul 75	7-6-5-4-3-2-1 (BLOW YOUR WHISTLE) All Platinum 6146 304		26	5 wks

Miguel RIOS — Spain, male vocalist — 12 wks

Date	Title	Label	Pos	Wks
11 Jul 70	SONG OF JOY	A & M AMS 790	16	12 wks

Waldo de los RIOS — Argentina, orchestra — 16 wks

Date		Title	Pos	Wks
10 Apr 71	●	MOZART SYMPHONY NO.40 IN G MINOR K550 1ST MOVEMENT (ALLEGRO MOLTO). A & M AMS 836	5	16 wks

Minnie RIPERTON — US, female vocalist — 10 wks

Date		Title	Label	Pos	Wks
12 Apr 75	●	LOVING YOU	Epic EPC 3121	2	10 wks

RITCHIE FAMILY
US, female vocal group — 19 wks

Date		Title	Label	Pos	Wks
23 Aug 75		BRAZIL	Polydor 2058 625	41	4 wks
18 Sep 76	●	THE BEST DISCO IN TOWN	Polydor 2058 777	10	9 wks
17 Feb 79		AMERICAN GENERATION	Mercury 6007 199	49	6 wks

Tex RITTER — US, male vocalist — 14 wks

Date		Title	Label	Pos	Wks
22 Jun 56	●	WAYWARD WIND	Capitol CL 14581	8	14 wks

Danny RIVERS — UK, male vocalist — 3 wks

Date	Title	Label	Pos	Wks
12 Jan 61	CAN'T YOU HEAR MY HEART	Decca F 11294	36	3 wks

Kate ROBBINS — UK, female vocalist — 10 wks

Date		Title	Label	Pos	Wks
30 May 81	●	MORE THAN IN LOVE	RCA 69	2	10 wks

Marty ROBBINS — US, male vocalist — 32 wks

Date		Title	Label	Pos	Wks
29 Jan 60		EL PASO	Fontana H 233	19	7 wks
7 Apr 60		EL PASO (re-entry)	Fontana H 233	44	1 wk
26 May 60		BIG IRON	Fontana H 229	48	1 wk
27 Sep 62	●	DEVIL WOMAN	CBS AAG 114	5	17 wks
17 Jan 63		RUBY ANN	CBS AAG 128	24	6 wks

Austin ROBERTS — US, male vocalist — 7 wks

Date	Title	Label	Pos	Wks
25 Oct 75	ROCKY	Private Stock PVT 33	22	7 wks

Malcolm ROBERTS — UK, male vocalist — 29 wks

Date		Title	Label	Pos	Wks
11 May 67		TIME ALONE WILL TELL	RCA 1578	45	2 wks
30 Oct 68	●	MAY I HAVE THE NEXT DREAM WITH YOU Major Minor MM 581		8	14 wks
12 Feb 69		MAY I HAVE THE NEXT DREAM WITH YOU (re-entry) Major Minor MM 581		45	1 wk
22 Nov 69		LOVE IS ALL	Major Minor MM 637	12	12 wks

B.A. ROBERTSON — UK, male vocalist — 47 wks

Date		Title	Label	Pos	Wks
28 Jul 79	●	BANG BANG	Asylum K 13152	2	12 wks
27 Oct 79	●	KNOCKED IT OFF	Asylum K 12396	8	12 wks
1 Mar 80		KOOL IN THE KAFTAN	Asylum K 12427	17	12 wks
31 May 80	●	TO BE OR NOT TO BE	Asylum K 12449	9	11 wks

See also B.A. Robertson and Maggie Bell; Frida and B.A. Robertson.

B.A. ROBERTSON and Maggie BELL
UK, male/female vocal duo — 8 wks

Date	Title	Label	Pos	Wks
17 Oct 81	HOLD ME	Swansong BAM 1	11	8 wks

See also B.A. Robertson; Maggie Bell; Frida and B.A. Robertson.

Don ROBERTSON
US, male instrumentalist - piano and whistler — 9 wks

Date		Title	Label	Pos	Wks
11 May 56	●	THE HAPPY WHISTLER	Capitol CL 14575	8	9 wks

Ivo ROBIC *Germany, male vocalist* *1 wk*

6 Nov 59	**MORGEN** *Polydor 23 923*	**23**	1 wk

Floyd ROBINSON *US, male vocalist* *9 wks*

16 Oct 59 ●	**MAKIN' LOVE** *RCA 1146*	**9**	9 wks

Smokey ROBINSON *US, male vocalist* *23 wks*

23 Feb 74	**JUST MY SOUL RESPONDING**		
	Tamla Motown TMG 883	**35**	6 wks
9 May 81 ★	**BEING WITH YOU** *Motown TMG 1223*	**1**	13 wks
13 Mar 82	**TELL ME TOMORROW** *Motown TMG 1255* ...	**51**	4 wks

See also Smokey Robinson and the Miracles; Diana Ross, Marvin Gaye, Smokey Robinson and Stevie Wonder.

Smokey ROBINSON and the MIRACLES *US, male vocal group* *71 wks*

24 Feb 66	**GOING TO A GO-GO** *Tamla Motown TMG 547*	**44**	5 wks
22 Dec 66	**(COME 'ROUND HERE) I'M THE ONE YOU**		
	NEED *Tamla Motown TMG 584*	**45**	2 wks
27 Dec 67	**I SECOND THAT EMOTION**		
	Tamla Motown TMG 631	**27**	11 wks
3 Apr 68	**IF YOU CAN WANT** *Tamla Motown TMG 648*	**50**	1 wk
7 May 69 ●	**TRACKS OF MY TEARS**		
	Tamla Motown TMG 696	**9**	13 wks
1 Aug 70 ★	**TEARS OF A CLOWN** *Tamla Motown TMG 745*	**1**	14 wks
30 Jan 71	**(COME 'ROUND HERE) I'M THE ONE YOU**		
	NEED (re-issue) *Tamla Motown TMG 761*	**13**	9 wks
5 Jun 71	**I DON'T BLAME YOU AT ALL**		
	Tamla Motown TMG 774	**11**	10 wks
2 Oct 76	**TEARS OF A CLOWN** (re-issue)		
	Tamla Motown TMG 1048	**34**	6 wks

See also Miracles; Smokey Robinson; Diana Ross, Marvin Gaye, Smokey Robinson and Stevie Wonder.

Tom ROBINSON *UK, male vocalist* *18 wks*

25 Jun 83 ●	**WAR BABY** *Panic NIC 2*	**6**	9 wks
12 Nov 83	**LISTEN TO THE RADIO: ATMOSPHERICS**		
	Panic NIC 3	**39**	6 wks
15 Sep 84	**RIKKI DON'T LOSE THAT NUMBER**		
	Castaway/RCA TR 2	**58**	3 wks

See also Tom Robinson Band.

Tom ROBINSON BAND *UK, male vocal/instrumental group* *23 wks*

22 Oct 77 ●	**2-4-6-8 MOTORWAY** *EMI 2715*	**5**	9 wks
18 Feb 78	**DON'T TAKE NO FOR AN ANSWER** *EMI 2749*	**18**	6 wks
13 May 78	**UP AGAINST THE WALL** *EMI 2787*	**33**	6 wks
17 Mar 79	**BULLY FOR YOU** *EMI 2916*	**68**	2 wks

See also Tom Robinson.

ROCK CANDY *UK, male vocal/instrumental group* *6 wks*

11 Sep 71	**REMEMBER** *MCA MK 5069*	**32**	6 wks

ROCK GODDESS *UK, female vocal/instrumental group* *5 wks*

5 Mar 83	**MY ANGEL** *A & M AMS 8311*	**64**	2 wks

---

24 Mar 84	**I DIDN'T KNOW I LOVED YOU (TILL I SAW**		
	YOU ROCK 'N' ROLL) *A & M AMS 185* ...	**57**	3 wks

Sir Monti ROCK III - *See DISCO TEX and the SEX-O-LETTES*

ROCKER'S REVENGE *US, male/female vocal/instrumental group* *20 wks*

14 Aug 82 ●	**WALKING ON SUNSHINE** *London LON 11*	**4**	13 wks
29 Jan 83	**THE HARDER THEY COME** *London LON 18* ..	**30**	7 wks

First hit has credit: 'Featuring Donnie Calvin'.

ROCKETS - *See Tony CROMBIE and his ROCKETS.*

ROCKIN' BERRIES *UK, male vocal/instrumental group* *41 wks*

1 Oct 64	**I DIDN'T MEAN TO HURT YOU**		
	Piccadilly 7N 35197	**43**	1 wk
15 Oct 64 ●	**HE'S IN TOWN** *Piccadilly 7N 35203*	**3**	13 wks
21 Jan 65	**WHAT IN THE WORLD'S COME OVER YOU**		
	Piccadilly 7N 35217	**23**	7 wks
13 May 65 ●	**POOR MAN'S SON** *Piccadilly 7N 35236*	**5**	11 wks
26 Aug 65	**YOU'RE MY GIRL** *Piccadilly 7N 35254*	**40**	7 wks
6 Jan 66	**THE WATER IS OVER MY HEAD**		
	Piccadilly 7N 35270	**43**	1 wk
20 Jan 66	**THE WATER IS OVER MY HEAD** (re-entry)		
	Piccadilly 7N 35270	**50**	1 wk

Lord ROCKINGHAM'S XI *UK, male instrumental group* *20 wks*

24 Oct 58 ★	**HOOTS MON** *Decca F 11059*	**1**	17 wks
6 Feb 59	**WEE TOM** *Decca F 11104*	**16**	3 wks

Both of the group's hits contain a little spoken Scottish.

ROCKNEY - *See CHAS and DAVE*

ROCKSTEADY CREW *US, male/female vocal group* *16 wks*

1 Oct 83 ●	**(HEY YOU) THE ROCKSTEADY CREW**		
	Charisma/Virgin RSC 1	**6**	12 wks
5 May 84	**UPROCK** *Charisma/Virgin RSC 2*	**64**	4 wks

ROCKWELL *US, male vocalist* *11 wks*

4 Feb 84 ●	**SOMEBODY'S WATCHING ME**		
	Motown TMG 1331	**6**	11 wks

Clodagh RODGERS *Ireland, female vocalist* *59 wks*

26 Mar 69 ●	**COME BACK AND SHAKE ME** *RCA 1792*	**3**	14 wks
9 Jul 69 ●	**GOODNIGHT MIDNIGHT** *RCA 1852*	**4**	11 wks
4 Oct 69	**GOODNIGHT MIDNIGHT** (re-entry) *RCA 1852*	**48**	1 wk
8 Nov 69	**BILJO** *RCA 1891*	**22**	9 wks
4 Apr 70	**EVERYBODY GO HOME THE PARTY'S OVER**		
	RCA 1930	**47**	2 wks
20 Mar 71 ●	**JACK IN THE BOX** *RCA 2066*	**4**	10 wks
9 Oct 71	**LADY LOVE BUG** *RCA 2117*	**28**	12 wks

Jimmie RODGERS *US, male vocalist* *37 wks*

1 Nov 57	**HONEYCOMB** *Columbia DB 3986*	**30**	1 wk

20 Dec 57 ●	KISSES SWEETER THAN WINE			
	Columbia DB 4052		7	11 wks
28 Mar 58	OH OH, I'M FALLING IN LOVE AGAIN			
	Columbia DB 4078		18	6 wks
19 Dec 58	WOMAN FROM LIBERIA Columbia DB 4206		18	6 wks
14 Jun 62 ●	ENGLISH COUNTRY GARDEN			
	Columbia DB 4847		5	13 wks

Tommy ROE US, male vocalist · 74 wks

6 Sep 62 ●	SHEILA HMV POP 1060	3	14 wks
6 Dec 62	SUSIE DARLIN' HMV POP 1092	37	5 wks
21 Mar 63 ●	THE FOLK SINGER HMV POP 1138	4	13 wks
26 Sep 63 ●	EVERYBODY HMV POP 1207	9	11 wks
19 Dec 63	EVERYBODY (re-entry) HMV POP 1207	49	3 wks
16 Apr 69 ★	DIZZY Stateside SS 2143	1	19 wks
23 Jul 69	HEATHER HONEY Stateside SS 2152	24	9 wks

Julie ROGERS UK, female vocalist · 38 wks

13 Aug 64 ●	THE WEDDING Mercury MF 820	3	23 wks
10 Dec 64	LIKE A CHILD Mercury MF 838	21	9 wks
25 Mar 65	HAWAIIAN WEDDING SONG Mercury MF 849	31	6 wks

Kenny ROGERS US, male vocalist · 87 wks

18 Oct 69 ●	RUBY DON'T TAKE YOUR LOVE TO TOWN		
	Reprise RS 20829	2	23 wks
7 Feb 70 ●	SOMETHING'S BURNING Reprise RS 20888	8	14 wks
30 Apr 77 ★	LUCILLE United Artists UP 36242	1	14 wks
17 Sep 77	DAYTIME FRIENDS United Artists UP 36289	39	4 wks
2 Jun 79	SHE BELIEVES IN ME United Artists UP 36533	42	7 wks
26 Jan 80 ★	COWARD OF THE COUNTY		
	United Artists UP 614	1	12 wks
15 Nov 80	LADY United Artists UP 635	12	12 wks
22 Oct 83	EYES THAT SEE IN THE DARK RCA 358	61	1 wk

First two hits credit Kenny Rogers and the First Edition, US, male/female vocal/instrumental group. See also Kenny Rogers and Sheena Easton; Kenny Rogers and Dolly Parton.

Kenny ROGERS and Dolly PARTON US, male/female vocal duo · 15 wks

12 Nov 83 ●	ISLANDS IN THE STREAM RCA 378	7	15 wks

See also Kenny Rogers; Dolly Parton; Kenny Rogers and Sheena Easton.

Kenny ROGERS and Sheena EASTON US/UK, male/female vocal duo · 7 wks

12 Feb 83	WE'VE GOT TONIGHT Liberty UP 658	28	7 wks

See also Kenny Rogers; Sheena Easton; Kenny Rogers and Dolly Parton.

ROKOTTO
UK, male vocal/instrumental group · 10 wks

22 Oct 77	BOOGIE ON UP State STAT 62	40	4 wks
10 Jun 78	FUNK THEORY State STAT 80	49	6 wks

ROLLING STONES
UK, male vocal/instrumental group · 313 wks

25 Jul 63	COME ON Decca F 11675	21	14 wks
14 Nov 63	I WANNA BE YOUR MAN Decca F 11764	12	16 wks
27 Feb 64 ●	NOT FADE AWAY Decca F 11845	3	15 wks
2 Jul 64 ★	IT'S ALL OVER NOW Decca F 11934	1	15 wks
19 Nov 64 ★	LITTLE RED ROOSTER Decca F 12014	1	12 wks
4 Mar 65 ★	THE LAST TIME Decca F 12104	1	13 wks

26 Aug 65 ★	(I CAN'T GET NO) SATISFACTION		
	Decca F 12220	1	12 wks
28 Oct 65 ★	GET OFF OF MY CLOUD Decca F 12263	1	12 wks
10 Feb 66 ●	NINETEENTH NERVOUS BREAKDOWN		
	Decca F 12331	2	8 wks
19 May 66 ★	PAINT IT BLACK Decca F 12395	1	10 wks
29 Sep 66 ●	HAVE YOU SEEN YOUR MOTHER BABY		
	STANDING IN THE SHADOW Decca F 12497	5	8 wks
19 Jan 67 ●	LET'S SPEND THE NIGHT TOGETHER/RUBY		
	TUESDAY Decca F 12546	3	10 wks
23 Aug 67 ●	WE LOVE YOU/DANDELION Decca F 12654	8	8 wks
29 May 68 ★	JUMPING JACK FLASH Decca F 12782	1	11 wks
9 Jul 69 ★	HONKY TONK WOMEN Decca F 12952	1	17 wks
24 Apr 71 ●	BROWN SUGAR/BITCH/LET IT ROCK		
	Rolling Stones RS 19100	2	13 wks
3 Jul 71	STREET FIGHTING MAN Decca F 13195	21	8 wks
29 Apr 72 ●	TUMBLING DICE Rolling Stones RS 19103	5	8 wks
1 Sep 73 ●	ANGIE Rolling Stones RS 19105	5	10 wks
3 Aug 74 ●	IT'S ONLY ROCK AND ROLL		
	Rolling Stones RS 19114	10	7 wks
20 Sep 75	OUT OF TIME Decca F 13597	45	2 wks
1 May 76 ●	FOOL TO CRY Rolling Stones RS 19131	6	10 wks
3 Jun 78 ●	MISS YOU /FAR AWAY EYES		
	Rolling Stones EMI 2802	3	13 wks
30 Sep 78	RESPECTABLE Rolling Stones EMI 2861	23	9 wks
5 Jul 80 ●	EMOTIONAL RESCUE Rolling Stones RSR 105	9	8 wks
4 Oct 80	SHE'S SO COLD Rolling Stones RSR 106	33	6 wks
29 Aug 81 ●	START ME UP Rolling Stones RSR 108	7	9 wks
12 Dec 81	WAITING ON A FRIEND Rolling Stones RSR 109	50	6 wks
12 Jun 82	GOING TO A GO GO Rolling Stones RSR 110	26	6 wks
2 Oct 82	TIME IS ON MY SIDE Rolling Stones RSR 111	62	2 wks
12 Nov 83	UNDERCOVER OF THE NIGHT		
	Rolling Stones RSR 113	11	9 wks
11 Feb 84	SHE WAS HOT Rolling Stones RSR 114	42	4 wks
21 Jul 84	BROWN SUGAR (re-entry)		
	Rolling Stones SUGAR 1	58	2 wks

Far Away Eyes credited from 15 Jul 78 until end of record's run.

ROMAN HOLLIDAY
UK, male vocal/instrumental group · 19 wks

2 Apr 83	STAND BY Jive JIVE 31	61	3 wks
2 Jul 83	DON'T TRY TO STOP IT Jive JIVE 39	14	9 wks
24 Sep 83	MOTORMANIA Jive JIVE 49	40	7 wks

ROMANTICS - *See RUBY and the ROMANTICS*

Max ROMEO Jamaica, male vocalist · 25 wks

28 May 69 ●	WET DREAM Unity UN 503	10	24 wks
29 Nov 69	WET DREAM (re-entry) Unity UN 503	50	1 wk

RONDO VENEZIANA Italy, orchestra · 3 wks

22 Oct 83	LA SERENISSIMA (THEME FROM 'VENICE IN		
	PERIL') Ferroway 7 RON 1	58	3 wks

RONETTES US, female vocal group · 34 wks

17 Oct 63 ●	BE MY BABY London HLU 9793	4	13 wks
9 Jan 64	BABY I LOVE YOU London HLU 9826	11	14 wks
27 Aug 64	BEST PART OF BREAKING UP		
	London HLU 9905	43	3 wks
8 Oct 64	DO I LOVE YOU London HLU 9922	35	4 wks

Linda RONSTADT US, female vocalist · 9 wks

8 May 76	TRACKS OF MY TEARS Asylum K 13034	42	3 wks
28 Jan 78	BLUE BAYOU Asylum K 13106	35	4 wks
26 May 79 ★	ALISON Asylum K 13149	66	2 wks

ROOFTOP SINGERS
US, male/female vocal group   *12 wks*

31 Jan 63	● WALK RIGHT IN Fontana TF 271700	10	12 wks

ROSE OF ROMANCE ORCHESTRA
UK, orchestra   *1 wk*

9 Jan 82	TARA'S THEME FROM 'GONE WITH THE WIND' BBC RESL 108	71	1 wk

ROSE ROYCE
US, male/female vocal/instrumental group   *100 wks*

25 Dec 76	● CAR WASH MCA 267	9	12 wks
22 Jan 77	PUT YOUR MONEY WHERE YOUR MOUTH IS MCA 259	44	5 wks
2 Apr 77	I WANNA GET NEXT TO YOU MCA 278	14	8 wks
24 Sep 77	DO YOUR DANCE Whitfield K 17006	30	6 wks
14 Jan 78	● WISHING ON A STAR Warner Bros. K 17060	3	14 wks
6 May 78	IT MAKES YOU FEEL LIKE DANCIN' Warner Bros. K 17148	16	10 wks
16 Sep 78	● LOVE DON'T LIVE HERE ANYMORE Whitfield K 17236	2	10 wks
3 Feb 79	I'M IN LOVE (AND I LOVE THE FEELING) Whitfield K 17291	51	4 wks
17 Nov 79	IS IT LOVE YOU'RE AFTER Whitfield K 17456	13	13 wks
8 Mar 80	OOH BOY Whitfield K 17575	46	7 wks
21 Nov 81	EXPRESS Warner Bros. K 17875	52	3 wks
1 Sep 84	MAGIC TOUCH Streetwave KHAN 2	43	8 wks

ROSE TATTOO
Australia, male vocal/instrumental group   *4 wks*

11 Jul 81	ROCK'N'ROLL OUTLAW Carrere CAR 200	60	4 wks

Jimmy ROSELLI *US, male vocalist*   *5 wks*

5 Mar 83	WHEN YOUR OLD WEDDING RING WAS NEW A1/Satril A1 282	51	5 wks

Diana ROSS *US, female vocalist*   *270 wks*

18 Jul 70	REACH OUT AND TOUCH Tamla Motown TMG 743	33	5 wks
12 –Sep 70	● AIN'T NO MOUNTAIN HIGH ENOUGH Tamla Motown TMG 751	6	12 wks
3 Apr 71	● REMEMBER ME Tamla Motown TMG 768	7	12 wks
31 Jul 71	★ I'M STILL WAITING Tamla Motown TMG 781	1	14 wks
30 Oct 71	● SURRENDER Tamla Motown TMG 792	10	11 wks
13 May 72	DOOBEDOOD'NDOOBE DOOBEDOOD'NDOOBE Tamla Motown TMG 812	12	9 wks
14 Jul 73	● TOUCH ME IN THE MORNING Tamla Motown TMG 861	9	12 wks
13 Oct 73	TOUCH ME IN THE MORNING (re-entry) Tamla Motown TMG 861	50	1 wk
5 Jan 74	● ALL OF MY LIFE Tamla Motown TMG 880	9	13 wks
4 May 74	LAST TIME I SAW HIM Tamla Motown TMG 893	35	4 wks
28 Sep 74	LOVE ME Tamla Motown TMG 917	38	5 wks
29 Mar 75	SORRY DOESN'T ALWAYS MAKE IT RIGHT Tamla Motown TMG 941	23	9 wks
3 Apr 76	● THEME FROM MAHOGANY (DO YOU KNOW WHERE YOU'RE GOING TO) Tamla Motown TMG 1010	5	8 wks
24 Apr 76	● LOVE HANGOVER Tamla Motown TMG 1024 ..	10	10 wks
10 Jul 76	I THOUGHT IT TOOK A LITTLE TIME Tamla Motown TMG 1032	32	5 wks

16 Oct 76	I'M STILL WAITING (re-issue) Tamla Motown TMG 1041	41	4 wks
19 Nov 77	GETTIN' READY FOR LOVE Motown TMG 1090	23	7 wks
22 Jul 78	LOVIN' LIVIN' AND GIVIN' Motown TMG 1112	54	6 wks
21 Jul 79	THE BOSS Motown TMG 1150	40	7 wks
6 Oct 79	NOONE GETS THE PRIZE Motown TMG 1160	59	3 wks
24 Nov 79	IT'S MY HOUSE Motown TMG 1169	32	10 wks
19 Jul 80	● UPSIDE DOWN Motown TMG 1195	2	12 wks
20 Sep 80	● MY OLD PIANO Motown TMG 1202	5	9 wks
15 Nov 80	I'M COMING OUT Motown TMG 1210	13	10 wks
17 Jan 81	IT'S MY TURN Motown TMG 1217	16	8 wks
28 Mar 81	ONE MORE CHANCE Motown TMG 1227	49	5 wks
13 Jun 81	CRYIN' MY HEART OUT FOR YOU Motown TMG 1233	58	3 wks
7 Nov 81	● WHY DO FOOLS FALL IN LOVE Capitol CL 226	4	12 wks
23 Jan 82	TENDERNESS Motown TMG 1248	73	1 wk
30 Jan 82	MIRROR MIRROR Capitol CL 234	36	5 wks
6 Feb 82	TENDERNESS (re-entry) Motown TMG 1248 ...	75	1 wk
29 May 82	● WORK THAT BODY Capitol CL 241	7	11 wks
7 Aug 82	IT'S NEVER TOO LATE Capitol CL 256	41	4 wks
23 Oct 82	MUSCLES Capitol CL 268	15	9 wks
15 Jan 83	SO CLOSE Capitol CL 277	43	4 wks
23 Jul 83	PIECES OF ICE Capitol CL 298	46	3 wks
15 Sep 84	TOUCH BY TOUCH Capitol CL 337	47	6 wks

See also Supremes; Supremes and the Four Tops; Diana Ross and Michael Jackson; Diana Ross and the Supremes and the Temptations; Diana Ross and Marvin Gaye; Diana Ross, Marvin Gaye, Smokey Robinson and Stevie Wonder; Diana Ross and Lionel Richie.

Diana ROSS and Marvin GAYE
US, female/male vocal duo   *20 wks*

23 Mar 74	● YOU ARE EVERYTHING Tamla Motown TMG 890	5	12 wks
20 Jul 74	STOP LOOK LISTEN (TO YOUR HEART) Tamla Motown TMG 906	25	8 wks

See also Marvin Gaye; Diana Ross; Marvin Gaye and Tammi Terrell; Marvin Gaye and Mary Wells; Marvin Gaye and Kim Weston; Diana Ross and the Supremes and the Temptations; Diana Ross, Marvin Gaye, Smokey Robinson and Stevie Wonder; Diana Ross and Michael Jackson; Diana Ross and Lionel Richie.

Diana ROSS, Marvin GAYE, Smokey ROBINSON and Stevie WONDER *US, female/male vocal group*   *5 wks*

24 Feb 79	POPS, WE LOVE YOU Motown TMG 1136	66	5 wks

See also Diana Ross; Diana Ross and the Supremes and the Temptations; Diana Ross and Michael Jackson; Diana Ross and Marvin Gaye; Diana Ross and Lionel Richie; Marvin Gaye and Tammi Terrell; Marvin Gaye and Mary Wells; Marvin Gaye and Kim Weston; Stevie Wonder; Smokey Robinson; Smokey Robinson and the Miracles; Paul McCartney and Stevie Wonder.

Diana ROSS and Michael JACKSON *US, female/male vocal duo*   *4 wks*

18 Nov 78	EASE ON DOWN THE ROAD MCA 396	45	4 wks

See also Diana Ross and the Supremes and the Temptations; Diana Ross and Marvin Gaye; Michael Jackson; Jackson Five; Jacksons; Diana Ross, Marvin Gaye, Smokey Robinson and Stevie Wonder; Diana Ross and Lionel Richie; Michael Jackson and Paul McCartney.

Diana ROSS and Lionel RICHIE
US, female/male vocal duo   *12 wks*

12 Sep 81	● ENDLESS LOVE Motown TMG 1240	7	12 wks

See also Lionel Richie; Diana Ross; Supremes; Diana Ross and Michael Jackson; Diana Ross and The Supremes and the Temptations; Diana Ross and Marvin Gaye; Diana Ross, Marvin Gaye, Smokey Robinson and Stevie Wonder.

Diana ROSS and the SUPREMES and the TEMPTATIONS
US, female and male vocal groups 27 wks

29 Jan 69	●	I'M GONNA MAKE YOU LOVE ME	Tamla Motown TMG 685	3	11 wks
23 Apr 69		I'M GONNA MAKE YOU LOVE ME (re-entry)	Tamla Motown TMG 685	49	1 wk
20 Sep 69		I SECOND THAT EMOTION	Tamla Motown TMG 709	18	8 wks
21 Mar 70		WHY (MUST WE FALL IN LOVE)	Tamla Motown TMG 730	31	7 wks

See also Diana Ross; Supremes; Diana Ross and Marvin Gaye; Supremes and the Four Tops; Temptations; Diana Ross, Marvin Gaye, Smokey Robinson and Stevie Wonder; Diana Ross and Michael Jackson; Diana Ross and Lionel Richie.

Laurent ROSSI - *See BIMBO JET*

Nini ROSSO
Italy, male instrumentalist - trumpet 14 wks

26 Aug 65	●	IL SILENZIO	Durium DRS 54000	8	14 wks

ROULETTES - *See Adam FAITH*

Robert ROUNSEVILLE - *See VARIOUS ARTISTS (Carousel Soundtrack)*

Demis ROUSSOS *Greece, male vocalist* 44 wks

22 Nov 75	●	HAPPY TO BE ON AN ISLAND IN THE SUN	Philips 6042 033	5	10 wks
28 Feb 76		CAN'T SAY HOW MUCH I LOVE YOU	Philips 6042 114	35	5 wks
26 Jun 76	★	THE ROUSSOS PHENOMENON (EP)	Philips DEMIS 001	1	12 wks
2 Oct 76	●	WHEN FOREVER HAS GONE	Philips 6042 186	2	10 wks
19 Mar 77		BECAUSE Philips 6042 245		39	4 wks
18 Jun 77		KYRILA (EP) Philips DEMIS 002		33	3 wks

Tracks on The Roussos Phenomen on EP: Forever And Ever/ Sing An Ode To Love/So Dreamy/My Friend The Wind. Tracks on Kyrila EP: Kyrila/I'm Gonna Fall in Love/I Dig You/ Sister Emilyne.

ROUTERS *US, male instrumental group* 7 wks

27 Dec 62		LET'S GO	Warner Bros. WB 77	32	7 wks

John ROWLES *New Zealand, male vocalist* 28 wks

13 Mar 68	●	IF I ONLY HAD TIME	MCA MU 1000	3	18 wks
19 Jun 68		HUSH NOT A WORD TO MARY	MCA MU 1023	12	10 wks

ROXY MUSIC
UK, male vocal/instrumental group 153 wks

19 Aug 72	●	VIRGINIA PLAIN	Island WIP 6144	4	12 wks
10 Mar 73	●	PYJAMARAMA	Island WIP 6159	10	12 wks
17 Nov 73	●	STREET LIFE	Island WIP 6173	9	12 wks
12 Oct 74		ALL I WANT IS YOU	Island WIP 6208	12	8 wks
11 Oct 75	●	LOVE IS THE DRUG	Island WIP 6248	2	10 wks
27 Dec 75		BOTH ENDS BURNING	Island WIP 6262	25	7 wks
22 Oct 77		VIRGINIA PLAIN (re-issue)	Polydor 2001 739	11	6 wks
3 Mar 79		TRASH	Polydor POSP 32	40	6 wks
28 Apr 79	●	DANCE AWAY	Polydor POSP 44	2	14 wks
11 Aug 79	●	ANGEL EYES	Polydor POSP 67	4	11 wks
17 May 80	●	OVER YOU	Polydor POSP 93	5	9 wks

2 Aug 80	●	OH YEAH (ON THE RADIO)	Polydor 2001 972	5	8 wks
8 Nov 80		THE SAME OLD SCENE	Polydor ROXY 1	12	7 wks
21 Feb 81	★	JEALOUS GUY	EG/Polydor ROXY 2	1	11 wks
3 Apr 82	●	MORE THAN THIS	EG/Polydor ROXY 3	6	8 wks
19 Jun 82		AVALON	EG/Polydor ROXY 4	13	6 wks
25 Sep 82		TAKE A CHANCE WITH ME	E.G./Polydor ROXY 5	26	6 wks

Roy 'C' *US, male vocalist* 24 wks

21 Apr 66	●	SHOTGUN WEDDING	Island WI 273	6	11 wks
25 Nov 72	●	SHOTGUN WEDDING (re-issue)	UK 19	8	13 wks

Billy Joe ROYAL *US, male vocalist* 4 wks

7 Oct 65	DOWN IN THE BOONDOCKS	CBS 201802	38	4 wks

The Central Band of the ROYAL AIR FORCE, Conductor W/CDR. A.E. SIMS O.B.E. *UK, military band* 1 wk

21 Oct 55	THE DAMBUSTERS MARCH	HMV B 10877	18	1 wk

ROYAL GUARDSMEN
US, male vocal/instrumental group 17 wks

19 Jan 67	●	SNOOPY VS. THE RED BARON	Stateside SS 574	8	13 wks
6 Apr 67		RETURN OF THE RED BARON	Stateside SS 2010	37	4 wks

ROYAL PHILHARMONIC ORCHESTRA arranged and conducted by Louis CLARK
UK, orchestra and conductor 19 wks

25 Jul 81	●	HOOKED ON CLASSICS	RCA 109	2	11 wks
24 Oct 81		HOOKED ON CAN-CAN	RCA 151	47	3 wks
10 Jul 82		BBC WORLD CUP GRANDSTAND	BBC RESL 116	61	3 wks
7 Aug 82		IF YOU KNEW SOUSA (AND FRIENDS)	RCA 256	71	2 wks

See also Elvis Costello. Louis Clark not conductor for third hit.

The Pipes and Drums and Military Band of the ROYAL SCOTS DRAGOON GUARDS
UK, military band 43 wks

1 Apr 72	★	AMAZING GRACE	RCA 2191	1	24 wks
19 Aug 72		HEYKENS SERENADE/THE DAY IS OVER	RCA 2251	30	7 wks
2 Dec 72		LITTLE DRUMMER BOY	RCA 2301	13	9 wks
23 Dec 72		AMAZING GRACE (re-entry)	RCA 2191	42	3 wks

Lita ROZA *UK, female vocalist* 18 wks

13 Mar 53	★	(HOW MUCH IS) THAT DOGGIE IN THE WINDOW	Decca F 10070	1	11 wks
7 Oct 55		HEY THERE	Decca F 10611	17	2 wks
23 Mar 56		JIMMY UNKNOWN	Decca F 10679	15	5 wks

See also Various Artists - All Star Hit Parade.

NEIL REID (left) His number one mum was denied being number one pop by the New Seekers 'I'd Like To Teach The World To Sing'.

TODD RUNDGREN (centre) He has worked in the studio with a list of musicians that include The Band, Janis Joplin, Badfinger, Grand Funk Railroad, New York Dolls, Sparks, Steve Hillage, Tom Robinson, Patti Smith, Johnny Winter and Hall and Oates.

DEBBIE REYNOLDS (right) Miss Burbank 1948.

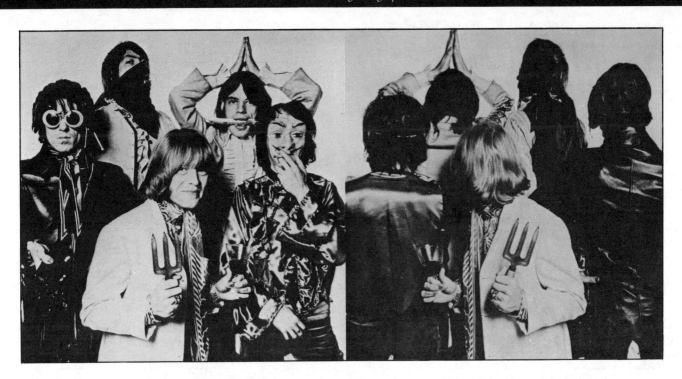

ROLLING STONES relaxing during a private moment.

RUBETTES
UK, male vocal/instrumental group — *68 wks*

4 May 74	★ SUGAR BABY LOVE *Polydor 2058 442*	1	10 wks
13 Jul 74	TONIGHT *Polydor 2058 499*	12	9 wks
16 Nov 74	● JUKE BOX JIVE *Polydor 2058 529*	3	12 wks
8 Mar 75	● I CAN DO IT *State STAT 1*	7	9 wks
21 Jun 75	FOE-DEE-O-DEE *State STAT 7*	15	6 wks
22 Nov 75	LITTLE DARLING *State STAT 13*	30	5 wks
1 May 76	YOU'RE THE REASON WHY *State STAT 20*	28	4 wks
25 Sep 76	UNDER ONE ROOF *State STAT 27*	40	3 wks
12 Feb 77	● BABY I KNOW *State STAT 37*	10	10 wks

RUBY and the ROMANTICS
US, female vocalist, male vocal backing group — *6 wks*

28 Mar 63	OUR DAY WILL COME *London HLR 9679*	38	6 wks

RUDIES - *See Freddie NOTES and the RUDIES*

Bruce RUFFIN
Jamaica, male vocalist — *23 wks*

1 May 71	RAIN *Trojan TR 7814*	19	11 wks
24 Jun 72	● MAD ABOUT YOU *Rhino RNO 101*	9	12 wks

David RUFFIN
US, male vocalist — *8 wks*

17 Jan 76	● WALK AWAY FROM LOVE *Tamla Motown TMG 1017*	10	8 wks

Jimmy RUFFIN
US, male vocalist — *105 wks*

27 Oct 66	● WHAT BECOMES OF THE BROKEN HEARTED *Tamla Motown TMG 577*	10	15 wks
9 Feb 67	I'VE PASSED THIS WAY BEFORE *Tamla Motown TMG 593*	29	7 wks
20 Apr 67	GONNA GIVE HER ALL THE LOVE I'VE GOT *Tamla Motown TMG 603*	26	6 wks
9 Aug 69	I'VE PASSED THIS WAY BEFORE (re-issue) *Tamla Motown TMG 703*	33	6 wks
28 Feb 70	● FAREWELL IS A LONELY SOUND *Tamla Motown TMG 726*	8	16 wks
4 Jul 70	● I'LL SAY FOREVER MY LOVE *Tamla Motown TMG 740*	7	12 wks
17 Oct 70	● IT'S WONDERFUL *Tamla Motown TMG 753* ...	6	14 wks
27 Jul 74	● WHAT BECOMES OF THE BROKEN HEARTED (re-issue) *Tamla Motown TMG 603*	4	12 wks
2 Nov 74	FAREWELL IS A LONELY SOUND (re-issue) *Tamla Motown TMG 922*	30	5 wks
16 Nov 74	TELL ME WHAT YOU WANT *Polydor 2058 433*	39	4 wks
3 May 80	● HOLD ON TO MY LOVE *RSO 57*	7	8 wks

RUFUS and Chaka KHAN
US, male instrumental group — *12 wks*

31 Mar 84	● AIN'T NOBODY *Warner Bros. RCK 1*	8	12 wks

See also Chaka Khan.

Barbara RUICK - *See VARIOUS ARTISTS (carousel soundtrack)*

RUMOUR - *See Graham PARKER and the RUMOUR*

RUMPLE-STILTS-SKIN
US, male/female vocal/instrumental group — *4 wks*

24 Sep 83	I THINK I WANT TO DANCE WITH YOU *Montage/Polydor POSP 649*	51	4 wks

Todd RUNDGREN
US, male vocalist — *6 wks*

30 Jun 73	I SAW THE LIGHT *Bearsville K 15506*	36	6 wks

RUSH
Canada, male vocal/instrumental group — *33 wks*

11 Feb 78	CLOSER TO THE HEART *Mercury RUSH 7* ...	36	3 wks
15 Mar 80	SPIRIT OF RADIO *Mercury RADIO 7*	13	7 wks
28 Mar 81	VITAL SIGNS/A PASSAGE TO BANGKOK *Mercury VITAL 7*	41	4 wks
31 Oct 81	TOM SAWYER *Exit EXIT 7*	25	6 wks
4 Sep 82	NEW WORLD MAN *Mercury/Phonogram RUSH 8*	42	3 wks
30 Oct 82	SUBDIVISIONS *Mercury/Phonogram RUSH 9*	53	2 wks
7 May 83	COUNTDOWN/NEW WORLD MAN *Mercury/Phonogram RUSH 10*	36	5 wks
26 May 84	THE BODY ELECTRIC *Vertigo/Phonogram RUSH 11*	56	3 wks

New World Man on RUSH 10 is a live version of RUSH 8.

Patrice RUSHEN
US, female vocalist — *25 wks*

1 Mar 80	HAVEN'T YOU HEARD *Elektra K 12414*	62	3 wks
24 Jan 81	NEVER GONNA GIVE YOU UP (WON'T LET YOU BE) *Elektra K 12494*	66	3 wks
24 Apr 82	● FORGET ME NOTS *Elektra K 13173*	8	11 wks
10 Jul 82	I WAS TIRED OF BEING ALONE *Elektra K 13184*	39	5 wks
9 Jun 84	FEELS SO REAL (WON'T LET GO) *Elektra E 9742*	51	3 wks

Brenda RUSSELL
US, female vocalist — *5 wks*

19 Apr 80	SO GOOD SO RIGHT/IN THE THICK OF IT *A & M AMS 7515*	51	5 wks

RUTLES
UK, male vocal group — *4 wks*

15 Apr 78	I MUST BE IN LOVE *Warner Bros. K 17125*	39	3 wks
13 May 78	I MUST BE IN LOVE (re-entry) *Warner Bros. K 17125*	64	1 wk

RUTS
UK, male vocal/instrumental group — *28 wks*

16 Jun 79	● BABYLON'S BURNING *Virgin VS 271*	7	11 wks
8 Sep 79	SOMETHING THAT I SAID *Virgin VS 285*	29	5 wks
19 Apr 80	STARING AT THE RUDE BOYS *Virgin VS 327*	22	8 wks
30 Aug 80	WEST ONE (SHINE ON ME) *Virgin VS 370* ...	43	4 wks

Barry RYAN
UK, male vocalist — *33 wks*

23 Oct 68	● ELOISE *MGM 1442*	2	12 wks
19 Feb 69	LOVE IS LOVE *MGM 1464*	25	4 wks
4 Oct 69	HUNT *Polydor 56 348*	34	5 wks
21 Feb 70	MAGICAL SPIEL *Polydor 56 370*	49	1 wk
16 May 70	KITSCH *Polydor 2001 035*	37	6 wks
15 Jan 72	CAN'T LET YOU GO *Polydor 2001 256* ...	32	5 wks

See also Paul and Barry Ryan.

Marion RYAN
UK, female vocalist — *11 wks*

24 Jan 58	● LOVE ME FOREVER *Pye Nixa N 15121*	5	11 wks

Paul and Barry RYAN
UK, male vocal duo — *43 wks*

11 Nov 65	DON'T BRING ME YOUR HEARTACHES *Decca F 12260*	13	9 wks

3 Feb 66	**HAVE PITY ON THE BOY** *Decca F 12319*	**18**	6 wks
12 May 66	**I LOVE HER** *Decca F 12391*	**17**	8 wks
14 Jul 66	**I LOVE HOW YOU LOVE ME** *Decca F 12445* ..	**21**	7 wks
29 Sep 66	**HAVE YOU EVER LOVED SOMEBODY**		
	Decca F 12494	**49**	1 wk
8 Dec 66	**MISSY MISSY** *Decca F 12520*	**43**	4 wks
2 Mar 67	**KEEP IT OUT OF SIGHT** *Decca F 12567*	**30**	6 wks
29 Jun 67	**CLAIRE** *Decca F 12633*	**47**	2 wks

See also Barry Ryan.

Bobby RYDELL   US, male vocalist   *56 wks*

10 Mar 60	● **WILD ONE** *Columbia DB 4429*	**7**	14 wks
23 Jun 60	**WILD ONE** (re-entry) *Columbia DB 4429*	**47**	1 wk
30 Jun 60	**SWINGING SCHOOL** *Columbia DB 4471* ...	**44**	1 wk
1 Sep 60	**VOLARE** *Columbia DB 4495*	**46**	1 wk
15 Sep 60	**VOLARE** (re-entry) *Columbia DB 4495*	**22**	5 wks
15 Dec 60	**SWAY** *Columbia DB 4545*	**12**	13 wks
23 Mar 61	**GOOD TIME BABY** *Columbia DB 4600* ...	**42**	7 wks
23 May 63	**FORGET HIM** *Cameo Parkway C 108*	**13**	14 wks

See also Chubby Checker and Bobby Rydell.

Mitch RYDER and the DETROIT WHEELS   US, male vocalist, male
vocal/instrumental backing group   *5 wks*

10 Feb 66	**JENNY TAKE A RIDE** *Stateside SS 481*	**44**	1 wk
24 Feb 66	**JENNY TAKE A RIDE** (re-entry) *Stateside SS 481*	**33**	4 wks

S

SABRES - *See Denny SEYTON and the SABRES*

SAD CAFÉ
UK, male vocal/instrumental group   *44 wks*

22 Sep 79	● **EVERY DAY HURTS** *RCA PB 5180*	**3**	12 wks
19 Jan 80	**STRANGE LITTLE GIRL** *RCA PB 5202*	**32**	5 wks
15 Mar 80	**MY OH MY** *RCA SAD 3*	**14**	11 wks
21 Jun 80	**NOTHING LEFT TOULOUSE** *RCA SAD 4* ...	**62**	4 wks
27 Sep 80	**LA-DI-DA** *RCA SAD 5*	**41**	6 wks
20 Dec 80	**I'M IN LOVE AGAIN** *RCA SAD 6*	**40**	6 wks

SADE
UK, female/male vocal/instrumental group   *27 wks*

25 Feb 84	● **YOUR LOVE IS KING** *Epic A 4137*	**6**	11 wks
19 May 84	**YOUR LOVE IS KING** (re-entry) *Epic A 4137* ...	**75**	1 wk
26 May 84	**WHEN AM I GONNA MAKE A LIVING**		
	Epic A 4437	**36**	5 wks
15 Sep 84	**SMOOTH OPERATOR** *Epic A 4655*	**19**	10 wks

Staff Sergeant Barry SADLER
US, male vocalist   *8 wks*

24 Mar 66	**BALLAD OF THE GREEN BERETS** *RCA 1506*	**24**	8 wks

SAFFRONS - *See CINDY and the SAFFRONS*

Mike SAGAR   UK, male vocalist   *5 wks*

8 Dec 60	**DEEP FEELING** *HMV POP 819*	**44**	5 wks

Carole Bayer SAGER
US, female vocalist   *9 wks*

28 May 77	● **YOU'RE MOVING OUT TODAY**		
	Elektra K 12257	**6**	9 wks

SAILOR   UK, male vocal/instrumental group   *24 wks*

6 Dec 75	● **GLASS OF CHAMPAGNE** *Epic EPC 3770*	**2**	12 wks
27 Mar 76	● **GIRLS GIRLS GIRLS** *Epic EPC 3858*	**7**	8 wks
19 Feb 77	**ONE DRINK TOO MANY** *Epic EPC 4804*	**35**	4 wks

ST. ANDREWS CHORALE
UK, church choir   *5 wks*

14 Feb 76	**CLOUD 99** *Decca F 13617*	**31**	5 wks

ST. CECILIA
UK, male vocal/instrumental group   *17 wks*

19 Jun 71	**LEAP UP AND DOWN (WAVE YOUR**		
	KNICKERS IN THE AIR) *Polydor 2058 104* ...	**12**	17 wks

Barry ST. JOHN   UK, female vocalist   *1 wk*

9 Dec 65	**COME AWAY MELINDA** *Columbia DB 7783* ...	**47**	1 wk

ST. LOUIS UNION
UK, male vocal/instrumental group   *10 wks*

13 Jan 66	**GIRL** *Decca F 12318*	**11**	10 wks

Crispian ST. PETERS   UK, male vocalist   *31 wks*

6 Jan 66	● **YOU WERE ON MY MIND** *Decca F 12287*	**2**	14 wks
31 Mar 66	● **PIED PIPER** *Decca F 12359*	**5**	13 wks
15 Sep 66	**CHANGES** *Decca F 12480*	**49**	1 wk
29 Sep 66	**CHANGES** (re-entry) *Decca F 12480*	**47**	3 wks

ST. WINIFRED'S SCHOOL CHOIR
UK, school choir   *11 wks*

22 Nov 80	★ **NO ONE QUITE LIKE GRANDMA**		
	MFP FP 900	**1**	11 wks

General SAINT - *See Clint EASTWOOD and General SAINT*

Buffy SAINTE-MARIE
US, female vocalist   *23 wks*

17 Jul 71	● **SOLDIER BLUE** *RCA 2081*	**7**	18 wks
18 Mar 72	**I'M GONNA BE A COUNTRY GIRL AGAIN**		
	Vanguard VRS 35143	**34**	5 wks

SAINTS
Australia, male vocal/instrumental group   *4 wks*

16 Jul 77	**THIS PERFECT DAY** *Harvest HAR 5130*	**34**	4 wks

Kyu SAKAMOTO   Japan, male vocalist   *13 wks*

27 Jun 63	● **SUKIYAKI** *HMV POP 1171*	**6**	13 wks

SAKKARIN

UK, Jonathan King under a false name   14 wks

| 3 Apr 71 | SUGAR SUGAR | RCA 2064 | 12 | 14 wks |

See also Jonathan King.

SALFORD JETS

UK, male vocal/instrumental group   2 wks

| 31 May 80 | WHO YOU LOOKING AT | RCA PB 5239 | 72 | 2 wks |

SALSOUL ORCHESTRA - See CHARO and the SALSOUL ORCHESTRA

SAM and DAVE   US, male vocal duo   39 wks

16 Mar 67	SOOTHE ME	Stax 601 004	48	2 wks
13 Apr 67	SOOTHE ME	(re-entry) Stax 601 004	35	6 wks
1 Nov 67	SOUL MAN	Stax 601 023	24	14 wks
13 Mar 68	I THANK YOU	Stax 601 030	34	9 wks
29 Jan 69	SOUL SISTER BROWN SUGAR	Atlantic 584 237	15	8 wks

SAM THE SHAM and the PHARAOHS

US, male vocal/instrumental group   18 wks

24 Jun 65	WOOLY BULLY	MGM 1269	11	15 wks
4 Aug 66	LIL' RED RIDING HOOD	MGM 1315	48	1 wk
18 Aug 66	LIL' RED RIDING HOOD	(re-entry) MGM 1315	46	2 wks

Mike SAMMES SINGERS

UK, male/female vocal group   38 wks

| 15 Sep 66 | SOMEWHERE MY LOVE | HMV POP 1546 | 22 | 19 wks |
| 12 Jul 67 | SOMEWHERE MY LOVE | (re-entry) HMV POP 1546 | 14 | 19 wks |

Dave SAMPSON   UK, male vocalist   6 wks

| 19 May 60 | SWEET DREAMS | Columbia DB 4449 | 48 | 1 wk |
| 2 Jun 60 | SWEET DREAMS | (re-entry) Columbia DB 4449 | 29 | 5 wks |

SAMSON   UK, male vocal/instrumental group   6 wks

4 Jul 81	RIDING WITH THE ANGELS	RCA 67	55	3 wks
24 Jul 82	LOSING MY GRIP	Polydor POSP 471	63	2 wks
5 Mar 83	RED SKIES	Polydor POSP 554	65	1 wk

SAN JOSE   UK, male instrumental group   8 wks

| 17 Jun 78 | ARGENTINE MELODY (CANCION DE ARGENTINA) | MCA 369 | 14 | 8 wks |

Hit has credit 'featuring Rodriguez Argentina'.

SAN REMO STRINGS   US, orchestra   8 wks

| 18 Dec 71 | FESTIVAL TIME | Tamla Motown TMG 795 | 39 | 8 wks |

Chris SANDFORD   UK, male vocalist   9 wks

| 12 Dec 63 | NOT TOO LITTLE NOT TOO MUCH | Decca F 11778 | 17 | 9 wks |

SANDPIPERS   US, male vocal group   33 wks

15 Sep 66	● GUANTANAMERA	Pye International 7N 25380	7	17 wks
5 Jun 68	QUANDO M'INNAMORO (A MAN WITHOUT LOVE)	A & M AMS 723	33	6 wks
26 Mar 69	KUMBAYA	A & M AMS 744	39	1 wk
9 Apr 69	KUMBAYA	(re-entry) A & M AMS 744	49	1 wk
27 Nov 76	HANG ON SLOOPY	Satril SAT 114	32	8 wks

Jodie SANDS   US, female vocalist   10 wks

| 17 Oct 58 | SOMEDAY | HMV POP 533 | 14 | 10 wks |

Tommy SANDS   US, male vocalist   7 wks

| 4 Aug 60 | OLD OAKEN BUCKET | Capitol CL 15143 | 25 | 7 wks |

Samantha SANG   Australia, female vocalist   13 wks

| 4 Feb 78 | EMOTIONS | Private stock PVT 128 | 11 | 13 wks |

SANTA CLAUS and the CHRISTMAS TREES

UK, male vocal/instrumental group   10 wks

| 11 Dec 82 | SINGALONG-A-SANTA | Polydor IVY 1 | 19 | 5 wks |
| 10 Dec 83 | SINGALONG-A-SANTA AGAIN | Polydor IVY 2 | 39 | 5 wks |

SANTA ESMERALDA and Leroy GOMEZ

US/France, male/female vocal/instrumental group   5 wks

| 12 Nov 77 | DON'T LET ME BE MISUNDERSTOOD | Philips 6042 325 | 41 | 5 wks |

SANTANA

US, male vocal/instrumental group   25 wks

28 Sep 74	SAMBA PA TI	CBS 2561	27	7 wks
15 Oct 77	SHE'S NOT THERE	CBS 5671	11	12 wks
25 Nov 78	WELL ALL RIGHT	CBS 6755	53	3 wks
22 Mar 80	ALL I EVER WANTED	CBS 8160	57	3 wks

SANTO and JOHNNY

US, male instrumental duo, steel and electric guitars   5 wks

| 16 Oct 59 | SLEEP WALK | Pye International 7N 25037 | 22 | 4 wks |
| 31 Mar 60 | TEARDROP | Parlophone R 4619 | 50 | 1 wk |

Mike SARNE   UK, male vocalist   43 wks

10 May 62	★ COME OUTSIDE	Parlophone R 4902	1	19 wks
30 Aug 62	WILL I WHAT	Parlophone R 4932	18	10 wks
10 Jan 63	JUST FOR KICKS	Parlophone R 4974	22	7 wks
28 Mar 63	CODE OF LOVE	Parlophone R 5010	29	7 wks

Come Outside - Mike Sarne with Wendy Richard; Will I What with Billie Davis. See also Billie Davis.

Joy SARNEY   UK, female vocalist   6 wks

| 7 May 77 | NAUGHTY NAUGHTY NAUGHTY | Alaska ALA 2005 | 26 | 6 wks |

SARR BAND   *Italy, female vocalist;*
England/France, male instrumental group.   *1 wk*

16 Sep 78		MAGIC MANDRAKE *Calendar DAY 115*		68	1 wk

Peter SARSTEDT   *UK, male vocalist*   *25 wks*

5 Feb 69	★	WHERE DO YOU GO TO MY LOVELY			
		United Artists UP 2262		1	16 wks
4 Jun 69	●	FROZEN ORANGE JUICE			
		United Artists UP 35021		10	9 wks

Robin SARSTEDT   *UK, male vocalist*   *9 wks*

8 May 76	●	MY RESISTANCE IS LOW *Decca F 13624*		3	9 wks

SATURDAY NIGHT BAND
US, male vocal/instrumental group   *9 wks*

1 Jul 78		COME ON DANCE DANCE *CBS 6367*		16	9 wks

Edna SAVAGE   *UK, female vocalist*   *1 wk*

13 Jan 56		ARRIVEDERCI DARLING *Parlophone R 4097* ...		19	1 wk

Telly SAVALAS   *US, male vocalist*   *12 wks*

22 Feb 75	★	IF *MCA 174*		1	9 wks
31 May 75		YOU'VE LOST THAT LOVIN' FEELING			
		MCA 189		47	3 wks

SAVANNAH
US, male vocalist/instrumentalist-guitar   *4 wks*

10 Oct 81		I CAN'T TURN AWAY *R & B RBS 203*		61	4 wks

SAXON   *UK, male vocal/instrumental group*   *52 wks*

22 Mar 80		WHEELS OF STEEL *Carrere CAR 143*		20	11 wks
21 Jun 80		747 (STRANGERS IN THE NIGHT)			
		Carrere CAR 151		13	9 wks
28 Jun 80		BIG TEASER/RAINBOW THEME *Carrere HM 5*		66	2 wks
28 Jun 80		BACKS TO THE WALL *Carrere HM 6*		64	2 wks
29 Nov 80		STRONG ARM OF THE LAW *Carrere CAR 170*		63	3 wks
11 Apr 81		AND THE BANDS PLAYED ON			
		Carrere CAR 180		12	8 wks
18 Jul 81		NEVER SURRENDER *Carrere CAR 204*		18	6 wks
31 Oct 81		PRINCESS OF THE NIGHT *Carrere CAR 208* ..		57	3 wks
23 Apr 83		POWER AND THE GLORY *RCA SAXON 1* ..		32	5 wks
30 Jul 83		NIGHTMARE *Carrere CAR 284*		50	3 wks

Al SAXON   *UK, male vocalist*   *10 wks*

16 Jan 59		YOU'RE THE TOP CHA *Fontana H 164*		17	4 wks
28 Aug 59		ONLY SIXTEEN *Fontana H 205*		24	3 wks
22 Dec 60		BLUE-EYED BOY *Fontana H 278*		39	2 wks
7 Sep 61		THERE I'VE SAID IT AGAIN *Piccadilly 7N 35011*		48	1 wk

Leo SAYER   *UK, male vocalist*   *142 wks*

15 Dec 73	●	THE SHOW MUST GO ON *Chrysalis CHS 2023*		2	13 wks
15 Jun 74	●	ONE MAN BAND *Chrysalis CHS 2045*		6	9 wks
14 Sep 74	●	LONG TALL GLASSES *Chrysalis CHS 2052* ..		4	9 wks
30 Aug 75	●	MOONLIGHTING *Chrysalis CHS 2076*		2	8 wks
30 Oct 76	●	YOU MAKE ME FEEL LIKE DANCING			
		Chrysalis CHS 2119		2	12 wks
29 Jan 77	★	WHEN I NEED YOU *Chrysalis CHS 2127*		1	13 wks
9 Apr 77	●	HOW MUCH LOVE *Chrysalis CHS 2140*		10	8 wks
10 Sep 77		THUNDER IN MY HEART *Chrysalis CHS 2163*		22	8 wks
16 Sep 78	●	I CAN'T STOP LOVIN' YOU (THOUGH I TRY)			
		Chrysalis CHS 2240		6	11 wks
25 Nov 78	●	RAINING IN MY HEART *Chrysalis CHS 2277* ...		21	10 wks
5 Jul 80	●	MORE THAN I CAN SAY *Chrysalis CHS 2442* ..		2	11 wks
13 Mar 82	●	HAVE YOU EVER BEEN IN LOVE			
		Chrysalis CHS 2596		10	9 wks
19 Jun 82		HEART (STOP BEATING IN TIME)			
		Chrysalis CHS 2616		22	10 wks
12 Mar 83		ORCHARD ROAD *Chrysalis CHS 2677*		16	8 wks
15 Oct 83		TILL YOU COME BACK TO ME			
		Chrysalis LE 01		51	3 wks

Alexei SAYLE   *UK, male vocalist*   *8 wks*

25 Feb 84		'ULLO JOHN GOT A NEW MOTOR?			
		Springtime/Island IS 162		15	8 wks

SCAFFOLD   *UK, male vocal group*   *62 wks*

22 Nov 67	●	THANK U VERY MUCH *Parlophone R 5643*		4	12 wks
27 Mar 68		DO YOU REMEMBER *Parlophone R 5679* ..		34	5 wks
6 Nov 68	★	LILY THE PINK *Parlophone R 5734* ..		1	24 wks
1 Nov 69		GIN GAN GOOLIE *Parlophone R 5812* ..		38	11 wks
24 Jan 70		GIN GAN GOOLIE (re-entry) *Parlophone R 5812*		50	1 wk
1 Jun 74	●	LIVERPOOL LOU *Warner Bros. K 16400* ..		7	9 wks

Boz SCAGGS   *US, male vocalist*   *31 wks*

30 Oct 76		LOWDOWN *CBS 4563*		28	4 wks
22 Jan 77	●	WHAT CAN I SAY *CBS 4869*		10	10 wks
14 May 77		LIDO SHUFFLE *CBS 5136*		13	9 wks
10 Dec 77		HOLLYWOOD *CBS 5836*		33	8 wks

SCARLET PARTY
UK, male vocal/instrumental group   *5 wks*

16 Oct 82		101 DAM-NATIONS *Parlophone R 6058*		44	5 wks

Michael SCHENKER GROUP
Germany/UK, male vocal/instrumental group   *9 wks*

13 Sep 80		ARMED AND READY *Chrysalis CHS 2455*		53	3 wks
8 Nov 80		CRY FOR THE NATIONS *Chrysalis CHS 2471* ..		56	3 wks
11 Sep 82		DANCER *Chrysalis CHS 2636*		52	3 wks

Lalo SCHIFRIN   *US, orchestra*   *9 wks*

9 Oct 76		JAWS *CTI CTSP 005*		14	9 wks

Peter SCHILLING
Germany, male vocalist   *6 wks*

5 May 84		MAJOR TOM (COMING HOME)			
		PSP/WEA X 9438		42	5 wks
16 Jun 84		MAJOR TOM (COMING HOME) (re-entry)			
		PSP/WEA X 9438		73	1 wk

SCORPIONS
Germany, male vocal/instrumental group   *15 wks*

26 May 79		IS THERE ANYBODY THERE/ANOTHER PIECE			
		OF MEAT *Harvest HAR 5185*		39	4 wks

ROCKIN' BERRIES Jefferson (centre) left to have a solo hit with the 'Colour Of My Love'.

ROXY MUSIC air their flares.

ROCK GODDESS Their second hit was a cover of Gary Glitter's second hit.

25 Aug 79	LOVEDRIVE *Harvest HAR 5188*	69	2 wks
31 May 80	MAKE IT REAL *Harvest HAR 5206*	72	2 wks
20 Sep 80	THE ZOO *Harvest HAR 5212*	75	1 wk
3 Apr 82	NO ONE LIKE YOU *Harvest HAR 5219*	65	3 wks
1 May 82	NO ONE LIKE YOU (re-entry) *Harvest HAR 5219*	64	1 wk
17 Jul 82	CAN'T LIVE WITHOUT YOU *Harvest HAR 5221*	63	2 wks

SCOTLAND WORLD CUP SQUAD
UK, male football team vocalists   *13 wks*

22 Jun 74	EASY EASY *Polydor 2058 452*	20	4 wks
1 May 82	● WE HAVE A DREAM *WEA K 19145*	5	9 wks

Jack SCOTT   *Canada, male vocalist*   *28 wks*

10 Oct 58	● MY TRUE LOVE *London HLU 8626*	9	10 wks
25 Sep 59	THE WAY I WALK *London HLL 8912*	30	1 wk
10 Mar 60	WHAT IN THE WORLD'S COME OVER YOU *Top Rank JAR 280*	11	15 wks
2 Jun 60	BURNING BRIDGES *Top Rank JAR 375*	32	2 wks

Linda SCOTT   *US, female vocalist*   *14 wks*

18 May 61	● I'VE TOLD EVERY LITTLE STAR *Columbia DB 4638*	7	13 wks
14 Sep 61	DON'T BET MONEY HONEY *Columbia DB 4692*	50	1 wk

Simon SCOTT   *UK, male vocalist*   *8 wks*

13 Aug 64	MOVE IT BABY *Parlophone R 5164*	37	8 wks

SCRITTI POLITTI
UK, male vocal/instrumental group   *35 wks*

21 Nov 81	THE SWEETEST GIRL *Rough Trade RT 091* ...	64	3 wks
22 May 82	FAITHLESS *Rough Trade RT 101*	56	4 wks
7 Aug 82	ASYLUMS IN JERUSALEM/JACQUES DERRIDA *Rough Trade RT 111*	43	5 wks
10 Mar 84	● WOOD BEEZ (PRAY LIKE ARETHA FRANKLIN) *Virgin VS 657*	10	12 wks
9 Jun 84	ABSOLUTE *Virgin VS 680*	17	9 wks
17 Nov 84	HYPNOTISE *Virgin VS 725*	68	2 wks

Earl SCRUGGS - *See Lester FLATT and Earl SCRUGGS*

SEA LEVEL   *US, male instrumental group*   *4 wks*

17 Feb 79	FIFTY-FOUR *Capricorn POSP 28*	63	4 wks

SEARCHERS
UK, male vocal/instrumental group   *128 wks*

27 Jun 63	★ SWEETS FOR MY SWEET *Pye 7N 15533*	1	16 wks
10 Oct 63	SWEET NOTHINS *Philips BF 1274*	48	2 wks
24 Oct 63	● SUGAR AND SPICE *Pye 7N 15566*	2	13 wks
16 Jan 64	★ NEEDLES AND PINS *Pye 7N 15594*	1	15 wks
16 Apr 64	★ DON'T THROW YOUR LOVE AWAY *Pye 7N 15630*	1	11 wks
16 Jul 64	SOMEDAY WE'RE GONNA LOVE AGAIN *Pye 7N 15670*	11	8 wks
17 Sep 64	● WHEN YOU WALK IN THE ROOM *Pye 7N 15694*	3	12 wks
3 Dec 64	WHAT HAVE THEY DONE TO THE RAIN *Pye 7N 15739*	13	11 wks
4 Mar 65	● GOODBYE MY LOVE *Pye 7N 15794*	4	11 wks
8 Jul 65	HE'S GOT NO LOVE *Pye 7N 15878*	12	10 wks

14 Oct 65	WHEN I GET HOME *Pye 7N 15950*	35	3 wks
16 Dec 65	TAKE ME FOR WHAT I'M WORTH *Pye 7N 15992*	20	8 wks
21 Apr 66	TAKE IT OR LEAVE IT *Pye 7N 17094*	31	6 wks
13 Oct 66	HAVE YOU EVER LOVED SOMEBODY *Pye 7N 17170*	48	2 wks

SEASHELLS   *UK, female vocal group*   *5 wks*

9 Sep 72	MAYBE I KNOW *CBS 8218*	32	5 wks

Harry SECOMBE   *UK, male vocalist*   *35 wks*

9 Dec 55	ON WITH THE MOTLEY *Philips PB 523*	16	3 wks
3 Oct 63	IF I RULED THE WORLD *Philips BF 1261*	44	2 wks
21 Nov 63	IF I RULED THE WORLD (re-entry) *Philips BF 1261*	18	15 wks
23 Feb 67	● THIS IS MY SONG *Philips BF 1539*	2	15 wks

SECOND CITY SOUND
UK, male instrumental group   *8 wks*

20 Jan 66	TCHAIKOVSKY ONE *Decca F 12310*	22	7 wks
2 Apr 69	DREAM OF OLWEN *Major Minor MM 600*	43	1 wk

SECOND IMAGE
UK, male vocal/instrumental group   *9 wks*

24 Jul 82	STAR *Polydor POSP 457*	60	2 wks
2 Apr 83	BETTER TAKE TIME *Polydor POSP 565*	67	2 wks
26 Nov 83	DON'T YOU *MCA 848*	68	2 wks
11 Aug 84	SING AND SHOUT *MCA MCA 882*	53	3 wks

SECRET AFFAIR
UK, male vocal/instrumental group   *34 wks*

1 Sep 79	TIME FOR ACTION *I-Spy SEE 1*	13	10 wks
10 Nov 79	LET YOUR HEART DANCE *I-Spy SEE 3*	32	6 wks
8 Mar 80	MY WORLD *I-Spy SEE 5*	16	9 wks
23 Aug 80	SOUND OF CONFUSION *I-Spy SEE 8*	45	5 wks
17 Oct 81	DO YOU KNOW *I-Spy SEE 10*	57	4 wks

Neil SEDAKA   *US, male vocalist*   *190 wks*

24 Apr 59	● I GO APE *RCA 1115*	9	13 wks
13 Nov 59	● OH CAROL *RCA 1152*	3	17 wks
14 Apr 60	● STAIRWAY TO HEAVEN *RCA 1178*	8	15 wks
1 Sep 60	YOU MEAN EVERYTHING TO ME *RCA 1198*	45	3 wks
2 Feb 61	● CALENDAR GIRL *RCA 1220*	8	14 wks
18 May 61	● LITTLE DEVIL *RCA 1236*	9	12 wks
21 Dec 61	● HAPPY BIRTHDAY SWEET SIXTEEN *RCA 1266*	3	18 wks
19 Apr 62	KING OF CLOWNS *RCA 1282*	23	11 wks
19 Jul 62	● BREAKING UP IS HARD TO DO *RCA 1298*	7	16 wks
22 Nov 62	NEXT DOOR TO AN ANGEL *RCA 1319*	29	4 wks
30 May 63	LET'S GO STEADY AGAIN *RCA 1343*	42	1 wk
13 Jun 63	LET'S GO STEADY AGAIN (re-entry) *RCA 1343*	43	2 wks
7 Oct 72	OH CAROL /BREAKING UP IS HARD TO DO/LITTLE DEVIL (re-issue) *RCA Maximillion 2259*	19	14 wks
4 Nov 72	BEAUTIFUL YOU *RCA 2269*	43	3 wks
24 Feb 73	THAT'S WHEN THE MUSIC TAKES ME *RCA 2310*	18	10 wks
2 Jun 73	STANDING ON THE INSIDE *MGM 2006 267*	26	9 wks
25 Aug 73	OUR LAST SONG TOGETHER *MGM 2006 307*	31	8 wks
9 Feb 74	A LITTLE LOVIN' *Polydor 2058 434*	34	6 wks
22 Jun 74	LAUGHTER IN THE RAIN *Polydor 2058 494*	15	9 wks
22 Mar 75	THE QUEEN OF 1964 *Polydor 2058 546*	35	5 wks

SEEKERS
Australia/Ceylon, male/female vocal group 120 wks

7 Jan 65	★	I'LL NEVER FIND ANOTHER YOU	Columbia DB 7431	**1**	23 wks
15 Apr 65	●	A WORLD OF OUR OWN Columbia DB 7532		**3**	18 wks
28 Oct 65	★	THE CARNIVAL IS OVER Columbia DB 7711		**1**	17 wks
24 Mar 66		SOMEDAY ONE DAY Columbia DB 7867		**11**	11 wks
8 Sep 66	●	WALK WITH ME Columbia DB 8000		**10**	12 wks
24 Nov 66	●	MORNINGTOWN RIDE Columbia DB 8060		**2**	15 wks
23 Feb 67	●	GEORGY GIRL Columbia DB 8134		**3**	11 wks
20 Sep 67		WHEN WILL THE GOOD APPLES FALL Columbia DB 8273		**11**	12 wks
13 Dec 67		EMERALD CITY Columbia DB 8313		**50**	1 wk

Bob SEGER AND THE SILVER BULLET BAND
US, male vocal/instrumental group 21 wks

30 Sep 78	HOLLYWOOD NIGHTS Capitol CL 16004	**42**	6 wks
3 Feb 79	WE'VE GOT TONITE Capitol CL 16028	**41**	6 wks
24 Oct 81	HOLLYWOOD NIGHTS (re-issue) Capitol CL 223	**49**	3 wks
6 Feb 82	WE'VE GOT TONITE (re-issue) Capitol CL 235	**60**	4 wks
9 Apr 83	EVEN NOW Capitol CL 284	**73**	2 wks

The SELECTER
UK, male/female vocal/instrumental group 28 wks

13 Oct 79	●	ON MY RADIO 2 Tone CHSTT 4	**8**	9 wks
2 Feb 80		THREE MINUTE HERO 2 Tone CHS TT 8	**16**	6 wks
29 Mar 80		MISSING WORDS 2 Tone CHS TT 10	**23**	8 wks
23 Aug 80		THE WHISPER Chrysalis CHSS 1	**36**	5 wks

Peter SELLERS *UK, male vocalist* 18 wks

2 Aug 57	ANY OLD IRON Parlophone R 4337	**21**	3 wks
6 Sep 57	ANY OLD IRON (re-entry) Parlophone R 4337	**17**	8 wks
23 Dec 65	A HARD DAY'S NIGHT Parlophone R 5393	**14**	7 wks

See also Peter Sellers and Sophia Loren.

Peter SELLERS and Sophia LOREN
UK/Italy, male/female vocal duo 19 wks

10 Nov 60	●	GOODNESS GRACIOUS ME Parlophone R 4702	**4**	14 wks
12 Jan 61		BANGERS AND MASH Parlophone R 4724	**22**	5 wks

See also Peter Sellers.

Michael SEMBELLO *US, male vocalist* 6 wks

20 Aug 83	MANIAC Casablanca/Phonogram CAN 1017	**43**	6 wks

SEMPRINI *UK, orchestra* 8 wks

16 Mar 61	THEME FROM 'EXODUS' HMV POP 842	**25**	8 wks

SET THE TONE
UK, male vocal/instrumental group 6 wks

22 Jan 83	DANCE SUCKER Island WIP 6836	**62**	2 wks
26 Mar 83	RAP YOUR LOVE Island IS 110	**67**	4 wks

SETTLERS
UK, male/female vocal/instrumental group 5 wks

16 Oct 71	THE LIGHTNING TREE York SYK 505	**36**	5 wks

SEVERINE *France, female vocalist* 11 wks

24 Apr 71	●	UN BANC, UN ARBRE, UNE RUE Philips 6009 135	**9**	11 wks

David SEVILLE *US, male vocalist* 6 wks

23 May 58	WITCH DOCTOR London HLU 8619	**11**	6 wks

See also Chipmunks; Alfi and Harry.

SEX PISTOLS
UK, male vocal/instrumental group 80 wks

11 Dec 76		ANARCHY IN THE U. K. EMI 2566	**38**	4 wks
4 Jun 77	●	GOD SAVE THE QUEEN Virgin VS 181	**2**	9 wks
9 Jul 77	●	PRETTY VACANT Virgin VS 184	**6**	8 wks
22 Oct 77	●	HOLIDAYS IN THE SUN Virgin VS 191	**8**	6 wks
8 Jul 78	●	NO ONE IS INNOCENT/MY WAY Virgin VS 220	**7**	10 wks
3 Mar 79	●	SOMETHING ELSE/FRIGGIN' IN THE RIGGIN' Virgin VS 240	**3**	12 wks
7 Apr 79		SILLY THING/WHO KILLED BAMBI Virgin VS 256	**6**	8 wks
30 Jun 79	●	C'MON EVERYBODY Virgin VS 272	**3**	9 wks
13 Oct 79		THE GREAT ROCK'N'ROLL SWINDLE/ROCK AROUND THE CLOCK Virgin VS 290	**21**	6 wks
14 Jun 80		(I'M NOT YOUR) STEPPING STONE Virgin VS 339	**21**	8 wks

Rock Around The Clock *and* Who Killed Bambi *credited to Ten Pole Tudor. No One Is Innocent is described as a 'Punk Prayer By Ronald Biggs'. See also Ten Pole Tudor.*

SEX-O-LETTES - *See DISCO TEX and the SEX-O-LETTES*

Denny SEYTON and the SABRES
UK, male vocal/instrumental group 1 wk

17 Sep 64	THE WAY YOU LOOK TONIGHT Mercury MF 824	**48**	1 wk

SHADOWS
UK, male instrumental/vocal group 359 wks

21 Jul 60	★	APACHE Columbia DB 4484	**1**	21 wks
10 Nov 60	●	MAN OF MYSTERY/THE STRANGER Columbia DB 4530	**5**	15 wks
9 Feb 61	●	F. B. I. Columbia DB 4580	**6**	19 wks
11 May 61	●	FRIGHTENED CITY Columbia DB 4637	**3**	20 wks
7 Sep 61	●	KON-TIKI Columbia DB 4698	**1**	10 wks
16 Nov 61	●	THE SAVAGE Columbia DB 4726	**10**	8 wks
23 Nov 61		KON-TIKI (re-entry) Columbia DB 4698	**37**	2 wks
1 Mar 62	★	WONDERFUL LAND Columbia DB 4790	**1**	19 wks
2 Aug 62	●	GUITAR TANGO Columbia DB 4870	**4**	15 wks
13 Dec 62	★	DANCE ON Columbia DB 4948	**1**	15 wks
7 Mar 63	★	FOOT TAPPER Columbia DB 4984	**1**	16 wks
6 Jun 63		ATLANTIS Columbia DB 7047	**2**	17 wks
19 Sep 63		SHINDIG Columbia DB 7106	**6**	12 wks
5 Dec 63		GERONIMO Columbia DB 7163	**11**	12 wks
5 Mar 64		THEME FOR YOUNG LOVERS Columbia DB 7231	**12**	10 wks
7 May 64	●	THE RISE & FALL OF FLINGEL BUNT Columbia DB 7261	**5**	14 wks
3 Sep 64		RHYTHM & GREENS Columbia DB 7342	**22**	7 wks
3 Dec 64		GENIE WITH THE LIGHT BROWN LAMP Columbia DB 7416	**17**	10 wks

SEARCHERS (above) Their debut hit knocked Elvis off the top spot to become the fourth Merseybeat charttopper of 1963.

SAMSON (left) The Chain Kang.

SADE (right) This smooth operator registered 27 weeks in her first chart year.

11 Feb 65	**MARY ANNE** *Columbia DB 7476*	17	10 wks
10 Jun 65	**STINGRAY** *Columbia DB 7588*	19	7 wks
5 Aug 65	● **DON'T MAKE MY BABY BLUE** *Columbia DB 7650*	10	10 wks
25 Nov 65	**WAR LORD** *Columbia DB 7769*	18	9 wks
17 Mar 66	**I MET A GIRL** *Columbia DB 7853*	22	5 wks
7 Jul 66	**A PLACE IN THE SUN** *Columbia DB 7952*	24	6 wks
3 Nov 66	**THE DREAMS I DREAM** *Columbia DB 8034*	42	6 wks
13 Apr 67	**MAROC 7** *Columbia DB 8170*	24	8 wks
8 Mar 75	**LET ME BE THE ONE** *EMI 2269*	12	9 wks
16 Dec 78	● **DON'T CRY FOR ME ARGENTINA** *EMI 2890*	5	14 wks
28 Apr 79	● **THEME FROM THE DEER HUNTER (CAVATINA)** *EMI 2939*	9	14 wks
26 Jan 80	**RIDERS IN THE SKY** *EMI 5027*	12	12 wks
23 Aug 80	**EQUINOXE (PART V)** *Polydor POSP 148*	50	3 wks
2 May 81	**THE THIRD MAN** *Polydor POSP 255*	44	4 wks

All the above hits were instrumentals except for Mary Anne, Don't Make My Baby Blue, I Met A Girl, The Dreams I Dream and Let Me Be The One. See also Cliff Richard.

SHAG
UK, male vocalist, Jonathan King under a false name   *13 wks*

14 Oct 72	● **LOOP DI LOVE** *UK 7*	4	13 wks

See also Jonathan King; 53rd and 3rd.

SHAKATAK
UK, male/female vocal/instrumental group   *79 wks*

8 Nov 80	**FEELS LIKE THE RIGHT TIME** *Polydor POSP 188*	41	5 wks
7 Mar 81	**LIVING IN THE U.K.** *Polydor POSP 230*	52	4 wks
25 Jul 81	**BRAZILIAN DAWN** *Polydor POSP 282*	48	3 wks
21 Nov 81	**EASIER SAID THAN DONE** *Polydor POSP 375*	12	17 wks
3 Apr 82	● **NIGHT BIRDS** *Polydor POSP 407*	9	8 wks
19 Jun 82	**STREETWALKIN'** *Polydor POSP 452*	38	6 wks
4 Sep 82	**INVITATIONS** *Polydor POSP 502*	24	7 wks
6 Nov 82	**STRANGER** *Polydor POSP 530*	43	3 wks
4 Jun 83	**DARK IS THE NIGHT** *Polydor POSP 595*	15	8 wks
27 Aug 83	**IF YOU COULD SEE ME NOW** *Polydor POSP 635*	49	4 wks
7 Jul 84	● **DOWN ON THE STREET** *Polydor POSP 688*	9	11 wks
15 Sep 84	**DON'T BLAME IT ON LOVE** *Polydor POSP 699*	55	3 wks

SHAKY and BONNIE
UK, male/female vocal duo   *9 wks*

7 Jan 84	● **A ROCKIN' GOOD WAY** *Epic A 4071*	5	9 wks

See also Shakin' Stevens; Bonnie Tyler.

SHALAMAR
US, male/female vocal group   *127 wks*

14 May 77	**UPTOWN FESTIVAL** *Soul Train FB 0885*	30	5 wks
9 Dec 78	**TAKE THAT TO THE BANK** *RCA FB 1379*	20	12 wks
24 Nov 79	**THE SECOND TIME AROUND** *Solar FB 1709*	45	9 wks
9 Feb 80	**RIGHT IN THE SOCKET** *Solar SO2*	44	6 wks
30 Aug 80	**I OWE YOU ONE** *Solar SO 11*	13	10 wks
28 Mar 81	**MAKE THAT MOVE** *Solar SO 17*	30	10 wks
27 Mar 82	● **I CAN MAKE YOU FEEL GOOD** *Solar K 12599*	7	11 wks
12 Jun 82	★ **A NIGHT TO REMEMBER** *Solar K 13162*	5	12 wks
4 Sep 82	● **THERE IT IS** *Solar K 13194*	5	10 wks
27 Nov 82	**FRIENDS** *Solar CHUM 1*	12	10 wks
11 Jun 83	● **DEAD GIVEAWAY** *Solar E 9818*	8	10 wks
13 Aug 83	**DISAPPEARING ACT** *Solar E 9807*	18	8 wks
15 Oct 83	**OVER AND OVER** *Solar E 9792*	23	6 wks
24 Mar 84	**DANCING IN THE SHEETS** *CBS A 4171*	41	3 wks
31 Mar 84	**DEADLINE USA** *MCA MCA 866*	52	3 wks
24 Nov 84	**AMNESIA** *Solar/MCA SHAL 1*	61	2 wks

SHAM 69
UK, male vocal/instrumental group   *53 wks*

13 May 78	**ANGELS WITH DIRTY FACES** *Polydor 2059 023*	19	10 wks
29 Jul 78	● **IF THE KIDS ARE UNITED** *Polydor 2059 050*	9	9 wks
14 Oct 78	● **HURRY UP HARRY** *Polydor POSP 7*	10	8 wks
24 Mar 79	**QUESTIONS AND ANSWERS** *Polydor POSP 27*	18	9 wks
4 Aug 79	● **HERSHAM BOYS** *Polydor POSP 64*	6	9 wks
27 Oct 79	**YOU'RE A BETTER MAN THAN I** *Polydor POSP 82*	49	5 wks
12 Apr 80	**TELL THE CHILDREN** *Polydor POSP 136*	45	3 wks

Jimmy SHAND
UK, male dance band   *2 wks*

23 Dec 55	**BLUEBELL POLKA** *Parlophone F 3436*	20	2 wks

Paul SHANE and the YELLOWCOATS
UK, male vocalist with male/female vocal group   *5 wks*

16 May 81	**HI DE HI (HOLIDAY ROCK)** *EMI 5180*	36	5 wks

SHANGRI-LAS
US, female vocal group   *57 wks*

8 Oct 64	**REMEMBER (WALKIN' IN THE SAND)** *Red Bird RB 10008*	14	13 wks
14 Jan 65	**LEADER OF THE PACK** *Red Bird RB 10014*	11	9 wks
14 Oct 72	● **LEADER OF THE PACK** (re-issue) *Kama Sutra 2013 024*	3	14 wks
5 Jun 76	● **LEADER OF THE PACK** (2nd re-issue) *Charly CS 1009*	7	11 wks
12 Jun 76	● **LEADER OF THE PACK** (3rd re-issue) *Contempo CS 9032*	7	10 wks

From 19 Jun 76 until 14 Aug 76, the last week of the disc's chart run, the Charly and Contempo releases of Leader Of The Pack were bracketed together on the chart.

SHANNON
US, female vocalist   *30 wks*

19 Nov 83	**LET THE MUSIC PLAY** *Club/Phonogram LET 1*	51	3 wks
28 Jan 84	**LET THE MUSIC PLAY** (re-entry) *Club/Phonogram LET 1*	14	12 wks
7 Apr 84	**GIVE ME TONIGHT** *Club/Phonogram JAB 1*	24	7 wks
30 Jun 84	**SWEET SOMEBODY** *Club/Phonogram JAB 3*	25	8 wks

Del SHANNON
US, male vocalist   *147 wks*

27 Apr 61	★ **RUNAWAY** *London HLX 9317*	1	22 wks
14 Sep 61	● **HATS OFF TO LARRY** *London HLX 9402*	6	12 wks
7 Dec 61	**SO LONG BABY** *London HLX 9462*	10	11 wks
15 Mar 62	● **HEY LITTLE GIRL** *London HLX 9515*	2	15 wks
6 Sep 62	**CRY MYSELF TO SLEEP** *London HLX 9587*	29	6 wks
11 Oct 62	● **SWISS MAID** *London HLX 9609*	2	17 wks
17 Jan 63	● **LITTLE TOWN FLIRT** *London HLX 9653*	4	13 wks
25 Apr 63	● **TWO KINDS OF TEARDROPS** *London HLX 9710*	5	13 wks
22 Aug 63	**TWO SILHOUETTES** *London HLX 9761*	23	8 wks
24 Oct 63	**SUE'S GONNA BE MINE** *London HLU 9800*	21	8 wks
12 Mar 64	**MARY JANE** *Stateside SS 269*	35	5 wks
30 Jul 64	**HANDY MAN** *Stateside SS 317*	36	4 wks
14 Jan 65	● **KEEP SEARCHIN' (WE'LL FOLLOW THE SUN)** *Stateside SS 368*	3	11 wks
18 Mar 65	**STRANGER IN TOWN** *Stateside SS 395*	40	2 wks

Helen SHAPIRO
UK, female vocalist   *119 wks*

23 Mar 61	● **DON'T TREAT ME LIKE A CHILD** *Columbia DB 4589*	3	20 wks
29 Jun 61	★ **YOU DON'T KNOW** *Columbia DB 4670*	1	23 wks
28 Sep 61	★ **WALKIN' BACK TO HAPPINESS** *Columbia DB 4715*	1	19 wks

15 Feb 62	● TELL ME WHAT HE SAID Columbia DB 4782 ..	2	15 wks
3 May 62	LET'S TALK ABOUT LOVE Columbia DB 4824	23	7 wks
12 Jul 62	● LITTLE MISS LONELY Columbia DB 4869	8	11 wks
18 Oct 62	KEEP AWAY FROM OTHER GIRLS		
	Columbia DB 4908	40	6 wks
7 Feb 63	QUEEN FOR TONIGHT Columbia DB 4966 ...	33	5 wks
25 Apr 63	WOE IS ME Columbia DB 7026	35	6 wks
24 Oct 63	LOOK WHO IT IS Columbia DB 7130	47	3 wks
23 Jan 64	FEVER Columbia DB 7190	38	4 wks

Feargal SHARKEY *UK, male vocalist* *7 wks*

13 Oct 84	LISTEN TO YOUR FATHER		
	Zarjazz/Virgin JAZZ 1	23	7 wks

SHARONETTES *UK, female vocal group* *8 wks*

26 Apr 75	PAPA OOM MOW MOW Black Magic BM 102 ..	26	5 wks
12 Jul 75	GOING TO A GO-GO Black Magic BM 104	46	3 wks

Dee Dee SHARP *US, female vocalist* *2 wks*

25 Apr 63	DO THE BIRD Cameo Parkway C 244	46	2 wks

See also Philadelphia All-Stars.

Rocky SHARPE and the REPLAYS
UK, male/female vocal group *41 wks*

16 Dec 78	RAMA LAMA DING DONG Chiswick CHIS 104	17	10 wks
24 Mar 79	IMAGINATION Chiswick CHIS 110	39	6 wks
25 Aug 79	LOVE WILL MAKE YOU FAIL IN SCHOOL		
	Chiswick CHIS 114	60	4 wks
9 Feb 80	MARTIAN HOP Chiswick CHIS 121	55	4 wks
17 Apr 82	SHOUT SHOUT (KNOCK YOURSELF OUT)		
	Chiswick DKE 3	19	9 wks
7 Aug 82	CLAP YOUR HANDS RAK 345	54	3 wks
26 Feb 83	IF YOU WANNA BE HAPPY Polydor POSP 560	46	5 wks

Third and fourth hits feature the Top Liners.

Sandie SHAW *UK, female vocalist* *162 wks*

8 Oct 64	★ (THERE'S) ALWAYS SOMETHING THERE TO		
	REMIND ME Pye 7N 15704	1	11 wks
10 Dec 64	● GIRL DON'T COME Pye 7N 15743	3	12 wks
18 Feb 65	● I'LL STOP AT NOTHING Pye 7N 15783 ...	4	11 wks
13 May 65	★ LONG LIVE LOVE Pye 7N 15841	1	14 wks
23 Sep 65	● MESSAGE UNDERSTOOD Pye 7N 15940 ...	6	10 wks
18 Nov 65	HOW CAN YOU TELL Pye 7N 15987	21	9 wks
27 Jan 66	● TOMORROW Pye 7N 17036	9	9 wks
19 May 66	NOTHING COMES EASY Pye 7N 17086	14	9 wks
8 Sep 66	RUN Pye 7N 17163	32	5 wks
24 Nov 66	THINK SOMETIMES ABOUT ME Pye 7N 17212	32	4 wks
19 Jan 67	I DON'T NEED ANYTHING Pye 7N 17239	50	1 wk
16 Mar 67	★ PUPPET ON A STRING Pye 7N 17272	1	18 wks
12 Jul 67	TONIGHT IN TOKYO Pye 7N 17346	21	6 wks
4 Oct 67	YOU'VE NOT CHANGED Pye 7N 17378	18	12 wks
7 Feb 68	TODAY Pye 7N 17441	27	7 wks
12 Feb 69	● MONSIEUR DUPONT Pye 7N 17615	6	15 wks
14 May 69	THINK IT ALL OVER Pye 7N 17726	42	4 wks
21 Apr 84	HAND IN GLOVE Rough Trade RT 130	27	5 wks

Winifred SHAW *US, female vocalist* *4 wks*

14 Aug 76	LULLABY OF BROADWAY		
	United Artists UP 36131	42	4 wks

George SHEARING
UK, male instrumentalist - piano *1 wk*

4 Oct 62	BAUBLES BANGLES & BEADS		
	Capitol CL 15269	49	1 wk

See also Nat 'King' Cole.

Gary SHEARSTON
Australia, male vocalist *8 wks*

5 Oct 74	● I GET A KICK OUT OF YOU Charisma CB 234	7	8 wks

SHEER ELEGANCE
UK, male vocal group *23 wks*

20 Dec 75	MILKY WAY Pye International 7N 25697	18	10 wks
3 Apr 76	● LIFE IS TOO SHORT GIRL		
	Pye International 7N 25703	9	9 wks
24 Jul 76	IT'S TEMPTATION Pye International 7N 25715 ..	41	4 wks

SHEILA and B. DEVOTION
France/US/Jamaica, female vocalist and male vocal/instrumental group *33 wks*

11 Mar 78	SINGIN' IN THE RAIN PART 1		
	Carrere EMI 2751	11	13 wks
22 Jul 78	YOU LIGHT MY FIRE Carrere EMI 2828	44	6 wks
24 Nov 79	SPACER Carrere CAR 128	18	14 wks

First two hits have no 'and' in the act's name.

Doug SHELDON *UK, male vocalist* *15 wks*

9 Nov 61	RUNAROUND SUE Decca F 11398	36	3 wks
4 Jan 62	YOUR MA SAID YOU CRIED IN YOUR SLEEP		
	LAST NIGHT Decca F 11416	29	6 wks
7 Feb 63	I SAW LINDA YESTERDAY Decca F 11564	36	6 wks

Pete SHELLEY *UK, male vocalist* *1 wk*

12 Mar 83	TELEPHONE OPERATOR Genetic XX1	66	1 wk

Peter SHELLEY *UK, male vocalist* *20 wks*

14 Sep 74	● GEE BABY Magnet MAG 12	4	10 wks
22 Mar 75	● LOVE ME LOVE MY DOG Magnet MAG 22 ...	3	10 wks

Anne SHELTON *UK, female vocalist* *31 wks*

16 Dec 55	ARRIVEDERCI DARLING HMV POP 146	17	4 wks
13 Apr 56	SEVEN DAYS Philips PB 567	20	4 wks
24 Aug 56	★ LAY DOWN YOUR ARMS Philips PB 616	1	14 wks
20 Nov 59	VILLAGE OF ST. BERNADETTE Philips PB 969	27	1 wk
26 Jan 61	● SAILOR Philips PB 1096	10	8 wks

SHEPHERD SISTERS
US, female vocal group *6 wks*

15 Nov 57	ALONE HMV POP 411	14	5 wks
3 Jan 58	ALONE (re-entry) HMV POP 411	22	1 wk

SHERBET

Australia, male vocal/instrumental group   *10 wks*

25 Sep 76	● HOWZAT	*Epic EPC 4574*	4	10 wks

Tony SHERIDAN and the BEATLES

UK, male vocalist, male instrumental backing group   *1 wk*

6 Jun 63	MY BONNIE	*Polydor NH 66833*	48	1 wk

See also Beatles.

Allan SHERMAN   *US, male vocalist*   *10 wks*

12 Sep 63	HELLO MUDDAH HELLO FADDAH			
	Warner Bros. WB 106		14	10 wks

Bobby SHERMAN   *US, male vocalist*   *4 wks*

31 Oct 70	JULIE DO YA LOVE ME	*CBS 5144*	28	4 wks

Pluto SHERVINGTON

Jamaica, male vocalist   *20 wks*

7 Feb 76	● DAT	*Opal PAL 5*	6	8 wks
10 Apr 76	RAM GOAT LIVER	*Trojan TR 7978*	43	4 wks
6 Mar 82	YOUR HONOUR	*KR KR 4*	19	8 wks

Your Honour credited to Pluto.

Holly SHERWOOD   *US, female vocalist*   *7 wks*

5 Feb 72	DAY BY DAY	*Bell 1182*	29	7 wks

Tony SHEVETON   *UK, male vocalist*   *1 wk*

13 Feb 64	MILLION DRUMS	*Oriole CB 1895*	49	1 wk

SHIRELLES   *US, female vocal group*   *29 wks*

9 Feb 61	● WILL YOU LOVE ME TOMORROW			
	Top Rank JAR 540		4	15 wks
31 May 62	SOLDIER BOY	*HMV POP 1019*	23	9 wks
23 May 63	FOOLISH LITTLE GIRL	*Stateside SS 181*	38	5 wks

SHIRLEY and COMPANY   *US, female vocalist/male vocal/instrumental backing group*   *9 wks*

8 Feb 75	● SHAME SHAME SHAME	*All Platinum 6146 301*	6	9 wks

SHO NUFF

US, male vocal/instrumental group   *4 wks*

24 May 80	IT'S ALRIGHT	*Ensign ENY 37*	53	4 wks

SHOCKING BLUE

Holland, male/female vocal/instrumental group   *14 wks*

17 Jan 70	● VENUS	*Penny Farthing PEN 702*	8	11 wks
25 Apr 70	MIGHTY JOE	*Penny Farthing PEN 713*	43	3 wks

Troy SHONDELL   *US, male vocalist*   *11 wks*

2 Nov 61	THIS TIME	*London HLG 9432*	22	11 wks

SHONDELLS - *See Tommy JAMES and the SHONDELLS*

SHOWADDYWADDY

UK, male vocal/instrumental group   *209 wks*

18 May 74	● HEY ROCK AND ROLL	*Bell 1357*	2	14 wks
17 Aug 74	ROCK 'N' ROLL LADY	*Bell 1374*	15	9 wks
30 Nov 74	HEY MR. CHRISTMAS	*Bell 1387*	13	8 wks
22 Feb 75	SWEET MUSIC	*Bell 1403*	14	9 wks
17 May 75	● THREE STEPS TO HEAVEN	*Bell 1426*	2	11 wks
6 Sep 75	● HEARTBEAT	*Bell 1450*	7	7 wks
15 Nov 75	HEAVENLY	*Bell 1460*	34	6 wks
29 May 76	TROCADERO	*Bell 1476*	32	3 wks
6 Nov 76	★ UNDER THE MOON OF LOVE	*Bell 1495*	1	15 wks
5 Mar 77	● WHEN	*Arista 91*	3	11 wks
23 Jul 77	● YOU GOT WHAT IT TAKES	*Arista 126*	2	10 wks
5 Nov 77	● DANCIN' PARTY	*Arista 149*	4	11 wks
25 Mar 78	● I WONDER WHY	*Arista 174*	2	11 wks
24 Jun 78	● A LITTLE BIT OF SOAP	*Arista 191*	5	12 wks
4 Nov 78	● PRETTY LITTLE ANGEL EYES			
	Arista ARIST 222		5	12 wks
31 Mar 79	REMEMBER THEN	*Arista 247*	17	8 wks
28 Jul 79	SWEET LITTLE ROCK 'N' ROLLER	*Arista 278*	15	9 wks
10 Nov 79	A NIGHT AT DADDY GEE'S	*Arista 314*	39	5 wks
27 Sep 80	WHY DO LOVERS BREAK EACH OTHER'S			
	HEARTS	*Arista ARIST 359*	22	10 wks
29 Nov 80	BLUE MOON	*Arista ARIST 379*	32	9 wks
13 Jun 81	MULTIPLICATION	*Arista ARIST 416*	39	4 wks
28 Nov 81	FOOTSTEPS	*Bell BELL 1499*	31	9 wks
28 Aug 82	WHO PUT THE BOMP (IN THE			
	BOMP-A-BOMP-A-BOMP)	*RCA 236*	37	6 wks

SHOWDOWN

US, male vocal/instrumental group   *3 wks*

17 Dec 77	KEEP DOIN' IT	*State STAT 63*	41	3 wks

SHOWSTOPPERS   *US, male vocal group*   *25 wks*

13 Mar 68	AIN'T NOTHING BUT A HOUSEPARTY			
	Beacon 3-100		11	15 wks
13 Nov 68	EENY MEENY	*MGM 1346*	33	7 wks
30 Jan 71	AIN'T NOTHING BUT A HOUSEPARTY			
	(re-issue) *Beacon BEA 100*		43	1 wk
13 Feb 71	AIN'T NOTHING BUT A HOUSEPARTY			
	(re-entry of re-issue) *Beacon BEA 100*		33	1 wk
27 Feb 71	AIN'T NOTHING BUT A HOUSEPARTY			
	(2nd re-entry of re-issue) *Beacon BEA 100*		36	1 wk

SHRIEKBACK

UK, male vocal/instrumental group   *4 wks*

28 Jul 84	HAND ON MY HEART	*Arista SHRK 1*	52	4 wks

SHY   *UK, male vocal/instrumental group*   *3 wks*

19 Apr 80	GIRL (IT'S ALL I HAVE)	*Gallery GA 1*	60	3 wks

Labi SIFFRE   *UK, male vocalist*   *27 wks*

27 Nov 71	IT MUST BE LOVE	*Pye International 7N 25572* ..	14	12 wks
25 Mar 72	CRYING LAUGHING LOVING LYING			
	Pye International 7N 25576		11	9 wks
29 Jul 72	WATCH ME	*Pye International 7N 25586*	29	6 wks

SILKIE
UK, male/female vocal/instrumental group   *6 wks*

23 Sep 65	**YOU'VE GOT TO HIDE YOUR LOVE AWAY**					
	Fontana TF 603				**28**	6 wks

SILVER BULLET BAND - *See Bob SEGER and the SILVER BULLET BAND*

SILVER CONVENTION
Germany/US, female vocal group   *35 wks*

5 Apr 75	**SAVE ME** *Magnet MAG 26*	**30**	7 wks
15 Nov 75	**FLY ROBIN FLY** *Magnet MAG 43*	**28**	8 wks
3 Apr 76	● **GET UP & BOOGIE** *Magnet MAG 55*	**7**	11 wks
19 Jun 76	**TIGER BABY/NO NO JOE** *Magnet MAG 69*	**41**	4 wks
29 Jan 77	**EVERYBODY'S TALKIN' 'BOUT LOVE**		
	Magnet MAG 81	**25**	5 wks

Dooley SILVERSPOON
US, male vocalist   *3 wks*

31 Jan 76	**LET ME BE THE NUMBER ONE**		
	Seville SEV 1020	**44**	3 wks

Harry SIMEONE CHORALE
US, choir   *14 wks*

13 Feb 59	**LITTLE DRUMMER BOY** *Top Rank JAR 101*	**13**	7 wks
22 Dec 60	**ONWARD CHRISTIAN SOLDIERS**		
	Ember EMBS 118	**35**	1 wk
5 Jan 61	**ONWARD CHRISTIAN SOLDIERS** (re-entry)		
	Ember EMBS 118	**38**	1 wk
21 Dec 61	**ONWARD CHRISTIAN SOLDIERS** (2nd re-entry)		
	Ember EMBS 118	**36**	3 wks
20 Dec 62	**ONWARD CHRISTIAN SOLDIERS** (re-issue)		
	Ember EMBS 144	**38**	2 wks

Gene SIMMONS
US, male vocalist   *4 wks*

27 Jan 79	**RADIOACTIVE** *Casablanca CAN 134*	**41**	4 wks

SIMON and GARFUNKEL
US, male vocal duo   *80 wks*

24 Mar 66	● **HOMEWARD BOUND** *CBS 202045*	**9**	12 wks
16 Jun 66	**I AM A ROCK** *CBS 202303*	**17**	10 wks
10 Jul 68	● **MRS. ROBINSON** *CBS 3443*	**4**	12 wks
8 Jan 69	● **MRS. ROBINSON** (EP) *CBS EP 6400*	**9**	5 wks
30 Apr 69	● **THE BOXER** *CBS 4162*	**6**	14 wks
21 Feb 70	★ **BRIDGE OVER TROUBLED WATER** *CBS 4790*	**1**	19 wks
15 Aug 70	**BRIDGE OVER TROUBLED WATER** (re-entry)		
	CBS 4790	**45**	1 wk
7 Oct 72	**AMERICA** *CBS 8336*	**25**	7 wks

See also Paul Simon; Art Garfunkel. Titles on Mrs. Robinson EP: Mrs. Robinson/Scarborough Fair-Canticle/Sounds Of Silence/April Come She Will. This EP would have stayed more than 5 weeks on chart had a decision to exclude EP from the chart not been taken in Feb 69.

Carly SIMON
US, female vocalist   *49 wks*

16 Dec 72	● **YOU'RE SO VAIN** *Elektra K 12077*	**3**	15 wks
31 Mar 73	**THE RIGHT THING TO DO** *Elektra K 12095*	**17**	9 wks
6 Aug 77	● **NOBODY DOES IT BETTER** *Elektra K 12261*	**7**	12 wks
21 Aug 82	● **WHY** *WEA K 79300*	**10**	13 wks

See also Carly Simon and James Taylor.

Carly SIMON and James TAYLOR
US, female/male vocal duo   *5 wks*

16 Mar 74	**MOCKINGBIRD** *Elektra K 12134*	**34**	5 wks

See also Carly Simon; James Taylor.

Joe SIMON
US, male vocalist   *10 wks*

16 Jun 73	**STEP BY STEP** *Mojo 2093 030*	**14**	10 wks

Paul SIMON
US, male vocalist   *52 wks*

19 Feb 72	● **MOTHER & CHILD REUNION** *CBS 7793*	**5**	12 wks
29 Apr 72	**ME & JULIO DOWN BY THE SCHOOLYARD**		
	CBS 7964	**15**	9 wks
16 Jun 73	● **TAKE ME TO THE MARDI GRAS** *CBS 1578*	**7**	11 wks
22 Sep 73	**LOVES ME LIKE A ROCK** *CBS 1700*	**39**	4 wks
10 Jan 76	**50 WAYS TO LEAVE YOUR LOVER** *CBS 3887*	**23**	6 wks
3 Dec 77	**SLIP SLIDIN' AWAY** *CBS 5770*	**36**	5 wks
6 Sep 80	**LATE IN THE EVENING** *Warner Bros. K 17666*	**58**	4 wks

See also Simon and Garfunkel.

Tito SIMON
Jamaica, male vocalist   *4 wks*

8 Feb 75	**THIS MONDAY MORNING FEELING**		
	Horse HOSS 57	**45**	4 wks

Nina SIMONE
US, female vocalist   *32 wks*

5 Aug 65	**I PUT A SPELL ON YOU** *Philips BF 1415*	**49**	1 wk
16 Oct 68	● **AIN'T GOT NO - I GOT LIFE/DO WHAT YOU GOTTA DO** *RCA 1743*	**2**	18 wks
15 Jan 69	● **TO LOVE SOMEBODY** *RCA 1779*	**5**	9 wks
15 Jan 69	**I PUT A SPELL ON YOU** (re-issue)		
	Philips BF 1736	**28**	4 wks

Do What You Gotta Do was only credited on the charts for 8 weeks of the 18, its highest position being 7.

SIMPLE MINDS
UK, male vocal/instrumental group   *58 wks*

12 May 79	**LIFE IN A DAY** *Zoom ZUM 10*	**62**	2 wks
23 May 81	**THE AMERICAN** *Virgin VS 410*	**59**	3 wks
15 Aug 81	**LOVE SONG** *Virgin VS 434*	**47**	4 wks
7 Nov 81	**SWEAT IN BULLET** *Virgin VS 451*	**52**	3 wks
10 Apr 82	**PROMISED YOU A MIRACLE** *Virgin VS 488*	**13**	11 wks
28 Aug 82	**GLITTERING PRIZE** *Virgin VS 511*	**16**	11 wks
13 Nov 82	**SOMEONE SOMEWHERE (IN SUMMERTIME)**		
	Virgin VS 538	**36**	5 wks
26 Nov 83	**WATERFRONT** *Virgin VS 636*	**13**	10 wks
28 Jan 84	**SPEED YOUR LOVE TO ME** *Virgin VS 649*	**20**	4 wks
24 Mar 84	**UP ON THE CATWALK** *Virgin VS 661*	**27**	5 wks

SIMPLICIOUS
US, male vocal group   *3 wks*

29 Sep 84	**LET HER FEEL IT** *Fourth and Broadway BRW 13*	**65**	3 wks

SIMPSON - *See ASHFORD and SIMPSON*

W/CDR. A. E. SIMS - *See Central Band of the ROYAL AIR FORCE, conductor W/CDR. A. E. SIMS, OBE*

Frank SINATRA
US, male vocalist   *391 wks*

9 Jul 54	**YOUNG AT HEART** *Capitol CL 14064*	**12**	1 wk

Date	Title	Catalogue	Pos	Wks
16 Jul 54	★ THREE COINS IN THE FOUNTAIN *Capitol CL 14120*		1	19 wks
10 Jun 55	YOU MY LOVE *Capitol CL 14240*		13	3 wks
22 Jul 55	YOU MY LOVE (re-entry) *Capitol CL 14240*		17	2 wks
5 Aug 55	● LEARNIN' THE BLUES *Capitol CL 14296*		2	13 wks
12 Aug 55	YOU MY LOVE (2nd re-entry) *Capitol CL 14240*		17	2 wks
2 Sep 55	NOT AS A STRANGER *Capitol CL 14326*		18	1 wk
13 Jan 56	● LOVE AND MARRIAGE *Capitol CL 14503*		3	8 wks
20 Jan 56	● THE TENDER TRAP *Capitol CL 14511*		2	9 wks
15 Jun 56	SONGS FOR SWINGING LOVERS (LP) *Capitol LCT 6106*		12	8 wks
22 Nov 57	ALL THE WAY *Capitol CL 14800*		29	1 wk
29 Nov 57	CHICAGO *Capitol CL 14800*		25	1 wk
6 Dec 57	ALL THE WAY (re-entry)/CHICAGO *Capitol CL 14800*		21	1 wk
13 Dec 57	● ALL THE WAY (re-entry) *Capitol CL 14800*		3	17 wks
7 Feb 58	WITCHCRAFT *Capitol CL 14819*		12	8 wks
14 Nov 58	MR. SUCCESS *Capitol CL 14956*		29	1 wk
12 Dec 58	MR. SUCCESS (re-entry) *Capitol CL 14956*		25	2 wks
2 Jan 59	MR. SUCCESS (2nd re-entry) *Capitol CL 14956*		26	1 wk
10 Apr 59	FRENCH FOREIGN LEGION *Capitol CL 14997*		18	5 wks
15 May 59	COME DANCE WITH ME (LP) *Capitol LCT 6179*		30	1 wk
28 Aug 59	HIGH HOPES *Capitol CL 15052*		28	1 wk
11 Sep 59	● HIGH HOPES (re-entry) *Capitol CL 15052*		6	13 wks
10 Mar 60	HIGH HOPES (2nd re-entry) *Capitol CL 15052*		42	1 wk
7 Apr 60	IT'S NICE TO GO TRAV'LING *Capitol CL 15116*		48	2 wks
16 Jun 60	RIVER STAY 'WAY FROM MY DOOR *Capitol CL 15135*		18	9 wks
8 Sep 60	NICE 'N EASY *Capitol CL 15150*		15	12 wks
24 Nov 60	OL' MACDONALD *Capitol CL 15168*		11	8 wks
20 Apr 61	MY BLUE HEAVEN *Capitol CL 15193*		33	7 wks
28 Sep 61	GRANADA *Reprise R 20010*		15	8 wks
23 Nov 61	THE COFFEE SONG *Reprise R 20035*		39	3 wks
5 Apr 62	EVERYBODY'S TWISTING *Reprise R 20063*		22	12 wks
7 Mar 63	MY KIND OF GIRL *Reprise R 20148*		35	6 wks
24 Sep 64	HELLO DOLLY *Reprise R 20351*		47	1 wk
12 May 66	★ STRANGERS IN THE NIGHT *Reprise R 23052*		1	20 wks
29 Sep 66	SUMMER WIND *Reprise RS 20509*		36	5 wks
15 Dec 66	THAT'S LIFE *Reprise RS 20531*		46	5 wks
23 Aug 67	THE WORLD WE KNEW *Reprise RS 20610*		33	11 wks
2 Apr 69	● MY WAY *Reprise RS 20817*		5	42 wks
4 Oct 69	● LOVE'S BEEN GOOD TO ME *Reprise RS 20852*		8	18 wks
31 Jan 70	MY WAY (re-entry) *Reprise RS 20817*		49	1 wk
28 Feb 70	MY WAY (2nd re-entry) *Reprise RS 20817*		30	5 wks
11 Apr 70	MY WAY (3rd re-entry) *Reprise RS 20817*		33	9 wks
27 Jun 70	MY WAY (4th re-entry) *Reprise RS 20817*		28	21 wks
28 Nov 70	MY WAY (5th re-entry) *Reprise RS 20817*		18	16 wks
6 Mar 71	I WILL DRINK THE WINE *Reprise RS 23487*		16	12 wks
27 Mar 71	MY WAY (6th re-entry) *Reprise RS 20817*		22	19 wks
4 Sep 71	MY WAY (7th re-entry) *Reprise RS 20817*		39	8 wks
1 Jan 72	MY WAY (8th re-entry) *Reprise RS 20817*		50	1 wk
20 Dec 75	I BELIEVE I'M GONNA LOVE YOU *Reprise K 14400*		34	7 wks
9 Aug 80	THEME FROM NEW YORK, NEW YORK *Reprise K 14502*		59	4 wks

See also Frank Sinatra and Sammy Davis Jr.; Nancy Sinatra and Frank Sinatra. My Kind Of Girl and Hello Dolly *with Count Basie*. Tracks on Songs For Swinging Lovers LP: You Make Me Feel So Young/It Happened In Monterey/You're Getting To Be A Habit With Me/You Brought A New Kind Of Love To Me/Too Marvellous For Words/Old Devil Moon/Pennies From Heaven/ Love Is Here To Stay/I've Got You Under My Skin/I Thought About You/We'll Be Together Again/Making Whoopee/Swingin' Down The Lane/Anything Goes/How About You. On Come Dance With Me *LP: Something's Gotta Give/Just In Time/Dancing In The Dark/Too Close For Comfort/I Could Have Danced All Night/Saturday Night Is The Loneliest Night Of The Week/Day In Day Out/Cheek To Cheek/Baubles Bangles And Beads/The Song Is You/The Last Dance. All The Way and Chicago, *Capitol CL 14800*, were at first billed separately, then together for one week, then All The Way on its own.

Frank SINATRA and Sammy DAVIS JR. *US, male vocal duo* — 9 wks

13 Dec 62	ME AND MY SHADOW *Reprise R 20128*		20	7 wks

7 Feb 63	ME AND MY SHADOW (re-entry) *Reprise R 20128*		47	2 wks

See also Frank Sinatra; Sammy Davis Jr.; Nancy Sinatra and Frank Sinatra; Sammy Davis Jr. and Carmen McRae.

Nancy SINATRA *US, female vocalist* — 61 wks

27 Jan 66	★ THESE BOOTS ARE MADE FOR WALKIN' *Reprise R 20432*		1	14 wks
28 Apr 66	HOW DOES THAT GRAB YOU DARLIN' *Reprise R 20461*		19	8 wks
19 Jan 67	● SUGAR TOWN *Reprise RS 20527*		8	10 wks
5 Jul 67	YOU ONLY LIVE TWICE/JACKSON *Reprise RS 20595*		11	19 wks
29 Nov 69	HIGHWAY SONG *Reprise RS 20869*		21	10 wks

See also Nancy Sinatra and Frank Sinatra; Nancy Sinatra and Lee Hazlewood. Jackson *was billed together with* You Only Live Twice *from 12 Jul 67. Jackson is by Nancy Sinatra and Lee Hazlewood.*

Nancy SINATRA and Lee HAZLEWOOD *US, female/vocal duo* — 20 wks

8 Nov 67	LADYBIRD *Reprise RS 20629*		47	1 wk
21 Aug 71	● DID YOU EVER *Reprise K 14093*		2	19 wks

See also Nancy Sinatra; Nancy Sinatra and Frank Sinatra. Did You Ever *bills the duo simply as Nancy and Lee.*

Nancy SINATRA and Frank SINATRA *US, female/male vocal duo* — 18 wks

23 Mar 67	★ SOMETHIN' STUPID *Reprise RS 23166*		1	18 wks

See also Nancy Sinatra; Nancy Sinatra and Lee Hazlewood; Frank Sinatra; Frank Sinatra and Sammy Davis Jr.

SINE *US, Disco aggregation* — 9 wks

10 Jun 78	● JUST LET ME DO MY THING *CBS 6351*		33	9 wks

SINGING DOGS *US, canine vocal group* — 4 wks

25 Nov 55	THE SINGING DOGS (MEDLEY) *Nixa N 15009*		13	4 wks

Medley Songs: Pat-a-cake/Three Blind Mice/Jingle Bells/ Oh Susanna.

SINGING NUN (Soeur Sourire) *Belgium, female vocalist* — 14 wks

5 Dec 63	● DOMINIQUE *Philips BF 1293*		7	14 wks

SINGING SHEEP *UK, computerised sheep noises* — 5 wks

18 Dec 82	BAA BAA BLACK SHEEP *Sheep/Virgin BAA 1*		42	5 wks

Maxine SINGLETON *US, female vocalist* — 3 wks

2 Apr 83	YOU CAN'T RUN FROM LOVE *Creole CR 50*		57	3 wks

SIOUXSIE and the BANSHEES *UK, female/male vocal/instrumental group* — 99 wks

26 Aug 78	● HONG KONG GARDEN *Polydor 2059 052*		7	10 wks
31 Mar 79	THE STAIRCASE (MYSTERY) *Polydor POSP 9*		24	8 wks

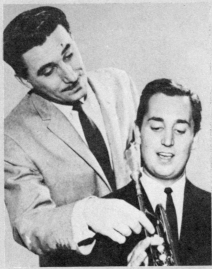

SAM THE SHAM (above left) Sham '65.

NEIL SEDAKA (centre) Trad Jazzman Kenny Ball demonstrates his trumpet fingering technique to the classically trained pianist Sedaka.

PAUL and BARRY RYAN (right) Their mother Marion charted 7 years before them. Despite their seven hits as a duo it took the first of Barry Ryan's six solo hits to better her peak position.

RINGO STARR (left) In the garden of Sunny Heights, his mock tudor home in Surrey.

CONNIE STEVENS A magazine questionnaire revealed the Brooklyn born singer's personal secret – 'Peanut butter and banana sandwiches make me drool!'

ROD STEWART (right) His career was unchecked during the seventies.

7 Jul 79	PLAYGROUND TWIST	Polydor POSP 59	28	6 wks
29 Sep 79	MITTAGEISEN (METAL POSTCARD) Polydor 2059 151		47	3 wks
15 Mar 80	HAPPY HOUSE	Polydor POSP 117	17	8 wks
7 Jun 80	CHRISTINE	Polydor 2059 249	24	8 wks
6 Dec 80	ISRAEL	Polydor POSP 205	41	8 wks
30 May 81	SPELLBOUND	Polydor POSP 273	22	8 wks
1 Aug 81	ARABIAN KNIGHTS	Polydor POSP 309	32	7 wks
29 May 82	FIRE WORKS	Polydor POSPG 450	22	6 wks
9 Oct 82	SLOWDIVE	Polydor POSP 510	41	4 wks
4 Dec 82	MELT/IL EST NE LE DIVIN ENFANT Polydor POSP 539		49	5 wks
1 Oct 83	● DEAR PRUDENCE	Wonderland/Polydor SHE 4	3	8 wks
24 Mar 84	SWIMMING HORSES	Wonderland/Polydor SHE 6	28	4 wks
2 Jun 84	DAZZLE	Wonderland/Polydor SHE 7	33	3 wks
27 Oct 84	THE THORN (EP)	Wonderland/Polydor SHEEP 8	47	3 wks

See also Creatures. Tracks on EP: Overground/Voices/Pacebo Effect/ Red Over White.

SIR DOUGLAS QUINTET
US, male vocal/instrumental group · 10 wks

17 Jun 65	SHE'S ABOUT A MOVER	London HLU 9964	15	10 wks

SISTER SLEDGE
US, female vocal group · 75 wks

21 Jun 75	MAMA NEVER TOLD ME	Atlantic K 10619	20	6 wks
17 Mar 79	● HE'S THE GREATEST DANCER Atlantic/Cotillion K 11257		6	11 wks
26 May 79	● WE ARE FAMILY	Atlantic/Cotillion K 11293	8	10 wks
11 Aug 79	LOST IN MUSIC	Atlantic/Cotillion K 11337	17	10 wks
19 Jan 80	GOT TO LOVE SOMEBODY Atlantic/Cotillion K 11404		34	4 wks
28 Feb 81	ALL AMERICAN GIRLS	Atlantic K 11656	41	5 wks
26 May 84	THINKING OF YOU	Cotillion/Atlantic B 9744	11	13 wks
8 Sep 84	LOST IN MUSIC	(re-issue) Cotillion/Atlantic B 9718	4	12 wks
17 Nov 84	WE ARE FAMILY	(E.REMIX) Cotillion/Atlantic B 9692	33	4 wks

The 12-inch of B 9718 was a Remix of K 11337.

SISTERS OF MERCY
UK, male vocal/instrumental group · 6 wks

16 Jun 84	BODY AND SOUL TRAIN Merciful Release/WEA MR 029		46	3 wks
20 Oct 84	WALK AWAY	Merciful Release/WEA MR 033	45	3 wks

SISTERS OF SOUL - *See Steve WRIGHT.*

SIVUCA
Brazil, male vocalist · 3 wks

28 Jul 84	AIN'T NO SUNSHINE	London LON 51	56	3 wks

SKATALITES
Jamaica, male instrumental group · 6 wks

20 Apr 67	GUNS OF NAVARONE	Island WI 168	36	6 wks

Peter SKELLERN
UK, male vocalist · 24 wks

23 Sep 72	● YOU'RE A LADY	Decca F 13333	3	11 wks
29 Mar 75	HOLD ON TO LOVE	Decca F 13568	14	9 wks
28 Oct 78	LOVE IS THE SWEETEST THING Mercury 6008 603		60	4 wks

Last hit has credit: Featuring Grimethorpe Colliery Band.

SKIDS
UK, male vocal/instrumental group · 60 wks

23 Sep 78	SWEET SUBURBIA	Virgin VS 227	70	1 wk
7 Oct 78	SWEET SUBURBIA	(re-entry) Virgin VS 227	71	2 wks
4 Nov 78	THE SAINTS ARE COMING	Virgin VS 232	48	3 wks
17 Feb 79	● INTO THE VALLEY	Virgin VS 241	10	11 wks
26 May 79	MASQUERADE	Virgin VS 262	14	9 wks
29 Sep 79	CHARADE	Virgin VS 288	31	6 wks
24 Nov 79	WORKING FOR THE YANKEE DOLLAR Virgin VS 306		20	11 wks
1 Mar 80	ANIMATION	Virgin VS 323	56	3 wks
16 Aug 80	CIRCUS GAMES	Virgin VS 359	32	7 wks
18 Oct 80	GOODBYE CIVILIAN	Virgin VS 373	52	4 wks
6 Dec 80	WOMEN IN WINTER	Virgin VSK 101	49	3 wks

SKY
UK/Australia, male instrumental group · 11 wks

5 Apr 80	● TOCCATA	Ariola ARO 300	5	11 wks

SKYHOOKS
Australia, male vocal/instrumental group · 1 wk

9 Jun 79	WOMEN IN UNIFORM	United Artists UP 36508	73	1 wk

SLADE
UK, male vocal/instrumental group · 247 wks

19 Jun 71	GET DOWN AND GET WITH IT Polydor 2058 112		16	14 wks
30 Oct 71	★ COZ I LUV YOU	Polydor 2058 155	1	15 wks
5 Feb 72	● LOOK WOT YOU DUN	Polydor 2058 195	4	10 wks
3 Jun 72	★ TAKE ME BAK 'OME	Polydor 2058 231	1	13 wks
2 Sep 72	★ MAMA WEER ALL CRAZEE NOW Polydor 2058 274		1	10 wks
25 Nov 72	● GUDBUY T'JANE	Polydor 2058 312	2	13 wks
3 Mar 73	★ CUM ON FEEL THE NOIZE	Polydor 2058 339	1	12 wks
30 Jun 73	★ SKWEEZE ME PLEEZE ME	Polydor 2058 377	1	10 wks
6 Oct 73	● MY FREND STAN	Polydor 2058 407	2	8 wks
15 Dec 73	★ MERRY XMAS EVERYBODY	Polydor 2058 422	1	9 wks
6 Apr 74	● EVERYDAY	Polydor 2058 453	3	7 wks
6 Jul 74	● BANGIN' MAN	Polydor 2058 492	3	7 wks
19 Oct 74	● FAR FAR AWAY	Polydor 2058 522	2	6 wks
15 Feb 75	HOW DOES IT FEEL	Polydor 2058 547	15	7 wks
17 May 75	● THANKS FOR THE MEMORY (WHAM BAM THANK YOU MAM) Polydor 2058 585		7	7 wks
22 Nov 75	IN FOR A PENNY	Polydor 2058 663	11	8 wks
7 Feb 76	LET'S CALL IT QUITS	Polydor 2058 690	11	7 wks
5 Feb 77	GYPSY ROAD HOG	Barn 2014 105	48	2 wks
29 Oct 77	MY BABY LEFT ME-THAT'S ALL RIGHT (MEDLEY) Barn 2014 114		32	4 wks
18 Oct 80	SLADE ALIVE AT READING '80 (EP) Cheapskate CHEAP 5		44	5 wks
27 Dec 80	MERRY XMAS EVERYBODY Cheapskate CHEAP 11		70	2 wks
31 Jan 81	● WE'LL BRING THE HOUSE DOWN Cheapskate CHEAP 16		10	9 wks
4 Apr 81	WHEELS AIN'T COMING DOWN Cheapskate CHEAP 21		60	3 wks
19 Sep 81	LOCK UP YOUR DAUGHTERS	RCA 124	29	8 wks
19 Dec 81	MERRY XMAS EVERYBODY	(re-entry) Polydor 2058 422	32	4 wks
27 Mar 82	RUBY RED	RCA 191	51	3 wks
27 Nov 82	(AND NOW - THE WALTZ) C'EST LA VIE RCA 291		50	6 wks
25 Dec 82	MERRY XMAS EVERYBODY	(2nd re-entry) Polydor 2058 422	64	2 wks
19 Nov 83	● MY OH MY	RCA 373	2	11 wks
10 Dec 83	MERRY XMAS EVERBODY	(3rd re-entry) Polydor 2058 422	20	5 wks
4 Feb 84	● RUN RUN AWAY	RCA 385	7	10 wks
17 Nov 84	ALL JOIN HANDS	RCA 455	15†	7 wks

15 Dec 84	**MERRY XMAS EVERYBODY**	(4th re-entry)		
	Polydor 2058 422		**47†**	3 wks

Tracks on Slade Alive at Reading '80 EP: When I'm Dancin' I Ain't Fightin'/Born To Be Wild/Somethin' Else/Pistol Packin' Mama/Keep A Rollin'. Merry Xmas Everybody on Cheapskate is credited to Slade and the Reading Choir and is a re-recording.

SLAVE US, *male vocal/instrumental group*   *3 wks*

8 Mar 80	**JUST A TOUCH OF LOVE**		
	Atlantic/Cotillion K 11442	**64**	3 wks

Percy SLEDGE US, *male vocalist*   *24 wks*

12 May 66	● **WHEN A MAN LOVES A WOMAN**		
	Atlantic 584 001	**4**	17 wks
4 Aug 66	**WARM & TENDER LOVE** *Atlantic 584 034*	**34**	7 wks

SLICK
US, *male/female vocal/instrumental group*   *15 wks*

16 Jun 79	**SPACE BASS** *Fantasy FTC 176*	**16**	10 wks
15 Sep 79	**SEXY CREAM** *Fantasy FTC 182*	**47**	5 wks

Grace SLICK US, *female vocalist*   *4 wks*

24 May 80	**DREAMS** *RCA PB 9534*	**50**	4 wks

SLIK UK, *male vocal/instrumental group*   *18 wks*

17 Jan 76	★ **FOREVER & EVER** *Bell 1464*	**1**	9 wks
8 May 76	**REQUIEM** *Bell 1478*	**24**	9 wks

SLIM CHANCE - *See Ronnie LANE*

SLITS UK, *female vocal/instrumental group*   *3 wks*

13 Oct 79	**TYPICAL GIRLS/I HEARD IT THROUGH THE GRAPEVINE** *Island WIP 6505*	**60**	3 wks

P. F. SLOAN US, *male vocalist*   *3 wks*

4 Nov 65	**SINS OF THE FAMILY** *RCA 1482*	**38**	3 wks

SLY and the FAMILY STONE US,
male/female vocal/instrumental group, Sly Stone, vocals and keyboards   *42 wks*

10 Jul 68	● **DANCE TO THE MUSIC** *Direction 58 3568*	**7**	14 wks
2 Oct 68	**M'LADY** *Direction 58 3707*	**32**	7 wks
19 Mar 69	**EVERYDAY PEOPLE** *Direction 58 3938*	**36**	1 wk
9 Apr 69	**EVERYDAY PEOPLE** (re-entry) *Direction 58 3938*	**37**	4 wks
8 Jan 72	**FAMILY AFFAIR** *Epic EPC 7632*	**15**	8 wks
15 Apr 72	**RUNNIN' AWAY** *Epic EPC 7810*	**17**	8 wks

SMALL ADS
UK, *male vocal/instrumental group*   *3 wks*

18 Apr 81	**SMALL ADS** *Bronze BRO 115*	**63**	3 wks

SMALL FACES
UK, *male vocal/instrumental group*   *137 wks*

2 Sep 65	**WHATCHA GONNA DO ABOUT IT?**		
	Decca F 12208	**14**	12 wks
10 Feb 66	● **SHA LA LA LA LEE** *Decca F 12317*	**3**	11 wks
12 May 66	● **HEY GIRL** *Decca F 12393*	**10**	9 wks
11 Aug 66	★ **ALL OR NOTHING** *Decca F 12470*	**1**	12 wks
17 Nov 66	● **MY MIND'S EYE** *Decca F 12500*	**4**	11 wks
9 Mar 67	**I CAN'T MAKE IT** *Decca F 12565*	**26**	7 wks
8 Jun 67	**HERE COMES THE NICE** *Immediate IM 050*	**12**	10 wks
9 Aug 67	● **ITCHYCOO PARK** *Immediate IM 057* . . .	**3**	14 wks
6 Dec 67	● **TIN SOLDIER** *Immediate IM 062*	**9**	12 wks
17 Apr 68	● **LAZY SUNDAY** *Immediate IM 064*	**2**	11 wks
10 Jul 68	**UNIVERSAL** *Immediate IM 069*	**16**	11 wks
19 Mar 69	**AFTERGLOW OF YOUR LOVE**		
	Immediate IM 077	**36**	1 wk
13 Dec 75	● **ITCHYCOO PARK** (re-issue) *Immediate IMS 102*	**9**	11 wks
20 Mar 76	**LAZY SUNDAY** (re-issue) *Immediate IMS 106*	**39**	5 wks

See also Faces.

Hurricane SMITH UK, *male vocalist*   *35 wks*

12 Jun 71	● **DON'T LET IT DIE** *Columbia DB 8785*	**2**	12 wks
29 Apr 72	● **OH BABE WHAT WOULD YOU SAY?**		
	Columbia DB 8878	**4**	16 wks
2 Sep 72	**WHO WAS IT** *Columbia DB 8916*	**23**	7 wks

Jimmy SMITH
US, *male instrumentalist - organ*   *3 wks*

28 Apr 66	**GOT MY MOJO WORKING** *Verve VS 536*	**48**	2 wks
19 May 66	**GOT MY MOJO WORKING** (re-entry)		
	Verve VS 536	**48**	1 wk

Keely SMITH US, *female vocalist*   *10 wks*

18 Mar 65	**YOU'RE BREAKIN' MY HEART** *Reprise R 20346*	**14**	10 wks

Muriel SMITH UK, *female vocalist*   *17 wks*

15 May 53	● **HOLD ME THRILL ME KISS ME** *Philips PB 122*	**3**	17 wks

O. C. SMITH US, *male vocalist*   *23 wks*

29 May 68	● **SON OF HICKORY HOLLER'S TRAMP**		
	CBS 3343	**2**	15 wks
26 Mar 77	**TOGETHER** *Caribou CRB 4910*	**25**	8 wks

Rex SMITH and Rachel SWEET
US, *male/female vocal duo*   *7 wks*

22 Aug 81	**EVERLASTING LOVE** *CBS A 1405*	**35**	7 wks

See also Rachel Sweet.

Whistling Jack SMITH
UK, *male whistler*   *12 wks*

2 Mar 67	● **I WAS KAISER BILL'S BATMAN**		
	Deram DM 112	**5**	12 wks

Patti SMITH GROUP
US, *female vocalist, male instrumental backing group*   *16 wks*

29 Apr 78	● **BECAUSE THE NIGHT** *Arista 181*	**5**	12 wks

19 Aug 78	PRIVILEGE (SET ME FREE) *Arista 197*		72	1 wk
2 Jun 79	FREDERICK *Arista 264*		63	3 wks

Richard Jon SMITH
South Africa, male vocalist *2 wks*

16 Jul 83	SHE'S THE MASTER OF THE GAME		
	Jive JIVE 38	63	2 wks

SMITHS *UK, male vocal/instrumental band* *35 wks*

12 Nov 83	THIS CHARMING MAN *Rough Trade RT 136*	25	12 wks
28 Jan 84	WHAT DIFFERENCE DOES IT MAKE		
	Rough Trade RT 146	12	9 wks
2 Jun 84 ●	HEAVEN KNOWS I'M MISERABLE NOW		
	Rough Trade RT 156	10	8 wks
1 Sep 84	WILLIAM, IT WAS REALLY NOTHING		
	Routh Trade RT 166	17	6 wks

SMOKE *UK, male vocal/instrumental group* *3 wks*

9 Mar 67	MY FRIEND JACK *Columbia DB 8115*	45	3 wks

SMOKIE *UK, male vocal/instrumental group* *106 wks*

19 Jul 75 ●	IF YOU THINK YOU KNOW HOW TO LOVE ME *RAK 206*	3	9 wks
4 Oct 75 ●	DON'T PLAY YOUR ROCK'N ROLL TO ME *RAK 217*	8	7 wks
31 Jan 76	SOMETHING'S BEEN MAKING ME BLUE *RAK 227*	17	8 wks
25 Sep 76	I'LL MEET YOU AT MIDNIGHT *RAK 241*	11	9 wks
4 Dec 76 ●	LIVING NEXT DOOR TO ALICE *RAK 244*	5	11 wks
19 Mar 77	LAY BACK IN THE ARMS OF SOMEONE *RAK 251*	12	9 wks
16 Jul 77 ●	IT'S YOUR LIFE *RAK 260*	5	9 wks
15 Oct 77 ●	NEEDLES AND PINS *RAK 263*	10	9 wks
28 Jan 78	FOR A FEW DOLLARS MORE *RAK 267*	17	6 wks
20 May 78 ●	OH CAROL *RAK 276*	5	13 wks
23 Sep 78	MEXICAN GIRL *RAK 283*	19	9 wks
19 Apr 80	TAKE GOOD CARE OF MY BABY *RAK 309*	34	7 wks

Group were spelt Smokey for first two hits.

SMURFS - *See Father ABRAHAM and the SMURFS*

SMURPS - *See Father ABRAPHART and the SMURPS*

SNIFF 'N' THE TEARS
UK, male vocal/instrumental group *5 wks*

23 Jun 79	DRIVER'S SEAT *Chiswick CHIS 105*	42	5 wks

Phoebe SNOW *US, female vocalist* *7 wks*

6 Jan 79	EVERY NIGHT *CBS 6842*	37	7 wks

SNOWMEN
UK, male vocal/instrumental group *12 wks*

12 Dec 81	HOKEY COKEY *Stiff ODB 1*	18	8 wks
18 Dec 82	XMAS PARTY *Solid STOP 006*	44	4 wks

Gino SOCCIO
Canada, male instrumentalist - keyboards *5 wks*

28 Apr 79	DANCER *Warner Bros. LV23/K 17357*	46	5 wks

SOFT CELL
UK, male vocal/instrumental duo *90 wks*

1 Aug 81 ★	TAINTED LOVE *Some Bizzarre BZS 2*	1	16 wks
14 Nov 81 ●	BED SITTER *Some Bizzarre BZS 6*	4	12 wks
9 Jan 82	TAINTED LOVE (re-entry) *Some Bizzarre BZS 2*	43	10 wks
6 Feb 82 ●	SAY HELLO WAVE GOODBYE *Some Bizzarre BZS 7*	3	9 wks
29 May 82	TORCH *Some Bizzarre BZS 9*	2	9 wks
24 Jul 82	TAINTED LOVE (2nd re-entry) *Some Bizzarre BZS 2*	50	4 wks
21 Aug 82 ●	WHAT *Some Bizzarre BZS 11*	3	8 wks
4 Dec 82	WHERE THE HEART IS *Some Bizzarre BZS 16*	21	7 wks
5 Mar 83	NUMBERS/BARRIERS *Some Bizzarre/Phonogram BZS 17*	25	4 wks
24 Sep 83	SOUL INSIDE *Some Bizzarre/Phonogram BZS 20*	16	5 wks
25 Feb 84	DOWN IN THE SUBWAY *Some Bizzarre/Phonogram BZS 22*	24	6 wks

Sal SOLO *UK, male vocalist* *3 wks*

15 Dec 84	SAN DAMIANO (HEART AND SOUL) *MCA MCA 930*	47†	3 wks

SONNY *US, male vocalist* *11 wks*

19 Aug 65 ●	LAUGH AT ME *Atlantic AT 4038*	9	11 wks

See also Sonny and Cher.

SONNY and CHER
US, male/female vocal duo *77 wks*

12 Aug 65 ★	I GOT YOU BABE *Atlantic AT 4035*	1	12 wks
16 Sep 65	BABY DON'T GO *Reprise R 20309*	11	9 wks
21 Oct 65	BUT YOU'RE MINE *Atlantic AT 4047*	17	8 wks
17 Feb 66	WHAT NOW MY LOVE *Atlantic AT 4069*	13	11 wks
30 Jun 66	HAVE I STAYED TOO LONG *Atlantic 584 018*	42	3 wks
8 Sep 66 ●	LITTLE MAN *Atlantic 584 040*	4	10 wks
17 Nov 66	LIVING FOR YOU *Atlantic 584 057*	44	4 wks
2 Feb 67	THE BEAT GOES ON *Atlantic 584 078*	29	8 wks
15 Jan 72 ●	ALL I EVER NEED IS YOU *MCA MU 1145*	8	12 wks

See also Sonny; Cher.

SORROWS
UK, male vocal/instrumental group *8 wks*

16 Sep 65	TAKE A HEART *Piccadilly 7N 35260*	21	8 wks

S.O.S. BAND
US, male/female vocal/instrumental group *28 wks*

19 Jul 80	TAKE YOUR TIME (DO IT RIGHT) PART 1 *Tabu TBU 8564*	51	4 wks
26 Feb 83	GROOVIN' (THAT'S WHAT WE'RE DOIN') *Tabu TBU A3120*	72	1 wk
7 Apr 84	JUST BE GOOD TO ME *Tabu/Epic A 3626*	13	11 wks
4 Aug 84	JUST THE WAY YOU LIKE IT *Tabu/Epic A 4621*	32	7 wks
13 Oct 84	WEEKEND GIRL *Tabu/Epic A 4785*	51	5 wks

David SOUL *US, male vocalist* *56 wks*

18 Dec 76 ★	DON'T GIVE UP ON US *Private Stock PVT 84*	1	16 wks
26 Mar 77 ●	GOING IN WITH MY EYES OPEN *Private Stock PVT 99*	2	8 wks
27 Aug 77 ★	SILVER LADY *Private Stock PVT 115*	1	14 wks
17 Dec 77 ●	LET'S HAVE A QUIET NIGHT IN *Private Stock PVT 130*	8	9 wks

27 May 78	**IT SURE BRINGS OUT THE LOVE IN YOUR EYES** *Private Stock PVT 137*		**12**	9 wks

Jimmy SOUL *US, male vocalist*   *2 wks*

11 Jul 63	**IF YOU WANNA BE HAPPY** *Stateside SS 178*	**39**	2 wks

SOUL BROTHERS
UK, male vocal/instrumental group   *3 wks*

22 Apr 65	**I KEEP RINGING MY BABY** *Decca F 12116*	**42**	3 wks

SOUL SONIC FORCE - *See Afrika BAMBAATA and SOUL SONIC FORCE*

SOUND 9418 *Jonathan King again*   *3 wks*

7 Feb 76	**IN THE MOOD** *UK 121*	**46**	3 wks

See also Jonathan King.

SOUNDS INCORPORATED
UK, male instrumental group   *11 wks*

23 Apr 64	**THE SPARTANS** *Columbia DB 7239*	**30**	6 wks
30 Jul 64	**SPANISH HARLEM** *Columbia DB 7321*	**35**	5 wks

SOUNDS NICE
UK, male instrumental group   *11 wks*

6 Sep 69	**LOVE AT FIRST SIGHT (JE T'AIME ... MOI NON PLUS)** *Parlophone R 5797*	**18**	11 wks

Has credit: Tim Mycroft on organ.

SOUNDS ORCHESTRAL
UK, orchestra   *18 wks*

3 Dec 64 ●	**CAST YOUR FATE TO THE WIND** *Piccadilly 7N 35206*	**5**	16 wks
8 Jul 65	**MOONGLOW** *Piccadilly 7N 35248*	**43**	2 wks

Joe SOUTH *US, male vocalist*   *11 wks*

5 Mar 69 ●	**GAMES PEOPLE PLAY** *Capitol CL 15579*	**6**	11 wks

Jeri SOUTHERN *US, female vocalist*   *3 wks*

21 Jun 57	**FIRE DOWN BELOW** *Brunswick 05665*	**22**	3 wks

SOUTHLANDERS *UK, male vocal group*   *10 wks*

22 Nov 57	**ALONE** *Decca F 10946*	**17**	10 wks

SOVEREIGN COLLECTION
UK, orchestra   *6 wks*

3 Apr 71	**MOZART 40** *Capitol CL 15676*	**27**	6 wks

Red SOVINE *US, male vocalist*   *8 wks*

13 Jun 81 ●	**TEDDY BEAR** *Starday SD 142*	**4**	8 wks

Bob B SOXX and the BLUE JEANS *US, male/female vocal group*   *2 wks*

31 Jan 63	**ZIP-A-DEE-DOO-DAH** *London HLU 9646*	**45**	2 wks

SPACE *France, male instrumental group*   *12 wks*

13 Aug 77 ●	**MAGIC FLY** *Pye International 7N 25746*	**2**	12 wks

SPACE MONKEY *US, male vocal group*   *4 wks*

8 Oct 83	**CAN'T STOP RUNNING** *Innervision A 3742*	**53**	4 wks

SPANDAU BALLET
UK, male vocal/instrumental group   *127 wks*

15 Nov 80 ●	**TO CUT A LONG STORY SHORT** *Reformation/Chrysalis CHS 2473*	**5**	11 wks
24 Jan 81	**THE FREEZE** *Reformation/Chrysalis CHS 2486*	**17**	8 wks
4 Apr 81 ●	**MUSCLEBOUND/GLOW** *Reformation/Chrysalis CHS 2509*	**10**	10 wks
18 Jul 81 ●	**CHANT NO.1 (I DON'T NEED THIS PRESSURE ON)** *Reformation/Chrysalis CHS 2528*	**3**	10 wks
14 Nov 81	**PAINT ME DOWN** *Chrysalis CHS 2560*	**30**	5 wks
30 Jan 82	**SHE LOVED LIKE DIAMOND** *Chrysalis CHS 2585*	**49**	4 wks
10 Apr 82 ●	**INSTINCTION** *Chrysalis CHS 2602*	**10**	11 wks
2 Oct 82 ●	**LIFELINE** *Chrysalis CHS 2642*	**7**	9 wks
12 Feb 83	**COMMUNICATION** *Chrysalis CHS 2662*	**12**	10 wks
23 Apr 83 ★	**TRUE** *Reformation/Chrysalis SPAN 1*	**1**	12 wks
13 Aug 83 ●	**GOLD** *Reformation/Chrysalis SPAN 2*	**2**	9 wks
9 Jun 84 ●	**ONLY WHEN YOU LEAVE** *Reformation/Chrysalis SPAN 3*	**3**	9 wks
18 Aug 84	**ONLY WHEN YOU LEAVE** (re-entry) *Reformation/Chrysalis SPAN 3*	**74**	1 wk
25 Aug 84 ●	**I'LL FLY FOR YOU** *Reformation/Chrysalis SPAN 4*	**9**	9 wks
20 Oct 84	**HIGHLY STRUNG** *Reformation/Chrysalis SPAN 5*	**15**	5 wks
8 Dec 84	**ROUND AND ROUND** *Reformation/Chrysalis SPAN 6*	**19†**	4 wks

SPARKS
US/UK, male vocal/instrumental group   *70 wks*

4 May 74 ●	**THIS TOWN AIN'T BIG ENOUGH FOR BOTH OF US** *Island WIP 6193*	**2**	10 wks
20 Jul 74 ●	**AMATEUR HOUR** *Island WIP 6203*	**7**	9 wks
19 Oct 74	**NEVER TURN YOUR BACK ON MOTHER EARTH** *Island WIP 6211*	**13**	7 wks
18 Jan 75	**SOMETHING FOR THE GIRL WITH EVERYTHING** *Island WIP 6221*	**17**	7 wks
19 Jul 75	**GET IN THE SWING** *Island WIP 6236*	**27**	7 wks
4 Oct 75	**LOOKS LOOKS LOOKS** *Island WIP 6249*	**26**	4 wks
21 Apr 79	**THE NUMBER ONE SONG IN HEAVEN** *Virgin VS 244*	**14**	12 wks
21 Jul 79 ●	**BEAT THE CLOCK** *Virgin VS 270*	**10**	9 wks
27 Oct 79	**TRYOUTS FOR THE HUMAN RACE** *Virgin VS 289*	**45**	5 wks

SPEAR OF DESTINY
UK, male vocal/instrumental group   *10 wks*

21 May 83	**THE WHEEL** *Epic A 3372*	**59**	5 wks
21 Jan 84	**PRISONER OF LOVE** *Burning Rome/CBS A 4068*	**59**	3 wks
14 Apr 84	**LIBERATOR** *Burning Rome/Epic A 4310*	**67**	2 wks

Billie Jo SPEARS   US, female vocalist   40 wks

12 Jul 75 ● BLANKET ON THE GROUND		
United Artists UP 35805	6	13 wks
17 Jul 76 ● WHAT I'VE GOT IN MIND		
United Artists UP 36118	4	13 wks
11 Dec 76 SING ME AN OLD FASHIONED SONG		
United Artists UP 36179	34	9 wks
21 Jul 79 I WILL SURVIVE United Artists UP 601	47	5 wks

SPECIAL A.K.A.
UK, male/female vocal/instrumental group   17 wks

3 Sep 83 RACIST FRIEND 2 Tone CBS TT 25	60	3 wks
17 Mar 84 ● NELSON MANDELA 2 Tone/Chrysalis TT 26 ...	9	10 wks
8 Sep 84 WHAT I LIKE MOST ABOUT YOU IS YOUR		
GIRLFRIEND 2 Tone/Chrysalis TT 27	51	4 wks

See also the Specials. After the Specials split up in 1981, certain members of the group stayed together to form the Specials A.K.A.

SPECIALS
UK, male vocal/instrumental group   78 wks

28 Jul 79 ● GANGSTERS 2 Tone TT 1	6	12 wks
27 Oct 79 ● A MESSAGE TO YOU RUDY/NITE CLUB		
2 Tone CHS TT 5	10	14 wks
26 Jan 80 ★ TOO MUCH TOO YOUNG (EP)		
2 Tone CHS TT 7	1	10 wks
24 May 80 ● RAT RACE/RUDE BUOYS OUTA JAIL		
2 Tone CHS TT 11	5	9 wks
20 Sep 80 ● STEREOTYPE/INTERNATIONAL JET SET		
2 Tone CHS TT 13	6	8 wks
13 Dec 80 ● DO NOTHING/MAGGIE'S FARM		
2 Tone CHS TT 16	4	11 wks
20 Jun 81 ★ GHOST TOWN 2 Tone CHS TT 17	1	14 wks

Gangsters credited to the Specials A.K.A. Second hit billed as Specials (featuring Rico+). The number one EP was actually entitled The Special AKA Live! but Too Much Too Young was the main track. The full track listing of the EP is: Too Much Too Young/Guns of Navarone/Long Shot Kick De Bucket/Liquidator/Skinhead Moonstomp. Maggie's Farm only listed with Do Nothing from 10 Jan 81. See also Special AKA

Chris SPEDDING
UK, male vocalist/instrumentalist - guitar   8 wks

23 Aug 75 MOTOR BIKING RAK 210	14	8 wks

Johnny SPENCE   UK, orchestra   15 wks

1 Mar 62 THEME FROM DR. KILDARE Parlophone R 4872	15	15 wks

Don SPENCER   UK, male vocalist   12 wks

21 Mar 63 FIREBALL HMV POP, 1087	32	11 wks
13 Jun 63 FIREBALL (re-entry) HMV POP 1087	49	1 wk

SPIDER   UK, male vocal/instrumental group   5 wks

5 Mar 83 WHY D'YA LIE TO ME RCA 313	65	2 wks
10 Mar 84 HERE WE GO ROCK 'N' ROLL		
A & M AM 180	57	3 wks

SPINNERS   - See DETROIT SPINNERS

SPLINTER   UK, male vocal/instrumental duo   10 wks

2 Nov 74 COSTAFINE TOWN Dark Horse AMS 7135	17	10 wks

SPLIT ENZ
New Zealand/UK, male vocal/instrumental group   15 wks

16 Aug 80 I GOT YOU A & M AMS 7546	12	11 wks
23 May 81 HISTORY NEVER REPEATS A & M AMS 8128	63	4 wks

SPLODGENESSABOUNDS
UK, male vocal/instrumental group   17 wks

14 Jun 80 ● SIMON TEMPLAR/TWO PINTS OF LAGER AND		
A PACKET OF CRISPS PLEASE		
Deram BUM 1	7	8 wks
6 Sep 80 TWO LITTLE BOYS/HORSE Deram ROLF 1	26	7 wks
13 Jun 81 COWPUNK MEDLUM Deram BUM 3	69	2 wks

SPOTNICKS
Sweden, male instrumental group   37 wks

14 Jun 62 ORANGE BLOSSOM SPECIAL Oriole CB 1724	29	10 wks
6 Sep 62 ROCKET MAN Oriole CB 1755	38	9 wks
31 Jan 63 HAVA NAGILA Oriole CB 1790	13	12 wks
25 Apr 63 JUST LISTEN TO MY HEART Oriole CB 1818	36	6 wks

Dusty SPRINGFIELD
UK, female vocalist   172 wks

21 Nov 63 ● I ONLY WANT TO BE WITH YOU		
Philips BF 1292	4	18 wks
20 Feb 64 STAY AWHILE Philips BF 1311	13	10 wks
2 Jul 64 ● I JUST DON'T KNOW WHAT TO DO WITH		
MYSELF Philips BF 1348	3	12 wks
22 Oct 64 ● LOSING YOU Philips BF 1369	9	13 wks
18 Feb 65 YOUR HURTIN' KIND OF LOVE		
Philips BF 1396	37	4 wks
1 Jul 65 ● IN THE MIDDLE OF NOWHERE		
Philips BF 1418	8	10 wks
16 Sep 65 ● SOME OF YOUR LOVIN' Philips BF 1430	8	12 wks
27 Jan 66 LITTLE BY LITTLE Philips BF 1466	17	9 wks
31 Mar 66 ★ YOU DON'T HAVE TO SAY YOU LOVE ME		
Philips BF 1482	1	13 wks
7 Jul 66 ● GOING BACK Philips BF 1502	10	10 wks
15 Sep 66 ● ALL I SEE IS YOU Philips BF 1510	9	12 wks
23 Feb 67 I'LL TRY ANYTHING Philips BF 1553	13	9 wks
25 May 67 GIVE ME TIME Philips BF 1577	24	6 wks
10 Jul 68 ● I CLOSE MY EYES AND COUNT TO TEN		
Philips BF 1682	4	12 wks
4 Dec 68 ● SON OF A PREACHER MAN Philips BF 1730 ..	9	9 wks
20 Sep 69 AM I THE SAME GIRL Philips BF 1811	43	3 wks
18 Oct 69 AM I THE SAME GIRL (re-entry) Philips BF 1811	46	1 wk
19 Sep 70 HOW CAN I BE SURE Philips 6006 045	36	4 wks
20 Oct 79 BABY BLUE Mercury DUSTY 4	61	5 wks

See also Springfields.

Rick SPRINGFIELD   Australia, male vocalist   13 wks

14 Jan 84 HUMAN TOUCH RCA RICK 1	23	7 wks
24 Mar 84 JESSIE'S GIRL RCA RICK 2	43	6 wks

SPRINGFIELDS
UK, male/female vocal/instrumental group   66 wks

31 Aug 61 BREAKAWAY Philips BF 1168	31	8 wks
16 Nov 61 BAMBINO Philips BF 1178	16	11 wks
13 Dec 62 ● ISLAND OF DREAMS Philips 326557 BF	5	26 wks
28 Mar 63 ● SAY I WON'T BE THERE Philips 326577 BF ...	5	15 wks
25 Jul 63 COME ON HOME Philips BF 1263	31	6 wks

See also Dusty Springfield.

SECOND IMAGE (left) Why are they all on second base?

SHAM 69 (right) Sham's Jimmy Pursey: spokesman for a punk generation 1978–1980.

SHAKATAK (centre left) Nightbirds on the boards.

SHALAMAR (bottom left) 'A Night To Remember' an 'Uptown Festival' with the three 'friends' snapped backstage at London's Dominion Theatre.

ROCKY SHARPE AND THE REPLAYS (bottom right) Their chart debut was a 1961 American hit for the Edsels, their fourth hit a '63 success Stateside for the Randells and the fifth Ernie Maresca's 1962 USA smash.

Bruce SPRINGSTEEN
US, male vocalist   22 wks

22 Nov 80	HUNGRY HEART	CBS 9309	44	4 wks
13 Jun 81	THE RIVER	CBS A 1179	35	6 wks
26 May 84	DANCING IN THE DARK	CBS A 4436	28	7 wks
6 Oct 84	COVER ME	CBS 4662	38	5 wks

SPRINGWATER UK, male instrumentalist,
Phil Cordell under a false group name   12 wks

| 23 Oct 71 | ● I WILL RETURN | Polydor 2058 141 | 5 | 12 wks |

SPYRO GYRA
US, male instrumental group   10 wks

| 21 Jul 79 | MORNING DANCE | Infinity INF 111 | 17 | 10 wks |

SQUADRONAIRES - See Joan REGAN

SQUEEZE
UK, male vocal/instrumental group   92 wks

8 Apr 78	TAKE ME I'M YOURS	A & M AMS 7335	19	9 wks
10 Jun 78	BANG BANG	A & M AMS 7360	49	5 wks
18 Nov 78	GOODBYE GIRL	A & M AMS 7398	63	2 wks
24 Mar 79	● COOL FOR CATS	A & M AMS 7426	2	11 wks
2 Jun 79	● UP THE JUNCTION	A & M AMS 7444	2	11 wks
8 Sep 79	SLAP AND TICKLE	A & M AMS 7466	24	8 wks
1 Mar 80	ANOTHER NAIL IN MY HEART A & M AMS 7507	17	9 wks
10 May 80	PULLING MUSSELS (FROM THE SHELL) A & M AMS 7523	44	6 wks
16 May 81	IS THAT LOVE	A & M AMS 8129	35	8 wks
25 Jul 81	TEMPTED	A & M AMS 8147	41	5 wks
10 Oct 81	● LABELLED WITH LOVE	A & M AMS 8166	4	10 wks
24 Apr 82	BLACK COFFEE IN BED	A & M AMS 8219	51	4 wks
23 Oct 82	ANNIE GET YOUR GUN	A & M AMS 8259	43	4 wks

Billy SQUIER US, male vocalist   3 wks

| 3 Oct 81 | THE STROKE | Capitol CL 214 | 52 | 3 wks |

Dorothy SQUIRES UK, female vocalist   46 wks

5 Jun 53	I'M WALKING BEHIND YOU	Polygon P 1068	12	1 wk
20 Sep 69	FOR ONCE IN MY LIFE	President PT 267	24	10 wks
20 Dec 69	FOR ONCE IN MY LIFE (re-entry) President PT 267	48	1 wk
21 Feb 70	TILL	President PT 281	25	10 wks
9 May 70	TILL (re-entry) President PT 281	48	1 wk
8 Aug 70	MY WAY	President PT 305	25	5 wks
19 Sep 70	MY WAY (re-entry) President PT 305	34	8 wks
28 Nov 70	MY WAY (2nd re-entry) President PT 305	25	10 wks

See also Dorothy Squires and Russ Conway.

Dorothy SQUIRES and Russ CONWAY
UK, female vocalist, male instrumentalist - piano   10 wks

| 24 Aug 61 | SAY IT WITH FLOWERS | Columbia DB 4665 | 23 | 10 wks |

See also Dorothy Squires; Russ Conway.

Jim STAFFORD US, male vocalist   16 wks

| 27 Apr 74 | SPIDERS & SNAKES | MGM 2006 374 | 14 | 8 wks |
| 6 Jul 74 | MY GIRL BILL | MGM 2006 423 | 20 | 8 wks |

Jo STAFFORD US, female vocalist   28 wks

14 Nov 52	★ YOU BELONG TO ME	Columbia DB 3152	1	19 wks
19 Dec 52	JAMBALAYA	Columbia DB 3169	11	2 wks
7 May 54	● MAKE LOVE TO ME	Philips PB 233	8	1 wk
9 Dec 55	SUDDENLY THERE'S A VALLEY Philips PB 509	12	5 wks
3 Feb 56	SUDDENLY THERE'S A VALLEY (re-entry) Philips PB 509	19	1 wk

Terry STAFFORD US, male vocalist   9 wks

| 7 May 64 | SUSPICION | London HLU 9871 | 31 | 9 wks |

STAIFFI and his MUSTAFAS
France, male vocal/instrumental group   1 wk

| 28 Jul 60 | MUSTAFA | Pye International 7N 25057 | 43 | 1 wk |

Frank STALLONE US, male vocalist   2 wks

| 22 Oct 83 | FAR FROM OVER | RSO 95 | 68 | 2 wks |

STAMFORD BRIDGE
UK, male vocal group   1 wk

| 16 May 70 | CHELSEA | Penny Farthing PEN 715 | 47 | 1 wk |

STAPLE SINGERS
US, male/female vocal group   14 wks

| 10 Jun 72 | I'LL TAKE YOU THERE | Stax 2025 110 | 30 | 8 wks |
| 8 Jun 74 | IF YOU'RE READY (COME GO WITH ME) Stax 2025 224 | 34 | 6 wks |

Cyril STAPLETON UK, orchestra   27 wks

27 May 55	ELEPHANT TANGO	Decca F 10488	20	2 wks
1 Jul 55	ELEPHANT TANGO (re-entry) Decca F 10488	20	1 wk
22 Jul 55	ELEPHANT TANGO (2nd re-entry) Decca F 10488	19	1 wk
23 Sep 55	● BLUE STAR	Decca F 10559	2	12 wks
6 Apr 56	THE ITALIAN THEME	Decca F 10703	18	2 wks
1 Jun 56	THE HAPPY WHISTLER	Decca F 10735	22	4 wks
19 Jul 57	FORGOTTEN DREAMS	Decca F 10912	27	5 wks

STARDUST
Sweden, male/female vocal/instrumental group   3 wks

| 8 Oct 77 | ARIANA | Satril SAT 120 | 42 | 3 wks |

Alvin STARDUST UK, male vocalist   114 wks

3 Nov 73	● MY COO-CA-CHOO	Magnet MAG 1	2	21 wks
16 Feb 74	★ JEALOUS MIND	Magnet MAG 5	1	11 wks
4 May 74	● RED DRESS	Magnet MAG 8	7	8 wks
31 Aug 74	● YOU YOU YOU	Magnet MAG 13	6	10 wks
30 Nov 74	TELL ME WHY	Magnet MAG 19	16	8 wks
1 Feb 75	GOOD LOVE CAN NEVER DIE Magnet MAG 21	11	9 wks

12 Jul 75	SWEET CHEATIN' RITA *Magnet MAG 32*	37	4 wks
5 Sep 81 ●	PRETEND *Stiff BUY 124*	4	10 wks
21 Nov 81	A WONDERFUL TIME UP THERE *Stiff BUY 132*	56	8 wks
5 May 84 ●	I FEEL LIKE BUDDY HOLLY *Chrysalis CHS 2784*	7	11 wks
4 Aug 84	I FEEL LIKE BUDDY HOLLY (re-entry) *Chrysalis CHS 2784*	75	1 wk
27 Oct 84 ●	I WON'T RUN AWAY *Chrysalis CHS 2829*	7†	10 wks
15 Dec 84	SO NEAR TO CHRISTMAS *Chrysalis CHS 2835*	29†	3 wks

Alvin started his career as Shane Fenton. See also Shane Fenton and the Fentones.

STARGARD   US, *female vocal group*   14 wks

28 Jan 78	THEME FROM 'WHICH WAY IS UP' *MCA 346*	19	7 wks
15 Apr 78	LOVE IS SO EASY *MCA 354*	45	1 wk
9 Sep 78	WHAT YOU WAITING FOR *MCA 382*	39	6 wks

STARGAZERS
UK, *male/female vocal group*   53 wks

13 Feb 53	BROKEN WINGS *Decca F 10047*	11	1 wk
27 Feb 53 ★	BROKEN WINGS (re-entry) *Decca F 10047*	1	11 wks
19 Feb 54 ★	I SEE THE MOON *Decca F 10213*	1	15 wks
9 Apr 54	HAPPY WANDERER *Decca F 10259*	12	1 wk
4 Mar 55	SOMEBODY *Decca F 10437*	20	1 wk
3 Jun 55	CRAZY OTTO RAG *Decca F 10523*	18	3 wks
9 Sep 55 ●	CLOSE THE DOOR *Decca F 10594*	6	9 wks
11 Nov 55 ●	TWENTY TINY FINGERS *Decca F 10626*	4	11 wks
22 Jun 56	HOT DIGGITY *Decca F 10731*	28	1 wk

STARGAZERS
UK, *male vocal/instrumental group*   3 wks

6 Feb 82	GROOVE BABY GROOVE (EP) *Epic EPC A 1924*	56	3 wks

Tracks on Groove Baby Groove EP: Groove Baby Groove/ Jump Around/La Rock 'N' Roll (Quelques Uns A La Lune)/Red Light Green Light.

STARJETS
UK, *male vocal/instrumental group*   5 wks

8 Sep 79	WAR STORIES *Epic EPC 7770*	51	5 wks

STARLAND VOCAL BAND
US, *male/female vocal group*   10 wks

7 Aug 76	AFTERNOON DELIGHT *RCA 2716*	18	10 wks

STARLITERS - *See Joey DEE and the STARLITERS*

Edwin STARR   US, *male vocalist*   64 wks

12 May 66	STOP HER ON SIGHT (SOS) *Polydor BM 56 702*	35	8 wks
18 Aug 66	HEADLINE NEWS *Polydor 56 717*	39	3 wks
11 Dec 68	STOP HER ON SIGHT (SOS)/HEADLINE NEWS (re-issue) *Polydor 56 153*	11	11 wks
13 Sep 69	25 MILES *Tamla Motown TMG 672*	36	6 wks
24 Oct 70 ●	WAR *Tamla Motown TMG 754*	3	12 wks
20 Feb 71	STOP THE WAR NOW *Tamla Motown TMG 764*	33	1 wk
27 Jan 79 ●	CONTACT *20th Century BTC 2396*	6	12 wks
26 May 79 ●	H.A.P.P.Y. RADIO *RCA TC 2408*	9	11 wks

Headline News *not listed with SOS from 22 Jan 69 to 19 Feb 69.*

Freddie STARR   UK, *male vocalist*   14 wks

23 Feb 74 ●	IT'S YOU *Tiffany 6121 501*	9	10 wks

---

20 Dec 75	WHITE CHRISTMAS *Thunderbird THE 102*	41	4 wks

Kay STARR   US, *female vocalist*   58 wks

5 Dec 52 ★	COMES A-LONG A-LOVE *Capitol CL 13808* ...	1	16 wks
24 Apr 53 ●	SIDE BY SIDE *Capitol CL 13876*	7	4 wks
19 Mar 54 ●	CHANGING PARTNERS *Capitol CL 14050*	4	14 wks
15 Oct 54	AM I A TOY OR A TREASURE *Capitol CL 14151*	17	3 wks
12 Nov 54	AM I A TOY OR A TREASURE (re-entry) *Capitol CL 14151*	20	1 wk
17 Feb 56 ★	ROCK AND ROLL WALTZ *HMV POP 168* ...	1	20 wks

Ringo STARR   UK, *male vocalist*   55 wks

17 Apr 71 ●	IT DON'T COME EASY *Apple R 5898*	4	11 wks
1 Apr 72 ●	BACK OFF BOOGALOO *Apple R 5944*	2	10 wks
27 Oct 73 ●	PHOTOGRAPH *Apple R 5992*	8	13 wks
23 Feb 74 ●	YOU'RE SIXTEEN *Apple R 5995*	4	10 wks
30 Nov 74	ONLY YOU *Apple R 6000*	28	11 wks

STARSHIP TROOPERS - *See Sarah BRIGHTMAN*

STARSOUND   Holland, *producer Jaap*
Eggermont *with male/female session singers*   37 wks

18 Apr 81 ●	STARS ON 45 *CBS 1102*	2	14 wks
4 Jul 81 ●	STARS ON 45 VOL.2 *CBS A 1407*	2	10 wks
19 Sep 81	STARS ON 45 VOL.3 *CBS A 1521*	17	6 wks
27 Feb 82	STARS ON STEVIE *CBS A 2041*	14	7 wks

STARTRAX   UK, *male/female session group*   8 wks

1 Aug 81	STARTRAX CLUB DISCO *Picksy KSY 1001* ...	18	8 wks

STARTURN ON 45 (PINTS)
UK, *male vocal group*   4 wks

24 Oct 81	STARTURN ON 45 (PINTS) *V Tone V TONE 003*	45	4 wks

STATLER BROTHERS
US, *male vocal group*   4 wks

24 Feb 66	FLOWERS ON THE WALL *CBS 201976*	38	4 wks

Candi STATON   US, *female vocalist*   42 wks

29 May 76 ●	YOUNG HEARTS RUN FREE *Warner Bros. K 16730*	2	13 wks
18 Sep 76	DESTINY *Warner Bros. K 16806*	41	3 wks
23 Jul 77 ●	NIGHTS ON BROADWAY *Warner Bros. K 16972*	6	12 wks
3 Jun 78	HONEST I DO LOVE YOU *Warner Bros. K 17164*	48	5 wks
24 Apr 82	SUSPICIOUS MINDS *Sugarhill SH 112*	31	9 wks

STATUS IV   US, *male vocal group*   3 wks

9 Jul 83	YOU AIN'T REALLY DOWN *TMT TMT 4* ...	56	3 wks

STATUS QUO
UK, *male vocal/instrumental group*   300 wks

24 Jan 68 ●	PICTURES OF MATCHSTICK MEN *Pye 7N 17449*	7	12 wks

21 Aug 68	● ICE IN THE SUN *Pye 7N 17581*	**8**	12 wks
28 May 69	ARE YOU GROWING TIRED OF MY LOVE		
	Pye 7N 17728	**46**	2 wks
18 Jun 69	ARE YOU GROWING TIRED OF MY LOVE		
	(re-entry) *Pye 7N 17728*	**50**	1 wk
2 May 70	● DOWN THE DUSTPIPE *Pye 7N 17907*	**12**	17 wks
7 Nov 70	IN MY CHAIR *Pye 7N 17998*	**21**	14 wks
13 Jan 73	● PAPER PLANE *Vertigo 6059 071*	**8**	11 wks
14 Apr 73	MEAN GIRL *Pye 7N 45229*	**20**	11 wks
8 Sep 73	● CAROLINE *Vertigo 6059 085*	**5**	13 wks
4 May 74	● BREAK THE RULES *Vertigo 6059 101*	**8**	8 wks
7 Dec 74	★ DOWN DOWN *Vertigo 6059 114*	**1**	11 wks
17 May 75	● ROLL OVER LAY DOWN *Vertigo QUO 13*	**9**	8 wks
14 Feb 76	● RAIN *Vertigo 6059 133*	**7**	7 wks
10 Jul 76	MYSTERY SONG *Vertigo 6059 146*	**11**	9 wks
11 Dec 76	● WILD SIDE OF LIFE *Vertigo 6059 153*	**9**	9 wks
8 Oct 77	● ROCKIN' ALL OVER THE WORLD		
	Vertigo 6059 184	**3**	16 wks
2 Sep 78	● AGAIN AND AGAIN *Vertigo 6059 1*	**13**	9 wks
25 Nov 78	ACCIDENT PRONE *Vertigo QUO 2*	**36**	8 wks
22 Sep 79	● WHATEVER YOU WANT *Vertigo 6059 242*	**4**	9 wks
24 Nov 79	LIVING ON AN ISLAND *Vertigo 6059 248*	**16**	10 wks
11 Oct 80	● WHAT YOU'RE PROPOSING *Vertigo QUO 3* ...	**2**	11 wks
6 Dec 80	LIES /DON'T DRIVE MY CAR *Vertigo QUO 4*	**11**	10 wks
28 Feb 81	● SOMETHING 'BOUT YOU BABY I LIKE		
	Vertigo QUO 5	**9**	7 wks
28 Nov 81	● ROCK'N'ROLL *Vertigo QUO 6*	**8**	11 wks
27 Mar 82	● DEAR JOHN *Vertigo/Phonogram QUO 7*	**10**	8 wks
12 Jun 82	SHE DONT FOOL ME *Vertigo/Phonogram QUO 8*	**36**	5 wks
30 Oct 82	CAROLINE (LIVE AT THE N.E.C.)		
	Vertigo/Phonogram QUO 10	**13**	7 wks
10 Sep 83	● OL' RAG BLUES *Vertigo/Phonogram QUO 11*	**9**	8 wks
5 Nov 83	A MESS OF THE BLUES		
	Vertigo/Phonogram QUO 12	**15**	6 wks
10 Dec 83	● MARGUERITA TIME *Vertigo/Phonogram QUO 14*	**3**	11 wks
19 May 84	GOING DOWN TOWN TONIGHT		
	Vertigo/Phonogram QUO 15	**20**	6 wks
27 Oct 84	● THE WANDERER *Vertigo/Phonogram QUO 16* ...	**7†**	10 wks

Don't Drive My Car listed from 20 Dec 80 only.

STEALER'S WHEEL

UK, male vocal/instrumental group **22 wks**

26 May 73	● STUCK IN THE MIDDLE WITH YOU		
	A & M AMS 7036	**8**	10 wks
1 Sep 73	EVERYTHING'L TURN OUT FINE		
	A & M AMS 7079	**33**	6 wks
26 Jan 74	STAR *A & M AMS 7094*	**25**	6 wks

STEAM *US, male vocal/instrumental group* **14 wks**

31 Jan 70	● NA NA HEY HEY KISS HIM GOODBYE		
	Fontana TF 1058	**9**	14 wks

Anthony STEEL and the RADIO REVELLERS

UK, male vocalist/male instrumental group **6 wks**

10 Sep 54	WEST OF ZANZIBAR *Polygon P 1114*	**11**	6 wks

STEEL PULSE

UK, male vocal/instrumental group **12 wks**

1 Apr 78	KU KLUX KLAN *Island WIP 6428*	**41**	4 wks
8 Jul 78	PRODIGAL SON *Island WIP 6449*	**35**	6 wks
23 Jun 79	SOUND SYSTEM *Island WIP 6490*	**71**	2 wks

Tommy STEELE *UK, male vocalist* **145 wks**

26 Oct 56	ROCK WITH THE CAVEMAN *Decca F 10795* ..	**13**	4 wks
30 Nov 56	ROCK WITH THE CAVEMAN (re-entry)		
	Decca F 10795	**23**	1 wk
14 Dec 56	★ SINGING THE BLUES *Decca F 10819*	**1**	13 wks
15 Feb 57	KNEE DEEP IN THE BLUES *Decca F 10849*	**15**	9 wks
19 Apr 57	SINGING THE BLUES (re-entry) *Decca F 10819*	**24**	1 wk
3 May 57	BUTTERFINGERS *Decca F 10877*	**25**	1 wk
17 May 57	● BUTTERFINGERS (re-entry) *Decca F 10877*	**8**	17 wks
17 May 57	SINGING THE BLUES (2nd re-entry)		
	Decca F 10849	**29**	1 wk
16 Aug 57	WATER WATER/HANDFUL OF SONGS		
	Decca F 10923	**5**	16 wks
30 Aug 57	SHIRALEE *Decca F 10896*	**11**	4 wks
22 Nov 57	HEY YOU *Decca F 10941*	**28**	1 wk
13 Dec 57	WATER WATER/HANDFUL OF SONGS		
	(re-entry) *Decca F 10923*	**28**	1 wk
7 Mar 58	● NAIROBI *Decca F 10991*	**3**	11 wks
25 Apr 58	HAPPY GUITAR *Decca F 10976*	**20**	5 wks
18 Jul 58	THE ONLY MAN ON THE ISLAND		
	Decca F 11041	**16**	8 wks
14 Nov 58	● COME ON LET'S GO *Decca F 11072*	**10**	13 wks
14 Aug 59	TALLAHASSEE LASSIE *Decca F 11152*	**16**	4 wks
28 Aug 59	GIVE GIVE GIVE *Decca F 11152*	**28**	2 wks
25 Sep 59	TALLAHASSEE LASSIE (re-entry) *Decca F 11152*	**25**	1 wk
4 Dec 59	● LITTLE WHITE BULL *Decca F 11177*	**6**	12 wks
10 Mar 60	LITTLE WHITE BULL (re-entry) *Decca F 11177*	**30**	5 wks
23 Jun 60	● WHAT A MOUTH *Decca F 11245*	**5**	11 wks
29 Dec 60	MUST BE SANTA *Decca F 11299*	**40**	1 wk
17 Aug 61	WRITING ON THE WALL *Decca F 11372*	**30**	5 wks

Handful Of Songs listed together with Water Water from week of 23 Aug 57. See also Various Artists - All Star Hit Parade No. 2.

STEELEYE SPAN

UK, male/female vocal/instrumental group **18 wks**

8 Dec 73	GAUDETE *Chrysalis CHS 2007*	**14**	9 wks
15 Nov 75	● ALL AROUND MY HAT *Chrysalis CHS 2078* ...	**5**	9 wks

STEELY DAN

US, male vocal/instrumental group **21 wks**

30 Aug 75	DO IT AGAIN *ABC 4075*	**39**	4 wks
11 Dec 76	HAITIAN DIVORCE *ABC 4152*	**17**	9 wks
29 Jul 78	FM (NO STATIC AT ALL) *MCA 374*	**49**	4 wks
2 Sep 78	FM (NO STATIC AT ALL) (re-entry) *MCA 374*	**75**	1 wk
10 Mar 79	RIKKI DON'T LOSE THAT NUMBER		
	ABC 4241	**58**	3 wks

Jim STEINMAN *US, male vocalist* **9 wks**

4 Jul 81	ROCK'N'ROLL DREAMS COME THROUGH		
	Epic/Cleveland EPC A 1236	**52**	7 wks
23 Jun 84	TONIGHT IS WHAT IT MEANS TO BE YOUNG		
	MCA MCA 889	**67**	2 wks

Second hit has credit: Jim Steinman and Fire Inc.

Mike STEIPHENSON - *See BURUNDI STEIPHENSON BLACK*

Doreen STEPHENS - *See Billy COTTON and his BAND*

STEPPENWOLF

US, male vocal/instrumental group **9 wks**

11 Jun 69	BORN TO BE WILD *Stateside SS 8017*	**30**	7 wks
9 Aug 69	BORN TO BE WILD (re-entry) *Stateside SS 8017*	**50**	2 wks

STEVE and EYDIE
US, male/female vocal duo   *13 wks*

22 Aug 63 ● **I WANT TO STAY HERE**   *CBS AAG 163* .....   **3**   13 wks

See also Steve Lawrence; Eydie Gorme.

April STEVENS - *See Nino TEMPO and April STEVENS*

Cat STEVENS   *UK, male vocalist*   *96 wks*

20 Oct 66		**I LOVE MY DOG** *Deram DM 102*	**28**	7 wks
12 Jan 67	●	**MATTHEW AND SON** *Deram DM 110*	**2**	10 wks
30 Mar 67	●	**I'M GONNA GET ME A GUN** *Deram DM 118* ..	**6**	10 wks
2 Aug 67		**A BAD NIGHT** *Deram DM 140*	**20**	8 wks
20 Dec 67		**KITTY** *Deram DM 156*	**47**	1 wk
27 Jun 70	●	**LADY D'ARBANVILLE** *Island WIP 6086*	**8**	13 wks
28 Aug 71		**MOON SHADOW** *Island WIP 6092*	**22**	11 wks
1 Jan 72	●	**MORNING HAS BROKEN** *Island WIP 6121*	**9**	13 wks
9 Dec 72		**CAN'T KEEP IT IN** *Island WIP 6152*	**13**	12 wks
24 Aug 74		**ANOTHER SATURDAY NIGHT** *Island WIP 6206*	**19**	8 wks
2 Jul 77		**(REMEMBER THE DAYS OF THE) OLD SCHOOL YARD** *Island WIP 6387*	**44**	3 wks

Connie STEVENS   *US, female vocalist*   *12 wks*

5 May 60	●	**SIXTEEN REASONS** *Warner Bros. WB 3*	**9**	11 wks
4 Aug 60		**SIXTEEN REASONS** (re-entry) *Warner Bros. WB 3*	**45**	1 wk

See also Edward Byrnes and Connie Stevens.

Ray STEVENS   *US, male vocalist*   *64 wks*

16 May 70	●	**EVERYTHING IS BEAUTIFUL** *CBS 4953*	**6**	16 wks
13 Mar 71	●	**BRIDGET THE MIDGET (THE QUEEN OF THE BLUES)** *CBS 7070*	**2**	14 wks
25 Mar 72		**TURN YOUR RADIO ON** *CBS 7634*	**33**	4 wks
25 May 74	★	**THE STREAK** *Janus 6146 201*	**1**	12 wks
21 Jun 75	●	**MISTY** *Janus 6146 204*	**2**	10 wks
27 Sep 75		**INDIAN LOVE CALL** *Janus 6146 205*	**34**	4 wks
5 Mar 77		**IN THE MOOD** *Warner Bros. K 16875*	**31**	4 wks

In the Mood does not feature Ray Stevens as a conventional vocalist, but as a group of chickens. In the US, he billed himself on this record as Henhouse Five Plus Two.

Ricky STEVENS   *UK, male vocalist*   *7 wks*

14 Dec 61   **I CRIED FOR YOU**   *Columbia DB 4739* ....   **34**   7 wks

Shakin' STEVENS   *UK, male vocalist*   *153 wks*

16 Feb 80		**HOT DOG** *Epic EPC 8090*	**24**	9 wks
16 Aug 80		**MARIE MARIE** *Epic EPC 8725*	**19**	10 wks
28 Feb 81	★	**THIS OLE HOUSE** *Epic EPC 9555*	**1**	17 wks
2 May 81	●	**YOU DRIVE ME CRAZY** *Epic A1165*	**2**	12 wks
25 Jul 81	★	**GREEN DOOR** *Epic A1354*	**1**	12 wks
10 Oct 81	●	**IT'S RAINING** *Epic A1643*	**10**	9 wks
16 Jan 82	★	**OH JULIE** *Epic EPC A1742*	**1**	12 wks
24 Apr 82	●	**SHIRLEY** *Epic EPC A2087*	**6**	6 wks
21 Aug 82		**GIVE ME YOUR HEART TONIGHT** *Epic EPC A2656*	**11**	10 wks
16 Oct 82	●	**I'LL BE SATISFIED** *Epic EPC A2846*	**10**	8 wks
11 Dec 82	●	**THE SHAKIN' STEVENS EP** *Epic SHAKY 1* ...	**2**	7 wks
23 Jul 83		**IT'S LATE** *Epic A 3565*	**11**	7 wks
5 Nov 83	●	**CRY JUST A LITTLE BIT** *Epic A 3774*	**3**	12 wks
24 Mar 84	●	**A LOVE WORTH WAITING FOR** *Epic A 4291*	**2**	10 wks
15 Sep 84	●	**A LETTER TO YOU** *Epic A 4677*	**10**	8 wks
24 Nov 84	●	**TEARDROPS** *Epic A 4882*	**5†**	6 wks

Tracks on The Shakin' Stevens EP: Blue Christmas/ Que Sera Sera/Josephine/Lawdy Miss Clawdy. See also Shaky and Bonnie.

STEVENSON'S ROCKET   *UK, male vocal/instrumental group*   *5 wks*

29 Nov 75		**ALRIGHT BABY** *Magnet MAG 47*	**37**	2 wks
20 Dec 75		**ALRIGHT BABY** (re-entry) *Magnet MAG 47* ...	**45**	3 wks

Al STEWART   *UK, male vocalist*   *6 wks*

29 Jan 77   **YEAR OF THE CAT**   *RCA 2771* ....   **31**   6 wks

Amii STEWART   *US, female vocalist*   *31 wks*

7 Apr 79	●	**KNOCK ON WOOD** *Atlantic/Hansa K 11214*	**6**	12 wks
16 Jun 79	●	**LIGHT MY FIRE/137 DISCO HEAVEN (MEDLEY)** *Atlantic/Hansa K 11278*	**5**	11 wks
3 Nov 79		**JEALOUSY** *Atlantic/Hansa K 11386*	**58**	3 wks
19 Jan 80		**PARADISE BIRD/THE LETTER** *Atlantic/Hansa K 11424*	**39**	4 wks
29 Dec 84		**FRIENDS** *RCA 471*	**73†**	1 wk

Amii STEWART and Johnny BRISTOL   *US, female/male vocal duo*   *5 wks*

19 Jul 80   **MY GUY - MY GIRL (MEDLEY)**   *Atlantic/Hansa K 11550* ....   **39**   5 wks

See also Amii Stewart; Johnny Bristol.

Andy STEWART   *UK, male vocalist*   *59 wks*

15 Dec 60	**DONALD WHERE'S YOUR TROOSERS** *Top Rank JAR 427*	**37**	1 wk
12 Jan 61	**A SCOTTISH SOLDIER** *Top Rank JAR 512*	**19**	38 wks
1 Jun 61	**THE BATTLE'S O'ER** *Top Rank JAR 565*	**28**	13 wks
12 Oct 61	**A SCOTTISH SOLDIER** (re-entry) *Top Rank JAR 512*	**43**	2 wks
12 Aug 65	**DR. FINLAY** *HMV POP 1454*	**50**	1 wk
26 Aug 65	**DR. FINLAY** (re-entry) *HMV POP 1454*	**43**	4 wks

Billy STEWART   *US, male vocalist*   *2 wks*

8 Sep 66   **SUMMERTIME**   *Chess CRS 8040* ....   **39**   2 wks

Dave STEWART
UK, instrumentalist - keyboards   *10 wks*

14 Mar 81   **WHAT BECOMES OF THE BROKENHEARTED?**   *Stiff BROKEN 1* ....   **13**   10 wks

Guest vocals: Colin Blunstone. See also Colin Blunstone; Neil MacArthur; Dave Stewart with Barbara Gaskin.

Dave STEWART with Barbara GASKIN   *UK, male instrumentalist-keyboard, with female vocalist*   *17 wks*

19 Sep 81	★	**IT'S MY PARTY** *Stiff/Broken BROKEN 2*	**1**	13 wks
13 Aug 83		**BUSY DOING NOTHING** *Broken BROKEN 5* ..	**49**	4 wks

See also Dave Stewart.

John STEWART   *US, male vocalist*   *6 wks*

30 Jun 79   **GOLD**   *RSO 35* ....   **43**   6 wks

Rod STEWART   *UK, male vocalist*   296 wks

Date		Title	Label	Pos	Wks
4 Sep 71		REASON TO BELIEVE	Mercury 6052 097	19	2 wks
18 Sep 71	★	MAGGIE MAY	Mercury 6052 097	1	19 wks
12 Aug 72	★	YOU WEAR IT WELL	Mercury 6052 171	1	12 wks
18 Nov 72	●	ANGEL /WHAT MADE MILWAUKEE FAMOUS (HAS MADE A LOSER OUT OF ME) *Mercury 6052 198*		4	11 wks
8 Sep 73	●	OH NO NOT MY BABY	Mercury 6052 371	6	9 wks
5 Oct 74	●	FAREWELL/BRING IT ON HOME TO ME/YOU SEND ME *Mercury 6167 033*		7	7 wks
16 Aug 75	★	SAILING	Warner Bros. K 16600	1	11 wks
15 Nov 75	●	THIS OLD HEART OF MINE	Riva 1	4	9 wks
5 Jun 76	●	TONIGHT'S THE NIGHT	Riva 3	5	9 wks
21 Aug 76	●	THE KILLING OF GEORGIE	Riva 4	2	10 wks
4 Sep 76	●	SAILING (re-entry)	Warner Bros. K 16600	3	20 wks
20 Nov 76	●	GET BACK	Riva 6	11	9 wks
4 Dec 76		MAGGIE MAY (re-issue)	Mercury 6160 006	31	7 wks
23 Apr 77	★	I DON'T WANT TO TALK ABOUT IT/FIRST CUT IS THE DEEPEST *Riva 7*		1	13 wks
15 Oct 77	●	YOU'RE IN MY HEART	Riva 11	3	10 wks
28 Jan 78	●	HOTLEGS/I WAS ONLY JOKING	Riva 10	5	8 wks
27 May 78	●	OLE OLA (MUHLER BRASILEIRA)	Riva 15	4	6 wks
18 Nov 78	★	DA YA THINK I'M SEXY?	Riva 17	1	13 wks
3 Feb 79		AIN'T LOVE A BITCH	Riva 18	11	8 wks
5 May 79		BLONDES (HAVE MORE FUN)	Riva 19	63	3 wks
31 May 80		IF LOVING YOU IS WRONG (I DON'T WANT TO BE RIGHT) *Riva 23*		23	9 wks
8 Nov 80		PASSION	Riva 26	17	10 wks
20 Dec 80		MY GIRL	Riva 28	32	7 wks
17 Oct 81	●	TONIGHT I'M YOURS (DON'T HURT ME) *Riva 33*		8	13 wks
12 Dec 81		YOUNG TURKS	Riva 34	11	9 wks
27 Feb 82		HOW LONG	Riva 35	41	4 wks
4 Jun 83	★	BABY JANE	Warner Bros. W 9608	1	14 wks
27 Aug 83	●	WHAT AM I GONNA DO	Warner Bros. W 9564	3	8 wks
10 Dec 83		SWEET SURRENDER	Warner Bros. W 9440	23	9 wks
26 May 84		INFATUATION	Warner Bros. W 9256	27	7 wks
28 Jul 84		SOME GUYS HAVE ALL THE LUCK *Warner Bros. W 9204*		15	10 wks

See also Faces; Jeff Beck and Rod Stewart. Ole Ola also features the Scottish World Cup Football Squad.

STIFF LITTLE FINGERS
UK, male vocal/instrumental group   39 wks

Date	Title	Label	Pos	Wks
29 Sep 79	STRAW DOGS	Chrysalis CHS 2368	44	4 wks
16 Feb 80	AT THE EDGE	Chrysalis CHS 2406	15	9 wks
24 May 80	NOBODY'S HERO/TIN SOLDIERS *Chrysalis CHS 2424*		36	5 wks
2 Aug 80	BACK TO FRONT	Chrysalis CHS 2447	49	4 wks
28 Mar 81	JUST FADE AWAY	Chrysalis CHS 2510	47	6 wks
30 May 81	SILVER LINING	Chrysalis CHS 2517	68	6 wks
23 Jan 82	LISTEN (EP)	Chrysalis CHS 2580	33	6 wks
18 Sep 82	BITS OF KIDS	Chrysalis CHS 2637	73	2 wks

Tracks on Listen EP: That's When Your Blood Bumps/Two Guitars Clash/Listen/Sad-Eyed People.

Stephen STILLS   *US, male vocalist*   4 wks

Date	Title	Label	Pos	Wks
13 Mar 71	LOVE THE ONE YOU'RE WITH *Atlantic 2091 046*		37	4 wks

See also Crosby, Stills and Nash.

STING   *UK, male vocalist*   8 wks

Date	Title	Label	Pos	Wks
14 Aug 82	SPREAD A LITTLE HAPPINESS *A & M AMS 8217*		16	8 wks

STINGERS - See B. BUMBLE and the STINGERS

Rhet STOLLER
UK, male instrumentalist - guitar   8 wks

Date	Title	Label	Pos	Wks
12 Jan 61	CHARIOT	Decca F 11302	26	8 wks

Morris STOLOFF   *US, orchestra*   11 wks

Date		Title	Label	Pos	Wks
1 Jun 56	●	MOONGLOW/THEME FROM PICNIC *Brunswick 05553*		7	11 wks

R & J STONE   *UK, male/female vocal duo*   9 wks

Date		Title	Label	Pos	Wks
10 Jan 76	●	WE DO IT	RCA 2616	5	9 wks

STONEBRIDGE McGUINNESS
UK, male vocal/instrumental duo   2 wks

Date	Title	Label	Pos	Wks
14 Jul 79	OO-EEH BABY	RCA PB 5163	54	2 wks

STORM
UK, male/female vocal/instrumental group   10 wks

Date	Title	Label	Pos	Wks
17 Nov 79	IT'S MY HOUSE	Scope SC 10	36	10 wks

Danny STORM   *UK, male vocalist*   4 wks

Date	Title	Label	Pos	Wks
12 Apr 62	HONEST I DO	Piccadilly 7N 35025	42	4 wks

STORYVILLE JAZZ BAND - See Bob WALLIS and his STORYVILLE JAZZ BAND

Peter STRAKER and the HANDS OF DR. TELENY
UK, male vocalist, male vocal/instrumental group   4 wks

Date	Title	Label	Pos	Wks
19 Feb 72	THE SPIRIT IS WILLING	RCA 2163	40	4 wks

Nick STRAKER BAND
UK, male vocal/instrumental group   15 wks

Date	Title	Label	Pos	Wks
2 Aug 80	A WALK IN THE PARK	CBS 8525	20	12 wks
15 Nov 80	LEAVING ON THE MIDNIGHT TRAIN *CBS 9088*		61	3 wks

STRANGE BEHAVIOUR - See Jane KENNAWAY and STRANGE BEHAVIOUR

STRANGLERS
UK, male vocal/instrumental group   141 wks

Date		Title	Label	Pos	Wks
19 Feb 77		(GET A) GRIP (ON YOURSELF) *United Artists UP 36211*		44	4 wks
21 May 77	●	PEACHES /GO BUDDY GO *United Artists UP 36248*		8	14 wks
30 Jul 77	●	SOMETHING BETTER CHANGE/STRAIGHTEN OUT *United Artists UP 36277*		9	8 wks
24 Sep 77	●	NO MORE HEROES	United Artists UP 36300	8	9 wks
4 Feb 78		FIVE MINUTES	United Artists UP 36350	11	9 wks
6 May 78		NICE 'N SLEAZY	United Artists UP 36379	18	8 wks
12 Aug 78		WALK ON BY	United Artists UP 36429	21	8 wks
18 Aug 79		DUCHESS	United Artists BP 308	14	9 wks
20 Oct 79		NUCLEAR DEVICE (THE WIZARD OF AUS) *United Artists BP 318*		36	4 wks

1 Dec 79	**DON'T BRING HARRY** (EP)		
	United Artists STR 1	**41**	3 wks
22 Mar 80	**BEAR CAGE** *United Artists BP 344*	**36**	5 wks
7 Jun 80	**WHO WANTS THE WORLD**		
	United Artists BPX 355	**39**	4 wks
31 Jan 81	**THROWN AWAY** *Liberty BP 383*	**42**	4 wks
14 Nov 81	**LET ME INTRODUCE YOU TO THE FAMILY**		
	United Artists BP 405	**42**	3 wks
9 Jan 82 ●	**GOLDEN BROWN** *Liberty BP 407*	**2**	12 wks
24 Apr 82	**LA FOLIE** *Liberty BP 410*	**47**	3 wks
24 Jul 82 ●	**STRANGE LITTLE GIRL** *Liberty BP 412* ...	**7**	9 wks
8 Jan 83 ●	**EUROPEAN FEMALE** *Epic EPC A 2893*	**9**	6 wks
26 Feb 83	**MIDNIGHT SUMMER DREAM**		
	Epic EPC A 3167	**35**	4 wks
6 Aug 83	**PARADISE** *Epic A 3387*	**48**	3 wks
6 Oct 84	**SKIN DEEP** *Epic A 4738*	**15**	7 wks
1 Dec 84	**NO MERCY** *Epic A 4921*	**37†**	5 wks

Go Buddy Go *credited with* Peaches *from 11 Jun 77.* Straighten Out *credited with* Something Better Change *from 13 Aug 77. Tracks on* Don't Bring Harry EP: *Don't Bring Harry/Wired/Crabs (live)/In the Shadows (live).*

STRAWBERRY SWITCHBLADE
UK, female vocal duo   7 wks

17 Nov 84	**SINCE YESTERDAY** *Korova KOW 38*	**47†**	7 wks

STRAWBS
UK, male vocal/instrumental group   27 wks

28 Oct 72	**LAY DOWN** *A & M AMS 7035*	**12**	13 wks
27 Jan 73 ●	**PART OF THE UNION** *A & M AMS 7047*	**2**	11 wks
6 Oct 73	**SHINE ON SILVER SUN** *A & M AMS 7082*	**34**	3 wks

STRAY CATS
US, male vocal/instrumental group   40 wks

29 Nov 80 ●	**RUNAWAY BOYS** *Arista SCAT 1*	**9**	10 wks
7 Feb 81 ●	**ROCK THIS TOWN** *Arista SCAT 2*	**9**	8 wks
25 Apr 81	**STRAY CAT STRUT** *Arista SCAT 3*	**11**	10 wks
7 Nov 81	**YOU DON'T BELIEVE ME** *Arista SCAT 4*	**57**	3 wks
6 Aug 83	**(SHE'S) SEXY AND 17** *Arista SCAT 6*	**29**	9 wks

See also Dave Edmunds and Stray Cats.

STREETBAND
UK, male vocal/instrumental group   6 wks

4 Nov 78	**TOAST/HOLD ON** *Logo GO 325*	**18**	6 wks

Barbra STREISAND *US, female vocalist*   71 wks

20 Jan 66	**SECOND HAND ROSE** *CBS 202025*	**14**	13 wks
30 Jan 71	**STONEY END** *CBS 5321*	**46**	1 wk
13 Feb 71	**STONEY END** (re-entry) *CBS 5321*	**27**	10 wks
30 Mar 74	**THE WAY WE WERE** *CBS 1915*	**31**	6 wks
9 Apr 77 ●	**LOVE THEME FROM A STAR IS BORN**		
	(EVERGREEN) *CBS 4855*	**3**	19 wks
4 Oct 80 ★	**WOMAN IN LOVE** *CBS 8966*	**1**	13 wks
30 Jan 82	**COMIN' IN AND OUT OF YOUR LIFE**		
	CBS A 1789	**66**	3 wks
20 Mar 82	**MEMORY** *CBS A 1903*	**34**	6 wks

See also Barbra Streisand and Barry Gibb; Barbra and Neil; Donna Summer and Barbra Streisand.

Barbra STREISAND and Barry GIBB *US/UK, female/male vocal duo*   10 wks

6 Dec 80	**GUILTY** *CBS 9315*	**34**	10 wks

See also Barbra Streisand; Donna Summer and Barbra Streisand; Barbra and Neil.

STRETCH
UK, male vocal/instrumental group   9 wks

8 Nov 75	**WHY DID YOU DO IT** *Anchor ANC 1021*	**16**	9 wks

STRIKERS
US, male vocal/instrumental group   5 wks

6 Jun 81	**BODY MUSIC** *Epic EPC A 1290*	**45**	5 wks

STRING-A-LONGS
US, male instrumental group   16 wks

23 Feb 61 ●	**WHEELS** *London HLU 9278*	**8**	16 wks

Chad STUART and Jeremy CLYDE
UK, male vocal duo   7 wks

28 Nov 63	**YESTERDAY'S GONE** *Ember EMB S 180*	**37**	7 wks

STUTZ BEARCATS and the Denis KING ORCHESTRA
UK, male/female vocal group with orchestra   6 wks

24 Apr 82	**THE SONG THAT I SING (THEME FROM 'WE'LL MEET AGAIN')**		
	Multi-Media Tapes MMT 6	**36**	6 wks

See also King Brothers.

STYLE COUNCIL
UK, male vocal instrumental duo   55 wks

19 Mar 83 ●	**SPEAK LIKE A CHILD** *Polydor TSC 1*	**4**	8 wks
28 May 83	**MONEY GO ROUND** (PART 1) *Polydor TSC 2*	**11**	6 wks
13 Aug 83 ●	**LONG HOT SUMMER** *Polydor TSC 3*	**3**	9 wks
20 Aug 83	**MONEY GO ROUND** (PART 1) (re-entry)		
	Polydor TSC 2	**74**	1 wk
19 Nov 83	**SOLID BOND IN YOUR HEART** *Polydor TSC 4*	**11**	8 wks
18 Feb 84 ●	**MY EVER CHANGING MOODS** *Polydor TSC 5*	**5**	7 wks
26 May 84	**GROOVIN' (YOU'RE THE BEST THING/BIG BOSS GROOVE)** *Polydor TSC 6*	**5**	8 wks
13 Oct 84 ●	**SHOUT TO THE TOP** *Polydor TSC 7*	**7**	8 wks

STYLISTICS *US, male vocal group*   143 wks

24 Jun 72	**BETCHA BY GOLLY WOW** *Avco 6105 011* ...	**13**	12 wks
4 Nov 72 ●	**I'M STONE IN LOVE WITH YOU**		
	Avco 6105 015	**9**	10 wks
17 Mar 73	**BREAK UP TO MAKE UP** *Avco 6105 020*	**34**	5 wks
30 Jun 73	**PEEK-A-BOO** *Avco 6105 023*	**35**	5 wks
19 Jan 74 ●	**ROCKIN' ROLL BABY** *Avco 6105 026*	**6**	9 wks
13 Jul 74 ●	**YOU MAKE ME FEEL BRAND NEW**		
	Avco 6105 028	**2**	14 wks
19 Oct 74	**LET'S PUT IT ALL TOGETHER** *Avco 6105 032*	**9**	9 wks
25 Jan 75	**STAR ON A TV SHOW** *Avco 6105 035*	**12**	8 wks
10 May 75 ●	**SING BABY SING** *Avco 6105 036*	**3**	10 wks
26 Jul 75 ★	**CAN'T GIVE YOU ANYTHING (BUT MY LOVE)**		
	Avco 6105 039	**1**	11 wks

NINA SIMONE (left) Her deeply emotional tribute to Martin Luther King, 'Why? (The King of Love Is Dead)' was recorded in concert at the Westbury Music Fair just 48 hours after his assassination.

SIMON AND GARFUNKEL (right) Slipping away un-noticed from Buckingham Palace.

SIMPLE MINDS (left) In 1984 frontman Jim Kerr (centre) married The Pretenders' Chrissie Hynde. (Photo: Peter Ashworth.)

FRANK SINATRA (below) Playing disc-jockey in the Radio Luxembourg studios.

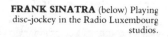

Date		Title	Label	Pos	Wks

15 Nov 75 ● **NA NA IS THE SADDEST WORD**
Avco 6105 041 . . . . **5** 10 wks

14 Feb 76 ● **FUNKY WEEKEND** *Avco 6105 044* . . . . **10** 7 wks

24 Apr 76 ● **CAN'T HELP FALLING IN LOVE**
Avco 6105 050 . . . . **4** 7 wks

7 Aug 76 ● **16 BARS** *H & L 6105 059* . . . . **7** 9 wks

27 Nov 76 **YOU'LL NEVER GET TO HEAVEN** (EP)
H & L STYL 001 . . . . **24** 9 wks

26 Mar 77 **7000 DOLLARS AND YOU** *H & L 6105 073* . . . **24** 7 wks

Tracks on You'll Never Get To Heaven EP: You'll Never Get To Heaven/Country Living/You Are Beautiful/The Miracle.

STYX *US, male vocal/instrumental group* *18 wks*

5 Jan 80 ● **BABE** *A & M AMS 7489* . . . . **6** 10 wks

24 Jan 81 **THE BEST OF TIMES** *A & M AMS 8102* . . . . . **42** 5 wks

18 Jun 83 **DON'T LET IT END** *A & M AM 120* . . . . **56** 3 wks

SUGAR CANE
US, male/female vocal group *5 wks*

30 Sep 78 **MONTEGO BAY** *Ariola Hansa AHA 524* . . . . **54** 5 wks

SUGARHILL GANG
US, male spoken word group *14 wks*

1 Dec 79 ● **RAPPER'S DELIGHT** *Sugarhill SHL 101* . . . . **3** 11 wks

11 Sep 82 **THE LOVER IN YOU** *Sugarhill SH 116* . . . . **54** 3 wks

Donna SUMMER *US, female vocalist* *219 wks*

17 Jan 76 ● **LOVE TO LOVE YOU BABY** *GTO GT 17* . . . **4** 9 wks

29 May 76 **COULD IT BE MAGIC** *GTO GT 60* . . . . **40** 7 wks

25 Dec 76 **WINTER MELODY** *GTO GT 76* . . . . **27** 6 wks

9 Jul 77 ★ **I FEEL LOVE** *GTO GT 100* . . . . **1** 11 wks

20 Aug 77 ● **DOWN DEEP INSIDE (THEME FROM 'THE DEEP')** *Casablanca CAN 111* . . . . **5** 10 wks

24 Sep 77 **I REMEMBER YESTERDAY** *GTO GT 107* . . . **14** 7 wks

3 Dec 77 ● **LOVE'S UNKIND** *GTO GT 113* . . . . **3** 13 wks

10 Dec 77 ● **I LOVE YOU** *Casablanca CAN 114* . . . . **10** 9 wks

25 Feb 78 **RUMOUR HAS IT** *Casablanca CAN 122* . . . . . **19** 8 wks

22 Apr 78 **BACK IN LOVE AGAIN** *GTO GT 117* . . . . **29** 7 wks

10 Jun 78 **LAST DANCE** *Casablanca TGIF 2* . . . . **70** 1 wk

24 Jun 78 **LAST DANCE** (re-entry) *Casablanca TGIF 2* . . **51** 5 wks

14 Oct 78 ● **MACARTHUR PARK** *Casablanca CAN 131* . . . . **5** 10 wks

17 Feb 79 **HEAVEN KNOWS** *Casablanca CAN 141* . . . . . **34** 8 wks

12 May 79 **HOT STUFF** *Casablanca CAN 151* . . . . **11** 10 wks

7 Jul 79 **BAD GIRLS** *Casablanca CAN 155* . . . . **14** 10 wks

1 Sep 79 **DIM ALL THE LIGHTS** *Casablanca CAN 162* . . . **29** 9 wks

16 Feb 80 **ON THE RADIO** *Casablanca NB 2236* . . . . **32** 6 wks

21 Jun 80 **SUNSET PEOPLE** *Casablanca CAN 198* . . . . . . **46** 5 wks

27 Sep 80 **THE WANDERER** *Warner Bros./Geffen K 79180* . . **48** 6 wks

17 Jan 81 **COLD LOVE** *Geffen K 79193* . . . . **44** 3 wks

10 Jul 82 **LOVE IS IN CONTROL (FINGER ON THE TRIGGER)** *Warner Bros. K 79302* . . . . **18** 11 wks

6 Nov 82 **STATE OF INDEPENDENCE**
Warner Bros. K 79344 . . . . **14** 11 wks

4 Dec 82 **I FEEL LOVE** *Casablanca/Phonogram FEEL 7* . . . . **21** 10 wks

5 Mar 83 **THE WOMAN IN ME** *Warner Bros. W 9983* . . . . **62** 2 wks

18 Jun 83 **SHE WORKS HARD FOR MONEY**
Mercury/Phonogram DONNA 1 . . . . **25** 8 wks

24 Sep 83 **UNCONDITIONAL LOVE**
Mercury/Phonogram DONNA 2 . . . . **14** 12 wks

21 Jan 84 **STOP LOOK AND LISTEN** *Mercury DONNA 3* . . **57** 2 wks

I Feel Love on Casablanca/Phonogram FEEL 7 is a re-mixed version of GTO GT 100. See also Donna Summer and Barbra Streisand.

Donna SUMMER and Barbra STREISAND *US, female vocal duo* *13 wks*

3 Nov 79 ● **NO MORE TEARS (ENOUGH IS ENOUGH)**
Casablanca/CAN 174 and CBS 8000 . . . . **3** 13 wks

See also Donna Summer; Barbra Streisand; Barbra and Neil. This hit was released simultaneously on two different labels, 7 inch single on Casablanca and 12 inch single on CBS.

SUNDRAGON
UK, male vocal/instrumental duo *1 wk*

21 Feb 68 **GREEN TAMBOURINE** *MGM 1380* . . . . . **50** 1 wk

SUNFIRE *US, male vocal/instrumental group* *11 wks*

12 Mar 83 **YOUNG, FREE AND SINGLE**
Warner Bros. W 9897 . . . . **20** 11 wks

SUNNY *UK, female vocalist* *10 wks*

30 Mar 74 ● **DOCTOR'S ORDERS** *CBS 2068* . . . . **7** 10 wks

SUNSHINE BAND - *See K. C. and the SUNSHINE BAND*

SUPERTRAMP
UK/US, male vocal/instrumental group *53 wks*

15 Feb 75 **DREAMER** *A & M AMS 7152* . . . . **13** 10 wks

25 Jun 77 **GIVE A LITTLE BIT** *A & M AMS 7293* . . . . . . **29** 7 wks

31 Mar 79 ● **THE LOGICAL SONG** *A & M AMS 7427* . . . . . **7** 11 wks

30 Jun 79 ● **BREAKFAST IN AMERICA** *A & M AMS 7451* . . **9** 10 wks

27 Oct 79 **GOODBYE STRANGER** *A & M AMS 7481* . . . . . **57** 3 wks

30 Oct 82 **IT'S RAINING AGAIN** *A & M AMS 8255* . . . . . **26** 12 wks

It's Raining Again is 'featuring vocals by Roger Hodgson'.

SUPREMES *US, female vocal group* *258 wks*

3 Sep 64 ● **WHERE DID OUR LOVE GO** *Stateside SS 327* . . **3** 14 wks

22 Oct 64 ★ **BABY LOVE** *Stateside SS 350* . . . . **1** 15 wks

21 Jan 65 **COME SEE ABOUT ME** *Stateside SS 376* . . . **27** 6 wks

25 Mar 65 ● **STOP IN THE NAME OF LOVE**
Tamla Motown TMG 501 . . . . **7** 12 wks

10 Jun 65 **BACK IN MY ARMS AGAIN**
Tamla Motown TMG 516 . . . . **40** 5 wks

9 Dec 65 **I HEAR A SYMPHONY** *Tamla Motown TMG 543* **50** 1 wk

23 Dec 65 **I HEAR A SYMPHONY** (re-entry)
Tamla Motown TMG 543 . . . . **39** 4 wks

8 Sep 66 ● **YOU CAN'T HURRY LOVE**
Tamla Motown TMG 575 . . . . **3** 12 wks

1 Dec 66 ● **YOU KEEP ME HANGIN' ON**
Tamla Motown TMG 585 . . . . **8** 10 wks

2 Mar 67 **LOVE IS HERE AND NOW YOU'RE GONE**
Tamla Motown TMG 597 . . . . **17** 10 wks

11 May 67 ● **THE HAPPENING** *Tamla Motown TMG 607* . . . **6** 12 wks

30 Aug 67 ● **REFLECTIONS** *Tamla Motown TMG 616* . . . . . . **5** 14 wks

29 Nov 67 **IN AND OUT OF LOVE**
Tamla Motown TMG 632 . . . . **13** 13 wks

10 Apr 68 **FOREVER CAME TODAY**
Tamla Motown TMG 650 . . . . **28** 8 wks

3 Jul 68 **SOME THINGS YOU NEVER GET USED TO**
Tamla Motown TMG 662 . . . . **34** 6 wks

20 Nov 68 **LOVE CHILD** *Tamla Motown TMG 677* . . . . **15** 14 wks

23 Apr 69 **I'M LIVING IN SHAME** *Tamla Motown TMG 695* **14** 9 wks

2 Jul 69 **I'M LIVING IN SHAME** (re-entry)
Tamla Motown TMG 695 . . . . **50** 1 wk

16 Jul 69 **NO MATTER WHAT SIGN YOU ARE**
Tamla Motown TMG 704 . . . . **37** 7 wks

13 Dec 69 **SOMEDAY WE'LL BE TOGETHER**
Tamla Motown TMG 721 . . . . **13** 13 wks

2 May 70 ●	UP THE LADDER TO THE ROOF	Tamla Motown TMG 735	6	15 wks
16 Jan 71 ●	STONED LOVE	Tamla Motown TMG 760	3	13 wks
21 Aug 71 ●	NATHAN JONES	Tamla Motown TMG 782	5	11 wks
4 Mar 72 ●	FLOY JOY	Tamla Motown TMG 804	9	10 wks
15 Jul 72 ●	AUTOMATICALLY SUNSHINE	Tamla Motown TMG 821	10	9 wks
21 Apr 73	BAD WEATHER	Tamla Motown TMG 847	37	4 wks
24 Aug 74	BABY LOVE (re-issue)	Tamla Motown TMG 915	12	10 wks

Diana Ross is lead singer on all the hits up to and including Someday We'll Be Together and on the re-issue of Baby Love. From Reflections up to and including Someday We'll Be Together, and on the re-issue of Baby Love, the group is billed as Diana Ross and the Supremes. See also Diana Ross; Supremes and the Four Tops; Diana Ross and the Supremes and the Temptations; Diana Ross and Michael Jackson; Diana Ross and Lionel Richie; Diana Ross and Marvin Gaye.

SUPREMES and the FOUR TOPS
US, female and male vocal groups — 20 wks

26 Jun 71	RIVER DEEP MOUNTAIN HIGH	Tamla Motown TMG 777	11	10 wks
20 Nov 71	YOU GOTTA HAVE LOVE IN YOUR HEART	Tamla Motown TMG 793	25	10 wks

See also Diana Ross and the Supremes and the Temptations; Supremes; Four Tops.

SURFACE
US, male vocal/instrumental duo — 7 wks

23 Jul 83	FALLING IN LOVE	Salsoul SAL 104	67	3 wks
23 Jun 84	WHEN YOUR 'EX' WANTS YOU BACK	Salsoul SAL 106	52	4 wks

SURFACE NOISE
UK, male instrumental group — 11 wks

31 May 80	THE SCRATCH	WEA K 18291	26	8 wks
30 Aug 80	DANCIN' ON A WIRE	Groove GP102	59	3 wks

SURFARIS
US, male instrumental group — 14 wks

25 Jul 63 ●	WIPE OUT	London HLD 9751	5	14 wks

SURPRISE SISTERS
UK, female vocal group — 3 wks

13 Mar 76	LA BOOGA ROOGA	Good Earth GD 1	38	3 wks

SURVIVOR
US, male vocal/instrumental group — 15 wks

31 Jul 82 ★	EYE OF THE TIGER	Scotti Brothers SCT A 2411	1	15 wks

SUTHERLAND BROTHERS
UK, male vocal/instrumental duo — 20 wks

3 Apr 76 ●	ARMS OF MARY	CBS 4001	5	12 wks
20 Nov 76	SECRETS	CBS 4668	35	4 wks
2 Jun 79	EASY COME EASY GO	CBS 7121	50	4 wks

First two hits credited to Sutherland Brothers and Quiver.

Pat SUZUKI
US, female vocalist — 1 wk

14 Apr 60	I ENJOY BEING A GIRL	RCA 1171	49	1 wk

Billy SWAN
US, male vocalist — 13 wks

14 Dec 74 ●	I CAN HELP	Monument MNT 2752	6	9 wks
24 May 75	DON'T BE CRUEL	Monument MNT 3244	42	4 wks

SWANSWAY
UK, male/female vocal/instrumental group — 12 wks

4 Feb 84	SOUL TRAIN	Exit/Phonogram EXT 3	20	7 wks
26 May 84	ILLUMINATIONS	Balgier/Phonogram PH 5	57	5 wks

SWEET
UK, male vocal/instrumental group — 154 wks

13 Mar 71	FUNNY FUNNY	RCA 2051	13	14 wks
12 Jun 71 ●	CO-CO	RCA 2087	2	15 wks
16 Oct 71	ALEXANDER GRAHAM BELL	RCA 2121	33	5 wks
5 Feb 72	POPPA JOE	RCA 2164	11	12 wks
10 Jun 72 ●	LITTLE WILLY	RCA 2225	4	14 wks
9 Sep 72 ●	WIG-WAM BAM	RCA 2260	4	13 wks
13 Jan 73 ★	BLOCKBUSTER	RCA 2305	1	15 wks
5 May 73 ●	HELL RAISER	RCA 2357	2	11 wks
22 Sep 73 ●	BALLROOM BLITZ	RCA 2403	2	9 wks
19 Jan 74 ●	TEENAGE RAMPAGE	RCA LPBO 5004	2	8 wks
13 Jul 74 ●	THE SIX TEENS	RCA LPBO 5037	9	7 wks
9 Nov 74	TURN IT DOWN	RCA 2480	41	2 wks
15 Mar 75 ●	FOX ON THE RUN	RCA 2524	2	10 wks
12 Jul 75	ACTION	RCA 2578	15	6 wks
24 Jan 76	LIES IN YOUR EYES	RCA 2641	35	4 wks
28 Jan 78 ●	LOVE IS LIKE OXYGEN	Polydor POSP 1	9	9 wks

Rachel SWEET
US, female vocalist — 8 wks

9 Dec 78	B-A-B-Y	Stiff BUY 39	35	8 wks

See also Rex Smith and Rachel Sweet.

SWEET DREAMS
UK, male/female vocal duo — 12 wks

20 Jul 74 ●	HONEY HONEY	Bradley's BRAD 7408	10	12 wks

SWEET DREAMS
UK, male/female vocal duo — 7 wks

9 Apr 83	I'M NEVER GIVING UP	Ariola ARO 333	21	7 wks

SWEET PEOPLE
France, male instrumental feathered vocal group — 8 wks

4 Oct 80 ●	ET LES OISEAUX CHANTAIENT (AND THE BIRDS WERE SINGING)	Polydor POSP 179	4	8 wks

SWEET SENSATION
UK, male vocal group — 17 wks

14 Sep 74 ★	SAD SWEET DREAMER	Pye 7N 45385	1	10 wks
18 Jan 75	PURELY BY COINCIDENCE	Pye 7N 45421	11	7 wks

SWINGING BLUE JEANS
UK, male vocal/instrumental group — 57 wks

20 Jun 63	IT'S TOO LATE NOW	HMV POP 1170	30	6 wks
8 Aug 63	IT'S TOO LATE NOW (re-entry)	HMV POP 1170	46	3 wks
12 Dec 63 ●	HIPPY HIPPY SHAKE	HMV POP 1242	2	17 wks
19 Mar 64	GOOD GOLLY MISS MOLLY	HMV POP 1273	11	10 wks

THE VINTAGE ROCK 'N' ROLL APPRECIATION SOCIETY

TERRY BURNS AND WALLACE CHADWICK

Present

SHAKIN STEVENS & THE SUNSETS

and

ROCK 'N' ROLL DISCO

at BRUNSHAW OLD BOYS LAWN TENNIS CLUB
BELVEDERE ROAD, BURNLEY

ON WEDNESDAY, JUNE 27th, at 8.00 p.m.

Admission 50p

STING In the days before he could afford clothes.

SPARKS Marx and Sparks!

4 Jun 64 ●	**YOU'RE NO GOOD** *HMV POP 1304*	**3**	13 wks
20 Jan 66	**DON'T MAKE ME OVER** *HMV POP 1501*	**31**	8 wks

SYLVESTER *US, male vocalist* — 37 wks

19 Aug 78 ●	**YOU MAKE ME FEEL (MIGHTY REAL)** *Fantasy FTC 160*	**8**	15 wks
18 Nov 78	**DANCE (DISCO HEAT)** *Fantasy FTC 163*	**29**	12 wks
31 Mar 79	**I (WHO HAVE NOTHING)** *Fantasy FTC 171* ..	**46**	5 wks
7 Jul 79	**STARS** *Fantasy FTC 177*	**47**	3 wks
3 Sep 83	**BAND OF GOLD** *London LON 33*	**67**	2 wks

SYLVESTER with Patrick COWLEY *US, male vocal duo* — 8 wks

11 Sep 82	**DO YA WANNA FUNK** *London LON 13*	**32**	8 wks

SYLVIA *US, female vocalist* — 11 wks

23 Jun 73	**PILLOW TALK** *London HL 10415*	**14**	11 wks

SYLVIA *Sweden, female vocalist* — 33 wks

10 Aug 74 ●	**Y VIVA ESPANA** *Sonet SON 2037*	**4**	19 wks
4 Jan 75	**Y VIVA ESPANA** (re-entry) *Sonet SON 2037*	**35**	9 wks
26 Apr 75	**HASTA LA VISTA** *Sonet SON 2005*	**38**	5 wks

David SYLVIAN *UK, male vocalist* — 10 wks

2 Jun 84	**RED GUITAR** *Virgin VS 633*	**17**	5 wks
18 Aug 84	**THE INK IN THE WELL** *Virgin VS 700*	**36**	3 wks
3 Nov 84	**PULLING PUNCHES** *Virgin VS 717*	**56**	2 wks

See also Sylvian Sakamoto.

SYLVIAN SAKAMOTO
UK/Japan, male vocal/instrumental duo — 12 wks

7 Aug 82	**BAMBOO HOUSES/BAMBOO MUSIC** *Virgin VS 510*	**30**	4 wks
2 Jul 83	**FORBIDDEN COLOURS** *Virgin VS 601*	**16**	8 wks

Second hit credited to the fuller act names of David Sylvian and Riuichi Sakamoto. See also David Sylvian.

SYMARIP *UK, male vocal/instrumental group* — 3 wks

2 Feb 80	**SKINHEAD MOONSTOMP** *Trojan TRO 9062* ..	**54**	3 wks

SYMBOLS *UK, male vocal/instrumental group* — 15 wks

2 Aug 67	**BYE BYE BABY** *President PT 144*	**44**	3 wks
3 Jan 68	**BEST PART OF BREAKING UP** *President PT 173*	**25**	12 wks

SYREETA *US, female vocalist* — 15 wks

21 Sep 74	**SPINNIN' & SPINNIN'** *Tamla Motown TMG 912*	**49**	3 wks
1 Feb 75	**YOUR KISS IS SWEET** *Tamla Motown TMG 933*	**12**	8 wks
12 Jul 75	**HARMOUR LOVE** *Tamla Motown TMG 954*	**32**	4 wks

See also Billy Preston and Syreeta.

SYSTEM *US, male vocal/instrumental duo* — 2 wks

9 Jun 84	**I WANNA MAKE YOU FEEL GOOD** *Polydor POSP 685*	**73**	2 wks

T

T. REX *UK, male vocal/instrumental group* — 213 wks

8 May 68	**DEBORA** *Regal Zonophone RZ 3008*	**34**	7 wks
4 Sep 68	**ONE INCH ROCK** *Regal Zonophone RZ 3011*	**28**	7 wks
9 Aug 69	**KING OF THE RUMBLING SPIRES** *Regal Zonophone RZ 3022*	**44**	1 wk
24 Oct 70 ●	**RIDE A WHITE SWAN** *Fly BUG 1*	**2**	20 wks
27 Feb 71 ★	**HOT LOVE** *Fly BUG 6*	**1**	17 wks
10 Jul 71 ★	**GET IT ON** *Fly BUG 10*	**1**	13 wks
13 Nov 71 ●	**JEEPSTER** *Fly BUG 16*	**2**	15 wks
29 Jan 72 ★	**TELEGRAM SAM** *T. Rex 101*	**1**	12 wks
1 Apr 72 ●	**DEBORA/ONE INCH ROCK** (re-issues) *Magnifly ECHO 102*	**7**	10 wks
13 May 72 ★	**METAL GURU** *EMI MARC 1*	**1**	14 wks
16 Sep 72 ●	**CHILDREN OF THE REVOLUTION** *EMI MARC 2*	**2**	10 wks
9 Dec 72 ●	**SOLID GOLD EASY ACTION** *EMI MARC 3* ..	**2**	11 wks
10 Mar 73 ●	**20TH CENTURY BOY** *EMI MARC 4*	**3**	9 wks
16 Jun 73 ●	**THE GROOVER** *EMI MARC 5*	**4**	9 wks
24 Nov 73	**TRUCK ON (TYKE)** *EMI MARC 6*	**12**	11 wks
9 Feb 74	**TEENAGE DREAM** *EMI MARC 7*	**13**	5 wks
13 Jul 74	**LIGHT OF LOVE** *EMI MARC 8*	**22**	5 wks
16 Nov 74	**ZIP GUN BOOGIE** *EMI MARC 9*	**41**	3 wks
12 Jul 75	**NEW YORK CITY** *EMI MARC 10*	**15**	8 wks
11 Oct 75	**DREAMY LADY** *EMI MARC 11*	**30**	5 wks
6 Mar 76	**LONDON BOYS** *EMI MARC 13*	**40**	3 wks
19 Jun 76	**I LOVE TO BOOGIE** *EMI MARC 14*	**13**	9 wks
2 Oct 76	**LASER LOVE** *EMI MARC 15*	**41**	4 wks
2 Apr 77	**THE SOUL OF MY SUIT** *EMI MARC 16*	**42**	3 wks
27 Mar 82	**TELEGRAM SAM** (re-entry) *T. Rex 101*	**69**	2 wks

Regal Zonophone and Magnifly hits bill the group as Tyrannosaurus Rex. Teenage Dream is by Marc Bolan and T. Rex. Dreamy Lady is by T. Rex Disco Party.

TALK TALK
UK, male vocal/instrumental group — 42 wks

24 Apr 82	**TALK TALK** *EMI 5284*	**52**	4 wks
24 Jul 82	**TODAY** *EMI 5314*	**14**	13 wks
13 Nov 82	**TALK TALK** *EMI 5352*	**23**	10 wks
19 Mar 83	**MY FOOLISH FRIEND** *EMI 5373*	**57**	3 wks
14 Jan 84	**IT'S MY LIFE** *EMI 5443*	**46**	5 wks
7 Apr 84	**SUCH A SHAME** *EMI 5433*	**49**	6 wks
11 Aug 84	**DUM DUM GIRL** *EMI 5480*	**74**	1 wk

EMI 5352 is a remixed version of EMI 5284.

TALKING HEADS
UK, male vocal/instrumental group — 18 wks

7 Feb 81	**ONCE IN A LIFETIME** *Sire SIR 4048*	**14**	10 wks
9 May 81	**HOUSES IN MOTION** *Sire SIR 4050*	**50**	3 wks
21 Jan 84	**THIS MUST BE THE PLACE** *Sire W 9451*	**51**	3 wks
3 Nov 84	**SLIPPERY PEOPLE** *EMI 5504*	**68**	2 wks

TAMS *US, male vocal group* — 24 wks

14 Feb 70	**BE YOUNG BE FOOLISH BE HAPPY** *Stateside SS 2123*	**32**	7 wks
31 Jul 71 ★	**HEY GIRL DON'T BOTHER ME** *Probe PRO 532*	**1**	17 wks

Norma TANEGA *US, female vocalist* — 8 wks

7 Apr 66	**WALKING MY CAT NAMED DOG** *Stateside SS 496*	**22**	8 wks

The Children of TANSLEY SCHOOL *UK, children's choir* *4 wks*

28 Mar 81	MY MUM IS ONE IN A MILLION *EMI 5151* ..	27	4 wks

TARRIERS
US, male vocal/instrumental group *5 wks*

1 Mar 57	BANANA BOAT SONG *Columbia DB 3891*	15	5 wks

A TASTE OF HONEY
US, female vocal duo *16 wks*

17 Jun 78	● BOOGIE OOGIE OOGIE *Capitol CL 15988*	3	16 wks

TAVARES *US, male vocal group* *64 wks*

10 Jul 76	● HEAVEN MUST BE MISSING AN ANGEL		
	Capitol CL 15876	4	11 wks
9 Oct 76	● DON'T TAKE AWAY THE MUSIC		
	Capitol CL 15886	4	10 wks
5 Feb 77	MIGHTY POWER OF LOVE *Capitol CL 15905*	25	6 wks
9 Apr 77	WHODUNIT *Capitol CL 15914*	5	10 wks
2 Jul 77	ONE STEP AWAY *Capitol CL 15930*	16	7 wks
18 Mar 78	THE GHOST OF LOVE *Capitol CL 15968*	29	6 wks
6 May 78	● MORE THAN A WOMAN *Capitol CL 15977* ...	7	11 wks
12 Aug 78	SLOW TRAIN TO PARADISE *Capitol CL 15996*	62	3 wks

Felice TAYLOR *US, female vocalist* *13 wks*

25 Oct 67	I FEEL LOVE COMIN' ON *President PT 155*	11	13 wks

James TAYLOR *US, male vocalist* *18 wks*

21 Nov 70	FIRE AND RAIN *Warner Bros. WB 6104*	42	3 wks
28 Aug 71	● YOU'VE GOT A FRIEND		
	Warner Bros. WB 16085	4	15 wks

See also Carly Simon and James Taylor.

Johnny TAYLOR *US, male vocalist* *7 wks*

24 Apr 76	DISCO LADY *CBS 4044*	25	7 wks

R. Dean TAYLOR *US, male vocalist* *48 wks*

19 Jun 68	GOTTA SEE JANE *Tamla Motown TMG 656* ...	17	12 wks
3 Apr 71	● INDIANA WANTS ME *Tamla Motown TMG 763*	2	15 wks
11 May 74	● THERE'S A GHOST IN MY HOUSE		
	Tamla Motown TMG 896	3	12 wks
31 Aug 74	WINDOW SHOPPING *Polydor 2058 502*	36	5 wks
21 Sep 74	GOTTA SEE JANE (re-issue)		
	Tamla Motown TMG 918	41	4 wks

Roger TAYLOR *UK, male vocalist* *6 wks*

18 Apr 81	FUTURE MANAGEMENT *EMI 5157*	49	4 wks
16 Jun 84	MAN ON FIRE *EMI 5478*	66	2 wks

T-CONNECTION
US, male vocal/instrumental group *27 wks*

18 Jun 77	DO WHAT YOU WANNA DO *TK XC 9109* ..	11	8 wks
14 Jan 78	ON FIRE *TK TKR 6006*	16	5 wks
10 Jun 78	LET YOURSELF GO *TK TKR 6024*	52	3 wks

24 Feb 79	AT MIDNIGHT *TK TKR 7517*	53	5 wks
5 May 79	SATURDAY NIGHT *TK TKR 7536*	41	6 wks

TEACH-IN
Holland, male/female vocal/instrumental group *7 wks*

12 Apr 75	DING-A-DONG *Polydor 2058 570*	13	7 wks

TEARDROP EXPLODES
UK, male vocal/instrumental group *50 wks*

27 Sep 80	WHEN I DREAM *Mercury TEAR 1*	47	6 wks
31 Jan 81	● REWARD *Vertigo TEAR 2*	6	13 wks
2 May 81	TREASON (IT'S JUST A STORY)		
	Mercury TEAR 3	18	8 wks
29 Aug 81	PASSIONATE FRIEND *Zoo TEAR 5*	25	10 wks
21 Nov 81	COLOURS FLY AWAY *Mercury TEAR 6*	54	3 wks
19 Jun 82	TINY CHILDREN *Mercury/Phonogram TEAR 7* ..	44	7 wks
19 Mar 83	YOU DISAPPEAR FROM VIEW		
	Mercury/Phonogram TEAR 8	41	3 wks

TEARS - *See SNIFF 'N' THE TEARS*

TEARS FOR FEARS
UK, male vocal/instrumental duo *54 wks*

2 Oct 82	● MAD WORLD *Mercury/Phonogram IDEA 3*	3	16 wks
5 Feb 83	● CHANGE *Mercury/Phonogram IDEA 4*	4	9 wks
30 Apr 83	● PALE SHELTER *Mercury/Phonogram IDEA 5*	5	8 wks
3 Dec 83	THE WAY YOU ARE *Mercury/Phonogram IDEA 6*	24	8 wks
18 Aug 84	MOTHER'S TALK *Mercury/Phonogram IDEA 7* ..	14	8 wks
1 Dec 84	● SHOUT *Mercury/Phonogram IDEA 8*	10†	5 wks

TECHNO TWINS
US, male/female vocal duo *2 wks*

16 Jan 82	FALLING IN LOVE AGAIN *PRT 7P 224*	75	1 wk
30 Jan 82	FALLING IN LOVE AGAIN (re-entry)		
	PRT 7P 224	70	1 wk

TEDDY BEARS
US, male/female vocal group *17 wks*

19 Dec 58	● TO KNOW HIM IS TO LOVE HIM		
	London HL 8733	2	16 wks
14 Apr 79	TO KNOW HIM IS TO LOVE HIM (re-issue)		
	Lightning LIG 9015	66	1 wk

To Know Him Is To Love Him *re-issue was coupled with* Endless Sleep *by Jody Reynolds as a double A-side. See also Jody Reynolds.*

TEENAGERS - *See Frankie LYMON and the TEENAGERS*

TEICHER - *See FERRANTE and TEICHER*

TELEVISION
US, male vocal/instrumental group *10 wks*

16 Apr 77	MARQUEE MOON *Elektra K 12252*	30	4 wks
30 Jul 77	PROVE IT *Elektra K 12262*	25	4 wks
22 Apr 78	FOXHOLE *Elektra K 12287*	36	2 wks

TELEX *Belgium, male vocal/instrumental duo* *7 wks*

21 Jul 79	ROCK AROUND THE CLOCK *Sire SIR 4020* ..	34	7 wks

TEMPERANCE SEVEN
UK, male vocal/instrumental band 45 wks

30 Mar 61	★ YOU'RE DRIVING ME CRAZY			
	Parlophone R 4757		**1**	16 wks
15 Jun 61	● PASADENA *Parlophone R 4781*		**4**	17 wks
28 Sep 61	HARD HEARTED HANNAH/CHILI BOM BOM			
	Parlophone R 4823		**28**	4 wks
7 Dec 61	CHARLESTON *Parlophone R 4851*		**22**	8 wks

Chili Bom Bom only listed with Hard Hearted Hannah for the weeks of 12 and 19 Oct 61.

Nino TEMPO and April STEVENS
US, male/female vocal duo 19 wks

7 Nov 63	DEEP PURPLE *London HLK 9785*		**17**	11 wks
16 Jan 64	WHISPERING *London HLK 9829*		**20**	8 wks

TEMPTATIONS *US, male vocal group* 153 wks

18 Mar 65	MY GIRL *Stateside SS 395*		**43**	1 wk
1 Apr 65	IT'S GROWING *Tamla Motown TMG 504*		**49**	1 wk
15 Apr 65	IT'S GROWING (re-entry)			
	Tamla Motown TMG 504		**45**	1 wk
14 Jul 66	AIN'T TOO PROUD TO BEG			
	Tamla Motown TMG 565		**21**	11 wks
6 Oct 66	BEAUTY IS ONLY SKIN DEEP			
	Tamla Motown TMG 578		**18**	10 wks
15 Dec 66	(I KNOW) I'M LOSING YOU			
	Tamla Motown TMG 587		**19**	9 wks
6 Sep 67	YOU'RE MY EVERYTHING			
	Tamla Motown TMG 620		**26**	15 wks
6 Mar 68	I WISH IT WOULD RAIN			
	Tamla Motown TMG 641		**45**	1 wk
12 Jun 68	I COULD NEVER LOVE ANOTHER			
	Tamla Motown TMG 658		**47**	1 wk
5 Mar 69	● GET READY *Tamla Motown TMG 688*		**10**	9 wks
23 Aug 69	CLOUD NINE *Tamla Motown TMG 707*		**15**	10 wks
17 Jan 70	I CAN'T GET NEXT TO YOU			
	Tamla Motown TMG 722		**13**	9 wks
13 Jun 70	PSYCHEDELIC SHACK			
	Tamla Motown TMG 741		**33**	7 wks
19 Sep 70	● BALL OF CONFUSION *Tamla Motown TMG 749*		**7**	12 wks
19 Dec 70	BALL OF CONFUSION (re-entry)			
	Tamla Motown TMG 749		**48**	3 wks
22 May 71	● JUST MY IMAGINATION (RUNNING AWAY			
	WITH ME) *Tamla Motown TMG 773*		**8**	16 wks
5 Feb 72	SUPERSTAR (REMEMBER HOW YOU GOT			
	WHERE YOU ARE) *Tamla Motown TMG 800*		**32**	5 wks
15 Apr 72	TAKE A LOOK AROUND			
	Tamla Motown TMG 808		**13**	10 wks
13 Jan 73	PAPA WAS A ROLLIN' STONE			
	Tamla Motown TMG 839		**14**	8 wks
29 Sep 73	LAW OF THE LAND *Tamla Motown TMG 866*		**41**	4 wks
12 Jun 82	STANDING ON THE TOP (PART 1)			
	Motown TMG 1263		**53**	3 wks
17 Nov 84	TREAT HER LIKE A LADY *Motown TMG 1365*		**12†**	7 wks

See also; Diana Ross and the Supremes and the Temptations. Standing On The Top is 'featuring Rick James'. See Rick James; Teena Marie.

10 C. C. *UK, male vocal/instrumental group* 131 wks

23 Sep 72	● DONNA *UK 6*		**2**	13 wks
19 May 73	★ RUBBER BULLETS *UK 36*		**1**	15 wks
25 Aug 73	● THE DEAN AND I *UK 48*		**10**	8 wks
15 Jun 74	● WALL STREET SHUFFLE *UK 69*		**10**	10 wks
14 Sep 74	SILLY LOVE *UK 77*		**24**	7 wks
5 Apr 75	● LIFE IS A MINESTRONE *Mercury 6008 010*		**7**	8 wks
31 May 75	★ I'M NOT IN LOVE *Mercury 6008 014*		**1**	11 wks
29 Nov 75	● ART FOR ART'S SAKE *Mercury 6008 017*		**5**	10 wks
20 Mar 76	● I'M MANDY FLY ME *Mercury 6008 019*		**6**	9 wks
11 Dec 76	● THINGS WE DO FOR LOVE *Mercury 6008 022*		**6**	11 wks
16 Apr 77	● GOOD MORNING JUDGE *Mercury 6008 025*		**5**	12 wks

12 Aug 78	★ DREADLOCK HOLIDAY *Mercury 6008 035*		**1**	13 wks
7 Aug 82	RUN AWAY *Mercury/Phonogram MER 113*		**50**	4 wks

From Dreadlock Holiday, 10 C.C. are a male vocal/instrumental duo.

TEN POLE TUDOR
UK, male vocal/instrumental group 26 wks

25 Apr 81	● SWORDS OF A THOUSAND MEN			
	Stiff BUY 109		**6**	12 wks
1 Aug 81	WUNDERBAR *Stiff BUY 120*		**16**	9 wks
14 Nov 81	THROWING MY BABY OUT WITH THE			
	BATHWATER *Stiff BUY 129*		**49**	5 wks

See also Sex Pistols.

TEN YEARS AFTER
UK, male vocal/instrumental group 18 wks

6 Jun 70	● LOVE LIKE A MAN *Deram DM 299*		**10**	18 wks

TENNESSEE THREE - *See Johnny CASH*

TENNILLE - *See CAPTAIN and TENNILLE*

Tammi TERRELL - *See Marvin GAYE and Tammi TERRELL*

Helen TERRY *UK, female vocalist* 6 wks

12 May 84	LOVE LIES LOST *Virgin VS 678*		**34**	6 wks

Joe TEX *US, male vocalist* 11 wks

23 Apr 77	● AIN'T GONNA BUMP NO MORE (WITH NO			
	BIG FAT WOMAN) *Epic EPC 5035*		**2**	11 wks

The THE *UK, male vocalist* 6 wks

4 Dec 82	UNCERTAIN SMILE *Epic EPC A 2787*		**68**	3 wks
17 Sep 83	THIS IS THE DAY *Epic A 3710*		**71**	3 wks

THEATRE OF HATE
UK, male vocal/instrumental group 9 wks

23 Jan 82	DO YOU BELIEVE IN THE WESTWORLD			
	Burning Rome BRR 2		**40**	7 wks
29 May 82	THE HOP *Burning Rome BRR 3*		**70**	2 wks

THEM *UK, male vocal/instrumental group* 21 wks

7 Jan 65	● BABY PLEASE DON'T GO *Decca F 12018*		**10**	9 wks
25 Mar 65	● HERE COMES THE NIGHT *Decca F 12094*		**2**	12 wks

THIN LIZZY
Ireland, male vocal/instrumental group 124 wks

20 Jan 73	● WHISKY IN THE JAR *Decca F 13355*		**6**	12 wks
29 May 76	● THE BOYS ARE BACK IN TOWN			
	Vertigo 6059 139		**8**	10 wks
14 Aug 76	JAILBREAK *Vertigo 6059 150*		**31**	4 wks
15 Jan 77	DON'T BELIEVE A WORD *Vertigo LIZZY 001*		**12**	7 wks
13 Aug 77	DANCIN' IN THE MOONLIGHT (IT'S CAUGHT			
	ME IN THE SPOTLIGHT) *Vertigo 6059 177*		**14**	8 wks
13 May 78	ROSALIE - COWGIRLS' SONG (MEDLEY)			
	Vertigo LIZZY 2		**20**	13 wks
3 Mar 79	● WAITING FOR AN ALIBI *Vertigo LIZZY 003*		**9**	8 wks

16 Jun 79		DO ANYTHING YOU WANT TO			
		Vertigo LIZZY 004	14	9 wks
20 Oct 79		SARAH Vertigo LIZZY 5	24	13 wks
24 May 80		CHINATOWN Vertigo LIZZY 6	21	9 wks
27 Sep 80	●	KILLER ON THE LOOSE Vertigo LIZZY 7	10	7 wks
2 May 81		KILLERS LIVE (EP) Vertigo LIZZY 8	19	7 wks
8 Aug 81		TROUBLE BOYS Vertigo LIZZY 9	53	4 wks
6 Mar 82		HOLLYWOOD (DOWN ON YOUR LUCK)		
		Vertigo/Phonogram LIZZY 10	53	3 wks
12 Feb 83		COLD SWEAT Vertigo/Phonogram LIZZY 11	27	5 wks
7 May 83		THUNDER AND LIGHTNING		
		Vertigo/Phonogram LIZZY 12	39	2 wks
6 Aug 83		THE SUN GOES DOWN		
		Vertigo/Phonogram LIZZY 13	52	3 wks

Tracks on Killers Live EP: Bad Reputation/Are You Ready/Dear Miss Lonely Hearts.

THIRD WORLD
Jamaica, male vocal/instrumental group   45 wks

23 Sep 78	●	NOW THAT WE'VE FOUND LOVE		
		Island WIP 6457	10	9 wks
6 Jan 79		COOL MEDITATION Island WIP 6469	17	10 wks
16 Jun 79		TALK TO ME Island WIP 6496	56	5 wks
6 Jun 81	●	DANCING ON THE FLOOR (HOOKED ON		
		LOVE) CBS A 1214	10	15 wks
17 Apr 82		TRY JAH LOVE CBS A 2063	47	6 wks

THIS MORTAL COIL
UK, male/female vocal/instrumental group   3 wks

22 Oct 83	SONG TO THE SIREN 4AD AD 310	66	2 wks
12 Nov 83	SONG TO THE SIREN (re-entry) 4AD AD 310	75	1 wk

THIS YEAR'S BLONDE
UK, male/female vocal/instrumental group   5 wks

10 Oct 81	PLATINUM POP Creole CR 19	46	5 wks

B. J. THOMAS US, male vocalist   4 wks

21 Feb 70	RAINDROPS KEEP FALLING ON MY HEAD		
	Wand WN1	38	3 wks
2 May 70	RAINDROPS KEEP FALLING ON MY HEAD		
	(re-entry) Wand WN1	49	1 wk

Carla THOMAS - See Otis REDDING and Carla THOMAS

Evelyn THOMAS US, female vocalist   29 wks

24 Jan 76	WEAK SPOT 20th Century BTC 1014	26	7 wks
17 Apr 76	DOOMSDAY 20th Century BTC 1019	41	1 wk
1 May 76	DOOMSDAY (re-entry) 20th Century BTC 1019	45	1 wk
21 Apr 84	● HIGH ENERGY Record Shack SOHO 18	5	17 wks
25 Aug 84	MASQUERADE Record Shack SOHO 25	60	3 wks

Jamo THOMAS US, male vocalist   2 wks

26 Feb 69	I SPY FOR THE FBI Polydor 56755	48	1 wk
12 Mar 69	I SPY FOR THE FBI (re-entry) Polydor 56755	44	1 wk

Nicky THOMAS Jamaica, male vocalist   14 wks

13 Jun 70	●	LOVE OF THE COMMON PEOPLE		
		Trojan TR 7750	9	14 wks

Rufus THOMAS US, male vocalist   12 wks

11 Apr 70	DO THE FUNKY CHICKEN Stax 144	18	12 wks

Tasha THOMAS US, female vocalist   3 wks

20 Jan 79	SHOOT ME (WITH YOUR LOVE) Atlantic LV 4	59	3 wks

Timmy THOMAS US, male vocalist   11 wks

24 Feb 73	WHY CAN'T WE LIVE TOGETHER		
	Mojo 2027 012	12	11 wks

Chris THOMPSON UK, male vocalist   5 wks

27 Oct 79	IF YOU REMEMBER ME Planet K 12389	42	5 wks

Sue THOMPSON US, female vocalist   9 wks

2 Nov 61	SAD MOVIES Polydor NH 66967	46	1 wk
16 Nov 61	SAD MOVIES (re-entry) Polydor NH 66967	48	1 wk
21 Jan 65	PAPER TIGER Hickory 1284	50	1 wk
11 Feb 65	PAPER TIGER (re-entry) Hickory 1284	30	6 wks

THOMPSON TWINS
UK/New Zealand, male/female vocal/instrumental group   77 wks

6 Nov 82		LIES Arista ARIST 486	67	3 wks
29 Jan 83	●	LOVE ON YOUR SIDE Arista ARIST 504	9	12 wks
16 Apr 83	●	WE ARE DETECTIVE Arista ARIST 526	7	9 wks
16 Jul 83		WATCHING Arista TWINS 1	33	6 wks
19 Nov 83	●	HOLD ME NOW Arista TWINS 2	4	15 wks
4 Feb 84	●	DOCTOR DOCTOR Arista TWINS 3	3	10 wks
31 Mar 84	●	YOU TAKE ME UP Arista TWINS 4	2	9 wks
7 Jul 84		SISTER OF MERCY Arista TWINS 5	11	8 wks
8 Sep 84		SISTER OF MERCY (re-entry) Arista TWINS 5	66	1 wk
8 Dec 84		LAY YOUR HANDS ON ME Arista TWINS 6	19†	4 wks

David THORNE US, male vocalist   8 wks

24 Jan 63	ALLEY CAT SONG Stateside SS 141	21	8 wks

Ken THORNE UK, orchestra   15 wks

18 Jul 63	●	THEME FROM THE FILM 'THE LEGION'S LAST		
		PATROL' HMV POP 1176	4	15 wks

THREE DEGREES
US, female vocal group   97 wks

13 Apr 74		YEAR OF DECISION		
		Philadelphia International PIR 2073	13	10 wks
13 Jul 74	★	WHEN WILL I SEE YOU AGAIN		
		Philadelphia International PIR 2155	1	16 wks
2 Nov 74		GET YOUR LOVE BACK		
		Philadelphia International PIR 2737	34	4 wks
12 Apr 75	●	TAKE GOOD CARE OF YOURSELF		
		Philadelphia International PIR 3177	9	9 wks
5 Jul 75		LONG LOST LOVER		
		Philadelphia International PIR 3352	40	4 wks
1 May 76		TOAST OF LOVE Epic EPC 4215	36	4 wks
7 Oct 78		GIVIN' UP GIVIN' IN Ariola ARO 130	12	10 wks
13 Jan 79	●	WOMAN IN LOVE Ariola ARO 141	3	11 wks
24 Mar 79	●	THE RUNNER Ariola ARO 154	10	10 wks
23 Jun 79		THE GOLDEN LADY Ariola ARO 170	56	3 wks
29 Sep 79		JUMP THE GUN Ariola ARO 183	48	5 wks

NINO TEMPO AND APRIL STEVENS (above left) The American duo model the latest Feb '63 sweater designs.

TALKING HEADS (above right) 'Once In A Lifetime' shot of Franz, Byrne, Harrison and Weymouth (Photo: Lynn Goldsmith/Rockshots.)

TEN POLE TUDOR (above) Out on bale! as they arrive at Broadcasting House singing 'Three Wheels On My Wogan'.

HELEN TERRY (right) Played a considerable part in Culture Club's success and obtained solo recognition with 'Love Lies Lost'. (Photo: David Levine.)

24 Nov 79 ● **MY SIMPLE HEART** *Ariola ARO 202* .... **9** 11 wks
See also MFSB.

THREE DOG NIGHT
US, male vocal/instrumental group *23 wks*

8 Aug 70 ●	**MAMA TOLD ME NOT TO COME**			
	Stateside SS 8052	**3**	14 wks
29 May 71	**JOY TO THE WORLD** *Probe PRO 523*	**24**	9 wks

THREE GOOD REASONS
UK, male vocal/instrumental group *3 wks*

10 Mar 66	**NOWHERE MAN** *Mercury MF 899*	**47**	3 wks

THREE KAYES *UK, female vocal group* *5 wks*

25 May 56	**IVORY TOWER** *HMV POP 209*	**20**	5 wks

The Three Kayes became The Kaye Sisters. See also Kaye Sisters; Frankie Vaughan and the Kaye Sisters.

THREE TONS OF JOY - *See Johnny OTIS Show*

THS-THE HORN SECTION
US, male/female vocal/instrumental group *3 wks*

18 Aug 84	**LADY SHING (SHINE ON)**		
	Fourth and Broadway/Island BRW 10	**54**	3 wks

Harry THUMANN
Germany, male instrumentalist - keyboards *6 wks*

21 Feb 81	**UNDERWATER** *Decca F 13901*	**41**	6 wks

THUNDERCLAP NEWMAN
UK, male vocal/instrumental group *13 wks*

11 Jun 69 ★	**SOMETHING IN THE AIR** *Track 604-031*	**1**	12 wks
27 Jun 70	**ACCIDENTS** *Track 2094 001*	**46**	1 wk

THUNDERTHIGHS
UK, female vocal group *5 wks*

22 Jun 74	**CENTRAL PARK ARREST** *Philips 6006 386*	**30**	5 wks

Bobby THURSTON *US, male vocalist* *10 wks*

29 Mar 80 ●	**CHECK OUT THE GROOVE** *Epic EPC 8348* ...	**10**	10 wks

TICH - *See Dave DEE, DOZY, BEAKY, MICK and TICH*

TIGHT FIT *UK, male/female vocal group.* *49 wks*

18 Jul 81 ●	**BACK TO THE SIXTIES** *Jive JIVE 002*	**4**	11 wks
26 Sep 81	**BACK TO THE SIXTIES PART 2** *Jive JIVE 005*	**33**	5 wks
23 Jan 82 ★	**THE LION SLEEPS TONIGHT** *Jive JIVE 9*	**1**	15 wks
1 May 82 ●	**FANTASY ISLAND** *Jive JIVE 13*	**5**	12 wks
31 Jul 82	**SECRET HEART** *Jive JIVE 20*	**41**	6 wks

TIJUANA BRASS - *See Herb ALPERT and the TIJUANA BRASS*

TIK and TOK *UK, male vocal duo* *2 wks*

8 Oct 83	**COOL RUNNING** *Survival SUR 016*	**69**	2 wks

TILBROOK - *See DIFFORD and TILBROOK*

Johnny TILLOTSON *US, male vocalist* *50 wks*

1 Dec 60 ★	**POETRY IN MOTION** *London HLA 9231*	**1**	15 wks
2 Feb 61	**JIMMY'S GIRL** *London HLA 9275*	**50**	1 wk
16 Feb 61	**JIMMY'S GIRL** (re-entry) *London HLA 9275*	**43**	1 wk
12 Jul 62	**IT KEEPS RIGHT ON A HURTIN'**		
	London HLA 9550	**31**	10 wks
4 Oct 62	**SEND ME THE PILLOW YOU DREAM ON**		
	London HLA 9598	**21**	10 wks
27 Dec 62	**I CAN'T HELP IT** *London HLA 9642*	**42**	1 wk
10 Jan 63	**I CAN'T HELP IT** (re-entry) *London HLA 9642* ..	**47**	1 wk
24 Jan 63	**I CAN'T HELP IT** (2nd re-entry)		
	London HLA 9642	**41**	4 wks
9 May 63	**OUT OF MY MIND** *London HLA 9695*	**34**	5 wks
14 Apr 79	**POETRY IN MOTION** (re-issue)/**PRINCESS**		
	PRINCESS *Lightning LIG 9016*	**67**	2 wks

TIMEBOX
UK, male vocal/instrumental group *4 wks*

24 Jul 68	**BEGGIN'** *Deram DM 194*	**38**	4 wks

TIME UK *UK, male vocal/instrumental group* *3 wks*

8 Oct 83	**THE CABARET** *Red Bus/Aroadia TIM 123*	**63**	3 wks

TIN TIN *UK, male vocalist* *4 wks*

9 Jul 83	**HOLD IT** *Curve/WEA X 9763*	**55**	4 wks

TINY TIM *US, male vocalist* *1 wk*

5 Feb 69	**GREAT BALLS OF FIRE** *Reprise RS 20802*	**45**	1 wk

TITANIC *Holland, male instrumental group* *12 wks*

25 Sep 71 ●	**SULTANA** *CBS 5365*	**5**	12 wks

Art and Dotty TODD
US, male/female vocal duo *7 wks*

13 Feb 53 ●	**BROKEN WINGS** *HMV B 10399*	**6**	7 wks

TOK - *See TIK and TOK*

TOKENS *US, male vocal group* *12 wks*

21 Dec 61	**THE LION SLEEPS TONIGHT** *RCA 1263*	**11**	12 wks

TOM TOM CLUB
US, female/male vocal/instrumental group *20 wks*

20 Jun 81 ●	**WORDY RAPPINGHOOD** *Island WIP 6694* ...	**7**	9 wks
10 Oct 81	**GENIUS OF LOVE** *Island WIP 6735*	**65**	2 wks
7 Aug 82	**UNDER THE BOARDWALK** *Island WIP 6762* ..	**22**	9 wks

TONIGHT
UK, male vocal/instrumental group — 10 wks

28 Jan 78		DRUMMER MAN	Target TDS 1	14	8 wks
20 May 78		MONEY THAT'S YOUR PROBLEM			
		Target TDS 2		66	2 wks

TOPOL
Israel, male vocalist — 20 wks

20 Apr 67	●	IF I WERE A RICH MAN	CBS 202651	9	20 wks

Mel TORME
US, male vocalist — 32 wks

27 Apr 56		MOUNTAIN GREENERY	Vogue/Coral Q 72150	15	11 wks
27 Jul 56	●	MOUNTAIN GREENERY	(re-entry)		
		Vogue/Coral Q 72150		4	13 wks
3 Jan 63		COMING HOME BABY	London HLK 9643	13	8 wks

TORNADOS
UK, male instrumental group — 59 wks

30 Aug 62	★	TELSTAR	Decca F 11494	1	25 wks
10 Jan 63	●	GLOBETROTTER	Decca F 11562	5	11 wks
21 Mar 63		ROBOT	Decca F 11606	17	12 wks
6 Jun 63		THE ICE CREAM MAN	Decca F 11662 ...	18	9 wks
10 Oct 63		DRAGONFLY	Decca F 11745	41	2 wks

Mitchell TOROK
US, male vocalist — 19 wks

28 Sep 56	●	WHEN MEXICO GAVE UP THE RUMBA			
		Brunswick 05586		6	17 wks
11 Jan 57		RED LIGHT GREEN LIGHT	Brunswick 05626 ...	29	1 wk
1 Feb 57		WHEN MEXICO GAVE UP THE RUMBA			
		(re-entry) Brunswick 05586		30	1 wk

Peter TOSH
Jamaica, male vocalist — 12 wks

21 Oct 78		(YOU GOTTA WALK) DON'T LOOK BACK			
		EMI 2859		43	7 wks
2 Apr 83		JOHNNY B. GOODE	EMI RIC 115	48	5 wks

TOTO
US, male vocal/instrumental group — 34 wks

10 Feb 79		HOLD THE LINE	CBS 6784	14	11 wks
5 Feb 83	●	AFRICA	CBS A 2510	3	10 wks
9 Apr 83		ROSANNA	CBS A 2079	12	8 wks
18 Jun 83		I WON'T HOLD YOU BACK	CBS A 3392	37	5 wks

TOTO COELO
UK, female vocal group — 14 wks

7 Aug 82	●	I EAT CANNIBALS PART 1			
		Radialchoice/Virgin TIC 10		8	10 wks
13 Nov 82		DRACULA'S TANGO/MUCHO MACHO			
		Radialchoice/Virgin TIC 11		54	4 wks

TOTTENHAM HOTSPUR F.A. CUP FINAL SQUAD
UK, male football team vocalists — 15 wks

9 May 81	●	OSSIE'S DREAM (SPURS ARE ON THEIR WAY TO WEMBLEY)	Rockney SHELF 1	5	8 wks
1 May 82		TOTTENHAM TOTTENHAM	Rockney SHELF 2	19	7 wks

Both hits feature the uncredited vocal and instrumental talents of Chas and Dave. See Chas and Dave.

TOURISTS
UK, male/female vocal/instrumental group — 40 wks

9 Jun 79		BLIND AMONG THE FLOWERS	Logo GO 350	52	5 wks
8 Sep 79		THE LONELIEST MAN IN THE WORLD			
		Logo GO 360		32	7 wks
10 Nov 79	●	I ONLY WANT TO BE WITH YOU			
		Logo GO 370		4	14 wks
9 Feb 80	●	SO GOOD TO BE BACK HOME AGAIN			
		Logo TOUR 1		8	9 wks
18 Oct 80		DON'T SAY I TOLD YOU SO	RCA TOUR 2	40	5 wks

Pete TOWNSHEND
UK, male vocalist — 17 wks

5 Apr 80		ROUGH BOYS	Atco K 11460	39	6 wks
21 Jun 80		LET MY LOVE OPEN YOUR DOOR			
		Atco K 11486		46	6 wks
21 Aug 82		UNIFORMS (CORPS D'ESPRIT)	Atco K 11751	48	5 wks

TOYAH
UK, female vocalist — 73 wks

14 Feb 81	●	FOUR FROM TOYAH (EP)	Safari TOY 1	4	14 wks
16 May 81	●	I WANT TO BE FREE	Safari SAFE 34	8	11 wks
3 Oct 81	●	THUNDER IN THE MOUNTAINS			
		Safari SAFE 38		4	9 wks
28 Nov 81		FOUR MORE FROM TOYAH (EP)	Safari TOY 2	14	9 wks
22 May 82		BRAVE NEW WORLD	Safari SAFE 45	21	8 wks
17 Jul 82		IEYA	Safari SAFE 28	48	5 wks
9 Oct 82		BE LOUD BE PROUD (BE HEARD)			
		Safari SAFE 52		30	7 wks
24 Sep 83		REBEL RUN	Safari SAFE 56	24	5 wks
19 Nov 83		THE VOW	Safari SAFE 58	50	5 wks

Tracks on Four From Toyah EP: It's A Mystery/Revelations/ War Boys/Angels and Demons. Tracks on Four More From Toyah EP: Good Morning Universe/Urban Tribesman/In The Fairground/The Furious Futures.

TOYS
US, female vocal group — 17 wks

4 Nov 65	●	A LOVER'S CONCERTO	Stateside SS 460	5	13 wks
27 Jan 66		ATTACK	Stateside SS 483	36	4 wks

TRACIE
UK, female vocalist — 22 wks

26 Mar 83	●	THE HOUSE THAT JACK BUILD			
		Respond KOB 701		9	8 wks
16 Jul 83		GIVE IT SOME EMOTION	Respond KOB 704 ...	24	9 wks
14 Apr 84		SOUL'S ON FIRE	Respond KOB 708	73	2 wks
9 Jun 84		(I LOVE YOU) WHEN YOU SLEEP			
		Respond KOB 710		59	3 wks

TRAFFIC
UK, male vocal/instrumental group — 40 wks

1 Jun 67	●	PAPER SUN	Island WIP 6002	5	10 wks
6 Sep 67	●	HOLE IN MY SHOE	Island WIP 6017	2	14 wks
29 Nov 67	●	HERE WE GO ROUND THE MULBERRY BUSH			
		Island WIP 6025		8	12 wks
6 Mar 68		NO FACE, NO NAME, NO NUMBER			
		Island WIP 6030		40	4 wks

TRAMMPS
US, male vocal group — 50 wks

23 Nov 74		ZING WENT THE STRINGS OF MY HEART			
		Buddah BDS 405		29	10 wks
1 Feb 75		SIXTY MINUTE MAN	Buddah BDS 415	40	4 wks
11 Oct 75	●	HOLD BACK THE NIGHT	Buddah BDS 437 ...	5	8 wks
13 Mar 76		THAT'S WHERE THE HAPPY PEOPLE GO			
		Atlantic K 10703		35	8 wks
24 Jul 76		SOUL SEARCHIN' TIME	Atlantic K 10797 ...	42	3 wks
14 May 77		DISCO INFERNO	Atlantic K 10914	16	7 wks
24 Jun 78		DISCO INFERNO	(re-issue) Atlantic K 11135	47	10 wks

TRASH UK, male vocal/instrumental group 3 wks

25 Oct 69	**GOLDEN SLUMBERS/CARRY THAT WEIGHT** Apple 17	35	3 wks

John TRAVOLTA US, male vocalist 24 wks

7 Oct 78	● **SANDY** Polydor POSP 6	2	15 wks
2 Dec 78	**GREASED LIGHTNIN'** Polydor/Midsong POSP 14	11	9 wks

See also John Travolta and Olivia Newton-John.

John TRAVOLTA and Olivia NEWTON-JOHN
US/UK, male/female vocal duo 45 wks

20 May 78	★ **YOU'RE THE ONE THAT I WANT** RSO 006	1	26 wks
16 Sep 78	★ **SUMMER NIGHTS** RSO 18	1	19 wks

See also John Travolta; Olivia Newton-John; Olivia Newton-John and Electric Light Orchestra; Olivia Newton-John and Cliff Richard. Second hit has credit: and cast (being the cast of the film 'Grease').

TREMELOES
UK, male vocal/instrumental group 131 wks

2 Feb 67	● **HERE COMES MY BABY** CBS 202519	4	11 wks
27 Apr 67	★ **SILENCE IS GOLDEN** CBS 2723	1	15 wks
2 Aug 67	● **EVEN THE BAD TIMES ARE GOOD** CBS 2930	4	13 wks
8 Nov 67	**BE MINE** CBS 3043	39	2 wks
17 Jan 68	● **SUDDENLY YOU LOVE ME** CBS 3234	6	11 wks
8 May 68	**HELULE HELULE** CBS 2889	14	9 wks
18 Sep 68	● **MY LITTLE LADY** CBS 3443	6	12 wks
11 Dec 68	**I SHALL BE RELEASED** CBS 3873	29	5 wks
19 Mar 69	**HELLO WORLD** CBS 4065	14	8 wks
1 Nov 69	● **(CALL ME) NUMBER ONE** CBS 4582	2	15 wks
21 Mar 70	**BY THE WAY** CBS 4815	35	6 wks
12 Sep 70	● **ME AND MY LIFE** CBS 5139	4	18 wks
10 Jul 71	**HELLO BUDDY** CBS 7294	32	7 wks

See also Brian Poole and the Tremeloes.

Jackie TRENT UK, female vocalist 17 wks

22 Apr 65	★ **WHERE ARE YOU NOW (MY LOVE)** Pye 7N 15776	1	11 wks
1 Jul 65	**WHEN THE SUMMERTIME IS OVER** Pye 7N 15865	39	2 wks
2 Apr 69	**I'LL BE THERE** Pye 7N 17693	38	4 wks

Tony TRIBE Jamaica, male vocalist 2 wks

16 Jul 69	**RED RED WINE** Downtown DT 419	50	1 wk
9 Aug 69	**RED RED WINE** (re-entry) Downtown DT 419	46	1 wk

TRINIDAD OIL COMPANY
Trinidad, male/female vocal/instrumental group 5 wks

21 May 77	**THE CALENDAR SONG** Harvest HAR 5122	34	5 wks

TRINITY - See Julie DRISCOLL, Brian AUGER and the TRINITY

TRIO Germany, male vocal/instrumental group 10 wks

3 Jul 82	● **DA DA DA** Mobile Suit Corporation/Phonogram CORP 5	2	10 wks

TRISTRAM - See NEW VAUDEVILLE BAND

TRIUMPH
Canada, male vocal/instrumental group 2 wks

22 Nov 80	**I LIVE FOR THE WEEKEND** RCA 13	59	2 wks

TROGGS UK, male vocal/instrumental group 85 wks

5 May 66	● **WILD THING** Fontana TF 689	2	12 wks
14 Jul 66	★ **WITH A GIRL LIKE YOU** Fontana TF 717	1	12 wks
29 Sep 66	● **I CAN'T CONTROL MYSELF** Page One POF 001	2	14 wks
15 Dec 66	● **ANY WAY THAT YOU WANT ME** Page One POF 010	8	10 wks
16 Feb 67	**GIVE IT TO ME** Page One POF 015	12	10 wks
1 Jun 67	**NIGHT OF THE LONG GRASS** Page One POF 022	17	6 wks
26 Jul 67	**HI HI HAZEL** Page One POF 030	42	3 wks
18 Oct 67	● **LOVE IS ALL AROUND** Page One POF 040	5	14 wks
28 Feb 68	**LITTLE GIRL** Page One POF 056	37	4 wks

TROUBADOURS DU ROI BAUDOUIN Zaire, male/female vocal group 11 wks

19 Mar 69	**SANCTUS (MISSA LUBA)** Philips BF 1732	28	6 wks
7 May 69	**SANCTUS (MISSA LUBA)** (re-entry) Philips BF 1732	37	5 wks

Doris TROY US, female vocalist 12 wks

19 Nov 64	**WHATCHA GONNA DO ABOUT IT** Atlantic AT 4011	37	7 wks
21 Jan 65	**WHATCHA GONNA DO ABOUT IT** (re-entry) Atlantic AT 4011	38	5 wks

TRUCKIN' CO. - See Garnet MIMMS and TRUCKIN' CO.

Andrea TRUE CONNECTION
US, female vocalist, male instrumental backing group 16 wks

17 Apr 76	● **MORE MORE MORE** Buddah BDS 442	5	10 wks
4 Mar 78	**WHAT'S YOUR NAME WHAT'S YOUR NUMBER** Buddah BDS 467	34	6 wks

TRUSSEL US, male vocal/instrumental group 4 wks

8 Mar 80	**LOVE INJECTION** Elektra K 12412	43	4 wks

TRUTH UK, male vocal duo 6 wks

3 Feb 66	**GIRL** Pye 7N 17035	27	6 wks

TRUTH UK, male vocal/instrumental group 16 wks

11 Jun 83	**CONFUSION (HITS US EVERYTIME)** Formation/WEA TRUTH 1	22	7 wks
27 Aug 83	**A STEP IN THE RIGHT DIRECTION** Formation/WEA TRUTH 2	32	7 wks
4 Feb 84	**NO STONE UNTURNED** Formation/WEA YZ 1	66	2 wks

TUBES US, male vocal/instrumental group 18 wks

19 Nov 77	**WHITE PUNKS ON DOPE** A & M AMS 7323	28	4 wks
28 Apr 79	**PRIME TIME** A & M AMS 7423	34	10 wks
12 Sep 81	**DON'T WANT TO WAIT ANYMORE** Capitol CL 208	60	4 wks

TUBEWAY ARMY - See Gary NUMAN

Louise TUCKER *UK, female vocalist* *5 wks*

| 9 Apr 83 | MIDNIGHT BLUE *Ariola ARO 289* .... | 59 | 5 wks |

Tommy TUCKER *US, male vocalist* *10 wks*

| 26 Mar 64 | HI-HEEL SNEAKERS *Pye 7N 25238* ...... | 23 | 10 wks |

Claramae TURNER - See VARIOUS ARTISTS (Carousel Soundtrack)

Ike and Tina TURNER
US, male instrumentalist - guitar, and female vocalist *44 wks*

9 Jun 66	● RIVER DEEP MOUNTAIN HIGH *London HL 10046*	3	13 wks
28 Jul 66	TELL HER I'M NOT HOME *Warner Bros. WB 5753*	48	1 wk
27 Oct 66	A LOVE LIKE YOURS *London HL 10083*	16	10 wks
12 Feb 69	RIVER DEEP MOUNTAIN HIGH (re-issue) *London HLU 10242*	33	7 wks
8 Sep 73	● NUTBUSH CITY LIMITS *United Artists UP 35582*	4	13 wks

See also Tina Turner.

Sammy TURNER *US, male vocalist* *2 wks*

| 13 Nov 59 | ALWAYS *London HLX 8963* .... | 26 | 2 wks |

Tina TURNER *US, female vocalist* *52 wks*

19 Nov 83	● LET'S STAY TOGETHER *Capitol CL 316*	6	20 wks
25 Feb 84	HELP *Capitol CL 325*	40	4 wks
16 Jun 84	● WHAT'S LOVE GOT TO DO WITH IT *Capitol CL 334*	3	16 wks
15 Sep 84	BETTER BE GOOD TO ME *Capitol CL 338* ...	45	5 wks
17 Nov 84	PRIVATE DANCER *Capitol CL 343*	26†	7 wks

See also Ike and Tina Turner.

TURTLES *US, male vocal/instrumental group* *39 wks*

23 Mar 67	HAPPY TOGETHER *London HL 10115*	12	12 wks
15 Jun 67	● SHE'D RATHER BE WITH ME *London HLU 10135*	4	15 wks
30 Oct 68	● ELENORE *London HL 10223*	7	12 wks

TUXEDOS - See Bobby ANGELO and the TUXEDOS

TWEETS *UK, male instrumental group* *34 wks*

12 Sep 81	● THE BIRDIE SONG (BIRDIE DANCE) *PRT 7P 219*	2	23 wks
5 Dec 81	LET'S ALL SING LIKE THE BIRDIES SING *PRT 7P 226*	44	6 wks
18 Dec 82	THE BIRDIE SONG (BIRDIE DANCE) (re-entry) *PRT 7P 219*	46	5 wks

TWICE AS MUCH *UK, male vocal duo* *9 wks*

| 16 Jun 66 | SITTIN' ON A FENCE *Immediate IM 033* ...... | 25 | 9 wks |

TWIGGY *UK, female vocalist* *10 wks*

| 14 Aug 76 | HERE I GO AGAIN *Mercury 6007 100* ...... | 17 | 10 wks |

TWINKLE *UK, female vocalist* *20 wks*

| 26 Nov 64 | ● TERRY *Decca F 12013* .... | 4 | 15 wks |
| 25 Feb 65 | ● GOLDEN LIGHTS *Decca F 12076* .... | 21 | 5 wks |

TWISTED SISTER
US, male vocal/instrumental group *25 wks*

26 Mar 83	I AM (I'M ME) *Atlantic A 9854*	18	9 wks
28 May 83	THE KIDS ARE BACK *Atlantic A 9827*	32	6 wks
20 Aug 83	YOU CAN'T STOP ROCK 'N' ROLL *Atlantic A 9792*	43	4 wks
2 Jun 84	WE'RE NOT GONNA TAKE IT *Atlantic A 9657*	58	6 wks

Conway TWITTY *US, male vocalist* *36 wks*

14 Nov 58	★ IT'S ONLY MAKE BELIEVE *MGM 992*	1	15 wks
27 Mar 59	STORY OF MY LOVE *MGM 1003*	30	1 wk
21 Aug 59	● MONA LISA *MGM 1029*	5	14 wks
21 Jul 60	IS A BLUE BIRD BLUE *MGM 1082*	43	3 wks
23 Feb 61	C'EST SI BON *MGM 1118*	40	3 wks

TWO MAN SOUND
Belgium, male vocal/instrumental group *7 wks*

| 20 Jan 79 | QUE TAL AMERICA *Miracle M 1* | 46 | 7 wks |

TYGERS OF PAN TANG
UK, male vocal/instrumental group *15 wks*

14 Feb 81	HELLBOUND *MCA 672*	48	3 wks
27 Mar 82	LOVE POTION NO. 9 *MCA 769*	45	6 wks
10 Jul 82	RENDEZVOUS *MCA 777*	49	4 wks
11 Sep 82	PARIS BY AIR *MCA 790*	63	2 wks

Bonnie TYLER *UK, female vocalist* *53 wks*

30 Oct 76	● LOST IN FRANCE *RCA 2734*	9	10 wks
19 Mar 77	MORE THAN A LOVER *RCA PB 5008*	27	6 wks
3 Dec 77	IT'S A HEARTACHE *RCA PB 5057*	4	12 wks
30 Jun 79	MARRIED MEN *RCA PB 5164*	35	6 wks
19 Feb 83	★ TOTAL ECLIPSE OF THE HEART *CBS TYLER 1*	1	12 wks
7 May 83	FASTER THAN THE SPEED OF LIGHT *CBS A 3338*	43	4 wks
25 Jun 83	HAVE YOU EVER SEEN THE RAIN *CBS A 3517*	47	3 wks

See also Shaky and Bonnie.

TYMES *US, male vocal group* *41 wks*

25 Jul 63	SO MUCH IN LOVE *Cameo Parkway P 871*	21	8 wks
15 Jan 69	PEOPLE *Direction 58 3903*	16	10 wks
21 Sep 74	YOU LITTLE TRUST MAKER *RCA 2456*	18	9 wks
21 Dec 74	★ MS GRACE *RCA 2493*	1	11 wks
17 Jan 76	GOD'S GONNA PUNISH YOU *RCA 2626*	41	3 wks

TYPICALLY TROPICAL
UK, male vocal/instrumental duo *11 wks*

| 5 Jul 75 | ★ BARBADOS *Gull GULS 14* .... | 1 | 11 wks |

Judie TZUKE *UK, female vocalist* *10 wks*

| 14 Jul 79 | STAY WITH ME TILL DAWN *Rocket XPRES 17* | 16 | 10 wks |

EVELYN THOMAS (right) '76 and '84 were great years but she didn't go high in between.

THIN LIZZY (centre) 'Listen, if Petula Clark, Donovan and Suzi Quatro can pose with Cliff why can't I . . .?' (T.M.B. Rice and B.A. Robertson caught trying to sneak a piece of the action). (Photo: Rex features.)

TRACIE (below) The first single for Paul Weller's protégée was written by The Questions.

B. J. THOMAS (above) Sacha Distel fell on his head.

THOMPSON TWINS (left) Named after characters in *Tin Tin*

U

U. K.   *UK, male vocal/instrumental group*   *2 wks*

30 Jun 79	**NOTHING TO LOSE** *Polydor POSP 55*	67	2 wks

U2   *Ireland, male vocal/instrumental group*   *38 wks*

8 Aug 81	**FIRE** *Island WIP 6679*	35	6 wks
17 Oct 81	**GLORIA** *Island WIP 6733*	55	4 wks
3 Apr 82	**A CELEBRATION** *Island WIP 6770*	47	4 wks
22 Jan 83	● **NEW YEARS DAY** *Island UWIP 6848*	10	8 wks
2 Apr 83	**TWO HEARTS BEAT AS ONE** *Island IS 109* ...	18	5 wks
15 Sep 84	● **PRIDE (IN THE NAME OF LOVE)** *Island IS 202*	3	11 wks

U.B.40   *UK, male vocal/instrumental group*   *128 wks*

8 Mar 80	● **KING/FOOD FOR THOUGHT** *Graduate GRAD 6*	4	13 wks
14 Jun 80	● **MY WAY OF THINKING/I THINK IT'S GOING TO RAIN** *Graduate GRAD 8*	6	10 wks
1 Nov 80	● **THE EARTH DIES SCREAMING/DREAM A LIE** *Graduate GRAD 10*	10	12 wks
23 May 81	**DON'T LET IT PASS YOU BY/DON'T SLOW DOWN** *Dep International DEP 1*	16	9 wks
8 Aug 81	● **ONE IN TEN** *Dep International DEP 2*	7	10 wks
13 Feb 82	**I WON'T CLOSE MY EYES** *Dep International DEP 3*	32	6 wks
15 May 82	**LOVE IS ALL IS ALRIGHT** *Dep International DEP 4*	29	7 wks
28 Aug 82	**SO HERE I AM** *Dep International DEP 5*	25	9 wks
5 Feb 83	**I'VE GOT MINE** *Dep International 7 DEP 6*	45	4 wks
20 Aug 83	★ **RED RED WINE** *Dep International 7 DEP 7*	1	14 wks
15 Oct 83	● **PLEASE DON'T MAKE ME CRY** *Dep International 7 DEP 8*	10	8 wks
10 Dec 83	**MANY RIVERS TO CROSS** *Dep International 7 DEP 9*	16	8 wks
17 Mar 84	**CHERRY OH BABY** *Dep International/Virgin DEP 10*	12	8 wks
22 Sep 84	● **IF IT HAPPENS AGAIN** *Dep International/Virgin DEP 11*	9	8 wks
1 Dec 84	**RIDDLE ME** *Dep International/Virgin DEP 15*	59	2 wks

UFO   *UK, male vocal/instrumental group*   *31 wks*

5 Aug 78	**ONLY YOU CAN ROCK ME** *Chrysalis CHS 2241*	50	4 wks
27 Jan 79	**DOCTOR DOCTOR** *Chrysalis CHS 2287*	35	6 wks
31 Mar 79	**SHOOT SHOOT** *Chrysalis CHS 2318*	48	5 wks
12 Jan 80	**YOUNG BLOOD** *Chrysalis CHS 2399*	36	5 wks
17 Jan 81	**LONELY HEART** *Chrysalis CHS 2482*	41	5 wks
30 Jan 82	**LET IT RAIN** *Chrysalis CHS 2576*	62	3 wks
19 Mar 83	**WHEN IT'S TIME TO ROCK** *Chrysalis CHS 2672*	70	3 wks

U.K. PLAYERS
UK, male vocal/instrumental group   *3 wks*

14 May 83	**LOVE'S GONNA GET YOU** *RCA 326*	52	3 wks

U.K. SUBS
UK, male vocal/instrumental group   *39 wks*

23 Jun 79	**STRANGLEHOLD** *Gem GEMS 5*	26	8 wks
8 Sep 79	**TOMORROW'S GIRLS** *Gem GEMS 10*	28	6 wks
1 Dec 79	**SHE'S NOT THERE/KICKS** (EP) *Gem GEMS 14*	36	7 wks
8 Mar 80	**WARHEAD** *Gem GEMS 23*	30	4 wks
17 May 80	**TEENAGE** *Gem GEMS 30*	32	5 wks
25 Oct 80	**PARTY IN PARIS** *Gem GEMS 42*	37	4 wks

18 Apr 81	**KEEP ON RUNNIN' (TILL YOU BURN)** *Gem GEMS 45*	41	5 wks

Tracks on EP: She's Not There/Kicks/Victim/The Same Thing.

Tracey ULLMAN   *UK, female vocalist*   *49 wks*

19 Mar 83	● **BREAKAWAY** *Stiff BUY 168*	4	11 wks
24 Sep 83	● **THEY DON'T KNOW** *Stiff BUY 180*	2	11 wks
3 Dec 83	● **MOVE OVER DARLING** *Stiff BUY 195*	8	9 wks
3 Mar 84	**MY GUY** *Stiff BUY 197*	23	6 wks
28 Jul 84	**SUNGLASSES** *Stiff BUY 205*	18	9 wks
27 Oct 84	**HELPLESS** *Stiff BUY 211*	61	3 wks

ULTRAVOX
UK, male vocal/instrumental group   *130 wks*

5 Jul 80	**SLEEPWALK** *Chrysalis CHS 2441*	29	11 wks
18 Oct 80	**PASSING STRANGERS** *Chrysalis CHS 2457*	57	4 wks
17 Jan 81	● **VIENNA** *Chrysalis CHS 2481*	2	14 wks
28 Mar 81	**SLOW MOTION** *Island WIP 6691*	33	4 wks
6 Jun 81	**ALL STOOD STILL** *Chrysalis CHS 2522*	8	10 wks
2 Aug 81	**THE THIN WALL** *Chrysalis CHS 2540*	14	8 wks
7 Nov 81	**THE VOICE** *Chrysalis CHS 2559*	16	12 wks
25 Sep 82	**REAP THE WILD WIND** *Chrysalis CHS 2639* .	12	9 wks
27 Nov 82	**HYMN** *Chrysalis CHS 2657*	11	11 wks
19 Mar 83	**VISIONS IN BLUE** *Chrysalis CHS 2676*	15	6 wks
4 Jun 83	**WE CAME TO DANCE** *Chrysalis VOX 1*	18	7 wks
11 Feb 84	**ONE SMALL DAY** *Chrysalis VOX 2*	27	6 wks
19 May 84	● **DANCING WITH TEARS IN MY EYES** *Chrysalis UV 1*	3	10 wks
7 Jul 84	**LAMENT** *Chrysalis UV 2*	22	6 wks
14 Jul 84	**DANCING WITH TEARS IN MY EYES** (re-entry) *Chrysalis UV 1*	65	2 wks
25 Aug 84	**LAMENT** (re-entry) *Chrysalis UV 2*	73	1 wk
20 Oct 84	**LOVE'S GREAT ADVENTURE** *Chrysalis UV 3*	12	9 wks

Piero UMILIANI
Italy, orchestra and chorus   *8 wks*

30 Apr 77	● **MAH NA MAH NA** *EMI International INT 530* ..	8	8 wks

UNDERTAKERS
UK, male vocal/instrumental group   *1 wk*

9 Apr 64	**JUST A LITTLE BIT** *Pye 7N 15607*	49	1 wk

UNDERTONES
UK, male vocal/instrumental group   *67 wks*

21 Oct 78	**TEENAGE KICKS** *Sire SIR 4007*	31	6 wks
3 Feb 79	**GET OVER YOU** *Sire SIR 4010*	57	4 wks
28 Apr 79	**JIMMY JIMMY** *Sire SIR 4015*	16	10 wks
21 Jul 79	**HERE COMES THE SUMMER** *Sire SIR 4022* ..	34	6 wks
20 Oct 79	**YOU'VE GOT MY NUMBER (WHY DON'T YOU USE IT?)** *Sire SIR 5024*	32	6 wks
5 Apr 80	● **MY PERFECT COUSIN** *Sire SIR 4038*	9	10 wks
5 Jul 80	**WEDNESDAY WEEK** *Sire SIR 4042*	11	9 wks
2 May 81	**IT'S GOING TO HAPPEN!** *Ardeck AROS 8*	18	9 wks
25 Jul 81	**JULIE OCEAN** *Ardeck ARDS 9*	41	5 wks
9 Jul 83	**TEENAGE KICKS** (re-issue) *Ardeck ARDS 1*	60	2 wks

UNDISPUTED TRUTH
US, male/female vocal/instrumental group   *4 wks*

22 Jan 77	**YOU + ME = LOVE** *Warner Bros. K 16804*	43	4 wks

UNION GAP   -   *See Gary PUCKETT and the UNION GAP*

UNIQUE
US, male/female vocal/instrumental group · *7 wks*

10 Sep 83	WHAT I GOT IS WHAT YOU NEED		
	Prelude A 3707	27	7 wks

UNIT FOUR PLUS TWO
UK, male vocal/instrumental group · *29 wks*

13 Feb 64	GREEN FIELDS *Decca F 11821*	48	2 wks
25 Feb 65	★ CONCRETE AND CLAY *Decca F 12071*	1	15 wks
13 May 65	YOU'VE NEVER BEEN IN LOVE LIKE THIS BEFORE *Decca F 12144*	14	11 wks
17 Mar 66	BABY NEVER SAY GOODBYE *Decca F 12333*	49	1 wk

UNITONE - *See Laurel AITKEN and the UNITONE*

Phil UPCHURCH COMBO *US, male*
instrumental group, Phil Upchurch bass guitar · *2 wks*

5 May 66	YOU CAN'T SIT DOWN *Sue WI 4005*	39	2 wks

UPSETTERS
Jamaica, male instrumental group · *15 wks*

4 Oct 69	● RETURN OF DJANGO/DOLLAR IN THE TEETH		
	Upsetter US 301	5	15 wks

Midge URE *UK, male vocalist* · *10 wks*

12 Jun 82	● NO REGRETS *Chrysalis CHS 2618*	9	10 wks

See also Midge Ure and Mick Karn.

Midge URE and Mick KARN
UK, male vocal/instrumental duo - guitar and bass · *4 wks*

9 Jul 83	AFTER A FASHION *Musicfest/Chrysalis FEST 1* ..	39	4 wks

See also Midge Ure.

V

VAGABONDS - *See Jimmy JAMES and the VAGABONDS*

Ricky VALANCE *UK, male vocalist* · *16 wks*

25 Aug 60	★ TELL LAURA I LOVE HER *Columbia DB 4493*	1	16 wks

Ritchie VALENS *US, male vocalist* · *1 wk*

6 Mar 59	DONNA *London HL 8803*	29	1 wk

Caterina VALENTE
France, female vocalist · *14 wks*

19 Aug 55	● THE BREEZE AND I *Polydor BM 6002*	5	14 wks

Dickie VALENTINE *UK, male vocalist* · *92 wks*

20 Feb 53	BROKEN WINGS *Decca F 9954*	12	1 wk
13 Mar 53	● ALL THE TIME AND EVERYWHERE		
	Decca F 10038	9	3 wks
5 Jun 53	● IN A GOLDEN COACH *Decca F 10098*	7	1 wk
5 Nov 54	ENDLESS *Decca F 10346*	19	1 wk
17 Dec 54	★ FINGER OF SUSPICION *Decca F 10394*	1	15 wks
17 Dec 54	MR. SANDMAN *Decca F 10415*	5	12 wks
18 Feb 55	● A BLOSSOM FELL *Decca F 10430*	9	9 wks
29 Apr 55	A BLOSSOM FELL (re-entry) *Decca F 10430*	18	1 wk
3 Jun 55	● I WONDER *Decca F 10493*	4	15 wks
25 Nov 55	★ CHRISTMAS ALPHABET *Decca F 10628*	1	7 wks
16 Dec 55	OLD PIANNA RAG *Decca F 10645*	15	5 wks
7 Dec 56	● CHRISTMAS ISLAND *Decca F 10798*	8	5 wks
27 Dec 57	SNOWBOUND FOR CHRISTMAS *Decca F 10950*	28	1 wk
13 Mar 59	VENUS *Pye Nixa 7N 15192*	28	1 wk
3 Apr 59	VENUS (re-entry) *Pye Nixa 7N 15192*	25	1 wk
17 Apr 59	VENUS (2nd re-entry) *Pye Nixa 7N 15192*	20	4 wks
22 May 59	VENUS (3rd re-entry) *Pye Nixa 7N 15192*	25	1 wk
19 Jun 59	VENUS (4th re-entry) *Pye Nixa 7N 15192*	28	1 wk
23 Oct 59	ONE MORE SUNRISE (MORGEN)		
	Pye 7N 15215	14	8 wks

See also Various Artists - All Star Hit Parade.

VALENTINE BROTHERS
US, male vocal duo · *1 wk*

23 Apr 83	MONEY'S TOO TIGHT (TO MENTION)		
	Energy NRG 1	73	1 wk

Joe VALINO *US, male vocalist* · *2 wks*

18 Jan 57	GARDEN OF EDEN *HMV POP 283*	23	2 wks

Frankie VALLI *US, male vocalist* · *50 wks*

12 Dec 70	YOU'RE READY NOW *Philips 320226*	11	13 wks
1 Feb 75	● MY EYES ADORED YOU *Private Stock PVT 1*	5	11 wks
21 Jun 75	SWEARIN' TO GOD *Private Stock PVT 21*	31	5 wks
17 Apr 76	FALLEN ANGEL *Private Stock PVT 51*	11	7 wks
26 Aug 78	● GREASE *RSO 012*	3	14 wks

See also Four Seasons.

David VAN DAY *UK, male vocalist* · *3 wks*

14 May 83	YOUNG AMERICANS TALKING *WEA DAY 1*	43	3 wks

Leroy VAN DYKE *US, male vocalist* · *20 wks*

4 Jan 62	● WALK ON BY *Mercury AMT 1166*	5	17 wks
26 Apr 62	BIG MAN IN A BIG HOUSE *Mercury AMT 1173*	34	3 wks

VAN HALEN
US/Holland, male vocal/instrumental group · *18 wks*

28 Jun 80	RUNNIN' WITH THE DEVIL		
	Warner Bros. HM 10	52	3 wks
4 Feb 84	● JUMP *Warner Bros. W 9384*	7	13 wks
19 May 84	PANAMA *Warner Bros. W 9273*	61	2 wks

VANDELLAS - *See Martha REEVES and the VANDELLAS*

Luther VANDROSS *US, male vocalist* · *6 wks*

19 Feb 83	NEVER TOO MUCH *Epic EPC A 3101*	44	6 wks

VANGELIS
Greece, male instrumentalist - keyboards   23 wks

9 May 81	CHARIOTS OF FIRE - TITLES *Polydor POSP 246*	12	10 wks
11 Jul 81	HEAVEN AND HELL, THIRD MOVEMENT (THEME FROM THE BBC-TV SERIES, THE COSMOS) *BBC 1*	48	6 wks
24 Apr 82	CHARIOTS OF FIRE - TITLES (re-entry) *Polydor POSP 246*	41	7 wks

See also Jon and Vangelis.

VANILLA FUDGE
US, male vocal/instrumental group   11 wks

| 9 Aug 67 | YOU KEEP ME HANGIN' ON *Atlantic 584 123* | 18 | 11 wks |

VANITY FARE
UK, male vocal/instrumental group   34 wks

28 Aug 68	I LIVE FOR THE SUN *Page One POF 075*	20	9 wks
23 Jul 69	● EARLY IN THE MORNING *Page One POF 142*	8	12 wks
27 Dec 69	HITCHIN' A RIDE *Page One POF 158*	16	13 wks

Randy VANWARMER
US, male vocalist   11 wks

| 4 Aug 79 | ● JUST WHEN I NEEDED YOU MOST *Bearsville WIP 6516* .... | 8 | 11 wks |

VAPORS *UK, male vocal/instrumental group*   23 wks

9 Feb 80	● TURNING JAPANESE *United Artists BP 334*	3	13 wks
5 Jul 80	NEWS AT TEN *United Artists BP 345*	44	4 wks
11 Jul 81	JIMMIE JONES *Liberty BP 401*	44	6 wks

VARDIS *UK, male vocal/instrumental group*   4 wks

| 27 Sep 80 | LET'S GO *Logo VAR 1* .... | 59 | 4 wks |

VARIOUS ARTISTS   18 wks

29 Jun 56	● ALL STAR HIT PARADE *Decca F 10752*	2	9 wks
15 Jun 56	CAROUSEL - ORIGINAL SOUNDTRACK (LP) *Capitol LCT 6105*	27	1 wk
6 Jul 56	CAROUSEL - ORIGINAL SOUNDTRACK (LP) (re-entry) *Capitol LCT 6105*	26	1 wk
26 Jul 57	ALL STAR HIT PARADE NO. 2 *Decca F 10915*	15	7 wks

All Star Hit Parade on Decca F 10752 featured the following artists with the following songs: Winifred Atwell - Theme From The Threepenny Opera; Dave King - No Other Love; Joan Regan - My September Love; Lita Roza - A Tear Fell; Dickie Valentine - Out Of Town; David Whitfield - It's Almost Tomorrow. See also the separate hit lists of each of these artists. Tracks and artists on Carousel are as follows: Carousel Waltz - Orchestra conducted by Alfred Newman; You're A Queer One Julie Jordan - Barbara Ruick and Shirley Jones; Mister Snow - Barbara Ruick; If I Loved You - Shirley Jones and Gordon MacRae; June Is Busting Out All Over - Claramae Turner; Soliloquy - Gordon MacRae; Blow High Blow Low - Cameron Mitchell; When The Children Are Asleep - Robert Rounseville and Barbara Ruick; This Was A Real Nice Clambake - Barbara Ruick, Claramae Turner, Robert Rounseville and Cameron Mitchell; Stonecutters Cut It On Stone (There's Nothing So Bad For A Woman) - Cameron Mitchell; What's The Use Of Wonderin' - Shirley Jones; You'll Never Walk Alone - Claramae Turner; If I Loved You - Gordon MacRae; You'll Never Walk Alone - Shirley Jones. The cast are American and the sex of each performer should be obvious. See also Partridge Family starring Shirley Jones. All Star Hit Parade 2 featured the following artists with the following songs: Johnston Brothers - Around The World; Billy Cotton - Puttin' On The Style; Jimmy Young - When I Fall In Love; Max Bygraves - A White Sport Coat; Beverley Sisters - Freight Train; Tommy Steele - Butterfly. See also the separate hit lists of each of these artists.

Frankie VAUGHAN *UK, male vocalist*   212 wks

29 Jan 54	ISTANBUL *HMV B 10599*	11	1 wk
28 Jan 55	HAPPY DAYS & LONELY NIGHTS *HMV B 10783*	12	3 wks
22 Apr 55	TWEEDLE DEE *Philips PB 423*	17	1 wk
2 Dec 55	SEVENTEEN *Philips PB 511*	18	3 wks
3 Feb 56	MY BOY FLAT TOP *Philips PB 544*	20	2 wks
9 Nov 56	● GREEN DOOR *Philips PB 640*	2	15 wks
11 Jan 57	★ GARDEN OF EDEN *Philips PB 660*	1	13 wks
4 Oct 57	● MAN ON FIRE/WANDERIN' EYES *Philips PB 729*	6	12 wks
20 Dec 57	● KISSES SWEETER THAN WINE *Philips PB 775*	8	11 wks
7 Mar 58	CAN'T GET ALONG WITHOUT YOU/WE'RE NOT ALONE *Philips PB 793*	11	6 wks
9 May 58	● KEWPIE DOLL *Philips PB 825*	10	12 wks
1 Aug 58	WONDERFUL THINGS *Philips PB 834*	22	3 wks
12 Sep 58	WONDERFUL THINGS (re-entry) *Philips PB 834*	27	3 wks
10 Oct 58	AM I WASTING MY TIME ON YOU *Philips PB 865*	25	2 wks
9 Jan 59	AM I WASTING MY TIME ON YOU (re-entry) *Philips PB 865*	27	2 wks
30 Jan 59	THAT'S MY DOLL *Philips PB 895*	28	2 wks
24 Jul 59	● THE HEART OF A MAN *Philips PB 930*	5	14 wks
18 Sep 59	WALKIN' TALL *Philips PB 931*	28	1 wk
2 Oct 59	WALKIN' TALL (re-entry) *Philips PB 931*	29	1 wk
29 Jan 60	WHAT MORE DO YOU WANT *Philips PB 985*	25	2 wks
22 Sep 60	KOOKIE LITTLE PARADISE *Philips PB 1054* ..	31	5 wks
27 Oct 60	MILORD *Philips PB 1066*	34	6 wks
9 Nov 61	★ TOWER OF STRENGTH *Philips PB 1195*	1	13 wks
1 Feb 62	DON'T STOP TWIST *Philips PB 1219*	22	7 wks
27 Sep 62	HERCULES *Philips 326542 BF*	42	4 wks
24 Jan 63	● LOOP-DE-LOOP *Philips 326566 BF*	5	12 wks
20 Jun 63	HEY MAMA *Philips BF 1254*	21	9 wks
4 Jun 64	HELLO DOLLY *Philips BF 1339*	18	11 wks
11 Mar 65	SOMEONE MUST HAVE HURT YOU A LOT *Philips BF 1394*	46	1 wk
23 Aug 67	● THERE MUST BE A WAY *Columbia DB 8248* ..	7	21 wks
15 Nov 67	SO TIRED *Columbia DB 8298*	21	9 wks
28 Feb 68	NEVERTHELESS *Columbia DB 8354*	29	5 wks

See also Frankie Vaughan and the Kaye Sisters.

Frankie VAUGHAN and The KAYE SISTERS
UK, male vocalist, female vocal group   20 wks

| 1 Nov 57 | ● GOTTA HAVE SOMETHING IN THE BANK FRANK *Philips PB 751* .... | 8 | 11 wks |
| 1 May 59 | ● COME SOFTLY TO ME *Philips PB 913* .... | 9 | 9 wks |

See also Frankie Vaughan; Kaye Sisters; Three Kayes.

Malcolm VAUGHAN *UK, male vocalist*   106 wks

1 Jul 55	● EVERY DAY OF MY LIFE *HMV B 10874*	5	16 wks
27 Jan 56	WITH YOUR LOVE *HMV POP 130*	20	1 wk
10 Feb 56	WITH YOUR LOVE (re-entry) *HMV POP 130* ..	18	1 wk
2 Mar 56	WITH YOUR LOVE (2nd re-entry) *HMV POP 130*	20	1 wk
26 Oct 56	ST. THERESE OF THE ROSES *HMV POP 250*	27	1 wk
16 Nov 56	● ST. THERESE OF THE ROSES (re-entry) *HMV POP 250*	3	19 wks
12 Apr 57	THE WORLD IS MINE *HMV POP 303*	30	1 wk
3 May 57	THE WORLD IS MINE (re-entry) *HMV POP 303*	29	2 wks
10 May 57	CHAPEL OF THE ROSES *HMV POP 325*	13	8 wks
31 May 57	THE WORLD IS MINE (2nd re-entry) *HMV POP 303*	26	1 wk
29 Nov 57	● MY SPECIAL ANGEL *HMV POP 419*	3	14 wks
21 Mar 58	TO BE LOVED *HMV POP 459*	14	12 wks
17 Oct 58	● MORE THAN EVER (COME PRIMA) *HMV POP 538*	5	14 wks
27 Feb 59	WAIT FOR ME/WILLINGLY *HMV POP 590*	28	1 wk
13 Mar 59	WAIT FOR ME (re-entry) *HMV POP 590*	13	14 wks

Norman VAUGHAN　*UK, male vocalist*　　*5 wks*

| 17 May 62 | SWINGING IN THE RAIN　*Pye 7N 15438* ...... | 34 | 5 wks |

Sarah VAUGHAN　*US, female vocalist*　　*17 wks*

11 Sep 59	● BROKEN HEARTED MELODY		
	Mercury AMT 1057	7	13 wks
29 Dec 60	LET'S/SERENATA　*Columbia DB 4542*	37	3 wks
2 Feb 61	LET'S/SERENATA　(re-entry) *Columbia DB 4542*	47	1 wk

See also Billy Eckstine and Sarah Vaughan.

Billy VAUGHN　*US, orchestra and chorus*　　*8 wks*

27 Jan 56	SHIFTING WHISPERING SANDS		
	London HLD 8205	20	1 wk
23 Mar 56	THEME FROM THE 'THREEPENNY OPERA'		
	London HLD 8238	12	7 wks

Bobby VEE　*US, male vocalist*　　*134 wks*

19 Jan 61	● RUBBER BALL　*London HLG 9255*	4	11 wks
13 Apr 61	● MORE THAN I CAN SAY　*London HLG 9316* ...	4	16 wks
3 Aug 61	● HOW MANY TEARS　*London HLG 9389*	10	13 wks
26 Oct 61	● TAKE GOOD CARE OF MY BABY		
	London HLG 9438	3	16 wks
21 Dec 61	● RUN TO HIM　*London HLG 9470*	6	15 wks
8 Mar 62	PLEASE DON'T ASK ABOUT BARBARA		
	Liberty LIB 55419	29	9 wks
7 Jun 62	● SHARING YOU　*Liberty LIB 55451*	10	13 wks
27 Sep 62	A FOREVER KIND OF LOVE　*Liberty LIB 10046*	13	19 wks
7 Feb 63	● THE NIGHT HAS A THOUSAND EYES		
	Liberty LIB 10069	3	12 wks
20 Jun 63	BOBBY TOMORROW　*Liberty LIB 55530*	21	10 wks

Tata VEGA　*US, female vocalist*　　*4 wks*

| 26 May 79 | GET IT UP FOR LOVE/I JUST KEEP THINKING | | |
| | ABOUT YOU BABY　*Motown TMG 1140* .... | 52 | 4 wks |

VELVELETTES　*US, female vocal group*　　*7 wks*

| 31 Jul 71 | THESE THINGS WILL KEEP ME LOVING YOU | | |
| | *Tamla Motown TMG 780* .... | 34 | 7 wks |

VELVETS　*US, male vocal group*　　*2 wks*

11 May 61	THAT LUCKY OLD SUN　*London HLU 9328* ...	46	1 wk
17 Aug 61	TONIGHT (COULD BE THE NIGHT)		
	London HLU 9372	50	1 wk

VENTURES　*US, male instrumental group*　　*31 wks*

8 Sep 60	● WALK DON'T RUN　*Top Rank JAR 417*	8	13 wks
1 Dec 60	● PERFIDIA　*London HLG 9232*	4	13 wks
9 Mar 61	RAM-BUNK-SHUSH　*London HLG 9292*	45	1 wk
11 May 61	LULLABY OF THE LEAVES　*London HLG 9344*	43	4 wks

Al VERLANE　-　*See PING PING and Al VERLANE*

VERNONS GIRLS
UK, female vocal group　　*31 wks*

17 May 62	LOVER PLEASE　*Decca F 11450*	16	9 wks
23 Aug 62	LOVER PLEASE/YOU KNOW WHAT I MEAN		
	(re-entry) *Decca F 11450*	39	7 wks
6 Sep 62	LOCO-MOTION　*Decca F 11495*	47	1 wk

18 Oct 62	YOU KNOW WHAT I MEAN　(re-entry)		
	Decca F 11450	37	3 wks
15 Nov 62	YOU KNOW WHAT I MEAN　(2nd re-entry)		
	Decca F 11450	50	1 wk
3 Jan 63	FUNNY ALL OVER　*Decca F 11549*	31	8 wks
18 Apr 63	DO THE BIRD　*Decca F 11629*	50	1 wk
2 May 63	DO THE BIRD　(re-entry) *Decca F 11629*	44	1 wk

You Know What I Mean was not coupled with Lover Please on the chart of 23 Aug 62, but both sides of this record were listed for the following 6 weeks.

VIBRATIONS　-　*See Tony JACKSON and the VIBRATIONS*

VIBRATORS
UK, male vocal/instrumental group　　*8 wks*

18 Mar 78	AUTOMATIC LOVER　*Epic EPC 6137*	35	5 wks
17 Jun 78	JUDY SAYS (KNOCK YOU IN THE HEAD)		
	Epic EPC 6393	70	3 wks

VICE SQUAD
UK, male/female vocal/instrumental group　　*1 wk*

| 13 Feb 82 | OUT OF REACH　*Zonophone Z 26* ...... | 68 | 1 wk |

VICIOUS PINK
UK, male/female vocal/instrumental duo　　*4 wks*

| 15 Sep 84 | CCCAN'T YOU SEE　*Parlophone R 6074* ...... | 67 | 4 wks |

Mike VICKERS　-　*See Kenny EVERETT and Mike VICKERS*

VIDEO SYMPHONIC　*UK, orchestra*　　*3 wks*

| 24 Oct 81 | THE FLAME TREES OF THIKA　*EMI EMI 5222* | 42 | 3 wks |

VIENNA PHILHARMONIC
ORCHESTRA　*Austria, orchestra*　　*14 wks*

| 18 Dec 71 | THEME FROM THE 'ONEDIN LINE' | | |
| | *Decca F 13259* .... | 15 | 14 wks |

VILLAGE PEOPLE
US, male vocal/instrumental group　　*49 wks*

3 Dec 77	SAN FRANCISCO (YOU'VE GOT ME)		
	DJM DJS 10817	45	5 wks
25 Nov 78	★ Y.M.C.A.　*Mercury 6007 192*	1	16 wks
17 Mar 79	◉ IN THE NAVY　*Mercury 6007 209*	2	9 wks
16 Jun 79	GO WEST　*Mercury 6007 221*	15	8 wks
9 Aug 80	CAN'T STOP THE MUSIC　*Mercury MER 16* ...	11	11 wks

Gene VINCENT　*US, male vocalist*　　*51 wks*

13 Jul 56	BE BOP A LULA　*Capitol CL 14599*	30	2 wks
24 Aug 56	BE BOP A LULA　(re-entry) *Capitol CL 14599*	16	3 wks
28 Sep 56	BE BOP A LULA　(2nd re-entry) *Capitol CL 14599*	23	2 wks
12 Oct 56	RACE WITH THE DEVIL　*Capitol CL 14628*	28	1 wk
19 Oct 56	BLUE JEAN BOP　*Capitol CL 14637*	16	5 wks
8 Jan 60	WILD CAT　*Capitol CL 15099*	21	3 wks
10 Mar 60	WILD CAT　(re-entry) *Capitol CL 15099*	39	3 wks
10 Mar 60	MY HEART　*Capitol CL 15115*	16	6 wks
28 Apr 60	MY HEART　(re-entry) *Capitol CL 15115*	47	1 wk
19 May 60	MY HEART　(2nd re-entry) *Capitol CL 15115*	36	1 wk
16 Jun 60	PISTOL PACKIN' MAMA　*Capitol CL 15136*	15	9 wks
1 Jun 61	SHE SHE LITTLE SHEILA　*Capitol CL 15202* ...	22	10 wks

17 Aug 61	SHE SHE LITTLE SHEILA (re-entry)			
	Capitol CL 15202		44	1 wk
31 Aug 61	I'M GOING HOME Capitol CL 15215		36	4 wks

Bobby VINTON *US, male vocalist* — *18 wks*

2 Aug 62	ROSES ARE RED Columbia DB 4878	15	8 wks
19 Dec 63	THERE I'VE SAID IT AGAIN Columbia DB 7179	34	10 wks

VIOLINSKI *UK, male instrumental group* — *9 wks*

17 Feb 79	CLOG DANCE Jet 136	17	9 wks

VIPERS SKIFFLE GROUP
UK, male vocal/instrumental group — *18 wks*

25 Jan 57	● DON'T YOU ROCK ME DADDY-O		
	Parlophone R 4261	10	9 wks
22 Mar 57	● CUMBERLAND GAP Parlophone R 4289	10	6 wks
31 May 57	STREAMLINE TRAIN Parlophone R 4308	23	3 wks

V.I.P.S *UK, male vocal/instrumental group* — *4 wks*

6 Sep 80	THE QUARTER MOON Gem GEMS 39	55	4 wks

VISAGE *UK, male vocal/instrumental group* — *55 wks*

20 Dec 80	● FADE TO GREY Polydor POSP 194	8	15 wks
14 Mar 81	MIND OF A TOY Polydor POSP 236	13	8 wks
11 Jul 81	VISAGE Polydor POSP 293	21	7 wks
13 Mar 82	DAMNED DON'T CRY Polydor POSP 390	11	8 wks
26 Jun 82	NIGHT TRAIN Polydor POSP 441	12	10 wks
13 Nov 82	PLEASURE BOYS Polydor POSP 523	44	3 wks
1 Sep 84	LOVE GLOVE Polydor POSP 697	67	4 wks

VISCOUNTS *UK, male vocal group* — *18 wks*

13 Oct 60	SHORT'NIN' BREAD Pye 7N 15287	16	8 wks
14 Sep 61	WHO PUT THE BOMP Pye 7N 15379	21	10 wks

VISION *UK, male vocal/instrumental group* — *1 wk*

9 Jul 83	LOVE DANCE MVM MVM 2886	74	1 wk

VOGGUE *Canada, female vocal duo* — *6 wks*

18 Jul 81	DANCIN' THE NIGHT AWAY Mercury MER 76	39	6 wks

VOYAGE *UK/France, disco aggregation* — *27 wks*

17 Jun 78	FROM EAST TO WEST/SCOTS MACHINE		
	GTO/Hansa GT 224	13	13 wks
25 Nov 78	SOUVENIRS GTO GT 241	56	7 wks
24 Mar 79	LET'S FLY AWAY GTO/Hansa GT 245	38	7 wks

'Scots Machine' credited from 24 Jun 78 until end of record's chart run.

VOYAGER
UK, male vocal/instrumental group — *8 wks*

26 May 79	HALFWAY HOTEL Mountain VOY 001	33	8 wks

Adam WADE *US, male vocalist* — *6 wks*

8 Jun 61	TAKE GOOD CARE OF HER HMV POP 843	38	1 wk
22 Jun 61	TAKE GOOD CARE OF HER (re-entry)		
	HMV POP 843	38	5 wks

WAH!
UK, male/female vocal/instrumental group — *17 wks*

25 Dec 82	● THE STORY OF THE BLUES Eternal JF 1	3	12 wks
19 Mar 83	HOPE (I WISH YOU'D BELIEVE ME)		
	WEA X 9880	37	5 wks

See also Mighty Wah.

WAIKIKIS *US, male instrumental group* — *2 wks*

11 Mar 65	HAWAIIAN TATTOO Palette PG 9025	41	2 wks

WAILERS - See Bob MARLEY and the WAILERS

John WAITE *UK, male vocalist* — *11 wks*

29 Sep 84	● MISSING YOU EMI America EA 182	9	11 wks

WAITRESSES *UK, female vocal group* — *4 wks*

18 Dec 82	CHRISTMAS WRAPPING Ze/Island WIP 6821	45	4 wks

Johnny WAKELIN *UK, male vocalist* — *20 wks*

18 Jan 75	● BLACK SUPERMAN (MUHAMMAD ALI)		
	Pye 7N 45420	7	10 wks
24 Jul 76	● IN ZAIRE Pye 7N 45595	4	10 wks

Black Superman by Johnny Wakelin and the Kinshasa Band.

Narada Michael WALDEN
US, male vocalist/instrumentalist-drums — *18 wks*

23 Feb 80	TONIGHT I'M ALL RIGHT Atlantic K 11437	34	9 wks
26 Apr 80	● I SHOULDA LOVEDYAH Atlantic K 11413	8	9 wks

Gary WALKER *US, male vocalist* — *12 wks*

24 Feb 66	YOU DON'T LOVE ME CBS 202036	26	6 wks
26 May 66	TWINKIE LEE CBS 202081	26	6 wks

See also Walker Brothers.

John WALKER *US, male vocalist* — *6 wks*

5 Jul 67	ANNABELLA Philips BF 1593	48	1 wk
19 Jul 67	ANNABELLA (re-entry) Philips BF 1593	24	5 wks

See also Walker Brothers.

Junior WALKER and the ALL-STARS *US, male instrumental/vocal group, Junior Walker tenor sax* — *59 wks*

18 Aug 66	HOW SWEET IT IS Tamla Motown TMG 571	22	10 wks

TINA TURNER Her 1984 hit 'What's Love Got To Do With It' topped the classic 'River Deep Mountain High' by 3 weeks on chart. Both made the number three position.

JACKIE TRENT AND TONY HATCH (below) Celebrating her 1965 hit with a small Tot of the Pops.

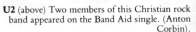

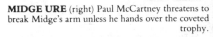

U2 (above) Two members of this Christian rock band appeared on the Band Aid single. (Anton Corbin).

MIDGE URE (right) Paul McCartney threatens to break Midge's arm unless he hands over the coveted trophy.

FRANKIE VAUGHAN (far right) Churned out Merseybeat hits long before The Beatles and Frankie Goes to Hollywood.

2 Apr 69	**(I'M A) ROAD RUNNER**		**12**	12 wks
	Tamla Motown TMG 691			
18 Oct 69	**WHAT DOES IT TAKE (TO WIN YOUR LOVE)**		**13**	12 wks
	Tamla Motown TMG 712			
26 Aug 72	**WALK IN THE NIGHT** *Tamla Motown TMG 824*		**16**	11 wks
27 Jan 73	**TAKE ME GIRL I'M READY**		**16**	9 wks
	Tamla Motown TMG 840			
30 Jun 73	**WAY BACK HOME** *Tamla Motown TMG 857* ..		**35**	5 wks

Scott WALKER   *US, male vocalist*   *30 wks*

8 Dec 67	**JACKIE** *Philips BF 1628*		**22**	9 wks
1 May 68 ●	**JOANNA** *Philips BF 1662*		**7**	11 wks
11 Jun 69	**LIGHTS OF CINCINATTI** *Philips BF 1793*		**13**	10 wks

See also Walker Brothers.

WALKER BROTHERS
US, male vocal group   *93 wks*

29 Apr 65	**LOVE HER** *Philips BF 1409*		**20**	13 wks
19 Aug 65 ★	**MAKE IT EASY ON YOURSELF** *Philips BF 1428*		**1**	14 wks
2 Dec 65 ●	**MY SHIP IS COMING IN** *Philips BF 1454*		**3**	12 wks
3 Mar 66 ★	**THE SUN AIN'T GONNA SHINE ANYMORE**		**1**	11 wks
	Philips BF 1473			
14 Jul 66	**(BABY) YOU DON'T HAVE TO TELL ME**		**13**	8 wks
	Philips BF 1497			
22 Sep 66	**ANOTHER TEAR FALLS** *Philips BF 1514*		**12**	8 wks
15 Dec 66	**DEADLIER THAN THE MALE** *Philips BF 1537*		**34**	6 wks
9 Feb 67	**STAY WITH ME BABY** *Philips BF 1548*		**26**	6 wks
18 May 67	**WALKING IN THE RAIN** *Philips BF 1576*		**26**	6 wks
17 Jan 76 ●	**NO REGRETS** *GTO GT 42*		**7**	9 wks

See also Gary Walker; John Walker; Scott Walker.

WALL OF VOODOO
US, male vocal/instrumental group   *3 wks*

19 Mar 83	**MEXICAN RADIO** *Illegal ILS 36*		**64**	3 wks

Jerry WALLACE   *US, male vocalist*   *1 wk*

23 Jun 60	**YOU'RE SINGING OUR LOVE SONG TO**			
	SOMEBODY ELSE *London HLH 9110*		**46**	1 wk

Bob WALLIS and his STORYVILLE JAZZ BAND
UK, male jazz band, Bob Wallis trumpet   *7 wks*

6 Jul 61	**I'M SHY MARY ELLEN I'M SHY**		**44**	2 wks
	Pye Jazz 7NJ 2043			
4 Jan 62	**COME ALONG PLEASE** *Pye Jazz 7NJ 2048* ...		**33**	5 wks

Joe WALSH   *US, male vocalist*   *15 wks*

16 Jul 77	**ROCKY MOUNTAIN WAY** (EP)		**39**	4 wks
	ABC ABE 12002			
8 Jul 78	**LIFE'S BEEN GOOD** *Asylum K 13129*		**14**	11 wks

Tracks on Rocky Mountain Way EP: Rocky Mountain Way/Turn To Stone/Meadows/Walk Away.

Sheila WALSH and Cliff RICHARD   *UK, female/male vocal duo*   *2 wks*

4 Jun 83	**DRIFTING** *DJM SHEIL 1*		**64**	2 wks

See also Cliff Richard; Phil Everly and Cliff Richard.

Trevor WALTERS   *UK, male vocalist*   *22 wks*

24 Oct 81	**LOVE ME TONIGHT** *Magnet MAG 198*		**27**	8 wks
21 Jul 84 ●	**STUCK ON YOU** *Sanity IS 002*		**9**	12 wks
1 Dec 84	**NEVER LET HER SLIP AWAY**			
	Polydor POSP 716		**73**	2 wks

WANG CHUNG
UK, male vocal/instrumental group   *12 wks*

28 Jan 84	**DANCE HALL DAYS** *Geffen A 3837*		**21**	12 wks

Dexter WANSELL
US, male instrumentalist - keyboards   *3 wks*

20 May 78	**ALL NIGHT LONG**			
	Philadelphia International PIR 6255		**59**	3 wks

WAR   *US, male vocal/instrumental group*   *27 wks*

24 Jan 76	**LOW RIDER** *Island WIP 6267*		**12**	7 wks
26 Jun 76	**ME AND BABY BROTHER** *Island WIP 6303* ...		**21**	7 wks
14 Jan 78	**GALAXY** *MCA 339*		**14**	7 wks
15 Apr 78	**HEY SENORITA** *MCA 359*		**40**	2 wks
10 Apr 82	**YOU GOT THE POWER** *RCA 201*		**58**	4 wks

Anita WARD   *US, female vocalist*   *11 wks*

2 Jun 79 ★	**RING MY BELL** *TK TKR 7543*		**1**	11 wks

Billy WARD   *US, male vocalist*   *13 wks*

13 Sep 57	**STARDUST** *London HLU 8465*		**13**	11 wks
29 Nov 57	**DEEP PURPLE** *London HLU 8502*		**30**	1 wk
3 Jan 58	**STARDUST** (re-entry) *London HLU 8465*		**26**	1 wk

Clifford T. WARD   *UK, male vocalist*   *16 wks*

30 Jun 73 ●	**GAYE** *Charisma CB 205*		**8**	11 wks
26 Jan 74	**SCULLERY** *Charisma CB 221*		**37**	5 wks

Michael WARD   *UK, male vocalist*   *13 wks*

29 Sep 73	**LET THERE BE PEACE ON EARTH (LET IT**			
	BEGIN WITH ME) *Philips 6006 340*		**15**	10 wks
15 Dec 73	**LET THERE BE PEACE ON EARTH (LET IT**			
	BEGIN WITH ME) (re-entry) *Philips 6006 340*		**50**	3 wks

WARM SOUNDS   *UK, male vocal duo*   *6 wks*

4 May 67	**BIRDS AND BEES** *Deram DM 120*		**27**	6 wks

Jennifer WARNES - *See Joe COCKER and Jennifer WARNES*

Dionne WARWICK   *US, female vocalist*   *83 wks*

13 Feb 64	**ANYONE WHO HAD A HEART**			
	Pye International 7N 25234		**42**	3 wks
16 Apr 64 ●	**WALK ON BY** *Pye International 7N 25241*		**9**	14 wks
30 Jul 64	**YOU'LL NEVER GET TO HEAVEN**			
	Pye International 7N 25256		**20**	8 wks
8 Oct 64	**REACH OUT FOR ME** *Pye International 7N 25265*		**23**	7 wks
1 Apr 65	**YOU CAN HAVE HIM** *Pye International 7N 25290*		**37**	5 wks
13 Mar 68	**VALLEY OF THE DOLLS**			
	Pye International 7N 25445		**28**	8 wks

15 May 68 ● DO YOU KNOW THE WAY TO SAN JOSE			
Pye International 7N 25457		8	10 wks
23 Oct 82 ● HEARTBREAKER Arista ARIST 496		2	13 wks
11 Dec 82 ● ALL THE LOVE IN THE WORLD			
Arista ARIST 507		10	10 wks
26 Feb 83 YOURS Arista ARIST 518		66	2 wks
28 May 83 I'LL NEVER LOVE THIS WAY AGAIN			
Arista ARIST 530		62	3 wks

See also Dionne Warwick and the Detroit Spinners.

Dionne WARWICKE and the DETROIT SPINNERS
US, female vocalist, male vocal group   *6 wks*

19 Oct 74 THEN CAME YOU Atlantic K 10495		29	6 wks

See also Dionne Warwick; Detroit Spinners.

WAS (NOT WAS)
US, male vocal/instrumental duo   *5 wks*

3 Mar 84 OUT COME THE FREAKS ZE/Geffen A 4178 ..		41	5 wks

Dinah WASHINGTON
US, female vocalist   *4 wks*

30 Nov 61 SEPTEMBER IN THE RAIN Mercury AMT 1162		35	3 wks
18 Jan 62 SEPTEMBER IN THE RAIN (re-entry)			
Mercury AMT 1162		49	1 wk

Geno WASHINGTON and the RAM JAM BAND
UK, male vocalist, male instrumental backing group   *20 wks*

19 May 66 WATER Piccadilly 7N 35312		39	8 wks
21 Jul 66 HI HI HAZEL Piccadilly 7N 35329		45	3 wks
25 Aug 66 HI HI HAZEL (re-entry) Piccadilly 7N 35329		48	1 wk
6 Oct 66 QUE SERA SERA Piccadilly 7N 35346		43	3 wks
2 Feb 67 MICHAEL Piccadilly 7N 35359		39	5 wks

Grover WASHINGTON JR.
US, male instrumentalist - saxophone   *7 wks*

16 May 81 JUST THE TWO OF US Elektra K 12514		34	7 wks

Dennis WATERMAN and George COLE
UK, male vocal duo   *5 wks*

17 Dec 83 WHAT ARE WE GONNA GET 'ER INDOORS			
EMI MIN 101		21	5 wks

See also Dennis Waterman with the Dennis Waterman Band.

Dennis WATERMAN with the DENNIS WATERMAN BAND
UK, male vocalist/male instrumental group   *12 wks*

25 Oct 80 ● I COULD BE SO GOOD FOR YOU EMI 5009		3	12 wks

See also Dennis Waterman and George Cole.

Peter WATERMAN - See 14–18

Johnny 'Guitar' WATSON
US, male vocalist, instrumentalist - guitar   *8 wks*

28 Aug 76 I NEED IT DJM DJS 20694		35	5 wks
23 Apr 77 A REAL MOTHER FOR YA DJM DJT 10762 ..		44	3 wks

WAVELENGTH   *UK, male vocal group*   *12 wks*

10 Jul 82 HURRY HOME Ariola ARO 281		17	12 wks

WAY OF THE WEST
UK, male vocal/instrumental group   *5 wks*

25 Apr 81 DON'T SAY THAT'S JUST FOR WHITE BOYS			
Mercury MER 66		54	5 wks

Jeff WAYNE   *US/UK, orchestra*   *3 wks*

10 Jul 82 MATADOR CBS A 2493		57	3 wks

See also Jeff Wayne's War Of The Worlds.

Jeff WAYNE'S WAR OF THE WORLDS
US/UK, male/female vocal/instrumental cast   *8 wks*

9 Sep 78 EVE OF THE WAR CBS 6496		36	8 wks

See also Jeff Wayne.

WEATHER GIRLS
US, female vocal group   *14 wks*

27 Aug 83 IT'S RAINING MEN CBS A 2924		73	3 wks
3 Mar 84 ● IT'S RAINING MEN (re-entry) CBS A 2924		2	11 wks

WEATHERMEN
UK, male vocalist, Jonathan King under a false name   *9 wks*

16 Jan 71 IT'S THE SAME OLD SONG B and C CB 139		19	9 wks

See also Jonathan King.

Marti WEBB   *UK, female vocalist*   *18 wks*

9 Feb 80 ● TAKE THAT LOOK OFF YOUR FACE			
Polydor POSP 100		3	12 wks
19 Apr 80 TELL ME ON A SUNDAY Polydor POSP 111 ..		67	2 wks
20 Sep 80 YOUR EARS SHOULD BE BURNING NOW			
Polydor POSP 166		61	4 wks

Joan WEBER   *US, female vocalist*   *1 wk*

18 Feb 55 LET ME GO LOVER Philips PB 389		16	1 wk

Max WEBSTER
Canada, male vocal/instrumental group   *3 wks*

19 May 79 PARADISE SKIES Capitol CL 16079		43	3 wks

Fred WEDLOCK   *UK, male vocalist*   *10 wks*

31 Jan 81 ● OLDEST SWINGER IN TOWN Rocket XPRES 46		6	10 wks

Bert WEEDON
UK, male instrumentalist - guitar   *38 wks*

15 May 59	●	GUITAR BOOGIE SHUFFLE	*Top Rank JAR 117*	10	9 wks
20 Nov 59		NASHVILLE BOOGIE	*Top Rank JAR 221*	29	2 wks
10 Mar 60		BIG BEAT BOOGIE	*Top Rank JAR 300*	37	3 wks
7 Apr 60		BIG BEAT BOOGIE (re-entry)	*Top Rank JAR 300*	49	1 wk
9 Jun 60		TWELFTH STREET RAG	*Top Rank JAR 360*	47	2 wks
28 Jul 60		APACHE	*Top Rank JAR 415*	44	1 wk
11 Aug 60		APACHE (re-entry)	*Top Rank JAR 415*	24	3 wks
27 Oct 60		SORRY ROBBIE	*Top Rank JAR 517*	28	11 wks
2 Feb 61		GINCHY	*Top Rank JAR 537*	35	5 wks
4 May 61		MR. GUITAR	*Top Rank JAR 559*	47	1 wk

Frank WEIR   *UK, orchestra*   *4 wks*

15 Sep 60	CARIBBEAN HONEYMOON	*Oriole CB 1559*	42	4 wks

Eric WEISSBERG   -   *See DELIVERANCE SOUNDTRACK*

Brandi WELLS   *US, female vocalist*   *1 wk*

20 Feb 82	WATCH OUT	*Virgin VS 479*	74	1 wk

Houston WELLS   *UK, male vocalist*   *10 wks*

1 Aug 63	ONLY THE HEARTACHES	*Parlophone R 5031*	22	10 wks

Mary WELLS   *US, female vocalist*   *24 wks*

21 May 64	●	MY GUY	*Stateside SS 288*	5	14 wks
8 Jul 72		MY GUY (re-issue)	*Tamla Motown TMG 820*	14	10 wks

See also Marvin Gaye and Mary Wells.

Terri WELLS   *US, female vocalist*   *9 wks*

2 Jul 83	YOU MAKE IT HEAVEN	*Phillyworld PWS 111*	53	2 wks
5 May 84	I'LL BE AROUND	*Phillyworld LON 48*	17	7 wks

Alex WELSH
UK, male instrumentalist - trumpet   *4 wks*

10 Aug 61	TANSY	*Columbia DB 4686*	45	4 wks

Dodie WEST   *UK, female vocalist*   *4 wks*

14 Jan 65	GOING OUT OF MY HEAD	*Decca F 12046*	39	4 wks

Keith WEST   *UK, male vocalist*   *18 wks*

9 Aug 67	●	EXCERPT FROM A TEENAGE OPERA	*Parlophone R 5623*	2	15 wks
22 Nov 67		SAM	*Parlophone R 5651*	38	3 wks

WEST HAM UNITED CUP SQUAD
UK, male football team vocalists   *2 wks*

10 May 75	I'M FOREVER BLOWING BUBBLES	*Pye 7N 45470*	31	2 wks

WEST STREET MOB
US, male vocal group   *3 wks*

8 Oct 83	BREAK DANCIN'-ELECTRIC BOOGIE	*Sugarhill SH 128*	71	1 wk
22 Oct 83	BREAK DANCIN'-ELECTRIC BOOGIE (re-entry)	*Sugarhill SH 128*	64	2 wks

Kim WESTON   -   *See Marvin GAYE and Kim WESTON*

WHALERS   -   *See Hal PAGE and the WHALERS*

WHAM!
UK, male/female vocal/instrumental group   *92 wks*

16 Oct 82	●	YOUNG GUNS (GO FOR IT) *Innervision IVL A2766*		3	17 wks
15 Jan 83	●	WHAM RAP *Innervision IVL A2442*		8	11 wks
14 May 83	●	BAD BOYS *Innervision A 3143*		2	14 wks
30 Jul 83	●	CLUB TROPICANA *Innervision A 3613*		4	11 wks
3 Dec 83		CLUB FANTASTIC MEGAMIX *Innervision A 3586*		15	8 wks
26 May 84	★	WAKE ME UP BEFORE YOU GO GO *Epic A 4440*		1	16 wks
13 Oct 84	★	FREEDOM *Epic A 4743*		1†	12 wks
15 Dec 84	●	LAST CHRISTMAS/EVERYTHING SHE WANTS *Epic A 4949*		2†	3 wks

WHATNAUTS   -   *See MOMENTS and WHATNAUTS*

Nancy WHISKEY   -   *See Charles McDEVITT Skiffle Group featuring Nancy WHISKEY*

WHISPERS   *US, male vocal group*   *37 wks*

2 Feb 80	●	AND THE BEAT GOES ON	*Solar SO 1*	2	12 wks
10 May 80		LADY	*Solar SO 4*	55	3 wks
12 Jul 80		MY GIRL	*Solar SO 8*	26	6 wks
14 Mar 81		IT'S A LOVE THING	*Solar SO 16*	9	11 wks
13 Jun 81		I CAN MAKE IT BETTER	*Solar SO 19*	44	5 wks

WHITE and TORCH
UK, male vocal/instrumental duo   *4 wks*

2 Oct 82	PARADE	*Chrysalis CHS 2641*	54	4 wks

Barry WHITE   *US, male vocalist*   *117 wks*

9 Jun 73	I'M GONNA LOVE YOU JUST A LITTLE BIT MORE BABY *Pye International 7N 25610*		23	7 wks
26 Jan 74	NEVER NEVER GONNA GIVE YA UP *Pye International 7N 25633*		14	11 wks
17 Aug 74 ●	CAN'T GET ENOUGH OF YOUR LOVE BABE *Pye International 7N 25661*		8	12 wks
2 Nov 74 ★	YOU'RE THE FIRST THE LAST MY EVERYTHING *20th Century BTC 2133*		1	14 wks
8 Mar 75 ●	WHAT AM I GONNA DO WITH YOU *20th Century BTC 2177*		5	8 wks
24 May 75	I'LL DO ANYTHING YOU WANT ME TO *20th Century BTC 2208*		20	6 wks
27 Dec 75 ●	LET THE MUSIC PLAY *20th Century BTC 2265*		9	8 wks
6 Mar 76 ●	YOU SEE THE TROUBLE WITH ME *20th Century BTC 2277*		2	10 wks
21 Aug 76	BABY WE BETTER TRY AND GET IT TOGETHER *20th Century BTC 2298*		15	7 wks
13 Nov 76	DON'T MAKE ME WAIT TOO LONG *20th Century BTC 2309*		17	8 wks
5 Mar 77	I'M QUALIFIED TO SATISFY *20th Century BTC 2328*		37	5 wks

15 Oct 77		IT'S ECSTASY WHEN YOU LAY DOWN NEXT TO ME *20th Century BTC 2350*	40	3 wks
16 Dec 78		JUST THE WAY YOU ARE *20th Century BTC 2380*	12	12 wks
24 Mar 79		SHA LA LA MEANS I LOVE YOU *20th Century BTC 1041*	55	6 wks

Chris WHITE *UK, male vocalist*   *4 wks*

20 Mar 76	SPANISH WINE *Charisma CB 272*	37	4 wks

Snowy WHITE
UK, male vocalist/instrumentalist - guitar   *10 wks*

24 Dec 83	●	BIRD OF PARADISE *Towerbell TOW 42*	6	10 wks

Tam WHITE *UK, male vocalist*   *4 wks*

15 Mar 75	WHAT IN THE WORLD'S COME OVER YOU *RAK 193*	36	4 wks

Tony Joe WHITE *US, male vocalist*   *10 wks*

6 Jun 70	GROUPIE GIRL *Monument MON 1043*	22	10 wks

WHITE PLAINS *UK, male vocal group*   *56 wks*

7 Feb 70	●	MY BABY LOVES LOVIN' *Deram DM 280*	9	11 wks
18 Apr 70		I'VE GOT YOU ON MY MIND *Deram DM 291*	17	11 wks
24 Oct 70	●	JULIE DO YA LOVE ME *Deram DM 315*	8	14 wks
12 Jun 71		WHEN YOU ARE A KING *Deram DM 333*	13	11 wks
17 Feb 73		STEP INTO A DREAM *Deram DM 371*	21	9 wks

WHITEHEAD - *See McFADDEN and WHITEHEAD*

WHITESNAKE
UK, male vocal/instrumental group   *58 wks*

24 Jun 78		SNAKE BITE (EP) *EMI International INEP 751*	61	3 wks
10 Nov 79		LONG WAY FROM HOME *United Artists BP 324*	55	2 wks
26 Apr 80		FOOL FOR YOUR LOVING *United Artists BP 352*	13	9 wks
12 Jul 80		READY AN' WILLING (SWEET SATISFACTION) *United Artists BP 363*	43	4 wks
22 Nov 80		AIN'T NO LOVE IN THE HEART OF THE CITY *Sunburst/Liberty BP 381*	51	4 wks
11 Apr 81		DON'T BREAK MY HEART AGAIN *Liberty BP 395*	17	9 wks
6 Jun 81		WOULD I LIE TO YOU *Liberty BP 399*	37	6 wks
6 Nov 82		HERE I GO AGAIN /BLOODY LUXURY *Liberty BP 416*	34	10 wks
13 Aug 83		GUILTY OF LOVE *Liberty BP 420*	31	5 wks
14 Jan 84		GIVE ME MORE TIME *Liberty BP 422*	29	4 wks
28 Apr 84		STANDING IN THE SHADOW *Liberty BP 423*	62	2 wks

Tracks on Snake Bite EP: Bloody Mary/Steal Away/Ain't No Love In The Heart Of The City/Come On. This EP and Long Way From Home were credited to David Coverdale's Whitesnake.

David WHITFIELD *UK, male vocalist*   *181 wks*

2 Oct 53	●	BRIDGE OF SIGHS *Decca F 10129*	9	1 wk
16 Oct 53	★	ANSWER ME *Decca F 10192*	1	13 wks
11 Dec 53		RAGS TO RICHES *Decca F 10207*	12	1 wk
8 Jan 54	●	RAGS TO RICHES (re-entry) *Decca F 10207*	3	10 wks
29 Jan 54		ANSWER ME (re-entry) *Decca F 10192*	12	1 wk
19 Feb 54	●	THE BOOK *Decca F 10242*	5	12 wks
28 May 54	●	THE BOOK (re-entry) *Decca F 10242*	10	3 wks
18 Jun 54	★	CARA MIA *Decca F 10327*	1	25 wks
12 Nov 54	●	SANTO NATALE *Decca F 10399*	2	10 wks
11 Feb 55	●	BEYOND THE STARS *Decca F 10458*	8	9 wks
27 May 55		MAMA *Decca F 10515*	20	1 wk
24 Jun 55		MAMA (re-entry) *Decca F 10515*	19	2 wks
8 Jul 55	●	EV'RYWHERE *Decca F 10515*	3	20 wks
29 Jul 55		MAMA (2nd re-entry) *Decca F 10515*	12	8 wks
25 Nov 55	●	WHEN YOU LOSE THE ONE YOU LOVE *Decca F 10627*	7	11 wks
2 Mar 56		MY SEPTEMBER LOVE *Decca F 10690*	19	2 wks
23 Mar 56		MY SEPTEMBER LOVE (re-entry) *Decca F 10690*	18	1 wk
6 Apr 56	◉	MY SEPTEMBER LOVE (2nd re-entry) *Decca F 10690*	3	20 wks
24 Aug 56		MY SON JOHN *Decca F 10769*	22	4 wks
31 Aug 56		MY UNFINISHED SYMPHONY *Decca F 10769*	29	1 wk
7 Sep 56		MY SEPTEMBER LOVE (3rd re-entry) *Decca F 10690*	25	1 wk
25 Jan 57	●	ADORATION WALTZ *Decca F 10833*	9	11 wks
5 Apr 57		I'LL FIND YOU *Decca F 10864*	28	2 wks
7 Jun 57		I'LL FIND YOU (re-entry) *Decca F 10864*	27	2 wks
14 Feb 58		CRY MY HEART *Decca F 10978*	22	3 wks
16 May 58		ON THE STREET WHERE YOU LIVE *Decca F 11018*	16	14 wks
8 Aug 58		THE RIGHT TO LOVE *Decca F 11039*	30	1 wk
24 Nov 60		I BELIEVE *Decca F 11289*	49	1 wk

Slim WHITMAN *US, male vocalist*   *75 wks*

15 Jul 55	★	ROSE MARIE *London HL 8061*	1	19 wks
29 Jul 55	●	INDIAN LOVE CALL *London L 1149*	7	12 wks
23 Sep 55		CHINA DOLL *London L 1149*	15	2 wks
9 Mar 56		TUMBLING TUMBLEWEEDS *London HLU 8230*	19	2 wks
13 Apr 56		I'M A FOOL *London HLU 8252*	16	3 wks
11 May 56		I'M A FOOL (re-entry) *London HLU 8252*	29	1 wk
22 Jun 56		SERENADE *London HLU 8287*	24	3 wks
27 Jul 56		SERENADE (re-entry) *London HLU 8287*	8	12 wks
12 Apr 57	●	I'LL TAKE YOU HOME AGAIN KATHLEEN *London HLP 8403*	7	13 wks
5 Oct 74		HAPPY ANNIVERSARY *United Artists UP 35728*	14	10 wks

Roger WHITTAKER
Kenya, male vocalist   *75 wks*

8 Nov 69		DURHAM TOWN (THE LEAVIN') *Columbia DB 8613*	12	18 wks
11 Apr 70	●	I DON'T BELIEVE IN IF ANYMORE *Columbia DB 8664*	8	18 wks
10 Oct 70		NEW WORLD IN THE MORNING *Columbia DB 8718*	17	14 wks
3 Apr 71		WHY *Columbia DB 8752*	47	1 wk
2 Oct 71		MAMMY BLUE *Columbia DB 8822*	31	10 wks
26 Jul 75	●	THE LAST FAREWELL *EMI 2294*	2	14 wks

WHO *UK, male vocal/instrumental group*   *243 wks*

18 Feb 65	Ⓖ	I CAN'T EXPLAIN *Brunswick 05926*	8	13 wks
27 May 65	●	ANYWAY ANYHOW ANYWHERE *Brunswick 05935*	10	12 wks
4 Nov 65	●	MY GENERATION *Brunswick 05944*	2	13 wks
10 Mar 66	●	SUBSTITUTE *Reaction 591 001*	5	13 wks
24 Mar 66		A LEGAL MATTER *Brunswick 05956*	32	6 wks
1 Sep 66	●	I'M A BOY *Reaction 591 004*	2	13 wks
1 Sep 66		THE KIDS ARE ALRIGHT *Brunswick 05965*	41	2 wks
22 Sep 66		THE KIDS ARE ALRIGHT (re-entry) *Brunswick 05965*	48	1 wk
15 Dec 66	●	HAPPY JACK *Reaction 591 010*	3	11 wks
27 Apr 67	●	PICTURES OF LILY *Track 604 002*	4	10 wks
26 Jul 67		THE LAST TIME/UNDER MY THUMB *Track 604 006*	44	3 wks
18 Oct 67	●	I CAN SEE FOR MILES *Track 604 011*	10	12 wks
19 Jun 68		DOGS *Track 604 023*	25	5 wks
23 Oct 68		MAGIC BUS *Track 604 024*	26	6 wks
19 Mar 69	●	PINBALL WIZARD *Track 604 027*	4	13 wks
4 Apr 70		THE SEEKER *Track 604 036*	19	11 wks
8 Aug 70		SUMMERTIME BLUES *Track 2094 002*	38	4 wks
10 Jul 71	●	WON'T GET FOOLED AGAIN *Track 2094 009*	9	12 wks

23 Oct 71		LET'S SEE ACTION *Track 2094 012*		**16**	12 wks
24 Jun 72	●	JOIN TOGETHER *Track 2094 102*		**9**	9 wks
13 Jan 73		RELAY *Track 2094 106*		**21**	5 wks
13 Oct 73		5:15 *Track 2094 115*		**20**	6 wks
24 Jan 76		SQUEEZE BOX *Polydor 2121 275*		**10**	9 wks
30 Oct 76	●	SUBSTITUTE (re-issue) *Polydor 2058 803*		**7**	7 wks
22 Jul 78		WHO ARE YOU *Polydor WHO 1*		**18**	12 wks
28 Apr 79		LONG LIVE ROCK *Polydor WHO 2*		**48**	5 wks
7 Mar 81	●	YOU BETTER YOU BET *Polydor WHO 004*		**9**	8 wks
9 May 81		DON'T LET GO THE COAT *Polydor WHO 005*		**47**	4 wks
2 Oct 82		ATHENA *Polydor WHO 6*		**40**	4 wks
26 Nov 83		READY STEADY WHO (EP) *Reaction/Polydor WHO 7*		**58**	2 wks

See also High Numbers. Tracks on EP: Disguises/Circles/Batman/Bucket 'T'/Barbara Ann.

WHODINI
US, male rapping and scratching duo   *10 wks*

25 Dec 82		MAGIC'S WAND *Jive JIVE 28*		**47**	6 wks
17 Mar 84		MAGIC'S WAND (THE WHODINI ELECTRIC EP) (re-issue) *Jive JIVE 61*		**63**	4 wks

Tracks on EP: (re-issue) Jive Magic Wand/Nasty Lady/Rap Machine/ The Haunted House of Rock.

WIGAN'S CHOSEN FEW
US, instrumental track plus UK crowd vocal   *11 wks*

18 Jan 75	●	FOOTSEE *Pye Disco Demand DDS 111*		**9**	11 wks

WIGAN'S OVATION
UK, male vocal/instrumental group   *19 wks*

15 Mar 75		SKIING IN THE SNOW *Spark SRL 1122*		**12**	10 wks
28 Jun 75		PER-SO-NAL-LY *Spark SRL 1129*		**38**	6 wks
29 Nov 75		SUPER LOVE *Spark SRL 1133*		**41**	3 wks

Jack WILD *UK, male vocalist*   *2 wks*

2 May 70		SOMETHING BEAUTIFUL *Capitol CL 15635*		**46**	2 wks

WILD CHERRY
US, male vocal/instrumental group   *11 wks*

9 Oct 76	●	PLAY THAT FUNKY MUSIC *Epic EPC 4593*		**7**	11 wks

Eugene WILDE *US, male vocalist*   *9 wks*

13 Oct 84		GOTTA GET YOU HOME TONIGHT *Fourth and Broadway/Island BRW 15*		**18**	9 wks

Kim WILDE *UK, female vocalist*   *72 wks*

21 Feb 81	●	KIDS IN AMERICA *RAK 327*		**2**	13 wks
9 May 81	●	CHEQUERED LOVE *RAK 330*		**4**	9 wks
1 Aug 81		WATER ON GLASS/BOYS *RAK 334*		**11**	8 wks
14 Nov 81		CAMBODIA *RAK 336*		**12**	12 wks
17 Apr 82		VIEW FROM A BRIDGE *RAK 342*		**16**	7 wks
16 Oct 82		CHILD COME AWAY *RAK 352*		**43**	4 wks
30 Jul 83		LOVE BLONDE *RAK 360*		**23**	8 wks
12 Nov 83		DANCING IN THE DARK *RAK 365*		**67**	2 wks
13 Oct 84		THE SECOND TIME *MCA KIM 1*		**29**	6 wks
8 Dec 84		THE TOUCH *MCA KIM 2*		**56**	3 wks

Marty WILDE *UK, male vocalist*   *117 wks*

11 Jul 58	●	ENDLESS SLEEP *Philips PB 835*		**4**	14 wks
6 Mar 59	●	DONNA *Philips PB 902*		**3**	16 wks
5 Jun 59	●	A TEENAGER IN LOVE *Philips PB 926*		**2**	17 wks
3 Jul 59		DONNA (re-entry) *Philips PB 902*		**25**	2 wks
25 Sep 59		SEA OF LOVE *Philips PB 959*		**3**	12 wks
11 Dec 59		BAD BOY *Philips PB 972*		**7**	8 wks
10 Mar 60		JOHNNY ROCCO *Philips PB 1002*		**30**	4 wks
19 May 60		THE FIGHT *Philips PB 1022*		**47**	1 wk
22 Dec 60		LITTLE GIRL *Philips PB 1078*		**16**	9 wks
26 Jan 61	●	RUBBER BALL *Philips PB 1101*		**9**	9 wks
27 Jul 61		HIDE AND SEEK *Philips PB 1161*		**47**	2 wks
9 Nov 61		TOMORROW'S CLOWN *Philips PB 1191*		**33**	5 wks
24 May 62		JEZEBEL *Philips PB 1240*		**19**	11 wks
25 Oct 62		EVER SINCE YOU SAID GOODBYE *Philips 326546 BF*		**31**	7 wks

Matthew WILDER *US, male vocalist*   *11 wks*

21 Jan 84	●	BREAK MY STRIDE *Epic A 3908*		**4**	11 wks

Sue WILKINSON *UK, female vocalist*   *8 wks*

2 Aug 80		YOU GOTTA BE A HUSTLER IF YOU WANNA GET ON *Cheapskate CHEAP 2*		**25**	8 wks

Andy WILLIAMS *US, male vocalist*   *228 wks*

19 Apr 57	★	BUTTERFLY *London HLA 8399*		**1**	15 wks
21 Jun 57		I LIKE YOUR KIND OF LOVE *London HLA 8437*		**16**	10 wks
30 Aug 57		BUTTERFLY (re-entry) *London HLA 8399*		**29**	1 wk
14 Jun 62		STRANGER ON THE SHORE *CBS AAG 103*		**30**	10 wks
21 Mar 63	●	CAN'T GET USED TO LOSING YOU *CBS AAG 138*		**2**	18 wks
27 Feb 64		A FOOL NEVER LEARNS *CBS AAG 182*		**40**	4 wks
16 Sep 65	●	ALMOST THERE *CBS 201813*		**2**	17 wks
24 Feb 66		MAY EACH DAY *CBS 202042*		**19**	8 wks
22 Sep 66		IN THE ARMS OF LOVE *CBS 202300*		**33**	7 wks
4 May 67		MUSIC TO WATCH GIRLS BY *CBS 2675*		**33**	6 wks
2 Aug 67		MORE AND MORE *CBS 2886*		**45**	1 wk
13 Mar 68	●	CAN'T TAKE MY EYES OFF YOU *CBS 3928*		**5**	18 wks
7 May 69		HAPPY HEART *CBS 4062*		**47**	1 wk
21 May 69		HAPPY HEART (re-entry) *CBS 4062*		**19**	9 wks
14 Mar 70	●	CAN'T HELP FALLING IN LOVE *CBS 4818*		**3**	17 wks
1 Aug 70		IT'S SO EASY *CBS 5113*		**13**	13 wks
7 Nov 70		IT'S SO EASY (re-entry) *CBS 5113*		**49**	1 wk
21 Nov 70		HOME LOVIN' MAN *CBS 5267*		**7**	12 wks
20 Mar 71	●	(WHERE DO I BEGIN) LOVE STORY *CBS 7020*		**4**	17 wks
24 Jul 71		(WHERE DO I BEGIN) LOVE STORY (re-entry) *CBS 7020*		**49**	1 wk
5 Aug 72		LOVE THEME FROM THE GODFATHER *CBS 8166*		**50**	1 wk
2 Sep 72		LOVE THEME FROM THE GODFATHER (re-entry) *CBS 8166*		**44**	3 wks
30 Sep 72		LOVE THEME FROM THE GODFATHER (2nd re-entry) *CBS 8166*		**42**	5 wks
8 Dec 73	●	SOLITAIRE *CBS 1824*		**4**	18 wks
18 May 74		GETTING OVER YOU *CBS 2181*		**35**	5 wks
31 May 75		YOU LAY SO EASY ON MY MIND *CBS 3167*		**32**	7 wks
6 Mar 76		THE OTHER SIDE OF ME *CBS 3903*		**42**	3 wks

Andy and David WILLIAMS
US, male vocal duo   *5 wks*

24 Mar 73		I DON'T KNOW WHY *MCA MUS 1183*		**37**	5 wks

Do not see Andy Williams. This Andy and the other Andy are not the same, although they are related.

Billy WILLIAMS *US, male vocalist*   *9 wks*

2 Aug 57		I'M GONNA SIT RIGHT DOWN AND WRITE MYSELF A LETTER *Vogue Coral Q 72266*		**22**	8 wks

18 Oct 57	**I'M GONNA SIT RIGHT DOWN AND WRITE MYSELF A LETTER** (re-entry) *Vogue Coral Q 72266*	**28**	1 wk

Danny WILLIAMS *UK, male vocalist* — 74 wks

25 May 61	**WE WILL NEVER BE AS YOUNG AS THIS AGAIN** *HMV POP 839*	**44**	3 wks
6 Jul 61	**THE MIRACLE OF YOU** *HMV POP 885*	**41**	8 wks
2 Nov 61	★ **MOON RIVER** *HMV POP 932*	**1**	19 wks
18 Jan 62	**JEANNIE** *HMV POP 968*	**14**	14 wks
12 Apr 62	● **WONDERFUL WORLD OF THE YOUNG** *HMV POP 1002*	**8**	13 wks
5 Jul 62	**TEARS** *HMV POP 1035*	**22**	7 wks
28 Feb 63	**MY OWN TRUE LOVE** *HMV POP 1112*	**45**	3 wks
30 Jul 77	**DANCIN' EASY** *Ensign ENY 3*	**30**	7 wks

Deniece WILLIAMS *US, female vocalist* — 38 wks

2 Apr 77	★ **FREE** *CBS 4978*	**1**	10 wks
30 Jul 77	● **THAT'S WHAT FRIENDS ARE FOR** *CBS 5432*	**8**	11 wks
12 Nov 77	**BABY BABY MY LOVE'S ALL FOR YOU** *CBS 5779*	**32**	5 wks
5 May 84	● **LET'S HEAR IT FOR THE BOY** *CBS A 4319*	**2**	12 wks

See also Johnny Mathis and Deniece Williams.

Diana WILLIAMS *US, female vocalist* — 3 wks

25 Jul 81	**TEDDY BEAR'S LAST RIDE** *Capitol CL 207*	**54**	3 wks

Don WILLIAMS *US, male vocalist* — 16 wks

19 Jun 76	**I RECALL A GYPSY WOMAN** *ABC 4098*	**13**	10 wks
23 Oct 76	**YOU'RE MY BEST FRIEND** *ABC 4144*	**35**	6 wks

Iris WILLIAMS *UK, female vocalist* — 8 wks

27 Oct 79	**HE WAS BEAUTIFUL (CAVATINA) (THE THEME FROM THE DEER HUNTER)** *Columbia DB 9070*	**18**	8 wks

John WILLIAMS
UK, male instrumentalist – guitar — 11 wks

19 May 79	**CAVATINA** *Cube BUG 80*	**13**	11 wks

John WILLIAMS
US, orchestra leader with US orchestra — 10 wks

18 Dec 82	**THEME FROM 'E.T.' (THE EXTRA-TERRESTRIAL)** *MCA 800*	**17**	10 wks

Kenny WILLIAMS *US, male vocalist* — 7 wks

19 Nov 77	**(YOU'RE) FABULOUS BABE** *Decca FR 13731*	**35**	7 wks

Larry WILLIAMS *US, male vocalist* — 18 wks

20 Sep 57	**SHORT FAT FANNY** *London HLN 8472*	**21**	8 wks
17 Jan 58	**BONY MORONIE** *London HLU 8532*	**11**	10 wks

Lenny WILLIAMS *US, male vocalist* — 7 wks

5 Nov 77	**SHOO DOO FU FU OOH** *ABC 4194*	**38**	4 wks

16 Sep 78	**YOU GOT ME BURNING** *ABC 4228*	**67**	3 wks

Mason WILLIAMS
US, male instrumentalist – guitar — 13 wks

28 Aug 68	● **CLASSICAL GAS** *Warner Bros. WB 7190*	**9**	13 wks

Maurice WILLIAMS and the ZODIACS *US, male vocal group* — 9 wks

5 Jan 61	**STAY** *Top Rank JAR 526*	**14**	9 wks

Viola WILLS *US, female vocalist* — 10 wks

6 Oct 79	● **GONNA GET ALONG WITHOUT YOU NOW** *Ariola/Hansa AHA 546*	**8**	10 wks

Al WILSON *US, male vocalist* — 5 wks

23 Aug 75	**THE SNAKE** *Bell 1436*	**41**	5 wks

Dooley WILSON *US, male vocalist* — 9 wks

3 Dec 77	**AS TIME GOES BY** *United Artists UP 36331*	**15**	9 wks

Disc has credit 'with the voices of Humphrey Bogart and Ingrid Bergman'.

Jackie WILSON *US, male vocalist* — 62 wks

15 Nov 57	● **REET PETITE** *Coral Q 72290*	**6**	14 wks
14 Mar 58	**TO BE LOVED** *Coral Q 72306*	**27**	1 wk
28 Mar 58	**TO BE LOVED** (re-entry) *Coral Q 72306*	**23**	6 wks
16 May 58	**TO BE LOVED** (2nd re-entry) *Coral Q 72306*	**23**	1 wk
15 Sep 60	**ALL MY LOVE** *Coral Q 72407*	**33**	6 wks
3 Nov 60	**ALL MY LOVE** (re-entry) *Coral Q 72407*	**47**	1 wk
22 Dec 60	**ALONE AT LAST** *Coral Q 72412*	**50**	1 wk
14 May 69	**(YOUR LOVE KEEPS LIFTING ME) HIGHER AND HIGHER** *MCA BAG 2*	**11**	11 wks
29 Jul 72	● **I GET THE SWEETEST FEELING** *MCA MU 1160*	**9**	13 wks
3 May 75	**I GET THE SWEETEST FEELING/HIGHER AND HIGHER** (re-issue) *Brunswick BR 18*	**25**	8 wks

Higher and Higher was not listed together with I Get The Sweetest Feeling on Brunswick until 17 May 75.

Mari WILSON *UK, female vocalist* — 34 wks

6 Mar 82	**BEAT THE BEAT** *Compact PINK 2*	**59**	3 wks
8 May 82	**BABY IT'S TRUE** *Compact PINK 3*	**42**	6 wks
11 Sep 82	● **JUST WHAT I ALWAYS WANTED** *Compact PINK 4*	**8**	10 wks
13 Nov 82	**(BEWARE) BOYFRIEND** *Compact/London PINK 5*	**51**	4 wks
19 Mar 83	**CRY ME A RIVER** *Compact/London PINK 6*	**27**	7 wks
11 Jun 83	**WONDERFUL** *Compact Organisation PINK 7*	**47**	4 wks

Meri WILSON *US, female vocalist* — 10 wks

27 Aug 77	● **TELEPHONE MAN** *Pye International 7N 25747*	**6**	10 wks

Chris WILTSHIRE - *See CLASS ACTION featuring Chris WILTSHIRE*

WINDJAMMER
US, male vocal/instrumental group — 12 wks

30 Jun 84	**TOSSING AND TURNING** *MCA MCA 897*	**18**	12 wks

WOMACK AND WOMACK (right) An oxymoron introduced this married couple to the charts.

BERT WEEDON (right) Showing Mike Read and Belle Star Sara Jane the guitar boogie shuffle. (Photo: Dave Marriott.)

WAITRESSES (below) They Christmas wrapped in their spare time.

STEVE WRIGHT (above) Radio 1's Afternoon Show D.J. had by the end of 1984 notched up three times as many hits as John Denver.

WING AND A PRAYER Fife and Drum Corps
US, male/female vocal/instrumental group *7 wks*

24 Jan 76		**BABY FACE** *Atlantic K 10705*	**12**	7 wks

Pete WINGFIELD *UK, male vocalist* *7 wks*

28 Jun 75	●	**EIGHTEEN WITH A BULLET** *Island WIP 6231*	**7**	7 wks

WINGS
UK/US, male/female vocal/instrumental group *192 wks*

26 Feb 72		**GIVE IRELAND BACK TO THE IRISH** *Apple R 5936*	**16**	8 wks
27 May 72	●	**MARY HAD A LITTLE LAMB** *Apple R 5949* ..	**9**	11 wks
9 Dec 72	●	**HI HI HI/C MOON** *Apple R 5973*	**5**	13 wks
7 Apr 73	●	**MY LOVE** *Apple R 5985*	**9**	11 wks
9 Jun 73		**LIVE AND LET DIE** *Apple R 5987* ..	**9**	13 wks
15 Sep 73		**LIVE AND LET DIE** (re-entry) *Apple R 5987* ...	**49**	1 wk
3 Nov 73		**HELEN WHEELS** *Apple R 5993*	**12**	12 wks
2 Mar 74	●	**JET** *Apple R 5996*	**7**	9 wks
6 Jul 74	●	**BAND ON THE RUN** *Apple R 5997* .	**3**	11 wks
9 Nov 74		**JUNIOR'S FARM** *Apple R 5999* ..	**16**	10 wks
31 May 75	●	**LISTEN TO WHAT THE MAN SAID** *Capitol R 6006*	**6**	8 wks
18 Oct 75		**LETTING GO** *Capitol R 6008*	**41**	3 wks
15 May 76	●	**SILLY LOVE SONGS** *Parlophone R 6014* ..	**2**	11 wks
7 Aug 76	●	**LET 'EM IN** *Parlophone R 6015* ..	**2**	10 wks
19 Feb 77		**MAYBE I'M AMAZED** *Parlophone R 6017* ..	**28**	5 wks
19 Nov 77	★	**MULL OF KINTYRE/GIRL'S SCHOOL** *Capitol R 6018*	**1**	17 wks
1 Apr 78	●	**WITH A LITTLE LUCK** *Parlophone R 6019*	**5**	9 wks
1 Jul 78		**I'VE HAD ENOUGH** *Parlophone R 6020*	**42**	7 wks
9 Sep 78		**LONDON TOWN** *Parlophone R 6021*	**60**	4 wks
7 Apr 79	●	**GOODNIGHT TONIGHT** *Parlophone R 6023*	**5**	10 wks
16 Jun 79		**OLD SIAM SIR** *MPL R 6026*	**35**	6 wks
1 Sep 79		**GETTING CLOSER/BABY'S REQUEST** *R 6027*	**60**	3 wks

My Love, Helen Wheels, Jet, Band On The Run *and* Junior's Farm *are credited to Paul McCartney and Wings. R 6027 credited no label at all, although the number is a Parlophone one. See also Paul McCartney.*

Edgar WINTER GROUP
US, male instrumental group *9 wks*

26 May 73		**FRANKENSTEIN** *Epic EPC 1440*	**18**	9 wks

Ruby WINTERS *US, female vocalist* *35 wks*

5 Nov 77	●	**I WILL** *Creole CR 141*	**4**	13 wks
29 Apr 78		**COME TO ME** *Creole CR 153*	**11**	12 wks
26 Aug 78		**I WON'T MENTION IT AGAIN** *Creole CR 160* ..	**45**	5 wks
16 Jun 79		**BABY LAY DOWN** *Creole CR 171*	**43**	5 wks

Steve WINWOOD *UK, male vocalist* *9 wks*

17 Jan 81		**WHILE YOU SEE A CHANCE** *Island WIP 6655*	**45**	5 wks
9 Oct 82		**VALERIE** *Island WIP 6818*	**51**	4 wks

WIRE *UK, male vocal/instrumental group* *3 wks*

27 Jan 79		**OUTDOOR MINER** *Harvest HAR 5172*	**51**	3 wks

Norman WISDOM *UK, male vocalist* *20 wks*

19 Feb 54	●	**DON'T LAUGH AT ME** *Columbia DB 3133*	**3**	15 wks

---

15 Mar 57		**WISDOM OF A FOOL** *Columbia DB 3903*	**13**	5 wks

Bill WITHERS *US, male vocalist* *17 wks*

12 Aug 72		**LEAN ON ME** *A & M AMS 7004*	**18**	9 wks
14 Jan 78	●	**LOVELY DAY** *CBS 5773*	**7**	8 wks

WIZZARD
UK, male vocal/instrumental group *76 wks*

9 Dec 72	●	**BALL PARK INCIDENT** *Harvest HAR 5062*	**6**	12 wks
21 Apr 73	★	**SEE MY BABY JIVE** *Harvest HAR 5070*	**1**	17 wks
1 Sep 73	★	**ANGEL FINGERS** *Harvest HAR 5076* ..	**1**	10 wks
8 Dec 73	●	**I WISH IT COULD BE CHRISTMAS EVERYDAY** *Harvest HAR 5079*	**4**	9 wks
27 Apr 74	●	**ROCK 'N ROLL WINTER** *Warner Bros. K 16357*	**6**	7 wks
10 Aug 74		**THIS IS THE STORY OF MY LOVE (BABY)** *Warner Bros. K 16434*	**34**	4 wks
21 Dec 74	●	**ARE YOU READY TO ROCK** *Warner Bros. K 16497*	**8**	10 wks
19 Dec 81		**I WISH IT COULD BE CHRISTMAS EVERY DAY** (re-issue) *Harvest HAR 5173*	**41**	4 wks
15 Dec 84		**I WISH IT COULD BE CHRISTMAS EVERY DAY** (re-entry of re-issue) *Harvest HAR 5173*	**23†**	3 wks

I Wish It Could Be Christmas Everyday *features vocal backing by the Suedettes plus Stockland Green Bilateral School First Year Choir with additional noises Miss Snob and Class 3C.*

Terry WOGAN *Ireland, male vocalist* *5 wks*

7 Jan 78		**FLORAL DANCE** *Philips 6006 592*	**21**	5 wks

Bobby WOMACK *US, male vocalist* *3 wks*

16 Jun 84		**TELL ME WHY** *Motown TMG 1339*	**60**	3 wks

See also Wilton Felder.

WOMACK and WOMACK
US, male/female vocal duo *12 wks*

28 Apr 84		**LOVE WARS** *Elektra E 9799*	**14**	10 wks
30 Jun 84		**BABY I'M SCARED OF YOU** *Elektra E 9733* ...	**72**	2 wks

WOMBLES *UK, Mike Batt, male vocalist,*
arranger and producer under group name *87 wks*

26 Jan 74	●	**THE WOMBLING SONG** *CBS 1794*	**4**	23 wks
6 Apr 74	●	**REMEMBER YOU'RE A WOMBLE** *CBS 2241*	**3**	16 wks
22 Jun 74	●	**BANANA ROCK** *CBS 2465*	**9**	13 wks
12 Oct 74		**MINUETTO ALLEGRETTO** *CBS 2710* ..	**16**	9 wks
7 Dec 74	●	**WOMBLING MERRY CHRISTMAS** *CBS 2842*	**2**	8 wks
10 May 75		**WOMBLING WHITE TIE AND TAILS** *CBS 3266*	**22**	7 wks
9 Aug 75		**SUPER WOMBLE** *CBS 3480*	**20**	6 wks
13 Dec 75		**LET'S WOMBLE TO THE PARTY TONIGHT** *CBS 3794*	**34**	5 wks

See also Mike Batt.

Stevie WONDER
US, male vocalist - multi-instrumentalist *322 wks*

3 Feb 66		**UPTIGHT** *Tamla Motown TMG 545*	**14**	10 wks
18 Aug 66		**BLOWIN' IN THE WIND** *Tamla Motown TMG 570*	**36**	5 wks
5 Jan 67		**A PLACE IN THE SUN** *Tamla Motown TMG 588*	**20**	5 wks
26 Jul 67	●	**I WAS MADE TO LOVE HER** *Tamla Motown TMG 613*	**5**	15 wks
25 Oct 67		**I'M WONDERING** *Tamla Motown TMG 626*	**22**	8 wks

8 May 68	SHOO BE DOO BE DOO DA DAY			
	Tamla Motown TMG 653		46	4 wks
18 Dec 68 ●	FOR ONCE IN MY LIFE			
	Tamla Motown TMG 679		3	13 wks
19 Mar 69	I DON'T KNOW WHY Tamla Motown TMG 690		14	10 wks
9 Jul 69	I DON'T KNOW WHY (re-entry)			
	Tamla Motown TMG 690		43	1 wk
16 Jul 69 ●	MY CHERIE AMOUR Tamla Motown TMG 690		4	15 wks
15 Nov 69 ●	YESTER-ME YESTER-YOU YESTERDAY			
	Tamla Motown TMG 717		2	13 wks
28 Mar 70 ●	NEVER HAD A DREAM COME TRUE			
	Tamla Motown TMG 731		6	12 wks
18 Jul 70	SIGNED SEALED DELIVERED I'M YOURS			
	Tamla Motown TMG 744		15	9 wks
26 Sep 70	SIGNED SEALED DELIVERED I'M YOURS			
	(re-entry) Tamla Motown TMG 744		49	1 wk
21 Nov 70	HEAVEN HELP US ALL			
	Tamla Motown TMG 757		29	11 wks
15 May 71	WE CAN WORK IT OUT			
	Tamla Motown TMG 772		27	7 wks
22 Jan 72	IF YOU REALLY LOVE ME			
	Tamla Motown TMG 798		20	7 wks
3 Feb 73	SUPERSTITION Tamla Motown TMG 841		11	9 wks
19 May 73 ●	YOU ARE THE SUNSHINE OF MY LIFE			
	Tamla Motown TMG 852		7	11 wks
13 Oct 73	HIGHER GROUND Tamla Motown TMG 869 ...		29	5 wks
12 Jan 74	LIVING FOR THE CITY			
	Tamla Motown TMG 881		15	9 wks
13 Apr 74 ●	HE'S MISSTRA KNOW IT ALL			
	Tamla Motown TMG 892		10	9 wks
19 Oct 74	YOU HAVEN'T DONE NOTHIN'			
	Tamla Motown TMG 921		30	5 wks
11 Jan 75	BOOGIE ON REGGAE WOMAN			
	Tamla Motown TMG 928		12	8 wks
18 Dec 76 ●	I WISH Tamla Motown TMG 1054		5	10 wks
9 Apr 77 ●	SIR DUKE Motown TMG 1068		2	9 wks
10 Sep 77	ANOTHER STAR Motown TMG 1083		29	5 wks
24 Nov 79	SEND ONE YOUR LOVE Motown TMG 1149 ..		52	3 wks
26 Jan 80	BLACK ORCHID Motown TMG 1173		63	3 wks
29 Mar 80	OUTSIDE MY WINDOW Motown TMG 1179 ..		52	4 wks
13 Sep 80 ●	MASTERBLASTER (JAMMIN')			
	Motown TMG 1204		2	10 wks
27 Dec 80 ●	I AIN'T GONNA STAND FOR IT			
	Motown TMG 1215		10	10 wks
7 Mar 81 ●	LATELY Motown TMG 1226		3	13 wks
25 Jul 81 ●	HAPPY BIRTHDAY Motown TMG 1235		2	11 wks
23 Jan 82	THAT GIRL Motown TMG 1254		39	6 wks
5 Jun 82 ●	DO I DO Motown TMG 1269		10	7 wks
25 Sep 82	RIBBON IN THE SKY Motown TMG 1280		45	4 wks
25 Aug 84 ★	I JUST CALLED TO SAY I LOVE YOU			
	Motown TMG 1349		1†	19 wks
1 Dec 84	LOVE LIGHT IN FLIGHT Motown TMG 1364 ..		44†	5 wks
29 Dec 84	DON'T DRIVE DRUNK Motown TMG 1372 ...		71†	1 wk

See also Diana Ross, Marvin Gaye, Smokey Robinson and Stevie Wonder; Paul McCartney with Stevie Wonder and also Jackson Five. You Haven't Done Nothing has credit: Doo Doo Wopsssss by the Jackson Five.

WONDER DOGS *UK, canine vocal group* *7 wks*

21 Aug 82	RUFF MIX Flip FLIP 001		31	7 wks

Brenton WOOD *US, male vocalist* *14 wks*

27 Dec 67 ●	GIMME LITTLE SIGN Liberty LBF 15021		8	14 wks

Roy WOOD *UK, male vocalist/multi-instrumentalist* *35 wks*

11 Aug 73	DEAR ELAINE Harvest HAR 5074		18	8 wks
1 Dec 73 ●	FOREVER Harvest HAR 5078		8	13 wks
15 Jun 74	GOING DOWN THE ROAD Harvest HAR 5083		13	7 wks
31 May 75	OH WHAT A SHAME Jet 754		13	7 wks

Edward WOODWARD *UK, male vocalist* *2 wks*

16 Jan 71	THE WAY YOU LOOK TONIGHT			
	DJM DJS 232		50	1 wk
30 Jan 71	THE WAY YOU LOOK TONIGHT (re-entry)			
	DJM DJS 232		42	1 wk

Sheb WOOLEY *US, male vocalist* *8 wks*

20 Jun 58	PURPLE PEOPLE EATER MGM 981		12	8 wks

WORKING WEEK *UK, male/female vocal/instrumental group* *2 wks*

9 Jun 84	VENCEREMOS-WE WILL WIN			
	Paladin/Virgin VS 684		64	2 wks

WORLD FAMOUS SUPREME TEAM *US, male vocal group* *5 wks*

25 Feb 84	HEY DJ Charisma/Virgin TEAM 1		52	5 wks

See also Malcolm McLaren, where act is billed World's Famous Supreme Team.

WORLD PREMIERE *US, male vocal instrumental group* *4 wks*

28 Jan 84	SHARE THE NIGHT Epic A 4133		64	4 wks

Betty WRIGHT *US, female vocalist* *14 wks*

25 Jan 75	SHOORAH SHOORAH RCA 2491		27	7 wks
19 Apr 75	WHERE IS THE LOVE RCA 2548		25	7 wks

Ruby WRIGHT *UK, female vocalist* *15 wks*

16 Apr 54 ●	BIMBO Parlophone R 3816		7	4 wks
21 May 54	BIMBO (re-entry) Parlophone R 3816		12	1 wk
22 May 59	THREE STARS Parlophone R 4556		19	10 wks

Steve WRIGHT *UK, male vocalist* *10 wks*

27 Nov 82	I'M ALRIGHT RCA 296		40	6 wks
15 Oct 83	GET SOME THERAPY RCA RCA 362		75	1 wk
1 Dec 84	THE GAY CAVALIEROS (THE STORY SO FAR)			
	MCA 925		61	3 wks

Second hit credited to Steve Wright and the Sisters of Soul (UK, female vocalists). First hit credited to Young Steve and the Afternoon Boys (UK, male vocal instrumental group).

WURZELS *UK, male vocal/instrumental group* *27 wks*

15 May 76 ★	COMBINE HARVESTER (BRAND NEW KEY)			
	EMI 2450		1	13 wks
11 Sep 76 ●	I AM A CIDER DRINKER (PALOMA BLANCA)			
	EMI 2520		3	9 wks
25 Jun 77	FARMER BILL'S COWMAN (I WAS KAISER			
	BILL'S BATMAN) EMI 2637		32	5 wks

See also Adge Cutler and the Wurzels.

Robert WYATT *UK, male vocalist* *11 wks*

28 Sep 74	I'M A BELIEVER Virgin VS 114		29	5 wks

7 May 83	**SHIPBUILDING** *Rough Trade RT 115*	**35**	6 wks

Michael WYCOFF *US, male vocalist* — 2 wks

23 Jul 83	**(DO YOU REALLY LOVE ME) TELL ME LOVE** *RCA 348*	**60**	2 wks

Bill WYMAN *UK, male vocalist* — 13 wks

25 Jul 81	**(SI SI) JE SUIS UN ROCK STAR** *A & M AMS 8144*	**14**	9 wks
20 Mar 82	**A NEW FASHION** *A & M AMS 8209*	**37**	4 wks

Jane WYMAN - *See Bing CROSBY and Jane WYMAN*

Tammy WYNETTE *US, female vocalist* — 23 wks

26 Apr 75	★ **STAND BY YOUR MAN** *Epic EPC 7137*	**1**	12 wks
28 Jun 75	**D. I. V. O. R. C. E.** *Epic EPC 3361*	**12**	7 wks
12 Jun 76	**I DON'T WANNA PLAY HOUSE** *Epic EPC 4091*	**37**	4 wks

Mark WYNTER *UK, male vocalist* — 80 wks

25 Aug 60	**IMAGE OF A GIRL** *Decca F 11263*	**11**	10 wks
10 Nov 60	**KICKING UP THE LEAVES** *Decca F 11279*	**24**	10 wks
9 Mar 61	**DREAM GIRL** *Decca F 11323*	**27**	5 wks
8 Jun 61	**EXCLUSIVELY YOURS** *Decca F 11354*	**32**	7 wks
4 Oct 62	● **VENUS IN BLUE JEANS** *Pye 7N 15466*	**4**	15 wks
13 Dec 62	● **GO AWAY LITTLE GIRL** *Pye 7N 15492*	**6**	11 wks
6 Jun 63	**SHY GIRL** *Pye 7N 15525*	**28**	6 wks
14 Nov 63	**IT'S ALMOST TOMORROW** *Pye 7N 15577*	**12**	12 wks
9 Apr 64	**ONLY YOU** *Pye 7N 15626*	**38**	4 wks

X

Malcolm X *US, male orator* — 4 wks

7 Apr 84	**NO SELL OUT** *Tommy Boy/Island IS 165*	**60**	4 wks

Hit features credit: Music by Keith Le Blanc.

Miss X *UK, female vocalist* — 6 wks

1 Aug 63	**CHRISTINE** *Ember S 175*	**37**	6 wks

Miss X was Joyce Blair.

XAVIER *US, male vocal/instrumental group* — 3 wks

20 Mar 82	**WORK THAT SUCKER TO DEATH** *Liberty UP 651*	**53**	3 wks

X-RAY SPEX *UK, male/female vocal/instrumental group* — 32 wks

29 Apr 78	**THE DAY THE WORLD TURNED DAY-GLOW** *EMI International INT 533*	**23**	7 wks
22 Jul 78	**IDENTITY** *EMI International INT 563*	**24**	10 wks
4 Nov 78	**GERM-FREE ADOLESCENCE** *EMI International INT 573*	**19**	11 wks
21 Apr 79	**HIGHLY INFLAMMABLE** *EMI International INT 583*	**45**	4 wks

XTC *UK, male vocal/instrumental group* — 59 wks

12 May 79	**LIFE BEGINS AT THE HOP** *Virgin VS 259*	**54**	4 wks

22 Sep 79	**MAKING PLANS FOR NIGEL** *Virgin VS 282* ..	**17**	11 wks
6 Sep 80	**GENERALS AND MAJORS/DON'T LOSE YOUR TEMPER** *Virgin VS 365*	**32**	8 wks
18 Oct 80	**TOWERS OF LONDON** *Virgin VS 372*	**31**	5 wks
24 Jan 81	**SGT ROCK (IS GOING TO HELP ME)** *Virgin VS 384*	**16**	9 wks
23 Jan 82	● **SENSES WORKING OVERTIME** *Virgin VS 462*	**10**	9 wks
27 Mar 82	**BALL AND CHAIN** *Virgin VS 482*	**58**	4 wks
15 Oct 83	**LOVE ON A FARMBOY'S WAGES** *Virgin VS 613*	**50**	4 wks
29 Sep 84	**ALL YOU PRETTY GIRLS** *Virgin VS 709*	**55**	5 wks

Y

Y & T *US, male vocal/instrumental group* — 4 wks

13 Aug 83	**MEAN STREAK** *A & M AM 135*	**41**	4 wks

YAN - *See YIN and YAN*

Weird Al YANKOVIC
US, male vocalist — 7 wks

7 Apr 84	**EAT IT** *Scotti Bros./Epic A 4257*	**36**	7 wks

YARBROUGH and PEOPLES
US, male/female vocal/instrumental duo — 15 wks

27 Dec 80	● **DON'T STOP THE MUSIC** *Mercury MER 53* ...	**7**	12 wks
5 May 84	**DON'T WASTE YOUR TIME** *Total Experience/RCA XE 501*	**60**	3 wks

YARDBIRDS
UK, male vocal/instrumental group — 62 wks

12 Nov 64	**GOOD MORNING LITTLE SCHOOLGIRL** *Columbia DB 7391*	**44**	4 wks
18 Mar 65	● **FOR YOUR LOVE** *Columbia DB 7499*	**3**	12 wks
17 Jun 65	● **HEART FULL OF SOUL** *Columbia DB 7594*	**2**	13 wks
14 Oct 65	● **EVIL HEARTED YOU/STILL I'M SAD** *Columbia DB 7706*	**3**	10 wks
3 Mar 66	● **SHAPES OF THINGS** *Columbia DB 7848*	**3**	9 wks
2 Jun 66	● **OVER UNDER SIDEWAYS DOWN** *Columbia DB 7928*	**10**	9 wks
27 Oct 66	**HAPPENINGS TEN YEARS TIME AGO** *Columbia DB 8024*	**43**	5 wks

YAZOO
UK, female/male vocal/instrumental duo — 45 wks

17 Apr 82	● **ONLY YOU** *Mute MUTE 020*	**2**	14 wks
17 Jul 82	● **DON'T GO** *Mute YAZ 001*	**3**	11 wks
20 Nov 82	**THE OTHER SIDE OF LOVE** *Mute YAZ 002* ..	**13**	9 wks
21 May 83	● **NOBODY'S DIARY** *Mute YAZ 003*	**3**	11 wks

YELLO *Switzerland, male instrumental group* — 5 wks

25 Jun 83	**I LOVE YOU** *Stiff BUY 176*	**41**	4 wks
26 Nov 83	**LOST AGAIN** *Stiff BUY 191*	**73**	1 wk

YELLOW DOG
US/UK, male vocal/instrumental group — 13 wks

4 Feb 78	● **JUST ONE MORE NIGHT** *Virgin VS 195*	**8**	9 wks
22 Jul 78	**WAIT UNTIL MIDNIGHT** *Virgin VS 217*	**54**	4 wks

YELLOW MAGIC ORCHESTRA
Japan, male instrumental group   *11 wks*

14 Jun 80	**COMPUTER GAME (THEME FROM THE INVADERS)** *A & M AMS 7502*	**17** 11 wks

YELLOWCOATS - *See Paul SHANE and the YELLOWCOATS*

YES
UK, male vocal/instrumental group   *30 wks*

17 Sep 77 ●	**WONDEROUS STORIES** *Atlantic K 10999*	**7** 9 wks
26 Nov 77	**GOING FOR THE ONE** *Atlantic K 11047*	**24** 4 wks
9 Sep 78	**DON'T KILL THE WHALE** *Atlantic K 11184* ...	**36** 4 wks
12 Nov 83	**OWNER OF A LONELY HEART** *Acto B 9817* ..	**28** 9 wks
31 Mar 84	**LEAVE IT** *Acto B 9787*	**56** 4 wks

YIN and YAN
UK, male vocal duo   *5 wks*

29 Mar 75	**IF** *EMI 2282*	**25** 5 wks

YOUNG and COMPANY
US, male/female vocal/instrumental group   *12 wks*

1 Nov 80	**I LIKE (WHAT YOU'RE DOING TO ME)** *Excalibur EXC 501*	**20** 12 wks

Faron YOUNG
US, male vocalist   *23 wks*

15 Jul 72 ●	**IT'S FOUR IN THE MORNING** *Mercury 6052 140*	**3** 23 wks

Jimmy YOUNG
UK, male vocalist   *88 wks*

9 Jan 53	**FAITH CAN MOVE MOUNTAINS** *Decca F 9986*	**11** 1 wk
21 Aug 53 ●	**ETERNALLY** *Decca F 10130*	**8** 9 wks
6 May 55 ★	**UNCHAINED MELODY** *Decca F 10502* ..	**1** 19 wks
16 Sep 55 ★	**THE MAN FROM LARAMIE** *Decca F 10597*	**1** 12 wks
23 Dec 55	**SOMEONE ON YOUR MIND** *Decca F 10640* ...	**13** 5 wks
16 Mar 56 ●	**CHAIN GANG** *Decca F 10694*	**9** 6 wks
8 Jun 56	**WAYWARD WIND** *Decca F 10736*	**27** 1 wk
22 Jun 56	**RICH MAN POOR MAN** *Decca F 10736* ...	**25** 1 wk
28 Sep 56 ●	**MORE** *Decca F 10774*	**4** 17 wks
3 May 57	**ROUND AND ROUND** *Decca F 10875* ..	**30** 1 wk
10 Oct 63	**MISS YOU** *Columbia DB 7119*	**15** 13 wks
26 Mar 64	**UNCHAINED MELODY** *Columbia DB 7234*	**43** 3 wks

The versions of Unchained Melody *on Decca and on Columbia are different recordings of the same song.*

John Paul YOUNG
Australia, male vocalist   *13 wks*

29 Apr 78 ●	**LOVE IS IN THE AIR** *Ariola ARO 117*	**5** 13 wks

Karen YOUNG
UK, female vocalist   *21 wks*

6 Sep 69 ●	**NOBODY'S CHILD** *Major Minor MM 625*	**6** 21 wks

Karen YOUNG
US, female vocalist   *8 wks*

19 Aug 78	**HOT SHOT** *Atlantic K 11180*	**34** 7 wks
24 Feb 79	**HOT SHOT** (re-issue) *Atlantic LV 8*	**75** 1 wk

Neil YOUNG
Canada, male vocalist   *15 wks*

11 Mar 72 ●	**HEART OF GOLD** *Reprise K 14140*	**10** 11 wks
6 Jan 79	**FOUR STRONG WINDS** *Reprise K 14493*	**57** 4 wks

Paul YOUNG
UK, male vocalist   *48 wks*

18 Jun 83 ★	**WHEREVER I LAY MY HAT (THAT'S MY HOME)** *CBS A 3371*	**1** 15 wks
10 Sep 83 ●	**COME BACK AND STAY** *CBS A 3636*	**4** 9 wks
19 Nov 83 ●	**LOVE OF THE COMMON PEOPLE** *CBS A 3585*	**2** 13 wks
13 Oct 84 ●	**I'M GONNA TEAR YOUR PLAYHOUSE DOWN** *CBS A 4786*	**9** 7 wks
8 Dec 84 ●	**EVERYTHING MUST CHANGE** *CBS A 4972* ..	**9†** 4 wks

Retta YOUNG
US, female vocalist   *7 wks*

24 May 75	**SENDING OUT AN S. O. S.** *All Platinum 6146 305*	**28** 7 wks

YOUNG AND MOODY BAND
UK, male/female vocal/instrumental group   *4 wks*

10 Oct 81	**DON'T DO THAT** *Bronze BRO 130*	**63** 4 wks

Young and Moody Band comprises Motorhead and the Nolans. See Motorhead, Nolans.

YOUNG IDEA
UK, male vocal duo   *6 wks*

29 Jun 67 ●	**WITH A LITTLE HELP FROM MY FRIENDS** *Columbia DB 8205*	**10** 6 wks

YOUNG RASCALS
US, male vocal/instrumental group   *17 wks*

25 May 67 ●	**GROOVIN'** *Atlantic 584 111*	**8** 13 wks
16 Aug 67	**A GIRL LIKE YOU** *Atlantic 584 128*	**37** 4 wks

Leon YOUNG STRING CHORALE - *See Mr Acker BILK*

Z

Helmut ZACHARIAS
Germany, orchestra   *11 wks*

29 Oct 64 ●	**TOKYO MELODY** *Polydor YNH 52341*	**9** 11 wks

Pia ZADORA - *See Jermaine JACKSON and Pia ZADORA*

ZAGER and EVANS
US, male vocal duo   *13 wks*

9 Aug 69 ★	**IN THE YEAR 2525 (EXORDIUM AND TERMINUS)** *RCA 1860*	**1** 13 wks

Michael ZAGER BAND
US, male/female vocal/instrumental group   *12 wks*

1 Apr 78 ●	**LET'S ALL CHANT** *Private Stock PVT 143*	**8** 12 wks

Georghe ZAMFIR
Romania, male instrumentalist - pipes   *9 wks*

21 Aug 76 ●	**(LIGHT OF EXPERIENCE) DOINA DE JALE** *Epic EPC 4480*	**4** 9 wks

Tommy ZANG *US, male vocalist* *1 wk*

16 Feb 61	**HEY GOOD LOOKING** *Polydor NH 66957*	**45**	1 wk

Lena ZAVARONI *UK, female vocalist* *14 wks*

9 Feb 74 ●	**MA HE'S MAKING EYES AT ME** *Philips 6006 367*	**10**	11 wks
1 Jun 74	**PERSONALITY** *Philips 6006 391*	**33**	3 wks

ZEPHYRS
UK, male vocal/instrumental group *1 wk*

18 Mar 65	**SHE'S LOST YOU** *Columbia DB 7481*	**48**	1 wk

ZIGZAG JIVE FLUTES - *See ELIAS and his ZIGZAG JIVE FLUTES*

ZODIACS - *See Maurice WILLIAMS and the ZODIACS*

ZOMBIES *UK, male vocal/instrumental group* *16 wks*

13 Aug 64	**SHE'S NOT THERE** *Decca F 11940*	**12**	11 wks
11 Feb 65	**TELL HER NO** *Decca F 12072*	**42**	5 wks

ZZ TOP *US, male vocal/instrumental group* *25 wks*

3 Sep 83	**GIMME ALL YOUR LOVIN'** *Warner Bros. W 9693*	**61**	3 wks
26 Nov 83	**SHARP DRESSED MAN** *Warner Bros. W 9576* ..	**53**	3 wks
31 Mar 84	**TV DINNERS** *Warner Bros. W 9334*	**67**	3 wks
6 Oct 84 ●	**GIMME ALL YOUR LOVIN'** (re-entry) *Warner Bros. W 9693*	**10†**	13 wks
15 Dec 84	**SHARP DRESSED MAN** (re-entry) *Warner Bros. W 9576*	**45†**	3 wks

PART TWO

The British Hit Singles: Alphabetically by Title

Different songs/tunes with the same title (e.g. IT'S ALL OVER NOW which has been a hit title for both the Rolling Stones and for Shane Fenton and The Fentones) are indicated by [A], [B], etc. Where there is no letter in brackets after the title, all hit recordings are of just one number. Individual titles of songs or tunes on L.P.'s, E.P.'s or medley singles which made the singles chart are not included here, with the obvious exception of titles that are actually part of the overall title of the hit L.P., E.P. or medley single.

The recording act named alongside each song title is not necessarily exactly the same act that is billed on the record, but is the act under whose name all the information about the title can be found in Part One of this book. The year of chart entry column contains the year in which each disc made its very first appearance on the chart. Subsequent appearances are only listed here if they signify a period of success totally separate from the disc's first impact.

Title – Act (Position)	Year of Chart Entry
A BA NI BI - Izhar **Cohen** and **Alphabeta** (20)	78
'A' BOMB IN WARDOUR STREET - **Jam** (25)	78
'A' TEAM, THE - Mike **Post** (45)	84
ABACAB - **Genesis** (9)	81
ABC - **Jackson Five** (8)	70
ABIDE WITH ME - **Inspirational Choir** (44)	84
ABRACADABRA - Steve **Miller Band** (2)	82
ABRAHAM MARTIN & JOHN - Marvin **Gaye** (9)	70
ABSOLUTE - **Scritti Politti** (17)	84
ABSOLUTE BEGINNERS - **Jam** (4)	81
ACAPULCO 1922 - Kenny **Ball** and his **Jazzmen** (27)	63
ACCIDENT PRONE - **Status Quo** (36)	78
ACCIDENTS - **Thunderclap Newman** (46)	70
ACCIDENTS WILL HAPPEN - Elvis **Costello** and the **Attractions** (28)	79
ACE OF SPADES - **Motorhead** (15)	80
ACES HIGH - **Iron Maiden** (20)	84
ACKEE 1-2-3 - The **Beat** (54)	83
ACTION - **Sweet** (15)	75
ADIOS AMIGO - Jim **Reeves** (23)	62
ADORATION WALTZ - David **Whitfield** (9)	57
ADULT EDUCATION - Daryl **Hall** and John **Oates** (63)	84
ADVENTURES OF THE LOVE CRUSADER, THE - Sarah **Brightman** (53)	79
AFFAIR TO REMEMBER, AN - Vic **Damone** (29)	57
AFRICA - **Toto** (3)	83
AFRICAN AND WHITE - **China Crisis** (45)	82
AFRICAN WALTZ - Johnny **Dankworth** (9)	61
AFTER A FASHION - Midge **Ure** and Mick **Karn** (39)	83
AFTER THE GOLDRUSH - **Prelude** (21)	74,82
AFTER THE LOVE HAS GONE - **Earth Wind and Fire** (4)	79
AFTER YOU'VE GONE - Alice **Babs** (43)	63
AFTERGLOW OF YOUR LOVE - **Small Faces** (36)	69
AFTERNOON DELIGHT - **Starland Vocal Band** (18)	76
AFTERNOON OF THE RHINO - Mike **Post** (48)	75
AGADOO - **Black Lace** (2)	84
AGAIN AND AGAIN - **Status Quo** (13)	78
AGAINST ALL ODDS (TAKE A LOOK AT ME NOW) - Phil **Collins** (2)	84
AI NO CORRIDA (I-NO-KO-REE-DA) - Quincy **Jones** (14)	81
AIN'T DOIN' NOTHIN' - Jet **Bronx** and the **Forbidden** (49)	77
AIN'T GONNA BE THAT WAY - Marv **Johnson** (50)	63
AIN'T GONNA BUMP NO MORE (WITH NO BIG FAT WOMAN) - Joe **Tex** (2)	77
AIN'T GONNA WASH FOR A WEEK - **Brook Brothers** (13)	61
AIN'T GOT A CLUE - **Lurkers** (45)	78
AIN'T GOT NO - I GOT LIFE - Nina **Simone** (2)	68
AIN'T LOVE A BITCH - Rod **Stewart** (11)	79
AIN'T MISBEHAVIN' - Tommy **Bruce** (3)	60
AIN'T MISBEHAVIN' - Johnnie **Ray** (17)	56
AIN'T NO LOVE IN THE HEART OF THE CITY - **Whitesnake** (51)	80
AIN'T NO MOUNTAIN HIGH ENOUGH - **Boystown Gang** (46)	81
AIN'T NO MOUNTAIN HIGH ENOUGH - Diana **Ross** (6)	70
AIN'T NO PLEASING YOU - **Chas** and **Dave** (2)	82
AIN'T NO STOPPIN' US NOW - **McFadden Whitehead** (5)	79
AIN'T NO STOPPING - **Enigma** (11)	81
AIN'T NO SUNSHINE - Michael **Jackson** (8)	72
AIN'T NO SUNSHINE - **Sivuca** (56)	84
AIN'T NOBODY - **Rufus** and Chaka **Khan** (8)	84
AIN'T NOTHIN' (GONNA KEEP ME FROM YOU) - Terri **De Sario** (52)	78
AIN'T NOTHIN' LIKE THE REAL THING - Marvin **Gaye** and Tammi **Terrell** (34)	68
AIN'T NOTHING BUT A HOUSEPARTY - **Showstoppers** (11)	68,71
AIN'T SHE SWEET - **Beatles** (29)	64
AIN'T THAT A SHAME - Pat **Boone** (7)	55
AIN'T THAT A SHAME - Fats **Domino** (23)	57
AIN'T THAT A SHAME - **Four Seasons** (38)	63
AIN'T THAT ENOUGH FOR YOU - John **Davis** and the **Monster Orchestra** (70)	79
AIN'T THAT FUNNY - Jimmy **Justice** (8)	62
AIN'T THAT LOVIN' YOU BABY - Elvis **Presley** (15)	64
AIN'T TOO PROUD TO BEG - **Temptations** (21)	66
AIN'T WE FUNKIN' NOW - **Brothers Johnson** (43)	78
AIR THAT I BREATHE, THE - **Hollies** (2)	74
AIRPORT - **Motors** (4)	78
AL CAPONE - Prince **Buster** (18)	67
AL DI LA - Emilio **Pericoli** (30)	62
ALABAMA JUBILEE - **Ferko String Band** (20)	55
ALABAMA SONG - David **Bowie** (23)	80
ALBATROSS - **Fleetwood Mac** (1)	68,73
ALEXANDER GRAHAM BELL - **Sweet** (33)	71
ALFIE - Cilla **Black** (9)	66
ALISON - Linda **Ronstadt** (66)	79
ALL ALONE AM I - Brenda **Lee** (7)	63
ALL ALONG THE WATCHTOWER - Jimi **Hendrix Experience** (5)	68
ALL AMERICAN BOY - Bill **Parsons** (22)	59
ALL AMERICAN GIRLS - **Sister Sledge** (41)	81
ALL AROUND MY HAT - **Steeleye Span** (5)	75
ALL AROUND THE WORLD - **Jam** (13)	77
ALL BECAUSE OF YOU - **Geordie** (6)	73
ALL BY MYSELF - Eric **Carmen** (12)	76
ALL CRIED OUT - Alison **Moyet** (8)	84
ALL DAY AND ALL OF THE NIGHT - **Kinks** (2)	64
ALL FALL DOWN - **Lindisfarne** (34)	72
ALL FOR LEYNA - Billy **Joel** (40)	80
ALL I EVER NEED IS YOU - **Sonny** and **Cher** (8)	72
ALL I EVER WANTED - **Santana** (57)	80
ALL I HAVE TO DO IS DREAM - **Everly Brothers** (1)	58
ALL I HAVE TO DO IS DREAM - Bobbie **Gentry** and Glen **Campbell** (3)	69
ALL I NEED IS EVERYTHING - **Aztec Camera** (34)	84
ALL I NEED IS YOUR SWEET LOVIN' - Gloria **Gaynor** (44)	75
ALL I REALLY WANT TO DO - **Byrds** (4)	65
ALL I REALLY WANT TO DO - **Cher** (9)	65
ALL I SEE IS YOU - Dusty **Springfield** (9)	66
ALL I THINK ABOUT IS YOU - **Nilsson** (43)	77
ALL I WANT FOR CHRISTMAS IS A BEATLE - Dora **Bryan** (20)	63
ALL I WANT IS YOU - **Roxy Music** (12)	74
ALL JOIN HANDS - **Slade** (15)	84
ALL KINDS OF EVERYTHING - **Dana** (1)	70
ALL MY LIFE - Major **Harris** (61)	83
ALL MY LOVE [A] - Jackie **Wilson** (33)	60
ALL MY LOVE [B] - Cliff **Richard** (6)	67
ALL MY LOVING - **Dowlands** (33)	64
ALL NIGHT LONG [A] - **Cloud** (72)	81
ALL NIGHT LONG [B] - **Mary Jane Girls** (13)	83
ALL NIGHT LONG [C] - **Rainbow** (5)	80
ALL NIGHT LONG [D] - Dexter **Wansell** (59)	78
ALL NIGHT LONG (ALL NIGHT) - Lionel **Richie** (2)	83
(ALL OF A SUDDEN) MY HEART SINGS - Paul **Anka** (10)	59
ALL OF ME LOVES ALL OF YOU - **Bay City Rollers** (4)	74
ALL OF MY HEART - **ABC** (5)	82
ALL OF MY LIFE - Diana **Ross** (9)	74
ALL OF YOU [A] - Sammy **Davis Jr.** (28)	56
ALL OF YOU [B] - Julio **Iglesias** and Diana **Ross** (43)	84
ALL OR NOTHING - **Small Faces** (1)	66
ALL OUT OF LOVE - **Air Supply** (11)	80
ALL OUT TO GET YOU - The **Beat** (22)	81
ALL OVER THE WORLD [A] - **Electric Light Orchestra** (11)	80
ALL OVER THE WORLD [B] - Françoise **Hardy** (16)	65
ALL RIGHT - Christopher **Cross** (51)	83
ALL RIGHT NOW - **Free** (2)	70
ALL SHOOK UP - Elvis **Presley** (24)	57,77
ALL STAR HIT PARADE - **Various Artists** (2)	56
ALL STAR HIT PARADE NO. 2 - **Various Artists** (15)	57
ALL STOOD STILL - **Ultravox** (8)	81
ALL THAT GLITTERS - Gary **Glitter** (48)	81
ALL THAT I AM - Elvis **Presley** (18)	66
ALL THE LOVE IN THE WORLD [A] - **Consortium** (22)	69
ALL THE LOVE IN THE WORLD [B] - Dionne **Warwick** (10)	82
ALL THE TIME AND EVERYWHERE - Dickie **Valentine** (9)	53
ALL THE WAY - Frank **Sinatra** (21)	57
ALL THE WAY FROM AMERICA - Joan **Armatrading** (54)	80
ALL THE WAY FROM MEMPHIS - **Mott The Hoople** (10)	73
ALL THE YOUNG DUDES - **Mott The Hoople** (3)	72
ALL THOSE YEARS AGO - George **Harrison** (13)	81
ALL THROUGH THE NIGHT - Cyndi **Lauper** (64)	84
ALL TIME HIGH - Rita **Coolidge** (75)	83
ALL TOMORROW'S PARTIES - **Japan** (38)	83
ALL YOU NEED IS LOVE - **Beatles** (1)	67
ALL YOU PRETTY GIRLS - **XTC** (55)	84
ALLEY CAT SONG - David **Thorne** (21)	63
ALLEY OOP - **Hollywood Argyles** (24)	60
ALLY'S TARTAN ARMY - Andy **Cameron** (6)	78
ALMOST SATURDAY NIGHT - Dave **Edmunds** (58)	81
ALMOST THERE - Andy **Williams** (2)	65
ALONE - Petula **Clark** (8)	57
ALONE - Kaye **Sisters** (27)	58
ALONE - Shepherd **Sisters** (14)	57
ALONE - **Southlanders** (17)	57
ALONE AGAIN (NATURALLY) - Gilbert **O'Sullivan** (3)	72
ALONE AT LAST - Jackie **Wilson** (50)	60
ALONG CAME CAROLINE - Michael **Cox** (41)	60
ALRIGHT ALRIGHT ALRIGHT - Mungo **Jerry** (3)	73
ALRIGHT BABY - **Stevenson's Rocket** (37)	75
ALSO SPRACH ZARATHUSTRA (2001) - **Deodato** (7)	73
ALTERNATE TITLE - **Monkees** (2)	67
ALWAYS - Sammy **Turner** (26)	59
ALWAYS AND EVER - Johnny **Kidd** and the **Pirates** (46)	64
ALWAYS AND FOREVER - **Heatwave** (9)	78
ALWAYS ON MY MIND - Willie **Nelson** (49)	82
ALWAYS ON MY MIND - Elvis **Presley** (9)	72
ALWAYS SOMETHING THERE TO REMIND ME - **Naked Eyes** (60)	83
ALWAYS THE LONELY ONE - Alan **Drew** (48)	63
ALWAYS YOU AND ME - Russ **Conway** (33)	62
ALWAYS YOURS - Gary **Glitter** (1)	74
AM I A TOY OR A TREASURE - Kay **Starr** (17)	54
AM I THAT EASY TO FORGET - Engelbert **Humperdinck** (3)	68
AM I THE SAME GIRL - Dusty **Springfield** (43)	69
AM I WASTING MY TIME ON YOU - Frankie **Vaughan** (25)	58
AMANDA - Stuart **Gillies** (13)	73
AMATEUR HOUR - **Sparks** (7)	74
AMAZING GRACE - Judy **Collins** (5)	70

249

DON'T LET 'EM GRIND YOU DOWN - **Exploited** and **Anti-Pasti** (70) 81
DON'T LET GO - **Manhattan Transfer** (32) 77
DON'T LET GO THE COAT - **Who** (47) 81
DON'T LET HIM STEAL YOUR HEART AWAY - Phil **Collins** (45) 83
DON'T LET HIM TOUCH YOU - **Angelettes** (35) 72
DON'T LET IT DIE - Hurricane **Smith** (2) 71
DON'T LET IT END - **Styx** (56) 83
DON'T LET IT FADE AWAY - **Darts** (18) 78
DON'T LET IT PASS YOU BY - **U.B.40** (16) 81
DON'T LET ME BE MISUNDERSTOOD - **Animals** (3) 65
DON'T LET ME BE MISUNDERSTOOD - **Santa Esmeralda** and Leroy **Gomez** (41) 77
DON'T LET NOBODY HOLD YOU DOWN - L J **Reynolds** (53) 84
DON'T LET THE RAIN COME DOWN - Ronnie **Hilton** (21) 64
DON'T LET THE STARS GET IN YOUR EYES - Perry **Como** (1) 53
DON'T LET THE SUN CATCH YOU CRYING - **Gerry** and the **Pacemakers** (6) 64
DON'T LET THE SUN GO DOWN ON ME - Elton **John** (16) 74
DON'T LOOK ANY FURTHER - Dennis **Edwards** (45) 84
DON'T LOOK BACK - **Boston** (43) 78
DON'T LOOK DOWN - **Planets** (66) 80
DON'T LOSE YOUR TEMPER - **XTC** (32) 80
DON'T LOVE ME TOO HARD - **Nolans** (14) 82
DON'T MAKE ME - Babbity **Blue** (48) 65
DON'T MAKE ME OVER - **Swinging Blue Jeans** (31) 66
DON'T MAKE ME WAIT - **Peech Boys** (49) 82
DON'T MAKE ME WAIT TOO LONG [A] - Roberta **Flack** (44) 80
DON'T MAKE ME WAIT TOO LONG [B] - Barry **White** (17) 76
DON'T MAKE MY BABY BLUE - **Shadows** (10) 65
DON'T MAKE WAVES - **Nolans** (12) 80
DON'T PANIC - **Liquid Gold** (42) 81
DON'T PAY THE FERRYMAN - Chris **De Burgh** (48) 82
DON'T PLAY THAT SONG - Aretha **Franklin** (13) 70
DON'T PLAY YOUR ROCK'N ROLL TO ME - **Smokie** (8) 75
DON'T PUSH IT, DON'T FORCE IT - Leon **Haywood** (12) 80
DON'T SAY I TOLD YOU SO - **Tourists** (40) 80
DON'T SAY THAT'S JUST FOR WHITE BOYS - **Way Of The West** (54) 81
DON'T SET ME FREE - Ray **Charles** (37) 63
DON'T SING - **Prefab Sprout** (62) 84
DON'T SLEEP IN THE SUBWAY - Petula **Clark** (12) 67
DON'T SLOW DOWN - **U.B.40** (16) 81
DON'T STAND SO CLOSE TO ME - **Police** (1) 80
DON'T STAY AWAY TOO LONG - **Peters** and **Lee** (3) 74
DON'T STOP [A] - **Fleetwood Mac** (32) 77
DON'T STOP [B] - **K.I.D.** (49) 81
DON'T STOP [C] - **Mood** (59) 82
DON'T STOP [D] - Jeffrey **Osbourne** (61) 84
DON'T STOP BELIEVIN' - **Journey** (62) 82
DON'T STOP IT NOW - **Hot Chocolate** (11) 76
DON'T STOP LOVIN' ME BABY - **Pinkerton's Assorted Colours** (50) 66
DON'T STOP ME NOW - **Queen** (9) 79
DON'T STOP NOW - Gene **Farrow** and **G.F. Band** (71) 78
DON'T STOP THAT CRAZY RHYTHM - **Modern Romance** (14) 83
DON'T STOP THE CARNIVAL - Alan **Price** (13) 68
DON'T STOP THE FEELING - Roy **Ayers** (56) 80
DON'T STOP THE MUSIC - **Yarbrough** and **Peoples** (7) 80
DON'T STOP TILL YOU GET ENOUGH - Michael **Jackson** (3) 79
DON'T STOP TWIST - Frankie **Vaughan** (22) 62
DON'T TAKE AWAY THE MUSIC - **Tavares** (4) 76
DON'T TAKE IT LYIN' DOWN - **Dooleys** (60) 78
DON'T TAKE NO FOR AN ANSWER - Tom **Robinson Band** (18) 78
DON'T TALK - Hank **Marvin** (49) 82
DON'T TALK TO HIM - Cliff **Richard** (2) 63
DON'T TALK TO ME ABOUT LOVE - **Altered Images** (7) 83
DON'T TELL ME [A] - **Blancmange** (8) 84
DON'T TELL ME [B] - **Central Line** (55) 82
DON'T THAT BEAT ALL - Adam **Faith** (8) 62
DON'T THROW AWAY ALL THOSE TEARDROPS - Frankie **Avalon** (37) 60
DON'T THROW IT ALL AWAY - Gary **Benson** (20) 75
DON'T THROW YOUR LOVE AWAY - **Searchers** (1) 64
DON'T TREAT ME LIKE A CHILD - Helen **Shapiro** (3) 61
DON'T TRY TO CHANGE ME - **Crickets** (37) 63
DON'T TRY TO STOP IT - **Roman Holliday** (14) 83
DON'T TURN AROUND - **Merseybeats** (13) 64
DON'T WALK AWAY [A] - **Electric Light Orchestra** (21) 80
DON'T WALK AWAY [B] - **Four Tops** (16) 81
DON'T WALK AWAY TILL I TOUCH YOU - Elaine **Paige** (46) 78
DON'T WANNA SAY GOODNIGHT - **Kandidate** (47) 78
DON'T WANT TO WAIT ANYMORE - **Tubes** (60) 81
DON'T WASTE YOUR TIME - **Yarbrough** and **Peoples** (60) 84
DON'T WORRY [A] - Johnny **Brandon** (18) 55
DON'T WORRY [B] - Billy **Fury** (40) 61
DON'T YOU - **Second Image** (68) 83
DON'T YOU GET SO MAD - Jeffrey **Osbourne** (54) 83
DON'T YOU KNOW - **Butterscotch** (17) 70
DON'T YOU KNOW IT - Adam **Faith** (12) 61
DON'T YOU ROCK ME DADDY-O - Lonnie **Donegan** (4) 57
DON'T YOU ROCK ME DADDY-O - **Vipers Skiffle Group** (10) 57
DON'T YOU THINK IT'S TIME - Mike **Berry** (6) 63
DON'T YOU WANT ME - **Human League** (1) 81
DOOBEDOOD'NDOOBE DOOBEDOOD'NDOOBE - Diana **Ross** (12) 72
DOOMSDAY - Evelyn **Thomas** (41) 76
DOOR IS STILL OPEN TO MY HEART, THE - Dean **Martin** (42) 64
DOORS OF YOUR HEART - The **Beat** (33) 81
DOOT DOOT - **(Freur)** (59) 83
DOUBLE BARREL - Dave and Ansil **Collins** (1) 71
DOUBLE DUTCH [A] - **Fatback Band** (31) 77
DOUBLE DUTCH [B] - Malcolm **McLaren** (3) 83
DOWN AT THE DOCTOR'S - **Dr. Feelgood** (48) 78
DOWN BY THE LAZY RIVER - **Osmonds** (40) 72
DOWN DEEP INSIDE (THEME FROM 'THE DEEP') - Donna **Summer** (5) 77
DOWN DOWN - **Status Quo** (1) 74
DOWN IN THE BOONDOCKS - Billy Joe **Royal** (38) 65
DOWN IN THE SUBWAY - **Soft Cell** (24) 84
DOWN IN THE TUBE STATION AT MIDNIGHT - **Jam** (15) 78
DOWN ON THE BEACH TONIGHT - **Drifters** (7) 74
DOWN ON THE CORNER - **Creedence Clearwater Revival** (31) 70
DOWN ON THE STREET - **Shakatak** (9) 84
DOWN THE DUSTPIPE - **Status Quo** (12) 70
DOWN THE HALL - **Four Seasons** (34) 77
DOWN THE RIVER NILE - John **Leyton** (42) 62
DOWN UNDER - **Men At Work** (1) 83
DOWN YONDER - **Johnny** and the **Hurricanes** (8) 60
DOWNHEARTED - Eddie **Fisher** (3) 53
DOWNTOWN - Petula **Clark** (2) 64
DR BEAT - **Miami Sound Machine** (6) 84
DR MABUSE - **Propaganda** (27) 84
DR. HECKYLL AND MR. JIVE - **Men At Work** (31) 83
DRACULA'S TANGO - **Toto Coelo** (54) 82
DRAG ME DOWN - **Boomtown Rats** (50) 84
DRAGNET - Ray **Anthony** (7) 53
DRAGNET - Ted **Heath** (12) 53
DRAGON POWER - **JKD Band** (58) 78
DRAGONFLY - **Tornados** (41) 63
DRAW OF THE CARDS - Kim **Carnes** (49) 81
DREADLOCK HOLIDAY - **10 C. C.** (1) 78
DREAM A LIE - **U.B.40** (10) 80
DREAM A LITTLE DREAM OF ME - Mama **Cass** (11) 68
DREAM A LITTLE DREAM OF ME - Anita **Harris** (33) 68
DREAM BABY - Glen **Campbell** (39) 71
DREAM BABY - Roy **Orbison** (2) 62
DREAM GIRL - Mark **Wynter** (27) 61
DREAM LOVER - Bobby **Darin** (1) 59,79
DREAM OF OLWEN - **Second City Sound** (43) 69
DREAM SEQUENCE (ONE) - Pauline **Murray** and the **Invisible Girls** (67) 80
DREAM TO SLEEP - **H2O** (17) 83
DREAMBOAT [A] - Alma **Cogan** (1) 55
DREAMBOAT [B] - **Limmie** and the **Family Cookin'** (31) 73
DREAMER [A] - **Jacksons** (22) 77
DREAMER [B] - **Supertramp** (13) 75
DREAMIN' [A] - Johnny **Burnette** (5) 60
DREAMIN' [B] - **Liverpool Express** (40) 77
DREAMIN' [C] - Cliff **Richard** (8) 80
DREAMING - **Blondie** (2) 79
DREAMING, THE - Kate **Bush** (48) 82
DREAMING OF ME - **Depeche Mode** (57) 81
DREAMS [A] - **Fleetwood Mac** (24) 77
DREAMS [B] - Grace **Slick** (50) 80
DREAMS CAN TELL A LIE - Nat 'King' **Cole** (10) 56
DREAMS I DREAM, THE - **Shadows** (42) 66
DREAMS OF CHILDREN, THE - **Jam** (1) 80
DREAMS OF YOU - Ralph **McTell** (36) 75
DREAMY LADY - **T. Rex** (30) 75
DRIFTING - Sheila **Walsh** and Cliff **Richard** (64) 83
DRINK UP THY ZIDER - Adge **Cutler** and the **Wurzels** (45) 67
DRINKING SONG - Mario **Lanza** (13) 55
DRIVE - **Cars** (5) 84
DRIVE SAFELY DARLIN' - Tony **Christie** (35) 76
DRIVE-IN SATURDAY - David **Bowie** (3) 73
DRIVER'S SEAT - **Sniff 'N' The Tears** (42) 79
DRIVIN' HOME - Duane **Eddy** (30) 61
DRIVING IN MY CAR - **Madness** (4) 82
DROP THE PILOT - Joan **Armatrading** (11) 83
DROWNING - The **Beat** (22) 81
DROWNING IN BERLIN - **Mobiles** (9) 82
DRUMMER MAN - **Tonight** (14) 78
DRUMMIN' UP A STORM - Sandy **Nelson** (39) 62
DRUMS ARE MY BEAT - Sandy **Nelson** (30) 62
DRY COUNTY - **Blackfoot** (43) 82
DUCHESS [A] - **Genesis** (46) 80
DUCHESS [B] - **Stranglers** (14) 79
DUCK FOR THE OYSTER - Malcolm **McLaren** (54) 83
DUELLING BANJOS - **'Deliverance' Soundtrack** (17) 73
DUKE OF EARL - **Darts** (6) 79
DUM DUM - Brenda **Lee** (22) 61
DUM DUM GIRL - **Talk Talk** (74) 84
DUMB WAITERS - **Psychedelic Furs** (59) 81
DURHAM TOWN (THE LEAVIN') - Roger **Whittaker** (12) 69
DYNAMITE [A] - Cliff **Richard** (16) 59
DYNAMITE [B] - Stacy **Lattisaw** (51) 80
DYNA-MITE - **Mud** (4) 73
DYNOMITE (PART 1.) - Tony **Camillo's Bazuka** (28) 75
THEME FROM 'E.T.' (THE EXTRA-TERRESTRIAL) - John **Williams** (17) 82
EACH AND EVERYONE - **Everything But The Girl** (28) 84
EARLY IN THE MORNING [A] - **Gap Band** (55) 82
EARLY IN THE MORNING [B] - Buddy **Holly** (17) 58
EARLY IN THE MORNING [C] - **Vanity Fare** (8) 69
EARLY TO BED - **Poni-Tails** (26) 59
EARTH ANGEL - **Crew Cuts** (4) 55
EARTH DIES SCREAMING, THE - **U.B.40** (10) 80
EASE ON DOWN THE ROAD - Diana **Ross** and Michael **Jackson** (45) 78
EASIER SAID THAN DONE [A] - **Essex** (41) 63
EASIER SAID THAN DONE [B] - **Shakatak** (12) 81
EAST OF EDEN - **Big Country** (17) 84
EAST RIVER - **Brecker Brothers** (34) 78
EAST WEST - **Herman's Hermits** (37) 66
EASY - **Commodores** (9) 77
EASY COME EASY GO - **Sutherland Brothers** (50) 79
EASY EASY - **Scotland World Cup Squad** (20) 74
EASY GOING ME - Adam **Faith** (12) 61
EASY LIFE - **Bodysnatchers** (50) 80
EASY LIVIN' - **Fastway** (74) 83
EAT IT - Weird Al **Yankovic** (36) 84
EAT YOUR HEART OUT - Paul **Hardcastle** (59) 84
EBB TIDE - Frank **Chacksfield** (9) 54
EBB TIDE - **Righteous Brothers** (48) 66
EBONY AND IVORY - Paul **McCartney** Stevie **Wonder** (1) 82
ECHO BEACH - **Martha** and the **Muffins** (10) 80
EDDY VORTEX - Steve **Gibbons Band** (56) 78
EDELWEISS - Vince **Hill** (2) 67
EENY MEENY - **Showstoppers** (33) 68
EGO - Elton **John** (34) 78
EGYPTIAN REGGAE - Jonathan **Richman** and the **Modern Lovers** (5) 77
EIGHT BY TEN - Ken **Dodd** (22) 64
EIGHT MILES HIGH - **Byrds** (24) 66
18 CARAT LOVE AFFAIR - **Associates** (21) 82
EIGHTEEN WITH A BULLET - Pete **Wingfield** (7) 75
EIGHTEEN YELLOW ROSES - Bobby **Darin** (37) 63
EIGHTH DAY - Hazel **O'Connor** (5) 80
EIGHTIES - **Killing Joke** (60) 84
80'S ROMANCE - **Belle Stars** (71) 84
EINSTEIN A GO-GO - **Landscape** (5) 81
EL BIMBO - **Bimbo Jet** (12) 75
EL PASO - Marty **Robbins** (19) 60
ELEANOR RIGBY - **Beatles** (1) 66
ELEANOR RIGBY - Ray **Charles** (36) 68
ELECTED - Alice **Cooper** (4) 72
ELECTRIC AVENUE - Eddy **Grant** (2) 83
ELECTRIC LADY - **Geordie** (32) 73
ELENORE - **Turtles** (7) 68
ELEPHANT TANGO - Cyril **Stapleton** (20) 55
ELEPHANT'S GRAVEYARD (GUILTY), THE - **Boomtown Rats** (26) 81
ELISABETH SERENADE - Gunther **Kallman Choir** (45) 64
ELIZABETHAN REGGAE - Boris **Gardner** (48) 70
ELMO JAMES - **Chairmen Of The Board** (21) 72
ELO EP (EP) - **Electric Light Orchestra** (34) 78
ELOISE - Barry **Ryan** (2) 68
ELSTREE - **Buggles** (55) 80
ELUSIVE BUTTERFLY - Val **Doonican** (5) 66
ELUSIVE BUTTERFLY - Bob **Lind** (5) 66
EMBARRASSMENT - **Madness** (4) 80
EMERALD CITY - **Seekers** (50) 67
EMERGENCY (DIAL 999) - **Loose Ends** (41) 84
EMMA - **Hot Chocolate** (3) 74
EMOTIONAL RESCUE - **Rolling Stones** (9) 80
EMOTIONS - Brenda **Lee** (45) 61
EMOTIONS - Samantha **Sang** (11) 78
EMPIRE SONG - **Killing Joke** (43) 82
EMPIRE STATE HUMAN - **Human League** (62) 80
EMPTY GARDEN - Elton **John** (51) 82
EMPTY ROOMS - Gary **Moore** (51) 84
ENCORE - Cheryl **Lynn** (68) 84
END ... OR THE BEGINNING, THE - **Classix Nouveaux** (60) 82
END OF THE WORLD - Skeeter **Davis** (18) 63
ENDLESS - Dickie **Valentine** (19) 54
ENDLESS LOVE - Diana **Ross** and Lionel **Richie** (7) 81
ENDLESS SLEEP - Jody **Reynolds** (66) 79
ENDLESS SLEEP - Marty **Wilde** (4) 58
ENDLESSLY [A] - Brook **Benton** (28) 59
ENDLESSLY [B] - John **Foxx** (66) 83
ENGINE ENGINE NO. 9 - Roger **Miller** (33) 65
ENGLAND SWINGS - Roger **Miller** (45) 65
ENGLAND WE'LL FLY THE FLAG - **England World Cup Squad** (2) 82
ENGLISH CIVIL WAR (JOHNNY COMES MARCHING HOME) - **Clash** (25) 79
ENGLISH COUNTRY GARDEN - Jimmie **Rodgers** (5) 62
ENJOY YOURSELF - **Jacksons** (42) 77
ENOLA GAY - **Orchestral Manoeuvres** in the **Dark** (8) 80

255

GUITAR MAN [B] - **Bread** (16) 72
GUITAR TANGO - **Shadows** (4) 62
GUNS FOR HIRE - **AC/DC** (37) 83
GUNS OF NAVARONE - **Skatalites** (36) 67
GUNSLINGER - Frankie **Laine** (50) 61
GURNEY SLADE - Max **Harris** (11) 60
GYPSIES TRAMPS AND THIEVES - **Cher** (4) 71
GYPSY - **Fleetwood Mac** (46) 82
GYPSY BEAT - **Packabeats** (49) 61
GYPSY EYES - Jimi **Hendrix Experience** (35) 71
GYPSY ROAD HOG - **Slade** (48) 77
GYPSY ROVER - **Highwaymen** (41) 61
GYPSY WOMAN - Brian **Hyland** (45) 71
H.A.P.P.Y. RADIO - Edwin **Starr** (9) 79
HA CHA CHA (FUNKTION) - **Brass Construction** (37) 77
HA HA SAID THE CLOWN - **Manfred Mann** (4) 67
HAITIAN DIVORCE - **Steely Dan** (17) 76
HALEY'S GOLDEN MEDLEY - Bill **Haley** and his **Comets** (50) 81
HALF A BOY HALF A MAN - Nick **Lowe** (53) 84
HALF A MINUTE - **Matt Bianco** (23) 84
HALF AS MUCH - Rosemary **Clooney** (3) 52
HALF OF MY HEART - Emile **Ford** and the **Checkmates** (50) 61
HALF THE DAY'S GONE AND WE HAVN'T EARNED A PENNY - Kenny **Lynch** (50) 83
HALFWAY DOWN THE STAIRS - **Muppets** (7) 77
HALFWAY HOTEL - **Voyager** (33) 79
HALFWAY TO PARADISE - Billy **Fury** (3) 61
HALFWAY UP HALFWAY DOWN - Dennis **Brown** (56) 82
HALLELUJAH - **Milk and Honey** (5) 79
HALLELUJAH DAY - **Jackson Five** (20) 73
HALLELUJAH FREEDOM - Junior **Campbell** (10) 72
HALLELUJAH I LOVE HER SO - Eddie **Cochran** (28) 60
HALLELUJAH I LOVE HER SO - Dick **Jordan** (47) 60
HAMMER HORROR - Kate **Bush** (44) 78
HAMMER TO FALL - **Queen** (13) 84
HAND A HANDKERCHIEF TO HELEN - Susan **Maughan** (41) 63
HAND HELD IN BLACK AND WHITE - **Dollar** (19) 81
HAND IN GLOVE - Sandie **Shaw** (27) 84
HAND ON MY HEART - **Shriekback** (52) 84
HANDBAGS & GLADRAGS - Chris **Farlowe** (33) 67
HANDFUL OF SONGS - Tommy **Steele** (5) 57
HANDS OFF - SHE'S MINE - The **Beat** (9) 80
HANDS UP (GIVE ME YOUR HEART) - **Ottawan** (3) 81
HANDY MAN - Jimmy **Jones** (3) 60
HANDY MAN - Del **Shannon** (36) 64
HANG 'EM HIGH - Hugo **Montenegro** (50) 69
HANG ON IN THERE BABY - Johnny **Bristol** (3) 74
HANG ON NOW - **Kajagoogoo** (13) 83
HANG ON SLOOPY - **McCoys** (5) 65
HANG ON SLOOPY - **Sandpipers** (32) 76
HANG ON TO A DREAM - Tim **Hardin** (50) 67
HANG TOGETHER - **Odyssey** (36) 81
HANGIN' - **Chic** (64) 83
HANGIN' OUT - **Kool** and the **Gang** (52) 80
HANGING AROUND - Hazel **O'Connor** (45) 81
HANGING AROUND WITH THE BIG BOYS - **Bloomsbury Set** (56) 83
HANGING GARDEN - **Cure** (34) 82
HANGING ON THE TELEPHONE - **Blondie** (5) 78
HANKY PANKY - Tommy **James** and the **Shondells** (38) 66
HANNA HANNA - **China Crisis** (44) 84
HAPPENING, THE - **Supremes** (6) 67
HAPPENINGS TEN YEARS TIME AGO - **Yardbirds** (43) 66
HAPPINESS - Ken **Dodd** (31) 64
HAPPINESS IS JUST AROUND THE BEND - Cuba **Gooding** (72) 83
HAPPINESS IS ME AND YOU - Gilbert **O'Sullivan** (19) 74
HAPPY ANNIVERSARY [A] - Joan **Regan** (29) 60
HAPPY ANNIVERSARY [B] - Slim **Whitman** (14) 74
HAPPY BIRTHDAY [A] - **Altered Images** (2) 81
HAPPY BIRTHDAY [B] - Stevie **Wonder** (2) 81
HAPPY BIRTHDAY SWEET SIXTEEN - Neil **Sedaka** (3) 61
HAPPY DAYS - **Pratt** and **McLain** with **Brotherlove** (31) 77
HAPPY DAYS & LONELY NIGHTS - Suzi **Miller** (14) 55
HAPPY DAYS & LONELY NIGHTS - Ruby **Murray** (6) 55
HAPPY DAYS & LONELY NIGHTS - Frankie **Vaughan** (12) 55
HAPPY ENDING - Joe **Jackson** (58) 84
HAPPY FEELING - Hamilton **Bohannon** (49) 75
HAPPY GO LUCKY ME - George **Formby** (40) 60
HAPPY GUITAR - Tommy **Steele** (20) 58
HAPPY HEART - Andy **Williams** (47) 69
HAPPY HOUSE - **Siouxsie** and the **Banshees** (17) 80
HAPPY JACK - **Who** (3) 66
HAPPY (LOVE THEME FROM 'LADY SINGS THE BLUES') - Michael **Jackson** (52) 83
HAPPY SONG - Otis **Redding** (24) 68
HAPPY TALK - **Captain Sensible** (1) 82
HAPPY TO BE ON AN ISLAND IN THE SUN - Demis **Roussos** (5) 75
HAPPY TO MAKE YOUR ACQUAINTANCE - Sammy **Davis JR.** and Carmen **McRAE** (46) 60
HAPPY TOGETHER - **Turtles** (12) 67
HAPPY WANDERER - **Obernkirchen Children's Choir** (2) 54
HAPPY WANDERER - **Stargazers** (12) 54
HAPPY WHISTLER, THE - Don **Robertson** (8) 56
HAPPY WHISTLER, THE - Cyril **Stapleton** (22) 56
HAPPY XMAS (WAR IS OVER) - John **Lennon** (4) 72
HARBOUR LIGHTS - **Platters** (11) 60
HARD DAY'S NIGHT, A - **Beatles** (1) 64
HARD DAY'S NIGHT, A - Peter **Sellers** (14) 65
HARD HABIT TO BREAK - **Chicago** (8) 84
HARD HEADED WOMAN - Elvis **Presley** (2) 58
HARD HEARTED HANNAH - **Temperance Seven** (28) 61
HARD RAIN'S GONNA FALL, A - Bryan **Ferry** (10) 73
HARD ROAD - **Black Sabbath** (33) 78
HARD TO HANDLE - Otis **Redding** (15) 68
HARD TO SAY I'M SORRY - **Chicago** (4) 82
HARD WAY, THE - **Nashville Teens** (45) 66
HARDEN MY HEART - **Quarterflash** (49) 82
HARDER THEY COME, THE - **Rocker's Revenge** (30) 83
HARDROCK - Herbie **Hancock** (65) 84
HARE KRISHNA MANTRA - **Radha Krishna Temple** (12) 69
HARLEM SHUFFLE - **Bob** and **Earl** (7) 69
HARMONY IN MY HEAD - **Buzzcocks** (32) 79
HARMOUR LOVE - **Syreeta** (32) 75
HARPER VALLEY P. T. A. - Jeannie C. **Riley** (12) 68
ROBIN (THE HOODED MAN) - **Clannad** (42) 84
HARVEST FOR THE WORLD - **Isley Brothers** (10) 76
HARVEST OF LOVE - Benny **Hill** (20) 63
HASTA LA VISTA - **Sylvia** (38) 75
HATS OFF TO LARRY - Del **Shannon** (6) 61
HAVA NAGILA - **Spotnicks** (13) 63
HAVE A DRINK ON ME - Lonnie **Donegan** (8) 61
HAVE I STAYED TOO LONG - **Sonny** and **Cher** (42) 66
HAVE I THE RIGHT - **Dead End Kids** (6) 77
HAVE I THE RIGHT - **Honeycombs** (1) 64
HAVE PITY ON THE BOY - Paul and Barry **Ryan** (18) 66
HAVE YOU EVER BEEN IN LOVE - Leo **Sayer** (10) 82
HAVE YOU EVER LOVED SOMEBODY - Paul and Barry **Ryan** (49) 66
HAVE YOU EVER LOVED SOMEBODY - **Searchers** (48) 66
HAVE YOU EVER SEEN THE RAIN - **Creedence Clearwater Revival** (36) 71
HAVE YOU EVER SEEN THE RAIN - Bonnie **Tyler** (47) 83
HAVE YOU SEEN HER - **Chi-Lites** (3) 72,75
HAVE YOU SEEN YOUR MOTHER BABY STANDING IN THE SHADOW - **Rolling Stones** (5) 66
HAVEN'T STOPPED DANCING YET - **Gonzalez** (15) 79
HAVEN'T YOU HEARD - Patrice **Rushen** (62) 80
HAVING A PARTY - **Osmonds** (28) 75
HAWAIIAN TATTOO - **Waikikis** (41) 65
HAWAIIAN WEDDING SONG - Julie **Rogers** (31) 65
HAWKEYE - Frankie **Laine** (7) 55
HAZELL - Maggie **Bell** (37) 78
HE AIN'T HEAVY HE'S MY BROTHER - **Hollies** (3) 69
HE GOT WHAT HE WANTED - **Little Richard** (38) 62
HE IS SAILING - **Jon** and **Vangelis** (61) 83
HE KNOWS YOU KNOW - **Marillion** (35) 83
HE REMINDS ME - Randy **Crawford** (65) 83
HE WAS BEAUTIFUL (CAVATINA) (THE THEME FROM THE DEER HUNTER) - Iris **Williams** (18) 79
HEAD OVER HEELS - **Abba** (25) 82
HEAD OVER HEELS IN LOVE - Kevin **Keegan** (31) 79
HEADLINE NEWS - Edwin **Starr** (11) 66,68
HEADS DOWN NO NONSENSE MINDLESS BOOGIE - **Alberto Y Lost Trios Paranoias** (47) 78
HEART [A] - Max **Bygraves** (14) 57
HEART [A] - **Johnston Brothers** (23) 57
HEART [B] - Rita **Pavone** (27) 66
HEART AND SOUL - **Jan** and **Dean** (24) 61
HEART AND SOUL [B] - **Exile** (54) 81
HEART ATTACK - Olivia **Newton-John** (46) 82
HEART FULL OF SOUL - **Yardbirds** (2) 65
HEART OF A MAN, THE - Frankie **Vaughan** (5) 59
HEART OF A TEENAGE GIRL - George **Chakiris** (49) 60
HEART OF A TEENAGE GIRL, THE - Craig **Douglas** (10) 60
HEART OF GLASS - **Blondie** (1) 79
HEART OF GOLD - Neil **Young** (10) 72
HEART OF MY HEART - Max **Bygraves** (7) 54
HEART OF STONE [A] - **Kenny** (11) 73
HEART OF STONE [B] - Suzi **Quatro** (60) 82
HEART ON MY SLEEVE - **Gallagher** and **Lyle** (6) 76
HEART (STOP BEATING IN TIME) - Leo **Sayer** (22) 82
HEARTACHE - Roy **Orbison** (44) 68
HEARTACHE AVENUE - **Maisonettes** (7) 82
HEARTACHE TONIGHT - **Eagles** (40) 79
HEARTACHES - Patsy **Cline** (31) 62
HEARTACHES - Vince **Hill** (28) 66
HEARTACHES BY THE NUMBER - Guy **Mitchell** (26) 59
HEARTBEAT - **England Sisters** (33) 60
HEARTBEAT - Buddy **Holly** (30) 60
HEARTBEAT [A] - Ruby **Murray** (3) 54
HEARTBEAT [B] - Buddy **Holly** (30) 59
HEARTBEAT [B] - **Showaddywaddy** (7) 75
HEARTBEAT [C] - Sammy **Hagar** (67) 80
HEARTBREAK HOTEL [A] - Stan **Freberg** (24) 56
HEARTBREAK HOTEL [A] - Elvis **Presley** (2) 56,71
HEARTBREAK HOTEL [B] - **Jacksons** (44) 80
HEARTBREAKER [A] - **Musical Youth** (44) 83
HEARTBREAKER [B] - Dionne **Warwick** (2) 82
HEARTLIGHT - Neil **Diamond** (47) 82
HEARTSONG - Gordon **Giltrap** (21) 78
HEAT IS ON, THE - Agnetha **Faltskog** (36) 83
HEAT OF THE BEAT - Roy **Ayers** and Wayne **Henderson** (43) 79
HEAT OF THE MOMENT - **Asia** (46) 82
HEATHER HONEY - Tommy **Roe** (24) 69
HEAVEN - **Psychedelic Furs** (29) 84
HEAVEN AND HELL, THIRD MOVEMENT (THEME FROM THE BBC-TV SERIES, THE COSMOS) - **Vangelis** (48) 81
HEAVEN HELP US ALL - Stevie **Wonder** (29) 70
HEAVEN IS HERE - Julie **Felix** (22) 70
HEAVEN IS IN THE BACK SEAT OF MY CADILLAC - **Hot Chocolate** (25) 76
HEAVEN IS MY WOMAN'S LOVE - Val **Doonican** (34) 73
HEAVEN IS WAITING - **Danse Society** (60) 83
HEAVEN KNOWS - Donna **Summer** (34) 79
HEAVEN KNOWS I'M MISERABLE NOW - **Smiths** (10) 84
HEAVEN MUST BE MISSING AN ANGEL - **Tavares** (4) 76
HEAVEN MUST HAVE SENT YOU - **Elgins** (3) 71
HEAVEN ON THE 7TH FLOOR - Paul **Nicholas** (40) 77
HEAVEN SENT - Paul **Haig** (74) 83
HEAVENLY - **Showaddywaddy** (34) 75
HEAVEN'S ON FIRE - **Kiss** (43) 84
HEAVY MAKES YOU HAPPY - Bobby **Bloom** (31) 71
HEAVY VIBES - **Montana Sextet** (59) 83
HELEN WHEELS - **Wings** (12) 73
HELL HATH NO FURY - Frankie **Laine** (28) 56
HE'LL HAVE TO GO - Jim **Reeves** (36) 60
HE'LL HAVE TO STAY - Jeanne **Black** (41) 60
HELL RAISER - **Sweet** (2) 73
HELLBOUND - **Tygers of Pan Tang** (48) 81
HELLO - Lionel **Richie** (1) 84
HELLO AGAIN - Neil **Diamond** (51) 81
HELLO AMERICA - **Def Leppard** (45) 80
HELLO BUDDY - **Tremeloes** (32) 71
HELLO DOLLY - Louis **Armstrong** (4) 64
HELLO DOLLY - **Bachelors** (38) 66
HELLO DOLLY - Kenny **Ball** and his **Jazzmen** (30) 64
HELLO DOLLY - Frank **Sinatra** (47) 64
HELLO DOLLY - Frankie **Vaughan** (18) 64
HELLO GOODBYE - **Beatles** (1) 67
HELLO HAPPINESS - **Drifters** (12) 76
HELLO HEARTACHE GOODBYE LOVE - Little Peggy **March** (29) 63
HELLO HELLO I'M BACK AGAIN - Gary **Glitter** (2) 73
HELLO HOW ARE YOU - **Easybeats** (20) 68
HELLO HURRAY - Alice **Cooper** (6) 73
HELLO I AM YOUR HEART - Bette **Bright** (50) 80
HELLO I LOVE YOU - **Doors** (15) 79,68
HELLO JOSEPHINE - Wayne **Fontana** and the **Mindbenders** (46) 63
HELLO LITTLE GIRL - **Fourmost** (9) 63
HELLO MARY LOU - Rick **Nelson** (2) 61
HELLO MUDDAH HELLO FADDAH - Allan **Sherman** (14) 63
HELLO STRANGER - Yvonne **Elliman** (26) 77
HELLO SUMMERTIME - Bobby **Goldsboro** (14) 74
HELLO SUZIE - **Amen Corner** (4) 69
HELLO THIS IS JOANIE (THE TELEPHONE ANSWERING MACHINE SONG) - Paul **Evans** (6) 78
HELLO WORLD - **Tremeloes** (14) 69
HELLO YOUNG LOVERS - Paul **Anka** (44) 60
HELP - Tina **Turner** (40) 84
HELP, GET ME SOME HELP! - **Ottawan** (49) 81
HELP IT ALONG - Cliff **Richard** (29) 73
HELP ME GIRL - Eric **Burdon** (14) 66
HELP ME MAKE IT THROUGH THE NIGHT - John **Holt** (6) 74
HELP ME MAKE IT THROUGH THE NIGHT - Gladys **Knight** and the **Pips** (11) 72
HELP ME RHONDA - **Beach Boys** (27) 65
HELP YOURSELF - Tom **Jones** (5) 68
HELP! - **Beatles** (1) 65
HELPLESS - Tracey **Ullman** (61) 84
HELULE HELULE - **Tremeloes** (14) 68
HER ROYAL MAJESTY - James **Darren** (36) 62
HERCULES - Frankie **Vaughan** (42) 62
HERE COMES MY BABY - **Tremeloes** (4) 67
HERE COMES SUMMER - Dave **Clark Five** (44) 70
HERE COMES SUMMER - Jerry **Keller** (1) 59
HERE COMES THAT FEELING - Brenda **Lee** (5) 62
HERE COMES THE JUDGE [A] - Shorty **Long** (30) 68
HERE COMES THE JUDGE [B] - Pigmeat **Markham** (19) 68
HERE COMES THE NICE - **Small Faces** (12) 67
HERE COMES THE NIGHT [A] - **Beach Boys** (37) 79
HERE COMES THE NIGHT [B] - **Lulu** (50) 64
HERE COMES THE NIGHT [B] - **Them** (2) 65
HERE COMES THE RAIN AGAIN - **Eurythmics** (8) 84
HERE COMES THE STAR - **Herman's Hermits** (33) 69
HERE COMES THE SUMMER - **Undertones** (34) 79
HERE COMES THE SUN - Steve **Harley** and **Cockney Rebel** (10) 76
HERE I GO AGAIN [A] - Archie **Bell** and the **Drells** (11) 72
HERE I GO AGAIN [B] - **Guys** and **Dolls** (33) 75
HERE I GO AGAIN [C] - **Hollies** (4) 64
HERE I GO AGAIN [D] - **Twiggy** (17) 76
HERE I GO AGAIN [E] - **Whitesnake** (34) 82
HERE IN MY HEART - Al **Martino** (1) 52
HERE IS THE NEWS - **Electric Light Orchestra** (24) 82
HERE IT COMES AGAIN - **Fortunes** (4) 65
HERE THERE AND EVERYWHERE - Emmylou **Harris** (30) 76

LOVE MAN - Otis **Redding** (43) 69
LOVE ME [A] - Yvonne **Elliman** (6) 76
LOVE ME [B] - Diana **Ross** (38) 74
LOVE ME AS IF THERE WERE NO TOMORROW - Nat 'King' **Cole** (24) 56
LOVE ME BABY - Susan **Cadogan** (22) 75
LOVE ME DO - **Beatles** (17) 62
LOVE ME FOR A REASON - **Osmonds** (1) 74
LOVE ME FOREVER - **Four Esquires** (23) 58
LOVE ME FOREVER - Eydie **Gormé** (21) 58
LOVE ME FOREVER - Marion **Ryan** (5) 58
LOVE ME LIKE A LOVER - Tina **Charles** (28) 76
LOVE ME LIKE I LOVE YOU - **Bay City Rollers** (4) 76
LOVE ME LIKE THIS - **Real To Reel** (68) 84
LOVE ME LOVE MY DOG - Peter **Shelley** (3) 75
LOVE ME OR LEAVE ME - Sammy **Davis JR.** (8) 55
LOVE ME OR LEAVE ME - Doris **Day** (20) 55
LOVE ME TENDER - Richard **Chamberlain** (15) 62
LOVE ME TENDER - Elvis **Presley** (11) 56
LOVE ME TENDER - Roland **Rat Superstar** (32) 84
LOVE ME TO SLEEP - **Hot Chocolate** (50) 80
LOVE ME TONIGHT [A] - Tom **Jones** (9) 69
LOVE ME TONIGHT [B] - Trevor **Walters** (27) 81
LOVE ME WARM AND TENDER - Paul **Anka** (19) 62
LOVE ME WITH ALL YOUR HEART - Karl **Denver** (37) 64
LOVE MEETING LOVE - **Level 42** (61) 80
LOVE MY WAY - **Psychedelic Furs** (42) 82
LOVE NEEDS NO DISGUISE - Gary **Numan** (33) 81
LOVE OF MY LIFE [A] - **Dooleys** (9) 77
LOVE OF MY LIFE [B] - **Queen** (63) 79
LOVE OF THE COMMON PEOPLE - Nicky **Thomas** (9) 70
LOVE OF THE COMMON PEOPLE - Paul **Young** (2) 83
LOVE OF THE LOVED - Cilla **Black** (35) 63
LOVE ON A FARMBOY'S WAGES - **XTC** (50) 83
LOVE ON A MOUNTAIN TOP - Robert **Knight** (10) 73
LOVE ON A SUMMER NIGHT - **McCrarys** (52) 82
LOVE ON THE LINE - **Barclay James Harvest** (63) 80
LOVE ON THE ROCKS - Neil **Diamond** (17) 80
LOVE ON YOUR SIDE - **Thompson Twins** (9) 83
LOVE OR MONEY [A] - **Blackwells** (46) 61
LOVE OR MONEY [A] - Jimmy **Crawford** (49) 61
LOVE OR MONEY [A] - Billy **Fury** (57) 82
LOVE OR MONEY [B] - Sammy **Hagar** (67) 80
LOVE OVER GOLD (LIVE) - **Dire Straits** (50) 84
LOVE PATROL - **Dooleys** (29) 80
LOVE PLUS ONE - **Haircut 100** (3) 82
LOVE POTION NO. 9 - **Tygers of Pan Tang** (45) 82
LOVE REACTION - **Divine** (65) 83
LOVE REALLY HURTS WITHOUT YOU - Billy **Ocean** (2) 76
LOVE RESURRECTION - Alison **Moyet** (10) 84
LOVE SHADOW - **Fashion** (51) 82
LOVE SO RIGHT - **Bee Gees** (41) 76
LOVE SONG [A] - **Damned** (20) 79
LOVE SONG [B] - **Simple Minds** (47) 81
LOVE SONGS ARE BACK AGAIN (MEDLEY) - **Band Of Gold** (24) 84
LOVE STORY - **Jethro Tull** (29) 69
LOVE THE ONE YOU'RE WITH - Stephen **Stills** (37) 71
LOVE THEME FROM A STAR IS BORN (EVERGREEN) - Barbra **Streisand** (3) 77
LOVE THEME FROM THE GODFATHER - Andy **Williams** (50) 72
LOVE THEME FROM 'THE THORN BIRDS' - Juan **Martin** (10) 84
LOVE TIMES LOVE - **Heavy Pettin'** (69) 84
LOVE TO LOVE YOU BABY - Donna **Summer** (4) 76
LOVE TO STAY - **Altered Images** (46) 83
LOVE TOWN - Booker **Newbury III** (6) 83
LOVE TRAIN - **O'Jays** (9) 73
LOVE WARS - **Womack** and **Womack** (14) 84
LOVE WILL FIND A WAY - David **Grant** (24) 83
LOVE WILL KEEP US TOGETHER - **Captain** and **Tennille** (32) 75
LOVE WILL MAKE YOU FAIL IN SCHOOL - Rocky **Sharpe** and the **Replays** (60) 79
LOVE WILL TEAR US APART - **Joy Division** (13) 80
LOVE WON'T LET ME WAIT - Major **Harris** (37) 75
LOVE WORTH WAITING FOR, A - Shakin' **Stevens** (2) 84
LOVE X LOVE - George **Benson** (10) 80
LOVE YOU INSIDE OUT - **Bee Gees** (13) 79
LOVE YOU MORE - **Buzzcocks** (34) 78
LOVE YOU SAVE, THE - **Jackson Five** (7) 70
LOVEDRIVE - **Scorpions** (69) 79
LOVELY DAY - Bill **Withers** (7) 78
LOVELY MONEY - **Damned** (42) 82
LOVELY ONE - **Jacksons** (29) 80
LOVER IN YOU, THE - **Sugarhill Gang** (54) 82
LOVER PLEASE - **Vernons Girls** (16) 62
LOVER'S CONCERTO, A - **Toys** (5) 65
LOVER'S HOLIDAY, A - **Change** (14) 80
LOVERS OF THE WORLD UNITE - **David** and **Jonathan** (7) 66
LOVE'S A PRIMA DONNA - Steve **Harley** and **Cockney Rebel** (41) 76
LOVE'S BEEN GOOD TO ME - Frank **Sinatra** (8) 69
LOVE'S COMIN' AT YA - Melba **Moore** (15) 82
LOVE'S CRASHING WAVES - **Difford** and **Tilbrook** (57) 84
LOVE'S GONNA GET YOU - **U.K. Players** (52) 83
LOVE'S GOTTA HOLD ON ME - **Dollar** (4) 79
LOVE'S GREAT ADVENTURE - **Ultravox** (12) 84
LOVE'S JUST A BROKEN HEART - Cilla **Black** (5) 66
LOVE'S MADE A FOOL OF YOU - **Crickets** (26) 59
LOVE'S MADE A FOOL OF YOU - Buddy **Holly** (39) 64
LOVE'S MADE A FOOL OF YOU - **Matchbox** (63) 81
LOVES ME LIKE A ROCK - Paul **Simon** (39) 73
LOVE'S SUCH A WONDERFUL THING - **Real Thing** (33) 77
LOVE'S THEME - **Love Unlimited Orchestra** (10) 74
LOVE'S UNKIND - Donna **Summer** (3) 77
LOVESICK BLUES - Frank **Ifield** (1) 62
LOVIN' LIVIN' AND GIVIN' - Diana **Ross** (54) 78
LOVIN' THINGS - **Marmalade** (6) 68
LOVIN' UP A STORM - Jerry Lee **Lewis** (28) 59
LOVING AND FREE - Kiki **Dee** (13) 76
LOVING ARMS - Elvis **Presley** (47) 81
LOVING JUST FOR FUN - Kelly **Marie** (21) 80
LOVING ON THE LOSING SIDE - Tommy **Hunt** (28) 76
LOVING YOU [A] - Elvis **Presley** (24) 57
LOVING YOU [B] - Chris **Rea** (65) 82
LOVING YOU [C] - Minnie **Riperton** (2) 75
LOVING YOU AIN'T EASY - **Pagliaro** (31) 72
LOVING YOU HAS MADE ME BANANAS - Guy **Marks** (25) 78
LOVING YOU IS SWEETER THAN EVER - **Four Tops** (21) 66
LOW RIDER - **War** (12) 76
LOWDOWN - Boz **Scaggs** (28) 76
LUCILLE [A] - **Everly Brothers** (4) 60
LUCILLE [A] - **Little Richard** (10) 57
LUCILLE [B] - Kenny **Rogers** (1) 77
LUCKY DEVIL - Carl **Dobkins Jr.** (44) 60
LUCKY DEVIL - Frank **Ifield** (22) 60
LUCKY FIVE - Russ **Conway** (14) 60
LUCKY LIPS - Cliff **Richard** (4) 63
LUCKY NUMBER - Lene **Lovich** (3) 79
LUCKY ONE, THE - Laura **Branigan** (56) 84
LUCKY STAR - **Madonna** (14) 84
LUCKY STARS - Dean **Friedman** (3) 78
LUCY IN THE SKY WITH DIAMONDS - Elton **John** (10) 74
LULLABY OF BROADWAY - Winifred **Shaw** (42) 76
LULLABY OF THE LEAVES - **Ventures** (43) 61
LUMBERED - Lonnie **Donegan** (6) 61
LUNATICS (HAVE TAKEN OVER THE ASYLUM), THE - **Funboy Three** (20) 81
EL LUTE - **Boney M** (12) 79
LUTON AIRPORT - **Cats U.K.** (22) 79
LYDIA - Dean **Friedman** (31) 78
LYIN' EYES - **Eagles** (23) 75
MA BAKER - **Boney M** (2) 77
MA HE'S MAKING EYES AT ME - Johnny **Otis Show** (2) 57
MA HE'S MAKING EYES AT ME - Lena **Zavaroni** (10) 74
MA SAYS PA SAYS - Doris **Day** and Johnnie **Ray** (12) 53
MACARTHUR PARK - Richard **Harris** (4) 68,72
MACARTHUR PARK - Donna **Summer** (5) 78
MACDONALD'S CAVE - **Piltdown Men** (14) 60
MACHINE GUN - **Commodores** (20) 74
MACHINERY - Sheena **Easton** (38) 82
MACK THE KNIFE - Louis **Armstrong** (24) 59
MACK THE KNIFE - Bobby **Darin** (1) 59,79
MACK THE KNIFE - Ella **Fitzgerald** (19) 60
MACK THE KNIFE - **King Kurt** (55) 84
MAD ABOUT YOU - Bruce **Ruffin** (9) 72
MAD EYED SCREAMER - **Creatures** (24) 81
MAD PASSIONATE LOVE - Bernard **Bresslaw** (6) 58
MAD WORLD - **Tears For Fears** (3) 82
MADAM BUTTERFLY - Malcolm **Mclaren** (13) 84
MADE TO LOVE (GIRLS GIRLS GIRLS) - Eddie **Hodges** (37) 62
MADE YOU - Adam **Faith** (5) 60
MADISON, THE - Ray **Ellington** (41) 62
MADNESS (IS ALL IN THE MIND) - **Madness** (8) 83
MAGGIE - **Foster** and **Allen** (27) 83
MAGGIE MAY - Rod **Stewart** (1) 71,76
MAGGIE'S FARM - Bob **Dylan** (22) 65
MAGGIE'S FARM - **Specials** (4) 80
MAGIC [A] - Olivia **Newton-John** (32) 80
MAGIC [B] - **Pilot** (11) 74
MAGIC BUS - **Who** (26) 68
MAGIC FLY - **Space** (2) 77
MAGIC MANDRAKE - **Sarr Band** (68) 78
MAGIC MIND - **Earth Wind and Fire** (75) 78
MAGIC MOMENTS - Perry **Como** (1) 58
MAGIC MOMENTS - Ronnie **Hilton** (22) 58
MAGIC ROUNDABOUT - Jasper **Carrott** (5) 75
MAGIC TOUCH [A] - **Odyssey** (41) 82
MAGIC TOUCH [B] - **Rose Royce** (43) 84
MAGICAL MYSTERY TOUR (DOUBLE EP) - **Beatles** (2) 67
MAGICAL SPIEL - Barry **Ryan** (49) 70
MAGIC'S WAND - **Whodini** (47) 82
MAGIC'S WAND (THE WHODINI ELECTRIC EP) - **Whodini** (63) 84
MAGNIFICENT SEVEN, THE [A] - John **Barry** (48) 61
MAGNIFICENT SEVEN, THE [B] - Al **Caiola** (34) 61
MAGNIFICENT SEVEN, THE [B] - **Clash** (34) 81
MAGNUM (DOUBLE SINGLE) - **Magnum** (47) 80
MAH NA MAH NA - Piero **Umiliani** (8) 77
MAID OF ORLEANS (THE WALTZ JOAN OF ARC) - **Orchestral Manoeuvres** in the **Dark** (4) 82
MAIDEN JAPAN - **Iron Maiden** (43) 81
MAIGRET THEME, THE - Joe **Loss** (20) 62
MAIN ATTRACTION, THE - Pat **Boone** (12) 62
MAIN THEME FROM 'THE THORNBIRDS' - Henry **Mancini** (23) 84
MAIN TITLE THEME FROM 'MAN WITH THE GOLDEN ARM' - Jet **Harris** (12) 62
MAIN TITLE THEME FROM MAN WITH THE GOLDEN ARM - Billy **May** (9) 56
MAIS OUI - **King Brothers** (16) 60
MAJOR TOM (COMING HOME) - Peter **Schilling** (42) 84
MAJORCA - Petula **Clark** (12) 55
MAKE A DAFT NOISE FOR CHRISTMAS - **Goodies** (20) 75
MAKE A MOVE ON ME - Olivia **Newton-John** (43) 82
MAKE BELIEVE IT'S YOUR FIRST TIME - **Carpenters** (60) 83
MAKE HER MINE - Nat 'King' **Cole** (11) 54
MAKE IT A PARTY - Winifred **Atwell** (7) 56
MAKE IT EASY ON YOURSELF - **Walker Brothers** (1) 65
MAKE IT REAL - **Scorpions** (72) 80
MAKE IT SOON - Tony **Brent** (9) 53
MAKE IT WITH YOU - **Bread** (5) 70
MAKE LOVE TO ME - John **Leyton** (49) 64
MAKE LOVE TO ME - Jo **Stafford** (8) 54
MAKE ME AN ISLAND - Joe **Dolan** (3) 69
MAKE ME SMILE (COME UP AND SEE ME) - Steve **Harley** and **Cockney Rebel** (1) 75
MAKE THAT MOVE - **Shalamar** (30) 81
MAKE THE WORLD GO AWAY - Eddy **Arnold** (8) 66
MAKE THE WORLD GO AWAY - Donny and Marie **Osmond** (18) 75
MAKE YOURS A HAPPY HOME - Gladys **Knight** and the **Pips** (35) 76
MAKIN' IT - David **Naughton** (44) 79
MAKIN' LOVE - Floyd **Robinson** (9) 59
MAKIN' WHOOPEE - Ray **Charles** (42) 65
MAKING PLANS FOR NIGEL - **XTC** (17) 79
MAKING TIME - **Creation** (49) 66
MAKING UP AGAIN - **Goldie** (7) 78
MAKING YOUR MIND UP - **Bucks Fizz** (1) 81
MALT AND BARLEY BLUES - **McGuinness Flint** (5) 71
MAMA [A] - Dave **Berry** (5) 66
MAMA [B] - Connie **Francis** (2) 60
MAMA [B] - David **Whitfield** (12) 55
MAMA [C] - **Genesis** (4) 83
MAMA NEVER TOLD ME - **Sister Sledge** (20) 75
MAMA TOLD ME NOT TO COME - **Three Dog Night** (3) 70
MAMA USED TO SAY (AMERICAN REMIX) - **Junior** (7) 82
MAMA WEER ALL CRAZEE NOW - **Slade** (1) 72
MA-MA-MA-BELLE - **Electric Light Orchestra** (22) 74
MAMA'S BOY - Suzi **Quatro** (34) 80
MAMA'S PEARL - **Jackson Five** (25) 71
MAMBO ITALIANO - Rosemary **Clooney** (1) 54
MAMBO ITALIANO - Dean **Martin** (14) 55
MAMBO ROCK - Bill **Haley** and his **Comets** (14) 55
MAMMA MIA - **Abba** (1) 75
MAMMY BLUE - Roger **Whittaker** (31) 71
MAMY BLUE - **Pop Tops** (34) 71
MAN - Rosemary **Clooney** (7) 54
MAN FROM LARAMIE, THE - Al **Martino** (19) 55
MAN FROM LARAMIE, THE - Jimmy **Young** (1) 55
MAN FROM MADRID - Tony **Osborne Sound** (50) 61
MAN FROM NAZARETH - John Paul **Joans** (41) 70
MAN IN BLACK, THE - Cozy **Powell** (18) 74
MAN OF MYSTERY - **Shadows** (5) 60
MAN OF THE WORLD - **Fleetwood Mac** (2) 69
MAN ON FIRE [A] - Roger **Taylor** (66) 84
MAN ON FIRE [B] - Frankie **Vaughan** (6) 57
MAN ON THE CORNER - **Genesis** (41) 82
MAN OUT OF TIME - Elvis **Costello** and the **Attractions** (58) 82
MAN THAT GOT AWAY, THE - Judy **Garland** (18) 55
MAN TO MAN - **Hot Chocolate** (14) 76
MAN WHO PLAYS THE MANDOLINO, THE - Dean **Martin** (21) 57
MAN WHO SOLD THE WORLD, THE - **Lulu** (3) 74
MAN WITH THE CHILD IN HIS EYES - Kate **Bush** (6) 78
MAN WITHOUT LOVE [A], A - Engelbert **Humperdinck** (2) 68
MAN WITHOUT LOVE [B], A - Kenneth **McKellar** (30) 66
MANCHESTER UNITED - **Manchester United Football Club** (50) 76
MANDOLINS IN THE MOONLIGHT - Perry **Como** (13) 58
MANDY [A] - Eddie **Calvert** (9) 58
MANDY [B] - Barry **Manilow** (11) 75
MANEATER - Daryl **Hall** and John **Oates** (6) 82
MANGOS - Rosemary **Clooney** (25) 57
MANHATTAN SPIRITUAL - Reg **Owen** (20) 59
MANIAC - Michael **Sembello** (43) 83
MANNEQUIN - **Kids From 'Fame'** (50) 82
MANY RIVERS TO CROSS - **U.B.40** (16) 83
MANY TEARS AGO - Connie **Francis** (12) 61
MANY TOO MANY - **Genesis** (43) 78
MARBLE BREAKS IRON BENDS - Peter **Fenton** (46) 66
MARCH OF THE MODS - Joe **Loss** (35) 64
MARCH OF THE SIAMESE CHILDREN - Kenny **Ball** and his **Jazzmen** (4) 62
MARCHETA - Karl **Denver** (8) 61
MARGATE - **Chas** and **Dave** (46) 82
MARGIE - Fats **Domino** (18) 59
MARGOT - Billy **Fury** (28) 59

MARGUERITA TIME - Status Quo (3) 83
MARIA - P. J. Proby (8) 65
MARIA ELENA [A] - Los Indios Tabajaras (5) 63
MARIA ELENA [B] - Gene Pitney (25) 65
MARIANA - Gibson Brothers (11) 80
MARIANNE [A] - Hilltoppers (20) 57
MARIANNE [B] - Cliff Richard (22) 68
MARIE - Bachelors (9) 65
MARIE CELESTE - Polecats (53) 81
MARIE MARIE - Shakin' Stevens (19) 80
MARJORINE - Joe Cocker (48) 68
MARKET SQUARE HEROES - Marillion (60) 82
MARQUEE MOON - Television (30) 77
MARRAKESH EXPRESS - Crosby, Stills and Nash (17) 69
MARRIED MEN - Bonnie Tyler (35) 79
MARRY ME - Mike Preston (14) 61
MARTA - Bachelors (20) 67
MARTIAN HOP - Rocky Sharpe and the Replays (55) 80
MARVIN THE PARANOID ANDROID - Marvin (53) 81
MARY ANN - Black Lace (42) 79
MARY ANNE - Shadows (17) 65
MARY HAD A LITTLE LAMB - Wings (9) 72
MARY JANE - Del Shannon (35) 64
MARY OF THE FOURTH FORM - Boomtown Rats (15) 77
MARY'S BOY CHILD - Harry Belafonte (1) 57
MARY'S BOY CHILD - Nina and Frederick (26) 59
MARY'S BOY CHILD - OH MY LORD - Boney M (1) 78
MASQUERADE [A] - Skids (14) 79
MASQUERADE [B] - Evelyn Thomas (60) 84
MASSACHUSETTS - Bee Gees (1) 67
MASTER AND SERVANT - Depeche Mode (9) 84
MASTERBLASTER (JAMMIN') - Stevie Wonder (2) 80
MATADOR - Jeff Wayne (57) 82
MATCHSTALK MEN AND MATCHSTALK CATS AND DOGS - Brian and Michael (1) 78
MATTHEW AND SON - Cat Stevens (2) 67
MATT'S MOOD [A] - Breakout Krew (51) 84
MATT'S MOOD [B] - Matt Bianco (44) 84
MAY EACH DAY - Andy Williams (19) 66
MAY I HAVE THE NEXT DREAM WITH YOU - Malcolm Roberts (8) 68
MAY THE SUN SHINE - Nazareth (22) 79
MAY YOU ALWAYS - McGuire Sisters (15) 59
MAY YOU ALWAYS - Joan Regan (9) 59
MAYBE - Thom Pace (14) 79
MAYBE BABY - Crickets (4) 58
MAYBE I KNOW - Lesley Gore (20) 64
MAYBE I KNOW - Seashells (32) 72
MAYBE I'M AMAZED - Wings (28) 77
MAYBE TOMORROW [A] - Chords (40) 80
MAYBE TOMORROW [B] - Billy Fury (22) 59
ME & JULIO DOWN BY THE SCHOOLYARD - Paul Simon (15) 72
ME & MRS JONES - Billy Paul (12) 73
ME AND BABY BROTHER - War (21) 76
ME AND MR SANCHEZ - Blue Rondo a la Turk (40) 81
ME AND MY GIRL (NIGHT-CLUBBING) - David Essex (13) 82
ME AND MY LIFE - Tremeloes (4) 70
ME AND MY SHADOW - Frank Sinatra and Sammy Davis JR. (20) 62
ME AND YOU AND A DOG NAMED BOO - Lobo (4) 71
ME MYSELF I - Joan Armatrading (21) 80
ME NO POP I - Kid Creole and the Coconuts (32) 81
ME OR YOU? - Killing Joke (57) 83
ME THE PEACEFUL HEART - Lulu (9) 68
MEAN GIRL - Status Quo (20) 73
MEAN MEAN MAN - Wanda Jackson (46) 61
MEAN STREAK [A] - Cliff Richard (10) 59
MEAN STREAK [B] - Y & T (43) 83
MEAN TO ME - Shaye Cogan (43) 60
MEAN WOMAN BLUES - Roy Orbison (3) 63
MEANING OF LOVE, THE - Depeche Mode (12) 82
MECCA - Cheetahs (36) 64
MEDAL SONG, THE - Culture Club (32) 84
MEDICINE SONG, THE - Stephanie Mills (29) 84
MEET ME ON THE CORNER [A] - Max Bygraves (2) 55
MEET ME ON THE CORNER [B] - Lindisfarne (5) 72
MELLOW MELLOW RIGHT ON - Lowrell (37) 79
MELLOW YELLOW - Donovan (8) 67
MELODY OF LOVE - Ink Spots (10) 55
MELT - Siouxsie and the Banshees (49) 82
MELTING POT - Blue Mink (3) 69
MEMO FROM TURNER - Mick Jagger (32) 70
MEMORIES [A] - Mike Berry (55) 81
MEMORIES [B] - Public Image Ltd. (60) 79
MEMORIES ARE MADE OF THIS - Val Doonican (11) 67
MEMORIES ARE MADE OF THIS - Dave King (5) 56
MEMORIES ARE MADE OF THIS - Dean Martin (1) 56
MEMORY - Elaine Paige (6) 81
MEMORY - Barbra Streisand (34) 82
MEMPHIS - Lonnie Mack (47) 79
MEMPHIS TENNESSEE - Chuck Berry (6) 63
MEMPHIS TENNESSEE - Dave Berry (19) 63
LA MER (BEYOND THE SEA) - Bobby Darin (8) 60
MERCI CHERI - Vince Hill (36) 66
MERRY CHRISTMAS DARLING - Carpenters (45) 72

MERRY GENTLE POPS - Barron Knights (9) 65
MERRY JINGLE, A - Greedies (28) 79
MERRY PLOUGHBOY, THE - Dermot O'Brien (46) 66
MERRY XMAS EVERYBODY - Slade (1) 73,80
MESS OF BLUES, A - Elvis Presley (2) 60
MESS OF THE BLUES, A - Status Quo (15) 83
MESSAGE, THE - Grandmaster Flash, Melle Mel and the Furious Five (8) 82
MESSAGE II (SURVIVAL) - Melle Mel and Duke Bootee (74) 83
MESSAGE IN A BOTTLE - Police (1) 79
MESSAGE OF LOVE - Pretenders (11) 81
MESSAGE TO MARTHA - Lou Johnson (36) 64
MESSAGE TO MARTHA (KENTUCKY BLUEBIRD) - Adam Faith (12) 64
MESSAGE TO YOU RUDY, A - Specials (10) 79
MESSAGE UNDERSTOOD - Sandie Shaw (6) 65
MESSAGES - Orchestral Manoeuvres in the Dark (13) 80
MESSAGES FROM THE STARS - Rah Band (42) 83
METAL GURU - T. Rex (1) 72
METAL HEALTH - Quiet Riot (45) 83
METEOR MAN - Dee D. Jackson (48) 78
MEXICALI ROSE - Karl Denver (8) 61
MEXICAN, THE - Fentones (41) 62
MEXICAN GIRL - Smokie (19) 78
MEXICAN RADIO - Wall of Voodoo (64) 83
MEXICO - Long John Baldry (15) 68
MICHAEL - Highwaymen (1) 61
MICHAEL - Geno Washington and the Ram Jam Band (39) 67
MICHAEL & THE SLIPPER TREE - Equals (24) 69
MICHAEL CAINE - Madness (11) 84
MICHAEL JACKSON MEDLEY - Ashaye (45) 83
MICHAEL ROW THE BOAT - Lonnie Donegan (6) 61
MICHELLE - David and Jonathan (11) 66
MICHELLE - Overlanders (1) 66
MICKEY - Toni Basil (2) 82
MICRO KIDS - Level 42 (37) 83
MIDDLE OF THE NIGHT - Brotherhood Of Man (41) 78
MIDNIGHT - Paul Anka (26) 58
MIDNIGHT AT THE LOST AND FOUND - Meat Loaf (17) 83
MIDNIGHT AT THE OASIS - Maria Muldaur (21) 74
MIDNIGHT BLUE - Louise Tucker (59) 83
MIDNIGHT COWBOY - Midnight Cowboy Soundtrack (47) 80
MIDNIGHT FLYER - Nat 'King' Cole (23) 62
MIDNIGHT GROOVIN' - Light of the World (72) 79
MIDNIGHT IN MOSCOW - Kenny Ball and his Jazzmen (2) 61
MIDNIGHT RIDER - Paul Davidson (10) 76
MIDNIGHT SHIFT - Buddy Holly (26) 59
MIDNIGHT SPECIAL - Paul Evans (41) 60
MIDNIGHT SUMMER DREAM - Stranglers (35) 83
MIDNIGHT TO SIX MAN - Pretty Things (46) 66
MIDNIGHT TRAIN TO GEORGIA - Gladys Knight and the Pips (10) 76
MIDNITE DYNAMOS - Matchbox (14) 80
MIGHTY JOE - Shocking Blue (43) 70
MIGHTY POWER OF LOVE - Tavares (25) 77
MIGHTY QUINN - Manfred Mann (1) 68
MIKE OLDFIELD'S SINGLE (THEME FROM TUBULAR BELLS) - Mike Oldfield (31) 74
MILES AWAY - John Foxx (51) 80
MILK AND ALCOHOL - Dr. Feelgood (9) 79
MILKY WAY - Sheer Elegance (18) 75
MILLION DRUMS - Tony Sheveton (49) 64
MILLIONS LIKE US - Purple Hearts (57) 79
MILLY MOLLY MANDY - Glyn Poole (35) 73
MILORD - Edith Piaf (41) 60
MILORD - Frankie Vaughan (34) 60
MIND BLOWING DECISIONS - Heatwave (12) 78
MIND GAMES - John Lennon (26) 73
MIND OF A TOY - Visage (13) 81
MIND UP TONIGHT - Melba Moore (22) 83
MINDLESS BOOGIE - Hot Chocolate (46) 79
MINE - Everything But The Girl (58) 84
MINEFIELD - I-Level (52) 83
MINUETTO ALLEGRETTO - Wombles (16) 74
MINUTE BY MINUTE - Doobie Brothers (47) 79
MINUTE OF YOUR TIME, A - Tom Jones (14) 68
MINUTE YOU'RE GONE, THE - Cliff Richard (1) 65
MIRACLE OF YOU, THE - Danny Williams (41) 61
MIRROR IN THE BATHROOM - The Beat (4) 80
MIRROR MAN - Human League (2) 82
MIRROR MIRROR [A] - Pinkerton's Assorted Colours (9) 66
MIRROR MIRROR [B] - Diana Ross (36) 82
MIRROR MIRROR (MON AMOUR) - Dollar (4) 81
MIRRORS - Sally Oldfield (19) 78
MISS HIT AND RUN - Barry Blue (26) 74
MISS THE GIRL - Creatures (21) 83
MISS YOU [A] - Rolling Stones (3) 78
MISS YOU [B] - Jimmy Young (15) 63
MISS YOU NIGHTS - Cliff Richard (15) 76
MISSING WORDS - The Selecter (23) 80
MISSING YOU - John Waite (9) 84
MISSISSIPPI - Pussycat (1) 76
MISSY MISSY - Paul and Barry Ryan (43) 66
MR. BASS MAN - Johnny Cymbal (24) 63
MR. BLUE - David MacBeth (18) 59
MR. BLUE - Mike Preston (12) 59
MR. BLUE SKY - Electric Light Orchestra (6) 78

MR. CROWLEY - Ozzy Osbourne Blizzard Of Ozz (46) 80
MR. CUSTER - Charlie Drake (12) 60
MR. GUDER - Carpenters (12) 74
MR. GUITAR - Bert Weedon (47) 61
MISTER PORTER - Mickie Most (45) 63
MR. PRESIDENT - D, B, M and T (33) 70
MR. RAFFLES (MAN IT WAS MEAN) - Steve Harley and Cockney Rebel (13) 75
MR. SANDMAN - Max Bygraves (16) 55
MR. SANDMAN - Chordettes (11) 54
MR. SANDMAN - Four Aces (9) 55
MR. SANDMAN - Dickie Valentine (5) 54
MR. SECOND CLASS - Spencer Davis Group (35) 68
MR. SOFT - Steve Harley and Cockney Rebel (8) 74
MR. SOLITAIRE - Animal Nightlife (25) 84
MR. SUCCESS - Frank Sinatra (29) 58
MR. TAMBOURINE MAN - Byrds (1) 65
MR. WONDERFUL - Peggy Lee (5) 57
MR. ZERO - Keith Relf (50) 66
MRS MILLS' MEDLEY - Mrs. Mills (18) 61
MRS. ROBINSON (EP) - Simon and Garfunkel (9) 69
MRS. ROBINSON - Simon and Garfunkel (4) 68
MS GRACE - Tymes (1) 74
MISTY - Johnny Mathis (12) 60
MISTY - Ray Stevens (2) 75
MISTY BLUE - Dorothy Moore (5) 76
MISUNDERSTANDING - Genesis (42) 80
MITTAGEISEN (METAL POSTCARD) - Siouxsie and the Banshees (47) 79
M'LADY - Sly and the Family Stone (32) 68
MOANIN' - Chris Farlowe (46) 67
MOB RULES - Black Sabbath (46) 81
MOBILE - Ray Burns (4) 55
MOCKINGBIRD - Belle Stars (51) 82
MOCKINGBIRD - Inez and Charlie Foxx (36) 69
MOCKINGBIRD - Carly Simon and James Taylor (34) 74
MOCKINGBIRD HILL - Migil Five (10) 64
MODEL, THE - Kraftwerk (1) 82
MODERN GIRL [A] - Sheena Easton (56) 80
MODERN GIRL [B] - Meat Loaf (17) 84
MODERN LOVE - David Bowie (2) 83
MODERN WORLD, THE - Jam (36) 77
MONA LISA - Conway Twitty (5) 59
MONDAY MONDAY - Mamas and the Papas (3) 66
MONEY - Bern Elliott and the Fenmen (14) 63
MONEY - Flying Lizards (5) 79
MONEY GO ROUND (PART 1) - Style Council (11) 83
MONEY HONEY - Bay City Rollers (3) 75
MONEY IN MY POCKET - Dennis Brown (14) 79
MONEY MONEY MONEY - Abba (3) 76
MONEY THAT'S YOUR PROBLEM - Tonight (66) 78
MONEY'S TOO TIGHT (TO MENTION) - Valentine Brothers (73) 83
MONKEES EP - Monkees (33) 80
MONKEY CHOP - Dan-I (30) 79
MONKEY MAN - Maytals (47) 70
MONKEY SPANNER - Dave and Ansil Collins (7) 71
MONSIEUR DUPONT - Sandie Shaw (6) 69
MONSTER MASH - Bobby 'Boris' Pickett and the Crypt-Kickers (3) 73
MONTEGO BAY - Bobby Bloom (3) 70
MONTEGO BAY - Freddie Notes and the Rudies (45) 70
MONTEGO BAY - Sugar Cane (54) 78
MONY MONY - Tommy James and the Shondells (1) 68
MOODY BLUE - Elvis Presley (6) 77
MOODY RIVER - Pat Boone (18) 61
MOON HOP - Derrick Morgan (49) 70
MOON RIVER - Greyhound (12) 72
MOON RIVER - Henry Mancini (46) 61
MOON RIVER - Danny Williams (1) 61
MOON SHADOW - Cat Stevens (22) 71
MOON TALK - Perry Como (17) 58
MOONGLOW - Sounds Orchestral (43) 65
MOONGLOW - Morris Stoloff (7) 56
MOONLIGHT & ROSES - Jim Reeves (34) 71
MOONLIGHT AND MUZAK - M (33) 79
MOONLIGHT GAMBLER - Frankie Laine (13) 56
MOONLIGHT SERENADE - Glenn Miller (12) 54,76
MOONLIGHT SHADOW - Mike Oldfield (4) 83
MOONLIGHTING - Leo Sayer (2) 75
MOONSHINE SALLY - Mud (10) 75
MORE - Perry Como (10) 56
MORE - Jimmy Young (4) 56
MORE AND MORE - Andy Williams (45) 67
MORE AND MORE PARTY POPS - Russ Conway (5) 59
MORE GOOD OLD ROCK 'N ROLL - Dave Clark Five (34) 70
MORE I SEE (THE LESS I BELIEVE), THE - Funboy Three (68) 83
MORE I SEE YOU, THE - Joy Marshall (34) 66
MORE I SEE YOU, THE - Chris Montez (3) 66
MORE LIKE THE MOVIES - Dr. Hook (14) 78
MORE MONEY FOR YOU AND ME (MEDLEY) - Four Preps (39) 61
MORE, MORE, MORE [A] - Carmel (23) 84
MORE MORE MORE [B] - Andrea True Connection (5) 76
MORE PARTY POPS - Russ Conway (2) 58
MORE THAN A FEELING - Boston (22) 77

NEVER ON SUNDAY - **Manuel** and his **Music Of The Mountains** (29) 60
NEVER SAY DIE - **Black Sabbath** (21) 78
NEVER SAY DIE (GIVE A LITTLE BIT MORE) - Cliff **Richard** (15) 83
NEVER STOP - **Echo** and the **Bunnymen** (15) 83
NEVER SURRENDER - **Saxon** (18) 81
NEVER TOO MUCH - Luther **Vandross** (44) 83
NEVER TURN AWAY - **Orchestral Manoeuvres** in the **Dark** (70) 84
NEVER TURN YOUR BACK ON MOTHER EARTH - **Sparks** (13) 74
NEVER WED AN OLD MAN - **Dubliners** (43) 67
NEVERTHELESS - **New Seekers** (34) 73
NEVERTHELESS - Frankie **Vaughan** (29) 68
NEW AMSTERDAM - Elvis **Costello** and the **Attractions** (36) 80
NEW DAY, A - **Killing Joke** (56) 84
NEW DIMENSIONS - **Imagination** (56) 83
NEW FASHION, A - Bill **Wyman** (37) 82
NEW GRANGE - **Clannad** (65) 83
NEW GUITAR IN TOWN - **Lurkers** (72) 79
NEW KID IN TOWN - **Eagles** (20) 77
NEW LIFE - **Depeche Mode** (11) 81
NEW LIVE AND RARE - **Deep Purple** (31) 77
NEW LIVE AND RARE II (EP) - **Deep Purple** (45) 78
NEW LIVE AND RARE VOLUME 3 - **Deep Purple** (48) 80
NEW MOON ON MONDAY - **Duran Duran** (9) 84
NEW ORLEANS - Gary 'U.S.' **Bonds** (16) 61
NEW ORLEANS - Bern **Elliott** and the **Fenmen** (24) 64
NEW ORLEANS - **Gillan** (17) 81
NEW ORLEANS - **Harley Quinne** (19) 72
NEW SONG - Howard **Jones** (3) 83
NEW TOY - Lene **Lovich** (53) 81
NEW WORLD IN THE MORNING - Roger **Whittaker** (17) 70
NEW WORLD MAN - **Rush** (36) 82,83
NEW YEARS DAY - **U2** (10) 83
NEW YORK CITY - **T. Rex** (15) 75
NEW YORK GROOVE - **Hello** (9) 75
NEW YORK MINING DISASTER 1941 - **Bee Gees** (12) 67
NEW YORK, NEW YORK - Gerard **Kenny** (43) 78
NEWS AT TEN - **Vapors** (44) 80
NEWS OF THE WORLD - **Jam** (27) 78
NEXT DOOR TO AN ANGEL - Neil **Sedaka** (29) 62
NEXT TIME, THE - Cliff **Richard** (1) 62
NICE AND SLOW - Jesse **Green** (17) 76
NICE LEGS SHAME ABOUT HER FACE - **Monks** (19) 79
NICE 'N EASY - Frank **Sinatra** (15) 60
NICE 'N SLEAZY - **Stranglers** (18) 78
NICE ONE CYRIL - **Cockerel Chorus** (14) 73
NIGHT - **Four Seasons** (7) 75
NIGHT AT DADDY GEE'S, A - **Showaddywaddy** (39) 79
NIGHT BIRDS - **Shakatak** (9) 82
NIGHT CHICAGO DIED, THE - **Paper Lace** (3) 74
NIGHT DANCING - Joe **Farrell** (57) 78
NIGHT FEVER [A] - **Bee Gees** (1) 78
NIGHT FEVER [A] - Carol **Douglas** (66) 78
NIGHT FEVER [B] - **Fatback Band** (38) 76
NIGHT GAMES - Graham **Bonnet** (6) 81
NIGHT HAS A THOUSAND EYES, THE - Bobby **Vee** (3) 63
NIGHT IN NEW YORK, A - Elbow **Bones** and the **Racketeers** (33) 84
NIGHT IS YOUNG, THE - Gary **Miller** (29) 61
NIGHT LADIES - **Crusaders** (55) 84
NIGHT LINE - Randy **Crawford** (51) 83
NIGHT OF FEAR - **Move** (2) 67
NIGHT OF THE LONG GRASS - **Troggs** (17) 67
NIGHT OF THE VAMPIRE - **Moontrekkers** (50) 61
NIGHT OWL - Gerry **Rafferty** (5) 79
NIGHT PORTER - **Japan** (29) 82
NIGHT THE WINE AND THE ROSES, THE - **Liquid Gold** (32) 80
NIGHT THEY DROVE OLD DIXIE DOWN, THE - Joan **Baez** (6) 71
NIGHT TO REMEMBER, A - **Shalamar** (5) 82
NIGHT TRAIN [A] - Buddy **Morrow** (12) 53
NIGHT TRAIN [B] - **Visage** (12) 82
NIGHTMARE [A] - **Gillan** (36) 81
NIGHTMARE [B] - **Saxon** (50) 83
NIGHTMARES - **A Flock of Seagulls** (53) 83
NIGHTS IN WHITE SATIN - Elkie **Brooks** (33) 82
NIGHTS IN WHITE SATIN - **Dickies** (39) 79
NIGHTS IN WHITE SATIN - **Moody Blues** (9) 67,72,79
NIGHTS ON BROADWAY - Candi **Staton** (6) 77
NINE TIMES OUT OF TEN - Cliff **Richard** (3) 60
9 TO 5 [A] - Sheena **Easton** (3) 80
9 TO 5 [B] - Dolly **Parton** (47) 81
1999 - **Prince** (25) 83
NINETEENTH NERVOUS BREAKDOWN - **Rolling Stones** (2) 66
98.6 - **Bystanders** (45) 67
98.6 - **Keith** (24) 67
99 WAYS - Tab **Hunter** (5) 57
99 RED BALLOONS - **Nena** (1) 84
96 TEARS - **? (Question Mark)** and the **Mysterians** (37) 66
99 1/2 - Carol **Lynn Townes** (47) 84
NIPPLE TO THE BOTTLE - Grace **Jones** (50) 82
NITE CLUB - **Specials** (10) 79
NO ARMS CAN EVER HOLD YOU - **Bachelors** (7) 64
NO CHANCE (NO CHARGE) - Billy **Connolly** (24) 76
NO CHARGE - J. J. **Barrie** (1) 76
NO CLASS - **Motorhead** (61) 79
NO DOUBT ABOUT IT - **Hot Chocolate** (2) 80
NO FACE, NO NAME, NO NUMBER - **Traffic** (40) 68
NO GETTING OVER YOU - **Paris** (49) 82
NO GOODBYES - Curtis **Mayfield** (65) 78
NO HIDING PLACE - Ken **Mackintosh** (45) 60
NO HONESTLY - Lynsey **De Paul** (7) 74
NO LAUGHING IN HEAVEN - **Gillan** (31) 81
NO LOVE - Joan **Armatrading** (50) 82
NO MATTER HOW I TRY - Gilbert **O'Sullivan** (5) 71
NO MATTER WHAT - **Badfinger** (5) 71
NO MATTER WHAT SIGN YOU ARE - **Supremes** (37) 69
NO MERCY - **Stranglers** (37) 84
NO MILK TODAY - **Herman's Hermits** (7) 66
NO MORE - **McGuire Sisters** (20) 55
NO MORE HEROES - **Stranglers** (8) 77
NO MORE LONELY NIGHTS - Paul **McCartney** (2) 84
(NO MORE) LOVE AT YOUR CONVENIENCE - Alice **Cooper** (44) 77
NO MORE MR. NICE GUY - Alice **Cooper** (10) 73
NO MORE TEARS (ENOUGH IS ENOUGH) - Donna **Summer** and Barbra **Streisand** (3) 79
NO MULE'S FOOL - **Family** (29) 69
NO NO JOE - **Silver Convention** (41) 76
NO NO NO - Nancy **Nova** (63) 82
NO ONE - Ray **Charles** (35) 63
NO ONE BUT YOU - Billy **Eckstine** (3) 54
NO ONE CAN BREAK A HEART LIKE YOU - Dave **Clark Five** (28) 68
NO ONE CAN MAKE MY SUNSHINE SMILE - **Everly Brothers** (11) 62
NO ONE IS INNOCENT - **Sex Pistols** (7) 78
NO ONE LIKE YOU - **Scorpions** (65) 82
NO ONE QUITE LIKE GRANDMA - **St. Winifred's School Choir** (1) 80
NO ONE TO CRY TO - Ray **Charles** (38) 64
NO ONE WILL EVER KNOW - Frank **Ifield** (25) 66
NO OTHER BABY - Bobby **Helms** (30) 58
NO OTHER LOVE - Ronnie **Hilton** (1) 56
NO OTHER LOVE - Edmund **Hockridge** (24) 56
NO OTHER LOVE - **Johnston Brothers** (22) 56
NO PARTICULAR PLACE TO GO - Chuck **Berry** (3) 64
NO REGRETS [A] - Shirley **Bassey** (39) 65
NO REGRETS [B] - Midge **Ure** (9) 82
NO REGRETS [B] - **Walker Brothers** (7) 76
NO SELF CONTROL - Peter **Gabriel** (33) 80
NO SELL OUT - Malcolm **X** (60) 84
NO STONE UNTURNED - **Truth** (66) 84
NO SURVIVORS - **GBH** (63) 82
NO TIME TO BE 21 - **Adverts** (38) 78
NO WOMAN NO CRY - Bob **Marley** and the **Wailers** (22) 75
NOBODY - Toni **Basil** (52) 82
NOBODY BUT YOU - Gladys **Knight** and the **Pips** (34) 77
NOBODY DOES IT BETTER - Carly **Simon** (7) 77
NOBODY I KNOW - **Peter** and **Gordon** (10) 64
NOBODY MADE ME - Randy **Edelman** (60) 82
NOBODY NEEDS YOUR LOVE - Gene **Pitney** (2) 66
NOBODY TOLD ME - John **Lennon** (6) 84
NOBODY WINS - Elton **John** (42) 81
NOBODY'S CHILD - Karen **Young** (6) 69
NOBODY'S DARLIN' BUT MINE - Frank **Ifield** (4) 63
NOBODY'S DIARY - **Yazoo** (3) 83
NOBODY'S FOOL [A] - **Haircut 100** (9) 82
NOBODY'S FOOL [B] - Jim **Reeves** (32) 70
NOBODY'S HERO - **Stiff Little Fingers** (36) 80
NON HO L'ETA PER AMARTI - Gigliola **Cinquetti** (17) 64
NO-ONE DRIVING - John **Foxx** (32) 80
NO ONE GETS THE PRIZE - Diana **Ross** (59) 79
NO ONE TO CRY TO - Ray **Charles** (38) 64
NORA MALONE - Teresa **Brewer** (26) 57
NORMAN - Carol **Deene** (24) 62
NORMAN BATES - **Landscape** (40) 81
NORTH TO ALASKA - Johnny **Horton** (23) 61
NORTHERN LIGHTS - **Renaissance** (10) 78
NOT AS A STRANGER - Frank **Sinatra** (18) 55
NOT FADE AWAY - **Rolling Stones** (3) 64
NOT NOW JOHN - **Pink Floyd** (30) 83
NOT RESPONSIBLE - Tom **Jones** (18) 66
NOT TOO LITTLE NOT TOO MUCH - Chris **Sandford** (17) 63
NOT UNTIL THE NEXT TIME - Jim **Reeves** (13) 65
NOTHIN' TO DO - Michael **Holliday** (20) 56
NOTHING CAN STOP ME - Gene **Chandler** (41) 68
NOTHING COMES EASY - Sandie **Shaw** (14) 66
NOTHING LEFT TOULOUSE - **Sad Café** (62) 80
NOTHING RHYMED - Gilbert **O'Sullivan** (8) 70
NOTHING TO LOSE - **U. K.** (67) 79
NOW - Val **Doonican** (43) 68
NOW - Al **Martino** (3) 53
NOW I'M HERE - **Queen** (11) 75
NOW IS THE TIME - Jimmy **James** and the **Vagabonds** (5) 76
NOW IT'S GONE - **Chords** (63) 79
NOW THAT WE'VE FOUND LOVE - **Third World** (10) 78
NOW THOSE DAYS ARE GONE - **Bucks Fizz** (8) 82
NOW WE'RE THRU - **Poets** (31) 64
NOWHERE FAST - **Meat Loaf** (67) 84
NOWHERE GIRL - **B-Movie** (67) 82
NOWHERE MAN - **Three Good Reasons** (47) 66
NOWHERE TO RUN - Martha **Reeves** and the **Vandellas** (26) 65,69
NUCLEAR DEVICE (THE WIZARD OF AUS) - **Stranglers** (36) 79
NUMBER 9 DREAM - John **Lennon** (23) 75
NUMBER OF THE BEAST, THE - **Iron Maiden** (18) 82
NUMBER ONE DEE JAY - **Goody Goody** (55) 78
NUMBER ONE SONG IN HEAVEN, THE - **Sparks** (14) 79
NUMBERS - **Soft Cell** (25) 83
NUNC DIMITTIS - Paul **Phoenix** (56) 79
NUT ROCKER - B. **Bumble** and the **Stingers** (1) 62,72
NUTBUSH CITY LIMITS - Ike and Tina **Turner** (4) 73
007 - Desmond **Dekker** and the **Aces** (14) 67
007 - **Musical Youth** (26) 83
O SUPERMAN - Laurie **Anderson** (2) 81
O.K. FRED - Erroll **Dunkley** (11) 79
O.K? - Julie **Covington, Rula Lenska,** Charlotte **Cornwell** and Sue **Jones-Davies** (10) 77
OB-LA-DI OB-LA-DA - **Bedrocks** (20) 68
OB-LA-DI OB-LA-DA - **Marmalade** (1) 68
OBLIVIOUS - **Aztec Camera** (18) 83
OBSESSED - **999** (71) 81
OBSESSION - Reg **Owen** (43) 60
OCEAN DEEP - Cliff **Richard** (27) 84
ODE TO BILLY JOE - Bobbie **Gentry** (13) 67
OFF THE WALL - Michael **Jackson** (7) 79
OFFICIAL SECRETS - **M** (64) 80
OFFSHORE BANKING BUSINESS - **Members** (31) 79
OH BABE WHAT WOULD YOU SAY? - Hurricane **Smith** (4) 72
OH BOY - **Crickets** (3) 57
OH BOY - **Mud** (1) 75
OH BOY (THE MOOD I'M IN) - **Brotherhood Of Man** (8) 77
OH CAROL [A] - Neil **Sedaka** (3) 59,72
OH CAROL [B] - **Smokie** (5) 78
OH DIANE - **Fleetwood Mac** (9) 82
OH GIRL - **Chi-Lites** (14) 72,75
OH HAPPY DAY [A] - Edwin **Hawkins Singers** (2) 69
OH HAPPY DAY [B] - **Johnston Brothers** (4) 53
OH HOW I MISS YOU - **Bachelors** (30) 67
OH JULIE - Shakin' **Stevens** (1) 82
OH LONESOME ME - Craig **Douglas** (15) 62
OH LORI - **Alessi** (8) 77
OH ME OH MY (I'M A FOOL FOR YOU BABY) - **Lulu** (47) 69
OH MEIN PAPA - Eddie **Calvert** (1) 53
OH MEIN PAPA - Eddie **Fisher** (9) 54
OH NO - **Commodores** (44) 81
OH NO NOT MY BABY - **Manfred Mann** (11) 65
OH NO NOT MY BABY - Rod **Stewart** (6) 73
OH OH, I'M FALLING IN LOVE AGAIN - Jimmie **Rodgers** (18) 58
OH PRETTY WOMAN - Roy **Orbison** (1) 64
OH WELL - **Fleetwood Mac** (2) 69
OH WHAT A CIRCUS - David **Essex** (3) 78
OH WHAT A SHAME - Roy **Wood** (13) 75
OH YEAH (ON THE RADIO) - **Roxy Music** (5) 80
OH YES! YOU'RE BEAUTIFUL - Gary **Glitter** (2) 74
OH YOU PRETTY THING - Peter **Noone** (12) 71
OH! WHAT A DAY - Craig **Douglas** (43) 60
L'OISEAU ET L'ENFANT - Marie **Myriam** (42) 77
OKAY! - Dave **Dee, Dozy, Beaky, Mick** and **Tich** (4) 67
OL' MACDONALD - Frank **Sinatra** (11) 60
OL' RAG BLUES - **Status Quo** (9) 83
OLD - **Dexy's Midnight Runners** (17) 82
OLD & WISE - Alan **Parsons Project** (74) 83
OLD FASHIONED WAY, THE - Charles **Aznavour** (50) 73
OLD FLAMES - **Foster** and **Allen** (51) 82
OLD OAKEN BUCKET - Tommy **Sands** (25) 60
OLD PIANNA RAG - Dickie **Valentine** (15) 55
OLD RIVERS - Walter **Brennan** (38) 62
OLD RUGGED CROSS, THE - Ethna **Campbell** (33) 75
OLD SHEP - Clinton **Ford** (27) 59
OLD SIAM SIR - **Wings** (35) 79
OLD SMOKEY - **Johnny** and the **Hurricanes** (24) 61
OLD SONGS, THE - Barry **Manilow** (48) 81
OLDEST SWINGER IN TOWN - Fred **Wedlock** (6) 81
OLE OLA (MUHLER BRASILEIRA) - Rod **Stewart** (4) 78
OLIVE TREE - Judith **Durham** (33) 67
OLIVER'S ARMY - Elvis **Costello** and the **Attractions** (2) 79
OLYMPIC RECORD, AN - **Barron Knights** (35) 68
ON A CAROUSEL - **Hollies** (4) 67
ON A LITTLE STREET IN SINGAPORE - **Manhattan Transfer** (20) 78
ON A SATURDAY NIGHT - Terry **Dactyl** and the **Dinosaurs** (45) 73
ON A SLOW BOAT TO CHINA - Emile **Ford** and the **Checkmates** (3) 60
ON A SUNDAY - Nick **Heyward** (52) 83
ON FIRE - **T-Connection** (16) 78
ON HORSEBACK - Mike **Oldfield** (4) 75
ON MOTHER KELLY'S DOORSTEP - Danny **La Rue** (33) 68
ON MY RADIO - The **Selecter** (8) 79
ON MY WORD - Cliff **Richard** (12) 65
ON THE BEACH - Cliff **Richard** (7) 64
ON THE BEAT - **B, B,** and **Q Band** (41) 81

ON THE RADIO - Donna **Summer** (32) 80
ON THE REBOUND - Floyd **Cramer** (1) 61
ON THE ROAD AGAIN - **Canned Heat** (8) 68
ON THE STREET WHERE YOU LIVE - Vic **Damone** (1) 58
ON THE STREET WHERE YOU LIVE - David **Whitfield** (16) 58
ON THE WINGS OF A NIGHTINGALE - **Everly Brothers** (41) 84
ON THE WINGS OF LOVE - Jeffrey **Osbourne** (11) 84
ON WITH THE MOTLEY - Harry **Secombe** (16) 55
ONCE - **Genevieve** (43) 66
ONCE BITTEN TWICE SHY - Ian **Hunter** (14) 75
ONCE I HAD A SWEETHEART - **Pentangle** (46) 69
ONCE IN A LIFETIME - **Talking Heads** (14) 81
ONCE IN EVERY LIFETIME - Ken **Dodd** (28) 61
ONCE THERE WAS A TIME - Tom **Jones** (18) 66
ONCE UPON A DREAM - Billy **Fury** (7) 62
ONCE UPON A TIME [A] - Marvin **Gaye** and Mary **Wells** (50) 64
ONCE UPON A TIME [B] - Tom **Jones** (32) 65
ONE AND ONE IS ONE - **Medicine Head** (3) 73
ONE AND ONLY, THE - Gladys **Knight** and the **Pips** (32) 78
ONE BETTER DAY - **Madness** (17) 84
ONE BROKEN HEART FOR SALE - Elvis **Presley** (12) 63
ONE DAY AT A TIME - Lena **Martell** (1) 79
ONE DAY I'LL FLY AWAY - Randy **Crawford** (2) 80
ONE DAY IN YOUR LIFE - Michael **Jackson** (1) 81
ONE DRINK TOO MANY - **Sailor** (35) 77
ONE FINE DAY - **Chiffons** (29) 63
ONE FINE MORNING - Tommy **Hunt** (44) 76
ONE FOR YOU ONE FOR ME - La **Bionda** (54) 78
ONE FOR YOU ONE FOR ME - Jonathan **King** (29) 78
ONE HEART BETWEEN TWO - Dave **Berry** (41) 64
ONE HELLO - Randy **Crawford** (48) 82
ONE IN TEN - **U.B.40** (7) 81
ONE INCH ROCK - **T. Rex** (7) 68,72
ONE LAST KISS - J. **Geils Band** (74) 79
ONE LOVE - Bob **Marley** and the **Wailers** (5) 84
ONE LOVER (DON'T STOP THE SHOW) - **Forrest** (67) 83
ONE MAN BAND - Leo **Sayer** (6) 74
ONE MAN WOMAN - Sheena **Easton** (14) 80
ONE MIND, TWO HEARTS - **Paradise** (42) 83
ONE MORE CHANCE - Diana **Ross** (49) 81
ONE MORE DANCE - Esther and Abi **Ofarim** (13) 68
ONE MORE SATURDAY NIGHT - **Matchbox** (63) 82
ONE MORE SUNRISE (MORGEN) - Dickie **Valentine** (14) 59
ONE NATION UNDER A GROOVE - (PART 1) - **Funkadelic** (9) 78
ONE NIGHT - **Mud** (32) 75
ONE NIGHT - Elvis **Presley** (1) 59
ONE NIGHT IN BANGKOK - Murray **Head** (12) 84
ONE NINE FOR SANTA - Fogwell **Flax** and the **Anklebiters** from **Freehold Junior School** (68) 81
ONE OF THE LUCKY ONES - Joan **Regan** (47) 60
ONE OF THESE NIGHTS - **Eagles** (23) 75
ONE OF THOSE NIGHTS - **Bucks Fizz** (20) 81
ONE OF US - **Abba** (3) 81
ONE OF US MUST KNOW (SOONER OR LATER) - Bob **Dylan** (33) 66
ONE ON ONE - Daryl **Hall** and John **Oates** (63) 83
ONE PIECE AT A TIME - Johnny **Cash** (32) 76
ONE ROAD - **Love Affair** (16) 69
ONE RULE FOR YOU - **After The Fire** (40) 79
ONE SMALL DAY - **Ultravox** (27) 84
ONE STEP AWAY - **Tavares** (16) 77
ONE STEP BEYOND - **Madness** (7) 79
ONE STEP CLOSER (TO LOVE) - George **McCrae** (57) 84
ONE STEP FURTHER - **Bardo** (2) 82
137 DISCO HEAVEN (MEDLEY) - Amii **Stewart** (5) 79
ONE TO CRY, THE - **Escorts** (49) 64
1-2-3 [A] - Len **Barry** (3) 65
1-2-3 [B] - **Professionals** (43) 80
1-2-3 O'LEARY - Des **O'Connor** (4) 68
ONE WAY LOVE - Cliff **Bennett** and the **Rebel Rousers** (9) 64
ONE WAY TICKET - **Eruption** (9) 79
ONION SONG - Marvin **Gaye** and Tammi **Terrell** (9) 69
ONLY BOY IN THE WORLD, THE - Stevie **Marsh** (29) 59
ONLY CRYING - Keith **Marshall** (12) 81
ONLY FLAME IN TOWN, THE - Elvis **Costello** and the **Attractions** (71) 84
ONLY FOR LOVE - **Limahl** (16) 83
ONLY LOVE CAN BREAK YOUR HEART - Elkie **Brooks** (43) 78
ONLY LOVIN' DOES IT - **Guys** and **Dolls** (42) 78
ONLY MAN ON THE ISLAND, THE - Vic **Damone** (24) 58
ONLY MAN ON THE ISLAND, THE - Tommy **Steele** (16) 58
ONLY ONE WOMAN - **Marbles** (5) 68
ONLY SIXTEEN - Sam **Cooke** (23) 59
ONLY SIXTEEN - Craig **Douglas** (1) 59
ONLY SIXTEEN - Al **Saxon** (24) 59
ONLY THE HEARTACHES - Houston **Wells** (22) 63
ONLY THE LONELY - Roy **Orbison** (36) 60
ONLY THE LONELY - **Prelude** (55) 82
ONLY THE STRONG SURVIVE - Billy **Paul** (33) 77
ONLY TIME WILL TELL - **Asia** (54) 82
ONLY WAY OUT, THE - Cliff **Richard** (10) 82
ONLY WHEN YOU LEAVE - **Spandau Ballet** (3) 84
ONLY WOMEN BLEED - Julie **Covington** (12) 77
ONLY YESTERDAY - **Carpenters** (7) 75
ONLY YOU [A] - Jeff **Collins** (40) 72
ONLY YOU [A] - **Hilltoppers** (3) 56
ONLY YOU [A] - **Platters** (5) 56
ONLY YOU [A] - Ringo **Starr** (28) 74
ONLY YOU [A] - Mark **Wynter** (38) 64
ONLY YOU [B] - Teddy **Pendergrass** (41) 78
ONLY YOU [C] - **Flying Pickets** (1) 83
ONLY YOU [C] - **Yazoo** (2) 82
ONLY YOU (AND YOU ALONE) - **Child** (33) 79
ONLY YOU CAN - **Fox** (3) 75
ONLY YOU CAN ROCK ME - **UFO** (50) 78
ONWARD CHRISTIAN SOLDIERS - Harry **Simeone Chorale** (35) 60,62
OO-EEH BABY - **Stonebridge McGuinness** (54) 79
OOH BABY - Gilbert **O'Sullivan** (18) 73
OOH BOY - **Rose Royce** (46) 80
OOH I DO - Lynsey **De Paul** (25) 74
OOH LA LA - Joe 'Mr. Piano' **Henderson** (46) 60
OOH LA LA LA (LET'S GO DANCIN') - **Kool** and the **Gang** (6) 82
OOH MY SOUL - **Little Richard** (30) 58
OOH TO BE AH - **Kajagoogoo** (7) 83
OOH! WHAT A LIFE - **Gibson Brothers** (10) 79
OOH-WAKKA-DOO-WAKKA-DAY - Gilbert **O'Sullivan** (8) 72
OOPS UP SIDE YOUR HEAD - **Gap Band** (6) 80
OPEN UP - **Mungo Jerry** (21) 72
OPEN UP YOUR HEART - Joan **Regan** (19) 55
OPEN YOUR HEART - **Human League** (6) 81
OPUS 17 (DON'T YOU WORRY 'BOUT ME) - **Four Seasons** (20) 66
ORANGE BLOSSOM SPECIAL - **Spotnicks** (29) 62
ORCHARD ROAD - Leo **Sayer** (16) 83
ORIGINAL BIRD DANCE - **Electronicas** (22) 81
ORVILLE'S SONG - Keith **Harris** and **Orville** (4) 82
OSSIE'S DREAM (SPURS ARE ON THEIR WAY TO WEMBLEY) - **Tottenham Hotspur F.A. Cup Final Squad** (5) 81
OTHER MAN'S GRASS, THE - Petula **Clark** (20) 67
OTHER SIDE OF LOVE, THE - **Yazoo** (13) 82
OTHER SIDE OF ME, THE - Andy **Williams** (42) 76
OTHER SIDE OF THE SUN, THE - Janis **Ian** (44) 80
OTHER WOMAN, THE OTHER MAN, THE - Gerard **Kenny** (69) 84
OUR DAY WILL COME - **Ruby** and the **Romantics** (38) 63
OUR FAVOURITE MELODIES - Craig **Douglas** (9) 62
OUR HOUSE - **Madness** (5) 82
OUR LAST SONG TOGETHER - Neil **Sedaka** (31) 73
OUR LIPS ARE SEALED - **Funboy Three** (7) 83
OUR LIPS ARE SEALED - **Go-Gos** (47) 82
OUR LOVE - Elkie **Brooks** (43) 82
(OUR LOVE) DON'T THROW IT ALL AWAY - Andy **Gibb** (32) 79
OUR WORLD - **Blue Mink** (17) 70
OUT COME THE FREAKS - **Was (Not Was)** (41) 84
OUT DEMONS OUT - Edgar **Broughton Band** (39) 70
OUT HERE ON MY OWN - Irene **Cara** (58) 82
OUT IN THE DARK - **Lurkers** (72) 79
OUT OF CONTROL - **Angelic Upstarts** (58) 80
OUT OF MY MIND - Johnny **Tillotson** (34) 63
OUT OF REACH - **Vice Squad** (68) 82
OUT OF SIGHT, OUT OF MIND - **Level 42** (41) 83
OUT OF THIS WORLD - Tony **Hatch** (50) 62
OUT OF TIME - Chris **Farlowe** (1) 66,75
OUT OF TIME - Dan **McCafferty** (41) 75
OUT OF TIME - **Rolling Stones** (45) 75
OUT OF TOUCH - Daryl **Hall** and John **Oates** (48) 84
OUT OF TOWN - Max **Bygraves** (18) 56
OUT ON THE FLOOR - Dobie **Gray** (42) 75
OUTA SPACE - Billy **Preston** (44) 72
OUTDOOR MINER - **Wire** (51) 79
OUTSIDE MY WINDOW - Stevie **Wonder** (52) 80
OUTSIDE OF HEAVEN - Eddie **Fisher** (1) 53
OUTSTANDING - **Gap Band** (68) 83
OVER AND OVER [A] - **Dave Clark Five** (45) 65
OVER AND OVER [B] - **James Boys** (39) 73
OVER AND OVER [C] - **Shalamar** (23) 83
OVER THE RAINBOW - YOU BELONG TO ME (MEDLEY) - **Matchbox** (15) 80
OVER UNDER SIDEWAYS DOWN - **Yardbirds** (10) 66
OVER YOU [A] - **Freddie** and the **Dreamers** (13) 64
OVER YOU [B] - **Roxy Music** (5) 80
OVERKILL [A] - **Men At Work** (21) 83
OVERKILL [B] - **Motorhead** (39) 79
OWNER OF A LONELY HEART - **Yes** (28) 83
OXYGENE PART IV - Jean-Michel **Jarre** (4) 77
P.Y.T (PRETTY YOUNG THING) - Michael **Jackson** (11) 84
PABLO - Russ **Conway** (45) 61
PACK UP YOUR SORROWS - Joan **Baez** (50) 66
PAINT IT BLACK - **Modettes** (42) 80
PAINT IT BLACK - **Rolling Stones** (1) 66
PAINT ME DOWN - **Spandau Ballet** (30) 81
PAINTER MAN - **Boney M** (10) 79
PAINTER MAN - **Creation** (36) 66
PAL OF MY CRADLE DAYS - Ann **Breen** (69) 83
PALE BLUE EYES - Paul **Quinn** and Edwyn **Collins** (72) 84
PALE SHELTER - **Tears For Fears** (5) 83
PALISADES PARK - Freddy **Cannon** (20) 62
PALOMA BLANCA - George **Baker Selection** (10) 75
PAMELA PAMELA - Wayne **Fontana** (11) 66
PANAMA - **Van Halen** (61) 84
PANDORA'S BOX - **Procol Harum** (16) 75
PAPA LOVES MAMA - Joan **Regan** (29) 60
PAPA LOVES MAMBO - Perry **Como** (16) 54
PAPA OOM MOW MOW - Gary **Glitter** (38) 75
PAPA OOM MOW MOW - **Sharonettes** (26) 75
PAPA WAS A ROLLIN' STONE - **Temptations** (14) 73
PAPA'S GOT A BRAND NEW BAG - James **Brown** (25) 65
PAPA'S GOT A BRAND NEW PIGBAG - **Pigbag** (3) 82
PAPER DOLL - Windsor **Davies** and Don **Estelle** (41) 75
PAPER PLANE - **Status Quo** (8) 73
PAPER ROSES - Anita **Bryant** (49) 60
PAPER ROSES - Maureen **Evans** (40) 60
PAPER ROSES - **Kaye Sisters** (7) 60
PAPER ROSES - Marie **Osmond** (2) 73
PAPER SUN - **Traffic** (5) 67
PAPER TIGER - Sue **Thompson** (50) 65
PAPERBACK WRITER - **Beatles** (1) 66
PARADE - **White** and **Torch** (54) 82
PARADISE [A] - Frank **Ifield** (26) 65
PARADISE [B] - **Stranglers** (48) 83
PARADISE BIRD - Amii **Stewart** (39) 80
PARADISE LOST - **Herd** (15) 67
PARADISE SKIES - Max **Webster** (43) 79
PARALYSED - Elvis **Presley** (8) 57
PARANOID - **Black Sabbath** (4) 70,80
PARANOID - **Dickies** (45) 79
PARIS BY AIR - **Tygers of Pan Tang** (63) 82
PARIS IS ONE DAY AWAY - **Mood** (42) 82
PARISIENNE GIRL - **Incognito** (73) 80
PARISIENNE WALKWAYS - Gary **Moore** (8) 79
PART OF THE UNION - **Strawbs** (2) 73
PART TIME LOVE [A] - Elton **John** (15) 78
PART TIME LOVE [B] - Gladys **Knight** and the **Pips** (30) 75
PARTY - Elvis **Presley** (2) 57
PARTY DOLL - **Jets** (72) 84
PARTY DOLL - Buddy **Knox** (29) 57
PARTY FEARS TWO - **Associates** (9) 82
PARTY IN PARIS - **U.K. Subs** (37) 80
PARTY LIGHTS - **Gap Band** (30) 80
PARTY PARTY - Elvis **Costello** and the **Attractions** (48) 82
PARTY POPS - Russ **Conway** (24) 57
PARTY TIME - **Fatback Band** (41) 76
PARTYLINE - **Brass Construction** (56) 84
PARTY'S OVER, THE - Lonnie **Donegan** (9) 62
PASADENA - **Temperance Seven** (4) 61
PASS THE DUTCHIE - **Musical Youth** (1) 82
PASSAGE TO BANGKOK, A - **Rush** (41) 81
PASSENGERS - Elton **John** (5) 84
PASSING BREEZE - Russ **Conway** (16) 60
PASSING STRANGERS [A] - Billy **Eckstine** and Sarah **Vaughan** (20) 57,69
PASSING STRANGERS [B] - **Ultravox** (57) 80
PASSION - Rod **Stewart** (17) 80
PASSION IN DARK ROOMS - **Mood** (74) 82
PASSION KILLER - **One the Juggler** (71) 83
PASSIONATE FRIEND - **Teardrop Explodes** (25) 81
PASSIONS OF LOVERS, THE - **Bauhaus** (51) 81
PAST, PRESENT AND FUTURE - **Cindy** and the **Saffrons** (56) 83
PATCHES - Clarence **Carter** (2) 70
PATHS OF PARADISE - Johnnie **Ray** (20) 55
PATRICIA - Perez **Prado** (8) 58
PAY OFF, THE - Kenny **Ball** and his **Jazzmen** (23) 62
PAY TO THE PIPER - **Chairmen Of The Board** (34) 71
PEACE IN OUR TIME - **Imposter** (48) 84
PEACE ON EARTH - **Hi Tension** (8) 78
PEACE ON EARTH - LITTLE DRUMMER BOY - David **Bowie** and Bing **Crosby** (3) 82
PEACEFUL - Georgie **Fame** (16) 69
PEACHES [A] - **Darts** (66) 80
PEACHES [B] - **Stranglers** (8) 77
PEARL IN SHELL - Howard **Jones** (7) 84
PEARL'S A SINGER - Elkie **Brooks** (8) 77
PEARLY-DEW DROPS DROPS - **Cocteau Twins** (29) 84
PEEK-A-BOO [A] - **New Vaudeville Band** (7) 67
PEEK-A-BOO [B] - **Stylistics** (35) 73
PEGGY SUE - Buddy **Holly** (32) 57,68
PEGGY SUE GOT MARRIED - Buddy **Holly** (13) 59
PENNY ARCADE - Roy **Orbison** (40) 69
PENNY LANE - **Beatles** (2) 67
PENNY LOVER - Lionel **Richie** (18) 84
PENTHOUSE AND PAVEMENT - **Heaven 17** (57) 81
PEOPLE - **Tymes** (16) 69
PEOPLE ARE PEOPLE - **Depeche Mode** (4) 84
PEOPLE GET READY - Bob **Marley** and the **Wailers** (5) 84
PEOPLE LIKE YOU AND PEOPLE LIKE ME - **Glitter Band** (5) 76
PEPE - Russ **Conway** (19) 61
PEPE - Duane **Eddy** (2) 61
PEPPER BOX - **Peppers** (6) 74
PEPPERMINT TWIST [A] - Joey **Dee** (33) 62
PEPPERMINT TWIST [B] - Danny **Peppermint** and the **Jumping Jacks** (26) 62
PERFECT SKIN - Lloyd **Cole** and the **Commotions** (71) 84

PERFECT TIMING - Kiki **Dee** (66) 81
PERFIDIA - **Ventures** (4) 60
PERFUMED GARDEN - **Rah Band** (45) 82
PERHAPS LOVE - Placido **Domingo** with John **Denver** (46) 81
PER-SO-NAL-LY - **Wigan's Ovation** (38) 75
PERSONALITY - Anthony **Newley** (6) 59
PERSONALITY - Lloyd **Price** (9) 59
PERSONALITY - Lena **Zavaroni** (33) 74
PERSUADERS, THE - John **Barry** (13) 71
PETER AND THE WOLF - **Clyde Valley Stompers** (25) 62
PETER GUNN THEME - Duane **Eddy** (6) 59
PETITE FLEUR - Chris **Barber's Jazz Band** (3) 59
PHEW WOW - **Farmers Boys** (59) 84
PHILADELPHIA FREEDOM - Elton **John** (12) 75
PHONE HOME - Johnny **Chingas** (43) 83
PHOTOGRAPH [A] - **Def Leppard** (66) 83
PHOTOGRAPH [B] - Ringo **Starr** (8) 73
PHYSICAL - Olivia **Newton-John** (7) 81
PIANISSIMO - Ken **Dodd** (21) 62
PIANO MEDLEY NO. 114 - Charlie **Kunz** (20) 54
PIANO PARTY - Winifred **Atwell** (10) 59
PICK A BALE OF COTTON - Lonnie **Donegan** (11) 62
PICK ME UP I'LL DANCE - Melba **Moore** (48) 79
PICK UP THE PIECES [A] - **Average White Band** (6) 75
PICK UP THE PIECES [B] - **Hudson-Ford** (8) 73
PICKIN' A CHICKEN - Eve **Boswell** (9) 55
PICKNEY GAL - Desmond **Dekker** and the **Aces** (42) 70
PICTURE OF YOU, A - Joe **Brown** (2) 62
PICTURE THIS - **Blondie** (12) 78
PICTURES OF LILY - **Who** (4) 67
PICTURES OF MATCHSTICK MEN - **Status Quo** (7) 68
PIECE OF MY HEART - Sammy **Hagar** (67) 82
PIECE OF THE ACTION - **Bucks Fizz** (12) 81
PIECES OF ICE - Diana **Ross** (46) 83
PIED PIPER - **Bob** and **Marcia** (11) 71
PIED PIPER - Crispian **St. Peters** (5) 66
PIED PIPER (THE BEEJE) - Steve **Race** (29) 63
PILLOW TALK - **Sylvia** (14) 73
PILLS AND SOAP - **Imposter** (16) 83
PILOT OF THE AIRWAVES - Charlie **Dore** (66) 79
PILTDOWN RIDES AGAIN - **Piltdown Men** (14) 61
PINBALL - Brian **Protheroe** (22) 74
PINBALL WIZARD - Elton **John** (7) 76
PINBALL WIZARD - **Who** (4) 69
PINBALL WIZARD - SEE ME FEEL ME (MEDLEY) - **New Seekers** (16) 73
PINK PARKER (EP), THE - Graham **Parker** and the **Rumour** (24) 77
PINKY BLUE - **Altered Images** (35) 82
PIPELINE - **Chantays** (16) 63
PIPELINE - Bruce **Johnston** (33) 77
PIPES OF PEACE - Paul **McCartney** (1) 83
PISTOL PACKIN' MAMA - Gene **Vincent** (15) 60
PLACE IN THE SUN [A], A - **Shadows** (24) 66
PLACE IN THE SUN [B], A - Stevie **Wonder** (20) 67
PLACE IN YOUR HEART - **Nazareth** (70) 78
PLAN B - **Dexy's Midnight Runners** (58) 81
PLANET EARTH - **Duran Duran** (12) 81
PLANET ROCK - Afrika **Bambaata** and the **Soul Sonic Force** (53) 82
PLASTIC AGE, THE - **Buggles** (16) 80
PLASTIC MAN - **Kinks** (31) 69
PLATINUM BLONDE - **Prelude** (45) 80
PLATINUM POP - **This Year's Blonde** (46) 81
PLAY ME LIKE YOU PLAY YOUR GUITAR - Duane **Eddy** (9) 75
PLAY THAT FUNKY MUSIC - **Wild Cherry** (7) 76
PLAY THE GAME - **Queen** (14) 80
PLAY TO WIN - **Heaven 17** (46) 81
PLAYGROUND - Anita **Harris** (46) 67
PLAYGROUND TWIST - **Siouxsie** and the **Banshees** (28) 79
PLAYTHING - **Linx** (48) 82
PLEASANT VALLEY SUNDAY - **Monkees** (11) 67
PLEASE COME HOME FOR CHRISTMAS - **Eagles** (30) 78
PLEASE DON'T ASK ABOUT BARBARA - Bobby **Vee** (29) 62
PLEASE DON'T FALL IN LOVE - Cliff **Richard** (7) 83
PLEASE DON'T GO [A] - Donald **Peers** (3) 68
PLEASE DON'T GO [B] - **KC** and **The Sunshine Band** (3) 79
PLEASE DON'T MAKE ME CRY - **U.B.40** (10) 83
PLEASE DON'T TEASE - Cliff **Richard** (1) 60
PLEASE DON'T TOUCH - Johnny **Kidd** and the **Pirates** (26) 59
PLEASE HELP ME I'M FALLING - Hank **Locklin** (9) 60
PLEASE MR. POSTMAN - **Carpenters** (2) 75
PLEASE PLEASE ME - **Beatles** (2) 63
PLEASE PLEASE ME - David **Cassidy** (16) 74
PLEASE STAY - **Cryin' Shames** (26) 66
PLEASE TELL HIM THAT I SAID HELLO - **Dana** (8) 75
PLEASURE BOYS - **Visage** (44) 82
PLENTY GOOD LOVIN' - Connie **Francis** (18) 59
LA PLUME DE MA TANTE - **Hugo** and **Luigi** (29) 59
POACHER, THE - Ronnie **Lane** (36) 74
POCKET CALCULATOR - **Kraftwerk** (39) 81
POETRY IN MOTION - Johnny **Tillotson** (1) 60,79
POINT OF VIEW - **Matumbi** (35) 79
POISON ARROW - **ABC** (6) 82
POISON IVY - **Coasters** (15) 59
POISON IVY - **Lambrettas** (7) 80
POISON IVY - **Paramounts** (35) 64
POLICE AND THIEVES - Junior **Murvin** (23) 80
POLICE OFFICER - Smiley **Culture** (40) 84
POLITICS OF DANCING, THE - **Re-Flex** (28) 84
POLK SALAD ANNIE - Elvis **Presley** (23) 73
PONY TIME - Chubby **Checker** (27) 61
POOL HALL RICHARD - **Faces** (8) 73
POOR JENNY - **Everly Brothers** (14) 59
POOR LITTLE FOOL - Rick **Nelson** (4) 58
POOR MAN'S SON - **Rockin' Berries** (5) 65
POOR ME - Adam **Faith** (1) 60
POOR PEOPLE OF PARIS - Winifred **Atwell** (1) 56
POP GO THE WORKERS - **Barron Knights** (5) 65
POP GOES MY LOVE - **Freeez** (26) 83
POP GOES THE WEASEL - Anthony **Newley** (12) 61
POP MUZIK - **M** (2) 79
POPCORN - **Hot Butter** (5) 72
POPCORN LOVE - **New Edition** (44) 83
POPPA JOE - **Sweet** (11) 72
POPPA PICCOLINO - Diana **Decker** (2) 53
POPS, WE LOVE YOU - Diana **Ross**, Marvin **Gaye**, Smokey **Robinson** and Stevie **Wonder** (66) 79
PORT AU PRINCE - Winifred **Atwell** (18) 56
PORTRAIT OF MY LOVE - Matt **Monro** (3) 60
PORTSMOUTH - Mike **Oldfield** (3) 76
PORTUGUESE WASHERWOMAN - Joe 'Fingers' **Carr** (20) 56
POSITIVELY FOURTH STREET - Bob **Dylan** (8) 65
POSTMAN PAT - Ken **Barrie** (44) 82
POWER AND THE GLORY - **Saxon** (32) 83
POWER OF LOVE, THE - **Frankie Goes To Hollywood** (1) 84
POWER TO ALL OUR FRIENDS - Cliff **Richard** (4) 73
POWER TO THE PEOPLE - John **Lennon** (7) 71
PRANCE ON - Eddie **Henderson** (44) 78
PRECIOUS - **Jam** (1) 82
PRETEND - Nat 'King' **Cole** (2) 53
PRETEND - Alvin **Stardust** (4) 81
PRETTY BLUE EYES - Craig **Douglas** (4) 60
PRETTY BROWN EYES - Jim **Reeves** (33) 68
PRETTY FLAMINGO - **Manfred Mann** (1) 66
PRETTY IN PINK - **Psychedelic Furs** (43) 81
PRETTY JENNY - Jess **Conrad** (50) 62
PRETTY LITTLE ANGEL EYES - Curtis **Lee** (47) 61
PRETTY LITTLE ANGEL EYES - **Showaddywaddy** (5) 78
PRETTY LITTLE BLACK EYED SUSIE - Guy **Mitchell** (2) 53
PRETTY PAPER - Roy **Orbison** (6) 64
PRETTY THING - Bo **Diddley** (34) 63
PRETTY VACANT - **Sex Pistols** (6) 77
PRETTY WOMAN - **Juicy Lucy** (45) 70
PRICE OF LOVE, THE - **Everly Brothers** (2) 65
PRICE YOU PAY - **Questions** (56) 83
PRIDE (IN THE NAME OF LOVE) - **U2** (3) 84
PRIMARY - **Cure** (43) 81
PRIME TIME - **Haircut 100** (46) 83
PRIME TIME - **Mtume** (57) 84
PRIME TIME - **Tubes** (34) 79
PRIMROSE LANE - Dickie **Pride** (28) 59
PRINCE, THE - **Madness** (16) 79
PRINCE CHARMING - **Adam** and The **Ants** (1) 81
PRINCE OF DARKNESS - **Bow Wow Wow** (58) 81
PRINCESS IN RAGS - Gene **Pitney** (9) 65
PRINCESS OF THE NIGHT - **Saxon** (57) 81
PRINCESS PRINCESS - Johnny **Tillotson** (67) 79
PRISONER OF LOVE - **Spear of Destiny** (59) 84
PRIVATE DANCER - Tina **Turner** (26) 84
PRIVATE EYES - Daryl **Hall** and John **Oates** (32) 82
PRIVATE INVESTIGATIONS - **Dire Straits** (2) 82
PRIVATE LIFE - Grace **Jones** (17) 80
PRIVATE NUMBER - Judy **Clay** and William **Bell** (8) 68
PRIVILEGE (SET ME FREE) - Patti **Smith Group** (72) 78
PRIZE OF GOLD - Joan **Regan** (6) 55
PROBLEMS - **Everly Brothers** (6) 59
PROCESSION - **New Order** (38) 81
PRODIGAL SON - **Steel Pulse** (35) 78
PROMISE, A - **Echo** and the **Bunnymen** (49) 81
PROMISED LAND - Chuck **Berry** (26) 65
PROMISED LAND - Elvis **Presley** (9) 75
PROMISED YOU A MIRACLE - **Simple Minds** (13) 82
PROMISES [A] - **Buzzcocks** (20) 78
PROMISES [B] - Eric **Clapton** (37) 78
PROMISES [C] - Ken **Dodd** (6) 66
PROUD MARY - **Checkmates Ltd.** (30) 69
PROUD MARY - **Creedence Clearwater Revival** (8) 69
PROUD ONE, THE - **Osmonds** (5) 75
PROVE IT - **Television** (25) 77
PSYCHEDELIC SHACK - **Temptations** (33) 70
PUB WITH NO BEER, A - Slim **Dusty** (3) 59
PUBLIC IMAGE - **Public Image Ltd.** (9) 78
PUCKWUDGIE - Charlie **Drake** (47) 72
PUFF - Kenny **Lynch** (33) 62
PULL UP TO THE BUMPER - Grace **Jones** (53) 81
PULLING MUSSELS (FROM THE SHELL) - **Squeeze** (44) 80
PULLING PUNCHES - David **Sylvian** (56) 84
PUMP IT UP - Elvis **Costello** and the **Attractions** (24) 78
PUNCH AND JUDY - **Marillion** (29) 84
PUNKY REGGAE PARTY - Bob **Marley** and the **Wailers** (9) 77
PUPPET MAN - Tom **Jones** (49) 71
PUPPET ON A STRING - Sandie **Shaw** (1) 67
PUPPY LOVE - Paul **Anka** (33) 60
PUPPY LOVE - Donny **Osmond** (1) 72
PUPPY SONG, THE - David **Cassidy** (1) 73
PURELY BY COINCIDENCE - **Sweet Sensation** (11) 75
PURGATORY - **Iron Maiden** (52) 81
PURPLE HAZE - Jimi **Hendrix Experience** (3) 67
PURPLE PEOPLE EATER - Jackie **Dennis** (29) 58
PURPLE PEOPLE EATER - Sheb **Wooley** (12) 58
PURPLE RAIN - **Prince** (8) 84
PUSHBIKE SONG, THE - **Mixtures** (2) 71
PUSS 'N BOOTS - **Adam** and The **Ants** (5) 83
PUT A LIGHT IN THE WINDOW - **King Brothers** (29) 58
PUT A LITTLE LOVE IN YOUR HEART - Dave **Clark Five** (31) 69
PUT HIM OUT OF YOUR MIND - **Dr. Feelgood** (73) 79
PUT OUR HEADS TOGETHER - **O'Jays** (45) 83
PUT YOUR HEAD ON MY SHOULDER - Paul **Anka** (17) 60
PUT YOUR LOVE IN ME - **Hot Chocolate** (10) 77
PUT YOUR MONEY WHERE YOUR MOUTH IS - **Rose Royce** (44) 77
PUT YOURSELF IN MY PLACE - **Elgins** (28) 71
PUT YOURSELF IN MY PLACE - **Isley Brothers** (13) 69
PUTTING ON THE STYLE - Lonnie **Donegan** (1) 57
PYJAMARAMA - **Roxy Music** (10) 73
QUANDO M'INNAMORO (A MAN WITHOUT LOVE) - **Sandpipers** (33) 68
QUANDO QUANDO QUANDO - Pat **Boone** (41) 62
QUARTER MOON, THE - **V.I.P.s** (55) 80
QUARTER TO THREE - Gary 'U.S.' **Bonds** (7) 61
QUE SERA MI VIDA (IF YOU SHOULD GO) - **Gibson Brothers** (5) 79
QUE SERA SERA - Geno **Washington** and the **Ram Jam Band** (43) 66
QUE TAL AMERICA - **Two Man Sound** (46) 79
QUEEN FOR TONIGHT - Helen **Shapiro** (33) 63
QUEEN OF 1964, THE - Neil **Sedaka** (35) 75
QUEEN OF CLUBS - **KC** and **The Sunshine Band** (7) 74
QUEEN OF HEARTS - Dave **Edmunds** (11) 79
QUEEN OF MY SOUL - **Average White Band** (23) 76
QUEEN OF THE HOP - Bobby **Darin** (24) 59
QUEEN OF THE RAPPING SCENE (NOTHING EVER GOES THE WAY YOU PLAN) - **Modern Romance** (37) 82
QUEEN'S FIRST EP - **Queen** (17) 77
QUESTION - **Moody Blues** (2) 70
QUESTIONS AND ANSWERS - **Sham 69** (18) 79
QUESTIONS I CAN'T ANSWER - **Heinz** (39) 64
QUICK JOEY SMALL (RUN JOEY RUN) - **Kasenetz-Katz Singing Orchestral Circus** (19) 68
QUIEREME MUCHO (YOURS) - Julio **Iglesias** (3) 82
QUIET LIFE - **Japan** (19) 81
QUIT THIS TOWN - **Eddie** and the **Hotrods** (36) 78
QUITE A PARTY - **Fireballs** (29) 61
QUITE RIGHTLY SO - **Procol Harum** (50) 68
QUOTE GOODBYE QUOTE - Carolyne **Mas** (71) 80
RABBIT - **Chas** and **Dave** (8) 80
RACE IS ON, THE [A] - Dave **Edmunds** and the **Stray Cats** (34) 81
RACE IS ON, THE [B] - Suzi **Quatro** (43) 78
RACE WITH THE DEVIL [A] - **Girlschool** (49) 80
RACE WITH THE DEVIL [A] - **Gun** (8) 68
RACE WITH THE DEVIL [B] - Gene **Vincent** (28) 56
RACHEL - Al **Martino** (10) 53
RACHMANINOFF'S 18TH VARIATION ON A THEME BY PAGANINI - Winifred **Atwell** (9) 54
RACIST FRIEND - **Special A.K.A.** (60) 83
RADANCER - **Marmalade** (6) 72
RADAR LOVE - **Golden Earring** (44) 77,73
RADIO GAGA - **Queen** (2) 84
RADIO RADIO - Elvis **Costello** and the **Attractions** (29) 78
RADIOACTIVE - Gene **Simmons** (41) 79
RAG DOLL - **Four Seasons** (2) 64
RAG MAMA RAG - **Band** (16) 70
RAGAMUFFIN MAN - **Manfred Mann** (8) 69
RAGS TO RICHES - Elvis **Presley** (9) 71
RAGS TO RICHES - David **Whitfield** (12) 53
RAGTIME COWBOY JOE - **Chipmunks** (11) 59
RAIN [A] - Bruce **Ruffin** (19) 71
RAIN [B] - **Status Quo** (7) 76
RAIN AND TEARS - **Aphrodite's Child** (30) 68
RAIN FOREST [A] - **Biddu** (39) 76
RAIN FOREST [B] - Paul **Hardcastle** (41) 84
RAIN RAIN RAIN - Frankie **Laine** (8) 54
RAINBOW [A] - **Marmalade** (3) 70
RAINBOW [B] - **Peters** and **Lee** (17) 74
RAINBOW CHASER - **Nirvana** (34) 68
RAINBOW IN THE DARK - **Dio** (46) 83
RAINBOW THEME - **Saxon** (66) 80
RAINBOW VALLEY - **Love Affair** (5) 68
RAINDROPS KEEP FALLING ON MY HEAD - Sacha **Distel** (50) 70
RAINDROPS KEEP FALLIN' ON MY HEAD - Bobbie **Gentry** (40) 70
RAINDROPS KEEP FALLING ON MY HEAD - B. J. **Thomas** (38) 70
RAININ' THROUGH MY SUNSHINE - **Real Thing** (40) 78
RAINING IN MY HEART - Leo **Sayer** (21) 78
RAINY DAY WOMEN NOS. 12 & 35 - Bob **Dylan** (7) 66

273

275

283

PART THREE
The British Hit Singles: Facts and Feats

This section should not be used to suggest that the music of the Archies is superior to that of the Beatles, nor vice versa. We are not trying to prove that Jess Conrad's singing voice is better than neil's, nor that the music of Dean Martin and Sweet have anything in common, other than they have both been on the British charts for the same length of time. The statistics record quantity rather than quality.

MOST WEEKS ON CHART

The following table lists all the recording acts that have spent 100 weeks or more on the British singles chart from the first chart on 14 Nov 52 up to and including the chart for 29 Dec 1984. It is of course possible for an act to be credited with two or more chart weeks in the same week from simultaneous hits. Double-sided hits, EPs, LPs and double singles only count as 1 week each week.

	Weeks
ELVIS PRESLEY	1124
CLIFF RICHARD	902

(+ 9 with Phil Everly, 7 with Olivia Newton-John and 2 with Sheila Walsh)

BEATLES	419

(+ 1 with Tony Sheridan)

FRANK SINATRA	391

(+ 18 with Nancy Sinatra and 9 with Sammy Davis Jnr)

SHADOWS	359

(+ 404 backing Cliff Richard)

EVERLY BROTHERS	337

(Phil Everly 6 more and 9 more with Cliff Richard)

STEVIE WONDER	323

(+ 10 with Paul McCartney and 5 with Diana Ross, Marvin Gaye and Smokey Robinson)

JIM REEVES	322
LONNIE DONEGAN	321
DAVID BOWIE	317

(+ 11 with Queen and 8 with Bing Crosby)

ROLLING STONES	313
SHIRLEY BASSEY	313
ROY ORBISON	309
ELTON JOHN	306

(+ 14 with Kiki Dee and 4 with John Lennon)

TOM JONES	306
HOLLIES	300
STATUS QUO	300
PAT BOONE	296
ROD STEWART	296

(+ 46 with Faces and 6 with Jeff Beck)

PERRY COMO	294
BILLY FURY	281
PAUL McCARTNEY/WINGS	277

(86 as Paul McCartney, 192 as Wings. Paul McCartney + 25 with Michael Jackson and 10 with Stevie Wonder)

David Bowie 6 years 63 days in space

DIANA ROSS	270

(+ 196 as a Supreme, 20 with Supremes and Temptations, 20 with Marvin Gaye, 12 with Lionel Richie, 8 with Julio Iglesias, 5 with Marvin Gaye, Smokey Robinson and Stevie Wonder and 4 with Michael Jackson)

BEE GEES	266
FOUR TOPS	265

(+ 20 with Supremes)

SUPREMES	258

(+ 27 with Temptations, 20 with Four Tops)

HOT CHOCOLATE	255
BEACH BOYS	253
FRANKIE LAINE	253

(+ 16 with Jimmy Boyd, 8 with Doris Day and 4 with Johnnie Ray)

ADAM FAITH	251
ABBA	247
SLADE	247
WHO	243

(+ 4 as High Numbers)

CONNIE FRANCIS	241
PETULA CLARK	236
ELECTRIC LIGHT ORCHESTRA	236

(+ 11 with Olivia Newton-John)

ENGELBERT HUMPERDINCK	235
KEN DODD	233
QUEEN	230

(+ 11 with David Bowie)

ANDY WILLIAMS	228
NAT 'KING' COLE	225
JACKSON FIVE/JACKSONS	219

(104 as Jackson Five, 115 as Jacksons)

DONNA SUMMER	219

(+ 13 with Barbra Streisand)

KINKS	213
T. REX	213
FRANKIE VAUGHAN	212

(+ 20 with Kaye Sisters)

HERMAN'S HERMITS	211
BRENDA LEE	210
SHOWADDYWADDY	209
JAM	201

Bust of **John Lennon** by Scottish sculptor John Somerville

Ultravox The only team with four goalkeepers

Marty Wilde All set for a nite at the 2 I's coffee bar. From left to right: Ian Samwell and Terry Smart (members of the British Drifters, the group that became the Shadows), Michael Cox, Marty Wilde and country and western singer Rick Richards.

Buck's Fizz Definitely not a mixture of Orange Juice and Evelyn 'Champagne' King

Neil Diamond Thirteen American hits before charting in Britain

Other performers who have spent more than 100 weeks on the chart in a combination of disguises include:

For the first time since *The Guinness Book Of British Hit Singles* was published in 1977, a new name has broken into the Top Ten of the Most Weeks on Chart table. In fact, two new names have arrived, Stevie Wonder and the Rolling Stones, replacing Shirley Bassey and Roy Orbison. David Bowie, Elton John, Status Quo, Rod Stewart and Paul McCartney have all closed in on the Top Ten during the past 2 years, so even the Shadows may slip before the eighties are finished.

It is extremely difficult to list in correct order the individuals who have spent most weeks on the chart under all guises, groups and other pseudonyms. However, a Top Ten of the individuals who have spent most weeks on the charts whether alone or as fully paid up members of duos or groups, looks like this:

ELVIS PRESLEY 1124 weeks, CLIFF RICHARD 920 weeks, HANK B. MARVIN 784 weeks, BRUCE WELCH 763 weeks, PAUL McCARTNEY 733 weeks, JOHN LENNON 597 weeks, DIANA ROSS 535 weeks, GEORGE HARRISON 479 weeks, RINGO STARR 476 weeks, MICHAEL JACKSON 446 weeks.

MOST WEEKS ON CHART IN EACH YEAR

Year	Artist	Weeks
1952	Vera Lynn	10
1953	Frankie Laine	66
1954	Frankie Laine	67
1955	Ruby Murray	80
1956	Bill Haley	110
1957	Elvis Presley	108
1958	Elvis Presley	70
1959	Russ Conway	79
1960	Cliff Richard	78
1961	Elvis Presley	88
1962	Mr. Acker Bilk	71
1963	Beatles	67
	Cliff Richard	67
1964	Jim Reeves	73
1965	Seekers	51
1966	Dave Dee, Dozy, Beaky, Mick and Tich	50
1967	Engelbert Humperdinck	97
1968	Tom Jones	58
1969	Fleetwood Mac	52
	Frank Sinatra	52
1970	Elvis Presley	59
1971	Elvis Presley	66
1972	T.Rex	58
1973	David Bowie	55

MOST WEEKS ON CHART IN ONE YEAR

110	Bill Haley and his Comets	1956
108	Elvis Presley	1957
97	Engelbert Humperdinck	1967
91	Adam and The Ants	1981
88	Elvis Presley	1961
84	Pat Boone	1957
80	Ruby Murray	1955
79	Russ Conway	1959
78	Cliff Richard	1960
77	Adam Faith	1960
73	Jim Reeves	1964
72	Beatles	1964
71	Mr. Acker Bilk	1962
70	Bachelors	1964
	Chubby Checker	1962
	Elvis Presley	1958

MOST WEEKS ON CHART: 1983

55	JAM
47	WHAM!
46	MICHAEL JACKSON
	(+ 14 with Paul McCartney)
41	EURYTHMICS
	NEW ORDER
39	CULTURE CLUB
37	ELTON JOHN
36	KAJAGOOGOO
	MADNESS
34	MEN AT WORK
	LIONEL RICHIE
	THOMPSON TWINS

Jam created a number of records by becoming the top act of the year despite breaking up at the end of 1982, releasing no new singles during the year, enjoying only one week in the Top Ten all year and appearing for the final time on the chart on 26 February. Paul Weller then went on to form Style Council, who enjoyed a further 31 chart weeks in 1983.

Madness enjoyed a fourth consecutive year in the Top Ten acts, but no other act remained from 1982. Michael Jackson reappeared among the Top Ten acts for the first time since 1972, and Elton John for the first time since 1974.

MOST WEEKS ON CHART: 1984

68	FRANKIE GOES TO HOLLYWOOD
53	GRANDMASTER FLASH AND MELLE MEL
50	NIK KERSHAW
44	POINTER SISTERS
	QUEEN
	(Freddie Mercury 9 more weeks solo)
43	HOWARD JONES
	LIONEL RICHIE
40	THOMPSON TWINS
	TINA TURNER
39	MICHAEL JACKSON
	(+ 3 with Paul McCartney)

(George Michael had 17 weeks on the chart solo, and 34 with Wham!, total 51)

Michael Jackson, Lionel Richie and the Thompson Twins remain from the Top Ten acts of 1983, but Madness disappear for the first time since 1979. Queen, amazingly, appear among the top acts of the year for the first time ever.

MOST HITS

Double-sided hits, double singles, EPs and LPs only count as one hit each time. Re-issues and re-entries do not count as new hits, but re-recordings of the same song by the same act do count as two hits. Re-mixes also count as two hits provided they are not in the chart at the same time. For example, the re-mix of Wham's 'Everything She Wants' is not a second hit because it shared a chart placing with the original release, but the re-mix of Sister Sledge's 'Lost In Music' does count as a second hit because it was distinct in time and chart placing from the original version, as well as sounding significantly different.

A record is a hit if it makes the chart, even if only for 1 week at number 75.

106	ELVIS PRESLEY
84	CLIFF RICHARD
	(+ 1 with Olivia Newton-John, 1 with Phil Everly and 1 with Sheila Walsh)
37	DAVID BOWIE
	(+ 1 with Queen and 1 with Bing Crosby)
	STEVIE WONDER
	(+ 1 with Paul McCartney, and 1 with Diana Ross, Marvin Gaye and Smokey Robinson)
36	ELTON JOHN
	(+ 1 with Kiki Dee, 1 with John Lennon)
34	DIANA ROSS
	(+ 18 with Supremes, 2 with Supremes and Temptations, 2 with Marvin Gaye, 1 with Lionel Richie, 1 with Michael Jackson, 1 with Julio Iglesias and 1 with Marvin Gaye, Stevie Wonder and Smokey Robinson)

Elvis Presley 106 hits – This is Elvis in the film that gave him his 7th

Rolling Stones More hits than any other British group

33 FRANK SINATRA
(+ 1 with Nancy Sinatra, 1 with Sammy Davis Jnr)
32 ROLLING STONES
31 PAUL McCARTNEY/WINGS
(21 Wings, 10 McCartney. McCartney 1 more with
Stevie Wonder, 2 with Michael Jackson)
SHADOWS
(+ 30 with Cliff Richard)
STATUS QUO
30 LONNIE DONEGAN
HOT CHOCOLATE
29 EVERLY BROTHERS
(Phil Everly 1 more with Cliff Richard)
BILLY FURY
HOLLIES
SLADE
FRANKIE VAUGHAN
(+ 2 with Kaye Sisters)
28 BEATLES
(+ 1 with Tony Sheridan)

Beatles Landing at London Airport after another
successful trip. Now four hits behind their rivals, the
Stones

NAT 'KING' COLE
ROY ORBISON
28 ROD STEWART
(+ 5 with Faces, 1 with Jeff Beck and 1 as part of
Python Lee Jackson)
WHO
(+ 1 as High-Numbers)
27 PETULA CLARK
DONNA SUMMER
(+ 1 with Barbra Streisand)
26 SHIRLEY BASSEY
BEACH BOYS
PAT BOONE
ELECTRIC LIGHT
ORCHESTRA
(+ 1 with Olivia Newton-John)
TOM JONES
QUEEN
(+ 1 with David Bowie)
JIM REEVES
25 ABBA
BEE GEES
FOUR TOPS
(+ 2 with Supremes)
JACKSON FIVE/JACKSONS
(11 as Jackson 5, 14 as Jacksons)
24 ADAM FAITH
SUPREMES
(+ 3 with Temptations, 2 with Four Tops)
23 PERRY COMO
CONNIE FRANCIS
FRANKIE LAINE
(+ 1 with Jimmy Boyd, 1 with Doris Day and 1 with
Johnnie Ray)
SHOWADDYWADDY
T. REX
22 DAVE CLARK FIVE
DAVID ESSEX

KINKS
BRENDA LEE
STRANGLERS
21 ELVIS COSTELLO
(+ 2 as the Imposter)
DUANE EDDY
GENE PITNEY
ANDY WILLIAMS
20 FATS DOMINO
HERMAN'S HERMITS
GLADYS KNIGHT AND THE
PIPS
(Gladys Knight + 1 with Johnny Mathis)
TEMPTATIONS
(+ 3 with Supremes)
19 CILLA BLACK
19 RUSS CONWAY
(+ 1 with Dorothy Squires)
KEN DODD
DRIFTERS
GARY GLITTER
MICHAEL JACKSON
(+ 2 with Paul McCartney, 1 with Diana Ross, 25 as
a Jackson)
MADNESS
18 BUDDY HOLLY
(+ 4 as a Cricket)
JAM
NEIL SEDAKA
SANDIE SHAW
DUSTY SPRINGFIELD
(+ 5 as a Springfield)
17 ADAM AND THE
ANTS/ADAM ANT
BACHELORS
MAX BYGRAVES
(+ 1 as part of All Star Hit Parade)
CARPENTERS
ALMA COGAN
BOBBY DARIN
FOUR SEASONS
RONNIE HILTON
JONATHAN KING
(9 under his own name, 8 under pseudonyms)
MANFRED MANN
(+ 5 as Manfred Mann's Earth Band)
THIN LIZZY
DAVID WHITFIELD
(+ 1 as part of All Star Hit Parade)
16 RAY CHARLES
CLASH
BOB DYLAN
SHANE FENTON/ALVIN
STARDUST
(4 as Shane Fenton, 12 as Alvin Stardust)
FLEETWOOD MAC
KOOL AND THE GANG
JOHN LENNON
(+ 1 with Elton John)
BARRY MANILOW
DEAN MARTIN
OLIVIA NEWTON-JOHN
(+ 2 with John Travolta, 1 with E L O and 1 with
Cliff Richard)
POLICE

ROXY MUSIC
SHALAMAR
SIOUXSIE AND THE
  BANSHEES
TOMMY STEELE
(+ 1 as part of All Star Hit Parade)
SHAKIN' STEVENS
(+ 1 with Bonnie Tyler)
STYLISTICS
SWEET

15 WINIFRED ATWELL
(+ 1 as part of All Star Hit Parade)
EARTH WIND AND FIRE
(+ 1 with Emotions)
FRANK IFIELD
LULU
MUD
RICK NELSON
GARY NUMAN/TUBEWAY
  ARMY
GILBERT O'SULLIVAN
SUZI QUATRO
(+ 1 with Chris Norman)
LEO SAYER
SPANDAU BALLET
U.B. 40
ULTRAVOX

Mention should also be made of the Osmonds who as a family have enjoyed 25 hits: ten by the Osmonds, seven by Donny, four by Donny and Marie, three by Little Jimmy and one by Marie. Marvin Gaye has now hit ten times solo and eleven other times with various girls. Eric Burdon has fronted 15 hits, nine as an uncredited member of the Animals and six more under his own name. Otis Redding's 14 solo hits are boosted by two more with Carla Thomas. Three quarters of the Small Faces participated in the five Faces hits as well as the 12 Small Faces successes. The Tremeloes had 13 hits on their own and another eight with Brian Poole. Eric Stewart featured on 13 hits by 10 C.C. one by Hotlegs, six by Wayne Fontana and the Mindbenders and four by the Mindbenders after their split from Wayne Fontana, a total of 24. The Boomtown Rats have had 14 hits, and Bob Geldof also organised the Band Aid hit 'Do They Know It's Christmas?'.

MOST TOP TEN HITS

The same rules apply as for the Most Hits list, except that a disc must have made the Top Ten for at least one week to qualify.

55 ELVIS PRESLEY
49 CLIFF RICHARD
(+ 1 more with Phil Everly)
25 BEATLES
21 ROLLING STONES
19 ABBA
PAUL McCARTNEY/WINGS
(Wings 12, Paul McCartney 7, + 1 more with Stevie Wonder, 2 with Michael Jackson)
18 DAVID BOWIE
(+ 1 with Queen, 1 with Bing Crosby)
STATUS QUO
17 LONNIE DONEGAN
HOLLIES
FRANKIE LAINE
(+ 1 with Jimmy Boyd, 1 with Doris Day)
ROD STEWART
(+ 3 with Faces, 1 with Python Lee Jackson)
16 SHADOWS
(+ 25 with Cliff Richard)
SLADE
15 MADNESS
STEVIE WONDER
(+ 1 with Paul McCartney)
14 BEE GEES
ELECTRIC LIGHT
ORCHESTRA
(+ 1 with Olivia Newton-John)
MICHAEL JACKSON
(+ 11 with Jacksons, 2 with Paul McCartney)
ELTON JOHN
(+ 1 with Kiki Dee)
13 NAT 'KING' COLE
EVERLY BROTHERS
(Phil Everly 1 more with Cliff Richard)
TOM JONES
KINKS
MANFRED MANN
(+ 3 as Manfred Mann's Earth Band)
QUEEN
(+ 1 with David Bowie)
WHO
12 SHIRLEY BASSEY
BEACH BOYS
GARY GLITTER
GUY MITCHELL
DIANA ROSS
(+ 1 with Marvin Gaye, 1 with Lionel Richie)
SHAKIN' STEVENS
(+ 1 with Bonnie Tyler)
SUPREMES
DAVID WHITFIELD
(+ 1 as part of All Star Hit Parade)
11 WINIFRED ATWELL
(+ 1 as part of All Star Hit Parade)
CILLA BLACK
PAT BOONE
PETULA CLARK
ADAM FAITH

Elvis Presley when the first *Guinness Book of British Hit Singles* was published in 1977. Elvis was leading Cliff by 50–4 in the most Top Ten hits section – his lead has since been narrowed.

BILLY FURY
HOT CHOCOLATE
JACKSON FIVE/JACKSONS
(6 as Jackson Five, 5 as Jacksons)
MUD
T. REX
10 C.C.
(+ 1 more as Hotlegs, more or less)
10 ADAM AND THE
  ANTS/ADAM ANT
BAY CITY ROLLERS
BLONDIE
DAVID ESSEX
FOUR TOPS
CONNIE FRANCIS
HERMAN'S HERMITS
ROY ORBISON
GENE PITNEY
POLICE
ROXY MUSIC
LEO SAYER
SHOWADDYWADDY
DUSTY SPRINGFIELD
STYLISTICS
SWEET

The Osmond clan have reached the Top Ten 16 times in various combinations. Frank Sinatra has had only nine solo Top Ten hits, but one more with his daughter Nancy. Frankie Vaughan has had nine solo Top Tenners, plus two more with the Kaye Sisters. Johnnie Ray's nine Top Ten entries are augmented by one more in duet with Doris Day, who herself has had seven solo Top Ten hits, two more with Frankie Laine and that one with Johnnie Ray.

Most Top Ten Hits Without a Number One Hit

14	ELTON JOHN
	ELECTRIC LIGHT ORCHESTRA
13	NAT 'KING' COLE
	WHO
11	BILLY FURY
10	GENE PITNEY

A great loss to music – the death of **Billy Fury** in January 1983

Most Hits Without a Top Ten Hit

It took Barry Manilow 12 hits to reach the Top Ten for the first time, but he is the only act so far who has taken more than ten hits to reach the Top Ten for the first time. Three acts have already had ten or more hits without reaching the Top Ten, as follows:

CLASH	16 hits
AC/DC	13 hits
WHITESNAKE	11 hits
SIMPLE MINDS	10 hits
SAXON	10 hits

Fats Domino had 18 more hits after his only Top Ten hit, 'Blueberry Hill'.

36	ELTON JOHN	(who has reached the very top in duet with Kiki Dee)
29	BILLY FURY	(who has spent 2 weeks at number two)
28	NAT 'KING' COLE	(who has spent a record 9 weeks at number two)
	WHO	(who have spent 3 weeks at number two)
26	ELECTRIC LIGHT ORCHESTRA	(who have reached the very top with Olivia Newton-John)
22	BRENDA LEE	(who has never climbed higher than number three)
	STRANGLERS	(who have spent 2 weeks at number two)
21	DUANE EDDY	(who has spent 2 weeks at number two)
	GENE PITNEY	(who has spent 3 weeks at number two)
20	FATS DOMINO	(who has never climbed higher than number six)
	GLADYS KNIGHT AND THE PIPS	(who have twice reached number four, but never higher)
	TEMPTATIONS	(who have never climbed higher than number seven)

THE NUMBER ONE HITS

Date disc hit the top	Title/Artist/Label	Number of weeks at no. 1

1952 (Top Twelve – *N.M.E.* Chart)

14 Nov	HERE IN MY HEART Al Martino (Capitol)	9

1953

16 Jan	YOU BELONG TO ME Jo Stafford (Columbia)	1
23 Jan	COMES A-LONG A-LOVE Kay Starr (Capitol)	1
30 Jan	OUTSIDE OF HEAVEN Eddie Fisher (HMV)	1
6 Feb	DON'T LET THE STARS GET IN YOUR EYES Perry Como (HMV)	5
13 Mar	SHE WEARS RED FEATHERS Guy Mitchell (Columbia)	4
10 Apr	BROKEN WINGS Stargazers (Decca)	1
17 Apr	(HOW MUCH IS) THAT DOGGIE IN THE WINDOW Lita Roza (Decca)	1
24 Apr	I BELIEVE Frankie Laine (Philips)	9
26 Jun	I'M WALKING BEHIND YOU Eddie Fisher (HMV)	1
3 Jul	I BELIEVE Frankie Laine (Philips)	6
14 Aug	MOULIN ROUGE Mantovani (Decca)	1
21 Aug	I BELIEVE Frankie Laine (Philips	3
11 Sep	LOOK AT THAT GIRL Guy Mitchell (Philips)	6
23 Oct	HEY JOE Frankie Laine (Philips)	2
6 Nov	ANSWER ME David Whitfield (Decca)	1
13 Nov	ANSWER ME Frankie Laine (Philips)	8
	(ANSWER ME by David Whitfield returned to number one for one week to share the top spot with Frankie Laine's version on 11 Dec 1953)	

1954

8 Jan	OH MEIN PAPA Eddie Calvert (Columbia)	9
12 Mar	I SEE THE MOON Stargazers (Decca)	5
16 Apr	SECRET LOVE Doris Day (Philips)	1
23 Apr	I SEE THE MOON Stargazers (Decca)	1
30 Apr	SUCH A NIGHT Johnnie Ray (Philips)	1
7 May	SECRET LOVE Doris Day (Philips)	8
2 Jul	CARA MIA David Whitfield with chorus and Mantovani and his orchestra (Decca)	10
10 Sep	LITTLE THINGS MEAN A LOT Kitty Kallen (Brunswick)	1
17 Sep	THREE COINS IN THE FOUNTAIN Frank Sinatra (Capitol)	3

Top Twenty began 1 Oct 1954

8 Oct	HOLD MY HAND Don Cornell (Vogue)	4
5 Nov	MY SON MY SON Vera Lynn (Decca)	2
19 Nov	HOLD MY HAND Don Cornell (Vogue)	1
26 Nov	THIS OLE HOUSE Rosemary Clooney (Philips)	1
3 Dec	LET'S HAVE ANOTHER PARTY Winifred Atwell (Philips)	5

1955

7 Jan	FINGER OF SUSPICION Dickie Valentine (Decca)	1
14 Jan	MAMBO ITALIANO Rosemary Clooney (Philips)	1
21 Jan	FINGER OF SUSPICION Dickie Valentine (Decca)	2
4 Feb	MAMBO ITALIANO Rosemary Clooney (Philips)	2
18 Feb	SOFTLY SOFTLY Ruby Murray (Columbia)	3
11 Mar	GIVE ME YOUR WORD Tennessee Ernie Ford (Capitol)	7
29 Apr	CHERRY PINK AND APPLE BLOSSOM WHITE Perez Prado (HMV)	2
13 May	STRANGER IN PARADISE Tony Bennett (Philips)	2
27 May	CHERRY PINK AND APPLE BLOSSOM WHITE Eddie Calvert (Columbia)	4
24 Jun	UNCHAINED MELODY Jimmy Young (Decca)	3
15 Jul	DREAMBOAT Alma Cogan (HMV)	2
29 Jul	ROSE MARIE Slim Whitman (London)	11
14 Oct	THE MAN FROM LARAMIE Jimmy Young (Decca)	4
11 Nov	HERNANDO'S HIDEAWAY Johnston Brothers (Decca)	2
25 Nov	ROCK AROUND THE CLOCK Bill Haley and his Comets (Brunswick)	3
16 Dec	CHRISTMAS ALPHABET Dickie Valentine (Decca)	3

On 30 Dec 1955 the chart was extended to 25 records for one week only

1956

6 Jan	ROCK AROUND THE CLOCK Bill Haley and his Comets (Brunswick)	2
20 Jan	SIXTEEN TONS Tennessee Ernie Ford (Capitol)	4
17 Feb	MEMORIES ARE MADE OF THIS Dean Martin (Capitol)	4
16 Mar	IT'S ALMOST TOMORROW Dreamweavers (Brunswick)	2
30 Mar	ROCK AND ROLL WALTZ Kay Starr (HMV)	1
6 Apr	IT'S ALMOST TOMORROW Dreamweavers (Brunswick)	1

Top Thirty began 13 Apr 1956

13 Apr	POOR PEOPLE OF PARIS Winifred Atwell (Decca)	3
4 May	NO OTHER LOVE Ronnie Hilton (HMV)	6
15 Jun	I'LL BE HOME Pat Boone (London)	5
20 Jul	WHY DO FOOLS FALL IN LOVE Teenagers featuring Frankie Lymon (Columbia)	
10 Aug	WHATEVER WILL BE WILL BE Doris Day (Philips)	6
21 Sep	LAY DOWN YOUR ARMS Anne Shelton (Philips)	4
19 Oct	A WOMAN IN LOVE Frankie Laine (Philips)	4
16 Nov	JUST WALKIN' IN THE RAIN Johnnie Ray (Philips)	7

1957

4 Jan	SINGING THE BLUES Guy Mitchell (Philips)	1
11 Jan	SINGING THE BLUES Tommy Steele (Decca)	1
18 Jan	SINGING THE BLUES Guy Mitchell (Philips)	1
25 Jan	GARDEN OF EDEN Frankie Vaughan (Philips)	4

(SINGING THE BLUES by Guy Mitchell returned to number one for one week to share the top spot with GARDEN OF EDEN by Frankie Vaughan on 1 Feb 1957)

22 Feb	YOUNG LOVE Tab Hunter (London)	7
12 Apr	CUMBERLAND GAP Lonnie Donegan (Pye Nixa)	5
17 May	ROCK-A-BILLY Guy Mitchell (Philips)...............	1
24 May	BUTTERFLY Andy Williams (London)	2
7 Jun	YES TONIGHT JOSEPHINE Johnnie Ray (Philips)	3
28 Jun	GAMBLIN' MAN/PUTTING ON THE STYLE Lonnie Donegan (Pye Nixa)	2
12 Jul	ALL SHOOK UP Elvis Presley (HMV)...............	7
30 Aug	DIANA Paul Anka (Columbia)	9
1 Nov	THAT'LL BE THE DAY Crickets (Vogue-Coral) ...	3
22 Nov	MARY'S BOY CHILD Harry Belafonte (RCA)	7

1958

10 Jan	GREAT BALLS OF FIRE Jerry Lee Lewis (London)	2
24 Jan	JAILHOUSE ROCK Elvis Presley (RCA)	3
14 Feb	THE STORY OF MY LIFE Michael Holliday (Columbia)....................................	2
28 Feb	MAGIC MOMENTS Perry Como (RCA)	8
25 Apr	WHOLE LOTTA WOMAN Marvin Rainwater (MGM)	3
16 May	WHO'S SORRY NOW Connie Francis (MGM).....	6
27 Jun	ON THE STREET WHERE YOU LIVE Vic Damone (Philips)...................................	2

(On 4 Jul 1958 ON THE STREET WHERE YOU LIVE by Vic Damone and ALL I HAVE TO DO IS DREAM/CLAUDETTE by the Everly Brothers shared the top spot)

4 Jul	ALL I HAVE TO DO IS DREAM/CLAUDETTE Everly Brothers (London)	7
22 Aug	WHEN Kalin Twins (Brunswick).....................	5
26 Sep	CAROLINA MOON/STUPID CUPID Connie Francis (MGM)	6
7 Nov	IT'S ALL IN THE GAME Tommy Edwards (MGM)	3
28 Nov	HOOTS MON Lord Rockingham's XI (Decca)......	3
19 Dec	IT'S ONLY MAKE BELIEVE Conway Twitty (MGM)	5

1959

23 Jan	THE DAY THE RAINS CAME Jane Morgan (London)....................................	1
30 Jan	ONE NIGHT/I GOT STUNG Elvis Presley (RCA)	3
20 Feb	AS I LOVE YOU Shirley Bassey (Philips).............	4

20 Mar	SMOKE GETS IN YOUR EYES Platters (Mercury)...................................	1
27 Mar	SIDE SADDLE Russ Conway (Columbia).............	4
24 Apr	IT DOESN'T MATTER ANYMORE Buddy Holly (Coral)...................................	3
15 May	A FOOL SUCH AS I/I NEED YOUR LOVE TONIGHT Elvis Presely (RCA)	5
19 Jun	ROULETTE Russ Conway (Columbia)...............	2
3 Jul	DREAM LOVER Bobby Darin (London)	4
31 Jul	LIVING DOLL Cliff Richard and the Shadows (Columbia)..................................	6
11 Sep	ONLY SIXTEEN Craig Douglas (Top Rank)	4
9 Oct	HERE COMES SUMMER Jerry Keller (London)...	1
16 Oct	MACK THE KNIFE Bobby Darin (London)	2
30 Oct	TRAVELLIN' LIGHT Cliff Richard and the Shadows (Columbia)	5
4 Dec	WHAT DO YOU WANT Adam Faith (Parlophone)	3

(On 18 Dec 1959 WHAT DO YOU WANT by Adam Faith and WHAT DO YOU WANT TO MAKE THOSE EYES AT ME FOR by Emile Ford and the Checkmates shared the top spot)

18 Dec	WHAT DO YOU WANT TO MAKE THOSE EYES AT ME FOR Emile Ford and the Checkmates (Pye)	6

1960

29 Jan	STARRY EYED Michael Holliday (Columbia).......	1
5 Feb	WHY Anthony Newley (Decca)	4

Record Retailer, now *Music and Video Week*, **began publication of a Top Fifty on 10 Mar 1960. From this point on their charts are used. The final** *New Musical Express* **chart used is that of 26 Feb 1960, as the chart published in** *Record Retailer* **on 10 Mar 1960 was dated 5 Mar 1960 and clearly corresponded with the** *N.M.E.* **chart of 4 Mar 1960.**

10 Mar	POOR ME Adam Faith (Parlophone)	1
17 Mar	RUNNING BEAR Johnny Preston (Mercury)	2
31 Mar	MY OLE MAN'S A DUSTMAN Lonnie Donegan (Pye)....................................	4
28 Apr	DO YOU MIND Anthony Newley (Decca)	1
5 May	CATHY'S CLOWN Everly Brothers (Warner Brothers)...................................	7
23 Jun	THREE STEPS TO HEAVEN Eddie Cochran (London)....................................	2
7 Jul	GOOD TIMIN' Jimmy Jones (MGM).................	3
28 Jul	PLEASE DON'T TEASE Cliff Richard and the Shadows (Columbia)	1
4 Aug	SHAKIN' ALL OVER Johnny Kidd and the Pirates (HMV).....................................	1
11 Aug	PLEASE DON'T TEASE Cliff Richard and the Shadows (Columbia)	2
25 Aug	APACHE Shadows (Columbia)......................	5
29 Sep	TELL LAURA I LOVE HER Ricky Valance (Columbia)...................................	3
20 Oct	ONLY THE LONELY Roy Orbison (London)	2
3 Nov	IT'S NOW OR NEVER Elvis Presley (RCA)	8
29 Dec	I LOVE YOU Cliff Richard and the Shadows (Columbia)...................................	2

1961

12 Jan	POETRY IN MOTION Johnny Tillotson (London)	2
26 Jan	ARE YOU LONESOME TONIGHT? Elvis Presley (RCA)	4
23 Feb	SAILOR Petula Clark (Pye)	1
2 Mar	WALK RIGHT BACK Everly Brothers (Warner Brothers)	3
23 Mar	WOODEN HEART Elvis Presley (RCA)	6
4 May	BLUE MOON Marcels (Pye International)	2
18 May	ON THE REBOUND Floyd Cramer (RCA)	1
25 May	YOU'RE DRIVING ME CRAZY Temperance Seven (Parlophone)	1
1 Jun	SURRENDER Elvis Presley (RCA)	4
29 Jun	RUNAWAY Del Shanon (London)	3
20 Jul	TEMPTATION Everly Brothers (Warner Brothers)	2
3 Aug	WELL I ASK YOU Eden Kane (Decca)	1
10 Aug	YOU DON'T KNOW Helen Shapiro (Columbia)	3
31 Aug	JOHNNY REMEMBER ME John Leyton (Top Rank)	3
21 Sep	REACH FOR THE STARS/CLIMB EV'RY MOUNTAIN Shirley Bassey (Columbia)	1
28 Sep	JOHNNY REMEMBER ME John Leyton (Top Rank)	1
5 Oct	KON-TIKI Shadows (Columbia)	1
12 Oct	MICHAEL Highwaymen (HMV)	1
19 Oct	WALKIN' BACK TO HAPPINESS Helen Shapiro (Columbia)	3
9 Nov	LITTLE SISTER/HIS LATEST FLAME Elvis Presley (RCA)	4
7 Dec	TOWER OF STRENGTH Frankie Vaughan (Philips)	3
28 Dec	MOON RIVER Danny Williams (HMV)	2

1962

11 Jan	THE YOUNG ONES Cliff Richard and the Shadows (Columbia)	6
22 Feb	ROCK-A-HULA BABY/CAN'T HELP FALLING IN LOVE Elvis Presley (RCA)	4
22 Mar	WONDERFUL LAND Shadows (Columbia)	8
17 May	NUT ROCKER B. Bumble and the Stingers (Top Rank)	1
24 May	GOOD LUCK CHARM Elvis Presley (RCA)	5
28 Jun	COME OUTSIDE Mike Sarne with Wendy Richard (Parlophone)	2
12 Jul	I CAN'T STOP LOVING YOU Ray Charles (HMV)	2
26 Jul	I REMEMBER YOU Frank Ifield (Columbia)	7
13 Sep	SHE'S NOT YOU Elvis Presley (RCA)	3
4 Oct	TELSTAR Tornados (Decca)	5
8 Nov	LOVESICK BLUES Frank Ifield (Columbia)	5
13 Dec	RETURN TO SENDER Elvis Presley (RCA)	3

1963

3 Jan	THE NEXT TIME/BACHELOR BOY Cliff Richard and the Shadows (Columbia)	3
24 Jan	DANCE ON Shadows (Columbia)	1
31 Jan	DIAMONDS Jet Harris and Tony Meehan (Decca)	3
21 Feb	WAYWARD WIND Frank Ifield (Columbia)	3
14 Mar	SUMMER HOLIDAY Cliff Richard and the Shadows (Columbia)	2
28 Mar	FOOT TAPPER Shadows (Columbia)	1
4 Apr	SUMMER HOLIDAY Cliff Richard and the Shadows (Columbia)	1
11 Apr	HOW DO YOU DO IT? Gerry and the Pacemakers (Columbia)	3
2 May	FROM ME TO YOU Beatles (Parlophone)	7
20 Jun	I LIKE IT Gerry and the Pacemakers (Columbia)	4
18 Jul	CONFESSIN' Frank Ifield (Columbia)	2
1 Aug	(YOU'RE THE) DEVIL IN DISGUISE Elvis Presley (RCA)	1
8 Aug	SWEETS FOR MY SWEET Searchers (Pye)	2
22 Aug	BAD TO ME Billy J. Kramer and the Dakotas (Parlophone)	3
12 Sep	SHE LOVES YOU Beatles (Parlophone)	4
10 Oct	DO YOU LOVE ME Brian Poole and the Tremeloes (Decca)	3
31 Oct	YOU'LL NEVER WALK ALONE Gerry and the Pacemakers (Columbia)	4
28 Nov	SHE LOVES YOU Beatles (Parlophone)	2
12 Dec	I WANT TO HOLD YOUR HAND Beatles (Parlophone)	5

1964

16 Jan	GLAD ALL OVER Dave Clark Five (Columbia)	2
30 Jan	NEEDLES AND PINS Searchers (Pye)	3
20 Feb	DIANE Bachelors (Decca)	1
27 Feb	ANYONE WHO HAD A HEART Cilla Black (Parlophone)	3
19 Mar	LITTLE CHILDREN Billy J. Kramer and the Dakotas (Parlophone)	2
2 Apr	CAN'T BUY ME LOVE Beatles (Parlophone)	3
23 Apr	WORLD WITHOUT LOVE Peter and Gordon (Columbia)	2
7 May	DON'T THROW YOUR LOVE AWAY Searchers (Pye)	2
21 May	JULIET Four Pennies (Philips)	1
28 May	YOU'RE MY WORLD Cilla Black (Parlophone)	4
25 Jun	IT'S OVER Roy Orbison (London)	2
9 Jul	HOUSE OF THE RISING SUN Animals (Columbia)	1
16 Jul	IT'S ALL OVER NOW Rolling Stones (Decca)	1
23 Jul	A HARD DAY'S NIGHT Beatles (Parlophone)	3
13 Aug	DO WAH DIDDY DIDDY Manfred Mann (HMV)	2
27 Aug	HAVE I THE RIGHT Honeycombs (Pye)	2
10 Sep	YOU REALLY GOT ME Kinks (Pye)	2
24 Sep	I'M INTO SOMETHING GOOD Herman's Hermits (Columbia)	2
8 Oct	OH PRETTY WOMAN Roy Orbison (London)	2
22 Oct	(THERE'S) ALWAYS SOMETHING THERE TO REMIND ME Sandie Shaw (Pye)	3
12 Nov	OH PRETTY WOMAN Roy Orbison (London)	1
19 Nov	BABY LOVE Supremes (Stateside)	1
3 Dec	LITTLE RED ROOSTER Rolling Stones (Decca)	1
10 Dec	I FEEL FINE Beatles (Parlophone)	5

1965

14 Jan	YEH YEH Georgie Fame with the Blue Flames (Columbia)	2
28 Jan	GO NOW Moody Blues (Decca)	1
4 Feb	YOU'VE LOST THAT LOVIN' FEELIN' Righteous Brothers (London)	2
18 Feb	TIRED OF WAITING FOR YOU Kinks (Pye)	1
25 Feb	I'LL NEVER FIND ANOTHER YOU Seekers (Columbia)	2
11 Mar	IT'S NOT UNUSUAL Tom Jones (Decca)	1
18 Mar	THE LAST TIME Rolling Stones (Decca)	3
8 Apr	CONCRETE AND CLAY Unit Four Plus Two (Decca)	1
15 Apr	THE MINUTE YOU'RE GONE Cliff Richard (Columbia)	1
22 Apr	TICKET TO RIDE Beatles (Parlophone)	3
13 May	KING OF THE ROAD Roger Miller (Philips)	1
20 May	WHERE ARE YOU NOW (MY LOVE) Jackie Trent (Pye)	1
27 May	LONG LIVE LOVE Sandie Shaw (Pye)	3
17 Jun	CRYING IN THE CHAPEL Elvis Presley (RCA)	1
24 Jun	I'M ALIVE Hollies (Parlophone)	1
1 Jul	CRYING IN THE CHAPEL Elvis Presley (RCA)	1
8 Jul	I'M ALIVE Hollies (Parlophone)	2
22 Jul	MR. TAMBOURINE MAN Byrds (CBS)	2
5 Aug	HELP! Beatles (Parlophone)	3
26 Aug	I GOT YOU BABE Sonny and Cher (Atlantic)	2
9 Sep	(I CAN'T GET NO) SATISFACTION Rolling Stones (Decca)	2
23 Sep	MAKE IT EASY ON YOURSELF Walker Brothers (Philips)	1
30 Sep	TEARS Ken Dodd (Columbia)	5
4 Nov	GET OFF OF MY CLOUD Rolling Stones (Decca)	3
25 Nov	THE CARNIVAL IS OVER Seekers (Columbia)	3
16 Dec	DAY TRIPPER/WE CAN WORK IT OUT Beatles (Parlophone)	5

1966

20 Jan	KEEP ON RUNNING Spencer Davis Group (Fontana)	1
27 Jan	MICHELLE Overlanders (Pye)	3
17 Feb	THESE BOOTS ARE MADE FOR WALKIN' Nancy Sinatra (Reprise)	4
17 Mar	THE SUN AIN'T GONNA SHINE ANYMORE Walker Brothers (Philips)	4
14 Apr	SOMEBODY HELP ME Spencer Davis Group (Fontana)	2
28 Apr	YOU DON'T HAVE TO SAY YOU LOVE ME Dusty Springfield (Philips)	1
5 May	PRETTY FLAMINGO Manfred Mann (HMV)	3
26 May	PAINT IT BLACK Rolling Stones (Decca)	1
2 Jun	STRANGERS IN THE NIGHT Frank Sinatra (Reprise)	3
23 Jun	PAPERBACK WRITER Beatles (Parlophone)	2
7 Jul	SUNNY AFTERNOON Kinks (Pye)	2
21 Jul	GET AWAY Georgie Fame with the Blue Flames (Columbia)	1

28 Jul	OUT OF TIME Chris Farlowe and the Thunderbirds (Immediate)	1
4 Aug	WITH A GIRL LIKE YOU Troggs (Fontana)	2
18 Aug	YELLOW SUBMARINE/ELEANOR RIGBY Beatles (Parlophone)	4
15 Sep	ALL OR NOTHING Small Faces (Decca)	1
22 Sep	DISTANT DRUMS Jim Reeves (RCA)	5
27 Oct	REACH OUT I'LL BE THERE Four Tops (Tamla Motown)	3
17 Nov	GOOD VIBRATIONS Beach Boys (Capitol)	2
1 Dec	GREEN GREEN GRASS OF HOME Tom Jones (Decca)	7

1967

19 Jan	I'M A BELIEVER Monkees (RCA)	4
16 Feb	THIS IS MY SONG Petula Clark (Pye)	2
2 Mar	RELEASE ME Engelbert Humperdinck (Decca)	6
13 Apr	SOMETHING STUPID Nancy Sinatra and Frank Sinatra (Reprise)	2
27 Apr	PUPPET ON A STRING Sandie Shaw (Pye)	3
18 May	SILENCE IS GOLDEN Tremeloes (CBS)	3
8 Jun	A WHITER SHADE OF PALE Procol Harum (Deram)	6
19 Jul	ALL YOU NEED IS LOVE Beatles (Parlophone)	3
9 Aug	SAN FRANCISCO (BE SURE TO WEAR SOME FLOWERS IN YOUR HAIR) Scott McKenzie (CBS)	4
6 Sep	THE LAST WALTZ Engelbert Humperdinck (Decca)	5
11 Oct	MASSACHUSETTS Bee Gees (Polydor)	4
8 Nov	BABY NOW THAT I'VE FOUND YOU Foundations (Pye)	2
22 Nov	LET THE HEARTACHES BEGIN Long John Baldry (Pye)	2
6 Dec	HELLO GOODBYE Beatles (Parlophone)	7

1968

24 Jan	THE BALLAD OF BONNIE AND CLYDE Georgie Fame (CBS)	1
31 Jan	EVERLASTING LOVE Love Affair (CBS)	2
14 Feb	MIGHTY QUINN Manfred Mann (Fontana)	2
28 Feb	CINDERELLA ROCKEFELLA Esther and Abi Ofarim (Philips)	3
20 Mar	THE LEGEND OF XANADU Dave Dee, Dozy, Beaky, Mick and Tich (Fontana)	1
27 Mar	LADY MADONNA Beatles (Parlophone)	2
10 Apr	CONGRATULATIONS Cliff Richard (Columbia)	2
24 Apr	WHAT A WONDERFUL WORLD/CABARET Louis Armstrong (HMV)	4
22 May	YOUNG GIRL Union Gap featuring Gary Puckett (CBS)	4
19 Jun	JUMPING JACK FLASH Rolling Stone (Decca)	2
3 Jul	BABY COME BACK Equals (President)	3
24 Jul	I PRETEND Des O'Connor (Columbia)	1
31 Jul	MONY MONY Tommy James and the Shondells (Major Minor)	2
14 Aug	FIRE Crazy World of Arthur Brown (Track)	1
21 Aug	MONY MONY Tommy James and the Shondells (Major Minor)	1

Date	Song	Weeks
28 Aug	DO IT AGAIN Beach Boys (Capitol)	1
4 Sep	I'VE GOTTA GET A MESSAGE TO YOU Bee Gees (Polydor)	1
11 Sep	HEY JUDE Beatles (Apple)	2
25 Sep	THOSE WERE THE DAYS Mary Hopkin (Apple)	6
6 Nov	WITH A LITTLE HELP FROM MY FRIENDS Joe Cocker (Regal-Zonophone)	1
13 Nov	THE GOOD THE BAD AND THE UGLY Hugo Montenegro and his Orchestra and chorus (RCA)	4
11 Dec	LILY THE PINK Scaffold (Parlophone)	3

1969

Date	Song	Weeks
1 Jan	OB-LA-DI OB-LA-DA Marmalade (CBS)	1
8 Jan	LILY THE PINK Scaffold (Parlophone)	1
15 Jan	OB-LA-DI OB-LA-DA Marmalade (CBS)	2
29 Jan	ALBATROSS Fleetwood Mac (Blue Horizon)	1
5 Feb	BLACKBERRY WAY Move (Regal-Zonophone)	1
12 Feb	(IF PARADISE IS) HALF AS NICE Amen Corner (Immediate)	2
26 Feb	WHERE DO YOU GO TO MY LOVELY Peter Sarstedt (United Artists)	4
26 Mar	I HEARD IT THROUGH THE GRAPEVINE Marvin Gaye (Tamla Motown)	3
16 Apr	THE ISRAELITES Desmond Dekker and the Aces (Pyramid)	1
23 Apr	GET BACK Beatles with Billy Preston (Apple)	6
4 Jun	DIZZY Tommy Roe (Stateside)	1
11 Jun	THE BALLAD OF JOHN AND YOKO Beatles (Apple)	3
2 Jul	SOMETHING IN THE AIR Thunderclap Newman (Track)	3
23 Jul	HONKY TONK WOMEN Rolling Stones (Decca)	5
30 Aug	IN THE YEAR 2525 (EXORDIUM AND TERMINUS) Zager and Evans (RCA)	3
20 Sep	BAD MOON RISING Creedence Clearwater Revival (Liberty)	3
11 Oct	JE T'AIME MOI NON PLUS Jane Birkin and Serge Gainsbourg (Major Minor)	1
18 Oct	I'LL NEVER FALL IN LOVE AGAIN Bobbie Gentry (Capitol)	1
25 Oct	SUGAR SUGAR Archies (RCA)	8
20 Dec	TWO LITTLE BOYS Rolf Harris (Columbia)	6

1970

Date	Song	Weeks
31 Jan	LOVE GROWS (WHERE MY ROSEMARY GOES) Edison Lighthouse (Bell)	5
7 Mar	WAND'RIN' STAR Lee Marvin (Paramount)	3
28 Mar	BRIDGE OVER TROUBLED WATER Simon and Garfunkel (CBS)	3
18 Apr	ALL KINDS OF EVERYTHING Dana (Rex)	2
2 May	SPIRIT IN THE SKY Norman Greenbaum (Reprise)	2
16 May	BACK HOME England World Cup Squad (Pye)	3
6 Jun	YELLOW RIVER Christie (CBS)	1
13 Jun	IN THE SUMMERTIME Mungo Jerry (Dawn)	7
1 Aug	THE WONDER OF YOU Elvis Presley (RCA)	6
12 Sep	TEARS OF A CLOWN Smokey Robinson and the Miracles (Tamla Motown)	1

Date	Song	Weeks
19 Sep	BAND OF GOLD Freda Payne (Invictus)	6
31 Oct	WOODSTOCK Matthews' Southern Comfort (Uni)	3
21 Nov	VOODOO CHILE Jimi Hendrix Experience (Track)	1
28 Nov	I HEAR YOU KNOCKIN' Dave Edmunds (MAM)	6

1971

Date	Song	Weeks
9 Jan	GRANDAD Clive Dunn (Columbia)	3
30 Jan	MY SWEET LORD George Harrison (Apple)	5
6 Mar	BABY JUMP Mungo Jerry (Dawn)	2
20 Mar	HOT LOVE T. Rex (Fly)	6
1 May	DOUBLE BARREL Dave and Ansil Collins (Technique)	2
15 May	KNOCK THREE TIMES Dawn (Bell)	5
19 Jun	CHIRPY CHIRPY CHEEP CHEEP Middle of the Road (RCA)	5
24 Jul	GET IT ON T. Rex (Fly)	4
21 Aug	I'M STILL WAITING Diana Ross (Tamla Motown)	4
18 Sep	HEY GIRL DON'T BOTHER ME Tams (Probe)	3
9 Oct	MAGGIE MAY Rod Stewart (Mercury)	5
13 Nov	COZ I LUV YOU Slade (Polydor)	4
11 Dec	ERNIE (THE FASTEST MILKMAN IN THE WEST) Benny Hill (Columbia)	4

1972

Date	Song	Weeks
8 Jan	I'D LIKE TO TEACH THE WORLD TO SING New Seekers (Polydor)	4
5 Feb	TELEGRAM SAM T. Rex (T. Rex)	2
19 Feb	SON OF MY FATHER Chicory Tip (CBS)	3
11 Mar	WITHOUT YOU Nilsson (RCA)	5
15 Apr	AMAZING GRACE Pipes and Drums and Military Band of the Royal Scots Dragoon Guards (RCA)	5
20 May	METAL GURU T. Rex (EMI)	4
17 Jun	VINCENT Don McLean (United Artists)	2
1 Jul	TAKE ME BAK 'OME Slade (Polydor)	1
8 Jul	PUPPY LOVE Donny Osmond (MGM)	5
12 Aug	SCHOOL'S OUT Alice Cooper (Warner Brothers)	3
2 Sep	YOU WEAR IT WELL Rod Stewart (Mercury)	1
9 Sep	MAMA WEER ALL CRAZEE NOW Slade (Polydor)	3
30 Sep	HOW CAN I BE SURE David Cassidy (Bell)	2
14 Oct	MOULDY OLD DOUGH Lieutenant Pigeon (Decca)	4
11 Nov	CLAIR Gilbert O'Sullivan (MAM)	2
25 Nov	MY DING-A-LING Chuck Berry (Chess)	4
23 Dec	LONG HAIRED LOVER FROM LIVERPOOL Little Jimmy Osmond (MGM)	5

1973

Date	Song	Weeks
27 Jan	BLOCKBUSTER Sweet (RCA)	5
3 Mar	CUM ON FEEL THE NOIZE Slade (Polydor)	4
31 Mar	THE TWELFTH OF NEVER Donny Osmond (MGM)	1
7 Apr	GET DOWN Gilbert O'Sullivan (MAM)	2

Date	Song	Weeks
21 Apr	TIE A YELLOW RIBBON ROUND THE OLD OAK TREE Dawn featuring Tony Orlando (Bell) ..	4
19 May	SEE MY BABY JIVE Wizzard (Harvest)	4
16 Jun	CAN THE CAN Suzi Quatro (RAK)	1
23 Jun	RUBBER BULLETS 10 cc (UK)	1
30 Jun	SKWEEZE ME PLEEZE ME Slade (Polydor)	3
21 Jul	WELCOME HOME Peters and Lee (Philips)	1
28 Jul	I'M THE LEADER OF THE GANG (I AM) Gary Glitter (Bell)	4
25 Aug	YOUNG LOVE Donny Osmond (MGM)	4
22 Sep	ANGEL FINGERS Wizzard (Harvest)	1
29 Sep	EYE LEVEL Simon Park Orchestra (Columbia)	4
27 Oct	DAYDREAMER/THE PUPPY SONG David Cassidy (Bell)	3
17 Nov	I LOVE YOU LOVE ME LOVE Gary Glitter (Bell)	4
15 Dec	MERRY XMAS EVERYBODY Slade (Polydor)	5

1974

Date	Song	Weeks
19 Jan	YOU WON'T FIND ANOTHER FOOL LIKE ME New Seekers (Polydor)	1
26 Jan	TIGER FEET Mud (Rak)	4
23 Feb	DEVIL GATE DRIVE Suzi Quatro (Rak)	2
9 Mar	JEALOUS MIND Alvin Stardust (Magnet)	1
16 Mar	BILLY DON'T BE A HERO Paper Lace (Bus Stop)	3
6 Apr	SEASONS IN THE SUN Terry Jacks (Bell)	4
4 May	WATERLOO Abba (Epic)	2
18 May	SUGAR BABY LOVE Rubettes (Polydor)	4
15 Jun	THE STREAK Ray Stevens (Janus)	1
22 Jun	ALWAYS YOURS Gary Glitter (Bell)	1
29 Jun	SHE Charles Aznavour (Barclay)	4
27 Jul	ROCK YOUR BABY George McCrae (Jayboy)	3
17 Aug	WHEN WILL I SEE YOU AGAIN Three Degrees (Philadelphia International)	2
31 Aug	LOVE ME FOR A REASON Osmonds (MGM)	3
21 Sep	KUNG FU FIGHTING Carl Douglas (Pye)	3
12 Oct	ANNIE'S SONG John Denver (RCA)	1
19 Oct	SAD SWEET DREAMER Sweet Sensation (Pye)	1
26 Oct	EVERYTHING I OWN Ken Boothe (Trojan)	3
16 Nov	GONNA MAKE YOU A STAR David Essex (CBS)	3
7 Dec	YOU'RE THE FIRST THE LAST MY EVERYTHING Barry White (20th Century)	2
21 Dec	LONELY THIS CHRISTMAS Mud (Rak)	4

1975

Date	Song	Weeks
18 Jan	DOWN DOWN Status Quo (Vertigo)	1
25 Jan	MS. GRACE Tymes (RCA)	1
1 Feb	JANUARY Pilot (EMI)	3
22 Feb	MAKE ME SMILE (COME UP AND SEE ME) Steve Harley and Cockney Rebel (EMI)	2
8 Mar	IF Telly Savalas (MCA)	2
22 Mar	BYE BYE BABY Bay City Rollers (Bell)	6
3 May	OH BOY Mud (Rak)	2
17 May	STAND BY YOUR MAN Tammy Wynette (Epic)	3
7 Jun	WHISPERING GRASS Windsor Davies and Don Estelle (EMI)	3

Date	Song	Weeks
28 Jun	I'M NOT IN LOVE 10 cc (Mercury)	2
12 Jul	TEARS ON MY PILLOW Johnny Nash (CBS)	1
19 Jul	GIVE A LITTLE LOVE Bay City Rollers (Bell)	3
9 Aug	BARBADOS Typically Tropical (Gull)	1
16 Aug	I CAN'T GIVE YOU ANYTHING (BUT MY LOVE) Stylistics (Avco)	3
6 Sep	SAILING Rod Stewart (Warner Brothers)	4
4 Oct	HOLD ME CLOSE David Essex (CBS)	3
25 Oct	I ONLY HAVE EYES FOR YOU Art Garfunkel (CBS)	2
8 Nov	SPACE ODDITY David Bowie (RCA)	2
22 Nov	D.I.V.O.R.C.E. Billy Connolly (Polydor)	1
29 Nov	BOHEMIAN RHAPSODY Queen (EMI)	9

1976

Date	Song	Weeks
31 Jan	MAMMA MIA Abba (Epic)	2
14 Feb	FOREVER AND EVER Slik (Bell)	1
21 Feb	DECEMBER '63 (OH WHAT A NIGHT) Four Seasons (Warner Brothers)	2
6 Mar	I LOVE TO LOVE (BUT MY BABY LOVES TO DANCE) Tina Charles (CBS)	3
27 Mar	SAVE YOUR KISSES FOR ME Brotherhood of Man (Pye)	6
8 May	FERNANDO Abba (Epic)	4
5 June	NO CHARGE J. J. Barrie (Power Exchange)	1
12 Jun	COMBINE HARVESTER (BRAND NEW KEY) Wurzels (EMI)	2
26 Jun	YOU TO ME ARE EVERYTHING Real Thing (Pye International)	3
17 Jul	THE ROUSSOS PHENOMENON (EP) Demis Roussos (Philips)	1
24 Jul	DON'T GO BREAKING MY HEART Elton John and Kiki Dee (Rocket)	6
4 Sep	DANCING QUEEN Abba (Epic)	6
16 Oct	MISSISSIPPI Pussycat (Sonet)	4
13 Nov	IF YOU LEAVE ME NOW Chicago (CBS)	3
4 Dec	UNDER THE MOON OF LOVE Showaddywaddy (Bell)	3
25 Dec	WHEN A CHILD IS BORN (SOLEADO) Johnny Mathis (CBS)	3

1977

Date	Song	Weeks
15 Jan	DON'T GIVE UP ON US David Soul (Private Stock)	4
12 Feb	DON'T CRY FOR ME ARGENTINA Julie Covington (MCA)	1
19 Feb	WHEN I NEED YOU Leo Sayer (Chrysalis)	3
12 Mar	CHANSON D'AMOUR Manhattan Transfer (Atlantic)	3
2 Apr	KNOWING ME KNOWING YOU Abba (Epic)	5
7 May	FREE Deniece Williams (CBS)	2
21 May	I DON'T WANT TO TALK ABOUT IT/FIRST CUT IS THE DEEPEST Rod Stewart (Riva)	4
18 Jun	LUCILLE Kenny Rogers (United Artists)	1
25 Jun	SHOW YOU THE WAY TO GO Jacksons (Epic)	1
2 Jul	SO YOU WIN AGAIN Hot Chocolate (Rak)	3
23 Jul	I FEEL LOVE Donna Summer (GTO)	4
20 Aug	ANGELO Brotherhood of Man (Pye)	1

27 Aug	FLOAT ON Floaters (ABC)..........................	1
3 Sep	WAY DOWN Elvis Presley (RCA)	5
8 Oct	SILVER LADY David Soul (Private Stock)	3
29 Oct	YES SIR I CAN BOOGIE Baccara (RCA)	1
5 Nov	NAME OF THE GAME Abba (Epic)	4
3 Dec	MULL OF KINTYRE/GIRLS' SCHOOL Wings (Capitol)	9

1978

4 Feb	UP TOWN TOP RANKING Althia and Donna (Lightning)	1
11 Feb	FIGARO Brotherhood of Man (Pye)	1
18 Feb	TAKE A CHANCE ON ME Abba (Epic)............	3
11 Mar	WUTHERING HEIGHTS Kate Bush (EMI)	4
8 Apr	MATCHSTALK MEN AND MATCHSTALK CATS AND DOGS Brian and Michael (Pye)	3
29 Apr	NIGHT FEVER Bee Gees (RSO)	2
13 May	RIVERS OF BABYLON Boney M. (Atlantic/Hansa)	5
17 Jun	YOU'RE THE ONE THAT I WANT John Travolta and Olivia Newton-John (RSO)	9
19 Aug	THREE TIMES A LADY Commodores (Motown)	5
23 Sep	DREADLOCK HOLIDAY 10 cc (Mercury)	1
30 Sep	SUMMER NIGHTS John Travolta and Olivia Newton-John (RSO)................................	7
18 Nov	RAT TRAP Boomtown Rats (Ensign)	2
2 Dec	DA YA THINK I'M SEXY Rod Stewart (Riva)	1
9 Dec	MARY'S BOY CHILD – OH MY LORD Boney M. (Atlantic/Hansa)	4

1979

6 Jan	Y.M.C.A. Village People (Mercury)...................	3
27 Jan	HIT ME WITH YOUR RHYTHM STICK Ian and the Blockheads (Stiff)	1
3 Feb	HEART OF GLASS Blondie (Chrysalis)	4
3 Mar	TRAGEDY Bee Gees (RSO)	2
17 Mar	I WILL SURVIVE Gloria Gaynor (Polydor)..........	4
14 Apr	BRIGHT EYES Art Garfunkel (CBS)	6
26 May	SUNDAY GIRL Blondie (Chrysalis)	3
16 Jun	RING MY BELL Anita Ward (TK)...................	2
30 Jun	ARE 'FRIENDS' ELECTRIC? Tubeway Army (Beggars Banquet).................................	4
28 Jul	I DON'T LIKE MONDAYS Boomtown Rats (Ensign)	4
25 Aug	WE DON'T TALK ANYMORE Cliff Richard (EMI)	4
22 Sep	CARS Gary Numan (Beggars Banquet)	1
29 Sep	MESSAGE IN A BOTTLE Police (A & M)	3
20 Oct	VIDEO KILLED THE RADIO STAR Buggles (Island)	1
27 Oct	ONE DAY AT A TIME Lena Martell (Pye)	3
17 Nov	WHEN YOU'RE IN LOVE WITH A BEAUTIFUL WOMAN Dr Hook (Capitol)	3
8 Dec	WALKING ON THE MOON Police (A & M)	1
15 Dec	ANOTHER BRICK IN THE WALL (PART II) Pink Floyd (Harvest)	5

1980

19 Jan	BRASS IN POCKET Pretenders (Real)	2
2 Feb	THE SPECIAL AKA LIVE (EP) Specials (2 Tone) ..	2
16 Feb	COWARD OF THE COUNTY Kenny Rogers (United Artists)	2
1 Mar	ATOMIC Blondie (Chrysalis).........................	2
15 Mar	TOGETHER WE ARE BEAUTIFUL Fern Kinney (WEA)	1
22 Mar	GOING UNDERGROUND/DREAMS OF CHILDREN Jam (Polydor)	3
12 Apr	WORKING MY WAY BACK TO YOU Detroit Spinners (Atlantic)	2
26 Apr	CALL ME Blondie (Chrysalis)	1
3 May	GENO Dexy's Midnight Runners (Parlophone)	2
17 May	WHAT'S ANOTHER YEAR Johnny Logan (Epic)	2
31 May	THEME FROM M*A*S*H (SUICIDE IS PAINLESS) Mash (CBS)	3
21 Jun	CRYING Don McLean (EMI)	3
12 Jul	XANADU Olivia Newton-John and Electric Light Orchestra (Jet)...................................	2
26 Jul	USE IT UP AND WEAR IT OUT Odyssey (RCA)	2
9 Aug	THE WINNER TAKES IT ALL Abba (Epic)	2
23 Aug	ASHES TO ASHES David Bowie (RCA).............	2
6 Sep	START Jam (Polydor)...............................	1
13 Sep	FEELS LIKE I'M IN LOVE Kelly Marie (Calibre) ..	2
27 Sep	DON'T STAND SO CLOSE TO ME Police (A & M)	4
25 Oct	WOMAN IN LOVE Barbra Streisand (CBS)	3
15 Nov	THE TIDE IS HIGH Blondie (Chrysalis)	2
29 Nov	SUPER TROUPER Abba (Epic)	3
20 Dec	(JUST LIKE) STARTING OVER John Lennon (WEA/Geffen)	1
27 Dec	THERE'S NO ONE QUITE LIKE GRANDMA St. Winifred's School Choir (MFP)	2

1981

10 Jan	IMAGINE John Lennon (Parlophone)	4
7 Feb	WOMAN John Lennon (Geffen)	2
21 Feb	SHADDUP YOU FACE Joe Dolce (Epic)	3
14 Mar	JEALOUS GUY Roxy Music (Polydor/EG)	2
28 Mar	THIS OLE HOUSE Shakin' Stevens (Epic)	3
18 Apr	MAKING YOUR MIND UP Bucks Fizz (RCA)....	3
9 May	STAND AND DELIVER Adam and The Ants (CBS)	5
13 Jun	BEING WITH YOU Smokey Robinson (Motown)	2
27 Jun	ONE DAY IN YOUR LIFE Michael Jackson (Motown)	2
11 Jul	GHOST TOWN Specials (2 Tone)	3
1 Aug	GREEN DOOR Shakin' Stevens (Epic)	4
29 Aug	JAPANESE BOY Aneka (Hansa/Ariola)	1
5 Sep	TAINTED LOVE Soft Cell (Some Bizzare)..........	2
19 Sept	PRINCE CHARMING Adam & The Ants (CBS) ..	4
17 Oct	IT'S MY PARTY Dave Stewart with Barbara Gaskin (Stiff/Broken)	4
14 Nov	EVERY LITTLE THING SHE DOES IS MAGIC Police (A & M)	
21 Nov	UNDER PRESSURE Queen and David Bowie (EMI)..	2

5 Dec	BEGIN THE BEGUINE (VOLVER A EMPEZAR) Julio Iglesias (CBS)	1
12 Dec	DON'T YOU WANT ME Human League (Virgin)	5

1982

16 Jan	THE LAND OF MAKE BELIEVE Bucks Fizz (RCA)	2
30 Jan	OH JULIE Shakin' Stevens (Epic)........................	1
6 Feb	THE MODEL/COMPUTER LOVE Kraftwerk (EMI)	1
13 Feb	A TOWN CALLED MALICE/PRECIOUS Jam (Polydor)	3
6 Mar	THE LION SLEEPS TONIGHT Tight Fit (Jive)	3
27 Mar	SEVEN TEARS Goombay Dance Band (Epic)	3
17 Apr	MY CAMERA NEVER LIES Bucks Fizz (RCA)	1
24 Apr	EBONY AND IVORY Paul McCartney with Stevie Wondder (Parlophone)............................	3
15 May	A LITTLE PEACE Nicole (CBS)	2
29 May	HOUSE OF FUN Madness (Stiff)	2
12 Jun	GOODY TWO SHOES Adam Ant (CBS)...........	2
26 Jun	I'VE NEVER BEEN TO ME Charlene (Motown) ..	1
3 Jul	HAPPY TALK Captain Sensible (A & M)	2
17 Jul	FAME Irene Cara (RSO)	3
7 Aug	COME ON EILEEN Dexy's Midnight Runners and Emerald Express (Mercury/Phonogram)	4
4 Sep	EYE OF THE TIGER Survivor (Scotti Brothers)....	4
2 Oct	PASS THE DUTCHIE Musical Youth (MCA)	3
23 Oct	DO YOU REALLY WANT TO HURT ME Culture Club (Virgin)	3
13 Nov	I DON'T WANNA DANCE Eddy Grant (Ice)	3
4 Dec	BEAT SURRENDER Jam (Polydor)...................	2
18 Oct	SAVE YOUR LOVE Renée and Renato (Hollywood)	4

1983

15 Jan	YOU CAN'T HURRY LOVE Phil Collins (Virgin)	2
29 Jan	DOWN UNDER Men At Work (Epic)	3
19 Feb	TOO SHY Kajagoogoo (EMI)	2
5 Mar	BILLIE JEAN Michael Jackson (Epic)...................	1
12 Mar	TOTAL ECLIPSE OF THE HEART Bonnie Tyler (CBS)...	2
26 Mar	IS THERE SOMETHING I SHOULD KNOW Duran Duran (EMI)	2
9 Apr	LET'S DANCE David Bowie (EMI America)	3
30 Apr	TRUE Spandau Ballet (Reformation/Chrysalis)	4
28 May	CANDY GIRL New Edition (London).................	1
4 Jun	EVERY BREATH YOU TAKE Police (A & M)	4
2 Jul	BABY JANE Rod Stewart (Warner Bros)	3
23 Jul	WHEREVER I LAY MY HAT (THAT'S MY HOME) Paul Young (CBS)............................	3
13 Aug	GIVE IT UP KC and the Sunshine Band (Epic)	3
3 Sep	RED RED WINE U.B. 40 (DEP International)	3
24 Sep	KARMA CHAMELEON Culture Club (Virgin)	6
5 Nov	UPTOWN GIRL Billy Joel (CBS)	5
10 Dec	ONLY YOU Flying Pickets (10 Records/Virgin)	5

1984

14 Jan	PIPES OF PEACE Paul McCartney (Parlophone) ...	2
28 Jan	RELAX Frankie Goes to Hollywood (ZTT/Island) ..	5
3 Mar	99 RED BALLOONS Nena (Epic)	3
24 Mar	HELLO Lionel Richie (Motown)	6
5 May	THE REFLEX Duran Duran (EMI)	4
2 Jun	WAKE ME UP BEFORE YOU GO GO Wham! (Epic)	2
16 Jun	TWO TRIBES Frankie Goes to Hollywood (ZTT/Island)	9
18 Aug	CARELESS WHISPER George Michael (Epic).......	3
8 Sep	I JUST CALLED TO SAY I LOVE YOU Stevie Wonder (Motown)	6
20 Oct	FREEDOM Wham! (Epic)..............................	3
10 Nov	I FEEL FOR YOU Chaka Khan (Warner Bros)	3
1 Dec	I SHOULD HAVE KNOWN BETTER Jim Diamond (A & M)	1
8 Dec	THE POWER OF LOVE Frankie Goes to Hollywood (ZTT/Island)	1
15 Dec	DO THEY KNOW IT'S CHRISTMAS? Band Aid (Mercury/Phonogram)	3

MOST NUMBER ONE HITS

17	BEATLES, Elvis PRESLEY
10	Cliff RICHARD
9	ABBA
8	ROLLING STONES
6	SLADE, Rod STEWART
5	BLONDIE, POLICE, SHADOWS (+ 7 with Cliff RICHARD)
4	BEE GEES, EVERLY BROTHERS, Frank IFIELD, JAM, Frankie LAINE, Guy MITCHELL, T. REX
3	ADAM AND THE ANTS, David BOWIE (+ 1 with QUEEN) BROTHERHOOD OF MAN, BUCKS FIZZ, Lonnie DONEGAN, Georgie FAME, FRANKIE GOES TO HOLLYWOOD, GERRY AND THE PACEMAKERS, Gary GLITTER, KINKS, John LENNON, MANFRED MANN, MUD, Roy ORBISON, Donny OSMOND, Johnnie RAY, Sandie SHAW, SEARCHERS, Shakin' STEVENS, 10 C.C.

Olivia Newton-John has had two number ones with John Travolta and one with Electric Light Orchestra. Frank Sinatra has had two solo number ones and one with Nancy Sinatra. Art Garfunkel has had two solo number ones and one with Paul Simon. Michael Jackson has had two solo number ones and one with the Jacksons. George Michael has had one solo number one and two more as half of Wham! Paul McCartney has had 17 number ones as one quarter of the Beatles, one more as one third of Wings, another as half of his duet with Stevie Wonder and one more as a soloist.

Most Weeks at Number One

By Artist
73	Elvis PRESLEY
69	BEATLES

(Paul McCartney 9 more with Wings, 3 more with Stevie Wonder and 2 more solo, total 83 weeks. John Lennon 7 more solo, total 76 weeks. George Harrison 5 more solo, total 74 weeks.)

35	Cliff RICHARD
32	Frankie LAINE

(1 week top equal)

31	ABBA
20	SLADE
19	EVERLY BROTHERS

(1 week top equal)

18	ROLLING STONES, Rod STEWART
17	Frank IFIELD
16	SHADOWS

(+ 28 weeks backing Cliff Richard, total 44 weeks)

T. REX, John TRAVOLTA and Olivia NEWTON-JOHN

(Olivia Newton-John 2 more weeks with Electric Light Orchestra, total 18 weeks)

John Travolta minus Olivia Newton-John in a scene from *Grease*, the film that provided the couple with two number ones in 1978.

15	Doris DAY, FRANKIE GOES TO HOLLYWOOD
14	Guy MITCHELL *(1 week top equal)*
13	Eddie CALVERT, Perry COMO, POLICE
12	BLONDIE, Connie FRANCIS, David WHITFIELD *(1 week top equal)*
11	ADAM AND THE ANTS, Lonnie DONEGAN, Tennessee Ernie FORD, GERRY AND THE PACEMAKERS, Engelbert HUMPERDINCK, Johnnie RAY, Slim WHITMAN
10	MUD, Donny OSMOND

(+ 3 weeks with Osmonds, total 13 weeks)

Queen have been number one for 9 weeks, plus 2 weeks with David Bowie. Art Garfunkel has been at number one for 8 weeks, plus 3 weeks with Simon and Garfunkel. Mantovani has been on top for 1 week, plus 10 more backing David Whitfield. Lionel Richie has had 6 weeks at number one, plus 5 more as one of the Commodores.

Most Weeks at Number One

By Artist in one Calendar Year
27	Frankie LAINE	1953
	(1 week top equal)	
18	Elvis PRESLEY	1961
16	BEATLES	1963
	John TRAVOLTA and Olivia NEWTON-JOHN	1978
15	Elvis PRESLEY	1962
	FRANKIE GOES TO HOLLYWOOD	1984
12	Connie FRANCIS	1958
	Frank IFIELD	1962
	BEATLES	1964
	ABBA	1976

Frankie Goes To Hollywood Their first three singles topped the chart and they equalled the 20-year-old record by Gerry and the Pacemakers.

MOST WEEKS AT NUMBER ONE

By One Disc – in Total

18	I BELIEVE/Frankie LAINE	1953
11	ROSE MARIE/Slim WHITMAN	1955
10	CARA MIA/David WHITFIELD	1954
9	HERE IN MY HEART/Al MARTINO	1952–3
	OH MEIN PAPA/Eddie CALVERT	1954
	SECRET LOVE/Doris DAY	1954
	DIANA/Paul ANKA	1957
	BOHEMIAN RHAPSODY/QUEEN	1975–6
	MULL OF KINTYRE/GIRLS' SCHOOL/WINGS	1977–8
	YOU'RE THE ONE THAT I WANT/John TRAVOLTA and Olivia NEWTON-JOHN	1978
	TWO TRIBES/FRANKIE GOES TO HOLLYWOOD	1984

MOST WEEKS AT NUMBER ONE

By One Disc – Consecutive Weeks

11	ROSE MARIE/Slim WHITMAN	1955
10	CARA MIA/David WHITFIELD	1954
9	HERE IN MY HEART/Al MARTINO	1952–3
	I BELIEVE/Frankie LAINE	1953
	OH MEIN PAPA/Eddie CALVERT	1954
	DIANA/Paul ANKA	1957
	BOHEMIAN RHAPSODY/QUEEN	1975–6
	MULL OF KINTYRE/GIRLS'SCHOOL/WINGS	1977–8
	YOU'RE THE ONE THAT I WANT/John TRAVOLTA and Olivia NEWTON-JOHN	1978
	TWO TRIBES/FRANKIE GOES TO HOLLYWOOD	1984
8	ANSWER ME/Frankie LAINE	1953–4
	(1 week top equal)	
	SECRET LOVE/Doris DAY	1954
	MAGIC MOMENTS/Perry COMO	1958
	IT'S NOW OR NEVER/Elvis PRESLEY	1960
	WONDERFUL LAND/SHADOWS	1962
	SUGAR SUGAR/ARCHIES	1969

Between 'Bright Eyes' by Art Garfunkel in 1979 and 'Karma Chameleon' by Culture Club in 1983, there were 90 number ones none of which stayed on top for more than 5 weeks.

MOST CONSECUTIVE NUMBER ONES

11 in a row   **BEATLES**
(from FROM ME TO YOU through to YELLOW SUBMARINE/ELEANOR RIGBY, 1963 to 1966)

6 in a row   **BEATLES**
(from ALL YOU NEED IS LOVE through to THE BALLAD OF JOHN AND YOKO, 1967 to 1969)

5 in a row   **Elvis PRESLEY**
(from HIS LATEST FLAME through to RETURN TO SENDER, 1961 to 1962)

5 in a row   **ROLLING STONES**
(from IT'S ALL OVER NOW through to GET OFF OF MY CLOUD, 1964 to 1965)

4 in a row   **Elvis PRESLEY**
(from IT'S NOW OR NEVER through to SURRENDER, 1960 to 1961). The first number one hat-trick.

4 in a row   **T. REX**
(from HOT LOVE through to METAL GURU, 1971 to 1972)

3 in a row   **Frank IFIELD**
(I REMEMBER YOU, LOVESICK BLUES and WAYWARD WIND, 1962 to 1963). The first number one hat trick by a British artist.

3 in a row   **GERRY AND THE PACEMAKERS**
(HOW DO YOU DO IT, I LIKE IT and YOU'LL NEVER WALK ALONE, 1963)

3 in a row   **ABBA**
(MAMMA MIA, FERNANDO and DANCING QUEEN, 1975 to 1976)

3 in a row   **ABBA**
(KNOWING ME KNOWING YOU, THE NAME OF THE GAME and TAKE A CHANCE ON ME, 1977 to 1978)

3 in a row   **POLICE**
(MESSAGE IN A BOTTLE, WALKING ON THE MOON and DON'T STAND SO CLOSE TO ME, 1979 to 1980) The only instance of the third record of a hat-trick coming on to the chart at number one.

3 in a row   **BLONDIE**
(ATOMIC, CALL ME and THE TIDE IS HIGH, 1980)

3 in a row   **John LENNON**
(IMAGINE, (JUST LIKE) STARTING OVER and WOMAN, 1980) Both the fastest and the slowest hat-trick depending on whether it started when IMAGINE first entered the chart in November 1975, or when (JUST LIKE) STARTING OVER came in late in 1980)

3 in a row   **FRANKIE GOES TO HOLLYWOOD**
(RELAX, TWO TRIBES and THE POWER OF LOVE, 1984)

Successive releases for the purpose of this table are successive official single releases. The Beatles' two runs of number ones were each interrupted by irregular releases. An old single with Tony Sheridan reached number 29 in the midst of their eleven number ones, and their double EP 'Magical Mystery Tour' made number two while 'Hello Goodbye' was becoming the second of their six chart-toppers on the trot. An LP track, 'Jeepster' and an old recording 'Debora/One Inch Rock' were released during T. Rex's run of number ones, while the group were changing labels. An EP by Elvis, 'Follow That Dream', pottered about the lower reaches of the charts during Elvis' run of five consecutive number ones. During Police's hat-trick, one single on another label, one old single re-issued and a six-pack of singles hit the chart in an attempt to distract the compilers of this table. John Lennon's 'Imagine' was the first of the three singles of his hat-trick (his last single for 5 years) but the second of the three to reach the top. During his hat-trick, a flood of old Lennon hits swarmed back on to the chart.

SLOWEST NUMBER ONE

By Artist

If an artist is going to have a number one hit, it usually comes along within a year or two of the artist's first chart hit. Band Aid were the 350th act ever to top the British charts, and like about half their predecessors, they did so with their first chart hit. The acts listed below are the only ones to have had to wait more than 10 years after their chart debut to chalk up their first number one hit.

18 years 218 days	STEVIE WONDER	(3 Feb 66 to 8 Sep 84)
18 years 217 days	JOHNNY MATHIS	(23 May 58 to 25 Dec 76)
15 years 157 days	CHUCK BERRY	(21 Jun 57 to 25 Nov 72)
15 years 127 days	LOUIS ARMSTRONG	(19 Dec 52 to 24 Apr 68)
14 years 279 days	BARBRA STREISAND	(20 Jan 66 to 25 Oct 80)
13 years 140 days	FOUR SEASONS	(4 Oct 62 to 21 Feb 76)
12 years 321 days	PAUL McCARTNEY	(27 Feb 71 to 14 Jan 84)
12 years 260 days	PINK FLOYD	(30 Mar 67 to 15 Dec 79)
11 years 184 days	TYMES	(25 Jul 63 to 25 Jan 75)
11 years 164 days	JOHN LENNON	(9 Jul 69 to 20 Dec 80)
10 years 298 days	BENNY HILL	(16 Feb 61 to 11 Dec 71)

Stevie Wonder, John Lennon and Paul McCartney had all reached the very top in combination with other people before their first solo number ones. Stevie Wonder's first week at number one was his 301st week on the chart, and with his 34th hit.

Stevie Wonder had to wait 18 years 218 days from his chart debut to his first solo number one.

SLOWEST NUMBER ONE

By Disc

Only five records have taken longer than 200 days to hit the top after their first appearance on the chart.

6 years 63 days	SPACE ODDITY by David Bowie	(6 Sep 69 to 8 Nov 75)
5 years 70 days	IMAGINE by John Lennon	(1 Nov 75 to 10 Jan 81)
322 days	ROCK AROUND THE CLOCK by Bill Haley and his Comets	(7 Jan 55 to 25 Nov 55)
308 days	EYE LEVEL by Simon Park Orchestra	(25 Nov 72 to 29 Sep 73)
210 days	THE MODEL/COMPUTER LOVE by Kraftwerk	(11 Jul 81 to 6 Feb 82)

FASTEST NUMBER ONE HIT

At the other end of Stevie Wonder's scale, these are the acts who moved from chart debut to the number one slot in the shortest time.

0 days Al Martino (14 Nov 52 – the first chart of all), Band Aid (15 Dec 84)
7 days Edison Lighthouse (24 to 31 Jan 70), Mungo Jerry (6 to 13 Jun 70), Dave Edmunds (21 to 28 Nov 70), George Harrison (23 to 30 Jan 71), Queen and David Bowie (14 to 21 Nov 81), Nicole (8 to 15 May 82), Captain Sensible (26 June to 3 July 82), Musical Youth (25 Sep to 3 Oct 82)
14 days 24 different acts

Biggest Jump to Number One

There have been 26 records that have jumped from outside the Top Ten straight to the top spot.

33 to 1	HAPPY TALK	Captain Sensible	3 Jul 82
27 to 1	SURRENDER	Elvis Presley	27 May 61
26 to 1	PASS THE DUTCHIE	Musical Youth	2 Oct 82
22 to 1	GREEN DOOR	Shakin' Stevens	1 Aug 81
21 to 1	HEY JUDE	Beatles	11 Sep 68
	(JUST LIKE) STARTING OVER	John Lennon	20 Dec 80
19 to 1	ARE YOU LONESOME TONIGHT	Elvis Presley	21 Jan 61
	HALF AS NICE	Amen Corner	12 Feb 69
	LOVE ME FOR A REASON	Osmonds	31 Aug 74
17 to 1	GET OFF OF MY CLOUD	Rolling Stones	4 Nov 65
16 to 1	I HEAR YOU KNOCKING	Dave Edmunds	28 Nov 70
	CHIRPY CHIRPY CHEEP CHEEP	Middle Of The Road	19 Jun 71
	YOUNG LOVE	Donny Osmond	25 Aug 73
	DANCING QUEEN	Abba	4 Sep 76
15 to 1	I DON'T LIKE MONDAYS	Boomtown Rats	28 Jul 79
	THE SPECIAL AKA LIVE EP	Specials	2 Feb 80
14 to 1	EYE LEVEL	Simon Park Orchestra	29 Sep 73
13 to 1	IN THE SUMMERTIME	Mungo Jerry	13 Jun 70
12 to 1	LOVE GROWS	Edison Lighthouse	31 Jan 70
11 to 1	(THERE'S) ALWAYS SOMETHING THERE TO REMIND ME	Sandie Shaw	22 Oct 64
	TICKET TO RIDE	Beatles	22 Apr 65
	MICHELLE	Overlanders	27 Jan 66
	LADY MADONNA	Beatles	20 Mar 68
	SUGAR SUGAR	Archies	25 Oct 69
	SHE	Charles Aznavour	29 Jun 74
	SUMMER NIGHTS	John Travolta and Olivia Newton-John	30 Sep 78

The biggest jump within the chart is a leap of 55 places, from 62 to 7 on 26 April 80 by Paul McCartney's aptly named 'Coming Up'. It never reached number one, but had to be content with the number two slot. The biggest chart leap by a disc that later went to number one is a jump of 51 places (60 to 9) by 'Only You' by the Flying Pickets on 3 December 83. The lowest initial chart entry by a record that eventually reached number one is 73, which is the position at which Charlene's 'I've Never Been To Me' entered the chart on 15 May 82.

Captain Sensible In 1982 the Captain outjumped the Kings 21-year-old record.

Biggest Falls from Number One

Only 18 records have ever fallen out of the top five directly from the very top spot, as follows:

1 to 12	MARY'S CHILD	Harry Belafonte	10 Jan 58
1 to 10	ONLY YOU	Flying Pickets	14 Jan 84
1 to 9	YOU'RE DRIVING ME CRAZY	Temperance Seven	1 Jun 61
	THESE BOOTS ARE MADE FOR WALKING	Nancy Sinatra	17 Mar 66
1 to 8	HELLO GOODBYE	Beatles	24 Jan 68
	LONELY THIS CHRISTMAS	Mud	18 Jan 75
1 to 7	WAYWARD WIND	Frank Ifield	14 Mar 63
	YOUNG LOVE	Donny Osmond	22 Sep 73
	KNOWING ME KNOWING YOU	Abba	7 May 77

Last Hit at Number One

Chart history shows that once an act has scored its first number one it is far more likely to hit the top again with its next release than to have no more chart hits at all. Disappearing without trace, chartwise, after a number one hit is comparatively rare, and apart from the one-hit wonders, listed separately, only seven acts have failed to follow up a number one.

Charles AZNAVOUR, Rolf HARRIS, Benny HILL, Tommy JAMES and the SHONDELLS, Kay STARR, TAMS, John TRAVOLTA and Olivia NEWTON-JOHN.

Both John Travolta and Olivia Newton-John have had solo hits that left the chart after the final disappearance of their last chart-topper together, but as a duo they share with Kay Starr the unlikely distinction of hitting number one with both their first and their last British hit singles.

1 to 6	HERE IN MY HEART	Al Martino	16 Jan 53
	ROCK AROUND THE CLOCK	Bill Haley and his Comets	20 Jan 56
	CATHY'S CLOWN	Everly Brothers	23 Jun 60
	SUMMER HOLIDAY	Cliff Richard and the Shadows	11 Apr 63
	SUGAR BABY LOVE	Rubettes	15 Jun 74
	YOU TO ME ARE EVERYTHING	Real Thing	17 Jul 76
	BRIGHT EYES	Art Garfunkel	26 May 79
	IT'S MY PARTY	Dave Stewart with Barbara Gaskin	14 Nov 81
	LET'S DANCE	David Bowie	30 Apr 83

FIRST TWO HITS AT NUMBER ONE

Only 11 acts in the 32-year history of the charts have hit the top with each of their first two chart hits.

EDDIE CALVERT (his number ones were consecutive chart hits but not consecutive releases), ADAM FAITH, TENNESSEE ERNIE FORD (not consecutive releases), FRANKIE GOES TO HOLLYWOOD, ART GARFUNKEL (not consecutive releases), GERRY AND THE PACEMAKERS, MUNGO JERRY, GARY NUMAN/TUBEWAY ARMY, STARGAZERS (not consecutive releases), ROD STEWART, JOHN TRAVOLTA AND OLIVIA NEWTON-JOHN.

Of these acts, only FRANKIE GOES TO HOLLYWOOD, GERRY AND THE PACEMAKERS, MUNGO JERRY and JOHN TRAVOLTA AND OLIVIA NEWTON-JOHN hit the top with their first two *releases*.

FIRST THREE HITS AT NUMBER ONE

On 31 October 1963, GERRY AND THE PACEMAKERS' third single release became their third number one hit, and thus established a record that was long considered impossible to equal. On 8 December 1984, 21 years and 38 days later, FRANKIE GOES TO HOLLYWOOD's third single release became their third number one hit. It is a curious coincidence that both acts come from Liverpool and both acts' third number one was a pseudo-religious song. In Gerry's case the third hit was 'You'll Never Walk Alone'. Frankie's third number one was the Nativity video hit 'The Power of Love', following up their controversial chart-toppers dealing with sex ('Relax') and politics ('Two Tribes'). The days of Gerry's sexual ('How Do You Do It?') and political ('I Like It') innocence were long ago. To complete the coincidence one track on the 12 inch version of 'Relax' was Frankie's interpretation of Gerry's seventh hit 'Ferry Cross The Mersey'.

Seventeen solo chart toppers have also hit the number one spot as part of a group, as follows:

David BOWIE
also with QUEEN and David BOWIE, BAND AID
Art GARFUNKEL
also with SIMON and GARFUNKEL
Eddy GRANT
EQUALS
George HARRISON
BEATLES
Buddy HOLLY
CRICKETS
Michael JACKSON
Jacksons
John LENNON
BEATLES
Paul McCARTNEY
BEATLES, WINGS, Paul McCARTNEY and Stevie WONDER, BAND AID
George MICHAEL
WHAM!, BAND AID
Donny OSMOND
OSMONDS
Lionel RICHIE
COMMODORES
Diana ROSS
SUPREMES
Frank SINATRA
Nancy SINATRA and Frank SINATRA
Nancy SINATRA
Nancy SINATRA and Frank SINATRA
Stevie WONDER
Paul McCARTNEY and Stevie WONDER
Paul YOUNG
BAND AID

Gary Numan's first number one was under the group name Tubeway Army, but the disc is listed under Numan's name in this book. Similarly, Adam and the Ants became Adam Ant with the release of 'Goody Two Shoes' in 1982, but there was no significant change in the personnel responsible for the hits. 'Goody Two Shoes' was marketed as the follow-up to 'Ant Rap', the final Adam and the Ants release.

This list does not include those people who were part of more than one chart-topping group unless they also had a solo number one. Thus Denny Laine (part of Wings and Moody Blues) or Roy Wood (Move and Wizzard) are not included.

THE ONE-HIT WONDERS

Qualification: One number one hit, and nothing else – ever

Year	Act	Song
1954	KITTY KALLEN	Little Things Mean A Lot
1956	DREAMWEAVERS	It's Almost Tomorrow
1958	KALIN TWINS	When
1959	JERRY KELLER	Here Comes Summer
1960	RICKY VALANCE	Tell Laura I Love Her
1962	B. BUMBLE AND THE STINGERS	Nut Rocker
1966	OVERLANDERS	Michelle
1968	CRAZY WORLD OF ARTHUR BROWN	Fire
1969	ZAGER AND EVANS	In The Year 2525
1969	JANE BIRKIN AND SERGE GAINSBOURG	Je T'Aime . . .Moi Non Plus
1969	ARCHIES	Sugar Sugar
1970	LEE MARVIN	Wand'rin' Star
1970	NORMAN GREENBAUM	Spirit In The Sky
1970	MATTHEWS' SOUTHERN COMFORT	Woodstock
1971	CLIVE DUNN	Grandad
1973	SIMON PARK ORCHESTRA	Eye Level
1975	TYPICALLY TROPICAL	Barbados
1976	J.J. BARRIE	No Charge
1977	FLOATERS	Float On
1978	ALTHIA AND DONNA	Up Town Top Ranking
1978	BRIAN AND MICHAEL	Matchstalk Men and Matchstalk Cats and Dogs
1979	ANITA WARD	Ring My Bell
1979	LENA MARTELL	One Day At A Time
1980	FERN KINNEY	Together We Are Beautiful
1980	JOHNNY LOGAN	What's Another Year
1980	MASH	Theme From M★A★S★H
1980	ST WINIFRED'S SCHOOL CHOIR	There's No-One Quite Like Grandma
1981	JOE DOLCE	Shaddup You Face
1982	CHARLENE	I've Never Been To Me
1982	SURVIVOR	Eye Of The Tiger

Apart from these 30 acts, nine other one-hit wonders exist, made up of acts who have had hits in other guises, as follows:

Year	Act	Song
1967	NANCY SINATRA AND FRANK SINATRA	Something Stupid (both have had solo number one hits)
1974	JOHN DENVER	Annie's Song (has also hit with Placido Domingo)
1976	ELTON JOHN AND KIKI DEE	Don't Go Breaking My Heart (both have had solo hits)
1980	OLIVIA NEWTON-JOHN AND ELECTRIC LIGHT ORCHESTRA	Xanadu (both acts have had solo hits)
1981	QUEEN AND DAVID BOWIE	Under Pressure (both acts have had solo number one hits)
1982	PAUL McCARTNEY AND STEVIE WONDER	Ebony And Ivory (both acts have had solo number one hits)
1984	GEORGE MICHAEL	Careless Whisper (half of Wham!)
1984	JIM DIAMOND	I Should Have Known Better (a graduate of Ph.D)
1984	BAND AID	Do They Know It's Christmas? (a conglomeration of hitmakers)

Brian and, above, **Michael**

The backing singers on Brian and Michael's 'Matchstalk Men and Matchstalk Cats and Dogs' were the St Winifred's School Choir, who are not only the largest and the youngest act ever to reach number one, but also the only people to be one-hit wonders twice!

The least successful of all the one-hit wonders is Johnny Logan, whose Eurovision Song Contest winner of 1980 stayed on the charts for only 8 weeks. The longest stay at number one by a one-hit wonder is 8 weeks by the Archies. The only one to fall from the top and then climb back again is 'It's Almost Tomorrow' by the Dreamweavers. The longest stay on the chart by any one-hit wonder is 34 weeks by Jane Birkin and Serge Gainsbourg. The only million-selling one-hit wonder until 1984 was 'Eye Level' by the Simon Park Orchestra, but in 1984 both George Michael's 'Carless Whisper' and Band Aid's 'Do They Know It's Christmas?' hit the seven-figure mark.

Cliff Richard discusses his gap of 11 years at the top with three ladies who all share the distinction of having topped the charts twice.

GAP BETWEEN NUMBER ONE HITS

Of all the acts that have enjoyed two or more number one hits, only four acts have suffered through a gap of more than 7 years between consecutive number ones. The Beatles crammed all 17 of their chart-toppers into a period of 6 years 54 days.

11 years 238 days   Frank SINATRA (7 Oct 54 to 2 Jun 66)

11 years 124 days   Cliff RICHARD (23 Apr 68 to 25 Aug 79)

9 years 231 days   BEE GEES (10 Sep 68 to 29 Apr 78)

7 years 357 days   Don McLEAN (30 Jun 72 to 21 Jun 80)

There was a gap of 14 years 113 days between the day the Equals dropped from number one to the day when one of their number, Eddy Grant, took his solo hit 'I Don't Wanna Dance' to the top. 'Tears Of A Clown' by Smokey Robinson and the Miracles dropped from number one 10 years and 268 days before Smokey's solo number one 'Being With You' reached the very top.

STRAIGHT IN AT NUMBER ONE

Seventeen records have come straight in to the chart at number one.

14 Nov 52	HERE IN MY HEART	Al Martino
24 Jan 58	JAILHOUSE ROCK	Elvis Presley
3 Nov 60	IT'S NOW OR NEVER	Elvis Presley
11 Jan 62	THE YOUNG ONES	Cliff Richard and the Shadows
23 Apr 69	GET BACK	Beatles with Billy Preston
3 Mar 73	CUM ON FEEL THE NOIZE	Slade
30 Jun 73	SKWEEZE ME PLEEZE ME	Slade
17 Nov 73	I LOVE YOU LOVE ME LOVE	Gary Glitter
15 Dec 73	MERRY XMAS EVERYBODY	Slade
22 Mar 80	GOING UNDERGROUND/DREAMS OF CHILDREN	Jam
27 Sep 80	DON'T STAND SO CLOSE TO ME	Police
9 May 81	STAND AND DELIVER	Adam and the Ants
13 Feb 82	A TOWN CALLED MALICE/PRECIOUS	Jam
4 Dec 82	BEAT SURRENDER	Jam
26 Mar 83	IS THERE SOMETHING I SHOULD KNOW	Duran Duran
16 June 84	TWO TRIBES	Frankie Goes To Hollywood
15 Dec 84	DO THEY KNOW IT'S CHRISTMAS?	Band Aid

Slade remain the only act to enter the chart at number one with consecutive releases. Five acts, Al Martino, Jam, Adam and the Ants, Duran Duran and Band Aid, went straight to number one with their first chart-topper. Changes in the way the chart is compiled have made this feat easier to achieve in recent years.

This table shows which acts had to wait the longest between successive hits. The definition of a 'hit' is the same as in other lists in this section, i.e. re-issues and re-entries do not count as new hits. The gap is calculated as the period between the last day of one chart run and the first day of the chart run of the next hit.

Twelve acts have waited patiently for over 15 years between hits, as follows:

Eartha KITT	28 years 170 days	(16 Jun 55 to 3 Dec 83)
Gary U.S. BONDS	19 years 223 days	(18 Oct 61 to 30 May 81)
Paul EVANS	18 years 254 days	(6 Apr 60 to 16 Dec 78)
Kenny LYNCH	18 years 16 days	(4 Aug 65 to 20 Aug 83)
Bing CROSBY	17 years 338 days	(5 Sep 57 to 9 Aug 75)
Slim WHITMAN	17 years 86 days	(11 Jul 57 to 5 Oct 74)
Mike BERRY	17 years 73 days	(22 May 63 to 2 Aug 80)
Dorothy SQUIRES	16 years 99 days	(11 Jun 53 to 20 Sep 69)
EVERLY BROTHERS	16 years 96 days	(18 Jun 68 to 22 Sep 84)
Dee CLARK	16 years 3 days	(8 Oct 59 to 11 Oct 75)
Billy FURY	15 years 349 days	(21 Sep 66 to 4 Sep 82)
Johnny TILLOTSON	15 years 306 days	(12 Jun 63 to 14 Apr 79)

Dorothy Squires appeared on the charts during her long solo absence, in 1961 with Russ Conway. Phil Everly had a hit with Cliff Richard in 1983. Johnny Tillotson's return to the charts in 1979 was by virtue of a re-issue of 'Poetry In Motion' backed by 'Princess Princess', which was enjoying its first run on the British charts and therefore qualifies as a new hit. Only Paul Evans and Dee Clark came back with their biggest chart hit ever.

26 other acts have been off the charts for over 10 years between hits. They are, in order of time off the chart,

Sandie SHAW (14 yrs 315 days), Trini LOPEZ (14 yrs 223 days), Danny WILLIAMS (14 years 132 days), Dionne WARWICK (14 years 92 days), Robin GIBB (13 years 349 days), Mr Acker BILK (13 years 167 days), LITTLE RICHARD (12 yrs 345 days), Murray HEAD (12 yrs 280 days), Marianne FAITHFULL (12 yrs 247 days), EXCITERS (12 yrs 219 days), Duncan BROWNE (12 yrs 84 days), PINK FLOYD (12 yrs 79 days), Paul ANKA (12 yrs 37 days), Tony OSBORNE (11 yrs 339 days), Henry MANCINI (11 yrs 314 days), Johnny MATHIS (11 yrs 290 days), ENGLAND WORLD CUP SQUAD (11 yrs 232 days), Duane EDDY (11 yrs 185 days), Millie JACKSON (11 yrs 107 days) Robert JOHN (11 yrs 61 days), Gene CHANDLER (10 yrs 216 days), Dobie GRAY (10 yrs 166 days), CHAKACHAS (10 yrs 130 days), BOOKER T. & M.G.'s (10 yrs 80 days), Wayne GIBSON (10 yrs 68 days), Charlie DRAKE (10 yrs 12 days).

Dionne Warwick and Robin Gibb both appeared on the charts during their long solo absences, Miss Warwick as Dionne Warwicke with the Detroit Spinners and Robin Gibb as a Bee Gee.

There was a gap of 11 years 59 days between Shane Fenton's final day on the charts and Alvin Stardust's first appearance.

Having two hits in the Top Ten in the same week is not as rare as you might think, although most instances occurred in the 1950s and 1960s. It has been achieved 275 times to the end of 1984, by a total of 41 acts. Those who have enjoyed more than 10 weeks with at least two Top Ten hits are:

Frankie LAINE	33 weeks
Elvis PRESLEY	25 weeks
Guy MITCHELL	20 weeks
BEATLES	17 weeks
Ruby MURRAY	15 weeks
Bill HALEY and his COMETS	14 weeks
Eddie FISHER	13 weeks

Five or more consecutive weeks with two Top Ten hits has been achieved 21 times, as follows:

13 weeks	Frankie LAINE	from 11 Sep 53
	Ruby MURRAY	from 28 Jan 55
11 weeks	Eddie FISHER	from 22 May 53
	Elvis PRESLEY	from 19 Jul 57
9 weeks	Perry COMO	from 25 Jun 54
	Frankie LAINE	from 5 Aug 55
	FRANKIE GOES TO HOLLYWOOD	from 23 Jun 84
8 weeks	Shirley BASSEY	from 23 Jan 59
	BEATLES	from 5 Dec 63
	John LENNON	from 27 Dec 80
7 weeks	Frankie LAINE	from 8 Jan 54
	Doris DAY	from 27 Aug 54
	Bill HALEY and his COMETS	from 12 Oct 56
	Guy MITCHELL	from 22 Feb 57
6 weeks	Dickie VALENTINE	from 7 Jan 55
	Dean MARTIN	from 5 Sep 58
	Russ CONWAY	from 29 May 59
	BEATLES	from 20 Dec 67
5 weeks	Al MARTINO	from 30 Jan 53
	Frank SINATRA	from 20 Jan 56
	Ken DODD	from 9 Dec 65

STRAIGHT IN TO THE TOP FIVE

A total of 75 records have entered the charts in one of the Top Five positions, including the 17 that have hit the very top spot in their first week of chart action. Those discs are listed separately.

These 75 records featured only 33 acts in all. The Beatles crashed into the Top Five in their first chart week nine times (and John Lennon did it once more solo), while Jam, Elvis Presley and Slade have each done it six times. Duran Duran have had four singles which have started chart life at five or above, while Adam Ant, Gary Glitter and Wham! have had three.

Of the 58 records that came in at numbers two to five, 35 made it to number one, but 23 did not. Six of them never went any higher than their original chart position. The full list is:

Date	Title	Highest Position
STRAIGHT IN AT NUMBER TWO		
14 Nov 52	YOU BELONG TO ME Jo Stafford	1
9 Dec 65	DAY TRIPPER/WE CAN WORK IT OUT Beatles	1
16 Jun 66	PAPERBACK WRITER Beatles	1
12 Jul 67	ALL YOU NEED IS LOVE Beatles	1
14 Mar 70	LET IT BE Beatles	2
2 Sep 72	MAMA WEER ALL CRAZEE NOW Slade	1
21 Jul 73	I'M THE LEADER OF THE GANG (I AM) Gary Glitter	1
22 Sep 73	BALLROOM BLITZ Sweet	2
12 Sep 81	PRINCE CHARMING Adam and the Ants	1
15 Dec 84	LAST CHRISTMAS/EVERYTHING SHE WANTS Wham!	2
STRAIGHT IN AT NUMBER THREE		
14 Nov 52	SOMEWHERE ALONG THE WAY Nat 'King' Cole	3
16 Oct 53	HEY JOE Frankie Laine	1
30 Oct 53	ANSWER ME Frankie Laine	1
23 Jan 59	ONE NIGHT/I GOT STUNG Elvis Presley	1
16 Jul 64	A HARD DAY'S NIGHT Beatles	1
29 Jan 72	TELEGRAM SAM T. Rex	1
10 Mar 73	20TH CENTURY BOY T. Rex	3
19 Oct 74	FAR FAR AWAY Slade	2
23 Feb 80	ATOMIC Blondie	1
23 Aug 80	START Jam	1
24 Jan 81	WOMAN John Lennon	1
17 Sep 83	KARMA CHAMELEON Culture Club	1
25 Aug 84	I JUST CALLED TO SAY I LOVE YOU Stevie Wonder	1
6 Oct 84	THE WAR SONG Culture Club	2
13 Oct 84	FREEDOM Wham!	1
1 Dec 84	THE POWER OF LOVE Frankie Goes to Hollywood	1
STRAIGHT IN AT NUMBER FOUR		
14 Nov 52	ISLE OF INNISFREE Bing Crosby	3
24 Apr 53	PRETTY LITTLE BLACK EYED SUSIE Guy Mitchell	2
10 Feb 56	MEMORIES ARE MADE OF THIS Dean Martin	1
24 Apr 59	A FOOL SUCH AS I/I NEED YOUR LOVE TONIGHT Elvis Presley	1
2 Nov 61	LITTLE SISTER/HIS LATEST FLAME Elvis Presley	1
4 Jun 69	THE BALLAD OF JOHN AND YOKO Beatles	1
5 May 73	HELL RAISER Sweet	2
6 Jul 74	BANGIN' MAN Slade	3
27 Nov 76	SOMEBODY TO LOVE Queen	2
16 Aug 80	ASHES TO ASHES David Bowie	1
6 June 81	FUNERAL PYRE Jam	4
29 Oct 83	UNION OF THE SNAKE Duran Duran	3

THREE TOP TEN HITS IN ONE WEEK

This far more rare achievement has been only achieved 15 times, by only four acts.

14 Nov 52   **Vera LYNN**
7 Forget Me Not
9 Homing Waltz
10 Auf Wiedersehen
16 Oct 53   **Frankie LAINE**
2 I Believe
3 Hey Joe
4 Where The Wind Blows
23 Oct 53   **Frankie LAINE**
1 Hey Joe
3 Where The Wind Blows
4 I Believe
20 Nov 53   **Frankie LAINE**
1 Answer Me
4 I Believe
6 Hey Joe
27 Nov 53   **Frankie LAINE**
1 Answer Me
5 Hey Joe
6 I Believe
4 Dec 53   **Frankie LAINE**
1 Answer Me
8 Hey Joe
10 I Believe
25 Feb 55   **Ruby MURRAY**
1 Softly Softly
4 Heartbeat
6 Happy Days And Lonely Nights
4 Mar 55   **Ruby MURRAY**
1 Softly Softly
4 Heartbeat
7 Happy Days And Lonely Nights
11 Mar 55   **Ruby MURRAY**
2 Softly Softly
7 Heartbeat
8 Happy Days And Lonely Nights
25 Mar 55   **Ruby MURRAY**
2 Softly Softly
6 Let Me Go Lover
10 If Anyone Finds This I Love You
27 Dec 80   **John LENNON**
2 Starting Over
4 Happy Xmas (War Is Over)
9 Imagine
3 Jan 81   **John LENNON**
2 Starting Over
4 Happy Xmas (War Is Over)
9 Imagine
10 Jan 81   **John LENNON**
1 Imagine
2 Happy Xmas (War Is Over)
5 Starting Over
17 Jan 81   **John LENNON**
1 Imagine

| 4 Feb 84 | RADIO GAGA Queen | 2 |
| 26 May 84 | WAKE ME UP BEFORE YOU GO GO Wham! | 1 |

STRAIGHT IN AT NUMBER FIVE

14 Nov 52	FEET UP Guy Mitchell	2
2 Jul 54	LITTLE THINGS MEAN A LOT Kitty Kallen	1
24 Jul 59	BIG HUNK O' LOVE Elvis Presley	4
24 Mar 60	MY OLD MAN'S A DUSTMAN Lonnie Donegan	1
29 Jul 65	HELP Beatles	1
19 May 66	PAINT IT BLACK Rolling Stones	1
23 Feb 67	PENNY LANE/STRAWBERRY FIELDS FOREVER Beatles	2
15 June 74	ALWAYS YOURS Gary Glitter	1
26 Mar 77	GOING IN WITH MY EYES OPEN David Soul	2
1 Dec 79	WALKING ON THE MOON Police	1
8 Nov 80	THE TIDE IS HIGH Blondie	1
22 May 82	GOODY TWO SHOES Adam Ant	1
18 Sep 82	THE BITTEREST PILL (I EVER HAD TO SWALLOW) Jam	2
26 Mar 83	LET'S DANCE David Bowie	1
28 Apr 84	THE REFLEX Duran Duran	1
9 Jun 84	ONLY WHEN YOU LEAVE Spandau Ballet	3
14 Jul 84	HOLE IN MY SHOE neil	2
3 Nov 84	THE WILD BOYS Duran Duran	2

Apart from the first chart of all (14 Nov 52), only two charts have ever included two new entries in the Top Five. These were the charts of 26 March 83, when 'Is There Something I Should Know' by Duran Duran came in at number one, and 'Let's Dance' by David Bowie came in at number five; and 15 December 84, when Band Aid's 'Do They Know It's Christmas?' came in at number one, and 'Last Christmas'/'Everything She Wants' by Wham! was the new number two.

Only three acts after the first chart week have ever had their first hit come into the chart in one of the top five positions. They are:

2 Jul 54	Kitty KALLEN	Little Things Mean A Lot	**no. 5**
14 Jul 84	neil	Hole In My Shoe	**no. 5**
15 Dec 84	BAND AID	Do They Know It's Christmas?	**no. 1**

Band Aid consisted solely of acts who had already had chart hits, and most of them had already experienced life at the very top.

'Get Back', which debuted at number one on 23 April 69, was credited to 'The Beatles with Billy Preston'. This was Billy Preston's first week on the chart.

Since 1 October 1954, when the chart became a Top 20 for the first time, the only other acts whose first week on the charts was in the Top Ten are:

			1st wk pos'n
4 Feb 55	AMES BROTHERS	Naughty Lady Of Shady Lane	9
15 Apr 55	Tony BENNETT	Stranger In Paradise	10
15 Jul 55	Slim WHITMAN	Rose Marie	10
7 Oct 55	Mitch MILLER	Yellow Rose Of Texas	9
4 Apr 58	CHAMPS	Tequila	10
23 Jan 71	George HARRISON	My Sweet Lord	7
11 Nov 78	CARS	My Best Friend's Girl	10
14 Nov 81	QUEEN and David BOWIE	Under Pressure	8
8 May 82	NICOLE	A Little Peace	8
19 Mar 83	STYLE COUNCIL	Speak Like a Child	6

Between 14 Nov 52 and 1 Oct 54, when the chart was only a Top Twelve, no fewer than 40 acts spent their first chart week in the Top Ten. Among these were the Mills Brothers, whose only week ever on the charts was the week of 30 Jan 53, when their 'Glow Worm' was at number ten.

3 Happy Xmas (War Is Over)
5 Starting Over
24 Jan 81   **John LENNON**
1 Imagine
3 Woman
9 Happy Xmas (War Is Over)

Ruby Murray's 'Let Me Go Lover' and 'Happy Days And Lonely Nights' were both on Columbia DB 3577, but were listed separately. They did not feature in the Top Ten in the same week.

FOUR TOP TEN HITS IN ONE WEEK

This amazing and unlikely to be repeated feat was performed by Frankie Laine for three consecutive weeks late in 1953, as follows:

30 Oct 1953   **Frankie LAINE**
1 Hey Joe
3 Answer Me
5 Where The Wind Blows
6 I Believe
6 Nov 53   **Frankie LAINE**
2 Answer Me
3 Hey Joe
5 I Believe
7 Where The Wind Blows
13 Nov 53   **Frankie LAINE**
1 Answer Me
4 Hey Joe
7 I Believe
9 Where The Wind Blows

Frankie Laine therefore enjoyed 8 consecutive weeks in 1953 with three or more Top Ten hits. For the first four of these weeks, he had three top five hits, a record not equalled until 10 January 81, by John Lennon.

Two Top Three Hits in One Week

Eight acts have between them performed this extraordinary feat of chart domination a total of thirty times, as follows:

1 May 53 Guy MITCHELL
2 Pretty Little Black Eyed Susie
3 She Wears Red Feathers

2 Oct 53 Frankie LAINE
2 Where The Wind Blows
3 I Believe

9 October 53 Frankie LAINE
2 I Believe
3 Where The Wind Blows

16 Oct 53 Frankie LAINE
2 I Believe
3 Hey Joe

23 Oct 53 Frankie LAINE
1 Hey Joe
3 Where The Wind Blows

30 Oct 53 Frankie LAINE
1 Hey Joe
3 Answer Me

6 Nov 53 Frankie LAINE
2 Answer Me
3 Hey Joe

27 Jan 56 Tennessee Ernie FORD
1 Sixteen Tons
3 The Ballad of Davy Crockett

2 Aug 57 Elvis PRESLEY
1 All Shook Up
3 Teddy Bear

16 Aug 57 Elvis PRESLEY
1 All Shook Up
3 Teddy Bear

6 Feb 59 Shirley BASSEY
3= As I Love You
3= Kiss Me Honey Honey Kiss Me

13 Feb 59 Shirley BASSEY
2 As I Love You
3 Kiss Me Honey Honey Kiss Me

12 Dec 63 BEATLES
1 I Want To Hold Your Hand
2 She Loves You

19 Dec 63 BEATLES
1 I Want To Hold Your Hand
2 She Loves You

26 Dec 63 BEATLES
1 I Want To Hold Your Hand
2 She Loves You

2 Jan 64 BEATLES
1 I Want To Hold Your Hand
3 She Loves You

20 Dec 67 BEATLES
1 Hello Goodbye
3 Magical Mystery Tour EP

27 Dec 67 BEATLES
1 Hello Goodbye
2 Magical Mystery Tour EP

3 Jan 68 BEATLES
1 Hello Goodbye
2 Magical Mystery Tour EP

10 Jan 68 BEATLES
1 Hello Goodbye
2 Magical Mystery Tour EP

10 Jan 81 John LENNON
1 Imagine
2 Happy Xmas (War Is Over)

17 Jan 81 John LENNON
1 Imagine
3 Happy Xmas (War Is Over)

24 Jan 81 John LENNON
1 Imagine
3 Woman

31 Jan 81 John LENNON
1 Imagine
2 Woman

30 Jun 84 FRANKIE GOES TO HOLLYWOOD
1 Two Tribes
3 Relax

7 Jul 84 FRANKIE GOES TO HOLLYWOOD
1 Two Tribes
2 Relax

14 Jul 84 FRANKIE GOES TO HOLLYWOOD
1 Two Tribes
2 Relax

21 Jul 84 FRANKIE GOES TO HOLLYWOOD
1 Two Tribes
3 Relax

28 Jul 84 FRANKIE GOES TO HOLLYWOOD
1 Two Tribes
3 Relax

4 Aug 84 FRANKIE GOES TO HOLLYWOOD
1 Two Tribes
3 Relax

The first act ever to take the top two places in 1 week were the Beatles, on 12 Dec 63. They have spent a total of 6 weeks holding the top two places. John Lennon spent 2 weeks in the top two slots, as did Frankie Goes To Hollywood in 1984. Holly and the boys equalled Frankie Laine's 1953 record by spending 6 consecutive weeks with two hits in the Top Three.

Most 'Unsuccessful' Number Two Hits

No record that climbs to number two can really be described as unsuccessful, but since the British singles charts began, there have been 415 records to the end of 1984 which reached number two, but failed to climb that all-important final rung up the ladder to the top. The following acts have had three or more number two hits.

		Weeks
9	Cliff RICHARD	20
	Elvis PRESLEY	19
5	SWEET	13
	QUEEN	10
4	Pat BOONE	17
	BEATLES	10
	Gary GLITTER	9
	Tom JONES	9
	T. REX	9
	SLADE	8
	HOLLIES	7
	Dean MARTIN	7
	EVERLY BROTHERS	6
	Leo SAYER	5
	SHOWADDYWADDY	4
	Stevie WONDER	4
3	Frankie LAINE	11
	Nat 'King' COLE	9
	Shakin' STEVENS	8
	KINKS	5
	Paul McCARTNEY	4
	David BOWIE	3
	DARTS	3
	Guy MITCHELL	3

All these acts except Nat 'King' Cole and Darts did reach number one with other hits. Paul McCartney has had a further two number twos with Wings and one more in a duet with Michael Jackson, bringing to ten the number of number two hits he has performed on.

MOST WEEKS AT NUMBER TWO

By an 'unsuccessful' single

8	Theme from 'Limelight' .... FRANK CHACKSFIELD
7	Love Letters In The Sand .... PAT BOONE
6	The Smurf Song FATHER ABRAHAM AND THE SMURFS
	Are You Sure .... ALLISONS
	Floral Dance BRIGHOUSE AND RASTRICK BRASS BAND
	Ruby Don't Take Your Love To Town KENNY ROGERS and the FIRST EDITION

The most *consecutive* weeks at number two is 6, a record jointly held by 'The Smurf Song' and 'The Floral Dance'.

Only one record has ever reached number two on two totally separate occasions. 'Honey' by Bobby Goldsboro reached number two on 29 May 68 for 1 week. It returned to number two as a re-issue on 26 April 75, almost 7 years later.

LEAST SUCCESSFUL CHART ACT

During the period from 10 March 1960 to 6 May 78, when a Top Fifty was published, there were thirteen acts whose entire chart career consisted of 1 week at number 50. As Manchester United FC removed themselves from this list on 21 May 83 and Millie JACKSON did the same on 10 Mar 84 it is worth recording the other eleven for posterity:

ANGELS, CHAQUITO, Jimmy CLANTON, COOKIES, Marvin GAYE and Kim WESTON, Tim HARDIN, Tony HATCH, MOONTREKKERS, Hal PAGE and the WHALERS, Keith RELF, and SUNDRAGON.

Since 13 May 78, when the Top 75 was first published, four acts have enjoyed only 1 week of chart glory, and that at number 75. They are

ADICTS	Bad Boy	14 May 83
ANGELWITCH	Sweet Danger	7 June 80
DAYTON	The Sound Of Music	10 Dec 83
GRAND PRIX	Keep On Believing	27 Feb 82

Steve Wright and the Sisters Of Soul spent only 1 week at number 75 with their mind-expanding 'Get Some Therapy', but as Steve Wright has hit the Top 75 on two other occasions under two other names, this particular line-up is not considered to be as unsuccessful as the four acts listed above. Even those four acts should not be too downhearted. One week on the charts is more than the Led Zeppelin ever managed, while major worldwide hits like Ray Charles' 'What'd I Say' and Rufus' 'Tell Me Something Good' never hit the charts at all.

MOST WEEKS ON CHART

By Recording

a) Total Weeks On Chart regardless of the number of re-issues and re-entries

Chart Weeks	Chart Runs	
122	9	MY WAY .... Frank Sinatra
67	8	AMAZING GRACE .... Judy Collins
57	8	ROCK AROUND THE CLOCK★ Bill Haley and his Comets
56	1	RELEASE ME★ .... Engelbert Humperdinck
55	1	STRANGER ON THE SHORE Mr Acker Bilk
48	1	RELAX★ .... Frankie Goes To Hollywood
47	2	I LOVE YOU BECAUSE .... Jim Reeves
44	5	LET'S TWIST AGAIN .... Chubby Checker
42	3	WHITE LINES (DON'T DON'T DO IT) ....Grandmaster Flash and Melle Mel
41	5	DECK OF CARDS .... Wink Martindale
40	1	RIVERS OF BABYLON/BROWN GIRL IN THE RING★ .... Boney M
40	2	TIE A YELLOW RIBBON ROUND THE OLD OAK TREE★ ....Dawn
40	2	A SCOTTISH SOLDIER .... Andy Stewart
39	3	HE'LL HAVE TO GO .... Jim Reeves
38	2	SOMEWHERE MY LOVE ...... Mike Sammes Singers
38	3	BLUE MONDAY .... New Order
36	1	I BELIEVE★ .... Frankie Laine
36	1	I PRETEND★ .... Des O'Connor
36	3	SHE LOVES YOU★ .... Beatles
35	2	AND I LOVE YOU SO .... Perry Como
35	2	ALBATROSS★ ....Fleetwood Mac
35	2	HOUND DOG .... Elvis Presley
35	4	ALL RIGHT NOW..............................Free
34	1	CHIRPY CHIRPY CHEEP CHEEP★.. Middle Of The Road
34	3	HEARTBREAK HOTEL........... Elvis Presley
34	3	JE T'AIME . . .MOI NON PLUS★ Jane Birkin and Serge Gainsbourg
34	3	LEADER OF THE PACK .... Shangri-Las
34	3	NIGHTS IN WHITE SATIN ..... Moody Blues
32	2	LET'S DANCE .... Chris Montez
32	2	OH CAROL .... Neil Sedaka
31	2	SAILING★ ....Rod Stewart
30	1	AS LONG AS HE NEEDS ME Shirley Bassey
30	1	SIDE SADDLE★ .... Russ Conway
30	1	THEME FROM 'A SUMMER PLACE' Percy Faith Orchestra
30	1	JUST LOVING YOU .... Anita Harris
30	2	BREAKING UP IS HARD TO DO ....Neil Sedaka
30	2	YOUNG GIRL★ ....Gary Puckett and the Union Gap
30	2	PARANOID........................ Black Sabbath
30	2	TRUE LOVE .... Bing Crosby and Grace Kelly
30	3	TAINTED LOVE★ .... Soft Cell

Only fifteen of the 39 records that have spent 30 or more weeks in the charts reached number one (indicated by asterisk).
'Rock Around The Clock' enjoyed a further 5 weeks chart success in shortened form as part of 'Haley's Golden Medley'.

b) Consecutive weeks on chart

56	RELEASE ME	Engelbert Humperdinck
55	STRANGER ON THE SHORE	Mr Acker Bilk
48	RELAX	Frankie Goes To Hollywood
42	MY WAY	Frank Sinatra
40	RIVERS OF BABYLON/BROWN GIRL IN THE RING	Boney M
39	TIE A YELLOW RIBBON ROUND THE OLD OAK TREE	Dawn
39	I LOVE YOU BECAUSE	Jim Reeves
38	WHITE LINES (DON'T DON'T DO IT)	Grandmaster Flash and Melle Mel
38	A SCOTTISH SOLDIER	Andy Stewart
36	I BELIEVE	Frankie Laine
36	I PRETEND	Des O'Connor
34	CHIRPY CHIRPY CHEEP CHEEP Middle Of The Road	
32	AMAZING GRACE	Judy Collins
31	SHE LOVES YOU	Beatles
31	AND I LOVE YOU SO	Perry Como
30	AS LONG AS HE NEEDS ME	Shirley Bassey
30	SIDE SADDLE	Russ Conway
30	THEME FROM 'A SUMMER PLACE'	Percy Faith Orchestra
30	JUST LOVING YOU	Anita Harris

MOST WEEKS ON CHART

By a Song in all its Recorded Versions

This list shows the most successful songs chart-wise from 1952 to 1984. Only complete recordings of the song count – parts of songs in medley discs are disqualified.

Weeks Chart versions

163	MY WAY	4 versions, all vocal
94	AMAZING GRACE	2 versions, one vocal, one instrumental
70	ROCK AROUND THE CLOCK	3 versions, all vocal
70	MACK THE KNIFE	7, six vocal, one instrumental
67	ONLY YOU	6 versions, all vocal
65	STRANGER ON THE SHORE	2, one vocal, one instrumental
61	UNCHAINED MELODY	6, five vocal, one instrumental
56	DECK OF CARDS	2, both vocal
56	RELEASE ME	1, vocal
54	I BELIEVE	3, all vocal
54	JE T'AIME . . . MOI NON PLUS/LOVE AT FIRST SIGHT	3, two vocal, one instrumental
51	IT'S ONLY MAKE BELIEVE	4, all vocal
50	LET'S TWIST AGAIN	2, both vocal

'It's Only Make Believe' (written by Conway Twitty and Jack Nance) is the only song in British chart history to have been a Top Ten hit in four different versions, at four different times.

Five songs have hit the chart in six different versions. They are:

'Unchained Melody', written by Alex North and Hy Zaret
'Mack The Knife', written by Kurt Weill and Bertholt Brecht, English lyrics by Marc Blitzstein
'Only You', written by Buck Ram and Ande Rande
'Stranger In Paradise', written by Robert Wright and George Forrest, based on a theme by Aleksandr Borodin
'White Christmas', written by Irving Berlin

'White Christmas' is one of two songs to have been a hit in five different years. The other is '(I Can't Get No) Satisfaction', written by Mick Jagger and Keith Richard.

Six songs have reached number one in two different versions: 'Answer Me' (Frankie Laine and David Whitfield), 'Cherry Pink And Apple Blossom White' (Perez Prado and Eddie Calvert), 'Singing The Blues' (Guy Mitchell and Tommy Steele), 'Young Love' (Tab Hunter and Donny Osmond) 'Mary's Boy Child' (Harry Belafonte and Boney M) and 'This Ole House' (Rosemary Clooney and Shakin' Stevens).

The most commonly used title for a hit single is 'Tonight'. There have now been nine different hit songs using this title, recorded by Shirley BASSEY, BOOMTOWN RATS, David BOWIE, Zaine GRIFF, Steve HARVAY, KOOL AND THE GANG, MODETTES, MOVE and RUBETTES. Of all these songs, only Kool and the Gang's made the Top Ten, and then only as part of the double-sided 1984 number 2 hit 'Joanna/Tonight'. The title 'Joanna' had already been used by Scott Walker for a hit song in 1968, so Kool's hit could be described as having the most unoriginal pair of titles of all time.

'Woman In Love' (Frankie LAINE and Barbra STREISAND) and 'Forever and Ever' (Demis ROUSSOS and SLIK) are the only titles used more than once for different number one hits. Two different songs called 'Only You' have been Top Ten hits for two different acts each.